CORPORATE FINANCIAL
MANAGEMENT

GLEN ARNOLD BSc(Econ), PhD
DEBORAH LEWIS BA, MBA, FCA, SFHEA

CORPORATE FINANCIAL
MANAGEMENT

SIXTH EDITION

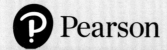 Pearson

Harlow, England • London • New York • Boston • San Francisco • Toronto • Sydney • Dubai • Singapore • Hong Kong
Tokyo • Seoul • Taipei • New Delhi • Cape Town • São Paulo • Mexico City • Madrid • Amsterdam • Munich • Paris • Milan

PEARSON EDUCATION LIMITED
KAO Two
KAO Park
Harlow CM17 9NA
United Kingdom
Tel: +44 (0)1279 623623
Web: www.pearson.com/uk

First published in Great Britain under the Financial Times Pitman Publishing imprint in 1998 (print)
Second edition published 2002 (print)
Third edition published 2005 (print)
Fourth edition published 2008 (print)
Fifth edition published 2013 (print and electronic)
Sixth edition published 2019 (print and electronic)

The Financial Times. With a worldwide network of highly respected journalists, *The Financial Times*
provides global business news, insightful opinion and expert analysis of business, finance
and politics. With over 500 journalists reporting from 50 countries worldwide, our in-depth
coverage of international news is objectively reported and analysed from an independent, global
perspective. To find out more, visit www.ft.com/pearsonoffer.

ISBN: 978-1-292-14044-5 (print)
        978-1-292-14047-6 (PDF)
        978-1-292-14048-3 (ePub)

British Library Cataloguing-in-Publication Data
A catalogue record for the print edition is available from the British Library

Library of Congress Cataloging-in-Publication Data
Names: Arnold, Glen, author. | Lewis, Deborah S., author.
Title: Corporate financial management / Glen Arnold, BSc(Econ), PhD, Deborah
Lewis, BA, MBA, FCA, SFHEA.
Description: Sixth edition. | Harlow, England ; New York : Pearson, 2019
Identifiers: LCCN 2018025913| ISBN 9781292140445 (print) | ISBN 9781292140476
(PDF) | ISBN 9781292140483 (ePub)
Subjects: LCSH: Corporations--Finance--Management. | Corporations--Finance.
Classification: LCC HG4026 .A755 2019 | DDC 658.15--dc23
LC record available at https://urldefense.proofpoint.com/v2/url?u=https-3A__lccn.loc.gov_2018025913&d=DwIFAg&c=
0YLnzTkWOdJlub_y7qAx8Q&r=Q1huLr_hfN5hBmNklTyEbqNkqKPJUy4ujVI9zNDFILM&m=
VR8NGw69pHRJJiX5cv67FTKvTLiw9fgpvabMVzd01eQ&s=txGOpxXfVn_XxRZdc9gyeJ1E49b5sHATBL82A3QixTI&e=

10 9 8 7 6 5 4 3 2 1
23 22 21 20 19

Cover image © Andy Brandl/Moment Select/Getty Images

Print edition typeset in 10/11.5 pt Sabon MT Pro by Pearson CSC
Printed and bound by L.E.G.O. S.p.A., Italy

NOTE THAT ANY PAGE CROSS REFERENCES REFER TO THE PRINT EDITION

Dedicated to Lesley my wife, for her loving support and encouragement. Glen Arnold

Brief contents

Contents

Part 3 Risk and return | 173

Part 6   Managing risk   923

21   Derivatives   924

22   Managing exchange-rate risk   972

APPENDICES   A:1

Lecturer Resources

For password-protected online resources tailored to support the use of this textbook in teaching, please visit
www.pearsoned.co.uk/arnold

Topics covered in the book

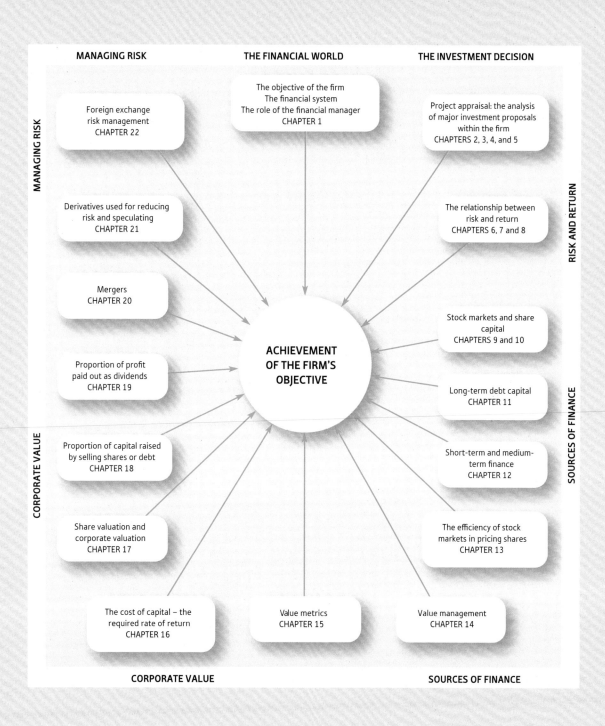

Introduction to the book

Aims of the book

If there is one lesson that the 2008 financial crisis and the Great Recession taught us, it is that there is good and bad financial practice. Unfortunately, many of the basic tenets of finance get forgotten by corporate managers, bankers and leaders of financial institutions from time to time. Important financial issues, such as adopting sensible levels of debt, or simply being aware of risk levels, or checking the validity of the assumptions made when investing in the business, valuing a financial security or embarking on a merger, can be very badly handled.

This book has been updated to emphasise the basic lessons from hundreds of years of finance practice and theory, so that you might be more aware of the difference between good practice and what is plain stupid; so that you can avoid the errors made by countless business leaders.

The book assumes no knowledge of finance. It is comprehensive and provides the key elements needed by business management, accounting and other undergraduates, postgraduates and practising managers. Finance theory and practice are integrated throughout the text, reflecting the extent to which real-world practice has been profoundly shaped by theoretical developments.

Some of the features in this sixth edition are listed below.

- While the underlying principles of finance have not altered since the publication of the fifth edition some further changes have occurred for example in regulation, legislation and the operation of financial markets. These are explained.

- Where appropriate, illustrations from more recent corporate events, many of which draw on *Financial Times* articles, have been incorporated.

- The evidence gathered in the twenty-first century on the usefulness of beta as defined by the Capital Asset Pricing Model has been overwhelmingly negative. When this is combined with the theoretical problems, a much more sceptical line on the CAPM-beta is called for.

- Trillions of pounds are now placed with investment funds buying share portfolios drawing on stock market inefficiency evidence – called 'smart beta' funds. The academic work providing the impetus for this (even though it has now been taken too far) is examined.

- Fintech developments, including crowdfunding and peer-to-peer lending, have brought new ways of raising funds for businesses.

- Surveys of business practice are used through the text, not least in the cost of capital and share valuation sections, where the deviations from pure theory illustrate the compromises that must be made in the real world.

- Statistics on the financial markets and instruments, have been updated.

- The jargon-busting glossary has been extended and updated.

Themes in the book

Practical orientation

Every chapter describes and illustrates how financial techniques are used in the practical world of business. Throughout the text insight is offered into how and why practice may sometimes differ from sound theory. For example, in making major investment decisions, managers still use techniques with little theoretical backing (e.g. payback) alongside the more theoretically accept-able approaches. We explore the reasons for the retention of these simple rule-of-thumb methods. This book uses theory, algebra and economic models where these are considered essential to assist learning about better decision making. Where these are introduced, however, they must always have passed the practicality test: 'Is this knowledge sufficiently useful out there, in the real world, to make it worthwhile for the reader to study it?' If it is not, then it is not included.

Clear, accessible style

Great care has been taken to explain sometimes difficult topics in an interesting and comprehensible way. An informal language style, and an incremental approach, which builds knowledge in a series of easily achieved steps, leads the reader to a high level of knowledge with as little pain as possible. The large panel of reviewers of the book assisted in the process of developing a text that is, we hope, comprehensive and easy to read.

Integration with other disciplines

Finance should never be regarded as a subject in isolation, separated from the workings of the rest of the organisation. This text, when considering the link between theoretical methods and practical financial decision making, recognises a wide range of other influences, from strategy to psychology.

Real-world relevance

Experience of teaching finance to undergraduates, postgraduates and managers on short courses has led to the conclusion that, in order to generate enthusiasm and commitment to the subject, it is vital continually to show the relevance of the material to what is going on in the world beyond the textbook. Therefore, this book incorporates vignettes/short case studies as well as examples of real companies making decisions drawing on the models, concepts and ideas of financial management.

A UK/international perspective

There is a primary focus on the UK, but also regular reference to international financial markets and institutions. The international character of the book has been enhanced by the detailed evaluation of each chapter by a number of respected academics teaching at universities in Europe, Asia, Australasia and Africa. The global world of modern finance requires that a text of this nature reflects the commonality of financial principles in all countries, as well as interactions and the impact of vast capital flows across borders.

A re-evaluation of classical finance theory

There is considerable debate about the validity of the theories of the 1950s and 1960s upon which much of modern finance was developed, stimulated by fresh evidence generated over the last two decades. For example, the theories concerning the relationship between the risk of a financial security and its expected return are under dispute, with some saying the old measure of risk, beta, is dead or dying. This issue and other financial economics theories are presented along with their assumptions and a consideration of recent revisions.

Real-world case examples

It has been possible to include much more than the usual quantity of real-world case examples in this book by drawing on material from the *Financial Times*. The aim of these extracts is to bring the subject of finance to life for readers. A typical example is shown in Exhibit 1, which is used to illustrate some of the financial issues explored in the book. This article touches on many of the financial decisions which are examined in greater detail later in the book. Expanding a retail empire requires a lot of money. In the summer of 2017, Quiz Clothing raised more money

Exhibit 1

Quiz Clothing soars on IPO to reach £245m market value

By Hannah Murphy

Quiz Clothing, the womenswear retailer, jumped more than 20 per cent on its trading debut on Friday. The company, which was founded in Glasgow in 1993, priced its initial public offering at 161p. The shares leapt 22 per cent to 197p in early trading, pushing its market value up to £245m from £200m.

Quiz said it had raised £102.7m from the float, £92.1m of which it earmarked for selling shareholders, while the remaining £10.6m it said would be used to "accelerate growth".

The successful listing is the latest by a new breed of fashion retailers aimed at millennials. Quiz describes itself as focused on women's "occasion wear and dressy casual wear" for 16-35-year-olds and says it has adopted "fast fashion" processes that allow it to bring designs into shops quickly.

While small in comparison, it will rival the likes of online retailers Asos, now up more than 30,000 per cent to £58.53 since its listing in 2001, and Boohoo, whose shares have risen 360 per cent to 233p since it first floated in 2014. Asos and Boohoo are valued at £4.85bn and £2.68bn respectively.

Unlike the two larger retailers, Quiz has 73 standalone stores in the UK, more than 165 concessions in the regions and Republic of Ireland and 65 franchise stores across 19 countries. But it is focused on boosting its online offering.

"There's still good growth in stores ... but the real growth story over the next few years will be international and online," founder and chief executive Tarak Ramzan said.

The company had chosen to float partly as a way to "bring in new talent", he added, citing the appointment of Peter Cowgill, chair of sportswear retailer JD Sports, to the board as part of its entry to the stock market.

Still, the company believes there is life in bricks and mortar, and said earlier this year that it saw potential for 40-50 more stores across the UK in "the medium to long term".

Just over half of the company, 51.2 per cent, is now in public hands.

to invest in the next stage of its development. There are four vital financial issues facing management:

1 *Raising finance and knowledge of financial markets.* Quiz grew its business using family money for 24 years until it turned to the London Stock Exchange (LSE) to sell newly created shares raising £9.4m (after expenses) to invest in the business. Also, the Ramzan family sold a proportion of their shares, thus benefiting from their hard work. Being listed on the LSE will enhance its ability to raise more capital in the future because of the additional credibility that flows from being on the exchange. Companies have a wide range of options when it comes to raising finance to allow growth – sources of finance are considered in Chapters 9–13.

2 *Investment in real assets, tangible or intangible.* The directors of Quiz believe that they have investment opportunities in online retailing as well as high street stores. The company intends to invest in new websites in Spain, Australia and the USA, to open six stores in Spain and 20 in the UK in the months following the flotation. Around £6m is earmarked for online marketing and advertising and £2m for capital expenditure on physical items to go in shops. It will also invest in its people and bring in new talent. There are sound techniques which help in the process of deciding whether to make a major investment – these are discussed early in the book (Chapters 2–6).

3 *Creating and measuring shareholder value.* Quiz will need to consider the strategic implications of its actions, such as the current and likely future return on capital in the markets it may

choose to enter. Will Quiz have a competitive edge over its rivals in those markets? Value-based management draws on the analytical techniques developed in finance and combines them with disciplines such as strategy and resource management to analyse whether value is being/will be created or destroyed (Chapters 14 and 15). At the centre of value-based management is recognition of the need to produce a return on capital devoted to an activity commensurate with the risk. Establishing the minimum required return is the 'cost of capital' issue (Chapter 16). Quiz might consider buying another company (mergers are covered in Chapter 20) and so being able to value business units, companies and shares is very useful (Chapter 17). Then there is the question of the proportion of annual profits that should be paid out as dividends or retained for reinvestment (Chapter 19).

4   *Managing risk*. Quiz is faced with many operational risks, e.g. perhaps it will fail to strike a chord with consumers in Spain or America. There are some risks the firm has to accept, including these operational risks. However, there are many others that can be reduced by taking a few simple steps. For example, the risk of a rise in interest rates increasing the cost of borrowings, thus wiping out profits, can be reduced/eliminated by changing the capital structure; raising additional equity and using this to reduce debt (Chapter 18). Derivative financial instruments can be used to reduce interest rate risk (Chapter 21) or exchange rate risk. Quiz will be selling a significant proportion of its clothing in currencies other than sterling but may have costs in other currencies. Currency shifts can have a large impact on profits (Chapter 22).

These are just a few of the financial issues that have to be tackled by the modern finance manager and trying to understand and then answer these questions forms the basis for this book.

Student learning features

Each chapter has the following elements to help the learning process:

- *Learning objectives* This section sets out the competencies expected to be gained by reading the chapter.
- *Introduction* Intended to engage the attention of the reader, this discusses the importance and relevance of the topic to real business decisions.
- *Worked examples* New techniques are illustrated in the text, with sections which present problems, followed by detailed answers.
- *Mathematical explanations* Students with limited mathematical ability should not be put off by this text. The basics are covered early and in a simple style. New skills are fully explained and illustrated, as and when required.
- *Case studies and articles* Extracts from recent articles from the *Financial Times,* company annual reports and other sources are used to demonstrate the arguments in the chapter, to add a different dimension to an issue, or to show that this sort of decision is being made in day-to-day business.
- *Key points and concepts* An outline is given of the essentials of what has been covered; new concepts, jargon and equations are summarised for easy reference.
- *References and further reading* One of the features of this text is the short commentaries included with the list of articles and books referred to. These allow students to be selective in their follow-up reading. Whether a particular article takes a high-level, algebraic and theoretical approach or is an easy-to-read introduction to the subject is highlighted, permitting the student to decide whether the article is of interest.
- *Websites* A useful list of websites is also included.
- *Self-review questions* These short questions are designed to prompt the reader to recall the main elements of the topic. They can act as a revision aid and highlight areas requiring more attention.
- *Questions and problems* These vary in the amount of time required, from 5 minutes to 45 minutes or more. Many are taken from university second year and final year undergraduate

examinations, and MBA module examinations. They allow the student to demonstrate a thorough understanding of the material presented in the chapter. Some of these questions necessitate the integration of knowledge from previous chapters with the present chapter. The answers to many of the questions can be found on the website for the book www.pearsoned.co.uk/arnold.

- *Assignments* These are projects which require the reader to investigate real-world practice in a firm and relate this to the concepts and techniques learned in the chapter. These assignments can be used both as learning aids and as a way of helping students to examine the relationship between current practice and finance theory and frameworks.

- *Recommended case studies* A list of case studies relevant to the chapter material is provided. These are drawn from the Harvard Business School website.

At the end of the book there are also the following elements:

- *Appendices* Appendices give a future value table (Appendix I), present value table (Appendix II), present value of annuity table (Appendix III), future value of an annuity (Appendix IV), areas under the standardised normal distribution (Appendix V), answers to questions in Chapter 2, and Appendix 2.1 reviewing mathematical tools for finance (Appendix VI).

- *Glossary* There is an extensive Glossary of terms, allowing the student quickly to find the meaning of new technical terms or jargon.

- *Bibliography* There is also a Bibliography of references for further reading.

Also on the Companion Website (found at www.pearsoned.co.uk/arnold) there are the following downloadable resources:

- Answers to the numerical questions and problems – with the exception of those question numbers followed by an asterisk (*) which are answered in the instructor's manual.

- Supporting spreadsheets for Chapters 2, 3, 6, 7, 11 & 19

Support for lecturers

Go to www.pearsoned.co.uk/arnold to access:

- Over 800 PowerPoint slides.
- Instructor's manual.
- A link to **MyLab Finance.**

Instructor's manual

This contains:

- Supplementary material for chapters, including learning objectives and key points and concepts listings.
- A multiple-choice question bank (also available on the website).
- Answers to the questions and problems marked with an asterisk * in the book.

Target readership

The book is aimed at second/final year undergraduates of accounting and finance, business/management studies, banking and economics, as well as postgraduate students on MBA/MSc courses in the UK, Europe and the rest of the world. It would be helpful if the student has an elementary knowledge of statistics, algebra, accounting and microeconomics, but this is not essential.

The practising manager, whether or not a specialist in financial decision making, should find the book useful – not least to understand the language and concepts of business and financial markets.

Students studying for examinations for the professional bodies will benefit from this text. The material is valuable for those working towards a qualification of one of the following organisations:

- CFA Institute
- Association of Corporate Treasurers
- Institute of Chartered Accountants in England and Wales
- Institute of Chartered Accountants of Scotland
- Chartered Institute of Public Finance and Accountancy
- Association of Chartered Certified Accountants
- Chartered Institute of Management Accountants
- Institute of Chartered Secretaries and Administrators
- The London Institute of Banking & Finance
- British Bankers Association

The applicability of finance knowledge for all organisations

Most of the theories and practical examples in the book are directed at businesses operating in a competitive market environment. However, the fundamental principles revealed by the logic and frameworks of finance are applicable to organisations other than commercial firms such as non-profit organisations and public sector bodies, ranging from schools and hospitals to charities and churches. The principles contained within the book have validity and applicability to any organisation needing to make decisions involving finance.

Acknowledgements

Our grateful thanks to the publishing team at Pearson Education for their help in the preparation of this book. In particular, thanks to Rebecca Pedley, Carole Drummond, Richard Townrow, Archana Makhija, Wendy Telfer, Sangeetha Rajan, Prasanna Kalyanaraman and my personal assistant Susan Henton, whose knowledge, skills and intelligence are a great blessing to me.

We thank the following reviewers for their valuable feedback on this book over its various editions:

Ian Jackson, Staffordshire University
Ruth Bender, Cranfield University
Vijay Lee, London South Bank University
Jean Bellemans, United Business Institutes, Belgium
Lars Vangaard, University of Southern Denmark
Dr Jan Jakobsen, Copenhagen Business School
Rob Jones, Newcastle University
Dr Stuart Hyde, Manchester Business School, University of Manchester
Heather Tarbert, Glasgow Caledonian University
Tony Boczko, University of Hull
Roger Henderson, Leeds Metropolitan University
David Bence, University of West England
Kay Pollock, Kingston University
Alex Stremme, Warwick University
Victor Murinde, University of Birmingham
Edel Barnes, National University of Cork
Edwards Jones, Heriot Watt University
Per Hiller, Stockholm School of Economics
Roger Lister, University of Salford
Robert Major, University of Portsmouth
Dr Liang Han, University of Hull
Dr Pornsawan Evans, Swansea University
Ruth Mattimoe, Dublin City University
Dr Jean Chen, University of Surrey

Publisher's acknowledgements

We are grateful to the following for permission to reproduce copyright material:

Text

Extract on page 938 from Blas, J. (2012) Reading the corn time-spreads. Financial Times, 25 September. © The Financial Times Limited 2018. All rights reserved; Extract on page 894 from Masters, B. and Burgess, K. (2009) FSA spells out rules for activist investors. Financial Times, 19 August. © The Financial Times Limited 2018. All rights reserved; Extract on page 905 from Stern, S. (2005) Making a corporate marriage work. Financial Times, 6 February. © The Financial Times Limited 2018. All rights reserved; Extract on page 908 from Johnson, L. (2011) Empire builders fall prey to their vanity. Financial Times, 4 May. © The Financial Times Limited 2018. All rights reserved; Extract on page 910 from Lucas, L. (2011) Cadbury people still chewing on Kraft culture.

junk amid reports retailer has hired advisers. Financial Times, 8 September. © The Financial Times Limited 2018. All rights reserved; Extract on page 849 from The Lex Column (2010) Pole position in the EU growth race, p. 16. Financial Times, 05 April. © The Financial Times Limited 2018. All rights reserved; Extract on page 927 from Call options on Unilever shares. Financial Times, 1 August. © The Financial Times Limited 2018. All rights reserved. Reprinted with permission; Extract on page 956 from (2007) Financial Times: Money. Financial Times, 30 June. © The Financial Times Limited 2018. All rights reserved; Extract on page 1003 from Pooler, M. (2016) Engineer Weir considers moving production to UK after Brexit. Financial Times, 28 December. © The Financial Times Limited 2018. All rights reserved; Extract on page 348 from Reproduced with permission from the ADVFN. http://uk.advfn.com/Help/what-does-the-seaq-aim-window-show-59.html; Extract on page 250 from Solnik, H Bruno, 'Why Not Diversify Internationally Rather than Domestically?' Financial Analysts Journal Vol. 30, No. 4, pp. 48–54; Extract on page 251 from Solnik, H Bruno, 'Why Not Diversify Internationally Rather than Domestically?' Financial Analysts Journal Vol. 30, No. 4, pp. 48-54; Extract on page 252 from Solnik, H Bruno, 'Why Not Diversify Internationally Rather than Domestically?' Financial Analysts Journal Vol. 30, No. 4, pp. 48–54; Extract on page 303 from Baker, Malcolm; Bradley, Brendan and Wurgler, Jeffrey, 'Benchmarks as Limits to Arbitrage: Understanding the Low-Volatility Anomaly', Financial Analysts Journal, Vol. 67, No. 1, pp. 40–54; Extract on page 276 from Graham, John R. and Harvey, Campbell R. (2016) The Equity Risk Premium in 2016; Extract on page 276 from Fernandez, Pablo and Ortiz Pizarro, Alberto and Fernández Acín, Isabel (2016). Market Risk Premium Used in 71 Countries in 2016: A Survey with 6,932 Answers; Extract on page 277 from Fernandez, Pablo and Ortiz Pizarro, Alberto and Fernández Acín, Isabel (2016). Market Risk Premium Used in 71 Countries in 2016: A Survey with 6,932 Answers; Extract on page 340 from www.londonstockexchange.com, statistics section. Reproduced courtesy of London Stock Exchange plc; Extract on page 12 from From The good company by Economist Times. Copyright © 22 January 2005, All Rights Reserved.

PART 1
Introduction

1   The financial world

The financial world

LEARNING OUTCOMES

At the end of this chapter the reader will have a balanced perspective on the purpose and value of the finance function, at both the corporate and the national level. More specifically, the reader should be able to:

■ describe alternative views on the purpose of the business and show the importance to any organisation of clarity on this point;

■ describe the impact of the divorce of corporate ownership from day-to-day managerial control;

■ explain the role of the financial manager;

■ detail the value of financial intermediaries;

■ show an appreciation of the function of the major financial institutions and markets.

Introduction

Before getting carried away with specific financial issues and technical detail, it is important to gain a broad perspective by looking at the fundamental questions and the place of finance in the overall scheme of things. The finance function is a vital one, both within an individual organisation and for society as a whole. In the UK, for example, the financial services industry accounts for a larger proportion of national output than the whole of manufacturing industry. Banking, finance, insurance and other finance-related businesses produce about 12% of output. This compares with manufacturing's 10% share, which is down from 30% of all production in 1970. There has been an enormous shift in demand and resources in recent decades. To some this is a cause of great alarm and regret but, given that this trend occurred at a time when free choice in the marketplace largely dictates what is produced, presumably there must be something useful that financial firms are providing. We will examine the key role played by financial intermediaries and markets in a modern economy, and how an efficient and innovative financial sector contributes greatly to the ability of other sectors to produce goods and services. One of the vital roles of the financial sector is to encourage the mobilisation of savings to put them to productive use through investment. Without a vibrant and adaptable financial sector all parts of the economy would be starved of investment and society would be poorer.

This chapter also considers the most fundamental question facing anyone trying to make decisions within an organisation: what is the objective of the business? Without clarity on this point it is very difficult to run a business in a purposeful and effective manner. The resolution of this question is somewhat clouded in the large, modern corporation by the tendency for the owners to be distant from the running of the enterprise. Professional managers are usually left in control and they have objectives which may or may not match those of the owners.

Finally, to help the reader become orientated, a brief rundown is given of the roles, size and activities of the major types of financial institutions and markets. A little bit of jargon busting early on will no doubt be welcomed.

The objective of the firm

Experian, widely regarded as one of the best-managed companies in the world, has a clear statement of its objective in its 2016 Annual Report – *see* **Case study 1.1.**

Case study 1.1   Experian

'Our business model is based on a set of substantial competitive advantages. Our strategy builds on and reinforces these advantages, so we can maximise the value we create for our shareholders in the long term.'

There follows a description of how they attempt to 'maximise the value we create for shareholders in the long term' by creating 'significant value for society' through offering services, including:

- Holding credit data on 918 million people and 107 million businesses. Thus, for example, credit reports can be obtained if an individual or a business is applying for a bank loan.

- Marketing data on 700 million people held and analysed so that companies can better understand customers.

Strategy follows clarity on the objective: 'Our strategy is centred on delivering world-class expertise . . . [to] become the world leader in powering data-driven opportunities.'

Aims follow the strategy:

- To deliver . . . revenue growth consistently

- To operate our business efficiently and cost effectively

▶

Case study 1.1 *(continued)*

- To generate good returns

- To deliver profit growth, while balancing investment in the business and shareholder returns

- To covert at least 90% of [profit] into operating cash flow

- To ensure Experian is a great place to work, attracting and retaining the best people

- To minimize as far as possible our impact on the environment

Source: Experian plc Annual Report 2016.

Notice that there is not a confusion of objectives (as there is in many companies) with no one knowing which of a long list of desirable outcomes is the dominant purpose of the firm. Experian does not confuse the objective with the strategy to be employed to achieve the objective. Many managerial teams believe that it is their objective to operate within a particular market or take particular actions. They seem unable to distinguish market positions or actions from the ultimate purpose for the existence of the organisation. This will not only lead to poor strategic decisions but frequently makes intelligent financial decisions impossible.

This book is all about practical decision making in the real world. When people have to make choices in the harsh environment in which modern businesses have to operate, it is necessary to be clear about the purpose of the organisation; to be clear about what objective is set for management to achieve. A multitude of small decisions is made every day; more importantly, every now and then major strategic commitments of resources are made. It is imperative that the management teams are aware of, respect and contribute to the fundamental objective of the firm in all these large and small decisions. Imagine the chaos and confusion that could result from the opposite situation where there is no clear, accepted objective. The outcome of each decision, and the direction of the firm, will become random and rudderless. One manager on one occasion will decide to grant long holidays and a shorter working week, believing that the purpose of the institution's existence is to benefit employees; while on another occasion a different manager sacks 'surplus' staff and imposes lower wages, seeing the need to look after the owner's interests as a first priority. So, before we can make decisions in the field of finance we need to establish what it is we are trying to achieve.

You have probably encountered elsewhere the question, 'In whose interests is the firm run?' This is a political and philosophical as well as an economic question and many books have been written on the subject. Here we will provide a brief overview of the debate because of its central importance to making choices in finance. The list of interested parties in **Exhibit 1.1** could be extended,

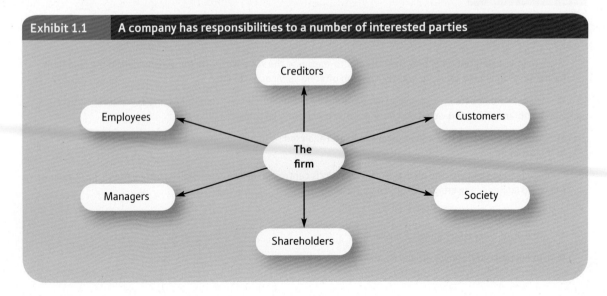

Exhibit 1.1   A company has responsibilities to a number of interested parties

but no doubt you can accept the point from this shortened version that there are a number of claimants on a firm.

Sound financial management is necessary for the survival of the firm and for its growth. Therefore all of these stakeholders, to some extent, have an interest in seeing sensible financial decisions being taken. Many business decisions do not involve a conflict between the objectives of each of the stakeholders. However, there are occasions when someone has to decide which claimants are to have their objectives maximised, and which are merely to be satisficed – that is, given just enough of a return to make their contributions.

There are some strong views held on this subject. The pro-capitalist economists, such as Friedrich Hayek and Milton Friedman, believe that making shareholders' interests the paramount objective will benefit both the firm and society at large. This approach is not quite as extreme as it sounds because these thinkers generally accept that unbridled pursuit of shareholder returns, to the point of widespread pollution, murder and extortion, will not be in society's best interest and so add the proviso that maximising shareholder wealth is the desired objective provided that firms remain within 'the rules of the game'. This includes obeying the laws and conventions of society, and behaving ethically and honestly.

At the opposite end of the political or philosophical spectrum are the left-wing advocates of the primacy of workers' rights and rewards. The belief here is that labour should have its rewards maximised. The employees should have all that is left over, after the other parties have been satisfied. Shareholders are given just enough of a return to provide capital, suppliers are given just enough to supply raw materials and so on.

Standing somewhere in the middle are those keen on a balanced stakeholder approach. Here the (often conflicting) interests of each of the claimants are somehow maximised but within the constraints set by the necessity to compromise in order to provide a fair return to the other stakeholders.

Some possible objectives

A firm can choose from an infinitely long list of possible objectives. Some of these will appear noble and easily justified; others remain hidden, implicit, embarrassing, even subconscious. The following represent some of the most frequently encountered.

- *Achieving a target market share* In some industrial sectors to achieve a high share of the market gives high rewards. These may be in the form of improved profitability, survival chances or status. Quite often the winning of a particular market share is set as an objective because it acts as a proxy for other, more profound objectives, such as generating the maximum returns to shareholders. On other occasions matters can get out of hand and there is an obsessive pursuit of market share with only a thin veneer of shareholder wealth espousement.

- *Keeping employee agitation to a minimum* Here, return to the organisation's owners is kept to a minimum necessary level. All surplus resources are directed to mollifying employees. Managers would be very reluctant to admit publicly that they place a high priority on reducing workplace tension, encouraging peace by appeasement and thereby, it is hoped, reducing their own stress levels, but actions tend to speak louder than words.

- *Survival* There are circumstances where the overriding objective becomes the survival of the firm. Severe economic or market shock may force managers to focus purely on short-term issues to ensure the continuance of the business. In firefighting they end up paying little attention to long-term growth and return to owners. However, this focus is clearly inadequate in the long run – there must be other goals. If survival were the only objective then putting all the firm's cash reserves into a bank savings account might be the best option. When managers say that their objective is survival, what they generally mean is the avoidance of large risks which endanger the firm's future. This may lead to a greater aversion to risk, and a rejection of activities that shareholders might wish the firm to undertake. Shareholders are in a position to diversify their investments: if one firm goes bankrupt they may be disappointed but they have other companies' shares to fall back on. However, the managers of that one firm may have the majority of their income, prestige and security linked to the continuing existence of that firm.

These managers may deliberately avoid high-risk/high-return investments and therefore deprive the owners of the possibility of large gains.

- *Creating an ever-expanding empire* This is an objective which is rarely discussed openly, but it seems reasonable to propose that some managers drive a firm forward, via organic growth or mergers, because of a desire to run an ever-larger enterprise. Often these motives become clearer with hindsight; when, for instance, a firm meets a calamitous end the post-mortem often reveals that profit and efficiency were given second place to growth. The volume of sales, number of employees or overall stock market value of the firm have a much closer correlation with senior executive salaries, perks and status than do returns to shareholder funds. This may motivate some individuals to promote growth.

- *Maximisation of profit* This is a much more acceptable objective, although not everyone would agree that maximisation of profit should be the firm's purpose.

- *Maximisation of long-term shareholder wealth* While many commentators concentrate on profit maximisation, finance experts are aware of a number of drawbacks of profit. The maximisation of the returns to shareholders in the long term is considered to be a superior goal. We look at the differences between profit maximisation and wealth maximisation later.

This list of possible objectives can easily be extended but it is not possible within the scope of this book to examine each of them. Suffice it to say, there can be an enormous variety of objectives and significant potential for conflict and confusion. We have to introduce some sort of order.

The assumed objective for finance

The company should make investment and financing decisions with the aim of maximising long-term shareholder wealth. Throughout the remainder of this book we will assume that the firm gives primacy of purpose to the wealth of shareholders. This assumption is made mainly on practical grounds, but there are respectable theoretical justifications too.

The practical reason

If one may assume that the decision-making agents of the firm (managers) are acting in the best interests of shareholders then decisions on such matters as which investment projects to undertake, or which method of financing to use, can be made much more simply. If the firm has a multiplicity of objectives, imagine the difficulty in deciding whether to introduce a new, more efficient machine to produce the firm's widgets, where the new machine will both be more labour efficient (thereby creating redundancies) and eliminate the need to buy from one half of the firm's suppliers. If one focuses solely on the benefits to shareholders, a clear decision can be made. This entire book is about decision-making tools to aid those choices. These range from whether to produce a component in-house, to whether to take over another company. If for each decision scenario we have to contemplate a number of different objectives or some vague balance of stakeholder interests, the task is going to be much more complex. Once the basic decision-making frameworks are understood within the tight confines of shareholder wealth maximisation, we can allow for complications caused by the modification of this assumption. For instance, shareholder wealth maximisation is clearly not the only consideration motivating actions of organisations such as the Co-operative Group, with publicly stated ethical principles and a goal of benefiting its members. The John Lewis Partnership has been a very successful employee-owned company, but recognises the need for a rational financial decision-making framework with a lot of power given to the Board and the executive directors – *see* **Exhibit 1.2**.

The theoretical reasons

The 'contractual theory' views the firm as a network of contracts, actual and implicit, which specifies the roles to be played by various participants in the organisation. For instance, the workers make both an explicit (employment contract) and an implicit (show initiative, reliability, etc.) deal with the firm to provide their services in return for salary and other benefits, and suppliers deliver necessary inputs in return for a known payment. Each party has well-defined rights and pay-offs. Most of the participants bargain for a limited risk and a fixed pay-off. Banks, for

Exhibit 1.2

John Lewis: trouble in store

by Michael Skapinker and Andrea Felsted

Joanne Griffiths has come from St Albans to do some shopping. "I like John Lewis a lot," she says. "Everyone seems to be very civilised." She knows the staff own the company. "They have a vested interest," she says.

John Lewis, founded in 1864 is one of the UK's best-loved companies. In the past year, it was named most admired British company for honesty and trust in an Ipsos Mori survey. It regularly comes at or near the top of customer satisfaction surveys. It sees itself, and is widely seen, as courteous, organised, high-quality but good value.

It is the UK's largest employee-owned business and one of the most successful in the world. Its central purpose is painted on the wall of the Cambridge branch as you walk up the stairs from what, in any other company, would be the staff entrance. Here it is the partners' entrance. The 93,800 people who work in the organisation are called partners.

Managers remind you of the partnership's purpose whenever they talk about the business. They recite it reverentially, parsing its component phrases. "The partnership's ultimate purpose is the happiness of all its members through their worthwhile and satisfying employment in a successful business."

Many of the John Lewis partners are happy enough to stay for decades. Some wear badges showing their last decade of completed service: a "10" badge or a "20". David Mayo wears a "50" badge. . . . he remembers a sign in his early days that said "The customer is always right". But the partners are not there principally for the customers. The partners are there to be happy — and their happiness comes from working in a business that is successful because you, the customer, are so pleased with the quality and the

service the partners provide. Except the partners' happiness has taken a dip. In this year's confidential online survey, 71 per cent of those who responded said they were satisfied with their jobs, down a percentage point from last year, and 81 per cent said John Lewis was a good place to work, down from 86 per cent. To most employers, these would be outstanding results. But this is not a company owned by outside shareholders or a distant founding family. This is a partnership — and 29 per cent, nearly one-third, were not satisfied working at the company they owned.

Charlie Mayfield, chairman: "I think people sometimes view the partnership as some land of milk and honey where nothing bad ever happens," he says of staff complaints. "And it always makes me smile in a wry way because it really, really does a disservice to the vigorous and constant debate that goes on within the partnership about how we're performing and where we need to do better. This is a very self-critical organisation and that's actually an enormous strength."

John Lewis's democratic structures hold the top managers to account, he says. The chairman is appointed by his predecessor but partners elect five members of the 15-member partnership board, which approves big policy decisions, and they vote for 66 members of the 85-member partnership council, which holds the chairman to account. "Fundamentally, we own this business and so we're all concerned about how it's performing," Mayfield says. "That sometimes makes for slightly uncomfortable times but, much more importantly, it's a strength which ensures that we don't get complacent and sit back and think we're very clever and we've got it all."

FT *Financial Times,* 16 October 2015.
All Rights Reserved.

example, when they lend to a firm, often strenuously try to reduce risk by making sure that the firm is generating sufficient cash flow to repay, that there are assets that can be seized if the loan is not repaid. The bankers' bargain, like that of many of the parties, is a low-risk one and so, the argument goes, they should be rewarded with just the bare minimum for them to provide their service to the firm. Shareholders, on the other hand, are asked to put money into the business at high risk. The deal here is, 'You give us your £10,000 nest egg that you need for your retirement and we, the directors of the firm, do not promise that you will receive a dividend or even see your capital again. We will try our hardest to produce a return on your money but we cannot give any guarantees. Sorry.' Thus the firm's owners are exposed to the possibilities that the firm may become bankrupt and all will be lost. Because of this unfair balance of risk between the different potential claimants on a firm's resources it seems reasonable that the owners should be entitled to any surplus returns which result after all the other parties have been satisfied.

Another theoretical reason hinges on the practicalities of operating in a free market system. In such a capitalist system, it is argued, if a firm chooses to reduce returns to shareholders because, say, it wishes to direct more of the firm's surplus to the workers, then this firm will find it difficult to survive. Some shareholders will sell their shares and invest in other firms more orientated towards their benefit. In the long run those individuals who do retain their shares may be amenable to a take-over bid from a firm which does concentrate on shareholder wealth creation. The acquirer will antici-pate being able to cut costs, not least by lowering the returns to labour. In the absence of a takeover the company would be unable to raise more finance from shareholders and this might result in slow growth and liquidity problems and possibly corporate death, throwing all employees out of work.

For over 200 years it has been argued that society is best served by businesses focusing on returns to the owner. Adam Smith (1776) expressed the argument very effectively:

> The businessman by directing . . . industry in such a manner as its produce may be of the greatest value, intends only his own gain, and he is in this, as in many other cases, led by an invisible hand to promote an end which was no part of his intention. Nor is it always the worse for society that it was no part of it. By pursuing his own interest he frequently promotes that of the society more effectually than when he really intends to promote it. I have never known much good done by those who affected to trade for the public good. It is an affectation, indeed, not very common among merchants.
>
> *Source*: Adam Smith, *The Wealth of Nations,* 1776, p. 400.

Adam Smith's objection to businessmen affecting to trade for the public good is echoed in Michael Jensen's writings in which he attacks the stakeholder approach (and its derivative, the Balanced Scorecard of Kaplan and Norton (1996)). His main worry is the confusion that results from having a multiplicity of targets to aim for, but he also takes a sideswipe at managers who are able to use the smokescreen of the stakeholder approach to cloak their actions in pursuit of benefits for themselves, or their pet 'socially beneficial' goals:

> Stakeholder theory effectively leaves managers and directors unaccountable for their steward-ship of the firm's resources . . . [it] plays into the hands of managers by allowing them to pursue their own interests at the expense of the firm's financial claimants and society at large. It allows managers and directors to devote the firm's resources to their own favorite causes – the environment, arts, cities, medical research – without being held accountable . . . it is not surprising that stakeholder theory receives substantial support from them.
>
> *Source*: Jensen, 2001.

However, Jensen goes on to say that companies cannot create shareholder value if they ignore important constituencies. They must have good relationships with customers, employees, sup-pliers, government and so on. This is a form of corporate social responsibility (CSR), within an overall framework of shareholder wealth maximisation. (Some of the CSR officers, consultants and departments take this a stage further to a belief that the firm must balance all the stakeholder interests to fulfil its social role – something Jensen disagrees with.) **Exhibit 1.3** illustrates one of the outcomes of the pressure applied by shareholders, who, despite being keenly interested in the returns generated from the shares they hold, nevertheless want companies to act responsibly with regard to educating the poorest, climate change, access by African malaria patients to medicines, etc. They are acutely aware of reputational risk, the potential backlash against 'heartless capital-ists', and litigation, but there are more positive reasons for the shift: people working within organ-isations are more committed if they feel the firm is 'a force for good in the world'. This is a way to attract and retain good staff, leading to improved business performance. A similar positive opinion about the firm can be generated in the minds of customers, encouraging sales.

Also, simply to tell people to maximise shareholder value may not be enough to motivate them to deliver value. They must be turned on by a vision or a strategy, e.g. to put a PC on every desk, to produce a drug to cure AIDs or to build a state-of-the-art aeroplane. Shareholder value can measure how successful you are, but it does not create superior vision or strategy – you need additional (but subsidiary) goals and measures.

Exhibit 1.3

Fortune 500 companies spend more than $15bn on corporate responsibility

by: Alison Smith

US and UK companies in the Fortune Global 500 spend $15.2bn a year on corporate social responsibility (CSR) activities, according to the first report to quantify this spending.

The research, carried out by economic consulting firm EPG, found that there was a clear difference in how US and British companies approached CSR.

In-kind donations, such as donating free drugs to health programmes or giving free software to universities, accounted for 71 per cent of the $11.95bn US spending on CSR.

Oracle, for example, which is one of the biggest CSR spenders, grants its software to secondary schools, colleges and universities in about 100 countries.

Cash contributions were just 16 per cent of the US total, with employee involvement and fundraising making up the remaining 13 per cent.

In the UK, while donating goods and services in kind was the largest component of the $3.25bn CSR activity, it totalled just 46 per cent of the total. Employee volunteering and fundraising made up 34 per cent and cash contributions 20 per cent.

Life assurance group Prudential involved employee volunteers in delivering an education programme to children in an impoverished community in central Jakarta.

Drugs companies are particularly prominent in CSR activity, with Merck and Johnson & Johnson being among the six groups providing almost two-thirds of the US CSR spend, while London-listed AstraZeneca and GlaxoSmithKline were two of the four companies accounting for more than three-quarters of the British total.

The findings will give fresh impetus to the debate about how far companies can persuade investors to see the value in CSR activity.

A survey last year of 1,000 chief executives by the UN Global Compact and Accenture, the consultancy, suggested that the landscape had become harsher. In 2013, 37 per cent of bosses said the lack of a clear link to business value was a critical factor in deterring them from faster action on sustainability – about twice the number who had cited the failure to identify such a link back in 2007. Mr Ioannou says there can be a wide range of investor reaction to sustainability initiatives, but sees some grounds for encouragement.

"Transient investors may not care, but long-term shareholders increasingly see environmental and social governance as a key indicator in terms of investment.

"Back in the 1990s, analysts might put a "sell" recommendation on companies with a strong CSR rating as they saw it as wasting investors' money. But that negative impact has been neutralised in more recent years, and some analysts now view CSR activity more positively."

Mr Pota argues that provided CSR spending is aligned to the company's business model, investors can see it is a matter of enlightened self-interest. "It's a matter of how you articulate it to shareholders," he says, adding that talking about it in terms of "global citizenship and sustainability" can help investors appreciate its value

John Kay also points out that firms going directly for 'shareholder value' may actually do less well for shareholders than those that focus on vision and excellence first and find themselves shareholder wealth maximisers in an oblique way. He argues that Boeing, in the 1990s, sacrificed its vision of being a company always on the cutting edge of commercial plane design, breaking through technological and marketplace barriers. This reduced the vibrancy of the pioneering spirit of the organisation, as it refocused on short-term financial performance measures – *see* **Exhibit 1.4.** However, it is possible to argue that Boeing's managers in the 1990s were not, in fact, shareholder wealth maximisers because they forgot the crucial 'long-term' focus. Being daring

Exhibit 1.4

Forget how the crow flies

If you want to go in one direction, the best route may involve going in the other. Paradoxical as it sounds, goals are more likely to be achieved when pursued indirectly. So the most profitable companies are not the most profit-oriented, and the happiest people are not those who make happiness their main aim. The name of this idea? Obliquity

By John Kay

. . . I once said that Boeing's grip on the world civil aviation market made it the most powerful market leader in world business. Bill Allen was chief executive from 1945 to 1968, as the company created its dominant position. He said that his spirit and that of his colleagues was to eat, breathe, and sleep the world of aeronautics. 'The greatest pleasure life has to offer is the satisfaction that flows from participating in a difficult and constructive undertaking', he explained . . .

The company's largest and riskiest project was the development of the 747 jumbo jet. When a non-executive director asked about the expected return on investment, he was brushed off: there had been some studies, he was told, but the manager concerned couldn't remember the results.

It took only 10 years for Boeing to prove me wrong in asserting that its market position in civil aviation was impregnable. The decisive shift in corporate culture followed the acquisition of its principal US rival, McDonnell Douglas, in 1997. The transformation was exemplified by the CEO, Phil Condit. The company's previous preoccupation with meeting 'technological challenges of supreme magnitude' would, he told Business Week, now have to change. 'We are going into a value-based environment where unit cost, return on investment and shareholder return are the measures by which you'll be judged. That's a big shift.'

The company's senior executives agreed to move from Seattle, where the main production facilities were located, to Chicago. More importantly, the more focused business reviewed risky investments in new civil projects with much greater scepticism. The strategic decision was to redirect resources towards projects for the US military that involved low financial risk. Chicago had the advantage of being nearer to Washington, where government funds were dispensed.

So Boeing's civil order book today lags behind that of Airbus, the European consortium whose aims were not initially commercial but which has, almost by chance, become a profitable business. . . . And what was the market's verdict on the company's performance in terms of unit cost, return on investment and shareholder return? Boeing stock, $48 when Condit took over, rose to $70 as he affirmed the commitment to shareholder value; by the time of his enforced resignation in December 2003 it had fallen to $38 . . .

At Boeing, the attempt to focus on simple, well defined objectives proved less successful than management with a broader, more comprehensive conception of objectives . . .

Obliquity gives rise to the profit-seeking paradox: the most profitable companies are not the most profit-oriented. Boeing illustrates how a greater focus on shareholder returns was self-defeating in its own narrow terms . . .

Collins and Porras compared the philosophy of George Merck ('We try never to forget that medicine is for the people. It is not for the profits. The profits follow, and if we have remembered that, they have never failed to appear. The better we have remembered it, the larger they have been') with that of John McKeen of Pfizer ('So far as humanly possible, we aim to get profit out of everything we do').

The individuals who are most successful at making money are not those who are most interested in making money. This is not surprising. The principal route to great wealth is the creation of a successful business, and building a successful business demands exceptional talents and hard work. There is no reason to think these characteristics are associated with greed and materialism: rather the opposite. People who are obsessively interested in money are drawn to get-rich-quick schemes rather than to business opportunities, and when these schemes come off, as occasionally they do, they retire to their villas in the sun ...

Although we crave time for passive leisure, people engaged in watching television reported low levels of contentment. Csikszentmihalyi's systematic finding is that the activities that yield the highest for satisfaction with life require the successful performance of challenging tasks.

(Also see Kay, J. (2010) *Obliquity*, Profile Books.)

FT   John Kay, *Financial Times Magazine*, 17 January 2004, pp. 17–21. Reproduced with kind permission of the *Financial Times*.

and at the cutting edge may be risky, but it often leads to the highest long-term shareholder wealth. Concentrating on short-term financial goals and presenting these as shareholder wealth-maximising actions can lead to slow pace and market irrelevance. So, being too fastidious in requiring immediately visible and quantifiable returns in an uncertain world can result in the rejection of extremely valuable projects that require a leap into the unknown by a team of enthusiasts. Where would Google be today if, when it was starting out, it had required a positive number popping out of a rigorous financial analysis of the prospects for its search engine when the internet was relatively primitive? John Mackey, founder of Whole Foods Market, is an obliquity man – *see* **Exhibit 1.5.**

In an interview in 2003 Milton Friedman focused on the main benefit of encouraging businesses to pursue high returns for owners. He said that this results in the best allocation of investment capital among competing industries and product lines. This is good for society because consumers end up with more of what they want because scarce investment money is directed to the best uses, producing the optimum mix of goods and services. 'The self-interest of employees in retaining their jobs will often conflict with this overriding objective.' He went on:

> the best system of corporate governance is one that provides the best incentives to use capital efficiently. . . . You want control . . . in the hands of those who are residual recipients [i.e. shareholders bear the residual risk when a company fails] because they are the ones with the direct interest in using the capital of the firm efficiently.

Source: Simon London, *Financial Times Magazine*, 7 June 2003, p. 13.

Exhibit 1.5

John Mackey, Whole Foods Market

by: Andrew Hill

In his Patagonia-brand fleece, purple shirt and trainers, you might easily guess that 59-year-old Mr Mackey had devoted his hippy-era sense of purpose to three and a half decades running just the natural foods store he and his girlfriend set up in Austin, Texas, after college. But he went far further. That small store was the precursor to what is now a global network, still expanding, of nearly 350 shops – cornucopian temples, stuffed with a variety of carefully sourced and lovingly displayed produce – in the US, Canada and the UK, that employ 80,000 staff.

An increasing amount of his energy is also feeding into "conscious capitalism", a non-profit "movement", in Mr Mackey's words, to persuade businesses to adopt "a higher purpose" and create value for suppliers, staff and local communities, not just shareholders.

Critics, who include some devotees of the shops, find it hard to stomach the contradiction between a voraciously acquisitive and highly profitable Nasdaq-listed retailer with annual sales of $12bn and an idealistic philosophy that insists profit should be only one of several goals of business. But Mr Mackey

▶

Exhibit 1.5 *(continued)*

insists "conscious" businesses grow faster, are more efficient and outperform their less self-aware peers because they foster greater loyalty among employees, suppliers and customers. In any case, he has long made clear that contradictions are part of his, and human, nature; and in person he comes across as both a visionary and a pragmatist. On a visit to Whole Foods' largest store, in London's Kensington, he talks about "trying to do something that helps and contributes, so that humanity and this planet can continue to evolve in a constructive way".

As for profits, he and co-author Raj Sisodia explain in their book Conscious Capitalism that they provide "the capital our world needs to innovate and progress – no profits, no progress". For Mr Mackey, size is a real asset in his quest. He reacts strongly to the suggestion companies such as Whole

Foods risk losing their values as they get larger: "It's not true: it's the exact opposite. People that want to believe that do so because they think big corporations are evil . . . If you have a mental model that says big corporations are fundamentally greedy and selfish and exploitative, you don't really want to have an exception to that model. It's much easier to say, yes, Whole Foods has been corrupted. But the fact is, it's exactly the opposite: we are more conscious as an organisation, we have a much more positive impact in the world today than we did 10 years ago."

Mr Mackey continues to have faith in the group's decentralised structure: self-managed teams – a dozen in a big store such as Kensington – that "elect" new members by a two-thirds vote, share productivity gains and regulate behaviour within the team.

One final and powerful reason for advancing shareholders' interests above all others (subject to the rules of the game) is very simple: they own the firm and therefore deserve any surplus it produces. The Companies Act 2006 reinforces this by stating that directors' primary duty is to promote the success of the company for the benefit of its members, that is, the shareholders. Yet in the fulfilment of that duty directors should have regard to the interests of employees, suppliers, customers, the environment and corporate reputation. Thus in closing a factory, say, the interests of shareholders trump those of employees, but the latter concerns should not be completely ignored. *The Economist* presents a series of arguments in favour of shareholder supremacy in **Exhibit 1.6.**

Exhibit 1.6

The good company

Companies today are exhorted to be 'socially responsible'. What, exactly, does this mean?

It will no longer do for a company to go quietly about its business, telling no lies and breaking no laws, selling things that people want, and making money. That is so passé. Today, all companies, but especially big ones, are enjoined from every side to worry less about profits and be socially responsible instead. Surprisingly, perhaps, these demands have elicited a willing, not to say avid, response in enlightened boardrooms everywhere. Companies at every opportunity now pay elaborate obeisance to the principles of corporate social responsibility. They have CSR officers, CSR consultants, CSR

departments, and CSR initiatives coming out of their ears. A good thing, too, you might think. About time. What kind of idiot or curmudgeon would challenge the case for businesses to behave more responsibly? Thank you for asking.

Cynics and believers

The practices that caring, progressive CEOs mention when speaking at conferences on CSR come in all shapes and sizes. Treat your employees well; encourage loyalty among your customers and suppliers; avoid investing in 'unethical' industries, or in countries where workers are paid low wages or denied decent benefits; take care to save energy and recycle used envelopes; and so on. The range of such policies makes it hazardous to generalise. Some of them advance the interests of shareholders and of the wider world as well; others make everyone, except the office bureaucrats paid to dream them up, worse off. Motives vary too. Some CSR advocates are cynics: they pay lip service to the idea but are chuckling quietly. Others are true believers, born-again champions of a kinder, gentler capitalism.

The one thing that all the nostrums of CSR have in common is that they are based on a faulty – and dangerously faulty – analysis of the capitalist system they are intended to redeem. Admittedly, CSR is now so well entrenched and amply funded that to complain about it may be pointless. We are concerned that it may even be a socially irresponsible use of scarce newsprint. Nonetheless, if businessmen had a clearer understanding of the CSR mindset and its defects, they would be better at their jobs and everybody else would be more prosperous.

Simply put, advocates of CSR work from the premise that unadorned capitalism fails to serve the public interest. The search for profit, they argue, may be a regrettable necessity in the modern world, a sad fact of life if there is to be any private enterprise. But the problem is that the profits of private enterprise go exclusively to shareholders. What about the public good? Only if corporations recognise their obligations to society – to 'stakeholders' other than the owners of the business – will that broader social interest be advanced. Often, governments can force such obligations on companies, through taxes and regulation. But that does not fully discharge the enlightened company's debt to society. For that, one requires CSR.

This is wrong. The goal of a well-run company may be to make profits for its shareholders, but merely in doing that – provided it faces competition in its markets, behaves honestly and obeys the law – the company, without even trying, is doing good works. Its employees willingly work for the company in exchange for wages; the transaction makes them better off. Its customers willingly pay for the company's products; the transaction makes them better off also. All the while, for strictly selfish reasons, well-run companies will strive for friendly long-term relations with employees, suppliers and customers. There is no need for selfless sacrifice when it comes to stakeholders. It goes with the territory.

Thus, the selfish pursuit of profit serves a social purpose. And this is putting it mildly. The standard of living people in the West enjoy today is due to little else but the selfish pursuit of profit. It is a point that Adam Smith emphasised in 'The Wealth of Nations': 'It is not from the benevolence of the butcher, the brewer, or the baker, that we expect our dinner, but from their regard to their own interest.' This is not the fatal defect of capitalism, as CSR-advocates appear to believe; it is the very reason capitalism works.

Maybe so, those advocates might reply, but perhaps the system would work even better if there were a bit more benevolence in the boardroom and a bit less self-interest. In some cases, that might be so, but in general (as Smith also noted) one should be wary of businessmen proclaiming their benevolence. A question to ask of all outbreaks of corporate goodness is, who is paying? Following the Indian Ocean tsunami, many companies made generous donations to charities helping the victims. There could be no worthier cause – but keep in mind that, in the case of public companies, the managers authorising those donations were giving other people's money, not their own. Philanthropy at others' expense, even in a cause as good as that one, is not quite the real thing.

All things considered, there is much to be said for leaving social and economic policy to governments. They, at least, are accountable to voters. Managers lack the time for such endeavours, or should do. Lately they have found it a struggle even to discharge their obligations to shareholders, the people who are paying their wages. If they want to make the world a better place – a commendable aim, to be sure – let them concentrate for the time being on that.

This is not the place to advocate one philosophical approach or another which is applicable to all organisations at all times. Many organisations are clearly not shareholder wealth maximisers and are quite comfortable with that. Charities, government departments and other non-profit organisations are fully justified in emphasising a different set of values to those espoused by the commercial firm. The reader is asked to be prepared for two levels of thought when using this book.

While it focuses on corporate shareholder wealth decision making, it may be necessary to make small or large modifications to be able to apply the same frameworks and theories to organisations with different goals.

However, beware of organisations that try to balance a number of objectives. Take, for example, football clubs that have floated on the stock market. They have at least two parties to satisfy: (i) shareholders looking for good return on their savings: (ii) fans looking for more spending on players and lower ticket prices. It is very difficult to satisfy both – hence the dramatic tensions and suspicions at so many clubs.

What is shareholder wealth?

Maximising wealth can be defined as maximising purchasing power. The way in which an enterprise enables its owners to indulge in the pleasures of purchasing and consumption is by paying them dividends. The promise of a flow of cash in the form of dividends is what prompts investors to sacrifice immediate consumption and hand over their savings to a management team through the purchase of shares. Shareholders are interested in a flow of dividends over a long time horizon and not necessarily in a quick payback. Take the electronics giant Philips: it could raise vast sums for short-term dividend payouts by ceasing all research and development (R&D) and selling off surplus sites. But this would not maximise shareholder wealth because, by retaining funds within the business, it is believed that new products and ideas, springing from the R&D programme, will produce much higher dividends in the future. Maximising shareholder wealth means maximising the flow of dividends to shareholders *through time* – there is a long-term perspective.

Profit maximisation is not the same as shareholder wealth maximisation

Profit is a concept developed by accountants to aid decision making, one decision being to judge the quality of stewardship shown over the owner's funds. The accountant has to take what is a continuous process, a business activity stretching over many years, and split this into accounting periods of, say, a year, or six months. To some extent this exercise is bound to be artificial and fraught with problems. There are many reasons why accounting profit may not be a good proxy for shareholder wealth. Here are five of them:

- *Prospects* Imagine that there are two firms that have reported identical profits but one firm is more highly valued by its shareholders than the other. One possible reason for this is that recent profit figures fail to reflect the relative potential of the two firms. The stock market will give a higher share value to the company which shows the greater future growth outlook. Perhaps one set of managers has chosen a short-term approach and raised profits in the near term but have sacrificed long-term prospects. One way of achieving this is to raise prices and slash marketing spend – over the subsequent year profits might be boosted as customers are unable to switch suppliers immediately. Over the long term, however, competitors will respond and profits will fall.

- *Risk* Again two firms could report identical historic profit figures and have future prospects which indicate that they will produce the same average annual returns. However, one firm's returns are subject to much greater variability and so there will be years of losses and, in a particularly bad year, the possibility of bankruptcy. **Exhibit 1.7** shows two firms which have identical average profit but Volatile Joe's profit is subject to much greater risk than that of Steady Eddie. Shareholders are likely to value the firm with stable income flows more highly than one with high risk.

- *Accounting problems* Drawing up a set of accounts is not as scientific and objective as some people try to make out. There is plenty of scope for judgement, guesswork or even cynical manipulation. Imagine the difficulty facing the company accountant and auditors of a clothes retailer when trying to value a dress which has been on sale for six months. Let us suppose the dress cost the firm £50. Perhaps this should go into the balance sheet and then the profit and loss account will not be affected. But what if the store manager says that he can sell that dress

Exhibit 1.7   Two firms with identical average profits but different risk levels

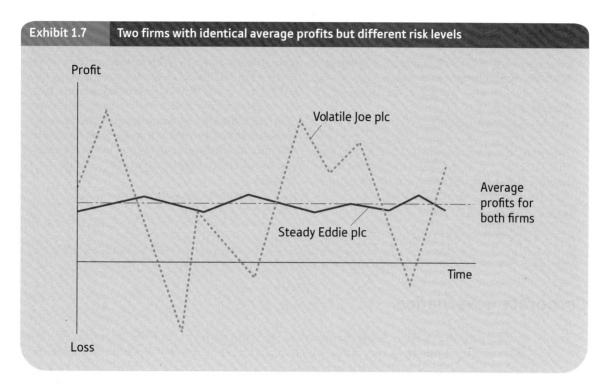

only if it is reduced to £30, and contradicting him the managing director says that if a little more effort was made £40 could be achieved? Which figure is the person who drafts the financial accounts going to take? Profits can vary significantly depending on a multitude of small judgements like this.

- *Communication* Investors realise and accept that buying a share is risky. However, they like to reduce their uncertainty and nervousness by finding out as much as they can about the firm. If the firm is reluctant to tell shareholders about such matters as the origin of reported profits, then investors generally will tend to avoid those shares. Fears are likely to arise in the minds of poorly informed investors: did the profits come from the most risky activities and might they therefore disappear next year? Is the company being used to run guns to unsavoury regimes abroad? The senior executives of large quoted firms spend a great deal of time explaining their strategies, sources of income and future investment plans to the large institutional shareholders to make sure that these investors are aware of the quality of the firm and its prospects. Firms that ignore the importance of communication and image in the investment community may be doing their shareholders a disservice as the share price might fall.

- *Additional capital* Profits can be increased simply by making use of more shareholders' money. If shareholders inject more money into the company or the firm merely retains profits (which belong to shareholders) their future profits can rise, but the *return* on shareholders' money may fall to less than what is available elsewhere for the same level of risk. This is shareholder wealth destructive. For more on this see Chapter 14.

Exhibit 1.8 shows what some leading European companies say about their objectives.

Exhibit 1.8

What companies state as their objective

'We are focussed on returning to growth in our chosen therapy areas through a science-led innovation strategy. This strategy is based on investing in three therapy areas, building a strong and balanced portfolio of primary care and speciality care medicines, and accelerating key R&D

▶

Exhibit 1.8 *(continued)*

programmes. It also involves engaging in targeted business development and leveraging our strong global commercial presence, particularly in Emerging Markets.'

AstraZeneca Annual Report 2015

'We focus on speciality food ingredients [and] bulk ingredients. . . .to deliver growing earnings, improving cash flow and rigorous capital allocation, and create value for shareholders.'

Tate and Lyle Annual Report 2016

'Our strategy seeks to reinforce our position as a leader in the oil and gas industry, while helping to meet global energy demand in a responsible way. We aim to balance growth with returns, by growing our cash flow and delivering competitive returns through economic cycles, to finance a competitive dividend and fund future growth. Safety and environmental and social responsibility are at the heart of our activities.'

Royal Dutch Shell Annual Report 2015

Author's note: This section took longer to complete than expected because most annual reports examined failed to state any objective for the organisation so the search for something to quote was extended. Perhaps this is the most telling fact to emerge!

Corporate governance

In theory the shareholders, being the owners of the firm, control its activities. In practice, the large modern corporation has a very diffuse and fragmented set of shareholders and control often lies in the hands of directors. It is extremely difficult to marshal thousands of shareholders, each with a small stake in the business, to push for change. Thus in many firms we have what is called a separation, or a divorce, of ownership and control. In times past the directors would usually be the same individuals as the owners. Today, however, less than 1% of the shares of most of the largest quoted firms is owned by the directors.

The separation of ownership and control raises worries that the management team may pursue objectives attractive to them, but which are not necessarily beneficial to the shareholders – this is termed 'managerialism' or 'managementism' – for example, raising their own pay or perks, expanding their empire, avoiding risky projects, boosting short-term results at the expense of long-term performance. This conflict is an example of the principal–agent problem. The principals (the shareholders) have to find ways of ensuring that their agents (the managers) act in their interests. This means incurring costs, 'agency costs', to (a) monitor managers' behaviour, and (b) create incentive schemes and controls for managers to encourage the pursuit of shareholders' wealth maximisation. These costs arise in addition to the agency cost of the loss of wealth caused by the extent to which prevention measures do not work and managers continue to pursue non-shareholder wealth goals.

Corporate governance means the system by which companies are managed and controlled. Its main focus is on the responsibilities and obligations placed on the executive directors and the non-executive directors, and on the relationships between the firm's owners, the board of directors and the top tier of managers. The interaction between these groups leads to the defining of the corporate objective, the placing of constraints on managerial behaviour and the setting of targets and incentive payments based on achievement.

The board of directors has the responsibility of overseeing the company, acting as a check on managerialism, so that shareholders' best interests are appropriately prioritised. The board sets company-wide policy and strategic direction, leaving the executive directors to manage day-to-day activities. It also decides who will be an executive director (subject to shareholder vote) and sets their pay. In addition, the board oversees the reporting of accounting results to shareholders. The board should also take a keen interest in the ethical behaviour of senior managers.

Annual general meeting

The board is expected to organise an annual general meeting (AGM) at which shareholders are encouraged by the directors to engage in dialogue with the directors, and can vote to change the board of directors if they are dissatisfied. Proxy votes may be assigned if a shareholder cannot attend, i.e. they ask someone else, usually the chairman of the company, to vote in a particular way on their behalf. In theory the shareholders can strongly influence the strategic and operational decisions. However, this power is usually weakened:

- The cost of attending a meeting (or even sending in a proxy form) outweighs the benefit for many shareholders, leading to many (most) votes being unused. (As an investor I attend AGMs, but I'm often the only shareholder there, other than company staff – Glen Arnold.)

- Many fund managers do not take their 'ownership' of stakes in a corporation seriously, and given that most shares quoted on public stock markets are now owned by institutional investors (e.g. pension funds, insurance funds), when faced with the issue of what to do with a poor board of directors and senior management, rather than acting to remove them, most fund managers find it easier simply to sell the shares and move on.

Corporate governance regulations

There is a considerable range of legislation and other regulatory pressures designed to encourage directors to act in shareholders' interests. In the UK the Companies Act 2006 requires certain minimum standards of behaviour, as does the London Stock Exchange (LSE). For example, directors are forbidden to use their position to profit at the expense of shareholders, e.g. they cannot buy shares in their own company just before announcing unexpectedly high profits. There is the back-up of the financial industry regulator, the Financial Conduct Authority (FCA) and the Financial Reporting Council (FRC), an accounting body.

Following a number of financial scandals, guidelines of best practice in corporate governance were issued. These are now consolidated in the UK Corporate Governance Code, which is backed by the FCA, the LSE and the FRC.

Under the code, directors of companies with a premium listing[1] on the Main Market of the LSE are required to state in the annual report how the principles of the code have been applied. If the principles have not been followed they have to state why – the 'comply or explain' approach. The principles include:

- The board should include a balance of executive and non-executive directors (and in particular independent[2] non-executive directors) such that no individual or small group of individuals can dominate the board's decision taking. For large companies (the largest 350 on the LSE) at least half the board, excluding the chairman, should comprise non-executive directors determined by the board to be independent. Smaller companies should have at least two independent non-executive directors. The independent non-executive directors can act as a powerful counterweight to the executive directors. These directors are not full-time and not concerned with day-to-day management. They may be able to take a broader view than executive directors, who may become excessively focused on detail. The experienced individuals who become non-executive directors are not expected to be dependent on the director's fee for income and can therefore afford to be independently minded. They are expected to 'constructively challenge and help develop proposals on strategy . . . scrutinize the performance of management in meeting agreed goals and objectives and monitor the reporting of performance' (The UK Code at www.frc.org.uk, p. 9).

- No one individual on the board should be able to dominate and impose their will. The running of the board of directors (by a chairman) should be a separate responsibility conducted by a person who is not also responsible for running the business, i.e. the chief executive officer

---

1 A premium listing is the most rigorous requiring high levels of disclosure and behaviour – see Chapter 9 for more.

2 The board should determine whether the director is independent in character and judgement and whether there are relationships or circumstances which are likely to affect, or could appear to affect, the director's judgement. To be independent the non-executive directors generally should not, for example, be a customer, ex-employee, supplier, or a friend of the founding family or the chief executive.

(CEO) or managing director (MD). This is frequently ignored in practice, which is permitted, if a written justification is presented to shareholders.

- There should be transparency on directors' remuneration, requiring a remuneration committee consisting exclusively of non-executive directors, independent of management. No director should be involved in deciding his or her remuneration. A significant proportion of remuneration can be linked to corporate and individual performance.

- The procedure for the appointment of board directors should be formal (nomination committee), rigorous, objective (based on merit) and transparent (information on the terms and conditions made available). FTSE 350 company directors should be subject to annual elecion by shareholders. All other directors should be submitted for election at intervals of no more than three years (after nine years of service non-executives are required to be subject to annual elections).

- The audit committee (responsible for validating financial figures, e.g. by appointing effective external auditors, and for the system of corporate reporting, risk management and internal control principles) should consist exclusively of independent non-executive directors; otherwise the committee would not be able to act as a check and balance to the executive directors.

- Directors are required to communicate with shareholders, e.g. meetings arranged between major shareholders and directors or using the annual general meeting to explain the company's performance and encourage discussion.

The 'comply or explain' approach is in contrast to many other systems of regulation of corporate governance around the world – these are often strict rule-based systems with lawyers to the fore (e.g. Sarbanes–Oxley regulations in the US). The code specifically allows companies to deviate from the guideline, so long as this can be justified with reference to shareholder well-being: 'It is recognised that an alternative to following a provision [of the code] may be justified in particular circumstances if good governance can be achieved by other means. A condition of doing so is that the reasons for it should be explained clearly and carefully to shareholders, who may wish to discuss the position with the company and whose voting intentions may be influenced as a result' (The UK Code at www.frc.org.uk, p. 4). However, failure to comply or explain properly will result in suspension from the stock exchange. **Exhibit 1.9** discusses how small companies frequently do not comply, preferring to explain, even if poorly.

Exhibit 1.9

Juniors too must learn the lessons of good governance

By Kate Burgess

Now sit up, and pay attention, the outgoing headmistress of the school of good governance tells small companies. There is no excuse for sloppy financial reporting. And size is no defence, so junior companies can stop looking out of the window on the false assumption that the UK's corporate governance code does not apply to them.

There is a touch of exasperation in Lady Hogg's last annual report as the Financial Reporting Council's chairman on the quality of compliance with the UK's governance code.

On the whole, adherence to the code's comply-or-explain provisions has improved. Most companies, including the titches, put their directors up for annual re-election, for example.

But where companies do not comply, too many can't even come up with a decent dog-ate-my-homework excuse, says Baronness Hogg. "Many still struggle to articulate clearly why they have chosen to deviate from the code." Just because compliance levels have risen, doesn't mean explanations for not doing so should be worse, she says.

It is no surprise perhaps that the worst culprits are small companies. Their reporting is generally "less informative," says the FRC, and the quality noticeably lags behind FTSE 100 companies.

That is understandable – the juniors have more limited resources. However, size should not justify poor transparency, says Lady Hogg sternly.

The most common cause of non-compliance with the code is too few independent non-executive directors or Neds, according to Grant Thornton. A fifth of the smallest 150 companies in the UK's top 350 corporates did not meet code requirements that at least half of

board directors should be independent. That compares with 4 per cent of the FTSE 100.

Again, governance prefects acknowledge that companies in the nursery and infant school may find it harder to recruit Neds. That is why smaller companies below the FTSE 350 are only asked to have two independent Neds on their boards.

But companies could do much better explaining themselves. The FRC worries non-compliance on board balance is a symptom of poor succession planning. Companies, whatever their size, need to anticipate board changes, says headteacher.

To broaden understanding of corporate governance you could look at www.ecgi.org which displays corporate governance codes in a range of countries. There are various other (complementary) methods used to try to align the actions of senior managers with the interests of shareholders, that is, to achieve 'goal congruence':

- *Linking rewards to shareholder wealth improvements* A technique widely employed in industry is to grant directors and other senior managers share options. These permit managers to purchase shares at some date in the future at a price which is fixed now. If the share price rises significantly between the date when the option was granted and the date when the shares can be bought, the manager can make a fortune by buying at the pre-arranged price and then selling in the marketplace. For example, in 2019 managers might be granted the right to buy shares in 2024 at a price of £1.50. If the market price moves to, say, £2.30 in 2024, the managers can buy and then sell the shares, making a gain of 80p. The managers under such a scheme have a clear interest in achieving a rise in share price and thus congruence comes about to some extent. An alternative method is to allot shares to managers if they achieve certain performance targets, for example growth in earnings per share or return on assets. Many companies have long-term incentive plans (LTIPs) for senior executives which at the end of three years or more pay bonuses if certain targets are surpassed, e.g. share price rise or high profit achieved. **Exhibit 1.10** discusses share option schemes and other ways of encouraging managers to promote the interests of shareholders.

Exhibit 1.10

How to encourage managers to act more like owners

By Stefan Stern

What would your customers say if they could see your expenses claim? The abstemious can rest easy. But extravagant restaurant receipts, first-class travel and accommodation, huge taxi fares – such things might not endear you to the people you are supposed to be serving. You should expect a tough conversation

about the prices you charge if customers get the impression you are enjoying the high life with their money.

That is why smart business leaders advise their colleagues to imagine they are spending their own

▶

Exhibit 1.10 *(continued)*

money when they are out on company business. Act like an owner, the adage goes. Be responsible. Think before you splash the company's cash about.

This is a micro-level example of what has been called the 'principal-agent problem'. Even the most senior managers are not, usually, the owners of the business they are working for. It may not be easy for them to think and act like an owner. At the same time, can owners be confident that managers are working in the company's best interests and not simply pursuing their own selfish agenda?

This question was explored by two academics, Michael Jensen and William Meckling, in a famous 1976 paper, which popularised so-called agency theory. Their answer to the problem? Among other things, try to align the interests of managers and shareholders. Use share options to give managers 'skin in the game', a personal interest in the success – or failure – of the company. Incentives work: they should be deployed to get people working towards the same end.

There have been, to put it at its gentlest, regrettable unintended consequences to the spread of this theory. It turns out that the simple solution of share options does not solve the complicated problem of how to encourage and reward effective, responsible management.

For one thing, senior managers may not have the same time horizons as owners. A chief executive might reasonably calculate that he or she will be given no more than three or four years to run the business before their time is up. You would understand it if that CEO worked pretty hard to get the share price up fast in order to make those share options more valuable. And the longer-term consequences for the business in engineering such a rapid share price rise? Not necessarily the CEO's problem.

The shareholder base will, in any case, reflect a wide range of characters with varying priorities. There will be long-term institutional investors and hedge funds working in their own unique way. You can't easily be aligned with all of these people at the same time.

Prof Jensen conceded in 2002, in the wake of the dotcom crash, that the incentives he regarded as crucial could do terrible harm. 'In the bubble, the carrots (options) became managerial heroin, encouraging a focus on short-term prices with destructive long-term consequences,' he said. 'It also encouraged behaviour that actually reduced the value of some firms to their shareholders.'

Stewardship – steady, long-term leadership that may not be reflected in rapid rises in the share price – is harder to reward with remuneration schemes based on stock markets.

In an important critique published in 2004 ('Bad management theories are destroying good management practices'), Sumantra Ghoshal condemned agency theory as an example of all that was wrong with modern management. Amoral theories taught in business schools, he said, had 'actively freed their students from any sense of moral responsibility'. Agency theory served to convert 'collective pessimism about managers into realised pathologies in management behaviours'.

According to this critique, the theory seems to launch a cycle of distrust. Managers are knaves, out for themselves, who have to be tied in with share options. But managers who feel regarded in this way can become unmotivated and in the end untrustworthy. Why has executive pay exploded over the past 20 years? Partly, Prof Ghoshal suggested, because managers have sunk to reach the low expectations people have for them.

So is the idea of managers acting like owners a futile dream? Not necessarily. Drawing on pointers given to him by a former boss, Phil Gerbyshak, a management blogger, has posted some apparently humdrum but, in fact, sensible thoughts on how managers could live up to that goal (my paraphrasing):

- Always act professionally. You never know who is going to hear what you're saying or see what you're doing.

- Treat everyone you talk to with respect, regardless of their position. Nothing and nobody is beneath you.

- A little overtime won't hurt. Work until the job is done.

- If you're the last one in the room, turn out the light.

- Be on time for meetings. Time is money. Why would you waste time?

Less exciting, perhaps, than holding plenty of in-the-money options. But more likely to do long-term good to a business.

- *Sackings* The threat of being sacked with the accompanying humiliation and financial loss may encourage managers not to diverge too far from the shareholders' wealth path. However, this method is employed in extreme circumstances only. It is sometimes difficult to implement because of the difficulties of making a coordinated shareholder effort. It is made easier if the majority of directors are independent of the executives.

- *Selling shares and the takeover threat* Shareholders, particularly financial institutions, are often not prepared to put resources into monitoring and controlling all the hundreds of firms of which they own a part. Quite often their first response, if they observe that management is not acting in what they regard as their best interest, is to sell the share rather than intervene. This will result in a lower share price, making the raising of funds more difficult. It may also lower rewards to managers whose remuneration partly depends on the share price level. If this process continues the firm may become vulnerable to a merger bid by another group of managers, resulting in a loss of top management posts. Fear of being taken over can establish some sort of backstop position to prevent shareholder wealth considerations being totally ignored.

- *Information flow* The accounting profession, the stock exchange and the investing institutions have conducted a continuous battle to encourage or force firms to release more accurate, timely and detailed information concerning their operations. The quality of corporate accounts and annual reports has generally improved, as has the availability of other forms of information flowing to investors and analysts, such as company briefings and company announcements (which are available from financial websites, e.g. www.uk.advfn.com). All this helps to monitor firms, and identify early any wealth-destroying actions by wayward managers, but as a number of recent scandals have shown, matters are still far from perfect.

In some countries the interests of shareholders are often placed far below those of powerful people – *see* **Exhibit 1.11**. The shareholder with the largest percentage holding often exploits his/her dominant power, disadvantaging other shareholders. They can select their preferred board of directors, often resulting in a distortion of the firm's objective to benefit themselves. Rules and regulations are of limited value in countering the problem. As an investor in small companies that often come with dominant shareholders Glen Arnold finds the most effective approach is to assess the character of the key person(s), and only invest if satisfied on integrity, especially a sense of fairness, honour and duty to all shareholders.

Exhibit 1.11

Corporate malfeasance continues apace in Asia

By Jeremy Grant

Conflicts of interest, weak reporting standards, company boards packed with family insiders and outright fraud – Europe and the US have their fair share of corporate malfeasance but this has been a banner year for poor corporate governance in Asia.

You only have to look at the blow-up at Japan's Olympus, where this week three former executives at the camera company pleaded guilty to filing false financial reports in connection with a $1.7bn accounting fraud. In Malaysia an independent director is battling charges of insider dealing at Sime Darby, the palm oil producer. And even in supposedly squeaky clean Singapore a handful of Chinese companies listed on the exchange – so-called

S chips – have undergone special audits after questions were raised over basic governance failures.

Some of them have at least raised a smile. In one case an S-chip tried to claim it had lost all its records in a stolen lorry.

Now the region's annual corporate governance report card is out. With a few notable exceptions, you would struggle to give the region a grade of B minus.

In fact, things have slid backwards after years of gradual improvement – mainly in China and Indonesia – according to the report, by broker CLSA and the Asian Corporate Governance Association (ACGA).The report examined 864 listed companies in

▶

Exhibit 1.11 *(continued)*

11 countries, scoring them on things such as independence of boards (generally horrible) and the composition of audit committees (don't even go there).

Much of this has its roots in the fact that in many Asian businesses, the controlling shareholder is a family. About 40 per cent of companies in Taiwan, Hong Kong, Singapore and the Philippines have three or more family members sitting on the board. Generally, investors have faced issues ranging from relatively minor corporate transgressions to growing concerns about the reliability of financial statements and, at the extreme, outright fraud. Corporate governance can no longer be taken for granted, the report warns.

Six countries saw their scores fall or remain flat, while the rest saw only modest improvement. China was the worst performer, dragged down by deep structural problems including conflict between government agencies over the interest of the state versus minorities in key enterprises.

Persistent problems elsewhere include companies holding on to cash on their balance sheets, diluting returns to shareholders.

Jamie Allen, ACGA secretary-general, believes the "systemic quality" of corporate governance in Asia is gradually improving in spite of malfeasance and fraud. It is precisely those factors that spur regulators and investors to take governance more seriously, he says.

That may be true. But it is also true that there is scant incentive for companies to improve governance at a time when US and European investors are piling into the region.

This week it emerged that companies in Asia had issued a total of $57.4bn worth of bonds so far this year . . . Asian stock markets are among the world's top performers.

Much of the investment is coming from within Asia itself, where investors can be more forgiving of corporate governance weakness than someone sitting in the compliance department in New York. This means the outlook for any improvement in governance is surely pretty poor.

A chink of hope may come from Southeast Asia. The report noted that most of the markets with falling corporate governance ratings were in North Asia.

Yet Singapore has jumped ahead of Hong Kong in having an independent audit regulator.

Indonesia remains a black spot, with a woeful record on enforcement of securities regulation. Yet it and its regional peers should realise that there is a link between improved corporate governance and more predictable investment flows, and the long-term competitiveness of capital markets.

Looking north to China, where the picture is rather different, this starts to look like a competitive advantage for the Association of Southeast Asian Nations. It should seize that opportunity now.

 Financial Times, 25 September 2012.

Primitive and modern economies

A simple economy

Before we proceed to discuss the role of the financial manager and the part played by various financial institutions it is useful to gain an overview of the economy and the place of the financial system within society. To see the role of the financial sector in perspective it is, perhaps, of value to try to imagine a society without any financial services. Imagine how people would go about their daily business in the absence of either money or financial institutions. This sort of economy is represented in **Exhibit 1.12.** Here there are only two sectors in society. The business sector produces goods and services, making use of the resources of labour, land and commodities which are owned by the household sector. The household sector is paid with the goods and services produced by the business sector.

In this economy there is no money and therefore there are two choices open to the household sector upon receipt of the goods and services:

1   *Consumption* Commodities can be consumed now either by taking those specific items provided from the place of work and enjoying their consumption directly, or, under a barter system, by exchanging them with other households to widen the variety of consumption.

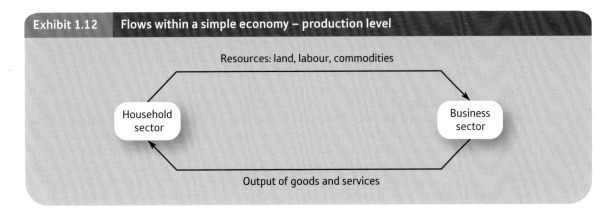

Exhibit 1.12 **Flows within a simple economy – production level**

Resources: land, labour, commodities

Household sector

Business sector

Output of goods and services

2 *Investment* Some immediate consumption could be forgone so that resources can be put into building assets which will produce a higher level of consumption in the future. For instance, a worker takes payment in the form of a plough so that in future years when he enters the productive (business) sector he can produce more food per acre.

The introduction of money

Under a barter system much time and effort is expended in searching out other households interested in trade. It quickly becomes apparent that a tool is needed to help make transactions more efficient. People will need something into which all goods and services received can be converted. That something would have to be small and portable, it would have to hold its value over a long period of time and have general acceptability. This will enable people to take the commodities given in exchange for, say, labour and then avoid the necessity of, say, carrying the bushels of wheat to market to exchange them for bricks. Instead money could be paid in exchange for labour, and money taken to the market to buy bricks. Various things have been used as a means of exchange ranging from cowry shells to cigarettes (in prisons particularly) but the most popular used to be a metal, usually gold or silver. (Now it is less tangible such as credit and debit card transactions.) The introduction of money into the system creates monetary as well as real flows of goods and services – *see* **Exhibit 1.13.**

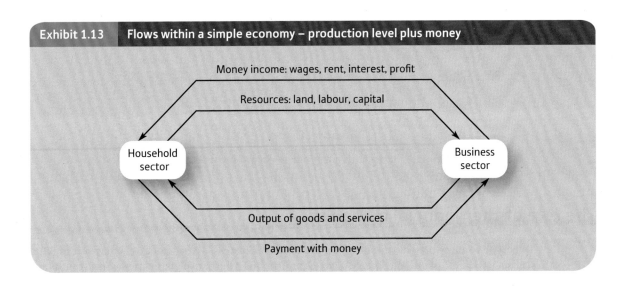

Exhibit 1.13 **Flows within a simple economy – production level plus money**

Money income: wages, rent, interest, profit

Resources: land, labour, capital

Household sector

Business sector

Output of goods and services

Payment with money

Investment in a money economy

Investment involves resources being laid aside now to produce a return in the future; for instance, today's consumption is reduced in order to put resources into building a factory and the creation of machine tools to produce goods in later years. Most investment is made in the business sector but it is not the business sector consumption which is reduced if investment is to take place, as all resources are ultimately owned by households. Society needs individuals who are prepared to sacrifice consumption now and to wait for investments to come to fruition. These capitalists are willing to defer consumption and put their funds at risk within the business sector but only if they anticipate a suitable return. In a modern, sophisticated economy there are large-scale flows of investment resources from the ultimate owners (individuals who make up households) to the business sector. Even the profits of previous years' endeavours retained within the business belong to households – they have merely permitted firms to hold on to those resources for further investments on their behalf.

Investment in the twenty-first century is on a grand scale and the time gap between sacrifice and return has in many cases grown very large. This has increased the risks to any one individual investor and so investments tend to be made via pooled funds drawing on the savings of many thousands of households. A capital market has developed to assist the flow of funds between the business and household sectors. Among their other functions the financial markets reduce risk through their regulatory regimes and insistence on a high level of disclosure of information. In these more advanced financial structures businesses issue securities which give the holder the right to receive income in specified circumstances. Those that hold debt securities have a relatively high certainty of receiving a flow of interest. Those that buy a security called a share have less certainty about what they will receive but, because the return is based on a share of profit, they expect to gain a higher return than if they had merely lent money to the firm.

In **Exhibit 1.14** we can see household savings going into business investment. In exchange for this investment the business sector issues securities which show the claims that households have over firms. This exhibit shows three interconnected systems. The first is the flow of real goods and services. The second is a flow of money. The third is the investment system which enables production and consumption to be increased in the future. It is mainly in facilitating the flow of investment finance that the financial sector has a role in our society. The financial system increases the efficiency of the real economy by encouraging the flow of funds to productive uses.

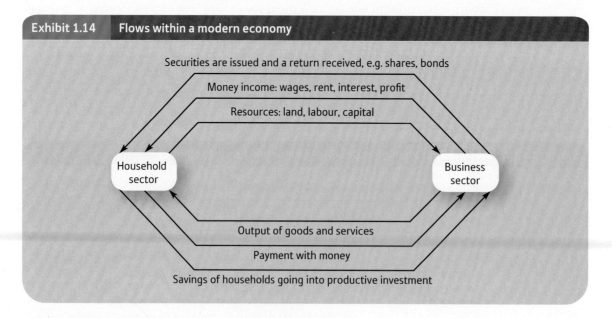

Exhibit 1.14   Flows within a modern economy

Securities are issued and a return received, e.g. shares, bonds

Money income: wages, rent, interest, profit

Resources: land, labour, capital

Household sector

Business sector

Output of goods and services

Payment with money

Savings of households going into productive investment

The role of the financial manager

To be able to carry on a business a company needs **real assets**. These real assets may be tangible, such as buildings, plant, machinery, vehicles and so on. Alternatively a firm may invest in intangible real assets, for example patents, expertise, licensing rights, etc. To obtain these real assets corporations sell financial claims to raise money; to lenders a bundle of rights are sold within a loan contract, to shareholders rights over the ownership of a company are sold as well as the right to receive a proportion of profits produced. The financial manager has the task of both raising finance by selling financial claims and advising on the use of those funds within the business. This is illustrated in **Exhibit 1.15**.

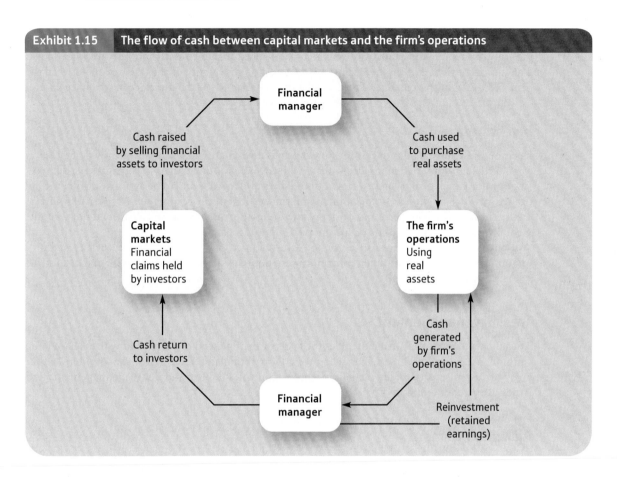

Exhibit 1.15   The flow of cash between capital markets and the firm's operations

The financial manager plays a pivotal role in the following:

Interaction with the financial markets

In order to raise finance, knowledge is needed of the financial markets and the way in which they operate. To raise share (equity) capital, awareness of the rigours and processes involved in 'taking a new company to market' might be useful. For instance, what is the role of an issuing house? What services do brokers, accountants, solicitors, etc. provide to a company wishing to float? Once a company is quoted on a stock market it is going to be useful to know about ways of raising additional equity capital – what about rights issues and open offers? Knowledge of exchanges such as the Alternative Investment Market (AIM) (UK) or the European market Euronext might be valuable. If the firm does not wish to have its shares quoted on an exchange perhaps an investigation needs to be made into the possibility of raising money through the private equity industry.

Understanding how shares are priced and what it is that shareholders are looking for when sacrificing present consumption to make an investment could help the firm to tailor its strategy, operations and financing decisions to suit its owners. These, and dozens of other equity finance questions, are part of the remit of the finance expert within the firm. All other managers need a working knowledge of these issues too.

Another major source of finance comes from banks. Understanding the operation of banks and what concerns them when lending to a firm may enable you to present your case better, to negotiate improved terms and obtain finance which fits the cash-flow patterns of the firm.

Then there are ways of borrowing which by-pass banks. Bonds could be issued either domestically or internationally. Medium-term notes, commercial paper, leasing, hire purchase and factoring are other possibilities (all described in Chapters 11 and 12).

Once a knowledge has been gained of each of these alternative financial instruments and of the operation of their respective financial markets, then the financial manager has to consider the issue of the correct balance between the different types. What proportion of debt to equity? What proportion of short-term finance to long-term finance and so on?

Perhaps you can already appreciate that the finance function is far from a boring 'bean-counting' role. It is a dynamic function with a constant need for up-to-date and relevant knowledge. The success or failure of the entire business may rest on the quality of the interaction between the firm and the financial markets. The financial manager stands at the interface between the two.

Investment

Decisions have to be made concerning how much to invest in real assets and which specific projects to undertake (capital budgeting decisions or capital expenditure (capex)). Managers need knowledge of both analytical techniques to aid these sorts of decisions and to be aware of a wide variety of factors which might have some influence on the wisdom of proceeding with a particular investment. These range from corporate strategy and budgeting restrictions to culture and the commitment of individuals likely to be called upon to support an activity.

There is also the opposite of investment – divestment or disinvestment. Assets, such as a factory or subsidiary, that are no longer contributing to shareholder wealth need to be disposed of to release capital.

Treasury management

The management of cash may fall under the aegis of the financial manager. Many firms have large sums of cash which need to be managed properly to obtain a high return for shareholders. Other areas of responsibility might include inventory control, creditor and debtor management, and issues of solvency and liquidity.

Risk management

Companies that enter into transactions abroad, for example exporters, are often subject to risk: they may be uncertain about the sum of money (in their own currency) that they will actually receive on the deal. Three or four months after sending the goods they may receive a quantity of yen or dollars but at the time the deal was struck they did not know the quantity of the home currency that could be bought with the foreign currency. Managing and reducing exchange rate risk is yet another area calling on the skills of the finance director.

Likewise, exposure to interest rate changes and commodity price fluctuations can be reduced by using hedging techniques. These often employ instruments such as futures, options, swaps and forward agreements. Failure to understand these derivatives and their appropriate employment can lead to disaster.

Strategy and value-based management

Managers need to formulate and implement long-term plans to maximise shareholder wealth. This means selecting markets and activities in which the firm, given its resources, has a competitive edge. Managers need to distinguish between those products or markets that generate value for the firm and those that destroy value. At the centre of value-based management is recognition of the need to produce a return on money invested in an activity commensurate with the risk taken. The financial manager has a pivotal role in this strategic analysis.

Financial knowledge is essential to perform well as a chief executive (CEO) – *see* **Exhibit 1.16.** Even those directors who have not held a finance post will be aware of their need for a sound understanding of the discipline.

Exhibit 1.16

Finance remains most common route to the top at FTSE 100 groups

By Brian Groom

A career in finance remains the most common route to the top of FTSE 100 companies, research by a recruitment firm has found.

Robert Half's annual FTSE 100 CEO Tracker found that 52 per cent of current chief executives have an accountancy or financial management background.

That compares with 21 per cent with credentials in engineering or natural resources, 9 per cent in retail or hospitality, 8 per cent in marketing or advertising and 4 per cent in technology.

More than one in 10 moved from a finance role, such as chief financial officer, straight to the chief executive's post in the same company.

The proportion of chiefs with a finance background is unchanged on last year but up from 31 per cent in 2008, underlining the fact that strong financial management skills have been seen as vital by boards since the economic downturn.

The trend has continued, with 10 of the past year's 18 new FTSE 100 chief executives – whether promoted or heading companies that have joined the index – having finance credentials.

FT *Financial Times,* 7 May 2013.
All Rights Reserved.

The flow of funds and financial intermediation

Exhibit 1.15 looked at the simple relationship between a firm and investors. Unfortunately the real world is somewhat more complicated and the flow of funds within the financial system involves a number of other institutions and agencies. **Exhibit 1.17** is a more realistic representation of the financial interactions between different groups in society.

Households generally place the largest proportion of their savings with financial institutions. These organisations then put that money to work. Some of it is lent back to members of the household sector in the form of, say, a mortgage to purchase a house, or as a personal loan. Some of the money is used to buy securities issued by the business sector. The institutions will expect a return on these loans and shares, which flows back in the form of interest and dividends. However, they are often prepared for businesses to retain profit within the firm for further investment in the hope of greater returns in the future. The government sector enters into the financial system in a number of ways, two of which are shown in Exhibit 1.17. Taxes are taken from businesses and this adds a further dimension to financial decisions – for example, taking taxation into account when selecting sources of finance and when analysing investment proposals. Second, governments usually fail to match their revenues with their expenditure and therefore borrow significant sums from the financial institutions. The diagram in Exhibit 1.17 remains a gross simplification – it has not allowed for overseas financial transactions, for example – but it does demonstrate a crucial role for financial institutions in an advanced market economy.

Primary investors

Typically the household sector is in financial surplus. This sector contains the savers of society. It is these individuals who become the main providers of funds used for investment in the business sector. Primary investors tend to prefer to exchange their cash for financial assets which (a) allow them to get their money back quickly should they need to (with low transaction cost of doing so) and (b) have a high degree of certainty over the amount they will receive back. That is, primary investors like high liquidity and low risk. Lending directly to a firm with a project proposal to

Exhibit 1.17	The flow of funds and financial intermediation

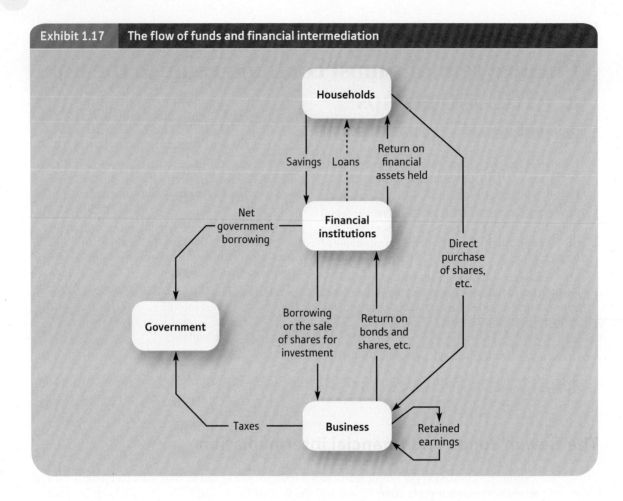

build a toll road which will not be sold until five years have passed is not a high-liquidity and low-risk investment. However, putting money into a sock under the bed is (if we exclude the possibility of the risk of sock theft).

Ultimate borrowers

In our simplified model the ultimate borrowers are in the business sector. These firms are trying to maximise the wealth generated by their activities. To do this companies need to invest in real plant, equipment and other assets, often for long periods of time. The firms, in order to serve their social function, need to attract funds for use over many years. Also these funds are to be put at risk, sometimes very high risk. (Here we are using the term 'borrower' broadly to include all forms of finance, even 'borrowing' by selling shares.)

Conflict of preferences

We have a conflict of preferences between the primary investors wanting low-cost liquidity and certainty, and the ultimate borrowers wanting long-term risk-bearing capital. A further complicating factor is that savers usually save on a small scale, £100 here or £200 there, whereas businesses are likely to need large sums of money. Imagine some of the problems that would occur in a society which did not have any financial intermediaries. Here lending and share buying will occur only as a result of direct contact and negotiation between two parties. If there were no organised market where financial securities could be sold on to other investors the fund provider, once committed, would be trapped in an illiquid investment. Also the costs that the two parties might incur in searching to find each other in the first place might be considerable. Following contact a thorough agreement would need to be drawn up to safeguard the investor, and additional expense would be incurred obtaining information to monitor the firm and its progress. In sum, the obstacles to putting saved funds to productive use would lead many to give up and to retain their cash. Those that do persevere will demand exceptionally high rates of return from the borrowers to compensate them for poor liquidity, risk, search costs, agreement costs and monitoring costs. This will mean that few firms will be able to justify investments because they cannot obtain those high levels of return when the funds are invested in real assets. As a result few investments take place and the wealth of society fails to grow. **Exhibit 1.18** shows (by the top arrow) little money flowing from saving into investment.

The introduction of financial intermediaries

The problem of under-investment can be alleviated greatly by the introduction of financial institutions (e.g. banks) and financial markets (e.g. a stock exchange). Their role is to facilitate the flow of funds from primary investors to ultimate borrowers at a low cost. They do this by solving the conflict of preferences. There are two types of financial intermediation: the first is an agency or brokerage type operation which brings together lenders and firms, the second is an asset-transforming type of intermediation, in which the conflict is resolved by creating intermediate securities which have the risk, liquidity and volume characteristics which the investors prefer. The financial institution raises money by offering these securities, and then uses the acquired funds to purchase primary securities issued by firms.

Brokers

At its simplest an intermediary is a 'go-between', someone who matches up a provider of finance with a user of funds. This type of intermediary is particularly useful for reducing the search costs for both parties. Stockbrokers, for example, make it easy for investors wanting to buy shares in a newly floated company. Brokers may also have some skill at collecting information on a firm and monitoring its activities, saving the investor time. They also act as middlemen when an investor wishes to sell to another, thus enhancing the liquidity of the fund providers. Another example is the mortgage broker who can advise on and arrange the best mortgage for a client.

Asset transformers

Intermediaries, by creating a completely new security, the intermediate security, increase the opportunities available to savers, encouraging them to invest and thus reducing the cost of finance for the productive sector. The transformation function can act in a number of different ways.

Risk transformation

For example, instead of an individual lending directly to a business with a great idea, such as installing wind turbines in the English Channel, a bank creates a deposit or current account with relatively low risk for the investor's savings. Lending directly to the firm the saver would demand compensation for the probability of default on the loan and therefore the business would have to pay a very high rate of interest which would inhibit investment. The bank, acting as an intermediary, creates a special kind of security called a bank account agreement. The intermediary then uses the funds attracted by the new financial asset to buy a security issued by the wind farm owner (the primary security) when it obtains long-term debt capital. Because of the extra security that a lender has by holding a bank account as a financial asset rather than by making a loan direct to a firm, the lender is prepared to accept a lower rate of interest and the ultimate borrower obtains funds at a relatively low cost. The bank is able to reduce its risk exposure to any one project by diversifying its loan portfolio among a number of firms. It can also reduce risk by building up expertise in assessing and monitoring firms and their associated risk. Another example of risk transformation is when unit or investment companies (*see* later in this chapter) take savers' funds and spread these over a wide range of company shares.

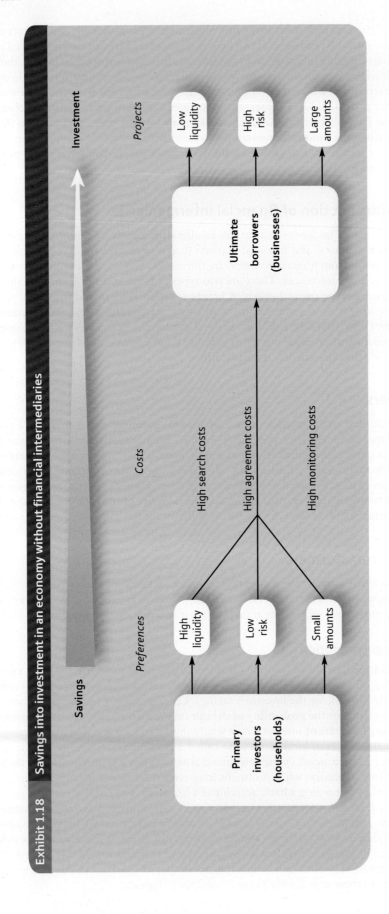

Exhibit 1.18   Savings into investment in an economy without financial intermediaries

Maturity (liquidity) transformation

The fact that a bank lends long term for a risky venture does not mean that the primary lender is subjected to illiquidity. Liquidity is not a problem because banks maintain sufficient liquid funds to meet their liabilities when they arise. You can walk into a bank and take the money from your account at short notice because the bank, given its size, exploits economies of scale and anticipates that only a small fraction of its customers will withdraw their money on any one day. Banks and building societies play an important role in borrowing 'short' and lending 'long'.

Volume transformation

Many institutions gather small amounts of money from numerous savers and re-package these sums into larger bundles for investment in the business sector. Apart from the banks and building societies, unit trusts are important here. It is uneconomic for an investor with, say, £50 per month, who wants to invest in shares, to buy small quantities periodically. Unit trusts gather together hundreds of individuals' monthly savings and invest them in a broad range of shares, thereby exploiting economies in transaction costs.

Intermediaries' economies of scale

An intermediary, such as a bank, is able to accept lending to (and investing in shares of) companies at a relatively low rate of return because of the economies of scale enjoyed compared with the primary investor. These economies of scale include:

(a) *Efficiencies in gathering information* on the riskiness of lending to a particular firm. Individuals do not have access to the same data sources or expert analysis.

(b) *Risk spreading* Intermediaries are able to spread funds across a large number of borrowers and thereby reduce overall risk. Individual investors may be unable to do this.

(c) *Transaction costs* They are able to reduce the search, agreement and monitoring costs that would be incurred by savers and borrowers in a direct transaction. Banks, for example, are convenient, safe locations with standardised types of securities. Savers do not have to spend time examining the contract they are entering upon when, say, they open a bank account. How many of us read the small print when we opened a bank account?

The reduced information costs, convenience and passed-on benefits from the economies of operating on a large scale mean that primary investors are motivated to place their savings with intermediaries.

Apart from linking savers with ultimate borrowers there are financial services within the household sector and within the business sector. For example, transferring money between bank accounts or providing financial advice.

Financial markets

A financial market, such as a stock exchange, has two aspects: there is the primary market where funds are raised from investors by the firm, and there is the secondary market in which investors buy and sell securities, such as shares and bonds, between each other. The securities sold into the primary market are generally done so on the understanding that repayment will not be made for many years, if ever, and so it is beneficial for the original buyer to be able to sell on to other investors in the secondary market. In this way the firm achieves its objective of raising finance that will stay in the firm for a lengthy period and the investor has retained the ability to liquidate (turn into cash) a holding by selling to another investor. In addition a well-regulated exchange encourages investment by reducing search, agreement and monitoring costs – *see* **Exhibit 1.19.**

Exhibit 1.19   Savings into investment in an economy with financial intermediaries and financial markets

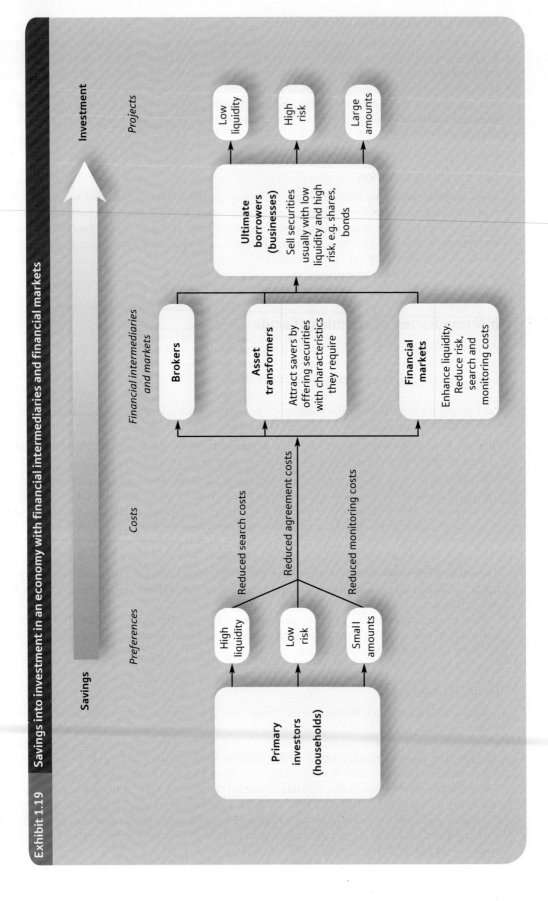

Growth in the financial services sector

The financial services sector has grown rapidly over the last 60 years. We define the core of the financial sector as banking (including building societies), insurance and various investment services. There are one or two other activities, such as accounting, which may or may not be included depending on your perspective. Firms operating in the financial services sector have, arguably, been the most dynamic, innovative and adaptable companies in the world.

Some reasons for the growth of financial services in the UK

There are a number of reasons for the growth of the financial services sector. These include:

1 *High income elasticity*. This means that as consumers' incomes rise the demand for financial services grows by a disproportionate amount. Thus a larger share of national income is devoted to paying this sector fees etc. to provide services because people desire the benefits offered. Firms have also bought an ever-widening range of financial services from the institutions which have been able to respond quickly to the needs of corporations.

2 *International comparative advantage*. London is the world's leading financial centre in a number of markets, for instance cross-border lending and international bond dealing. It is the place where the most currency transactions take place – about £2,440bn per day. It is also a major player in the fund management, insurance and derivatives markets. It is certainly Europe's leading financial centre. One of the reasons for London maintaining this dominance is that it possesses a comparative advantage in providing global financial services. This advantage stems, not least, from the critical mass of collective expertise which is difficult for rivals to emulate.

Dynamism, innovation and adaptation – five decades of change

Since the 1970s there has been a remarkably proactive response by the financial sector to changes in the market environment. New financial instruments, techniques of intermediation and markets have been developed with impressive speed. Instruments which even in the 1990s did not exist have sprung to prominence to create multi-billion-pound markets, with thousands of employees serving that market. *See* **Exhibit 1.20.**

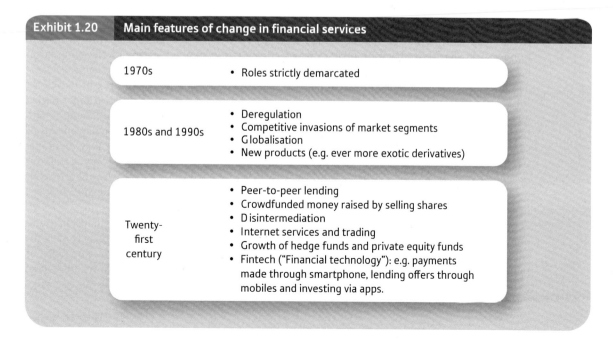

Exhibit 1.20   Main features of change in financial services

1970s	• Roles strictly demarcated
1980s and 1990s	• Deregulation • Competitive invasions of market segments • Globalisation • New products (e.g. ever more exotic derivatives)
Twenty-first century	• Peer-to-peer lending • Crowdfunded money raised by selling shares • Disintermediation • Internet services and trading • Growth of hedge funds and private equity funds • Fintech ("Financial technology"): e.g. payments made through smartphone, lending offers through mobiles and investing via apps.

From the 1970s until the financial crisis of 2008 there was a general trend towards deregulation and liberalisation for institutions, while recognising that individual investors need protection. Since then there have been moves to tighten regulatory control in certain areas, while still encouraging innovation.

Until the mid-1970s there were clearly delineated roles for different types of financial institutions. Banks did banking, insurance firms provided insurance, building societies granted mortgages and so on. There was little competition between the different sectors, and cartel-like arrangements meant that there was only limited competition within each sector. Some effort was made in the 1970s to increase the competitive pressures, particularly for banks. The arrival of large numbers of foreign banks in London helped the process of reform in the UK but the system remained firmly bound by restrictions, particularly in defining the activities firms could undertake.

The real breakthrough came in the 1980s. The guiding philosophy of achieving efficiency through competition led to large-scale deregulation of activities and pricing. There was widespread competitive invasion of market segments. Banks became much more active in the mortgage market and set up insurance operations, stockbroking arms, unit trusts and many other services. Building societies, meanwhile, started to invade the territory of the banks and offered personal loans, credit cards, cheque accounts. They even went into estate agency, stockbroking and insurance underwriting. The Stock Exchange was deregulated in 1986 (in what is known as the 'Big Bang') and this move enabled it to compete more effectively on a global scale and reduce the costs of dealing in shares, particularly for the large institutional investors.

The 1970s and early 1980s were periods of volatile interest rates and exchange rates. This resulted in greater uncertainty for businesses. New financial instruments were developed to help manage risk, such as swaps, options, futures traded in the informal 'over-the-counter' market (i.e. not on a regulated exchange).

The trend towards globalisation in financial product trading and services continued apace. Increasingly a worldwide market was established. It became unexceptional for a company to have its shares quoted in New York, London, Frankfurt and Tokyo as well as its home exchange in Africa. Bond selling and trading became global and currencies were traded 24 hours a day. International banking took on an increasingly high profile, not least because the multinational corporations demanded that their banks provide multifaceted services ranging from borrowing in a foreign currency to helping manage cash.

Vast investments were made in computing and telecommunications systems to cut costs and provide improved services. Automated teller machines (ATMs), banking by telephone and Internet, and payment by smartphone are now commonplace. A more advanced use of technological innovation is in the global trading of the ever-expanding range of financial instruments. You can sit on a beach in the Caribbean and trade pork belly futures in Chicago, interest rate options in London and shares in Singapore. There was a continuation of the blurring of the boundaries between different types of financial institutions to the point where organisations such as JPMorgan Chase and Barclays are referred to as 'financial supermarkets' (or 'universal banks' or 'financial services companies') offering a wide range of services. Interestingly, food supermarket giants such as Sainsbury's and Tesco set up comprehensive banking services, following a path trodden by a number of other non-banking corporations. The Internet provided a new means of supplying financial services and lowered the barrier to entry into the industry. New banking, stockbroking and insurance services have sprung up. The Internet allows people to trade millions of shares at the touch of a button from the comfort of their home, to transfer the proceeds between bank accounts and to search websites for data, company reports, newspaper reports, insurance quotations and so on – all much more cheaply than ever before.

The globalisation of business and investment decisions has continued, making national economies increasingly interdependent. Borrowers use the international financial markets to seek the cheapest funds, and investors look in all parts of the globe for the highest returns. Some idea of the extent of global financial flows can be gained by contrasting the *daily* turnover of foreign exchange (approximately £5,100bn)[3] with the *annual* output of all the goods and services

---

3 Bank for International Settlement: www.BIS.org

produced by the people in the UK of less than this. Another effect of technological change is the increased mobility of activities within firms. For example, banks have transferred a high proportion of their operations to India, as have insurance companies and other financial firms.

Another feature of recent years has been the development of disintermediation – in other words, cutting out the middleman. This means borrowing firms bypassing the banks and obtaining debt finance by selling debt securities, such as bonds, in the market. The purchasers can be individuals (who might buy bonds or lend via a peer-to-peer website) but are more usually the large savings institutions such as pension funds, insurance funds and hedge funds. Banks, having lost some interest income from lending to these large firms, have concentrated instead on fee income gained by arranging the sale and distribution of these securities as well as underwriting their issue (guaranteeing to buy if no one else will). Hedge funds, for example, (free from most regulatory control) now account for a high proportion of financial market trading whereas they were barely heard of 30 years ago. Private equity funds, which invest in shares and other securities of companies outside a stock exchange, have grown tremendously over the last 30 years, owning stakes in companies which employ millions of workers.

The financial system

To assist with orientating the reader within the financial system and to carry out more jargon busting, a brief outline of the main financial services sectors and markets is given here.

The institutions

The banking sector

Retail banks

Put at its simplest, the retail banks take (small) deposits from the public or borrow from the financial markets. This money is re-packaged and lent to businesses and households. This is generally high-volume and low-value business which contrasts with wholesale (investment) banking which is low volume but each transaction is for high value. The distinction between retail and investment banks has become blurred over recent years as the large institutions have diversified their operations. The big retail banks operate nationwide branch networks; but there are many 'challenger banks' which currently only operate in a few towns or only on the Internet, which are determined to draw customers from the established giants of the industry. A subset of banks provides a cheque-clearance system (transferring money from one account to another) – these are the clearing banks. The five largest UK clearing banks are Barclays, Lloyds (including Bank of Scotland), Royal Bank of Scotland (including NatWest), HSBC and Santander. Loans, overdrafts and mortgages are the main forms of retail bank lending. The trend up until 2009 was for retail banks to reduce their reliance on retail deposits and raise more wholesale funds from the financial markets. But this has partially been reversed as banks found wholesale funding less reliable than obtaining funds to lend from deposits in bank accounts. They get together with other banks if a large loan is required by a borrower (say £150m) rather than provide the full amount themselves as this would create an excessive exposure to one customer – this is called syndicate lending, discussed in Chapter 11.

Investment banks[4]

The terms wholesale bank, merchant bank and investment bank are often used interchangeably. There are subtle differences but for most practical purposes they can be regarded as the same. These institutions tend to deal in large sums of money – at least £250,000 – although some have set up retail arms. They concentrate on dealing with other large organisations, corporations,

---

4 There is much more on investment banks as well as many other financial organisations in Arnold (2012) and Arnold (2014b).

institutional investors and governments. While they undertake some lending their main focus is on generating commission or trading income by providing advice and facilitating deals. There are five main areas of activity:

- *Raising external finance for companies* These banks provide advice and arrange finance for corporate clients. Sometimes they provide loans themselves, but more often they assist the setting up of a bank syndicate or make arrangements with other institutions. They will advise and assist a firm issuing a bond, they have expertise in helping firms float on a stock exchange and make rights issues. They may 'underwrite' a bond or share issue, which assures the corporation that it will receive the funds it needs for its investment programme.

- *Broking and dealing* They act as agents for the buying and selling of securities on the financial markets, including shares and bonds. Some also have market-making arms which quote prices they are willing to buy or sell from or to, say, a shareholder or a bond holder, thus assisting the operation of secondary markets (see Chapter 9). They also trade in the markets on their own account and assist companies with export finance.

- *Fund management (asset management)* The investment banks offer services to rich individuals who lack the time or expertise to deal with their own investment strategies. They also manage unit and investment trusts as well as the portfolios of some pension funds and insurance companies. In addition corporations often have short-term cash flows which need managing efficiently (treasury management).

- *Assistance in corporate restructuring* Investment banks earn large fees from advising acquirers on mergers and assisting with the merger process. They also gain by helping target firms avoid being taken over too cheaply. Corporate disposal programmes, such as selling off a division, may also need the services of an investment bank.

- *Assisting risk management using derivatives* Risk can be reduced through hedging strategies using futures, options, swaps and the like. However, this is a complex area with large room for error and terrible penalties if a mistake is made (*see* Chapters 21 and 22). The banks may have specialist knowledge to offer in this area.

International banks

There are two main types of international banking in the UK:

- Foreign banking transactions (lending/borrowing, etc.) in the host country currency with overseas residents and companies, e.g. transactions in sterling with non-UK residents by UK banks.

- Eurocurrency banking for transactions in a currency outside the jurisdiction of the country of that currency, e.g. yen transactions in Canada (Chapter 11 considers this further).

The major part of international banking these days is borrowing and lending in foreign currencies. There are about 240 non-UK banks operating in London, hailing from 180 countries, the most prominent of which are American, German, Swiss and Japanese. Their initial function was mainly to provide services for their own nationals, for example for export and import transactions, but nowadays their main emphasis is in the short-term borrowing market and international securities (shares, bonds, etc.) trading. Often funds are held in the UK for the purpose of trading and speculation on the foreign exchange market.

Building societies

Building societies collect funds from millions of savers by enticing them to put their money in interest-bearing accounts. The vast majority of that deposited money is then lent to people wishing to buy a home – in the form of a mortgage. Thus, they take in short-term deposits (although they also borrow on the wholesale financial markets) and they lend money for long periods, usually for 25 years. More recently building societies have diversified their sources of finance (e.g. using the wholesale financial markets) and increased the range of services they offer.

Finance houses[5]

Finance houses are responsible for the financing of hire purchase agreements and other instalment credit, for example leasing. If you buy a large durable good such as a car or a washing machine you often find that the sales assistant also tries to get you interested in taking the item on credit, so you pay for it over a period of, say, three years. It is usually not the retailer that provides the finance for the credit. The retailer usually works with a finance house which pays the retailer the full purchase price of the good and therefore becomes the owner. You, the customer, get to use the good, but in return you have to make regular payments to the finance house, including interest. Under a hire purchase agreement, when you have made enough payments you will become the owner. Under leasing the finance house retains ownership (for more detail *see* Chapter 12). Finance houses also provide factoring services – providing cash to firms in return for receiving income from the firms' debtors when they pay up. Most of the large finance houses are subsidiaries of the major conglomerate banks.

Long-term savings institutions

Pension funds

Pension funds are set up to provide pensions for members. For example, the University Superannuation Scheme (USS), to which university lecturers belong, takes 8% of working members' salaries each month and puts it into the fund. In addition the employing organisation pays money into the scheme. When a member retires the USS will pay a pension. Between the time of making a contribution and payment in retirement, which may be decades, the pension trustees oversee the management of the fund. They may place some or all of the fund with specialist investment managers. This is a particularly attractive form of saving because of the generous tax relief provided. The long time horizon of the pension business means that large sums are built up and available for investment – currently over £2tn in the UK funds. A typical allocation of a fund is:

- 10–30% in UK shares;
- 40–50% lending to the UK government by buying bonds and bills and by lending via corporate bonds issued by UK firms;
- 20–30% overseas company shares;
- 3–6% in bonds issued by foreign organisations;
- 5–15% other (e.g. property, cash, private equity, hedge funds and overseas bonds).

Insurance funds

Insurance companies engage in two types of activities:

- General insurance This is insurance against specific contingencies such as fire, theft, accident, generally for a one-year period. The money collected in premiums is mostly held in financial assets which are relatively short term and liquid so that short-term commitments can be met (totalling around £150bn in the UK).
- Life assurance With term assurance, your life is assured for a specified period. If you die your beneficiaries get a payout. If you live you get nothing at the end of the period. With whole-of-life policies, the insurance company pays a capital sum upon death whenever this occurs. Endowment policies are more interesting from a financial systems perspective because they act as a savings vehicle as well as cover against death. The premium will be larger but after a number of years have passed the insurance company pays a substantial sum of money even if you are still alive. The life company has to take the premiums paid over, say, 10 or 25 years, and invest them wisely to satisfy its commitment to the policy holder.

---

5 The term 'finance house' is also used for broadly based financial service companies carrying out a wide variety of financial activities from share brokerage to corporate lending. However, we will confine the term to instalment credit and related services.

Life assurance companies also provide annuities. Here a policy holder pays an initial lump sum and in return receives regular payments in subsequent years. They have also moved into pensions. Indeed, the majority of their business is now pension related.

UK life assurance companies have over £1,700bn under management. A typical fund allocation is:

- 10–15% UK shares;
- 15–20% overseas shares;
- 15–20% lending to the UK government;
- 20–25% corporate bonds and other non-government debt;
- 5–10% property;
- 15–20% unit trusts;
- 5–10% other.

The risk spreaders

These institutions allow small savers a stake in a large diversified portfolio.

Unit trusts

Unit trusts are 'open-ended' funds, so the size of the fund and the number of units depend on the amount of money investors wish to put into the fund. If a fund of one million units suddenly doubled in size because of an inflow of investor funds it would become a fund of two million units through the creation and selling of more units. The buying and selling prices of the units are determined by the value of the fund. So if a two-million unit fund is invested in £2m worth of shares in the UK stock market, the value of each unit will be £1. If over a period the value of the shares rises to £3m, the units will be worth £1.50 each. Unit holders sell units back to the managers of the unit trust if they want to liquidate their holding. The manager will then either sell the units to another investor or sell some of the underlying investments to raise cash to pay the unit holder. The units are usually quoted at two prices depending on whether you are buying (higher) or selling. There is also an ongoing management charge for running the fund. Trustees supervise the funds to safeguard the interests of unit holders but employ managers to make the investment decisions.

There is a wide choice of unit trusts specialising in different types of investments ranging from Japanese equities to small European companies. Of the £1,000bn or so invested in unit trusts and their cousins, OEICs, 50–60% is devoted to shares (one-half of which are non-UK) with 15–20% devoted to bonds. Instruments similar to unit trusts are called mutual funds in other countries.

Investment trusts

Investment trusts differ from unit trusts because they are companies able to issue shares and other securities. Investors can purchase these securities when the investment company is launched or purchase shares in the secondary market from other investors. These are known as closed-ended funds because the company itself is closed to new investors – if you wished to invest your money you would go to an existing investor (via a broker) and not buy from the company. Investment trusts usually spread the investors' funds across a range of other companies' shares. They are also more inclined to invest in a broader range of assets than unit trusts – even property and shares not listed on a stock market. Approximately one-half of the money devoted to the 380 or so UK investment companies (£160bn) is put into UK securities and property, with the remainder placed in overseas securities. The managers of these funds are able to borrow in order to invest. This has the effect of increasing returns to shareholders when things go well. Correspondingly, if the value of the underlying investments falls, the return to shareholders falls even more, because of the obligation to meet interest charges.

Open-ended investment companies (OEICs)

Open-ended investment companies are hybrid risk-spreading instruments which allow an investment in an open-ended fund. Designed to be more flexible and transparent than either investment companies or unit trusts, OEICs have just one price. However, as with unit trusts, OEICs can issue more shares, in line with demand from investors, and they can borrow.[6]

Exchange-traded funds (ETFs)

ETFs are set up as companies issuing shares, and the money raised is used to buy a range of securities such as a collection of shares in a particular stock market index or sector, say the FTSE 100 or pharmaceutical shares. Thus if BP comprises 8% of the total value of the FTSE 100 and the ETF has £100m to invest, it will buy £8m of BP shares; if Whitbread is 0.15% of the FTSE, the ETF buys £150,000 of Whitbread shares. (Alternatively, many ETFs do not buy the actual shares but gain exposure to the share returns through the purchase of derivatives of the shares.) They are open-ended funds – the ETF shares are created and cancelled as demand rises or falls. However, they differ from unit trusts and OEICs in that the pricing of ETF shares is left up to the marketplace. ETFs are quoted companies and you can buy and sell their shares at prices subject to change throughout the day (unlike unit trusts and OEICs, where prices are set by a formula once a day). Globally, there are more than 4,400 different ETFs listed on over 60 exchanges with a total value over $3,000bn. They have become so significant that around 30% of US share trading is in ETFs.

The risk takers

Private equity funds

These are funds that invest in companies that do not have a stock market trading quote for their shares. The firms are often young and on a rapid growth trajectory, but private equity companies also supply finance to well-established companies. The funds usually buy shares in these companies and occasionally supply debt finance. Frequently the private equity funds are themselves funded by other financial institutions, such as a group of pension funds. Private equity has grown tremendously over the last 20 years to the point where now over one-fifth of non-government UK workers are employed by a firm financed by private equity. Private equity is discussed in Chapter 10.

Hedge funds

Hedge funds gather together investors' money and invest it in a wide variety of financial strategies largely outside of the control of the regulators, being created either outside the major financial centres or as private investment partnerships. The investors include wealthy individuals as well as institutions, such as pension funds, insurance funds and banks. By being somewhat outside normal regulatory control hedge funds are not confined to investing in particular types of security, or to using particular investment methods. For example, they have far more freedom than unit trusts in 'going short', i.e. selling a security first and then buying it later, hopefully at a lower price. They can also borrow many times the size of the fund to punt on a small movement of currency rates, or share movements, orange juice futures, or whatever they judge will go up (or go down). If the punt goes well (or rather, a series of punts over the year) the fund managers earn million-pound bonuses (often on the basis of 2% of funds under management fee plus 20% of the profit made for client investors).

Originally, the term 'hedge' made some sense when applied to these funds. They would, through a combination of investments, including derivatives, try to hedge (lower or eliminate) risk while seeking a high absolute return (rather than a return relative to an index). Today the word 'hedge' is misapplied to most of these funds because they generally take aggressive bets on the movements of currencies, equities, interest rates, bonds, etc. around the world. Their activities would not be a concern if they had remained a relatively small part of the investment scene. However, today they command enormous power and billions more are being placed in these funds every week. Already over £2,500bn is invested in these funds. Add to that the borrowed money – sometimes ten times the fund's base capital – and you can see why they are to be taken very seriously.

---

6 There is much more on unit trusts, investment trusts, OEICs and ETFs in Arnold (2014a).

The markets

The money markets

The money markets are wholesale markets (usually involving transactions of £500,000 or more) which enable borrowing on a short-term basis (usually less than one year). The banks are particularly active in this market – both as lenders and as borrowers. Large corporations, local government bodies and non-banking financial institutions also lend when they have surplus cash and borrow when short of money.

The bond markets

While the money markets are concerned with short-term lending the capital markets deal with longer-term (> 1 year) debt (e.g. bond) and equity instruments. A bond is merely a document which sets out the borrower's promise to pay sums of money in the future – usually regular interest plus a capital amount upon the maturity of the bond. These are securities issued by a variety of organisations including governments and corporations. The UK bond markets are over three centuries old and during that time they have developed very large and sophisticated primary and secondary sub-markets encompassing gilts (UK government bonds), corporate bonds, local authority bonds and international bonds, among others. Bonds as a source of finance for firms will be examined in Chapter 11.

The foreign exchange markets (forex or FX)

The foreign exchange markets are the markets in which one currency is exchanged for another. They include the spot market where currencies are bought and sold for 'immediate' delivery (in reality, one or two days later) and the forward markets, where the deal is agreed now to exchange currencies at some fixed point in the future. Also currency futures and options and other forex derivatives are employed to hedge risk and to speculate. The forex markets are dominated by the major banks, with dealing taking place 24 hours a day around the globe. Chapter 22 looks at how a company could use the forex market to facilitate international trade and reduce the risk attached to business transactions abroad.

The share markets

All major economies now have share markets. The London Stock Exchange, for example, is an important potential source of long-term equity (ownership) capital for UK companies and for hundreds of overseas companies. Chapters 9 and 10 examine stock markets and the raising of equity capital.

The derivative markets

A derivative is a financial instrument the value of which is derived from other financial securities or some other underlying asset. For example, a future is the right to buy something (e.g. currency, shares, bonds) at some date in the future at an agreed price. This *right* becomes a saleable derived financial instrument. The performance of the derivative depends on the behaviour of the underlying asset. Companies can use these markets for the management and transfer of risk. They can be used to reduce risk (hedging) or to speculate. ICE Futures Europe (formerly Liffe) trades options and futures in shares, bonds, commodities and interest rates. This used to be the only one of the markets listed here to have a trading floor where face-to-face dealing took place on an open outcry system (traders shouting and signalling to each other, face to face in a trading pit, the price at which they are willing to buy and sell). Now all the financial markets (money, bond, forex, derivatives and share markets) are conducted using computers (and telephones) from isolated trading rooms located in the major financial institutions. In the derivative markets a proportion of trade takes place on what is called the over-the-counter (OTC) market rather than on a regulated exchange. The OTC market flexibility allows the creation of tailor-made derivatives to suit a client's risk situation. The practical use of derivatives is examined in Chapters 21 and 22.

Concluding comments

We now have a clear guiding principle set as our objective for the myriad financial decisions discussed later in this book: maximise shareholder wealth. Whether we are considering a major investment programme, or trying to decide on the best kind of finance to use, the criterion of creating value for shareholders over the long run will be paramount. A single objective is set primarily for practical reasons to aid exposition in this text; however, many of the techniques described in later chapters will be applicable to organisations with other purposes as they stand; others will need slight modification.

There is an old joke about financial services firms: they just shovel money from one place to another, making sure that some of it sticks to the shovel. The implication is that they contribute little to the well-being of society. Extremists even go so far as to regard these firms as parasites on the 'really productive' parts of the economies. And yet very few people avoid extensive use of financial services. Most have bank and building society accounts, pay insurance premiums and contribute to pension schemes. People do not put their money into a bank account unless they get something in return. Likewise building societies, insurance companies, pension funds, unit trusts, investment banks and so on can survive only if they offer a service people find beneficial and are willing to pay for. Describing the mobilisation and employment of money in the service of productive investment as pointless or merely 'shovelling it around the system' is as logical as saying that the transport firms which bring goods to the high street do not provide a valuable service because of the absence of a tangible 'thing' created by their activities.

Key points and concepts

- Firms should clearly define the **objective** of the enterprise to provide a focus for decision making.

- **Sound financial management** is necessary for the achievement of all **stakeholder** goals.

- Some stakeholders will have their returns **satisficed** – given just enough to make their contribution. One (or more) group(s) will have their returns **maximised** – given any surplus after all others have been satisfied.

- The assumed objective of the firm for finance is to **maximise shareholder wealth**. Reasons:

  - **practical,** a single objective leads to clearer decisions;
  - the contractual theory;
  - **survival** in a competitive world;
  - it is better for **society**;
  - counters the tendency of managers to pursue goals for their own benefit;
  - they **own** the firm.

- **Maximising shareholder wealth is maximising purchasing power** or **maximising the flow of discounted cash flow** to shareholders over a long time horizon.

- **Profit maximisation** is not the same as shareholder wealth maximisation. Some factors a profit comparison does not allow for:

  - future prospects;
  - risk;
  - accounting problems;
  - communication;
  - additional capital.

- **Corporate governance.** Large corporations usually have a **separation of ownership and control**. This may lead to **managerialism** where the agents (the managers) take decisions primarily with their interests in mind rather than those of the principals (the shareholders). This is a **principal–agent problem**. Some solutions:

  - corporate governance regulation;
  - link managerial rewards to shareholder wealth improvement;
  - sackings;
  - selling shares and the takeover threat;
  - improve information flow.

- **Financial institutions and markets** encourage growth and progress by **mobilising savings** and encouraging investment.

▶

- Financial managers contribute to firms' success primarily through **investment and finance decisions.** Their knowledge of financial markets, investment appraisal methods, treasury, risk management and value analysis techniques is vital for company growth and stability.

- Financial institutions encourage the flow of saving into investment by acting as **brokers** and **asset transformers,** thus alleviating the **conflict of preferences** between the **primary investors** (households) and the **ultimate borrowers** (firms).

- **Asset transformation** is the creation of an intermediate security with characteristics appealing to the primary investor to attract funds, which are then made available to the ultimate borrower in a form appropriate to them. Types of asset transformation:

  - risk transformation;
  - maturity transformation;
  - volume transformation.

- Intermediaries are able to transform assets and encourage the flow of funds because of their **economies of scale** *vis-à-vis* the individual investor:

  - efficiencies in gathering information;
  - risk spreading;
  - transaction costs.

- The **secondary markets** in financial securities encourage investment by enabling investor liquidity (being able to sell quickly and cheaply to another investor) while providing the firm with long-term funds.

- The **financial services sector** has grown to be of great economic significance in the UK. Reasons:

  - high income elasticity;
  - international comparative advantage.

- The financial sector has shown remarkable **dynamism, innovation and adaptability** over the last four decades. Deregulation, new technology, globalisation and the rapid development of new financial products have characterised this sector.

- **Banking sector:**

  - **Retail banks** – high-volume and low-value business.

  - **Wholesale investment banks** – low-volume and high-value business. Mostly fee based.
  - **International banks** – mostly Eurocurrency transactions.
  - **Building societies** – still primarily small deposits aggregated for mortgage lending.
  - **Finance houses** – hire purchase, leasing, factoring.

- **Long-term savings institutions:**

  - **Pension funds** – major investors in financial assets.
  - **Insurance funds** – life assurance and endowment policies provide large investment funds.

- **The risk spreaders:**

  - **Unit trusts** – genuine trusts which are open-ended investment vehicles.
  - **Investment trusts** – companies which invest in other companies' financial securities, particularly shares, and other assets.
  - **Open-ended investment companies** (OEICs) – a hybrid between unit and investment trusts.
  - **Exchange traded funds (ETFs)** – set up as companies to invest in a range of securities.

- **The risk takers:**

  - **Private equity funds** – invest in companies not quoted on a stock exchange.
  - **Hedge funds** – wide variety of investment or speculative strategies outside regulators' control.

- **The markets:**

  - **The money markets** are short-term wholesale lending and/or borrowing markets.
  - **The bond markets** deal in long-term bond debt issued by corporations, governments, local authorities and so on, and usually have a secondary market.
  - **The foreign exchange market** – one currency is exchanged for another.
  - **The share market** – primary and secondary trading in companies' shares takes place.
  - **The derivatives market** – ICE Futures Europe dominates the 'exchange-traded' derivatives market in options and futures in the UK. However, there is a flourishing over-the-counter (OTC) market.

References and further reading

Students of finance, or any managerial discipline, should get into the habit of reading the *Financial Times* and *The Economist* to (a) reinforce knowledge gained from a course, and (b) appreciate the wider business environment.

Adams, R.B., Licht, A.N. and Sagiv, L. (2011) Shareholders and Stakeholders: How do directors decide? *Strategic Management Journal,* 32(12).

  Shareholderism and stakeholderism are the extremes, but this empirical study finds 'Most decision-makers . . . find a middle ground in the light of context.'

Aggarwal, R., Erel, I., Stulz, R. and Williamson, R. (2010) 'Differences in governance practices between U.S. and foreign firms: measurement, causes, and consequences', *Review of Financial Studies,* 23(3), pp. 3131–69.

  The higher the level of protection afforded to shareholders with only a small percentage of a company (minority shareholders) the greater the firm value.

Andreadakis, S. (2012) 'Enlightened Shareholder Value: Is it the new modus operandi for modern corporations?' In S. Boubaker et al. (eds), *Corporate Governance,* Springer-Verlag, Berlin.

  A call to maintain focus on shareholder value but also pay attention to other stakeholder needs, leading to better long-term financial performance.

Ang, J., Cole, R. and Lin, J. (2000) 'Agency costs and ownership structure', *Journal of Finance,* 55(1), pp. 81–106.

  Examines 1,708 companies and finds higher agency costs when an outsider (low shareholding by managers) rather than an insider manages the firm.

Anthony, R.N. (1960) 'The trouble with profit maximisation', *Harvard Business Review,* Nov.–Dec., pp. 126–34.

  Challenges the conventional economic view of profit maximisation on grounds of realism and morality.

Arnold, G. (2000) 'Tracing the development of value-based management'. In Glen Arnold and Matt Davies (eds), *Value-based Management: Context and Application.* London: Wiley.

  A more detailed discussion of the objective of the firm is presented.

Arnold, G. (2012) *Modern Financial Markets and Institutions.* Harlow: FT Prentice Hall.

  A textbook describing financial instruments, markets and institutions.

Arnold, G. (2014a) *The Financial Times Guide to Investing.* 3rd edn. Harlow: FT Prentice Hall.

This provides much more on the financial system and instruments.

Arnold G. (2014b) *The Financial Times Guide to Banking.* Harlow: FT Prentice Hall.

  Over 400 pages on banking.

Atanassov, J. and Kim, E.H. (2009) 'Labor and corporate governance: international evidence from restructuring decisions', *Journal of Finance,* 64(1), pp. 341–74.

  The effect of strong union laws on corporate governance with greater benefits to the workforce and managers. Easy to follow.

Bebchuk, L., Cohen, A. and Ferrell, A. (2009) 'What matters in corporate governance?' *Review of Financial Studies,* 22(2), pp. 783–827.

  Six governance factors seem to have a great impact on firm valuation.

Becht, M., Mayer, C. and Rossi, S. (2010) 'Returns to shareholder activism: evidence from a clinical study of the Hermes UK Focus Fund', *Review of Financial Studies,* 23(3), pp. 3093–129.

  Describes the extent of intervention by a fund in its investee companies. It outperforms, and the authors attribute this to the high level of engagement with management in companies.

Berle, A.A. and Means, G.C. (1932) *The Modern Corporation and Private Property.* New York: Macmillan.

  An early discussion of the principal–agent problem and corporate governance.

Cuňat, V., Gine, M. and Guadalupe (2012) 'The vote is cast: The effect of corporate governance on shareholder value', *Journal of Finance,* 67, pp. 1943–77.

  Shareholders passing a vote for corporate governance generates share price rises and longer term performance benefit – a US study.

Doidge, C., Andrew Karolyi, G. and Stulz, R. (2007) 'Why do countries matter so much for corporate governance?' *Journal of Financial Economics,* 86(1), pp. 1–39.

  Tests a model of how protections for minority shareholders at the national legal level influence firms' costs and benefits in implementing corporate governance improvements.

Donaldson, G. (1963) 'Financial goals: management vs. stockholders', *Harvard Business Review,* May–June, pp. 116–29.

  Clear and concise discussion of the conflict of interest between managers and shareholders.

Donghui L., Moshirian, F., Pham, P. and Zein, J. (2006) 'When financial institutions are large shareholders: the role of macro corporate governance environments', *Journal of Finance,* 61(6), pp. 2975–3007.

In countries with strong shareholder rights, effective legal enforcement and extensive financial disclosure there are larger percentage holdings of shares in companies.

Dyck, A. and Zingales, L. (2004) 'Private benefits of control: an international comparison', *Journal of Finance,* 59(2), pp. 537–600.

Someone who controls a company (without owning all the shares) can appropriate value for him/herself.

Fama, E.F. (1980) 'Agency problems and the theory of the firm', *Journal of Political Economy,* Spring, pp. 288–307.

Explains how the separation of ownership and control can lead to an efficient form of economic organisation.

Fich, E.M. and Shivdasani, A. (2006) 'Are busy boards effective monitors?' *Journal of Finance,* LXI(2), April.

Evidence that if non-executive directors hold three or more directorships then weaker governance occurs.

Fox, J. and Lorsch, J. W. (2012) 'What good are shareholders?' *Harvard Business Review,* July–August, pp. 48–57.

An opinion piece on the state of play of corporate governance in the US.

Friedman, M. (1970) 'The social responsibility of business is to increase its profits', *New York Times Magazine,* 30 Sept.

A viewpoint on the objective of the firm.

Galbraith, J. (1967) 'The goals of an industrial system' (excerpt from *The New Industrial State*). Reproduced in H.I. Ansoff, *Business Strategy.* London: Penguin, 1969.

Survival, sales and expansion of the 'technostructure' are emphasised as the goals in real-world corporations.

Ghoshal, S. (2005) 'Bad management theories are destroying good management practices', *Academy of Management's Learning and Education,* 4(1), pp. 75–91.

Argues that the encouragement of shareholder wealth maximisation is wrong.

Girerd-Potin, I., Jimenez-Garcès, S. and Louvet, P.J. (2014) 'Which dimensions of social responsibility concern financial investors', *Journal of Business Ethics,* 121(4), pp. 777–98.

Shareholders seem to penalize (lower share price) of those companies with worst behaviour regarding other stakeholders.

Hart, O.D. (1995a) *Firms, Contracts and Financial Structure.* Oxford: Clarendon Press.

A clear articulation of the principal–agent problem.

Hart, O.D. (1995b) 'Corporate governance: some theory and implications', *Economic Journal,* 105, pp. 678–9.

Principal–agent problem discussed.

Hayek, F.A. (1969) 'The corporation in a democratic society: in whose interests ought it and will it be run?' Reprinted in H.I. Ansoff, *Business Strategy.* London: Penguin, 1969.

Objective should be long-run return on owners' capital subject to restraint by general legal and moral rules.

Jensen, M.C. (1986) 'Agency costs of free cash flow, corporate finance and takeovers', *American Economic Review,* 76, pp. 323–9.

Agency cost theory applied to the issue of the use to which managers put business cash inflows.

Jensen, M.C. (2001) 'Value maximisation, stakeholder theory, and the corporate objective function', *Journal of Applied Corporate Finance,* 14(3), Fall.

Cogently argues against simple stakeholder balancing or a Balance Scorecard approach to directing a company because of the violation of the proposition that a single-valued objective is a prerequisite for purposeful or rational behaviour by any organisation, thus politicising the corporation and leaving managers empowered to exercise their own preferences.

Jensen, M.C. and Meckling, W.H. (1976) 'Theory of the firm: managerial behavior, agency costs and ownership structure', *Journal of Financial Economics,* Oct., 3, pp. 305–60.

Seminal work on agency theory.

John, K., Litov, L. and Yeung, B. (2008) 'Corporate governance and risk-taking', *Journal of Finance,* 63(4), pp. 1679–1728.

Some evidence that better investor protection mitigates against managers' natural tendency to reduce firm risk and slow down its growth.

Kaplan, R. and Norton, D.P. (1996) *The Balanced Scorecard.* Boston, MA: Harvard Business School Press.

The managerial equivalent of stakeholder theory in which multiple measures are used to evaluate performance.

Kay, J. (2004) 'Forget how the crow flies', *Financial Times Magazine,* 17–18 January, pp. 17–21.

An important argument on obliquity is presented.

Kay, J. (2010) *Obliquity: Why our goals are best achieved indirectly.* London: Profile Books.

An excellent set of ideas on obliquity with frequent reference to companies and other aspects of our lives where obliquity can be applied. Very easy to read.

Kim, K., Kitsabunnarat-Chatjuthamard, P. and Nofsinger, J. (2007) 'Large shareholders, board independence, and minority shareholder rights: evidence from Europe', *Journal of Corporate Finance,* 13(5), pp. 859–80.

Countries with stronger shareholder protection rights have firms with more independent directors. Also ownership concentration and board independence are negatively related.

Klein, A. and Zur, E. (2009) 'Entrepreneurial shareholder activism: hedge funds and other private investors', *Journal of Finance*, LXIV(1), pp. 187–229.

If the funds are pushing for change they lift the target share price and often gain seats on the board.

La Porta, R., Lopez-de-Silanes, F., Shleifer, A. and Vishny, R. (2000) 'Investor protection and corporate governance', *Journal of Financial Economics*, 58(1/2), pp. 3–27.

Describes the differences in laws and their effectiveness across countries.

Leuz, C., Lins, K. and Warnock, F. (2009) 'Do foreigners invest less in poorly governed firms?' *Review of Financial Studies*, 22(8), pp. 3245–85.

The answer is 'Yes'.

London, S. (2003) 'The long view: lunch with the FT, Milton Friedman', *Financial Times Magazine*, 7–8 June, pp. 12–13.

A famous pro-capitalist economist puts his case forward.

Masulis, R., Wang, C. and Xie, F. (2009) 'Agency problems at dual-class companies', *Journal of Finance*, 64(4), pp. 1697–1727.

Managers with more control over the cash of the firm are more prone to pursue their own benefits at shareholders' expense – higher pay, etc., and empire-building.

Maury, B. (2006) 'Family ownership and firm performance: empirical evidence from Western European corporations', *Journal of Corporate Finance*, 12(2), pp. 321–41.

Active family control is associated with higher profitability.

McKinsey and Company: Koller, T., Goedhart, M. and Wessels, D. (2015) *Valuation*. 6th edn. New York: John Wiley & Sons Ltd.

Contends that shareholder wealth should be the focus of managerial actions.

Rappaport, A. (2006) 'Ten ways to create shareholder value', *Harvard Business Review*, September, pp. 66–77.

Short-term goals can destroy long-term value; here are rules for compatibility.

Simon, H.A. (1959) 'Theories of decision making in economics and behavioural science', *American Economic Review*, June.

Traditional economic theories are challenged, drawing on psychology. Discusses the goals of the firm: satisficing vs. maximising.

Simon, H.A. (1964) 'On the concept of organisational goals', *Administrative Science Quarterly*, 9(1), June, pp. 1–22.

Discusses the complexity of goal setting.

Smith, A. (1776) *The Wealth of Nations*. Reproduced in 1910 in two volumes by J.M. Dent, London.

An early viewpoint on the objective of the firm.

The Economist (2005) 'A survey of corporate social responsibility', 22 January.

A forcefully argued piece on the dangers of advocating corporate social responsibility if that means less attention to shareholder wealth.

The Economist (2015) 'The business of business', 21 March.

Debates whether the purpose of a company is to maximize shareholder value or pursue broader social ends.

The Economist (2017) 'Six sects of shareholder value', 21 January.

The sects are 1. Corporate fundamentalists boosting immediate profits and share price, 2. Corporate toilers patiently aiming at shareholder value, 3. Corporate Oracles maximize shareholder wealth but anticipate changes in the rules of the game, 4. Corporate kings' success brings licence to ignore shareholder value occasionally, 5. Corporate socialists put social goals first, 6. Corporate apostates don't care about shareholders.

Tirole, J. (2005) *The Theory of Corporate Finance*. Princeton: Princeton University Press.

Provides a thorough overview of the principal–agent problem and corporate governance.

Tricker, R. I. (2015) *Corporate Governance: Principles, Policies, and Practices Paperback*. Third Edition. Oxford University Press.

A wide-ranging discussion of corporate governance, from academic models to practice in various countries.

UK Corporate Governance Code (2016) Available at the Financial Reporting Council website (www.frc.org.uk).

A clearly and concisely written set of principles, updated regularly.

Wen, S. and Zhao, J. (2011) 'Exploring the rationale of enlightened shareholder value in the realm of UK company law – the path dependence perspective', *International Trade and Business Law Review*, XIV, pp. 153–73.

A discussion of the impact of the Companies Act 2006 on the primacy of shareholder interests in the British company.

Williamson, O. (1963) 'Managerial discretion and business behaviour', *American Economic Review*, 53, pp. 1033–57.

Managerial security, power, prestige, etc. are powerful motivating forces. These goals may lead to less than profit-maximising behaviour.

Case study recommendations

Please see www.pearsoned.co.uk/arnold for case study synopses. Also, there is another list of useful case studies in the fifth edition.

- The Answer to Short-Termism isn't asking Investors to be Patient
  Author: Alex Edmans. Harvard Business School. Available at www.cb.hbsp.harvard.edu

- Cutting through the Fog: Finding a Future with Fintech
  Authors: Yiorgos Allayannis; Kayla Cartwright. Darden School of Business. Available at www. cb.hbsp. harvard.edu
- Fintech: Ecosystem, Business Models, Investment Decisions, and Challenges
  Authors: In Lee; Yong Jae Shin. Business Horizons. Available at www. cb.hbsp.harvard.edu

Websites

Alternative Investment Management Association (Hedge funds) www.aima.org
Association of British Insurers www.abi.org.uk
Association of Investment Companies www.theaic.co.uk
Bank for International Settlements www.bis.org
Bank of England www.bankofengland.co.uk
British Bankers Association www.bba.org.uk
British Venture Capital Association www.bvca.co.uk
Building Societies Association www.bsa.org.uk
City of London financial and business information www. cityoflondon.gov.uk
Companies House www.companieshouse.gov.uk
European Corporate Governance Institute www.ecgi.org
Finance and Leasing Association www.fla.org.uk
Financial Times www.FT.com

Financial Reporting Council www.frc.org.uk
ICE Futures Europe www.theice.com/futures-europe
Investment Management Association www.theinvestment-managementasociation.org
London Stock Exchange www.londonstockexchange.com
Pensions and Lifetime Savings Association www.plsa.co.uk
Securities Industry and Financial Markets Association www.sifma.org
The Banker www.thebanker.com
The City UK www.thecityuk.com
The London Institute of Banking and Finance www.libf.ac.uk
UK Corporate Governance Code www.frc.org.uk

Self-review questions

1 Why is it important to specify a goal for the corporation?

2 How can 'goal congruence' for managers and shareholders be encouraged?

3 How does money assist the well-being of society?

4 What are the economies of scale of intermediaries?

5 Distinguish between a primary market and a secondary market. How does the secondary market aid the effectiveness of the primary market?

6 Illustrate the flow of funds between primary investors and ultimate borrowers in a modern economy. Give examples of intermediary activity.

7 List as many financial intermediaries as you can. Describe the nature of their intermediation and explain the intermediate securities they create.

8 What is the principal–agent problem?

9 What is the 'contractual theory'? Do you regard it as a strong argument?

10 What difficulties might arise in state-owned industries in making financial decisions?

11 Briefly describe the following types of decisions (give examples):
   a   Financing
   b   Investment
   c   Treasury
   d   Risk management
   e   Strategic.

12 Briefly explain the role of the following:
   a   The money markets
   b   The bond markets
   c   The foreign exchange markets
   d   The share markets
   e   The derivatives markets.

Questions and problems

1 Explain the rationale for selecting shareholder wealth maximisation as the objective of the firm. Include a consideration of profit maximisation as an alternative goal.

2 What benefits are derived from the financial services sector which have led to its growth over recent years in terms of employment and share of gross domestic product (GDP)?

3 What is managerialism and how might it be incompatible with shareholder interests?

4 Why has an increasing share of household savings been channelled through financial intermediaries?

5 Discuss the relationship between economic growth and the development of a financial services sector.

6 Firm A has a stock market value of £20m (number of shares in issue × share price), while firm B is valued at £15m. The firms have similar profit histories:

	Firm A £m	Firm B £m
2014	1.5	1.8
2015	1.6	1.0
2016	1.7	2.3
2017	1.8	1.5
2018	2.0	2.0

Provide some potential reasons why, despite the same total profit over the last five years, shareholders regard firm A as being worth £5m more (extend your thoughts beyond the numbers in the table).

7 The chief executive of Geight plc receives a salary of £80,000 plus 4% of sales. Will this encourage the adoption of decisions which are shareholder wealth enhancing? How might you change matters to persuade the chief executive to focus on shareholder wealth in all decision making?

Assignments

1   Consider the organisations where you have worked in the past and the people you have come into contact with. List as many objectives as you can, explicit or implicit, that have been revealed to, or suspected by, you. To what extent was goal congruence between different stakeholders achieved? How might the efforts of all individuals be channelled more effectively?

2   Review all the financial services you or your firm purchase. Try to establish a rough estimate of the cost of using each financial intermediary and write a balanced report considering whether you or your firm should continue to pay for that service.

PART 2

The investment decision

Project appraisal:
net present value and internal rate of return

LEARNING OUTCOMES

By the end of this chapter the reader should be able to explain the theoretical justifications for using discounted cash flow techniques in analysing major investment decisions, based on the concepts of the time value of money and the opportunity cost of capital. More specifically, the reader should be able to:

■ calculate net present value and internal rate of return;

■ explain the relationship between net present value and internal rate of return;

■ describe and explain three potential problems that can arise with internal rate of return;

■ discuss why managers favour a percentage measure of investment performance;

■ discuss the use of a modified internal rate of return.

Introduction

Shareholders supply funds to a firm for a reason: to receive a return on their investment. Management uses the funds provided by the shareholders to invest in real assets such as property, plant and equipment which are then used in business operations to generate revenue and profit. No matter how large the company, there is always a limit to the funds available and so it is vital that management employs the best techniques available when analysing which of all the possible investment opportunities will give the best return.

Management has to decide whether it is better to build a new factory or extend the old; whether it is wiser to use an empty piece of land for a multi-storey car park or to invest a larger sum and build a shopping centre. Alternatively, would the shareholders be better off if the firm returned their money in the form of dividends because the shareholders could obtain a better return elsewhere?

Decisions about the allocation of funds require informed and skilled personnel plus information on many factors – the market environment, the level of demand, internal resources and capabilities, costs, and, of course, an understanding of the risk associated with the project. Hitachi presumably considered these factors before making their investment in train building in the UK – *see* **Exhibit 2.1**.

Exhibit 2.1

Hitachi to open £82m train plant in Durham this year

By Chris Tighe and Tanya Powley

A newly completed track from one of the UK's biggest new factories links rail transport in the 21st century to the industrial revolution of the 19th.

The track connects Hitachi Rail Europe's new County Durham plant to a nearby branch line it will use to deliver its trains into the intercity network. The same branch carried the first paying passenger train as it began its journey in 1825 on the Stockton and Darlington line.

A strong regional engineering tradition was one of the reasons that Hitachi chose the Newton Aycliffe site in 2012 from 40 potential UK locations. Darren Cumner, manager of the manufacturing plant, is focused on the future. "We have to be very careful with playing the heritage card," he said.

The £82m plant, which will open this year, will be one of northeast England's most significant industrial investments since Nissan's arrival in 1984.

The opening is an important moment for Britain's train building industry. It is the first train manufacturing plant built in the UK for decades, bringing hope that one of the country's oldest industries can be revived.

The industry that pioneered the steam train almost 200 years ago has been laid low by years of neglect and under-investment. It came close to extinction three years ago when the Bombardier plant in Derby lost out on a large contract to Siemens of Germany.

Bombardier's Derby train plant can also trace its roots back to the early days of rail. The plant was established in 1839 as the Derby Midland Railway Workshops just around the corner from where it stands today. But after being privatised as part of British Rail in 1989, the site has passed between various overseas owners before being bought by Bombardier of Canada.

After coming under heavy criticism for selecting Siemens to build trains for Thameslink, ministers have tried to develop a strong UK-based rail manufacturing industry to maximise the benefit to the economy of the huge expansion taking place in the network, such as Crossrail, Thameslink and the High Speed 2 project.

The government in 2013 launched a rail industry supply chain forum to support UK small and medium enterprises. Last year it awarded Bombardier a £1bn contract to supply Crossrail trains.

Hitachi's decision last year to make London the headquarters of its global train business bolstered hopes that the UK was at the start of a new rail industry boom.

▶

Exhibit 2.1 *(continued)*

The Newton Aycliffe site, the Japanese company's first European train factory, was given the go-ahead after the government awarded Hitachi Rail Europe the contract to supply the intercity express programme, the next generation of trains for the East Coast and Great Western main lines. Under this £5.7bn contract, which includes maintenance and runs for 27.5 years, Hitachi will build 122 trains comprising 866 carriages. Twelve trains are being manufactured at its Kasado works in Japan and the rest at Newton Aycliffe. Hitachi has also been named by Abellio, an arm of the Dutch state rail operator, as preferred bidder for 70 trains for ScotRail.

This month sees the start of recruiting of technicians, craftsmen and engineers who will fill most of the 730 jobs being created at the plant, ready for production to begin in January 2016.

Champions of the plant estimate the supply chain could support another 6,000 jobs. Hitachi has used a number of UK companies for its key systems and is now looking for tier-two suppliers, a key moment for companies hoping to enter the rail sector. More than 1,000 businesses attended one Durham supply chain event early in the project.

"We had an overwhelming, huge, response," said Jamie Foster, procurement director. "The rail industry is a new opportunity for many tier-two suppliers."

October's topping out of the 460,000 sq ft plant was marked with an announcement that Hitachi Rail Europe would open its design office at Newton Aycliffe, a clear signal that this is not merely an assembly plant.

"We aren't going to rely on the Japanese supplier base for components. We are going to Europeanise as much of this plant as we can," Mr Foster said. The company said it was working with 56 suppliers in Europe, 32 of them based in the UK.

In contrast to Nissan's high-volume, "just in time" Sunderland operation, which requires some suppliers to be located next to, or even in, the plant, Hitachi, with its longer manufacturing timescales, does not need them on the doorstep.

"We aren't stipulating it as a requirement", Mr Foster said.

Even so, the decision to build the plant at Newton Aycliffe has brought a "Hitachi effect", said Geoff Hunton, a director of Merchant Anglo Property Holdings, owner of Merchant Park which includes Hitachi's site. "It's the catalyst for everything we've been trying to achieve."

FT *Financial Times,* 11 January 2015.
All Rights Reserved.

Even when managers have full information about the competing investment opportunities, they need an investment appraisal technique which allows them to compare the opportunities and which leads to a 'good' decision.

This chapter examines two approaches to evaluating investments.[1] Both emphasise the central importance of the time value of money and are described as discounted cash flow (DCF) techniques. Net present value (NPV) and internal rate of return (IRR) are used in most large commercial organisations and are regarded as more complete than the traditional techniques of payback and accounting rate of return. These alternative methods are discussed in Chapter 4 alongside a consideration of some of the practical issues of project implementation. In this chapter, we concentrate on the calculation of net present value and internal rate of return and their theoretical underpinnings.

Value creation and corporate investment

If we accept that the objective of investment within the firm is to create value for its owners then the purpose of allocating money to a particular project is to generate future cash inflows significantly greater than the amount invested. The project appraisal decision compares the amount of cash put into an investment with the amount of cash returned. The key phrase and tricky issue is 'significantly greater than'.

A company offers you shares for £10,000. The management team intends to invest that £10,000 and return to you, in five years, the £10,000 plus £1,000. Would you accept? Is this a significant return? If you were aware that by investing the £10,000 yourself, by lending to the government, you could receive a 5% return per year or that you could obtain a return of 10% per annum by

---

1 The selection of investment projects is called capital expenditure – 'capex' – or capital budgeting.

investing in other shares on the stock market, you would not invest in an opportunity that offered a return of less than 2% per year.

Investors have alternative uses for their funds and therefore, if they invest in a company, they have an opportunity cost. The *investor's* opportunity cost is the sacrifice of the return available on the best forgone alternative. A company's investments must generate at least enough cash for all investors to obtain their required returns. If they produce less than the investor's opportunity cost, then the wealth of shareholders will decline. This idea of opportunity cost can perhaps be better explained by a diagram (*see* **Exhibit 2.2**).

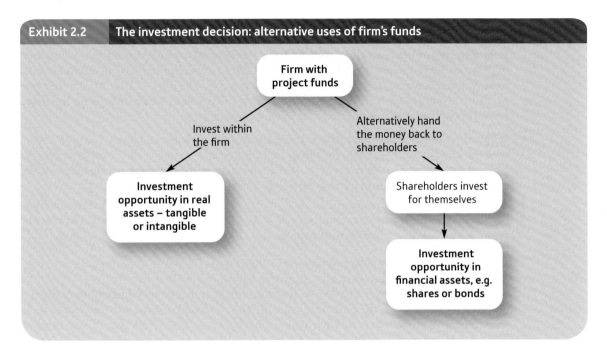

Exhibit 2.2   The investment decision: alternative uses of firm's funds

Wealth creation is determined not only by the future cash flows derived from a project but also by the timing of those cash flows. Future cash flows do not have the same value as today's cash flows – there is a time value of money – and this must be taken into account in decision making. **Exhibit 2.3** summarises the process of good investment appraisal.

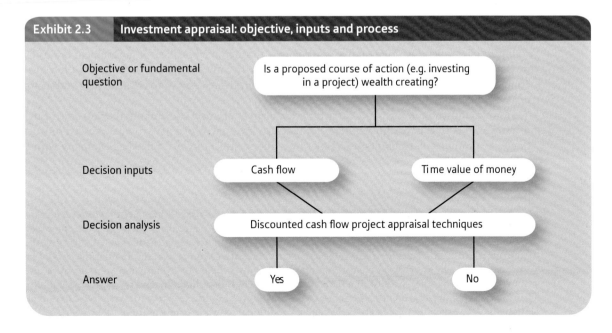

Exhibit 2.3   Investment appraisal: objective, inputs and process

The time value of money

When people invest, they give up the opportunity to use their money now. If an investor buys shares in a firm or lends to a business they sacrifice consumption today. One of the incentives to save is the possibility of higher future consumption from sacrificing some present consumption. Compensation is required to induce people to make that consumption sacrifice. Compensation will be required for at least three things:

● *Impatience to consume* Individuals generally prefer £1.00 today rather than £1.00 in five years' time. To put this formally: the utility of £1.00 now is greater than £1.00 received five years hence. Individuals are impatient to consume, thus they need an appropriate reward for saving. The rate of exchange between certain future consumption and certain current consumption is the pure rate of interest – this occurs even in a world of no inflation and no risk. If you lived in such a world you might be willing to sacrifice £100 of consumption today in return for £102 to be received in one year, your pure rate of interest is 2%. The price of time (the interest rate needed to compensate for impatience to consume) exists even when there is no inflation, because people prefer consumption now to consumption later.

● *Inflation* As inflation increases prices, the investor will be unable to buy, in one year's time, with the same quantity of cash, the things that they could buy today; their purchasing power (their ability to buy) has been reduced. If there is inflation, the providers of finance must be compensated for that loss in purchasing power over time.

● *Risk* The promise of the receipt of a sum of money in the future carries risk; the pay-out may not take place or the future amount may be less than expected. Risk simply means that the future return has a variety of possible values.

The firm seeking investment must be prepared to compensate the investor for impatience to consume, inflation and risk involved; otherwise no one will be willing to invest.[2]

An investor is considering a £1,000 one-year investment and requires compensation. First, a return of 2% is required for the pure time value of money. Second, inflation is anticipated to be 3% over the year. At time zero (t_0) £1,000 buys one basket of goods and services. To buy the same basket of goods and services at time t_1 (one year later) £1,030 is needed. To compensate the investor for impatience to consume and inflation the investment needs to generate a return of 5.06%, that is:

$$(1 + 0.02)(1 + 0.03) - 1 = 0.0506$$

The figure of 5.06% here is the risk-free return (RFR), the interest rate which is sufficient to induce investment assuming no uncertainty about cash flows. The RFR forms the bedrock for time value of money calculations as the pure time value and the expected inflation rate affect all investments equally.

Investors view lending to reputable governments through the purchase of government bonds or treasury bills as the nearest they are going to get to risk-free investing, because these select few governments have an almost unlimited ability to raise income from taxes or to create money and so are unlikely to default.

However, different investments carry different degrees of uncertainty about the outcome of the investment, i.e. they have different levels of risk. An investment in a new company based on cutting-edge or unproven technology is riskier than an investment in an established company with a

---

2 A further factor (which to some extent could be seen as a form of risk) is that once the lender has committed the funds to a borrower for a set period of time they have to face the risk that at some point they may need the funds. With some investments, there are ways of releasing the money – converting the instrument to cash – quickly, at low transaction cost and with certainty over the amount that would be released. This can be achieved by insisting that the borrower repays or from selling the right to receive interest, etc. to another investor in a market. That is, there is high liquidity and therefore low liquidity risk. If lenders/investors do not have access to the possibility of quick, low-cost conversion to cash – high liquidity risk – then they are likely to demand an additional return in compensation.

proven product and steady growth prospects. Investors require different risk premiums on top of the RFR to reflect the perceived level of extra risk.

Required return = RFR + Risk premium

The risk premium pushes up the total return required, thus compensating for all three elements of the time value of money.

Discounted cash flow

The net present value and internal rate of return techniques, both being discounted cash flow methods, consider the time value of money. **Exhibit 2.4**, which presents Project Alpha, suggests that on a straightforward analysis, Project Alpha generates more cash inflows than outflows. An outlay of £2,000 produces £2,400.

Exhibit 2.4	Project Alpha, simple cash flow	
	Points in time (yearly intervals)	**Cash flows (£)**
0	Now	−2,000
1	(1 year from now)	+600
2		+600
3		+600
4		+600

However, the £600 cash flows occur at different times and are therefore worth different amounts to an investor evaluating this investment at time zero. The investor would value the £600 received in one year more highly than the £600 received after four years. The present value of the pounds (at time zero) depends on when they are received.

It would be useful to convert all these different pounds to a common currency – their present value. The conversion is achieved by discounting all future cash flows, thereby expressing them as a present value, a comparable value at time zero. The process of discounting relies on a variant of the compounding formula:

$$F = P(1 + i)^n$$

where
F = future value
P = present value
i = interest rate
n = number of years over which compounding takes place

Note   Readers may need to turn to Appendix 2.1 at the end of this chapter to get to grips with the key mathematical tools which will be used. Readers are strongly advised to attempt the Appendix 2.1 exercises (answers are provided in Appendix VI at the end of the book).

If a saver deposited £100 in a bank account paying interest at 8% per annum, after three years the account will contain £125.97:

$$F = 100 (1 + 0.08)^3 = £125.97$$

This formula can be changed so that we can answer the following question: 'How much must I deposit in the bank now to receive £125.97 in three years?' We need to rearrange the formula so that we are calculating for present value, P.

$$P = \frac{F}{(1 + i)^n} \text{ or } F \times \frac{1}{(1 + i)^n}$$

$$P = \frac{125.97}{(1 + 0.08)^3} = 100$$

We have discounted the £125.97 back to a present value of £100. If this technique is now applied to Project Alpha to convert all the future cash flows into their present value equivalents the result is as follows (the time value of money is 10%) – **Exhibit 2.5**.

Exhibit 2.5	Project Alpha, discounted cash flow	

Points in time (yearly intervals)	Cash flows (£)	Discounted cash flows (£)
0	−2,000	−2,000.00
1	+600	$\frac{600}{1 + 0.10}$ = +545.45
2	+600	$\frac{600}{(1 + 0.10)^2}$ = +495.87
3	+600	$\frac{600}{(1 + 0.10)^3}$ = +450.79
4	+600	$\frac{600}{(1 + 0.10)^4}$ = +409.81

When the future pounds are converted to a common present value, this investment involves a larger outflow (£2,000) than inflow (£1,901.92). The cash flows in are worth less than the cash flows out, discounted at 10%. In other words, the return on the £2,000 investment is less than 10%.

Technical aside

If your calculator has a 'powers' function (usually represented by x^y or y^x) then compounding and discounting can be accomplished quickly. Alternatively, discount factors are in Appendix II. Taking the discounting of the fourth year's cash flow as an illustration:

$$\frac{1}{(1 + 0.10)^4} \times 600$$

Calculator: Input 1.10
Press y^x (or x^y)
Input 4
Press =
Display 1.4641
Press 1/x
Display 0.6830
Multiply by 600
Answer 409.81

Using Appendix II, look down the column 10% and along the row 4 years to find discount factor of 0.683. Calculating 0.683 × £600 = £409.81

Net present value and internal rate of return

Net present value: examples and definitions

The conceptual justification for, and the mathematics of, the net present value and internal rate of return methods of project appraisal will be illustrated through an imaginary but realistic decision-making process at the firm of Hard Decisions plc. This example, in addition to describing techniques, demonstrates the centrality of some key concepts such as opportunity cost and time value of money and shows the wealth-destroying effect of ignoring these issues.

You are the finance director of a large publicly quoted company called Hard Decisions plc, which has shareholder wealth maximisation as its primary objective. Recently, the board appointed a new director, Mr Spark, who has been hired to seek out avenues for expansion and ways to make better use of existing assets. Mr Spark has been reviewing a derelict ten-acre site that the company owns and has proposed three alternative investment opportunities.

Proposal 1 is to clean and decontaminate a site, previously used for chemical production, for £5m and then sell it to developers for £12m in one year's time, giving a profit of £7m.

Proposal 1:   Clean up and sell

Clearing the site plus decontamination, payable t_0	−£5m
Sell the site in one year, t_1	£12m
Profit	£7m

The chairman of the board turns to you, in your capacity as the financial expert on the board, to ask what you think. You make the following observations:

Point 1   This company is valued by the stock market at £100m because our investors are content that the rate of return they receive from us is consistent with the going rate for our risk class of shares: that is, 15% per annum. The opportunity cost for our shareholders of buying shares in this firm is 15% and is our minimum required return from any project of the same risk class that we undertake.

Point 2   We have received numerous offers for the ten-acre site over the past year. A reasonable estimate of its immediate sale value would be £6m. This £6m is an opportunity cost of the project, in that it is the value of the best alternative use. Thus, we should add to Mr Spark's £5m of clean-up costs the £6m of opportunity cost because we are sacrificing £11m to put this proposal into operation. If we did not go ahead with Mr Spark's proposal, but sold the site as it is, we could raise our bank balance by £6m; additionally we would not have to pay out the £5m for clean-up costs.

Proposal 1:   Clean up and sell – Year t_0 cash flows

Immediate sale value (opportunity cost)	£6m
Clean-up, etc.	£5m
Total sacrifice at t_0	£11m

Point 3   Mr Spark's final selling price of £12m is valid and supported by external experts, but we cannot compare the initial outlay *directly* with the final cash flow on a *nominal* basis. The £12m is to be received in one year's time, whereas the £5m for clean-up costs and the £6m opportunity cost sacrifice are being made immediately.

If we were to take the £11m initial cost of the project and invest it in financial assets of the same risk class as this firm, giving a return of 15%, then the value of that investment at the end of one year would be £12.65m. The calculation for this:

$$F = P(1 + k)$$

where k = the opportunity cost of capital:

$$11 (1 + 0.15) = £12.65m$$

This is more than the return promised by Mr Spark.

Another way of looking at this problem is to calculate the net present value of the project. We start with the classic formula for net present value:

$$NPV = CF_0 + \frac{CF_1}{(1 + k)^n}$$

where CF_0 = cash flow at time zero (t_0), and
CF_1 = cash flow at time one (t_1), one year after time zero:

$$NPV = -11 + \frac{12}{1 + 0.15} = -11 + 10.435 = -£0.565m$$

All cash flows are expressed in the common currency of present value – pounds at time zero. When the positives and negatives are netted out we have the *net* present value. The decision rules for net present value are:

NPV ≥ 0   Accept
NPV < 0   Reject

Project 1's negative NPV indicates that the present value of the cash inflows is less than the present value of the cash outflows and that a return of less than 15% per annum will be achieved from this project.

An investment proposal's net present value is derived by discounting all project cash flows, both in and out, to present value and summing them. The discount rate used, reflects the opportunity cost of the funds.

In conclusion given the choice between selling the site immediately raising £6m and saving £5m of expenditure – a total of £11m, or developing the site along the lines of Mr Spark's proposal, I would choose to sell it immediately and invest the £11m elsewhere.

Proposal 2: Office complex

Proposal 2 concerns a 6-year project. Paying £5m clean-up costs immediately and then, over the next two years, spending another £14m building an office complex, which, once complete, would be let gradually to tenants over years 3–6. When the office complex is fully let, in six years' time, it would be sold to an institution, such as a pension fund, for the sum of £40m (*see* **Exhibit 2.6**).

Mr Spark's figures show an almost doubling of the money invested (£25m invested over the first two years leads to an inflow of £47m).

The chairman asks: Is this project beneficial to our shareholders?

You reply: The best method of assessing whether a project is shareholder wealth enhancing is to discount all its cash flows to present value at the opportunity cost of capital. This requires a calculation of the net present value.

$$NPV = CF_0 + \frac{CF_1}{1 + k} + \frac{CF_2}{(1 + k)^2} + \frac{CF_3}{(1 + k)^3} \cdots + \frac{CF_n}{(1 + k)^n}$$

The NPV of Proposal 2 is negative – *see* **Exhibit 2.7**. Note that we again use a 15% discount rate, which implies that this project is at the same level of risk as project 1 and the same as the average of the existing set of risk projects carried out by the firm. If it is subject to higher risk an increased rate of return would be demanded (the calculation of the required rate of return is discussed in Chapter 16).

Exhibit 2.6	Project 2: Mr Spark's figures	

Points in time (yearly intervals)	Cash flows (£m)	Event
0 (now)	−11	Clean-up and opportunity costs
1	−4	Building cost
2	−10	Building cost
3	+1	Net rental income $-\frac{1}{4}$ of offices let
4	+2	Net rental income $-\frac{1}{2}$ of offices let
5	+4	Net rental income – all offices let
6	+40	Office complex sold
Total	+22	Inflow £47m / Outflow £25m

Note: *Mr Spark has added the opportunity cost of −£6m to his figures.*

Exhibit 2.7	Proposal 2: Net present value	

Points in time (yearly intervals)	Cash flows (£m)		Discounted cash flows (£m)
0	−11		−11.00
1	−4	$\dfrac{-4}{(1+0.15)}$	−3.48
2	−10	$\dfrac{-10}{(1+0.15)^2}$	−7.56
3	1	$\dfrac{1}{(1+0.15)^3}$	0.66
4	2	$\dfrac{2}{(1+0.15)^4}$	1.14
5	4	$\dfrac{4}{(1+0.15)^5}$	1.99
6	40	$\dfrac{40}{(1+0.15)^6}$	17.29
Net present value			−0.96

(An Excel spreadsheet version of this calculation is shown at www.pearsoned.co.uk/arnold.)

Proposal 2: Net present value

NPV is negative so we would serve our shareholders better by selling the site, saving the money spent on clearing and building and either investing in projects yielding more than 15% or returning the money to the shareholders.

The chairman thanks you and asks Mr Spark for his third proposal.

Proposal 3: World-beater manufacturing plant

Proposal 3 involves the use of the site for a factory to manufacture the product 'World-beater'. We have been producing 'World-beater' from our Liverpool factory for the past ten years and selling to the UK market. I propose the setting up of a second 'World-beater' factory which will serve the European market. The figures are as follows (*see* **Exhibit 2.8**).

Exhibit 2.8	Proposal 3: Mr Spark's figures	
Points in time (yearly intervals)	**Cash flows (£m)**	**Event**
0	−11	Clean-up and opportunity costs
1	−10	Factory building
2	0	
3 to infinity	+5	Net income from additional sales of 'World-beater'

Note: Revenue is earned in Year 2 from sales but is exactly offset by the cash outflows. The figures for Year 3 and all subsequent years are net cash flows that is, cash outflows are subtracted from cash inflows generated by sales.

You reply: World-beater is a well-established product and has been very successful. Taking the cash flow figures given by Mr Sparks, I have calculated the NPV for Project 3 (**Exhibit 2.9**).

Exhibit 2.9	Proposal 3: Net present value		
Points in time (yearly intervals)	**Cash flows (£m)**		**Discounted cash flows (£m)**
0	−11		−11
1	−10	$\dfrac{-10}{(1 + 0.15)}$	−8.7
		Value of perpetuity at time t_2:	
3 to infinity	5	$P = \dfrac{F}{k} = \dfrac{5}{0.15} = 33.33.$	

The present value of the perpetuity has to be discounted back two years to get present value of the perpetuity at $t_{0\,\sim\,\text{(see note below)}}$

$$\dfrac{33.33}{(1 + 0.15)^2} \qquad = \underline{25.20}$$

| Net present value | | | +5.5 |

(An Excel spreadsheet version of this calculation is shown at www.pearsoned.co.uk/arnold.)

Note	The perpetuity formula can be used on the assumption that the first payment arises one year from the time at which we are valuing. So, if the first inflow arises at time 3 we are valuing the perpetuity as though we are standing at time 2. The objective of this exercise is to convert all cash flows to time 0 value. Therefore, it is necessary to discount the perpetuity value at time 2 by two years to get the value at time 0.

This project gives a positive NPV and is shareholder wealth enhancing. Project 3 has a return greater than 15%; it provides a return of 15% plus an additional present value of £5.5m. I would recommend that the board considers Proposal 3 in more detail.

Mr Spark (interrupts): Our finance expert has stated that the way to evaluate these proposals is by using the NPV method, but in the firms where I have worked in the past, the internal rate of return (IRR) method of investment appraisal was used. I would like to see how these three proposals shape up when the IRR calculations are done.

The chairman asks you to explain the IRR method, and to apply it to the figures provided by Mr Spark.

Before continuing this boardroom drama, it might be useful at this point to broaden the understanding of NPV by considering two worked examples.

Worked example 2.1	**Camrat plc**

Camrat plc requires a return on investment of at least 10% per annum over the life of any proposed project with the same risk as its existing projects to meet the opportunity cost of its shareholders. The strategic development team have been examining the possibility of entering the new market area of mosaic floor tiles. This will require an immediate outlay of £1m for factory purchase and tooling-up, which will be followed by **net** (i.e. after all cash outflows, e.g. wages, variable costs, etc.) cash inflows of £0.2m in one year, and £0.3m in two years' time. Thereafter, annual net cash inflows will be £180,000.

Required

Given these cash flows, will this investment provide a 10% return (per annum) over the life of the project? Assume for simplicity that all cash flows arise on anniversary dates and the project has the same risk level as the existing set of projects.

Answer

First, lay out the cash flows:

Time (yearly)	0	1	2	3 to infinity
Cash flows (£)	−1m	0.2m	0.3m	0.18m

Second, discount these cash flows to their present value equivalents.

Points in time	0	1	2	3 to infinity
	CF_0	$\dfrac{CF_1}{1+k}$	$\dfrac{CF_2}{(1+k)^2}$	$\dfrac{CF_3}{k} \times \dfrac{1}{(1+k)^2}$
	−1m	$\dfrac{0.2}{1+0.1}$	$\dfrac{0.3}{(1+0.1)^2}$	$\dfrac{0.18}{0.1}$

This discounts back two years:

$$\frac{0.18/0.1}{(1+0.1)^2}$$

	−1m	0.1818	0.2479	$\dfrac{1.8}{(1.1)^2} = 1.4876$

Third, calculate the net present value:

$$-1.0000 + 0.1818 + 0.2479 + 1.4876 = +0.9173$$

▶

Worked example 2.1 *(continued)*

Conclusion

The positive NPV demonstrates that this project provides a return of more than 10% per annum. This is an attractive project: on a £1m investment the surplus generated beyond the opportunity cost of the shareholders (their time value of money) is £917,300; by accepting this project, we would increase shareholder wealth by this amount.

(An Excel spreadsheet version of this calculation is shown at www.pearsoned.co.uk/arnold.)

Worked example 2.2   Actarm plc

Actarm plc is examining two projects, A and B. The cash flows are as follows:

	A £	B £
Initial outflow, t_0	240,000	240,000
Cash inflows:		
Time 1 (one year after t_0)	200,000	20,000
Time 2	100,000	120,000
Time 3	20,000	220,000

Using discount rates of 8% and then 16%, calculate the NPVs and state which project is superior. Why do you get a different preference depending on the discount rate used?

Answer

Using 8% as the discount rate

$$NPV = CF_0 + \frac{CF_1}{1 + k} + \frac{CF_2}{(1 + k)^2} + \frac{CF_3}{(1 + k)^3}$$

Project A

$$-240,000 + \frac{200,000}{1 + 0.08} + \frac{100,000}{(1 + 0.08)^2} + \frac{20,000}{(1 + 0.08)^3}$$

$$-240,000 + 185,185 + 85,734 + 15,877 = +£46,796$$

Project B

$$-240,000 + \frac{20,000}{1 + 0.08} + \frac{120,000}{(1 + 0.08)^2} + \frac{220,000}{(1 + 0.08)^3}$$

$$-240,000 + 18,519 + 102,881 + 174,643 = +£56,043$$

Using an 8% discount rate both projects produce positive NPVs and therefore would enhance shareholder wealth. However, Project B is superior because it creates more value than Project A. Thus, if the accepting of one project excludes the possibility of accepting the other then B is preferred.

Using 16% as the discount rate

Project A

$$-240,000 + \frac{200,000}{1.16} + \frac{100,000}{(1.16)^2} + \frac{20,000}{(1.16)^3}$$

$$-240,000 + 172,414 + 74,316 + 12,813 = +£19,543$$

Project B

$$-240,000 + \frac{20,000}{1.16} + \frac{120,000}{(1.16)^2} + \frac{220,000}{(1.16)^3}$$

$$-240,000 + 17,241 + 89,180 + 140,945 = +£7,366$$

With a 16% discount rate Project A generates more shareholder value and so would be preferred to Project B. This is despite the fact that Project B, in pure undiscounted cash flow terms, produces an additional £40,000.

The different ranking (order of superiority) occurs because Project B has the bulk of its cash flows occurring towards the end of the project's life. These large distant cash flows, when discounted at a high discount rate, become relatively small compared with those of Project A, which has its high cash flows discounted by only one year.

(An Excel spreadsheet showing these calculations is available at www.pearsoned.co.uk/arnold.)

Internal rate of return

We now return to Hard Decisions plc. The chairman has asked you to explain internal rate of return (IRR).

You respond: The internal rate of return is a very popular method of project appraisal and, like NPV, it takes into account the time value of money. The IRR tells you the rate of return you will receive by putting your money into a project. It describes by how much the cash inflows exceed the cash outflows on an annualised percentage basis, taking account of the timing of those cash flows.

The internal rate of return is the rate of return which equates the present value of future cash flows with the outlay (or, for some projects, it equates discounted future cash outflows with initial inflow):

Outlay = Future cash flows discounted at rate r

Thus:

$$CF_0 = \frac{CF_1}{1 + r} + \frac{CF_2}{(1 + r)^2} + \frac{CF_3}{(1 + r)^3} \cdots \frac{CF_n}{(1 + r)^n}$$

IRR is also referred to as the 'yield' of a project.

Alternatively, the internal rate of return, r, can be viewed as the discount rate at which the net present value is zero. It is the value for r which makes the following equation hold:

$$CF_0 + \frac{CF_1}{1 + r} + \frac{CF_2}{(1 + r)^2} + \frac{CF_3}{(1 + r)^3} \cdots \frac{CF_n}{(1 + r)^n} = 0$$

(Note: in the first formula CF_0 is expressed as a positive number, whereas in the second it is usually a negative.)

These two equations amount to the same thing. They both require knowledge of the cash flows and their timings. The element which is unknown is the rate of return (r) which will make the time-adjusted outflows and inflows equal.

Calculation of IRR for each proposal

Proposal 1: Internal rate of return

Our objective is to find an r which makes the discounted inflow at time 1 of £12m plus the initial £11m outflow equal to zero:

$$CF_0 + \frac{CF_1}{1 + r} = 0$$

$$-11 + \frac{12}{1 + r} = 0$$

The recommended method for establishing r is trial and error; simply pick a discount rate and plug it into the formula. You can pick any (reasonable) discount rate to begin with. Let us try 5 per cent:

$$-11 + \frac{12}{1 + 0.05} = \text{£0.42857m or £428,571}$$

A 5% rate is not correct because the discounted cash flows do not total to zero. The surplus of approximately £0.43m suggests that a higher interest rate will be more suitable. This will reduce the present value of the future cash inflow.

Try 10 %:

$$-11 + \frac{12}{1 + 0.1} = -0.0909 \text{ or } -£90,909$$

Again we have not hit on the correct discount rate.

Try 9%:

$$-11 + \frac{12}{1 + 0.09} = + 0.009174 \text{ or } £9,174$$

The last two calculations tell us that the discount rate which causes the discounted future cash flow to equal the initial outflow lies somewhere between 9% and 10%. The precise rate is found through interpolation.

Interpolation for Proposal 1

First, display all the facts so far established (*see* **Exhibit 2.10**).

Exhibit 2.10	Interpolation			
Discount rate	9%	?		10%
Net present value	+£9,174	0		−£90,909
Point	A	B		C

Exhibit 2.10 illustrates that there is a rate (r) which lies between 9% and 10% which will produce an NPV of zero. The way to find that discount rate is to first find the distance between points A and B as a proportion of the entire distance between points A and C.

$$\frac{A \rightarrow B}{A \rightarrow C} = \frac{9.174 - 0}{9,174 + 90,909} = 0.0917$$

Thus rate (r) lies at a distance of 0.0917 of the distance between 9 and 10% above the 9% point.

$$IRR = 9 + \left(\frac{9,174}{100,083}\right) \times (10 - 9) = 9.0917 \text{ per cent}$$

To double-check our result:

$$-11 + \frac{12}{1 + 0.090917}$$
$$-11 + 11 = 0$$

Internal rate of return decision rules

The rule for internal rate of return decisions is:

If $k > r$ reject

If the opportunity cost of capital (k) for the project is greater than the internal rate of return (r) on a project, then the investor is better served by rejecting the project and applying the money to the best alternative use. However, if $k \leq r$, then accept the project.

The IRR of Proposal 1 is 9.091%, which is below the 15% opportunity cost of capital used by Hard Decisions plc for projects of this risk class. Therefore, using the IRR method gives the same decisions as the NPV method; this project should be rejected.

It might be enlightening to consider the relationship between NPV and IRR. **Exhibit 2.11** shows what happens to NPV as the discount rate is varied between zero and 10% for Proposal 1. At a zero discount rate the £12m received in one year is not discounted at all, so the NPV of £1m is simply the difference between the two cash flows. When the discount rate is raised to 10% the present value of the year 1 cash flow becomes less than the current outlay. Where the line crosses the x axis, i.e. when NPV is zero, we can read off the internal rate of return. It should be noted that in the case of Project proposal 1 the NPV/discount rate relationship is nearly a straight line. This is an unusual case. When cash flows occur over several years the line is likely to be more curved and concave to the origin.

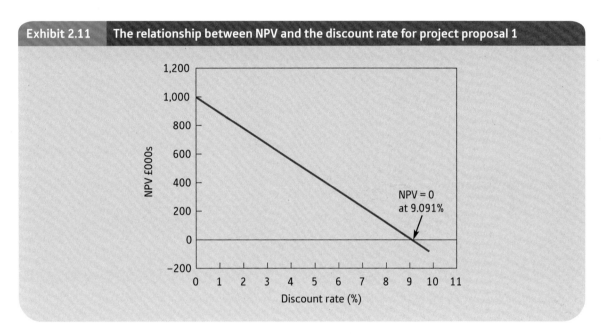

Exhibit 2.11 The relationship between NPV and the discount rate for project proposal 1

Proposal 2: IRR

To calculate the IRR for Proposal 2 we first lay out the cash flows in the discount formula:

$$-11 + \frac{-4}{(1+r)} + \frac{-10}{(1+r)^2} + \frac{1}{(1+r)^3} + \frac{2}{(1+r)^4} + \frac{4}{(1+r)^5} + \frac{40}{(1+r)^6} = 0$$

Then we try alternative discount rates to find a rate, r, that gives a zero NPV:
At 14 %:

NPV (approximately) $= -£43,000$

At 13%:

NPV (approximately) $= £932,000$

Interpolation is required to find an internal rate of return (*see* **Exhibit 2.12**).

Exhibit 2.12 Interpolation

Discount rate	13%		?	14%
NPV	+932,000		0	−43,000

$$13 + \frac{932,000}{975,000} \times (14 - 13) = 13.96\%$$

This project produces an IRR (13.96%) which is less than the opportunity cost of shareholders' funds (15%); therefore the project should be rejected. The curvature of the line (in **Exhibit 2.13**) is exaggerated to demonstrate the absence of linearity and emphasise the importance of having a small gap in trial and error interest rates for interpolation. The interpolation formula assumes a straight line between the two discount rates chosen and this may lead to a false result if the gap between the rates is too big. The effect of taking a wide range of rates can be illustrated if we calculate 5% and 30% – *see* **Exhibit 2.14**.

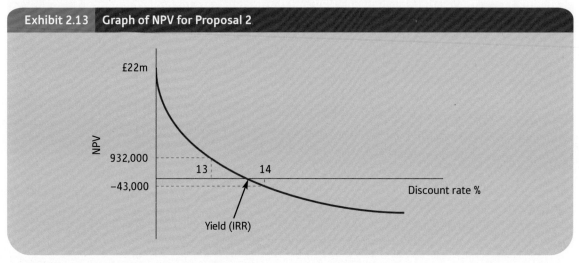

Exhibit 2.13   Graph of NPV for Proposal 2

(An Excel spreadsheet showing the IRR calculation for Proposal 2 is available at www.pearsoned.co.uk/arnold.)

At 5%, NPV of Project 2 £11.6121m.
At 30%, NPV of Project 2 –£9.4743m.

$$5 + \left(\frac{11.6121}{11.6121 + 9.4743} \right)(30 - 5) = 18.77\%$$

From Exhibit 2.14 we see that the non-linearity of the relationship between NPV and the discount rate has created an IRR almost 5% removed from the true IRR. This could lead to an erroneous acceptance of this project given the company's hurdle rate of 15%.

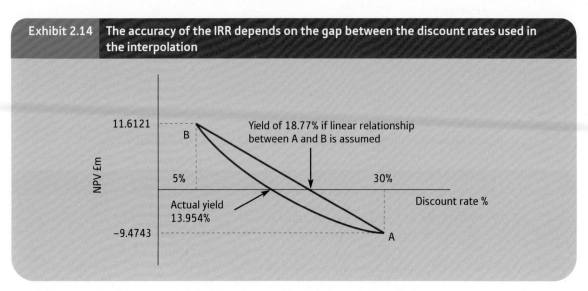

Exhibit 2.14   The accuracy of the IRR depends on the gap between the discount rates used in the interpolation

Proposal 3: IRR – *see* Exhibit 2.9 for cash flows

$$CF_0 + \frac{CF_1}{1 + r} + \frac{CF_3/r}{(1 + r)^2} = 0$$

Try 19%:

$$-11 + \frac{-10}{1 + 0.19} + \frac{5/0.19}{(1 + 0.19)^2} = -£0.82m$$

Try 18%:

$$-11 + \frac{-10}{1 + 0.18} + \frac{5/0.18}{(1 + 0.18)^2} = +£0.475m$$

Project 3 produces an internal rate of return of 18.37% which is higher than the opportunity cost of capital and therefore the investment is to be commended (**Exhibit 2.15**).

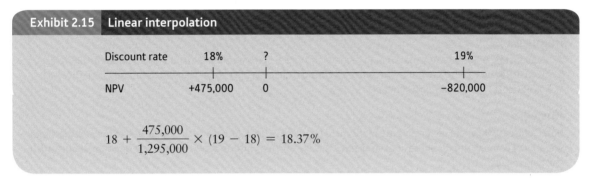

| Exhibit 2.15 | Linear interpolation |

Discount rate	18%	?		19%
NPV	+475,000	0		−820,000

$$18 + \frac{475,000}{1,295,000} \times (19 - 18) = 18.37\%$$

(An Excel spreadsheet is available at www.pearsoned.co.uk/arnold.)

IRR is a commonly used metric in business. Gerald Ronson, one of the richest people in the property business, uses it to make decisions – *see* **Exhibit 2.16**.

Exhibit 2.16

Bullish Ronson defies slump to carry on building apace

By Daniel Thomas

Mr Ronson says that most deals cross his large mahogany desk early on, but so far there have been few of interest. He has almost £140m to spend when the time is right.

'There will be interesting opportunities over the next 18–24 months but I have yet to see a deal that I consider we want to do. This is not the time to overpay, and you need to see a respectable return. We [want] to see a return over 20 per cent on an IRR basis with low gearing,' he adds.

We temporarily leave the saga of Mr Spark and his proposals to reinforce understanding of NPV and IRR through the worked example of Martac plc.

Worked example 2.3   Martac plc

Two new machines, the CAM and the ATR, are available. Both will give cost savings over existing processes and Martac needs to decide which machine to invest in:

£000s	CAM	ATR
Initial cost of machine and installation	120	250
Cash flow savings:		
Time 1 (1 year after initial outflow)	48	90
Time 2	48	90
Time 3	48	90
Time 4	48	90

All other factors remain constant and the firm has access to large amounts of capital. The required return on projects is 8%. Production ceases after four years and the machines will then have a zero scrap value.

Required

a   Calculate the IRR for CAM and ATR and recommend which machine should be purchased using the IRR rule.
b   Calculate the NPV for CAM and ATR and recommend which machine should be purchased using the NPV rule.
c   Is IRR or NPV the better decision tool?

Answers

Note: Total cash flows are not given. Instead the incremental cash flows (those which change due to the new machine) are provided, for example, the savings available. This is sufficient information to make the decision about which machine to purchase.

(a) IRR for CAM

$$CF_0 + \frac{CF_1}{1 + r} + \frac{CF_2}{(1 + r)^2} + \frac{CF_3}{(1 + r)^3} + \frac{CF_4}{(1 + r)^4} = 0$$

Try 22 %:

$$-120{,}000 + 48{,}000 \times \text{annuity factor (af) for 4 years @ 22\%}$$

(*See* Appendix 2.1 to this chapter for annuity calculations and Appendix III at the end of the book for an annuity table.)

The annuity factor tells us the present value of four lots of £1 received at four annual intervals. This is 2.4936, meaning that the £1 received per year for four years is worth, in present value terms, £2.49 (£1 x 2.4936 = £2.49). This allows us to calculate the value of the annual savings

$$-120{,}000 + (48{,}000 \times 2.4936) = -£307.20$$

Try 21 %:

$$-120{,}000 + 48{,}000 \times \text{annuity factor (af) for 4 years @ 21\%}$$

$$-120{,}000 + (48{,}000 \times 2.5404) = +£1{,}939.20$$

See Exhibit 2.17.

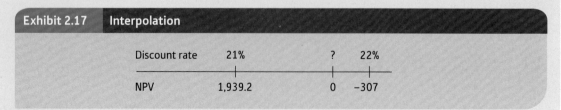

Exhibit 2.17   Interpolation

Discount rate	21%		?	22%
NPV	1,939.2		0	-307

$$21 + \left(\frac{1939.2}{1939.2 + 307}\right) \times (22 - 21) = 21.86\%$$

IRR for ATR
Try 16%:

$$-250{,}000 + (90{,}000 \times 2.7982) = +£1{,}838$$

Try 17%:

$$-250{,}000 + (90{,}000 \times 2.7432) = -£3{,}112$$

See **Exhibit 2.18.**

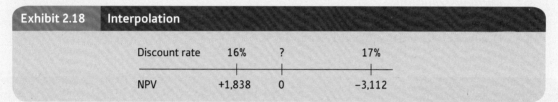

Exhibit 2.18	Interpolation			
Discount rate		16%	?	17%
NPV		+1,838	0	−3,112

$$16 + \left(\frac{1{,}838}{1{,}838 + 3{,}112}\right) \times (17 - 16) = 16.37\%$$

Choice of machine on basis of IRR

If IRR is the only decision tool available, then as long as the IRRs exceed the discount rate (or cost of capital) of 8% the project with the higher IRR might appear to be the preferred choice. In this case CAM (21.9%) ranks higher than ATR (16.4%).

(b) NPV for CAM at 8%: CAM

$$-120{,}000 + (48{,}000 \times 3.3121) = +£38{,}981$$

NPV for ATR at 8%

$$-250{,}000 + (90{,}000 \times 3.3121) = +£48{,}089$$

Choice of machine on basis of NPV

ATR generates a return which has a present value of £48,089 in addition to the minimum return on capital required. This is larger than for CAM and therefore ATR ranks higher than CAM if NPV is used as the decision tool.

(c) Choice of decision tool

This problem has produced conflicting recommendations, depending on the appraisal method employed. NPV is the better decision-making technique because it measures in absolute amounts of money, giving the increase in shareholder wealth available by accepting a project. IRR expresses its return as a percentage which may result in an inferior low-scale project being preferred to a higher-scale project: 10% of £5,000 is not as good as 2% of £1 million. So, if you cannot undertake both projects, the one that returns most to shareholders is the one with the higher NPV rather than the higher IRR.

(An Excel spreadsheet showing this calculation is shown at www.pearsoned.co.uk/arnold.)

Problems with internal rate of return

We now return to Hard Decisions plc.

Mr Spark: I have noticed your tendency to prefer NPV to any other method. Yet, in the three projects we have been discussing, NPV and IRR give the same decision recommendation. That is, reject Projects 1 and 2 and accept Project 3. So, why not use IRR more often?

You reply: It is true that the NPV and IRR methods of capital investment appraisal are closely related. Both are 'time-adjusted' measures of profitability. The NPV and IRR methods gave the same result in the cases we have considered because problems associated with the IRR method are not present in the figures we have been working with. In the appraisal of other projects, we may encounter the limitations of the IRR method and therefore I prefer to stick to the theoretically superior NPV technique. I will illustrate three of the most important problems, **multiple solutions, ranking** and confusion between **investing-type decisions** and **financing-type decisions**.

Multiple solutions

There may be a number of possible IRRs. This can be explained by examining the problems Deadhead is having (*see* Worked example 2.4).

Worked example 2.4   Deadhead plc

Deadhead plc has always used the IRR method of project appraisal. The CFO has started to have doubts about its usefulness after examining the proposal, 'Project Oscillation'.

Project Oscillation

Points in time (yearly intervals)	0	1	2
Cash flow	−3,000	+15,000	−13,000

Internal rates of return are found at 11.56% *and* 288.4%.

Given that Deadhead has a required rate of return of 20%, it is impossible to decide whether to implement Project Oscillation using an unadjusted IRR methodology. If there are a number of possible IRRs, you are unable to use IRR to make the investment decision.

The cause of multiple solutions is unconventional cash flows. Conventional cash flows occur when an original outflow is followed by a series of inflows or an original inflow is followed by a series of cash outflows. Unconventional cash flows are a series of cash flows with more than one change in direction of flow. In the case of Project Oscillation the flow changes from outflow to inflow and then from inflow to outflow. Multiple yields can be adjusted for while still using the IRR method, but the simplest approach is to use the NPV method.

Ranking

The IRR decision rule does not always rank projects in the same way as the NPV method. Sometimes it is important to find out not only which project gives a positive return, but which one gives the greater positive return. Projects may be mutually exclusive. If both have positive NPV but only one may be undertaken, then the company has to choose between them. IRR alone sometimes leads to a poor choice (*see* **Exhibit 2.19**).

From **Exhibit 2.20**, it is clear that the ranking of the projects by their IRRs is constant at 75% and 100%, regardless of of the opportunity cost of capital (discount rate). Project A is always better. On the other hand, ranking the projects by the NPV method is not fixed. The NPV ranking depends on the discount rate used. Thus if the discount rate used in the NPV calculation is higher than 50%, the ranking under both IRR and NPV would be the same, i.e. Project A is superior. If the discount rate falls below 50%, Project B is the better choice. A key factor leading to the theoretical dominance of NPV is that it takes into account the scale of investment. At a 15% discount rate,

Exhibit 2.19	Illustration of the IRR ranking problem

| Project | Cash flows £m | | IRR% | NPV (at 15%) |
	Time 0	One year later		£
A	−20	+40	100%	+14.78m
B	−40	+70	75%	+20.87m

NPV at different discount rates

Discount rate (%)	Project A	Project B
0	20	30
20	13	18
50	7	7
75	3	0
100	0	−5
125	−2	−9

Exhibit 2.20	NPV at different discount rates

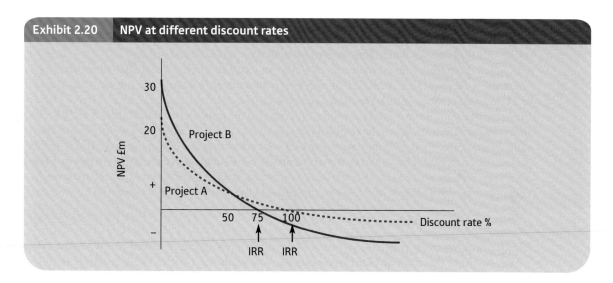

shareholders are better off by undertaking Project B because the initial size of the project was larger (making £20.87m above the 15% annual return). NPVs are measured in absolute amounts, whereas IRR is a % measure.

John Kay discusses the ranking problem of IRR in a FT article – *see* **Exhibit 2.21**.

Exhibit 2.21

How not to measure a business

By John Kay

Would you rather have a 20% return on £1,000 or a 25% return on £500? Ideally, you would like to find a company that would offer a 25% yield on any capital you invested in it, but such opportunities do not exist. If you could not do that, you would like to have both the 20% and the 25% projects, but you will often have to choose between alternative routes to the same objective, or different financial models for the same business. So should you always choose the higher return on equity? The answer is not obvious.

▶

Exhibit 2.21 (continued)

If you can expect to earn at least a 15% return on your other investments, then you will be better off taking the 25% proposition. If you cannot – and you probably cannot – then the lower, but still exhilarating, 20% return on the larger amount is a better choice.

All good introductory finance texts explain that ranking projects by their rate of return is not an appropriate means of choosing between them. Most suggest an alternative way of approaching the problem. Measure the opportunity cost of funds, based on the risk adjusted returns available elsewhere. In a world in which even long-term

borrowing by the US Treasury costs less than 4%, that figure is unlikely to be very high – let's put it at 7%. Then investing £1,000 at 20% yields £200 a year, and investing £500 at 25% and £500 at 7% only £160. And £200 is always better than £160. Money, not percentages (or relative performance), pays the grocer and the yacht chandler.

But that simple message has not got through. Large companies think their investment appraisal techniques are sophisticated if they compute internal rates of return. It is more and more common for them to highlight the rate of return on their equity in their annual reports.

Confusion over investing decisions versus financing decisions

Hard Decisions plc's Proposal 1 required a cash outflow of £11m at time zero followed by a cash inflow of £12m one year later. This resulted in an IRR of 9.0917% and negative NPV of –£0.565m, thus, given the stated required return of 15%, the project was rejected under both methods. This is an investing decision, because the initial cash flow is an outflow. Now consider a project that resulted in £11m being *received* at time zero and £12m *flowing out* at time 1 (one year later). Here we have a financing decision. You need to be careful in interpreting the results of a financing decision IRR. The IRR is again 9.09% and given the opportunity cost of capital of 15% there is a danger of automatically rejecting the project if you have it stuck in your mind that the IRR must exceed 15% for the project to be accepted. This would be wrong because you are being offered the chance to receive £11m, which can then be invested at 15% per year at that risk level. This will outweigh the outflow that occurs at time 1 of £12m. In other words, this project gives a positive NPV and should be accepted.

$$\text{NPV} = \pounds11m - \pounds12m/(1.15) = +\pounds0.565m$$

This leads us to reverse the IRR rules for a financing-type situation. To avoid confusion use NPV.

The board of directors of Hard Decisions are now ready for a coffee break and time to digest these concepts and techniques. The chairman thanks you for your clarity and rigorous analysis. He also thanks Mr Spark for originating three imaginative and thought-provoking proposals to take the business forward towards its goal of shareholder wealth enhancement.

Modified internal rate of return

The preference of managers for a percentage measure (see **Exhibit 2.22**) is a powerful force driving the adoption of IRR in the practical world of business where managers may not comprehend NPV. These issues are examined in more detail in Chapter 4, but it is perhaps worth explaining now the consequences of sticking rigidly to IRR.

One problem centres on the reinvestment assumption. With NPV it is assumed that cash inflows arising during the life of the project are reinvested at the opportunity cost of capital. In contrast the IRR implicitly assumes that the cash inflows that are received can be reinvested at a rate equal to the IRR until the end of the project's life. This is intuitively unacceptable. In the real world, if a firm invested in a very high-yielding project and cash was returned, this firm would be unlikely to be able to deposit this cash elsewhere until the end of the project for the same high yield, and yet this is what the IRR assumes. The more likely outcome is that any cash inflows will be invested at the 'going rate' or the opportunity cost of capital. In other words, the firm's normal discount rate is the better estimate of the reinvestment rate. The effect of this erroneous reinvestment assumption is to inflate the IRR of the project under examination.

Exhibit 2.22   Characteristics of NPV and IRR

NPV

- It recognises that £1 today is worth more than £1 tomorrow.

- In conditions where all worthwhile projects can be accepted (i.e. no mutual exclusivity) it maximises shareholder utility. Projects with a positive NPV should be accepted since they increase shareholder wealth, while those with negative NPVs decrease shareholder wealth.

- It takes into account investment size – absolute amounts of wealth change.

- It is not as intuitively understandable as a percentage measure.

- It can handle non-conventional cash flows.

- Additivity is possible: because present values are all measured in today's £s they can be added together. Thus the returns (NPVs) of a group of projects can be calculated.

- NPV assumes that cash inflows arising during the life of a project are reinvested at the opportunity cost of capital – a reasonable assumption.

IRR

- Also takes into account the time value of money.

- In situations of non-mutual exclusivity, shareholder wealth is maximised if all projects with IRR higher than the opportunity cost of capital are accepted, while those with a return less than the time value of money are rejected.

- Fails to measure in terms of absolute amounts of wealth change. It measures percentage returns and this may cause ranking problems in conditions of mutual exclusivity, i.e. the wrong project may be rejected.

- It is easier to communicate a percentage return than NPV to other managers and employees, who may not be familiar with the details of project appraisal techniques. The appeal of quick recognition and understanding should not be underestimated.

- Non-conventional cash flows cause problems, e.g. multiple solutions.
- Additivity is not possible.

- Financing decisions may result in misinterpretation of IRR results.

- IRR implicitly assumes that cash flows received can be invested elsewhere at a rate equal to the IRR until the end of the project's life – see next section for more detail on this problem.

For example, Project K below has a very high IRR, at 61.8%; thus the £1,000 received after one year is assumed to be taken back into the firm and then placed in another investment, again yielding 61.8% until time 2. This is obviously unlikely. If such an investment existed, why has the firm not already invested in it, given its cost of capital is only 15%?

Project K *(required rate of return 15%)*

Points in time (yearly intervals)	0	1	2
Cash flows (£)	−1,000	+1,000	+1,000

IRR
Try 60%: NPV = 15.63.
Try 62%: NPV = −1.68.

Interpolation

Exhibit 2.23   Project K

Discount rate	60%		?	62%
NPV	15.63		0	−1.68

$$60 + \left(\frac{15.63}{15.63 + 1.68}\right) \times (62 - 60) = 61.8\%$$

The reinvestment assumption of 61.8%, for the £1,000 receivable at time 1, is clearly unrealistic, especially in the light of the fact that most investors can obtain a return of only 15% for taking this level of risk.

The IRR of Project K assumes the following:

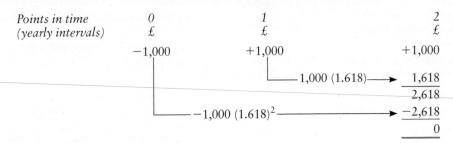

The £2,618 compounded cash flows at the terminal date of the project are equivalent to taking the original investment of £1,000 and compounding it for two years at 61.8%. However, an NPV calculation assumes that the intra-project cash inflow is invested at 15%:

Points in time (yearly intervals)	0 £	1 £	2 £
	−1,000	+1,000.00	+1,000.00
		1,000 (1.15) →	1,150.00
			2,150.00
	−1,000 (1.15)²	→	−1,322.50
			827.50

Discounting £827.50 back two years at 15% gives the NPV of £625.71.

If it is necessary to describe a project appraisal in percentage terms , then the **modified internal rate of return (MIRR)** should be used. For the sake of consistency with NPV, this assumes that any cash inflows arising during the project are reinvested at the opportunity cost of funds. That is, at the rate of return available on the next best alternative use of the funds in either financial or real assets. The MIRR is the rate of return, m, which, if used to compound the initial investment amount (the original cash outlay), produces the same terminal value as the project's cash inflows. The value of the project's cash inflows at the end of the project's life after they have been expressed in the terminal date's £s is achieved through compounding at the opportunity cost of funds. In other words, the common currency this time is not time 0 £s but time 4, or time 6, or time 'n' £s.

What we are attempting to do is find that rate of compounding which will equate the terminal value of the intra-project cash flows with the terminal value of the initial investment.

Modified internal rate of return for Project K

First, calculate the terminal value of the cash flows excluding the t_0 investment using the opportunity cost of capital.

	Terminal value (£)
t_1 1,000 (1.15)	1,150.00
t_2 1,000 already expressed as a terminal value because it occurs on the date of termination	1,000.00
Total terminal value	2,150.00

The modified internal rate of return is the rate of compounding applied to the original investment necessary to produce a future (terminal) value of £2,150.00 two years later.

$$1,000 (1 + m)^2 = 2,150$$

Solve for m. (The mathematical tools – *see* Appendix 2.1 – may be useful here.) Divide both sides of the equation by 1,000:

$$(1 + m)^2 = \frac{2,150}{1,000}$$

Then, take roots to the power of 2 of both sides of the equation:

$$\sqrt[2]{(1 + m)^2} = \sqrt[2]{\frac{2,150}{1,000}}$$

$$m = \sqrt[2]{\frac{2,150}{1,000}} - 1 = 0.466 \text{ or } 46.6\%$$

or more generally:

$$m = \sqrt[n]{\frac{F}{P}} - 1 \quad \text{(where F is the future terminal value and P the initial outlay)}$$

The MIRR is 46.6% compared with the IRR of 61.8%. In the case of Project K this reduced rate is still high and the project is accepted under either rule. However, in a number of situations, the calculation of the MIRR may alter the decision given under the IRR method. This is true in the worked example of Switcharound plc for projects Tic and Cit. As mutually exclusive projects, ranking is important.

Worked example 2.5   **Switcharound plc**

Switcharound plc needs to find a use for a vacated factory. The two projects it has selected for further consideration have a life of only three years, because the site will be flattened in three years when a new motorway is constructed. On the basis of IRR the company favours Cit but it knows that the key senior manager is aware of MIRR and therefore feels it is necessary to present the data calculated through both techniques. The opportunity cost of capital is 10%.

Cash flows

Points in time (yearly intervals)	0	1	2	3	IRR
Tic (£m)	−1	0.5	0.5	0.5	23.4%
Cit (£m)	−1	1.1	0.1	0.16	27.7%

However, on the basis of MIRR, a different preference emerges.

Tic: MIRR

		Terminal value £m
t_1	$0.5 \times (1.1)^2$	0.605
t_2	0.5×1.1	0.550
t_3	0.5	0.500
Total terminal value		1.655

$$1,000,000 (1 + m)^3 = 1,655,000$$

$$m = \sqrt[n]{\frac{F}{P}} - 1$$

$$m = \sqrt[3]{\frac{1,655,000}{1,000,000}} - 1 = 0.183 \text{ or } 18.3\%$$

▶

Worked example 2.5 *(continued)*

Cit: MIRR

		Terminal value £m
t_1	$1.1 \times (1.1)^2$	1.331
t_2	0.1×1.1	0.110
t_3	0.16	0.16
Total terminal value		1.601

$$1,000,000 \, (1 + m)^3 = 1,601,000$$

$$m = \sqrt[n]{\frac{F}{P}} - 1$$

$$m = \sqrt[3]{\frac{1,601,000}{1,000,000}} - 1 = 0.17 \text{ or } 17\%$$

A more satisfactory answer can be obtained by calculating NPVs, if the senior management team understands NPV.

NPVs for Tic and Cit

Tic $\quad -1 + 0.5 \times$ annuity factor, 3 years @ 10%
$\quad\quad -1 + 0.5 \times 2.4869 = 0.24345$ or £243,450

Cit $\quad -1 + \dfrac{1.1}{1 + 0.1} + \dfrac{0.1}{(1 + 0.1)^2} + \dfrac{0.16}{(1 + 0.1)^3} = 0.202855$ or £202,855

Therefore, Tic contributes more towards shareholder wealth.

Summary table

Ranking

	NPV	IRR	MIRR
Tic	£243,450 (1)	23.4% (2)	18.3% (1)
Cit	£202,855 (2)	27.7% (1)	17.0% (2)

Concluding comments

This chapter has concentrated on the key factors for consideration when an organisation is contemplating using financial (or other) resources for investment. The analysis has been based on the assumption that the objective of any such investment is to maximise economic benefits to the owners of the enterprise. To achieve such an objective requires allowance for the opportunity cost of capital or time value of money as well as analysis of relevant cash flows. Given that time has a value, the timing of cash flows is important for project analysis. The net present value (NPV) and internal rate of return (IRR) methods of project appraisal are both discounted cash flow techniques and therefore allow for the time value of money. However, the IRR method presents problems in a few special circumstances and so the theoretically preferred method is NPV. NPV requires studying and thought to be fully understood, and therefore it is not surprising to find in the workplace a bias in favour of communicating a project's viability in terms of percentages. Most large organisations use three or four methods of project appraisal, rather than rely on only one – *see* Chapter 4 for more detail. If a percentage approach is regarded as essential in a particular organisational setting then the MIRR is preferred to the IRR. The MIRR ranks projects more appropriately and so is useful in mutual exclusivity situations and avoids biasing upward expectations of returns from an investment. The fundamental conclusion of this chapter is that the best method for maximising shareholder wealth in assessing investment projects is net present value.

Key points and concepts

- ***Time value of money*** has three component parts each requiring compensation for a delay in the receipt of cash:

  - the pure time value, or impatience to consume,
  - inflation,
  - risk.

- ***Opportunity cost of capital*** is the yield forgone on the best available investment alternative – the risk level of the alternative being the same as for the project under consideration.

- Taking account of the time value of money and opportunity cost of capital in project appraisal leads to **discounted cash flow analysis** (DCF).

- **Net present value** (NPV) is the present value of the future cash flows after netting out the initial cash flow. Present values are achieved by discounting at the opportunity cost of capital.

$$NPV = CF_0 + \frac{CF_1}{1+k} + \frac{CF_2}{(1+k)^2} + \cdots \frac{CF_n}{(1+k)^n}$$

- **The net present value decision rules** are:

  NPV $\geq$ 0 accept
  NPV $<$ 0 reject

- **Internal rate of return** (IRR) is the discount rate which, when applied to the cash flows of a project, results in a zero net present value. It is an '*r*' which results in the following formula being true:

$$CF_0 + \frac{CF_1}{1+r} + \frac{CF_2}{(1+r)^2} + \cdots \frac{CF_n}{(1+r)^n} = 0$$

- **The internal rate of return decision rule** is:

  IRR $\geq$ opportunity cost of capital $-$ accept
  IRR $<$ opportunity cost of capital $-$ reject

- IRR is poor at handling situations with unconventional cash flows.

- There are circumstances when IRR and NPV rank projects differently. This **ranking problem** becomes an important issue in situations of mutual exclusivity.

- The IRR decision rule is reversed for financing decisions.

- NPV measures in **absolute amounts of money**. IRR is a percentage measure.

- IRR assumes that intra-project cash flows can be invested at a rate of return equal to the IRR.

- If a percentage measure is required, perhaps for communication within an organisation, then the **modified internal rate of return** (MIRR) is to be preferred to the IRR.

Appendix 2.1 Mathematical tools for finance

The purpose of this appendix is to explain essential mathematical skills that will be needed for this book. The authors have no love of mathematics for its own sake and so only those techniques of direct relevance to the subject matter of this textbook will be covered in this section.

Simple and compound interest

When there are time delays between receipts and payments of financial sums we need to make use of the concepts of simple and compound interest.

Simple interest

Interest is paid only on the original principal. No interest is paid on the accumulated interest payments.

Example 1

Suppose that a sum of £10 is deposited in a bank account that pays 12% per annum. At the end of year 1 the investor has £11.20 in the account. That is:

$$F = P(1 + i)$$

$$11.20 = 10(1 + 0.12)$$

where F = Future value, P = Present value, i = Interest rate.

The initial sum, called the principal, is multiplied by the interest rate to give the annual return. At the end of five years:

$$F = P(1 + in)$$

where n = number of years. Thus,

$$16 = 10(1 + 0.12 \times 5)$$

Note from the example that the 12% return is a constant amount each year. Interest is not earned on the interest already accumulated from previous years.

Compound interest

The more usual situation in the real world is for interest to be paid on the sum which accumulates – whether or not that sum comes from the principal or from the interest received in previous periods.

Example 2

An investment of £10 is made at an interest rate of 12% with the interest being compounded. In one year the capital will grow by 12% to £11.20. In the second year the capital will grow by 12%, but this time the growth will be on the accumulated value of £11.20 and thus will amount to an extra £1.34. At the end of two years:

$$F = P(1 + i)(1 + i)$$
$$F = 11.20(1 + i)$$
$$F = 12.54$$

Alternatively,

$$F = P(1 + i)^2$$

Exhibit 2.24 displays the future value of £1 invested at a number of different interest rates and for alternative numbers of years. This is extracted from Appendix I at the end of the book.

From the second row of the table in Exhibit 2.24 we can read that £1 invested for two years at 12% amounts to £1.2544. Thus, the investment of £10 provides a future capital sum 1.2544 times the original amount:

$$£10 \times 1.2544 = £12.54$$

Exhibit 2.24	The future value of £1				
			interest rate (% per annum)		
Year	1	2	5	12	15
1	1.0100	1.0200	1.0500	1.1200	1.1500
2	1.0201	1.0404	1.1025	1.2544	1.3225
3	1.0303	1.0612	1.1576	1.4049	1.5209
4	1.0406	1.0824	1.2155	1.5735	1.7490
5	1.0510	1.1041	1.2763	1.7623	2.0114

Over five years the result is:

$$F = P(1 + i)^n$$
$$17.62 = 10(1 + 0.12)^5$$

The interest on the accumulated interest is therefore the difference between the total arising from simple interest and that from compound interest:

£17.62 − £16.00 = £1.62

Almost all investments pay compound interest and so we will be using compounding throughout the book.

Present values

There are many occasions in financial management when you are given future sums and need to find out what those future sums are worth in present-value terms today. For example, you wish to know how much you would have to put aside today which will accumulate, with compounded interest, to a defined sum in the future; or you are given the choice between receiving £200 in five years or £100 now and wish to know which is the better option, given anticipated interest rates; or a project gives a return of £1m in three years for an outlay of £800,000 now and you need to establish if this is the best use of the £800,000. By the process of discounting, a sum of money to be received in the future is given a monetary value today.

Example 3

If we anticipate the receipt of £17.62 in five years' time we can determine its present value. Rearrangement of the compound formula, and assuming a discount rate of 12%, gives:

$$P = \frac{F}{(1 + i)^n} \text{ or } P = F \times \frac{1}{(1 + i)^n}$$

$$10 = \frac{17.62}{(1 + 0.12)^5}$$

Alternatively, discount factors may be used, as shown in **Exhibit 2.25** (this is an extract from Appendix II at the end of the book). The factor needed to discount £1 receivable in five years when the discount rate is 12% is 0.5674.

Therefore the present value of £17.62 is:

0.5674 × £17.62 = £10

Exhibit 2.25	The present value of £1					
			Interest rate (% per annum)			
Year	1	5	10	12	15	17
1	0.9901	0.9524	0.9091	0.8929	0.8696	0.8547
2	0.9803	0.9070	0.8264	0.7972	0.7561	0.7305
3	0.9706	0.8638	0.7513	0.7118	0.6575	0.6244
4	0.9610	0.8227	0.6830	0.6355	0.5718	0.5337
5	0.9515	0.7835	0.6209	0.5674	0.4972	0.4561
20	0.8195	0.3769	0.1486	0.1037	0.0611	0.0433

Examining the present value table in Exhibit 2.25 you can see that as the discount rate increases, the present value goes down. Also the further into the future the money is to be received, the less valuable it is in today's terms. Distant cash flows discounted at a high rate have a small present value; for instance, £1,000 receivable in 20 years when the discount rate is 17% has a present value of £43.30. Viewed from another angle, if you invested £43.30 for 20 years it would accumulate to £1,000 if interest compounds at 17%.

Determining the rate of interest

Sometimes you wish to calculate the rate of return that a project is earning. For instance, a savings company may offer to pay you £10,000 in five years if you deposit £8,000 now, when interest rates on accounts elsewhere are offering 6% per annum. In order to make a comparison you need to know the annual rate being offered by the savings company. Thus, we need to find i in the discounting equation.

To be able to calculate i it is necessary to rearrange the compounding formula. Since:

$$F = P(1 + i)^n$$

first, divide both sides by P:

$$F/P = (1 + i)^n$$

(The Ps on the right side cancel out.)

Second, take the root to the power n of both sides and subtract 1 from each side:

$$i = \sqrt[n]{[F/P]} - 1 \text{ or } i = [F/P]^{1/n} - 1$$

$$i = \sqrt[5]{£10,000/£8,000} - 1 = 0.046 \text{ or } 4.6\%$$

Not a good deal compared with accounts offering 6%.

Example 4

In the case of a five-year investment requiring an outlay of £10 and having a future value of £17.62 the rate of return is:

$$i = \sqrt[5]{\frac{17.62}{10}} - 1 \quad i = 12\%$$

$$i = [17.62/10]^{1/5} - 1 \quad i = 12\%$$

Alternatively, use the future value table, an extract of which is shown in Exhibit 2.24. In our example, the return on £1 worth of investment over five years is:

$$\frac{17.62}{10} = 1.762$$

In the body of the future value table look at the year 5 row for a future value of 1.762. Read off the interest rate of 12%.

The investment period

Rearranging the standard equation so that we can find n (the number of years of the investment), we create the following equation:

$$F = P(1 + i)^n$$

$$F/P = (1 + i)^n$$

$$\log(F/P) = \log(1 + i)n$$

$$n = \frac{\log(F/P)}{\log(1 + i)}$$

Example 5

How many years does it take for £10 to grow to £17.62 when the interest rate is 12%?

$$n = \frac{\log(17.62/10)}{\log(1 + 0.12)} \text{ Therefore } n = 5 \text{ years}$$

An application outside finance During the last 25 years, China's real national income grew by around 10% per annum, meaning that its income doubled every 7.3 years (see calculation below) and quadrupled in less than 14 years. It has gone from poverty to having an economy larger than that of the USA.

$$n = \frac{\log(2/1)}{\log(1 + 0.1)} = 7.3 \text{ years}$$

Annuities

Quite often there is not just one payment at the end of a certain number of years. There can be a series of identical payments made over a period of years. For instance:

- bonds usually pay a regular rate of interest;
- individuals can buy, from saving plan companies, the right to receive a number of identical payments over a number of years;
- a business might invest in a project which, it is estimated, will give regular cash inflows over a period of years;
- a typical house mortgage is an annuity.

An annuity is a series of payments or receipts of equal amounts. We are able to calculate the present value of this set of payments.

Example 6

For a regular payment of £10 per year, starting one year from now at time 1, for five years, when the interest rate is 12%, we can calculate the present value of the annuity by three methods.

Method 1

$$P_{an} = \frac{A}{(1 + i)} + \frac{A}{(1 + i)^2} + \frac{A}{(1 + i)^3} + \frac{A}{(1 + i)^4} + \frac{A}{(1 + i)^5}$$

where A = the periodic receipt.

$$P_{10,5} = \frac{10}{(1.12)} + \frac{10}{(1.12)^2} + \frac{10}{(1.12)^3} + \frac{10}{(1.12)^4} + \frac{10}{(1.12)^5} = £36.05$$

Method 2

Using the derived formula:

$$P_{an} = \frac{1 - 1/(1 + i)^n}{i} \times A$$

$$P_{10,5} = \frac{1 - 1/(1 + 0.12)^5}{0.12} \times 10 = £36.05$$

Method 3

Use the 'present value of an annuity' table. (*See* **Exhibit 2.26**, an extract from the more complete annuity table at the end of the book in Appendix III.) Here we simply look along the year 5 row and

12% column to find the figure of 3.6048. This refers to the present value of five annual receipts of £1 (the first of which is received in one year), which comes to £3.6048. Therefore we multiply by £10:

$$3.6048 \times £10 = £36.05$$

| Exhibit 2.26 | The present value of an annuity of £1 per annum |

	Interest rate (% per annum)				
Year	1	5	10	12	15
1	0.9901	0.9524	0.9091	0.8929	0.8696
2	1.9704	1.8594	1.7355	1.6901	1.6257
3	2.9410	2.7232	2.4869	2.4018	2.2832
4	3.9020	3.5460	3.1699	3.0373	2.8550
5	4.8534	4.3295	3.7908	3.6048	3.3522

Perpetuities

Some contracts run indefinitely and there is no end to a series of identical payments. Perpetuities are rare in the private sector, but certain government securities do not have an end date: that is, the amount paid when the bond was purchased by the lender will never be repaid, only interest payments are made. For example, the UK government has issued Consolidated Stocks or War Loans which may never be redeemed. Also, in a number of project appraisals or share valuations it is useful to assume that regular annual payments go on for ever. Perpetuities are annuities which continue indefinitely. The value of a perpetuity is simply the annual amount received divided by the interest rate when the latter is expressed as a decimal.

$$P = \frac{A}{i}$$

If £10 is to be received as an indefinite annual payment then the present value, at a discount rate of 12%, is:

$$P = \frac{10}{0.12} = £83.33$$

It is very important to note that in order to use this formula we are assuming that the first payment arises 365 days after the time at which we are standing (the present time or time zero).

Discounting semi-annually, monthly and daily

Sometimes financial transactions take place on the basis that interest will be calculated more frequently than once a year. If a bank account paid 12% nominal return per year, but credited 6% after half a year, in the second half of the year interest could be earned on the interest from the first six months. This will mean that the true annual rate of interest will be greater than 12%.

The greater the frequency with which interest is earned, the higher the future value of the deposit.

Example 7

If you put £10 in a bank account earning 12% per annum, then your return after one year is:

$$10(1 + 0.12) = £11.20$$

If the interest is compounded semi-annually (at a nominal annual rate of 12%):

$$10(1 + [0.12/2])(1 + [0.12/2]) = 10(1 + [0.12/2])^2 = £11.236$$

In Example 7 the difference between annual compounding and semi-annual compounding is an extra 3.6 p. With semi-annual compounding, after six months the bank credits the account with 60p in interest; in the following six months the investor earns 6% on the £10.60.

Compounded quarterly: $10(1 + [0.12/4])^4 = £11.255$
Daily compounding: $10(1 + [0.12/365])^{365} = £11.2747$

Example 8

If £10 is deposited in a bank account that compounds interest quarterly and the nominal return per year is 12%, how much will be in the account after eight years?

$$10(1 + [0.12/4])^{4 \times 8} = £25.75$$

Continuous compounding

If the compounding frequency is taken to the limit we say that there is continuous compounding. When the number of compounding periods approaches infinity the future value is found by $F = Pe^{in}$ where e is the value of the exponential function. This is set as 2.71828 (to five decimal places, as shown on a scientific calculator). So, the future value of £10 deposited in a bank paying 12% nominal compounded continuously after eight years is:

$$10 \times 2.71828^{0.12 \times 8} = £26.12$$

Converting monthly and daily rates to annual rates

Sometimes you are presented with a monthly or daily rate of interest and wish to know what that is equivalent to in terms of annual percentage rate (APR) (or effective annual rate (EAR)).

If m is the monthly interest or discount rate, then over 12 months:

$$(1 + m)^{12} = 1 + i$$

where i is the annual compound rate.

$$i = (1 + m)^{12} - 1$$

Thus, if a credit card company charges 1.5 % per month, the APR is:

$$i = (1 + 0.015)^{12} - 1 = 19.56\%$$

If you want to find the monthly rate when you are given the APR:

$$m = (1 + i)^{1/12} - 1 \text{ or } m = \sqrt[12]{(1 + i)} - 1$$

$$m = (1 + 0.1956)^{1/12} - 1 = 0.015 = 1.5\%$$

Daily rate:

$$(1 + d)^{365} = 1 + i$$

where d is the daily discount rate.

The following exercises will consolidate the knowledge gained by reading through this appendix (answers are provided at the end of the book in Appendix VI).

Exercise   Mathematical tools exercises

1   What will a £100 investment be worth in three years' time if the rate of interest is 8%, using: (a) simple interest? (b) annual compound interest?   **?**

2   You plan to invest £10,000 in the shares of a company.

  a If the value of the shares increases by 5% a year, what will be the value of the shares in 20 years?

  b If the value of the shares increases by 15% a year, what will be the value of the shares in 20 years?   **?**

3   How long will it take you to double your money if you invest it at: (a) 5%? (b) 15%?   **?**

4 As a winner of a lottery you can choose one of the following prizes:

   a £1,000,000 now.

   b £1,700,000 at the end of five years.

   c £135,000 a year for ever, starting in one year.

   d £200,000 for each of the next 10 years, starting in one year.

   If the time value of money is 9%, which is the most valuable prize? **?**

5 A bank lends a customer £5,000. At the end of 10 years he repays this amount plus interest. The amount he repays is £8,950. What is the rate of interest charged by the bank? **?**

6 The Memorial Garden Company will maintain a garden plot around your grave for a payment of £50 now, followed by annual payments, in perpetuity, of £50. How much would you have to put into an account to make these payments if the account guaranteed an interest rate of 8%? **?**

7 If the flat (nominal annual) rate of interest is 14% and compounding takes place monthly, what is the effective annual rate of interest (the annual percentage rate)? **?**

8 What is the present value of £100 to be received in 10 years' time when the interest rate (nominal annual) is 12% and (a) annual discounting is used? (b) semi-annual discounting is used? **?**

9 What sum must be invested now to provide an amount of £18,000 at the end of 15 years if interest is to accumulate at 8% for the first 10 years and 12% thereafter? **?**

10 How much must be invested now to provide an amount of £10,000 in six years' time assuming interest is compounded quarterly at a nominal annual rate of 8%? What is the effective annual rate? **?**

11 A company offers you an annuity of £800 per annum for 10 years. The price is £4,800. Assuming you could earn 11% on alternative investments, would you buy the annuity? **?**

12 Punter buys a car on hire purchase paying five annual instalments of £1,500, the first being an immediate cash deposit. Assuming an interest rate of 8% is being charged by the hire purchase company, what is the current price of the car? **?**

References and further reading

Andor, G. et al. (2015) 'Capital budgeting practices: A survey of Central and Eastern European firms', *Emerging Markets Review*, 23: 148–172.

   A survey of 400 executives in 10 countries in Central and Eastern Europe.

Bierman, H. and Smidt, S. (2006) *The Capital Budgeting Decision,* 9th edn. London: Routledge.

   A clear introductory exposition of the concepts discussed in this chapter.

Bierman, H. and Smidt, S. (2006) *Advanced Capital Budgeting.* London: Routledge.

   A book for those interested in pursuing the technical issue in depth.

Fama, E.F. and Miller, M.H. (1972) *The Theory of Finance.* New York: Holt, Rinehart & Winston.

   A more detailed consideration of IRR and NPV.

Fisher, I. (1930) *The Theory of Interest.* Reprinted in 1977 by Porcupine Press.

   Originator of the present value rule.

Frezatti, F., et al. (2013) 'Investment decisions on long-term assets: Integrating strategic and financial Perspectives', *European Accounting Review*, 22(2): 297–336.

   Looks at how companies formalise the decisions and control on long-term investments.

Hirshleifer, J. (1958) 'On the theory of optimal investment decision', *Journal of Political Economy*, 66 (August), pp. 329–52.

Early theory.

Hirshleifer, J. (1961) 'Risk, the discount rate and investment decisions', *American Economic Review*, May, pp. 112–20.

Theoretical justification for the use of net present value.

McDaniel, W.R., McCarty, D.E. and Jessell, K.A. (1988) 'Discounted cash flow with explicit reinvestment rates: Tutorial and extension', *The Financial Review*, August.

Modified internal rate of return discussed in more detail as well as other theoretical developments.

Solomon, E. (1963) *The Theory of Financial Management*. New York: Columbia University Press.

An early advocate of net present value.

Wilkes, F.M. (1980) 'On multiple rates of return', *Journal of Business Finance and Accounting*, 7(4).

Theoretical treatment of a specific issue.

Wnuk-Pel, T. (2014) 'The practice and factors determining the selection of capital budgeting methods – evidence from the field', *Procedia – Social and Behavioral Sciences*, 156, pp. 612–16.

Research based in Poland which considers the capital budget methods used and the reasons for selection.

Case study recommendations

Please see www.pearsoned.co.uk/arnold for case study synopses. Also, there is another list of useful case studies in the fifth edition.

- New Heritage Doll Company (Brief Case)
  Authors: Timothy A. Luehrman; Heide Abelli. Harvard Business School. Available at www.cb.hbsp.harvard.edu.

- Time Value of Money: A Home Investment Decision Dilemma
  Authors: Arit Chaudhury; Varun Dawar; Rakesh Arrawatia. Harvard Business School. Available at www.cb.hbsp.harvard.edu.

- Wonder Kidz Fran Chise
  Authors: Sachin Mittal; Nitin Tanted; Vinay Goyal .Ivey Publishing. Available at www.cb.hbsp.harvard.edu.

Websites

Investopedia www.investopedia.com
As well as tutorials on finance this website has quick definitions and quick calculators, e.g. for NPV.

Self-review questions

1　What are the theoretical justifications for the NPV decision rules?

2　Explain what is meant by conventional and unconventional cash flows and what problems they might cause in investment appraisal.

3　Define the time value of money.

4　What is the reinvestment assumption for project cash flows under IRR? Why is this problematical? How can it be corrected?

5　Rearrange the compounding equation to solve for: (a) the annual interest rate, and (b) the number of years over which compounding takes place.

6　What is the 'yield' of a project?

7　Explain why it is possible to obtain an inaccurate result using the trial and error method of IRR when a wide difference of two discount rates is used for interpolation.

Questions and problems

Answers to most questions can be found at www.pearsoned.co.uk/arnold.
Answers to questions marked with an asterisk are to be found only in the Lecturer's Guide.

1   Proast plc is considering two investment projects whose cash flows are:

Points in time (yearly intervals)	Project A	Project B
0	−120,000	−120,000
1	60,000	15,000
2	45,000	45,000
3	42,000	55,000
4	18,000	60,000

The company's required rate of return is 15%.

a   Advise the company whether to undertake the two projects.
b   Indicate the maximum outlay at time 0 for each project before it ceases to be viable.

(An Excel spreadsheet solution to the question is at www.pearsoned.co.uk/arnold.)

2   Highflyer plc has two possible projects to consider. It cannot do both – they are mutually exclusive. The cash flows are:

Points in time (yearly intervals)	Project A	Project B
0	−420,000	−100,000
1	150,000	75,000
2	150,000	75,000
3	150,000	0
4	150,000	0

Highflyer's cost of capital is 12%. Assume unlimited funds. These are the only cash flows associated with the projects.

a   Calculate the internal rate of return (IRR) for each project.
b   Calculate the net present value (NPV) for each project.
c   Compare and explain the results in (a) and (b) and indicate which project the company should undertake and why.

(An Excel spreadsheet solution to the question is at www.pearsoned.co.uk/arnold.)

3* Mr Baffled, the managing director of Confused plc, has heard that the internal rate of return (IRR) method of investment appraisal is the best modern approach. He is trying to apply the IRR method to two new projects.

	Cash flows		
Year	0	1	2
Project C	−3,000	+14,950	−12,990
Project D	−3,000	+7,500	−5,000

a   Calculate the IRRs of the two projects.
b   Explain why Mr Baffled is having difficulties with the IRR method.
c   Advise Confused whether to accept either or both projects. (Assume a discount rate of 25%.)

4   Using a 13% discount rate, find the NPV of a project with the following cash flows:

Points in time (yearly intervals)	t_0	t_1	t_2	t_3
Cash flow (£)	−300	+260	−200	+600

Explain the difficulties you might have analysing this project using the IRR method.

5   a   Find the total terminal value of the following cash flows when compounded at 15%. Cash flows occur at annual intervals and the fourth year's cash flow is the last.

Points in time (yearly intervals)	t_1	t_2	t_3	t_4
Cash flow (£)	+200	+300	+250	+400

b   If £900 is the initial cash outflow at time 0, calculate the compounding rate that will equate the initial cash outflow with the terminal value as calculated in (a) above.
c   You have calculated the modified internal rate of return (MIRR), now calculate the IRR for comparison.

6   a   If the cost of capital is 14%, find the modified internal rate of return for the following investment and state if you would implement it.

Points in time (yearly intervals)	t_0	t_1	t_2	t_3	t_4
Cash flow	−9,300	5,400	3,100	2,800	600

b   Is this project to be accepted under the internal rate of return method?

7* Seddet International is considering four major projects which have either two- or three-year lives. The firm has raised all of its capital in the form of equity and has never borrowed money. This is partly due to the success of the business in generating income and partly due to an insistence by the dominant managing director that borrowing is to be avoided if at all possible. Shareholders in Seddet International regard the firm as relatively risky, given its existing portfolio of projects. Other firms' shares in this risk class have generally given a return of 16% per annum and this is taken as the opportunity cost of capital for the investment projects. The risk level for the proposed projects is the same as that of the existing range of activities.

Project		Net cash flows		
Points in time (yearly intervals)	t_0	t_1	t_2	t_3
A	−5,266	2,500	2,500	2,500
B	−8,000	0	0	10,000
C	−2,100	200	2,900	0
D	−1,975	1,600	800	0

Ignore taxation and inflation.

a   The managing director has been on a one-day intensive course to learn about project appraisal techniques. Unfortunately, during the one slot given over to NPV he had to leave the room to deal with a business crisis, and therefore does not understand it. He vaguely understands IRR and insists that you use this to calculate which of the four projects should be proceeded with, if there are no limitations on the number which can be undertaken.

b   State which is the best project if they are mutually exclusive (i.e. accepting one excludes the possibility of accepting another), using IRR.

c   Use the NPV decision rule to rank the projects and explain why, under conditions of mutual exclusivity, the selected project differs from that under (b).

d   Write a report for the managing director, detailing the value of the net present value method for shareholder wealth enhancement and explaining why it may be considered of greater use than IRR

Assignments

1   Try to discover the extent to which NPV, IRR and MIRR are used in your organisation. Also try to gauge the degree of appreciation of the problems of using IRR.

2   If possible, obtain data on a real project, historical or proposed, and analyse it using the techniques learned in this chapter.

Project appraisal:
cash flow and applications

LEARNING OUTCOMES

By the end of this chapter the reader will be able to identify and apply relevant and incremental cash flows in net present value calculations. The reader will also be able to recognise and deal with sunk costs, incidental costs and allocated overheads and be able to employ this knowledge to the following:

■ the replacement decision/the replacement cycle;

■ the calculation of annual equivalent annuities;

■ the make or buy decision;

■ optimal timing of investment;

■ fluctuating output situations.

Introduction

The last chapter outlined the process of project evaluation. This required consideration of the fundamental elements; first, recognition of the fact that time has a value and that money received in the future must be discounted at the opportunity cost of capital; second, the identification of relevant cash flows that are to be subject to the discounting procedure. It is to this second issue that we now turn.

This chapter examines the estimation of the cash flows appropriate for good decision making. The relevant cash flows are not always obvious and easy to obtain and therefore diligent data collection and rigorous analysis are required. Defining and measuring future receipts and outlays accurately are central to successful project appraisal.

In **Case study 3.1** Toyota would have had to consider carefully which projected cash flows are, and are not, relevant to the decision to invest further in the UK.

Case study 3.1   Toyota invests £240m to upgrade car plant in boost for Brexit Britain

Investment in Burnaston supported by £21.3m cash injection from government

By Peter Campbell

Toyota is to invest £240m in upgrading its UK car plant, in a sign the Japanese carmaker will keep manufacturing in Britain after the country's departure from the EU.

The move is supported by an investment of up to £21.3m from the UK government, which has said it will do all it can to maintain the competitiveness of Britain's automotive sector following the Brexit vote.

The upgrades are essential for Toyota's site in Burnaston, Derbyshire, to win work in the future, as carmakers' plants compete against each other to build new models.

The UK site produces the Auris hatchback and the Avensis saloon, and makes about 180,000 cars a year at Burnaston. Toyota also manufacturers engines at Deeside in Wales.

Toyota said the extra government funding would be used to promote training, research and development, and improvements to the Burnaston plant's environmental performance.

About three-quarters of the cars that Toyota produces at Burnaston are exported to the EU. The company is also heavily dependent on the European single market for components that are used in its vehicles.

Toyota has said it will use the investment to install new equipment at the site, train its workforce and improve the productivity of the plant.

The company is already working to attract more suppliers to the local area to help insulate it from the potential impact of tariffs on parts imported to a UK outside the single market.

The investment in Burnaston will be seen as a vote of confidence in the British car industry, and comes after Nissan pledged to make new vehicles in the UK despite uncertainty over the future relationship with the EU.

Nissan made its commitment after it was offered assurances by the government that the trading conditions at its plant would not change after the UK leaves the EU.

Johan van Zyl, Toyota's European president, said on Thursday that the carmaker's investment in Burnaston was a "sign of confidence in our employees and suppliers and their focus on superior quality and greater efficiency".

He added: "Our investment demonstrates that, as a company, we are doing all we can to raise the competitiveness of our Burnaston plant in Derbyshire. Continued tariff-and-barrier free market access between the UK and Europe that is predictable and uncomplicated will be vital for future success."

The UK car industry has warned that losing access to the EU single market and customs union will hurt its competitiveness.

In the event of a so-called "hard Brexit" that sees the UK fall back on World Trade Organization rules, exported cars will face a tariff of 10 per cent, while imported car parts will face a levy of between 2 and 4.5 per cent.

Mr van Zyl had previously said the long-term future of its two UK plants was dependent on the outcome of trade negotiations with the EU, although the company has always stressed that it is "committed" to Britain.

The UK car industry has been enjoying a renaissance on the back of international investment from companies such as Toyota, Nissan and Tata Motors, which owns Jaguar Land Rover.

Output hit 1.7m cars last year, and the country is on track to produce a record 2m by 2020.

Having completed the essential groundwork, the chapter moves on to demonstrate the practical application of the net present value (NPV) method. This deals with important business decisions, such as whether to replace a machine with a new more efficient (but expensive) version or whether it is better to persevere with the old machine for a few more years despite its rising maintenance costs and higher raw material inputs. Another area examined is replacement cycles, that is, if you have machinery which costs more to run as it gets older and you know that you will continue to need this type of machine and therefore have to replace it at some stage, should you regularly replace after one year or two, three or four years? An example is a car hire company that replaces its fleet of cars on a regular cycle. Other topics include the make or buy decision and optimal timing for the implementation of a project.

Quality of information

Good decisions are born of good information. This principle applies to all business decisions but is especially appropriate in the case of capital investment decisions in which a substantial proportion of the firm's assets can be put at risk. Obtaining relevant and high-quality information reduces the extent of the risk for the enterprise. Information varies greatly in its reliability, which often depends upon its source. The financial manager or analyst is often dependent on the knowledge and experience of other specialists within the organisation to supply data. For example, the marketing team may be able to provide an estimate of likely demand while the production team could help establish the costs per unit. Allowance will have to be made for any bias that may creep into the information passed on; for instance, a manager who is particularly keen on encouraging the firm to expand in a geographical area might tend to be over-optimistic concerning market demand. For some elements of a project there might be high-quality information, whereas other aspects have a lower quality. Take the case of the investment in a new lorry for a courier firm; the cost of purchase can be estimated with high precision, whereas the reaction of competitor firms is subject to much more uncertainty.

The sources of information which are useful as inputs for decision making vary widely; from accounting systems and special investigations, to those of the informal, 'just-between-you-and-me-and-the-gatepost' type. Whatever its source all information should, as far as possible, have the following characteristics:

- relevance;
- completeness;
- consistency;
- accuracy;
- reliability;
- timeliness;
- low cost of collection compared with benefit to be gained by gathering more detail.

Are profit calculations useful for estimating project viability?

Accountants often produce a wealth of numerical information about an organisation and its individual operations. It is tempting to simply take the profit figures for a project and put these into the NPV formula as a substitute for cash flow. A further reason advanced for favouring profit-based evaluations is that managers are often familiar with the notion of 'the bottom line' and frequently their performance is judged using profit. However, as was noted in Chapter 1, determining whether a project is 'profitable' is not the same as achieving shareholder wealth maximisation.

Profit is a concept developed by accountants to assist them with auditing and reporting. Profit figures are derived by taking what is a continuous process, a change in a company's worth over time, and allocating these changes to discrete periods of time, say a year (*see* **Exhibit 3.1**). This is a difficult task. It is a complex task with rules, principles and conventions in abundance.

Profit uses two carefully defined concepts: income and expenses. Income is not cash inflow, it is the amount earned from business activity whether or not the cash has been handed over. So, if a £1,000 sofa has been sold on two years' credit the accountant's income arises in the year of sale despite the fact that cash flows in two years later. Expense relates the use of an asset to a particular time period whether or not any cash outflow relating to that item occurs in that period. If a firm pays immediately for a machine which will have a ten-year useful life it does not write off the full cost of the machine against the first year's profit, but allocates a proportion of the cost to each of the ten years. The cash outflow occurs in the first year but the expense (use) of the asset occurs over ten years.

Shareholders make current consumption sacrifices, or they give up the return available elsewhere when they choose to invest their money in a firm. They do this in anticipation of receiving more £s in the future than they originally invested. Hence what is of interest to them are the future cash flows and the precise timing of these cash flows. The accountant does a difficult and important job but the profit figures produced are not suitable for project appraisal. Profit is a poor approach for two main reasons, first, depreciation and second, working capital.

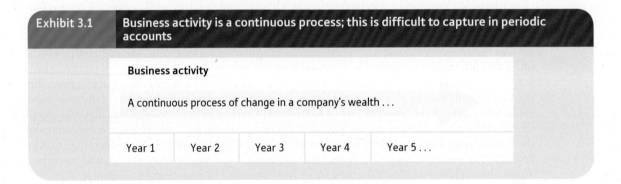

Exhibit 3.1	Business activity is a continuous process; this is difficult to capture in periodic accounts

Business activity

A continuous process of change in a company's wealth . . .

Year 1	Year 2	Year 3	Year 4	Year 5 . . .

Depreciation

Accounting profit is calculated after deducting depreciation, whereas what we are interested in is net cash inflows for a year. Depreciation should not be deducted to calculate net cash inflows, because although it is a business expense reflecting the cost of using the non-current assets, it does not result in a cash flow. For example, if a firm buys a machine for £20,000 which is expected to be productive for four years and have a zero-scrap value, the firm's accountant may allocate the depreciation on the machine over the four years to give the profit figures of, say, a stable £7,000 per year (*see* **Exhibit 3.2**). The reason for doing this may be so that the full impact of the £20,000 payout in the first year is not allocated solely to that year's profit and loss account, but is spread over the economic life of the asset. This makes good sense for calculating accounting profit. However, this is not appropriate for project appraisal based on NPV because these figures are not true cash flows. We need to focus on the cash flows at the precise time they occur and should not discount back to time zero the figure of £7,000, but rather the actual cash flows at the time they occur.

Exhibit 3.2	ABC plc: an example of adjustment to a profit and loss projection

Machine cost £20,000, at time 0.   Productive life of four years.

Accountant's figures

Year	1	2	3	4
	£	£	£	£
Profit before depreciation	12,000	12,000	12,000	12,000
Depreciation	5,000	5,000	5,000	5,000
Profit after depreciation	7,000	7,000	7,000	7,000

Cash flow

Point in time (yearly intervals)	t_0 £	t_1 £	t_2 £	t_3 £	t_4 £
Cash outflow	−20,000				
Cash inflow		12,000	12,000	12,000	12,000

Working capital

When a project is accepted and implemented the firm may have to invest in more than the large and obvious depreciable assets such as machines, buildings, vehicles and so forth. Investment in a new project often requires an additional investment in working capital, that is, the difference between short-term assets and liabilities. The main short-term assets are cash, stock (inventories) and debtors (receivables). The principal short-term liabilities are creditors (trade payables).

So, a firm might take on a project which involves an increase in the requirements for one of these types of working capital. Each of these will be taken in turn.

Cash floats

It may be that the proposed project requires the firm to have a much higher amount of cash float. For instance, a firm setting up a betting shop may have to consider not only the cash outflow for building or refurbishment, but also the amount of extra cash float needed to meet minute-by-minute betting payouts. Thus, we have to take into account this additional aspect of cash inputs when evaluating the size of the initial investment. This is despite the fact that the cash float will be recoverable at some date in the future (for instance, when the shop is closed in, e.g., three years' time). The fact that this cash is being used to lubricate day-to-day business and is therefore not available to shareholders means that a sacrifice has been made at a particular point. The owners of that money rightfully expect to receive a suitable return while that money is tied up and unavailable for them to use as they wish.

Stock (inventories)

Examples of stock are raw materials and finished goods. If a project is undertaken which raises the level of inventories then this additional cash outflow has to be allowed for. So, for a retail business opening a number of new shops the additional expenditure on stock is a form of investment. This extra cash being tied up will not be recognised by the profit and loss accounts because all that has happened is that one asset, cash, has been swapped for another, inventory. However, the cash use has to be recognised in any NPV calculation. With some projects there may be a reduction in inventory levels. This may happen in the case of the replacement of an inefficient machine with a new piece of equipment. In this case the stock reduction releases cash and so results in a positive cash flow.

Debtors (receivables)

Accounting convention dictates that if a sale is made during a year it is brought into the profit and loss account for that year. But in many cases a sale might be made on credit and all the firm has is a promise that cash will be paid in the future; the cash inflow has not materialised in the year the sale was recorded. Also, at the start of the financial year this firm may have had some outstanding debtors, that is, other firms or individuals owing this firm money, and in the early months of the year cash inflow is boosted by those other firms paying off their debt.

If we want to calculate the cash flow for the year then the annual profit figure has to be adjusted to exclude the closing balance of debtors (cash owed by customers at the end of the year but not yet paid over), and include the opening balance of debtors (cash owed by the customers at the beginning of the year which is received in this year for sales that took place the previous year).

Creditors (trade payables)

Whether suppliers send input goods and services to this firm for payment on 'cash on delivery terms' or 'credit terms' the accountant, rightly, records the value of these as an expense (if they are used up this year), and deducts this from the profit and loss account, in the year of delivery. The cash flow analyst needs to make an adjustment here because the full amount of the expense may not yet have flowed out in cash. So, if creditor balances increase we need to recognise that the profit and loss account has overstated the outflow of cash. We need then to add back the extent to which the creditor amount outstanding has increased from the beginning of the year to the end to arrive at the cash flow figure.

Thus, we may have four working capital adjustments to make to the profit and loss account figures to arrive at cash flow figures. The value of the firm's investment in net working capital, associated with a project, is found by the:

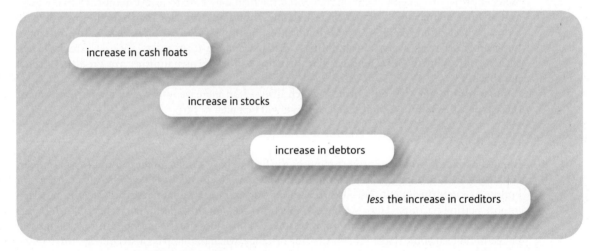

Net operating cash flow

The **net operating cash flow** associated with a new investment is equal to the profit, with depreciation[1] added back plus or minus any change in working capital. If the project results in an increase in working capital then:

---

1 Other non-cash deductions such as for amortisation of intangible assets may also be added back.

An example of the differences between profit and cash flow

We now turn to an example of the firm, ABC plc, carrying out a project appraisal. The finance manager has been provided with forecast profit and loss accounts and has to adjust these figures to arrive at cash flow (*see* **Exhibit 3.3**). This project will require investment in machinery of £20,000 at the outset. The machinery will have a useful life of four years and a zero-scrap value when production ceases at the end of the fourth year.

ABC's business involves dealing with numerous customers and the cash flows within any particular week are unpredictable. It therefore needs to maintain a cash float of £5,000 to be able to pay for day-to-day expenses. (Note: this cash float is not used up, and cannot therefore be regarded as a cost – in some weeks cash outflows are simply greater than cash inflows and to provide adequate liquidity £5,000 is needed for the firm to operate efficiently. The £5,000 will not be needed when output ceases.)

To produce the product, it will be necessary to have a stock of raw materials close to hand. The investment in this form of inventory together with the cash committed to work in progress and finished goods amounts to £2,000 at the beginning of production. However, more cash (an extra £1,000) is expected to be required for this purpose at the end of the second year. When the new business is begun a large proportion of raw materials will come from suppliers who will grant additional credit. Therefore, the level of creditors will rise by £1,000 over the period of the project.

To illustrate some of the differences between profit and cash flow there follows a conversion from projected accounting figures to cash flow. First it is necessary to add back the depreciation and instead account for the cost of the machine at time 0, the start date for the project when the cash left the firm. To capture the cash flow effect of the investment in inventories (stock) we need to see if any additional cash has been required between the beginning of the year and its end. If cash has been invested in inventory then the net stock adjustment to the cash flow calculation is negative. If cash has been released by the running down of inventory the cash flow effect is positive.

Now we turn to creditors. The accounting profit is derived after subtracting the expense of all inputs in a period, whether or not the payment for those inputs has been made in that period. If at the start ABC's suppliers provide goods and services to the value of £1,000 without requiring immediate payment then £1,000 needs to be added to the accountant's figures for true cash flow at that point. If the creditor's adjustment is not made then we are denying that of the £2,000 of stock delivered on the first day of trading half is bought on credit. It is not necessary for ABC to pay £2,000 at the start to suppliers; they pay only £1,000 and thus the creditor adjustment shows a positive cash flow at time 0, offsetting the outflow on stock. (In other examples, later in the book, it may be assumed that all stock is bought on trade credit and therefore there would not be a cash outflow for stock payments at time 0. In these examples, all creditor and debtor adjustments are made at the year ends and not at time 0.) In subsequent years the prior year's creditor debts actually paid match the amount outstanding at the year end, thus no net cash flow effect adjustment is necessary.

In this simplified example, it is assumed that after exactly four years all production ceases and outstanding creditors and debtors are settled on the last day of the fourth year. Also on the last day of the fourth year the money tied up in cash float and stock is released. Furthermore, the net cash flows from each year's trading all arrive on the last day of the respective year. These assumptions are obviously slightly unrealistic, but to make the example more realistic would add unnecessarily to its complexity.

Strictly speaking we should allow for the fact that a business generally receives and pays cash flows evenly through the year rather than assume that all cash flows occur at the end of the year. So, in theory, we should discount cash flows weekly or even daily (365 discount calculations per year!). The practice of simplifying to one net cash flow per year, followed by most managers, is justified on the grounds of practical necessity to avoid over-complicated calculations. Furthermore, by assuming cash comes in at the end of the year, and not any earlier, managers are, if anything, underestimating NPV. This more conservative estimate of project viability encourages greater confidence in the likelihood of project acceptance boosting shareholder wealth. An alternative is to assume cash inflows half-way through the year, in which case the discount factor becomes $\dfrac{1}{(1 + r)^{0.5}}, \dfrac{1}{(1 + r)^{1.5}}$, etc.

| Exhibit 3.3 | ABC plc: an example of profit to cash flow conversion |

- Machinery cost £20,000 at time 0, life of four years, zero scrap value.
- Extra cash floats required: £5,000, at time 0.
- Additional stock: £2,000 at time 0, £3,000 at time 2.
- Increase in creditors: £1,000.

ABC plc			Accounting year		
Point in time (yearly intervals)	**0**	**1**	**2**	**3**	**4**
	£	£	£	£	£
Accounting profit		7,000	7,000	7,000	7,000
Add back depreciation		5,000	5,000	5,000	5,000
		12,000	12,000	12,000	12,000
Initial machine cost	− 20,000				
Cash float	− 5,000				5,000
Stock					
Closing stock	2,000	2,000	3,000	3,000	0
Opening stock		2,000	2,000	3,000	3,000
Net stock adjustment	− 2,000	0	− 1,000	0	+ 3,000
(Outflow −tive, Inflow +tive)					
Creditors					
End of year	1,000	1,000	1,000	1,000	0
Start of year		1,000	1,000	1,000	−1,000
Cash flow effect of creditors	+ 1,000	0	0	0	− 1,000
(Outflow −tive, Inflow +tive)					
Net operating cash flow	− 26,000	12,000	11,000	12,000	19,000
Point in time (yearly intervals)	**0**	**1**	**2**	**3**	**4**
Cash flow	−26,000	12,000	11,000	12,000	19,000

Cost of capital 12%

$$NPV = -26{,}000 + \frac{12{,}000}{(1 + 0.12)} + \frac{11{,}000}{(1 + 0.12)^2} + \frac{12{,}000}{(1 + 0.12)^3} + \frac{19{,}000}{(1 + 0.12)^4} = +£14{,}099$$

This project produces a positive NPV, i.e. it generates a return which is more than the required rate of 12%, and therefore should be accepted.
(An Excel spreadsheet version of this calculation is available at www.pearsoned.co.uk/arnold.)

Incremental cash flows

A fundamental principle in project appraisal is to include only incremental cash flows. These are defined as the cash flows dependent on the project's implementation. Only those cash flows that are induced by the investment at time 0 and in subsequent years are regarded as incremental. Some of these cash flows are easy to establish but others are much more difficult to pin down.

Incremental cash flow	=	Cash flow for firm with the project	−	Cash flow for firm without the project

Here are some guideposts for finding relevant/incremental cash flows.

Include all opportunity costs

The direct inputs into a project are generally easy to understand and measure. However, quite often a project uses resources which already exist within the firm but which are in short supply and which cannot be replaced in the immediate future. That is, the project under consideration may be taking resources away from other projects. The loss of net cash flows from these other projects is termed an opportunity cost. For example, a firm may be considering a project that makes use of a factory which at present is empty. Because it is empty we should not automatically assume that the opportunity cost is zero. Perhaps the firm could engage in the alternative project of renting out the factory to another firm. The forgone rental income is a cost of the project under consideration.

Likewise, if a project uses the services of specialist personnel this may be regarded as having an opportunity cost. The loss of these people to other parts of the organisation may reduce cash flows on other projects. If they cannot be replaced with equally able individuals then the opportunity cost will be the lost net cash flows. If equally able hired replacements are found then the extra cost imposed, by the additional salaries, etc., on other projects should be regarded as an opportunity cost of the new project under consideration.

For a third example of opportunity cost, imagine your firm bought, when the price was low, a stock of platinum to use as a raw material. The total cost was £1m. It would be illogical to sell the final manufactured product at a price based on the old platinum value if the same quantity would now cost £3m. An alternative course of action would be to sell the platinum in its existing state, rather than to produce the manufactured product. The current market value of the raw platinum (£3m) then is the opportunity cost.

Include all incidental effects

It is possible for a new project to either increase or reduce sales of other products of the company. Take the case of an airline company trying to decide whether to go ahead with a project to fly between the USA and Japan. The direct cash flows of selling tickets, etc. on these flights may not give a positive NPV. However, it could be that the new service generates additional net revenue not only for USA–Japan flights but also on existing routes as customers switch to this airline because it now offers a more complete worldwide service. If this additional net cash flow is included the project may be viable.

On the other hand, if a clothes retailer opens a second or a third outlet in the same town, it is likely to find custom is reduced at the original store. This loss elsewhere in the organisation becomes a relevant cash flow in the appraisal of the *new* project, that is, the new shop.

In the soft drink business, the introduction of a new brand can reduce the sales of the older brands. This is not to say that a company should never risk any cannibalisation, only that if a new product is to be launched it should not be viewed in isolation. All incidental effects have to be allowed for, including those effects not directly associated with the new product or service.

In the article in **Exhibit 3.4a** Sir David Rowlands makes a plea for attention to be paid to incidental effects of a new high-speed rail route (HS2) in the UK. The importance of these incidental effects in the political decision-making process are further considered in John Kay's article from 2015 (**Exhibit 3.4b**).

Exhibit 3.4a

New lines needed to justify second high-speed rail route

By Robert Wright

A new, high-speed rail line in the UK 'may struggle' to justify itself under traditional measures, the man in charge of investigating options for a route admits.

Sir David Rowlands nevertheless looks poised to recommend building a high-speed route from London to Manchester via Birmingham, based on more sophisticated assessment techniques.

His comments in an interview underline the challenge facing backers of a second dedicated high-speed line in the UK following the completion in 2007

▶

Exhibit 3.4a *(continued)*

of High Speed 1 from the Channel Tunnel to London St Pancras. As the country's largest population centres are relatively near each other and rapid, frequent trains already have substantial market shares on many routes, traditional economic models produce too few benefits to justify the economic and social costs of construction.

Sir David says: 'Building a business case on a very traditional basis in terms of how transport projects are appraised, it may struggle.'

However, he adds, London Underground's Jubilee Line Extension also failed to justify itself in cost-benefit terms until civil servants started using novel analysis techniques. These measured 'agglomeration benefits' – the improved efficiency and competitiveness gained by connecting people better to each other. That project is now widely recognised as a success.

The case for a high-speed line is likely to be based on factors similar to those for the Jubilee Line, Sir David says, including a new route's ability to free up the existing west coast main line for more freight and commuter traffic.

'For HS2, you need to explore how sensibly you can go beyond existing appraisal techniques,' Sir David says. 'It's something to do with capturing the benefits of reliable train services; it's something to do with the benefits to the existing west coast; and it's something to do with the connectivity benefits that we may generate by drawing Scotland, Yorkshire, the north-west, Midlands and London closer together.'

FT *Financial Times,* 15 June 2009, p. 2.

Subsequent comment shows that political as well as economic facts can be relevant in project decisions.

Exhibit 3.4b

How modern politics gives HS2 plan an easy ride

By John Kay

In the 1980s privatisation was the big new idea in economic policy. I posed a question over a drink one evening to a friend who worked in 10 Downing Street. What is this policy really about, I asked? Is it aimed at improving the efficiency of nationalised companies or curbing union power? Is it intended to widen share ownership or just a means of raising revenue? I have never forgotten his response. You misunderstand, he said, the nature of modern politics. The policy is the policy because it is the policy. There is no more and no less to it than that.

Projects acquire political momentum of their own. The original rationale is forgotten, if indeed it ever existed. Even those whose support was only lukewarm respond to criticism by becoming ever more committed advocates. They seize on whatever arguments are to hand to justify their position.

And so it has been with HS2, the project to build a high-speed rail link from London to Birmingham and then to the north of England. Peter Mandelson has explained that the plan first won support from the Labour government of which he was part as an infrastructure project to lift the economy out of the recession created by the global financial crisis, although it is hard to see how a scheme that could not be "shovel ready" for a decade could have met that requirement.

The Conservative opposition, hoping to attract support in marginal constituencies in southwest London, backed the project as an alternative to the expansion of Heathrow airport, although the most cursory of calculations shows that only an insignificant proportion of users of that facility could be induced aboard Birmingham-bound trains.

So the plan acquired bipartisan political support. A government-owned company, HS2, was established, which in practice acted as an advocacy group. The cost-benefit analysis it commissioned confirmed, as its sponsors hoped, that the scheme would yield substantial benefits. Most of these benefits, however, were time savings to business travellers. Critics pointed out that modern business people are able to use the travel time productively — count the number of laptops on any train — and that, if these time savings were a real benefit, they were a benefit for which business travellers should pay.

The focus of argument shifted to claims that HS2 was the only effective means of dealing with potential excess demand for the West Coast lines out of London. On investigation, it appeared that the evidence of congestion on existing services mostly related to commuter traffic and the first evening trains on which long-distance travellers could use cheap tickets.

So more emphasis was put on the potential economic regeneration of the West Midlands, and the other provincial centres that might benefit from faster connections to the capital.

But this is a double-edged argument. The pull of London is strong. Would better access to the capital help or hinder economic growth in the regions? While there are examples of developments around the poles created by new stations, reducing the time it takes to travel between Birmingham and London may do more to encourage residents of Birmingham to go to London than to encourage London residents to go to Birmingham.

Britain's archaic House of Lords gains lustre, even justification, from its economic affairs committee, whose work has provided models of bipartisan investigation by intelligent people genuinely trying to ascertain the truth. The committee's report on the HS2 project, published just before the election in May and overwhelmed by it, is fully in this tradition. Members concluded, not that HS2 was a bad idea, but that no properly argued case had been made. They were right. The policy is the policy because it is the policy. There is no more or less to it than that.

Ignore sunk costs

Do not include sunk costs. The investors in Eurotunnel had, on several occasions, to decide whether to continue with the project. At the decision point the historic costs of design and development became irrelevant. Only future incremental flows should be considered. The design/development costs are in the past and should be ignored. The money spent on design/development is irrecoverable, whatever the decision. The fact that the overspend ran into billions of pounds and it was unclear whether the tunnel service would make a profit overall did not mean that the incremental cost of using some electricity to power the trains and the cost of employing some train drivers should not be incurred. The £9bn+ already spent was irrelevant to the decision on whether to transport passengers and freight between France and the UK. So long as the incremental future costs were less than incremental future benefits (cash flows when discounted) then the service should operate.

A common mistake in this area is to regard work already carried out or committed to (market demand screening, scientific study, geological survey, etc.) as relevant costs. They would not have been incurred but for the *possibility* of going ahead with the project. However, at the point of decision on whether to proceed, the costs are sunk. They have been incurred whether or not implementation takes place; they are therefore not incremental.

Sunk costs can be either costs for intangibles (e.g. research and development expenses) or costs for tangibles that cannot be used for other purposes (such as the cost of the Eurotunnel). When dealing with sunk costs, and being accused of throwing good money after bad, remember the 'bad' money outflow happened in the past and is no longer an input factor into a rigorous decision-making process.

Be careful with overheads

Overheads consist of salaries, rent, electricity etc. These costs, not directly associated with any one item produced, are usually allocated across products or projects. Project appraisal should only include the incremental expenses incurred as a result of project implementation. General overhead expenses, incurred regardless of whether the project takes place or not, are not incremental.

There are two types of overhead. The first involves incremental costs resulting from a project; e.g. extra costs incurred by going ahead rather than abstaining. The second type consists of such items as head office managerial salaries, legal expertise, public relations, research and development and even the corporate jet. These costs are not directly associated with any one part of the firm or one project and will be incurred regardless of whether the project under consideration is embarked upon. The accountant generally charges a proportion of this overhead to particular divisions and projects. When trying to assess the viability of a project only the incremental costs incurred by going ahead are relevant. Those costs which will be incurred whether or not the project is undertaken are irrelevant.

Dealing with interest

Interest on funds borrowed to invest is a cash outflow. However, it should not be included in cash flow calculations. **To repeat, interest should not be deducted from the net cash flows.** This is because, if it were subtracted, this would amount to double counting because the opportunity cost of capital used to discount the cash flows already incorporates the cost of these funds. The net cash flows are discounted to a present value by allowing for the weighted average cost of finance which is equal to the weighted average return required by shareholders and lenders. If the undiscounted cash flows also had interest deducted there would be double counting leading to an understatement of NPV. For more details see Chapter 16 on the calculation of the firm's discount rate (cost of capital).

Worked example 3.1   Tamcar plc

The accountants at Tamcar plc, manufacturers of sugar-coated candies, are analysing the viability of a new division, 'Sweet Heaven'. They estimate that this project will have a life of four years before the market disappears due to the imposition of an EU ban on sugar-coated candy. The estimated sales, made on three months' credit, are as follows:

Year	Sales (£)	There are no bad debts.
20X1	1.5m	
20X2	2.0m	
20X3	2.5m	
20X4	3.0m	

Year	Costs (£)	
20X1	0.75m	Costs of production are paid for on the last day of the year.
20X2	1.00m	There are no creditors. An investment in plant of £1m is required.
20X3	1.25m	The plant will have zero scrap value at the end of this project.
20X4	1.50m	The accountants depreciate the buildings and machinery
		at 25% per annum on a straight-line basis.

A cash float of £0.5m will be required at the start and stocks will increase by £0.3m. These are both recoverable at the end of the project life.

A £1m invoice for last year's scientific study of 'Sweet Heaven' technology has yet to be paid.

The head office allocates a proportion of central expenses to all divisions and projects. The share to be borne by 'Sweet Heaven' is £500,000 per annum. The head office costs are unaffected by the new project.

The accountants have produced the following projected profit and loss accounts:

Year	20X1 £m	20X2 £m	20X3 £m	20X4 £m
Sales	1.50	2.00	2.50	3.00
Costs of production	0.75	1.00	1.25	1.50
Depreciation	0.25	0.25	0.25	0.25
Scientific survey	0.25	0.25	0.25	0.25
Head office	0.50	0.50	0.50	0.50
Profit/loss	−0.25	0.00	0.25	0.50

Accountants' summary

Investment: £2m   Return: £0.5m over 4 years

$$\text{Average Return on Investment (ROI)} = \frac{\text{Average profit}}{\text{Investment}} = \frac{0.5 \div 4}{2} = 0.0625 \text{ or } 6.25\%$$

Recommendation: do not proceed with this project as 6.25% is a poor return.

Required

Calculate the net present value and recommend whether to accept this project or invest elsewhere.

Assume

- No tax.
- The return required on projects of this risk class is 11%.
- Start date of the project is 1.1.20X1.

Answer

- Depreciation is not a cash flow and should be excluded.
- The scientific survey is a sunk cost. This will not alter whether Tamcar chooses to go ahead or refuses to invest – it is irrelevant to the NPV calculation.
- Head office costs will be constant regardless of the decision to accept or reject the project, they are not incremental.

The sales figures shown in the first line of the table below are not the true cash receipts for each of those years because three months' credit is granted. Thus, in year 1 only three-quarters of £1.5m is received. An adjustment for debtors shows that one-quarter of the first year's sales are deducted. Thus £375,000 is received in the second year and therefore this is added to time 2's cash flow. However, one-quarter of the £2m of time 2's sales is subtracted because this is not received until the following year.

An assumption has been made concerning the receipt of debtor payments after production and distribution has ceased. In 20X4 sales are on the last day and given the three months' credit, cash is received after three months at time 4.25.

Time (annual intervals)	Tamcar cash flows					
	0	1	2	3	4	4.25
	start	end	end	end	end	mid
Year	20x1	20x1	20x2	20x3	20x4	20x5
Sales		+1.5	+2.0	+2.5	+3.0	
Buildings, plant, machinery	−1.0					
Cash float	−0.5				+0.5	
Stocks	−0.3				+0.3	
Costs of production		−0.75	−1.0	−1.25	−1.50	
Adjustment for debtors:						
Opening debtors	*0*	*0*	*0.375*	*0.500*	*0.625*	*0.75*
Closing debtors	*0*	*0.375*	*0.500*	*0.625*	*0.750*	*0*
Cash flow adjustment for debtors		−0.375	−0.125	−0.125	−0.125	+0.75
Cash flow	−1.8	+0.375	+0.875	+1.125	+2.175	+0.75

Net present value

$$-1.8 \; + \; \frac{0.375}{(1.11)} \; + \; \frac{0.875}{(1.11)^2} \; + \; \frac{1.125}{(1.11)^3} \; + \; \frac{2.175}{(1.11)^4} \; + \; \frac{0.75}{(1.11)^{4.25}}$$

−1.8	+0.338	+0.710	+0.823	+1.433	+0.481

NPV = + £1.985m

This is a project that adds significantly to shareholder wealth, producing £1.985m more than the minimum rate of return of 11 per cent required by the firm's finance providers.

(An Excel spreadsheet version of the calculation is available at www.pearsoned.co.uk/arnold.)

Worked example 3.2   The International Seed Company (TISC)

As the financial manager of TISC you analyse a proposal for the sale of genetically engineered vegetable seeds developed by a bio-technology firm. This firm will supply the seeds and permit TISC to sell them under licence.

Market research, costing £100,000, has been carried out to establish the likely demand. After three years TISC will withdraw from the market because these products will be superseded by further bio-technological developments.

The annual payment to the bio-technology firm will be £1m for the licence, payable at the end of each accounting year.

£500,000 will be needed initially to buy a fleet of vehicles for distribution which will be sold at the end of the third year for £200,000.

There will be a need for a packaging and administrative facility. TISC has a suitable factory with offices, which at present are empty. Head office has stated that they will let this space to your project at a reduced rent of £200,000 per annum payable at the end of the accounting year (the open market rental value is £1m p.a.).

The project would start on 1.1.20X1 and would not be subject to any taxation because of its special status as a growth industry. An inexperienced accountant has prepared forecast profit and loss accounts for the project as shown in the following table.

Year	20X1	20X2	20X3
	£m	£m	£m
Sales	5	6	6
Costs			
Market research	0.1		
Raw material (seeds)	2.0	2.4	2.4
Licence	1.0	1.0	1.0
Vehicle fleet depreciation	0.1	0.1	0.1
Direct wages	0.5	0.5	0.5
Rent	0.2	0.2	0.2
Overhead	0.5	0.5	0.5
Variable transport costs	0.5	0.5	0.5
Profit	0.1	0.8	0.8

The firm expects to attract a great deal of publicity which will improve its market position, and thus the profitability, of its other products. The benefit is estimated at £100,000 for each of the three years.

Head office allocates a proportion of its costs to any new project. This will be £100,000 for this project and has been included in the above overhead figures. The remainder of the overhead is directly related to the project.

All costs can be assumed to be paid at the end of each year. Most of the sales revenue may be assumed to be received at the end of each year. However, the firm will grant two months' credit to its customers which means that for some of the sales recorded by the accountant for a year the actual cash is received in the following year. An initial cash float of £1m will be needed. This will be returned at the end of the third year.

Assume no inflation. An appropriate discount rate is 15%.

Required

Assess the viability of the proposed project using the discounted cash flow technique you feel to be most appropriate.

Suggestion

Try to answer this question before reading the model answer.

Answer

Notes

- Market research cost is non-incremental.
- Opportunity cost of factory is £1m per annum.
- Vehicle depreciation does not belong in a cash flow calculation.
- The effect on TISC's other products is an incidental benefit.
- Head office cost apportionment should be excluded.

Cash flows						
£m	20X1 start	20X1 end	20X2 end	20X3 end	20X3 end	20X4 2 months
Inflows						
Sales		5.0	6.0	6.0		
Benefit to divisions		0.1	0.1	0.1		
Cash at end					1.0	
Vehicles					0.2	
Total inflows	0	5.1	6.1	6.1	1.2	0
Outflows						
Licence		1.0	1.0	1.0		
Vehicles	0.5					
Property rent (opportunity cost)		1.0	1.0	1.0		
Raw materials		2.0	2.4	2.4		
Direct wages		0.5	0.5	0.5		
Overheads		0.4	0.4	0.4		
Variable transport		0.5	0.5	0.5		
Initial cash	1.0					
Cash flows after outflows	−1.5	−0.3	0.3	0.3	1.2	0
Adjustment for debtors						
Debtor: start		0	0.833	1.00		1.0
end		0.833	1.000	1.00		0
Cash flow effect of debtors		−0.833	−0.167	0	0	+1.0
Cash flows	**−1.5**	**−1.133**	**+0.133**	**+0.3**	**+1.2**	**+1.0**
Net present value						

$$\text{NPV} = -1.5 + \frac{-1.133}{(1.15)} + \frac{0.133}{(1.15)^2} + \frac{0.3}{(1.15)^3} + \frac{1.2}{(1.15)^3} + \frac{1.0}{(1.15)^{3.167}}$$

$$\text{NPV} = -1.5 - 0.985 + 0.101 + 0.197 + 0.789 + 0.642 = -£0.756$$

Conclusion

Do not proceed with the project as it returns less than 15 per cent.

(An Excel spreadsheet version of the calculation is available at www.pearsoned.co.uk/arnold.)

Samsung had to consider relevant cash flows when deciding to expand production of chips (*see* **Exhibit 3.5**).

Exhibit 3.5

Samsung to spend $14.7bn on memory chip plant

S Korean group moves to meet demand for components used in mobile devices

By Song Jung-a

Samsung Electronics is to spend Won15.6tn ($14.7bn) building a new semiconductor plant in South Korea, the biggest single expenditure on a memory chip factory, to meet growing demand for components used in mobile devices.

Construction of the world's biggest state of the art chipmaking plant will begin in the first half of next year and complete in the second half of 2017, the South Korean company said. The plant will be built in Pyeongtaek, south of Seoul.

▶

Exhibit 3.5 *(continued)*

Samsung has been on a falling cycle of capital expenditure, which dropped to 10 per cent of sales last fiscal year from 14 per cent in 2010. It plans to devote the bulk of its capex to semiconductors, or Won14.4tn, to semiconductors this year.

The investment plan comes as Samsung struggles to maintain its leadership in the smartphone market, with Apple recently launching bigger-screen iPhones and Xiaomi grabbing market share from Samsung in China.

But the semiconductor unit has been a bright spot for Samsung, as chip prices stay firm amid tight supply after five years of brutal price competition whittled back the number of major D-Ram suppliers to three: Samsung, SK Hynix and Micron Technology.

"Our investment into the new fabrication plant will influence the shaping of Samsung's future semiconductor business," said Kwon Oh-hyun, Samsung's chief executive.

Part of that is through enhanced flexibility. The new plant could manufacture memory or processor chips, depending on demand, the world's largest memory chipmaker said. Memory chips are used in all smartphones, tablets and PCs, while processor chips power mobile devices.

Samsung's operating profit slid 25 per cent to Won7.2tn in the second quarter amid intense competition in the smartphone market. However, the group's semiconductor business was a standout for Samsung, reporting a 6 per cent year-on-year operating profit increase for the quarter.

"Demand for mobile D-Ram and processor chips used in smartphones continues to grow so this new plant is aimed at cementing its leadership in the future market," said Park Kang-ho, analyst at Daishin Securities.

"There is not much concern about oversupply as the chip market is pretty good, at the moment and other producers are not ramping up capacity much."

However, analysts remain downbeat on Samsung's earnings in the coming quarters.

The world's leading smartphone producer by sales has lost market share in China over the past two years to cheaper homegrown rivals and in the second quarter gave up the top spot, according to leading research firms.

Last month, Samsung launched the Galaxy Note 4, an upgraded model of its large-screen "phablet" to steal a march on Apple's new iPhones.

Analysts expect Samsung to report Won5.6tn of operating profit for the three months to September, which would be the group's weakest performance since the fourth quarter of 2011.

The company will reveal its guidance for the third-quarter earnings on Tuesday. Samsung shares gained 0.6 per cent to Won1.148m in morning trade, having fallen 17 per cent in the year-to-date.

 Financial Times, 6 October 2014.
All Rights Reserved.

The replacement decision

In the dynamic and competitive world of business, it is important to review operations to ensure efficient production. Technological change can offer cost reductions and a competitor, investing in new technology, can gain a cost advantage. Considering whether the machinery used in production should be replaced with an improved version is a continual process. Even if an existing machine has years of useful life left in it, the right decision may be to dispose of the old and bring in the new; if your firm does not produce at the lowest cost, another one will.

In making a replacement decision the costs associated with the purchase and installation of the new machine have to be weighed against the savings from switching to the new method of production. The incremental cash flows, the ones which change as a result of the decision, are the focus of attention (see Worked example 3.3).

Replacement cycles

Many business assets become increasingly expensive to operate and maintain as they become older. There is a point when it is better to buy a replacement than to face rising repair bills. Assets such as vehicles are often replaced on a regular cycle, say every two or three years, depending on

Worked example 3.3	Amtarc plc

Amtarc plc produces Tarcs with a machine which is now four years old. The management team estimates that this machine has a useful life of four more years before it will be sold for scrap, raising £10,000.

Q-leap, a manufacturer of machines suitable for Tarc production, has offered its new computer-controlled Q-2000 to Amtarc for a cost of £800,000 payable immediately.

If Amtarc sold its existing machine now, on the secondhand market, it would receive £70,000. (Its book (accounting) value, after depreciation, is £150,000.) The Q-2000 will have a life of four years before being sold for scrap for £20,000.

The attractive features of the Q-2000 are its lower raw material wastage and its reduced labour requirements. Selling price and variable overhead will be the same as for the old machine.

The accountants have prepared the figures shown below on the assumption that output will remain constant at last year's level of 100,000 Tarcs per annum.

	Profit per unit of Tarc	
	Old machine	Q-2000
	£	£
Sale price	45	45
Costs		
Labour	10	9
Materials	15	14
Variable overhead	7	7
Fixed overhead		
Factory admin., etc.	5	5
Depreciation	0.35	1.95
Profit per Tarc	7.65	8.05

The depreciation per unit has been calculated as follows:

$$\frac{\text{Total depreciation for a year}}{\text{Output for a year}}$$

Old machine: $\dfrac{(150{,}000 - 10{,}000)/4}{100{,}000} = £0.35$

Q-2000: $\dfrac{(800{,}000 - 20{,}000)/4}{100{,}000} = £1.95$

An additional benefit of the Q-2000 will be the reduction in required raw material buffer stocks – releasing £120,000 at the outset. However, because of the lower labour needs, redundancy payments of £50,000 will be necessary after one year.

Assume

● No inflation or tax.
● The required rate of return is 10%.
● To simplify the analysis sales, labour costs, raw material costs and variable overhead costs all occur on the last day of each year.

Required

Using the NPV method decide whether to continue using the old machine or to purchase the Q-2000.

Hints

Remember to undertake incremental analysis. That is, analyse only the difference in cash flow which will result from the decision to go ahead with the purchase. Remember to include the £10,000 opportunity cost of scrapping the old machine in four years if the Q-2000 is purchased.

▶

Worked example 3.3 *(continued)*

Answers

Stage 1
Note the irrelevant information:

1 Depreciation is not a cash flow and should not be included.
2 The book value of the machine is merely an accounting entry and has little relationship with the market value. Theoretically book value has no influence on the decision. (In practice, however, senior management may be reluctant to write off the surplus book value through the profit and loss account as this may prejudice an observer's view of their performance – despite there being no change in the underlying economic position.)

Stage 2
Work out the annual incremental cost savings.

	Savings per Tarc		
	Old machine **£**	**Q-2000** **£**	**Saving** **£**
Labour	10	9	1
Materials	15	14	1
Total saving			$\frac{2}{}$

Total annual saving £2 × 100,000 = £200,000.

Stage 3 Incremental cash flow table

Time £000s	0	1	2	3	4
Purchase of Q-2000	−800				
Scrap of old machine	+70				
Raw material stocks	+120				
Opportunity cost (old machine)					−10
Redundancy payments		−50			
Sale of Q-2000					+20
Annual cost savings		+200	+200	+200	+200
	−610	+150	+200	+200	+210

Stage 4 Calculate NPV

Discounted cash flows $\qquad -610 + \dfrac{150}{1.1} + \dfrac{200}{(1.1)^2} + \dfrac{200}{(1.1)^3} + \dfrac{210}{(1.1)^4}$

NPV = −£14,651.

The negative NPV indicates that shareholder wealth will be higher if the existing machine is retained.

the comparison between the benefit to be derived by delaying the replacement decision (that is, the postponed cash outflow associated with the purchase of new assets) and the cost in terms of higher maintenance costs (and lower secondhand value achieved with the sale of the used asset).

Consider the case of a car rental firm which is considering a switch to a new type of car. The cars cost £10,000 and a choice has to be made between four alternative (mutually exclusive) projects (four alternative regular replacement cycles).

Project	*Dispose after*	*Disposal proceeds* *£*	*Maintenance costs for year* *£*
1	1 year	7,000	500
2	2 years	5,000	900
3	3 years	3,000	1,200
4	4 years	1,000	2,500

The cars are not worth keeping for more than four years because of the bad publicity associated with breakdowns. The revenue streams and other costs are unaffected by which cycle is selected. We will focus on achieving the lowest present value of the costs.

If all the cash flows occur at annual intervals then the relevant cash flows are as set out in **Exhibit 3.6**. At first sight the figures suggest that the first project is the best, based on the normal rule, with mutually exclusive projects, of selecting the one with the lowest present value of costs.

Exhibit 3.6	Relevant cash flows						
	Point in time (yearly intervals)	**0**	**1**	**2**	**3**	**4**
Project 1		£	£	£	£	£
Replace after	Purchase cost	−10,000				
one year	Maintenance		−500			
	Sale proceeds		+7,000			
	Net cash flow	−10,000	+6,500			
Project 2						
Replace after	Purchase cost	−10,000				
two years	Maintenance		−500	−900		
	Sale proceeds			+5,000		
	Net cash flow	−10,000	−500	+4,100		
Project 3						
Replace after	Purchase cost	−10,000				
three years	Maintenance		−500	−900	−1,200	
	Sale proceeds				+3,000	
	Net cash flow	−10,000	−500	−900	+1,800	
Project 4						
Replace after	Purchase cost	−10,000				
four years	Maintenance		−500	−900	−1,200	−2,500
	Sale proceeds					+1,000
	Net cash flow	−10,000	−500	−900	−1,200	−1,500

Assuming a discount rate of 10% the present values (PVs) of costs of one cycle of the projects are:

$$PV_1 \quad -10,000 \quad + \quad \frac{6,500}{1.1} \qquad\qquad\qquad\qquad = -4,090.90$$

$$PV_2 \quad -10,000 \quad - \quad \frac{500}{1.1} \quad + \quad \frac{4,100}{(1.1)^2} \qquad\qquad = -7,066.12$$

$$PV_3 \quad -10,000 \quad - \quad \frac{500}{1.1} \quad - \quad \frac{900}{(1.1)^2} \quad + \quad \frac{1,800}{(1.1)^3} \qquad = -9,845.98$$

$$PV_4 \quad -10,000 \quad - \quad \frac{500}{1.1} \quad - \quad \frac{900}{(1.1)^3} \quad - \quad \frac{1,200}{(1.1)^3} \quad - \quad \frac{1,500}{(1.1)^4} = -13,124.44$$

However, purchases and sales of vehicles have to be allowed for beyond the first replacement cycle. If we assume that there are no increases in costs and the cars can be replaced with identical models on regular cycles in the future[2] then the pattern of cash flows for the third project, for example, are as shown in **Exhibit 3.7**.

---

2 This is a bold assumption. More realistic assumptions could be made, e.g. allowing for inflation, but the complexity that this produces is beyond the scope of this book.

Exhibit 3.7	Cash flows for project 3							
Time (years)	**0**	**1**	**2**	**3**	**4**	**5**	**6**	**7 . . .**
Cash flows (£)								
1st generation	−10,000	−500	−900	+1,800				
2nd generation				−10,000	−500	−900	+1,800	
3rd generation							−10,000	−500 . . .

One way of dealing with a long-lived project of this kind would be to calculate the present values of numerous cycles stretching into the future and compare the outcome with each project's present values calculated in a similar fashion. Fortunately, there is a quicker technique available called the annual equivalent annuity method (AEA). This third project involves three cash outflows followed by a cash inflow within one cycle as shown in **Exhibit 3.8**.

Exhibit 3.8	Cash outflows and cash inflow in one cycle			
Time (years)	**0**	**1**	**2**	**3**
Cash flows (£)	−10,000	−500	−900	+1,800

This produces a one-cycle present value of −£9,845.98. The annual equivalent annuity (AEA)[3] method finds the annuity (the amount that would be paid in each of the next three years if each annual payment were identical) that gives the same (equivalent) present value of −£9,845.98. That is, the constant amount which would replace the ? in **Exhibit 3.9**.

Exhibit 3.9	Using the AEA				
Time (years)	**0**	**1**	**2**	**3**	**Present value**
Actual cash flows (£)	−10,000	−500	−900	+1,800	−9,845.98
Annual equivalent annuity (£)		?	?	?	−9,845.98

(Recall that the first cash flow under an 'immediate' annuity arises after one year.)

To find the AEA we need to employ the annuity table in Appendix III. This table gives the value of a series of £1 cash flows occurring at annual intervals in terms of present money. Normally the annuity (A) – the amount of the cash flow that is received regularly – is multiplied by the annuity factor (af) from the table to obtain the present value, PV, of that annuity. In this case we already know the PV (−£9,845.98) and we can obtain the annuity factor by looking at the three-year row and the 10% column. The missing element is the annual annuity.

$$PV = A \times af \quad \text{or} \quad A = \frac{PV}{af}$$

In the case of the three-year replacement:

$$A = \frac{-£9,845.98}{2.4869} = -£3,959.14$$

---

3 Also called equivalent annual annuity and equivalent annual cash flow.

Thus, two alternative sets of cash flows give the same present value of −£9,845.98 (*see* **Exhibit 3.10**).

Exhibit 3.10	Cash flow 1 and cash flow 2			
Time (years)	**0** £	**1** £	**2** £	**3** £
Cash flow 1	−10,000	−500	−900	+1,800
Cash flow 2		−3,959.14	−3,959.14	−3,959.14

The second generation of cars bought at the end of the third year will have a cost of −£9,845.98 when discounted to the end of the third year (assuming both zero inflation and that the discount rate remains at 10%). The present value of the costs of this second generation of vehicle is equivalent to the present value of an annuity of −£3,959.14. Thus, replacing the car every three years is equivalent to a cash flow of −£3,959.14 every year to infinity (*see* **Exhibit 3.11**).

Exhibit 3.11	Replacing the car every three years							
Time (years)	**0**	**1**	**2**	**3**	**4**	**5**	**6**	**7 . . .**
Cash flows (£)								
First generation	−10,000	−500	−900	+1,800				
Second generation				−10,000	−500	−900	+1,800	
Third generation							−10,000	−500 . . .
Annual equivalent annuity	0	−3,959.14	−3,959.14	−3,959.14	−3,959.14	−3,959.14	−3,959.14	−3,959.14

If all the other projects are converted to their annual equivalent annuities a comparison can be made (*see* **Exhibit 3.12**).

Exhibit 3.12	Using AEAs for all projects		
Cycle	**Present value of one cycle (PV)**	**Annuity factor (af)**	**Annual equivalent annuity (PV/af)**
1 year	−4,090.90	0.9091	−4,499.95
2 years	−7,066.12	1.7355	−4,071.52
3 years	−9,845.98	2.4869	−3,959.14
4 years	−13,124.44	3.1699	−4,140.33

Thus Project 3 requires the lowest equivalent annual cash flow and is the optimal replacement cycle. This is over £540 per year cheaper than replacing the car every year.

A valid alternative to the annual equivalent annuity is the lowest common multiple (LCM) method, where the 'lowest common multiple' refers to the lowest common multiple of the alternative cycle lengths. The alternatives are compared using the present value of the costs over a timespan equal to the lowest common multiple. The lowest common multiple of 1, 2, 3 and 4 is 12 so the cash flow for 12 cycles of Project 1 would be discounted and compared with six cycles of Project 2, four cycles of Project 3 and three cycles of Project 4. The AEA method is the simplest and quickest method in cases where the lowest common multiple is high. For instance, the LCM of 5, 6 and 7 year cycles is 210 years, and would involve a great many calculations.

Worked example 3.4	Brrum plc

Suppose the firm Brrum has to decide between two machines, A and B. Whichever new machine is chosen it will be replaced on a regular cycle. Both machines produce the same level of output so we do not need to examine the cash inflows to choose between the machines; we can concentrate solely on establishing the lower-cost machine.

Brrum plc

- Machine A costs £30m, lasts three years and costs £8m a year to run.
- Machine B costs £20m, lasts two years and costs £12m a year to run.

Cash flows

Point in time (yearly intervals)	0	1	2	3	PV (6%)
Machine A (£m)	−30	−8	−8	−8	−51.38
Machine B (£m)	−20	−12	−12	−	−42.00

Because Machine B has a lower PV of cost, should we jump to the conclusion that this is the better option? Well, Machine B will have to be replaced one year before Machine A and, therefore, there are further cash flows to consider and discount.

Assuming a constant discount rate of 6% and no change in costs over future years, we can make a comparison between the two machines by converting the total PV of the costs to a cost per year. We convert the PV of the costs associated with each machine to the equivalent annuity.

Machine A

Machine A has a PV of −£51.38m. We need to find an annuity with a PV of −£51.38 m which has regular equal costs occurring at years 1, 2 and 3.

Look in the annuity table along the row of 3 years and down the column of 6% to get the three-year annuity factor.

PV = Annual annuity payment (A) × 3-year annuity factor (af)

$$-51.38 = A \times 2.673$$
$$A = -51.38/2.673 = -£19.22\text{m per year}$$

Point in time (yearly intervals)	0	1	2	3	PV (6%)
Cash flows (£m)	−30	−8	−8	−8	−51.38
Equivalent 3-year annuity (£m)		−19.22	−19.22	−19.22	−51.38

When Machine A needs to be replaced at the end of the third year, if we can assume it is replaced by a machine of equal cost we again have a PV of costs for the end of year 3 of £51.38m. This too has an equivalent annuity of −£19.22m. Thus, the −£19.22m annual costs is an annual cost for many years beyond year 3.

Machine B

$$PV = A \times af$$
$$-42 = A \times 1.8334$$
$$A = -42/1.8334 = -£22.908\text{m}$$

Point in time (yearly intervals)	0	1	2	PV (6%)
Cash flows (£m)	−20	−12	−12	−42
Equivalent 2-year annuity (£m)		−22.91	−22.91	−42

Again, if we assume that at the end of two years the machine is replaced with an identical one, with identical costs, then the annuity of −£22.91m can be assumed to be continuing into the future.

Comparing the annual annuities

> Machine A: −£19.22m.
> Machine B: −£22.91m.

When we compare the annual annuities, we see that Machine A, in fact, has the lower annual cost and is therefore the better buy.

When to introduce a new machine

Businesses, when switching from one kind of a machine to another, have to decide on the timing of that switch. The best option may not be to dispose of the old machine immediately. It may be better to wait for a year or two because the costs of running the old machine may amount to less than the equivalent annual cost of starting a regular cycle with replacements. However, eventually the old machine is going to become more costly due to its lower efficiency, increased repair bills or declining secondhand value. Let us return to the case of the car rental firm. It has been established that when a replacement cycle is begun for the new type of car, it should be a three-year cycle. The existing type of car used by the firm has a potential further life of two years. The firm is considering three alternative courses of action. The first is to sell the old vehicles immediately, raising £7,000 per car, and then begin a three-year replacement cycle with the new type of car. The second possibility is to spend £500 now to service the vehicles ready for another year's use. At the end of the year the cars could be sold for £5,200 each. The third option is to pay £500 for servicing now, followed by a further £2,000 in one year to maintain the vehicles on the road for a second year, after which they would be sold for £1,800. The easiest approach for dealing with a problem of this nature is to calculate NPVs for all the possible alternatives. We will assume that the revenue aspect of this car rental business can be ignored as this will not change regardless of which option is selected. The relevant cash flows are shown in **Exhibit 3.13**. Note that the annual equivalent annuity cash flow, rather than the actual cash flows for the three-year cycle of new cars, is incorporated and is assumed to continue to infinity. It is therefore a perpetuity.

(Note that the sums of £3,959.14 are perpetuities starting at times 1, 2 and 3, and so are valued at times 0, 1 and 2. The latter two therefore have to be discounted back one and two years respectively.) The net present value calculations are as set out in **Exhibit 3.14**.

Exhibit 3.13	Cash flow per car (excluding operating revenues, etc.)				
Point in time (yearly intervals)		0 £	1 £	2 £	3 → ∞ £
Option 1 – sell old car at time 0	Secondhand value	+7,000			
	New car		−3,959.14	−3,959.14	−3,959.14
	Net cash flow	+7,000	−3,959.14	−3,959.14	−3,959.14
Option 2 – sell old car after one year	Secondhand value		+5,200		
	Maintenance	−500			
	New car			−3,959.14	−3,959.14
	Net cash flow	−500	+5,200	−3,959.14	−3,959.14
Option 3 – sell old car after two years	Secondhand value			+1,800	
	Maintenance	−500	−2,000		
	New car				−3,959.14
	Net cash flow	−500	−2,000	+1,800	−3,959.14

Exhibit 3.14	Present value calculations

Option 1	$+ \quad 7{,}000$		$- \quad \dfrac{3{,}959.14}{0.1}$	$= -£32{,}591.40$
Option 2	$-500 \quad + \quad \dfrac{5{,}200}{1.1}$		$- \quad \dfrac{3{,}959.14}{0.1} \quad \times \quad \dfrac{1}{1.1}$	$= -£31{,}764.91$
Option 3	$-500 \quad - \quad \dfrac{2{,}000}{1.1}$	$+ \quad \dfrac{1{,}800}{(1.1)^2}$	$- \quad \dfrac{3{,}959.14}{0.1} \quad \times \quad \dfrac{1}{(1.1)^2}$	$= -£33{,}550.74$

The switch to the new cars should take place after one year. Thereafter the new cars should be replaced every three years. This policy is over £800 cheaper than selling off the old cars immediately.

Drawbacks of the annual equivalent annuity method

It is important to note that annual equivalent annuity analysis relies on there being a high degree of predictability of cash flows stretching into the future. While the technique can be modified reasonably satisfactorily for the problems caused by inflation we may encounter severe problems if the assets in question are susceptible to a high degree of technical change and associated cash flows. An example here would be computer hardware where simultaneously over short time periods both technical capability increases and cost of purchase decreases. The absence of predictability means that the AEA approach is not suitable in a number of situations. The requirement that identical replacement takes place can be a severe limitation but the AEA approach can be used for approximate analysis, which is sufficient for practical decisions in many situations – provided the analyst does not become too preoccupied with mathematical preciseness and remembers that good judgement is also required.

Timing of projects

In some industries, the mutually exclusive projects facing the firm may simply be whether to take a particular course of action now or to make shareholders better off by considering another possibility, for instance, to implement the action in a future year. It may be that taking action now would produce a positive NPV and is therefore attractive. However, by delaying action an even higher NPV can be obtained. Take the case of Lochglen distillery. Ten years ago, it laid down a number of vats of whisky. The older the whisky becomes, the higher the market value. The issue facing the management team is to decide in which of the next seven years to bottle and sell it. The table in **Exhibit 3.15** gives the net cash flows available for each of the seven alternative projects.

Exhibit 3.15	Lochglen distillery's choices

	Year of bottling						
Point in time (yearly intervals)	0	1	2	3	4	5	6
Net cash flow £000s per vat	60	75	90	103	116	129	139
Percentage change on previous year		25%	20%	14.4%	12.6%	11.2%	7.8%

The longer the firm refrains from bottling, the greater the inflow. However, this does not necessarily imply that shareholders will be best served by delaying as long as possible. They have an opportunity cost for their funds and therefore the firm must produce an adequate return over a period of time. In the case of Lochglen the assumption is that the firm requires a 9% return on projects. The calculation of the NPVs for each project is easy (*see* **Exhibit 3.16**).

Exhibit 3.16	NPVs for Lochglen distillery's choices						

	Year of bottling						
Point in time (yearly intervals)	0	1	2	3	4	5	6
£000s per vat		$\frac{75}{1.09}$	$\frac{90}{(1.09)^2}$	$\frac{103}{(1.09)^3}$	$\frac{116}{(1.09)^4}$	$\frac{129}{(1.09)^5}$	$\frac{139}{(1.09)^6}$
Net present value	60	68.8	75.8	79.5	82.2	83.8	82.9

As shown in Exhibit 3.16, the optimal point is at Year 5 when the whisky has reached the ripe old age of 15. Note also that prior to the fifth year the value increased at an annual rate greater than 9%. After Year 5 (or 15 years old) the rate of increase is less than the cost of capital. Another way of viewing this is to say that if the whisky was sold when at 15 years old, the cash received could be invested elsewhere (for the same level of risk) and receive a return of 9%, which is more than the 7.8% available by holding the whisky one more year.

The make or buy decision

A perennial issue that many organisations need to address is whether it is better to buy a particular item, such as a component, from a supplier or to produce the item in-house. If the firm produces for itself it will incur the costs of set-up as well as the ongoing annual costs. These costs can be avoided by buying in but this has the potential drawback that the firm may be forced to pay a high market price. This is essentially an incremental cash flow problem. We need to establish the difference between the costs of set-up and production in-house and the costs of purchase. Take the case of Davis and Davies plc which manufactures it fishing rods. At the moment, it buys in the 'eyes' for the rods from I'spies plc at £1 per set. It expects to make use of 100,000 sets per annum for the next few years. If Davis and Davies were to produce its own 'eyes' it would have to spend £40,000 immediately on machinery, setting up and training. The machinery will have a life of four years and the annual cost of production of 100,000 sets will be £80,000, £85,000, £92,000 and £100,000 respectively over the four years of production. The cost of bought-in components is not expected to remain at £1 per set. The more realistic estimates are £105,000 for year 1, followed by £120,000, £128,000 and £132,000 for years 2 to 4 respectively, for 100,000 sets per year. The new machinery will be installed in an empty factory, the open market rental value of which is £20,000 per annum and the firm's cost of capital is 11%. The extra cash flows associated with in-house production compared with buying in are as set out in **Exhibit 3.17**.

Exhibit 3.17	Cash flows for producing 'eyes' in-house				

Points in time (yearly intervals) £000s	0	1	2	3	4
1 Cash flows of self-production	40	80	85	92	100
2 Plus opportunity costs		20	20	20	20
3 Relevant cash flows of making	40	100	105	112	120
4 Costs of purchasing component		105	120	128	132
Incremented cash flow due to making (line 4 – line 3)	−40	5	15	16	12

▶

Exhibit 3.17 *(continued)*

Net present value of incremental cash flows

$$NPV = -\pounds 3,717 \qquad\qquad -40 + \frac{5}{1.11} + \frac{15}{(1.11)^2} + \frac{16}{(1.11)^3} + \frac{12}{(1.11)^4}$$

As the incremental NPV is negative Davis and Davies should continue to purchase 'eyes'. The present values of the future annual savings are worth less than the initial investment for self-production.

An example of this sort of buy-in or build decision is shown for JCB in **Exhibit 3.18**.

Exhibit 3.18

JCB to buck trend and build engines

By Dan Roberts, Industrial Editor

JCB is due to buck the trend in British engineering decline by launching one of the first new engines designed and built entirely in the UK for over a decade. The Staffordshire manufacturer of construction equipment says signs of recovery in several of its main export markets have encouraged it to commit £50m to replace existing diesel engines bought from foreign-owned suppliers.

Although the capital expenditure is small by global standards, it reflects growing confidence in one of the UK's biggest privately-owned companies and contradicts warnings that the specialist expertise required has been lost . . .

'Until recently we have never had the volume of sales to support the development of a new engine but we have been developing the project in secret for the last four years', said Mr Patterson . . .

JCB says annual vehicle sales are more than 30,000, up from 11,000 in 1993 . . .

Fluctuating output

Many businesses and individual machines operate at less than full capacity for long periods of time. Sometimes this is due to the nature of the firm's business. For instance, electricity demand fluctuates through the day and over the year. Fluctuating output can produce some interesting problems for project appraisal analysis. Take the case of the Potato Sorting Company, which grades and bags potatoes in terms of size and quality. During the summer and autumn its two machines work at full capacity, which is the equivalent of 20,000 bags per machine per year. However, in the six months of the winter and spring the machines work at half capacity because fewer home-grown potatoes need to be sorted. The operating cost of the machine per bag is 20 pence. The machines were installed over 50 years ago and can be regarded as still having a very long productive life. Despite this they have no secondhand value because modern machines called Fastsort now dominate the market. Fastsort has an identical capacity to the old machine but its running cost is only 10 pence per bag. These machines are also expected to be productive indefinitely, but they cost £12,000 each to purchase and install. The new production manager is keen on getting rid of the two old machines and replacing them with two Fastsort machines. She has presented the figures given in **Exhibit 3.19** to a board meeting on the assumption of a cost of capital of 10%.

Exhibit 3.19   Comparison of old machines with Fastsort

Cost of two old machines

Output per machine per year:

$=$ rate of 20,000 p.a. for six months 20,000 $\times$ 0.5 $=$ 10,000

$+$ rate of 10,000 p.a. for six months 10,000 $\times$ 0.5 $=$ $\dfrac{5,000}{15,000}$

15,000 bags @ 20p $\times$ 2 = £6,000.

Present value of a perpetuity of £6,000: $\dfrac{6,000}{0.1}$ $=$ £60,000

Cost of the Fastsorts

Annual output – same as under old machines, 30,000 bags p.a.

Annual operating cost 30,000 $\times$ 10p = £3,000

Present value of operating costs $\dfrac{3,000}{0.1}$ = £30,000

Plus initial investment   £24,000
Overall cost in present value terms   £54,000

The production manager has identified a way to save the firm £6,000 and is duly proud of her presentation. The newly appointed finance director thanks her for bringing this issue to the attention of the board but thinks that they should consider a third possibility. This is to replace only one of the machines. The virtue of this approach is that during the slack six months only the Fastsort will be used and can be supplemented with the old machine during the busy period, thus avoiding £12,000 of initial investment. The figures work out as set out in **Exhibit 3.20**.

The board decides to replace only one of the machines as this saves £8,000 compared with £6,000 under the production manager's proposal.

Exhibit 3.20   Replacing only one old machine

	Fastsort		Old machine	
Output	20,000 bags		10,000 bags	
Initial investment	£12,000			
Operating costs	10p $\times$ 20,000	= £2,000	20p $\times$ 10,000	= £2,000
Present value of operating costs	$\dfrac{2,000}{0.1}$	= £20,000	$\dfrac{2,000}{0.1}$	= £20,000
Total present value of costs	£12,000	+ £20,000	+ £20,000	= £52,000

Concluding comments

Finding appropriate cash flows to include in a project appraisal often involves some difficulty in data collection and requires some thoughtfulness in applying the concepts of incremental cash flow. The reader who has diligently worked through this chapter and has overcome the barriers to understanding may be more than a little annoyed at being told that the understanding of these issues is merely one of the stages leading to successful application of net present value to practical business problems. The logical, mathematical and conceptual knowledge presented above has to be married to an appreciation of real-world limitations imposed by the awkward fact that it is people who have to be persuaded to act to implement a plan. This is an issue examined in the next chapter. Further real-world complications such as the existence of risk, of inflation and taxation and of limits placed on availability of capital are covered in subsequent chapters.

Key points and concepts

- **Raw data** have to be checked for accuracy, reliability, timeliness, expense of collection, etc.

- **Depreciation** is not a cash flow and should be excluded.

- **Profit** is a poor substitute for cash flow. For example, working capital adjustments may be needed to modify the profit figures for NPV analysis.

- Analyse using **incremental cash flows**. That is the difference between the cash flows arising if the project is implemented and the cash flows if the project is not implemented:

  - **opportunity costs** associated with, say, using an asset which has an alternative employment are relevant;
  - **incidental effects,** that is, cash flow effects throughout the organisation, should be considered along with the obvious direct effects;
  - **sunk costs** – costs which will not change regardless of the decision to proceed are clearly irrelevant;

  - **allocated overhead** is a non-incremental cost and is irrelevant;
  - **interest** should not be double counted by both including interest as a cash flow and including it as an element in the discount rate.

- **The replacement decision** is an example of the application of incremental cash flow analysis.

- **Annual equivalent annuities (AEA)** can be employed to estimate the **optimal replacement cycle** for an asset under certain restrictive assumptions. The **lowest common multiple (LCM)** method is sometimes employed for short-lived assets.

- Whether to repair the old machine or sell it and buy a new machine is a very common business dilemma. Incremental cash flow analysis helps us to solve these types of problems. Other applications include **the timing of projects,** the issue of **fluctuating output** and the **make** or **buy decision.**

References and further reading

Bierman, H. and Smidt, S. (2006) *The Capital Budgeting Decision*, 9th edn. London: Routledge.
    Contains some good chapters for the beginner.

Bierman, H. and Smidt, S. (2006) *Advanced Capital Budgeting*. London: Routledge.
    Good for those wanting to pursue these topics in more depth.

Coulthurst, N.J. (1986) 'The application of the incremental principle in capital investment project evaluation', *Accounting and Business Research*, Autumn.
    A discussion of the theoretical and practical application of the incremental cash flow principle.

Ismail, T. and Cline, M. (2005) 'Investment appraisal under conditions of continuous and discrete cash flows and discounting', *Managerial Auditing Journal*, 20(1), pp. 30–35.

Discusses the most effective way to calculate investment returns under continuous and discrete cash flows. Discusses limitations of the assumption that cash flows occur at the start or end of the year.

Marco-Izquierdo, J.A. (2015) 'CEOs don't care enough about Capital Allocation', *Harvard Business Review Digital Articles 4/16/2015*, pp. 2–4.
    Discusses the shortage of CEOs who are skilled at capital allocation.

Mauboussin, M.J. and Callahan, D. (2014) 'Capital allocation: Evidence, Analytical Methods and Assessment Guidance', *Journal of Applied Corporate Finance*, 26(4), pp. 98–74.
    Examines the main sources and uses of capital by the largest 1,500 US companies during the last 30 years. Identifies capital allocated to seven alternatives,

including M&A, capital expenditures, R&D, and distributions of capital to investors. Summarizes the academic research on the effects on corporate values. Reports that US corporations fund most of their investments internally.

Pohlman, R.A., Santiago, E.S. and F. Lynn Markel (1988) 'Cash Flow Estimation Practices of Large Firms',

Financial Management, 17(2), pp. 71–9.

The study's findings reveal the importance of different factors on the cash flow forecasting process and provides insights on the weight firms give to information other than cash flows and discount rates when making capital investment decisions.

Case study recommendations

Please see www.pearsoned.co.uk/arnold for case study synopses. Also, there is another list of useful case studies in the fifth edition.

- Tottenham Hotspur PLC
  Authors: Joshua D Coval; Lauren H. Cohen; Christopher Malloy. Harvard Business School. Available at www.cb.hbsp.harvard.edu.

- Magic Timber and Steel: Investment Evaluation with Net Present Value
  Authors: Robert F. Bruner; Michael J. Schill. Ivey Publishing. Available at www. cb.hbsp.harvard.edu

- Fonderia Del Piemonte S.P.A.
  Authors: Robert F. Bruner; Michael J . Schill. Darden School of Business. Available at www. cb.hbsp. harvard.edu.

- Time Value of Money: The Buy Versus Rent Decision
  Authors: Sean Cleary; Stephen R. Foerster. Ivey Publishing. Available at www.cb.hbsp.harvard.edu

- Airbus A3xx: Developing the World's Largest Commercial Jet
  Authors: Benjamin C. Esty; Michael Kane. Harvard Business School. Available at www.cb.hbsp. harvard.edu

- Stryker Corp.: In-Sourcing PCBS
  Author: Timothy A. Luehrman. Harvard Business School. Available at www.cb.hbsp.harvard.edu

Self-review questions

1 Imagine the Ministry of Defence has spent £50m researching and developing a new guided weapon system. Explain why this fact may be irrelevant to the decision on whether to go ahead with production.

2 'Those business school graduates don't know what they are talking about. We have to allocate overheads to every department and activity. If we simply excluded this cost there would be a big lump of costs not written off. All projects must bear some central overhead.' Discuss this statement.

3 What is an annual equivalent annuity?

4 What are the two main techniques available for evaluating mutually exclusive repeated projects with different lengths of life? Why is it not valid simply to use NPVs?

5 Arcmat plc owns a factory which at present is empty. Mrs Hambicious, a business strategist, has been working on a proposal for using the factory for doll manufacture. This will require complete modernisation. Mrs Hambicious is a little confused about

project appraisal and has asked your advice about which of the following are relevant and incremental cash flows.

a The future cost of modernising the factory.

b The £100,000 spent two months ago on a market survey investigating the demand for these plastic dolls.

c Machines to produce the dolls – cost £10m payable on delivery.

d Depreciation on the machines.

e Arcmat's other product lines are expected to be more popular due to the complementary nature of the new doll range with these existing products – the net cash flow effect is anticipated at £1m.

f Three senior managers will be drafted in from other divisions for a period of a year.

g A proportion of the US head office costs.

h The tax saving due to the plant investment being offset against taxable income.

i The £1m of additional raw material stock required at the start of production.

j The interest that will be charged on the £20m bank loan needed to initiate this project.

k The cost of the utility services installed last year.

6 In a 'make or buy' type of decision should we also consider factors not easily quantified such as security of supply, convenience and the morale of the workforce? (This question is meant to start you thinking about the issues discussed in Chapter 4. You are not expected to give a detailed answer yet.)

7 'Depreciation is a cost recognised by tax authorities so why don't you use it in project appraisal?' Help the person who asked this question.

8 A firm is considering the implementation of a new project to produce slippers. The already owned equipment to be used has sufficient spare capacity to allow this new production without affecting existing product ranges. The production manager suggests that because the equipment has been paid for it is a sunk cost and should not be included in the project appraisal calculations. Do you accept his argument?

Questions and problems

Answers to most questions can be found at www.pearsoned.co.uk/arnold.
Answers to questions marked with an asterisk are to be found only in the Lecturer's Guide.

1 The Tenby-Saundersfoot Dock company is considering the reopening of one of its mothballed loading docks. Repairs and new equipment will cost £250,000 payable immediately. To operate the new dock will require additional dockside employees costing £70,000 per year. There will also be a need for additional administrative staff and other overheads such as extra stationery, insurance and telephone costs amounting to £85,000 per year. Electricity and other energy used on the dock is anticipated to cost £40,000 per year. The London head office will allocate £50,000 of its (unchanged) costs to this project. Other docks will experience a reduction in receipts of about £20,000 per year due to some degree of cannibalisation. Annual fees expected from the new dock are £255,000 per year.

Assume

– all cash flows arise at the year ends except the initial repair and equipment costs which are incurred at the outset;
– no tax or inflation;
– no sales are made on credit.

a   Lay out the net annual cash flow calculations. Explain your reasoning.
b   Assume an infinite life for the project and a cost of capital of 17%. What is the net present value?

2 A senior management team at Railcam, a supplier to the railway industry, is trying to prepare a cash flow forecast for the years 20X2–20X4. The estimated sales are:

Year	20X1	20X2	20X3	20X4	20X5
Sales (£)	20m	22m	24m	21m	25m

These sales will be made on three months' credit and there will be no bad debts.
There are only three cost elements. First, wages amounting to £6m per year. Second, raw materials costing one-half of sales for the year. Raw material suppliers grant three months of credit. Third, direct overhead (only incurred if the project is undertaken) at £5m per year. Start date: 1.1.20X1.
Calculate the net operating cash flow for the years 20X2–20X4.

3 (*Examination level*) Pine Ltd has spent £20,000 researching the prospects for a new range of products. If it were decided that production is to go ahead an investment of £240,000 in capital equipment on 1 January 20X1 would be required.
The accounts department has produced budgeted profit and loss statements for each of the next five years for the project. At the end of the fifth year the capital equipment will be sold and production will cease.

The capital equipment is expected to be sold for scrap on 31.12.20X5 for £40,000.

	Year end 31.12.20X1	Year end 31.12.20X2	Year end 31.12.20X3	Year end 31.12.20X4	Year end 31.12.20X5
Sales	400	400	400	320	200
Materials	240	240	240	192	120
Other variable costs	40	40	40	32	20
Overheads	20	20	24	24	24
Depreciation	40	40	40	40	40
Net profit/(loss)	60	60	56	32	(4)

(All figures in £000s)

When production is started it will be necessary to raise material stock levels by £30,000 and other working capital by £20,000.

Both the additional stock and other working capital increases will be released at the end of the project.

Customers receive one year's credit from the firm.

The overhead figures in the budgeted accounts have two elements – 60% is due to a reallocation of existing overheads, 40% is directly incurred because of the take-up of the project.

For the purposes of this appraisal you may regard all receipts and payments as occurring at the year end to which they relate, unless otherwise stated. The company's cost of capital is 12%.

Assume no inflation or tax.

Required

a   Use the net present value method of project appraisal to advise the company on whether to go ahead with the proposed project.

b   Explain to a management team unfamiliar with discounted cash flow appraisal techniques the significance and value of the NPV method.

(In addition to the standard solution given at www.pearsoned.co.uk/arnold there is an Excel spreadsheet solution available at www.pearsoned.co.uk/arnold.)   **?**

4*   *(Examination level)* Mercia plc owns two acres of derelict land near to the centre of a major UK city. The firm has received an invoice for £50,000 from consultants who were given the task of analysis, investigation and design of some project proposals for using the land. The consultants outline the two best proposals to a meeting of the board of Mercia.

Proposal 1 is to spend £150,000 levelling the site and then constructing a six-level car park at an additional cost of £1,600,000. The earthmoving firm will be paid £150,000 on the start date and the construction firm will be paid £1.4m on the start date, with the balance payable 24 months later.

It is expected that the car park will be fully operational as from the completion date (365 days after the earthmovers first begin).

The annual income from ticket sales will be £600,000 to an infinite horizon. Operational costs (attendants, security, power, etc.) will be £100,000 per annum. The consultants have also apportioned £60,000 of Mercia's central overhead costs (created by the London-based head office and the executive jet) to this project.

The consultants present their analysis in terms of a commonly used measure of project viability, that of payback.

This investment idea is not original; Mercia investigated a similar project two years ago and discovered that there are some costs which have been ignored by the consultants. First, the local council will require a payment of £100,000 one year after the completion of the construction for its inspection services and a trading and environmental impact licence. Second, senior management will have to leave aside work on other projects, resulting in delays and reduced income from these projects amounting to £50,000 per year once the car park is operational. Also, the proposal is subject to depreciation of one-fiftieth (1/50) of the earthmoving and construction costs each year.

Proposal 2 is for a health club. An experienced company will, for a total cost of £9m payable at the start of the project, design and construct the buildings and supply all the equipment. It will be ready for Mercia's use one year after construction begins. Revenue from customers will be £5m per annum and operating costs will be £4m per annum.

The consultants allocate £70,000 of central general head office overhead costs for each year from the start. After two years of operating the health club Mercia will sell it for a total of £11m.

Information not considered by the consultants for Proposal 2

The £9m investment includes £5m in buildings not subject to depreciation. It also includes £4m in equipment, 10% of which has to be replaced each year. This has not been included in the operating costs.

A new executive will be needed to oversee the project from the start of the project – costing £100,000 per annum. The consultants recommend that the board of Mercia accept the second proposal and reject the first.

Assume

- If the site was sold with no further work carried out it would fetch £100,000.
- No inflation or tax.
- The cost of capital for Mercia is 10% (this is the relevant rate for this project).
- It can be assumed, for simplicity of analysis, that all cash flows occur at year ends except those occurring at the start of the project.

Required

a   Calculate the net present value of each proposal.
    State whether you would recommend Proposal 1 or 2.
b   Calculate the internal rate of return for each proposed project.

(In addition to the solution given in the Lecturer's Guide there is an Excel spreadsheet solution available at www.pearsoned.co.uk/arnold (Lecturer's Guide).)   **?**

5*   (*Examination level*) Mines International plc
    The Albanian government is auctioning the rights to mine copper in the east of the country. Mines International plc (MI) is considering the amount they would be prepared to pay as a lump sum for the five-year licence. The auction is to take place very soon and the cash will have to be paid immediately following the auction.
    In addition to the lump sum the Albanian government will expect annual payments of £500,000 to cover 'administration'. If MI wins the licence, production would not start until one year later because it will take a year to prepare the site and buy in equipment. To begin production MI would have to commission the manufacture of specialist engineering equipment costing £9.5m, half of which is payable immediately, with the remainder due in one year.
    MI has already conducted a survey of the site which showed a potential productive life of four years with its new machine. The survey costs £300,000 which is payable immediately.
    The accounts department has produced the following projected profit and loss accounts.

Projected profit and loss (£m)	Year				
	1	2	3	4	5
Sales	0	8	9	9	7
Less expenses					
Materials and consumables	0.6	0.4	0.5	0.5	0.4
Wages	0.3	0.7	0.7	0.7	0.7
Overheads	0.4	0.5	0.6	0.6	0.5
Depreciation of equipment	0	2.0	2.0	2.0	2.0
Albanian govt. payments	0.5	0.5	0.5	0.5	0.5
Survey costs written off	0.3				
Profit (loss) excluding licence fee	(2.1)	3.9	4.7	4.7	2.9

The following additional information is available:
a   Payments and receipts arise at the year ends unless otherwise stated.
b   The initial lump sum payment has been excluded from the projected accounts as this is unknown at the outset.
c   The customers of MI demand and receive a credit period of three months.
d   The suppliers of materials and consumables grant a credit period of three months.
e   The overheads contain an annual charge of £200,000 which represents an apportionment of head office costs. This is an expense which would be incurred whether or not the project proceeds. The remainder of the overheads relate directly to the project.

f   The new equipment will have a resale value at the end of the fifth year of £1.5m.

g   During the whole of year 3 a specialised item of machinery will be needed, which is currently being used by another division of MI. This division will therefore incur hire costs of £100,000 for the period the machinery is on loan.

h   The project will require additional cash reserves of £1m to be held in Albania throughout the project for operational purposes. These are recoverable at the end of the project.

i   The Albanian government will make a one-off refund of 'administration' charges one and a half months after the end of the fifth year of £200,000.

The company's cost of capital is 12%.

Ignore taxation, inflation and exchange rate movements and controls.

Required

a   Calculate the maximum amount MI should bid in the auction.

b   What would be the internal rate of return on the project if MI did not have to pay for the licence?

c   The board of directors have never been on a finance course and do not understand any of the finance jargon. However, they have asked you to persuade them that the appraisal method you have used in (a) above can be relied on. Prepare a presentation for the board of directors explaining the reasoning and justification for using your chosen project appraisal technique and your treatment of specific items in the accounts. You will need to explain concepts such as the time value of money, opportunity cost and sunk cost in plain English. **?**

6   Find the annual equivalent annuity at 13% for the following cash flow:

Point in time (yearly intervals)	0	1	2	3
Cash flow (£)	−5,000	+2,000	+2,200	+3,500

?

7* *(Examination question if combined with Question 8)* Reds plc is attempting to decide a replacement cycle for new machinery. This machinery costs £10,000 to purchase. Operating and maintenance costs for the future years are:

Point in time (yearly intervals)	0	1	2	3
Operating and maintenance costs (£)	0	12,000	13,000	14,000

The values available from the sale of the machinery on the secondhand market are:

Point in time (yearly intervals)	0	1	2	3
Secondhand value (£)	0	8,000	6,500	3,500

Assume

−   replacement by an identical machine to an infinite horizon;
−   no inflation, tax or risk;
−   the cost of capital is 11%.

Should Reds replace this new machine on a one-, two- or three-year cycle? **?**

8* The firm Reds plc in Question 7 has not yet purchased the new machinery and is considering postponing such a cash outflow for a year or two. If it were to replace the existing machine now it could be sold immediately for £4,000. If the firm persevered with the old machine for a further year then £2,000 would have to be spent immediately to recondition it. The machine could then be sold for £3,000 in 12 months' time. The third possibility is to spend £2,000 now on reconditioning, and £1,000 on maintenance in one year, and finally sell the machine for £1,500, 24 months from now. Assuming all other factors remain constant regardless of which option is chosen, which date would you recommend for the commencement of the replacement cycle?

9   Quite plc has an ageing piece of equipment which is less efficient than more modern equivalents. This equipment will continue to operate for another 15 years but operating and maintenance costs will be £3,500 per year. Alternatively, it could be sold, raising £2,000 now, and replaced with its modern equivalent which costs £7,000 but has reduced operating and maintenance costs at £3,000 per year. This machine could be sold at the end of its 15-year life for scrap for £500. The third possibility is to spend £2,500 for an immediate overhaul of the old machine which will improve its efficiency for the rest of its life, so that operating and maintenance costs become £3,200 per annum. The old machine will have a zero-scrap value in 15 years, whether or not it is overhauled. Quite plc requires a return of 9% on projects in this risk class. Select the best course of action. (Assume that cash flows arise at the year ends.)

10*   The managing director of Curt plc is irritated that the supplier for the component widgets has recently increased prices by another 10% following similar rises for each of the last five years. Based on the assumption that this pattern will continue, the cost of these widgets will be:

Points in time (yearly intervals)	1	2	3	4	5
Payments for widgets (£)	100,000	110,000	121,000	133,100	146,410

The managing director is convinced that the expertise for the manufacture of widgets exists within Curt. He therefore proposes the purchase of the necessary machine tools and other items of equipment to produce widgets in-house, at a cost of £70,000. The net cash outflows associated with this course of action are:

Points in time (yearly intervals)	0	1	2	3	4	5
Cash outflows	70,000	80,000	82,000	84,000	86,000	88,000

Note: The figures include the £70,000 for equipment and operating costs, etc.

The machinery has a life of five years and can be sold for scrap at the end of its life for £10,000. This is not included in the £88,000 for year 5. The installation of the new machine will require the attention of the technical services manager during the first year. She will have to abandon other projects as a result, causing a loss of net income of £48,000 from those projects. This cost has not been included in the above figures.

The relevant discount rate is 16%, and all cash flows occur at year ends except the initial investment.

Help Curt plc to decide whether to produce widgets for itself. What other factors might influence this decision?

11   The Borough Company is to replace its existing machinery. It has a choice between two new types of machine having different lives. The machines have the following costs:

Points in time (yearly intervals)		Machine X	Machine Y
0	Initial investment	£20,000	£25,000
1	Operating costs	£5,000	£4,000
2	Operating costs	£5,000	£4,000
3	Operating costs	£5,000	£4,000
4	Operating costs		£4,000

Machine X ceases to operate and is worth nothing after three years. Machine Y ceases to operate and is worth nothing after four years.

Each machine will be replaced at the end of its life by identical machines with identical costs. This cycle will continue indefinitely. The cost of capital is 13%.

Which machine should Borough buy?

12*   Netq plc manufactures Qtrans, for which demand fluctuates seasonally. Netq has two machines, each with a productive capacity of 1,000 Qtrans per year. For four months of the year each machine operates at full capacity. For a further four months the machines operate at three-quarters of their full capacity and for the remaining months they produce at half capacity. The operating cost of producing a Qtran is £4 and the machines are expected to be productive to an indefinite horizon. Netq is considering scrapping the old machines (for which the firm will receive nothing) and replacing them with new improved versions. These machines are also expected to last forever if properly maintained but they cost £7,000 each. Each has an annual capacity of 1,000 Qtrans. Operating costs (including maintenance) will, however, fall to £1.80 per Qtran. The appropriate cost of capital is 13%. Should Netq replace both of its machines, one of them, or neither? Assume output is the same under each option and that the new machines have the same productive capacity as the old. **?**

13 Clipper owns 100 acres of mature woodland and is trying to decide when to harvest the trees. If it harvests immediately the net cash flow, after paying the professional loggers, will be £10,000. If it waits a year the trees will grow, so that the net cash flow will be £12,000. In two years, £14,000 can be obtained. After three years have elapsed, the cash flow will be £15,500, and thereafter will increase in value by £1,000 per annum.

Calculate the best time to cut the trees given a cost of capital of 10%. **?**

14* (*Examination level*) Opti plc operates a single machine to produce its output. The senior management are trying to choose between four possibilities. First, sell the machine on the secondhand market and buy a new one at the end of one year. Second, sell in the secondhand market and replace at the end of two years. The third is to replace after three years. Finally, the machine could be scrapped at the end of its useful life after four years. These replacement cycles are expected to continue indefinitely. The management team believe that all such replacements will be for financially identical equipment, i.e. the cash inflows produced by the new and old equipment are the same. However, the costs of maintenance and operations increase with the age of the machine. These costs are shown in the table, along with the secondhand and scrap values.

Points in time (yearly intervals)	0	1	2	3	4
Initial outlay (£)	20,000				
Operating and maintenance costs (£)		6,000	8,000	10,000	12,000
Secondhand/scrap value (£)		12,000	9,000	6,000	2,000

Assume

–   The cost of capital is 10%.
–   No inflation.
–   No technological advances.
–   No tax.
–   All cash flows occur on anniversary dates.

Required

Choose the length of the replacement cycle which minimises the present values of the costs of an infinite number of cycles. **?**

15 (*Examination level*) Hazel plc produces one of the components used in the manufacture of car bumpers. The production manager is keen on obtaining modern equipment and he has come to you, the finance director, with details concerning two alternative machines, A and B.

The cash flows and other assumptions are as follows.

Points in time (yearly intervals)	0	£000s 1	£000s 2	£000s 3
Machine A	−200	+220	+242	0
Machine B	−240	+220	+242	+266

Machine A would have to be replaced by an identical machine on a two-year cycle. Machine B would be replaced by an identical machine every three years.

It is considered reasonable to assume that the cash flows for the future replacements of A and B are the same as in the above table.

The opportunity cost of capital for Hazel is 15%.

Ignore taxation.

The acceptance of either project would leave the company's risk unchanged.

The cash flows occur on anniversary dates.

Required

a   Calculate the net present value of Machine A for its two-year life.
b   Calculate the net present value of Machine B for its three-year life.
c   Calculate the annual equivalent annuities for Machines A and B and recommend which machine should be selected.
d   You are aware that the production manager gets very enthusiastic about new machinery and this may cloud his judgement. You suggest the third possibility, which is to continue production with Machine C which was purchased five years ago for £400,000. This is expected to produce +£160,000 per year. It has a scrap value now of £87,000 and is expected to last another five years. At the end of its useful life it will have a scrap value of £20,000. Should C be kept for another five years?
e   The production manager asks why you are discounting the cash flows. Briefly explain the time value of money and its components.   **?**

Assignments

1   Try to obtain budgeted profit and loss accounts for a proposed project and by combining these with other data produce cash flow estimates for the project. Calculate the NPV and contrast your conclusions on the viability of the project with that suggested by the profit and loss projections.

2   Examine some items of machinery (e.g. shopfloor machine tools, vehicles, computers). Consider whether to replace these items with the modern equivalent, taking into account increased maintenance costs, loss or gain of customer sales, secondhand values, higher productivity, etc.

3   Apply the technique of annual equivalent annuities to an asset which is replaced on a regular cycle. Consider alternative cycle lengths.

The decision-making process for investment appraisal

LEARNING OUTCOMES

The main outcome expected from this chapter is that the reader is aware of both traditional and discounted cash flow investment appraisal techniques and the extent of their use. The reader should also be aware that these techniques are a small part of the overall capital-allocation planning process. The student is expected to gain knowledge of:

■ the empirical evidence on techniques used;

■ the calculation of payback, discounted payback and accounting rate of return (ARR);

■ the drawbacks and attractions of payback and ARR;

■ the balance to be struck between mathematical precision and imprecise reality;

■ the capital-allocation planning process.

Introduction

An organisation may be viewed as a collection of projects, some old, some new; many being major 'strategic' projects and others minor operating-unit-level schemes. It is in the nature of business for change to occur, and, through change, old activities, profit centres and methods die, to be replaced by the new. Without a continuous process of regeneration firms will cease to progress and be unable to compete in a dynamic environment. It is vital that the processes and systems that lead to the development of new production methods, new markets and products, and so on are efficient. That is, both the project appraisal techniques and the entire process of proposal creation and selection lead to the achievement of the objective of the organisation. Poor appraisal technique, set within the framework of an investment process that does not ask the right questions and which provides erroneous conclusions, will destroy the wealth of shareholders.

The payback and accounting rate of return (ARR) methods of evaluating capital investment proposals have historically been, and continue to be, very popular approaches. This is despite the best efforts of many writers to denigrate them. It is important to understand the disadvantages of these methods, but it is also useful to be aware of why practical business people still see a great deal of merit in observing the outcome of these calculations.

The employment of project appraisal techniques is merely one of the stages in the process of the allocation of resources within a firm. The appraisal stage can be reached only after ideas for the use of capital resources have been generated and those ideas have been filtered through a consideration of the strategic, budgetary and business resource capabilities of the firm. Following the appraisal stage are the approval, implementation and post-completion auditing stages.

Any capital allocation system has to be viewed in the light of the complexity of organisational life. This aspect has been ignored in Chapters 2 and 3, where mechanical analysis is applied. The balance is corrected in this chapter. Investment, as in the case of the oil business (*see* **Exhibit 4.1**), needs to be thoroughly evaluated. This chapter considers the process of project development, appraisal and post-investment monitoring.

Exhibit 4.1

Oil companies prepare to ramp up investment again

Energy groups are ready to revive spending following a partial crude price recovery

Crude oil glut frustrates Opec's price control moves

By: *Andrew Ward* in London and *Ed Crooks* in New York

Oil companies are preparing to ramp up spending this year as the recovery in crude prices gives them confidence to revive some of the projects postponed during the investment freeze of the past two years.

Brent crude has been trading at about $55 per barrel — double the 12-year low hit in early 2016 — after producer nations both inside and outside Opec, the oil producers' cartel, agreed last December to their first output cut for more than a decade.

This, coupled with deep cost cuts made by oil companies since prices crashed from more than $100 per barrel in 2014, has improved cash flow generation across the industry and made the economics of many prospective developments look more attractive.

"The industry has moved out of survival mode, through a phase of adaptation to lower prices and now it is beginning to think about renewed growth," says Malcolm Dickson, analyst at Wood Mackenzie, the energy consultancy.

Global capital spending by leading exploration and production companies will total $450bn in 2017, up 3 per cent compared to 2016 and ending two years of steep declines, according to Wood Mac forecasts published on Wednesday. Meanwhile, the number of final investment decisions by these 60 E&P companies — which range from large multinationals and independents to national oil groups — on new upstream projects will double to more than 20 in 2017, from nine last year.

Others have made similar projections. A survey of more than 100 E&P companies by Barclays analysts has predicted that their capital spending will rise by an average of 7 per cent this year. Rystad Energy, another energy research group, estimated that new offshore production capacity amounting to 15bn barrels of oil equivalent would be sanctioned in 2017, compared with 6bn last year.

"Companies can finally see a floor beneath oil prices and their [project] break-even points are coming down towards the same level," says Iain Reid, analyst at Macquarie.

Evidence on the employment of appraisal techniques

A number of surveys enquiring into the appraisal methods used in practice have been conducted. The results from surveys conducted in the UK by Pike (1996), by the author jointly with Panos Hatzopoulos (2000) and by Alkaraan and Northcott (2006) are displayed in **Exhibit 4.2**. These indicate that payback remains in wide use but with the increasing application of discounted cash

| Exhibit 4.2 | Appraisal techniques used |

	Proportion of companies using technique								
	Pike surveys[a]				Arnold and Hatzopoulos survey[b]				Alkaraan & Northcott[c]
	1975	1980	1986	1992	1997				2002
	%	%	%	%	Small %	Medium %	Large %	Total %	Large%
Payback	73	81	92	94	71	75	66	70	96
Accounting rate of return	51	49	56	50	62	50	55	56	60
Internal rate of return	44	57	75	81	76	83	84	81	89
Net present value	32	39	68	74	62	79	97	80	99

Capital budget (per year) for companies in Arnold and Hatzopoulos study approx. Small: £1–50m. Medium: £51–100m. Large: £100m+.

Notes
(a) Pike's studies focus on 100 large UK firms.
(b) In the Arnold and Hatzopoulos study (2000), 300 finance directors of UK companies taken from The Times 1000 (London: Times Books), ranked according to capital employed (excluding investment trusts), were asked dozens of questions about project appraisal techniques, sources of finance and performance measurement. The first 100 (Large size) of the sample are the top 100; another 100 are in the rankings at 250–400 (Medium size); the final 100 are ranked 820–1,000 (Small size). The capital employed ranges between £1.3bn and £24bn for the large firms, £207m and £400m for the medium-sized firms, and £40m and £60m for the small companies. Ninety-six usable replies were received: 38 large, 24 medium and 34 small.
(c) Alkaraan and Northcott focus on UK manufacturing companies each with at least a turnover of £100m, 1,000 employees and assets of £50m. 83 companies returned questionnaires.

Sources: Pike (1988 and 1996), Arnold and Hatzopoulos (2000) and Alkaraan and Northcott (2006)

flow techniques. Internal rate of return is popular, but net present value is the preferred method in large companies. Accounting rate of return is still used in over 50% of large firms in the UK. One observation that is emphasised in many studies is the tendency for decision makers to use several methods, with methods regarded as being complementary rather than competitors. International studies such as Hall and Millward (2010) in South Africa; Shinoda (2010) in Japan; Kester and Robbins (2011) in Ireland; Singh et al. (2012) in India and Daunfeldt and Hartwig (2014) in Sweden provide similar evidence of widespread but not total use of NPV and IRR along with the increasing use of real options (see Chapter 6)

There is an indication in the literature that while some methods have superior theoretical justification, other, simpler methods are used for purposes such as communicating project viability and gaining commitment throughout an organisation. It is also suggested that those who sponsor and advance projects within organisations like to have the option of presenting their case in an alternative form which shows the proposal in the best light.

Another clear observation from the literature is large firms use sophisticated formal procedures more than small- or medium-sized firms.

Payback

The payback period for a capital investment is the length of time before the cumulative stream of forecasted cash flows equals the initial investment. The decision rule is that if a project's payback period is less than or equal to a predetermined threshold figure it is acceptable.

Consider the case of Tradfirm's three mutually exclusive proposed investments (*see* **Exhibit 4.3**).

Exhibit 4.3	Tradfirm						
	Cash flows (£m)						
Points in time (yearly intervals)	**0**	**1**	**2**	**3**	**4**	**5**	**6**
Project A	−10	6	2	1	1	2	2
Project B	−10	1	1	2	6	2	2
Project C	−10	3	2	2	2	15	10

Note: Production ceases after six years, and all cash flows occur on anniversary dates.

There is a boardroom battle in Tradfirm, with some members preferring the payback rule with four years as the decision benchmark. For both A and B, the £10m initial outflow is recouped after four years. In the case of C, it takes five years. Thus, payback for the three projects is as follows:

Project A: 4 years
Project B: 4 years
Project C: 5 years

If the payback rule is rigidly applied, the board will reject the third project, and they still have to decide whether to accept A or B.

Other members understand and prefer the NPV rule and are thus able to offer a clear decision (see **Exhibit 4.4**).

As Exhibit 4.4 shows, Project A has a positive NPV and is therefore shareholder wealth enhancing. Project B has a negative NPV; the firm would be better served by investing the £10m in the alternative that offers a 10% return. Project C has the largest positive NPV and is therefore the one that creates most shareholder wealth.

Exhibit 4.4	Tradfirm: net present values (£M)

$$\text{Project A} \quad -10 + \frac{6}{1.1} + \frac{2}{(1.1)^2} + \frac{1}{(1.1)^3} + \frac{1}{(1.1)^4} + \frac{2}{(1.1)^5} + \frac{2}{(1.1)^6} = £0.913m$$

$$\text{Project B} \quad -10 + \frac{1}{1.1} + \frac{1}{(1.1)^2} + \frac{2}{(1.1)^3} + \frac{6}{(1.1)^4} + \frac{2}{(1.1)^5} + \frac{2}{(1.1)^6} = -£0.293m$$

$$\text{Project C} \quad -10 + \frac{3}{1.1} + \frac{2}{(1.1)^2} + \frac{2}{(1.1)^3} + \frac{6}{(1.1)^4} + \frac{15}{(1.1)^5} + \frac{10}{(1.1)^6} = £12.208m$$

Note: The discount rate is 10%.

Drawbacks of payback

The first drawback of payback is that it makes no allowance for the time value of money. It ignores the need to discount future cash flows to present values before comparing them with the initial investment. The second drawback is that receipts beyond the payback period are ignored. This problem is particularly obvious in the case of Project C. A third disadvantage is the arbitrary selection of the cut-off point. There is no theoretical basis for setting the appropriate time period and so guesswork, whim and manipulation take over.

Discounted payback

With discounted payback, the future cash flows are discounted prior to calculating the payback period. This is an improvement on the simple payback method in that it takes into account the time value of money. In **Exhibit 4.5** the *discounted* cash inflows are added together to calculate payback. In the case of Project B, the discounted cash inflows never reach the level of the cash outflow.

This modification tackles the first drawback of the simple payback method but it is still necessary to make an arbitrary decision about the cut-off date and it ignores cash flows beyond that date.

Exhibit 4.5	Discounted payback: Tradfirm plc (£m)

Points in time (yearly intervals)	0	1	2	3	4	5	6	Discounted payback
Project A								
Undiscounted cash flow	−10	6	2	1	1	2	2	
Discounted cash flow	−10	5.45	1.65	0.75	0.68	1.24	1.13	Year 6
Project B								
Undiscounted cash flow	−10	1	1	2	6	2	2	Outflow −10m
Discounted cash flow	−10	0.909	0.826	1.5	4.1	1.24	1.13	Inflow +£9.7m
Project C								
Undiscounted cash flow	−10	3	2	2	2	15	10	
Discounted cash flow	−10	2.73	1.65	1.5	1.37	9.3	5.64	Year 5

Note: The discount rate is 10%.

Reasons for the continuing popularity of payback

Payback remains a widely used project appraisal method despite its drawbacks. This requires some explanation. The first fact to note is that payback is rarely used as the primary investment technique, but rather as a secondary method which supplements the more sophisticated methods. Although it appears irrational to employ payback when the issue is examined in isolation, we may begin to see the logic behind its use if we take into account the organisational context and the complementary nature of alternative techniques. For example, payback may be used at an early stage to filter out projects which have clearly unacceptable risk and return characteristics. Identifying those projects at a preliminary stage avoids the need for more detailed evaluation through a discounted cash flow method, thus increasing the efficiency of the appraisal process. This early sifting has to be carefully implemented so as to avoid premature rejection.

Payback also has one extraordinarily endearing quality to busy managers and hard-pressed students alike – it is simple and easy to use. Executives admit that the payback rule, used indiscriminately, does not always give the best decision, but it is the simplest way to communicate an idea of project profitability. NPV is difficult to understand and so it is useful to have an alternative measure which all managers can follow. In the workplace, a project's success often relies on the gaining of widespread employee commitment. Discussion, negotiation and communication of ideas often need to be carried out in a simple form so that non-quantitative managers can make their contribution and, eventually, their commitment. Communication in terms of the sophisticated models may lead to alienation and exclusion and, ultimately, project failure.

Another argument advanced by practitioners is that projects which return their outlay quickly reduce the exposure of the firm to risk. In the world beyond the simplifications needed in academic exercises, as described in Chapters 2 and 3, there is a great deal of uncertainty about future cash flows. Managers often distrust forecasts for more distant years. Payback has an implicit assumption that the risk of cash flows is directly related to the time distance from project implementation date. By focusing on near-term returns this approach uses the data in which management has greatest faith. Take the case of the web-based music download industry. Here, competitive forces and technology are changing so rapidly that it is difficult to forecast for eight months ahead, let alone for eight years. Thus, managers may choose to ignore cash flow projections beyond a certain number of years. They accept only those projects immune to the risk of total market collapse a few years down the line or the risk of company failure due to an inability to meet debts as they become due. Those who advocate NPV counter this approach by saying that risk is accounted for in a better way in the NPV model than is done by simply excluding data – it certainly does not completely ignore cash flows beyond the payback period. Risk analysis applied to NPV is examined in Chapter 6.

There is some evidence that payback is more popular in companies which measure and reward executive performance through accounting profit numbers (payback tends to be high when near-term cash flows/profits are high).

A further advantage of payback, as perceived by many managers, is its use in situations of capital shortage. If funds are limited, there is an advantage in receiving a return on projects earlier rather than later, as this permits investment in other profitable opportunities. Theoretically this factor can be allowed for in a more satisfactory way with the NPV method; capital rationing is discussed in Chapter 5.

This section is not meant to promote the use of payback. It remains a theoretically inferior method to the discounted cash flow approaches. Payback has a number of valuable attributes, but the primary method of project appraisal in most organisations should take into account all of the relevant cash flows and then discount them.

Accounting rate of return

The accounting rate of return (ARR) method may be known to readers by other names such as the return on capital employed (ROCE) or return on investment (ROI). The ARR is a ratio of the accounting profit to the investment in the project, expressed as a percentage.

The *decision rule* is that if the ARR is greater than, or equal to, a hurdle rate then accept the project.

This ratio can be calculated in a number of ways but the most popular approach is to take profit after the deduction of depreciation. The investment figure is calculated as the initial investment plus any required increases in working capital. Three alternative versions of ARR are calculated for Timewarp plc which give markedly different results (*see* Worked example 4.1). Note: these are just three of all the possible ways of calculating ARR – there are many more.

Worked example 4.1	Timewarp plc

Timewarp is to invest £30,000 in machinery for a project which has a life of three years. The machinery will have a zero-scrap value and will be depreciated on a straight-line basis.

Accounting rate of return, version 1 (annual basis)

$$ARR = \frac{\text{Profit for the year}}{\text{Asset book value at start of year}} \times 100$$

Time (year)	1	2	3
	£	£	£
Profit before depreciation	15,000	15,000	15,000
Less depreciation	10,000	10,000	10,000
Profit after depreciation	5,000	5,000	5,000
Value of asset (book value)			
Start of year	30,000	20,000	10,000
End of year	20,000	10,000	0
Accounting rate of return	$\frac{5,000}{30,000} = 16.67\%$	$\frac{5,000}{20,000} = 25\%$	$\frac{5,000}{10,000} = 50\%$

On average the ARR is: $1/3 \times (16.67 + 25 + 50)\% = 30.55\%$.
Note the illusion of an annual rise in profitability despite profits remaining constant year on year.

Accounting rate of return, version 2 (total investment basis)

$$ARR = \frac{\text{Average annual profit}}{\text{Initial capital invested}} \times 100$$

$$ARR = \frac{(5,000 + 5,000 + 5,000)/3}{30,000} \times 100 = 16.67\%$$

Accounting rate of return, version 3 (average investment basis)

$$ARR = \frac{\text{Average annual profit}}{\text{Average capital invested}} \times 100$$

$$\text{Average capital invested: } \frac{30,000}{2} = 15,000$$

(At time 0 the machinery has a value of £30,000. Three years later it has a value of zero. If we assume constant devaluation then the average value of the machinery is £15,000.)

$$ARR = \frac{(5,000 + 5,000 + 5,000)/3}{15,000} \times 100 = 33.33\%$$

If we now make the example slightly more sophisticated by assuming that the machinery has a scrap value of £8,000 at the end of year 3, then the average capital invested figure becomes:

0.5 (initial outlay + scrap value)
0.5 (30,000 + 8,000) = 19,000

▶

Worked example 4.1 (continued)

The profit figures also change.

	Year 1 £	Year 2 £	Year 3 £
Profit before depreciation	15,000	15,000	15,000
Depreciation	7,333	7,333	7,333
Profit after depreciation	7,667	7,667	7,667

The ARR (version 3) is: $\dfrac{7,667}{19,000} \times 100 = 40.35\%$

Drawbacks of accounting rate of return

The number of alternative ARR calculations can be continued beyond the three possibilities described in Worked example 4.1. Each alternative would be a legitimate variant and would find favour with some managers and accountants. The almost wide-open field for selecting profit and asset definitions is a major weakness of ARR. This flexibility may tempt decision makers to abuse the technique to suit their purposes. Secondly, as explained in Chapter 3, the inflow and outflow of cash should be the focus of investment analysis appraisals. Profit figures are very poor substitutes for cash flow. The most important criticism of accounting rate of return is that it fails to take account of the time value of money. There is no allowance for the fact that cash received in year 1 is more valuable than an identical sum received in year 3. Also, there is a high degree of arbitrariness in defining the cut-off or hurdle rate. There is no reason for selecting 10, 15 or 20% as an acceptable ARR. This arbitrariness contrasts with NPV, which has a sound theoretical base to its decision rule: accept if the project's cash flows deliver more than the finance provider's opportunity cost of capital.

Accounting rate of return can lead to some perverse decisions. For example, suppose that Timewarp uses the second version, the total investment ARR, with a hurdle rate of 15%, and the appraisal teams discover that the machinery will in fact generate an additional profit of £1,000 in a fourth year. Common sense suggests that if all other factors remain constant this new situation is better than the old one, and yet the ARR declines to below the threshold level (15%) because the profits are averaged over four years rather than three and the project is therefore rejected.

The original situation is:

$$\text{ARR} = \frac{(5,000 + 5,000 + 5,000)/3}{30,000} = 16.67\%. \text{ Accepted}$$

The new situation is:

$$\text{ARR} = \frac{(5,000 + 5,000 + 5,000 + 1,000)/4}{30,000} = 13.33\%. \text{ Rejected}$$

An alternative way of viewing this problem is to think of two projects that are identical except that one offers the additional £1,000. If only one project can be accepted, which will the managers go for? If they are motivated by ARR (e.g. by bonuses related to ARR achieved) they may be inclined to accept the project that offers the higher ARR even if this means sacrificing £1,000 of shareholders' money.

Reasons for the continued use of accounting rate of returns

Exhibit 4.2 showed that over one-half of large firms calculate ARR when appraising projects and so the conclusion must be that, in the practical world of business, some merit is seen in this technique. One possible explanation is that managers are familiar with this ancient and extensively used profitability measure. The financial press regularly reports accounting rates of return. Divisional performance is often judged on a profit-to-assets-employed ratio. Indeed, the entire firm is often analysed and management evaluated on this ratio. Because performance is measured in this way, managers have a natural bias towards using it in appraising future projects. Conflicting signals are sometimes sent to managers controlling a division. They are expected to use a discounted cash flow approach for investment decisions, but find that their performance is being monitored on a profit-to-investment ratio basis. This dichotomy may produce a resistance to proposed projects which produce low returns in the early years and thus report a low ARR to head office. This may result in excellent long-term opportunities being missed. (Some additional reasons for the continued use of ARR and payback are given in the Arnold and Hatzopoulos (2000) paper.)

Exhibit 4.6 illustrates what can happen if too much emphasis is placed on accounting numbers.

Exhibit 4.6

More EU Lunacy?

By John Plender

Mrs Loyola de Palacio, the European Union's transport commissioner, complains bitterly that the International Accounting Standards Board and the European Financial Reporting Advisory Group pose a threat to the development of Europe's infrastructure. They are, she believes, too academic in dealing with the time gap between the vast negative cash flow incurred during construction and the subsequent revenue build-up.

The fear is that enormous accounting losses will have to be recognised in the early years of projects, while in the later years 'exaggerated' profits will appear.

The laughable assumption underlying this latest attempt by the European Commission to subvert standard setting in accountancy is that entrepreneurs and financial institutions are incapable of doing **net present value** calculations. So, to recognise what she calls the reality of 'the construction sector' Mrs de Palacio wants the accountants to distort economic reality and cook the books.

 Financial Times, 8 November 2004, p. 22.
All Rights Reserved.

Internal rate of return: reasons for continued popularity

Exhibit 4.2 showed that firms use IRR as much as the theoretically superior NPV which, given the problems associated with IRR described in Chapter 2, may seem strange. It is all the more perplexing as IRR is often more difficult to calculate manually than NPV (although, with modern computer programs, the computational difficulties disappear). Some possible explanations follow.

- *Psychological* Managers are familiar with expressing financial data in the form of a percentage. It is intuitively easier to grasp what is meant by an IRR of 15% than, say, an NPV of £2,000.

- *IRR can be calculated without knowledge of the required rate of return* Making a decision using the IRR involves two separate stages. Stage 1 involves gathering data and then computing the IRR. Stage 2 requires comparing this with the cut-off rate. By contrast, it is not possible to calculate NPV without knowing the required rate of return. The proposal has to be analysed in one stage only. In a large company it is possible for senior managers to request that profit centres and divisions appraise projects on the basis of their IRRs, while refusing to communicate in advance the rate of return required. This has at least two potential advantages. First, the required rate may change over time and it becomes a simple matter of changing the cut-off comparison rate at head office once the IRR computations are received from lower down the organisation. With NPV, each project's cash flows would need to be calculated again at the new discount rate. Secondly, managers are only human and there is a tendency to bias information passed upwards to achieve their personal goals. For instance, it has been known for ambitious managers to be excessively optimistic concerning the prospects for projects that would lead to an expansion of their domain. If they are provided with a cut-off rate prior to evaluating projects you can be sure that all projects they sponsor will have cash flows 'forecasted' to produce a return greater than the target. If the head office team chooses not to communicate a cut-off rate, this leaves it free to adjust the required return to allow for factors such as over-optimism. It may also adjust the minimum rate of return for perceived risk associated with projects or divisions.

● **Ranking** Some managers are not familiar with the drawbacks of IRR and believe that ranking projects to select between them is most accurately and most easily carried out using the percentage-based IRR method. This was, in Chapter 2, shown not to be the case.

The managerial 'art' of investment appraisal

This book places strong emphasis on the formal methods of project appraisal, so a word of warning is necessary at this point. Mathematical technique is merely one element needed for successful project appraisal. The quantitative analysis is only the starting point for decision making. In most real-world situations, there are many qualitative factors which need to be taken into account. The techniques described in Chapters 2 and 3 cannot be used in a mechanical fashion. Management is largely an art form with a few useful quantitative techniques to improve the quality of the art. For instance, in generating and evaluating major investments the firm has to take into account:

● **Strategy** The relationship between the proposed project and the strategic direction of the firm is very important. A business-unit investment isolated from the main thrust of the firm may be a distraction in terms of managerial attention and financial resources. A project that looks good at divisional level may not be appropriate when examined from the whole-firm perspective. It may even be contradictory to the firm's goals. For example, luxury goods companies are sometimes enticed to produce lower-priced items for the mass market or to stretch the brand into unrelated areas. The project, when judged on its own, appears to have a very high NPV. But there is the danger of losing the premium brand (expensive and exclusive) strategic position in the existing product ranges by association with something that does not quite fit the image the firm has nurtured.

● **Social context** The effect on individuals is a crucial consideration. Projects require people to implement them. Their enthusiasm and commitment will be of central importance. Neglecting this factor may lead to resentment and even sabotage. Discussion and consensus on major project proposals may matter more than selecting the mathematically correct option. In many cases, quantitative techniques are avoided because they are precise. It is safer to sponsor a project in a non-quantified or judgemental way at an early stage in its development. If, as a result of discussion with colleagues and superiors, the idea becomes more generally accepted and it fits into the pervading view on the firm's policy and strategy, the figures are presented in a report. Note here the order of actions. First, general acceptance. Second, quantification. A proposal is usually discussed at progressively higher levels of management before it is 'firmed up' into a project report. One reason for this is that continuing commitment and support from many people will be needed if the project is to succeed. In order to engender support and to improve the final report it is necessary to start the process in a rather vague way, making room for modifications in the light of suggestions. Some of these suggestions will be motivated by shareholder wealth considerations, others will be motivated by goals closer to the hearts of key individuals. Allowing adaptability in project development also means that if circumstances change, say, in the competitive environment, the final formal appraisal takes account of this. The sponsor or promoter of a capital investment has to be aware of, and to adjust for, social sub-systems within the organisation (see Ekanem (2005) for eight case studies showing the importance of social context).

● **Expense** Sophisticated project evaluation can cost a considerable amount of money. The financial experts' input is costly enough, but the firm also has to consider the time and trouble managers throughout the organisation might have to devote to provide good-quality data and make their contribution to the debate. In a firm of limited resources it may be more efficient to search for projects at an informal or judgement level, thus generating a multitude of alternative avenues for growth, rather than to analyse a few in greater quantitative depth.

- *Stifling the entrepreneurial spirit* Excessive emphasis on formal evaluatory systems may be demotivating to individuals who thrive on free thinking, fast decision making and action. The relative weights given to formal approaches and entrepreneurialism will depend on the context, such as the pace of change in the marketplace. A leading businessman describes the problems arising from overemphasis on accounting [or should that be finance?] numbers – *see* **Exhibit 4.7**.

Exhibit 4.7

Entrepreneur Fires Broad Attack

By Peter Marsh

British manufacturers have failed to invest enough in marketing and given too much management control to accountants, according to Edward Atkin, one of the country's most successful engineering entrepreneurs of the past decade.

Until recently Mr Atkin was the managing director and majority owner of Avent, one of the world's biggest makers of babies' bottles.

He sold Avent to a venture capital company for £300m, of which £225m (minus advisers' fees) came to Mr Atkin and his family. The entrepreneur is now weighing up several ideas about ways in which to invest some of the cash in innovative businesses.

In a speech to the Institution of Electrical Engineers Mr Atkin will say that most successful manufacturers require a stable investment climate and an interest in making world beating products.

These factors are more likely to be in place if the businesses are owned privately, and also have people with an interest in engineering at the helm, rather than accountants.

'As soon as financial criteria become the main method used for evaluating investment opportunities, the company is almost certainly doomed,' Mr Atkin will say.

'It is impossible to forecast variables like volumes, competitive pricing, raw material costs, interest rates or currencies three or five years out,' Mr Atkin will say. 'What is very easy, however, is to appreciate that speeding up a process, reducing waste, eliminating direct labour and improving tolerances and reliability will enhance both the products and their manufacturer, as well as the experience of the end-user. These benefits will be long-term and valid, irrespective of the output, exchange rate, raw material costs and all the other variables.'

Successful manufacturers such as US semiconductor maker Intel, and BMW and Toyota, two of the world's biggest car producers, have made as a centre of their businesses 'an unbroken trend of consistent [product] development, decade after decade.'

This is a culture, Mr Atkin will say, that makes it relatively easy to build up strong teams of engineering and marketing experts within the company that will stay for long periods. It also makes it easier to establish long-term brand loyalty.

FT   *Financial Times,* 17 January 2006, p. 5.
All Rights Reserved.

- *Intangible benefits* Frequently, many of the most important benefits that flow from an investment are difficult to measure in money terms. Improving customer satisfaction through better service, quality or image may lead to enhanced revenues, but it is often difficult to state precisely the quantity of the increased revenue flow. For example, new technology often provides a number of intangible benefits, such as reduced time needed to switch machine tools to the production of other products, thereby reducing risk in fluctuating markets, or a quicker response to customer choice. These non-quantifiable benefits can amount to a higher value than the more obvious tangible benefits (see Alkaraan and Northcott (2006) for a survey of just how important these factors are for UK firms). An example of how intangible benefits could be allowed for in project appraisal is shown through the example of Crowther Precision plc. *See* Worked example 4.2.

Worked example 4.2	Crowther Precision plc

Crowther Precision plc produces metal parts for the car industry, with machinery that is now more than 20 years old. With appropriate maintenance, these machines could continue producing indefinitely. However, developments in the machine tool industry have led to the creation of computer-controlled multi-use machines. Crowther is considering the purchase of the Z200 which would provide both quantifiable and non-quantifiable benefits over the old machine. The Z200 costs £1.2m but would be expected to last indefinitely if maintenance expenditure were increased by £20,000 every year forever.

The quantifiable benefits are:

(a) reduced raw material requirements, due to lower wastage, amounting to £35,000 in each future year;
(b) labour cost savings of £80,000 in each future year.

These quantifiable benefits are analysed using the NPV method (*see* **Exhibit 4.8**).

Exhibit 4.8	Incremental net present value analysis of Z200

		Present value £
Purchase of machine		−1,200,000
Present value of raw material saving	$\dfrac{35,000}{0.1}$	+350,000
Present value of labour saving	$\dfrac{80,000}{0.1}$	+800,000
Less present value of increased maintenance costs	$\dfrac{20,000}{0.1}$	−200,000
Net present value		−250,000

Note: Assume discount rate of 10%, all cash flows arise at the year ends, zero scrap value of old machine.

Examining the quantifiable elements in isolation will lead to a rejection of the project to buy the Z200. However, the non-quantifiable benefits are:

● reduced time required to switch the machine from producing one version of the car component to one of the other three versions Crowther presently produces;
● the ability to switch the machine over to completely new products in response to changed industry demands, or to take up, as yet unseen, market opportunities in the future;
● improved quality of output leading to greater customer satisfaction.

It is true that the discounted cash flow analysis has failed to take into account all the relevant factors, but this should not lead to its complete rejection. In cases where non-quantifiable elements are present, the problem needs to be separated into two stages.

1 Analyse those elements that are quantifiable using NPV.
2 If the NPV from Stage 1 is negative, then managerial judgement will be needed to subjectively assess the non-quantifiable benefits. If these are judged to be greater than the 'loss' signalled in Stage 1 then the project is viable. For Crowther, if the management team consider that the intangible benefits are worth more than £250,000 they should proceed with the purchase of the Z200.

This line of thought is continued in Chapter 6 (pp. 201–12), where operational and strategic decisions with options (real options) are considered. As the article in **Exhibit 4.9** shows, the decision to commit to an investment means the loss of options. Although this is an article from 1999, the basic arguments are more relevant than ever, especially as product cycles are shorter and market changes more rapid.

Exhibit 4.9

Tyranny of time

By their very nature capital investment decisions threaten to place a straitjacket on companies. There is no easy way out.

By Peter Martin

When you make a capital investment decision, you freeze time. In fast-moving industries, this may be the most important aspect of the decision – more important than its actual content. But it is rarely assessed in this light.

There is any amount of theory about how to take capital investment decisions.

All such approaches assume that there are financial and easily quantifiable costs of taking the decision; and less measurable benefits to set against it. The techniques all revolve around ways of making imponderable future benefits more tangible. There is a reason for this: managers usually want to take investment decisions while their superiors usually do not. So, the techniques are ever more elaborate ways of capturing the discounted value of blue sky.

But there are also intangible costs of taking the decision, and they are not given the attention they deserve. The cost of freezing time is one of the most important.

Here is how it works. When you make a big capital investment decision, it will usually take between 18 months and five years to bring the plant fully into operation. The cost of tying up capital for that time is reflected in the investment appraisal. But the broader implications of tying up the company are not.

When you have committed yourself to a big new plant, you have not just signed a cheque for the money. You have also sold your soul to this technology, on this scale, in this site. That is what freezing time means. Until the plant is complete, and it is clear whether it works and whether there is a market for its products, time stands still. For you, but not for your rivals.

They are free to react, to adjust technology, to play around with the pricing and volume. You are not. Unless you have built an implausibly flexible new plant, you are on a convergence course with a straitjacket.

Once your new plant is up and running, you can start to adjust the pattern of its output, and strive to reduce its costs. But until then, your options are more limited: press on, or give up.

The semiconductor industry illustrates this dilemma in a big way. In the mid-1990s, the UK looked like a good home for a bunch of new chip plants. Siemens, LG Group and Hyundai all targeted the British regions for big state-of-the-art factories. One of them – Siemens' factory on Tyneside – opened and promptly shut down again. The other two have never made it into production, and look more questionable by the moment: the Asian crisis undermined their parents and their markets simultaneously.

The decisions all three companies had to make were unenviable, because they were all or nothing. Technology had moved on while the plants were being prepared. Once the Siemens plant came into production, it was clear that it was the wrong plant, making the wrong sort of chip, in the wrong place.

So, the company shut it down, at vast cost – only to invest another huge sum in a different plant to make different chips in France. For LG and Hyundai, the moment of decision comes even before they have had the satisfaction of seeing their plants up and running.

The problem is not so much the risk that a plant's technology may prove inappropriate, or that its markets may not meet expectations: these are the normal risks of doing business in a capital-intensive industry. It is more that the process of building the factory shuts out other alternatives, freezing the company's options and its internal clock.

What can companies do to avoid this risk? First, look for investment decisions that can be made piece by piece, and implemented quickly, minimising the freezing effect. Engineers usually hate this approach, because it means they are never designing plants at the forefront of the technology, or at maximum efficient scale. That's tough.

Second, once an investment has been approved, managers must resist the temptation to make the decision sacrosanct. It needs revisiting, in the light of changing technology and markets, just as much as plants that are already operating. This is a difficult

▶

Exhibit 4.9 *(continued)*

balance to strike, because every big investment decision usually had to be made in the teeth of the opposition of a faction that wanted something bigger, smaller, older, newer, or somewhere else. This group of dissidents will never be happy with the decision, and they may even be right.

Third, keep a close eye on the relationship between the product cycle time in your industry and the time it takes to get a new plant commissioned.

If the former is shrinking while the latter is lengthening – a common feature of any high-technology industry that has to cater to retail consumers – there will come a point at which the price of freezing time will outstrip the benefits of new plant.

If you cannot keep going by patching the old factory, it is time to think of some revolutionary new process that will replace one big capital investment decision with a lot of small ones. Or give up.

The investment process

There is a great deal more to a successful investment programme than simply project appraisal. As **Exhibit 4.10** demonstrates, project appraisal is one of a number of stages in the investment process. The emphasis in the academic world on ever more sophistication in appraisal could be seriously misplaced. Attention paid to the evolution of investment ideas, their development and sifting may produce more practical returns. Marrying the evaluation of projects once screened with strategic, resource and human considerations may lead to avoidance of damaging decisions. Following through the implementation with a review of what went right, what went wrong, and why, may enable better decision making in the future.

Investment by a firm is a process often involving large numbers of individuals up and down an organisational hierarchy. It is a complex and infinitely adaptable process which is likely to differ from one organisation to another. However, we can identify some common threads.

Generation of ideas

A firm is more likely to founder because of a shortage of good investment ideas than because of poor methods of appraisal. A good investment planning process requires a continuous flow of ideas to regenerate the organisation through the exploitation of new opportunities. Thought needs to be given to mechanisms for idea generation and communication through the firm. Indeed, one of the central tasks of senior management is to nurture a culture of search for and sponsorship of ideas. In the absence of a well-functioning system, the danger remains that investment proposals only arise in a reactive manner. For example, a firm examines new product possibilities only when it is realised that the old product is becoming, or has become, obsolete or the latest technology is installed in reaction to its adoption by a competitor. A system and culture is needed to help the firm be proactive rather than reactive.

One of the main inputs into a more systematic search for ideas is likely to be an environment-scanning process. It is also helpful if all potential idea-generators are made aware of the general strategic direction of the firm and the constraints under which it operates. Idea-generators often become sponsors of their proposals within the organisation. These individuals, in a poorly operating system, can see themselves taking a high risk for very little reward. Their reputation and career prospects can be intimately associated with a project. If it goes badly then they may find themselves blamed for that failure. In a system with such poor incentives the natural response of most people would be to hold back from suggesting ideas and pushing them through, and concentrate on day-to-day management. This defensive attitude could be bad for the organisation and it is therefore incumbent on senior management to develop reward systems that do not penalise project idea-generators and sponsors.

Exhibit 4.10	The investment process

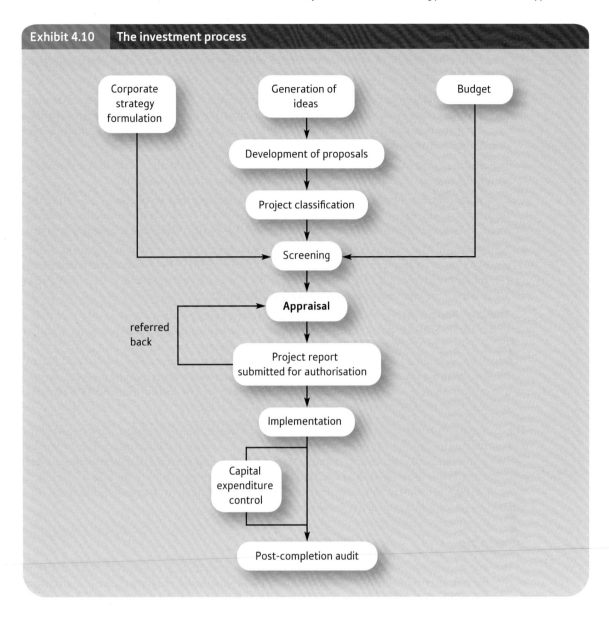

Development and classification

As the sponsor or the division-level team gathers more data and refines estimates, some degree of early filtering takes place. Ideas that may have looked good in theory do not necessarily look so good when examined more closely. In a well-functioning system, idea generation should be propagated in an unstructured, almost random manner, but the development phase starts to impose some degree of order. Many firms like to have a bottom-up approach, with ideas coming from plant level and being reviewed by divisional management before being presented to senior management. At the development stage the sponsor elaborates and hones ideas in consultation with colleagues. The divisional managers may add ideas, ask for information and suggest alternative scenarios. There may also be division-level projects which need further consideration. As the discussions and data gathering progress the proposal generally starts to gain commitment from a number of people who become drawn in and involved.

The classification stage involves matching projects to identified needs. Initially, there may be a long list of imaginative project ideas or solutions to a specific problem, but this may be narrowed down in these early stages to two or three. Detailed evaluation of all projects is expensive. Some types of project do not require the extensive search for data and complex evaluation that others do. The following classification may allow more attention to be directed at the type of project where the need is greatest:

1 *Equipment replacement* Equipment obsolescence can occur because of technological developments which create more efficient alternatives, because the old equipment becomes expensive to maintain or because of a change in the cost of inputs, making an alternative method cheaper (for example, if the oil price quadruples, taxi firms may shift to electric cars).

2 *Expansion or improvement of existing products* These investments relate to increasing the volume of output and/or improving product quality and market position.

3 *Cost reduction* A continuous process of search and analysis may be necessary to ensure that the firm is producing at lowest cost. Small modifications to methods of production or equipment, as well as the introduction of new machines, may bring valuable incremental benefits.

4 *New products* Many firms depend on a regular flow of innovatory products to permit continued expansion. Examples are Intel, GlaxoSmithKline and 3M. These firms have to make huge commitments to research and development, market research and promotion. Vast investments are needed in new production facilities around the world.

5 *Statutory and welfare* Investments may be required by law for such matters as safety, or pollution control. These do not, generally, give a financial return and so the focus is usually to satisfy the requirement at minimum cost. Welfare investments may lead to some intangible benefits which are difficult to quantify, such as a more contented workforce. The Arnold and Hatzopoulos (2000) survey showed that 78% of the firms undertook non-economic projects directed at health and safety issues; 74% accepted projects motivated by legislation; and 54% had paid for uneconomic projects for social and environmental reasons.

The management team need to weigh up the value of a more comprehensive analysis against the cost of evaluation. Regular equipment replacement, cost reduction and existing product expansion decisions are likely to require less documentation than a major strategic investment in a new product area. Also, the information needs are likely to rise in proportion to the size of the investment. A £100m investment in a new pharmaceutical plant is likely to be treated differently to a £10,000 investment in a new delivery vehicle.

Screening

At this stage, each proposal will be assessed to establish whether it is sufficiently attractive to receive further attention through the application of sophisticated analysis. Screening decisions should be made with an awareness of the strategic direction of the firm and the limitations imposed by the financial, human and other resources available. There should also be a check on the technical feasibility of the proposal and some preliminary assessment of risk.

Strategy

Capital allocation is a pivotal part of the overall strategic process. A good investment appraisal system must mesh with the firm's long-term plan. The managers at plant or division level may not be able to see opportunities at a strategic level, such as the benefits of combining two divisions, or the necessity for business-unit divestment. Thus, the bottom-up flow of ideas for investment at plant level should complement the top-down strategic planning from the centre. Each vantage point has a valuable contribution to make.

Budget

Most large firms prepare capital budgets stretching over many years. Often a detailed budget for capital expenditure in the forthcoming year is set within the framework of an outline plan for the next five years. Individual projects are required to conform to the corporate budget. However, the budget itself, at least in the long run, is heavily influenced by the availability of project proposals. The Arnold and Hatzopoulos (2000) survey shows the use of budgets by UK firms (*see* **Exhibit 4.11**).

Exhibit 4.11	Capital expenditure budgets for UK firms		
	Small firms %	**Medium-sized firms** %	**Large firms** %
Outline capital expenditure budgets are prepared for:			
1 year ahead	18	8	–
2 years ahead	18	25	13
3 years ahead	35	50	18
4 years ahead	9	–	5
More than 4 years ahead	21	13	61
Blank	–	4	3
Detailed capital expenditure budgets are prepared for:			
1 year ahead	70	79	55
2 years ahead	21	13	21
3 years ahead	9	4	8
4 years ahead	–	–	5
More than 4 years ahead	–	4	11

Note: 96 firms completed the survey questionnaire.

Source: Arnold and Hatzopoulos (2000).

Appraisal

It is at the appraisal stage that detailed cash flow forecasts are required as inputs to the more sophisticated evaluation methods, such as net present value. Manuals provide detailed checklists which help the project sponsor to ensure that all relevant costs and other factors have been considered. These manuals may explain how to calculate NPV and IRR and may also supply the firm's opportunity cost of capital. (If risk adjustment is made through the discount rate there may be more than one cost of capital and the sponsor then has to classify the project into, say, high-, medium- or low-risk categories – *see* Chapter 6.) The project promoter may seek the aid of specialists, such as engineers, accountants and economists, in the preparation of the formal analysis.

Report and authorisation

Many firms require that project proposals are presented in a specific manner through the use of capital appropriation request forms. Such forms will detail the nature of the project and the amount of finance needed, together with the forecasted cash inflows and the NPV, IRR, ARR and/or payback. Some analysis of risk and a consideration of alternatives to the proposed course of action may also be required.

Expenditure below a threshold, say £100,000, will gain authorisation at division level, while that above the threshold will need approval at corporate level. At head office, a committee consisting of the most senior officers (chairman, chief executive, finance director, etc.) will meet on a regular basis to consider major capital projects. Very few investment proposals are turned down by this committee, mainly because these project ideas will have already been through a number of stages of review and informal discussion up and down the organisation, and the obviously non-viable will have been eliminated. Also, even marginally profitable projects may get approval to give a vote of confidence to the sponsoring management team. The alternative of refusal may damage motivation and may cause loss of commitment to developing other projects. If the senior management had had doubts about a proposal they would have influenced the sponsoring division(s) long before the proposal reached the final report stage. In most cases there is a long period of consultation between head office and division managers, and informal pressures to modify or drop proposals can be both more efficient and politically astute ways of proceeding than refusal at the last hurdle.

Implementation

Capital expenditure controls

Firms must keep track of investment projects so as to be quickly aware of delays and cost differences compared with the plan. When a project is authorised, there is usually a specified schedule of expenditure, and the accountants and senior management will keep a watchful eye on cash outflows. During the installation, purchasing and construction phases, comparisons with original estimates will be made on a periodic basis. Divisions may be permitted to overspend by, say, 10% before a formal request for more funds is required. A careful watch is also kept on any changes to the projected start and completion dates. Deviations from projected cash flows are often caused by the following two factors:

a inaccuracy in the original estimate, that is, the proposal report did not reflect reality perfectly;

b poor control of costs.

It is often difficult to isolate each of these elements. However, deviations need to be identified and explained as the project progresses. This may permit corrective action to be taken to avoid further overspending and may, in extreme circumstances, lead to the cancellation of the project.

Post-completion audit

Post-completion auditing is the monitoring and evaluation of the progress of a capital investment project through a comparison of the actual cash flows and other costs and benefits with those forecasted at the time of authorisation. Companies need a follow-up procedure which examines the performance of projects over a long time span. It is necessary to isolate and explain deviations from estimated values.

Exhibit 4.12 shows the extent of the use of post-competition audits by UK companies.

Exhibit 4.12	Replies to the question: 'Does your company conduct post-audits of major capital expenditure?'			
	Small %	Medium-sized %	Large %	Composite %
Always	41	17	24	28
Sometimes/on major projects	41	67	71	59
Rarely	12	17	5	10
Never	6	–	–	2

Note: 96 companies responded to the survey.
Source: Arnold and Hatzopoulos (2000).

There are three main reasons for carrying out a post-completion audit:

1 *Financial control mechanism* This monitoring process helps to identify problems and errors evident in a particular project. A comparison with the original projections establishes whether the benefits claimed prior to approval actually materialise. If a problem is encountered then modifications or abandonment may be possible before it is too late.

2 *Insight gained may be useful for future capital investment decisions* One benefit of auditing existing projects is that it might lead to the identification of failings in the capital investment process generally. It may be discovered that data collection systems are inadequate or that appraisal methods are poor. Regular post-completion auditing helps to develop better decision making. For instance, past appraisals may have paid scant regard to likely competitor reaction; once recognised this omission will be corrected for in all future evaluations.

3   *The psychological effect* If potential project sponsors are aware that implemented proposals are monitored and reviewed they may be encouraged to increase their forecasting accuracy. They may also be dissuaded from playing 'numbers games' with their project submission, designed to draw more resources to their divisions or pet schemes unjustifiably. In addition, they may take a keener interest in the implementation phase.

Senior managers must conduct a careful balancing act because the post-completion audit may encourage another sort of non-optimal behaviour. For instance, if middle managers are judged on the extent to which project outcomes exceed original estimates, there will be a tendency to deliberately understate the forecast. Also, if the audit is too inquisitorial, or if it too forcefully apportions blame for results which are only partially under the control of managers, then they may be inclined to suggest only relatively safe projects with predictable outcomes. This may result in a loss of opportunities. Ideally, regular post-completion reviews are needed, but many firms settle for an audit one year after the asset has been put in place. This may be inadequate for projects producing returns over many years. Some firms do manage an annual review of progress, and some even go as far as monthly monitoring during the first year followed by annual reviews thereafter. On the other hand, many projects involve only minor commitment of resources and are routine in nature. The need for post-completion auditing is not as pressing for these as it would be for strategic projects requiring major organisational resource commitment. Given the costs involved in the auditing process, many firms feel justified in being highly selective and auditing only a small proportion. Another reason for not carrying out a post-completion audit in all cases is the difficulty of disentangling the costs and benefits of a specific project in a context of widespread interaction and interdependence.

Exhibit 4.13 describes the changes made by Reaction Engines to make progress with a risky project by adapting to environmental changes. They certainly have a system that encourages risk taking.

Exhibit 4.13

A space engine that could make flying into orbit commonplace

Britain's 'rocketeers' move closer to turning a near 30-year dream into reality

By: Peggy Hollinger, Industry Editor

The tiny metal tubes that sit at the heart of the Sabre engine seem too fragile to bear the weight of Britain's space ambitions. With walls half the thickness of a human hair, they will snap if bent too far.

Laid in sheets of overlapping spirals at the front of the engine they are the conduits of a unique air cooling system that could one day make flying to space and back again as commonplace as taking a flight from London to New York.

Reaction Engines has spent almost 30 years getting that magic to work, developing an engine concept that combines both conventional jet engine technology and rocket propulsion.

Founded in 1989 by a group of engineers known as the "three rocketeers", Alan Bond, Richard Varvill and the late John Scott-Scott gave up their day jobs to pursue their dreams of space travel. This is the year that their dream begins to become reality.

The company on Thursday announced plans to invest £10m to build its first proper ground test facility at Westcott, which for 70 years has been the home of British rocket research. This is a milestone development, one that marks the end of the experimental phase and the start of proving the Sabre concept.

"It is a big moment in the programme, says Mark Ford, head of propulsion engineering at the European Space Agency, which is administering some of the UK's £60m investment in Sabre technology.

"The stopwatch has started now. This is where we prove all the principles that Reaction has been saying. When that is done we can say this is very much a new type of engine."

▶

Exhibit 4.13 *(continued)*

The Sabre engine was conceived by the Three Rocketeers in tandem with a space plane, Skylon, to take an aircraft from earth to orbit and back again in a single stage, with no parts jettisoned in flight.

However, under Mark Thomas, chief executive since 2015, the company will focus on the engine and move towards its ultimate goal of single-stage-to-orbit propulsion in steps.

This means developing an intermediate solution to make the first stage of traditional two-stage launches more efficient.

Reaction has also cut the size of the engine under development by three-quarters and brought in BAE Systems, which injected £20.6m in exchange for a 20% stake. The impetus is a rising demand for lower cost re-usable satellite launch systems.

The advantage of scaling back ambitions in the near term, Mr Thomas says, is that this market can be accessed more quickly and the initial costs of development are significantly lower.

Now capable of being used in modular scaleable configurations, the technology can also be applied to a greater range of sectors to help generate revenue earlier.

"Single stage to orbit, full re-usable systems are the ideal state, the Holy Grail," he says from the company's headquarters at the Culham Science Centre near Abingdon. "But there has to be something between the two. Single stage to orbit is still on the road map.

"But we have pushed the horizon out slightly further, partly to enable us to exploit these earlier opportunities that we have seen through dialogue with government and industry."

Industry experts say Reaction's strategy makes sense — especially for a concept as ambitious as the Sabre engine. Reaction "is the only one in town doing this type of engine", says Phil Smith of US-based Bryce Space and Technology consultants.

"This iterative process is a very wise way to go. It demonstrates a maturity in the industry that didn't exist before." Rather than focusing on a goal that might fall victim to funding constraints, Reaction is seeking to demonstrate the utility of its innovation in more immediate ways, he says.

 Financial Times, 5 May 2017.
All Rights Reserved.

Concluding comments

The typical student of finance will spend time trying to cope with problems presented in a mathematical form. This is necessary because these are often the most difficult aspects of the subject to absorb. However, readers should not be misled into thinking that complex computations are at the centre of project investment in the practical world of business. Managers are often either ignorant of the principles behind discounted cash flow techniques or choose to stress more traditional rule-of-thumb techniques, such as payback and accounting rate of return, because of their communicatory or other perceived advantages. These managers recognise that good investment decision making and implementation require attention to be paid to the social and psychological factors at work within an organisation. They also know that formal technical appraisal takes place only after a long process of idea creation and development in a suitably nurturing environment. There is also a long period of discussion and commitment forming, and continuous re-examination and refinement. The real art of management is in the process of project creation and selection and not in the technical appraisal stage.

Key points and concepts

- **Payback and ARR** are widely used methods of project appraisal, but discounted cash flow methods are the most popular.

- Most large firms use **more than one appraisal method.**

- **Payback** is the length of time for cumulated future cash inflows to equal an initial outflow. Projects are accepted if this time is below an agreed cut-off point.

- **Payback has a few drawbacks:**

  - no allowance for the time value of money;
  - cash flows after the cut-off are ignored;
  - arbitrary selection of cut-off date.

- **Discounted payback** takes account of the time value of money.

- **Payback's attractions:**

  - it complements more sophisticated methods;
  - simple, and easy to use;
  - good for communication with non-specialists;
  - makes allowance for increased risk of more distant cash flows;
  - projects returning cash sooner are ranked higher. Thought to be useful when capital is in short supply.

- **Accounting rate of return** is the ratio of accounting profit to investment, expressed as a percentage.

- **Accounting rate of return has a few drawbacks:**

  - it can be calculated in a wide variety of ways;
  - profit is a poor substitute for cash flow;
  - no allowance for the time value of money;
  - arbitrary cut-off rate;
  - some perverse decisions can be made.

- **Accounting rate of return attractions:**

  - familiarity, ease of understanding and communication;
  - managers' performances are often judged using ARR and therefore they wish to select projects on the same basis.

- **Internal rate of return** is used more than NPV:

  - psychological preference for a percentage;
  - can be calculated without cost of capital;
  - thought (wrongly) to give a better ranking.

- **Mathematical technique is only one element** needed for successful project appraisal. Other factors to be considered are:

  - strategy;
  - social context;
  - expense;
  - entrepreneurial spirit;
  - intangible benefits.

- **The investment process** is more than appraisal. It has many stages:

  - generation of ideas;
  - development and classification;
  - screening;
  - appraisal;
  - report and authorisation;
  - implementation;
  - post-completion auditing.

References and further reading

Alkaraan, F. and Northcott, D. (2006) 'Strategic capital investment decision-making: a role for emergent analysis tools? A study of practice in large UK manufacturing companies', *British Accounting Review*, 38, pp. 149–73.
  As well as providing survey evidence on appraisal techniques used this paper considers the issue of using alternative techniques for strategic investments.

Arnold, G.C. and Hatzopoulos, P.D. (2000) 'The theory–practice gap in capital budgeting: evidence from the United Kingdom', *Journal of Business Finance and Accounting*, 27(5) and (6), June/July, pp. 603–26.
  Evidence of techniques used by UK firms, discussion of reasons for continued use of rule-of-thumb methods.

Arya, A., Fellingham, J.C. and Glover, J.C. (1998) 'Capital budgeting: some exceptions to the net present value rule', *Issues in Accounting Education*, 13(3), August, pp. 499–508.
  Discussion on the use of NPV.

Bennouna, K., Meredith, G.G. and Marchant, T. (2010) 'Improved capital budgeting decision making: evidence from Canada', *Management Decision*, 48(2), pp. 225–47.
  A survey of 88 large firms in Canada was conducted to evaluate current techniques in capital budget decision making including real options.

Bierman, H. and Smidt, S. (2006) *The Capital Budgeting Decision*, 9th edn. London: Routledge.
  Beginner's guide.

Bierman, H. and Smidt, S. (2006) *Advanced Capital Budgeting*. London: Routledge.
  For those who need more depth.

Boardman, C.M., Reinhard, W.J. and Celec, S.G. (1982) 'The role of the payback period in the theory and application of duration to capital budgeting', *Journal of Business Finance and Accounting*, 9(4), Winter, pp. 511–22.
  Payback critically assessed.

Bromwich, M. and Bhimani, A. (1991) 'Strategic investment appraisal', *Management Accounting*, March.
  Short article describing appraisal of non-quantifiable benefits of a project.

Brounen, D., de Jong, A. and Koedijk, K. (2004) 'Corporate finance in Europe: confronting theory with practice', *Financial Management,* Winter, pp. 71–101.

A pan-European survey of the use of appraisal techniques – payback is still popular (unfortunately < 5% surveyed replied).

Daunfeldt, S.O. and Hartwig, F. (2014), 'What determines the use of capital budgeting methods? Evidence from Swedish listed companies', *Journal of Finance and Economics,* 2(4), pp. 101–12.

The choice of capital budgeting methods used by companies listed on the Stockholm Stock Exchange (SSE) is examined using multivariate regression analysis. (2005–2008). The choice of capital budgeting methods is influenced by leverage, growth opportunities, dividend pay-out ratios, the choice of target debt ratio, the degree of management ownership, foreign sales, industry, and individual characteristics of the CEO.

Ekanem, I. (2005) '"Bootstrapping": the investment decision-making process in small firms', *British Accounting Review,* 37, pp. 299–318.

Describes how investment decisions are made in eight small firms – somewhat differently to textbook theory.

Elmassria, M.M., Harris, E.P. and Carter, D.B. (2016) 'Accounting for strategic investment decision-making under extreme uncertainly', *The British Accounting Review,* 48(2), pp. 151–68.

Illustrates how significant social, political and economic uncertainty impacts upon the utility of capital investment appraisal techniques employed in management accounting decision-making and how non-financial considerations and objectives take precedence over the technical 'accounting' measures.

Emmanuel, C., Harris, E. and Komakech, S. (2010) 'Towards a better understanding of capital investment decisions', *Journal of Accounting and Organizational Change,* 6(4), pp. 477–504.

This article investigates how managerial judgment can be detected by applying psychological concepts of heuristics, framing and consensus to the capital investment process.

Finnie, J. (1988) 'The role of financial appraisal in decisions to acquire advanced manufacturing technology', *Accounting and Business Research,* 18(70), pp. 133–9.

Argues that better management of the appraisal process is required for projects using advanced manufacturing technology.

Gadella, J.W. (1992) 'Post-project appraisal', *Management Accounting.* March, pp. 52 and 58.

Post-completion auditing discussion.

Gordon, L.A. and Myers, M.D. (1991) 'Post-auditing capital projects', *Management Accounting* (US), January, pp. 39–42.

Graham, J.R. and Harvey, C.R. (2001) 'The theory and practice of corporate finance: evidence from the field', *Journal of Financial Economics,* 60(2–3), May, pp. 187–243.

Provides evidence of US corporate use of project appraisal techniques together with an easy-to-follow discussion.

Hajdasinski, M.M. (1993) 'The payback period as a measure of profitability and liquidity', *Engineering Economist,* 38(3), Spring, pp. 177–91.

Payback's usefulness.

Hall, J. and Millard, S. (2010) 'Capital budgeting practices used by selected listed South African firms', *South African Journal of Economic Management Sciences,* 13(1), pp. 85–97.

Investigates the application of capital budgeting techniques and the incorporation of risk into the capital budgeting process among South African industrial firms listed on the JSE. Indicates that NPV and IRR are popular and that risk is incorporated. Sensitivity analysis is the most popular method but adjustments to the cash flows and discount rate are becoming more popular. The use of non-financial criteria to accept or reject a project has also increased in South Africa.

Hansen, H., Huhn, W., Legrand, O., Steiners, D. and Vahlenkamp, T. (2009) *Capex Excellence: Optimising fixed asset investing.* Chichester: John Wiley and Sons.

McKinsey consultants' perspective on capital expenditure decisions. Easy to read.

Ho, S.M. and Pike, R.H. (1991) 'Risk analysis techniques in capital budgeting contexts', *Accounting, and Business Research,* 21(83).

Survey of 146 UK firms' project risk analysis practices.

Kaplan, R.S. and Atkinson, A.A. (2013) *Advanced Management Accounting,* International Edition (3rd edition), Pearson.

Management accounting textbook that covers decision making.

Kee, R. and Bublitz, B. (1988) 'The role of payback in the investment process', *Accounting and Business Research,* 18(70), pp. 149–55.

Value of payback discussed.

Kennedy, A. and Mills, R. (1990) *Post Completion Audit of Capital Expenditure Projects.* London: CIMA. Management Accounting Guide 9.

Post-completion auditing evidence.

Kennedy, A. and Mills, R. (1992) 'Post completion auditing: a source of strategic direction?', *Management Accounting* (UK), May, pp. 26–8.

Post-completion auditing evidence.

Kennedy, A. and Mills, R. (1993a) 'Post completion auditing in practice', *Management Accounting,* October, pp. 22–5.

Post-completion auditing evidence.

Kennedy, A. and Mills, R. (1993b) 'Experiences in operating a post-audit system', *Management Accounting,* November.

Post-completion auditing evidence.

Kester, G. and Robbins, G. (2011) 'The capital budgeting practices of listed Irish companies: Insights from CFOs on their investment appraisal techniques', *Accountancy Ireland*, 43(1), pp. 28–30.

A survey of CFOs of companies listed on the Irish Stock Exchange on their companies' financial policies and practices in three major areas: capital structure policy and financing decisions, dividends, and capital budgeting.

Lawrence, A.G. and Myers, M.D. (1991) 'Post-auditing capital projects', *Management Accounting*, January, pp. 39–42.

Survey of 282 large US firms' post-auditing objectives, method and thoroughness.

Lefley, F. (1997) 'The sometimes-overlooked discounted payback method', *Management Accounting* (UK), November, p. 36.

Payback's virtues.

Lefley, F. (2013) 'The appraisal of ICT and non-ICT capital projects: A study of the current practices of large UK organisations', *International Journal of Managing Projects in Business*, Bingley, 6.3, pp. 505–533.

This research presents evidence of the financial and risk assessment models used by practitioners in the appraisal of both ICT and non-ICT capital projects. It shows that there was no significant difference between ICT and non-ICT appraisals.

Longmore, D.R. (1989) 'The persistence of the payback method: a time-adjusted decision rule perspective', *Engineering Economist*, 43(3), Spring, pp. 185–94.

Payback's use.

Lowenstein, L. (1991) *Sense and Nonsense in Corporate Finance*. Reading, MA: Addison Wesley.

Criticism of over-preciseness in project appraisal and the underplaying of unquantifiable elements.

Lumijärvi, O.P. (1991) 'Selling of capital investments to top management', *Management Accounting Research*, 2, pp. 171–88.

Describes a real-world case of a lower-level manager influencing superiors so that desired investment funds are received.

Pike, R.H. (1996) 'A longitudinal survey of capital budgeting practices', *Journal of Business Finance and Accounting*, 23(1), January.

Excellent, short and clear article surveying appraisal methods in UK large firms.

Ross, S.A. (1995) 'Uses, abuses, and alternatives to the net-present-value rule', *Financial Management*, 24(3), Autumn, pp. 96–102.

Discussion of the value of NPV.

Sangster, A. (1993) 'Capital investment appraisal techniques: a survey of current usage', *Journal of Business Finance and Accounting*, 20(3), April, pp. 307–33.

Evidence of use.

Shinoda, T. (2010) 'Capital budgeting management practices in Japan – a focus on the use of capital budgeting methods', *Economic Journal of Hokkaido University*, 39, no. 2010, pp. 39–50.

Results from a survey sent to 225 people in charge of capital budgeting at firms listed on the Tokyo Stock Exchange, with a focus on capital budgeting practices which show that Japanese firms manage their decision-making by a combination of payback period method and net present value method.

Singh, S., Jain, P.K and Yadav, S.S. (2012) 'Capital budgeting decisions: evidence from India', *Journal of Advances in Management Research*, 9(1), pp. 96–112.

Trends towards sophisticated techniques and sound capital budgeting decisions have continued in India but there remains a theory practice gap in the usage of IRR over NPV.

Statman, M. and Sepe, J.F. (1984) 'Managerial incentive plans and the use of the payback method', *Journal of Business Finance and Accounting*, 11(1), Spring, pp. 61–5.

Payback's usefulness.

Steele, R. and Albright, C. (2004) 'Games managers play at budget time', *MIT Sloan Management Review*, Spring, pp. 81–4.

Executive game-play tactics revealed.

Tyrrall, D.E. (1998) 'Discounted cash flow: rational calculation or psychological crutch?', *Management Accounting* (UK), February, pp. 46–8.

Discussion of theory–practice relationship.

Wooley, S. (2009) *Sources of Value: A practical guide to the art and science of valuation*. Cambridge University Press.

An easy-to-read introduction to traditional DCF, followed by distinct ideas on practical implementation.

Zimmerman, J.L. (2010) *Accounting for Decision Making and Control*, 7th edn. Boston: Irwin/McGraw-Hill.

Contains a useful discussion on discounted cash flow methods.

Case study recommendations

Please see www.pearsoned.co.uk/arnold for case study synopses. Also, there is another list of useful case studies in the fifth edition.

- Budgets and other Lies: Evidence of Bias in Financial Planning
  Author: Ron Messer. Business Horizons. Available at www.cb.hbsp.harvard.edu

- Gm's Capital Allocation Framework
  Authors: C. Fritz Foley; F. Katelynn Boland; Michael Lemm. Harvard Business School. Available at www.cb.hbsp.harvard.edu

Self-review questions

1 Payback is dismissed as unsound. Discuss.

2 Define accounting rate of return and compare it with net present value.

3 Describe discounted payback.

4 Do you believe the arguments for using IRR are strong enough to justify relying on this technique alone?

5 Why is investment project generation, selection and implementation closer to an art form than a science?

6 How would you appraise a project with a high proportion of non-quantifiable benefits?

7 If you were chief executive of a large corporation, how would you encourage project idea generation, communication and sponsorship?

8 Why is project screening necessary?

9 Invent five projects, each of which falls into a different project category.

10 Why are few projects rejected at the report stage?

11 When do capital expenditure controls and post-completion audits become an excessive burden, and when are they very important?

12 Comment on the following statement:

'The firm should choose the investment with a short payback rather than one with a larger net present value.'

Questions and problems

Answers to most questions can be found at www.pearsoned.co.uk/arnold.
Answers to questions marked with an asterisk are to be found only in the Lecturer's Guide.

1   For the following projects, calculate the payback and the discounted payback.

Point in time (yearly intervals)	0 £	1 £	2 £	3 £	4 £	5 £	6 £	7 £
A	−3,000	500	500	500	500	500	500	500
B	−10,000	2,000	5,000	3,000	2,000	–	–	–
C	−15,000	5,000	4,000	4,000	5,000	10,000	–	–
D	−4,000	1,000	1,000	1,000	1,000	7,000	7,000	7,000
E	−8,000	500	500	500	2,000	5,000	10,000	–

The cost of capital is 12%.

2   A project has a £10,000 initial investment and cash inflows of £3,334 per year over six years. What is the payback period? What will be the payback period if the receipts of £3,334 per year occur for only three years? Explain the significance of your answer.

3*   (*Examination level*) Oakland plc is considering a major investment project. The initial outlay of £900,000 will, in subsequent years, be followed by positive cash flows, as shown below. (These occur on the anniversary dates.)

Year	1	2	3	4	5
Cash flow (£)	+50,000	+120,000	+350,000	+80,000	+800,000

After the end of the fifth year this business activity will cease and no more cash flows will be produced.

The initial £900,000 investment in plant and machinery is to be depreciated over the five-year life of the project using the straight-line method. These assets will have no value after Year 5.

The management judge that the cash inflows shown above are also an accurate estimation of the profit before depreciation for each of the years. They also believe that the appropriate discount rate to use for the firm's projects is 10% per annum.

The board of directors is used to evaluating project proposals on the basis of a payback rule which requires that all investments achieve payback in four years.

As the newly appointed executive responsible for project appraisal you have been asked to assess this project using a number of different methods and to advise the board on the advantages and disadvantages of each. Do this in the following sequence.

(i)   a   Calculate the payback period.
     b   Calculate the discounted payback period.
     c   Calculate an accounting rate of return.
     d   Calculate the internal rate of return.
     e   Calculate the net present value.

(ii)   Compare the relative theoretical and practical merits and demerits of each of the methods used.
     Assume: No tax or inflation.

4   A firm is considering investing in a project with the following cash flows:

Year	1	2	3	4	5	6	7	8
Net cash flow (£)	1,000	1,500	2,000	1,750	1,500	1,000	500	500

The initial investment is £6,250. The firm has a required rate of return of 10%. Calculate:

a   the payback period;
b   the discounted payback;
c   the net present value.

What are the main objections to the use of payback? Why does it remain a very popular method?

5   Maple plc is considering which of two mutually exclusive projects to accept, each with a five-year life. Project A requires an initial expenditure of £2,300,000 and is forecast to generate annual cash flows before depreciation of £800,000. The equipment purchased at time zero has an estimated residual value after five years of £300,000. Project B costs £660,000 for equipment at the start. This has a residual value of £60,000 after five years. Cash inflows before depreciation of £250,000 per annum are anticipated. The company has a straight-line depreciation policy and a cost of capital of 15% (relevant for projects of this risk class). You can assume that the cash flows are also equal to the profits before depreciation. Calculate:

a   an accounting rate of return;
b   the net present value.

What are the disadvantages of using ARR?

6   Explain why empirical studies show that, in practice, firms often prefer to evaluate projects using traditional methods.

7   Camelia plc has been run in an autocratic style by the chief executive and main shareholder, Mr Linedraw, during its 40-year history. The company is now too large for Mr Linedraw to continue being involved in all decisions. As part of its reforms the firm intends to set up a structured programme of capital investment. You have been asked to compile a report which will guide management. This will detail the investment process and will not be confined to appraisal techniques.

8   'The making of good investment decisions is as much about understanding human psychology as it is about mathematics.' Explain this statement.

9   Explain how each of the following can lead to a sub-optimal investment process:

   a   relying on top-down idea generation;
   b   managers being judged solely on accounting rate of return;
   c   a requirement that projects have a quick payback;
   d   post-auditing once only, one year after completion;
   e   post-auditing conducted by managers from 'rival' divisions;
   f   over-optimism of project sponsors.

Assignment

Investigate the capital investment process in a firm you know well. Relate the stages and methods used to the process outlined in this chapter. Consider areas for improvement.

Project appraisal:
capital rationing, taxation and inflation

LEARNING OUTCOMES

By the end of this chapter the reader should be able to cope with investment appraisal in an environment of capital rationing, taxation and inflation and should be able to:

- explain why capital rationing exists;

- use the profitability ratio in one-period rationing situations;

- explain the influence of taxation on cash flows;

- discount money cash flows with a money discount rate, and real cash flows with a real discount rate.

Introduction

In the analysis conducted so far, simplifying assumptions have been made in order to convey the essential concepts and techniques of project appraisal. First, it was assumed that there are no limits placed on finance available (there is no capital rationing). Taxation was ignored and it was assumed that there was no inflation. Now we need to re-incorporate these ideas to allow more sophisticated and realistic analysis.

Capital rationing

Our discussion has rested on the assertion that if a project has a positive net present value then it should be undertaken; a positive NPV project increases the wealth of shareholders. However, in the practical world of business, there are limits placed on the availability of project finance and a choice has to be made between a number of positive NPV projects. This is the capital rationing problem.

Capital rationing occurs when funds are not available to finance all wealth-enhancing projects. There are two types of capital rationing: soft rationing and hard rationing.

Soft rationing

Soft capital rationing is internal management-imposed limits on investment expenditure. Such limits may be linked to the firm's financial control policy. Senior management may try to retain financial control over divisions by placing limits on the amount any division can spend on a set of projects. Some ambitious managers may be tempted to overstate the extent of investment opportunities within their sector of responsibility. To sort out the good projects from the bad, head office could examine each individually, but this would be bureaucratic and time consuming. The alternative is to impose a limit on the amount a division may invest in projects within a particular time frame. It is then the division's responsibility to decide which projects rank higher than others.

Some firms operate in dynamic sectors and have many potentially profitable expansion opportunities. Undertaking all of them would put pressure on the management and the organisation because of the excessive growth this might imply. For example, Microsoft's thousands of technically able employees might generate dozens of ideas for significant new businesses, ranging from new software and multimedia to links with television broadcasters and book publishers. Over-rapid expansion may lead to difficulties in planning and control. Capital rationing acts as a proxy for other types of resources in short supply, such as managerial talent or time, technical expertise or even equipment.

Firms may aim to avoid exceeding certain values for key financial ratios. One of the most important ratios examined is gearing or leverage, the relationship between borrowing and asset levels. Management may be concerned about the increasing risk associated with extensive borrowing and become reluctant to enter into the capital markets to borrow. Unwillingness to borrow more money has elements of soft and hard capital rationing. It is a form of self-imposed rationing, but it may have been prompted by signals from the capital markets that borrowing would be difficult or would be available only with onerous strings attached.

Another limit on the availability of finance can be created by the existing owner-manager or family shareholders who do not wish to lose control by permitting the firm to raise equity finance by selling new shares to outsiders.

Hard rationing

Hard capital rationing relates to capital limitations imposed from external sources. Agencies (e.g. shareholders) external to the firm will not supply unlimited amounts of investment capital, even though positive NPV projects are identified. In a perfect capital market hard rationing should never occur, because if a firm has positive NPV projects it will be able to raise any finance it needs.

However, companies continue to identify the lack of available funds as a constraint. This is a problem that has been evident since business activity first started and is a particular problem for smaller, less profitable and more high-risk firms. Governments have tried to improve the availability of funds available to firms. Stock exchanges have encouraged the development of equity markets specifically targeted at small firms trying to raise finance such as the Alternative Investment Market (AIM). In addition, the venture capital market provides for start-ups and early stage development in high-risk businesses. (Sources of equity capital are examined in Chapters 9 and 10.) Despite all these advances, companies still complain regularly about the gap between the amount of capital firms would like to use and that which is made available. Hard rationing, which as stated above, should not occur in a perfect market therefore implies market imperfections two elements of which might be the principal–agent problem and information asymmetry which lead to a lack of trust in managers' proposals.

One-period capital rationing

The simplest and most straightforward form of rationing occurs when limits are placed on finance availability for only one year; funds for all other years are unlimited. There are two possibilities within this one-period rationing situation.

1 *Divisible projects* The nature of the proposed projects means the company can undertake part of a project. For instance, if a project suggests opening a further 100 shops, it would be possible to undertake say 30% (30 shops) or any other fraction of the overall project. To simplify the calculations and the conceptual understanding it is usually assumed that all cash flows change in proportion to the fraction of the project implemented.

2 *Indivisible projects* With some projects it is impossible to undertake part of the project; the choice is between undertaking the whole of the investment or none (e.g., building a ship or a bridge).

Divisible projects

Worked example 5.1	Bigtasks plc

Bigtasks has four positive NPV projects to consider. Capital at time zero has been rationed to £4.5m because of head office planning and control policies, and because the holding company has been warned that another round of borrowing would not be welcomed by the financial institutions. However, funds are likely to be unlimited in future years. The four projects under consideration can each be undertaken once only and the acceptance of one of the projects does not exclude the possibility of accepting another one. The cash flows are as follows:

Point in time (yearly intervals)	0 £m	1 £m	2 £m	NPV at 10% £m
Project A	−2	6	1	4.281
Project B	−1	1	4	3.215
Project C	−1	1	3	2.388
Project D	−3	10	10	14.355

All these projects have positive NPVs and would therefore all be accepted in the absence of capital rationing. We need to determine the optimal combination of projects which will fit within the capital constraint. Ranking projects by the absolute NPV will be biased towards the selection of large projects. It may be better to invest in a number of smaller projects with lower individual NPVs. If we do select according to the highest absolute NPV, the total NPV produced is £17.566m, because we would allocate £3m first to Project D, and then the remaining £1.5m would be invested in 75% of Project A because this has the next highest absolute NPV.

▶

Worked example 5.1 (*continued*)

Ranking according to absolute NPV

	Initial outlay	NPV (£m)
All of Project D	3	14.355
3/4 of Project A	1.5	3.211
	4.5	Total NPV 17.566

To achieve an optimum allocation of the £4.5m we need to make use of either the profitability index (PI) or the benefit–cost ratio.[1]

$$\text{Profitability index} = \frac{\text{Gross present value}}{\text{Initial outlay}}$$

$$\text{Benefit} - \text{cost ratio} = \frac{\text{Net present value}}{\text{Initial outlay}}$$

The gross present value is the total present value of all the cash flows excluding the initial investment. Both ratios provide a measure of profitability per £ invested. For example, in **Exhibit 5.1**, for every £1 invested in Project A, £3.14 is returned in future cash flows when discounted. The benefit–cost ratio is, of course, closely related to the profitability index and for Project A shows that £1 committed at time zero will produce a *net* present value of £2.14.

Exhibit 5.1	Bigtasks plc: Profitability indices cost ratios

Project	NPV (@ 10%)	GPV (@ 10%)	Profitability index	Benefit–cost ratio
A	4.281	6.281	$\dfrac{6.281}{2} = 3.141$	$\dfrac{4.281}{2} = 2.141$
B	3.215	4.215	$\dfrac{4.215}{1} = 4.215$	$\dfrac{3.215}{1} = 3.215$
C	2.388	3.388	$\dfrac{3.388}{1} = 3.388$	$\dfrac{2.388}{1} = 2.388$
D	14.355	17.355	$\dfrac{17.355}{3} = 5.785$	$\dfrac{14.355}{3} = 4.785$

The use of profitability indices or benefit–cost ratios is a matter of personal choice. Whichever is used, the next stage is to arrange the projects in order of the highest profitability index or benefit–cost ratio. Then work down the list until the capital limit is reached. Here, the profitability index (PI) will be used (*see* **Exhibit 5.2**).

Exhibit 5.2	Bigtasks plc: Ranking according to the highest profitability index

Profit	Profitability index	Initial outlay £m	NPV £m
D	5.785	3	14.355
B	4.215	1	3.215
1/2 of C	3.388	0.5	1.194
Nothing of A	3.141	0	0
Total investment		4.5	18.764

---

1 The use of these terms is often muddled and they may be used interchangeably in the literature and in practice, so you should ensure that it is clearly understood how the ratio used in a particular situation is calculated.

With the profitability index, Project D gives the highest return and so is the best project in terms of return per £ of outlay. However, Project A no longer ranks second because this provides the lowest return per unit of initial investment. The smaller projects, B and C, give a higher PI.

The overall result for Bigtasks is that an extra £1.198m (£18.764 − £17.566m) is created for shareholders by selecting projects through one of the ratios rather than sticking rigidly to NPV.

Indivisible projects

In practice, few projects are divisible and so the profitability index is inappropriate. Now, assume that it is not possible to take a fraction of Bigtask's projects and that the capital limit at time zero is £3m. In these circumstances the easiest approach is to examine the total NPV values of all the feasible alternative combinations of whole projects, in other words, trial and error. (*See* **Exhibit 5.3**.)

Exhibit 5.3	Individual project with capital constraint of £3m

Feasible combination 1		NPV (£m)
£2m invested in Project A		4.281
£1m invested in Project B		3.215
	Total NPV	7.496

Feasible combination 2		NPV (£m)
£2m invested in Project A		4.281
£1m invested in Project C		2.388
	Total NPV	6.669

Feasible combination 3		NPV (£m)
£1m invested in Project B		3.215
£1m invested in Project C		2.388
	Total NPV	5.603

Feasible combination 4		NPV (£m)
£3m invested in Project D	Total NPV	14.355

Multi-period capital rationing

If capital constraints are likely in more than one time period, then the calculations to derive an optimal solution become more complicated. For example, Small Decisions Ltd (*see* **Exhibit 5.4**) is trying to decide how to allocate its resources between six projects. All the projects are independent (that is, not mutually exclusive) and no one project can be repeated. The firm is aware of a capital limit of £240,000 at time zero and a further constraint of £400,000 at time one.

Exhibit 5.4	Small decisions ltd: cash flows

Point in time (yearly intervals)	0 £000s	1 £000s	2 £000s	3 £000s
Project A	−200	−100	−20	500
Project B	0	−120	70	200
Project C	−10	0	−80	200
Project D	−80	−120	70	200
Project E	−30	−240	200	150
Project F	−60	−110	50	320

To find a solution to a problem like this, with fund constraints in more than one period, we cannot use a method based on the profitability index. A mathematical programme will be required and a computer would normally be employed. If the projects are divisible then linear programming is used. If the projects are indivisible the solution is found through integer programming. However, these techniques are beyond the scope of this book. The reader wishing to examine this issue in more detail is referred to the references and further reading list at the end of this chapter.

Taxation and investment appraisal

Taxation can have an important impact on project viability. If managers are implementing decisions that are shareholder wealth enhancing, they will focus on the cash flows available to shareholders. Therefore, they will evaluate the after-tax cash flows of a project. There are two rules to follow in investment appraisal in a world with taxation:

- **Rule 1** If acceptance of a project changes the tax liabilities of the firm then the incremental tax effects need to be included in the analysis.
- **Rule 2** Get the timing right. It is often the case (for small firms) that tax is paid one year or more after the receipt of the related cash flows. It is important to incorporate the cash outflow of tax into the analysis at the correct time.

Tax rates and systems change over time and any example presented using rules and rates applicable at the time of writing needs to be updated as changes occur. In this section we will concentrate on the general principles of how tax is taken into account in project appraisal.

In the UK HM Revenue and Customs collects corporation tax based on the taxable income of companies. Specific projects are not taxed separately, but if a project produces additional profits in a year, then this will generally increase the tax bill. If losses are made on a project, then the overall tax bill will generally be reduced. Taxable income is rarely the same as the profit reported in the annual reports and accounts because some of the expenses deducted to produce the reported profit are not permitted by HMRC when calculating taxable income. For example, depreciation is not an allowable cost. HMRC permits writing-down allowances or capital allowances rather than depreciation. So for most plant and machinery in the UK, a writing-down allowance of 18% on a declining balance is permitted. In a firm's accounts, such equipment may be depreciated by only, say, 10% a year, whereas the tax authorities permit the taxable income to be reduced by 18% of the equipment value. Thus, reported profit will often be higher than taxable income. Other types of long-lived assets, such as industrial buildings, have different percentage writing-down allowances – some assets carry a 100% writing-down allowance in the year of purchase.

Worked example 5.2	Snaffle

Snaffle is considering a project which will require the purchase of a machine for €1 million at time zero. This machine will have a scrap value at the end of its four-year life equal to its written-down value (this simplifying assumption will be dropped later). The tax authorities permit a 25% declining balance writing-down allowance on the machine each year. Corporation tax, at a rate of 30% of taxable income, is payable. Snaffle's required rate of return is 12%.[2] Operating cash flows, excluding depreciation, and before taxation, are forecast to be:

Time (year)	1 €	2 €	3 €	4 €
Cash flows before tax	400,000	400,000	220,000	240,000

Note: *All cash flows occur at year ends.*

---

2 If we are dealing with after-tax cash flows the discount rate will be the after-tax discount rate.

In order to calculate the net present value, first calculate the annual writing-down allowances (WDA). Note that each year the WDA is equal to 25% of the asset value at the start of the year. (*See* **Exhibit 5.5**.)

Exhibit 5.5	**Calculation of writing-down allowances**

Point in time (yearly intervals)	Annual writing-down allowance €	Written-down value €
0	0	1,000,000
1	$1{,}000{,}000 \times 0.25 = 250{,}000$	750,000
2	$750{,}000 \times 0.25 = 187{,}500$	562,500
3	$562{,}500 \times 0.25 = 140{,}625$	421,875
4	$421{,}875 \times 0.25 = 105{,}469$	316,406

The next step is to derive the project's incremental taxable income and to calculate the tax payments (**Exhibit 5.6**).

Exhibit 5.6	**Calculation of corporation tax**			

Year	1 €	2 €	3 €	4 €
Net income before writing-down allowance and tax	400,000	400,000	220,000	240,000
Less writing-down allowance	250,000	187,500	140,625	105,469
Incremental taxable income	150,000	212,500	79,375	134,531
Tax at 30% of incremental taxable income	45,000	63,750	23,813	40,359

Finally, the total cash flows and NPV are calculated (*see* **Exhibit 5.7**).

Exhibit 5.7	**Calculation of cash flows**				

Year	0 €	1 €	2 €	3 €	4 €
Incremental cash flow before tax	−1,000,000	400,000	400,000	220,000	240,000
Sale of machine					316,406
Tax		0	−45,000	−63,750	−23,813	−40,359
Net cash flow	−1,000,000	355,000	336,250	196,187	516,047
Discounted cash flow	$-1{,}000{,}000 \; +$	$\dfrac{355{,}000}{1.12} \; +$	$\dfrac{336{,}250}{(1.12)^2} \; +$	$\dfrac{196{,}187}{(1.12)^3} \; +$	$\dfrac{516{,}047}{(1.12)^4}$
	−1,000,000	+316,964	+268,056	+139,642	+327,957

Net present value $= +€52{,}619$

Note: Tax is payable in the same year that the income was earned in this case.

▶

Worked example 5.2 *(continued)*

The assumption that the machine can be sold at the end of the fourth year, for an amount equal to the written-down value, may be unrealistic. It may turn out that the machine is sold for the larger sum of €440,000. If this is the case, a *balancing charge* will need to be made, because by the end of the third year the tax authorities have already permitted write-offs against taxable profit such that the machine is shown as having a written-down value of €421,875. A year later its market value is found to be €440,000. The balancing charge is equal to the sale value at Time 4 minus the written-down book value at Time 3:

€440,000 − €421,875 = €18,125

Taxable profits for Year 4 are now:

	€
Pre-tax cash flows	240,000
Plus balancing charge	18,125
	258,125

This results in a tax payment of €258,125 × 0.30 = €77,438 rather than €40,359.

Of course, the analyst does not have to wait until the actual sale of the asset to make these modifications to a proposed project's projected cash flows. It may be possible to estimate a realistic scrap value at the outset.

An alternative scenario, where the scrap value is less than the Year 4 written-down value, will require a balancing allowance. If the disposal value is €300,000 then the machine cost the firm €700,000 (€1,000,000 − €300,000) but the tax writing-down allowances amount to only €683,594 (€1,000,000 − €316,406). The firm will effectively be overcharged by the tax authorities. In this case a balancing adjustment, amounting to €16,406 (€700,000 − €683,594), is made to reduce the tax payable (*see* **Exhibit 5.8**).

Exhibit 5.8	**Year 4 taxable profits**

	€
Pre-tax cash flows	240,000
Less annual writing-down allowance	105,469
Less balancing allowance	16,406
Taxable profits	118,125
Tax payable @ 30%	35,438

Taxation rates can have a great impact on the viability of investment projects – *see* **Exhibit 5.9**.

Exhibit 5.9

Xstrata 'suspends' £337m in projects

By Peter Smith in Sydney

Xstrata, the Anglo-Swiss miner, said it had 'suspended' A$586m (£337m) in spending on coal and copper projects in Australia in the weeks since Canberra announced plans for a new 40% resources super profits tax .

Nearly all miners operating in Australia have said they are reviewing their operations due to uncertainty about the proposed tax, which may yet be amended.

Fortescue Metals Group, Australia's third-biggest iron ore exporter, last month said it had put on hold two projects in development. It estimated the cost of developing those projects at A$15bn.

Mick Davis, Xstrata chief executive, said that the tax would impair the value of projects to the point that 'continued investment can no longer be justified'.

Xstrata has suspended A$400m of spending to extend the life of its Ernest Henry copper mine and a further A$91m earmarked for the Wandoan coal project.

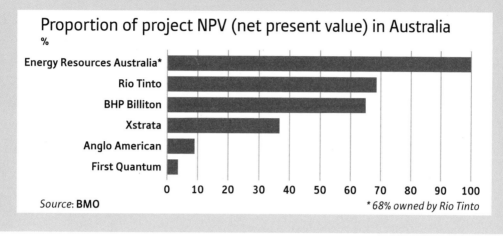

Proportion of project NPV (net present value) in Australia

Source: BMO   * 68% owned by Rio Tinto

The Australian tax which came into force in 2012 was significantly amended before being repealed in 2014 after a mining industry campaign to persuade voters that the tax was inhibiting investment. Ironically one of the reasons given for the repeal was the low present value of the expected tax revenue generated.

Inflation

Annual inflation has varied tremendously over the past 40 years. In the UK, for instance, it has varied from 1% to 26%. It is important to adapt investment appraisal methods to cope with price movements. Future rates of inflation are unlikely to be precisely forecasted; nevertheless, we will assume in the analysis that follows that we can anticipate inflation with reasonable accuracy. Unanticipated inflation is an additional source of risk and methods of dealing with this are described in the next chapter. **Exhibit 5.10** shows the importance of allowing for inflation.

Two types of inflation can be distinguished. Specific inflation refers to the price changes of an individual good or service. General inflation is the reduced purchasing power of money and is measured by an overall price index which follows the price changes of a 'basket' of goods and services through time. Even if there was no general inflation, specific items and sectors might experience price rises.

Exhibit 5.10

Anglo reveals $2bn overrun at Brazil site

by: Michael Kavanagh

Anglo American, the mining company hit by the resignation of its chief executive and continuing wildcat strikes at its South African operations, said costs at a large iron ore project in Brazil would be $2bn higher than expected.

Shares in the company fell by 3.15% to close at £17.70 on Tuesday, after Anglo American confirmed it now expected capital expenditure at its Minas-Rio development to exceed $8bn. The company's shares have lost over a quarter of their value since the start of the year.

Exhibit 5.10 *(continued)*

The company said its board had commissioned an external report into the causes of the cost overrun and delays at the project. Poor progress there has long been seen as a blot on Anglo's plans to lower its cost of production.

Last month the FTSE 100 miner said it was still confident that the resolution of legal disputes and other impediments could see production at the project begin by the end of 2014. But it also conceded that its last estimate of capital expenditure at Minas-Rio, which it put at $5.8bn, was too low.

It added that difficulties in bringing the multibillion-dollar project in within previous budgets reflected inflationary cost pressures within the Brazilian construction sector.

Inflation creates two problems for project appraisal. First, the estimation of future cash flows is made more troublesome. The project appraiser will have to estimate the degree to which future cash flows will be inflated. Second, the rate of return required by the firm's security holders, such as shareholders, will rise if inflation rises. Thus, inflation has an impact on the discount rate used in investment evaluation. We will look at the second problem in more detail first.

'Real' and 'money' rates of return

As stated in Chapter 2, the rate of return represented by the discount rate usually takes account of three types of compensation:

- the pure time value of money, or impatience to consume;
- risk;
- inflation.

Thus, the interest rates quoted in the financial markets are sufficiently high to compensate for all three elements. A 10-year loan to a reputable government (such as the purchase of a bond) may pay an interest rate of 5% per annum. Some of this is compensation for time preference and a little for risk, but the majority of that interest is likely to be compensation for future inflation. It is the same for the cost of capital for a business. When it issues financial securities, the returns offered include a large element of inflation compensation.

To illustrate: even in a situation of no inflation, given the choice between receiving goods and services now or receiving them some time in the future, shareholders would rather receive them now. If these pure time and risk preferences were valued, the value might turn out to be 3% per annum. That is, in a world without inflation, investors are indifferent as to whether they receive a given basket of commodities today or receive a basket of commodities which is 3% larger in one year's time.

The real rate of return is defined as the rate of return that would be required in the absence of inflation. In the example in **Exhibit 5.11**, the real rate of return is 3%.

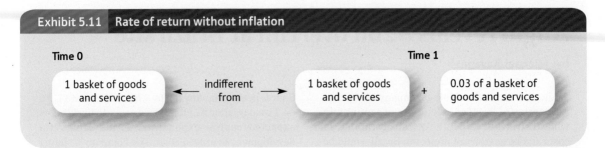

Exhibit 5.11   Rate of return without inflation

Time 0

1 basket of goods and services

← indifferent from →

Time 1

1 basket of goods and services

+ 0.03 of a basket of goods and services

If we change the assumption so that prices do rise, then investors will demand compensation for general inflation. They will require a larger monetary amount at Time 1 to buy 1.03 baskets. If inflation is 2%, then the money value of the commodities at Time 1, which would leave the investor indifferent when comparing it with one basket at Time 0, is:

$$1.03 \times 1.02 = 1.0506$$

That is, investors will be indifferent as to whether they hold £1,000 now or receive £1,050.60 one year hence. Since the money cash flow of £1,050.60 at Time 1 is financially equivalent to £1,000 now, the money rate of return is 5.06%. The money rate of return includes a return to compensate for inflation.

The generalised relationship between real rates of return and money (or market, or nominal) rates of return and inflation is expressed in Fisher's (1930) equation:

(1 + money rate of return) = (1 + real rate of return) $\times$ (1 + anticipated rate of inflation)
$$(1 + m) = (1 + h) \times (1 + i)$$
$$(1 + 0.506) = (1 + 0.03) \times (1 + 0.02)$$

'Money' cash flows and 'real' cash flows

We have now established two possible discount rates, the money discount rate and the real discount rate. There are two ways of adjusting for the effect of future inflation on cash flows. The first is to estimate the likely specific inflation rates for each of the inflows and outflows of cash and calculate the actual monetary amount paid or received in the year that the flow occurs. This is the money cash flow or the nominal cash flow.

With a *money cash flow*, all future cash flows are expressed in the prices expected to be paid or received when the cash flow occurs.

The other possibility is to measure the cash flows in terms of real prices. That is, all future cash flows are expressed in terms of, say, Time 0's prices.

With real cash flows, future cash flows are expressed in terms of constant purchasing power.

Adjusting for inflation

The two methods of adjusting for inflation when calculating net present value will lead to the same answer:

- *Approach 1* Estimate the cash flows in money terms and use a money discount rate.
- *Approach 2* Estimate the cash flows in real terms and use a real discount rate.

For now we will leave discussion of conversion to real prices and focus on the calculations using money cash flow. This will be done through the examination of an appraisal for Amplify plc.

Worked example 5.3	Amplify plc

Cash flow in money terms and money discount rate

Amplify plc is considering a project which would require an outlay of £2.4m at the outset. The money cash inflows from sales will depend on the specific inflation rate for Amplify's product. This is anticipated to be 6% per annum. Cash outflows consist of three elements: labour, materials and overheads. Labour costs are expected to increase at 9% per year, materials by 12% and overheads by 8%. The discount rate of 12.32% that Amplify uses is a money discount rate, including an allowance for inflation. One of the key rules of project appraisal is now followed: if the discount rate is stated in money terms, then consistency requires that the cash flows be estimated in money terms. (It is surprising how often this rule is broken.)

$$NPV = M_0 + \frac{M_1}{1 + m} + \frac{M_2}{(1 + m)^2} \cdots \frac{M_n}{(1 + m)^n}$$

▶

Worked example 5.3 (continued)

where M = actual or money cash flow
m = actual or money rate of return

Annual cash flows in present (Time 0) prices are as follows:

	£m	Inflation
Sales	2	6%
Labour costs	0.3	9%
Material costs	0.6	12%
Overheads	0.06	8%

All cash flows occur at year ends except for the initial outflow.

The first stage is to calculate the money cash flows. We need to restate the inflows and outflows for each of the years at the amount actually changing hands in money terms. (*See* **Exhibit 5.12**.)

Exhibit 5.12	Amplify plc: Money cash flow		

Point in time (yearly intervals)	Cash flow before allowing for price rises £m	Inflation adjustment	Money cash flow £m
0 Initial outflow	−2.4	1	−2.400
1 Sales	2	1.06	2.120
Labour	−0.3	1.09	−0.327
Materials	−0.6	1.12	−0.672
Overheads	−0.06	1.08	−0.065
Net money cash flow for Year 1			+1.056
2 Sales	2	$(1.06)^2$	2.247
Labour	−0.3	$(1.09)^2$	−0.356
Materials	−0.6	$(1.12)^2$	−0.753
Overheads	−0.06	$(1.08)^2$	−0.070
Net money cash flow for Year 2			+1.068
3 Sales	2	$(1.06)^3$	2.382
Labour	−0.3	$(1.09)^3$	−0.389
Materials	−0.6	$(1.12)^3$	−0.843
Overheads	−0.06	$(1.08)^3$	−0.076
Net money cash flow for Year 3			+1.074

Then we discount at the money rate of return (*see* **Exhibit 5.13**).

Exhibit 5.13	Amplify plc: Money cash flows discounted at the money discount rate			

Point in time (yearly intervals)	0 £m	1 £m	2 £m	3 £m
Undiscounted cash flows	−2.4	1.056	1.068	1.074
Discounting calculation	−2.4	$\dfrac{1.056}{1 + 0.1232}$	$\dfrac{1.068}{(1 + 0.1232)^2}$	$\dfrac{1.074}{(1 + 0.1232)^3}$
Discounted cash flows	−2.4	0.9402	0.8466	0.7579

Net present value = +£0.1447 million.

(*An Excel spreadsheet version of the calculation is available at* www.pearsoned.co.uk/arnold.)

This project produces a positive NPV and is therefore to be recommended.

Cash flow in real terms and real discount rate

The second approach is to calculate the net present value by discounting real cash flows by the real discount rate. A real cash flow is obtainable by discounting the money cash flow by the general rate of inflation, thereby converting it to its current purchasing power equivalent.

The general inflation rate is derived from Fisher's equation:

$$(1 + m) = (1 + h) \times (1 + i),$$

where m = money rate of return;
h = real rate of return;
i = inflation rate.

m is given as 0.1232, h as 0.08, i as 0.04.

$$i = \frac{(1 + m)}{(1 + h)} - 1 = \frac{1 + 0.1232}{1 + 0.08} - 1 = 0.04$$

Under this method net present value becomes:

$$NPV = R_0 + \frac{R_1}{1 + h} + \frac{R_2}{(1 + h_2)^2} + \frac{R_3}{(1 + h)^3} + \cdots$$

The net present value is equal to the sum of the real cash flows R_t discounted at a real required rate of return, h.

The first stage is to discount money cash flows by the general inflation rate to establish real cash flows (**Exhibit 5.14**).

The second task is to discount real cash flows at the real discount rate (**Exhibit 5.15**).

Note that the net present value is the same as before. To discount at the general inflation rate, i, followed by discounting at the real rate of return, h, is arithmetically the same as discounting money cash flows at the money rate, m. Often, in practice, to calculate future cash flows the analyst, instead of allowing for specific inflation rates, will make the simplifying assumption that all prices will stay the same, at Time 0's prices and then apply a real discount rate. This could lead to errors if a cost item (e.g. oil) is a major component and is subject to a very high specific inflation. However, in most cases reasonably accurate results can be obtained.

Note in the example of Amplify that the money cash flows are deflated by the general rate of inflation, not by the specific rates. This is because the ultimate beneficiaries of this project are interested in their ability to purchase a basket of goods generally and not their ability to buy any one good, and therefore the link between the real cost of capital and the money cost of capital is the general inflation rate.

Exhibit 5.14	Amplify plc: Discounting money cash flows by the general inflation rate		
Points in time (yearly intervals)	Cash flow £m	Calculation	Real cash flow £m
0	−2.4	–	−2.4
1	1.056	$\dfrac{1.056}{1 + 0.04}$	1.0154
2	1.068	$\dfrac{1.068}{(1 + 0.04)^2}$	0.9874
3	1.074	$\dfrac{1.074}{(1 + 0.04)^3}$	0.9548

▶

Worked example 5.3 *(continued)*

Exhibit 5.15	Amplify plc: Real cash flows discounted at the real discount rate			

Point in time (yearly intervals)	0 £m	1 £m	2 £m	3 £m
Real cash flow	−2.4	1.0154	0.9874	0.9548
Discounting calculation	−2.4	$\dfrac{1.0154}{1 + 0.08}$	$\dfrac{0.9874}{(1 + 0.08)^2}$	$\dfrac{0.9548}{(1 + 0.08)^3}$
Discounted cash flow	−2.4	0.9402	0.8465	0.7580

Net present value = +£0.1447 million.

The two methods for adjusting for inflation produce the same result and therefore it does not matter which method is used. The first method, using money discount rates, has the virtue of requiring only one stage of discounting.

Internal rate of return and inflation

The logic applied to the NPV analysis can be transferred to an internal rate of return approach. That is, two acceptable methods are possible, either:

(a) compare the IRR of the money cash flows with the opportunity cost of capital expressed in money terms; or

(b) compare the IRR of the real cash flows with the opportunity cost of capital expressed in real terms.

A warning

Never do either of the following:

1 Discount money cash flows with the real discount rate. This gives an apparent NPV much larger than the true NPV and so will result in erroneous decisions to accept projects which are not shareholder wealth enhancing.

2 Discount real cash flows with the money discount rate. This will reduce the NPV from its true value which causes the rejection of projects which will be shareholder wealth enhancing.

The treatment of inflation in practice

Exhibit 5.16 shows that UK companies generally either specify cash flow in constant prices and apply a real rate of return or express cash flows in inflated price terms and discount at the market rate of return.

Exhibit 5.16	Inflation adjustment methods used for investment appraisal by UK firms			
	Small %	Medium-sized %	Large %	Composite %
Specify cash flow in constant prices and apply a real rate of return	47	29	45	42
All cash flows expressed in inflated price terms and discounted at the market rate of return	18	42	55	39
Considered at risk analysis or sensitivity stage	21	13	16	17
No adjustment	18	21	3	13
Other	0	0	3	1

Source: Arnold and Hatzopoulos (2000).

Concluding comments

This chapter deals with some of the more technical aspects of project appraisal. These are issues that are of great concern to managers and should never be neglected in an investment evaluation. Serious misunderstanding and poor decision making can result from a failure to consider all relevant information.

Key points and concepts

- **Soft capital rationing** – internal management-imposed limits on investment expenditure despite the availability of positive NPV projects.

- **Hard capital rationing** – externally imposed limits on investment expenditure in the presence of positive NPV projects.

- For **divisible one-period capital rationing problems,** focus on the returns per £ of outlay:

$$\text{Profitability index} = \frac{\text{Gross present value}}{\text{Initial outlay}}$$

$$\text{Benefit–cost ratio} = \frac{\text{Net present value}}{\text{Initial outlay}}$$

- For **indivisible one-period capital rationing problems,** examine all the feasible alternative combinations.

- Two rules for **allowing for taxation** in project appraisal:

  - include incremental tax effects of a project as a cash outflow;
  - get the timing right.

- **Taxable profits are not the same as accounting profits.** For example, depreciation is not allowed for in the taxable profit calculation, but writing-down allowances are permitted.

- **Specific inflation** – price changes of an individual good or service over a period of time.

- **General inflation** – the reduced purchasing power of money.

- General inflation affects the rate of return required on projects:

  - **real rate of return** – the return required in the absence of inflation;
  - **money rate of return** – includes a return to compensate for inflation.

- **Fisher's equation**

  (1 + money rate of return) = (1 + real rate of return) × (1 + anticipated rate of inflation)

  $$(1 + m) = (1 + h) \times (1 + i)$$

- Inflation affects future cash flows:

  - **money cash flows** – all future cash flows are expressed in the prices expected to rule when the cash flow occurs;
  - **real cash flows** – future cash flows are expressed in constant purchasing power.

- **Adjusting for inflation in project appraisal:**

  - Approach 1 – Estimate the cash flows in money terms and use a money discount rate.
  - Approach 2 – Estimate the cash flows in real terms and use a real discount rate.

References and further reading

Arnold, G.C. and Hatzopoulos, P.D. (2000) 'The theory-practice gap in capital budgeting: evidence from the United Kingdom', *Journal of Business Finance and Accounting*, 27(5) and (6), June/July, pp. 603–26.

Empirical evidence on the treatment of inflation.

Bierman, H. and Smidt, S. (2006) *The Capital Budgeting Decision*, 9th edn. London: Routledge.

Some good chapters for the beginner.

Bierman, H. and Smidt, S. (2006) *Advanced Capital Budgeting*. London: Routledge.

Good for the reader who wishes to pursue these topics in more depth.

Coulthurst, N.J. (1986) 'Accounting for inflation in capital investment: state of the art and science', *Accounting and Business Research*, Winter, pp. 33–42.

A clear account of the impact of inflation on project appraisal. Also considers empirical evidence on the adjustments made in practice. Good for the beginner.

Fama, E.F. (1981) 'Stock returns, real activity, inflation and money', *American Economic Review*, 71 (Sept.), pp. 545–64.

On the complex relationship between returns on shares and inflation – high level economics.

Fisher, I. (1930) *The Theory of Interest*. New York: Macmillan.

    Early theory – interest rates and inflation.

Pike, R.H. (1983) 'The capital budgeting behaviour and corporate characteristics of capital-constrained firms',

Journal of Business Finance and Accounting, 10(4), Winter, pp. 663–71.

    Examines real-world evidence on capital rationing and its effects – easy to read.

Case study recommendations

Please see www.pearsoned.co.uk/arnold for case study synopses. Also, there is another list of useful case studies in the fifth edition.

- Finance Simulation: Capital Budgeting
  Author: Timothy A. Luehrman. Harvard Business School. Available at www.cb.hbsp.harvard.edu Capital budgeting; Present value; Project finance; Resource management; Risk

- Electrosteel Castings Ltd
  Authors: Robert Klassen; Nitish Bahl. Ivey Publishing. Available at www.cb.hbsp.harvard.edu

- Whirlpool Europe
  Authors: Richard S. Ruback; Sudhakar Balachandran; Aldo Sesia. Harvard Business School. Available at www.cb.hbsp.harvard.edu

Self-review questions

1 Explain why hard and soft rationing occur.

2 If the general rate of inflation is 5% and the market rate of interest is 9%, what is the real interest rate?

3 Explain the alternative methods of dealing with inflation in project appraisal.

4 Why not simply rank projects on the basis of the highest NPV in conditions of capital rationing?

5 Distinguish between a money cash flow and a real cash flow.

6 How should tax be allowed for in project appraisal?

7 Why is capital rationing impossible in perfect capital markets?

8 What are a balancing charge and a balancing allowance for capital items subject to a writing-down allowance?

9 Describe the two major effects inflation has on the evaluation of investments.

10 Name two great 'don'ts' in inflation adjustment for projects and explain the consequences of ignoring these.

11 What will be the effect of under-allowance for future inflation when using a money discount rate?

Questions and problems

Answers to most questions can be found at www.pearsoned.co.uk/arnold.
Answers to questions marked with an asterisk are to be found only in the Lecturer's Guide.

1 The washer division of Plumber plc is permitted to spend £5m on investment projects at Time 0. The cash flows for five proposed projects are:

	Points in time (yearly intervals)				
	0	*1*	*2*	*3*	*4*
Project	*£m*	*£m*	*£m*	*£m*	*£m*
A	−1.5	0.5	0.5	1.0	1.0
B	−2.0	0	0	0	4.0
C	−1.8	0	0	1.2	1.2
D	−3.0	1.2	1.2	1.2	1.2
E	−0.5	0.3	0.3	0.3	0.3

The cost of capital is 12%, all projects are divisible and none may be repeated. The projects are not mutually exclusive.

a   Which projects should be undertaken to maximise NPV in the presence of the capital constraint?
b   If the division was able to undertake all positive NPV projects, what level of NPV could be achieved?
c   If you now assume that these projects are indivisible, how would you allocate the available £5m?

2   The Telescope Company plc is considering five projects:

Project	Initial outlay	Profitability index
A	6,000	1.2
B	4,000	1.05
C	10,000	1.6
D	8,000	1.4
E	7,000	1.3

Projects C and D are mutually exclusive and the firm has £20,000 available for investment. All projects can only be undertaken once and are divisible. What is the maximum possible NPV?

3   The business insurance premiums of £20,000 for the next year have just been paid. What will these premiums be in three years' time, if the specific rate of inflation for insurance premiums is 8% per annum?
    If the money rate of return is 17% and the general inflation rate is anticipated to average 9% over three years, what is the present value of the insurance premiums payable at Time 3?

4* (*Examination level*) Wishbone plc is considering two mutually exclusive projects. Project X requires an immediate cash outflow of £2.5m and Project Y requires £2m. If there was no inflation then the cash flows for the three-year life of each of the projects would be:

Annual cash flows	Project X		Project Y	
	£	£	£	£
Inflow from sales		2,100,000		1,900,000
Cash outflows:				
Materials	800,000		200,000	
Labour	300,000		700,000	
Overheads	100,000		50,000	
		(1,200,000)		(950,000)
Net cash flow		900,000		950,000

These cash flows can be assumed to arise at the year ends of each of the three years.

Specific annual inflation rates have been estimated for each of the cash flow elements.

Sales	5%
Materials	4%
Labour	10%
Overheads	7%

The money cost of capital is 17% per annum.

a   Use the money cash flows and money cost of capital to calculate the NPV of the two projects and recommend the most appropriate course of action.

b   Now assume that the general inflation rate is anticipated to be 8% per annum. Calculate the real cash flows and the real cost of capital and use these to calculate the NPVs.

(In addition to the solution given in the Lecturer's Guide there is an Excel spreadsheet solution available at www. pearsoned.co.uk/arnold).   ?

5   Hose plc is trying to make a decision on whether to make a commitment of £800,000 now to a project with a life of seven years. At present prices the project will return net cash flows of £150,000 per annum at the year ends. Prices are not expected to remain constant and general inflation is anticipated at 6% per annum. The annual net cash inflows of this project are expected to rise in accordance with general inflation. The money rate of return is 13%. Advise Hose on the viability of this project.   ?

6   A machine costs £10,000 and has a five-year life. By how much can taxable profit be reduced through the writing-down allowance (WDA) in the third year, if the annual WDA is 25% on a declining balance? If the tax rate is 30%, what is the present value of the WDA in Year 4 to the machine's owners?

If the machine has a scrap value of £1,000 after five years, what will be the fifth year's adjustment to the WDA? The required rate of return is 10%.   ?

7* Bedford Onions plc is examining the possibility of purchasing a machine for a new venture. The machine will cost £50,000, have a four-year life and a scrap value of £10,000. An additional investment of £15,000 in working capital will be needed at the outset. This is recoverable at the end of the project. The accountant's figures for the annual trading accounts are as follows:

	£
Sales	100,000
Labour	(20,000)
Materials	(10,000)
Direct overhead	(20,000)
Allocated overhead	(15,000)
Depreciation	(10,000)
Annual profit	25,000

Allocated overhead consists of central administrative costs which are incurred with or without this project. The machine will be eligible for a 25% writing-down allowance (on a declining balance). Tax is payable at 30% in the year of profit creation.

For a project of this risk class a minimum return of 14% is considered acceptable.

Assume no inflation.

Required

Calculate the net present value of this investment.

8* (*Examination level*) Clipper plc is considering five project proposals. They are summarised below:

Project	Initial investment (£000)	Annual revenue (£000)	Annual fixed costs (cash outflows) (£000)	Life of project (years)
A	10	20	5	3
B	30	30	10	5
C	15	18	6	4
D	12	17	8	10
E	18	8	2	15

Variable costs (cash outflows) are 40% of annual revenue. Projects D and E are mutually exclusive. Each project can only be undertaken once and each is divisible.

Assume

– The cash flows are confined to within the lifetime of each project.
– The cost of capital is 10%.
– No inflation.
– No tax.
– All cash flows occur on anniversary dates.

If the firm has a limit of £40,000 for investment in projects at Time 0, what is the optimal allocation of this sum among these projects, and what is the maximum net present value obtainable?   **?**

9 (*Examination level*)

a   Oppton plc's managers are ambitious and wish to expand their range of activities. They have produced a report for the parent company's board of directors detailing five projects requiring large initial investments. After reading the report the main board directors say that they have a policy of permitting subsidiary managers to select investment projects without head office interference. However, they do set a limit on the amount spent in any one period. In the case of Oppton this limit is to be £110,000 at Time 0 for these projects, which if accepted will commence immediately. The five projects are not mutually exclusive (that is, taking on one does not exclude the possibility of taking on another), each one can only be undertaken once and they are all divisible.

The cash flow details are as follows:

	Point in time (yearly intervals)				
	0 (£000)	1 (£000)	2 (£000)	3 (£000)	4 (£000)
Project 1	−35	0	60	0	0
Project 2	−50	30	30	30	0
Project 3	−20	10	10	10	10
Project 4	−30	15	15	15	15
Project 5	−60	70	0	0	0

None of the projects lasts more than four years and cash flows are confined to within the four-year horizon.

Assume

– The cost of capital is 10%.
– No inflation.
– No tax.
– All cash flows occur on anniversary dates.

What is the optimal allocation of the £110,000 and the resulting net present value?

b   Distinguish between 'soft' and 'hard' capital rationing and explain why these forms of rationing occur.

10   Cartma plc's superb strategic planning group have identified five projects they judge to be shareholder wealth enhancing, and therefore feel that the firm should make these investment commitments.

The strategic planning group are keen on getting approval for the release of £42m to invest in all these projects. However, Cartma is a subsidiary of PQT and the holding company board has placed limits on the amount of funds available in any one year for major capital projects for each of its subsidiaries. They were prompted to do this by the poor response of debt holders to a recent capital raising exercise due to the already high borrowing levels. Also they feel a need to counteract the excessive enthusiasm in subsidiary strategic planning groups which could lead to over-rapid expansion if all positive NPV projects are accepted, placing a strain on management talent. The limit that has been imposed on Cartma for the forthcoming year is £38m.

The figures are:

Point in time (yearly intervals)	0 £m	1 £m	2 £m	3 £m	4 £m	5 £m	NPV
Project A							
Cash flow	−10	0	0	+20	0	0	
Discounted cash flows	−10	0	0	$20/(1.1)^3$	0	0	+5
Project B							
Cash flow	−15	5	5	5	5	5	
Discounted cash flow	−15	5 × Annuity factor for 5 years @ 10%					
	−15	+5 × 3.7908					+3.95
Project C							
Cash flow	−8	1	12	0	0	0	
Discounted cash flows	−8	1/1.1	$12/(1.1)^2$	0	0	0	+2.83
Project D							
Cash flow	−5	2	2	2	2	2	
Discounted cash flow	−5	2 × Annuity factor for 5 years @ 10%					
	−5	+2 × 3.7908					+2.58
Project E							
Cash flow	−4	0	0	3	3	3	
Discounted cash flow	−4	(3 × Annuity factor for 3 years @10%)/(1.1)²					
	−4	0	0	$\dfrac{3 \times 2.4869}{(1.1)^2}$			+2.17

Assume
–   No inflation or tax.
–   The rate of return required on projects of this risk class is 10%.
–   All project cash flows are confined within the five-year period.
–   All projects are divisible (a fraction of the project can be undertaken), and none can be undertaken more than once.

What is the maximum NPV available if projects are selected on the basis of NPV alone?

Now calculate profitability indices (or benefit–cost ratios) for each project and calculate the maximum potential NPV if the £38m limit is adhered to.

Assignments

1   Investigate the capital rationing constraints placed on a firm you are familiar with. Are these primarily soft or hard forms of rationing? Are they justified? What are the economic costs of this rationing? What actions do you suggest to circumvent irrational constraints?

2   Write a report on how inflation and tax are allowed for in project appraisal within a firm you know well. To what extent are the rules advocated in this chapter obeyed?

PART 3

Risk and return

CHAPTER

6

Risk and project appraisal

LEARNING OUTCOMES

Incorporating risk into investment appraisal ensures a more realistic and rounded view of a project's prospects and enables more informed decision making. By the end of Chapter 6, the reader should be able to:

- adjust for risk by varying the discount rate;

- present a sensitivity graph and discuss break-even NPV;

- undertake scenario analysis;

- make use of probability analysis to describe the extent of risk facing a project and thus make more enlightened choices;

- explain the nature of real options and the advantage in recognising their value;

- explain the appropriate use of and interpret the results of the four risk techniques described in this chapter;

- discuss the limitations of those four risk techniques.

Case study 6.1 **Camelot**

Camelot bid for, and won, the right to create the UK's national lottery. The company invested in a vast computer network linking 30,000 retail outlets and paid for 300 man years of specialised software development. Camelot also had to train 91,000 staff to operate the system, which can handle over 30,000 transactions a minute and spend large amounts on marketing. This investment was a huge gamble as the owners of Camelot had to persuade the public to participate in this new concept, the National Lottery. Camelot now runs lotteries around the world, and in the UK sold £7.6 billion of tickets in the year ended 31 March 2016 making profits of £97 million. It could have been so different; it could have made a multi-million pound investment followed by public indifference and enormous losses.

Introduction

Businesses operate in an environment of uncertainty. The Camelot example in **Case study 6.1** shows that managers can never be sure about what will happen in the future. There is the upside possibility of events turning out to be better than anticipated and the downside possibility of everything going wrong. Managers in telecommunications companies are currently having to deal with the risks associated with potential investment in 5G (*see* **Exhibit 6.1**).

Exhibit 6.1

Risk for 5G if no standard agreed

by: *Nic Fildes,* **Telecoms Correspondent**

Consumers may have only recently upgraded to the 4G standard on their mobile handsets, but telecoms carriers are already looking ahead to the next wave of wireless development, known as 5G. Many are openly discussing the possibility of rolling out this updated version commercially by 2019.

The telecoms industry is still struggling to define exactly what 5G technology is. The current generation of mobile transmission technology, 4G, has delivered on the promise of turning a mobile phone into a computer. Its predecessor, 3G, offered data services such as video calling. However, it is only since the advent of faster 4G networks that streaming video and live sports to a mobile phone has become a reality. The goal is that 5G should enable better delivery of streaming services and faster download times.

While there is much talk about the need for universal standards for 5G, Europe, the US and South Korea are racing to define the technology in potentially different ways.

All participants in the 5G chain — hardware makers, carriers and businesses developing software to take advantage of the internet of things — want to speed up the process and have formed numerous standards bodies to deliver on one common goal.

The industry is desperate to learn from history. Rolling out 3G was messy and took 10 years because of competition around standards, whereas 4G deployment, with only two variations were used, took place in half the time.

A global 5G event in Rome last November brought together engineers, European commissioners and standards experts to thrash out a plan.

Ryan Ding, executive director and president of products and solutions at Huawei, the Chinese telecoms equipment company, says that 5G "will be the cornerstone of the digital industries, and a global single standard is critical if all things are to be connected".

But there is a high risk of more fragmentation and some companies fear failure that to agree a common path quickly could jeopardise 5G's benefits.

The telecommunications managers cannot know, in advance, the outcome of making these investments. Implementing an investment project requires the decision makers to accept that the managers may have got it wrong; that the project or enterprise may fail. However, to avoid any possibility of failure means 'playing-safe' or 'doing-nothing', which may constitute a worse business sin, that of inertia, which could result in greater failure. There has to be an acceptance of risk and of the potential for getting decisions wrong, but this does not mean that risk cannot by analysed and action taken to minimise its impact.

What is risk?

A key feature of project appraisal is its orientation to the future. Management rarely has precise forecasts regarding the future return to be earned from an investment. The best management can do is to estimate the range of possible future inflows and outflows. There are two types of expectations individuals may have about the future: certainty and uncertainty.

1 *Certainty* Under certainty, future outcomes have only one value. There is not a variety of possible future eventualities – only one will occur. Such situations are rare, but there are some investments which are a reasonable approximation to certainty, for instance lending to a reputable government by purchasing three-month treasury bills. Unless you are very pessimistic and expect catastrophic change over the next three months, such as revolution, war or major earthquake, then you can be certain of receiving your original capital plus interest. Thus, a firm could undertake a project that had almost complete certainty by investing its funds in treasury bills, and receiving a return of, say, 2% per year. Shareholders may not, however, be very pleased with such a low return.

2 *Risk and uncertainty* describes a situation where there is not just one possible outcome, but an array of potential returns. Uncertainty applies in cases when it is not possible to identify all possible outcomes nor to assign probabilities to those outcomes. Risk occurs when specific probabilities can be estimated for the possible outcomes. The range and distribution of these possible outcomes may be estimated on the basis of either objective or subjective probabilities (or a combination of the two). While there is a strict theoretical difference it is usually very difficult to assign probabilities and people tend to use the terms risk and uncertainty interchangeably, which is what we'll do in the subsequent analysis.

Objective probabilities

An objective probability can be established mathematically or from historical data. The mathematical probability of a tossed coin showing a head is 0.5. The probability of taking the Ace of Hearts from a pack of 52 cards is 1/52 equal to 1.9%. A probability of 1 denotes that there is absolute certainty that this outcome will occur. A probability of 0 indicates no likelihood of that outcome. A probability of 0.3 indicates that in three times out of ten this outcome will occur. **The probabilities for all possible outcomes must sum to 1.**

We will now examine an example of an objective probability assessment based on historical data for a supermarket – Safebury's. If the firm is considering a project which is similar to numerous projects undertaken in the past it may be able to obtain probabilities for future outcomes by looking at historic outcomes. For instance, Safebury's is examining the proposal to build and operate a new supermarket in Birmingham. The firm has opened and operated 100 other supermarkets in the past and has observed their actual profitability; it is therefore able to use that historic data to assign realistic probabilities to the range of possible performance outcomes for the supermarket it is proposing to build (*see* **Exhibits 6.2** and **6.3**).

The examination of this sort of historical record is a useful first step in the decision-making process. However, the probabilities may have to be modified to take into account the particular circumstances surrounding the site in Birmingham. Management will use its knowledge and experience to adjust for differences in factors such as demographic trends, road connections and competitor activity which may influence the probabilities for profit or loss of this specific project. Even with large quantities of historical data there is room for subjective assessment in judging the range of possible outcomes.

Exhibit 6.2	Safebury's profitability frequency distribution of existing 100 supermarkets	

Profitability range (£m)	Frequency (Number of stores)	Probability
−30 to −20.01	1	0.01
−20 to −10.01	3	0.03
−10 to −0.01	11	0.11
0 to 9.99	19	0.19
10 to 19.99	30	0.30
20 to 29.99	20	0.20
30 to 39.99	10	0.10
40 to 49.99	6	0.06
TOTAL	100	1.00

Exhibit 6.3	Frequency distribution of supermarket profitability

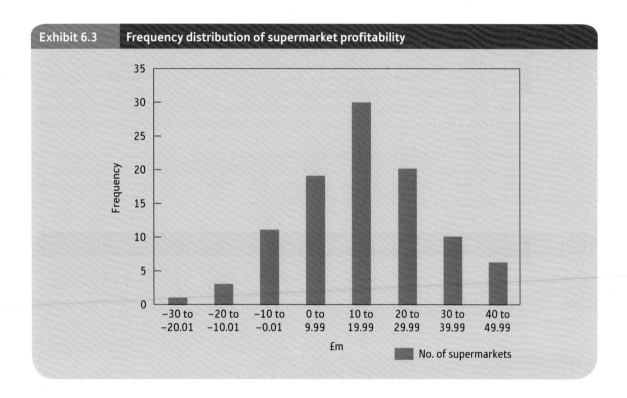

Subjective probabilities

In many project assessments there are no past records to help in the creation of the distribution of probabilities profile. For instance, the product or market may be new. In situations like these, subjective probabilities are likely to dominate. Managers, individually or collectively, use their personal judgement to assign probabilities to a range of outcomes.

The probabilities assigned to particular eventualities are unlikely to be entirely accurate and thus the decision making that follows may be subject to some margin of error. The alternative of merely stating the most likely outcomes could lead to less well-informed decisions and greater errors. For example, a firm might be considering two mutually exclusive projects, A and B (*see* **Exhibit 6.4**). Both projects are expected to be shareholder wealth enhancing, based on the estimate of the most likely outcome. The most likely outcome for A is for it to be shareholder wealth enhancing, with a 95% chance of occurrence. Similarly the most likely outcome for B is a shareholder wealth enhancing return, with a 55% chance of occurrence.

Exhibit 6.4	Probability outcome for two projects	

Outcome	Project A probability	Project B probability
Shareholder wealth enhancing	0.95	0.55
Not shareholder wealth enhancing	0.05	0.45

By using probabilities, a more informed decision is made. The project appraiser has been forced to consider the degree of confidence in the estimates. It is clear that Project A is unlikely to fail, whereas Project B has a fairly high likelihood of failure.

We will examine the use of probability distribution for considering risk later in the chapter. We now turn to more pragmatic, rule-of-thumb and intuitively easier methods for dealing with project risk.

Adjusting for risk through the discount rate

A traditional and still popular method of allowing for risk in project appraisal is the risk premium approach. The logic behind this is simple: investors require a greater reward for accepting a higher risk, thus the more risky the project the higher the minimum acceptable rate of return. In this approach a risk premium (an additional % return) is added to the risk-free discount rate. (The risk-free rate of return is usually taken from the rate available on government bonds.) The risk-adjusted discount rate is then used to calculate net present value in the normal manner.

An example is provided by Sunflower plc, which adjusts for risk through the discount rate by adding various risk premiums to the risk-free rate depending on whether the proposed project is judged to be low, medium or high risk (*see* **Exhibit 6.5**). This is an easy approach to understand and adopt, which explains its continued popularity.

Exhibit 6.5	Adjusting for risk – Sunflower plc		

Level of risk	Risk-free rate (%)	Risk premium (%)	Risk-adjusted rate (%)
Low	9	+3	12
Medium	9	+6	15
High	9	+10	19

The project currently being considered has the following cash flows:

Point in time (yearly intervals)	t_0	t_1	t_2
Cash flow (£)	−100	55	70

If the project is judged to be low risk, discount at 12%:

$$NPV = -100 + \frac{55}{1 + 0.12} + \frac{70}{(1+0.12)^2} = +£4.91 \text{ Accept.}$$

If the project is judged to be medium risk, discount at 15%:

$$NPV = -100 + \frac{55}{1 + 0.15} + \frac{70}{(1+0.15)^2} = +£0.76 \text{ Accept.}$$

If the project is judged to be high risk, discount at 19%

$$NPV = -100 + \frac{55}{1 + 0.19} + \frac{70}{(1+0.19)^2} = -£4.35 \text{ Reject.}$$

Drawbacks of the risk-adjusted discount rate method

The risk-adjusted discount rate method relies on an assessment of the riskiness of a project. Risk perception and judgement are subjective and susceptible to personal bias. There may also be a high degree of arbitrariness in the selection of risk premiums. In reality, it is extremely difficult to allocate projects to risk classes and identify appropriate risk premiums.

Sensitivity analysis

The net present values calculated in previous chapters gave one solution of the likely future outcome of an investment project, based on specific assumptions. In many business situations it is desirable to generate a more complete and realistic impression of what may happen to NPV (or IRR) in conditions of uncertainty. Net present value calculations rely on the appraiser making assumptions about crucial variables: for example, the sale price of the product, the cost of labour and the amount of initial investment are all set at single values for input into the NPV formula. It will be useful for managers to examine the degree to which the viability of the project, as measured by NPV, changes as the values of these key variables are altered. An interesting question to ask might be: if the sale price was raised by 10%, by how much would NPV increase? In other words, it would be useful to know how sensitive NPV is to changes in component values. Sensitivity analysis is essentially a 'what-if' analysis: for example what if labour costs are 5% lower? Or what if the raw materials double in price? By carrying out a series of calculations it is possible to build up a picture of the nature of the risks facing the project and their impact on project profitability. Sensitivity analysis can identify the extent to which variables may change before a negative NPV is produced.

> Sensitivity analysis **examines the impact of a change in the value of one variable on the project NPV.**

A series of 'what-if' questions are examined in the example of Acmart plc.

Worked example 6.1   **Acmart plc**

Acmart plc has developed a new product line called Marts. The marketing department, in partnership with senior managers from other disciplines, has estimated the likely demand for Marts at 1 million per year, at a price of £1, for the four-year life of the project.

If we can assume perfect certainty about the future then the cash flows associated with Marts are as set out in Exhibit 6.6.

Exhibit 6.6   **Cash flows of Marts**

Initial investment		£800,000
Cash flow per unit		£
Sale price		1.00
Costs		
Labour	0.20	
Materials	0.40	
Relevant overhead	0.10	
		0.70
Cash flow per unit		0.30

▶

Worked example 6.1 *(continued)*

The finance department has estimated that the appropriate required rate of return on a project of this risk class is 15%. It has also calculated the expected net present value.

Annual cash flow = 30p × 1,000,000 = £300,000.
Present value of annual cash flows   = 300,000 × annuity factor for 4 years @ 15%

		£
= 300,000 × 2.855	=	856,500
Less initial investment		− 800,000
Net present value		+ 56,500

The finance department is aware that when the proposal is placed before the capital investment committee it will want to know how the project NPV changes if certain key assumptions are altered. As part of the report the finance team asks some 'what-if' questions and draws a sensitivity graph.

- What if the price achieved is only 95p (5% below the expected £1) for sales of 1m units (all other factors remaining constant)?

  Annual cash flow = 25p × 1m = £250,000.

	£
250,000 × 2.855	713,750
Less initial investment	800,000
Net present value	−86,250

- What if the price rose by 1%?

  Annual cash flow = 31p × 1m = £310,000.

	£
310,000 × 2.855	885,050
Less initial investment	800,000
Net present value	+85,050

- What if the quantity demanded is 5% more than anticipated?

  Annual cash flow = 30p × 1.05m = £315,000.

	£
315,000 × 2.855	899,325
Less initial investment	800,000
Net present value	+99,325

- What if the quantity demanded is 10% less than expected?

  Annual cash flow = 30p × 900,000 = £270,000.

	£
270,000 × 2.855	770,850
Less initial investment	800,000
Net present value	−29,150

- What if the appropriate discount rate is 20% higher than originally assumed (that is, it is 18% rather than 15%)?

  Annual cash flows = 300,000 × annuity factor for 4 years @ 18%.

	£
300,000 × 2.6901	807,030
Less initial investment	800,000
	+7,030

● What if the discount rate is 10% lower than assumed (that is, it becomes 13.5%)?

300,000 × annuity factor for 4 years @ 13.5%.

	£
300,000 × 2.9438	883,140
Less initial investment	800,000
	+83,140

Exhibit 6.7   Sensitivity graph for Marts

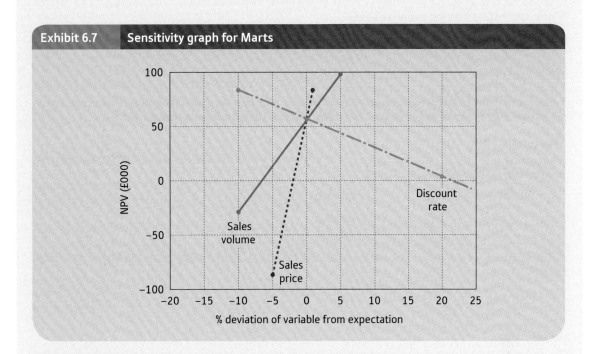

These findings can be summarised more clearly in a sensitivity graph (see **Exhibit 6.7**).

The sensitivity graph in Exhibit 6.7 clearly indicates those variables to which NPV is most responsive. This technique can be extended to consider the key factors that might cause a project to become unviable. This allows management to concentrate their attention on these key factors. By examining the probability of events occurring which would alter the most critical variables, management can identify ways of controlling the factors to which NPV is most sensitive. For example, if a small increase in material costs has a large negative impact on NPV, the managers can investigate ways of fixing the price of material inputs.

(An Excel spreadsheet version of the calculations is available at www.pearsoned.co.uk/arnold).

The break-even NPV

The break-even point, where NPV is zero, is a key concern of management. If the NPV is below zero the project is rejected; if it is above zero it is accepted.

The finance team at Acmart can calculate the extent to which the variables can change before the decision to accept switches to a decision to reject. (We will not go through all the possible variables.)

Initial investment

If this rises by £56,500, NPV will be at zero. A percentage increase of:

$$\frac{£56,500}{£800,000} \times 100 = 7.06\%$$

Worked example 6.1 (continued)

Sales price

The cash flow per unit (after costs), c, can fall to 28 pence before break-even is reached:

$$800,000 = c \times 1,000,000 \times 2.855$$

$$c = \frac{800,000}{2.855 \times 1,000,000} = 0.2802$$

If the final net cash inflow can only drop by 2 pence before the NPV becomes zero, then the selling price can decline by only 2 pence (2%) from the original price of £1.

An alternative approach to calculations is to look up the point at which the different lines in the sensitivity graph in Exhibit 6.7 cross with the zero NPV.

Material cost

If the cash flow per unit can fall to 28 pence before break-even is reached, 2 pence can be added to the price of materials before the project produces a negative net present value (assuming all other factors remain constant). In percentage terms, the material cost can rise by 5% ((2 ÷ 40) × 100) before break-even is reached.

Discount rate

One approach is to calculate the annuity factor that will lead to the four annual inflows of £300,000 equalling the initial outflow of £800,000 after discounting.

$$300,000 \times \text{annuity factor} = 800,000$$

$$\text{Annuity factor (four-year annuity)} = \frac{800,000}{300,000} = 2.667$$

The interest rate corresponding to a four-year annuity factor of 2.667 is approximately 18.5%. This is a percentage rise of 23.3%.

$$\frac{18.5 - 15}{15} \times 100 = 23.3$$

Overall

This project is relatively insensitive to a change in the discount rate but highly responsive to a change in the sales price. This observation may lead the managers to request further work to improve the level of confidence in the sales projections.

Advantages of using sensitivity analysis

Sensitivity analysis (SA) has the following advantages:

- *Information for decision making* SA allows the decision makers to be more informed about project sensitivities, to identify the room they have for judgmental error and to decide whether they are prepared to accept that risk.

- *To direct management effort* SA may indicate where further investigation might be worthwhile. Data collection can be time consuming and expensive; if sensitivity analysis points to some variables being more crucial than others, then search time and money can be concentrated.

- *To make contingency plans* During the implementation phase of the investment process SA can be used to highlight those factors which have the greatest impact on NPV. These factors can be actively monitored for variance from projected values and, if the key parameters differ significantly from the estimates, management can draw on contingency plans to deal with the variations. For example, a project may be highly sensitive to the price of a bought-in component. The management team, having identified this from the sensitivity analysis, prepares contingency plans to buy the component from an alternative supplier or to modify the product so that a substitute component can be used. Which alternative is implemented, if any, will be decided as events unfold.

As the UK entered into Brexit negotiations, many companies made contingency plans to protect their businesses. Beazley, a reinsurance company, made sure it had offices in both Dublin and London, for example – *see* **Exhibit 6.8**.

Exhibit 6.8

Contingency plans

By *Oliver Ralph*, Insurance Correspondent

Beazley will use Ireland as a base to increase European business as it prepares to operate across the region following Britain's decision to leave the EU.

The insurer had moved its domicile from **Dublin to London** this year but retains a presence in the Irish capital, which will give it a base to expand its operations in the EU.

The move comes as other London-based insurers consider post-Brexit options. Although many are hoping that existing "passporting" rights to operate across the EU will be maintained, they are also making contingency plans if this facility is lost for UK-based groups.

Those plans could involve setting up subsidiaries in other parts of the EU, although many insurers are still at the stage of working out which locations would be best.

Beazley said that the results of the referendum vote "will undoubtedly complicate planning for many businesses based in the City of London", although it added that "for Beazley we do not expect the impact to be greatly disruptive".

Drawbacks of sensitivity analysis

Sensitivity analysis identifies the key factors which, if they change, significantly impact the outcome. However it does not discuss the likelihood of these changes occurring. The absence of any assignment of probabilities to the variations of the parameters is a limitation of sensitivity analysis. For Marts, the discount rate can change by 23.3% before break-even NPV is reached, whereas the price can only change by 2%. Thus, at first glance, you could conclude that NPV is more vulnerable to the price changes than to variability in the discount rate. However, if you are then told that the market price for Marts is controlled by government regulations and therefore has a very low probability of changing, whereas the probability of the discount rate rising by more than 23.3% is high, you might change your assessment of the nature of the relative risks. This is another example where following the strict mathematical formula is a poor substitute for judgement. At the decision-making stage the formal sensitivity analysis must be read in the light of subjective or objective probabilities of the parameter changing.

The second major criticism of sensitivity analysis is that each variable is changed in isolation while all other factors remain constant. In the real world, a number of factors may change simultaneously. For example, if inflation is higher, both anticipated selling prices and input prices are likely to be raised. The next section presents a partial solution to this problem.

Scenario analysis

With sensitivity analysis we change one variable at a time and look at the result. Managers may be especially concerned about situations where a number of factors change. They are often interested in establishing a worst-case and a best-case scenario. That is, if all the initial assumptions turned out to be optimistic, what might the resultant NPV be? And what would be the result if matters went extremely well on all fronts?

Exhibit 6.9 describes only a worst-case and a best-case scenario for Marts but management may like to try alternative scenarios.

Exhibit 6.9	Acmart plc: Project proposal for the production of Marts – worst-case and best-case scenarios

Worst-case scenario

Sales	900,000 units
Price	90p
Initial investment	£850,000
Project life	3 years
Discount rate	17%
Labour costs	22p
Material costs	45p
Overhead	11p

Cash flow per unit		£
Sale price		0.90
Costs		
Labour	0.22	
Material	0.45	
Overhead	0.11	
		0.78
Cash flow per unit		0.12

Annual cash flow = 0.12 × 900,000 = £108,000

	£
Present value of cash flows 108,000 × 2.2096 =	238,637
Less initial investment	−850,000
Net present value	−611,363

Best-case scenario

Sales	1,200,000 units
Price	120p
Initial investment	£770,000
Project life	4 years
Discount rate	14%
Labour costs	19p
Material costs	38p
Overhead	9p

Cash flow per unit		£
Sale price		1.20
Costs		
Labour	0.19	
Material	0.38	
Overhead	0.09	
		0.66
Cash flow per unit		0.54

Annual cash flow = 0.54 × 1,200,000 = £648,000

	£
Present value of cash flows 648,000 × 2.9137 =	1,888,078
Less initial investment	−770,000
Net present value	1,118,078

Having carried out sensitivity, break-even NPV and scenario analysis the management team has a more complete picture of the project. It then needs to apply the vital element of judgement to make a sound decision.

Probability analysis

A further technique to assist the evaluation of the risk associated with a project is probability analysis. If management has obtained, through a mixture of objective and subjective methods, the probabilities of various outcomes this will help them to decide whether or not to go ahead with a project. We will look at this sort of decision making for the firm Pentagon plc, a firm trying to decide between five mutually exclusive one-year projects (*see* **Exhibit 6.10**).

Exhibit 6.10	Pentagon plc: Use of probability analysis	
	Return	**Probability of return occurring**
Project 1	16	1.0
Project 2	20	1.0
Project 3	−16	0.25
	36	0.50
	48	0.25
Project 4	−8	0.25
	16	0.50
	24	0.25
Project 5	−40	0.10
	0	0.60
	100	0.30

Projects 1 and 2 represent perfectly certain outcomes. For both projects the chance of not receiving the returns is so small as to be regarded as zero. These projects carry no risk. However, Project 2 has a higher return for the same level of risk and is therefore the obvious preferred choice. (These projects, with different returns for zero risk, only exist in an inefficient market environment. Normally you should find increased return is only available for accepting increased risk; market efficiency is discussed in Chapter 13.)

In comparing Project 2 with Projects 3, 4 and 5 we have a problem: which of the possible outcomes should we compare with Project 2's outcome of 20? Take Project 3 as an example. If the outcome is −16 then clearly Project 2 is preferred. However, if the outcome is 36, or even better, 48, then Project 3 is preferred to Project 2.

Expected return

A tool that will help Pentagon choose between these projects is the expected return.

The expected return is the mean or average outcome calculated by weighting each of the possible outcomes by the probability of occurrence and then summing the result (*see* **Exhibit 6.11**).

Algebraically:

$$\bar{x} = x_1 p_1 + x_2 p_2 + \cdots x_n p_n$$

Exhibit 6.11   Pentagon plc: Expected returns

Pentagon plc	Expected returns	
Project 1	16×1	16
Project 2	20×1	20
Project 3	$-16 \times 0.25 = -4$	
	$36 \times 0.50 = 18$	
	$48 \times 0.25 = \underline{12}$	
		26
Project 4	$-8 \times 0.25 = -2$	
	$16 \times 0.50 = 8$	
	$24 \times 0.25 = \underline{6}$	
		12
Project 5	$-40 \times 0.1 = -4$	
	$0 \times 0.6 = 0$	
	$100 \times 0.3 = \underline{30}$	
		26

or

$$\overline{x} = \sum_{i=1}^{i=n} (x_i p_i)$$

where $\overline{x}$ = the expected return

i = each of the possible outcomes (outcome 1 to outcome n)

p = probability of outcome i occurring

n = the number of possible outcomes

$\sum_{i=1}^{i=n}$ means add together the results for each of the possible outcomes i from the first to the nth outcome.

The preparation of probability distributions gives the management team some impression of likely outcomes. The additional calculation of expected returns adds a further dimension to the informed vision of the decision maker. Looking at expected returns is more enlightening than simply examining the single most likely outcome. For project 3, the most likely outcome of 36 is significantly different from the expected return of 26. For Project 5 the most likely outcome of 0 is not very informative and does not take into account the range of potential outcomes.

It is important to appreciate what these statistics are telling you. The expected return represents the outcome expected if the project is undertaken many times. If Project 4 was undertaken 1,000 times then on average the return would be 12. If the project was undertaken only once, as is the case in most business situations, there would be no guarantee that the actual outcome would equal the expected outcome. This is a significant limitation when you are evaluating one-off projects such as investments using probability analysis.

The projects with the highest expected returns turn out to be Projects 3 and 5, each with an expected return of 26. However, we cannot get any further in our decision making by using just the expected return formula. This is because the formula fails to take account of risk. **Risk is concerned with the likelihood that the actual performance might diverge from what is expected.** Note that risk in this context has both positive and negative possibilities of diverging from the mean, whereas in everyday speech 'risk' usually has only negative connotations. If we plot the possible outcomes for Projects 3 and 5 against their probabilities of occurrence we get an impression that the outcome of Project 5 is more uncertain than the outcome of Project 3 (see **Exhibit 6.12**). The range of possible outcomes is relatively narrow for Project 3 and therefore presents an impression of lower risk. This is only a general indication. We need a more precise measurement of the dispersion of possible outcomes. This is provided by the standard deviation.

Exhibit 6.12	Pentagon plc: Probability distribution for Projects 3 and 5

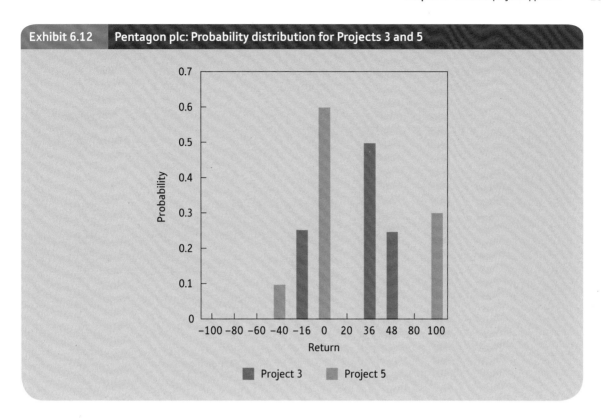

Standard deviation

The standard deviation, σ, is a statistical measure of the dispersion around the expected value. The standard deviation is the square root of the variance, σ^2.

Variance of $x = \sigma_x^2 = (x_1 - \overline{x})^2 p_1 + (x_2 - \overline{x})^2 p_2 + \cdots (x_n - \overline{x})^2 p_n$

or $\quad \sigma_x^2 = \sum_{i=1}^{i=n} \{(x_i - \overline{x})^2 p_i\}$

Standard deviation

$$\sigma_x = \sqrt{\sigma_x^2} \text{ or } \sqrt{\sum_{i=1}^{i=n} \{(x_i - \overline{x})^2 p_i\}}$$

Calculating the variance is straightforward if you take it in stages:

- **Stage 1.** Calculate the deviation of each potential outcome from the expected outcome $(x_i - \overline{x})$. So, in the case of Project 3 the first outcome is -16 (this is our x_i) and the expected outcome $(\overline{x})$ is 26. Subtracting the second number from the first we have -42.

- **Stage 2.** Square the result from Stage 1 for each of the outcomes $(x_i - \overline{x})^2$. So, for the first outcome of Project 3 we take the -42 and multiply it by itself: $-42 \times -42 = 1{,}764$. (We square to remove negative items as we are only interested in the size of the deviation and not whether it is positive or negative.)

- **Stage 3.** Multiply the number generated in Stage 2 by the probability of that outcome occurring. In the case of the first outcome of Project 3 we multiply 1,764 by $0.25 = 441$. That is, $(x_i - \overline{x})^2 p_i$.

- **Stage 4.** Finally, add together the results of all these calculations for that particular project. So, for Project 3 we add 441 to 50 to 121, which gives a variance of 612 (see **Exhibit 6.13**).

Note that the variances are very large numbers compared with the original potential outcomes. For Project 3 the outcomes are -16, 36 and 48 whereas the variance is over 600. This is because the variance measures are in pounds squared or returns squared, etc. Thus, the next stage is to obtain the standard deviation σ, by taking the square root of the variance. (This essentially undoes the squaring

Exhibit 6.13	Pentagon plc: Calculating the standard deviations for the five projects					
	Outcome (return)	Probability	Expected return	Deviation	Deviation squared	Deviation squared times probability
Project	x_i	p_i	$\bar{x}$	$x_i - \bar{x}$	$(x_i - \bar{x})^2$	$(x_i - \bar{x})^2 p_i$
1	16	1.0	16	0	0	0
2	20	1.0	20	0	0	0
3	−16	0.25	26	−42	1,764	441
	36	0.5	26	10	100	50
	48	0.25	26	22	484	121
					Variance =	612
					Standard deviation =	24.7
4	−8	0.25	12	−20	400	100
	16	0.5	12	4	16	8
	24	0.25	12	12	144	36
					Variance =	144
					Standard deviation =	12
5	−40	0.1	26	−66	4,356	436
	0	0.6	26	−26	676	406
	100	0.3	26	74	5,476	1,643
					Variance =	2,485
					Standard deviation =	49.8

(An Excel spreadsheet version of these calculations is available at www.pearson.co.uk/arnold).

that we carried out in Stage 2.) The standard deviation measures variability around the expected value in straightforward pound or return terms. The standard deviation provides a common yardstick to use when comparing the dispersions of possible outcomes for a number of projects. The more widely dispersed the outcomes, the greater the standard deviation; the greater the variation in possible outcomes, the greater the risk. For Project 3, the standard deviation is $\sqrt{612} = 24.7$.

If we now put together the two sets of measurements about the five projects, as shown in **Exhibit 6.14**, we might be able to make a decision on which one should be selected.

Exhibit 6.14	Pentagon plc: Expected return and standard deviation	
	Expected return $\bar{x}$	Standard deviation σ_x
Project 1	16	0
Project 2	20	0
Project 3	26	24.7
Project 4	12	12
Project 5	26	49.8

Project 1 would not, presumably, be chosen by anyone, because Project 2 offers a better return for the same level of risk. Also, Project 4 is obviously inferior to Project 2 because it has both a lower expected return and a higher standard deviation. That leaves us with Projects 2, 3 and 5. To choose between these we need to introduce a little utility theory in order to appreciate the significance of the standard deviation figures.

Risk and utility

Utility theory recognises that money in itself is unimportant to human beings. What is important is the well-being, satisfaction or utility to be derived from money. For most people a doubling of annual income will not double annual well-being. Money is used to buy goods and services. The first £8,000 of income will buy the most essential items – food, clothing, shelter, etc. Thus an individual going from an income of zero to one of £8,000 will experience a large increase in utility. If income is increased by a further £8,000 then utility will increase again, but the size of the increase will be less than for this first £8,000, because the goods and services bought with the second £8,000 provide less additional satisfaction. If the process of adding incremental amounts to annual income is continued then, when the individual has an income of, say, £150,000, the additional utility derived from a further £8,000 becomes very small. For most people the additional utility from consumption diminishes as consumption increases. This is the concept of diminishing marginal utility. Now consider the case of an individual who must choose between two alternative investments, A and B (*see* **Exhibit 6.15**).

Exhibit 6.15	Returns and utility				
		Investment A		**Investment B**	
	Return	**Probability**		**Return**	**Probability**
Poor economic conditions	2,000	0.5		0	0.5
Good economic conditions	6,000	0.5		8,000	0.5
Expected return		4,000			4,000

Both investments give an expected return of £4,000, but the outcomes of B are more widely dispersed. In other words, Investment B is more risky than Investment A. Suppose the individual has invested in A but is considering shifting all her money to B. As a result, in a poor year she will receive £2,000 less on Investment B than she would have received if she had stayed with A. In a good year Investment B will provide £2,000 more than if she had left her money in A. So the question is: is it worthwhile to shift from Investment A to Investment B? The answer hinges on the concept of diminishing marginal utility. While Investments A and B have the same expected returns they have different utilities. The extra utility associated with B in a good year is small compared with the loss of utility in a bad year when returns fall by an extra £2,000. Investment A is preferred because utility is higher for the first £2,000 of return than for the last £2,000 of return (increasing return from £6,000 to £8,000 by switching from A to B). Investors whose preferences are characterised by diminishing marginal utility are called risk averters.

A *risk averter* prefers a more certain return to an alternative with an equal but more risky expected outcome. The alternative to being a risk averter is to be a risk seeker. These investors have a preference rather than an aversion for risk. They are prepared to accept high uncertainty or volatility in the expectation of higher returns. For these people the marginal utility of each £ increases.

It is usually assumed that shareholders are risk averters. (However, some are less risk averse than others. Don't confuse this lower aversion with risk seeking.) When a risk averter is faced with two investments, each with the same expected return, he/she will select the one with the lower standard deviation or variance. This brings us to the mean-variance rule.

Mean-variance rule

Project X will be preferred to Project Y if at least one of the following conditions apply:

1   The expected return of X is at least equal to the expected return of Y, and the variance is less than that of Y.

2   The expected return of X exceeds that of Y and the variance is equal to or less than that of Y.

So, returning to Pentagon plc, we can see from **Exhibit 6.16** that Project 5 can be eliminated from any further consideration using the mean-variance rule because it has the same expected return as Project 3 but a wider dispersion of possible outcomes.

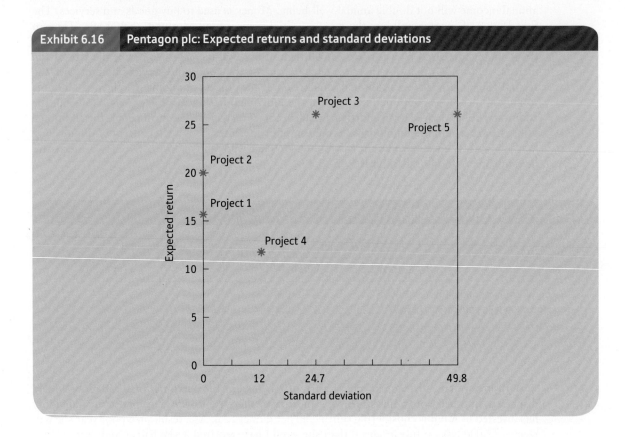

Exhibit 6.16	Pentagon plc: Expected returns and standard deviations

Projects 1, 4 and 5 are recognisably inferior, leaving a choice between Projects 2 and 3. From this point on there is no simple answer. The solution depends on the risk-return utility attitude of the decision maker. This is fundamentally a matter for subjective judgement and different management teams will make different choices. When the author has put the choice between Projects 2 and 3 to MBA classes of middle and senior managers approximately one-half take the safe option of Project 2. However, others in the class say that, for the sake of a little more risk, Project 3 gives a significantly higher return and so should be accepted. The board of directors of Pentagon needs to weigh up the risk preferences of the owners of the company and choose one project or the other. In doing so they may consider how this new project fits with the rest of the company's projects. If the firm already has other projects (operations, strategic business units, product lines, etc.) and many of these projects tend to do well in circumstances when Project 3 does badly, and vice versa, the benefits of diversification may incline them to accept this investment.

Another factor in the decision equation is that variability (standard deviation) may not be a worry if the project forms a small part of the firm's assets. If, however, choosing either Project 2 or Project 3 would entail the commitment of most of the company's assets the directors may take the safer option.

Expected net present values and standard deviation

In the example of Pentagon plc we have simply taken the potential returns of the projects as given. Now we will look at a project under circumstances of risk when you are not handed the *returns*, but have to calculate the NPV and the standard deviation of NPV using the cash flows associated with the investment. In addition, these cash flows will occur over a number of years and so the analysis becomes both more sophisticated and more challenging. First, the notation of the statistical formulae needs to be changed.

The expected net present value is:

$$\overline{NPV} = \sum_{i=1}^{i=n} (NPV_i p_i)$$

where

$\overline{NPV}$ = expected net present value

NPV_i = the NPV if outcome i occurs

p_i = probability of outcome i occurring

n = number of possible outcomes

$\sum_{i=1}^{i=n}$ = means add together the results of all the $NPV \times p$ calculations for each outcome i from the first to the nth outcome

The standard deviation of the net present value is:

$$\sigma_{NPV} = \sqrt{\sum_{i=1}^{i=n} \{(NPV_i - \overline{NPV})^2 \, p_i\}}$$

This more realistic application of probability analysis will be illustrated through the example of Horizon plc, which buys old pubs and invests in refurbishment and marketing. It then sells the pubs at the end of two years in what the firm hopes is a transformed and thriving state. The management are considering buying one of the pubs close to a university campus. The purchase of the freehold will cost, at Time 0, £500,000. The cost of refurbishment of £200,000 will be paid at the outset to the shop-fitting firm which Horizon always uses (in order to obtain a discount).

Purchase price, t_0	£500,000
Refurbishment, t_0	£200,000
	£700,000

Experience has taught the management team of Horizon that pub retailing is a very unpredictable business. Customers are fickle and the slightest change in fashion or trend can cause the level of customers to drop dramatically. Through a mixture of objective historical data analysis and subjective 'expert' judgement the managers have concluded that there is a 60% probability that the pub will become popular. There is a 40% chance that potential customers will not switch to this revamped hostelry within the first year.

The Year 1 cash flows are as follows:

	Probability	Cash flow at end of Year 1
Good customer response	0.6	£100,000
Poor customer response	0.4	£10,000

Note: For simplicity it is assumed that all cash flows arise at the year ends.

If the response of customers is good in the first year there are three possibilities for the second year:

1   The customer flow will increase further and the pub can be sold at the end of the second year for a large sum. The total of the net operating cash flows for the second year and the sale proceeds will be £2m. This eventuality has a probability of 0.1 or 10%.

2   Customer levels will be the same as in the first year and at the end of the second year the total cash flows will be £1.6m. The probability of this is 0.7 or 70%.

3   Many customers will abandon the pub. This may happen because of competitor action, for example other pubs in the area are relaunched, or perhaps the fashion changes. The result will be that the pub will have a net cash outflow on trading, and will have a much lower selling price. The result will be a cash inflow for the year of only £800,000. This has a 20% chance of occurring.

If, however, the response in the first year is poor then one of two eventualities may occur in the second year:

1   Matters continue to deteriorate and sales fall further. At the end of the second year the cash flows from trading and the sale of the pub total only £700,000. This has a probability of 50%, or a 50:50 chance.

2   In the second year sales rise, resulting in a total t_2 cash flow of £1.2m. Probability: 50%.

The conditional probabilities (conditional on what happens in the first year) for the second year are as follows:

If the first year elicits a *good response* then:

	Probability	Cash flow at end of Year 2
1 Sales increase in second year	0.1	£2m
or		
2 Sales are constant	0.7	£1.6m
or		
3 Sales decrease	0.2	£0.8m

If the first year elicits a *poor response* then:

	Probability	Cash flow at end of Year 2
1 Sales fall further	0.5	£0.7m
or		
2 Sales rise slightly	0.5	£1.2m

Note: All figures include net trading income plus sale of pub.

To be able to calculate the expected return and standard deviation for a project of this nature, we first need to establish the probability of each of the five possible outcomes (**Exhibit 6.17**). The probability that the initial expenditure is followed by a cash inflow of £100,000 after one year, and £2m after two years (outcome *a*) is very low. This is as we might expect given that this is an extreme, positive outcome. The overall probability of this path being followed is the first year's

Exhibit 6.17   An event tree showing the probabilities of the possible returns for Horizon plc

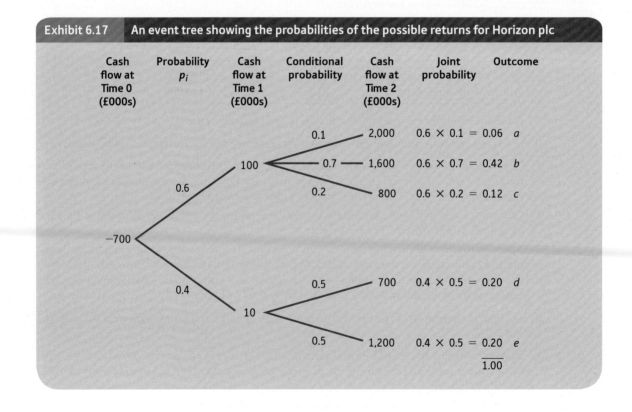

probability (0.6) multiplied by the second year's probability (0.1) to give 0.06 or a 6% chance of occurrence. The most likely outcome is for the first year to be successful (£100,000) followed by a continuation of the same sales level resulting in Year 2 cash flow of £1.6m (outcome *b*) with a probability of 42%.

The second stage is to calculate the expected return making use of the probabilities calculated in Exhibit 6.17 (*see* **Exhibit 6.18**). Then the standard deviation for this pub project can be calculated (*see* **Exhibit 6.19**).

Exhibit 6.18   Expected net present value, Horizon plc

Outcome							Net present values (£000s)	NPV × Probability	
a	−700	+	$\dfrac{100}{1.1}$	+	$\dfrac{2,000}{(1.1)^2}$	= 1,044		1,044 × 0.06 =	63
b	−700	+	$\dfrac{100}{1.1}$	+	$\dfrac{1,600}{(1.1)^2}$	= 713		713 × 0.42 =	300
c	−700	+	$\dfrac{100}{1.1}$	+	$\dfrac{800}{(1.1)^2}$	= 52		52 × 0.12 =	6
d	−700	+	$\dfrac{10}{1.1}$	+	$\dfrac{700}{(1.1)^2}$	= −112		−112 × 0.20 =	−22
e	−700	+	$\dfrac{10}{1.1}$	+	$\dfrac{1,200}{(1.1)^2}$	= 301		301 × 0.20 =	60
Expected net present value (£000)									407

Note: Assuming a 10% opportunity cost of capital.

Exhibit 6.19   Standard deviation for Horizon plc

Outcome £000s	Probability	Expected NPV	Deviation	Deviation squared	Deviation squared times probability
NPV_i	p_i	$\overline{NPV}$	$NPV_i - \overline{NPV}$	$(NPV_i - \overline{NPV})^2$	$(NPV_i - \overline{NPV})^2$
a	1,044	0.06	407	637	405,769	24,346
b	713	0.42	407	306	93,636	39,327
c	52	0.12	407	−355	126,025	15,123
d	−112	0.20	407	−519	269,361	53,872
e	301	0.20	407	−106	11,236	2,247
					Variance =	134,915
				Standard deviation =	$\sqrt{134,915}$ =	367
					or	£367,308

(An Excel spreadsheet version of all the calculations for Horizon is available at www.pearson.co.uk/arnold).

Now that the management team has calculated an expected NPV of £407,000 and a standard deviation of £367,000 it is in a position to make a more informed decision. The probability analysis can be taken on to further stages; for example, an additional dimension that may affect the management team's judgement of the worth of the project is the probability of certain extreme eventualities occurring, such as the project outcome being so bad as to lead to the insolvency of the company. This technique is described later. First, we broaden the application of probability analysis.

Independent probabilities

In the case of Horizon the possible outcomes in the second year depend upon what happens in the first year. That is, they are conditional probabilities. We now turn to a case where the second year's outcomes are independent of what happens in the first year, and therefore there can be any combination of first and second year outcomes (*see* **Exhibit 6.20**).

Exhibit 6.20	Independent probabilities		

Year 1		Year 2	
Cash flow (£000s)	Probability	Cash flow (£000s)	Probability
100	0.2	50	0.6
150	0.7	160	0.4
180	0.1		

The six possible overall outcomes are (£000s):

- 100 + 50
- 100 + 160
- 150 + 50
- 150 + 160
- 180 + 50
- 180 + 160

The initial cash outflow is £150,000. One method of calculating the expected NPV is to first calculate the expected cash flow in each year (*see* **Exhibit 6.21**).

Exhibit 6.21	Expected cash flow for each year		

Year 1

Cash flow (£000s)	Probability	Cash flow × probability (£000s)
100	0.2	20
150	0.7	105
180	0.1	18
		143

Year 2

Cash flow (£000s)	Probability	Cash flow × probability (£000s)
50	0.6	30
160	0.4	64
		94

Note: The discount rate is 10%.

The expected NPV is given by:

$$-150 + \frac{143}{1.1} + \frac{94}{(1.1)^2} = +57.69 \text{ or } £57,690$$

Expected NPV and standard deviation can be computed in one table as shown in **Exhibit 6.22**.

Exhibit 6.22		Expected NPV and standard deviation				
Cash flow (£000s)		**Probability**	**NPV**	**NPV $\times p_i$**	**Expected**	**$(NPV_i - \overline{NPV})^2 p_i$**
Year 1	**Year 2**	**p_i**			**NPV**	
100	50	$0.2 \times 0.6 = 0.12$	−17.77	−2.13	57.69	683.31
100	160	$0.2 \times 0.4 = 0.08$	73.14	5.85	57.69	19.10
150	50	$0.7 \times 0.6 = 0.42$	27.69	11.63	57.69	378.00
150	160	$0.7 \times 0.4 = 0.28$	118.59	33.21	57.69	1,038.47
180	50	$0.1 \times 0.6 = 0.06$	54.96	3.30	57.69	0.45
180	160	$0.1 \times 0.4 = 0.04$	145.87	5.83	57.69	311.03
		1.00	Expected NPV 57.69			

Variance $\sigma^2 = 2,430.36$

Standard deviation $\sigma = 49.3$

This project has an expected outcome of £57,690 but a fairly high standard deviation of £49,300. This means that there is a distinct possibility of the outcome being significantly under £57,690, at say £27,690, or £17,690, or even −£1,090. On the other hand, there are similar chances of obtaining £87,690, or £97,690, or even £116,470. To put more precise probability estimates on particular outcomes occurring we need to understand the Z statistic which will be explained by using it to tackle the probability of a project leading to insolvency.

The risk of insolvency

On occasions a project may be so large relative to the size of the firm that if the worst-case scenario occurred the firm would be made bankrupt. Managers need to know the probability that a project will have a sufficiently poor outcome as to threaten the survival of the company. We can estimate this probability if we know the shape of the probability distribution. We usually assume that the probability distribution of a project's potential return is 'normal, bell-shaped' (*see* **Exhibit 6.23**).

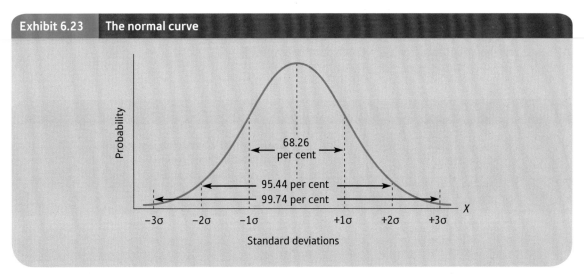

Exhibit 6.23   The normal curve

In a normal distribution, the distribution of possible outcomes is symmetrical about the expected return μ. The probability of an outcome, X, occurring between the expected return and one standard deviation away from the expected return in either a positive or negative direction is, in a normal distribution, 68.26%. The probability that the outcome lies between the expected return and +1 standard deviation is 34.13% (one half of 68.26%). That is, the chance of the outcome landing in the shaded area of **Exhibit 6.24** is 34.13%.

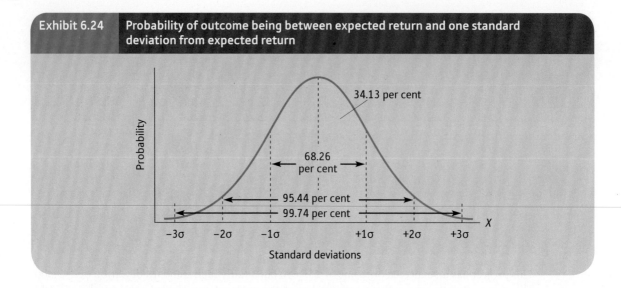

Exhibit 6.24   **Probability of outcome being between expected return and one standard deviation from expected return**

The probability of the outcome being within two standard deviations (positive or negative) of the expected return is 95.44%. The probability of being within +2 standard deviations of the expected return or −2 standard deviations of the expected return is 47.72% (one-half of 95.44%). To find the probability that the outcome will be between two particular values we first need to obtain the Z statistic. This simply shows the number of standard deviations from the expected return to the value that interests you.

$$Z = \frac{X - \mu}{\sigma}$$

where   Z   is the number of standard deviations from the mean
         X   is the outcome that you are concerned about
         μ is the mean of the possible outcomes
         σ is the standard deviation of the outcome distribution

We also need to use the standard normal distribution table. This is in Appendix V at the end of the book but an extract is presented in **Exhibit 6.25**.

Exhibit 6.25   **The standard normal distribution**

Value of the Z statistic	Probability that X lies within Z standard deviations above (or below) the expected value (%)
0.0	0.00
0.2	7.93
0.4	15.54
1.0	34.13
1.2	38.49
1.6	44.52
2.0	47.72
3.0	49.87

The use of the standard normal distribution table will be illustrated by the example of Roulette plc in Worked example 6.2.

Worked example 6.2   Roulette plc

Roulette plc is considering undertaking a large project and if the economy fails to grow there is a risk that the losses on this project will cause the liquidation of the firm. The company can take a maximum loss of £5m (NPV of –£5m) and still keep the rest of the business afloat. But if the loss is more than £5m the firm will become bankrupt. The managers are keen to know the probability that more than £5m will be lost.

The expected NPV has already been calculated at £8m but there is a wide variety of possible outcomes. If the economy booms the firm will make a fortune. If it is reasonably strong it will make a respectable return and if there is zero or negative growth large sums will be lost. These NPVs are judged to be normally distributed, that is, a bell-shaped distribution. The standard deviation is £6.5m.

To calculate the probability of insolvency we first calculate the Z statistic, when the X in which we are interested is at a value of −5.

$$Z = \frac{X - \mu}{\sigma}$$

$$Z = \frac{-5-8}{6.5} = -2$$

The value of −2 means that the distance between the expected outcome and the point of bankruptcy is two standard deviations. From the standardised normal distribution table (Appendix V) we can see that the probability that the return will lie between the mean and two standard deviations below the mean is 47.72% (*see* **Exhibit 6.26**).

Exhibit 6.26   Probability of outcome between μ and 2σ from μ

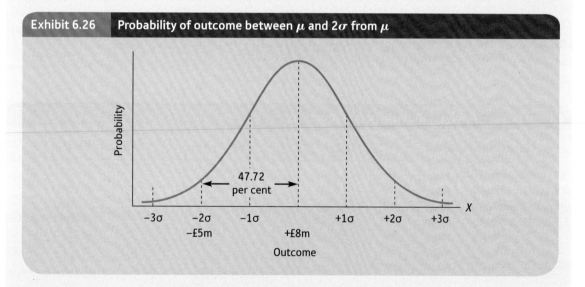

The probability distribution is symmetrical about the mean; therefore, the probability that the return will be above the mean (£8m) is 50%. Thus, the probability of the firm achieving an NPV greater than a loss of £5m is 97.72% (47.72% plus 50%). To make the final decision on whether to proceed with this project we need to consider the owners' and the managers' attitude to this particular level of risk of insolvency. This is likely to vary from one company to another. In some situations shareholders and managers will have well-diversified interests and so are reasonably sanguine about this risk. Other decision makers will not take a 2.28% (100% − 97.72%) chance of insolvency.

Interpreting probability distributions using different discount rates

In calculating NPVs and their standard deviations, two alternative discount rates may be used:

- the risk-free discount rate;

- a risk-adjusted discount rate (that is, with a risk premium added).

Regardless of which of these is used to calculate the probability of certain eventualities through the standard normal distribution, careful interpretation of the results is needed. This is illustrated through the example of Brightlight plc.

Brightlight plc is considering a project with the cash flows shown in **Exhibit 6.27**.

Exhibit 6.27 Brightlight plc: cash flows

Initial outlay 100

Economic conditions	Time (year)		Probability of economic event p_i
	1	2	
Economic boom	130	130	0.15
Good growth	110	110	0.20
Growth	90	90	0.30
Poor growth	70	70	0.20
Recession	50	50	0.15

The risk-free discount rate is 6%. Applying this the project produces an expected NPV of 65 and a standard deviation of 46.4 (*see* **Exhibit 6.28**).

Exhibit 6.28 Applying the risk-free discount rate

Economic conditions	NPV	NPV $\times$ p_i	$(NPV - \overline{NPV})^2 p_i$
Economic boom	138.342	20.7513	806.725
Good growth	101.674	20.3348	268.908
Growth	65.006	19.5018	0.000
Poor growth	28.338	5.6676	268.908
Recession	−8.330	−1.2495	806.725
		Expected NPV = 65.00	Variance = 2,151.27
			Standard deviation = $\sqrt{2,151.27}$ = 46.4

The management team is interested in discovering the probability of the project producing a negative NPV if the risk-free discount rate is used. Thus, in the Z statistic formula, X is set at a value of 0:

$$Z = \frac{X - \mu}{\sigma}$$

$$Z = \frac{0 - 65}{46.4} = -1.4$$

The probability of the outcome giving an NPV of between 0 and +65 is 1.4 standard deviations which, according to Appendix V, gives 0.4192 or 41.92%. Therefore, the probability of a negative NPV (the shaded area in **Exhibit 6.29**) is 8.08% (50% − 41.92%). The interpretation of this result is that there is an 8.08% probability of this project producing a return of *less than the risk-free rate*. The decision now has to be made as to whether this probability is acceptable, given that the rate set is merely the risk-free rate. If a number of mutually exclusive projects were being compared then to be consistent the risk-free rate must be used for all of them.

Exhibit 6.29	Probability distribution for Brightlight (risk-free discount rate)

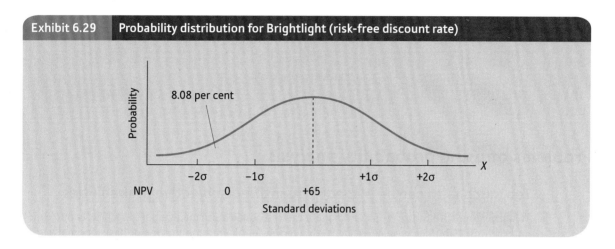

Brightlight also considers this project using a discount rate with a risk premium of 5% added to the risk-free rate, that is, 6 + 5 = 11% (*see* **Exhibit 6.30**).

Exhibit 6.30	Applying a discount rate including a risk premium of 5%

Economic conditions	NPV	NPV $\times$ p_i	$(NPV - \overline{NPV})^2 p_i$
Boom	122.625	18.394	703.8375
Good growth	88.375	17.675	234.6125
Growth	54.125	16.237	0
Poor growth	19.875	3.975	234.6125
Recession	−14.375	−2.156	703.8375

Expected NPV = 54.125   Variance = 1,876.90

Standard deviation = 43.3

The probability of a negative NPV is:

$$Z = \frac{X - \mu}{\sigma}$$

$$Z = \frac{0 - 54.125}{43.30} = -1.25$$

A standard deviation of 1.25 gives a probability of 39.44% of the outcome being between X and μ. Thus the probability of the project producing less than the required return of 11% is 10.56% (50% − 39.44%). Using the risk-adjusted discount rate tells the appraiser that this project is expected to produce a positive NPV of 54.125 when using a discount rate which takes account of risk. Also, if it is decided to implement this project, there is a 10.56% probability of the decision being incorrect, in the sense that the NPV will turn out to be negative and therefore will not be shareholder wealth enhancing (*see* **Exhibit 6.31**).

Exhibit 6.31	Probability distribution for Brightlight risk-adjusted discount rate

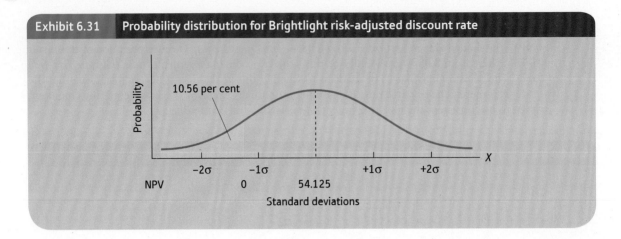

Problems of using probability analysis

Too much faith can be placed in quantified subjective probabilities

When dealing with future events, managers can only make informed guesses as to likely outcomes and their probabilities of occurrence. A danger lies in placing too much emphasis on analysis of these subjective estimates once they are converted to numerical form. It is all too easy to carry out detailed computations with accuracy to the nth degree, forgetting that the fundamental data usually have a small objective base. Again, mathematical purity is no substitute for thoughtful judgement.

The alternative to the assignment of probabilities, that of using only the most likely outcome estimates in the decision-making process, is more restricted in vision and equally subjective. At least probability analysis forces the decision maker to explicitly recognise a range of outcomes and the basis on which they are estimated, and to express the degree of confidence in those estimates.

Too complicated

Investment decision making and subsequent implementation often require the understanding and commitment of large numbers of individuals. It may be difficult to communicate the results of probability analysis if important employees do not understand what the numbers mean and there may be a need for education combined with good presentation.

Projects may be viewed in isolation

A project should never be viewed in isolation. The context of the firm is an important variable, determining whether a single project is too risky to accept. A firm with a large base of stable low-risk activities may be willing to accept a high-risk project because the overall profits might be very large and, even if the worst happened, the firm will survive. On the other hand a small firm that already has one risky activity may only accept further proposals if they are low risk.

The other aspect to consider is the extent to which a project increases or reduces the overall risk of the firm. This is based on the degree of negative covariance of project returns, an aspect of portfolio theory which is discussed in the next chapter.

Despite these drawbacks, probability analysis has an important advantage over scenario analysis. In scenario analysis the focus is on a few highly probable scenarios. In probability analysis consideration must be given to all possible outcomes (or at least an approximation of all outcomes) so that probabilities sum to one. This forces a more thorough consideration of the risks of the project.

Evidence of risk analysis in practice

Exhibit 6.32 summarises the risk analysis techniques used by UK firms.

Exhibit 6.32	Risk analysis techniques used in UK firms				
	Arnold and Hatzopoulos				**Alkaraan and Northcott**
	Small %	**Medium** %	**Large** %	**Total** %	%
Sensitivity/Scenario analysis	82	83	89	85	89
Reduced payback period	15	42	11	20	75
Risk-adjusted discount rate	42	71	50	52	82
Probability analysis	27	21	42	31	77
Beta analysis	3	0	5	3	43
Subjective assessment	44	33	55	46	–

Sources: Arnold and Hatzopoulos (2000) sample of 96 firms: 34 small, 24 medium, 38 large. Survey date July 1997. Alkaraan and Northcott (2006): 83 large companies returned questionnaires in 2002.

UK firms have increased the extent of risk analysis in project appraisal over the past 30 years (evident from surveys conducted by Pike (1988, 1996) and Ho and Pike (1991)). This trend has been encouraged by a greater awareness of the techniques and aided by the availability of computing software. Sensitivity and scenario analysis remain the most widely adopted approaches. Probability analysis is now used more widely but few smaller firms use it on a regular basis. Beta analysis, based on the capital-asset pricing model (discussed in Chapter 8) is rarely used. Simple, rule-of-thumb approaches have not been replaced by the more complex methods. Firms tend to be pragmatic and to use a multiplicity of techniques in a complementary fashion.

Real options (managerial options)

Traditional project appraisal, based on the calculation of NPV, implicitly assumes that the investment being analysed is a straightforward now or never decision; that you either accept the project in its entirety at the outset or forget about the whole idea. So, if a company is considering a project with cash flow spread over, say, eight years it would estimate the expected cash flows and discount all eight of them (usually following a probability analysis to allow for uncertainty). Under this view of decision making there is only the initial decision to accept or reject; and if accepted the project continues for the full term analysed (say, eight years).

Some business decisions are like this. For example, if the project is to build a bridge for a government, then once you have signed the contract, regardless of what happens in the future, you are obliged to deliver a bridge. You cannot delay the start date, nor can you abandon the project halfway through if new information is received indicating that the worst-case scenario is now likely to happen (say, building costs double).

However, with most projects the managers are not making all-or-nothing decisions at the outset. They are able to respond to changing circumstances as they unfold over the life of the project. For example, if events turn out badly they can react by abandoning the project. So a company that goes ahead with wind powered electricity machinery production, on the basis of a positive NPV given the government's current support for subsidising renewable energy, may abandon the project if government policy changes two years later. The option to abandon rather than be forced to persist has value. This value is usually ignored in traditional NPV analysis.

Sometimes it is the option to expand, if events turn out well, that is extremely valuable. On other occasions the decision to go ahead or not to go ahead is not now-or-never but the consideration of a range of dates for going ahead; this year, next year or the year after. That is, the company has the option to defer the project, e.g. developing a copper mine only when the world market price of copper rises sufficiently. Going ahead now would destroy value at current low copper prices (a negative NPV) but the *option* to develop has value. The ability to abandon, expand or defer a project can add considerable value compared with a project without these flexibilities. These are known as real options.

The real options perspective takes account of future managerial flexibility whereas the traditional NPV framework tends to ignore such flexibility.

Real options ('capital investment options') give the right, but not the obligation, to take an action in the future. In an uncertain future in which conditions change unpredictably, the ability to delay or change a choice has value. By holding a real option we have the right to select whatever decision suits the conditions best at the time. Real options differ from financial options traded in the market (*see* Chapter 21) in that their value does not depend on the movement in the price of an underlying financial security or instrument, such as a share, or currency rate, but on the cash flows of real investment projects within the firm.

Some simple examples of valuable real options

Firms sometimes undertake projects which apparently have negative NPVs. They do so because an option to expand, which may be desirable in the future, is created. The value of the option outweighs the loss of value on the project. For example, many Western firms have set up offices, marketing and production operations in China which run up losses. This has not led to a pull-out because of the long-term attraction to expand within the world's largest market. If companies withdrew they would find it very difficult to re-enter, and would therefore sacrifice the option to expand. This option is considered to be so valuable that some firms are prepared to pay the price of many years of losses. This kind of logic applied when Shell invested in an oil field in Iraq in 2009 – *see* **Exhibit 6.33**.

Exhibit 6.33

Winning move for Majnoon gives Shell a psychological boost

By Carola Hoyos, Chief energy correspondent

Royal Dutch Shell is counting its blessing that Baghdad has opened up the world's third-largest oil reserves more than 30 years after they were nationalised and six years after Saddam Hussein was overthrown by a US-led invasion force.

It must have been with some relief that Shell on Friday found it had put in the winning bid to develop Iraq's Majnoon oil field.

At 12.6bn barrels of reserves, Majnoon is not only one of Iraq's biggest untapped fields, it is one of the biggest in the world.

Investors are not exactly applauding the deal with gusto as it will do little to boost Shell's profitability.

That is because in the Iraq auctions, the winning bidders have agreed to service contracts, which give them no exposure to potential profit windfalls if the price of oil rises. Shell will only get $1.39 for every incremental barrel it produces.

To counter such complaints, the companies point out that they will not need to spend much capital on the projects because they can reinvest the cash flow from the fields as they expand production.

The main argument in favour of accepting such stringent financial terms to get Iraq's oil sector back on its feet is the long-term political upside.

They believe that entering Iraq now will give them a seat at the table when Baghdad decides to hand out the rights to explore for oil in the vast stretches of its desert that have remained untouched by geologists who were stopped in their tracks in 1972 when the country nationalised the oil sector.

'It's all about the future,' says Peter Hitchens [an analyst at Panmure Gordon in London], noting that the companies are counting on getting better terms for exploration contracts for taking on more geological risk.

The investment paid off as Iraq's oil production has developed post-war due to the large investments made by Western firms but there are still ongoing risks which Shell will have to consider when making further investment decisions. As illustrated in **Exhibit 6.34,** the long-term prospects still make this an attractive investment despite the short-term difficulties.

Exhibit 6.34

Storm clouds threaten Iraq oil's revival

By Guy Chazan

Iraq's oil production has increased by 1m barrels a day since 2002, the year before the US invasion, to about 3m b/d. Last year it hit a crucial milestone when it overtook Iran to become OPEC's second-biggest producer after Saudi Arabia.

And the trend is set to continue. The International Energy Agency says Iraq's output will more than double to 6.1m b/d by the end of the decade.

But storm clouds could threaten Iraq's revival. Bottlenecks are undermining continued production growth: weak government institutions mean contracts for crucial infrastructure projects are not being awarded quickly enough. A deficit of skilled workers is dogging the industry.

"There are a lot of issues that are out of the western oil companies' hands, such as Iraq's infrastructure constraints," Ms Brewer says. "There is a shortage of pipeline, storage and pumping station capacity."

As a result, the big ramp-up in output seen between 2010 and 2012 has now stalled. The continuing stand-off between Baghdad and the Kurdish regional government has not helped, and neither has the increase in sectarian violence.

Iraq's revival began after it signed a clutch of service contracts with international oil companies late last decade. As part of the bidding process, the majors committed themselves to hitting certain plateau production rates: combining these would give Iraq total capacity of 12m b/d by 2017, a huge number.

The majors won't risk huge investments in oil that might not make it to market because of export bottlenecks.

In the past four years, the westerners have moved in in force, deploying manpower and technology to revitalise production across the badly battered south. BP partnered China's CNPC in Rumaila, one of the world's largest oilfields. ExxonMobil signed up for West Qurna-1, Royal Dutch Shell for Majnoon and ENI for Zubair.

The companies were initially gung-ho. But the infrastructure challenges, the worsening security and the poor returns on their contracts – they receive a fee of just $1.15-$2 per barrel – have made them more cautious about pouring more money in.

One western consultant says: "The majors are entering a period of very large spending decisions as they move to full field development. But they won't risk huge investments in oil that might not make it to market because of export bottlenecks."

Analysts say more progress could have been achieved – both with the contract revisions and the infrastructure improvements – if Iraq was not so distracted by its constant political crises and the worsening security situation.

Despite all their private grumblings about poor returns, unrealistic targets, pipeline problems and geopolitical instability, the majors still have great deals in Iraq and are there for the long haul, Mr al Khateeb says.

"They signed up for producing fields, supergiants with billions of barrels of oil," he says. "And Iraq is the last place on planet Earth where you can still produce cheap oil."

Another example of real options would be where a firm has to decide whether to enter a new technological area which broadens the opportunities available to the firm. To refuse to enter on the basis of a crude NPV calculation could close off important future avenues for expansion. The pharmaceutical giants run dozens of research programmes showing apparent negative NPVs: they do so for what is often described as 'strategic reasons'. We might alternatively call this intuitive option analysis. Perhaps the drugs a company is currently developing in a field of medicine, say, for the treatment of Alzheimer's disease, show negative NPVs when taken in isolation. However, by undertaking this activity the firm builds capabilities within this specialism allowing the firm to stay in the game and participate in future generations of drugs which may have very high payoffs.

If a property developer purchases a prime site near a town centre there is, in the time it takes to draw up plans and gain planning permission, the alternative option of selling the land (abandonment option). Flexibility could also be incorporated into the construction process itself through the use of alternative materials if the price of the original material increases. Also, the buildings could be designed in such a way that they could be quickly and cheaply switched from one use to another (switching option), for example from offices to flats, or from hotel to shops. At each stage there is an option to abandon plan A and switch to plan B. Having plan B available has value. To have only plan A leaves the firm vulnerable to changing circumstances.

The property developer may create options that do not compel the firm to undertake investment at particular points in time. If there were an option to wait a year or two, then the prospects for rapid rental growth for office space *vis-à-vis* hotels, flats and shops could be more accurately assessed (deferral option or timing option). Thus a more informed, and in the long run more value-creating, decision can be made.

True NPV

We need to raise the sophistication of NPV analysis by allowing for the value of flexibility during the life of the project. A project in which there is the ability to take further action after uncertainty has been resolved or reduced significantly is more valuable than one that is rigid.

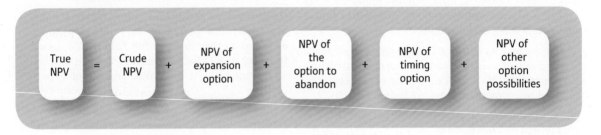

Option to abandon

Imagine that you are the chief executive of a company that designs, creates and sells computer games. A film studio is about to start shooting a major action thriller film which will reach the box office in one year. The film company have offered you the right to develop and market a game based on the film (with film clips and voice-overs from the principal actors). You would have to pay £10m now for this. From previous experience you estimate that there is a 50:50 chance of the film being a success or a flop. If it is a success, the present value of all the future cash flows for the game, excluding the initial investment, will amount to £50m. If, however, it is a flop the high costs of development and promotion will mean a present value of the future cash flows will be negative £50m.

Should you pay £10m now for the game rights?

Conventional NPV analysis is likely to mislead you in this decision. You would set out the cash flows and their probabilities and calculate an expected NPV from them, which will be −£10m (*see* **Exhibit 6.35**). Hence you would reject the project.

The fact that you would be purchasing an option to develop the game, without the obligation to do so, is very significant in the valuation of this project. You can abandon the whole plan in one year's time when you have some vital information: how the film performs at the box office after release. If it is a success then continue. If it is a failure then do not invest any more than the original £10m and save yourself £50m.

With this flexibility built in, your future cash flows are +£50m if the film is well received, and zero if it is hammered by the critics and audiences stay away. Each of these has a 50% chance of occurring (*see* **Exhibit 6.36**).

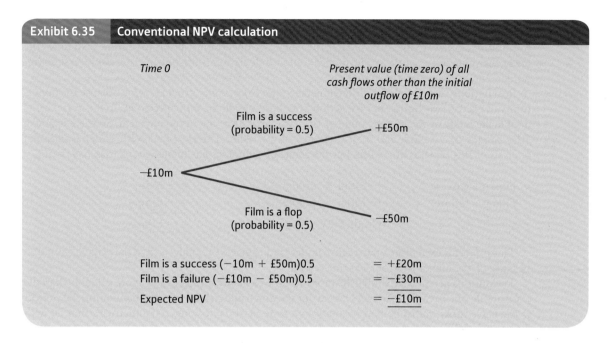

Exhibit 6.35   **Conventional NPV calculation**

Time 0

Present value (time zero) of all cash flows other than the initial outflow of £10m

Film is a success (probability = 0.5)   +£50m

−£10m

Film is a flop (probability = 0.5)   −£50m

Film is a success $(-10m + £50m)0.5$	=	+£20m
Film is a failure $(-£10m − £50m)0.5$	=	−£30m
Expected NPV	=	−£10m

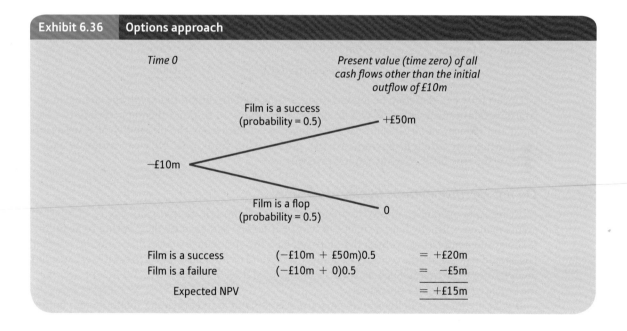

Exhibit 6.36   **Options approach**

Time 0

Present value (time zero) of all cash flows other than the initial outflow of £10m

Film is a success (probability = 0.5)   +£50m

−£10m

Film is a flop (probability = 0.5)   0

Film is a success	$(-£10m + £50m)0.5$	=	+£20m
Film is a failure	$(-£10m + 0)0.5$	=	−£5m
Expected NPV		=	+£15m

The important point is that we do not view the project as a take-it-now-in-its-entirety-or-forget-it deal, but rather consider the possibility of future managerial choices. Managers are not passive, but active over the life of the project. We need to allow for contingent future decisions which can boost NPV, when determining whether to buy the game rights.

The payoff when the real option to abandon is considered is +£15m and it is the right decision to pay £10m for the game rights now.

The value of the option to abandon is calculated as the difference between the NPV if obligated to go ahead with the entire project and the NPV with the option to abandon.

NPV with option − NPV if there is no option

$$+£15 − (−£10m) = £25m$$

Welcoming risk

In traditional NPV analysis the greater the degree of uncertainty about the future cash flows the lower the value of the project. The higher standard deviation is off-putting to a risk-averse shareholder, and their agents, the managers.

Real options analysis takes a different perspective. Uncertainty provides value because the opportunity to exercise the option to take action later becomes all the more precious. To illustrate, let us double the range of the present value of the cash flows after the initial payment. So there is now a 50% chance of +£100m and a 50% chance of −£100m. The expected NPV under traditional analysis of this remains at −£10m but the range of outcomes has increased, i.e. risk has risen.

Film is a success	(−£10m + £100m)0.5	= +£45m
Film is a failure	(−£10m − £100m)0.5	= −£55m
	Crude NPV	= −£10m

This project is even more unattractive under traditional NPV analysis than the original situation because of the higher risk for the same return.

The options perspective shows the more volatile cash flow project to be more valuable than the less volatile one because managers can avoid the downside risk by simply abandoning the project if the news turns out to be bad in one year's time. Risk is no longer symmetrical, that is, with equal probabilities of negative outcomes and positive outcomes around the expected return. It is asymmetrical: you benefit if things go well and do not lose if things go badly (at least you lose no more than you put down as a 'premium' to purchase the option in the first place).

Film is a success	(−£10m + £100m)0.5	= £45m
Film is a failure	(−£10m + 0)0.5	= −£5m
	Option perspective NPV	= £40m

Uncertainty can therefore be a good thing, if you hold an option to exploit the change in circumstances as time goes on. If you do not have flexibility to respond then uncertainty is a bad thing and reduces value. Traditional NPV analysis assumes away the possibility of response to contingencies, resulting in a symmetric risk profile. Thus traditional NPV can seriously underestimate the true NPV of many capital investments.

Do not sacrifice options lightly or cheaply

Most projects include an ability to abandon. If cash flows fall dramatically due to unforeseen events managers usually have a chance to 'cut their losses' and exercise their option to abandon. If you are contemplating a project that does not have the option to abandon then consider whether you should renegotiate the contract or adjust the method of implementation to see if you can build in an option to abandon. Such a clause or operational flexibility may be useful in a project with the potential for negative outcomes.

If your investment is in items with an active secondhand market then the abandonment option is easier to implement, e.g. purchase of a fleet of cars for car hire or a set of houses for rental. Building a specialist item with no secondhand market leaves you vulnerable, e.g. producing an information technology system for a government department. Think carefully in such situations about who bears the risk of future change in areas such as cost over-runs, delay and obsolescence if you are giving up the right to abandon.

In some cases the abandonment option may be better described as a switching option. For example, you might be contemplating the purchase of machinery to enable a project to go ahead. Even though machinery that is capable of producing many alternative products is more expensive than the dedicated version capable of producing only the products associated with this project, it may be worthwhile paying the extra because the option to switch from the manufacture of one item to another is so valuable. Thus car plants are often capable of producing more than one type of car on the assembly line. The assemblers can switch depending on the growth in demand of particular models. Electricity producers often build in the flexibility to switch from one type of fuel to another (e.g. oil or gas) in response to market prices.

Option to expand

A retail company has a plan to spend £200m now to open 50 branches across the country. There is a 50% chance that the venture will be a success and the present value of all future cash flows will be £300m. There is also a 50% chance that consumers will not flock to this new concept, in which case the present value of all future cash flows is £40m. Conducting a traditional NPV analysis leads the managers to reject the project (*see* **Exhibit 6.37**).

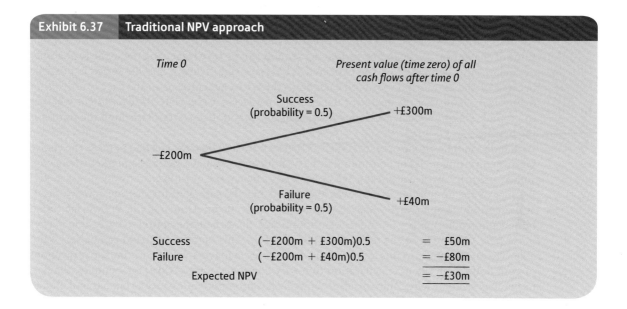

Exhibit 6.37   Traditional NPV approach

An alternative is to create an option to expand rather than commit fully at the outset. The managers could set up a pilot by opening five shops to test the market. This will resolve the uncertainty about the success of the concept. Full commitment only occurs after the information from the pilot is received. The cost of the pilot is £20m at time 0. There is a 50% chance of the five shops succeeding, which means there is a 50% chance of the entire 50 shops being successful (a suspect simplification for the sake of exposition). If the pilot is unsuccessful (50% probability) the option to expand is abandoned (*see* **Exhibit 6.38**).

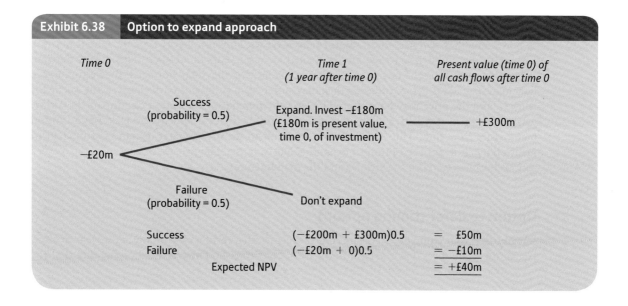

Exhibit 6.38   Option to expand approach

The *Lord of the Rings* trilogy was shot at the same time and then released as three separate films in three different years. In this case to produce the sequels at the same time as making the first film made sense. There were economies of scale and artistic quality would have been lowered by gathering actors, etc. together at a later date (and they might have exercised their option to ask for more pay for later films if the first film was a success). Also box office success was virtually assured and therefore risk of failure of the first or second film relatively low. However, in most cases sequels are not made at the same time as the first film. The studio produces one film while being very careful to hold on to the right, but not the obligation, to produce more in the series. By making the first film the studio creates value in the option. However, if the first film flops at the box office the studio can let the option to expand lapse. Analysing the NPV of the first film in isolation may give an artificially low NPV as the present value of the option to expand by producing sequels can be very large. So even if the probability of making the sequel is low the expected NPV rises significantly if a hit series is possible because of the extraordinarily high cash flows these can generate, as in the case of *Toy Story* or *Avengers*. Note that the degree of uncertainty of success is crucial to the decision of whether to produce simultaneously or to buy an option to expand. If uncertainty is high the option is the best bet.

In India, mobile phone operators such as Reliance Jio and Bharti Artel had to make the choice between investing in 4G or continuing to harvest income from 3G. India is a market where consumers are price sensitive and the 3G speeds are sufficient for most users. So why invest in 4G? Because of the option to expand. Even though 3G may be sufficient for their customers' needs at present, by engaging in 4G Bharti Artel, which made the investment, gains knowledge, capabilities and reputation (e.g. brand recognition) which allow them the option to be leading players in the next generation of the technology (4G and 5G). This option to expand can be very valuable. There is a danger in this argument: in some cases managers will use optimistic projections of cash flows from the next generation to justify continued losses. Take, for example, the biotechnology sector, where company after company has promised future profits but has had limited success after years of cash burn.

Alliances can be used to create options to expand. For example, Baidu is developing software for driverless cars. Chinese companies such as BYD and Cherry originally provided the cars in which Baidu tested its technology. Having met some challenges, Baidu determined that it needed to work with well-established global auto-manufacturing companies and entered into partnerships with Bosch and Continental in 2017.

Dirk Hoheisel, a member of Bosch's management board with responsibility for automotive systems integration, said in a *Financial Times* interview (1 June 2017) that the company was pleased to co-operate with Baidu. 'Combining the know-how of a high-tech internet corporation with our expertise as the world's biggest automotive supplier, the alliance will promote the development of smart mobility in China.' It also of course reduces the risk for both companies of operating outside their areas of expertise.

When airlines are considering ordering aircraft from manufacturers they are often uncertain as to how many they will need over, say, the next 30 years. However, because of the long lead times between order and delivery they are compelled to order years in advance. This means they are vulnerable to making the mistake of ordering planes that they may not need. By waiting to see how high demand is before ordering they may suffer from being put to the back of the queue for delivery and the price may have risen. However, by purchasing an option on aircraft the airline gets a fixed price and delivery date. It is up to the airline to decide whether to exercise the option many years from now. Thus the company can wait to see if passenger demand is sufficient to justify buying; if not the option to expand is left to lapse. The pricing of these options is very serious business for both the airlines and the manufacturers.

Option to defer (timing option)

Imagine that your company is considering a project with a certain cash inflow in one year of £4m. For all the years thereafter the cash flows are subject to risk. There is a 0.5 probability that the company will receive £6m for each of the future years, starting at time 2. There is a 0.5 probability that £2m is the annual cash flow from time 2 to infinity.

To undertake this project the company would need to spend £30m now (time 0). However, there is an option to defer for one year the initiation of the project. The advantage of doing so is that the uncertainty over the cash flow to be received after time 1 will be resolved. You can then decide whether to initiate the project (presumably you would do so if the cash flows will be £6m per year – but we will wait for the formal analysis below). Alternatively you could reject the project (presumably this would happen if the cash flow will be £2m per year).

The disadvantage of delaying one year is that the initial cash outflow rises to £33m. The time value of money is 10%.

If the project is started now the expected NPV is £10m (*see* **Exhibit 6.39**).

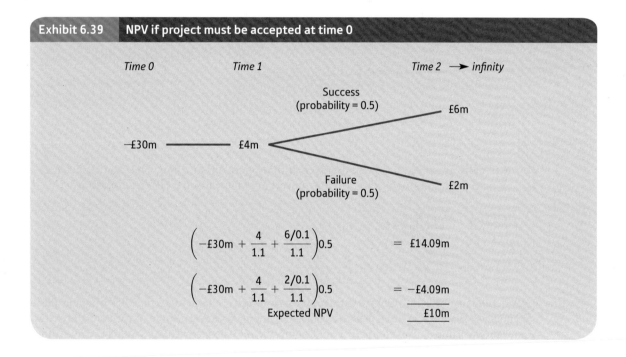

Exhibit 6.39   NPV if project must be accepted at time 0

This is a positive NPV and therefore, in the absence of a better mutually exclusive alternative, would be accepted. However, there is a more attractive alternative which is to defer the decision for one year until information on future demand has been received (*see* **Exhibit 6.40**).

Even though the delay of one year results in costs of implementing the project rising by £3m to £33m it is best to defer the project at time 0 so that if the information at time 1 suggests a poor level of sales the project idea can be rejected.

Naturally, if you were making the decision to invest at time 1 you would be faced with one of the future cash flows, either £6m or £2m per year, as the uncertainty is resolved. This would be an easy decision to make. However, this is not the decision you have to make at time 0. Right now you have to decide whether to go ahead or defer for one year. At time 0 you do not know what market demand will be so you still have to calculate expected NPV allowing for the equal probabilities of £6m or £2m being the outcome. What you do know at time 0 is that if the future cash flows are £2m p.a. then you would not go ahead. Thus there is a 50% chance of 'no-go' on the project.

The value of the option to defer is the difference between the NPV if there was no possibility of delay and the NPV with the deferment flexibility, that is £12.27 − £10m = £2.27m.

Greater uncertainty increases the value of the deferral option. If the cash flow for year 2 to infinity changes to £7m (probability 0.5) or £1m (probability 0.5) the expected NPV calculated

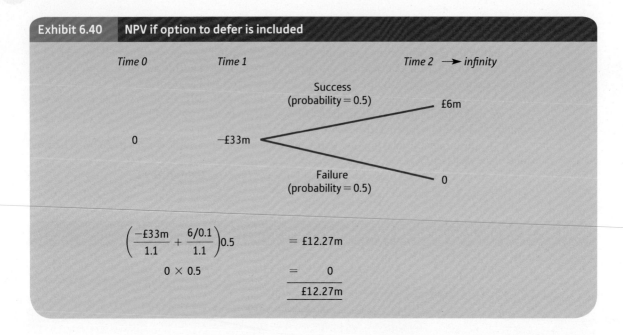

Exhibit 6.40   NPV if option to defer is included

conventionally as a project to be undertaken at time 0 remains at £10m. The value of being able to wait until the resolution of the cash flow uncertainty increases the NPV to £16.82m.

$$\left(\frac{-£33m}{1.1} + \frac{7/0.1}{1.1} \right)0.5 \quad = £16.82m$$
$$0 \times 0.5 \qquad = \qquad 0$$
$$\overline{£16.82m}$$

If a company owns the rights to extract oil (or some other commodity) the NPV of going ahead and doing so right now is often negative. This does not make the ownership of the land and extraction rights worthless. The company could pump the oil whenever it likes, and it is conceivable, given the volatility of the price of oil, that there will come a time when the oil field will become very valuable. Indeed, in order to retain their drilling or mining rights companies have been known to reject multi-million pound offers for unused land (from, say, property developers) because the real option to defer production is worth much more. An example of this idea is discussed in **Exhibit 6.41**.

Exhibit 6.41

Petro China to increase spending after oil price recovery

By Lucy Hornby

Chinese oil major PetroChina plans to raise capital investment to RMB191.3bn ($28bn) in response to recovering oil prices, up from RMB172.4bn last year, in the latest sign of recovery for the oil sector.

China's largest oil producer saw profits fall 78% in 2016 to RMB7.86bn ($1.1bn), its third consecutive decline due to the multi-year slump in oil prices that ended last year.

Revenues fell 6.3%, to RMB1.62tn, it said in a filing to the stock exchange on Thursday.

However, the company said it will increase its capital expenditure this year after a 15 per cent cut in 2016.

PetroChina said it expects the global economy "to continue to recover moderately", and will focus on developing key basins to "raise the exploration investment efficiency".

Difficulties with real option analysis

- *Complexity of the valuation process* This book has explained real options using very simple mathematical examples. Analysts in this field actually make use of complex models, e.g. the Black and Scholes option price model (*see* Appendix to Chapter 21). This complexity means that most managers, without extensive training, are unable to participate in the valuation process in an informed manner. The danger is that untrained managers treat the exercise as black box decision making: supplying some inputs, e.g. standard deviation of key cost or revenue components, then handing the numbers over to the financial wizards who put them into the model and out pops the answer. The managers are totally unable to assess critically the machinations within the black box. It may be necessary to question the assumptions behind the calculations but the key managers are not empowered to do so. This could lead to poor decision making because the quality of inputs is often poor (*see* next point) and to cynicism about the real options approach throughout the organisation.

- *Measuring uncertainty* There is a practical constraint of not being able to measure the degree of uncertainty, and therefore the value of an option. Historic data are usually used (where available), e.g. historic volatility of oil prices for an oil exploration and development project. A leap of faith is then made in assuming that future standard deviations will be like those in the past. In many cases the option valuer clutches at straws to provide inputs to the calculations – giving the impression of scientific rigour, when the foundations are in fact very weak. Standard deviation numbers are often derived from a source only tangentially related to the project, e.g. average standard deviation of technology share price movements may be used as a proxy for the standard deviation of outcomes for a new project initiated by a new company in a new technological field.

- *Over optimism* In circumstances of very high uncertainty, e.g. when there is brand new technology such as the Internet in the 1990s, there is a tendency to be overoptimistic about the value of expanding. In 1999 new 'dotcom' companies joined the stock market proclaiming that once their model was established the potential for scaling up was almost limitless. The market was so huge, they said, that even if the company had an 80% chance of complete failure it was still worth backing as it might be the one left standing with options to expand to control the industry standard (the one most visited by travellers, pet owners, book buyers, etc.). Similar arguments are currently being made about social networking sites, such as Snapchat. These companies presented analyses from 'independent' experts on the growth of user numbers (usually exponential) and the revenues in this field (again exponentially rising). Similar hype can be exhibited by junior and middle managers about a growth area they are particularly enthusiastic about. Senior managers need to view the high ranges of likely outcomes presented to them with scepticism. In particular they should ask whether the firm's competitors are really going to do nothing while they take all this market for themselves.

- *What is the life of an option?* It may not be clear how long the option value will be available to the firm. For example, a pharmaceutical company may have invested considerably in cardiovascular drug R & D, providing it with potential competitive advantages for many years to come through its options to expand to new generations of drugs. But it is impossible to be precise on how many years the option to develop more drugs in this field will be valuable: is it three years? Five or 20 years? The life of the option depends on so many variables, e.g. developments in surgery or competitors' actions.

Perhaps it is because of these difficulties that only 3.6% of large UK firms say that a real options approach to investment analysis is 'important' – none replied that it was 'very important' and 56.6% said it was 'not important' (Alkaraan and Northcott, 2006). It is a shame that over complexity has put managers off because the concept is very important.

Concluding comments

This chapter, and the previous one, have dealt with some of the more sophisticated aspects of project analysis. They have, it is hoped, encouraged the reader to consider a wider range of factors when embarking on investment appraisal. Taking into account more real-world influences such as inflation, rationing, tax and risk will enable the appraiser and the decision maker to obtain a clearer picture of the nature of the proposal being discussed. Greater realism and more information clears away some of the fog which envelops many capital investment decision-making processes.

However, this chapter has focused primarily on the technical/mathematical aspects of the appraisal stage of the investment process sequence. While these aspects should not be belittled, as we ought to improve the analysis wherever we can, it should be noted that a successful programme of investment usually rests far more on quality management of other stages in the process. Issues of human communication, enthusiasm and commitment are as vital to investment returns as, for example, assessing risk correctly.

Key points and concepts

- **Risk** – more than one possible outcome.

- **Objective probability** – likelihood of outcomes established mathematically or from historic data.

- **Subjective probability** – personal judgement of the likely range of outcomes along with the likelihood of their occurrence.

- **Risk can be allowed for by raising or lowering the discount rate:**

  Advantages:

  - easy to adopt and understand;
  - theoretical support.

  Drawbacks: susceptible to subjectivity in risk premium and risk class allocation.

- **Sensitivity analysis** views a project's NPV under alternative assumed values of variables, changed one at a time. It permits a broader picture to be presented, enables scarce resources to be more efficiently directed and allows contingency plans to be made.

  Drawbacks of sensitivity analysis:

  - does not assign probabilities and these may need to be added for a fuller picture;
  - each variable is changed in isolation.

- **Scenario analysis** permits a number of factors to be changed simultaneously. Allows best- and worst-case scenarios.

- **Probability analysis** allows for more precision in judging project viability.

- **Expected return** – the mean or average outcome is calculated by weighting each of the possible outcomes by the probability of occurrence and then summing the result:

$$\bar{x} = \sum_{i=1}^{i=n} (x_i p_i)$$

- **Standard deviation** – a measure of dispersion around the expected value:

$$\sigma_x = \sqrt{\sigma_x^2} \text{ or } \sqrt{\sum_{i=1}^{i=n} \{(x_i - \bar{x})^2 p_i\}}$$

- It is assumed that most people are **risk averters** who demonstrate **diminishing marginal utility**, preferring less risk to more risk.

- **Mean-variance rule:**

  Project X will be preferred to Project Y if at least one of the following conditions applies:

  1 The expected return of X is at least equal to the expected return of Y, and the variance is less than that of Y.

  2 The expected return of X exceeds that of Y and the variance is equal to or less than that of Y.

- If a normal, bell-shaped distribution of possible outcomes can be assumed, the probabilities of various events, for example insolvency, can be calculated using the **Z statistic**.

$$Z = \frac{X - \mu}{\sigma}$$

- **Careful interpretation** is needed when using a risk-free discount rather than a risk-adjusted discount rate for probability analysis.

- **Problems with probability analysis:**
  - undue faith can be placed in quantified results;
  - can be too complicated for general understanding and communication;

- projects may be viewed in isolation rather than as part of the firm's mixture of projects.

- Sensitivity analysis and scenario analysis are the most popular methods of allowing for project risk.

- The **real options** perspective takes account of future managerial flexibility whereas the traditional NPV framework tends to assume away such flexibility. Real options give the right, but not the obligation, to take action in the future.

References and further reading

Alkaraan, F. and Northcott, D. (2006) 'Strategic capital investment decision-making: a role for emergent analysis tools? A study of practice in large UK manufacturing companies', *British Accounting Review*, 38, pp. 149–73.

As well as providing survey evidence on appraisal techniques used, this paper considers the issue of using alternative techniques for strategic investments.

Amran, M. and Kulatilaka, N. (1999) *Real Options: Managing Strategic Investment in an Uncertain World.* Boston, MA: Harvard Business School Press.

Applies options thinking to non-financial assets, bringing a financial market discipline to the appraisal of company opportunities.

Arnold, G.C. and Hatzopoulos, P.D. (2000) 'The theory-practice gap in capital budgeting: evidence from the United Kingdom', *Journal of Business Finance and Accounting*, 27(5) and (6), June/July, pp. 603–26.

Discussion on the use of alternative risk adjustment methods is provided.

Bierman, H. and Smidt, S. (2006) *The Capital Budgeting Decision,* 9th edn. London: Routledge.

An introduction to risk in project appraisal.

Bierman, H. and Smidt, S. (2006) *Advanced Capital Budgeting.* London: Routledge.

Block, S. (2007) 'Are "Real Options" Actually Used in the Real World?' *The Engineering Economist,* 52(3), 255–68.

The author surveys Fortune 1,000 companies to see if they have picked up on the use of real options to complement traditional analysis.

Brennan, M.J. and Schwartz, E.S. (1985) 'Evaluating natural resource investments', *Journal of Business,* 58, pp. 135–57.

A pioneering paper in the field of real options.

Brennan, M.J. and Trigeorgis, L. (eds) (2000) *Project Flexibility, Agency, and Competition: New Developments in the Theory and Application of Real Options.* Oxford, New York: Oxford University Press.

Contains a number of important papers on real options.

Bulan, L., Mayer, C. and Somerville, S.T. (2009) 'Irreversible investment, real options and competition: evidence from real estate development', *Journal of Urban Development,* May, 65(3), pp. 237–51.

Evidence of property developers in Canada delaying real estate investments when faced with greater risk.

Childs, P.D., Ott, S.M. and Triantis, A.J. (1998) 'Capital budgeting for interrelated projects: a real options approach', *Journal of Financial and Quantitative Analysis,* 33(3), pp. 305–34.

Applications of the real options approach to the case of development-stage expenditure for mutually exclusive projects. Advanced level.

Chittenden, F. and Darregia, M. (2004) 'Capital Investment decision making: some results from studying entrepreneurial businesses', www.icaew.co.uk.

Many entrepreneurial firms rely more on qualitative assessments than formal capital budgeting. Also they build in options through leasing, hiring and renting because they are cheap to get out of.

Copeland, T. and Antikarov, V. (2001) *Real Options: A Practitioner's Guide.* New York: Texere.

A technical and mathematical approach to the subject.

Copeland, T. and Tufano, P. (2004) 'A real-world way to manage real options', *Harvard Business Review,* March, pp. 1–11.

A simplified use of option analysis.

Dixit, A. and Pindyck, R. (1994) *Investment Under Uncertainty*. Princeton, NJ: Princeton University Press.
An approach to the capital investment decisions of firms which deals with the difficulty of investment decisions in an uncertain economic environment. Recognises the option value of waiting.

Dixit, A.K. and Pindyck, R.S. (1995) 'The options approach to capital investment', *Harvard Business Review*, May–June. (Also reproduced in J. Rutterford (ed.) *Financial Strategy*. New York: John Wiley, 1998.)
An easy-to-follow discussion of inadequacy of the traditional simple NPV approach and an introduction to the real options perspective.

Espinoza R.D. (2014) 'Separating project risk from the time-value of money: A step toward integration of risk management and valuation of infrastructure investments', *International Journal of Project Management*, 32, pp. 1056–72.
The rationale for using heuristics to establish a risk premium that is added to the risk-free rate to obtain the value of an investment is questioned and an alternative method, termed decoupled net present value (DNPV), is proposed.

Graham, J.R. and Harvey, C.R. (2001) 'The theory and practice of corporate finance: evidence from the field', *Journal of Financial Economics*, 60(2–3), May, pp. 187–243.
It shows the use of risk techniques in US corporations.

Harchaoui, T.M. and Lasserre, P. (2001) 'Testing the option value theory of irreversible investment', *International Economic Review*, February, 42(1), pp. 141–66.
A model of option decision making tested on Canadian copper mine decisions.

Hertz, D.B. (1964) 'Risk analysis in capital investment', *Harvard Business Review*, January/ February, pp. 95–106.
Excellent discussion of risk and the use of probability analysis.

Hertz, D.B and Thomas, H. (1984) *Practical Risk Analysis: An Approach through Case Histories*. Chichester: Wiley.
Contains some interesting case studies of companies applying the principles and techniques discussed in this chapter.

Hillier, F.S. (1963) 'The derivation of probabilistic information for the evaluation of risky investments', *Management Science*, April, pp. 443–57.
The use of standard deviation in project appraisal.

Ho, S. and Pike, R.H. (1991) 'Risk analysis in capital budgeting contexts: simple or sophisticated', *Accounting and Business Research*, Summer, pp. 227–38.
Excellent survey of risk-handling techniques adopted in 146 large companies.

Howell, S., Stark, A., Newton, D., Paxson, D., Cavus, M. and Pereira, J. (2001) *Real Options: Evaluating Corporate Investment Opportunities in a Dynamic World*. Harlow: Financial Times Prentice Hall.
An intermediate-level book that tries to make mathematical real option analysis digestible.

Magee, J.F. (1964a) 'Decision trees for decision making', *Harvard Business Review*, July/August, pp. 126–38.
The use of decision trees is explained in clear terms.

Magee, J.F. (1964b) 'How to use decision trees in capital investment', *Harvard Business Review*, September/ October, pp. 79–96.
Decision trees applied to project appraisal.

Markowitz, H. (1959) *Portfolio Selection*. New York: Wiley.
Utility foundations of mean-variance analysis.

Merton, R.C. (1998) 'Application of option-pricing theory: twenty-five years later', *American Economic Review*, June, No. 3, pp. 323–49.
Mostly focused on option price theory. Advanced level.

Moel, A. and Tufano, P. (2002) 'When are real options exercised? An empirical study of mine closings', *The Review of Financial Studies*, Spring, 15(1), pp. 35–64.
The usefulness of real option analysis is demonstrated.

Pike, R.H. (1988) 'An empirical study of the adoption of sophisticated capital budgeting practices and decision-making effectiveness', *Accounting and Business Research*, 18(72), pp. 341–51.
Interesting evidence on the practical use of risk analysis techniques.

Pike, R.H. (1996) 'A longitudinal survey of capital budgeting practices', *Journal of Business Finance and Accounting*, 23(1), January.
Clearly described evidence on the capital investment appraisal practices of major UK companies.

Quigg, L. (1993) 'Empirical testing of real option pricing models', *Journal of Finance*, 48(2), pp. 621–40.
An early application of real option theory. Advanced level.

Rigopoulos, G. (2014b) 'Real options adoption in capital budgeting: A highlight of recent literature', *Journal of Economics and Business Research*, 20.2, pp. 41–51.
This paper presents a literature review of recent empirical surveys on capital budgeting methods.

Rigopoulos, G. (2015) 'A review on Real Options utilization in Capital Budgeting practice', *International Journal of Information, Business and Management*, 7(2).
This paper presents a literature review of empirical surveys on capital budgeting methods.

Schwartz, E.S. and Trigeorgis, L. (eds) (2001) *Real Options and Investment Under Uncertainty: Classical Readings and Recent Contributions*. London, Cambridge, MA: MIT Press.

The major articles in the field are included – dozens of them.

Swalm, R.O. (1966) 'Utility theory – insights into risk taking', *Harvard Business Review,* November/December, pp. 123–36.

An accessible account of utility theory.

Triantis, A. and Borison A. (2001) 'Real options: State of the practice', *Journal of Applied Corporate Finance,* 14(2), 8–24.

The companies that have shown the greatest interest in real options generally operate in industries where large investments with uncertain returns are commonplace, such as oil and gas, and life sciences.

Triantis, A.J. and Hodder, J.E. (1990) 'Valuing flexibility as a complex option', *Journal of Finance,* 45, pp. 545–66.

An application to manufacturing systems. Advanced level.

Trigeorgis, L. (1996) *Real Options: Managerial Flexibility and Strategy in Resource Allocation.* Cambridge, MA: MIT Press.

Reviews capital budgeting techniques and uses options to value management flexibility in uncertain markets.

Van Putten, A. B. and MacMillan I.C. (2004) 'Making real options really work', *Harvard Business Review,* December, pp. 1–8.

Easy-to-read article explaining the complementary use of real option analysis and DCF analysis.

Case study recommendations

Please see www.pearsoned.co.uk/arnold for case study synopses. Also, there is another list of useful case studies in the fifth edition

- Aestiete : Expansion Plant in Brazil
  Authors: Yiorgos Allayannis; Gerry Yemen; Roberson Oliveira. Darden School of Business. Available at www. cb.hbsp.harvard.edu

- County Line Markets: Real Options and Store Expansions

Authors: Tom J . Cook; Lou D'Antonio; Ron Rizzuto North. American Case Research Association (NACRA). Available at www.cb.hbsp.harvard.edu

- Measuring Risk in Investment Projects: Npv at Risk
  Author: Roberto Garcia Castro. IESE Available at www.cb.hbsp.harvard.edu

Self-review questions

1 Explain, with reference to probability and sensitivity analysis, why the examination of the most likely outcome of an investment in isolation can both be limiting and give a false impression.

2 What do you understand by the following?
   a   Risk-lover.
   b   Diminishing marginal utility.
   c   Standard deviation.

3 Discuss the consequences of the quantification of personal judgements about future eventualities. Are we right to undertake precise analysis on this sort of basis?

4 Explain the attraction of using more than one method to examine risk in project appraisal.

5 Why has the development of powerful computers helped the more widespread adoption of scenario analysis?

6 Suggest reasons why probability analysis is used so infrequently by major international corporations.

7 'The flatter the line on the sensitivity graph, the less attention we have to pay to that variable.' Is the executive who made this statement correct in all cases?

8 If one project has a higher standard deviation and a higher expected return than another, can we use the mean-variance rule?

9 What does it mean if a project has a probability of a negative NPV of 20% when (a) the risk-free discount rate is used, (b) the risk-adjusted discount rate is used?

10 What is the probability of an outcome being within 0.5 of a standard deviation from the expected outcome?

Questions and problems

Answers to most questions can be found at *www.pearsoned.co.uk/arnold*.
Answers to questions marked with an asterisk are to be found only in the Lecturer's Guide.

1   Calculate the NPV of the following project with a discount rate of 9%.

Point in time (yearly intervals)	0	1	2	3	4
Cash flow (£000s)	−800	300	250	400	500

Now examine the impact on NPV of raising the discount rate by the following risk premiums:

a   3 percentage points;
b   6 percentage points.

2*   (*Examination level*) Cashion International are considering a project that is susceptible to risk. An initial investment of £90,000 will be followed by three years each with the 'most likely' cash flows shown in the table (there is no inflation or tax).

The initial investment consists of £70,000 in machines, which have a zero scrap value at the end of the three-year life of the project and £20,000 in additional working capital which is recoverable at the end. The discount rate is 10%.

Required

a   Draw a sensitivity graph showing the sensitivity of NPV to changes in the following:

   – sales price;
   – labour costs;
   – material costs;
   – discount rate.

		£		£
Annual sales (volume of 100,000 units multiplied by estimated sales price of £2)				200,000
Annual costs				
Labour		100,000		
Materials		40,000		
Other		10,000		
		150,000		(150,000)
				50,000

b   For the four variables considered in (a) state the break-even point and the percentage deviation from 'most likely' levels before break-even NPV is reached (assuming all other variables remain constant).

(*An Excel spreadsheet version of these calculations is available in the Lecturers-only section at www.pearsoned. co.uk/arnold*).

3* Use the data in question 2 to calculate the NPV in two alternative scenarios:

Worst-case scenario		Best-case scenario	
Sales volume	90,000	Sales volume	110,000
Sales price	£1.90	Sales price	£2.15
Labour costs	£110,000	Labour costs	£95,000
Material costs	£44,000	Material costs	£39,000
Other costs	£13,000	Other costs	£9,000
Project life	3 years	Project life	3 years
Discount rate	13%	Discount rate	10%
Initial investment	£90,000	Initial investment	£90,000

4 (*Examination level*) A company is trying to decide whether to make a £400,000 investment in a new product area. The project will last 10 years and the £400,000 of machinery will have a zero scrap value. Other best estimate forecasts are:

 – sales volume of 22,000 units per year;
 – sales price £21 per unit;
 – variable direct costs £16 per unit.

There are no other costs and inflation and tax are not relevant.

a The senior management team have asked you to calculate the internal rate of return (IRR) of this project based on these estimates.

b To gain a broader picture they also want you to recalculate IRR on the assumption that each of the following variables changes adversely by 5% in turn:

 – sales volume;
 – sales price;
 – variable direct costs.

c Explain to the management team how this analysis can help to direct attention and further work to improve the likelihood of a successful project implementation.

(*An Excel spreadsheet version of these calculations is available at www.pearsoned.co.uk/arnold*).

5 Project W may yield a return of £2m with a probability of 0.3, or a return of £4m with a probability of 0.7. Project X may earn a negative return of £2m with a probability of 0.3 or a positive return of £8m with a probability of 0.7. Project Y yields a return of £2m which is certain. Compare the mean return and risk of the projects.

6 The returns from a project are normally distributed with a mean of £220,000 and a standard deviation of £160,000. If the project loses more than £80,000 the company will be made insolvent. What is the probability of insolvency?

7 (*Examination level*) Toughnut plc is considering a two-year project that has the following probability distribution of returns:

Year 1		Year 2	
Return	*Probability*	*Return*	*Probability*
8,000	0.1	4,000	0.3
10,000	0.6	8,000	0.7
12,000	0.3		

The events in each year are independent of other years (that is, there are no conditional probabilities). An outlay of £15,000 is payable at Time 0 and the other cash flows are receivable at the year ends. The risk-adjusted discount rate is 11%.

Calculate

a   The expected NPV.
b   The standard deviation of NPV.
c   The probability of the NPV being less than zero assuming a normal distribution of return – (bell shaped and symmetrical about the mean).
d   Interpret the figure calculated in (c).

8   A project with an initial outlay of £1m has a 0.2 probability of producing a return of £800,000 in Year 1 and a 0.8 probability of delivering a return of £500,000 in Year 1. If the £800,000 result occurs then the second year could return either £700,000 (probability of 0.5) or £300,000 (probability of 0.5). If the £500,000 result for Year 1 occurs then either £600,000 (probability 0.7) or £400,000 (probability 0.3) could be received in the second year. All cash flows occur on anniversary dates. The discount rate is 12%.

Calculate the expected return and standard deviation.

(An Excel spreadsheet version of the calculation is available at www.pearsoned.co.uk/arnold).

9   A project requires an immediate outflow of cash of £400,000 in return for the following probable cash flows:

State of economy	Probability	End of Year 1 (£)	End of Year 2 (£)
Recession	0.3	100,000	150,000
Growth	0.5	300,000	350,000
Boom	0.2	500,000	550,000

Assume that the state of the economy will be the same in the second year as in the first. The required rate of return is 8%. There is no tax or inflation.

a   Calculate the expected NPV.
b   Calculate the standard deviation of NPV.

10   (*Examination level*) RJW plc is a quoted firm which operates ten lignite mines in Wales. It has total assets of £50m and the value of its shares is £90m. RJW plc's directors perceive a great opportunity in the UK government's privatisation drive. They have held preliminary discussions with the government about the purchase of the 25 lignite mines in England. The purchase price suggested by the Treasury is £900m.

For two months the directors have been engaged in a fund-raising campaign to persuade City financial institutions to provide £500m of new equity capital for RJW and £400m of fixed interest rate debt capital in the form of bank loans.

You are a senior analyst with the fund management arm of Klein-Ben Wensons and last week you listened attentively to RJW's presentation. You were impressed by their determination, acumen and track record but have some concerns about their figures for the new project.

RJW's projections are as follows, excluding the cost of purchasing the mines:

Table 1: Cash flows for the English lignite mines: RJW's estimate

Time t	0	1	2	3	4	5 and all subsequent years
Sales (£m) (cash inflows)		1,200	1,250	1,300	1,320	1,350
Less operating costs (£m) (cash outflows)		1,070	1,105	1,150	1,190	1,200
Net cash flows (£m)		130	145	150	130	150

You believe the probability of RJW's projections being correct to be 50% (or 0.5). You also estimate that there is a chance that RJW's estimates are over-cautious. There is a 30% probability of the cash flows being as shown in Table 2 (excluding the cost of purchasing the mines).

Table 2: A more optimistic forecast

Time t	0	1	2	3	4	5 and all subsequent years
Sales (£m) (cash inflows)		1,360	1,416.7	1,473.33	1,496	1,530
Less operating costs (£m) (cash outflows)		1,100	1,140	1,190	1,225	1,250
Net cash flows (£m)		260	276.7	283.33	271	280

On the other hand, events may not turn out as well as RJW's estimates. There is a 20% probability that the cash flows will be as shown in Table 3.

Table 3: A more pessimistic scenario (excluding purchase cost of mines)

Time t	0	1	2	3	4	5 and all subsequent years
Sales (£m) (cash inflows)		1,166.67	1,216.7	1,266.67	1,144	1,170
Less operating costs (£m) (cash outflows)		1,070	1,105	1,150	1,165	1,150
Net cash flows (£m)		96.67	111.7	116.67	−21	20

Assume

1   The cost of capital can be taken to be 14%.

2   Cash flows will arise at year ends except the initial payment to the government which occurs at Time 0.

Required

a   Calculate the expected net present value (NPV) and the standard deviation of the NPV for the project to buy the English lignite mines if £900m is taken to be the initial cash outflow.

b   There is a chance that events will turn out to be much worse than RJW would like. If the net present value of the English operation turns out to be worse than negative £550m, RJW will be liquidated. What is the probability of avoiding liquidation?

c   If the NPV is greater than positive £100m then the share price of RJW will start to rise rapidly in two or three years after the purchase. What is the probability of this occurring?

11   (*Examination level*) Alder plc is considering four projects, for which the cash flows have been calculated as follows:

Project	Points in time (yearly intervals)					
	0	1	2	3	4	
A	−£500,000	+£600,000				Project ends after 1 year.
B	−£200,000	+£200,000	+£150,000			Project ends after 2 years.
C	−£700,000	0	£1million			Project ends after 2 years.
D	−£150,000	+£60,000	+£60,000	+£60,000	+£60,000	Project ends after 4 years.

The appropriate rate of discount is judged to be 10% for risk-free projects.

Accepting one of the projects does not exclude the possibility of accepting another one, and each can only be undertaken once.

Assume that the annual cash flows arise on the anniversary dates of the initial outlay and that there is no inflation or tax.

Required

a   Calculate the net present value for each of the projects on the assumption that the cash flows are not subject to any risk. Rank the projects on the basis of these calculations, assuming there is no capital rationing.

b   Briefly explain two reasons why you might regard net present value as being superior to internal rate of return for project appraisal.

c   Now assume that at Time 0 only £700,000 of capital is available for project investment. Calculate the wisest allocation of these funds to achieve the optimum return on the assumption that each of the projects is divisible (fractions may be undertaken). What is the highest net present value achievable using the risk free discount rate?

d   A change in the law now makes the outcome of Project D subject to risk because the cash flows depend upon the actions of central government. The project will still require an initial cash outflow of £150,000. If the government licensing agency decides at time 0 to permit Alder a licence for a one-year trial production and sale of the product, then the net cash inflow at the end of the first year will be +£50,000. If the agency decides to allow the product to go on sale from time 0 under a four-year licence without a trial run the cash inflow in at the end of Year 1 will be +£70,000. The probability of the government insisting on a trial run is 50% and the probability of full licensing is 50%.

If the trial run takes place then there are two possibilities for future cash flows. The first, with a probability of 30%, is that the product is subsequently given a full licence for the remaining three years, resulting in a net cash flow of +£60,000 per year. The second possibility, with a probability of 70%, is that the government does not grant a licence and production and sales cease after the first year.

If a full licence is granted at time 0 then there are two possible sets of cash flows for the subsequent three years. First, the product sells very well, producing an annual net cash flow of +£80,000 – this has a probability of 60%. Secondly, the product sells less well, producing annual cash flows of +£60,000 – this has a probability of 40%.

The management wants you to calculate the probability of this product producing a negative net present value (assume a normal distribution). The appropriate discount rate for a project of this risk class is 13%.

(?)

12*   (*Examination level*) The UK manufacturer of footwear, Willow plc, is considering a major investment in a new product area, novelty umbrellas. It hopes that these products will become fashion icons.

The following information has been collected:

–   The project will have a limited life of 11 years.

–   The initial investment in plant and machinery will be £1m and a marketing budget of £200,000 will be allocated to the first year.

–   The net cash flows before depreciation of plant and machinery and before marketing expenditure for each umbrella will be £1.

–   The products will be introduced both in the UK and in France.

–   The marketing costs in Years 2 to 11 will be £50,000 per annum.

–   If the product catches the imagination of the consumer in both countries then sales in the first year are anticipated at 1m umbrellas.

–   If the fashion press ignores the new products in one country but becomes enthusiastic in the other the sales will be 700,000 umbrellas in Year 1.

–   If the marketing launch is unsuccessful in both countries, first year sales will be 200,000 umbrellas.

The probability of each of these events occurring is:

- 1m sales: 0.3
- 0.7m sales: 0.4
- 0.2m sales: 0.3

If the first year is a success in both countries then two possibilities are envisaged:

a   Sales levels are maintained at 1m units per annum for the next 10 years – probability 0.3.
b   The product is seen as a temporary fad and sales fall to 100,000 units for the remaining 10 years – probability 0.7.

If success is achieved in only one country in the first year then for the remaining 10 years there is:

a   a 0.4 probability of maintaining the annual sales at 700,000 units; and
b   a 0.6 probability of sales immediately falling to 50,000 units per year.

If the marketing launch is unsuccessful in both countries then production will cease after the first year.
    The plant and machinery will have no alternative use once installed and will have no scrap value.
    The annual cash flows and marketing costs will be payable at each year end.

Assume

- Cost of capital: 10%.
- No inflation or taxation.
- No exchange rate changes.

Required

a   Calculate the expected net present value for the project.
b   Calculate the standard deviation for the project.
c   If the project produces a net present value less than minus £1m the directors fear that the company will be vulnerable to bankruptcy. Calculate the probability of the firm avoiding bankruptcy. Assume a normal distribution.   **?**

(An Excel spreadsheet version of these calculations is available in the Lecturers-only section at www.pearson. co.uk/arnold).

Assignments

1   Gather together sufficient data on a recent or forthcoming investment in a firm you know well to be able to carry out the following forms of risk analysis:

a   Sensitivity analysis.
b   Scenario analysis.
c   Risk-adjusted return analysis.
d   Probability analysis (expected return, standard deviation, probabilities of various eventualities).

Write a report giving as full a picture of the project as possible.

2   Comment on the quality of risk assessment for major investments within your firm. Provide implications and recommendations sections in your report.

CHAPTER

7

Portfolio theory

LEARNING OUTCOMES

This chapter should enable the reader to understand, describe and explain in a formal way the interactions between investments and the risk-reducing properties of portfolios. This includes:

- calculating two-asset portfolio expected returns and standard deviations;

- estimating measures of the extent of interaction – covariance and correlation coefficients;

- being able to describe dominance, identify efficient portfolios and then apply utility theory to obtain optimum portfolios;

- recognise the properties of the multi-asset portfolio set and demonstrate the theory behind the capital market line.

Introduction

The principles discussed in this chapter are as old as the hills. If you are facing a future which is uncertain, as most of us do, you will be vulnerable to negative shocks if you rely on a single source of income. It is less risky to have diverse sources of income or, to put it another way, to hold a portfolio of assets or investments. You do not need to study high-level portfolio theory to be aware of the common sense behind the adage 'don't put all your eggs in one basket'.

Here we examine the extent of risk reduction when an investor switches from complete commitment to one asset, for example shares in one company or one project, to the position where resources are split between two or more assets. By doing so it is possible to maintain returns while reducing risk. In this chapter we will focus on the use of portfolio theory particularly in the context of investment in financial securities, for instance shares in companies. The reader needs to be aware, however, that the fundamental techniques have much wider application – for example, observing the risk-reducing effect of having a diversity of projects within the firm.

The basis of portfolio theory was first developed in 1952 by Harry Markowitz. The thinking behind the explanation of the risk-reducing effect of spreading investment across a range of assets is that in a portfolio unexpected bad news concerning one company will be compensated for to some extent by unexpected good news about another. Markowitz gave us the tools for identifying portfolios which give the highest return for a particular level of risk. Investors can then select the optimum risk-return trade-off for themselves, depending on the extent of personal risk aversion – at least, that is the theory. For example, a retired person dependent on investments for income may prefer a low-risk and low-return portfolio, whereas a young person with alternative sources of income may prefer to choose a portfolio with a higher return and concomitant higher risk. The fundamental point is this: despite the different preferences, each investor will be able to invest in an efficient portfolio: that is, one that gives the highest return for a given level of risk.

Holding period returns

To invest in a share is to become part owner of a business. If the business performs well then high returns will be earned. If the business does less well the holders of other types of securities, for instance the lenders, have the right to demand their contractual return before the ordinary shareholders receive anything. This can result in the share investor receiving little or nothing. The return earned on a share is defined by the holding period returns: R. For one year this is:

$$\text{Return} = \frac{\text{Dividends received} + (\text{Share price at end of period} - \text{Purchase price})}{\text{Purchase price}}$$

$$R = \frac{D_1 + P_1 - P_0}{P_0}$$

The return is the money received less the cost, where P_0 is the purchase price, P_1 the securities value at the end of the holding period and D_1 the dividend paid during the period (usually assumed to occur at the end, for ease of calculations). Thus the return on a share consists of two parts: first, a dividend; and second, a capital gain (or loss), $P_1 - P_0$. For example if a share was bought for £2, and paid a dividend after one year of 10p and the share was sold for £2.20 after one year the return was:

$$\frac{0.10 + 2.20 - 2.00}{2} = 0.15 \text{ or } 15\%$$

If another share produced a holding period return of, say, 10% over a six-month period we cannot make a direct comparison between the two investments. However, a one-year return and a six-month return are related through the formula:

$$(1 + s)^2 = 1 + R$$

where: s = semi-annual rate
           R = annual rate[1]

Thus if the semi-annual return is converted to an annual rate we have a true comparison (*see* **Exhibit 7.1**).

Exhibit 7.1	Comparison of returns	
First investment		**Second investment**
		$(1 + 0.1)^2 = 1 + R$
		$R = (1 + 0.1)^2 - 1$
Return = 0.15 or 15%		Return = 0.21 or 21%

For a three-year holding period, with dividends received at Time 1, 2 and 3 (yearly intervals) the annual rate of return is obtained by solving for R in the following formula:

$$P_0 = \frac{D_1}{1 + R} + \frac{D_2}{(1 + R)^2} + \frac{D_3}{(1 + R)^3} + \frac{P_3}{(1 + R)^3}$$

So, for example, if the initial share price was £1 and the share price three years later (P_3) was £1.20 and a dividend of 6p was paid at the end of Year 1 (D_1), 7p was paid at the end of Year 2 (D_2) and 8p was paid at the end of Year 3 (D_3), the annual rate of return can be found by trial and error:[2]

Try 13%

	Pence	Discounted
D_1	6	5.31
D_2	7	5.48
D_3	8	5.54
P_3	120	83.17
		99.50

Try 12%

	Pence	Discounted
D_1	6	5.36
D_2	7	5.58
D_3	8	5.69
P_3	120	85.41
		102.04

---

1 See Appendix 2.1 for mathematical tools.
2 Normally a calculator or computer with an internal rate of return function would be used. We do this the long-winded way here to show the underlying logic. It can be found using the IRR or goal seek function in Excel – see www.pearsoned.co.uk/arnold.

```
12                                   ?      13
|————————————————————————————|——————|
102.04                             100    99.50
```

$$12 + \frac{2.04}{(102.04 - 99.50)}(13 - 12) = 12.8\%$$

If the annual rate of return was 12.8% then the three-year holding period return was (assuming dividend income was reinvested at the internal rate of return):

$$(1 + 0.128)^3 - 1 = 43.5\%$$

or

$$P(1 + i)^n = F$$
$$£1(1 + 0.128)^3 = £1.4352$$

(An Excel spreadsheet version of this calculation is available at www.pearsoned.co.uk/arnold).

Expected return and standard deviation for shares

The analysis so far has been backward looking, as it focused on the certain returns that have already been received. Given perfect hindsight it is easy to make a choice between investments. When making investment decisions we are concerned with the future. The only certain fact the investor has is the price P_0 to be paid. The uncertainty over the future dividend has to be taken into account and, in addition, the even more difficult task of estimating the market value of the share at the end of the period has to be undertaken. Next, the fashion retailer, has steadily raised its dividend year on year and therefore the estimation of the dividend one year hence can be predicted with a reasonable amount of confidence. However, forecasting the future share price is more formidable. This is subject to a number of influences ranging from the talent of the clothes buyers to the general sentiment in the stock market about macroeconomic matters.

So when dealing with the future we have to talk about expected returns. An expected return is derived by considering a variety of possibilities and weighting the possible outcomes by the probability of occurrence. The list of possible outcomes along with their probability of occurrence is called the frequency function.

A frequency function or probability distribution for shares in Ace plc is described in **Exhibit 7.2**. If the economy booms over the next year then the return will be 20%. If normal growth occurs the return will be 5%. A recession will produce a negative return, losing an investor 10% of the original investment.

Exhibit 7.2   Ace plc

A share costs 100p to purchase now and the estimates of returns for the next year are as follows.

Event	Estimated selling price, P_1	Estimated dividend, D_1	Return R_i	Probability
Economic boom	114p	6p	+20%	0.2
Normal growth	100p	5p	+5%	0.6
Recession	86p	4p	−10%	0.2
				1.0

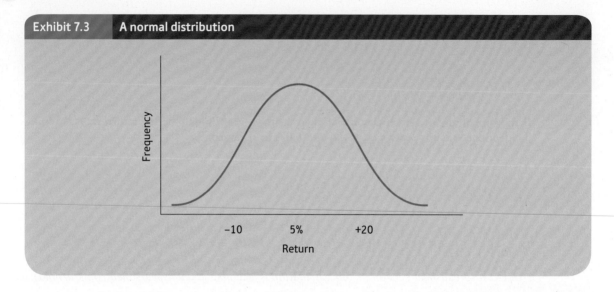

Exhibit 7.3   A normal distribution

The example shown in Exhibit 7.2 lists only three possibilities. This small number was chosen in order to simplify the analysis, but it is possible to imagine that in reality there would be a number of intermediate outcomes, such as a return of 6% or −2%. Each potential outcome would have a defined probability of occurrence but the probability of all the outcomes would sum to 1.0. This more sophisticated approach to probability distribution is illustrated in **Exhibit 7.3** where the distribution is assumed to be normal, symmetrical and bell shaped.

We could add to the three possible events shown in Exhibit 7.2, for example slow growth, bad recession, moderate recession and so on, and thereby draw up a more complete representation of the distribution of the probabilities of eventualities. However, to represent all the possibilities would be an enormous task and the table would become unwieldy. Furthermore, the data we are dealing with, namely, future events, do not form a suitable base for such precision. We are better off representing the possible outcomes in terms of two summary statistics, the expected return and standard deviation.

The expected return

The expected return is represented by the following formula:

$$\overline{R} = \sum_{i=1}^{n} R_i p_i$$

where:
$\overline{R}$ = expected return
R_i = return if event i occurs
p_i = probability of event i occurring
n = number of events

In the case of Ace plc the expected return is as set out in **Exhibit 7.4**.

Exhibit 7.4   Expected return, Ace plc

Event	Probability of event p_i	Return R_i	$R_i \times p_i$
Boom	0.2	+20	4
Growth	0.6	+5	3
Recession	0.2	−10	−2
		Expected return	5 or 5%

Standard deviation

The standard deviation gives a measure of the extent to which outcomes vary around the expected return, as set out in the following formula:

$$\sigma = \sqrt{\sum_{i=1}^{n} (R_i - \overline{R_i})^2 p_i}$$

In the case of Ace plc, the standard deviation is as set out in **Exhibit 7.5**.

Exhibit 7.5	Standard deviation, Ace plc			
Probability p_i	Return R_i	Expected return $\overline{R_i}$	Deviation $R_i - \overline{R_i}$	Deviation squared × probability $(R_i - \overline{R_i})^2 p_i$
0.2	20%	5%	15	45
0.6	5%	5%	0	0
0.2	−10%	5%	−15	45
			Variance σ^2	90
			Standard deviation σ	9.49%

Comparing shares

If we contrast the expected return and standard deviation of Ace with that for a share in a second company, Bravo, then using the mean-variance rule described in the previous chapter we would establish a preference for Ace (*see* **Exhibits 7.6** and **7.7**).

Exhibit 7.6	Returns for a share in Bravo plc	
Event	Return R_i	Probability p_i
Boom	−15%	0.2
Growth	+5%	0.6
Recession	+25%	0.2
		1.0

The expected return is:
$(-15 \times 0.2) + (5 \times 0.6) + (25 \times 0.2) = 5\%$.
The standard deviation for Bravo is as set out in Exhibit 7.7.

Exhibit 7.7	Standard deviation, Bravo plc			
Probability p_i	Return R_i	Expected return $\overline{R_i}$	Deviation $R_i - \overline{R_i}$	Deviation squared × probability $(R_i - \overline{R_i})^2 p_i$
0.2	−15%	5%	−20	80
0.6	+5%	5%	0	0
0.2	+25%	5%	+20	80
1.0			Variance σ^2	160
			Standard deviation σ	12.65%

If we had to choose between these two shares then we would say that Ace is preferable to Bravo for a risk-averse investor because both shares have an expected return of 5% but the standard deviation for Ace is lower at 9.49.

Combinations of investments

In the last section we confined our choice to two options – either invest all the money in Ace, or, alternatively, invest everything in Bravo. If the option were taken to invest in Ace then over a few years the returns might turn out to be as shown in **Exhibit 7.8**.

Note, in Exhibit 7.8, the large variability from one year to the next. The returns on Ace are high when the economy is doing well but fall dramatically when recession strikes. There are numerous industries which seem to follow this sort of pattern. For example, the luxury car market is vulnerable to the ups and downs of the economy, as are the hotel and consumer goods sectors.

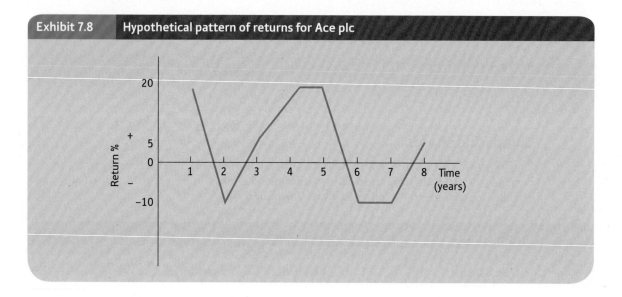

Exhibit 7.8   Hypothetical pattern of returns for Ace plc

If all funds were invested in Bravo in isolation then the patterns of future returns might turn out as shown in **Exhibit 7.9**.

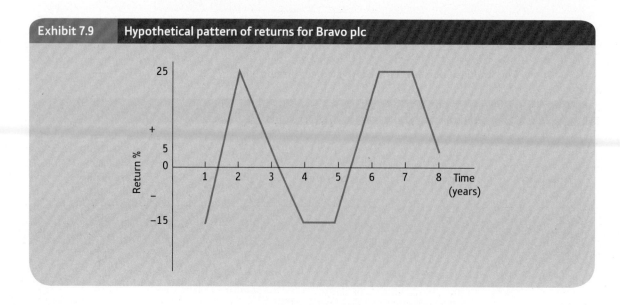

Exhibit 7.9   Hypothetical pattern of returns for Bravo plc

Bravo is in the sort of industry that performs best in recession years; for example, it could be an insolvency practice. Again, note the wild swings in returns from year to year.

Now assume that the investor is not confined to a pure investment in either Ace's shares or Bravo's shares. Another possibility is to buy a portfolio, in other words, to split the fund between the two companies. We will examine the effect on return and risk of placing £571 of a fund totalling £1,000 into Ace, and £429 into Bravo (*see* **Exhibits 7.10** and **7.11**).

Exhibit 7.10	Returns over one year from placing £571 in Ace and £429 in Bravo			
Event	Returns Ace £	Returns Bravo £	Overall returns on £1,000	Percentage returns
Boom	571(1.2) = 685	429 − 429(0.15) = 365	1,050	5%
Growth	571(1.05) = 600	429(1.05) = 450	1,050	5%
Recession	571 − 571(0.1) = 514	429(1.25) = 536	1,050	5%

Exhibit 7.11	Hypothetical pattern of returns for Ace, Bravo and the two-asset portfolio

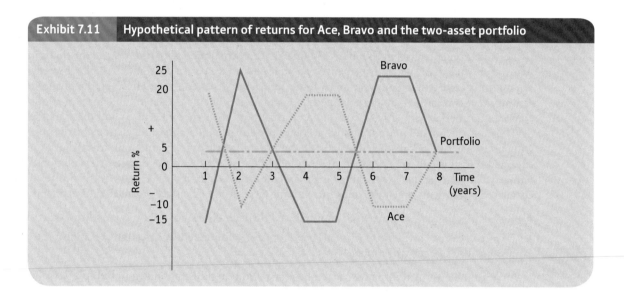

By spreading the investment between these two companies we have achieved complete certainty. Year after year a constant return of 5% is assured rather than the fluctuations experienced if only one share is chosen. Risk has been reduced to zero but average return has remained the same. This is a rare case of receiving something for nothing: without needing to sacrifice any gain we eliminate a 'bad', that is, variability in return.

Perfect negative correlation

Here we have a dramatic demonstration of how the risk (degree of deviation from the expected value) on a portfolio can be less than the risk of the individual constituents. The risk becomes zero because the returns on Bravo are highest in circumstances when the returns on Ace are at their lowest, and vice versa. The co-movement of the returns on Ace and Bravo is such that they exactly offset one another. That is, they exhibit perfect negative correlation.

Perfect positive correlation

By contrast to the relationship of perfect negative correlation between Ace and Bravo **Exhibit 7.12** shows that the returns on Ace and Clara move exactly in step. This is called perfect positive correlation.

Exhibit 7.12	Annual returns on Ace and Clara		
Event *i*	Probability p_i	Returns on Ace %	Returns on Clara %
Boom	0.2	+20	+50
Growth	0.6	+5	+15
Recession	0.2	−10	−20

If a portfolio were constructed from equal investments of Ace and Clara the result would be as shown in **Exhibit 7.13**.

Exhibit 7.13	Returns over a one-year period from placing £500 in Ace and £500 in Clara			
Event *i*	Outcome for Ace £	Outcome for Clara £	Overall outcome on £1,000 investment	Percentage return
Boom	600	750	1,350	35%
Growth	525	575	1,100	10%
Recession	450	400	850	−15%

The situation portrayed in Exhibit 7.13 indicates that, compared with investing all the funds in Ace, the portfolio has a wider dispersion of possible percentage return outcomes. A higher percentage return is earned in a good year and a lower return in a recession year. However, the portfolio returns are less volatile than an investment in Clara alone. There is a general rule for a portfolio consisting of perfectly positively correlated returns: both the expected returns and the standard deviation of the portfolio are weighted averages of returns and standard deviations of the constituents respectively. Thus because half of the portfolio is from Ace and half from Clara the expected return is half-way between the two individual shares. Also the degree of oscillation is half-way between the small variability of Ace and the large variability of Clara. Perfectly positively correlated investments are at the opposite extreme to perfectly negatively correlated investments.

● *Perfect positive correlation*: risk is not reduced through diversification, it is merely averaged.

● *Perfect negative correlation*: risk can be completely eliminated by selecting the appropriate proportions of each investment.

A typical pattern of returns over an eight-year period might be as shown in **Exhibit 7.14** for Ace and Clara and a 50 : 50 portfolio.

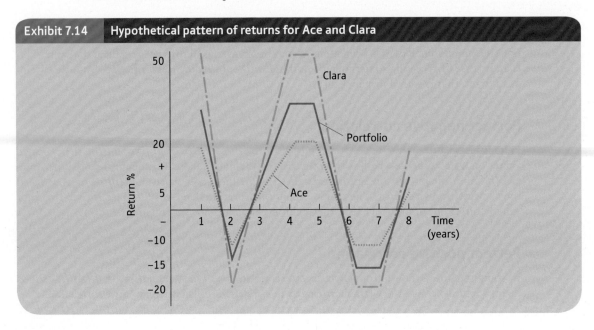

Exhibit 7.14   Hypothetical pattern of returns for Ace and Clara

Independent investments

A third possibility is that the returns on shares in two firms are completely unrelated. Within a portfolio of two statistically independent shares we find that when one firm gives a high return the other one may give a high return *or* it may give a low return: that is, we are unable to state any correlation between the returns. The example of X and Y in **Exhibits 7.15–7.18** shows the effect on risk of this kind of zero correlation situation when two shares are brought together in a portfolio. Shares in X have a 0.5 probability of producing a return of 35% and a 0.5 probability of producing a return of negative 25%. Shares in Y have exactly the same returns and probabilities but which of the two outcomes will occur is totally independent of the outcome for X.

Exhibit 7.15	Expected returns for shares in X and shares in Y

Expected return for shares in X	Expected returns for shares in Y
Return × Probability	Return × Probability
−25 × 0.5 = −12.5	−25 × 0.5 = −12.5
35 × 0.5 = 17.5	35 × 0.5 = 17.5
5.0%	5.0%

Exhibit 7.16	Standard deviations for X or Y as single investments

Return R_i	Probability p_i	Expected return $\overline{R}_i$	Deviation $R_i - \overline{R}_i$	Deviation squared × probability $(R_i - \overline{R}_i)^2 p_i$
−25%	0.5	5%	−30	450
35%	0.5	5%	30	450
			Variance σ^2	900
			Standard deviation σ	30%

If a 50:50 portfolio is created we see that the expected returns remain at 5%, but the standard deviation is reduced (*see* Exhibits 7.17 and 7.18).

Exhibit 7.17	A mixed portfolio: 50% of the fund invested in X and 50% in Y, expected return

Possible outcome combinations	Joint returns	Joint probability	Return × probability
Both firms do badly	−25	0.5 × 0.5 = 0.25	−25 × 0.25 = −6.25
X does badly Y does well	5	0.5 × 0.5 = 0.25	5 × 0.25 = 1.25
X does well Y does badly	5	0.5 × 0.5 = 0.25	5 × 0.25 = 1.25
Both firms do well	35	0.5 × 0.5 = 0.25	35 × 0.25 = 8.75
		1.00	Expected return 5.00%

The reason for the reduction in risk from a standard deviation of 30 (as shown in Exhibit 7.16) to one of 21.21 (as shown in Exhibit 7.18), is that there is now a third possible outcome.

Exhibit 7.18	Standard deviation, mixed portfolio			

Return R_i	Probability p_i	Expected return $\overline{R}_i$	Deviation $R_i - \overline{R}_i$	Deviation squared × probability $(R_i - \overline{R}_i)^2 p_i$
−25	0.25	5	−30	225
5	0.50	5	0	0
35	0.25	5	30	225
			Variance σ^2	450
			Standard deviation σ	21.21%

Previously the only outcomes were −25 and +35. Now it is possible that one investment will give a positive result and one will give a negative result. The overall effect is that there is a 50% chance of an outcome being +5. The diversified portfolio reduces the dispersion of the outcomes and the chance of suffering a major loss of 25% is lowered from a probability of 0.5 to only 0.25 for the mixed portfolio.

A correlation scale

We have examined three extreme positions which will provide the foundation for more detailed consideration of portfolios. The case of Ace and Bravo demonstrated that when investments produce good or bad outcomes which vary in exact opposition to each other, risk can be eliminated. This relationship, described as perfect negative correlation, can be assigned the number −1 on a correlation scale which ranges from −1 to +1. The second example, of Ace and Clara, showed a situation where returns on both shares were affected by the same events and these returns moved in lock-step with one another. This sort of perfect positive correlation can be assigned a value of +1 on a correlation scale. The third case, of X and Y where returns are independent, showed that risk is not entirely eliminated but it can be reduced. (Extreme outcomes are still possible, but they are less likely.) Independent investments are assigned a value of zero on the correlation scale (see **Exhibit 7.19**).

This leads to an important conclusion from portfolio theory:

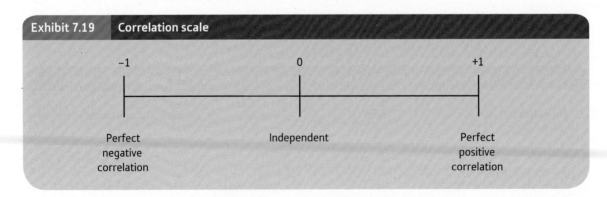

Exhibit 7.19	Correlation scale

Perfect negative correlation (−1)   Independent (0)   Perfect positive correlation (+1)

So long as the returns of constituent assets of a portfolio are not perfectly positively correlated, diversification can reduce risk. The degree of risk reduction depends on:

(a) the extent of statistical interdependence between the returns of the different investments: the more negative the better; and

(b) the number of securities over which to spread the risk: the greater the number, the lower the risk.

This is an amazing conclusion because it is only in the very extreme and rare situation of perfect positive correlation that risk is not reduced.

It is all very well focusing on these three unusual types of relationships but what about the majority of investments in shares, projects or whatever? Real-world assets tend to have returns which have some degree of correlation with other assets but this is neither perfect nor zero. It is to this slightly more complex situation we now turn.

Initially the mathematics of portfolio theory may seem daunting but they do break down into manageable components. The algebra and theory are necessary to gain a true appreciation of the uses of portfolio theory, but the technical aspects are kept to a minimum.

The effects of diversification when security returns are not perfectly correlated

We will now look at the risk-reducing effects of diversification when two financial securities, two shares, have only a small degree of interrelatedness between their returns. Suppose that an investor has a chance of either investing all funds in one company, A or B, or investing a fraction in one with the remainder purchasing shares in the other. The returns on these companies respond differently to the general activity within the economy. Company A does particularly well when the economy is booming. Company B does best when there is normal growth in the economy. Both do badly in a recession. There is some degree of 'togetherness' or correlation of the movement of the returns, but not much (*see* **Exhibit 7.20**).

Exhibit 7.20	Returns on shares A and B for alternative economic states		
Event *i* State of the economy	Probability p_i	Return on A R_A	Return on B R_B
Boom	0.3	20%	3%
Growth	0.4	10%	35%
Recession	0.3	0%	−5%

Before examining portfolio risk and returns we first calculate the expected return and standard deviation for each of the companies' shares as single investments (*see* **Exhibits 7.21–7.25**).

Exhibit 7.21	Company A: Expected return	
Probability p_i	Return R_A	$R_A \times p_i$
0.3	20	6
0.4	10	4
0.3	0	0
		10%

Exhibit 7.22	Company A: Standard deviation

Probability p_i	Return R_A	Expected return $\overline{R_A}$	Deviation $R_A - \overline{R_A}$	Deviation squared × probability $(R_A - \overline{R_A})^2 p_i$
0.3	20	10	10	30
0.4	10	10	0	0
0.3	0	10	−10	30
				$\overline{60}$
			Variance σ^2	60
			Standard deviation σ	7.75%

Exhibit 7.23	Company B: Expected return

Probability p_i	Return R_B	$R_B \times p_i$
0.3	3	0.9
0.4	35	14.0
0.3	−5	−1.5
		$\overline{13.4\%}$

Exhibit 7.24	Company B: Standard deviation

Probability p_i	Return R_B	Expected return $\overline{R_B}$	Deviation $R_B - \overline{R_B}$	Deviation squared × probability $(R_B - \overline{R_B})^2 p_i$
0.3	3	13.4	−10.4	32.45
0.4	35	13.4	21.6	186.62
0.3	−5	13.4	−18.4	101.57
			Variance σ^2	320.64
			Standard deviation σ	17.91%

Exhibit 7.25	Summary table: Expected returns and standard deviations for Companies A and B

	Expected return	Standard deviation
Company A	10%	7.75%
Company B	13.4%	17.91%

Compared with A, Company B is expected to give a higher return but also has a higher level of risk. If the results are plotted on a diagram we can give an impression of the relative risk-return profiles (*see* **Exhibit 7.26**).

From a first glance at Exhibit 7.26 it might be thought that it is possible to invest in different proportions of A and B and obtain a risk-return combination somewhere along the dotted line.

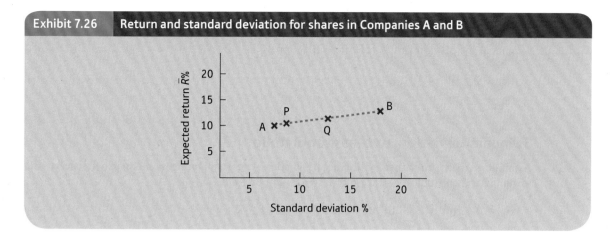

Exhibit 7.26   Return and standard deviation for shares in Companies A and B

That is, a two-asset portfolio of A and B has an expected return which is a weighted average of the expected returns on the individual investments *and* the standard deviation is a weighted average of the risk of A and B depending on the proportions of the portfolio devoted to A and B. So if point Q represented a 50:50 split of capital between A and B the expected return, following this logic, would be:

$$(10 \times 0.5) + (13.4 \times 0.5) = 11.7\%$$

and the standard deviation would be:

$$(7.75 \times 0.5) + (17.91 \times 0.5) = 12.83\%$$

Point P represents 90% of the fund in A and 10% in B. If this portfolio was on the dotted line the expected return would be:

$$(10 \times 0.9) + (13.4 \times 0.1) = 10.34\%$$

and the standard deviation would be:

$$(7.75 \times 0.9) + (17.91 \times 0.1) = 8.766\%$$

However, this would be **wrong** because the risk of any portfolio of A and B is less than the weighted average of the two individual standard deviations. You can, in fact, reduce risk at each level of return by investing in a portfolio of A and B. This brings us to a general rule in portfolio theory:

> Portfolio returns are a weighted average of the expected returns on the individual investments . . .
> BUT . . .
> Portfolio standard deviation is less than the weighted average risk of the individual investments, except for perfectly positively correlated investments.

Portfolio expected return and standard deviation

The rule stated above will now be illustrated by calculating the expected return and standard deviation when 90% of the portfolio funds are placed in A and 10% are placed in B.

Expected returns, two-asset portfolio

The expected returns from a two-asset portfolio are as follows.

Proportion of funds in A $= a = 0.90$
Proportion of funds in B $= 1 - a = 0.10$

The expected return of a portfolio R_p is solely related to the proportion of wealth invested in each constituent. Thus we simply multiply the expected return of each individual investment by their weights in the portfolio, 90% for A and 10% for B.

$$\overline{R_P} = a\overline{R_A} + (1 - a)\overline{R_B}$$
$$R_p = 0.90 \times 10 + 0.10 \times 13.4 = 10.34\%$$

Standard deviation, two-asset portfolio

Now comes the formula that for decades has made the hearts of students sink when first seen – the formula for the standard deviation of a two-asset portfolio. This is:

$$\sigma_p = \sqrt{a^2\sigma_A^2 + (1 - a)^2\sigma_B^2 + 2a(1 - a)\,\text{cov}\,(R_A, R_B)}$$

where:

σ_p = portfolio standard deviation

σ_A^2 = variance of investment A

σ_B^2 = variance of investment B

$\text{cov}\,(R_A, R_B)$ = covariance of A and B

The formula for the standard deviation of a two-asset portfolio may seem daunting at first. However, the component parts are fairly straightforward. To make the formula easier to understand it is useful to break it down to three terms:

1 The first term, $a^2\,\sigma_A^2$, is the variance for A multiplied by the square of its weight – in the example $a^2 = 0.90^2$.

2 The second term $(1 - a)^2\sigma_B^2$, is the variance for the second investment B multiplied by the square of its weight in the portfolio, 0.10^2.

3 The third term, $2a(1 - a)\,\text{cov}\,(R_A, R_B)$, focuses on the covariance of the returns of A and B, which is examined below.

When the results of all three calculations are added together the square root is taken to give the standard deviation of the portfolio. The only piece of information not yet available is the covariance. This is considered next.

Covariance

The covariance measures the extent to which the returns on two investments 'co-vary' or 'co-move'. If the returns tend to go up together and go down together then the covariance will be a positive number. If, however, the returns on one investment move in the opposite direction to the returns on another when a particular event occurs then these securities will exhibit negative covariance. If there is no co-movement at all, that is, the returns are independent of each other, the covariance will be zero. This positive–zero–negative scale should sound familiar, as covariance and the correlation coefficient are closely related. However, the correlation coefficient scale has a strictly limited range from −1 to +1 whereas the covariance can be any positive or negative value. The covariance formula is:

$$\text{cov}\,(R_A, R_B) = \sum_{i=1}^{n} \{(R_A - \overline{R_A})(R_B - \overline{R_B})p_i\}$$

To calculate covariance take each of the possible events that could occur in turn and calculate the extent to which the returns on investment A differ from expected return $(R_A - \overline{R_A})$– and note whether this is a positive or negative deviation. Follow this with a similar deviation calculation for an investment in B if those particular circumstances (that is, boom, recession, etc.)

prevail $(R_B - \overline{R_B})$. Then multiply the deviation of A by the deviation of B and the probability of that event occurring, p_i. (Note that if the deviations are both in a positive direction away from the mean, that is, a higher return than average, or both negative, then the overall calculation will be positive. If one of the deviations is negative while the other is positive the overall result is negative.) Finally the results from all the potential events are added together to give the covariance.

Applying the formula to A and B will help to clarify matters (*see* **Exhibit 7.27**).

Exhibit 7.27	Covariance							
Event and probability of event p_i		**Returns** R_A R_B		**Expected returns** $\overline{R_A}$ $\overline{R_B}$		**Deviations** $R_A - \overline{R_A}$ $R_B - \overline{R_B}$		**Deviation of A $\times$ deviation of B $\times$ probability** $(R_A - \overline{R_A})(R_B - \overline{R_B})p_i$
Boom	0.3	20	3	10	13.4	10	−10.4	10 × −10.4 × 0.3 = −31.2
Growth	0.4	10	35	10	13.4	0	21.6	0 × 21.6 × 0.4 = 0
Recession	0.3	0	−5	10	13.4	−10	−18.4	−10 × −18.4 × 0.3 = 55.2
							Covariance of A and B, cov (R_A, R_B) =	+24

(*An Excel spreadsheet showing these covariance calculations is available at www.pearsoned.co.uk/arnold*).

It is worth spending a little time dwelling on the covariance and seeing how a positive or negative covariance comes about. In the calculation for A and B the 'Boom' eventuality contributed a negative 31.2 to the overall covariance. This is because A does particularly well in boom conditions and the returns are well above expected returns, but B does badly compared with its expected return of 13.4 and therefore the co-movement of returns is a negative one. In a recession both firms experience poor returns compared with their expected values, thus the contribution to the overall covariance is positive because they move together. This second element of co-movement outweighs that of the boom possibility and so the total covariance is positive 24.

Now that we have the final piece of information to plug into the standard deviation formula we can work out the risk resulting from splitting the fund, with 90% invested in A and 10% in B.

$$\sigma_p = \sqrt{a^2\sigma_A^2 + (1 - a)^2\sigma_B^2 + 2a(1 - a)\,\text{cov}\,(R_A, R_B)}$$

$$\sigma_p = \sqrt{0.90^2 \times 60 + 0.10^2 \times 320.64 + 2 \times 0.90 \times 0.10 \times 24}$$

$$\sigma_p = \sqrt{48.6 + 3.206 + 4.32}$$

$$\sigma_p = 7.49\%$$

A 90 : 10 portfolio gives both a higher return and a lower standard deviation than a simple investment in A alone (*see* **Exhibit 7.28**).

Exhibit 7.28	Summary table: expected return and standard deviation		
		Expected return (%)	**Standard deviation (%)**
All invested in Company A		10	7.75
All invested in Company B		13.4	17.91
Invested in a portfolio (90% in A, 10% in B)		10.34	7.49

(*An Excel spreadsheet showing all the calculations for A and B is available at www.pearsoned.co.uk/arnold*).

In the example shown in **Exhibit 7.29** the degree of risk reduction is so slight because the returns on A and B are positively correlated. Later we will consider the example of Augustus and Brown, two shares which exhibit negative correlation. Before that, it will be useful to examine the relationship between covariance and the correlation coefficient.

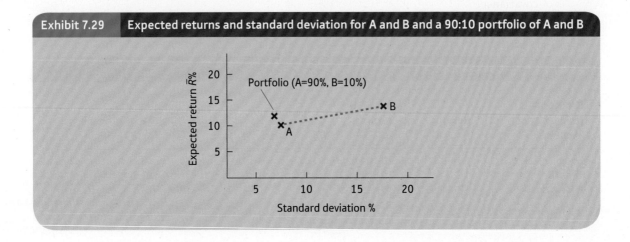

| Exhibit 7.29 | Expected returns and standard deviation for A and B and a 90:10 portfolio of A and B |

Correlation coefficient

Both the covariance and the correlation coefficient measure the degree to which returns move together. The covariance can take on any value and so it is difficult to use the covariance to compare relationships between pairs of investments. A 'standardised covariance' with a scale of interrelatedness is often more useful. This is what the correlation coefficient gives us. To calculate the correlation coefficient, R_{AB}, divide the covariance by the product (i.e. multiplied together) of the individual investment standard deviations.

So for investments A and B:

$$R_{AB} = \frac{\text{cov}\,(R_A, R_B)}{\sigma_A \sigma_B}$$

$$R_{AB} = \frac{24}{7.75 \times 17.91} = +0.1729$$

The correlation coefficient has the same properties as the covariance but it measures co-movement on a scale of -1 to $+1$ which makes comparisons easier. It also can be used in an alternative method of calculating portfolio standard deviation:

$$\text{If } R_{AB} = \frac{\text{cov}\,(R_A, R_B)}{\sigma_A \sigma_B} \text{ then cov}\,(R_A, R_B) = R_{AB}\sigma_A\sigma_B$$

This can then be used in the portfolio standard deviation formula:

$$\sigma_p = \sqrt{a^2\sigma_A^2 + (1 - a)^2\sigma_B^2 + 2a\,(1 - a)\,R_{AB}\sigma_A\sigma_B}$$

Exhibit 7.30 illustrates the case of perfect positively correlated returns ($R_{FG} = +1$) for the shares F and G. All the plot points lie on a straight upward-sloping line.

If the returns on G vary in an exactly opposite way to the returns on F we have perfect negative correlation, $R_{FG} = -1$ (*see* **Exhibit 7.31**).

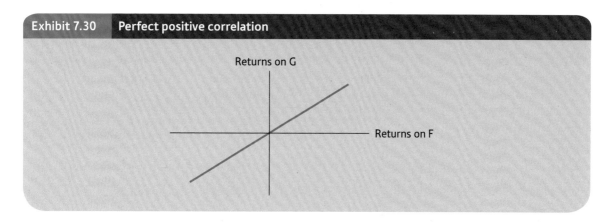

Exhibit 7.30   Perfect positive correlation

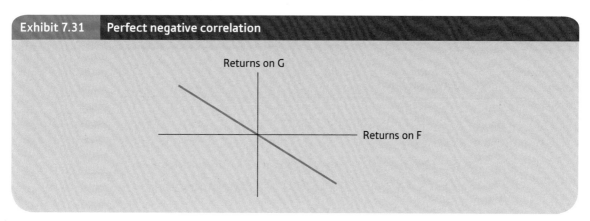

Exhibit 7.31   Perfect negative correlation

If the securities have a zero correlation coefficient ($R = 0$) we are unable to show a line representing the degree of co-movement (*see* **Exhibit 7.32**).

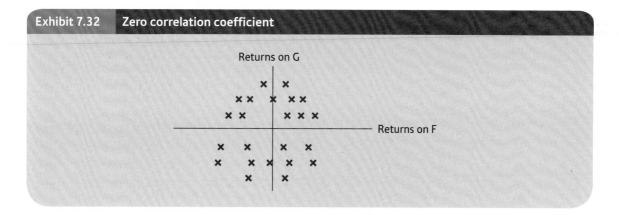

Exhibit 7.32   Zero correlation coefficient

Dominance and the efficient frontier

Suppose an individual is able to invest in shares of Augustus, in shares of Brown or in a portfolio made up from Augustus and Brown shares. Augustus is an ice cream manufacturer and so does well if the weather is warm. Brown is an umbrella manufacturer and so does well if it rains. Because the weather is so changeable from year to year an investment in one of these firms alone is likely to be volatile, whereas a portfolio will probably reduce the variability of returns (*see* **Exhibits 7.33–7.35**).

Exhibit 7.33   Returns on shares in Augustus and Brown

Event (weather for season)	Probability of event	Returns on Augustus	Returns on Brown
	p_i	R_A	R_B
Warm	0.2	20%	−10%
Average	0.6	15%	22%
Wet	0.2	10%	44%
Expected return		15%	20%

Exhibit 7.34   Standard deviation for Augustus and Brown

Probability p_i	Returns on Augustus R_A	$(R_A - \bar{R}_A)^2 p_i$	Returns on Brown R_B	$(R_B - \bar{R}_B)^2 p_i$
0.2	20	5	−10	180.0
0.6	15	0	22	2.4
0.2	10	5	44	115.2
	Variance, σ^2_A	10	Variance, σ^2_B	297.6
	Standard deviation, σ_A	3.162	Standard deviation, σ_B	17.25

Exhibit 7.35   Covariance

Probability p_i	Returns R_A	Returns R_B	Expected returns $\bar{R}_A$	Expected returns $\bar{R}_B$	Deviations $R_A - \bar{R}_A$	Deviations $R_B - \bar{R}_B$	Deviation of A × deviation of B × probability $(R_A - \bar{R}_A)(R_B - \bar{R}_B)p_i$
0.2	20	−10	15	20	5	−30	5 × −30 × 0.2 = −30
0.6	15	22	15	20	0	2	0 × 2 × 0.6 = 0
0.2	10	44	15	20	−5	24	−5 × 24 × 0.2 = −24
						Covariance (R_A, R_B) =	−54

The correlation coefficient is:

$$R_{AB} = \frac{\text{cov}\,(R_A, R_B)}{\sigma_A \sigma_B}$$

$$R_{AB} = \frac{-54}{3.162 \times 17.25} = -0.99$$

There are an infinite number of potential combinations of Augustus and Brown shares giving different levels of risk and return. To make the analysis easier we will examine only five portfolios. These are shown in **Exhibit 7.36**.

| Exhibit 7.36 | | Risk-return correlations: two-asset portfolios for Augustus and Brown | | |

Portfolio	Augustus weighting (%)	Brown weighting (%)	Expected return (%)	Standard deviation	
A	100	0	15		= 3.16
J	90	10	15.5	$\sqrt{0.9^2 \times 10 + 0.1^2 \times 297.6 + 2 \times 0.9 \times 0.1 \times -54}$	= 1.16
K	85	15	15.75	$\sqrt{0.85^2 \times 10 + 0.15^2 \times 297.6 + 2 \times 0.85 \times 0.15 \times -54}$	= 0.39
L	80	20	16.0	$\sqrt{0.8^2 \times 10 + 0.2^2 \times 297.6 + 2 \times 0.8 \times 0.2 \times -54}$	= 1.01
M	50	50	17.5	$\sqrt{0.5^2 \times 10 + 0.5^2 \times 297.6 + 2 \times 0.5 \times 0.5 \times -54}$	= 7.06
N	25	75	18.75	$\sqrt{0.25^2 \times 10 + 0.75^2 \times 297.6 + 2 \times 0.25 \times 0.75 \times -54}$	= 12.16
B	0	100	20		= 17.25

Exhibit 7.37 shows the risk-return profile for alternative portfolios. Portfolio K is very close to the minimum risk combination that actually occurs with a portfolio consisting of 84.6% in Augustus and 15.4% in Brown. The formula for calculating this minimum standard deviation point is shown in Worked example 7.1.

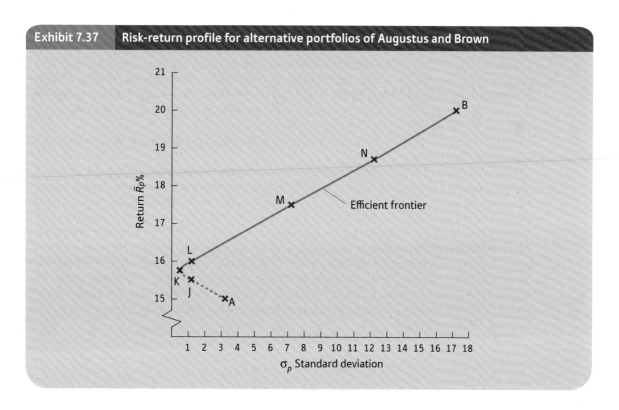

| Exhibit 7.37 | | Risk-return profile for alternative portfolios of Augustus and Brown |

Worked example 7.1   Finding the minimum standard deviation for combinations of two securities

If a fund is to be split between two securities, A and B, and a is the fraction to be allocated to A, then the value for a which results in the lowest standard deviation is given by:

$$a = \frac{\sigma_B^2 - \text{cov}(R_A, R_B)}{\sigma_A^2 + \sigma_B^2 - 2\text{cov}(R_A, R_B)}$$

In the case of Augustus and Brown:

$$a = \frac{297.6 - (-54)}{10 + 297.6 - 2 \times -54} = 0.846 \text{ or } 84.6\%$$

To obtain the minimum standard deviation (or variance) place 84.6% of the fund in Augustus and 15.4% in Brown. We can now calculate the minimum standard deviation:

$$\sigma_P = \sqrt{a^2\sigma_A^2 + (1-a)^2\sigma_B^2 + 2a(1-a)\text{cov}(R_A, R_B)}$$

$$\sigma_P = \sqrt{0.846^2 \times 10 + 0.154^2 \times 297.6 + 2 \times 0.846 \times 0.154 \times -54}$$

$$\sigma_P = 0.38\%$$

Thus, an extremely risk-averse individual who was choosing a combination of shares in Augustus and Brown can achieve a very low variation of income of a tiny standard deviation of 0.38% by allocating 84.6% of the investment fund to Augustus.[1]

The risk-return line drawn, sometimes called the opportunity set, or feasible set, has two sections. The first, with a solid line, from point K to point B, represents all the efficient portfolios. This is called the efficient frontier. Portfolios between K and A are dominated by the efficient portfolios. Take L and J as examples: they have (almost) the same risk levels but portfolio L dominates portfolio J because it has a better return. All the portfolios between K and A are *inefficient* because for each possibility there is an alternative combination of Augustus and Brown on the solid line K to B which provides a higher return for the same risk.

An efficient portfolio is a combination of investments which maximises the expected return for a given standard deviation.

Identifying the efficient portfolios helps in the quest to find the optimal portfolio for an investor as it eliminates a number of inferior possibilities from further consideration. However, there remains a large range of risk-return combinations available in the efficient zone and we need a tool to enable us to find the best portfolio for an individual given that person's degree of risk aversion. For instance a highly risk-averse person will probably select a portfolio with a high proportion of Augustus (but not greater than 84.6%), perhaps settling for the low-return and low-risk combination represented by portfolio L. A less risk-averse investor may be prepared to accept the high standard deviation of portfolio N if compensated by the expectation of greater reward. To be more accurate in choosing between efficient portfolios we need to be able to represent the decision makers' attitude towards risk. Indifference curve analysis is one tool which has been tried by economists.

---

1 An intriguing line of recent research has indicated that the minimum standard deviation (variance) portfolio produces future returns that are much higher than predicted by theory, thus indicating some degree of stock market inefficiency in share pricing. For example, Clarke et al. (2006) found over the period 1968–2005 that a US minimum variance share portfolio produced a risk three-quarters the size of the general market (to be expected) but also produced returns greater than the general market (not expected). Some fund managers switched to buying the shares in the proportions defined by a minimum-variance calculation. Unigestion, for example, claimed its European share minimum-variance portfolio outperformed the wider market by 4% points between 1999 and 2008 (*see* Johnson (2008)).

Chapter 7 • Portfolio theory

Indifference curves

Indifference curve analysis draws on the concept of utility to present alternative trade-offs between risk and return each equally acceptable to the investor. Every individual will exhibit unique preferences for risk and return and so everyone has a unique set of indifference curves. Consider Mr Chisholm who is hypothetically allocated portfolio W represented in **Exhibit 7.38**. This portfolio has a return of 10% and a standard deviation of 16%. Now imagine you asked Mr Chisholm, 'If we were to change the constituents of the portfolio so that the risk increased to a standard deviation of 20% how much extra return would you require to compensate for the increased risk to leave your overall utility unchanged?' According to this simple model an extra return of 4% is required. That is, Mr Chisholm is indifferent between W and the portfolio Z with a standard deviation of 20% and return of 14%. His utility (or well-being) is identical for each portfolio.

In fact all the risk-return combinations along the indifference curve I_{105} in Exhibit 7.38 have the same level of desirability to Mr Chisholm. (The 105 is just a label; it has no more significance than that.) Portfolio X has a higher risk than portfolio Y and is therefore less desirable on this factor. However, exactly offsetting this is the attraction of the increased return.

Exhibit 7.38	Indifference curve for Mr Chisholm

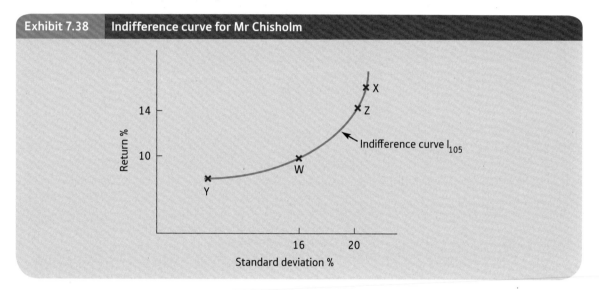

Now consider **Exhibit 7.39** where there are a number of indifference curves drawn for Mr Chisholm. Even though Mr Chisholm is indifferent between W and Z, he will not be indifferent between W and S. Portfolio S has the same level of risk as W but provides a higher level of return and is therefore preferable.

Exhibit 7.39	A map of indifference curves

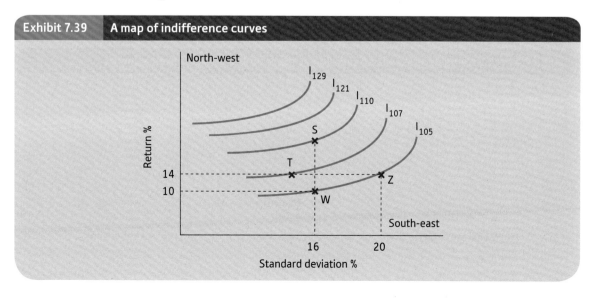

Likewise portfolio T is preferred to portfolio Z because for the same level of return a lower risk is obtainable. All portfolios along I_{110} provide a higher utility than any of the portfolios along I_{105}.

Similarly I_{121} portfolios are better than I_{110}. Indifference curve I_{129} gives the highest utility of all the curves represented in Exhibit 7.39, whereas I_{105} gives the lowest. The further 'north-west' the indifference curve, the higher the desirability, and therefore an investor will strive to obtain a portfolio which is furthest in this direction. Note that Exhibit 7.39 shows only five possible indifference curves whereas in reality there will be an infinite number, each representing alternative utility levels.

An important rule to bear in mind when drawing indifference curves is that they must never cross. To appreciate this rule consider point M in **Exhibit 7.40**. Remember that I_{105} represents alternative portfolios with the same level of utility for Mr Chisholm and he is therefore indifferent between the risk-return combinations offered along I_{105}. If M also lies on I_{101} this is saying that Mr Chisholm is indifferent between any of the I_{101} portfolios and point M. It is illogical to suppose that Mr Chisholm is indifferent between I_{105} and I_{101}. To the right of point M, I_{105} is clearly preferred. To the left of M, I_{101} gives the higher utility level. This logical contradiction is avoided by never allowing indifference curves to cross.

Exhibit 7.40   Intersecting indifference curves

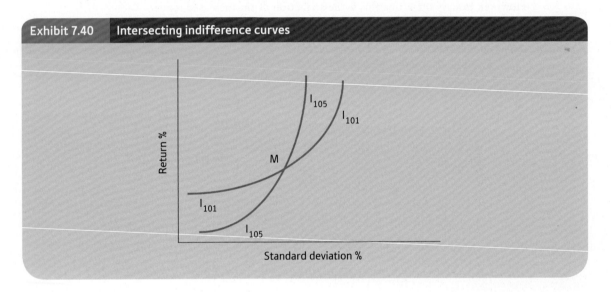

Mr Chisholm's personality and circumstances led to the drawing of his unique indifference curves with their particular slope. Other investors may be less risk averse than Mr Chisholm, in which case the increase in return required to compensate for each unit of increased risk will be less. That is, the indifference curves will have a lower slope. This is represented in **Exhibit 7.41(b)**. Alternatively, individuals may be less tolerant of risk and exhibit steeply sloped indifference curves, as demonstrated in **Exhibit 7.41(c)**. Here large increases in return are required for small increases in risk.

Exhibit 7.41   Varying degrees of risk aversion as represented by indifference curves

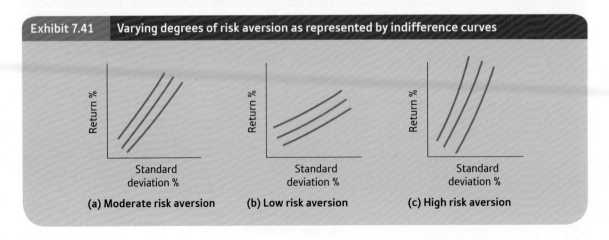

Choosing the optimal portfolio

We can now return to the investor considering investment in Augustus and Brown and apply indifference curve analysis to find the optimal portfolio. By assuming that this investor is moderately risk averse we can draw three of his indifference curves on to the risk-return profile diagram for two-asset portfolios of Augustus and Brown. This is shown in **Exhibit 7.42**. One option available is to select portfolio N, putting 25% of the fund into Augustus and the remainder in Brown. This will give a respectable expected return of 18.75% for a risk level of 12.16% for the standard deviation. It is interesting to note that this investor would be just as content with the return of 15.5% on portfolio J if risk were reduced to a standard deviation of 1.16%. I_1 represents quite a high level of utility and the investor would achieve a high level of well-being selecting either N or J. However, this is not the highest level of utility available – which is what the investor is assumed to be trying to achieve. By moving on to the indifference curve I_2, further to the north-west, the investor will increase his satisfaction. This curve touches the risk-return combination line at only one point, M, which represents an allocation of half of the funds to Augustus and half to Brown, giving a return of 17.5% and a standard deviation of 7.06%. This leads to a general rule when applying indifference curves to the risk-return combination line:

> Select the portfolio where the highest attainable indifference curve is tangential to (just touching) the efficient frontier.

Indifference curve I_3 is even more attractive than I_2 but this is impossible to obtain. The investor can dream of ever-increasing returns for low risk but will not achieve this level of utility.

Problems with indifference curve analysis

Obtaining indifference curves for individuals is time consuming and difficult. It is also subject to error. Try estimating your own risk-return preferences and your own degree of risk aversion to gain an impression involved in drawing up curves from subjective material such as thoughts and feelings. Even if you did arrive at firm conclusions at one specific time, are you confident that these will not change as your circumstances alter? It is plain that there are serious drawbacks to excessive

Exhibit 7.42   Optimal combination of Augustus and Brown

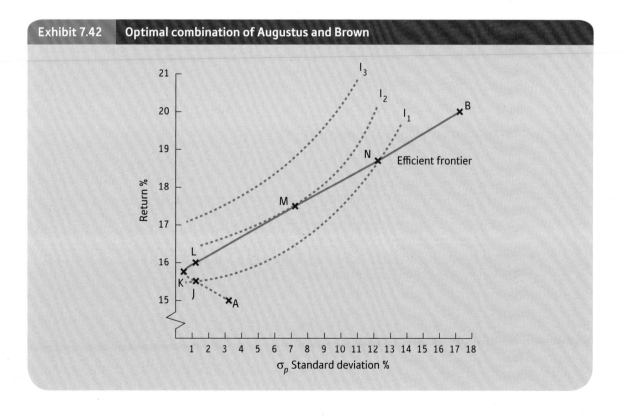

reliance on mathematically precise curves when they are based on imprecise opinion. However, it would be wrong to 'throw the baby out with the bathwater' and reject utility analysis completely. The model used does give us a representation of the different risk tolerances of individuals and permits us to come to approximate conclusions concerning likely optimal portfolios for particular individuals based on their risk-reward preferences. For instance, a highly risk-averse person is unlikely to elect to place all funds in Brown but will tend to select portfolios close to L or K. The exact allocation is less important than the general principles of (a) identifying efficient portfolios and (b) selecting an efficient portfolio which roughly matches the degree of risk aversion of the decision maker.

The boundaries of diversification

We can now consider the extreme circumstances of perfect negative, perfect positive and zero correlation to demonstrate the outer boundaries of the risk-return relationships.

Consider the two securities C and D, the expected returns and standard deviations for which are presented in **Exhibit 7.43**.

Exhibit 7.43	Expected return and standard deviation, Companies C and D	
	Company C	**Company D**
Expected return	$\overline{R_C} = 15\%$	$\overline{R_D} = 22\%$
Standard deviation	$\sigma_C = 3\%$	$\sigma_D = 9\%$

Perfect negative correlation

If we first assume that C and D are perfectly negatively correlated, $R_{CD} = -1$, then the point of minimum standard deviation is found as follows:

a = proportion of funds invested in C

$$a = \frac{\sigma_D^2 - \text{cov}(R_C, R_D)}{\sigma_C^2 + \sigma_D^2 - 2\,\text{cov}(R_C, R_D)}$$

or, given that $\text{cov}(R_C, R_D) = R_{CD}\sigma_C\sigma_D$:

$$a = \frac{\sigma_D^2 - R_{CD}\sigma_C\sigma_D}{\sigma_C^2 + \sigma_D^2 - 2R_{CD}\sigma_C\sigma_D}$$

$$a = \frac{9^2 - (-1 \times 3 \times 9)}{3^2 + 9^2 - (2 \times -1 \times 3 \times 9)} = 0.75$$

The portfolio which will reduce risk to zero is one which consists of 75% of C and 25% of D. The return available on this portfolio is:

$$R_P = aR_C + (1 - a)R_D$$
$$= 0.75 \times 15 + 0.25 \times 22 = 16.75\%$$

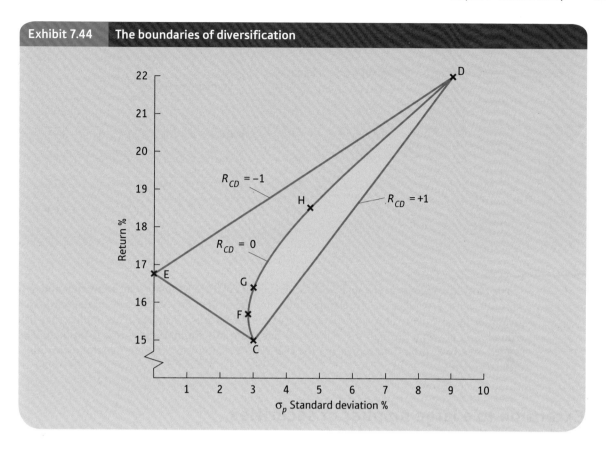

Exhibit 7.44   The boundaries of diversification

To confirm that this allocation will give the minimum risk the portfolio standard deviation could be calculated.

$$\sigma_P = \sqrt{a^2\sigma_C^2 + (1-a)^2\sigma_D^2 + 2a(1-a)R_{CD}\sigma_C\sigma_D}$$

$$\sigma_P = \sqrt{0.75^2 \times 3^2 + 0.25^2 \times 9^2 + 2 \times 0.75 \times 0.25 \times -1 \times 3 \times 9} = 0$$

This minimum variance portfolio has been labelled E in **Exhibit 7.44**. In the circumstances of a correlation coefficient of −1 all the other risk-return combinations are described by the dog-legged line CED. This describes the left boundary of the feasible set of portfolio risk-return lines.

Perfect positive correlation

The risk-return line for portfolios of C and D under the assumption of a correlation coefficient of +1 is a straight line joining C and D. This line forms the right boundary of possible portfolios. If the investment fund is evenly split between C and D both the expected return and the standard deviation will be weighted averages of those for single shares:

Expected return: $(15 \times 0.5) + (22 \times 0.5) = 18.5\%$
Standard deviation: $(3 \times 0.5) + (9 \times 0.5) = 6\%$

Zero correlation

The risk-return portfolio combinations for all correlation coefficients of less than +1 lie to the left of the line CD and exhibit non-linearity (that is, they are curved). The non-linearity becomes increasingly pronounced as the correlation coefficient approaches −1. The line CFGHD represents an intermediate level of the risk-reducing effect of diversification. For this line the correlation coefficient between C and D is set at 0. The plot points for the various portfolios are shown in **Exhibit 7.45**.

Exhibit 7.45	Risk-return combinations for C and D with a correlation coefficient of 0			
Portfolio	C weighting (%)	D weighting (%)	Expected return (%)	Standard deviation
C	100	0	15	3.00
F	90	10	15.7	$\sqrt{0.9^2 \times 3^2 + 0.1^2 \times 9^2 + 0}$ = 2.85
G	80	20	16.4	$\sqrt{0.8^2 \times 3^2 + 0.2^2 \times 9^2 + 0}$ = 3.00
H	50	50	18.5	$\sqrt{0.5^2 \times 3^2 + 0.5^2 \times 9^2 + 0}$ = 4.74
D	0	100	22	9.00

For most investments in the real world, correlation coefficients tend to lie between 0 and +1. This is because general economic changes influence the returns on securities in similar ways, to a greater or lesser extent. This is particularly true for the returns on shares. This implies that risk reduction is possible through diversification but the total elimination of risk is unlikely. The shaded area in Exhibit 7.44 represents the risk-return region for two-asset portfolios for most ordinary shares.

Extension to a large number of securities

To ensure that the analysis is manageable we have so far confined ourselves to two-asset portfolios. Investors rarely construct portfolios from shares in just two firms. Most realise that if risk can be reduced by moving from a single investment to a portfolio of two shares it can be further reduced by adding a third and fourth security, and so on. Consider the three securities represented in **Exhibit 7.46**. If the investor were to limit the extent of diversification by dividing the fund between two shares, three possible portfolio risk-return combination lines are possible. Curve 1 represents portfolios made by varying allocations of a fund between A and B. Curve 2 shows the alternative risk and return profiles available by investing in B and C; and Curve 3 represents A and C portfolios. With three securities the additional option arises of creating three-asset portfolios. Curve 4 shows the further reduction in return fluctuations resulting from adding the third share.

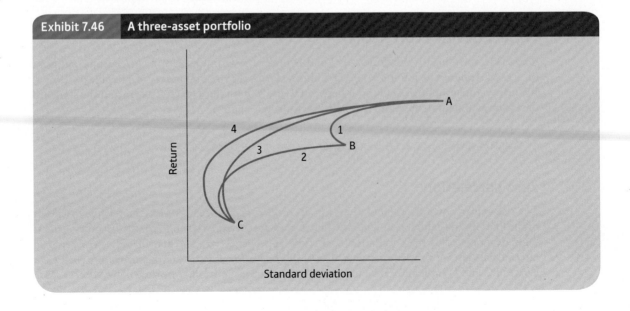

Exhibit 7.46   A three-asset portfolio

For two-asset portfolios the alternative risk-return combinations are shown by a line or curve. For a three- (or more) asset portfolio the possible combinations are represented by an area. Thus any risk-return combination within the shaded area of Exhibit 7.46 is potentially available to the investor. However, most of them will be unattractive because they are dominated by more efficient alternatives. In fact the rational investor will only be interested in portfolios lying on the upper part of Curve 4. This is the efficient frontier or efficient boundary. If the number of securities is raised the area representing the whole population of potential risk-return combinations comes to resemble an umbrella battling against a strong wind.

From Exhibit 7.46 it is not possible to establish which portfolio a rational investor would choose. This would depend on the individual's attitude to risk. Two types of investor attitudes are shown in **Exhibit 7.47** by drawing two sets of indifference curves. Indifference curves I_H are for a highly risk-averse person who would select the multi-asset portfolio U, which gives a relatively low return combined with a low risk. The less risk-averse person's attitude to risk is displayed in the indifference curves I_L. This person will buy portfolio V, accepting high risk but also anticipating high return. In this manner both investors achieve their optimum portfolios and the highest possible levels of utility.

Exhibit 7.47	The opportunity set for multi-security portfolios and portfolio selection for a highly risk-averse person and for a slightly risk-averse person

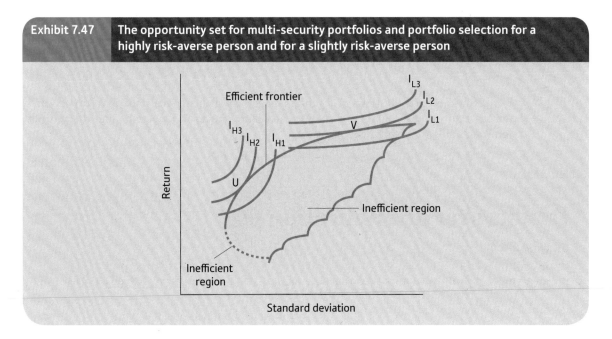

Evidence on the benefits of diversification

A crucial question for a risk-averse investor is: 'How many securities should be included in a portfolio to achieve a reasonable degree of risk reduction?' Obviously the greater the number of securities the lower the risk as measured by standard deviation (there are other types of risk – see later). But many investors, particularly small ones, are not keen on dividing their resources into ever smaller amounts, particularly given the transaction cost of buying financial securities. So it would be useful to know the extent to which standard deviation risk is reduced as additional securities are added to a portfolio. A long time ago Solnik (1974) investigated this issue for shares in eight countries. The result for the UK is shown in **Exhibit 7.48** – the overall picture is unlikely to alter much over time. The vertical axis measures portfolio risk (standard deviation) as a percentage of the risk of holding an individual security.

Solnik randomly generated portfolios containing between one and 50 shares. Risk is reduced in a dramatic manner by the addition of the first four securities to the portfolio. Most of the benefits of diversification are generated by a portfolio of 10–15 securities. Thus up to 90% of the benefit of diversification can be gained by holding a relatively small portfolio. Beyond this level the marginal risk reduction becomes relatively small. Also note that there is a level of risk below which the curve cannot fall even if larger numbers of securities are added to the portfolio. This is because there are certain risk factors common to all shares and these cannot be diversified away. This is called systematic (or market) risk and will be discussed in more detail in the next chapter.

Exhibit 7.48	The effect of increasing the number of securities in a portfolio – UK shares

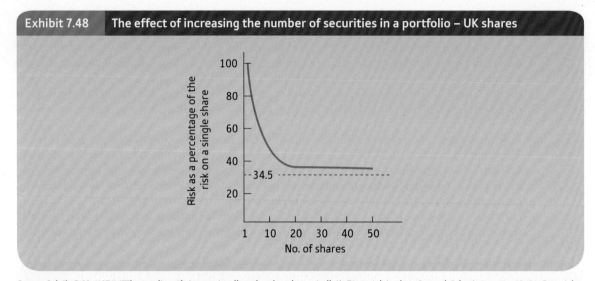

Exhibit 7.49 reports the views of a fund manager who believes that many investors diversify too much, thus losing the ability to analyse each share (stock) in a portfolio and the ability to concentrate funds on the top investment ideas.

Exhibit 7.49

Doubts over diversification use

By Chris Flood

Building a widely diversified equity portfolio merely raises transaction costs and turns a fund into an unnecessarily expensive index tracker, without significantly lowering risk, according to Senhouse Capital, a London-based asset manager.

Andrew Sykes, a fund manager at Senhouse, said research by Dresdner Kleinwort suggested the marginal benefit, in terms of reducing the volatility of a portfolio, of diversifying beyond 20 stocks was minimal.

However, a fund manager was unlikely to have an in-depth knowledge of every holding if there are 100 stocks or more in a portfolio, Mr Sykes argued, whereas a more concentrated fund allowed managers to focus more tightly on stocks they believed to be undervalued.

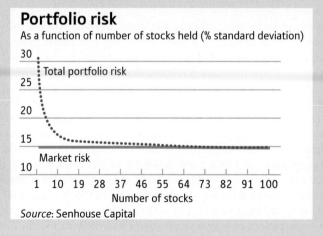

Portfolio risk
As a function of number of stocks held (% standard deviation)

Source: Senhouse Capital

'There are benefits to having fewer stocks in a fund than the formulas behind modern portfolio theory would suggest,' he said.

'It is reasonable to assume that it is going to be easier to find 20 undervalued stocks than it is to find 80.'

Mr Sykes said that because most funds' fee structures are based on assets under management, rather than performance, managers have a strong incentive to create more diversified vehicles, which are able to absorb more capital.

Senhouse's European Focus Fund currently holds just 16 'high conviction' ideas, although it can be expanded to a maximum of 25 stocks.

FT *Financial Times*, 19 April 2010, p. 2.

International diversification

We have seen that it is possible to reduce risk by diversifying within the boundaries of one country. It logically follows that further risk reduction is probably available by investing internationally. Exhibit 7.48 showed that there is a limit to the gains experienced by spreading investment across a range of shares in one country. This is because of the economy-wide risk factors such as interest rates and the level of economic activity, which influence all share returns simultaneously. Researchers have demonstrated that this limit can be side-stepped to some extent and that substantial further benefits can be attained through portfolio diversification into foreign shares. Solnik (1974) described a study for Germany, for example, in which 43.8% of risk remains even after complete diversification through buying shares within the domestic stock market; thus there was still a large amount of risk remaining, which could be reduced further by purchasing shares in other countries (*see* **Exhibit 7.50**).

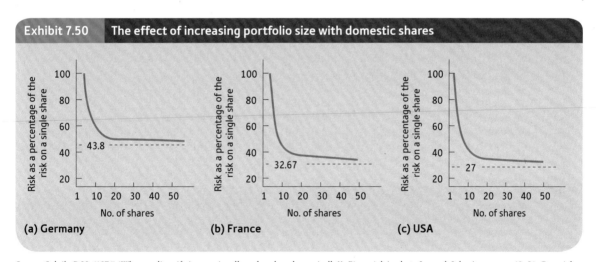

Exhibit 7.50   The effect of increasing portfolio size with domestic shares

(a) Germany

(b) France

(c) USA

Source: Solnik, B.H. (1974) 'Why not diversify internationally rather than domestically?', *Financial Analysts Journal*, July–August, pp. 48–54. Copyright 1974, Association for Investment Management and Research. Reproduced and republished from *Financial Analysts Journal* with permission from the Association for Investment Management and Research. All rights reserved.

The benefits of international diversification shown in **Exhibit 7.51** can be significant. In Solnik's collection of randomly produced portfolios the internationally diversified ones could reduce standard deviation risk to less than half the level of a domestically focused portfolio.

If the world economy were so intimately linked that stock markets in different countries moved together, there would be little to gain from diversifying abroad. Fortunately, this sort of perfect positive correlation of markets does not occur. **Exhibit 7.52** shows that the correlation coefficients between national stock markets are significantly less than +1. The correlation between the USA and Canada (0.8 over 101 years or 0.78 over 1996–2000) is quite strong because their economies

Exhibit 7.51	Benefits of international diversification

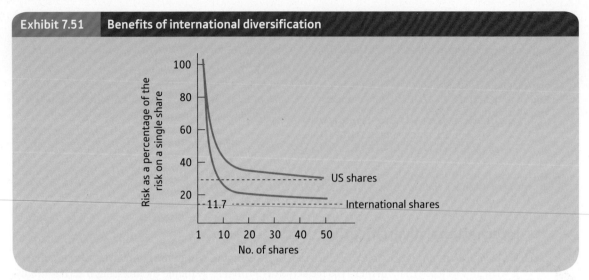

Exhibit 7.52	Correlation coefficients between world equity markets*

	Wld	US	UK	Swi	Swe	Spa	SAf	Neth	Jap	Ita	Ire	Ger	Fra	Den	Can	Bel	Aus
Wld		.93	.77	.59	.62	.67	.54	.73	.68	.52	.69	.69	.73	.57	.82	.54	.69
US	.85		.67	.44	.46	.53	.46	.57	.49	.40	.66	.56	.56	.46	.78	.45	.57
UK	.70	.55		.58	.44	.63	.31	.71	.42	.39	.73	.58	.59	.57	.57	.59	.56
Swi	.68	.50	.62		.39	.60	.19	.72	.36	.45	.57	.53	.64	.58	.35	.63	.37
Swe	.62	.44	.42	.54		.63	.38	.63	.34	.49	.27	.76	.76	.44	.61	.29	.44
Spa	.41	.25	.25	.36	.37		.35	.63	.32	.64	.50	.64	.75	.56	.51	.55	.54
SAf	.55	.43	.49	.39	.34	.26		.30	.44	.24	.31	.42	.37	.25	.62	.10	.66
Neth	.57	.39	.42	.51	.43	.28	.29		.39	.59	.63	.74	.77	.64	.55	.70	.46
Jap	.45	.21	.33	.29	.39	.40	.31	.25		.18	.33	.25	.36	.24	.50	.17	.59
Ita	.54	.37	.43	.52	.39	.41	.41	.32	.34		.33	.55	.71	.50	.40	.51	.38
Ire	.58	.38	.73	.70	.42	.35	.42	.46	.29	.43		.42	.45	.49	.54	.57	.50
Ger	.30	.12	−.01	.22	.09	−.03	.05	.27	.06	.16	.03		.83	.61	.57	.59	.46
Fra	.62	.36	.45	.54	.44	.47	.38	.48	.25	.52	.53	.19		.63	.60	.66	.48
Den	.57	.38	.40	.51	.56	.34	.31	.50	.46	.38	.55	.22	.45		.55	.54	.30
Can	.80	.80	.55	.48	.53	.27	.54	.34	.30	.37	.41	.13	.35	.46		.30	.65
Bel	.58	.38	.40	.57	.43	.40	.29	.60	.25	.47	.49	.26	.68	.42	.35		.30
Aus	.66	.47	.66	.51	.50	.28	.56	.41	.28	.43	.62	.04	.47	.42	.62	.35	

Correlations in bold (lower left-hand triangle) are based on 101 years of real dollar returns, 1900–2000. Correlations in roman (top right-hand triangle) are based on 60 months of real dollar returns, 1996–2000, from FTSE World (Ireland and South Africa) and MSCI (all others).

are closely linked whereas the correlation between Japan and European equity market returns has been relatively low.[3]

Plainly, risk can be reduced by international diversification but some risk remains even for the broadest portfolio. There is an increasing degree of economic integration across the globe.

---

3 These correlation coefficients need to be treated with great caution as they tend to vary from one study to another. They also change a great deal over time; for example, the correlation coefficient between the UK and the USA has varied from 0.67 to zero during the past century.

The linkages mean that the economic independence of nations is gradually being eroded and there is some evidence that stock markets are becoming more correlated. A poor performance on Wall Street often ricochets across the Pacific to Tokyo and other Far East markets and causes a wave of depression on the European exchanges – or vice versa. However, while short-term market crashes have shown increasingly high correlation, over long periods 'international diversification does an excellent job of protecting investors'.[4]

Around the world there is still a bias towards home investment. This disinclination to buy abroad is the result of many factors. These include: a lack of knowledge of companies and markets in faraway places; exchange rate problems; legal restrictions; cost; political risk. Choi et al. (2017) examined the performances of 10,771 institutional investor portfolios from 72 countries between 1999 and 2010 and found that greater home portfolio concentration generally led to higher return performance. They concluded that the bias towards investing in the home stock market was a rational optimization strategy, because investors have an informational advantage at home. This evidence is consistent with the model developed by Van Nieuwerburgh and Veldkamp (2009) which postulates that investors start with greater knowledge than non-domiciled investors about their home country shares; also that they go on to specialize and learn more about securities in which they have an initial comparative information advantage, leading to higher returns.

The capital market line

Consider Portfolio A on the efficient frontier of a multi-asset portfolio feasibility set in **Exhibit 7.53**. An investor could elect to place all funds into such a portfolio and achieve a particular risk-return trade-off. Alternatively, point B could be selected. Here the investor places half the funds invested in an efficient portfolio, C, and half in a risk-free asset such as bonds or Treasury bills issued by a reputable government. These bonds are represented by point r_f which demonstrates a relatively low return but a corresponding zero standard deviation. By purchasing government bonds the investor is lending to the government. Any combination containing a proportion of a share portfolio, such as C, and the risk-free asset will have an expected return which is a simple weighted average of the expected return of the share portfolio C and the risk-free asset r_f. More significantly, if the risk-free

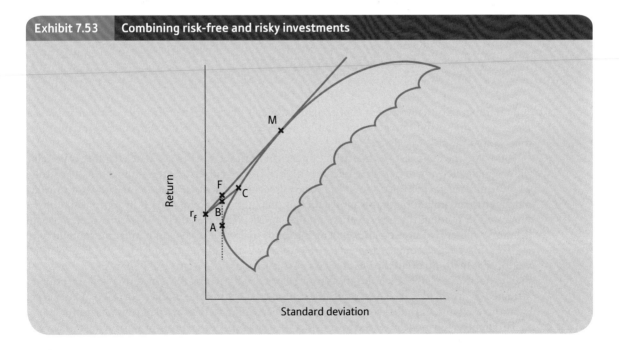

Exhibit 7.53   Combining risk-free and risky investments

---

4 Asness et al. (2011).

asset has a zero standard deviation, the standard deviation of a portfolio containing C and the risk-free asset will also be a simple weighted average. This results in the straight line between C and r_f representing all the possible allocations of a fund between these two types of investment.

Point B in Exhibit 7.53 is obviously a more efficient combination of investments than point A because for the same level of risk a higher return is achievable. However, this is not the best result possible. If a fund were split between a portfolio of shares represented by M and the risk-free investment then all possible allocations between r_f and M would dominate those on the line r_fC. If the fund were divided so that risk-free lending absorbed most of the funds, with approximately one-quarter going into shares of portfolio M, then point F would be reached. This dominates points B and A and is therefore more efficient. The schedule r_fM describes the best possible risk-return combinations. No other share portfolio when combined with a riskless asset gives such a steep slope as Portfolio M. Therefore the investor's interests will be best served by choosing investments comprising Portfolio M and selecting an optimum risk-return combination, by allocating appropriate proportions of a fund between M and the risk-free asset, r_f. This is demonstrated in **Exhibit 7.54**.

Exhibit 7.54   Indifference curves applied to combinations of the market portfolio and the risk-free asset

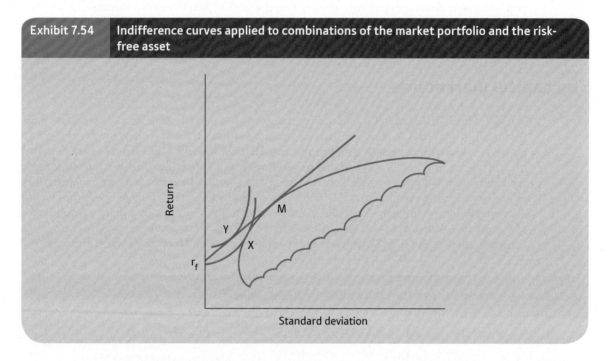

In Exhibit 7.54 an investment X is available which is on the efficient frontier of the feasible set. However, a higher indifference curve can be achieved if point Y is selected, comprising the portfolio M and the risk-free asset.

Following the logic of this theorising, under circumstances where risk-free lending is possible the original efficient frontier is significantly altered from a curve to a straight line (r_fM). Portfolio M is the most attractive portfolio of risk-bearing securities because it allows the investor to select a risk-return combination that is most efficient. In a perfect capital market investors will only be interested in holding the investments comprising M. Whatever their risk-return preference all investors will wish to invest some or all of the funds in Portfolio M. Combining this thought with the fact that someone must hold each risky asset, we are led to conclude that, in this idealised world, M is made up of all the possible risky assets available. Imagine if BT shares were not in the market portfolio. If nobody holds its shares the price will become zero. Investors will start to buy, attracted by its dividends. Thus, logically, it has to be held in the market portfolio. The market portfolio contains all traded securities weighted according to their market capitalisations.

To complete the model we need to consider the possibility of an investor borrowing rather than lending, that is, purchasing assets in Portfolio M to a value greater than the amount of money the investor has available from the existing fund. Borrowing to fund investment in risky assets is bound to lead to an overall increase in risk; but the corollary is that a higher return can be anticipated. This is shown in the line MN in **Exhibit 7.55** where it is assumed that all investors can borrow at the same interest rate as a reputable government.

All the risk-return combinations along MN in Exhibit 7.55 dominate those along the original efficient frontier. An investor who was only mildly risk averse might select point T, purchasing the market portfolio and being financed in part by borrowing at the risk-free rate. This is preferable to Portfolio S, purchased without borrowing. The line r_fMN is called the capital market line; it describes the expected return and risk of all efficient portfolios. This idealised model shows that even though investors have differences in their tolerance of risk all will purchase the market portfolio. The degree of risk aversion of individuals expresses itself by the investors either placing some of the fund into risk-free securities, as in the case of the relatively risk-intolerant investor who selects point G, or borrowing (at the risk-free rate of return) to invest in the market portfolio, thereby raising both risk and/or return, as in the case of the investor who selects point T. This is the Separation Theorem (after Tobin),[5] that is, the choice of the optimal Portfolio M is separated from the risk/return choice. Thus the investor, according to the model, would have two stages to the investment process. First, find the point of tangency on the original efficient frontier and thereby establish M; secondly, borrow or lend to adjust for preferred risk and return combinations.

Exhibit 7.55	The capital market line

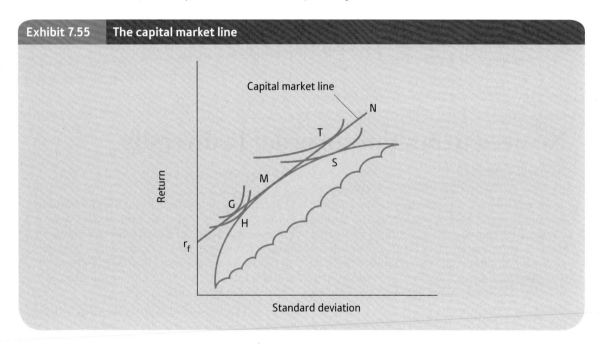

This theory is founded on a number of major (some say dubious) assumptions, for example:

1   There are no transaction costs or taxes.

2   Investors can borrow or lend at the risk-free rate of return.

3   Investors have all relevant information regarding the range of investment opportunities. They make their choices on the basis of known expected returns and standard deviations.

4   Maximisation of utility is the objective of all investors.

No less a figure than Harry M. Markowitz (2005) has strongly criticised this part of modern portfolio theory as taking things too far, because investors cannot borrow at the risk-free rate. Once this assumption is dropped, the capital market line is suspect and the conclusions of the theory built upon it (the Capital Asset Pricing Model discussed in the next chapter) 'no longer follow', says Markowitz.[6]

---

5   Tobin's Separation Theorem was first discussed in his 1958 article.

6   To be read after reading Chapter 8: Markowitz said that 'the original CAPM, with unlimited borrowing . . . impl[ies] that the expected return of a stock [share] depends in a simple (linear) way on its beta, and only on its beta. This conclusion has been used for estimating expected returns, but it has lost favour for this because of poor predictive results. It is still used routinely in "risk adjustment". However, for valuing assets and analysing investment strategies on a "risk-adjusted basis". . . the conclusion that expected returns are linear functions of beta does not hold when real-world limits on permitted portfolio holdings are introduced into the CAPM. This discussion will call into question the frequent use of beta in risk adjustment' (2005, p. 18).

Problems with portfolio theory

The portfolio theory model is usually implemented using *historical* returns, standard deviations and correlations to aid decision making about *future* investment. Generally, there is the implicit assumption that key statistical relationships will not alter over the life of the investment. The model relies on the predictability and stability of the probability profile of returns. If the returns have, historically, been volatile then the probability distribution for the anticipated returns will be given a correspondingly wide range; if they have been confined to small fluctuations in the past, then the forecasted variability will be similarly small. Predicting returns, standard deviations and covariances is a difficult and imprecise art. The past may guide to some degree, but there remain large margins for error. As well as standard deviations and covariances changing significantly over time, we have the problem that they change depending on whether the historical data used for their calculation are based on daily, weekly, monthly or quarterly observations.

In addition, the volume of computations for large portfolios can be inhibiting. If there are n securities then n expected returns have to be calculated along with n standard deviations and $n(n-1)/2$ covariances. Thus a portfolio of 30 shares will require 495 data items to be calculated. Even the great supporters of modern portfolio theory find the complexity unnecessary and off-putting – *see* **Exhibit 7.56**.

Exhibit 7.56

No need to multiply in order to diversify

By David Stevenson

A few months back, I had the good fortune to sit in on a customer panel session at a leading stockbroking firm. My primary purpose was to quiz the poor unfortunate clients on their behavioural vices for an up and coming book – I wanted the truth about their over-trading, and their overconfidence in their ability to pick shares in the style of Warren Buffett.

But what I actually got was a bunch of fairly level-headed folk who were largely terrified of making mistakes and who looked to people like me (sadly) to provide them with clues. More to the point, when I started talking about diversification they all said, 'How much is enough? We all understand that you have to diversify but how exactly should you do it?'

It was a cracking question to which there's a proper answer – and a real answer.

The proper answer is to listen to the collective wisdom of generations of investment academics and use modern portfolio theory, as devised by professor Harry Markowitz. This suggests that you look at risks and returns, alongside volatility, and then compute something called 'an efficient frontier' of different assets, allocated sensibly, in an optimised fashion. It's what the big wealth managers claim to do (although they actually don't, in most cases). It's also what many fine and upstanding financial planners will do for a very fair fee.

Unfortunately, its not what anyone I've ever talked to actually does. It's not the *real* answer. Here's Professor Markowitz at a conference in Chicago on what he invested in: 'I should have computed co-variances of the asset classes and drawn an efficient frontier – instead I split my contributions 50/50 between bonds and equities'.

He's not alone. Take the father of modern risk analysis in economics, Bill Sharpe, on the subject of how he builds his portfolio: 'I invest in various funds, large stocks, small stocks and international stocks'. Or Eugene Fama, the father of the index funds movement – when asked what he invested in, he replied by detailing a fund invested in the broad-based US Wilshire 5000 index, plus small cap and international index funds, and a just over a third in value-oriented stock indexes and short-term bond funds.

The vast majority of UK-based academics that I talk to also maintain a very sensible 60/40 split between equities and bonds, with just a couple of funds of each. The odd few go a little further, adding a few additional asset categories and maybe getting up to 6 funds – but that's it.

US analyst Rob Arnott says: 'Most of the advantage of diversifying happens with three or four significant positions in seriously cheap assets. If you go beyond ten, you're diluting the opportunity set. You're reducing your ability to add value.'

Tim Bond at BarCap also cautions against over-diversification, favouring a focus on China's infrastructure boom and the new carbon light economy. 'Under those circumstances, diversification is literally the worse possible solution to your investment needs... it's the worst possible thing to do. Actually, you need a really narrowly focused portfolio, where you're investing specifically on that theme'.

Also, the accurate estimation of indifference curves is probably an elusive goal and therefore the techniques used in this chapter can be criticised for trying to use unobtainable information. However, to counter this criticism it should be pointed out that utility analysis combined with an approximation of the efficient frontier provides a framework for thinking through the implications of portfolio selection. It is perhaps true that people cannot express their indifference curves exactly, but they will probably be able to state their risk preferences within broad categories, such as 'highly risk averse' or 'moderately risk averse' and so on. Through such approximate methods more appropriate portfolio selection can be made than would be the case without the framework. The model has been used in the fund management industry for constructing portfolios of different risk-return characteristics by weighting classes of investment assets differently, for example domestic shares, cash, bonds, foreign shares, property. Theorists have gone a stage further and developed 'portfolio optimisers'. These are mathematical computer programs designed to select an optimal portfolio. Relatively few investment managers have adopted these models, despite their familiarity with the principles and technical aspects of portfolio theory. It appears that traditional approaches to investment selection are valued more highly than the artificial precision of the optimisers. The problem seems to stem from the difficulty of finding high-quality data to put into the system on expected returns, standard deviations, covariances and so on – because of the necessity to rely on past returns. Extreme historical values such as an extraordinarily low standard deviation can lead the program to suggest counter-intuitive and uninvestable portfolios. They have a tendency to promote a high turnover of shares within the portfolio by failing to take into account transaction costs. Also there is a tendency to recommend the purchasing of shares in very small firms having impossibly poor liquidity. The use of portfolio optimisers fits a pattern in finance: entirely substituting mathematics for judgement does not pay off. John Kay makes this point very well in **Exhibit 7.57**. I particularly like the statement 'Financial models are indispensable. So is scepticism in their application.'

Exhibit 7.57

Financial models are no excuse for resting your brain

By John Kay

The model seems to be in question. But the idea behind it – that careful diversification can combine good returns with low risk – is as valid as ever. The problem is that some supporters of that approach put too much blame on sophisticated modelling techniques at the expense of their own knowledge and judgment.

Quantitative portfolio management relies on measures of correlations between asset classes. These historical correlations are not universal constants but the products of particular economic conditions. Unless you understand the behaviour that produced them, you cannot assess their durability. In 2007-08, assets that had been uncorrelated were strongly correlated and many portfolio managers were surprised when the diversification they sought proved illusory.

Underlying causal relations had changed, as they frequently do in business. In the new economy bubble of the 1990s, equities roared ahead while property languished. But during 2003-2008, the availability of

▶

Exhibit 7.57 *(continued)*

underpriced credit, followed by its abrupt withdrawal, affected property and shares in similar ways. Anyone in the financial world knew these things: but computers, churning through reams of data, did not.

Private equity was once a punt on small entrepreneurs. A manager with good judgment could make money from a few hits in a diversified portfolio. But by 2006 the sheer size of private-equity funds led them to focus on well established businesses. Such investments were a geared play on the stock market. They no longer spread risk: they concentrated it. Worse, many uncorrelated assets appeared uncorrelated in the past only because they were thinly traded and infrequently valued.

But, during the credit crunch, traditional forms of diversification have done what they are supposed to do. Gold, trading at about $650 per ounce before the credit crunch, is nearing $850. UK government stocks show a total return of 23 per cent from conventional bonds and 15 per cent from indexed bonds from July

2007 to December 2008: for global sovereign bonds, the sterling returns are 75 per cent and 41 per cent.

Diversification is a matter of judgment not statistics. A model will tell you only what you have already told the model and can never replace, though it can enhance, an understanding of market psychology and the factors that make for successful business. As a student of finance, I never expected to see the efficient risk-return frontiers I drew on the blackboard feature in *PowerPoint* presentations to meetings of trustees: or that these trustees would view the numbers that emerged as statements of fact rather than illustrations of possibilities.

People who were persuaded by these analyses have been badly hurt. Some will never pay heed to quantitative investment analysis again. Others will place equally blind faith in some new and fanciful construction. Both reactions are mistakes. Financial models are indispensable. So is scepticism in their application.

There are many financial market practitioners who do not believe that volatility (standard deviation) is a good measure of the real risks investors face, and therefore portfolio theory is of little value to them – *see* **Exhibit 7.58** and the 'Sceptics' views' section in Chapter 8. (Pablo Triana's (2009) book is a good antidote for those who think finance is about mathematical complexity.)

Exhibit 7.58

Challenging the notion volatility equals risk

By Pablo Triana

For decades, financial players, regulators, and academics have equated risk with volatility. The practice can probably be traced back to Harry Markowitz's fateful afternoon at the University of Chicago's library some 60 years ago, when the future Nobel laureate came up with his famous mean-variance model of portfolio selection. This stated that the standard deviation of an asset's returns (the statistical measure typically associated with volatility) is a pretty good indicator of its riskiness.

This idea has since become conventional wisdom in financial circles. Want to measure the 'risks'

of a market play? Open your Excel spreadsheet, collect some historical returns data, calculate the standard deviation and, voilà, that is the exposure you are facing. The more volatile an asset, so the argument goes, the higher the risk of investing in it. Or, put differently, the less volatile an asset the less we should worry about its future performance, thus entitling ourselves to accumulate tons of it without taking too many precautions.

The recent crisis has consigned all that conventional wisdom to the wastebasket.

Volatility has been revealed as a pretty poor measure of true exposures. What had been regarded as placid and dormant in the recent past suddenly revealed itself as destructively toxic. Assets with low standard deviations suddenly lost all their value.

The crux of the problem is that volatility can provide camouflage for lethal assets, thus acting as a Trojan Horse of the markets. With volatility as your main tool, it can be quite easy to hide the true risks of a play. All you have to do is find a historical time series containing nothing but good news for your standard deviation number to be very modest. Going back three years does not yield a volatility figure tame enough?

Just go back six years, since between year six and year three turbulence was negligible. Worried that the market meltdown of two years ago will categorise assets as wildly problematic? Just use the past 12 months, entirely dominated by rosy recovery.

If you want to gorge on exotic high-yielding assets in a highly leveraged way, data-dependent volatility can help a lot: just scour the asset universe until you find a decently toxic family member that happens to have enjoyed a privileged past life; the risk estimates and the capital requirements will be minimal, excusing your enthusiastic forays into toxic-land.

Finding daring assets with a sunny record might not be that hard. Toxic securities tend to be binary: either they are doing quite well (as the bubble gains strength) or they are worth zero (as they inevitably collapse into nothingness). For these securities there cannot be 'mildly bad' news: if the market turns sour, it means total destruction, not just a minor correction. It follows that, if they exist at all, their past performance must have been rosy.

It is thus quite easy to use standard deviation to categorise problematic stuff as non-problematic.

In fact, a troubling paradox is allowed to take place: obviously sounder assets (say, US Treasuries) can be labelled riskier than obviously slipperier alternatives (say, subprime collateralised debt obligations) if the former happened to have gone through a temporary rough patch while the latter still rode the crest of the bubble wave.

Commonsensical analysis is turned on its head when volatility is mechanistically equated with risk. The collateral damage from all this can be quite unpleasant, as the latest malaise can attest.

It is often told that fellow Chicago professor (and legendary economist) Milton Friedman had real hesitations when it came to rubber-stamping Mr Markowitz's portfolio theory all those years ago. With all due respect for Mr Markowitz, perhaps it would have been better if the notion that volatility is risk had not, Trojan-horse style, infiltrated the markets.

Pablo Triana is the author of Lecturing Birds On Flying: Can Mathematical Theories Destroy The Financial Markets?

Source: John Wiley & Sons

Concluding comments

The criticisms levelled at portfolio theory do strike at those who would use it in a dogmatic, mathematically precise and unquestioning manner. However, they do not weaken the fundamental truths revealed. Selecting shares (or other types of securities, projects or assets) on the basis of expected returns alone is inadequate. The additional dimensions of risk and the ability to reduce risk through diversification must be taken into account.

In trying to achieve a low standard deviation it is not enough to invest in a large number of securities. The fundamental requirement is to construct a portfolio in which the securities have low covariance between them. Thus to invest in the shares of 100 different engineering firms will not bring about as many benefits of diversification as the same sized portfolio spread between the sectors of paper manufacturers, retailers, media companies, telecommunications operators and computer software producers, etc. Returns on firms in the same industry are likely to respond in similar ways to economic and other events, to greater or lesser degrees, and so may all do badly at the same time. Firms in different industries are likely to have lower covariances than firms within an industry.

Key points and concepts

- The one-year holding period return:

$$R = \frac{D_1 + P_1 - P_0}{P_0}$$

  Use IRR-type calculations for multi-period returns.

- With **perfect negative correlation** the risk on a portfolio can fall to zero if an appropriate allocation of funds is made.

- With **perfect positive correlations** between the returns on investments, both the expected returns and the standard deviations of portfolios are weighted averages of the expected returns and standard deviations, respectively, of the constituent investments.

- In cases of **zero correlation** between investments risk can be reduced through diversification, but it will not be eliminated.

- The **correlation coefficient** ranges from -1 to $+1$. Perfect negative correlation has a correlation coefficient of -1. Perfect positive correlation has a correlation coefficient of $+1$.

- **The degree of risk reduction** for a portfolio depends on:

  a the extent of statistical interdependency between the returns on different investments; and
  b the number of securities in the portfolio.

- **Portfolio expected returns** are a weighted average of the expected returns on the constituent investments:

$$R_P = aR_A + (1 - a)R_B$$

- **Portfolio standard deviation** is less than the weighted average of the standard deviation of the constituent investments (except for perfectly positively correlated investments):

$$\sigma_p = \sqrt{a^2\sigma_A^2 + (1 - a)^2\sigma_B^2 + 2a(1 - a)\, \mathrm{cov}\,(R_A, R_B)}$$

$$\sigma_p = \sqrt{a^2\sigma_A^2 + (1 - a)^2\sigma_B^2 + 2a(1 - a)R_{AB}\sigma_A\sigma_B}$$

- **Covariance** means the extent to which the returns on two investments move together:

$$\mathrm{cov}\,(R_A, R_B) = \sum_{i=1}^{n}\{(R_A - \overline{R_A})(R_B - \overline{R_B})p_i\}$$

- **Covariance and the correlation coefficient** are related. Covariance can take on any positive or negative value. The correlation coefficient is confined to the range -1 to $+1$:

$$R_{AB} = \frac{\mathrm{cov}\,(R_A, R_B)}{\sigma_A\sigma_B}$$

  or $\mathrm{cov}\,(R_A, R_B) = R_{AB}\sigma_A\sigma_B$

- **Efficient portfolios** are on the **efficient frontier.** These are combinations of investments which maximise the expected returns for a given standard deviation. Such portfolios **dominate** all other possible portfolios in an **opportunity set** or **feasible set.**

- To find the proportion of the fund, a, to invest in investment C in a two-asset portfolio to achieve **minimum variance or standard deviation**:

$$a = \frac{\sigma_D^2 - \mathrm{cov}\,(R_C, R_D)}{\sigma_C^2 + \sigma_D^2 - 2\,\mathrm{cov}\,(R_C, R_D)}$$

- **Indifference curves** for risk and return:

  - are upward sloping;
  - do not intersect;
  - are preferred if they are closer to the 'north-west';
  - are part of an infinite set of curves;
  - have a slope which depends on the risk aversion of the individual concerned.

- **Optimal portfolios** are available where the highest attainable indifference curve is tangential to the efficient frontier.

- **Most securities** have correlation coefficients in the range of 0 to $+1$.

- The feasible set for **multi-asset portfolios** is an area that resembles an umbrella.

- **Diversification within a home stock market** can reduce risk to less than one-third of the risk on a typical single share. Most of this benefit is achieved with a portfolio of 10 securities.

- **International diversification** can reduce risk even further than domestic diversification.

- **Problems with portfolio theory:**

  - relies on past data to predict future risk and return, not taking into account the uniqueness of underlying conditions or human actions;
  - involves complicated calculations;
  - indifference curve generation is difficult;
  - few investment managers use computer programs because of the nonsense results they frequently produce.

References and further reading

Asness, C.S., Israelov, R. and Liew, J.M. (2011) 'International diversification works (eventually)', *Financial Analysts Journal,* 67(3), pp. 24–38.
  While international equity markets tend to be highly correlated during crashes, they have excellent diversification benefits over the long run.

Barry, C.B., Peavy J.W. (III) and Rodriguez, M. (1998) 'Performance characteristics of emerging capital markets', *Financial Analysts Journal,* January/February, pp. 72–80.
  Some useful evidence/data of relevance to international diversification.

Choi, N., Fedenia, M., Skiba, H. and Sokolyk, T. (2017) 'Portfolio concentration and performance of institutional investors worldwide', *Journal of Financial Economics,* 123, pp. 189–208.
  Evidence from 72 countries that home country bias in portfolio concentration tends to lead to higher returns, thus countering the argument for blindly following correlation logic to greater international diversification.

Clarke, R., de Silva, H. and Thorley, S. (2006) 'Minimum-variance portfolios in the US equity market: reducing volatility without sacrificing returns', *The Journal of Portfolio Management,* Fall, pp. 10–24.
  US shares in a minimum standard deviation portfolio subsequently perform much better than portfolio theory would indicate.

Cochrane, J.H. (2005) *Asset Pricing.* Princeton, NJ, and Oxford: Princeton University Press.
  An examination of asset pricing theory aimed at PhD students and academics.

Cooper, I. and Kaplanis, E. (1994) 'Home bias in equity portfolios, inflation hedging and international capital market equilibrium', *Review of Financial Studies,* 7(1), pp. 45–60.
  Examines the general bias of investors towards investing in their domestic stock market.

Dimson, E., Marsh, P. and Staunton, M. (2002) *Triumph of the Optimists: 101 Years of Global Investment Returns.* Princeton, NJ, and Oxford: Princeton University Press.
  An excellent source of data and thought-provoking discussion of equity risk premiums.

Divecha, A.B., Drach, J. and Stefek, D. (1992) 'Emerging markets: a quantitative perspective', *Journal of Portfolio Management,* Fall, pp. 41–50.
  An investigation of the risk-reducing benefits of international diversification.

Elton, E.J., Gruber, M.J., Brown, S.J. and Goetzmann, W.N. (2014) *Modern Portfolio Theory and Investment Analysis,* 9th edn. Chichester: John Wiley & Sons.
  From introductory to advanced portfolio theory.

Fama, E.F. and Miller, M.H. (1972) *The Theory of Finance.* Orlando, FL: Holt, Rinehart & Winston.
  Utility analysis and indifference curve theory.

Frost, P.A. and Savarino, J.E. (1986) 'Portfolio size and estimation risk', *Journal of Portfolio Management,* 12, Summer, pp. 60–4.
  Discussion of portfolio theory.

Goetzman, W.N., Lingfeng, L. and Rouwenhorst, K.G. (2005) 'Long-term global market correlations', *Journal of Business,* 78(1), pp. 1–38.
  Shows correlations of shares across countries over 150 years. Correlations shift overtime.

Johnson, S. (2008) "Magic formula" defies all the rules', *Financial Times,* FTfm section, 5 September, p. 3.
  A short article discussing the outperformance (in returns) of portfolios of minimum variance relative to the general share market.

Jorion, P. (1992) 'Portfolio optimisation in practice', *Financial Analysts Journal,* 48, January/February, pp. 68–74.
  The use of portfolio theory investigated.

Kaplanis, E. and Schaefer, S. (1991) 'Exchange risk and international diversification in bond and equity portfolios', *Journal of Economics and Business,* 43, pp. 287–307.
  Considers the problem of exchange-rate risk on internationally diversified portfolios.

Lewis, K. (1996) 'Consumption, stock returns, and the gains from international risk-sharing', *NBER Working Paper,* No. 5410, January.
  Advanced theoretical discussion of the gains from international diversification.

Lintner, J. (1965) 'The valuation of risky assets and the selection of risky investments in stock portfolios and capital budgets', *Review of Economics and Statistics,* 47, February, pp. 13–37.
  Theoretical paper contributing to the development of portfolio theory.

Markowitz, H.M. (1952) 'Portfolio selection', *Journal of Finance,* 7, pp. 77–91.
  Pioneering theory.

Markowitz, H.M. (1959) *Portfolio Selection: Efficient Diversification of Investments.* New York: John Wiley & Sons (1991); 2nd edn: Cambridge, MA: Basil Blackwell.
  The Nobel Prize winner explains his ideas.

Markowitz, H.M. (1991) 'Foundations of portfolio theory', *Journal of Finance,* June.
  Markowitz describes some of his thinking in the development of portfolio theory. Plus some advanced utility theory.

Markowitz, H.M. (2005) 'Market efficiency: a theoretical distinction and so what?', *Financial Analysts Journal*, Sept/Oct, pp. 17–30.
>   The assumptions behind the capital market line and thus the security market line of the Capital Asset Pricing Model are severely criticised.

Michaud, R.O. (1989) 'The Markowitz optimization enigma: Is "optimized" optimal?', *Financial Analysts Journal*, 45, January–February, pp. 31–42.
>   Discusses reasons for the low rate of adoption of portfolio optimiser programmes by the investment community.

Michaud, R.O., Bergstorm, G.L., Frashure, R.D. and Wolahan, B.K. (1996) 'Twenty years of international equity investment', *Journal of Portfolio Management*, Fall, pp. 9–22.
>   Diversifying into well-developed markets did not reduce risk substantially.

Mossin, J. (1966) 'Equilibrium in a capital asset market', *Econometrica*, 34, October, pp. 768–83.
>   Theoretical paper taking forward portfolio theory and discussing the 'market line'.

Roy, A. D. (1952) 'Safety First and the Holding of Assets', *Econometrica*, 20(3), July, pp. 431–49.
>   Concurrent with Markovitz, Roy developed a form of mean-variance optimization in portfolios by focusing on the probability of the portfolio return falling below a minimum specified percentage.

Sharpe, W.F. (1963) 'A simplified model for portfolio analysis', *Management Science*, 9, pp. 277–93.
>   Builds on Markowitz's work, focusing on the determination of the efficient set.

Solnik, B.H. (1974) 'Why not diversify internationally rather than domestically?', *Financial Analysts Journal*, July–August, pp. 48–54.
>   Empirical investigation on the effect of diversification for eight countries.

Solnik, B.H. and McLeavey, D. (2003) *International Investments*, 5th edn. Boston, MA: Pearson Education.
>   The benefits of international diversification are discussed in an accessible manner – some good data.

Spiedell, L.S. and Sappenfield, R. (1992) 'Global diversification in a shrinking world', *Journal of Portfolio Management*, Fall, pp. 57–67.
>   Diversifying into emerging markets enables significant risk reduction.

Tobin, J. (1958) 'Liquidity preference as behaviour toward risk', *Review of Economic Studies*, February, 26, pp. 65–86.
>   The first discussion of the separation of the selection of the efficient market portfolio and the individual's risk return choice.

Triana, P. (2009) *Lecturing Birds on Flying: Can Mathematical Theories Destroy the Financial Markets?* Hoboken, NJ: John Wiley & Sons.
>   A forceful attack on those who have an unreasonable faith in financial models and mathematical answers rather than taking into account human actions.

Van Nieuwerburgh, S. and Veldkamp, L. (2009) Informational immobility and the home bias puzzle, *Journal of Finance*, 64, pp. 1187–215.
>   A model of investor behaviour that explains why investors rationally tend to concentrate investment in their home markets, with little venturing abroad.

Wagner, W.H. and Lau, S. (1971) 'The effects of diversification on risk', *Financial Analysts Journal*, November–December.
>   Empirical evidence of the effect on standard deviation of increasing portfolio size.

Case study recommendations

Please see www.pearsoned.co.uk/arnold for case study synopses. Also, there is another list of useful case studies in the fifth edition.

- Innocents Abroad: Currencies and International Stock Returns
  Authors: Mihir A. De sai; Kathleen Luchs; Elizabeth A. Meyer; Mark F. Veblen. Harvard Business School. Available at www.cb.hbsp.harvard.edu

- Chris Lee's Investment Plan
  Authors: Hubert Pun; Lana Rao. Ivey Publishing. Available at www.cb.hbsp.harvard.edu

Self-review questions

1 How do you calculate the risk on a two-asset portfolio?

2 What is a dominant portfolio?

3 What are indifference curves and why can they never intersect?

4 How are holding-period returns calculated?

5 Show how the covariance and correlation coefficient are related.

6 Explain the necessary conditions for the standard deviation on a portfolio to be zero.

7 Illustrate the efficient frontier and explain why all portfolios on the frontier are not necessarily optimal.

8 A risk-averse investor currently holds low-risk shares in one company only. In what circumstances would it be wise to split the fund by purchasing shares in a high-risk and high-return share?

9 'The objective of portfolio investment is to minimise risk.' Do you agree?

10 Why is the standard deviation on a portfolio usually not a weighted average of the standard deviations of the constituent securities?

11 Describe why investors do not routinely calculate portfolio standard deviations and indifference curves.

12 How are the gains from diversification linked to correlation coefficients?

Questions and problems

Answers to most questions can be found at www.pearsoned.co.uk/arnold.
Answers to questions marked with an asterisk are to be found only in the Lecturer's Guide.

1 What is the holding-period return for a share which cost £2.50, was held for a year and then sold for £3.20, and which paid a dividend at the end of the holding period of 10p? **?**

2 Calculate the percentage holding-period return for a share which is held for three months and sold for £5. The purchase price was £4.80 and no dividend is payable. **?**

3 Shares in Whitchat plc can be purchased today for £1.20. The expected dividend in one year is 5p. This is expected to be followed by annual dividends of 6p and 7p respectively in the following two years. The shares are expected to be sold for £2 in three years. What is the average annual rate of return? What is the three-year holding-period return?

4* (Examination level if combined with Questions 5 and 6) The probability of a hot summer is 0.2. The probability of a moderately warm summer is 0.6, whereas the probability of a wet and cold summer is 0.2. If a hot summer occurs then the return on shares in the Ice Cream Manufacturing Company will be 30%. If moderately warm the return will be 15%, and if cold 2%.

  a   What is the expected return?
  b   What is the standard deviation of that return?

5* Splash plc owns a swimming pool near to a major seaside resort town. Holidaymakers boost the turnover of this firm when they are unable to use the beach on cold and wet days. Thus Splash's returns are best when the weather is poor. The returns on the shares are shown in the table below, together with the probability of when a particular weather 'event' may occur.

Event	Probability	Returns on shares in Splash plc (%)
Hot weather	0.2	5
Modestly warm	0.6	15
Cold weather	0.2	20
	1.0	

Calculate

  a   The expected return for a share in Splash plc.
  b   The standard deviation of a share in Splash plc.

6* a Given the data on the Ice Cream Manufacturing Company (ICMC) in Question 4 and Splash plc in Question 5, now calculate the expected returns and standard deviation of the following portfolios.

Portfolio	Proportion of funds invested in ICMC	Proportion of funds invested in Splash
A	0.80	0.20
B	0.50	0.50
C	0.25	0.75

b Calculate the correct allocation of resources between ICMC and Splash which will give the minimum standard deviation. Draw a risk-return line on graph paper using the data you have generated from Questions 4, 5 and 6a.

7 Given the following expected returns and standard deviations for shares X and Y,

$$\overline{R}_X = 25\%, \overline{R}_Y = 35\%, \sigma_X = 15\%, \sigma_Y = 20\%$$

a What is the expected return and standard deviation for a portfolio composed of 50% of X and 50% of Y assuming X and Y have a correlation coefficient of −0.7?

b What is the expected return and standard deviation for a portfolio composed of 30% of X and 70% of Y, assuming X and Y have a correlation coefficient of +0.5?

8 The returns on shares S and T vary depending on the state of economic growth.

State of economy	Probability of economic state occurring	Returns on S if economic state occurs (%)	Returns on T if economic state occurs (%)
Boom	0.15	45	18
Growth	0.70	20	17
Recession	0.15	−10	16

Required

a Calculate the expected return and standard deviation for share S.

b Calculate the expected return and standard deviation for share T.

c What is the covariance and the correlation coefficient between returns on S and returns on T?

d Determine a portfolio expected return and standard deviation if two-thirds of a fund are devoted to S and one-third devoted to T.

(An Excel spreadsheet showing the calculations for Question 8 is available at www.pearsoned.co.uk/arnold)

9 Using the results generated in Question 8 and three or four additional calculations, display the efficient frontier for a two-asset portfolio consisting of S and T.

Show a set of indifference curves for a highly risk-averse investor and select an optimal portfolio on the assumption that the investor can only invest in these two shares.

10 An investor has £100,000 to invest in shares of Trent or Severn the expected returns and standard deviations of which are as follows.

The correlation coefficient between those two shares is −0.2.

	$\bar{R}$	σ
Trent	10	5
Severn	20	12

Required

a   Calculate the portfolio expected returns and standard deviations for the following allocations.

Portfolio	Trent (%)	Severn (%)
A	100	0
B	75	25
C	50	50
D	25	75
E	0	100

b   Calculate the minimum standard deviation available by varying the proportion of Trent and Severn shares in the portfolio.

c   Create a diagram showing the feasible set and the efficient frontier.

d   Select an optimal portfolio for a slightly risk-averse investor using indifference curves.

11   Big Trucks plc is considering two major projects. The first is to expand production at the Midlands factory. The second is to start production in the Far East. The returns in terms of internal rates of return depend on world economic growth. These are as follows.

World growth	Probability of growth occurring	IRR for Midlands project (%)	IRR for Far East project (%)
High	0.3	20	50
Medium	0.4	18	30
Low	0.3	16	0

Calculate

a   The expected return and standard deviation of each project.

b   An alternative to selecting one project or the other is to split the available investment funds between the two projects. Now calculate the expected return and standard deviation if half of the funds were devoted to the Midlands project and half to the Far East. Assume returns per pound invested remain constant regardless of the size of the investment.

c   Calculate the expected return and standard deviation for a series of four other possible allocations of the funds and construct a risk-return line.

d   Suggest an approach for choosing the optimal allocation of funds assuming a highly risk-averse management and shareholders own shares in this one firm only.

12   Shares in F and G are perfectly negatively correlated.

	$\bar{R}$	σ
F	17	6
G	25	10

a   Calculate the expected return and standard deviation from a portfolio consisting of 50% of F and 50% of G.
b   How would you allocate the fund to achieve a zero standard deviation?

13   Suppose that Mrs Qureshi can invest all her savings in shares of Ihser plc, or all her savings in Resque plc. Alternatively she could diversify her investment between these two. There are three possible states of the economy, boom, growth or recession, and the returns on Ihser and Resque depend on which state will occur.

State of the economy	Probability of state of the economy occurring	Ihser return (%)	Resque return (%)
Boom	0.3	40	10
Growth	0.4	30	15
Recession	0.3	−10	20

Required

a   Calculate the expected return, variance and standard deviation for each share.
b   Calculate the expected return, variance and standard deviation for the following diversifying allocations of Mrs Qureshi's savings:

(i)   50% in Ihser, 50% in Resque;
(ii)   10% in Ihser, 90% in Resque.

c   Explain the relationship between risk reduction and the correlation between individual financial security returns.

14*   *(Examination level)* **Horace Investments**
Your Uncle Horace is a wealthy man with investments in a variety of businesses. He is also a generous person, especially to his nieces and nephews. He has written explaining that he will be distributing some of his shareholdings among the next generation. To your surprise, he has offered you £100,000 of shares in two firms of great sentimental value to him: Ecaroh and Acehar. You may allocate the £100,000 in any one of four ways. The first two options are to put all of the money into one of the firms. An alternative is to allocate half to Ecaroh and half to Acehar. Finally you may have £90,000 of Ecaroh shares and £10,000 of Acehar shares. During the week you are given to make your decision you contact a friend who is a corporate analyst with access to extensive brokers' and other reports on firms. The information he provides could help you to allocate this generous gift. He tells you that the market consensus is that Ecaroh is a relatively unexciting but steady, reliable firm producing profits which do not vary in an erratic fashion. If the economy is growing strongly then the returns on Ecaroh are expected to be 10% per year. If normal economic growth occurs then the returns will be 15% and if poor growth is the outcome the returns will be 16%.

Acehar, a consumer electronics firm, is a much more exciting and dynamic but risky firm. Profits vary in dramatic ways with the general level of activity in the economy. If growth is strong then Acehar will return 50%; if normal, 25%; and, if poor, there will be no return. You generate your own estimates of the probabilities of particular economic growth rates occurring by amalgamating numerous macroeconomic forecasts and applying a dose of scepticism to any one estimate. Your conclusions are that there is a 30% chance of strong growth, a 40% chance of normal growth and the probability of slow growth is put at 30%.

Because of Horace's emotional attachment to these firms he insists that these are the only investment(s) you hold, as he puts it, to 'engender commitment and interest in the success of his corporate babies'.

Required

a   For each of the alternatives on offer calculate returns and standard deviation.
b   Draw a risk and return diagram displaying the four options and then add a reasonable risk-return line for all possible allocations between Acehar and Ecaroh.
     State which of the four options are efficient portfolios and which are inefficient given your risk-return line.
c   You are young and not as risk averse as most people, because you feel you will be able to bounce back from a financial disaster should one occur. Draw indifference curves on the diagram for a person who is only slightly risk averse. Demonstrate an optimal risk-return point on the risk-return line by labelling it point 'J'.
d   Briefly discuss the benefits of greater diversification. Do these benefits continue to increase with ever greater diversification?

15 (*Examination level*) You have been bequeathed a legacy of £100,000 and you are considering placing the entire funds either in shares of company A or in shares in company B.

When you told your stock broker about this plan he suggested two alternative investment approaches.

a   Invest some of the money in A and some in B to give you at least a small degree of diversification. The proportions suggested are given in Table 2 below.

b   Invest the entire sum in a broad range of investments to reduce risk. This portfolio is expected to produce a return of 23% per year with a standard deviation of 6%.

To assist your final decision the broker provides you with forecasts for shares in A and B given various states of the economy – *see* Table 1.

Table 1

State of the economy	Probability of that state of the economy	Returns on A (%)	Returns on B (%)
Recession	0.25	10	15
Growth	0.50	20	55
Boom	0.25	30	−10

Table 2

Portfolio	Proportion of portfolio invested in A (%)	Proportion of portfolio invested in B (%)
1	25	75
2	75	25
3	90	10

Required

a   Compare the risk and return of the alternatives (including your original intention of putting all the money into either A or B).

b   Display the results on a graph and draw an estimated portfolio risk-return line based on the plot points for the two-share portfolio. (There is no requirement to calculate the minimum risk portfolio.)

c   Describe the efficient and inefficient region.

d   Use indifference curves to select the optimal portfolio to give the highest utility assuming that you are highly risk averse.

e   Define the Market Portfolio in Modern Portfolio Theory.

Assignments

1   If you have access to information on financial security return probability profiles then draw up a report showing the efficient frontier for a two-asset portfolio. Draw indifference curves based on canvassed opinion and/or subjective judgement and select an optimal portfolio.

2   If you have access to the estimated probability distribution of returns for some projects within the firm, consider the impact of accepting these projects on the overall risk-return profile of the firm. For instance, are they positively or negatively correlated with the existing set of activities?

The Capital Asset Pricing Model and multi-factor models

LEARNING OUTCOMES

The ideas, frameworks and theories surrounding the relationship between the returns on a security and its risk are pivotal to most of the issues discussed in this book. At times it may seem that this chapter is marching you up to the top of the hill only to push you down again. But remember, sometimes what you learn on a journey and what you see from new viewpoints are more important than the ultimate destination. By the end of this chapter the reader should be able to:

■ describe the fundamental features of the Capital Asset Pricing Model (CAPM);

■ show an awareness of the empirical evidence relating to the CAPM and the reasons why the academic community and practitioners are turning away from using the CAPM;

■ explain the key characteristics of multi-factor models, including the arbitrage pricing theory (APT) and the three-factor model;

■ express a reasoned and balanced judgement of the risk-return relationship in financial markets.

Introduction

One financial theory has dominated the academic literature and influenced greatly the practical world of finance and business for over five decades since it was first expounded by the Nobel prizewinner William Sharpe and other theoreticians.[1] This is the Capital Asset Pricing Model (CAPM). At its heart the CAPM (pronounced cap-em) has an old and common observation – the returns on a financial asset increase with risk. The 'breakthrough' in the 1960s was to define risk in a very precise way. It was no longer enough to rely on standard deviation after the work of Markowitz and others (see Chapter 7) had shown the benefits of diversification. The argument goes that it is illogical to be less than fully diversified so investors tend to create large portfolios. When a very large and diverse portfolio is formed one type of risk factor is eliminated – that which is specifically associated with the fortunes and misfortunes of particular companies. This is called unsystematic risk (it has other names: specific risk, idiosyncratic risk or unique risk). Once this is taken from the scene the investor merely has to concentrate on risks which cannot be eliminated by holding ever larger portfolios. This is systematic risk, an element of risk common to all firms to a greater or lesser extent (this too has other names: market risk, undiversifiable risk).

A central tenet of the CAPM is that systematic risk, as measured by beta, is the *only* factor affecting the level of return required on a share for a completely diversified investor. For practical use this risk factor is considered to be the extent to which a particular share's returns move when the stock market as a whole moves. Furthermore, the relationship between this beta factor and returns is described by a straight line (it is linear). This neat and, at first sight, apparently complete model changed the way people viewed the world of finance and influenced their actions.

Its far-reaching consequences changed the way in which portfolios were constructed for pension and insurance funds of millions of people. It contributed to the strengthening of the notion of stock market efficiency – the idea that the stock market 'correctly' prices shares (*see* Chapter 13). It has affected the investment philosophies of large numbers of investors. It has influenced the calculation of the cost of capital for a firm, or to express it another way, the required rate of return on projects. By providing a target figure of the return required by shareholders the CAPM has enabled management to vary the discount rate by which project cash flows were discounted, depending on the perceived level of systematic risk as defined by beta. Thus countless investment proposals have been accepted or rejected on the strength of what the CAPM has to say about the minimum return demanded by shareholders. In the view of many this is regrettable. Some see the CAPM as artificially restricting the investment opportunities undertaken by firms in national economies and this has led to charges of under-investment, economic backwardness and short-termism.

Far more damning criticism was to come for the CAPM in the 1980s and 1990s when researchers looked at the relationship between the CAPM's systematic risk measure, beta, and the returns on shares over the period since the mid-1960s. They discovered either that there was absolutely no relationship at all or that beta had only a weak influence on the return shareholders received. They commented that there were other factors determining the returns on shares. This opened up a raging debate within the academic community, with some saying beta was dead, some saying that it was only wounded, and some saying it was alive and well.

The irony is that just as the academic community was having serious doubts about the model, in the outside world the CAPM was reaching new heights of popularity. Hundreds of thousands, if not millions, have studied the CAPM in universities over the past five decades and are now placed in important positions around the world ready to make key decisions often under the subliminal influence of the CAPM. Indeed, a new industry has been built selling data and information which can be plugged into CAPM-based decision-making frameworks in the workplace. However, by the end of the noughties the weight of evidence against the use of CAPM-beta was so great that few academics or practitioners who had kept up their reading on the issue believed it was right to continue teaching the CAPM-beta as though it was *the* answer to the risk-return relationship.

As far back as the late 1970s, partly in response to the empirical evidence, and partly from theoretical doubts about the CAPM, academics began exploring models which were based on a number of explanatory factors influencing the returns on shares rather than the one solitary variable considered in the CAPM. The most prominent is the arbitrage pricing theory (APT) which permits factors other than beta to explain share returns. But wait! We are running ahead of the story. First we have to understand the workings of the CAPM, its theoretical

---

1 Sharpe (1964), Lintner (1965), Mossin (1966), Treynor (1965) and Black (1972).

underpinnings and the various items of jargon that have grown up within this area of finance. Only then will a full appreciation of its limitations be possible, along with a consideration of alternative risk-return approaches.

Some fundamental ideas and problems

To understand these risk-return models we need to remember, as discussed in Chapter 2, that people who sacrifice current consumption to invest in securities such as shares require the rate of return that is currently available on the safest type of investment (usually taken to be a debt security issued by a highly reputable government when it borrows from investors) plus a premium. This premium is an extra annual return to accept the higher levels of risk associated with share investing. After all, shares can lose money if the business performs badly or even become worthless if the company goes bust, as happened to British Home Stores and Lehman Brothers.

Thus we have:

Required return on share of company j	=	Risk-free rate of return	+	Risk premium
Or r_j	=	r_f	+	RP

So, we could have a situation where UK government bonds and Treasury bills (short-term lending to the government usually for three months) are both offering an annual rate of return of 4%. Any investor thinking about where to place savings would look at this 4% as the minimum obtainable – and for no (very little) risk! To be tempted to invest in a portfolio of shares, however, the investor will have to consider what extra percentage points of return are required on top of the 4%. Naturally different shares have different degrees of risk, so investors will ask for a greater risk premium for shares with higher than normal (average) risk.

But, it is very difficult for finance experts to figure out how big the risk premium is. Is 2% per year enough? Or is 7% extra required? Researchers usually break the problem down into two stages:

1 Estimate the risk premium for the averagely risky share on the stock market. The risk premium for the stock market as a whole may be termed the equity risk premium (ERP), market risk premium (MRP) or equity premium (EP).

2 Multiply this number by a risk-adjustment factor for each individual share. So, for example, if it is found that the average risk premium is 5% and shares in BHP are twice as risky as the average share, then the risk premium for BHP is 10%. This would be added to the current risk-free rate, say 4%, to give a required return of 14%.

But we have only kicked a major problem a little further down the road: how do we find out the average risk premium for shares?

One approach has been to speak to investors and potential investors and ask: how much extra annual return above the risk-free rate do you require to invest in an averagely risky share today? The reactions to this question are likely to be furrowed foreheads and puzzled expressions. Those few people who do respond with anything like a considered answer will very often go for a very large number: 'Well, I'm *hoping* for 20% per year so that I can retire in ten years' time.' Some respondents, however, will be aware of stock market and bond market history and so will have anchor points for their thinking. They know full well that over the past century there has not been one decade when average annual returns on UK shares have been as great as 15%, let alone 20%. Furthermore, they know that some decades produced negative returns, so that the average is significantly less than 10%. Government bonds have provided positive average annual returns and so the average risk premium for investing in shares above the return on bonds has been a lot less than 10%. So these (few very) informed individuals are likely to ask for a much lower risk premium than 10% as they know that a greater amount would be mere wishful thinking.

You can see the difficulty with simply asking people what their personal risk premium is – most don't know other than 'as high as possible'. However, those few informed participants anchoring on statistical data are on to something. We can move beyond a subjective view on RP by treating the extra return on shares over bonds in each of the last, say, 50 or 100 years as an indicator of what equity investors are generally willing to put up with and still keep investing in shares. If they had not been content with this amount to compensate for the extra volatility of shares over risk-free investments in past decades then it seems reasonable to suppose that they would have sold their shares. The selling pressure would lower prices of shares. And, if we can assume that the dividends flowing from the operations of Unilever, M&S, etc. remain the same for the subsequent years then a lowered share price indicates a higher rate of return on the money needed to buy some shares.

So rather than ask people what their RP is, we examine past RPs and make the admittedly bold assumption that the extra returns received in the past reflect their *required* returns, that is before the returns are actually received. Not every researcher agrees that we can simply take this raw difference between the return on the average share and the return on the reputable government debt security and state that as the RP. There are a few objections, for example:

- Investors in shares in past decades might have been lucky relative to investors in bonds and bills. Equity investors just happened to live through a charmed period, whereas bond/bill investors suffered high inflation, seeing their securities fall in price or return less than inflation. It is not that share investors demanded these high returns at the outset as their *required* return, merely that that is how it turned out. This is the line taken by Dimson et al. in their 2002 book, *Triumph of the Optimists* (the clue is in the title).

- We don't know how many years to look at; and the RP is different over 20, 50 and 117 years. However, we do know that you cannot take just a handful of years to estimate what investors require over bonds because freakish things happen in the markets. For example, over the seventeen years 2010 to the end of 2016, UK shares gave an average annual real (after knocking off inflation) return of 2.4%, whereas UK government bonds produced 4.6%. So if we were to use this difference as our risk premium for a calculation made in 2017 when UK government bonds (gilts) are offering a return of 1.2% (r_f) and the RP is $2.4 - 4.6 = -2.2\%$, the investor in an averagely risky share in 2017 will require $1.2 + (-2.2) = -1.0\%$ per year. That plainly does not make sense. Obviously to discover the revealed RP we need a long period of measuring share and bond returns. (Note that it is not as though share investors in 2000 expected (required) a negative risk premium; otherwise they would simply have avoided shares. This negative number simply tells us that investors in this period were 'unlucky' – they took a risk and lost.)

- There is a debate over whether to use the rate of return on a government bond with a high reputation for repaying its debts or its Treasury bills for the risk-free rate of return – we look at this issue later.

So, the risk premium is a crucial number in finance. It is needed so that we can value shares. It is also needed so that we can work out the discount rate to be used for project appraisal, and it is needed for judging the performance of an investment strategy in the financial markets, e.g. share portfolio management. It may be a crucial number, but as you are starting to realise, it is fiendishly difficult to pin down. In fact, I would go so far as to say that anybody using a number between 3 and 5 percentage points could find very plausible arguments supporting it – or even a number slightly beyond those boundaries. I will use 5% later in the chapter because I'm forced to select something to make the illustrations workable. But note that I would not be in dispute with others who chose 3.5 or 4%; there is just too much uncertainty in the practicalities of obtaining real-world numbers.

We will now look at some of the data that has been gathered to help us estimate the future equity risk premium.

A short history of shares, bonds and bills

Returns

We begin with an examination of the rate of return earned on shares and other classes of financial securities over the period since the end of 1899. Elroy Dimson, Paul Marsh and

Mike Staunton from the London Business School, in collaboration with the bank Credit Suisse, regularly produce analyses of the returns earned on shares, government bonds (lending to the UK government by buying long-term financial investments, often called 'gilts') and Treasury bills since the end of 1899. As can be seen from **Exhibit 8.1** shares have produced a much better return than the other two classes of investment. Even if the effects of inflation are removed, an investor placing £100 in a portfolio of shares at the end of 1899 would, by the beginning of 2017, be able to purchase 513 times as many goods and services as could be purchased in 1899 with the initial amount invested.

Exhibit 8.1	What a £100 investment in January 1900 would be worth at the end of 2016 with all income reinvested		
	If invested in equities (shares)	If invested in bonds (gilts)	If invested In Treasury bills
Money (nominal) return	£3m	£53,000	£22,000
Real return	£51,300	£806	£320

Source: from *Global Investment Returns Yearbook 2017*, Credit Suisse Research Institute (Dimson, E., Marsh, P. and Staunton, M. 2017) © Elroy Dimson, Paul Marsh and Mike Staunton.

Dimson, Marsh and Staunton's research shows that equities (shares) have produced average annual real returns (after reinvestment of dividends) higher than that on gilts or Treasury bills over both 50 years and 117 years (*see* **Exhibit 8.2**).

Exhibit 8.2	Real returns on UK financial securities (% per annum)		
Geometric means			
	117 years (Jan 1900– Jan 2017)	**50 years** (Jan 1967– Jan 2017)	**17 years** (Jan 2000–Jan 2017)
Equities	5.5	6.9	2.4
Gilts	1.8	3.8	4.6
Treasury bills	1.0	1.7	0.7
Inflation	3.7		2.0

Source: from *Global Investment Returns Yearbook 2017*, Credit Suisse Research Institute (Dimson, E., Marsh, P. and Staunton, M. 2017) © Elroy Dimson, Paul Marsh and Mike Staunton.

The DMS study shows an extra return for equities compared with gilts over 117 years of 3.6% (5.5% − 1.8%) on the basis of geometric means – we know this doesn't quite add up due to technical factors; 3.6% is the risk premium DMS state (For a discussion on geometric and arithmetic means, consult Appendix 8.1.)

If a 50-year history of financial security returns is examined then the premium received by share investors is only slightly over 3%. The premium over Treasury bills is larger at 5.2%. Clearly the size of the additional return achieved by equity investors compared with government bond or Treasury bill investors has varied over time and so to state definitively the return premium share investors generally receive over gilt and Treasury bill investors is obviously impossible as it depends on the period of time studied. What we can do is apply a principle when trying to establish a usable figure for the equity risk premium. We would look at data for a long time period because the relationship between the returns on shares and bonds (or bills) is subject to a great deal of fluctuation in the short term.

Some more return data

Estimating the returns on shares, government bonds and Treasury bills over the past few decades is far from easy. There are various problems to be overcome, such as poor data availability in the early years, and choosing which securities to include in an index as representative of that class of securities. The difficult judgements made mean that we find different results depending on the analysis undertaken. It is worth taking the time to look at some more historical data so that you can make up your own mind on the appropriate RP to use – or should that be a range of values for RP?

Exhibit 8.3 shows the average annual return on long-term government bonds, Treasury bills and shares for 21 countries over the 117-year period to the end of 2016. All the numbers are returns above (sometimes below) inflation. The key observation to make is that the extra return on shares over government-issued securities is generally in the region of 3–5%.

Exhibit 8.3	Real returns on equities, government bonds and bills, 1900–2016, 117 years,% (geometric means)

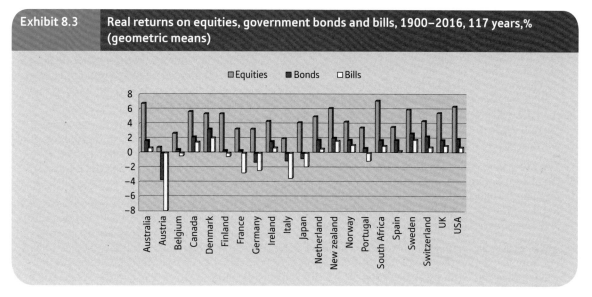

Source: from *Global Investment Returns Yearbook 2017,* Credit Suisse Research Institute (Dimson, E., Marsh, P. and Staunton, M. 2017) © Elroy Dimson, Paul Marsh and Mike Staunton.

Andrew Smithers calculated a US equity risk premium for 1800 to 2000 for his book *Wall Street Revalued* – the results are shown in **Exhibit 8.4**.

Exhibit 8.4	The US equity risk premium, 1800–2000

	1800–2000	1800–1900	1900–2000
US real equity returns % p.a.	7.0	7.5	6.5
US real bond returns % p.a.	3.4	5.0	1.8
Equity risk premium defined in terms of the outturn rather than in terms of expectation (i.e. 'ex-post') and after deducting 0.5% because equity costs more to trade	3.1	2.0	4.2

But note that Smithers is very sceptical about our ability to pin down the ERP because it has been so unstable. This is demonstrated in **Exhibit 8.5** where the difference between the returns on equities and the returns on government bonds over a number of 30-year periods has bounced around all over the place. This helps to reinforce the point that periods of 30 years of observations are too short. Smithers counters this as the main explanation for the variability by saying that the

ERP has not shown any clear indication of rotating around some stable long-term average – which, when you look at Exhibit 8.5, seems true, which is quite a challenge to those who glibly select a precise RP from a database.

Exhibit 8.5

The problem of the equity risk premium

By Andrew Smithers

In some of my more gamesome moments I have challenged my students to produce an article about the equity risk premium, which made a useful contribution to our understanding of the way **financial markets** work. So far the challenge has not been met. This may reflect the modesty and good manners of those I teach but also, I hope and believe, the fact they are too sensible to wish to defend the way this often ill-defined and generally useless concept has been habitually discussed. In practice, comments on the ERP seem to me to have been a source of confusion and error rather than illumination.

The ERP can be defined in at least two ways. One is the historic difference between the returns on bonds and equities and another is the expected difference in these returns. Alternatively, the "risk-free rate" [Treasury-bill rate] can be used in place of bonds.

Any of these concepts might be useful for something. For example, it might be useful for investors when making decisions about asset allocation. If the ERP

were stable, it might also be useful for valuing equities. In fact it is useless for making asset allocation decisions; and the ERP is far from stable, whether it is defined as a historic relationship or an expected one.

Chart one shows the long-term real returns in the US on cash, bonds and equities. Two things are obvious. The first is that the long-term real returns on equities have been stable; the second is that this has not been true of cash [bills] or bonds.

Chart two shows the historic differences between equity returns and those on cash and bonds. It underlines the conclusion that there has been no stable historic relationship between the returns on these different asset classes.

It is nonetheless possible that there has been such a relationship between expected returns but that this has not applied to realised returns because investors have been bad at forecasting. If this is the case, then the poor ability to forecast must apply to real returns on bonds and cash rather than equities. As the latter

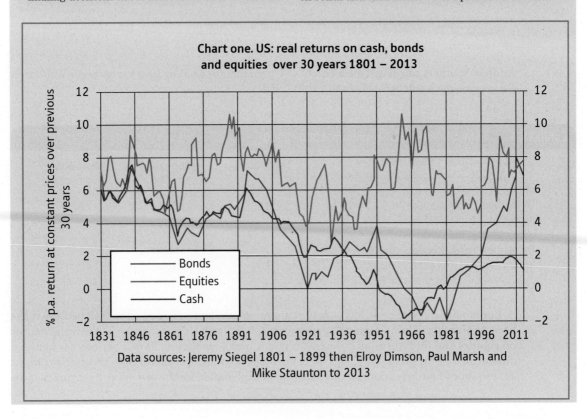

Chart one. US: real returns on cash, bonds and equities over 30 years 1801 – 2013

Bonds
Equities
Cash

% p.a. return at constant prices over previous 30 years

Data sources: Jeremy Siegel 1801 – 1899 then Elroy Dimson, Paul Marsh and Mike Staunton to 2013

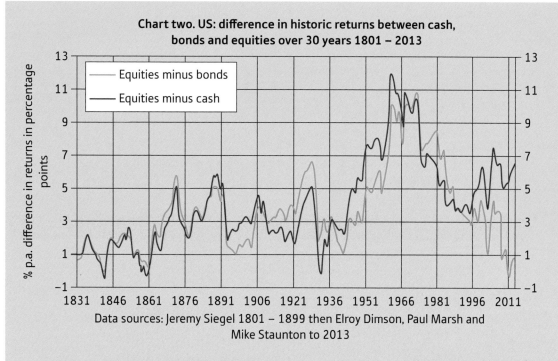

Chart two. US: difference in historic returns between cash, bonds and equities over 30 years 1801 – 2013

Data sources: Jeremy Siegel 1801 – 1899 then Elroy Dimson, Paul Marsh and Mike Staunton to 2013

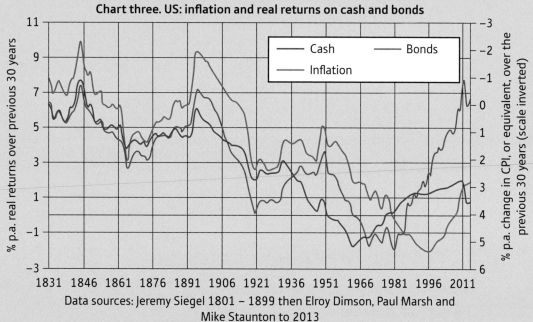

Chart three. US: inflation and real returns on cash and bonds

Data sources: Jeremy Siegel 1801 – 1899 then Elroy Dimson, Paul Marsh and Mike Staunton to 2013

is a title to ownership to real assets, and the value of cash and bonds is determined only in nominal terms, it is inherently likely that an inability to forecast inflation would be crucial.

Chart three shows that poor forecasting has clearly been a major factor in the variation in the realised returns from cash and bonds.

The absence of a stable relationship between real bond and equity yields does not mean that there is no relationship at all. But, if there is one, its exponents are yet, as far as I am aware, to set out what it is in a way that can be tested and be shown to be robust when tested.

Another approach to estimating the equity risk premium is to ask those who, on a day-to-day basis, need to give the issue some thought. One such survey is conducted by John Graham and Campbell Harvey, who ask US chief financial officers each quarter what they think the return for the US share market, represented by the S&P 500 index, will be over the next ten years. For the summer 2016 survey, for example, they asked the CFOs to complete the following sentence: 'On May 17, 2016 the annual yield on 10-yr treasury bonds was 1.8% . . . over the next 10 years, I expect the average annual S&P 500 return will be . . . ' The answers for a number of these surveys are graphed in **Exhibit 8.6**, which shows a remarkable degree of variability over quite short time periods, but generally stays within the range 2.5–4.5%.

In another regular survey Pablo Fernandez *et al.* ask not only managers of companies but also finance/economic professors and analysts working in the finance industry what market risk premium (same as average equity risk premiums) they are using. The spring 2016 survey 6,932 responses are summarized in **Exhibit 8.7**.

Exhibit 8.6

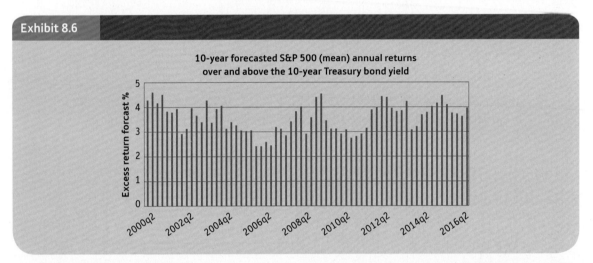

Source: Graham, J.R. and C. R.Harvey (2016).

Exhibit 8.7   Market risk premium used for 71 countries in 2016 by professors, analysts and managers of companies

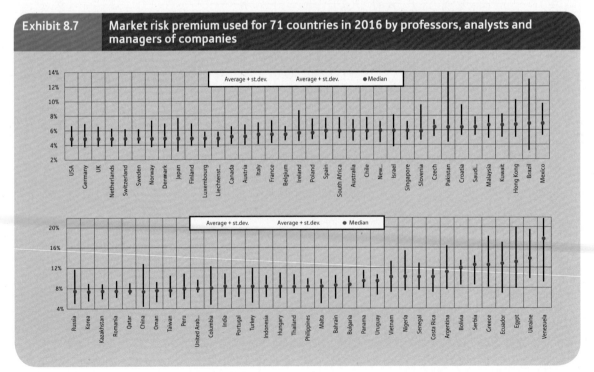

Source: Fernandez, Pablo and Ortiz Pizarro, Alberto and Fernández Acín, Isabel, (2016).

Clearly, within countries these users of the risk premium differ in the figures they choose, but most are within quite a narrow range, as shown in **Exhibit 8.8**.

Exhibit 8.8	Market risk premium used in 2016 for some countries – plot of answers

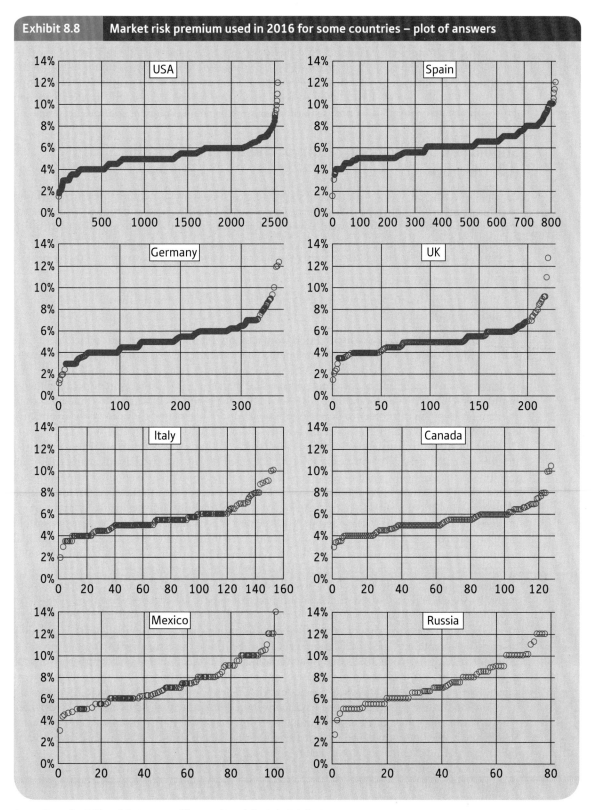

Source: Fernandez, Pablo and Ortiz Pizarro, Alberto and Fernández Acín, Isabel (2016).

Many informed thinkers (e.g. Dimson *et al.* (2006)) believe that an equity risk premium for US, UK and world equities today lies in the region of $3-3\frac{1}{2}\%$. Fama and French (2002) suggest an equity premium of 2.5% to 4.3% for US shares, Damodaran (2017) estimates 4.31%, while other textbooks (e.g. Brealey, Myers and Allen 2017) stick to higher numbers (5% to 8%). The regulators of the UK water industry (Ofwat), and the telecommunications industry (Ofcom) often control the amount that producers charge customers. This is meant to be calculated as high enough to allow a satisfactory rate of return to them without exploiting their captive customers. To do this, one of the estimates they make is the equity risk premium so that they can figure out the amount of return the shareholders should receive – the r_j for each company. Ofwat uses an ERP of 5%, with Ofcom opting for 5.3%. However, they do have a habit of regularly changing their minds. Ofgem (electricity and gas regulator) will not publish a precise figure because 'this would represent spurious accuracy'.[2]

Should you use the bond return or the bill return for the risk-free rate, r_f?

As you have gathered, we can examine the expected return on shares and other investments relative to either long-term highly reputable government securities (bonds, such as UK gilts) or to government securities with less than one year – usually three months – until they expire (Treasury bills). But which is best?

The risk-free rate is a completely certain return. For complete certainty two conditions are needed:

1 The risk of default is zero.
2 When intermediate cash flows are earned on a multi-year investment there is no uncertainty about reinvestment rates.

The return available on a zero coupon bond from a highly reputable government which has a time horizon equal to the investment under consideration is the closest we are going to get to the theoretically correct risk-free rate of return. A zero coupon bond is one with the promise of only one payment which is at the end of the bond's life, rather than a stream of interest (coupon) payments in the intervening years as on most bonds. Naturally such a bond will be sold for much less than the sum promised to the holder to be received, say, six or ten years later, thus providing an effective interest rate. *See* Chapter 11 for more on bonds.

Those business projects and investments in shares, etc. that we are evaluating using a required rate of return, r_j, usually involve cash flows arising at intervals, rather than all at the end of an investment. Theoretically, each of these separate cash flows should be discounted using different discount rates, the risk-free component of which varies from one year to the next. So, for the cash flows arising after one year on a multi-year investment, the rate on a one-year zero coupon government bond should be used as the relevant risk-free rate. The cash flows arising in year five should be discounted on the basis of a cost of capital calculated using the five-year zero coupon rate and so on. However, this approach is cumbersome. More significantly, it is difficult to find reputable government zero coupon bonds for more than a handful of time periods.

There is a practical alternative that gives a reasonable approximation to the theoretical optimum. It is considered by many thinkers and practitioners to be acceptable to use a long-term government rate on all the cash flows of a project/investment with a long-term horizon. Furthermore, the return on a government bond with coupons, rather than a zero coupon bond, is generally taken to be acceptable. The rule of thumb seems to be to use the return available on a reputable government security having the same time horizon as the project under consideration – thus for a short-term project one should use the discount rate which incorporates the short-term government security rate, but for a 20-year project use the 20-year government bond yield to maturity.

(Note that the risk-free rate used depends on whether the future cash flows expected to emanate from an investment are expressed in nominal or real terms. If they are in nominal (money) terms then the risk-free rate should also include the inflation element. If the cash flows are in real terms then the r_f should exclude an allowance for inflation.)

The above argument is the pragmatic response to the difficulties of real-world decision making. But bear in mind that the CAPM and other pricing models were founded on the idea that the nearest

---

2 Minutes of a Meeting of the Gas and Electricity Markets Authority, 13 November 2014.

asset to a totally risk-free investment is a Treasury bill issued by a highly dependable (low default risk) government. To use the long-term bond rate is to include a 'maturity premium'. This means that government securities which pay out over a number of years, rather than after three or six months, have an extra risk (and therefore higher return) because they are more volatile than short-term debt instruments due to their movements in price in response to changing investor perceptions of future inflation and interest rates. (This risk is discussed further in Chapter 11 under the liquidity preference hypothesis.[3]) Investors avoid this risk by preferring to invest in Treasury bills, thus the interest rate (the r_f) is generally lower on government bills than it is on government bonds.

However, the use of bills for rates of return calculations makes sense only if you need an r_f for an investment that lasts for less than one year. Investing in three-month Treasury bills does result in a guaranteed return over the next three months. But what if the risky investment you are evaluating lasts for five years? You would then need to assume that it was possible to keep rolling over (repaying then borrowing again) this type of risk-free investing every three months for the full five years at the same interest rate. This introduces a risk known as reinvestment risk: you may not be able to achieve the same rate on roll-overs. In contrast, investing in a reputable five-year government bond will generate a guaranteed return for the next five years (despite some volatility in bond prices from month to month during the five years).

So which to use? Some respected thinkers in this area prefer Treasury bills because 'bonds are subject to uncertainty about future inflation and real interest rates' (Dimson *et al.*, 2009, p. 7) while other respected thinkers prefer bonds because the argument of no price risk for bills makes sense only 'if we are interested in a single period equity risk premium (say, for the next year). If your time horizon is longer (say 5 or 10 years), it is the Treasury bond that provides the more predictable returns' (Damodaran, 2017, p. 22).

You have a choice in selecting your r_f. Which weighs more heavily on your mind: reinvestment risk of bills or the risk of bond volatility during the months of its life? Isn't it frustrating that finance is not about simple, precise number crunching? Welcome to reality – after all, you have to admit it is far more fun when judgement is required!

The *Financial Times* article in **Exhibit 8.9** stirs the pot a little bit more by discussing the diminishing possibilities of risk-free investing.

Exhibit 8.9

No such thing as risk-free assets

By John Plender

Is the global pool of safe assets shrinking? The question is hugely important for anyone involved in asset allocation. Yet the terminology in which the debate is conducted remains highly confusing.

Economists like to talk about risk-free assets. Yet that is close to being an oxymoron. No asset is risk-free, nor does it make much sense to talk of the risk-free rate when referring to the yield on top quality sovereign [government] debt.

Fixed-interest sovereign debt is subject to inflation risk. Meantime, the growing healthcare and pension liabilities of governments around the world mean that default risk is not negligible even in government debt of the most stable advanced economies.

Worse, supposedly risk-free rates on much sovereign debt now deliver a negative real return.

The issue is further confused by the conflicting perceptions of credit rating agencies and markets. The US was downgraded by the agencies last year, yet the US Treasury market remains the world's pre-eminent investment bolt-hole and repository of safe assets in periods of financial instability.

It is not, at least in this case, that the rating agencies are wrong. US public sector debt is above the level most mainstream economists would regard as sustainable. The reserve role of the dollar along with the breadth and depth of US financial markets nonetheless ensure that there is no safer haven – for the moment – for nervous money.

All this prompts the Bank for International Settlements, the central bankers' bank, to opt for a pragmatic definition.

▶

---

3 Bond volatility is discussed further in Arnold (2012) and Arnold (2015).

Exhibit 8.9 *(continued)*

It uses the term "risk-free" to describe assets associated with a sufficiently high probability of creditors being repaid to allow credit risk not to be explicitly taken into account in investment decisions by market participants. Not a bad basis on which to proceed to the substance of the argument.

The BIS remarks in its latest annual report, sovereign debtors have been losing their risk-free status at an alarming rate. Default risk on much eurozone government debt has soared, because eurozone members have given up the sovereign power to print their way out of excessive accumulations of debt.

The private sector has seen a long-term decline in the pool of safe assets. Credit ratings of both corporations and banks, few of which now command AAA ratings, have been on a secular declining trend for years.

 Financial Times, 8 July 2012.

Risk

It is highly unlikely that Treasury bills issued by the UK government will default and the fact they mature in a matter of days means that their prices do not vary a great deal.

Long-term government bonds issued by the UK government also have a low risk of default but they do suffer from uncertainty concerning the price that can be achieved in the market when selling to another investor prior to the maturity date. The prices fluctuate inversely to interest rates. If interest rates rise due to, say, a perceived increase in inflation, then the price of bonds will fall, resulting in a capital loss over a period of a year or so. Often these capital losses outweigh the gain from the interest paid, producing an overall negative annual return. Despite these yearly ups and downs, for practical purposes bonds issued by a reputable government such as the UK's may be viewed as being risk free if a long-term (to maturity) perspective is taken. This is because the promised payments by the government are highly unlikely to be missed, therefore the nominal return is virtually guaranteed (unexpected inflation may be a problem for real returns, but government bonds and bills are the nearest we are going to get to risk-free securities). Shares carry the highest risk because their payouts of dividends and capital gains and losses depend on the performance of the underlying businesses. We now examine the extent to which total returns (dividends or interest plus capital gain or loss) have varied over the years.

A general impression of the degree of volatility associated with each class of investment can be found by examining **Exhibits 8.10, 8.11** and **8.12**. An investor in UK Treasury bills in any year is unlikely to experience a real (after inflation) loss greater than 5%. The investor in gilts,

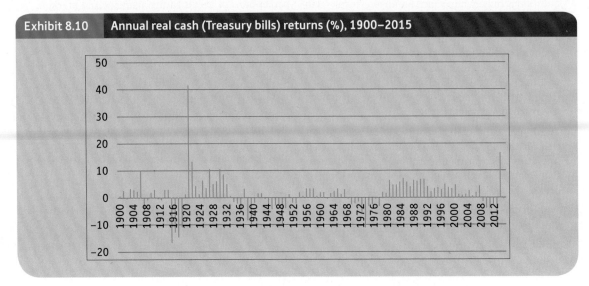

Exhibit 8.10   Annual real cash (Treasury bills) returns (%), 1900–2015

Source: Barclays Capital. Various Equity Gilt Studies. London: Barclays Capital.

Exhibit 8.11	Annual real gilt returns (%), 1900–2015

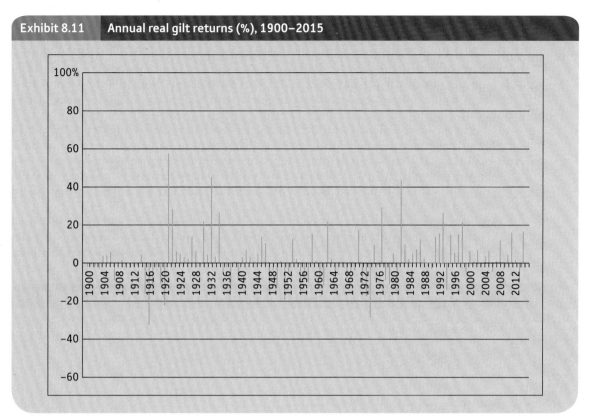

Source: Barclays Capital. Various Equity Gilt Studies. London: Barclays Capital.

Exhibit 8.12	Annual real equity returns (%), 1900–2015

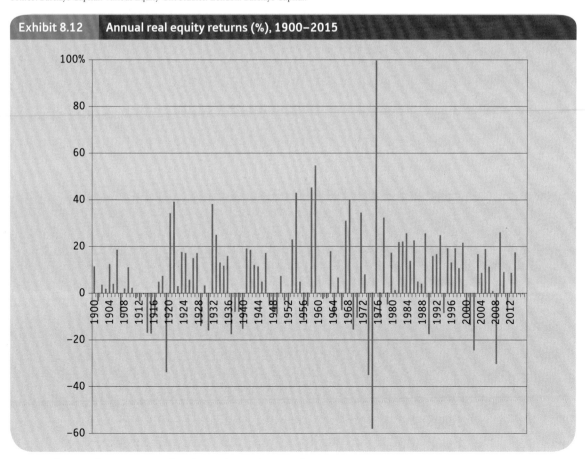

Source: Barclays Capital. Various Equity Gilt Studies. London: Barclays Capital.

on the other hand, has a fair chance of making a significant negative return over the period of a year. There is also the possibility of large gains, many of which are over 10%. Shares can show spectacular year-on-year gains and equally extraordinary losses. Take the years 1973 and 1974: a purchaser of shares at the start of 1973 lost 35% in the first year followed by 58.1% in 1974. The pain was offset by the bounce-back of 1975 but the fear and dislike of sharp stock market collapse is bound to haunt the experienced equity investor, given the history of stock market returns.

The frequency distribution of returns for the three asset classes is shown in **Exhibits 8.13, 8.14** and **8.15**. These show the number of years that each type of investment had a return within a particular range. For Treasury bills (cash) the returns vary from a negative 16% to a positive 14% (if we ignore the outlier at 41.5%). The range for bonds is much wider, and for equities wider still. (The two most extreme returns for shares −58.1% in 1974 and +99.6% in 1975, were excluded as outliers.)

We now have data for the average annual return on each class of asset, and some impression of the annual variability of those returns. *See* **Exhibit 8.16**, where standard deviation provides a measure of volatility. This confirms that equities are the most risky asset class of the three.

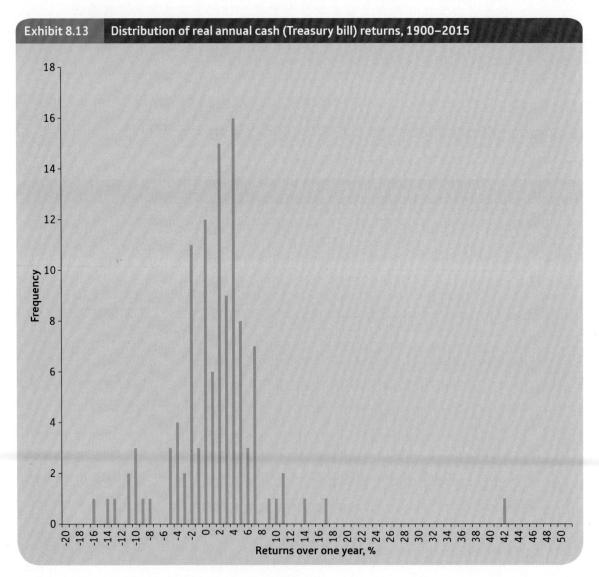

Exhibit 8.13   Distribution of real annual cash (Treasury bill) returns, 1900–2015

Source: Barclays Capital. Various Equity Gilt Studies. London: Barclays Capital.

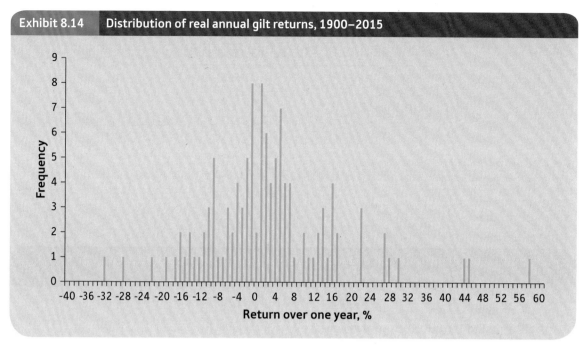

Exhibit 8.14   Distribution of real annual gilt returns, 1900–2015

Source: Barclays Capital. Various Equity Gilt Studies. London: Barclays Capital.

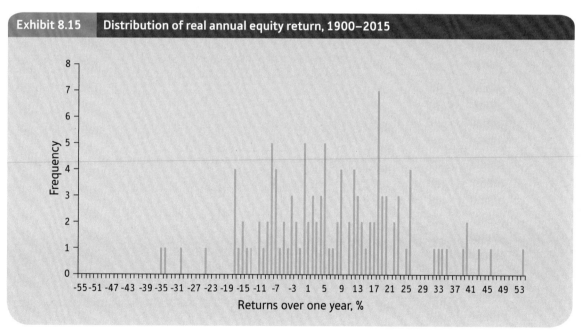

Exhibit 8.15   Distribution of real annual equity return, 1900–2015

Source: Barclays Capital, Various Equity Gilt Studies. London: Barclays Capital.

The standard deviation of equities is much larger than that for bonds, and at least three times that for Treasury bills. The exhibits examined so far endorse the belief in a positive relationship between return and risk. This is confirmed to be the case for a number of other countries in **Exhibit 8.17**.

The article excerpted in **Exhibit 8.18** describes the remarkable rewards for accepting additional risk by investing in shares (American, this time) rather than something safer.

Exhibit 8.16	A measure of risk on financial securities, 1900–2016[a]

	Standard deviation%
Equities	19.6
Gilts	13.7
Treasury bills	6.3

Note a – Based on real returns after inflation.

Source: from *Global Investment Returns Yearbook 2017*, Credit Suisse Research Institute (Dimson, E., Marsh, P. and Staunton, M. 2017) © Elroy Dimson, Paul Marsh and Mike Staunton

Exhibit 8.17	Standard deviations of annual real returns for financial securities in 20 countries, 1900–2016

Country	Equities	Bonds	Bills
	Standard deviation %	Standard deviation %	Standard deviation %
Australia	17.6	13.1	5.3
Austria	29.9	51.0	18.5
Belgium	23.5	15.0	12.6
Canada	17.0	10.3	4.8
Denmark	20.8	11.8	5.9
Finland	29.8	13.7	11.6
France	23.0	13.0	9.3
Germany	31.6	15.7	13.0
Ireland	22.9	15.0	6.5
Italy	28.5	14.7	11.2
Japan	29.4	19.6	13.6
Netherlands	21.3	9.8	4.9
New Zealand	19.3	9.0	4.6
Norway	26.8	12.0	7.0
Portugal	34.3	18.7	9.7
South Africa	22.1	10.5	6.1
Spain	21.9	12.5	5.7
Sweden	21.1	12.7	6.4
Switzerland	19.4	9.4	4.9
USA	20.0	10.4	4.6

Source: from *Global Investment Returns Yearbook 2017*, Credit Suisse Research Institute (Dimson, E., Marsh, P. and Staunton, M. 2017) © Elroy Dimson, Paul Marsh and Mike Staunton

Exhibit 8.18

Big bequest: Former Chicago secretary Gladys Holm, who never earned more than $15,000 (£9,202) a year, left $18m to a hospital in her will. She used to invest any spare earnings on the stock market.

FT   *Financial Times,* 1 August 1997.

The Capital Asset Pricing Model

From the capital market line (CML) to the security market line (SML)

The capital market line was described in Chapter 7 as an expression of the relationship between risk and return for a fully diversified investor. If an investor is able to first identify and invest in the *market portfolio*; and secondly, able to lend or borrow at the risk-free rate of return[4] then the alternative risk–return combinations available to the investor lie on a straight line – there is a positive linear association. An example of this relationship is shown in **Exhibit 8.19**.

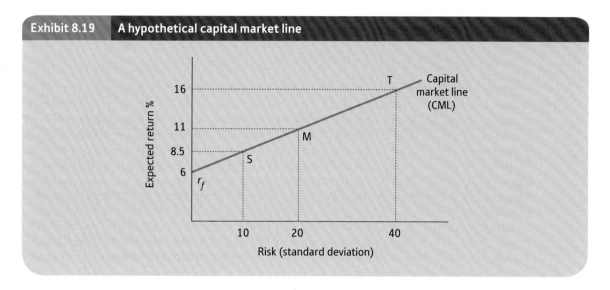

Exhibit 8.19   A hypothetical capital market line

Ideally, when referring to the market portfolio, we should include all assets, ranging from gold through to bonds, property and shares. In practice, to make the CAPM workable, we use a proxy for the market portfolio, usually a broadly based index of shares such as the FTSE Actuaries All-Share Index which contains about 600 shares.

At least two possible options are open to a potential investor. The first is to place all funds into risk-free securities.[5] In the example given in Exhibit 8.19 this would result in a return of 6% per year. (In reality the risk-free rate varies from day to day depending on supply and demand in the bond and bill markets.) The second option is to invest all the funds in the market portfolio. The share index proxies studied in empirical work such as the Barclays Capital and Dimson *et al.* studies generally show that over the past 50–117 years investors in shares have received a return of about 3 to 5% more than if they had invested in risk-free securities.[6] We will use a figure of 5% – thus, if anything, biasing the calculations upwards. Thus an investor in the market portfolio will expect, in this assumed model, a return of 6% plus, say, 5%. Having established the two benchmarks, of 11% return for a risk level with a standard deviation of 20% and a return of 6% for zero risk in this hypothetical but representative model, we can now calculate alternative risk-return combinations constructed by varying the amount of a fund going into each of these two types of investment. For example, if half of the fund were placed in the market portfolio and half in the

4 Ignore the doubts we might have about the ability of you or I, or any investor, being able to borrow at the risk-free rate for now, so that we can deal with the theory.

5 Real returns on government Treasury bills have not had a zero standard deviation when measured on a year-to-year basis, but over the three-month life of a Treasury bill the rate of return is fixed and the risk of default is virtually zero. Returns on government bonds may fluctuate from year to year, but the government is highly unlikely to default, and so they may be regarded as risk free for practical purposes (in nominal terms, at least) if they are held to maturity.

6 For illustrative purposes we are using data supplied by Barclays Capital and Dimson *et al.* while also referring to the FTSE All-Share Index. These data, while being based on share returns, are not identical. Also they are mere proxies for the true market portfolio (*see* the discussion of the market portfolio later in this chapter).

risk-free asset, the standard deviation on this new portfolio would be a weighted average of the two constituent standard deviations:

0.5 × (standard deviation of risk-free asset) + 0.5 × (standard deviation of market portfolio)

$$0.5 \times 0 + 0.5 \times 20 = 10\%$$

For calculating the expected return a slightly more complicated formula is needed because the CML does not start at a zero expected return. This is as follows:

$$\text{expected return} = \text{risk-free return} + \overset{\text{risk premium}}{\underset{\text{portfolio}}{\text{for market}}} \times \left[\frac{\text{risk of new portfolio, S}}{\text{risk of market portfolio}} \right]$$

$$r_j = 6 + 5 \times (10/20) = 8.5\%$$

These two formulae can be used to calculate any potential new portfolio along the capital market line. Between points r_f, the risk-free rate of return, and point M, the intuitive understanding of the creation of alternative risk-return conditions is fairly straightforward. Such conditions are created by using part of a fund to lend to a safe borrower (for example the UK government) and part for investment in risky assets as represented by the market portfolio. To the right of point M intuitive understanding is a little more difficult at first. In this region the investor achieves higher return and higher risk by not only investing the money available in a fund in the market portfolio but also borrowing more funds to invest in the market portfolio.

Take, for example, an investor who has a £1m fund fully invested in the market portfolio. The investor borrows at the risk-free rate of return of 6% another £1m to put into the market portfolio. The expected return on this investment will be twice the rate available from a £1m investment less the cost of the borrowing:

	£
11% return on shares (£110,000 × 2)	220,000
Less interest	60,000
	£160,000

This is a return of 16% for a fund belonging to the investor of £1m. Before everyone rushes out to gear up their portfolios in this way, note that this is the expected return – the statistical mean. We saw in the last section how volatile share returns can be. It could be that the investor will receive no return from the market portfolio at all and yet will still have to pay the interest. Investors such as this one expose themselves to a greater variation in possible outcomes, that is, risk. The standard deviation for portfolio T is:

$$\frac{(2,000,000 \times 20\%) - (1,000,000 \times 0\%)}{1,000,000} = 40\%$$

From this section we can conclude that if the conditions leading to the establishment of the CML are fulfilled (such as a perfect capital market with no taxes, no transaction costs, full information about future return distributions disclosed to all investors and the ability to borrow and lend at the risk-free rate of interest) then an investor can achieve any point along the CML simply by varying the manner in which the portfolio is constructed from the two components of the market portfolio and the risk-free asset.

To get to a full understanding of the CAPM the reader is recommended to temporarily suspend disbelief. Of course the simplifying assumptions do not match reality, but such extraordinary artificiality is necessary to make a model intelligible and usable. What matters is whether the CAPM explains and predicts reality accurately and this is something examined much later in the chapter. For now we need to introduce the concept of beta to provide a bridge between the capital market line analysis and the Capital Asset Pricing Model.

Beta

In the previous chapter a number of graphs demonstrated the risk-reducing effect of adding securities to a portfolio. If there is only one company's shares in a 'portfolio' then risk is very high. Adding a second reduces risk (except in the rare cases of perfect positive correlation). The addition of a third and fourth continues to reduce risk but by smaller amounts. This sort of effect is demonstrated in **Exhibit 8.20**.

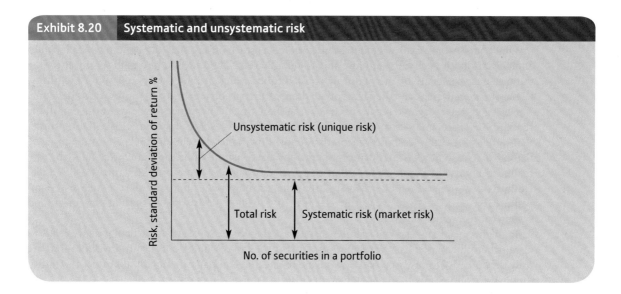

Exhibit 8.20   Systematic and unsystematic risk

The reason for the risk reduction is that security returns generally do not vary with perfect positive correlation. At any one time the good news about one share is offset to some extent by bad news about another – if one is shooting up, others are stable, going down or rising. Each share movement depends mostly on the news emanating from the company. News is generally particular to companies and so we should not expect them each to report good (or bad) news on the same day. So, if on one day a share in the portfolio reports the resignation of a brilliant chief executive we might expect that share to fall. But, because the portfolio owner is diversified the return on the portfolio will not move dramatically downward. Other companies are reporting marketing coups, big new contracts, etc., pushing up their share prices. Others (the majority) are not reporting any news and their share prices do not move much at all. The point is by not having all your eggs in one basket you reduce the chance of the collective value of your investments falling off a cliff (how is that for a mixed metaphor!).

So, despite the fact that returns on individual shares can vary dramatically, a portfolio will be relatively stable. The type of risk that is being reduced through diversification is called unique risk or unsystematic risk or idiosyncratic risk or specific risk. This element of variability in a share's return is due to the particular circumstances of the individual firm. In a portfolio these individual ups and downs tend to cancel out. Another piece of jargon applied to this type of risk is that it is 'diversifiable'. That is, it can be eliminated simply by holding a sufficiently large portfolio.

However, no matter how many shares are held, there will always be an element of risk that cannot be cancelled out by broadening the portfolio: **systematic** or **market risk**. There are some risk factors that are common to all firms to a greater or lesser extent. These include macroeconomic movements such as economic growth, inflation and exchange rate changes. No firm is entirely immune from these factors. For example, a deceleration in gross domestic product (GDP) growth or a rise in tax rates is likely to impact on the returns of all firms within an economy. Note, however, that while all shares respond to these system-wide risk factors they do not all respond equally. Some shares will exhibit a greater sensitivity to these systematic risk elements than others. The revenues of the consumer and luxury goods sectors, for example, are particularly sensitive to the ups and downs of the economy. Spending on expensive holidays and sports cars rises when the economy is in a strong growth phase but falls off significantly in recession. On the other hand, some sectors experience limited variations in demand as the economy booms and shrinks; the food-producing and food retailing sectors are prime examples here. People do not cut down significantly on food bought for home consumption even when their incomes fall.

It is assumed, quite reasonably, that investors do not like risk. If this is the case, then the logical course of action is going to be to eliminate as much unsystematic risk as is reasonable by diversifying. Most of the shares in UK companies are held by highly diversified institutional investors such as pension funds, insurance funds, unit trusts and investment trusts. While it is true that many small investors are not fully diversified, it is equally true that the market, and more importantly market returns, are dominated by the actions of highly diversified investors. These investors ensure that the market does not reward investors for bearing some unsystematic risk. To understand this, imagine that by some freak accident a share offered a return of, say, 50% per annum which includes compensation for both unsystematic and systematic risk. There would be a mad scramble to buy these shares, especially by the major diversified funds which are not concerned about the unsystematic risk on this share – they have other share returns to offset the oscillations of this new one. The buying pressure would result in a rise in the share price. This process would continue until the share offered the same return as other shares offering that level of systematic risk. (Don't forget that returns are future cash flows (e.g. dividends) flowing to shareholders relative to the price of the share. If cash flows from business operations are constant while the share price falls, the rate of return is raised.) Let us assume that the price doubles and therefore the return falls to 25%. Undiversified investors will be dismayed that they can no longer find any share which will compensate for what they perceive as the relevant risk for them, consisting of both unsystematic and systematic elements.

In the financial markets the risk that matters is the degree to which a particular share tends to move when the market as a whole moves. This is the only issue of concern to investors that are fully diversified, because ups and downs due to specific company events do not affect the return on the portfolio – only market-wide events affect the portfolio's return.

This is leading to a new way of measuring risk. For the diversified investor, the relevant measure of risk is no longer standard deviation, it is systematic risk.

The Capital Asset Pricing Model (CAPM) defined this systematic risk as beta.[7] Beta (β) measures the covariance between the returns on a particular share with the returns on the market as a whole (usually measured by a market index, e.g. the FTSE All-Share index).

In the CAPM model, because all investors are assumed to hold the market portfolio, an individual asset (e.g. a share) owned by an investor will have a risk that is defined as the amount of risk that it adds to the market portfolio. Assets that tend to move a lot when the market portfolio moves will be more risky to the fully diversified investor than those assets that move a little when the market portfolio moves. To the extent that asset movements are unrelated to the market portfolio's movement they can be ignored by the investor because, with full diversification, this unsystematic risk element will be eliminated when the asset is added to the portfolio. Therefore only co-movements with the market portfolio count. Statistically, risk is measured by the covariance of the asset with the market portfolio:

$$\text{Beta of asset, } j = \frac{\text{Covariance of asset } j \text{ with the market portfolio}}{\text{Variance of the market portfolio}}$$

$$\beta_j = \frac{\text{Cov } (R_j, R_M)}{\sigma^2_M}$$

The beta value for a share indicates the sensitivity of that share to general market movements. A share with a beta of 1.0 tends to have returns which move broadly in line with the market index.

---

7 Other models of risk and return define systematic risk in other ways. Some of these are discussed later in the chapter.

A share with a beta greater than 1.0 tends to exhibit amplified return movements compared to the index. For example, Premier Foods in 2017 had a beta of 2.63 and, according to the CAPM, when the market index return rises by, say, 10%, the returns on Premier Foods shares will tend to rise by 26.3%. Conversely, if the market falls by 10%, the returns on Premier Foods shares will tend to fall by 26.3%.

Shares with a beta of less than 1.0, such as Marks & Spencer with a beta of 0.72, will vary less than the market as a whole. So, if the market is rising, shares in M&S will not enjoy the same level of upswing. However, should the market ever suffer a downward movement, for every 10% decline in shares generally, M&S will, according to CAPM theory, give a return decline of only 7.2%. Note that these co-movements are to be taken as statistical expectations rather than precise predictions. Thus, over a large sample of return movements M&S's returns will move by 7.2% for a 10% market movement if CAPM-beta is a correct measure of company to market returns. On any single occasion the co-movements may not have this relationship. **Exhibit 8.21** displays the betas for four large UK companies.

Exhibit 8.21	Betas as measured in 2017		
Share	**Beta**	**Share**	**Beta**
Barclays Bank	1.09	Sainsbury's (J)	1.11
Marks and Spencer	0.72	BT	0.80

Source: www.yahoo finance.com.

When

$\beta = 1$ — A 1 per cent change in the market index return generally leads to a 1 per cent change in the return on a specific share.

$0 < \beta < 1$ — A 1 per cent change in the market index return generally leads to a less than 1 per cent change in the returns on a specific share.

$\beta > 1$ — A 1 per cent change in the market index return generally leads to a greater return than 1 per cent on a specific company's share.

The security market line (SML)

The return expected on a share J is $r_j = r_f + RP$, where RP is the risk premium. To calculate the expected return on an average share (or share market as a whole) we need two figures: (i) the current risk-free rate of return available to investors, and (ii) the RP for the average share. However, this is not enough information when we are examining shares that are not in the same risk category as the market as a whole. So, we must adjust (up or down) the RP for the averagely risky share to calculate the required return on a specific share.

Risk has been redefined for a fully diversified investor in an efficient market as systematic risk because this is the risk that cannot be diversified away and so a higher return is required if an investor is to bear it. In the CAPM the relationship between risk as measured by beta and expected return is shown by the security market line as in **Exhibit 8.22**. Shares perfectly correlated with the market return (r_m at point M) will have a beta of 1.0 and are expected to produce an annual return of 11% in the circumstances of a risk-free rate of return at 6% and the risk premium on the market portfolio of shares over safe securities at 5%. Shares which are twice as risky, with a beta of 2.0, will have an expected return of 16%; shares which vary half as much as the market index are expected to produce a return of 8.5% in this particular hypothetical risk-return line.

Exhibit 8.22   A hypothetical security market line (SML)

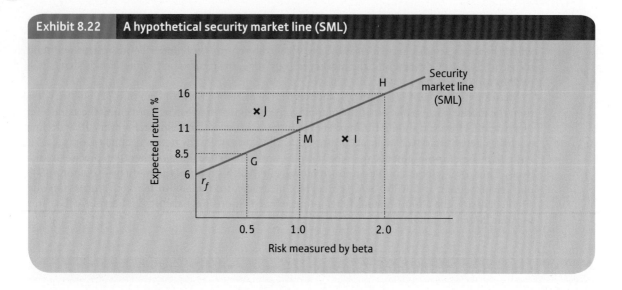

To find the level of return expected for a given level of CAPM-beta risk along the SML the following equation can be used:

| Expected return | = | risk-free rate | + beta × | The average risk premium for shares (expected return on the market minus the risk-free rate) |

or $r_j = r_f + \beta (r_m - r_f)$

Thus for a share with a beta of 1.31 the expected return will be:

$r_j = 6 + 1.31 (11 - 6) = 12.55\%$

The better way of presenting this is to place the risk premium (RP) in the brackets rather than r_m and r_f separately because this reminds us that what is important is the required extra return over the risk-free rate as revealed by investors over many years – not the current risk-free rate. It is amazing how often financial journalists get this wrong and fixate on the current r_m and r_f rather than the long-term historical difference between the two. The market risk premium $(r_m - r_f)$ is fairly stable over time as it is usually taken from a long-term historical relationship. Indeed, taking a short period to estimate this would result in wild fluctuations from year to year. None of these fluctuations would reflect the premiums that investors demand for holding a risky portfolio of shares compared with a risk-free security. It is only over long periods that we can get a clearer view of returns required by shareholders as an acceptable premium.

At any one time the position of the SML depends primarily on the risk-free rate of return. If the interest rate on government securities rises by, say, four percentage points, the SML lifts upwards by 4% (see **Exhibit 8.23**). Note that the slope of the SML does not change even though the r_f in $(r_m - r_f)$ changes because $r_m - r_f$ is the *long-term* historical risk premium for shares over the risk-free rate.

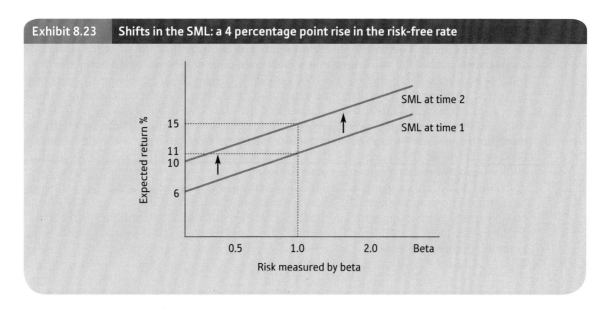

Exhibit 8.23   Shifts in the SML: a 4 percentage point rise in the risk-free rate

According to the CAPM all securities lie on the security market line, their exact position being determined by their beta. But what about shares J and I in Exhibit 8.22? These are shares that are not in equilibrium. J offers a particularly high level of return for the risk its holders have to bear. This will not last for long in an efficient market because investors are constantly on the prowl for shares like this. As they start to buy in large quantities the price will rise and correspondingly the expected return will fall (assuming that future cash flows attached to the share remain constant). This will continue until the share return is brought on to the SML. Conversely, share I will be sold until the price falls sufficiently to bring about equilibrium; that is, I is placed on the SML.

Estimating some expected returns

To calculate the returns investors require from particular shares it is necessary to obtain three numbers using the CAPM: (a) the risk-free rate of return, r_f, (b) the risk premium for the market portfolio (or proxy index), $(r_m - r_f)$, and (c) the beta of the share. Betas are available from many financial websites.

In 2017 the returns on UK long-term government securities were about 1.2%. For practical use we will take a risk premium of 5%. We could plump for a much lower figure if we accept the argument that investors were surprised by the size of the premium they actually received; they weren't demanding it *a priori*, it was just that the optimists (share investors) were lucky and got it anyway – see Shiller (2000) and Dimson, Marsh and Staunton (2002, 2006) for this view – in future, it is argued, they will get a smaller return above the government bond rate. **Exhibit 8.24** calculates the returns required on shares of some leading UK firms using beta as the only risk variable influencing returns, a risk-free rate of 1.2% and a risk premium of 5%.

Exhibit 8.24   Returns expected by investors based on the capital asset pricing model

Share	Beta (β)	Expected returns $r_f + \beta (r_m - r_f)$
BT	0.80	$1.2 + 0.8(5) = 5.2\%$
Sainsbury's (J)	1.11	$1.2 + 1.11(5) = 6.8\%$
Barclays Bank	1.09	$1.2 + 1.09(5) = 6.7\%$
Marks & Spencer	0.72	$1.2 + 0.72(5) = 4.8\%$

Calculating beta

To make the Capital Asset Pricing Model work for making decisions concerning the future it is necessary to calculate the *future* beta: that is, how much more or less volatile is a particular share going to be relative to the market. Investors want extra compensation for relative volatility over the period when they hold the share – i.e. time yet to come. Obviously, the future cannot be foreseen, and so it is difficult to obtain an estimate of the likely co-movements of the returns on a share and the market portfolio. One approach is to substitute subjective probability beliefs, but this has obvious drawbacks. The most popular method is to observe the historic relationship between returns and to assume that this covariance will persist into the future. This is called *ex-post* analysis because it takes place after the event.

Exhibit 8.25 shows a simplified and idealised version of this sort of analysis. Here are shown 12 monthly observations for, say, 2017. (Commercially supplied beta calculations are usually based on 60 monthly observations stretching back over five years.) Each plot point expresses the return on the market index portfolio for a particular month and the return on the specific shares being examined in that same month.

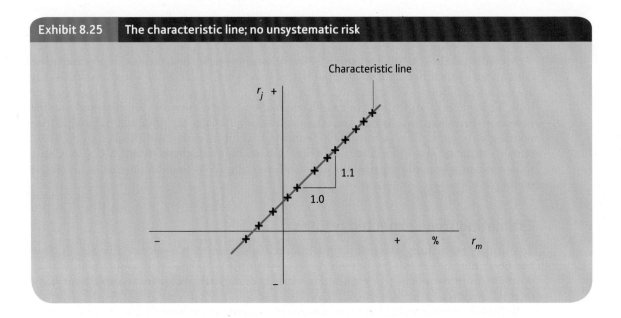

| Exhibit 8.25 | The characteristic line; no unsystematic risk |

In an analysis such as that presented in Exhibit 8.25 the market portfolio will be represented by some broad index containing many hundreds of shares. In this highly idealised example the relative returns plot along a straight line referred to as the characteristic line. Exhibit 8.25 shows a perfect statistical relationship, in that there is no statistical 'noise' causing the plot points to be placed off the line. The characteristic line has a form described by the following formula:

$$r_j = \alpha \cdot + \beta_j r_m + e$$

where: r_j = rate of return on the jth share
r_m = rate of return on the market index portfolio
$\alpha \cdot$ = regression line intercept
e = residual error about the regression line (in this simple case this has a value of zero because all the plot points are on a straight line)
β_j = the beta of security *j*

Thus the slope of the characteristic line is the beta for share *j*. That is:

$$\frac{\text{Change in } r_j}{\text{Change in } r_m} = \frac{\Delta r_j}{\Delta r_m} = \beta$$

In this case the slope is 1.1 and therefore $\beta = 1.1$.

A more realistic representation of the relationship between the monthly returns on the market and the returns on a specific share is shown in **Exhibit 8.26**. Here very few of the plot points fall on the fitted regression line (the line of best fit). The reason for this scatter of points is that the unsystematic risk effects in any one month may cause the returns on a specific share to rise or fall by a larger or smaller amount than they would if the returns on the market were the only influence. The slope of the best fit line is 1.2; therefore beta is 1.2.

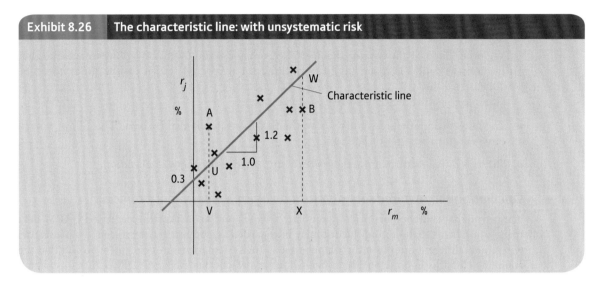

Exhibit 8.26   The characteristic line: with unsystematic risk

To gain an appreciation of what the model presented in Exhibit 8.26 reveals, we will examine two of the plot points. Take point A: this represents the returns for the market and for share j in the month of, say, August 2017. Part of the movement of j is explained by the general market changes – this is the distance UV. However, a large element of j's returns in that month is attributable to unsystematic risk factors – this is represented by the distance AU. Now consider point B for the month of November. If systematic risk was the only influence on the return of a single share then we would expect the change in j's return to be XW. However, unsystematic risk influences have reduced the extent of variation to only BX. The distances AU and WB make up part of the error term e in the market model formula.

Applications of the CAPM

In this section we present a few examples of how the CAPM has been employed.

Investment in the financial markets

Portfolio selection

The beta metric has been used to construct different types of portfolio. For highly risk-averse investors a portfolio consisting of low beta securities may be chosen. If the average beta of the portfolio is 0.7 then for every 1% change in the index the portfolio is expected to change by only 0.7%. Similarly a high-risk portfolio could be created which consisted of high beta stocks and this will be expected to outperform the market in an upswing but underperform in a market correction. We will look at evidence later that indicates that this has not worked: high-beta shares (established by looking at past returns) go on to produce *lower* returns than low-beta shares.

Mispriced shares

Investors have used beta estimates to identify shares with anomalous risk-return characteristics. A share with an unusually attractive expected return for its beta level would be a 'buy' opportunity and one with an unusually low anticipated return a 'sell'. Getting this analysis correct is easier said than done, even if the CAPM worked perfectly.

Measuring portfolio performance

If a fund manager produces a high annual return of, say, 15% how do you judge if this is due to good share selection? Well, one of the elements to consider is the systematic risk of the fund. If the 15% return has been achieved because particularly risky shares were selected then perhaps you would hesitate to congratulate the manager. For example, if the beta risk is 1.7, the risk-free rate of return is 8% and the historic risk premium for the market index over the risk-free investment $(r_m - r_f)$ has been 5% then you would expect a return of 16.5%:

$$r_j = r_f + \beta(r_m - r_f) = 8 + 1.7(5) = 16.5\%$$

On the other hand, if the beta of the portfolio is only 0.8 you might be willing to agree to that promotion the fund manager has been pushing for (expected return on the fund would be $8 + 0.8(5) = 12\%$).

A couple of performance measures used in practice:

- Treynor's ratio measures return above the risk-free rate divided by beta. This allows you to observe return per unit of beta risk.

- Sharpe's ratio is return above the risk-free rate divided by standard deviation.

Calculating the required rate of return on a firm's investment projects

If it is true that shareholders price a company's shares on the basis of the perceived CAPM-beta risk of the firm as a whole, and the firm may be regarded as a collection of projects, then investors will require different rates of return depending on the systematic risk of each new project that the company embarks upon. Consider a firm which at present has a beta of 1.1 because its existing projects produce returns which are vulnerable to systematic risk only slightly more than market average. If this firm now begins a major investment programme in a new area with a systematic risk of 1.8, the theory tells us that shareholders will demand higher levels of return to compensate for the increased risk. The management team cannot rely on the same rate of return for all projects because each has a different risk level. This application of the CAPM is discussed later in this chapter and in Chapter 16.

Accepted theory and controversial theory

This is a good point at which to recap, and to point out those issues that are generally accepted and those that are controversial.

- Shareholders demand a higher return for riskier assets – **uncontroversial**.

- Risk-averters are wise to diversify – **uncontroversial**.

- The risk of securities (for example shares) has two elements: (a) unsystematic risk factors specific to firms which can be diversified away; and (b) systematic risk caused by risk factors common to all firms – **uncontroversial**.

- Investors will not be rewarded for bearing unsystematic risk – **uncontroversial**.

- Different shares have different degrees of sensitivity to the systematic risk elements – **uncontroversial**.

- Systematic risk is measured by CAPM-beta which, in practice, is calculated as the degree of co-movement of a security's return with a market index return – **highly controversial**. As we will see later, there is a very convincing body of research indicating that CAPM-beta has no effect on the level of returns earned on shares (that is, there is no relationship, and the SML does not exist); others believe that CAPM-beta is one of a number of systematic risk factors influencing share returns.

- Beta, as calculated by examining past returns, is valid for decision making concerned about the future – **controversial**.

Technical problems with the CAPM

There are two issues that need to be addressed if the CAPM is to be a valid and useful tool in the commercial world. First, the CAPM has to be workable from the technical point of view. Second, the users have to be reassured that the CAPM, through its emphasis on beta, does accurately describe the returns witnessed on shares and securities. This second issue has been examined in scores of marketplace studies. The results of some of them are discussed in the next section; here we concentrate on the technical problems.

Measuring beta

The mathematics involved in obtaining a historical beta are straightforward enough; however, it is not clear whether it is more appropriate to use daily, weekly or monthly data, or whether the observation period should be three, five or ten years. (Some people observe market and share returns over a mere 30 days!) Each is likely to provide a different estimate of beta. This can be illustrated by drawing on the work of Pablo Fernández at IESE, Spain. In one paper (2009) he shows the betas of Coca-Cola calculated on each of the 30 days of the month of April 2009, using, firstly, monthly data (as in Exhibit 8.26) going back five years; secondly, using weekly data for the previous five years; and finally, using daily data for the previous five years – *see* **Exhibit 8.27**. Using daily data the betas change very little from a beta of around 0.2. However, with the weekly data the betas vary between 0.07 and 0.35. They are even more volatile for the monthly data, moving as low as 0.06 and as high as 0.57. So, what is the beta for Coca-Cola? It depends whether you use monthly, weekly or daily data.

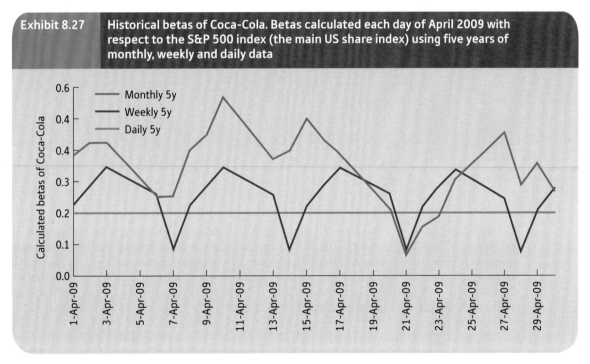

Exhibit 8.27 Historical betas of Coca-Cola. Betas calculated each day of April 2009 with respect to the S&P 500 index (the main US share index) using five years of monthly, weekly and daily data

Source: Fernández (2009).

The results in Exhibit 8.27 highlight another problem with calculating betas: they tend to be unstable over time. Even within one month and using 60 months of data, Coca-Cola's beta varies depending on whether we make the calculation on 6 April 2009 (using data for the sixth of each of 60 months) or 10 April 2009 (using data for the tenth of each month). To ensure that he has not just by chance come across a company with a particularly volatile beta, Fernández examined over 3,000 companies and found that the median percentage change in beta from one day to the next was 20% (using monthly data stretching back five years). The results for Walt Disney, Walmart and Coca-Cola are shown in **Exhibit 8.28**. The beta of Disney varies from 0.66 to 1.07, and the beta of Walmart varies from −0.05 to 0.5. Note that these companies have very stable operating business, the riskiness of which does not change much over decades, let alone over one month.

| Exhibit 8.28 | Historical betas of Walt Disney, Walmart And Coca-Cola. Betas calculated each day of April 2009 with respect to the S&P 500 using five years of monthly data, e.g. on 7 April 2009 the beta is calculated by running a regression of the 60 monthly returns of the company on the 60 monthly returns of the S&P 500 calculated on the 7th of each of the months |

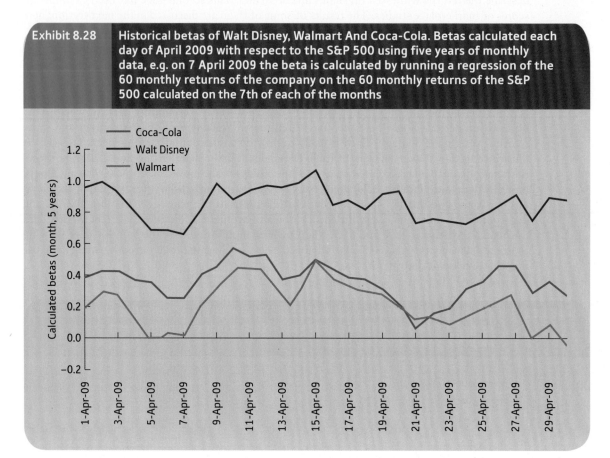

Source: Fernández (2009).

For the first edition of this book Marks & Spencer's beta was obtained from Datastream. It used data for the five years to 1997 and M&S's beta was 0.95. A mere three years later Datastream calculated (based on the five years to 2000) its value at less than half that, at 0.44. For the fourth edition the beta was 0.64, and for the current edition it was calculated at 0.97. For Sainsbury's the change is even more dramatic: 0.60 in 1997, 0.19 in 2000, 0.8 in 2004, 1.04 in 2007, 0.67 in 2011 and 0.68 in 2017 – *see* **Exhibit 8.29**.

Exhibit 8.29	Betas as measured for the five years to 1997, 2000, 2004, 2007, 2011 and 2017					
	1997	**2000**	**2004**	**2007**	**2011**	**2017**
Barclays	1.22	1.55	1.11	1.03	1.78	1.13
BT	0.91	0.94	1.62	0.94	0.91	0.98
Marks & Spencer	0.95	0.44	0.50	0.64	0.77	0.97
J. Sainsbury	0.60	0.19	0.80	1.04	0.67	0.68

Source: Thomson Financial Datastream.

One potential explanation for the shifting betas is that the risk of the security changes – firms change the way they operate, as do the markets they serve. A company that was relatively insensitive to general market change two years ago may now be highly responsive, for example. But can you really say that the risk of M&S's and Sainsbury's business has changed? Alternatively, the explanation may lie in measurement error – large random errors cause problems in producing comparable betas from one period to another.

Most people now download betas from free financial websites. For the same company on the same day these betas can vary tremendously – *see* **Exhibit 8.30**.

Exhibit 8.30	Betas of four companies according to website, 26 May 2017			
Website	**Barclays**	**BT**	**M&S**	**J. Sainsbury**
Datastream	1.13	0.98	0.97	0.68
ADVFN.com	0.87	0.08	0.99	0.61
FT.com	0.93	1.07	0.98	0.64
Yahoo Finance	1.09	0.80	0.72	1.11
Digitalook.com	1.29	0.71	0.62	0.69

Some very old research by Blume showed that betas tended to change towards a value of 1 over time, but the bouncing around we see in the beta values today means that if that was ever true it is not any longer. There is also a claim that the betas of industries are much more stable and reliable, and so they should be substituted for the beta calculated for a specific company within an industry. However, Fernández (2008) reports that industry betas also change significantly over a period of a few weeks. And anyway, many industries are so heterogeneous that it does not make sense to group those companies in the same systematic risk categories. Take the 'media' industry, for example, where newspapers are lumped in with Internet-based companies, book publishers and broadcasters. Are investors in these companies' shares really facing the same systematic risks?

To add to the problems there is a wide variety of market indices (e.g. FTSE All-Share, FTSE-100) to choose from when calculating the historical covariability of a share with the market (i.e. its beta). Fernández (2008) demonstrated this by calculating the betas of the 30 companies in the Dow Jones Industrial Average firstly by using the S&P 500 index as the 'market' and then on the same day the Dow Jones index was used to represent the market return. The ratio of the two betas for each company was displayed. If the market index choice made no difference to the beta, the ratios would all turn out to be 1. In fact, the ratios were far from 1. A random selection is shown in **Exhibit 8.31**.

Exhibit 8.31	The ratio of beta values as calculated first using the S&P 500 and then the Dow Jones Industrial Average indices				
3M Co.	0.65	Coca-Cola	0.90	McDonald's	0.93
Alcoa	0.66	Du Pont	0.70	Microsoft	1.34
AT&T	1.66	General Elec.	1.10	SBC Commu.	1.46

Source: Fernández (2008).

So, we are faced with the reality that using historical betas as a proxy for the expected future beta could lead to error because of the great uncertainties in being able to alight on a 'true' beta for the past. This is due to beta volatility and room for choice in selecting the period of calculation, the interval of calculation and the index representing the market return, r_m. Fernández (2009, p. 5) draws a pessimistic conclusion: 'We argue, as many professors mention [in survey replies], that historical betas (calculated from historical data) are useless to calculate the required return to equity, to rank portfolios with respect to systematic risk, and to estimate the expected return of companies.'

Ex ante theory with ex post testing

Applications of the CAPM tend to be focused on the future, for example deciding whether a share will provide a sufficiently high return to compensate for its risk level. Thus, it is investors' *expectations* that drive share prices. The CAPM follows this ex ante (before the event) line of reasoning; it describes *expected* returns and *future* beta. However, when it comes to testing the theory, we observe what has already occurred – these are ex post observations. There is usually a large difference between investors' expectations and the outcome. Therefore when we obtain, say, the risk premium for the market from historical data (*ex post*) we may be making an error in assuming that this is the appropriate rate today for calculating the required rate of return for an input to our *ex ante* (forward looking) analysis of say an investment project.

The market portfolio is unobtainable

A linchpin of the CAPM is the market portfolio, because all investors are assumed to hold this in combination with risk-free lending and borrowing. In theory the market portfolio consists of a portion of all the potential assets in the world weighted in proportion to their respective market values. In practice, just identifying, let alone obtaining, the market portfolio is pretty well impossible. Consider what you would need to do. It would be necessary to identify all possible assets: that is, all the securities issued by firms in every country of the world, as well as all government debt, buildings and other property, cash and metals. Other possibilities for inclusion would be consumer durables and what is called human capital – the skills and knowledge of people. The value of these assets is clearly very difficult to assess. Because of these difficulties practitioners of the CAPM use market portfolio proxies such as broad share indices. Richard Roll (1977) has put forward the argument that the impossibility of obtaining or even identifying the market portfolio means that the CAPM is untestable. Using proxies can lead to conflicting results and the CAPM not being properly employed.

One-period model

Investments usually involve a commitment for many years, whether the investment is made by a firm in real assets or by investors purchasing financial assets. However, the CAPM is based on parameters measured at one point in time. Key variables such as the risk-free rate of return might, in reality, change.

A strict interpretation of the CAPM would insist on the use of the three-month Treasury bill rate of return sold by a reputable government to investors. But sticking to the strict rule can lead to nonsense results. For example, in 2016 US Treasury bill interest rates were as low as 0.2%. If this is used for r_f the required rate of return for an average risk-level US share is about 5% $(0.2 + 1(5) = 5.2\%)$. For shares or projects within firms with a beta of 0.4 some analysts (and, it would seem, some textbook writers) would ask for a return of 2.2% $(0.2 + 0.4(5) = 2.2\%)$. This is odd given that many of these firms are investing in projects with lives of 5–30 years, not three months. Furthermore this was at a time when lending to the government could gain you a return of 3%, if you lent for 30 years. The practical solution is to use long-term government bond rates for r_f.

Very few government securities are close to being risk free

For investors and corporate managers in most countries their own government's bonds and bills ('sovereign debt') are regarded as having substantial risk. They are very far from risk free – just ask investors in Greek and Venezualan government bonds. This means that they usually pay interest rates significantly higher than those paid by corporations when borrowing by issuing bonds. So what should, say, a Greek company use as its r_f in calculating an appropriate discount rate for project appraisal, or an investor in Greek shares use as the risk-free rate in required return and valuation calculations? I can offer no satisfactory solution, sorry. A couple of options might be (a) use the interest on top-rated ('triple A-rated') bonds issued in that currency, even if that is by a company rather than the government, or (b) while Greece is in the eurozone use the interest rate paid by the safest euro borrower, the German government. But these options present difficulties of their own.

Unrealistic assumptions

The CAPM is created on the foundation of a number of assumptions about the behaviour of investors and the operation of capital markets. Here are some of them:

Exhibit 8.32

Irrational regard for economic models

By James Mackintosh

CAPM . . . makes several big assumptions, none of which even approximates to reality, yet is widely used by investors to design their portfolios.

The assumptions about investors include that they are rational, risk averse, do not influence market prices, hold diversified portfolios, pay no tax, have access to unlimited low-cost leverage and instant equal access to information.

The models also need a "risk-free rate", the return on a supposedly risk-free asset, to design a portfolio. Usually US Treasuries are used; but even before they were downgraded by Standard & Poor's this summer, the US government was not risk free.

Ask any investor why they use these models, and the response is typically: "It isn't perfect, but there isn't anything better."

The models are not just imperfect. They do not even approximate to reality, and contributed to widespread misallocation of capital. Academic economists can offer insights. But investors must realise that the results of economics are not like those of physics. A model from physics can be tested, its simplifications understood, and its results used by engineers to build bridges.

An economics model creates an abstract world, populated by synthetic beings with goals set by the economist. These can be interesting, but tell us little about the real world.

The danger comes from the unthinking application of the models to investment. In an uncertain world, a model that claims scientific rigour for its recommendation to hold so much in equities, bonds or property is appealing – and often wrong.

Politicians, investors and policymakers began to realise during the crisis that the models and assumptions they had relied on were no longer valid. There is, as yet, no reliable replacement model. It is time to realise that perhaps there never will be. Investors need to use their own judgment to build portfolios, not mechanical constructs.

- Investors are rational and risk averse.
- Investors are able to assess returns and standard deviations. Indeed they all have the same forecasts of returns and risk because of the free availability of information.
- There are no taxes or transaction costs.
- All investors can borrow or lend at the risk-free rate of interest.
- All assets are traded and it is possible to buy a fraction of a unit of an asset.

Clearly some of these assumptions do not reflect reality – see **Exhibit 8.32**. But then, that is the way of economic modelling – it is necessary to simplify in order to explain real-world behaviour. In a sense it is not of crucial importance whether the assumptions are realistic. The important consideration is whether the model describes market behaviour. If it has some degree of predictive power about real-world relationships then it would be reasonable to overlook some of its technical problems and absurd assumptions.

Does the CAPM work in practice?

Researchers have sidestepped or ignored the technical and theoretical problems to try to see if taking on higher risk, as measured by beta, is rewarded by higher return, as described by the CAPM. More significantly, they have tried to establish if beta is the *only* factor influencing returns.

Empirical research carried out in the 20 years or so following the development of the CAPM tended to support the model. Work by Black *et al.* (1972) and Fama and MacBeth (1973), among dozens of others,[8] demonstrated that risk when measured by beta did have an influence on return.

---

8 See References and further reading list at the end of this chapter for empirical studies.

Eugene Fama and James MacBeth, for instance, allocated all the shares listed on the New York Stock Exchange between 1935 and 1966 to 20 portfolios. Over a five-year period monthly returns on specific shares and the market index were observed to calculate each share's beta. The shares were then allocated to portfolios. Portfolio 1 contained the 5% of shares with the lowest betas. Portfolio 2 consisted of the second-lowest 5% of shares as measured by their betas, and so on. Then a comparison was made for each subsequent four-year period between the calculated betas and the rate of return earned on each portfolio. If beta explained returns completely then the expectation is that the graphical plot points of beta and returns would be described by a straight line. The results did not show a perfect relationship. However, the plot points were generally placed around a market line and Fama and MacBeth felt able to conclude that 'there seems to be a positive trade off between returns and risk'.

While the early empirical work helped to spread the acceptance of the CAPM a few nagging doubts remained because, in general, the results gave only limited support to the notion that beta completely explains returns. An overview of these studies (presented in diagram form in **Exhibit 8.33**) gives the following conclusions. First, the intercept value for the security market line (SML) tends to be higher than the risk-free rate of return, r_f; perhaps this indicates other risk factors at play, or perhaps investors expected to be compensated for accepting unsystematic risk. Second, the slope of the SML is much flatter than theory would imply – that is, low-risk shares tend to show rates of return higher than theory would suggest and high beta shares show lower returns than the CAPM predicts. Third, when individual shares are examined, the R^2 (coefficient of determination) of the characteristic line is low, suggesting that systematic risk as measured by

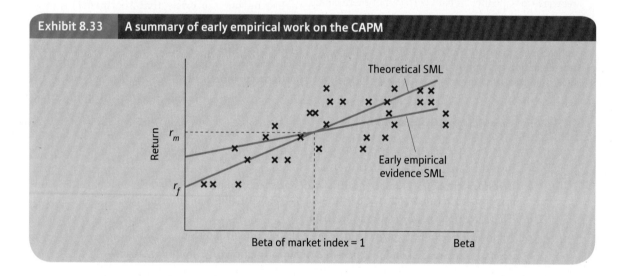

Exhibit 8.33   A summary of early empirical work on the CAPM

beta is only a very small part of the explanation of the overall variability in share returns. Unsystematic risk and other types of systematic risk have far more significant effects on returns.

Later work has generally caused more problems for the CAPM. For example, Fischer Black (1993) discovered major differences in the strength of the beta-return relationship in the period 1931–65 compared with the period 1966–91. Ironically, up until the time of the development of the CAPM in the mid-1960s, the model seems to work reasonably well; but following its development and subsequent implementation the relationship breaks down. Black simulates a portfolio strategy that investors might adopt. First US shares are allocated on an annual basis to 10 categories of different beta levels. Each year the betas are recalculated from the returns over the previous 60 months. The first investment portfolio is constructed by hypothetically purchasing all those shares within the top 10% of CAPM-beta values. As each year goes by the betas are recalculated and shares that are no longer in the top 10% are sold and replaced by shares which now have the highest levels of beta. The second portfolio consists of the 10% of shares with the next highest betas and this is reconstituted each year.

If ten portfolios with different levels of beta are created it should be possible to observe the extent to which beta risk is related to return in the period after formation. The relationship shown in

Exhibit 8.34 is not exactly as described by the SML for these ten portfolios held over the period 1931–91. The plot points are not placed precisely on the SML but it would be reasonable to conclude that higher-beta portfolios produce higher returns than lower-beta portfolios. The portfolio with a beta of 1.52 produces a return above the risk-free rate of 17% per annum compared with 9% for a portfolio having a beta of only 0.49. Also note that if a regression line is fitted to the observed data its shape would be flatter than the SML passing through the market portfolio plot point.

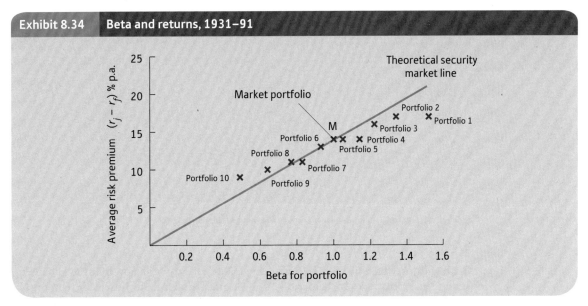

Exhibit 8.34   Beta and returns, 1931–91

Source: Data derived from Black, F. (1993) 'Beta and return', *Journal of Portfolio Management*, 20, Fall, pp. 8–18.

The problems start when the data are split into two time periods. The pre-1965 data confirm a risk-return relationship roughly corresponding to the CAPM but with a flatter line. However, the post-1965 data (in **Exhibit 8.35**) show a complete absence of a relationship. Both the high-beta portfolio and the low-beta portfolio show average annual returns over the risk-free rate of 6%.

A further blow to the CAPM came with the publication of Eugene Fama and Kenneth French's (1992) empirical study of US share returns over the period 1963–90. They found 'no reliable relation between β, and average return'.[9] They continue

> The asset-pricing model of Sharpe (1964), Lintner (1965), and Black (1972) [the CAPM] has long shaped the way academics and practitioners think about average returns and risk . . . In short, our tests do not support the most basic prediction of the SLB model, that average stock returns are positively related to market βs . . . Our bottom-line results are: (a) β does not seem to help explain the cross-section of average stock returns, and (b) the combination of size and book-to-market equity [does].

In other words, CAPM-beta has not been able to explain returns whereas two other factors have. A firm's total market value has had some effect on returns: the larger the firm (market capitalisation), the lower the return. Also the ratio of the firm's book (balance sheet) value to its market value (total value of all shares issued) has had some explanatory power: if book value is high *vis-à-vis* market value, then returns tend to be higher.[10] Fama and French's later (2006) paper also reports that higher beta did not lead to higher returns over the 77 years to 2004.

---

9   There is some controversy over their interpretation of the data, but nevertheless this is a very serious challenge to the CAPM.

10 In Fama and French's subsequent writing they describe size and book-to-market ratio as risk factors believing the market to be efficient at pricing shares. Other researchers (e.g. Daniel and Titman 1997, 2006) see these factors as elements that are not properly priced by investors, i.e. they underprice small companies and those with a high book value relative to market value. These shares subsequently produce high returns as investors slowly positively reappraise them. See Chapter 13 for a discussion on share mispricing.

| Exhibit 8.35 | Beta and returns, 1966–91 |

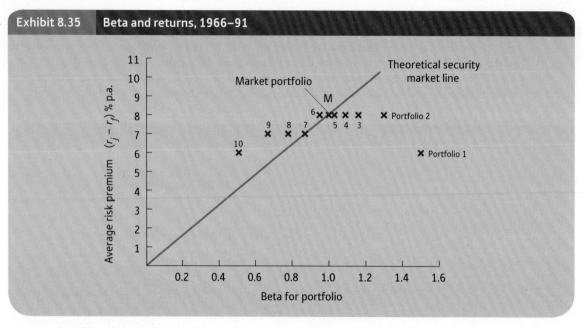

Louis Chan and Josef Lakonishok (1993) breathed a little life into the now dying CAPM-beta. They looked at share returns over the period 1926–91 and found a faint pulse of a relationship between CAPM-beta and returns, but were unable to show statistical significance because of the 'noisy' data. More vibrant life can be witnessed if the share return data after 1982 are excluded – but, then, shouldn't it work in all periods? They also argued that beta may be a more valid determinant of return in extreme market circumstances, such as a stock market crash, and therefore should not be written off as being totally 'dead'.

Beta has been brought to its knees by the punches delivered by American researchers; it was kicked again while it was down by the damaging evidence drawn from the European share markets. For example, Albert Corhay and co-researchers Gabriel Hawawini and Pierre Michel (1987) found that investors in shares trading in the United States, the United Kingdom and Belgium were not compensated with higher average returns for bearing higher levels of risk (as measured by beta) over the 13-year sample period. Investors in shares trading on the Paris Stock Exchange were actually penalised rather than rewarded, in that they received below-average rates of return for holding shares with above-average levels of beta risk. Rouwenhorst, Heston and Wessels (1999), however, found some relation between beta and returns in 12 European countries. Strong and Xu (1997) show that UK shares during the period 1973–92 displayed evidence consistent with a *negative* relationship between average returns and CAPM-beta!

The evidence is now mounting that far from investors requiring higher returns for higher CAPM-betas, they seem to be either indifferent or are content with *lower* rates of return. **Exhibit 8.36** shows the results of one piece of research, by Baker *et al.* (2011). For each month during the period 1968–2008 they placed all US shares into one of five groups based on the beta measured over the previous 60 months. They followed the subsequent returns for each of the five portfolios over the 41 years. A dollar invested in the lowest CAPM-beta ('bottom quintile') portfolio grew to $60.46 ($10.28 in real terms) and a dollar invested in the highest CAPM-beta portfolio ('top quintile') grew to $3.77 (64 cents in real terms). The high beta investor underperformed his low beta neighbour by 964%.

Frazzini and Pedersen (2014) state that 'The security market line is not only flatter than predicted by the standard CAPM for US equities . . . but we also find this relative flatness in 18 of 19 international equity markets [ranging from Australia to the UK between 1984 and 2012]'.

Exhibit 8.36   Returns for beta quintiles, January 1968 – December 2008

Source: Baker, Bradley and Wurgler (2011).

Fernández and Bermejo (2009) tested the question: Which gives the better correlation for the return performance of the 30 Dow Jones companies over the next year: the measured beta of the firm in the past or the market return, i.e. assuming each firm has a beta of 1? Answer: beta has a lower correlation with annual returns than assuming each firm has a beta of 1, thus using beta is a poorer predictor of returns than simply assuming they will be similar to the returns on the market taken as a whole.

In emerging markets Rouwenhorst (1999) finds no statistically significant evidence that high beta shares outperform low beta shares.

Factor models

The Capital Asset Pricing Model assumes that there is a single factor influencing returns on securities. This view has been difficult to sustain over recent years given the empirical evidence and theoretical doubts. It also seems to defy common sense; for example, it seems reasonable, and is observed in practice, that the returns on a share respond to industry or sector changes as well as to the general market changes.

Multi-factor models are based on the notion that a security's return may be sensitive to a variety of factors. Using these models the analyst attempts to first identify the important influences within the business and financial environment, and second, measure the degree of sensitivity of particular securities to these factors. We will see how this works by considering a one-factor model and building from there.

A one-factor model

Let us assume that we believe the main influence on the returns of shares in Rose plc (*see* **Exhibit 8.37**) is the economy-wide inflation rate. To test this hypothesis we have gathered data for the past six years.

Exhibit 8.37	Returns on Rose and changes in a single potential explanatory factor	
Year	Inflation (%)	Return on a share in Rose plc (%)
1	4	22.5
2	3.4	22.5
3	3.1	20.0
4	5.0	32.5
5	2.6	21.25
6	2.2	12.5

The fitted line in **Exhibit 8.38** has a positive slope of 5, indicating a positive relationship between Rose's returns and inflation. The relationship is not perfect (in that the plot points do not lie on the line), indicating that there are other influences on the return.

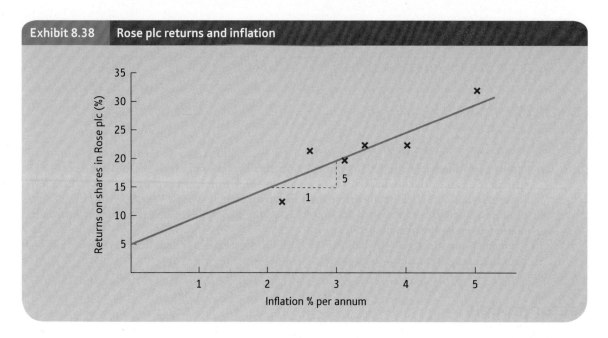

Exhibit 8.38   Rose plc returns and inflation

The kind of one-factor model shown in Exhibit 8.38 can be expressed in mathematical form:

$$r_j = a + b\,F_1 + e$$

where:
- r_j = return on share j
- a = intercept term when the Factor F_1 is zero
- F_1 = the factor under consideration
- b = the sensitivity of the return to the factor
- e = error term caused by other influences on return, e.g. unsystematic risk

In the example shown in Exhibit 8.38 the expected return on a share in Rose is given by

$$r_j = 5 + 5 \times F_1$$

so, if inflation is 1%, the expected return on Rose will be 10%; if it is 2%, Rose is expected to return 15%.

(Strictly speaking, many factor models focus on only the unexpected part of the change in F_1, F_2 etc. because returns on share j over a period are not going to respond to expected changes in F_1 or F_2 because in an efficient market the share would already have moved to the new level at the start of the period in anticipation.)

Of course, the CAPM is a type of one-factor model where F_1 is defined as the equity risk premium and b equates to CAPM-beta (representing sensitivity to the determining factor):

$$r_j = a + b F_1 + e$$

In the CAPM: $a = r_f$, $b = \beta$, $F_1 = (r_m - r_f)$. Thus:

$$r_j = r_f + \beta(r_m - r_f) + e$$

However, the useful characteristic of this factor model is that it permits F_1 to be any one of a number of explanatory influences, and does not restrict the researcher or practitioner to the market index premium.

An investment in Rose is an investment in a single company's shares; therefore both systematic and unsystematic risk will be present – or in the language of factor models, *factor risk* and *non-factor risk*. By diversifying, an investor can eliminate non-factor risk. Most factor model analysis takes place under the assumption that all non-factor (unsystematic) risk can be ignored because the investors are fully diversified and therefore this type of risk will not be rewarded with a higher return.

A two-factor model

The returns on Rose may be influenced by more than simply the general inflation rate. Perhaps the price of oil products has an effect. A two-factor model can be represented by the following equation:

$$r_j = a + b_1 F_1 + b_2 F_2 + e$$

where: F_1 = inflation rate
  b_1 = sensitivity of j to inflation rate growth
  F_2 = price of oil
  b_2 = sensitivity of j to price of oil

To establish the slope values of b_1 and b_2 as well as a, a multiple regression analysis could be carried out. The relationship of the returns on Rose and the influencing factors can no longer be represented by a two-dimensional graph. The level of return in any one period is determined by the following formula, which has been constructed on the assumption that for every (unexpected) $1 on the price of oil return increases by 0.3 of a percentage point and every (unexpected) 1% increase in inflation generates an extra 5% of return . . .

$$r_j = a + b_1 F_1 + b_2 F_2$$
$$r_j = 3 + 5 F_1 + 0.3 F_2$$

Of course, for a particular share in addition to this systematic risk-related return there is likely to be an unsystematic (specific to the firm) element of return in any period. This is the element e in the equation, which can often be much greater than the systematic elements in explaining a return for, say, a period of a year.

Multi-factor models

No doubt the reader can think of many other systematic risk factors that might influence the returns on a share, ranging from GDP growth to the exchange rate. These relationships have to be presented in a purely mathematical fashion. So, for a five-factor model the equation could look like this:

$$r_j = a + b_1 F_1 + b_2 F_2 + b_3 F_3 + b_4 F_4 + b_5 F_5 + e$$

where F_3 might be, say, the industrial group that firm j belongs to, F_4 is the growth in national GDP and F_5 is the size of the firm. This particular share will have a set of sensitivities (b_1, b_2, b_3, b_4 and b_5) to its influencing factors which is likely to be different from the sensitivity of other shares, even those within the same line of business.

The arbitrage pricing theory

As the CAPM has come under attack the arbitrage pricing theory (APT) has attracted more attention (at least in the academic world) since it was developed by Stephen Ross in 1976. In similar fashion to the CAPM it assumes that investors are fully diversified and therefore factor risks (systematic risks) are the only influence on long-term returns. However, the systematic factors permissible under the APT are many and various, compared with the CAPM's single determining variable. The returns on a share under the APT are found through the following formula:

$$\text{Expected returns} = \text{risk-free return} + \beta_1(r_1 - r_f) + \beta_2(r_2 - r_f) + \beta_3(r_3 - r_f) + \beta_4(r_4 - r_f) \ldots + \beta_n(r_n - r_f) + e$$

where β_1 stands for the security's beta with respect to the first factor, β_2 stands for the security's beta with respect to the second factor, and so on. The terms in brackets are the risk premiums for each of the factors in the model – $(r_1 - r_f)$ is the risk premium for the first factor for a security whose beta with respect to the first factor is 1 and whose beta with respect to all other factors is zero. Notice that the $(r_1 - r_f)$ etc. are the extra percentage annual returns on a share for bearing this type of risk. This is different from F_1, F_2, etc. above, which relate to, say, the unexpected change in the price of oil which may be expressed in dollars per barrel, or GDP growth, as they change year on year.

Arbitrage pricing theory does not specify what will be systematic risk factors, nor does it state the size or the sign (positive or negative) of the 'βs'. Each share or portfolio will have a different degree of sensitivity to each of the risk factors that happen to be included in the model tested.

Researchers have tried to identify the most frequently encountered systematic risk factors. Some studies have shown these to be changes in the macroeconomic environment such as inflation, interest rates, industrial production levels, personal consumption and money supply. This seems to make sense given that future profits are likely to be influenced by the state of the economy. All firms are likely to react to a greater or lesser extent to changes in those macroeconomic variables. Also, most firms will respond in the same way. For instance, if the economy is growing strongly then most firms' profits will rise; therefore these factors cannot be diversified away. However, some firms will be more sensitive to changes in the factors than others – this is measured by the 'βs'. Each of these risk factors has a risk premium because investors will only accept the risk if they are adequately rewarded with a higher return. It is the sum of these risk premiums when added to the risk-free rate that creates the return on a particular share or portfolio.

A major problem with the APT is that it does not tell us in advance what the risk factors are. In practice there have been two approaches to find these. The first is to specify those factors thought most likely to be important and then to test to see if they are relevant. The drawback here is that it is rather *ad hoc* and there will always be the nagging doubt that you failed to test some of the crucial factors. The second approach employs a complex statistical technique that simultaneously determines from a mass of factors which are relevant in a data set, as well as their coefficients.

Empirical research has demonstrated the value of the APT in highlighting where there is more than one factor influencing returns. Unfortunately there is disagreement about the key variables as the identified factors vary from study to study. This lack of specificity regarding the crucial factors has meant that the APT has not been widely adopted in the investment community despite its intuitive appeal. Investors are generally left to themselves to discover the risk factors if they can. Even if they are able to identify relevant factors and the degree of sensitivity is carefully worked out, the analyst is forced to recognise that the outcomes only explain past returns. The focus of most investors and business people is on the future and so judgement is needed to make these models valuable in a predictive role. Using historical information in a mechanical fashion to predict future returns may produce disappointing results.

The three-factor model

Fama and French (1996) have developed a three-factor model based on their previous work which showed that smaller companies produce higher returns than larger companies, and those with lots of net assets compared to the market value of the company outperform those with few net assets as a proportion of share market value of the firm. They interpreted size and the book-to-market value ratio as risk factors that require compensation in the form of higher returns (rather than share traders temporarily irrationally underpricing small companies and those with high book-to-market values – *see* Chapter 13 for this alternative view). In their model returns are determined by the risk-free rate plus:

- the excess return on a broad market portfolio $(r_m - r_f)$;
- the difference between the return on a portfolio of small shares (companies with a small market capitalisation) and the return on a portfolio of large shares (SMB, small minus big);
- the difference between the return on a portfolio of high book-to-market shares and the return on a portfolio of low book-to-market shares (HML, high minus low).

$$\text{Expected returns} = \text{risk-free rate} + \beta_1(r_m - r_f) + \beta_2(\text{SMB}) + \beta_3(\text{HML})$$

The model is attempting to pick up systematic risk factors not captured by the simple CAPM. In the Fama and French model, as well as being influenced by the general risk premium for shares $(r_m - r_f)$, the average small share is taken to be more risky than the average large share and so offers an additional risk premium, SMB. Also the share with a high balance sheet (book) value per share relative to the market value of each share is assumed to be more risky than a share with a low book value compared with the share price, and so offers a risk premium, HML. Fama and French tested this model on US shares and concluded that 'the model is a good description of returns' (Fama and French 1996).

To make the model useful you need to establish the risk premium associated with each factor $(r_m - r_f)$, (SMB) and (HML). For the purposes of illustration let us assume that the risk premium on the market portfolio $(r_m - r_f)$, is 5% and the annual risk premium for a small company share compared with a large company share is 2% and the extra return received on a share with a high book-to-market ratio compared with a low book-to-market ratio is 3%.

These are the risk premiums for averagely sensitive shares. Individual shares are more or less sensitive to the fluctuations in the returns on the three factors.

So, if we take the shares of an imaginary company, A, with a high sensitivity to market movements $(r_m - r_f)$, they will be observed to have a high β_1, say, 1.5. If the sensitivity to size (SMB) is small (in fact, negative) then β_2 will be, say, -0.02. If the sensitivity to HML is 0.25 then:

$$\begin{aligned}
\text{Expected risk premium} &= \beta_1(r_m - r_f) + \beta_2(\text{SMB}) + \beta_3(\text{HML}) \\
&= 1.5(5) - 0.02(2) + 0.25(3) \\
&= 8.21\%
\end{aligned}$$

If the risk-free rate of return is 4% the expected return is 12.21%.

The five-factor model

Fama and French go further in a 2015 paper. Having noticed that share returns seem to be greater for companies with higher profits-to-net-asset ratios, an observation seemingly unexplained by the three-factor model, they put this new factor in. Their new model includes the variable 'RMW', which means the returns on 'Robust' profitability firms Minus the returns on 'Weak' profitability firms.

While they were at it, they added another 'anomaly' not explained by the older risk factor models, i.e. that firms with a small change in total assets over the last year perform better than those with large increases in investment levels. They labelled this 'CMA': returns on

'Conservatively' investing firms Minus returns on 'Aggressively' investing firms. Thus we have two more hypothesised 'risk factors' and the model becomes:

$$\text{Expected} = \text{risk free rate} + \beta_1(r_m - r_f) + \beta_2(\text{SMB}) + \beta_3(\text{HML}) + \beta_4(\text{RMW}) + \beta_5(\text{CMA})$$

The arbitrage pricing theory, and the three- and five-factor models are complex answers to the flaws in the CAPM. However, they have serious flaws of their own. For example, the three- and five-factor models' assumptions of the efficient pricing of shares is very suspect. Perhaps it will be useful to step back from high academic theory and observe the techniques that some market practitioners use to see if they have greater predictive power.

Fundamental beta

Our forefathers, long before the development of the APT and the CAPM, had to grapple with the problem of quantifying risk. Perhaps some of these more traditional approaches based on commonsense risk influences provide greater insight and predictive power than the fancy theoretical constructs. For example, you do not need knowledge of high finance to realise that a firm that has a large amount of borrowing relative to its equity base will be subject to more risk than one with a lower level of borrowing (assuming all other factors are the same). Furthermore, if the geared-up firm is in a particularly volatile industry it will be subject to even more risk.

Instead of using CAPM-beta based on historical data, many analysts and company managers have switched to calculating a fundamental beta. This is based on the intuitive underpinning of the risk–return relationship: if the firm's (or project within the firm) cash flows are subject to more systematic variability then the required return should be higher. What causes systematic variability? Three factors have been advanced:

1 *The type of business undertaken.* Some businesses are more sensitive to market conditions than others. The turnover and profits of cyclical businesses change a great deal with the ups and downs of the economy. So, for example, the sales of yachts, cars or designer clothes rise in booms and crash in recessions. Non-cyclical industries, such as food retailing or tobacco, experience less variability with the economic cycle. Thus in a fundamental beta framework cyclical businesses would be allocated a higher beta than non-cyclical businesses – if the variability is systematic rather than specific to the firm. If the purchase of the product can be delayed for months, years or even indefinitely (i.e. it is discretionary) then the industry is likely to be more vulnerable to an economic downturn.

2 *Degree of operating gearing.* If the firm has high fixed costs compared with the variable costs of production, its profits are highly sensitive to output (turnover) levels. A small percentage fall in sales can result in a large percentage change in profits. The higher variability in profit means a higher beta should be allocated. (Chapter 18 discusses operating gearing.)

3 *Degree of financial gearing.* If the company has high borrowings, with a commitment to pay interest regularly, then profit attributable to shareholders is likely to be more vulnerable to shocks. The obligation to meet interest payments increases the variability of after-interest profits. In recession, profits can more easily turn into losses. So the beta will rise if the company has higher financial gearing (leverage). Financial gearing exacerbates the underlying business risk.

The obvious problem with using the fundamental beta approach is the difficulty of deriving the exact extent to which beta should be adjusted up or down depending on the strength of the three factors. I have to admit that this is subjective and imprecise, but as Warren Buffett points out, I'd rather be roughly right than precisely wrong.

Fernández (2009) has taken the fundamental beta idea a stage further with the MASCOFLA-PEC method (from the initials of the parameters used to evaluate risk). This is shown in **Exhibit 8.39**, where each parameter is scored from 1 to 5 according to the contribution to the overall risk. Each factor has to be weighted. The example shows the sum of the scores of each parameter after adjusting for weights is 3.5. This is multiplied by 0.5 to obtain a beta of 1.75. With

Exhibit 8.39		A fundamental beta calculation using the MASCOFLAPEC method						

Weight		Parameter (risk factor)	Risk level					Weighted risk
			Low	Average		High	V. High	
			1	2	3	4	5	
10%	M	Management	1					0.1
25%	A	Assets: Business: industry/product					5	1.2
3%	S	Strategy						0.1
15%	C	Country risk				4		0.6
10%	O	Operating leverage				4		0.4
15%	F	Financial leverage				4		0.3
5%	L	Liquidity of investment						0.2
5%	A	Access to sources of funds					5	0.1
2%	P	Partners			3			0.0
5%	E	Exposure to other risks (currencies...)		2		4		0.1
5%	C	Cash flow stability		2	3			0.1
100%								Total = 3.5

$$\text{Beta of equity} = 3.5 \times 0.5 = 1.75$$

Source: Fernández (2009).

this system, using 0.5 as the final multiplier, the betas can vary from 0.5 to 2.5. You could substitute other multipliers if you think a wider range is justified.

As Fernández says, these methods are simply an aid to common sense. They allow the user to value a company or a project depending on the risk that the valuer sees in the expected future cash flows.

Project appraisal and systematic risk

Senior managers are generally aware that the returns on their company's shares are set at a particular level by the collective buying and selling actions of shareholders adjusting the share price. They are further aware that adjustment continues until the investors are content that the prospective returns reflect the riskiness of the share. What determines the systematic risk of a share is the underlying activities of the firm. Some firms engage in high-risk ventures and so shareholders, in exchange for accepting the possibility of a large loss, will expect a high return. Other firms undertake relatively safe activities and so shareholders will be prepared to receive a lower return.

The overall risk and return on the equity finance of a firm is determined by the portfolio of projects and their associated systematic risk. If a firm undertook an additional capital investment which had a much higher degree of risk than the average in the existing set then it is intuitively obvious that a higher return than the normal rate for this company will be required. On the other hand, if an extraordinarily low-risk activity is contemplated this should require a lower rate of return than usual.

Situations of this type are illustrated in **Exhibit 8.40** for a representative all-equity financed firm. Given the firm's normal risk level the market demands a return of 8%. If another project were started with a similar level of risk then it would be reasonable to calculate NPV on the basis of a discount rate of 8%. This is the opportunity cost of capital for the shareholders – they could obtain 8% by investing their money in shares of other firms in a similar risk class. If, however, the firm were to invest in project A with a risk twice the normal level, management would be doing their shareholders a disservice if they sought a mere 8% rate of return. At this risk level shareholders can get 13% on their money elsewhere. This sort of economic decision making will result in projects being accepted when they should have been rejected. Conversely project B, if discounted at the standard rate of 8%, will be rejected when it should have been accepted. It produces a return of 7% when all that is required is a return of 5% for this risk class. It is clear that this firm should accept any project lying above the sloping line and reject any project lying below this line.

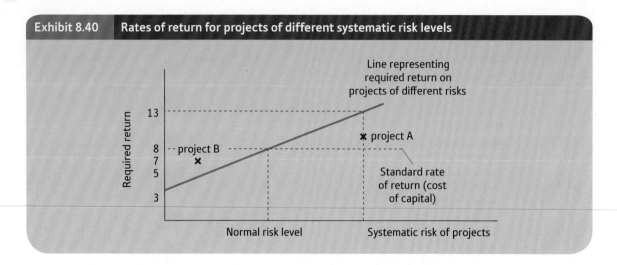

Exhibit 8.40   Rates of return for projects of different systematic risk levels

The rule taught in Chapter 2 that a firm should accept any project that gives a return greater than the firm's opportunity cost of capital now has to be refined. This rule can only be applied if the marginal project has the same risk level as the existing set of projects. Projects with different risk levels require different levels of return.

While the logic of adjusting for risk is impeccable a problem does arise when it comes to defining risk. The traditional approach, before the use of the CAPM, was to exercise judgement. It was, and still is, popular to allocate projects to three or more categories (low, medium and high) rather than to precisely state the risk level. Then in the 1960s the CAPM presented a very precise linear relationship between CAPM-beta risk as measured by the covariance of returns against the market index. Calculating the historical beta for a share quoted on a stock market is relatively straightforward because the analyst has access to share return data to construct the characteristic line. However, the estimation of the risk on a *proposed* project that is merely one part of a firm's suite of activities is more problematic. A suggested solution is to use the CAPM-beta values of quoted firms in a similar line of business. Thus if the new project were in food retailing, the betas from all the firms in the food retailing industry could be averaged to establish an estimate of this project's beta. Adjustments might have to be made to this to allow for differences in the riskiness of the average peer group firms and this particular project but the fundamental techniques will not change.

The doubts surrounding the CAPM have led to a questioning of this approach. An alternative is to factor in a range of macroeconomic influences. Here we would try to estimate the sensitivity of the project's cash flows to changes in the economy such as GDP, inflation and industrial output. Some projects will be highly sensitive to macroeconomic forces and so will be regarded as more risky; others will be relatively stable.

Sceptics' views – alternative perspectives on risk

David Dreman, an experienced investor, does not have a great deal of respect for the financial economists' models. In his book *Contrarian Investment Strategies: The Next Generation* he asks, "What is risk?". In answering he says that the academic response, derived from the efficient market hypothesis and modern portfolio theory, is that measuring risk is simple, "an A-B-C commodity"; it is all to do with the volatility of a share or portfolio whether that is measured by beta or standard deviation. But, how did the professors find out that investors in the real world measure risk by volatility? His answer is that they didn't; they didn't do any research investigating whether investors calculate and use beta. "The academics simply declared it as fact" he wrote "Importantly, this definition was easy to use to build complex models, and that's what the professors wanted to do." He says that some academics became obsessional about the neatness of the model, because a "rational" person would use it. Whether it is realistic is another matter. Then these academic enthusiasts trained the next generation to believe that risk is volatility.

But, he points out, it has been known for decades that there is no correlation between returns on shares and risk as the academics define it. These measures of volatility even fail to remain constant over time; the volatility in one period has little or no correlation with that in the following period, "a stock could pass from violent fluctuation to lamb like docility".

Dreman's preferred way of thinking about risk is for the investor to focus on the potential loss of money in terms of real purchasing power through the impact of both inflation and taxes. For this the following two factors are key:

> "1. The probability that the investment you choose will preserve your capital over the time you intend to invest your funds.
> 2. The probability the investments you select will outperform alternative investments for this period."

This way of looking at risk means considering an appropriate time period in the future, at least five years, but quite possibly decades; the time period when the savings put into investment will be required. Markets and individual shares may go up and down over the short run – periods of months or even years – but that is not of much concern to the true investor. Over 5-10 years volatility diminishes radically.

*See Eric N. Berg, 'Market Place: A study shakes confidence in volatile-stock theory', *New York Times*, 18 February 1992, p. 3.

Warren Buffett, the world's richest man, has little respect for the CAPM, as the following extract indicates. Note that these comments come from a man who started with very little capital and made all his money by selecting company shares for purchase:

> In our opinion, the real risk that an investor must assess is whether his aggregate after-tax receipts from an investment (including those he receives on sale) will, over his prospective holding period, give him at least as much purchasing power as he had to begin with, plus a modest rate of interest on that initial stake. Though this risk cannot be calculated with engineering precision, it can in some cases be judged with a degree of accuracy that is useful. The primary factors bearing upon this evaluation are:
>
> 1 The certainty with which the long-term economic characteristics of the business can be evaluated;
> 2 The certainty with which management can be evaluated, both as to its ability to realize the full potential of the business and to wisely employ its cash flows;
> 3 The certainty with which management can be counted on to channel the rewards from the business to the shareholders rather than to itself;
> 4 The purchase price of the business;
> 5 The levels of taxation and inflation that will be experienced and that will determine the degree by which an investor's purchasing-power return is reduced from his gross return.
>
> These factors will probably strike many analysts as unbearably fuzzy, since they cannot be extracted from a data base of any kind. But the difficulty of precisely quantifying these matters does not negate their importance nor is it insuperable. Just as Justice Stewart found it impossible to formulate a test for obscenity but nevertheless asserted, 'I know it when I see it', so also can investors – in an inexact but useful way – 'see' the risks inherent in certain investments without reference to complex equations or price histories.
>
> Is it really so difficult to conclude that Coca-Cola and Gillette possess far less business risk over the long-term than, say, *any* computer company or retailer? Worldwide, Coke sells about 44% of all soft drinks, and Gillette has more than a 60% share (in value) of the blade market. Leaving aside chewing gum, in which Wrigley is dominant, I know of no other significant businesses in which the leading company has long enjoyed such global power.
>
> Moreover, both Coke and Gillette have actually increased their worldwide shares of market in recent years. The might of their brand names, the attributes of their products, and the strength of their distribution systems give them an enormous competitive advantage, setting up a protective moat around their economic castles. The average company, in contrast, does battle daily without any such means of protection. As Peter Lynch says, stocks of companies selling commodity-like products should come with a warning label: 'Competition may prove hazardous to human wealth.'
>
> The competitive strengths of a Coke or Gillette are obvious to even the casual observer of business. Yet the beta of their stocks is similar to that of a great many run-of-the-mill companies who possess little or no competitive advantage. Should we conclude from this similarity that the competitive strength of Coke and Gillette gains them nothing when business risk is being measured? Or should we conclude that the risk in owning a piece of a company – its stock – is somehow divorced from the long-term risk inherent in its business operations? We believe neither conclusion makes sense and that equating beta with investment risk also makes no sense.

The theoretician bred on beta has no mechanism for differentiating the risk inherent in, say, a single-product toy company selling pet rocks or hula hoops from that of another toy company whose sole product is Monopoly or Barbie. But it's quite possible for ordinary investors to make such distinctions if they have a reasonable understanding of consumer behavior and the factors that create long-term competitive strength or weakness. Obviously, every investor will make mistakes. But by confining himself to a relatively few, easy-to-understand cases, a reasonably intelligent, informed and diligent person can judge investment risks with a useful degree of accuracy.

Buffett, W. (1993) Letter accompanying the Annual Report for Berkshire Hathaway Inc. for 1993 copyright © Warren E. Buffett and Berkshire Hathaway Inc., reproduced with permission.

Benjamin Graham, the father of security analysis, is equally scathing of the focus on short-term price movements as the form of risk. He taught his students (e.g. Warren Buffett) to examine the potential for loss over many years and even to welcome volatility as it gave people the chance to buy into good companies when the market was being unreasonably pessimistic. In his book *The Intelligent Investor* he wrote that people tend to apply "risk" and "safety" to shares in two senses. This can cause confusion. Clearly, a bond, if it defaults, is unsafe. Similarly, if a share is bought in the expectation of a particular dividend rate, and then, in the event, the dividend is reduced or stopped altogether it is proven unsafe. Furthermore, an investment exhibits risk if there is a fair possibility that the owner might need to sell at a time when it has drifted to below cost.

But, Graham observed, people extend the concept of risk to "a possible decline in the price of a security, even though the decline may be of a cyclical or temporary nature and even though the holder is unlikely to be forced to sell at such times." He declares that such a situation does not involve risk in any meaningful sense.

To explain he draws the analogy with someone who borrows to buy a building. That person might have to take a substantial loss if forced to sell at an unfavourable time. But this type of risk is not taken into account by the mortgage lender when judging its safety or risk. Here, the relevant factor is the certainty of payments on time.

Similarly, the risk associated with ownership of a commercial business is the "chance of losing money, not what would happen if the owner were forced to sell".

This leads his thoughts to the stock market investor. He/she does not lose money just because the market price of a share falls. What matters to the owner of a portfolio of well-selected shares is whether there is a "satisfactory overall return, as measured through a fair number of years, then this group investment has proved to be safe".

Yes, during the holding period the shares will fluctuate. There might even be periods when the market prices fall below what was paid for them. "If that fact makes the investment 'risky', it would then have to be called both risky and safe at the same time. This confusion may be avoided if we apply the concept of risk solely to a loss of value which either is realised through actual sale, or is caused by a significant deterioration in the company's position – or more frequently, perhaps, is the result of the payment of an excessive price in relation to the intrinsic worth of the security."

Concluding comments

So, where does all this grand theory leave people of a more practical persuasion, who simply want a tool that will help them to make better investment decisions? It is clear that we are far from the end of the road of discovery in this area. We have not yet reached *the* answer. However, the theoretical and empirical work has helped to clarify some important matters. The distinction between systematic and unsystematic risk is an important one. It seems reasonable to focus on the former when describing the relationship between risk and return.

Investors' buying and selling actions have given us two benchmarks by which to judge returns: if the investment is without systematic risk then the risk-free rate of return, approximated by the returns on high reputation government-issued securities, gives us the marker at the lower end of the risk spectrum; we also have a revealed demand for a risk premium of around 3–5% for investors accepting a risk level equivalent to that on the average ordinary share. The problem is that we cannot unequivocally, given the recent empirical evidence, draw a straight line between these two plot points with beta values placed on the x-axis. The relationship appears to be far more complex – the 'x-axis' probably consists of numerous risk factors.

Nevertheless a finding of sorts emerges: higher risk, however defined, requires higher return. Therefore, for a company trying to estimate the rate of return a shareholder will require from a project, it is right that the estimate is calculated after taking account of some measure of systematic risk. If the project has a systematic risk which is lower than that on the average share then it would seem sensible that the returns attributable to shareholders on this project should be somewhere between the risk-free rate and the risk-free rate plus, say, 3, 4 or 5%. If the project has a systematic risk greater than that exhibited by shares generally then the returns required for shareholders will be more than the risk-free rate plus, say, 3, 4 or 5%.

The tricky part is calculating the systematic risk level. In the heyday of the CAPM this was simple: beta was all that was necessary. Today we have to allow for a multiplicity of systematic risk factors. Not unnaturally, many business people shrug their shoulders at the prospect of such a burdensome approach and fall back on their 'judgement' to adjust for the risk of a project. In practice it is extremely difficult to state precisely the riskiness of a project – we are dealing with future uncertainties about cash flows from day-to-day business operations subject to sudden and unforeseen shocks. The pragmatic approach is to avoid precision and simply place each proposed project into one of three risk categories: low, medium or high. This neatly bypasses the complexities laid on by the theorists and also accurately reflects the fact that decisions made in the real world are made with less than complete knowledge. Mechanical decision making within the firm based on over-simplistic academic models is often a poor substitute for judgement recognising the imperfections of reality. Analogously, informed judgement about unquantifiable factors such as strength of competitive position and quality of management is a very important part of successful stock market investment.

When I (Glen) am making business and share investment decisions I do not adjust for CAPM-beta risk (my investment Newsletters describe the factors I do examine for particular investee companies). Apart from the strong evidence that past betas do not have any influence on future returns, correlations in share movements do not bother me in the slightest. I'm focused on a horizon years into the future. How a share moves over a period of a few days or weeks when the market as a whole moves is irrelevant to that. I am, however, intensely interested in the real risks facing the underlying business. These are the elements mentioned by many great investors,[11] particularly the strength of the competitive position of the firm within its industry, the industry economics (e.g. Michael Porter's five forces), and the competence and integrity of the managerial team. In addition, factors such as operating gearing and financial gearing can influence riskiness.

Although I do not undertake quantitative analysis similar to MASCOFLAPEC I try to qualitatively assess businesses using similar criteria, with particular emphasis on strategy and managerial quality. I still think in terms of risk-free rate plus a risk premium to have in mind a rough estimate of the required return on equity, but rarely make an adjustment to the risk premium for a specific share because of the fear of putting too much weight on subjective elements. Therefore, to stray from a beta of 1 I need a very firm justification. A great mental battle is to differentiate between firm-specific risk elements and systematic risk elements. For example, if a company strengthens its pricing power in the marketplace through creating a very strong brand in customers' minds, are the risks associated with those additional future cash flows specific to the firm? Or has it reduced its vulnerabilities to recessions and therefore lowered systematic risk? Domino's Pizza, Pepsi and Walker's crisps sell well through recessions due to both branding and (for the latter two) power vis-à-vis retailers.

I suspect most investors, like me, find the separation between systematic and unsystematic risk too difficult to cope with and usually end up evaluating the total risk in similar style to Warren Buffett with his five primary factors bearing on the overall risk to preserving and enhancing purchasing power over a number of years. But all of us should be properly diversified to reduce the risk coming from unsystematic elements.

Having been so critical of the theoretical models we have to be careful not to 'throw out the baby with the bathwater'. The academic debate has enabled us to ask the right questions and to focus on the key issues when enquiring what it is we should be doing to enhance shareholder value. It has also enabled a greater understanding of price setting in the financial markets and insight into the behaviour of investors.

---

11 For a summary please read Arnold (2009). Arnold (2011) discusses an additional three investors: George Soros, Sir John Templeton and Anthony Bolton.

The road is long and winding but the vistas revealed along the way provide enlightenment, if only of the kind captured in the following phrase: 'The fool says he is knowledgeable and has the answers, the wise man says he has much to learn.'

Key points and concepts

- Risky securities, such as shares quoted on the London Stock Exchange, have produced a much higher average annual return than relatively risk-free securities. However, the annual swings in returns are much greater for shares than for Treasury bills or bonds. **Risk and return** are positively related.

- **Total risk** consists of two elements:

  - **systematic risk** (or market risk, or non-diversifiable risk) – risk factors common to all firms;
  - **unsystematic risk** (or specific risk, diversifiable risk, or idiosyncratic risk).

- **Unsystematic risk can be eliminated by diversification.** An efficient market will not reward unsystematic risk.

- **Beta** measures the covariance between the returns on a particular share with the returns on the market as a whole.

- The **security market line (SML)** shows the relationship between risk as measured by CAPM-beta and expected returns.

- The equation for the **Capital Asset Pricing Model is**:

  $$r_j = r_f + \beta_j (r_m - r_f)$$

- The slope of the characteristic line represents beta

  $$r_j = \alpha + \beta_j r_m + e$$

- **Some examples of the CAPM's application**:

  - portfolio selection;
  - identifying mispriced shares;
  - measuring portfolio performance;
  - rate of return on firm's projects.

- **Technical problems with the CAPM**:

  - measuring beta;
  - *ex ante* theory but *ex post* testing and analysis;

  - unobtainability of the market portfolio;
  - one-period model;
  - few government securities are risk free;
  - unrealistic assumptions.

- **Early research** seemed to confirm the **validity of beta** as the measure of risk influencing returns. **Later work cast serious doubt** on this. Some researchers say beta has no influence on returns.

- **Beta is not the only determinant of return.**

- **Multi-factor models** allow for a variety of influences on share returns.

- Factor models refer to diversifiable risk as **non-factor risk** and non-diversifiable risk as **factor risk**.

- **Major problems with multi-factor models** include:

  - the difficulty of finding the influencing factors;
  - once found, the influencing factors only explain past returns.

- The **arbitrage pricing theory (APT)** is one possible multi-factor model:

  Expected returns = risk-free return + $\beta_1(r_1 - r_f) + \beta_2(r_2 - r_f) + \beta_3(r_3 - r_f) + \beta_4(r_4 - r_f) \ldots + \beta_n(r_n - r_f) + e$

- Fama and French have developed a **three-factor model**:

  Expected return = risk-free rate + $\beta_1(r_m - r_f) + \beta_2(\text{SMB}) + \beta_3(\text{HML})$

- **Traditional commonsense based measures of risk** seem to have more explanatory power over returns than beta or standard deviation.

- Projects of differing risks should be appraised using different discount rates.

Appendix 8.1: Note on arithmetic and geometric means

To understand the difference between arithmetic and geometric means, consider the case of an investment that only has capital gains and losses (there are no dividends).

At Time 0 the investment is worth £100. One year later (Time 1) it has risen to £200, an annual rate of return of 100%. In the next year the investment falls back to £100, a loss of 50% for the year. In the third year the value rises to £130, a 30% gain.

The arithmetic average annual rate of return is 26.67%:

$$
\begin{array}{l}
+\ 100\% \\
-\ \ 50\% \\
+\ \ 30\% \\
\hline
\ \ \ \ 80\% \qquad\quad 80/3\ =\ 26.67\%
\end{array}
$$

The arithmetic mean is the average of the annual returns. The geometric mean, on the other hand, is the compound annual return.

The geometric mean is the rate at which the beginning sum grows through the period of study. It depends on the initial and final values for the investment and not necessarily on any intermediate values.

So for our example:

Geometric
annual rate
of return $= \sqrt[n]{(1\ +\ \text{the first return})(1\ +\ \text{the second return})(1\ +\ \text{the third return})}\ -\ 1$

$\qquad\qquad = \sqrt[3]{(1\ +\ 1.0)(1\ +\ [-0.5])(1\ +\ 0.3)}\ -\ 1$

$\qquad\qquad = 0.0914 \text{ or } 9.14\%$

Alternatively:

$$F = P(1\ +\ r)^n$$
$$r = \sqrt[n]{(F/P)}\ -\ 1$$
$$\quad = \sqrt[3]{(130/100)}\ -\ 1$$
$$\quad = 0.0914 \text{ or } 9.14\%$$

For one-year periods arithmetic and geometric means will be identical. But over longer periods the geometric return is always less than the average returns (except when individual yearly returns are the same).

When examining past returns the geometric mean is more appropriate. However, for short-term forward-looking decisions the historical arithmetic mean is the more appropriate because it represents the mean of all the returns that may possibly occur over the investment holding period. For long-term forward-looking decisions the geometric mean is the more appropriate:

> Those who use the arithmetic mean argue that it is much more consistent with the mean-variance framework of the CAPM and a better predictor of the premium in the next period. The geometric mean is justified on the grounds that it takes into account compounding and that it is a better predictor of the average premium in the long term.
>
> (Damodaran, 2015, p. 69)

So, if the future-oriented decision is a short-term one (one year) then the arithmetic mean-based risk premium is appropriate. If the future-oriented decision is for more than one year then the geometric mean is more appropriate.

Appendix 8.2: Why professors do or do not use CAPM-beta

The following responses to a survey from finance and economics professors concerning their rationale for using or not using CAPM-beta administered by Fernández in 2009 are very interesting. Many professors have completely abandoned CAPM-beta. Within the cohort of those who continue to use it you might be able to detect a high degree of dissatisfaction. I have included the first 25 comments only to save space (but all of them are printed in the fifth edition so you are relieved of the suspicion that I have selected them).

Comments from professors who use calculated betas

1 We have to use historical data to estimate beta; therefore of necessity there is estimation error.

2 Professors should justify the beta information through regression analysis. Research indicates that five years' data provides more appropriate results. I used five years' monthly closing data to justify CitiBank, Wells Fargo and Bank of America beta and after regression the result is very close to beta (available in Reuters).

3 Betas are a useful tool to compare one stock with another. However, beta has a number of weaknesses and limitations. First, betas are based on historical data and may not be a good indication of the future. Second, there is an infinite number of ways to calculate beta because of the choices of time period (1, 3, 5, 20 years. . .), prices (open, high, low, close), interval (daily, weekly, monthly), and whether to use a moving average and over what period. Third, the choice of market to which your target company is to be compared is wide (S&P 500, DJIA, Wilshire 2000, etc.). Fourth, applying a beta based on historical observations to cash flow estimates of future operations invites problems, for example, changes in leverage (gearing). Using Adjusted Present Value calculations and adjusted betas can overcome some of these problems.

4 When using betas obtained from an Internet source, the same source should be used for all companies being compared to assure the same method was used to calculate each beta. A sensitivity analysis could be conducted by changing beta to determine the effect on the cost of equity, WACC and Net Present Value.

5 Indian betas vary from one year to another and from one source to another. I feel these are highly suspect.

6 I've used downside risk measures, as downside risk, tail measures and downside risk beta.

7 Betas are a primitive model (like a car from before 1900) and more sophisticated models are now available.

8 I explain how betas are computed and I show students how to find betas already computed, and we talk about what a particular beta means. We also discuss the fact that betas are not stable and that the CAPM assumes that the beta is the expected beta, not the historical beta.

9 I use betas. . . but I use all metrics that are available.

10 Students calculate their own betas about 15–20 different ways using regression. I discuss published sources and their use. In all cases, I point out the underlying volatility of beta depending on the specific calculation approach.

11 Beta use requires judgement. I demonstrate how to calculate betas and highlight the issues with time-line and independent variable selection.

12 Showing regression and sensitivities to choice of time window and sampling frequency to generate both raw and adjusted beta (i.e. Vasicek or Blume beta).

13 I justify the betas by computing them and proving that they are right. References are also made to financial webs.

14 I always emphasise that beta calculations have to be taken with some leeway.

15 I get students to download Thomson One Banker data and then get them to estimate betas via a single index model. Often they are required to compare the results from different frequencies and time spans of data. Also, we get them to produce adjusted betas (e.g. $2/3 \times$ estimate $+ 1/3 \times 1$).

16 I point out that returns on beta are much flatter than predicted by the CAPM.

17 I discuss the issues of betas and use a robust measure from a reliable source. I make reference to high-quality scholarship on the matter. I do *not* confuse beta with standard deviation.

18 If one does not use beta then what is there?

19 I do not use betas for personal investing, but I teach their use with both regressions and secondary sources.

20 It is a simplification of reality, but a useful one.

21 I tell my students to use an average published beta for the stock's systematic risk.

22 We use the equity betas in our text, based on reference to multiple articles – beginning with Sharpe (1964) and Hamada (1972) and going up through current research.

23 I usually look at a couple of sources before deciding what beta is appropriate.

24 I am becoming more and more sceptical of using betas and believe that the total return for an industry is just as good. I am also investigating the 'Total' beta concept. The problem with using betas is that the equity risk premium is suspect and has no standard interpretation. I do not believe that the historical ERP from Ibbotson from 1926 is valid.

25 Our students calculate betas for an industry. They unlever the individual companies; calculate betas using the Fama–French factors; test two hypotheses: that the unlevered betas are identical, and that the factors are priced; estimate the model subject to APT restrictions; and then lever the betas for the individual firms.

Comments from professors who use 'common sense'[12] betas

1 I use them in a general sense and I think many on the street do as well; 'high', 'low' or 'average' beta stocks. You can't measure them accurately.

2 I use regression, webs and the comments of financial analyst contacts to obtain betas. I may subjectively adjust them. For example, I do not believe the Pepsico beta of 0.6 in Value Line. So I use a 1.0 as I believe that Pepsico's systematic risk is = or > the market.

3 Regressions (1–5 years' daily data). Where no information available, ad hoc betas like 0.8, 1.0 and 1.2 for below average, average and above average risk.

4 I always use 1.

5 My own estimation combining regression, judgement and adjustment for specific reasons/events.

6 Common sense. I always emphasise that this is the most important ingredient. For example, if a regression tells me that Marks and Spencer has a lower beta than Tesco (note: they're both supermarkets), you should not trust the regression, and feel confident to overrule it.

7 Given the instability of estimated betas, I check the estimated beta of the company against leverage adjusted betas for 'comparables'. Also may use range of WACCs based on range of betas. However, the main impact of the uncertain estimates is to weight heavily the results of a competitive/strategic analysis.

8 I first decide on a required return and then I derive a beta to justify it.

Comments from professors who do not use betas

1 I have never believed the theory, which means that one is sampling from a fixed distribution. But where does that distribution come from?

2 Based on Fama and French (1998), beta is 'dead'. So, I don't use it.

3 I do not use the betas. Weak hypothesis of normality.

4 I do not use beta as a measure of risk. Beta, after all, does not consider price.

5 The beta calculation is deductively correct. However, our belief in beta, in any shape or form, is unjustified. The whole calculation is essentially a waste of time. As is the CAPM.

6 I teach CAPM in class, but I do not believe that betas are useful to determine the required return on equity. For that, you need an estimate of the market's future/expected return, which is as anyone's guess as the return on equity itself, so in my opinion you are only shifting the problem.

7 My method begins by an analysis of technology relationships and moves from that base into stock analysis. My method calls for me to sell an individual stock out of a client's account when it reaches a 40% gain.

8 I do not use betas when investing in individual stocks but find them useful when looking at mutual fund performance.

---

12 Also named by professors as personal judgement, qualitative betas, intuitive betas, logical magnitude betas and own judgement betas.

9 The use of betas is a completely arbitrary 'rule' in valuation. There's nothing that exists in nature that ties betas to the 'correct' cost of equity. One's cost of equity is a personal decision which should be based on assumed upside/downside, and one's tolerance for losing money (which is different from what beta defines). Valuation is an art as much as a science.

10 I don't use them in anything I do, but I do teach them to people who (some) will.

11 I do not use beta and I do not believe in it.

12 I do not use betas at all since I do not believe CAPM is a reliable model.

13 There is no 'required' return to equity. It is something that textbook authors write about, but they do that mainly because other textbook authors write about it, and they do not know what else to write about.

14 Real estate investment analysis is too local and the sample set size is too small for a reliable estimated beta.

15 I used to use betas in quantitative research years ago, with unsatisfactory results.

16 I do not research using betas. My research is related to asset pricing using martingale techniques.

17 Beta is bull-hockey. The underlying assumptions are not realistic or understood by most users. Moreover, most analysis misapplies the betas – even if there was a way to compute a meaningful number. The betas do not give an indication of investment risk. Better to approach risk from a different direction entirely.

18 I can't really answer this question as I believe the required return on equity is determined by a multi-factor model, not by the CAPM. As it has been argued by Campbell, Vuolteenaho and Polk, I think the cash-flow component of beta has a much higher price of risk than the discount-rate component.

19 I don't use betas because I work on non-traded companies. I use valuation models derived from the CCAPM.

20 I show why: (1) markets are inefficient [long term] because of economic externalities – government regulation, change of managers due to retirement and death, etc.; (2) betas are not stable over time, they are based on historical data which may change markedly in the future; and (3) when computing betas there is the problem of determining the frequency of the data, which can alter your results.

21 CAPM does not give any information. Roll (1977– two articles) has pointed out that using CAPM (beta) is tautological to market efficiency which means that the market value must be correct.

22 This is outside my domain entirely. It is like asking me about baptism or roller blading.

23 To calculate the cost of equity capital for the firms of one industry, I use the size-adjusted Capital Asset Pricing Model from Ibbotson Associates (2008), by assuming beta = 1 for every firm.

24 I think in general it's useless.

25 We do not calculate required returns to equity. But we calculate 'expected average returns', by using long-run risk premia (e.g. over money market) for various asset classes.

References and further reading

Arnold, G. (2009) *Financial Times Guide to Value Investing: How to become a disciplined investor.* 2nd edn. Harlow: FT Prentice Hall.
  A synthesis of investment philosophies and strategic/financial analysis.

Arnold, G. (2011) *The Great Investors.* Harlow: FT Prentice Hall.
  Describes the investment approaches of nine great investors.

Arnold, G. (2012) *Modern Financial Markets and Institutions.* FT Prentice Hall
  A comprehensive introduction to markets, instruments and institutions.

Arnold, G. (2015) *Financial Times Guide to Bond and Money Markets.* Harlow: FT Prentice Hall.
  An introduction to the markets in bonds and short-term wholesale money

Arnott, R. and Bernstein, P. (2002) 'What risk premium is normal?', *Financial Analysts Journal,* March/April.

Argues that investors were lucky to get a high equity premium in the past.

Baker, M., Bradley, B. and Wurgler, J. (2011) 'Benchmarks as limits to arbitrage: understanding the low-volatility anomaly', *Financial Analysts Journal,* 67(1) pp. 40–54.

Low CAPM-beta shares subsequently produce higher returns than high CAPM-beta shares.

Barclays Capital *Equity Gilt Studies.* London: Barclays.

Annual reports on security returns. Excellent data and discussion.

Black, F. (1972) 'Capital market equilibrium with restricted borrowing', *Journal of Business* (July), pp. 444–55.

Showed how the CAPM changes when there is no risk-free asset or investors face restrictions on, or extra cost of, borrowing.

Black, F. (1993) 'Beta and return', *Journal of Portfolio Management,* 20, Fall, pp. 8–18.

Estimating the relationship between beta and return on US shares, 1926–91. Relationship is poor after 1965.

Black, F., Jensen, M.C. and Scholes, M. (1972) 'The Capital Asset Pricing Model: some empirical tests', in M. Jensen (ed.), *Studies in the Theory of Capital Markets.* New York: Praeger.

Early empirical work supporting the CAPM.

Blume, M.E. (1971) 'On the assessment of risk', *Journal of Finance,* 26(1), March, pp. 1–10.

Betas change over time.

Blume, M.E. (1975) 'Betas and their regression tendencies', *Journal of Finance,* 30(3), June, pp. 785–95.

Betas tend to 1 over time.

Blume, M. and Friend, I. (1973) 'A new look at the Capital Asset Pricing Model', *Journal of Finance,* March, pp. 19–33.

The evidence in this paper seems to require a rejection of the capital asset pricing theory as an explanation of the observed returns on all financial assets.

Brealey, R.H., Myers, S.C. and Allen, F. (2017) *The Principles of Corporate Finance,* 12th edn. Boston: McGraw-Hill.

A time-honoured introductory finance text.

Chan, A. and Chui, A.P.L. (1996) 'An empirical re-examination of the cross-section of expected returns: UK evidence', *Journal of Business Finance and Accounting,* 23, pp. 1435–52.

In explaining returns beta is unimportant.

Chan, L.C.K. and J. Laskonishok (1993) 'Are the reports of betas' death premature?', Journal of Portfolio Management, Summer, 19, 4, p. 51.

Some indication of beta having an impact on share returns.

Cochrane, J.H. (2001) *Asset Pricing.* Princeton, NJ, and Oxford: Princeton University Press.

Advanced level.

Corhay, A., Hawawini, G. and Michel, P. (1987) 'Seasonality in the risk-return relationship: some international evidence', *Journal of Finance,* 42, pp. 49–68.

Evidence on the validity of the CAPM in the UK, France, Belgium and the USA. Not good news for the CAPM.

Damodaran, A. (2015) *Applied Corporate Finance: A User's Manual.* 4th Edition. New York: John Wiley & Sons.

A writer prepared to address the difficult practical issues rather than stay on the (often barren) high ground of theory – easy to read as well!

Damodaran, A. (2008) 'What is the risk free rate?' Working paper, available at http://papers.ssrn.com/sol3/papers.cfm?abstract_id=1317436

A critical discussion of how we obtain the risk-free rate.

Damodaran, A. (2009) 'Equity risk premiums (ERP): determinants, estimation and implications – a post-crisis update', *Financial Markets, Institutions & Instruments,* 18(5), pp. 289–370.

An excellent discussion of the difficulties in calculating an equity risk premium – clearly expressed, non-technical.

Damodaran, Aswath, (2017) 'Equity Risk Premiums (ERP): Determinants, Estimation and Implications – The 2017 Edition.' Available at SSRN: https://ssrn.com/abstract=2947861

An excellent, easy-to-follow discussion of the difficulties in estimating an equity risk premium. Updated regularly at SSRN.

Daniel, H. and Titman, S. (1997) 'Evidence on the characteristics of cross-sectional variation in common stock returns', *Journal of Finance,* 52, pp. 1–33.

Points out that Fama and French's empirical results are also consistent with mispricing-based (behavioural) models.

Daniel, H. and Titman, S. (2006) 'Market reactions to tangible and intangible information', *Journal of Finance,* 61(4), pp. 1605–43.

Disputes the interpretation that high returns to high book-to-market companies are due to these firms being in financial distress.

Dhrymes, P.J., Friend, I. and Gultekim, N.B. (1984) 'A critical reexamination of the empirical evidence on the arbitrage pricing theory', *Journal of Finance,* 39, June, pp. 323–46.

Attacks APT as not being markedly superior to the CAPM in explaining relevant empirical evidence.

Dimson, E., Marsh, P. and Staunton, M. (2002) *Triumph of the Optimists: 101 Years of Global Investment Returns*. Princeton, NJ, and Oxford: Princeton University Press.

Fascinating evidence on risk premiums. Updated each year via the Credit Suisse Global Investment Returns Yearbook

Dimson, E., Marsh, P. and Staunton, M. (2006) The Worldwide Equity Premium: a smaller puzzle (7 April 2006), EFA 2006 Zurich meetings papers available at SSRN: http://ssrn.com/abstract=891620

Equity risk premiums for 17 countries over 106 years – average 4%. But authors suggest that investors expect a premium of around $3–3\frac{1}{2}$%. Easy to follow.

Dimson, E., Marsh, P. and Staunton, M. (2009) Credit Suisse Global Investment Returns Yearbook 2009. Credit Suisse Research Institute, available at http://publications.credit-suisse.com/

Includes a view on whether to use the bill or the bond rate as the risk-free rate.

Dimson, E., Marsh, P. and Staunton, M. (2017) Credit Suisse Global Investment Returns Yearbook 2017. Credit Suisse Research Institute, available at http://publications.credit-suisse.com/

An excellent annual publication providing up-to-date data and discussion on returns of shares and interest-bearing instruments.

Dreman, D. (1998) *Contrarian Investment Strategies*: The Next Generation. New York: John Wiley & Sons.

A down-to-earth discussion of investment and the nature of risk and return.

Elton, E.J., Gruber, M.J. and Mei, J. (1994) 'Cost of capital using arbitrage pricing theory: a case study of nine New York utilities', *Financial Markets, Institutions and Instruments*, 3, August, pp. 46–73.

Interesting application.

Elton, E.J., Gruber, M.J. and Brown, S.J. (2014) *Modern Portfolio Theory and Investment Analysis*, 9th edn. New York: Wiley.

Detailed but clear description of the CAPM, APT and empirical evidence.

Fama, G. and French, K. (1992) 'The cross-section of expected stock return', *Journal of Finance*, 47, June, pp. 427–65.

The relationship between beta and return is flat. Size and book-to-market equity ratio are better predictors of share returns.

Fama, E.F. and French, K.R. (1993) 'Common risk factors in the returns on stocks and bonds', *Journal of Financial Economics*, 33, pp. 3–56.

Three-factor model.

Fama, E.F. and French, K.R. (1995) 'Size and book-to-market factors in earnings and returns', *Journal of Finance*, 50(1), March, pp. 131–55.

The relationship of stock prices, size and book-to-market equity with earnings behaviour.

Fama, E.F. and French, K.R. (1996) 'Multifactor explanations of asset pricing anomalies', *Journal of Finance*, 50 (1), March, pp. 55–84.

The three-factor model is discussed.

Fama, E.F. and French, K.R. (2002) 'The equity premium', *Journal of Finance*, 57(2), April, pp. 637–59.

A new look at judging the prospective equity risk premiums taking account of the lucky surprise US investors in equity had over the period 1951 to 2000.

Fama, E.F. and French, K.R. (2006) 'The Value premium and the CAPM', *Journal of Finance*, LXI (5) October, pp. 2163–85.

Higher returns for high book-to-market ratio and price-earnings ratio shares for US (and 14 other countries). The return premium is not explained by CAPM beta.

Fama, E.F. and French, K.R. (2015) 'The five-factor asset pricing model', *Journal of Financial Economics*, 116, pp. 1–22.

The additional risk factors of profitability and investment are put in to a model.

Fama, E.F. and MacBeth, J. (1973) 'Risk, return and equilibrium: empirical test', *Journal of Political Economy*, May/June, pp. 607–36.

Early empirical research. Shares on the NYSE grouped by beta and subsequent return is compared.

Fernández, P. (2007a) 'Equity premium: historical, expected, required and implied.' Working paper published on SSRN, available at www.ssrn.com/

A discussion on the differences between the concepts of historical equity risk premium, expected equity risk premium, required equity risk premium and implied equity risk premium, and the dangers arising from not recognising the differences. An easy read.

Fernández, P. (2008a) 'Are calculated betas worth anything?' Working paper published on SSRN, available at http://ssrn.com/abstract=504565

Industry betas are very unstable.

Fernández, P. (2009) 'Betas used by professors: A survey with 2,500 answers.' Working paper published on SSRN, available at http://papers.ssrn.com/sol3/papers.cfm?abstract_id=1407464

Evidence on what professors use around the world, but also a serious challenge to those who continue to use CAPM-beta.

Fernández, P. and Bermejo, V. (2009) 'Beta = 1 does a better job than calculated betas.' Working paper on SSRN, available at http://ssrn.com/abstract=1406923

Assuming betas are 1 for US companies has a higher correlation than calculated CAPM-betas.

Fernandez, P., Ortiz Pizarro, Alberto and Fernández Acín, Isabel (2016) 'Market Risk Premium Used in 71 Countries in 2016: A Survey with 6,932 Answers.' Available at SSRN: https://ssrn.com/abstract=2776636

A report on the RPs used by academics and business people.

Frazzini, A. and L.H. Pedersen (2014) 'Betting against beta', *Journal of Financial Economics,* 111, pp. 1–25.

In 18 out of 19 countries high beta shares gave lower returns than low beta shares.

Graham, B. (1973, 2003) *The Intelligent Investor.* Revised edition with commentary by Jason Zweig. New York: Harper Business.

Widely regarded as the best book ever written on investment principles.

Graham, John R. and Harvey, Campbell R. (2016) The Equity Risk Premium in 2016. Available at SSRN: https://ssrn.com/abstract=2816603 or http://dx.doi.org/10.2139/ssrn.2816603

Graham and Harvey report on the results of surveys of CFOs.

Gregory, A., Rajesh, T. and Christidis, A. (2013) 'Constructing and Testing Alternative Versions of the Fama-French and Carhart Models in the UK', *Journal of Business Finance & Accounting.* Jan/Feb 2013, 40(1/2), pp. 172–214.

'We do not find that risk factors are consistently and reliably priced.'

Hong, H. and D.A. Sraer (2016) 'Speculative betas', *Journal of Finance,* Oct, 71(5), pp. 2095–144.

More evidence that high beta shares give lower returns than low beta shares: 'Our explanation is that high-beta assets are prone to speculative overpricing. When investors disagree about the stock market's prospects, high-beta assets are more sensitive to this aggregate disagreement, experience greater divergence of opinion about their payoffs, and are overpriced due to short-sales constraints.'

Jorion, P. and Goetzmann, W.N. (1999) 'Global stock markets in the twentieth century', *Journal of Finance,* LIV(3) June, pp. 953–80.

The US equity risk premium is affected by survivorship bias – equity returns are higher than other countries because of the unusual success of US capitalism.

Levy, H. (1978) 'Equilibrium in an imperfect market: a constraint on the number of securities in the portfolio', *American Economic Review,* September, pp. 643–58.

The CAPM cannot be accepted since it performs quite poorly in explaining price behaviour.

Levy, R.A. (1971) 'On the short-term stationarity of beta coefficients', *Financial Analysts Journal, November–December,* pp. 55–62.

Betas change over time.

Lintner, J. (1965) 'The valuation of risky assets and the selection of risky investments in stock portfolios and capital budgets', *Review of Economics and Statistics,* February, 47, pp. 13–37.

Major contributor to the development of CAPM theory.

Markowitz, H.M. (2005) 'Market efficiency: a theoretical distinction and so what?' *Financial Analysts Journal,* September/October, pp. 17–30.

'I . . . show here that the conclusion that expected returns are linear functions of beta does not hold when real-world limits on permitted portfolio holdings are introduced into CAPM. This discussion will call into question the frequent use of beta in risk adjustment.'

Mehra, R. (2003) 'The equity premium puzzle?' Why is it a puzzle? *Financial Analysts Journal,* 59, pp. 54–69.

High returns on shares relative to risk-free investments may well continue.

Mehra, R. and Prescott, E.C. (1985) 'The Equity Premium: A Puzzle', *Journal of Monetary Economics,* 15, pp. 145–61.

Investors in shares appear to have received an excessively high return relative to risk-free securities.

Mehra, R. and Prescott, E. (2006) 'The equity premium: what have we learned in 20 years?' in R. Mehra (ed.) *Handbook of Investments: Equity risk premium* in the Handbook of Economics and Finance Series. Amsterdam: Elsevier.

An overview of the debate on the equity risk premium.

Miles, D. and Timmermann, A. (1996) 'Variations in expected stock returns: evidence on the pricing of equities from a cross-section of UK companies', *Economica,* 63, pp. 369–82.

Beta has no relationship with UK share returns.

Montier, J. (2007) *Behavioural Investing.* Chichester: John Wiley & Sons.

Full of insights about the reality of investing – challenges many of the theories of financial economists. Easy to read.

Mossin, J. (1966) 'Equilibrium in a capital asset market', *Econometrica,* 34, October, pp. 768–83.

Important early paper – technical.

Myers, S.C. (1996) 'Fischer Black's contributions to corporate finance', *Financial Management,* 25(4), Winter, pp. 95–103.

Acceptance of the CAPM: disillusionment expressed.

Nichols, N.A. (1993) 'Efficient? Chaotic? What's the New Finance?', *Harvard Business Review,* March–April, pp. 50–8.

Highly readable account of the 1990s disillusionment with the CAPM and market efficiency theory.

Reinganum, M.R. (1982) 'A direct test of Roll's conjecture on the firm size effect', *Journal of Finance,* 37, pp. 27–35.

Small firms' shares earn higher average rates of return than those of large firms, even after accounting for beta risk.

Roll, R. (1977) 'A critique of the Asset Pricing Theory's tests: Part 1: On past and potential testability of the theory', *Journal of Financial Economics,* 4 March, pp. 129–76.

Important, theoretical attack on CAPM testing methods.

Roll, R. and Ross, S.A. (1980) 'An empirical investigation of the Arbitrage Pricing Theory', *Journal of Finance,* 35, December, pp. 1073–103.

Testing of APT leads to at least three, possibly four, factors generating returns.

Rosenberg, B. and Rudd, A. (1986) 'The corporate uses of Beta', in J.M. Stern and D.H. Chew (eds), *The Revolution in Corporate Finance.* Oxford: Basil Blackwell.

Using the CAPM to find discount rate for projects. Incorporates other risk factors: growth, earnings variability, leverage and size. Easy-to-read article aimed at the novice.

Ross, S.A. (1974) 'Return, risk and arbitrage', in I. Friend and J.L. Bicksler (eds), *Risk and Return in Finance.* New York: Heath Lexington.

The arbitrage pricing theory – the early days.

Ross, S.A. (1976) 'The arbitrage theory of capital asset pricing', *Journal of Economic Theory,* 13, December, pp. 341–60.

Originator of the APT.

Rouwenhorst, K.G. (1999) 'Local return factors and turnover in emerging stock markets', *Journal of Finance,* 54, August, pp. 1439–64.

Share returns are related to size of company and value characteristics, but not beta.

Rouwenhorst, K.G., Heston, S. and Wessels, R.E. (1999) 'The role of beta and size in the cross-section of European stock returns', *European Financial Management,* 4.

Some evidence of relation between beta and share returns in 12 countries.

Sharpe, W.F. (1964) 'Capital asset prices: a theory of market equilibrium under conditions of risk', *Journal of Finance,* 19, September, pp. 425–42.

Pioneering paper – technical.

Siegal, J.J. (2005) 'Perspectives on the equity risk premium', *Financial Analysts Journal, Nov./Dec.,* pp. 61–73.

Discusses in an easy-to-read manner, the difficulties in fixing on a precise equity risk premium, and the 'equity premium puzzle'.

Smithers, A. (2009) *Wall Street Revalued: Imperfect markets and inept central bankers.* Chichester: John Wiley & Sons.

A thorough and thought-provoking consideration of the valuation of assets, with a wealth of historical data.

Strong, N. and Xu, X.G. (1997) 'Explaining the cross-section of UK expected stock returns', *British Accounting Review,* 29(1), pp. 1–23.

More evidence of the poor relationship between beta and returns.

Treynor, J. (1965) 'How to rate management of investment funds', *Harvard Business Review,* January–February.

Early theory.

Case study recommendations

Please see www.pearsoned.co.uk/arnold for case study synopses. Also, there is another list of useful case studies in the fifth edition can be found there.

- Alex Sharpe's Portfolio. Author: Colette Southam. Ivey Publishing. Available at www.cb.hbsp.harvard.edu
- Lyxor Chinah versus Lyxor Msindia: portfolio risk and return. Authors: Ruth S.K. Tan; Zsuzsa R. Huszar; Weina Zhang, Ivey Publishing. Available at www.cb.hbsp.harvard.edu
- Kapoor's portfolio. Authors: Miguel Angel Canela Campos; Ines Alegre Tort-Martorell; Melina Moleskis, IESE. Available at www. cb.hbsp.harvard.edu

Self-review questions

1 Outline the difference between systematic and unsystematic risk.

2 Explain the meaning of CAPM-beta.

3 State the equation for the security market line.

4 If a share lies under the security market line is it over- or under-valued by the market (assuming the CAPM to be correct)? What mechanism will cause the share return to move towards the security market line?

5 What problems are caused to the usefulness of the CAPM if betas are not stable over time?

6 What influences the CAPM-beta level for a particular share according to the theory?

7 Describe how the characteristic line is established.

8 What are the fundamental differences between the CAPM and the APT?

9 Is the firm's existing cost of capital suitable for all future projects? If not, why not?

10 List the theoretical and practical problems of the CAPM.

11 Discuss the potential problems with the implementation of the arbitrage pricing theory.

12 In 2011 and 2014 the return on UK shares was less than the return on UK Government bonds. Why don't we take the most recent returns for $r_m - r_f$ in the CAPM rather than the long-term historical average $r_m - r_f$?

Questions and problems

Answers to most questions can be found at www.pearsoned.co.uk/arnold.
Answers to questions marked with an asterisk are to be found only in the Lecturer's Guide.

1 Company X has a CAPM-beta value of 1.3, the risk-free rate of return is 8% and the historic risk premium for shares over the risk-free rate of return has been 5%. Calculate the return expected on shares in X assuming the CAPM applies. **?**

2 'Last year I bought some shares. The returns have not been as predicted by the CAPM.' Is this sufficient evidence to reject the CAPM?

3 Share A has a beta of 2, share B has a beta of 0.5 and C a beta of 1. The riskless rate of interest is 7% and the risk premium for the market index has been 5%. Calculate the expected returns on A, B and C (assuming the CAPM applies). **?**

4 The risk-free return is 9%, Company J has a beta of 1.5 and an expected return of 20%. Calculate the risk premium for the market index over the risk-free rate assuming J is on the security market line. **?**

5 Shares in M and N lie on the security market line.

	Share M	Share N
Expected return	18%	22%
Beta	1	1.5
(assume the CAPM holds)		

a   What is the riskless rate of return and the risk premium on the market index portfolio?
b   Share P has an expected return of 30% and a beta of 1.7. What is likely to happen to the price and return on shares in P?
c   Share Q has an expected return of 10% and a beta of 0.8. What is likely to happen to the price and returns on a share in Q? **?**

6 Explain from first principles the CAPM and how it may be used in financial markets and within a firm for determining the discount rate used in project appraisal. Why might you have doubts about actually using the model?

7 The directors of Frane plc are considering a project with an expected return of 23%, a beta coefficient of 1.4 and a standard deviation of 40%. The risk-free rate of return is 10% and the risk premium for shares generally has been 5%. (Assume the CAPM applies.)

a   Explain whether the directors should focus on beta or the standard deviation given that the shareholders are fully diversified.
b   Is the project attractive to those shareholders? Explain to the directors unfamiliar with the jargon of the CAPM the factors you are taking into account in your recommendation. **?**

8   The risk-free rate of return is 7% and the annual premium received on shares over Treasury bills has been 5%. A firm is considering the following investments (the CAPM applies):

Project	CAPM-beta	Project Expected return (%)
1	0.6	10
2	0.9	11
3	1.3	20
4	1.7	21

    a   Which projects should be accepted?
    b   Why doesn't the firm simply use its overall discount rate of 13% for all project appraisal?

9   True or false?

    a   A £1,000 investment in the market portfolio combined with a £500 investment in the risk-free security will have a CAPM-beta of 2.
    b   The risk premium on the market portfolio of shares has always been 5%.
    c   The CAPM states that systematic risk is the only factor influencing returns in a diversified portfolio.
    d   Beta has proved to be an excellent predictor of share returns over the past thirty years.
    e   Investors expect compensation for risk factors other than beta such as macroeconomic changes.
    f   The arbitrage pricing theory assumes unsystematic risk as a key input factor.

10   Mr Gill has inherited the following portfolio:

Share	Share price	No. of shares	CAPM-beta
ABC plc	£1.20	20,000	0.80
DEF plc	£2.00	10,000	1.20
GHI plc	£1.80	20,000	1.10

    a   What is the beta on this portfolio assuming that CAPM theory works?
    b   If the risk-free rate of return is 6.5% and the risk premium on shares over Treasury bills has been 5% what is the expected return on this portfolio over the next year?
    c   Why might the outcome be significantly different from the expected return?

11   'The arbitrage pricing theory has solved all the problems of estimating the relationship between risk and return.' Do you agree? Explain your reasoning.

Assignments

1   Find out your firm's beta from published sources and calculate the rate of return expected from your firm's shares on the assumption that the CAPM holds.

2   Investigate how systematic risk factors are taken into account when setting discount rates for projects of different risk levels in a firm you know well. Write a report detailing how this process might be improved.

PART 4

Sources of finance

Stock markets

LEARNING OUTCOMES

An appreciation of the rationale and importance of a well-organised stock market in a sophisticated financial system is a necessary precursor to understanding what is going on in the world around us. To this end the reader, having read this chapter, will be able to:

■ describe the scale of stock market activity around the world and explain the reasons for the widespread adoption of stock exchanges as one of the foci for a market-based economy;

■ explain the functions of stock exchanges and the importance of an efficiently operated stock exchange;

■ give an account of the stock markets available to UK firms;

■ demonstrate a grasp of the regulatory framework for the UK financial system;

■ be able to understand many of the financial terms expressed in the broadsheet newspapers (particularly the *Financial Times*);

■ outline the UK corporate taxation system.

Case study 9.1	**Using the stock market both to create wealth and to treat disease**

Oxford BioMedica

Alan and Sue Kingsman started an Oxford University-backed company called Oxford BioMedica in 1995. This company develops technologies to treat diseases including cancer, wet age-related muscular degeneration and Parkinson's disease. The aim is to replace faulty genes and target cancer cells.

Alan and Sue are biochemistry academics who lacked the finance needed for future research and development. They raised seed finance in June 1996 (small amounts of start-up money) and then raised £5.1m by floating on the UK's Alternative Investment Market (AIM) in December 1996. Later AIM shareholders bought another £23.6m of shares from the company which was then able to ramp up research.

Oxford BioMedica was upgraded to the Official List of the London Stock Exchange in 2001 following a successful £35.5m fund-raising. In 2003 a further £20.4 million was raised through a rights issue (selling more shares to existing shareholders) followed by £30.1m in 2005.

More share issues were to follow: £20m via a share placing and open offer in 2011; £10.1m in 2012, £21.6m in June 2014, $4.3m in October 2014 and £17.6m in 2016, bringing the total raised from outside investors to £190m.

Oxford BioMedica's proprietary gene delivery system, called the LentiVector® platform technology, was invented initially through pioneering work at Oxford University and then through in-house development. Lentiviruses can deliver a significant amount of genetic information into cells very efficiently. They transport genetically engineered cells into the human body. For example, Novartis is using LentiVector® to carry modified cells as part of its therapy for paediatric and young adult patients with B-cell acute lymphoblastic leukaemia.

The company has never made a profit, but shareholders are willing to wait. The potential rewards are huge, running into billions of pounds if successful treatments are created. The rewards to patients could be beyond price.

Sources: Based on various articles in the *Financial Times* and Oxford BioMedica's website.

Introduction

This chapter is concerned with the role and value of stock markets in the modern economy. It also looks more specifically at the workings of the London Stock Exchange. Imagine the difficulties Sue and Alan Kingsman would have getting their venture off the ground in a world without some form of market where long-term risk capital can be raised from investors, and where those investors are able to sell on their holdings to other risk takers whenever they wish. There would certainly be a much smaller pool of money made available to firms with brilliant ideas and society would be poorer.

Stock exchanges around the world

Stock exchanges are markets where government and industry can raise long-term capital and investors can buy and sell securities. Stock exchanges[1] grew in response to the demand for funds to finance investment and (especially in the early days) ventures in overseas trade. The risky sea-voyage trading businesses of the sixteenth, seventeenth and eighteenth centuries often required the raising of capital from large numbers of investors. Until the Napoleonic Wars the Dutch capital markets were pre-eminent, raising funds for investment abroad and loans for governments and businesses, and developing a thriving secondary market in which investors could sell their financial securities to other investors. This transferability of ownership of financial assets was an important breakthrough for the development of sophisticated financial systems. It offered the investor liquidity, which encouraged the flow of funds to firms, while leaving the capital in the business venture untouched.

---

1 Stock exchange and stock market will be used interchangeably. Bourse is an alternative word used particularly in Continental Europe.

The Napoleonic Wars led to a rapid rise in the volume of British government debt sold to the public. Trading in this debt tended to take place in coffee houses in London and other cities. Much of the early industrialisation was financed by individuals or partnerships, but as the capital requirements became larger it was clear that joint-stock enterprises were needed, in which the money of numerous investors was brought together to give joint ownership with the promise of a share of profits. Canal corporations, docks companies, manufacturing enterprises, railways and insurance companies were added to the list of firms with shares and bonds traded on the stock exchanges of Europe, America and a few places in Asia in the nineteenth century.

The second major breakthrough was the introduction of limited liability for shareholders in 1855.[2] This meant that the owners of shares were not responsible for the debts of the firm – once they had handed over the money to purchase the shares they could not be called on to contribute any further, regardless of the demands of creditors to a failed firm. This encouraged an even greater flow of funds into equity (ownership) capital and aided the rise of Victorian Britain as an economic powerhouse. Similar measures were taken in other European and North American countries to boost the flow of funds for investment. Outside the Western economies the value of limited liability and a stock exchange was quickly recognised – for example, Bombay and Johannesburg opened stock markets while still part of the British Empire.

Growth of stock markets

Stock markets have prospered and expanded globally. New markets have appeared in developing countries to join and rival the traditional stock markets. **Exhibit 9.1** details the relative size of stock markets around the world according to the total market capitalisation (number of shares multiplied by share price) of the companies traded on them.

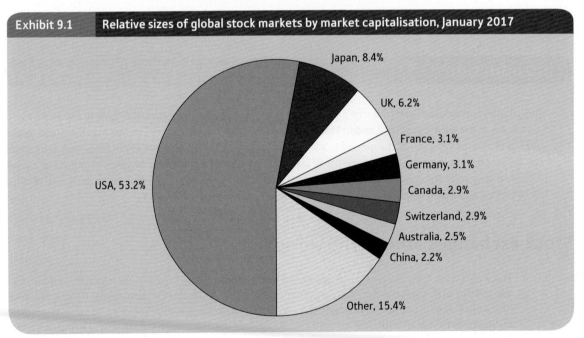

| Exhibit 9.1 | Relative sizes of global stock markets by market capitalisation, January 2017 |

Japan, 8.4%
UK, 6.2%
France, 3.1%
Germany, 3.1%
Canada, 2.9%
Switzerland, 2.9%
Australia, 2.5%
China, 2.2%
Other, 15.4%
USA, 53.2%

Source: from *Global Investment Returns Yearbook 2017*, Credit Suisse Research Institute (Dimson, E., Marsh, P. and Staunton, M. 2017) © Elroy Dimson, Paul Marsh and Mike Staunton.

The world has changed significantly in 30 years. Liberalisation towards greater free market capitalism and the accelerating wave of privatisation pushed stock markets to the forefront of developing countries' tools of economic progress. The ideological opposition to capitalism has been replaced with stock markets in Moscow, Warsaw and Sofia. Even countries which still espouse

2 The first limited liability law was introduced in the USA in 1811.

communism, such as China and Vietnam, now have thriving and increasingly influential stock exchanges designed to facilitate the mobilisation of capital and its employment in productive endeavour, with a return going to shareholders. China has two thriving stock exchanges, in Shanghai and Shenzhen, with over 3,000 companies listed. There are now tens of millions of Chinese investors who can only be properly described as 'capitalists' given that they put at risk their savings on the expectations of a reward on their capital.

Importance of stock exchanges

Today the important contribution of stock exchanges to economic well-being is recognised from Uzbekistan to Uruguay. There are over 140 countries with exchanges and many of these countries have more than one exchange. Many markets have joined forces with exchanges in other countries to gain economies and marketing muscle. The London Stock Exchange (LSE) merged with the Borsa Italiana in 2007. The NYSE merged in 2006 with the Euronext group, itself a merger of the Paris, Amsterdam, Brussels and Lisbon exchanges and in 2008 with the American Stock Exchange; then, in 2013 the whole group was bought by the American ICE (InterContinentalExchange) which also has energy, metals and other commodity exchanges. But in 2014 Euronext was demerged from ICE and its shares listed as an independent entity on the four European markets its serves (it also trades shares in London). ICE held onto the NYSE and the market for small companies formally the American Exchange (AMEX), now called NYSE MKT.

The US market Nasdaq merged in 2007 with OMX, the Scandanavian and Baltic group of exchanges in Stockholm, Helsinki, Copenhagen, Reykjavik , Riga, Tallinn, Vilnius and Armenia and also with the Boston and Philadelphia exchanges. Nasdaq Inc. lists over 3,100 companies in the US and over 700 are listed on its Nasdaq Nordic grouping.

Deutsche Börse tried a few times to merge with another large exchange, most recently with London in 2017, but has been either spurned or defeated by competition regulators worried about market dominance. At least it has a market-leading derivatives exchange (Eurex in Zurich and Frankfurt) to go with its Frankfurt stock market.

In addition to actual mergers, many stock exchanges have holdings in other exchanges or have mutual trading agreements. For instance, the Tokyo Stock Exchange has a 4.99 per cent shareholding in the Singapore exchange.

Exhibit 9.2 focuses on the share trading aspect of 20 of these markets, but most markets usually also trade bonds and other securities. Note the size and importance now of markets outside Europe and North America.

A comparison of the major markets

The London Stock Exchange is now only the eighth largest market as measured by market capitalisation of shares traded there, but it retains its place as one of the most important for deals in shares of overseas companies. The Chinese markets have leapt in importance with Shanghai, Shenzhen and Hong Kong collectively trading shares with a total market value greater than Nasdaq in America.

The outstanding leader in terms of market capitalisation remains the New York Stock Exchange, but it is pipped to the post by Nasdaq for number of companies listed, and also by Japan, Canada, India and Spain.

Clearly, stock markets are regarded as an important element in the intricate lattice work of a modern and sophisticated society. Not only are they a vital meeting place for investors and a source of investment capital for businesses, they permit a more appropriate allocation of resources within society – that is, an optimum mix of goods and services produced to satisfy people.

Multilateral trading facilities (MTFs)

Traditional stock exchanges tended to have monopoly or duopoly positions for the trading of shares and other securities in their home countries. They had little incentive to cut fees or to improve their trading technology. This resulted in the main users, institutional investment funds, banks, brokers and hedge funds, becoming frustrated with the raw deal they were getting.

Exhibit 9.2	The world's 20 largest stock exchanges 2016, ranked according to domestic market capitalisation of equities

| | Domestic equities market capitalisation[1] | Total share trading in year | Number of listed companies | | |
	$ billion	$ billion	Total	Domestic	Foreign
USA – New York SE	19,573	19,737	2,307	1,822	485
USA – Nasdaq	7,779	31,944	2,897	2,509	388
Japan	4,955	6,361	3,541	3,535	6
Shanghai	4,099	7,553	1,182	1,182	NA
Euronext	3,459	1,807	1,051	936	115
Shenzhen	3,213	11,681	1,870	1,870	NA
Hong Kong	3,193	1,350	1,973	1,872	101
London	3,127	1,651	2,213	1,602	611
TMX (Canada)	1,994	1,170	3,419	3,368	51
Deutsche Börse	1,716	1,328	592	531	61
Bombay (BSE)	1,567	111	5,821	5,820	1
National SE India	1,540	692	1,840	1,839	1
Swiss	1,403	873	264	227	37
Australia	1,268	907	2,095	1,969	126
Korea	1,254	1,680	2,059	2,039	20
Nasdaq Nordic	1,248	782	938	900	38
Johannesburg	951	401	376	303	73
Taiwan	844	521	911	833	78
BM&FBOVESPA (Brazil)	759	524	349	338	11
Spanish (BME)	704	716	3,506	3,480	26

[1] The total value, at market prices, of all issued shares of companies quoted on the stock market.

Sources: World Federation of Exchanges: www.worldexchanges.org. and London Stock Exchange, http://www.londonstockexchange.com/exchange/statistics

Starting in the US in the early 2000s they determined that the national stock exchanges could do with some competition, so they got together, chipped in a few million for start-up costs and created new trading platforms. These were equipped with nimbler technology and required far fewer staff than the traditional exchanges. They had narrower differences between the price to buy (bid) and the price to sell (offer) a share, lower execution (transaction) costs, and the time between sending an order and the order being complete was much faster than the traditional exchanges. Not only did the institutions now have a cheaper way of trading shares but they could also use the presence of the new trading platforms to force the old exchanges to change their ways.

North Americans called these platforms electronic communications networks (ECNs) (alternative trading systems is a broader term because it allows the possibility of non-electronic and automated trading). They are also known as multilateral trading facilities (MTFs) (a term more favoured in Europe) and they have certainly had an effect. As recently as 2004 about 80 per cent of the trading volume in the shares listed on the NYSE was handled by the NYSE itself. Today less than one-quarter of the trades go through the NYSE; the rest are traded through new trading systems, mostly ECNs including BATS, Instinet and NYSE-ArcaEx. NYSE is not alone; Nasdaq has also lost a lot of trade in the shares listed on its exchange to the new venues.

A major change occurred in 2007 with the introduction of the European Union's Markets in Financial Instruments Directive (Mifid), which had the aim of providing a 'harmonised regulatory regime for investment services across the 30 member states of the European Economic Area'. The main objectives of the Directive are 'to increase competition and consumer protection in investment services'. Following this Directive, brokers acting on behalf of share (and other security) buyers and sellers must now demonstrate that they are achieving the keenest price and using the most efficient, cost-effective trading venues.[3] This encouraged the establishment of cheaper and faster electronic trading platforms to challenge the old ones. And, of course, European institutional investors were just as keen as their US counterparts to have alternatives to the national exchanges.

Traditional stock markets have lost a lot of trade to the new generation of European MTFs (such as BATS Chi-X Europe and Aquis Exchange). These trade shares in companies listed/quoted on a variety of national exchanges across Europe, and they are far less strictly regulated than stock markets.

The proliferation of trading venues means that prices are increasingly being set for shares in a number of different places. A company like Rolls-Royce's might find its shares publicly traded on a dozen or more platforms.[4]

Globalisation of financial flows

Over the last 20 years of the twentieth century there was an increasing emphasis on share (equity) finance and stock exchanges. An 'equity culture' spread around the world. Given that stock markets have been around for centuries, what happened in those years to spark such a widespread interest? The first explanation is that a greatly increased number of companies sought a stock market quotation for their shares and there were deliberate attempts by governments to stimulate interest in share ownership. Following the Thatcher and Reagan privatisations, and the push for wider share ownership in 1980s Britain and the USA, hundreds of state-owned or privately held companies worldwide floated their shares on stock exchanges. Governments the world over, regardless of their position on the political spectrum, promoted share markets and other financial markets as enabling tools for economic progress. Secondly, it became apparent that equities had provided good long-term returns over the first eighty years of the twentieth century – returns significantly ahead of inflation and those on bonds. So, increasingly, those with responsibility for providing pensions decades in the future concentrated on buying shares. Thirdly, the 1980s and 1990s was one of the best periods ever for share returns. The bull market stimulated interest from millions of investors who previously preferred to hold less risky, lower-return securities, such as bonds.

Despite the drop-off in interest after the poor returns of the first decade of the twenty-first century, shares and the stock market remain very important for many people across the globe. In the USA, Japan, Australia and Canada for instance, about one-third of households now own shares (either directly or indirectly through mutual funds and pension funds). One-fifth of British households own shares directly. The equity culture is reasonably well established in Germany, with over 8 million people holding shares (13% of the population), but is stronger in Scandinavia and the Netherlands.

Financial globalisation means the integration of capital markets across the world. The extent of the internationalisation of the equity markets is illustrated by the volume of foreign equity trades in the major financial centres, now running into tens of billions every day. It is also evident in the fact that a substantial proportion of pension fund and insurance fund money is invested in foreign equities. And today a corporation is not limited to raising funds in a capital market where it is domiciled, but can sell its shares in many markets. Three of the major elements encouraging cross-border financial activity are shown in **Exhibit 9.3**.

Deregulation

The 1980s and 1990s was a period when government deregulation of financial markets was seen as a way of enabling financial and corporate entities to compete in the global marketplace and benefit consumers. The limits placed on the purchase and sale of foreign currency

---

3 'Best execution', a requirement of Mifid, of a trade means demonstrating that the broker obtained the best price, low cost of execution, speed and the likelihood of settlement of the trade going well.

4 For more on the consequences of the shift towards MTFs consult Arnold (2012a) Chapter 8.

(foreign exchange controls) were eliminated or lowered in most advanced economies. This encouraged the flow of investment capital. Cartel-like arrangements for fixing the minimum commissions paid by investors for buying and selling shares were eroded, as were the restrictions on ownership of financial firms and brokers by foreigners. Now, more than ever, domestic securities can be purchased by individuals and institutional funds from another country. Commercial banks have found the barriers preventing participation in particular markets being demolished. Tax laws have been modified so as not to discourage the flow of funds across borders for investment, and the previously statutorily enforced 'single-activity' financial institutions (in which, for example, banks did banking, building societies did mortgage lending) have ventured into each other's markets, increasing competition and providing a better deal for the consumer.

More recently there has been a reaction against relaxed regulation of international capital. This follows the 2008 financial crisis and the feeling that rogue bankers/financiers, encouraged by a lax regulatory environment, got away with grossly irresponsible behaviour, while innocent people suffered in the post-crisis austerity. Anti-internationalisation sentiment was vividly manifest in the 2016 Brexit vote. We wait to see how far down the road of tighter national regulation we go, driven as it is by politics; but, already banks are much more restricted in how they behave, manage risk and hold money in their overseas units.

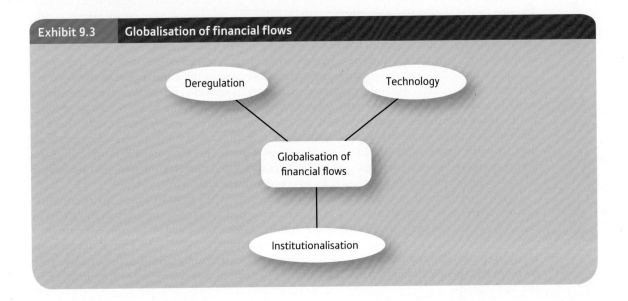

Exhibit 9.3 Globalisation of financial flows

Technology

The rapid transmission of vast quantities of financial information around the globe has transformed the efficiency of financial markets. Securities can be monitored, analysed and dealt in on hundreds of share, bond, commodity and derivative exchanges at the touch of a button from almost anywhere in the world. The advent of powerful smartphones and computers allows accelerated integration, bringing with it complex trading strategies and enormous daily capital flows.

Institutionalisation

Forty years ago most shares were owned by individuals. Today, the markets are dominated by financial institutions (pension funds, insurance companies, hedge funds, the 'mutual funds' such as unit and investment trusts and private equity funds (*see* Chapter 10)). Whereas the individual, as a shareholder, tended to be more parochial and to concentrate on national company shares, the institutions have sufficient knowledge and strength to seek out the rewards from overseas investments. They also appreciate the diversification benefits which accrue due to the low level of correlation of returns between some financial markets (*see* Chapter 7).

Why do companies list their shares on more than one exchange?

There are hundreds of companies paying for the privilege of having their shares listed for trading on stock exchanges in other countries instead of, or as well as, on their local exchange. Exhibit 9.2 shows that the most popular secondary listings locations are the USA and the UK. There are also substantial numbers of foreign shares listed on most of the northern European exchanges, as well as on those of Canada, Australia, and Japan. This dual or triple listing can be a costly business and the regulatory environment can be stringent so there must be some powerful motivating factors driving managers to globalise their investor base. Here are some reasons for listing abroad:

- **To *broaden the shareholder base*** Making it possible for a larger number of investors to trade the company's shares raises the options when it comes to selling more shares, now or in the future, for a higher price and thus raise capital more cheaply (that is, a lower return will be required per £ invested). See the case of The Bank of Cyprus in **Exhibit 9.4**.

Exhibit 9.4

Bank of Cyprus targets FTSE 250 place with listing move to London

By Martin Arnold

Bank of Cyprus is planning to shift its primary stock market listing to London as it seeks to attract new investors.

The group, the biggest lender on the crisis-hit Mediterranean island where it is to remain head-quartered, will keep a secondary listing in Cyprus, but plans to ditch its other listing in Athens, where it sold its operations several years ago.

Investors will be offered the option of transferring their shares to London or Cyprus.

"The listing and, subject to meeting the eligibility criteria, potential inclusion in the FTSE UK Index

series will enhance the group's visibility and share liquidity," the bank said.

It said a London listing would provide "access to a greater pool of international capital together with greater profile and visibility in the European financial markets".

The bank added that it hoped to boost confidence through "adherence to the high standards of corporate governance and transparency that is required for a premium listing on the LSE".

Financial Times, 31 March 2016.

- **The *domestic stock exchange is too small or the firm's growth is otherwise constrained*** Some companies are so large relative to their domestic stock markets that they have no choice but to obtain equity finance from abroad. When Ashanti Goldfields, the Ghanaian gold-mining company, was privatised it was valued at about $1.7bn, which was more than ten times the capitalisation of the Accra stock market. A listing in London was a great success and the company expanded its activities in other African countries; it also listed in New York, Toronto, Zimbabwe, Ghana and London.
- **To *reward employees*** Many employees of foreign-owned firms are rewarded with shares in the parent company. If these shares are locally listed the share-ownership plans can be better managed and are more appealing to employees.
- **Investors in that particular market may understand the firm better** This point is illustrated with the case of Caparo (**Exhibit 9.5**). AIM, discussed later in this chapter, is one of the markets organised by the London Stock Exchange.
- **To *raise awareness of the company*** For example, Standard Chartered listed on the Bombay Stock Exchange as well as London and Hong Kong to strengthen its brand (*see* **Exhibit 9.6**).

Exhibit 9.5

Indian Business Opts For Aim

By David Blackwell

Aim is enjoying an Indian summer as companies from the sub-continent opt to join the junior market.

On Tuesday, Caparo Energy will become the third Indian company in a month to float on Aim.

Caparo, which has raised about £50m ($80m), is planning to develop a portfolio of wind farms. Investors include Blackrock and Henderson.

Ravi Kailas, chief executive, said the company had looked at raising the money from private equity groups, but London's institutional investors were aware of the Indian energy sector on Aim and a flotation on the junior market would leave other options open.

 Financial Times, 11 October 2010.
All Rights Reserved.

Exhibit 9.6

Stanchart Eyes 'Small' Listings In China And India

By Sharlene Goff, Retail Banking Correspondent

Standard Chartered, the Asia-focused bank, is targeting stock market listings in Mumbai and Shanghai as it seeks to strengthen its brand in key local markets.

Peter Sands, chief executive, said a listing in India could be launched in the first half of next year, while plans for a listing in China were less advanced.

Speaking to the Financial Times following the bank's trading update, Mr Sands said: 'These two markets are incredibly important to us. We are actively pursuing a listing in India and how we could make it work effectively. Plans for China are at an earlier stage.'

He said the additional listings would be 'relatively small' and were 'not driven by the quantum of capital but what they would do to reinforce the profile and positioning of the bank'.

Mr Sands said he had no plans to relocate from London.

This differs to the strategy of HSBC, which is also primarily focused on Asia and recently decided to move its chief executive to Hong Kong.

Standard Chartered, which derives more than 90 per cent of earnings from Asia, Africa and the Middle East, is on track for record profits this year.

FT *Financial Times,* 30 October 2009.
All Rights Reserved.

- *Discipline* Not only have Chinese companies seen the benefit of tapping capitalistic share investors, they have also been made aware of the managerial rigour demanded by stock markets and their investors. Many Russian companies have also listed in London to gain respectability through the enforcement by Western investors of improved corporate governance and transparency of information (they have also listed in London to gain some protection against arbitrary actions by the Russian government).

- **To understand better the economic, social and industrial changes** occurring in major product markets. This is illustrated by the Toyota article (*see* **Exhibit 9.7**).

Exhibit 9.7

Toyota to list in New York and London

Toyota, Japan's third-largest company by market capitalisation, plans to list its shares in New York and London this month.

The issue is aimed at attracting international investors, meeting the needs of the increasingly global industry and boosting Toyota's image, said Yuji Araki, senior managing director.

The move is the latest in a series of global offers by Japanese companies, which are aimed at increasing the international element of their shareholder base . . .

Mr Araki said the company decided to list in New York and London not only to increase its investor base but also to be able to judge whether Toyota's performance met western standards.

'If they don't, we will have to change ourselves', he said.

Listing in the two cities would also help Toyota sense the changes in foreign stock markets more quickly and from those changes, the economic, social and industrial changes occurring in those markets, Mr Araki said.

Foreigners own a relatively low proportion of Toyota – just 8.8 per cent. But Mr Araki emphasised that the company had no fixed target for foreign shareholders . . .

In addition to New York, Toyota decided to list in London because 'in order to attract international investors it is essential to list in London', he added . . .

However, over the next two to three years, changes would be introduced in Japanese reporting requirements, which would bring them much closer to SEC standards, Mr Araki said.

FT Michiyo Nakamoto and Paul Abrahams, *Financial Times,* 8 September 1999, p. 26.
All Rights Reserved.

The importance of a well-run stock exchange

A well-run stock exchange has a number of characteristics. It is one where a 'fair game' takes place; that is, where it is not possible for some investors and fundraisers to benefit at the expense of other participants – all players are on 'a level playing field'. It is a market which is well regulated to avoid abuses, negligence and fraud in order to reassure investors who put their savings at risk. It is also one on which it is reasonably cheap to carry out transactions. In addition, a large number of buyers and sellers are likely to be needed for the efficient price setting of shares and to provide sufficient liquidity, allowing the investor to sell at any time without altering the market price. There are six main benefits of a well-run stock exchange.

1 *Firms can find funds and grow* Because investors in financial securities with a stock market quotation are assured that they are, generally, able to sell their shares quickly, cheaply and with a reasonable degree of certainty about the price, they are willing to supply funds to firms at a lower cost than they would if selling was slow, or expensive, or the sale price was subject to much uncertainty. Thus stock markets encourage investment by mobilising savings. As well as stimulating the investment of domestic savings, stock markets can be useful for attracting foreign savings and for aiding the privatisation process.

2 *Allocation of capital* One of the key economic problems for a nation is finding a mechanism for deciding what mixture of goods and services to produce. An extreme solution has been tried and shown to be lacking in sophistication – that of a totalitarian directed economy where bureaucratic diktat determines the exact quantity of each line of commodity produced. The alternative method favoured in most nations (for the majority of goods and services) is to let the market decide what will be produced and which firms will produce it.

An efficiently functioning stock market is able to assist this process through the flow of investment capital. If the stock market was poorly regulated and operated then the mis-pricing of shares and other financial securities could lead to society's scarce capital resources being put into sectors which are inappropriate given the objective of maximising economic well-being. If, for instance, the market priced the shares of a badly managed company in a declining industrial sector at a high level then that firm would find it relatively easy to sell shares and raise funds for further investment in its business or to take over other firms. This would deprive companies with better prospects and with a greater potential contribution to make to society of essential finance.

To take an extreme example: imagine the year is 1910 and on the stock market are some firms which manufacture horse-drawn carriages. There are also one or two young companies which have taken up the risky challenge of producing motor cars. Analysts will examine the prospects of the two types of enterprise before deciding which firms will get a warm reception when they ask for more capital in, say, a rights issue. The unfavoured firms will find their share prices falling as investors sell their shares, and will be unable to attract more savers' money. One way for the older firm to stay in business would be to shift resources within the firm to the production of those commodities for which consumer demand is on a rising trend.

History is rhyming one hundred years later: Elon Musk, who founded Tesla, raised tens of billion of dollars for electric car production and an enormous factory for battery manufacture. The stock market shifted resources from old technology to new. Tesla currently has a market value greater than Ford Motors, despite the absence of profit. At the same time, the older vehicle makers have shift billions into electric research and development, and into production lines for all-electric vehicles. Tesla and other big new players, such as BYD in China, will have a fight on their hands from the likes of General Motors, Nissan and VW. Despite the eye-watering 'bet the business' level of investment required, stock market investors are demanding that the capital expenditure takes place; otherwise their firms will become obsolete.

3 *For shareholders* Shareholders benefit from the availability of a speedy, cheap secondary market if they want to sell. Not only do shareholders like to know that they can sell shares when they want to, they may simply want to know the value of their holdings even if they have no intention of selling at present. By contrast, an unquoted firm's shareholders often find it very difficult to assess the value of their holding.

Founders of firms may be particularly keen to obtain a quotation for their firms. This will enable them to diversify their assets by selling a proportion of their holdings. Also, venture capital firms which fund unquoted firms during their rapid growth phase often press the manager to aim for a quotation to permit the venture capitalist to have the option of realising the gains made on the original investment, or simply to boost the value of their holding by making it more liquid.

4 *Status and publicity* The public profile of a firm can be enhanced by being quoted on an exchange. Banks and other financial institutions generally have more confidence in a quoted firm and therefore are more likely to provide funds at a lower cost. Their confidence is raised because the company's activities are now subject to detailed scrutiny. The publicity surrounding the process of gaining a quotation may have a positive impact on the image of the firm in the eyes of customers, suppliers and employees and so may lead to a beneficial effect on their day-to-day business.

5 *Mergers* Mergers can be facilitated better by a quotation. This is especially true if the payments offered to the target firm's shareholders for their holdings are shares in the acquiring firm. A quoted share has a value defined by the market, whereas shares in unquoted firms are difficult to assess.

The stock exchange also assists what is called 'the market in managerial control'. This is a mechanism in which teams of managers are seen as competing for control of corporate assets. Or, to put it more simply, mergers through the stock market permit the displacement of inefficient management with a more successful team. Thus, according to this line of reasoning, assets will be used more productively and society will be better off. This 'market in managerial control' is not as effective as is sometimes claimed (it tends to be over-emphasised by acquiring managers) (*see* Chapter 20 for further discussion).

6 *Improves corporate behaviour* If a firm's shares are traded on an exchange, the directors may be encouraged to behave in a manner conducive to shareholders' interests. This is achieved through a number of pressure points. For example, to obtain a quotation on a reputable

exchange, companies are required to disclose a far greater range and depth of information than is required by accounting standards or the Companies Acts. This information is then disseminated widely and can become the focus of much public and press comment. In addition, investment analysts ask for regular briefings from senior managers and continuously monitor the performance of firms. Before a company is admitted to the Stock Exchange the authorities insist on being assured that the management team are sufficiently competent and, if necessary, additional directors are appointed to supplement the board's range of knowledge and skills. Directors of quoted companies are required to consult shareholders on important decisions, such as mergers. They also have to be very careful to release price-sensitive information in a timely and orderly fashion and they are strictly forbidden to use inside information to make a profit by buying or selling the firm's shares.

The London Stock Exchange

The London Stock Exchange (LSE) started in the coffee houses of eighteenth-century London where the buying and selling of shares in joint stock companies took place. In 1773 the volume of trade was sufficiently great for the brokers to open a subscription room in Threadneedle Street. They called the building the Stock Exchange.[5] During the nineteenth century, over 20 other stock exchanges were formed in the rapidly expanding industrial towns of Britain. They amalgamated in 1973 to become a unified Stock Exchange. All of the old trading floors of the regional exchanges and in London, where market members would meet face to face to exchange shares, are now obsolete. Today, there is no physical marketplace. The dealing rooms of the various finance houses are linked via telephone and computer, and trading takes place without physical contact. Having abandoned floor trading in 1986 the LSE found itself with an overly large building. In 2004 it moved within the City's square mile to Paternoster Square next to St Paul's Cathedral.

Securities traded

The volume of trade has expanded enormously in recent years. **Exhibit 9.8** indicates the types of securities sold on the Exchange. There are many types of *fixed-interest securities* traded in London, including gilts, local authority bonds, sterling corporate bonds and Eurobonds. Also government bonds from over 40 countries are traded in London, e.g. China's Renminbi bonds. There is a wide range of international corporate bonds, such as the Indian companies' 'Masala' bonds. In addition, financial instruments complying with Islamic rules, giving a return but not interest, are issued and traded in London, such as sukuk.

The UK government bond or 'gilts' market is big, with an annual turnover of over £8.3tr in the year ended April 2018. In that year the UK government raised over £100bn through selling gilt-edged securities. Sterling bonds issued by companies (corporate bonds) comprise a relatively small market – just a few billion. During 2017, 1,759 new Eurobonds were listed in London by UK companies, raising a total of £251bn.

Specialist securities, such as covered warrants, are normally bought and traded by a few investors who are particularly knowledgeable in investment matters. Covered warrants are a type of derivative that allows the holder the right (but not obligation) to buy or sell an underlying, such as company shares, at a predetermined price on or before a certain date in the future (Warrants are discussed in Chapter 10 – the 'covered' element means those issued by an institution independent of the company whose shares/asset the warrant is based upon, whereas straightforward warrants are issued by the company that also issues the underlying shares.

The Specialist Fund Market was launched in 2007. It creates a market in shares of closed-ended investment funds such as hedge funds, emerging market funds, specialist property and private equity funds for institutional investors (not for individuals, who may be less aware of the risks of investing in these funds).

---

5 It moved in 1801 to Capel Court and in 1972 to Throgmorton Street.

Exhibit 9.8 **Exhibit 9.8** Types of financial securities sold on the London Stock Exchange

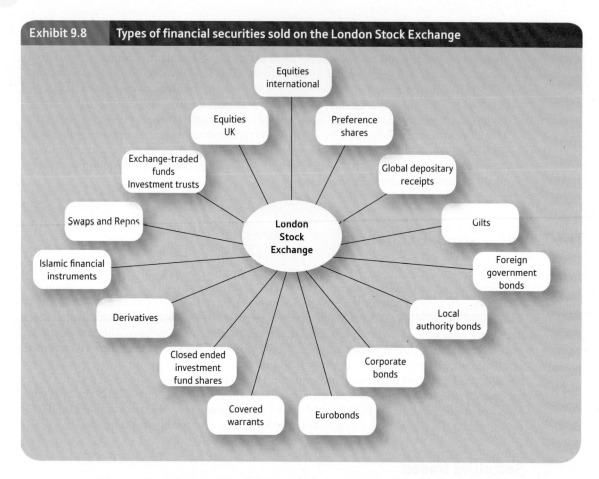

There has been the rapid development of the depositary receipt market over the last two decades. These are certificates which can be bought and sold, which represent evidence of ownership of a company's shares held by a depositary. Thus, an Indian company's shares could be packaged in, say, groups of five by a depositary (usually a bank) which then sells a certificate representing the bundle of shares. The depositary receipt can be denominated in a currency other than the corporation's domestic currency and dividends can be received in the currency of the depositary receipt (say, pounds) rather than the currency of the original shares. These are attractive securities for sophisticated international investors because they may be more liquid and more easily traded than the underlying shares. They may also be used to avoid settlement (*see* later) or foreign exchange and foreign ownership difficulties (government restrictions on investment by foreigners) which may exist in the company's home market. From the company's point of view depositary receipts are attractive because they allow a market in the company's shares (even though they are wrapped up in a depositary receipt) permitting fund raising and the other benefits of a quotation on a regulated global capital market without the company needing to jump the regulatory hurdles necessary to join the Main Market (Official List) in London. DRs have been very useful as a means for companies in emerging countries (such as Kazakhstan, Brazil or India) to raise capital from the developed world's exchanges. However, emerging nations have developed to such an extent that they now have wealthy investors looking to invest in the developed world – *see* **Exhibit 9.9**. In more recent times the London Stock Exchange has developed markets in derivative financial instruments such as futures, options and swaps. These types of instruments are discussed in Chapters 21 and 22.

Our main concern in this chapter is with the market in ordinary shares and it is to this we now turn. The London Stock Exchange is both a primary market and a secondary market. The primary market is where firms can raise new finance by selling shares to investors. The secondary market is where existing securities are sold by one investor to another.[6]

---

6 Confusion can arise here with the terms 'primary listing' (when a company's shares are traded on more than one market its primary listing is on its main market and it is subject to stringent regulations there) and 'secondary listing' where the shares are traded outside its main market.

Exhibit 9.9

Emerging Market Bourses Hunt Western Blue Chips

By Steve Johnson

A swathe of emerging market stock exchanges are lining up to launch depositary receipt programmes, allowing local investors to access foreign companies without leaving their home market.

The move would also ease the way for western companies to raise capital from increasingly wealthy emerging market investors.

Standard Chartered, the UK-headquartered but emerging market-focused bank, blazed a trail by listing the first Indian depositary receipt – raising $500m in the process.

Telefónica, the Spanish telecoms company, and Dufry Group, a Swiss retailer, have listed Brazilian depositary receipts, while a number of Indian companies have launched DRs in Singapore.

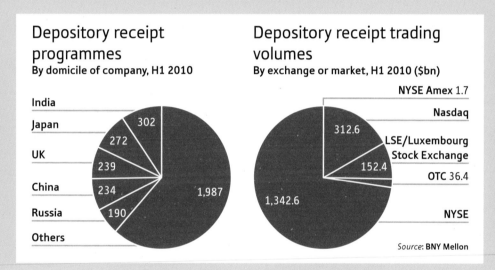

Depository receipt programmes
By domicile of company, H1 2010

India 302
Japan 272
UK 239
China 234
Russia 190
Others 1,987

Depository receipt trading volumes
By exchange or market, H1 2010 ($bn)

NYSE Amex 1.7
Nasdaq 312.6
LSE/Luxembourg Stock Exchange 152.4
OTC 36.4
NYSE 1,342.6

Source: BNY Mellon

The primary market (equities)

Large sums of money flow from the savers in society via the Stock Exchange to firms wanting to invest and grow. In 2017 there were over 900 UK companies on the Main Markets as well as over 400 foreign companies. There were also over 800 UK companies on the Exchange's market for smaller and younger companies, the Alternative Investment Market (AIM) together with 152 foreign companies. During 2017, UK-listed firms raised new capital amounting to over £96bn by selling equity and fixed interest securities on the LSE. Included in this figure was £5.3bn raised by companies coming to the Stock Exchange for the first time by selling shares. Companies already quoted on the Main Market (Official List of the LSE) sold a further £12.1bn of shares through events such as rights issues. AIM companies sold £6.37bn of shares. UK companies also regularly raised money by selling convertible bonds, debentures, loans and preference shares (*see* Chapters 10 and 11 for discussion on these securities and **Exhibit 9.10** for a summary of the money raised by UK companies).

Each year there is great interest and excitement inside dozens of companies as they prepare for flotation on the London Stock Exchange. The year 2017 was a watershed year for 64 UK companies which joined the Main Market and 80 which joined AIM. The requirements for joining the Main Market are stringent. The listing particulars should give a complete picture of the

Exhibit 9.10	Money raised by UK companies, 1999–2016							

	New companies issuing shares		Other issues of shares (e.g. rights issues) and other securities		Eurobonds		AIM	
	No. of co.'s	Money raised (£m)	No. of co.'s	Money raised (£m)	No. of co.'s	Money raised (£m)	No. of new companies joining AIM*	Money raised* (£m)
2007	73	7,613	477	8,995	2,025	165,924	284	16,184
2008	53	3,110	402	51,666	2,101	432,445	114	4,332
2009	17	458	378	73,907	1,858	254,571	36	5,602
2010	57	6,998	380	12,360	2096	184,465	102	6,850
2011	21	9,240	580	2,462	2,312	196,442	90	4,295
2012	26	1,879	572	3,817	2,167	139,481	73	3,163
2013	33	7,894	406	11,615	1,379	78,677	99	3,907
2014	57	9,497	486	13,096	933	98,422	118	5,727
2015	68	6,846	461	15,190	1,182	97,993	61	5,456
2016	41	3,526	375	10,900	777	107,906	64	4,766

*Includes non-UK companies

Source: London Stock Exchange. Taken from various statistical publications of London Stock Exchange plc. http://www.londonstockexchange.com/statistics/historic/

company: its trading history, financial record, management and business prospects. It should (normally) have at least a three-year trading history and has to make at least 25 per cent of its ordinary shares publicly available (*see* Chapter 10 for more detail). Given the costs associated with gaining a listing, it may be surprising to find that the total market capitalisation of more than half quoted UK companies is less than £100m (*see* **Exhibit 9.11**).

Exhibit 9.11	Distribution of UK companies by equity market value at May 2017 for Main Market and AIM. The AIM numbers include non-UK companies

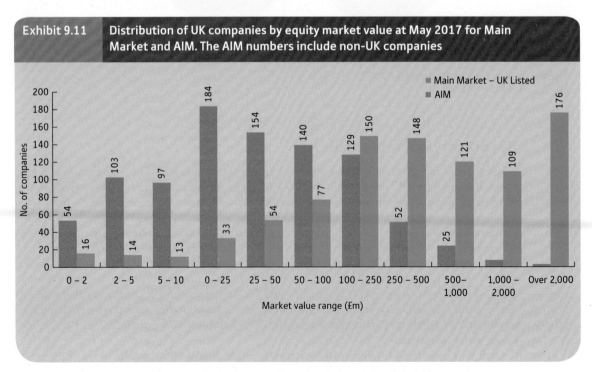

Source: www.londonstockexchange.com, statistics section. Reproduced courtesy of London Stock Exchange plc.

The LSE is clearly an important source of new finance for UK corporations and for companies around the world. However, it is not the most significant source, which is generally from within the firm itself (internal finance). This is the accumulated profits retained within the firm and not distributed as dividends. In an average year retained profits account for about one-half of the new funds for companies.

These retained earnings are also equity capital because this is money that belongs to shareholders – they have merely allowed companies to use it within the business rather than paying it out to the owners. Thus the amount of equity capital devoted to a firm can grow to be worth millions of pounds largely through the retention of profits, despite the fact that it might have raised only a few thousands by selling shares to investors at its start. The sale of new ordinary shares rarely accounts for a significant proportion of capital raised. Following retained earnings, bank loans are often very important for companies, but this does vary significantly. The sale of bonds and preference shares combined generally accounts for less than 5 per cent of new capital put into UK companies.

The secondary market in equities

The LSE operates and regulates a secondary market for the buying and selling of UK shares between investors in which an average of about 900,000 bargains, worth over £4,000m, are completed in a typical day. In addition to these domestic equities about £500m of foreign shares are traded on a typical day. The secondary market turnover far exceeds the primary market sales. This high level of activity ensures a liquid market enabling shares to change ownership speedily, at low cost and without large movements in price – one of the main objectives of a well-run exchange.

The UK equity markets available to companies

The Main Market (Official List)

Companies wishing to be listed have to sign a Listing Agreement which commits directors to certain high standards of behaviour and levels of reporting to shareholders. This is a market for medium and large established firms with a reasonably long trading history. The costs of launching even a modest new issue runs into hundreds of thousands of pounds and therefore small companies are unable to justify a full main market listing. The regulations and the process of floating on the Main Market are discussed in Chapter 10.

The Alternative Investment Market (AIM)

There is a long-recognised need for equity capital by small, young companies which are unable to afford the costs of full Official listing. Many stock exchanges have alternative equity markets that set less stringent rules and regulations for joining or remaining quoted (often called 'second-tier markets').

Lightly regulated or unregulated markets have a continuing dilemma. If the regulation is too lax scandals of fraud or incompetence will arise, damaging the image and credibility of the market, and thus reducing the flow of investor funds to companies. (This happened to the German market for small companies, Neuer Markt, which had to close in 2002 because of the loss in investor confidence.) On the other hand, if the market is too tightly regulated, with more company investigations, more information disclosure and a requirement for longer trading track records prior to flotation, the associated costs and inconvenience will deter many companies from seeking a quotation.

The driving philosophy behind AIM is to offer young and developing companies access to new sources of finance, while providing investors with the opportunity to buy and sell shares in a trading environment run, regulated and marketed by the LSE. Efforts are made to keep the costs down and make the rules as simple as possible. In contrast to the Main Market there is no requirement for AIM companies to be a minimum size, to have traded for a minimum period of three years or for a set proportion of their shares to be in public hands – if they wish to sell a mere 1 per cent or 5 per cent of the shares to outsiders then that is acceptable. They do not have to ensure that 25 per cent of the shares are in public hands (that is, not in the hands of dominant shareholders or connected persons). However, investors have some degree of reassurance about the quality of companies coming to the market. These firms have to appoint, and retain at all times, a nominated adviser and nominated broker. The nominated adviser ('nomad') is selected by the corporation from a Stock Exchange approved register. These advisers have demonstrated to the Exchange that they have sufficient experience and qualifications to act as a 'quality controller', confirming to the LSE that the company has complied with the rules. Unlike with Official List companies there is no pre-vetting of admission documents by the UK Listing Authority (or the Exchange) as a lot of weight is placed on the nominated advisers' investigations and informed opinion about the company.

Nominated brokers have an important role to play in bringing buyers and sellers of shares together. Investors in the company are reassured that at least one broker is ready to trade or do its best to match up buyers and sellers. They also represent the firm to the Market (public relations). The adviser and broker are to be retained throughout the company's life on AIM. They have high reputations and it is regarded as a very bad sign if either of them abruptly refuses further association with a firm. AIM companies are also expected to comply with strict rules regarding the publication of price-sensitive information (that which might have an impact on the share price) and the quality of annual and interim reports. **Exhibit 9.12** shows that companies have to be very careful to keep nomads, shareholders and potential shareholders informed.

Exhibit 9.12

Aim misses target again

By *Kate Burgess*

Last week, the disciplinarians at the Alternative Investment Market fined a company £75,000. The group — unnamed — had not taken its obligations to Aim seriously enough. It had not told its nominated adviser — also unnamed — what it was up to. It had merely sent over minutes of meetings without context or explanation. The Aim company did not ask advice on what it should disclose to the market. Not good enough, tutted the bods on Aim's disciplinary committee, also unnamed although we are told they are drawn from the great and good and are independent of the London Stock Exchange, which owns Aim.

But we do not know what the company should have told its nomad and why it did not. It is hard to see how a private censure will cause a sharp intake of breath among the other 1,000 or so companies on Aim. They would have to be small indeed for a fine of £75,000 to change behaviour. Maintaining a quote on Aim costs companies considerably more. This is regulation at its most opaque. The Aim team privately censors companies and nomads two or three times a year. The LSE has promised more clarity about its disciplinary system in the new year.

Upon flotation an 'AIM admission document' is required; this is similar to a prospectus required for companies floating on the Main Market, but less detailed (see Chapter 10). The admission documentation even goes so far as to state the directors' unspent convictions and all bankruptcies of companies where they were directors. The LSE charges companies an annual fee to maintain a quotation on AIM. If to this is added the cost of financial advisers, brokers and of management time spent communicating with institutions and investors the annual cost of being quoted on AIM runs into tens of thousands of pounds. This can be too expensive for some companies.

However, there are cost savings compared with the Main Market. The flotation admission document is less detailed and therefore cheaper than a prospectus. The annual expense of managing a quotation is less. For example AIM companies do not have to disclose as much information as companies on the Main Market. Price-sensitive information will have to be published but normally this will require only an electronic message from the adviser to the Exchange rather than a circular to shareholders. AIM companies are not bound by the Listing Rules administered by the UKLA but instead are subject to the AIM rules, written and administered by the LSE.

Note also that there are tax advantages for shareholders investing in AIM companies via venture capital trusts and the Enterprise Investment Scheme (*see* Chapter 10) or through the reduction in inheritance tax for some investors.

Offsetting the cost advantages AIM has over the Official List is the fact that the higher level of regulation and related enhanced image, prestige and security of Official List companies means that equity capital can usually be raised at a lower required rate of return (the shares can be sold for more per unit of projected profit).

AIM is not just a stepping-stone for companies planning to graduate to the Official List. It has many attractive features in its own right. Indeed, many Official List companies have moved to AIM in recent years. Some of the companies on AIM are very large, e.g. ASOS with a market capitalization of over £4bn, Boohoo worth over £1.5bn and Fevertree Drinks at £1.4bn.

NEX Exchange

Companies that do not want to pay the costs of a flotation on one of the markets run by the LSE (this can range from £100,000 to £1 million just for getting on the market in the first place) and the ongoing annual costs, could go for a quotation on London-based NEX Exchange (formerly ICAP Securities & Derivatives Exchange (ISDX)). By having their shares quoted on NEX Exchange companies provide a service to their shareholders, allowing them to buy and sell shares. It also allows the company to gain access to capital, for example, by selling more shares in a rights issue, without submitting to the rigour and expense of a quotation on LSE. The downside for investors is that trading in NEX Exchange shares can be illiquid (not many buyers and sellers), with high dealing costs. Buy and sell prices offered are frequently 20% or more apart, despite there often being a number of competing market makers making a market in a company's shares (see below for the role of market makers).

Companies must have at least 12 months of audited accounts to be admitted. Joining fees range from a minimum of £7,500 to a maximum of £50,000 (for the largest companies). There is an annual fee of £6,500. When companies join the market there are 'Corporate Adviser's' fees of around £20,000. If new capital is raised fees can climb above £100,000. Companies also pay an annual retainer fee to their Corporate Advisers. Companies are required to have one-tenth of their shares in public hands, in a 'free float'.

NEX Exchange companies are generally very small and often brand new, but there are also some long-established and well-known firms, such as Adnams, the brewers. Note that the criteria for companies gaining admission for a quote on NEX Exchange do not include compliance with the normal listing rules, so investors have far fewer quality assurances about these companies. However, these companies have to adhere to its code of conduct, e.g. insider trading by directors is prohibited; they must have a Corporate Adviser (e.g. an investment bank, corporate broker, accountant or lawyer) at all times; an 'admission document' must be produced for companies listing; the market must be properly informed of any developments or any information that may have an impact on the financial status of the company. The Corporate Adviser will advise on compliance with NEX Exchange rules and insist that good accounting systems are in place with annual audited accounts and semi-annual accounts. They also ensure that the company has at least one non-executive director, and adequate working capital.

There are 85 companies currently paying for NEX Exchange quote dealing facility. In addition NEX Exchange provides an alternative trading facility for 500 AIM companies.

NEX Exchange is often seen as a nursery market for companies that eventually grow big enough for AIM or the Main Market. Despite this many companies are happy to remain on NEX Exchange for several years and have no desire to increase their costs by moving up to the LSE markets.

Tasks for stock exchanges

Traditionally, exchanges perform the following tasks in order to play their valuable role in a modern society:

● Supervision of trading to ensure fairness and efficiency.

● The authorisation of market participants such as brokers and market makers.

- Creation of an environment in which prices are formed efficiently and without distortion (price discovery or price formation). This requires not only regulation of a high order and low transaction cost but also a liquid market in which there are many buyers and sellers, permitting investors to enter or exit quickly without moving the price.

- Organisation of the clearing and settlement of transactions (after the deal has been struck the buyer must pay for the shares and the shares must be transferred to the new owners).

- The regulation of the admission of companies to the exchange and the regulation of companies on the exchange.

- The dissemination of information, e.g. trading data, prices and company announcements. Investors are more willing to trade if prompt and complete information about trades, companies and prices is available.

In recent years there has been a questioning of the need for stock exchanges to carry out all these activities. In the case of the LSE the settlement of transactions was long ago handed over to CREST (discussed later in this chapter). Also the responsibility for authorising the listing of companies was transferred to the UK Listing Authority arm of the Financial Conduct Authority (the principal UK regulator). The LSE's Regulatory News Service (which distributes important company announcements and other price-sensitive news) now has to compete with other distribution platforms outside the LSE's control as listed companies are now able to choose between competing providers of news dissemination platforms. Despite all this upheaval the LSE still retains an important role in the distribution of trading and pricing information.

How stock exchanges work

Types of trading

Traditionally shares were traded between two traders, face to face. A few stock exchanges around the world still have a place where buyers and sellers (or at least their representatives) meet to trade. For example, the NYSE continues to make some use of a large trading floor, with thousands of face-to-face deals taking place every working day (open outcry trading). This is the traditional image of a stock market, and if television reporters have a story about what is going on in the world's security markets, they often show an image of traders rushing around, talking quickly amid a flurry of small slips of paper on the NYSE trading floor. Most trading now, however, is conducted silently in front of banks of computers, with deals being completed in nano-seconds. The stress levels for those dealing remain as high, if not higher, than ever, as now a slight mistake with a finger on a keyboard can cause mayhem.

Quote-driven trading is how most stock exchanges were operated. With this type of approach, market makers give a price at which they will buy (lower price) or sell (higher price), and they make their profits on the margins between buying and selling. Traditionally they operated in 'trading pits' and used an open outcry system of trading, i.e. shouting and using hand signals to make trades, much like you might see bookmakers doing at a horse race meeting. They were able to adjust their prices according to what other traders were doing. Although this type of trading does still take place, it has been superseded by electronic trading. Market makers input their prices ('bid' is the price at which they are willing to buy and 'offer' or 'ask' is the price at which they are willing to sell) to a computer system and dealing generally takes place electronically.

Market makers, also known as dealers, fulfil a crucial role in the markets: in those securities in which market makers agree to make a market there will always be (in trading hours) someone available who will quote a price at which they will buy or sell – as a purchaser or seller you may not like the price but at least someone is making a trade possible. To take share trading as an example, imagine if you wanted to invest in a small company's shares and there were no market makers, then you might hesitate because the shares would fail to have the important quality of liquidity. Investors in companies lacking an active secondary market will demand higher rates of return (lower share prices) to compensate for the inability to quickly find a counterparty willing to trade.

The idea is that in a market with competing market makers, if the gap between the bid and offer prices gets too wide then clients will be lured away by better prices being offered by other market makers in that security.[7] The difference between the prices is known as the trader's spread or bid–offer spread. Many of these prices are displayed on electronic systems so that clients can see them displayed on their computer screens throughout the day. Other security bid–offer prices are given to you only if you telephone the market maker and ask for a quote.

Market makers take a considerable risk: they have to hold inventories of shares and other securities to supply those who want to buy. Tying up a lot of money in inventories of shares, bonds, etc. can be very expensive, and there is always the possibility of downward movement in price while they hold millions of pounds or euros in inventory. The degree of risk varies from one security to another and this helps explain the differences in the size of the bid–offer spread. For some securities it is significantly less than 1 per cent of the value, in others it can be 20 per cent or more. The other major factor influencing the spread is the volume of trade that takes place relative to the amount that has to be held in inventory – high volume gives access to a liquid market for the market maker. Thus Marks & Spencer has millions of shares traded every day and so the market maker is not likely to have M&S shares on its hands for long because they are going out of the door as fast as they are coming in – spreads here can be around one-tenth of 1 per cent. Shares of a small engineering company, meanwhile, might trade in lots of only a few hundred at two- or three-day intervals. Thus the market maker has money tied up for days before selling and is fearful of a price fall between trading days.

We can see how the quote-driven system works through **Exhibit 9.13**. This could apply to markets in a wide variety of securities and instruments, from bonds to commodities, but we will assume that it is company shares. The demand curve shows that as the price declines, the amount demanded to buy from the market maker rises. The supply curve shows rising volume offered by investors with higher prices. The clearing price is 199p – this is where the demand from clients wanting to buy and supply of the securities from those wanting to sell are evenly matched. Naturally, the market makers in this security will be taking a spread around this clearing price, so the true price to the buying client might be 199.5p, whereas the price that a seller to the market makers can obtain is only 198.5p.

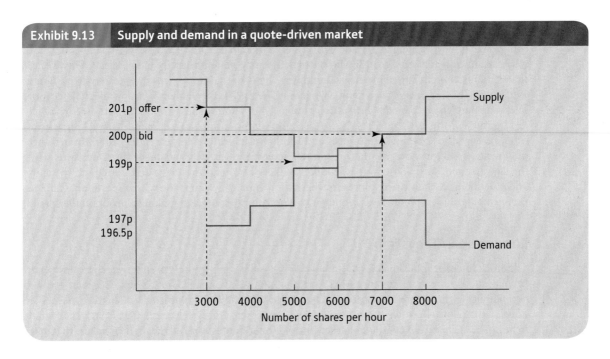

Exhibit 9.13 Supply and demand in a quote-driven market

If one of the market makers is currently quoting prices of 200p–201p (offering to buy at 200p and sell at 201p) then he will experience a flood of orders from sellers because investors are willing to sell 7,000 shares per hour if offered 200p. On the other hand, demand at 201p is a mere 3,000 shares. The market maker will thus end up buying a net 4,000 shares per hour if he takes all the trade. In fact, it is even worse than this for our market maker because the potential buyers can

---

7 Unfortunately, in many cases there is only one market maker willing to make a market in a security.

pick up their shares for only 199.5p from other market makers and so he ends up buying 7,000 per hour and not selling any.

Even if our market maker is exceptionally optimistic about the market equilibrium price rising significantly above 201p in the next few hours he is not doing himself any favours by quoting such high prices because he could buy a large number of the shares he wants at a price a lot less than this – there are 5,000 per hour going through other market makers at 199.5p, for example. Thus there is a strong incentive for our market maker to move his prices down towards the intersection of the supply and demand curves.

Now consider a market maker who quotes 197p–196.5p. She will experience a flood of buy orders from clients given the prices offered by other market makers in this competitive market. Under the rules governing market makers she is obliged to deal at the prices quoted up to a maximum number of shares (decided by the exchange that controls this particular market). Perhaps this obligation to sell 8,000 shares per hour to clients when she is attracting few (no) clients to sell to her may lead to problems in satisfying demand. She will thus be tempted (unless she has a lot of shares to shift) to move her bid and offer prices to around the market equilibrium price.

A market maker who tries to maintain a large bid–offer spread will fail when there are many market makers for a security. For example, consider the five market makers offering the following prices:

Market maker	Bid price	Offer price
1	198.5p	199.5p
2	197.3p	199.5p
3	197.0p	200.0p
4	198.5p	199.7p
5	198.3p	202.0p

Any potential seller (or broker for the seller) would look at the various market makers' prices and conclude that they would like to trade with either market maker 1 or 4 at 198.5p. Any buyer of shares would want to trade with 1 or 2. Market maker 4 may be temporarily under-stocked with these shares and is content to see inventory build up – he is not going to get many to buy from him at 199.7p when buyers can get away with paying only 199.5p. Market maker 2, meanwhile, will see more sales than purchases – perhaps she has excessive inventory and wishes to allow an outflow for a while.

Of course, for most securities the intersection of the supply and demand 'curves' moves over time. Perhaps the company announces at 2pm that it has won a large export order. Immediately the investors see this news on their computer screen and the demand curve shifts upwards while the supply curve shifts downwards. Market makers also read the news and anticipate the shifts and quickly move their price quotes to where they think they can trade with a reasonable balance between bid deals and offer deals, aiming for a large number of each making a profit on the spread.

London's SEAQ system

The Stock Exchange Automated Quotation (SEAQ) is the LSE's quote-driven service that allows market makers to quote prices in those AIM securities not traded on SETS or SETSqx – see later – as well as a number of fixed interest securities. Only those companies with at least two market makers are listed on the SEAQ electronic notice board where market makers display prices at which they are willing to buy or sell. The SEAQ computer gathers the bid–offer quotes from all the market makers that make a market in that particular share (there are about 36 approved market makers). These competing quotations are then available to brokers and other financial institutions linked up to the SEAQ system.

Exhibit 9.14 goes through the stages in buying or selling on the LSE's SEAQ system. What happens when you, as an investor, telephone your broker to buy shares is this: when you mentioned the company name the broker immediately punched into their computer the company code. So within a second of your mentioning your interest in the company the broker has on their screen all the prices that different market makers are willing to pay as well as all the prices at which they are willing to sell the shares – see **Exhibit 9.15** for an example of a screen.

It can be confusing and time consuming for the broker to look at all the prices to find the best current rates. Fortunately they do not have to do this as the screen displays a 'yellow strip' above the market makers' prices, which provides the identity of the market makers offering the best bid and offer prices (these are called touch prices). It is the price in the yellow strip that the broker will immediately report to you over the telephone. Market makers NMRA, WINS, MLSB and UBSW present the best price, at 37p, if you want to sell. There are four market makers offering 42p if you want to buy. So, your broker will tell you 37–42. If you were happy with 42p you would then instruct your broker to buy, say, 10,000 shares.

The screen shows that eight market makers are offering prices. The fact that there are a relatively large number of competing organisations willing to quote prices indicates that this is a fairly large company for SEAQ trading. Small companies may have only two or three market makers willing to display prices on SEAQ.

| Exhibit 9.14 | The SEAQ quote-driven system |

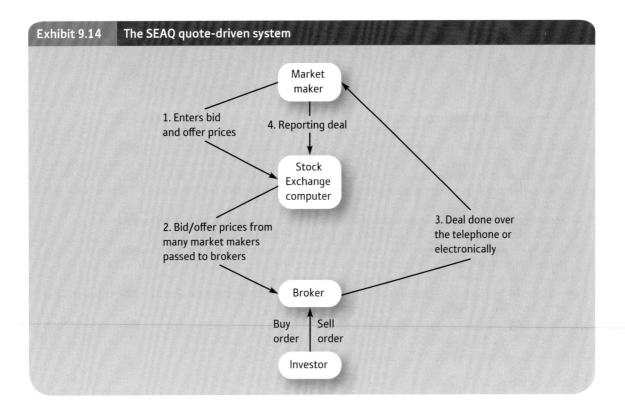

Market makers are obliged to deal (up to a certain number of shares defined by the Normal Market Size or Exchange Market Size at the price quoted, they are 'firm prices', but they have the freedom to adjust prices after deals are completed. Transactions may be completed by the broker speaking to the market maker on the telephone, but an increasing number of trades are completed electronically. All trades are reported to the exchange's central electronic computer and are disseminated to market participants (usually within three minutes) so that they are aware of the price at which recent trades were completed. Criticism of trading systems based on market makers quoting bid and offer prices focused on the size of the middleman's (the market maker's) margin led to the development of order-driven trading, where buyers trade with sellers at a single price so that there is no bid–offer spread. Most stock exchanges in the world now operate this type of system. These markets allow buy and sell orders to be entered on a central computer, and investors are automatically matched (they are sometimes called matched-bargain systems or order book trading). In 1997, the LSE introduced an order-driven service known as SETS (Stock Exchange Electronic Trading System) and I will use this as an example to explain how order-driven trading works.

| Exhibit 9.15 | A typical SEAQ screen |

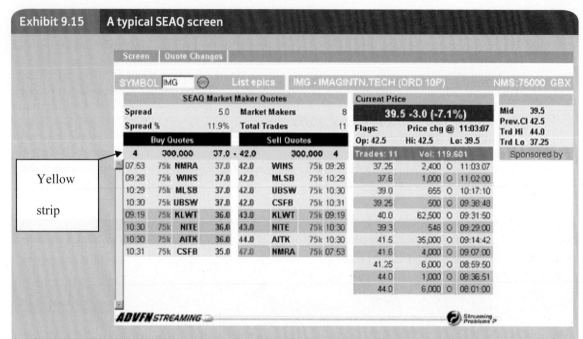

- **EPIC** or Symbol of "IMG" is the short 3 digit code/name for the company Imagination Technology.
- **NMS 75,000** The normal market size (NMS) for this stock is 75,000 shares. This is also called the **Exchange Market Size, EMS,** which is the minimum quote size at which market makers are obliged to trade. EMS is set by London Stock Exchange for each security at around 2% of the average daily trade (for SETS shares – see later – the EMS is 1% of average daily turnover).
- **Spread** This is the difference between bid and offer, in this case it is 5p or 11.9% of the share price.
- **Total Trades** is the total number of trades that have occurred so far today, there have been 11.
- **Current Price (MID) 39.5** This tells us what the current mid-price is. This is based on the middle price between the current bid and offer. The colour denotes the current mid-price compared with last night's close. Blue means up, Red means down and Green means no change.
- **− 3.0 (− 7.1 %)** This is a calculation based on the current mid-price compared to yesterday's closing price for this particular share. The mid-price is minus 3.0p, or −7.1% on the day so far.
- **Vol** Total number of shares that have traded today is 471,035.

Source: http://uk.advfn.com/Help/what-does-the-seaq-aim-window-show-59.html.

SETS

SETS electronic order book uses powerful computer systems to execute millions of trades a day in milliseconds for the shares in over 900 larger companies (including those on the Main Market and some big AIM firms). Traders (via brokers) enter the prices at which they are willing to buy or sell as well as the quantity of shares they want to trade. They can then wait for the market to move to the price they set as their limit. Alternatively they can instruct brokers to transact immediately at the best price currently available on the order book system. Trades are then executed by the system if there is a match between a buy order price and a sell order price. These prices are displayed anonymously to the entire market. An example of prices and quantities is shown in the lower half of **Exhibit 9.16** – a reproduction of a SETS screen as seen by brokers.

The buy orders are shown on the left and the sell orders on the right. So, we can observe for Lloyds Bank someone (or more than one person) has entered that they are willing to buy 100,000 shares at a maximum price of 69.92p (bottom line on screen). Someone else has entered that they would like to sell 6,930 shares at a minimum price of 70.53p. Clearly the computer cannot match these two orders and neither of these two investors will be able to trade. They will either have to adjust their limit prices or wait until the market moves in their favour.

As we travel up the screen we observe a closing of the gap between the prices buyers are willing to pay and the offering price of sellers. On the eighth line from the bottom we see that buyers want 36,060 shares at 70.17p whereas sellers are prepared to accept 70.20p for 87,116 shares. Now we are getting much closer to a match. Indeed, if we look above the yellow strip we can see the price where buyers and sellers were last matched – the 'last traded price' is 70.18p. These screens are available to market participants at all times and so they are able to judge where to pitch their price limits. For example, if I was a buyer of 5,000 shares entering the market I would not be inclined to offer more than 70.2p given the current state of supply and demand. However, if I was a seller of 5,000 shares I would recognise that the price offered would not have to fall below 70.17p to attract buyers. If I was a buyer of 110,000 shares rather than just 5,000 I have two options: I could set a maximum price of 70.2p, in which case I would transact for 87,116 immediately but would leave the other 22,884 unfilled order in the market hoping for a general market price decline; alternatively, I could set my limit at 70.44p, in which case I could transact with those investors prepared to sell at 70.2p, 70.23p, 70.43p and 70.44p. The unfilled orders of the sellers at 70.44p (118,170–110,000) are carried forward on SETS.

Exhibit 9.16   A typical SETS screen

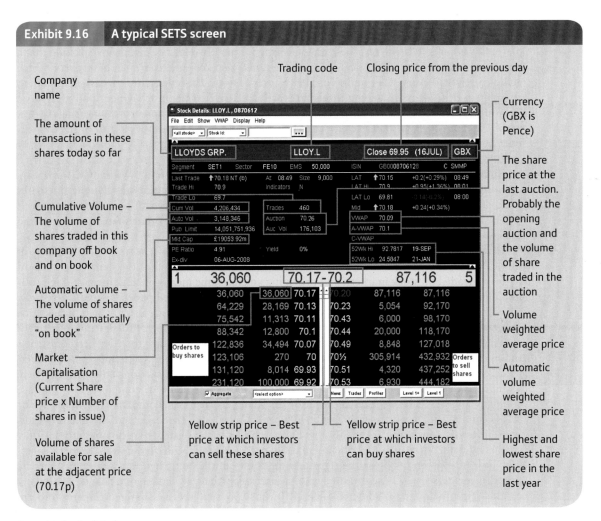

Source: London Stock Exchange.

Supporters of the older quote-driven system say that a major problem with the order-driven system is that there may be few or no shares offered at prices close to a market clearing rate and so little trade can take place. In other words, the market can be very illiquid. There may indeed be times when no sellers are posting sensible prices and other times when buyers are scarce. This is when the quote-driven system may be more liquid because market makers who make a book in a company's shares must continuously offer prices and are obliged to trade at the price shown (up to a certain quantity of shares). By way of counter-criticism, it is alleged there have been times when it has been difficult to contact market makers to trade at their displayed prices, even though in theory they are obliged to make themselves available to quote and trade at bid and offer prices throughout the trading day. To improve trading liquidity on SETS, in 2007 the system was modified so that market makers can now post prices on it. Thus it offers a continuous order book with automatic execution (via computer rather than market maker systems), but also has market makers providing continuous bid and offer prices for many shares (but these trades are executed through the automatic system). It is thought that by having the two systems combined there will be tighter bid–offer spreads, greater transparency of trades and improved liquidity.

Clearing and settlement

When a trade has been completed and reported to the exchange it is necessary to clear the trade. That is, the exchange ensures that all reports of the trade are reconciled to make sure all parties are in agreement as to the number and the price of shares traded. The exchange also checks that the buyer and seller have the cash and securities to do the deal. Also the company registrar is notified of the change in ownership. Later the transfer of ownership from seller to buyer has to take place; this is called settlement. These days clearing frequently does not just mean checking that a buyer and a seller agree on the deal; the clearing house also acts as a 'central counterparty' which acts as a buyer to every seller and as a seller to every buyer. This eliminates the risk of failure to complete a deal by guaranteeing that shares will be delivered against payment and vice versa. Clearing houses and central counterparties (CCPs in Europe, central counterparty clearing (CCCs) in the USA) provide an invaluable service – they execute and guarantee every aspect of the transaction. Instead of having to wait for cheque clearance, or for documents to be signed and arrive by post, traders set up accounts with clearing houses and CCPs, so that transactions can be carried out immediately, with the CCP absorbing any loss should either default. With a CCP, investors can also 'net' their trades, so that if one part of the investing institution has bought 1m shares while another has sold 1.5m, the trades are paired so that settlement is for only 500,000 shares.

The LSE recently moved to share settlement at T+2, which means that shares are transferred to new owners two working days after the trade takes place.

To facilitate settlement the CREST system is used. CREST acts as a central securities depository (CSD) enabling dematerialisation by keeping an electronic register of the shares and a record of shares traded on stock markets, and providing an electronic means of settlement and registration. This system is cheaper and quicker than the old one which used paper – ownership is now transferred with a few strokes on a keyboard. Under CREST shares are usually held in the name of a nominee company rather than in the name of the actual purchaser. Brokers and investment managers run these nominee accounts. Thus, when an investor trades, their broker holds their shares electronically in their (the broker's) nominee account and arranges settlement through their membership of the CREST system. This increases the speed of transactions enormously. There might be dozens of investors with shares held by a particular nominee company. The nominee company appears as the registered owner of the shares as far as the company (say, Sainsbury or BT) is concerned. Despite this, the beneficial owners receive all dividends and any sale proceeds. Some investors oppose the CREST system because under such a system they do not automatically receive annual reports and other documentation, such as an invitation to the annual general meeting. They also potentially lose the right to vote (after all, the company does not know who the beneficial owners are). Those investors who take seriously their ownership of a part of a company can insist on remaining outside of CREST. In this way they receive share certificates and are treated as the real owners of the business. This is more expensive when share dealing, but that is not a great concern for investors who trade infrequently.

There is a compromise position: personal membership of CREST. The investor is then both the legal owner and the beneficial owner of the shares, and also benefits from rapid (and cheap) electronic share settlement. The owner will be sent all company communications and retain voting rights. However, this is more expensive than the normal CREST accounts.

SETSqx

Trading on SETS is for companies whose trading is liquid, i.e. large companies with a high proportion of the shares held by a wide range of investors (a large free float), so there are plenty of shares traded each day.[8] There are other means of trading for less frequently traded shares. SETSqx

(Stock Exchange Electronic Trading Service – quotes and crosses) trades in Main Market (and a few AIM) shares which are less liquid and not traded on SETS. SETSqx combines order book technology (similar to the SETS method of trading) with the best of the LSE's existing quote-driven trading. On SETSqx a single market maker's quote can be displayed if a market maker is interested in quoting a price. (Ideally, the exchange would like many market makers quoting prices so that competition encourages keener prices for share owners.)

An investor wanting to trade with a market maker can do so in the normal way, but also can connect, usually via brokers, to the electronic system and put onto the system's screen display an order for shares stating a price at which they would like to trade, either to sell or to buy – particularly useful if there are no market makers in that share. If someone else on the system likes the displayed price, they can phone the originator and a deal is done.

This may still leave some orders for trades unexecuted (i.e. no one phones up and trades at the advertised price). To cope with this, or to trade shares anonymously, there are five auctions per day (at 08.00, 09.00, 11.00, 14.00 and 16.35) in which investors make bids and the system matches up buyers and sellers. In the first few minutes of the auction period traders can put in limit prices for buy or sell orders. They can keep withdrawing them or modifying them, while observing other limit prices, during this period. Then the computer moves to a new phase where it sets the prices at which trades will be automatically completed, informed by the most recent bids; a price permitting the maximum number of trades. Now all Main Market shares trade on either SETS or SETSqx.

The ownership of UK shares

The latest figures from the Office for National Statistics (ONS) give the ownership of UK shares from 1963 to 2016, and some dramatic changes can be seen – *see* **Exhibit 9.17**.

Individual investors used to dominate the market, holding 54% of UK quoted company shares in 1963. This sector showed a continuous gradual decline, falling to 10% in 2012. More recently it has picked up to reach 12.5% in 2016. The reason for the long-term decline was not just that individual investors became less interested in the stock market – not helped by the stock market downturns of 2000–2002 and 2007–2009 – but also the tendency to switch from direct investment to collective investment vehicles, such as unit trusts, or via insurance products or pension funds, where they gain benefits of diversification and skilled management. Unit trusts have been the big winners, growing in importance from 2% of UK shares in the 1980s to 9.5% today. Although the mode of investment has moved somewhat from direct to indirect, Britain remains a society with a deep interest in the stock market. Very few people are immune from the performance of the LSE. The vast majority of the UK population have a pension plan or endowment savings scheme, or a unit trust investment.

A major reason for the decline in the proportion held by UK individuals is the internationalization of financial markets. UK investors have diversified by buying more overseas shares, which they can now do very easily. More importantly for the ownership statistics of UK shares, has been the remarkable growth in the proportion held by investors from outside the UK: only 7% in 1963, but 53.9% in 2016. This increase partly reflects international mergers where the new company is listed in the UK. Take BHP Billiton for example: its origins are largely in Australia and so it has many investors there, and also attracts holders from a hundred other nations. Other foreign companies have floated their UK subsidiaries but retain a large shareholding.

The main factor influencing the rise in foreign ownership is the global phenomenon of the increased willingness to buy shares in overseas markets. It has become much easier for non-native individual and institutional investors to buy shares abroad, particularly in the UK, with its open equity markets, helped by electronic trading allowing long distance buying. Reinforcing that, we have lived through a remarkable time when the world, particularly the 'developing world', became wealthy at an amazingly fast rate. There are now hundreds of millions of investors in Asia for example, looking to save through share investing. Indeed, around 8% of UK shares are owned by Asians or their institutions. The greatest source of foreign investment comes from North

---

8 It trades FTSE 100, FTSE 250 and FTSE Small Cap constituents (see later) plus ETFs (*see* Chapter 1), liquid AIM and Irish company shares.

American investors, who account for half of overseas buyers. That is, roughly 26% of the value of all UK shares are owned by North American institutions or individual investors.

Large sovereign wealth funds are investing, say oil or gas money, in shares around the world. Qatar, for example, holds one-fifth of British Airways-owner International Airlines Group. The rising internationalisation of share ownership is not just manifest in the UK – for each of the following countries more than 30% of the domestic company shares are owned by overseas organisations: the Netherlands, Switzerland, Greece, Portugal, Poland, France, Norway, Sweden, Spain, Austria and Denmark.

UK insurance and pension funds used to dominate UK company share registers, with a combined 52% of listed UK shares in 1992. The tax-favoured status of pension funds made them a very attractive vehicle for savings, resulting in billions of pounds being put into them each year. However, in the last three decades they have been taking money out of UK quoted shares and placing it in other investments such as bonds, overseas shares and venture capital. They were prompted to reduce their high risk-exposure to UK equities, and so sought greater diversification and shifted more into 'safer' bonds, particular UK government bonds. Now the combined holding of insurance and pension funds is under 10% of UK shares.

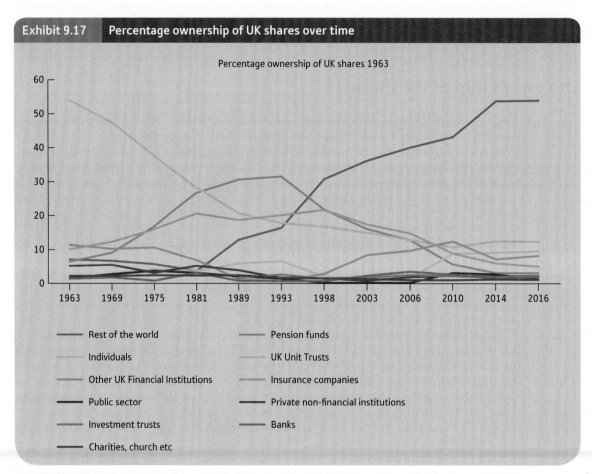

Exhibit 9.17   Percentage ownership of UK shares over time

Source: Office for National Statistics

'Chart that Tells a Story', 4 September 2015 (online version)

Regulation

Financial markets need high-quality regulation in order to induce investors to place their trust in them. There must be safeguards against unscrupulous and incompetent operators. There must be an orderly operation of the markets, fair dealing and integrity. However, the regulations must not be so restrictive as to stifle innovation and prevent the markets from being competitive internationally. London's financial markets have a unique blend of law, self-regulation and custom to regulate and supervise their members' activities.

The Financial Conduct Authority (FCA) oversees exchanges, conducts market surveillance and monitors transactions on many financial markets, covering:

- investor protection against wrong doing such as mis-selling, incompetence and fraud;
- market supervision and regulation;
- business conduct of banks and financial services, including approval of consumer-related managers and the supervision of investment managers and other firms;
- civil and criminal enforcement of market abuse rules, e.g. putting false information into the market to benefit from a rise or fall in a share price;
- UK Listing Authority – supervision of initial public offerings and subsequent monitoring of listed companies (*see* Chapter 10);
- Promoting effective competition in the interests of consumers;
- Helping people gain the knowledge, aptitude and skills to manage their financial affairs effectively by promoting public understanding of the financial system.

The Bank of England has the responsibility of ensuring the systemic safety of the banking system; that is, setting rules on capital and liquidity reserves (plenty of cash and near cash to cope with sudden outflows) for banks across the sector as a whole and imposing other rules to reduce the risk that the failure of one bank leads on to the failure of many. The Bank of England also has the Monetary Policy Committee to set interest rates and adjust the money supply.

The FCA can be described as semi-detached from government: it is financed by the industries it regulates, but its powers come from legislation; it often consults the financial services companies before deciding on principles, rules and codes of conduct, but it has basic principles approved by the government and it is answerable to the Treasury, which appoints its board, and through them to Parliament.[9]

With regard to the markets: the FCA supervises exchanges, conducts market surveillance and monitors transactions on nine Recognised Investment Exchanges (RIEs). The recognised exchanges work with the FCA to protect investors and maintain the integrity of markets. Much of the monitoring and enforcement is delegated to the RIEs – *see* Exhibit 9.18. The London Stock Exchange, LSE, for example, vets new stockbrokers and tries to ensure compliance with LSE rules, aimed at making sure members (e.g. market makers and brokers) act with the highest standards of integrity, fairness, transparency and efficiency. It monitors market makers' quotations and the price of actual trades to ensure compliance with its dealing rules. It is constantly on the lookout for patterns of trading that deviate from the norm with the aim of catching those misusing information (e.g. insider dealing), creating a false or misleading impression to the disadvantage of other investors or some other market-distorting action. The LSE in partnership with the FCA also requires companies to disseminate all information that could significantly affect their share prices.

Outside the FCA structure there are numerous ways in which the conduct of firms and financial institutions is put under scrutiny and constraint. The media keep a watchful stance – always looking to reveal stories of fraud, greed and incompetence. There is legislation prohibiting insider dealing, fraud and negligence. Companies Acts regulate the formation and conduct of companies and there are special Acts for building societies, insurance companies and unit trusts. The Competition and Markets Authority (CMA) attempts to prevent abuse of market power, such as monopoly pricing of goods. The Panel on Takeovers and Mergers determines the manner in which acquisitions are conducted for public companies (*see* Chapter 20). Accountants also function, to some extent, as regulators helping to ensure companies do not misrepresent their financial position. In addition any member of the public may access the accounts of any company easily and cheaply at Companies House (or via Companies House's website or the postal system). The Serious Fraud Office (SFO) investigates cases of serious or complex fraud.

---

9 For more on financial regulation consult Arnold (2012a).

Exhibit 9.18 **UK financial service industry regulation**

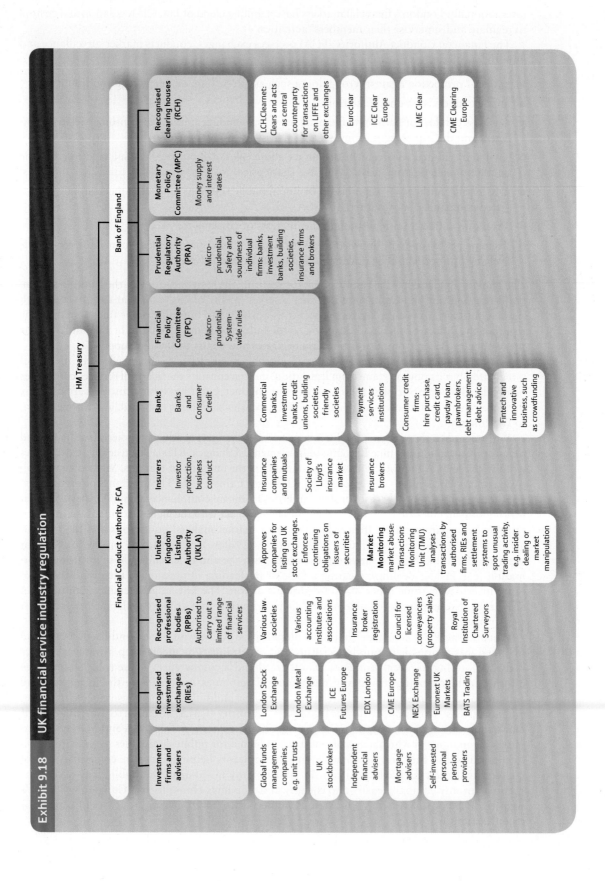

Understanding the figures in the financial pages

Financial managers and investors need to be aware of what is happening on the financial markets, how their shares are affected and which measures are used as key yardsticks in evaluating a company. The financial pages of the broadsheet newspapers, particularly the *Financial Times,* provide some important statistics on company share price performance and valuation ratios. These enable comparisons to be made between companies within the same sector and across sectors. **Exhibit 9.19** shows extracts from two issues of the *Financial Times.* The information provided in the Monday edition is different from that provided on the other days of the week.

Indices

Information on individual companies in isolation is less useful than information set in the context of the firm's peer group, or in comparison with quoted companies generally. For example, if Tesco's shares fall by 1 per cent on a particular day, an investor might be keen to learn whether the market as a whole rose or fell on that day, and by how much. The *Financial Times* (FT) joined forces with the Stock Exchange (SE) to create FTSE International which has taken over the calculation of a number of equity indices. These indicate the state of the market as a whole or selected sectors of the market and consist of 'baskets' of shares so that the value of that basket can be compared at different times. Senior managers are often highly sensitive to the relative performance of their company's share price. One reason for this is that their compensation package may be linked to the share price and in extreme circumstances managers are dismissed if they do not generate sufficiently high relative returns.

To calculate the indices shown in **Exhibit 9.20** each component share contributes to the index level. However, the shares do not have an equal weight in calculating the average. Rather, the average is derived by weighting each share by the size of the company; by its market capitalisation. Thus a 2 per cent movement in the share price of a large company has a greater effect on an index than a 2 per cent change in a small company's share price.[10] The characteristics of some of these indices are as follows.

- *FTSE 100* The 'Footsie™' index is based on the 100 largest companies with a premium listing (generally with over £4bn market capitalisation) which make up approximately 80% of the total market capitalisation of the LSEs Main Market. Large and relatively safe companies are referred to as 'blue chips'. This index has risen seven-fold since it was introduced at the beginning of 1984 at a value of 1,000. This is the measure most watched by investors. It is calculated in real time (every 15 seconds) and so changes can be observed throughout the day. The other international benchmarks are: for the USA, the Dow Jones Industrial average (DJIA) (30 share) index , the Standard & Poor's 500 index and the NASDAQ 100; for the Japanese market the Nikkei 225 index; for France the CAC-40; for Hong Kong the Hang Seng index; and for Germany the Xetra DAX index. For Europe as a whole there is FTSEurofirst 300 and Euro Stoxx 50 and for the world FTSE All-World.

- *FTSE All-Share* This index is the most representative in that it reflects the average movements of over 600 shares representing 98% of the value of the London market. This index is broken down into a number of industrial and commercial sectors, so that investors and companies can use sector-specific yardsticks, such as those for mining or chemicals. Companies in the FTSE All-Share index have market capitalisations (roughly) above £70m. It is an aggregation of the FTSE 100, FTSE 250 and the FTSE SmallCap.

- *FTSE 250* This index is based on 250 firms which are in the next size range after the top 100. Capitalisations are generally between £500m and £4bn. (It is also calculated with investment trusts excluded.)

- *FTSE 350* This index is based on the largest 350 quoted companies. It combines the FTSE 100 and the FTSE 250. This cohort of shares is also split into two to give high and low dividend yield groups. A second 350 index excludes investment trusts.

---

10 The weighting for some shares is reduced if a high proportion of the shares are held not in a free float but in the hands of people closely connected with the business, e.g. directors, major shareholders.

Exhibit 9.19

London Share Service Extracts: Aerospace and Defence

Wednesday Edition

Notes	Price	Chng	52 Week High	Low	Yld	P/E	Vol '000s
Aerospace & Defence							
AvonRub..†	259	−17.75	340	156	1	13	51
BAE Sys....	254	−6	372.90	241	7.1	7.4	19,439
Chemring.†	519	−9.50	740	470.30	2.4	10.8	557
Cobham...†	168.50	−4.50	247.40	167	3.7	12.4	3,109
Hampson...	9.43	+0.03	41	9.22	–	1.1	1,374
Meggitt...†	322.30	−8.10	400.90	124	3	13.4	16,880
RollsRyc.	571	−27	666.61	314.06	2.6	6.3	10,410
Senior.....†	137	−5.60	193.60	128.60	2.4	10.3	3,114
UltraElc...†	£15.32	+0.11	£19.03	£12.65	2.3	14.4	159
UMECO.....	310.75xd	−6.25	512.50	305.71	59	22.4	7

Monday Edition

Notes	Price	Wks% Chng	Div	Div Cov	Mcap £m	Last xd
Aerospace & Defence						
AvonRub.†	258	−2.0	2.50	8.0	87.6	10.8
BAE Sys....	267.30	−2.4	18	1.9	8,889.2	20.4
Chemring.†	528.50	+1.0	12.40-	3.9	1,025.5	13.7
Cobham...†	174.80	−2.6	6.17	2.2	1,912.9	4.5
Hampson...	9.50	−13.6	–	–	26.5	9.10
Meggitt...†	334.90	+5.7	9.55	2.5	2,603.0	10.8
RollsRyc.	595	−0.2	14.85	6.2	11,139.7	27.10
Senior.....†	144.50	+6.6	3.27	4.1	581.2	4.5
UltraElc...†	£15.05	+0.9	35.70	3.0	1,035.6	7.9
UMECO.....	319.25xd	+0.7	18.25	0.8	153.8	7.9

Annotations:

Price/earnings ratio (PER) – share price divided by the company's earnings (profits after tax) per share in the latest twelve-month period. A much examined and talked about measure

$$PER = \frac{\text{share price}}{\text{earnings per share}}$$

Market price – this is the mid-price (midway between the best buying and selling prices) quoted at 4.30 pm on the previous day

Change in closing price on day before (Tuesday) compared with previous trading day

The highest and lowest prices during the previous 52 weeks

Dividend yield – the dividend divided by the current share price expressed as a percentage

$$\frac{\text{dividend per share}}{\text{current share price}} \times 100$$

Volume of trade in those shares on the day

Share price change over the previous week

The dividend paid in the company's last full year – it is the cash payment in pence per share (after deduction of 10% tax for UK firms)

Dividend cover – profit after tax divided by the dividend payment, or earnings per share divided by dividend per share

$$\text{Dividend cover} = \frac{\text{earnings per share}}{\text{dividend per share}}$$

Market capitalisation is calculated by multiplying the number of shares by their market price

Ex-dividend date is the last date on which the share went ex-dividend (new buyers of the shares will not receive the recently announced dividend after this date) 17th August in this case

Exhibit 9.20

FTSE Actuaries Shares Indices

Produced in conjunction with the Institute and Faculty of Actuaries

	£ Strlg Jul 05	Day's chge%	Div yield%	P/E ratio	Total Return
FTSE 100 (100)	7367.80	0.14	3.81	29.11	6142.68
FTSE 250 (250)	19451.22	0.78	2.70	22.34	14124.09
FTSE 250 ex Inv Co (207)	20810.95	0.83	2.76	21.50	15417.53
FTSE 350 (350)	4084.25	0.25	3.62	27.67	6840.52
FTSE 350 ex Investment Trusts (306)	4049.56	0.25	3.66	27.57	3493.99
FTSE SmallCap (289)	5581.15	0.35	2.76	26.59	7994.94
FTSE SmallCap ex Inv Co (154)	4905.94	0.43	2.92	20.27	7390.35
FTSE All-Share (639)	4029.81	0.25	3.59	27.63	8824.08
FTSE All-Share ex Inv Co (460)	3973.84	0.25	3.65	27.37	3484.50
FTSE All-Share ex Multinationals (577)	1212.89	0.33	3.16	25.07	2172.91
FTSE Fledgling (97)	10019.79	0.18	2.96	24.16	18792.85
FTSE Fledgling ex Inv Co (47)	14128.80	0.35	3.94	13.09	25903.55
FTSE All-Small (386)	3883.84	0.34	2.77	26.46	7142.06
FTSE All-Small ex Inv Co Index (201)	3680.32	0.43	2.96	19.88	7024.39
FTSE AIM All-Share Index (804)	960.68	0.17	1.69	73.35	1057.58

Financial Times, 6 July 2017.

- **FTSE SmallCap** This index covers companies (289 of them in July 2017) included in the FTSE All-Share but excluded from the FTSE 350, with a market capitalisation of about £70m to £800m.

- **FTSE Fledgling** This includes companies listed on the Main Market but too small to be in the FTSE All-Share Index.

- **FTSE AIM All-Share** Index of all AIM companies (except those with a low free float and low liquidity).

- **FTSE All-small** Combines companies in FTSE SmallCap with those in the FTSE Fledgling (396 companies in July 2017).

The indices in the first column in Exhibit 9.20 are price indices only (share price movements only are reflected in the indices). The final column, 'Total return', shows the overall performance with both share price rises and dividends reinvested in the portfolio.

Taxation and corporate finance

Taxation impacts on financial decisions in at least three ways.

1 *Capital allowances* At one time it was possible for a firm to reduce its taxable profit by up to 100 per cent of the amount invested in certain fixed assets. So if a firm made a profit of £10m, and in the same year bought £10m worth of approved plant and equipment, HM Revenue and Customs would not charge any tax because the capital allowance of £10m could be subtracted from the profit to calculate taxable profit. The idea behind this generosity was to encourage investment and thus stimulate economic growth. Today, the type of expenditure subject to 100 per cent capital allowances is very restricted (to, for example energy saving investment and

some electric vehicles) and the capital allowance is generally 18 per cent of the value of the investment in the first year and 18 per cent on a declining balance for subsequent years. Capital allowances in project appraisal were discussed in Chapter 5.

2   *Selecting type of finance* The interest paid on borrowed capital can be used to reduce the taxable profit and thus lower the tax bill. On the other hand, payments to shareholders, such as dividends, cannot be used to reduce taxable profit. This bias against share capital may have some impact on the capital structure decision – *see* Chapter 18.

3   *Distribution of profit* UK Companies pay corporation tax on profits nine months after the end of the accounting period (except very large companies which pay quarterly instalments earlier than that). The profits are calculated after all costs have been deducted, including interest but excluding dividends. The proportion of taxable profit paid to the tax authorities is 19% of the profit

Standard-rate taxpayers (those with a marginal tax rate of 20% on normal income) are liable to pay 10% income tax on dividends, but the first £2,000 is tax free. The rate of income tax on dividends for higher rate taxpayers is 32.5%. The 10% rate is deemed to be paid by the company when it pays corporation tax. Therefore, standard-rate taxpayers do not have to pay tax on dividends received. The higher-rate taxpayer can offset the 10% tax paid against the total tax they are due to pay on dividends.

Concluding comments

Stock markets are major contributors to the well-being of a modern financially sophisticated society. They have great value to a wide variety of individuals and institutions. For savers they provide an environment in which savings can be invested in real productive assets to yield a return both to the saver and to society at large. The powerful pension and insurance funds rely on a well-regulated and broadly based stock exchange to enable the generation of income for their members. The mobilisation of savings for investment is a key benefit of a well-run exchange; so too is the improved allocation of scarce resources in society, and this results in a more beneficial mixture of goods and services being produced. The stock market has a part to play in directing investment to those parts of the economy which will generate the greatest level of utility for consumers. If people want cars rather than horse-drawn transport then savings will be directed to permit investment in factories and production lines for cars. If they demand smartphones rather than notebooks then tech firms supplying smartphones will find it easier to raise fresh finance than will the notebook firm.

Companies value stock markets for their capacity to absorb new issues of financial securities permitting firms to expand, innovate and produce wealth. Entrepreneurs can reap the rewards of their efforts by having access to a flourishing secondary share market and employees can be rewarded with shares which become more appealing because they can be quickly priced by looking at reports in the financial press. Managers often acknowledge the disciplinary benefits of a stock market which insists on high levels of information disclosure, integrity, competence and the upholding of shareholder interests. Governments are aware of the range of social benefits listed above and so should value an exchange on these grounds alone. However, they also see more direct advantages in a fit and proper market. For example, they are able to raise finance to cover the difference between taxes and expenditure, and they are able to tap the market in privatisations and thereby not only fill government coffers but encourage wider share ownership and allow the market to pressurise managers to run previously state-owned businesses in a more efficient manner.

Having gained some background knowledge of the workings of the London Stock Exchange, we now need to turn to the question of how equity funds are actually raised on the Main Market of the LSE and on AIM. The next chapter will examine this. It will also describe sources of equity finance available to firms which are not quoted.

Key points and concepts

- **Stock exchanges** are markets where government and industry can raise long-term capital and investors can buy and sell securities.

- **Two breakthroughs in the rise of capitalism**:
  - thriving secondary markets for securities;
  - limited liability.

- **Over 140 countries now have stock markets.** They have grown in significance due to:
  - disillusionment with planned economies;
  - recognition of the key role of stock markets in a liberal pro-market economic system in mobilising saving and allocating resources.

- The **largest** domestic stock markets are in the USA, Japan and China.

- **Electronic communication networks (ECNs)** or **multilateral trading facilities (MTFs)** are alternative trading venues for shares quoted on the major national stock exchanges of the USA and Europe.

- The **globalisation** of equity markets has been driven by:
  - deregulation;
  - technology;
  - institutionalisation.

- Companies **list on more than one exchange** for the following reasons:
  - to broaden the shareholder base and lower the cost of equity capital;
  - the domestic market is too small or the firm's growth is otherwise constrained;
  - to reward employees;
  - investors in particular markets may understand the firm better;
  - to raise awareness of the company;
  - to discipline the firm and learn to improve performance;
  - to understand better the economic, social and industrial changes occurring in major product markets.

- **A well-run stock exchange**:
  - allows a 'fair game' to take place;
  - is regulated to avoid negligence, fraud and other abuses;
  - allows transactions to take place cheaply;
  - has enough participants for efficient price setting and liquidity.

- **Benefits of a well-run stock exchange**:
  - firms can find funds and grow;
  - society can allocate capital better;
  - shareholders can sell speedily and cheaply. They can value their financial assets and diversify;
  - increase in status and publicity for firms;
  - mergers can be facilitated by having a quotation. The market in managerial control is assisted;
  - corporate behaviour can be improved.

- The **London Stock Exchange** regulates the trading of **equities** (domestic and international) and **debt instruments** (e.g. gilts, corporate bonds and Eurobonds, etc.) and **other financial instruments** (e.g. covered warrants, depositary receipts and preference shares).

- The **primary market** is where firms can raise finance by selling shares (or other securities) to investors.

- The **secondary market** is where existing securities are sold by one investor to another.

- **Internal funds** are generally the most important source of long-term capital for firms. **Bank borrowing** varies greatly and **new share or bond issues** account for a minority of the funds needed for corporate growth.

- LSE's **Main Market** is the most heavily regulated UK exchange.

- The **Alternative Investment Market (AIM)** is the lightly regulated exchange designed for small, young companies.

- NEX Exchange provides a share trading facility for companies, less costly than the LSE.

- Stock exchanges undertake most or all of the following **tasks** to play their role in a modern society:
  - supervise trading;
  - authorise market participants (e.g. brokers, market makers);
  - assist price formation;
  - clear and settle transactions;
  - regulate the admission of companies to and companies on the exchange;
  - disseminate information.

- A **quote-driven** share trading system is one in which **market makers** quote a bid and an offer price for shares. An **order-driven system** is one in which investors' buy and sell orders are matched without the intermediation of market makers.

▶

- The **ownership of quoted shares** has shifted from dominance by individual shareholders in the 1960s to dominance by institutions, many of which are from overseas.

- **High-quality regulation** generates confidence in the financial markets and encourages the flow of savings into investment.

- The **Financial Conduct Authority** is at the centre of UK financial regulation.

- **Dividend yield:**

$$\frac{\text{Dividend per share}}{\text{Share price}} \times 100$$

- **Price-earnings ratio (PER):**

$$\frac{\text{Share price}}{\text{Earnings per share}}$$

- Dividend cover:

$$\frac{\text{Earnings per share}}{\text{Dividend per share}}$$

- **Taxation** impacts on financial decisions in at least three ways:

  - capital allowances;
  - selecting type of finance;
  - corporation tax.

References and further reading

Arnold, G. (2014a) *The Financial Times Guide to Investing*. 3rd edn. Harlow: FT Prentice Hall.
   Contains more information on the financial markets.

Arnold, G. (2012a) *Modern Financial Markets and Institutions*. Harlow: FT Prentice Hall.
   Contains more on equity and other markets.

Arnold, G. (2012b) *The Financial Times Guide to Financial Markets*. Harlow: FT Prentice Hall.
   More on equity and other markets.

Credit Suisse Global Investment Returns Yearbook.
   An annual publication discussing returns on shares and other financial assets for leading exchanges over 117 years. www.credit-suisse.com/uk

London Stock Exchange Website.
   An excellent overview of the role and activities of the LSE. Great graphics and illustrations.

Office for National Statistics (2017) *Ownership of UK quoted shares 2016*. *www.ons.gov.uk*.
   The ONS is a great source of statistics – free on the Internet.

Case study recommendations

Please see www.pearsoned.co.uk/arnold for case study synopses. Also, another list of useful case studies from the fifth edition can be found there.

- The Bombay Stock Exchange: liquidity enhancement incentive programmes. Authors: Nupur Pavan Bang; Khemchand H. Sakaldeepi; Ramabhadran S. Thirumalai, Ivey Publishing. Available at www.cb.hbsp.harvard.edu

- Oriental fortune capital: building a better stock exchange. Authors: Josh Lerner; Keith Chi-ho Wong, Harvard Business School. Available at www.cb.hbsp.harvard.edu

- Melco Crown Entertainment: rolling the dice and other ways to raise capital. Authors: Stephen Sapp; Matthew Gray, Ivey Publishing. Available at www.cb.hbsp.harvard.edu

- Calpers' emerging equity in the markets principles. Authors: Robert G. Eccles; Aldo Sesia, Harvard Business School. Available at www.cb.hbsp.harvard.edu

Websites

ADVFN www.advfn.com
Companies House www.companieshouse.gov.uk
CREST ww.euroclear.com
Federation of European Securities Exchanges www.fese.eu
Financial Conduct Authority www.fca.org.uk
Financial Times www.ft.com
FTSE Russell www.ftserussell.com/
Investors Chronicle www.investorschronicle.co.uk
LCH Clearnet, www.lch.com
London Stock Exchange www.londonstockexchange.com
Morgan Stanley Capital www.msci.com
NASDAQ www.nasdaq.com
Euronext www.euronext.com
Office for National Statistics www.ons.gov.uk
NEX Exchanges www.nexexchange.com
World Federation of Exchanges www.world-exchanges.org

Video presentations

Chief executives and finance directors describe their current policy on raising funds on Merchant Cantos.com (video.merchantcantos.com) – this is free to view.

Self-review questions

1 Name the largest (by volume of share turnover on the secondary market) share exchanges in the USA, Europe and Asia.

2 What is a depositary receipt and why are they created?

3 Explain why finance has been 'globalised' over the past 30 years.

4 What are the characteristics of, and who benefits from, a well-run exchange?

5 What securities, other than shares, are traded on the London Stock Exchange?

6 Why is a healthy secondary market good for the primary share market?

7 Explain the acronyms AIM, SETS, SETSqx, RIE and FCA.

8 What is the most important source of long-term finance for companies generally?

9 Why has it been necessary to have more share exchanges than simply the Main Market of the London Stock Exchange in the UK?

10 Why is a nominated adviser appointed to a firm wishing to join AIM?

11 Why might you be more cautious about investing in a company listed on NEX Exchange, than a company on the Main Market of the London Stock Exchange?

12 What is CREST?

13 What have been the main trends in UK share ownership over the past 30 years?

14 Explain the following: FTSE 100, FT All-Share, FTSE Fledgling.

Questions and problems

1   'Stock markets are capitalist exploitative devices giving no benefit to ordinary people.' Write an essay countering this argument.

2   Describe what a badly run stock exchange would be like and explain how society would be poorer as a result.

3   Many countries, for example Peru and Germany, are encouraging small investors to buy quoted shares. Why are they doing this?

4   Explain why firms obtain a share listing in countries other than their own.

5   Describe the trading systems of the London Stock Exchange and outline the advantages and disadvantages of the alternative methods of trading shares.

6   In the USA some firms have bypassed the formal stock exchanges and have sold their shares directly to investors over the internet (e.g. Spring Street Brewing). What advantages are there to this method of raising funds compared with a regulated exchange? What are the disadvantages, for firms and shareholders?

7   Discuss some of the consequences you believe might follow from the shift in UK share ownership over the past 30 years.

8   Describe the network of controls and restraints on the UK financial system to prevent fraud, abuse, negligence, etc.

9   Frame-up plc is considering a flotation on the Official List of the London Stock Exchange. The managing director has asked you to produce a 1,000-word report explaining the advantages of such a move.

10 Collasus plc is quoted on the London Stock Exchange. It is a large conglomerate with factories and sales operations in every continent. Why might Collasus wish to consider obtaining additional quotations in other countries?

11 'The City is still far too clubby and gentlemanly. They are not rigorous enough in rooting out wrongdoing. What we need is an American type of system where the government takes a lead in setting all the detailed rules of behaviour.' Consider the advantages and disadvantages of a self-regulatory system so decried by this speaker.

Assignments

1   Carry out a comparative study in your firm (or any quoted firm) using information provided by the *Financial Times*. Compare PERs, dividend yields, dividend cover and other key factors, with a peer group of firms and the stock market as a whole. Try to explain the differences.

2   If your firm has made use of the stock market for any reason, put together a report to explain the benefits gained and some estimate of the costs of membership.

Raising equity capital

LEARNING OUTCOMES

By the end of this chapter the reader will have a firm grasp of the variety of methods of raising finance by selling shares and understand a number of the technical issues involved. More specifically the reader should be able to:

■ contrast equity finance with debt and preference shares;

■ explain the admission requirements and process for joining the Main Market of the London Stock Exchange and for the AIM;

■ describe the nature and practicalities of rights issues, scrip issues, vendor placings, open offers and warrants;

■ give an account of the options open to an unquoted firm wishing to raise external equity finance;

■ explain why some firms become disillusioned with quotation, and present balanced arguments describing the pros and cons of quotation.

Some firms are keen to float on a stock exchange . . .

Strix, the world leader in safety controls for kettles – switching them off when water is boiling – floated on the UK stock market in 2017. It sold 190m shares at £1 each. Its technology is in operation around 1bn times per day, stopping kettles boiling dry. The motivations for the float included enhancing its international profile with customers and suppliers; incentivising the managers and employees by offering share options for shares with a daily quoted market price; and providing permanent capital to enable the directors to invest in new products. But an additional very important reason was to provide its private equity backers with a way of cashing in on their investment – the money raised from stock market investors was mostly used to pay off investors who had helped it develop over the previous 12 years.

Some firms are desperate to leave a stock exchange . . .

Richard Branson, Alan Sugar and **Michael Dell** have demonstrated deep dissatisfaction with their companies' quotation. Sir Richard Branson first floated the Virgin Group in, then bought it back. Alan Sugar made plain his dislike of the City and its ways after his market experience with Amstrad. Michael Dell who started selling computers as a 19-year-old student, and now with a net worth of around $20bn, took his company off the stock market in 2013 by buying out other shareholders. He criticised the short-termist ethos of the public markets, arguing that only as a private company could Dell invest and grow. He also said that 20% of the time of a quoted company CEO's time was consumed by 'annoying' stock market related activity.

And some firms are content to raise equity finance without being quoted on an exchange

Innocent Drinks was started by three friends who met at Cambridge University. They developed other careers, but on a skiing holiday discussed starting a business together. 'In the summer of 1998 when we had developed our first smoothie recipes but were still nervous about giving up our proper jobs, we bought £500 worth of fruit, turned it into smoothies and sold them from a stall at a little music festival in London. We put up a big sign saying, "Do you think we should give up our jobs to make these smoothies?" and put out a bin saying "YES" and a bin saying "NO" and asked people to put the empty bottle in the right bin. At the end of the weekend the "YES" bin was full, so we went in the next day and resigned.' (Company website)

'After we left our jobs, we had no cash – just one month's salary each that we tried to eke out for two months. We each ran up debts of about £15,000 from overdrafts and credit cards. For the better part of 12 months, we had no income, then we started off on £15,000 a year. It took us four years before we were back to earning £40,000 – the same salary that we had left.' (Co-founder Richard Reed, interviewed in *Financial Times* 1 July 2011)

Eventually they secured £250,000 from US businessman Maurice Pinto for an 18% stake, with the remaining shares split between the founders. For the next decade they grew the business using retained earnings and bank borrowings.

However, the investment requirements needed to compete in the larger European market caused them to seek additional equity finance. In April 2009, for £30m, a 30% share stake was sold to Coca-Cola (later raised to 58%). Importantly, the founders retained operational control and a separate ethos. 'Coke have been the hands-off investor they promised to be. They've helped whenever we've asked, haven't interfered and have been great people to work with' (company website). Maurice Pinto, now in his seventies, saw this as the opportunity for him to realise the value he's helped create. The co-founders said: 'We're really happy for him.' He had taken a chance and made a lot of money. And all without the need for a stock market quotation.

Sources: Various *Financial Times* articles and company websites

Introduction

There are many ways of raising money by selling shares, and this chapter looks at the most important. It considers the processes that a firm would have to go through to gain a quotation on the Main Market of the London Stock Exchange (LSE) and raise fresh equity finance. We will examine the tasks and responsibilities of the various advisers and other professionals who assist a company like Strix to present itself to investors in a suitable fashion.

A firm wishing to become quoted may, in preference to the Main Market (Official List), choose to raise finance on the Alternative Investment Market (AIM), where the regulations and the costs are lower.

In addition to, or as an alternative to, a 'new issue' on a stock market, which usually involves raising finance by selling shares to a new group of shareholders, a company may make a rights issue, in which existing shareholders are invited to pay for new shares in proportion to their present holdings. This chapter explains the mechanics and technicalities of rights issues as well as some other methods, such as placings and open offers.

It is necessary to broaden our perspective beyond stock markets, to consider the equity finance-raising possibilities for firms which are not quoted on an exchange. There are over 3.6 million limited liability companies in the UK and less than 0.1% of them have shares traded on the recognised exchanges. For decades there has been a perceived financing gap for small- and medium-sized firms which has to a large extent been filled by the rapidly growing venture capital/private equity industry, which has supplied share and debt capital to thousands of companies on fast-growth trajectories.

Most companies are content to grow without the aid of either stock markets or venture capital. For example, J.C. Bamford (JCB) which manufactures earth-moving machines, has built a large, export award-winning company, without needing to bring in outside shareholders. This contentedness and absence of a burning desire to be quoted is reinforced by the stories which have emerged of companies which became disillusioned with being quoted. The pressures and strains of being quoted are considered by some (for example, Philip Green, owner of Arcadia (Burtons, Top Shop, etc.) and formally BHS) to be an excessively high price to pay for access to equity finance. So to round off this chapter we examine some of the arguments advanced against gaining a quotation and contrast these with the arguments a growing company might make for joining a market.

What is equity capital?

Ordinary shares

Ordinary shares represent the equity share capital of the firm. The holders of these securities share in the prosperity of a company. These investors, as owners of the firm, have the right to exercise control over the company. They can vote at shareholder meetings to determine such crucial matters as the composition of the team of directors. They can also approve or disapprove of major strategic and policy issues such as the type of activities that the firm might engage in, or the decision to merge with another firm. These ordinary shareholders have a right to receive a share of dividends distributed as well as, if the worst came to the worst, a right to share in the proceeds of a liquidation sale of the firm's assets, albeit after all other creditors such as banks, tax authorities, trade creditors, etc. have been paid. To exercise effective control over the firm the shareholders will need information; and while management are reluctant to put large amounts of commercially sensitive information useful to competitors into the public domain, they are required to make available to each shareholder a copy of the annual report and make timely formal announcements about key value-impacting events, such as a loss on the closing of a division.

There is no agreement between ordinary shareholders and the company that the investor will receive back the original capital invested. What ordinary shareholders receive depends on how well the company is managed. To regain invested funds an equity investor must either sell the shares to another investor (or in rare circumstances to the company – firms are allowed to repurchase their own shares under strict conditions) or force the company into liquidation, in which case all assets are sold and the proceeds distributed. Both courses of action may leave the investor with less than originally invested. There is a high degree of discretion left to the directors in proposing an annual or semi-annual dividend, and individual shareholders are often effectively powerless to influence the income from a share – not only because of the risk attached to the trading profits which generate the resources for a dividend, but also because of the relative power of directors in a firm with a disparate or divided shareholder body. If a shareholder owns 100 shares of a company with millions of shares in issue, there is little likelihood of this person exerting any influence; institutional shareholders who often own very large amounts of shares are able to bring more pressure to bear.

Debt

Debt is very different from equity finance. Usually the lenders to the firm have no official control; they are unable to vote at general meetings and therefore cannot choose directors and determine major strategic issues. However, there are circumstances in which lenders have significant influence.

For instance, they may insist that the company does not exceed certain liquidity or solvency ratio levels (*see* negative covenants in Chapter 11), or they may take a charge over a particular building as security for a loan, thus restricting the directors' freedom of action over the use and disposal of that building. Debt finance also contrasts with equity finance in that it usually requires regular cash outlays in the form of interest and the repayment of the capital sum. The firm will be obliged to maintain the repayment schedule through good years and bad or face the possibility of action being taken by the lender to recover their money by forcing the firm to sell assets or liquidate.

Disadvantages of ordinary shares for investors

The main disadvantage for investors holding ordinary shares compared to other securities is that they are the last in the queue to have their claims met. When the income for the year is being distributed others, such as debt holders and preference shareholders, get paid first. If there is a surplus after that, then ordinary shareholders may receive a dividend. Also when a company is wound up, employees, tax authorities, trade creditors and lenders all come before ordinary shareholders. Given these disadvantages there must be a very attractive feature to ordinary shares to induce individuals to purchase and keep them. The attraction is that if the company does well there are no limits to the size of the claim equity shareholders have on profit. There have been numerous instances of investors placing modest sums into the shares of young firms who find themselves millionaires. For example, if you had bought $1,000 shares in Facebook in 2007, your holding would now be worth millions.

Advantages and disadvantages of share issues

From the company's point of view there are two significant advantages of raising finance by selling shares rather than borrowing more:

1 *Usually there is no obligation to pay dividends* So when losses are made the company does not have the problem of finding money for a dividend. Equity acts as a kind of shock absorber.

2 *The capital does not have to be repaid* Shares do not have a redemption date, that is, a date when the original sum invested is repaid to the shareholder. The requirement to repay debt capital put into the business can put a severe strain on cash flow, to the point where there is a danger of the firm not being able to survive. By always having equity capital kept in the business it again acts as a shock absorber in bad times.

There are, however, disadvantages of this form of finance.

1 *High cost* The cost of issuing shares is usually higher than the cost of raising the same amount of money by obtaining additional loans. There are two types of cost. First, there are the direct costs of issue such as the costs of advice from an investment bank and/or broker, and the legal, accounting and prospectus costs, etc. These costs can absorb 5 to 25% of the amount of money raised. Secondly, and by far the most important, there is the cost represented by the return required to satisfy shareholders, which is greater than that on safer securities such as bonds issued by the firm. Equity holders demand a greater rate of return because they recognise that investing in a firm via equity is more risky because interest on debt is paid out before dividends are paid even if that means there is nothing left to pay the shareholders a dividend. Also, if the firm goes into liquidation, the holders of a debt type of financial security are paid back before shareholders receives anything. Thus, we say that debt holders 'rank' higher than equity holders for annual payouts and liquidation proceeds. (*See* Chapter 16 on cost of capital.)

2 *Loss of control* Entrepreneurs sometimes have a difficult choice to make – they need additional equity finance for the business and are unable to borrow more but dislike the notion of inviting external equity investors to buy shares. The choice is sometimes between slow/no growth or dilution of the entrepreneurs' control. External equity providers may impose conditions such as veto rights over important business decisions and the right to appoint a number of directors. In many instances, founders take the decision to forgo expansion in order to retain control.

3 *Dividends cannot be used to reduce taxable profit* Dividends are paid out of after-tax earnings, whereas interest payments on loans are tax deductible. This affects the relative costs to the company of financing by issuing interest-based securities and financing through ordinary shares. When a company pays interest the tax authorities regard this as a cost of doing business

and therefore it can be used to reduce the profit subject to tax. This lowers the effective cost to the firm of servicing the debt. Thus to the attractions of the low required return on debt we must add the benefit of tax deductibility. The effect of tax deductibility of interest is shown later in this chapter (in the section on preference shares).

Authorised, issued and par values

Until 2009, when the 2006 Companies Act came into force, the original shareholders decided the number of shares to be *authorised* (the authorised capital).[1] This is the maximum share capital the company can issue, unless shareholders vote to change the limit. Because most companies were formed before 2009 these rules remain in many company constitutions, although shareholders can now vote to abolish any such restriction. More recently established companies usually do not have a restriction, and directors may simply allot new shares, but the shareholders are entitled to impose an authorised total if they wish. In most cases firms do not issue up to the authorised amount specified. For example, Green plc has authorised capital of £5m, split between £1m of preference shares and £4m of ordinary shares. The company has issued all of the preference shares (at par) but the issued ordinary share capital is only £2.5m, leaving £1.5m as authorised but unissued ordinary share capital. This allows the directors to issue the remaining £1.5m of capital without being required to ask shareholders for further permission (subject to the rights issue or placing rules – see later in chapter).

Shares have a stated par value, say 25p or 5p. This nominal value usually bears no relation to the price at which the shares could be sold or their subsequent value. So let us assume Green has 10 million ordinary shares issued, each with a par value of 25p (£2.5m total nominal value divided by the nominal price per share, 25p = 10m shares); these were originally sold for £2 each, raising £20m, and the present market value is £3.80 per share.

The par value has no real significance[2] and for the most part can be ignored. However, a point of confusion can arise when one examines company accounts because issued share capital appears on the balance sheet at par value and so often seems pathetically small. This item has to be read in conjunction with the share premium account, which represents the difference between the price received by the company for the shares and the par value of those shares. Thus, in the case of Green the premium on each share was 200p − 25p = 175p. The total share premium in the balance sheet will be £17.5m.

Limited companies, plcs and listed companies

Limited liability means that the ordinary shareholders are only liable up to the amount they have invested or have promised to invest in purchasing shares. Lenders and other creditors are not able to turn to the ordinary shareholder should they find on a liquidation that the company, as a separate legal 'person', has insufficient assets to repay them in full. This contrasts with the position for a partner in a partnership who will be liable for all the debts of the business to the point where personal assets such as houses and cars can be seized to be sold to pay creditors.

Private companies, with the suffix 'Limited' or 'Ltd', are the most common form of company (over 95% of all UK companies). The less numerous, but more influential, form of company is a public limited company (or just public companies). These firms must display the suffix 'plc'. The private company has no minimum amount of share capital and there are restrictions on the type of purchaser who can be offered shares in the enterprise, whereas the plc has to have a minimum share capital of £50,000 paid up but is able to offer shares to a wide range of potential investors. Not all public companies are quoted on a stock market. This can be particularly confusing when the press talks about a firm 'going public' – it may have been a public limited company for years and has merely decided to 'come to the market' to obtain a quotation. Strictly speaking, the term

---

1 Note that not all businesses are incorporated, that is, set up as a separate legal 'person' with its own constitution (memorandum and articles of association), limited liability and ability to issue shares. Many businesses are set up in an unincorporated fashion, e.g. sole trader or partnership, in which one, two or more people share risks and profits. Each partner is liable for the debts and business actions of the others, to the full extent or his/her resources.

2 Except that it shows proportional voting and income rights.

'listed' should only be applied to those firms on the Official List (i.e. those accepted by the UK Listing Authority – most of which are on the Main Market of the London Stock Exchange) but the term is used rather loosely and shares on AIM are often referred to as being quoted or listed.

Preference shares

Preference shares usually offer their owners a fixed rate of dividend each year, unlike ordinary shares which offer no regular dividend. However, if the firm has insufficient profits the amount paid would be reduced, sometimes to zero. Thus, there is no guarantee that an annual income will be received, unlike with debt capital. The dividend on preference shares is paid before anything is paid out to ordinary shareholders – indeed, after the preference dividend obligation has been met there may be nothing left for ordinary shareholders. Preference shares are attractive to some invest-ors because they offer a regular income at a higher rate of return than that available on fixed interest securities, e.g. bonds. However, this higher return also comes with higher risk, as the preference dividend ranks after bond interest, and upon liquidation preference holders are further back in the queue as recipients of the proceeds of asset sell-offs.

Preference shareholders are not usually able to benefit from any extraordinarily good performance of the firm – any profits above expectations go to the ordinary shareholders. Also preference shares usually carry no voting rights, except if the dividend is in arrears or in the case of a liquidation (but some companies issue preference shares with the same voting rights are ordinary shares).

Advantages to the firm of preference share capital

1 *Dividend 'optional'* Preference dividends can be omitted for one or more years. This can give the directors more flexibility and a greater chance of surviving a downturn in trading. Although there may be no legal obligation to pay a dividend every year the financial community is likely to take a dim view of a firm which missed a dividend – this may have a deleterious effect on the ordinary share price as investors become nervous and sell (dividends cannot be paid to ordinary shareholders before preference dividend arrears are cleared).

2 *Influence over management* Preference shares are an additional source of capital which, because they do not (usually) confer voting rights, do not dilute the influence of the ordinary shareholders on the firm's direction. Thus, a family-run or small company wishing to raise shareholder capital may do so using preference shares, thereby retaining voting control.

3 *Extraordinary profits* The limits placed on the return to preference shareholders mean that the ordinary shareholders receive all the extraordinary profits when the firm is doing well (unless the preference shares are 'participating' – *see* below).

4 *Financial gearing considerations* There are limits to safe levels of borrowing. Preference shares are an alternative, if less effective, shock absorber to ordinary shares because of the possibility of avoiding the annual cash outflow due on dividends. In some circumstances a firm may be prevented from raising finance by borrowing as this increases the risk of financial distress (*see* Chapter 18), and the shareholders may be unwilling to provide more equity risk capital. If this firm is determined to grow by raising external finance, preference shares are one option.

Disadvantages to the firm of preference share capital

1 *High cost of capital* The higher risk attached to the annual returns and capital cause preference shareholders to demand a higher level of return than debt holders.

2 *Dividends are not tax deductible* Because preference shares are regarded as part of shareholders' funds the dividend is regarded as an appropriation of profits. Tax is payable on the firm's profit before the deduction of the preference dividend. In contrast, lender interest has to be paid whether or not a profit is made. This cost is regarded as a legitimate expense reducing taxable profit. In recent years preference shares have become a relatively unpopular method of raising finance because bonds and bank loans, rival types of long-term finance, have this tax advantage. This is illustrated by the example of companies A and B. Both firms have raised £1m, but

Company A sold bonds yielding 8%, Company B sold preference shares offering a dividend yield of 8%. (Here we assume the returns are identical for illustration purposes – in reality the return on preference shares will be a little higher than that on bonds.) *See* **Exhibit 10.1**.

Exhibit 10.1	The effect of the tax deductibility of interest and the non-tax deductibility of preference share dividends		
		Company A	**Company B**
Profits before tax, dividends and interest		200,000	200,000
Interest payable on bonds		80,000	0
Taxable profit		120,000	200,000
Tax payable @ 20% of taxable profit		24,000	40,000
		96,000	160,000
Preference dividend		0	80,000
Available for ordinary shareholders		96,000	80,000

Company A has a lower tax bill because its bond interest is used to reduce taxable profit, resulting in an extra £16,000 (£96,000 − £80,000) being available for the ordinary shareholders.

Types of preference shares

There are a number of variations on the theme of preference share. Here are some features which can be added:

- *Cumulative* If dividends are missed in any year the right to eventually receive a dividend is carried forward. These prior-year dividends have to be paid before any payout to ordinary shareholders.

- *Participating* As well as the fixed payment, the dividend may be increased if the company has high profits. (Usually the additional payment is a proportion of any ordinary dividend declared.)

- *Redeemable* These have a finite life, at the end of which the initial capital investment will be repaid. Irredeemables have no fixed redemption date.

- *Convertibles* These can be converted at the holder's request into ordinary shares at specific dates and on preset terms (for example, one ordinary share for every two preference shares). These shares often carry a lower yield (dividend as a proportion of share price) since there is the attraction of a potentially large capital gain.

- *Variable rate* A variable dividend is paid. The rate may be linked to general interest rates, e.g. LIBOR (*see* Chapter 11) or to some other variable factor.

Some unusual types of shares

In addition to ordinary shares and preference shares there are other, more unusual, types of shares.

1 **Non-voting shares** or **reduced voting shares** are sometimes issued by family-controlled firms which need additional equity finance but wish to avoid the diluting effects of an ordinary share issue. These shares are often called 'A' shares or 'B' shares (or N/V) and usually get the same dividends, and the same share of assets in a liquidation, as the ordinary shares. The issue of non-voting or reduced voting shares is contentious, with many saying that everyone who puts equity into a company should have a vote on how that money is spent: the 'one share one vote' principle. On the other hand, investors can buy 'non-voters' for less than 'voters' and thereby gain a higher dividend yield. Also, without the possibility of issuing non-voting shares, many companies would simply prefer to forgo expansion. Around one-third of Europe's largest businesses fail to observe the one share one vote principle. The Ford family own less than 2%

of the shares. However, when the motor company joined the NYSE in 1956 the family's shares were converted into a special class that guaranteed 40% of the voting power, no matter how many ordinary shares are in issue. When Google floated in 2004 Larry Page and Sergey Brin, the founders, held 'B' shares each with ten times as many votes per share as the 'A' shares issued to other investors – a dual-class share structure. Snap Inc (Snapchat) took things further in 2017 by issuing 200m 'A' shares at $17 without attaching any votes (the founders have the majority of votes through their C shares each with 10 votes; B shares, held by early investors, have one vote). In the UK there are a few companies with reduced voting rights, but Hong Kong is very strict, with Singapore currently deliberating the issue – *see* **Exhibit 10.2.**

2   **Deferred ordinary shares** rank lower than **ordinary shares** for an agreed rate of dividend, so in a poor year the ordinary holders might get their payment while deferred ordinary holders receive nothing, but in a good year the holders (often founders) may receive a large share of the profit Preferred ordinary shares usually rank ahead of ordinary shares for both income and capital but behind preference shares. Many have a right to a fixed dividend or share of profits.

3   **Golden shares** are shares with extraordinary special powers, for example the right to block a takeover. The UK government holds golden shares in a number of privatised firms, e.g. Rolls-Royce whose 'Special Share' bars it from selling 25% or more of its net assets or its nuclear division without consent; it also restricts foreign ownership to 15%. Golden shares are also useful if a company wishes to preserve certain characteristics it possesses such as a football club's golden share dictating that 80% of revenues from transfer fees be reinvested in new players.

Exhibit 10.2

Singapore weighs up dual-class shareholdings

By Jennifer Hughes

The city kicked off [a] debate . . . that could yet have as big a bearing on perceptions of the Lion City — that of introducing dual-class listings to the Singapore Exchange.

Proponents, led by bankers and lawyers, argue that dropping Singapore's one-share-one-vote rule would give it an edge in the region in attracting Asian stars like Alibaba and global headliners such as Manchester United. Both chose New York over Hong Kong and Singapore because the US was more receptive to their desire to weight voting rights in favour of small groups.

Both US exchanges have allowed dual-class shares since the 1980s when the New York Stock Exchange, faced with the threatened loss of such blue-chips as General Motors to Nasdaq, dropped its 60-year opposition to the practice. Today's opponents in Singapore argue that allowing more than one class of shares would start a race to the bottom among the region's exchanges. They contend that would exacerbate the governance problems inherent in sprawling family-run empires and state-owned groups.

"The SGX will look like a desperate dancer who hitches up their skirt at the end of the night to get attention," said David Smith, head of corporate governance for Aberdeen Asset Management in Asia. "The SGX is a commercial entity, I know. But many dual-class supporters do each transaction and move on. Investors are left holding the shares and I don't see why we should allow this."

Opponents of dual-class shares fear that Singapore's establishment will embrace the idea much as they have taken to fintech — making it harder to fight. As one investor put it: "What tycoon doesn't want cheap control of his company?"

Hong Kong just deliberated for two years on the same topic only to have its proposals shot down in short order by the regulator. If Singapore moved fast to implement new rules, it could steal a march since few in Hong Kong have the appetite to take up such a painful topic any time soon.

Singapore is expected to consider safeguards, such as each share class listing needing SGX approval, and sunset clauses to limit a family's control over generations.

The exchange has decided to consult more widely first. A quick process after that seems unlikely too, if the two-plus years taken by both New York and Hong Kong are any guide.

Floating on the Main Market (Official List)

To 'go public' and become a listed company is a major step for a firm; it is a major legal undertaking. The United Kingdom Listing Authority, UKLA (part of the Financial Conduct Authority) rigorously enforces a set of demanding rules and the directors will be put under the strain of new and greater responsibilities both at the time of flotation and in subsequent years. The UKLA is responsible for the approval of the prospectus, admission of companies to the Official List (most of which are on the Main Market of the London Stock Exchange) and enforcement of continuing obligations of company directors and their firms. The company is required to separately apply to the London Stock Exchange to have its securities admitted to trading. The LSE has its own set of admission and disclosure of information standards which are designed to sit alongside the UKLA's Listing Rules.

A new issue, can increase availability of equity finance to fund expansion and development programmes. It may also allow existing shareholders to sell a proportion of their investment and for employees to be rewarded through share reward schemes. In addition it can 'raise the profile' of a company both in the financial world and in its product markets, which may give it a competitive edge.

Prospectus

To create a stable market and encourage investors to place their money with companies the UKLA tries to reduce the risk of investing by ensuring that the firms obtaining a quotation abide by high standards. For example, the directors are required to prepare a detailed prospectus to inform potential shareholders about the company. This may contain far more information about the firm than it has previously dared to put into the public domain. Even without the stringent conditions laid down by the UKLA the firm has an interest in producing a stylish and informative prospectus. A successful flotation can depend on the prospectus acting as a marketing tool as the firm attempts to persuade investors to apply for shares.

The content and accuracy of this vital document is the responsibility of the directors, but they are assisted over the many weeks of its preparation by advisers – see later in the chapter. Contained within it must be three years of audited accounts, details of indebtedness and a statement as to the adequacy of working capital. Statements by experts are often required: valuers may be needed to confirm the current value of property, engineers to state the viability of processes or machinery and accountants to comment on the profit figures. All major contracts will be detailed and a description of the risks facing the firm provided. Any persons with a shareholding of more than 3% have to be named. A mass of operational data is required, ranging from an analysis of sales by geographic area and category of activity, to information on research and development and significant investments in other companies.

The Listing Rules state that the expected market value of the company's shares is to be at least £700,000 to allow for sufficient dealings to take place. However, this is an absurdly small number in this day and age. Given that the cost of advisers to the new issue will be at least £500,000 it is rarely worth floating on the Main Market unless the market capitalisation is at least £10m.

Conditions and responsibilities imposed

All companies obtaining a full listing must ensure that at least 25% of their share capital is in public hands, to ensure that the shares are capable of being traded actively on the market.[3] 'Public' generally means people or organisations not associated with the directors or major

---

3 If there is plenty of liquidity because, for example, the company is very large with hundreds of millions of shares and a wide range of shareholders the UKLA may, at its discretion, reduce the minimum free float – usually to around 20%.

shareholders. If a reasonably active secondary market is not established, trading may become stultified and the shares may become illiquid. Also, many crucial shareholder votes require a 75% majority and so allowing dominant owners more than 75% puts too much power in their hands.

Directors may find their room for discretion restricted when it comes to paying dividends. Stock market investors, particularly the major institutions, tend to demand regular dividends. Not only do they usually favour consistent cash flow, they also use dividend policy as a kind of barometer of corporate health (*see* Chapter 19). This can lead to pressure to maintain a growing dividend flow, which the unquoted firm may not experience.

There is also a loss of some privacy and autonomy, e.g. greater disclosure of directors' salaries and other remuneration. There are strict rules concerning the buying and selling of the company's shares by its own directors. The Criminal Justice Act 1993 and the Model Code for Director Dealings have to be followed. Directors are prevented from dealing for a minimum period (normally two months) prior to an announcement of regularly recurring information such as annual results. They are also forbidden to deal before the announcement of matters of an exceptional nature involving unpublished information which is potentially price sensitive. These rules also apply to any employee in possession of such information. When directors do buy or sell shares in their company they are required to disclose these dealings publicly.[4]

Suitability

The UKLA tries to ensure that the 'quality' of the company is sufficiently high to appeal to the investment community. The management team must have the necessary range and depth, and there must be a high degree of continuity and stability of management over recent years. Investors do not like to be over-reliant on the talents of one individual and so will expect a team of able directors and managers, including some non-executive directors and an appropriately qualified finance director.

The UKLA usually insists that a company has a track record (in the form of accounting figures) stretching back at least three years. This applies to companies that have a premium listing on the London Stock Exchange, the vast majority of listed companies. Recently, a standard listing regime has been introduced which does not necessarily require three years of figures and is far less tough on a number of other quality indicators and ongoing restraints, such as requiring shareholder approval for significant transactions. Given that few firms have opted for a standard listing we will concentrate on describing premium listings in the rest of the text.[5] It would seem that companies recognise the advantages of being under a regime of tight rules because the greater reassurance of public disclosure of information and scrupulousness encourages investors to buy and hold, and so firms generally stick with premium listings.

Companies at the forefront of innovative research and product development can be admitted to the techMARK or techMARK Medisceience (sub-sets of the Main Market), with only one year of accounts.

Another suitability factor is the timing of the flotation because investors often desire stability, a reasonable spread of activities and evidence of potential growth in the core business; if the underlying product market served by the firm is going through a turbulent period it may be wise to delay the flotation until investors can be reassured about long-run viability.

---

4 This disclosure rule applies to the buying and selling of financial instruments that derive their value from share price movements such as contracts for difference (see *The Financial Times Guide to Investing* (Arnold (2014a)) for a description).

5 In 2013 the LSE went even further and introduced 'Admission via the High Growth Segment'. This requires only 10% of the shares to be in free float (minimum £30m). It is even more lightly regulated. Again few, if any, companies are queuing at the door to join this.

The issuing process

The issuing process involves a number of specialist advisers. The process is summarised in Exhibit 10.3.

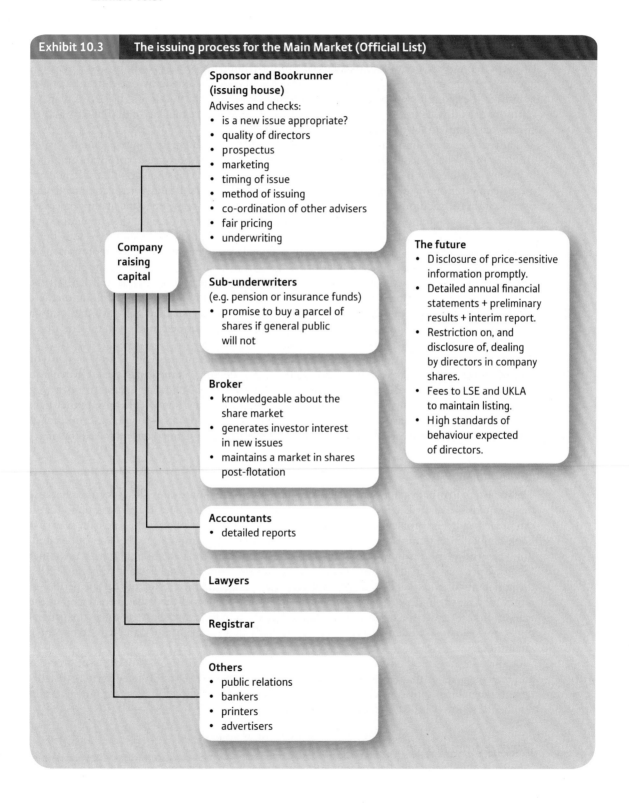

Exhibit 10.3   The issuing process for the Main Market (Official List)

Company raising capital

Sponsor and Bookrunner (issuing house)
Advises and checks:
- is a new issue appropriate?
- quality of directors
- prospectus
- marketing
- timing of issue
- method of issuing
- co-ordination of other advisers
- fair pricing
- underwriting

Sub-underwriters
(e.g. pension or insurance funds)
- promise to buy a parcel of shares if general public will not

Broker
- knowledgeable about the share market
- generates investor interest in new issues
- maintains a market in shares post-flotation

Accountants
- detailed reports

Lawyers

Registrar

Others
- public relations
- bankers
- printers
- advertisers

The future
- Disclosure of price-sensitive information promptly.
- Detailed annual financial statements + preliminary results + interim report.
- Restriction on, and disclosure of, dealing by directors in company shares.
- Fees to LSE and UKLA to maintain listing.
- High standards of behaviour expected of directors.

The sponsor and bookrunner

Given the vast range of matters directors consider in order to gain a place on the Official List it is clear that experts are required to guide firms through the complexities. The key adviser in a flotation is the sponsor. This may be an investment bank, stockbroker or other professional adviser. Directors, particularly of small companies, often first seek advice from their existing professional advisers, for example accountants and lawyers. But their expertise will probably need to be supplemented with specialist sponsoring organisations, those with the approval of the UKLA – (see www.fca.org.uk/markets/ukla/sponsor-regime/list or a list of approved sponsors). Sponsors are chosen with care as the relationship is likely to be a lengthy one during the tense months of the floatation process, and often continues long after the flotation. The UKLA requires sponsors to certify that a company has complied with all the regulatory requirements and to ensure that all necessary documentation is filed on time.

The sponsor (sometimes called the issuing house) will first examine the company and the aspirations of the management team to assess whether flotation is an appropriate corporate ambition by taking into account its structure, strategy and capital needs. The sponsor will also comment on the composition of the board and the calibre of the directors. It may even recommend supplementation with additional directors if the existing team do not come up to the quality expected. Sponsors can be quite forceful in this because they do not want to damage their reputation by bringing a poorly managed company to market. The sponsor will draw up a timetable – sometimes the planning period for a successful flotation may extend over two years, but a few months is more usual. There are various methods of floating, ranging from a placing to an offer to the public, and the sponsor will advise on the most appropriate. Another important function is to help draft the prospectus and provide input to the marketing strategy. Throughout the process of flotation there will be many other professional advisers involved and it is vital that their activities mesh into a coherent whole. It is the sponsor's responsibility to co-ordinate the activities of all the other professional advisers.

Bookrunners, often part of the sponsoring organisation but can be other investment banks or brokers, assist with selling the shares. They do this by conducting detailed analytical research into the company and then contacting dozens of investing institutions. Following a series of marketing presentations they build up an 'order book' of demand for the new shares. The insight they gain from conversations with institutions, including explicit messages of intent to purchase, mean they can help a company price its shares as well as go direct to the confirmed buyers to sell them.

Paying underwriters

The sponsor will usually underwrite the issue, guaranteeing the share sale. This is required because the company is usually keen to have certainty that it will receive money from the issue so that it can plan ahead. The problem of not selling all of the shares is lessened if the sale is by way of a book-building programme because the price can be adjusted in response to the level of demand. But when the method is by what is called an offer for sale to the general public with the issuer fixing the price early on in the process there can be doubt about the final demand, especially given the possibility of a market downturn between price-setting and the closing of the sale period. In return for a fee the underwriter guarantees to buy the proportion of the issue not taken up by the market. In most cases the underwriters do not have to purchase any shares because the general public are keen to take them up. However, occasionally they receive a shock and have to buy large quantities.

An investment bank sponsoring the issue will usually charge a fee of 2–4% of the issue proceeds and then pay part of that fee, say 1.25–3.0% of the issue proceeds, to sub-underwriters (usually large financial institutions such as pension funds and banks) who each agree to buy a certain number of shares if called on to do so.

The corporate broker

When a broker is employed as a sponsor/bookrunner the roles can be combined. If the sponsor is, say, an investment bank the UKLA requires that a broker is also appointed. However, most investment banks also have corporate broking arms and so can take on both roles. Brokers advise on share market conditions and the likely demand from investors for the company's shares. They also represent the company to investors to try to generate interest. When debating issues such as the method to be employed, the marketing strategy, the size of the issue, the timing or the pricing of the shares the company may value the market knowledge the broker has to offer. Brokers can also organise sub-underwriting. In the years following flotation the company's corporate broker may work with it to manage relations with the market, i.e. communicating with analysts, investors, the LSE, media, etc., by say organising investor-director meetings and collating feedback from investors. The broker will also advise on regulations to be abided by, and counsel on corporate transactions such as a merger with another firm or rights issues. A broker can be a useful sounding board for corporate strategy ideas and the establishment of a dividend policy. Market intelligence on share price movements, macroeconomic events and market themes and moods is another useful service.

Accountant

The reporting accountant in a flotation has to be different from the company's existing auditors, but can be a separate team in the same firm.

The accountant will be asked by the sponsor to prepare a detailed report on the firm's financial controls, track record, financing and forecasts (the 'long form' report). Not all of this information will be included in the prospectus but it does serve to reassure the sponsor that the company is suitable for flotation. Accountants may also have a role in tax planning from both the company's viewpoint and that of its shareholders. They also investigate working capital requirements. The UKLA insists that companies show they have enough working capital for current needs and for at least the next 12 months.

Lawyers

All legal requirements in the flotation preparation and in the information displayed in the prospectus must be complied with. Examples of other legal issues are directors' contracts, changes to the company's articles of association, re-registering the company as a plc, underwriting agreements and share option schemes. Lawyers also prepare the 'verification' questions which are used to confirm that every statement in the prospectus can be justified as fact. Directors bear the ultimate responsibility for the truthfulness of the documents.

Registrars

The record on the ownership of shares is maintained by registrars as shares are bought and sold; they keep the company's register and issue certificates. There are about two dozen major registrars linked up to CREST through which they are required to electronically adjust records of ownership of company shares within two hours of a trade.

After flotation

The UKLA insists on listed companies having 'continuing obligations'. One of these is that all price-sensitive information is given to the market as soon as possible and that there is 'full and accurate disclosure' to all investors at the same time. Information is price sensitive if it might influence the share price or the trading in the shares. Investors need to be sure that they are not disadvantaged by market distortions caused by some participants having the benefit of superior information. Public announcements will be required in a number of instances, for example: the development of major new products; the signing of major contracts; details of an acquisition; a sale of large assets; a change in directors or a decision to pay a dividend. Most free financial websites show major announcements made by companies going back many years.

Listed companies are also required to provide detailed financial statements in limited time frames. The full audited report and accounts for Main Market companies have to be available within four months of the year-end (six months for AIM companies). Firms usually choose to make preliminary profit announcements based on unaudited results for the year a few weeks before the audited results are published. Interim reports for the first half of each accounting year are also required (within three months). The penalty for non-compliance is suspension from the Exchange.

Other ongoing obligations include the need to inform the market about director dealings in the company's shares. The UKLA and the Exchange also encourage high standards of corporate governance, some of which are contained in the UK Corporate Governance Code (*see* Chapter 1). While these standards of behaviour are encouraged they are not required by the UKLA. However, if a company does not comply it must explain why not in the annual reports.

New issue statistics

The number of companies joining the Main Market and AIM varies from one year to the next; but as **Exhibit 10.4** shows, the numbers are considerable. Note that the AIM generally attracts more companies than the Main Market. The average amount raised by new issues is usually in the range £70m to £150m for the Main Market companies. For AIM the range is generally £10m to £22m.

Exhibit 10.4	Equity finance raised by companies through the new issue market for the Main Market and AIM					
Year	Main Market number	Main Market money raised (£m)	Main Market average (£m)	AIM number	AIM money raised (£m)	AIM average (£m)
2006	82	9,088	111	462	9,944	22
2007	73	7,613	104	284	6,581	23
2008	53	3,110	59	114	1,108	10
2009	17	458	27	36	740	21
2010	57	6,998	123	102	1,201	12
2011	21	9,240	440	90	614	7
2012	26	1,879	72	73	712	10
2013	33	7,894	239	99	1,191	12
2014	57	9,497	167	118	2,604	22
2015	68	6,846	101	61	1,240	20
2016	41	3,526	86	64	1,104	17
2017	64	5,280	83	80	1,586	20

The numbers for AIM include international companies whereas the numbers for the Main Market are for UK companies only.

Source: *London Stock Exchange*: www.londonstockexchange.com.

The new issue process

Thirty years ago the most common method of new issue was the offer for sale, in which the company sponsor offers shares to the public by inviting subscriptions from institutional and individual investors. Normally the shares are offered at a fixed price determined by the company's directors and their financial advisers.

But by far the most popular today is the cheaper placing method via a book-building process. In a placing, shares are offered to the public but the term 'public' is narrowly defined. Instead of engaging in advertising to the population at large, the sponsor or broker handling the issue sells the shares to institutions it is in contact with, such as pension and insurance funds. There are lower publicity costs and legal costs than with an offer for sale. A drawback of this method is that the spread of shareholders is going to be more limited. To alleviate this problem the Stock Exchange does insist on a large number of placees holding shares after the new issue.

Because of its current dominance we'll examine the placing with book building in some detail.

The start of the listing process

There is a pre-float preparation period, usually 12–24 weeks before admission to the Official List and trading on LSE, in which advisers are appointed, broad outlines on the procedure and object-ives of the float are discussed, and a timetable is agreed. Even at this early stage the UKLA is contacted and briefed on the plan.

Four to twelve weeks before admission

The accountant's long-form report is prepared and there is an initial consideration of the price of the shares, with the sponsor and broker having input. Draft documents are submitted to the UKLA, which raises questions to be answered by the directors. At an initial meeting with the LSE the business is described and ideas are developed on how to ensure an active market in the shares after the float. A draft prospectus is worked on by advisers and company managers. The sponsor and other advisers conduct a thorough check on the company and its performance, assets, etc., as well as a check of the facts stated in any flotation related document – a process called due diligence.

Later, there might be some 'pilot fishing', i.e. initial confidential meetings between the bookrun-ner and a small number of potential investors to obtain feedback on the likely market reaction and acceptable valuation of the company. This also helps to build relations with key potential investors.

Four to two weeks before admission

A big day is the Announcing the Intention to Float Day (AITF) which is the formal start of public marketing. The announcement will contain a summary of the company's investment case. A num-ber of meetings with media organisations follow to gain positive publicity. Bookrunners publish their notes on the company. This can be accompanied by a pathfinder prospectus which is a detailed description of the company, but does not state the price of the shares.

The AITF fires the starting gun on what is normally a two-week process of investor education. The bookrunner and equity sales people of the sponsor and other financial institutions assisting the sale engage in conversations with investing clients. These meetings can be in various regions, or for larger offers in a number of countries. Feedback is collated, presentation of the investment case improved, and pricing considered with the views of institutional investors having a strong impact.

Management Roadshow – just over two weeks to go

A management team from the floating company, usually the chief executive and the chief financial officer, meet potential investors usually over a two-week period. They explain the business, the investment and the rationale for the placing. Again, these meetings can be held in various regions or countries.

Pricing the offer

Bookrunners and senior company managers would have selected a price range for discussion before institutions have even met the directors at a roadshow. The range is likely to be quite wide, with the bottom price designed to hook investors' interest and the upper bound an ambitious aspiration. Orders from investors are taken during the management roadshow period. Investors may make different types of order. For example, some might set a price limit, refusing to buy any above that; others might make an unlimited order, i.e. with no price limit; yet others select stepped orders throughout the price range (precise amounts they will buy at different prices). At the end of the management roadshow bookrunners, company and major existing shareholders agree the price.

This will be designed to balance the desire to maximize the amount raised against the need to gain a strong group of committed shareholders (not dumping their shares at the first opportunity).

Completion meeting, impact day and the float

The key documents are presented in their final form at the company's completion meeting with advisers. The day after the completion meeting is called impact day, when the availability of the full prospectus is advertised and the listing is officially announced. The documents are sent to the UKLA for approval and formal application to trade on LSE is made. Usually, two days after impact day the shares are exchanged for cash and are traded on the market. The float is complete.

A retail offering

In a few (very few these days) instances the share offer is made to the general public, rather than just those institutions contacted by the bookrunner – an offer for sale. The LSE refers to this method as an initial public offering, IPO. But others use the term initial public offering to include any act of offering shares on a public stock exchange, including placings using a bookrunner. With a retail offer the price is normally the same as for the institutions, but occasionally a discount is offered, e.g. when a government in privatising a company it previous controlled it might want to encourage the wider population to hold shares and therefore offers say a 5% discount on the price charged to the institutions.

The greater complexity and cost of the retail offer can be worthwhile for some companies because they might be able to drum up a lot of demand from small investors and thereby push up the price, e.g. if they have a widely-recognised brand or strong customer loyalty. Private investors might buy the shares by filling in application forms or through a device known as an intermediaries offer; here the shares are offered for sale to financial institutions such as stockbrokers, and clients of these intermediaries can then apply to buy shares from them.

Other methods of floating

Introduction

Introductions do not raise any new money for the company. If the company's shares are already quoted on another stock exchange or there is a wide spread of shareholders, with more than 25% of the shares in public hands, the Exchange permits a company to be 'introduced' to the market. This method may allow companies trading on AIM to move up to the Main Market or for foreign corporations to gain a London listing. This is the cheapest method of flotation since there are no underwriting costs and relatively small advertising expenditures.

Reverse takeover

Sometimes a larger unquoted company makes a deal with a smaller quoted company whereby the smaller company 'takes over' the larger firm by swapping newly created shares in itself for the shares in the unquoted firm currently held by its owners. Because the quoted firm creates and issues more new shares in itself than it had to start with the unquoted firm's shareholders end up with the majority of the shares in the newly merged entity. They therefore now control a quoted company. The only task remaining is to decide on a name for the company – frequently the name of the previously unquoted company is chosen. A reverse takeover is a way for a company to gain a listing/quotation without the hassle of an official new issue.

In 2017 Escape Hunt gained a quotation through a reverse takeover (see **Exhibit 10.5**). Before the deal Dorcester plc had 10m shares. It created another 10.26m shares to buy out the shares in Escape Hunt. Following this the holders of the new shares in Dorcester had 51.2% of its ordinary shares. Escape Hunt's CEO, Richard Harpham became CEO of Dorcester which quickly changed its name to Escape Hunt. Other senior managers were drawn from the ranks of Escape Hunt's old hands.

Exhibit 10.5

'Escape room' gaming group set to float on Aim

By Chloe Cornish

Escape Hunt is set to become the first "escape room" company to list on the London Stock Exchange next month, ...The immersive gaming phenomenon, where players solve puzzles and crack codes in order to break out of locked rooms within a set time limit, has struck a chord with punters eager for unique experiences, and serves as a novel team-building activity. Some companies have even trapped candidates in the rooms as part of their recruitment processes. Escape Hunt, the biggest chain in the nascent market, is set to float through a reverse takeover by Dorcaster.

Founded in Bangkok by entrepreneur Paul Bartosik in 2013, Escape Hunt comprises 214 escape rooms in 28 franchises from Hyderabad to Dallas. Pre-tax profits are still small, at £400,000 in 2016 . . . Escape Hunt has no sites in the UK and is planning to open eight by the end of the year.

 Financial Times, 30 April 2017.

How does an AIM flotation differ from one on the Official List?

AIM's rules are kept as relaxed as possible to encourage a wide variety of companies to join and keep costs of membership and capital raising reasonably low. However, it is felt necessary to have some vetting process for firms wishing to float on AIM. This policing role is given to nominated advisers, Nomads, who are paid a fee by the company to act as an unofficial 'sponsor' in investigating and verifying its financial health. When the cost of the nominated advisers' time is added to those of the Stock Exchange fees, underwriters, accountants, lawyers, printers and so on, the (administrative) cost of capital raising are typically 9–10%, but can be as much as 30% of the amount being raised. AIM was designed so that the minimum cost of joining was in the region of £40,000–£50,000, but that is very out of date. It has now risen so that frequently more than £500,000 is paid. Most of the additional cost is for raising funds by selling shares rather than just joining AIM, which costs about £100,000 to £200,000, for professional help from nomads, brokers, etc. The nominated advisers' fees have risen because they now incur more investigatory costs due to the emphasis put on their policing role by the Stock Exchange. The cost of flotation on AIM (or the Main Market) varies significantly depending on the nature of the company and whether new capital is being raised, but a 'typical' breakdown for a company raising finance by selling shares (and therefore paying underwriters) might be as set out in **Exhibit 10.6**.

Exhibit 10.6	Typical costs associated with an AIM and Main Market company selling shares worth £20m

	£
Underwriters	400,000–1m
Financial advisers	200,000–400,000
Legal expenses	200,000–400,000
Accounting	100,000–300,000
Listing fees	<30,000
Printing, public relations, etc.	<100,000
	1,030,000–2,230,000

Companies floating on AIM need to be public limited companies and have accounts conforming to UK and other recognised international accounting standards. They need to produce an **AIM admission document**, but this is a little less detailed than the prospectus for a Main Market quotation and therefore cheaper.

There are a few savings by being on AIM rather than the Main Market; for example Main Market companies often complain that they are required to obtain shareholder approval for taking over another company[6] if the target is more than one-quarter its size. Issuing letters and accompanying information often costs over £100,000 on each occasion. The burden is lessened on AIM because a company only has to consult shareholders when it doubles in size through acquisition. Nevertheless, many AIM companies say they spend between £100,000 and £220,000 each year to belong to AIM, including fees for nomads, brokers, non-executive directors and more detailed audits – see **Exhibit 10.7**.

Exhibit 10.7

Anxious? Dreaming of a better life? You must be on Aim

By Andrew Bounds

Britain's small listed businesses are on the couch. They are fretful despite the growing economy, according to BDO and the Quoted Companies Alliance, the lobby group for small and mid-caps.

One nagging worry is the rising cost of being on the market at all. It is about £220,000 a year ... according to the survey. An auditor is about £85,000, stockbroker/nominated adviser £46,000, with investor relations and financial PR roughly £40,000 and £15,000 for the annual report and AGM.

Despite the "premium of membership", many companies do not tap the markets very often, the research finds. Just over half of quoted companies say the ability to access capital was the best reason to list.

However, of the companies surveyed only 43 per cent intend to raise any capital over the next 12 months and, of these, only 44 per cent would use the equity markets. Business would need £2m of benefits to make a listing worthwhile, BDO believes.

So what do they get out of it? Nearly a third consider the added cachet of being a quoted company added to their visibility and profile with customers and suppliers whereas 23 per cent wanted to attract and reward employees with shares.

Tim Ward, chief executive of the Quoted Companies Alliance, says: "It is a cost of capital and of being transparent." Mr Knight says many companies won overseas business because they were listed and therefore trusted. "It is a Kitemark."

Some of the 1,000 surveyed are also dreaming of bigger things. A fifth intended to move to the main market in the future. Some 4 per cent (about 40) expect to do so within the next couple of years.

It is a fantasy. Last year just six switched, with only 86 over the past 15 years. Although the top 25 Aim companies would fit within the FTSE 250 (requiring a market capitalisation of about £400m), attracting tracker funds, many do not move. Some 38 per cent said the reason was tax incentives for Aim shares. While the flotation fervour has faded, Mr Knight says investors are still hungry for secondary fundraisings. "They want to back trusted management teams that have delivered before."

Aim has been busier than the main market. Since 1998, it has had 1,777 new listings, compared with 561 on the international and main markets. There have been four times the number of cash calls [e.g. selling more shares] (8,573 compared to 2,188). In February alone, there were 42 cash calls.

The costs of new issues

There are three types of cost involved when a firm makes an issue of equity capital:

- administrative/transaction costs;
- the equity cost of capital;
- market pricing costs.

The first of these has already been discussed.

---

6 Shareholder approval is also required for disposal of a substantial asset.

The second cost is not something to be dealt with in detail here – this can be left to Chapter 16. However, we can say that shareholders suffer an opportunity cost. By holding shares in one company they are giving up the use of that money elsewhere. The firm therefore needs to produce a rate of return for those shareholders which is at least equal to the return they could obtain by investing in other shares of a similar risk class. Because ordinary shareholders face higher risks than debt or preference shareholders the rate of return demanded is higher. If the firm does not produce this return then shares will be sold and the firm will find raising capital difficult.

Market pricing cost is to do with the possibility of underpricing new issues. The firm is usually keen to have the offer fully taken up by public investors to make sure it can finance its planned growth. To have shares left with the underwriters gives the firm a bad image because it is perceived to have had an issue which 'flopped'. Furthermore, the underwriters, over the forthcoming months, will try to offload their shares and this action has the potential to depress the price for a long time. The sponsor also has an incentive to avoid leaving the underwriters with large blocks of shares. The sponsoring organisation consists of people who are professional analysts and dealmakers and an issue which flops can be very bad for their image. It might indicate that they are not reading the market signals correctly and that they have overestimated demand. They might have done a poor job in assessing the firm's riskiness or failed to communicate its virtues to investors. These bad images can stick, so both the firm and the sponsor have incentives to err on the side of caution and price a little lower to make sure that the issue will be fully subscribed.[7]

A major problem in establishing this discount is that with an offer for sale or placing the firm has to decide the price days before the close of the offer. Between then and the first trading day the market may decline dramatically. This makes potential investors nervous about committing themselves to a fixed price. To overcome this additional risk factor the issue price may have to be significantly less than the expected first day's trading price. Another incentive for underpricing is that the firm and its sponsors want to avoid being sued for overpricing by irate shareholders.

Giving a discount on new shares deprives the firm of money (incumbent shareholders) which it might have received in the absence of these uncertainties, and can therefore be regarded as a cost. In the case of the Metro Bank flotation in 2016, the shares moved to a first-day premium of 7.5% – *see* **Exhibit 10.8**. It could be argued that the existing shareholders sold a piece of the business too cheaply at the issue price.

Exhibit 10.8

Metro Bank shares up by 7.5% on first day

By Financial Times

A none-too-shabby first day on the stock market for Metro Bank so far. Shares have soared on the first day of trading, and they are up by 7.5 per cent to £21.64, above the IPO price of £20. The bank had initially planned to float at £24, but last month it slashed both the size of its initial public offering and the target price amid a sharp sell-off in banking stocks.

The challenger bank was launched in 2010 to take on large high street lenders. The London and South East-focused UK bank raised £400m in a move that valued it at £1.6bn.

 Financial Times, 7 March 2016.
All Rights Reserved.

---

7 It has also been suggested that when sponsors are underwriters they have an additional incentive to price the shares cheaply as this reduces the risk of being required to buy the shares. If they do buy them, they then obtain them at a good price.

Rights issues

A rights issue is an invitation to existing shareholders to purchase additional shares in the company. This is a very popular method of raising new funds. It is easy and relatively cheap (compared with new issues because there is less professional adviser involvement and no prospectus). Directors are not required to seek the prior consent of shareholders, and the London Stock Exchange will only intervene in larger issues (to adjust the timing so that the market does not suffer from too many issues in one period). The UK has particularly strong traditions and laws concerning pre-emption rights. These require that a company raising new equity capital by selling shares first offers those shares to the existing shareholders. The owners of the company are entitled to subscribe for the new shares in proportion to their existing holding. This will enable them to maintain the existing percentage ownership of the company – the only difference is that each slice of the company cake is bigger because it is part of a larger financial asset. **Exhibit 10.9** discusses rights issues in other countries.

The shares are usually offered at a significantly discounted price from the market price of the current shares – typically 10–40%. Shareholders can either buy these shares themselves or sell the 'right' to buy to another investor. For further reassurance that the firm will raise the anticipated finance, rights issues are usually underwritten by institutions.

Exhibit 10.9

Pre-emption: Knowing your rights is a serious issue

By Kate Burgess

Ask shareholders which rights they treasure most highly and many say it is their right to pre-emption, which protects their holdings from being diluted by new share issues.

Many countries impose rules on share issues, forcing companies to tell existing shareholders of their plans or give existing shareholders the right of first refusal of new shares.

But few shareholders elsewhere take these rights more seriously than those in the UK, where protections have developed over centuries to stop managers transferring wealth from the owners of companies to new investors.

Market historians have found references to rights issues in the UK in 1719 and they were going strong by 1900 and pre-emption is now enshrined in UK company law.

The UK system stands out in two ways. UK investors' rights are separately valued and even shareholders who do not take up their entitlements to new shares are paid something for their rights.

Second, the system is designed to treat all shareholders equally. The Association of British Insurers, which is responsible for the government-backed guidelines on rights issues, distinguishes between rights issues found in many parts of the

world and fully pre-emptive rights issues in the UK, which give existing shareholders first refusal of new shares.

The UK imposes some of the toughest constraints on companies raising funds. There are, for example, restrictions on how deeply new issues are discounted as well as a 5 per cent limit on 'disapplication' – the amount of shares a company can sell without talking to shareholders.

'Pre-emption is an article of faith in the UK,' says Daniel Epstein, a partner at law firm Allen & Overy. It contrasts sharply with the US, where pre-emption was restricted by state legislation in 1930 and does not feature in the company law of Delaware, where most US companies are incorporated.

In the US, managements can sell what they want to the highest bidder and investors have limited protection from their actions.

Elsewhere round the world, from Canada to Egypt and Australia, some form of pre-emption exists but the procedures and levels of protection differ.

In Egypt, say lawyers, companies can fulfil their obligations to investors by informing them of an issue in a local newspaper. Investors do not have tradeable rights. 'There is an entitlement understood as a right but there is no mechanism for monetising it,' says Mr Epstein. Even in Europe, pre-emption varies.

In the UK, regulators and shareholders argue that tight rules on pre-emption give investors confidence, which helps companies to raise capital at a lower cost, compared with share issues elsewhere.

Placing shares in the US costs an average of 5 per cent or more, compared with 3 to 4 per cent in the UK.

US bankers say they charge more because the market includes more private investors with small holdings – marketing to a diverse shareholder base costs more than to big investment groups based in one or two cities.

That said, the UK's rights issue process has not gone unchallenged. US bankers have long complained that the system is protracted and the requirement to send out wads of documents ahead of a shareholder vote and then give investors time to trade their rights introduces risk.

The pre-emption concept is gaining ground in other jurisdictions. In Japan, pre-emption rights issues were almost unknown. But as struggling companies found they needed to raise equity in more flexible ways, calls for share issues that protect shareholder rights have gained support, from the Tokyo stock exchange, among others.

 Financial Times, 3 February 2010.
All Rights Reserved.

An example

Take the case of the imaginary listed company Swell plc with 100 million shares in issue. It wants to raise £25m for expansion but does not want to borrow it. Given that its existing shares are quoted on the stock market at 120p, the new rights shares will have to be issued at a lower price to appeal to shareholders because there is a risk of the market share price falling in the period between the announcement and the purchasing of new shares. The offer must remain open for shareholders to send in applications with payment for at least ten working days.

Swell has decided that the £25m will be obtained by issuing 25 million shares at 100p each. Thus the ratio of new shares to old is 25:100. In other words, this issue is a 'one-for-four' rights issue. Each shareholder will be offered one new share for every four already held. The discount on these new shares is 20p or 16.7% of 120p.

If the market price before the issue is 120p valuing the entire company at £120m, and then another £25m of value is added in the form of cash by selling 25m shares for £1 then the market price of Swell shares will not be able to stay at 120p after the rights issue is complete. A company that was previously valued at £120m which then adds £25m should be worth £145m (disregarding stock market fluctuations and revaluations of the company). This company now has 125 million shares; therefore each share is worth £1.16 (i.e. £145m divided by 125m shares). An alternative way of calculating the ex-rights price, the price at which the shares should theoretically sell after the issue is as follows:

Four existing shares at a price of 120p	480p
One new share for cash at 100p	+100p
Value of five shares	= 580p
Value of one share ex-rights 580p/5	116p

Investors call this the theoretical ex-rights price, TERP.

Shareholders have experienced a decline in the price of their old shares from 120p to 116p. A fall of this magnitude necessarily follows from the introduction of new shares at a discounted price. However, the loss is exactly offset by the gain in share value on the new rights issue shares. They cost 100p but have a market price of 116p. This can be illustrated through the example of Sid, who owned 100 shares worth £120 prior to the rights announcement. Sid loses £4 on the old shares – their value is now £116. However, he makes a gain of £4 on the new shares:

Cost of rights shares (25 × £1)	£25
Ex-rights value (25 × £1.16)	£29
Gain	£4

When the press talks glibly of a rights offer being 'very attractively priced for shareholders' they are generally talking nonsense. Whatever the size of the discount, the same value will be removed from the old shares to leave the shareholder no worse or better off. Logically value cannot be handed over to the shareholders from the size of the discount decision. Shareholders own all the company's shares before and after the rights issue – they can't hand value to themselves without also taking value from themselves. Of course, if the prospects for the company's profits rise because it can now make brilliant capital expenditures, which lead to dominant market positions, then the value of shares will rise – for both the old and the new shares. But this is value creation that has nothing to do with the level of the discount.

What if a shareholder does not want to take up the rights?

As owners of the firm all shareholders must be treated in the same way. To make sure that some shareholders do not lose out because they are unwilling or unable to buy more shares the law requires that shareholders have a third choice, other than to buy or not buy the new shares. This is to sell the rights on to someone else on the stock market – selling the rights nil paid. Take the case of impoverished Sid, who is unable to find the necessary £25. He could sell the rights to subscribe for the shares to another investor and not have to go through the process of taking up any of the shares himself. Indeed, so deeply enshrined are pre-emption rights that even if the shareholder does nothing the company will sell his rights to the new shares on his behalf and send the proceeds to him.[8] Thus, Sid would benefit to the extent of 16p per share or a total of £4 (if the market price stays constant) which adequately compensates for the loss on the 100 shares he holds. But the extent of his control over the company has been reduced – his percentage share of the votes has decreased. The value of a right on one new share is:

Theoretical market value of share ex-rights − subscription price = 116p − 100p = 16p

The value of a right on one old share in Swell is:

$$\frac{\text{Theoretical market value of share ex-rights} - \text{subscription price}}{\text{No. of old shares required to purchase one new share}}$$

$$= \frac{116 - 100}{4} = 4\text{p}$$

In the case of Cobham's issue (*see* **Exhibit 10.10**) 98% of shareholders took up their rights. Those who did not had their share entitlement sold on their behalf. The premium over the 75p rights price was sent to them – this was just under 62p for each new share because they were placed with other investors at 137p (financial adviser expenses were deducted from the proceeds).

Exhibit 10.10

Cobham offers investors steep discount on rights issue

By Peggy Hollinger

Cobham is offering a steep 41 per cent discount on shares issued in a £512m rescue fundraising as it attempts to woo investors who have been buffeted by five profit warnings in less than two years.

The defence equipment company's announcement of a two for five rights issue at 75p a share comes the day after Cobham revealed that it is under investigation by the UK's Financial Conduct

---

8 For companies whose shares are not quoted on a recognised stock exchange it may be difficult to sell the rights to another investor.

Authority for the manner in which it handled sensitive information ahead of a previous £500m rights issue in 2016.

The company's shares held steady in midday trading at 127p.

David Lockwood, the chief executive said the funds would help to bring its debt down to sustainable levels. Cobham needs to bolster its balance sheet to fulfil promises on some big, but troublesome defence contracts.

Investors will have stumped up £1bn in just under a year when the rights issue closes on April 12.

Cobham has said the net proceeds of £496.6m, after fees and expenses, would not on its own take the company to its goal of net debt to earnings before interest, tax, amortisation and depreciation of 1.5 times. The balance would have to come from operational improvements and disposals from its diverse portfolio of wireless, electronic and air flight services divisions.

At 75p, the new shares will be issued at a 41 per cent discount to the close on Monday, and a 33 per cent reduction on the theoretical price of the shares after accounting for the enlarged equity base.

The rights issue has been underwritten by Bank of America Merrill Lynch, and JPMorgan Securities and Barclays Bank.

 Financial Times, 28 March 2017.
All Rights Reserved.

Ex-rights and cum-rights

Old shares bought in the stock market which are designated cum-rights carry with them to the new owner the right to subscribe for the new shares in the rights issue. After a cut-off date set by the company the shares go ex-rights, which means that any purchaser of old shares will not have the right to the new shares; they remain with the former shareholder.

The price discount decision

It does not matter greatly whether Swell raises £25m on a one-for-four basis at 100p or on a one-for-three basis at 75p per share, or on some other basis (*see* **Exhibit 10.11**).

Exhibit 10.11	Comparison of different rights bases		
Rights basis	**Number of new shares (m)**	**Price of new shares (p)**	**Total raised (£m)**
1 for 4	25	100	25
1 for 3	33.3	75	25
1 for 2	50	50	25
1 for 1	100	25	25

Whatever the basis of the rights issue, the company will receive £25m and shareholders will see the price of their old shares decrease, but this will be exactly offset by the value of the rights on the new shares. However, the ex-rights price will change. For a one-for-three basis it will be £108.75:

Three shares at 120p	360p
One share at 75p	75p
Value of four shares	435p
Value of one share (435/4)	108.75p

If Swell chose the one-for-one basis this would be regarded as a deep-discounted rights issue. With an issue of this sort there is only a minute probability that the market price will fall below the rights offer price and therefore there is almost complete certainty that the offer will be taken up. It seems reasonable to suggest that the underwriting service provided by the institutions is largely redundant here and that the firm can make a significant saving. Yet almost all rights issues are underwritten, usually involving many sub-underwriters. The underwriting fees used to be a flat 2% of the offer. Of this the issuing house received 0.5%, the broker received 0.25% and the sub-underwriter 1.25%. However, fees can rise to 3% or more. Even the London Stock Exchange, when it needed to raise money to take over Russell, paid 2.6% – see **Exhibit 10.12**. As an exercise you might like to calculate the theoretical ex-rights price based on this.

Exhibit 10.12

London Stock Exchange cash call supports underwriting cartel

Rights issue fees should be tackled by the exchange, not endorsed

By Neil Collins

The LSE is in the middle of a well-flagged, and generally well-received rights issue to pay for a sensible acquisition – a fine opportunity to show how efficiently capital can be raised on the exchange at a reasonable cost to the shareholders.

Pricing such issues is a demonstration of the investment banker's art. After all, much can happen between the fixing of the price and the moment the shareholders must choose whether to pay up. The LSE's experts decided that offering three new shares for every 11 was the right proportion, at a price of £12.95 a share.

This ridiculously complex piece of maths raises £963m, to go towards the $2.7bn purchase price of Russell Investments.

Unfortunately, not all the proceeds flow to the company. For all that erudite advice, and taking the risk that on September 25 all the shareholders turn the share offer down, the advisers (eight banks plus assorted hangers-on) are charging £25m. There is a

risk, of course, but the new shares are priced at a stonking 30.1 per cent discount to the market price immediately before the announcement on August 22 – this, you will recall, for a fundraising that had been well signalled beforehand and thus priced in by the market.

In order for the underwriters to be obliged to take the stock, markets everywhere would have to go into free fall in the next four weeks. Even if shares did collapse far enough to discourage some LSE shareholders, it is absurdly unlikely that none would subscribe, so the underwriters would be released from at least some of their obligations.

This level of costs, for this level of risk, is commonplace. It is a blight on the LSE, and when the LSE itself fails to take a golden opportunity to do something to break this monstrous cartel, it provides the answer to the question above. Mr Gibson-Smith is retiring after a hugely successful 11 years, but this is not his finest hour.

Exercise   **Premier Foods**

To consolidate knowledge gained from the rights issue section it is suggested that it be applied to the case of Premier Foods' one-for-one issue.

Premier Foods planned to raise a sum of money equivalent to 60% of its stock market value through a rights issue. This was to provide the funds needed to purchase the UK and Irish operations of Campbell's Soup. One new share was offered for each existing share held at 185p. The existing shares traded at 310p.

Calculate the following on the assumption that the market price of an old share in Premier Foods is 310p:

a   the ex-rights price;

b   the value of a right of a new share;

c   the value of a right of an old share;

d   the amount a holder of £8,000 worth of shares could receive if the rights were sold.

Other equity issues

Some companies argue that the lengthy procedures and expense associated with rights issues (e.g. the time and trouble it takes to get the documents prepared and approved by the UKLA) frustrate directors' efforts to take advantage of opportunities in a timely fashion. Firms in the USA have much more freedom to bypass pre-emption rights. They are able to sell blocks of shares to securities houses for distribution elsewhere in the market. This is fast and has low transaction costs. If this were permitted in the UK there would be a concern for existing shareholders: they could experience a dilution of their voting power and/or the shares could be sold at such a low price that a portion of the firm would be handed over to new shareholders too cheaply. The UK authorities have produced a compromise, under which firms must obtain shareholders' approval through a special resolution (a majority of 75% of those voting) at the company's annual general meeting, or at an extraordinary general meeting to waive ('disapply') the pre-emption right.

Even for Main Market companies under the premium listing UKLA rules the new shares must not be sold to outside investors at more than 10% discount to the share price. The guidelines produced by the major investing institutions via The Pre-Emption Group for these premium-listed companies are slightly different (standard listed and AIM companies 'are encouraged to adopt' the same rules). They state that the maximum discount should be 5%. It does not make any difference to existing shareholders if new shares are offered at a deep discount to the market price as long as they are offered to them, but if external investors get a discount there is a transfer of value from the current shareholders to the new.

The Pre-Emption Group also insists that disapplication of pre-emption rights should only be on 5% of the issued share capital in normal circumstances (with a rolling 7.5% aggregate limit on non-pre-emptive issues for cash over a three-year period). However, if the company is making a specified major capital investment or an acquisition of another company an additional 5% is allowed.

The Pre-Emption Group say that their Statement of Principles is not a rule book, but warn companies that if they do not comply they are likely to find themselves with upset and rebellious shareholders who will be less cooperative with future requests for a general disapplication of pre-emption rights.

Placings

In placings, new shares of companies already listed are sold directly to a narrow group of external investors. The institutions, as existing shareholders, have produced guidelines to prevent abuse, which normally allow a placing of only a small proportion of the company's capital (a maximum of 5% in a single year, and no more than 7.5% is to be added to the company's equity capital over a rolling three-year period) in the absence of a clawback. Companies can ask to go beyond these limits if they give appropriate justification, but this is rare.

Placings are usually structured so that a prospectus is not required, so this saves money. Placings can be completed in a matter of days rather than weeks or months for rights issues.

Under clawback, existing shareholders have the right to reclaim the placing shares as though they were entitled to them under a rights issue. They can buy them at the price they were offered to the external investors. With a clawback the issue becomes an 'open offer'. The major difference compared with a rights issue is that if they do not exercise this clawback right they receive no compensation for any reduction in the price of their existing shares – there are no nil-paid rights to sell.

Vendor placing

If a company wishes to pay for an asset such as a subsidiary of another firm or an entire company with newly issued shares, but the vendor does not want to hold the shares, the purchaser could arrange for the new shares to be bought by institutional investors for cash. In this way the buyer gets the asset, the vendor (e.g. shareholders in the target company in a merger or takeover) receives cash and the institutional investor makes an investment. There is usually a clawback arrangement for a vendor placing (if the issue is more than 10% of market capitalisation of the acquirer). Again, the price discount can be no more than 5 or 10% of the current share price.

Bought deal

Instead of selling shares to investors, companies are sometimes able to make an arrangement with a securities house whereby it buys all the shares being offered for cash. The securities house then sells the shares on to investors included in its distribution network, hoping to make a profit on the deal. Securities houses often compete to buy a package of shares from the company, with the highest bidder winning. The securities houses take the risk of being unable to sell the shares for at least the amount that they paid. Bought deals are limited by the 5 or 10% pre-emption rules.

Acquisition for shares

Shares are often issued in exchange for business assets or shares in another business. While these issues are subject to shareholder approval, the Pre-Emption Group's size restrictions are less onerous.

Scrip issues

Scrip issues do not raise new money: a company simply gives shareholders more shares in proportion to their existing holdings. In theory, the value of each shareholding does not change, because the share price drops in proportion to the additional shares. They are also known as capitalisation issues or bonus issues. The purpose is to make shares more attractive by bringing down the price. British investors are thought to consider a share price of £10 and above as less marketable than one in single figures. So a company with shares trading at £15 on the Exchange might distribute two 'free' shares for every one held – a two-for-one scrip issue. Since the amount of money in the firm and its economic potential remain the same the share price will theoretically fall to £5. Scrip issues are often regarded as indicating confidence in future earnings increases. If this new optimism is expressed in the share price it may not fall as much as theory would suggest.

With a scrip issue there will be some adjustment necessary to the balance sheet. If we suppose that the pre-scrip issued share capital was £200m (25p par value × 800m shares) and the profit and loss account reserves accumulated from previous years amounted to £500m, then after the two-for-one scrip issue the issued share capital figure rises to £600m (25p par value × 2,400m shares) and the profit and loss account reserve (revenue reserve) falls to £100m. Thus £400m of profit and loss reserves are 'capitalised' into issued share capital.

A number of companies have annual scrip issues while maintaining a constant dividend per share, effectively raising the level of profit distribution. For example, if a company pays a regular dividend of 20p per share but also has a one-for-ten scrip, the annual income will go up by 10%. (A holder of 10 shares who previously received 200p now receives 220p on a holding of 11 shares.)

Scrip dividends are slightly different: shareholders are offered a choice between receiving a cash dividend or receiving additional shares. This is more like a rights issue because the shareholders are making a cash sacrifice if they accept the scrip shares. Shareholders are able to add to their holdings without paying stockbrokers' commission. Companies are able to raise additional equity capital without the expense of a rights issue.

A share split (stock split) means that the nominal value of each share is reduced in proportion to the increase in the number of shares, so the book total nominal value of shares remains the same. So, for example, a company may have one million shares in issue with a nominal value of 50p each. It issues a further one million shares to existing shareholders with the nominal value of each share reducing to 25p, but total nominal value remains at £500,000. Of course, the share price will halve – assuming all else is constant.

If the share price goes too low, say 15p, a company may pursue consolidation of shares. This is the opposite of a split: the number of shares is reduced and the nominal value of each remaining share rises. If the nominal (par) value is 5p the company could consolidate on the basis of five shares for one. Every five 5p nominal share would be replaced by a 25p nominal share, which would then trade in the market at 75p: 15p × 5 (or slightly more if investors are more attracted to shares within a normal price range).

Warrants

Warrants give the holder the right to subscribe for a specified number of shares at a fixed price during or at the end of a specified time period. If a company has shares currently trading at £3 it might choose to sell warrants, each of which grants the holder the right to buy a share at, say, £4 over the next five years. If by the fifth year the share price has risen to £6 the warrant holders could exercise their rights and then sell the shares immediately, realising £2 per share, which is likely to be a considerable return on the original warrant price of a few pence. Warrants are frequently attached to bonds, and make the bond more attractive because the investor benefits from a relatively safe (but low) income on the bond if the firm performs in a mediocre fashion, but if the firm does very well and the share price rises significantly the investor will participate in some of the extra returns through the 'sweetener' or 'equity kicker' provided by the warrant.

There is no requirement for investors to hold warrants until exercised or they expire. There is an active secondary market on the London Stock Exchange.

Equity finance for unquoted firms

We have looked at some of the details of raising money on the Stock Exchange. In the commercial world there are millions of companies which do not have access to the Exchange. We now consider a few of the ways that unquoted firms can raise equity capital.

The financing gap

Small companies usually rely on retained earnings, capital injections from the founder family and bank borrowing for growth. More mature companies can turn to the stock market to raise debt or equity capital. In between these two, it is suggested, lies a financing gap. The intermediate businesses are too large or too fast growing to ask the individual shareholders for more funds or to obtain sufficient bank finance, and they are not ready to launch on the stock market. Also there are many small start-up businesses with great ideas which simply lack wealthy family and friends able to put up the large amounts of equity capital needed to get going in the first place. To help fill these gaps in financing there has been rapid development in the private equity industry over the past 40 years – a move welcomed by companies frustrated in their plans to exploit market opportunities due to lack of available funds. Private equity may also provide funding for under-performing companies or for those in financial difficulties which would prosper given adequate funds.

The costs and inconveniences of being on a stock market mean that many managers and share-holders prefer to obtain funds from private equity funds – even those that are perfectly capable of raising money on stock markets deliberately stay away from them. Private equity funds can be more long-term focused than stock market investors, allowing higher near-term investment in, say, research and development or marketing even at the expense of this year's or next year's earnings per share figures. The corporate managers also avoid the hassle of regular time-consuming meetings with institutional shareholders, so they are freer to get on with the job of creating long-term wealth for shareholders. They might also welcome the technical/managerial expertise and contacts that many private equity funds can draw on – many funds specialise in particular industries and develop a deep talent pool. Also, private equity shareholders are more likely to be in favour of granting directors and senior managers shares in the company if they perform well. This can make them very wealthy.

Private equity has a major impact in countries all over the world. In the UK, for instance, there are over 10,000 companies with over 3m employees (one in six of the non-government workforce) financed by private equity money, making private equity investment crucial to the UK economy. **Exhibit 10.13** provides a list of some well-known British companies backed by private equity. **Exhibit 10.14** looks at private equity's impact on Africa.

Exhibit 10.13	Well-known UK companies backed by private equity
Agent Provocateur	New Look
Alliance Boots	Odeon and UCI Cinemas
Autonomy	Phones4U
Birds Eye Iglo	Pizza Express/Zizzi/Ask – Gondola Group
Cambridge Silicon Radio	Plastic Logic
CenterParcs	Poundland
Deliveroo	Pret A Manger
Findus Group (Foodvest)	The AA/Saga
Funding Circle	Skyscanner
Jimmy Choo	Travelodge
Merlin Entertainments Group	Weetabix
Moto	West Cornwall Pasty Co.
National Car Parks	

Source: bvca.co.uk.

Exhibit 10.14

Private equity looks to east Africa for investment opportunities

By Maggie Fick

Buyout groups investing in Africa are turning east and shunning the oil-rich western part of the continent as they grapple with the effect of low commodity prices on private equity's final frontier. In the decade before oil prices plummeted, west Africa — particularly Nigeria — was the most attractive region on the continent for global private equity groups from Carlyle to Actis looking to tap the potential of the "emerging African consumer".

But with Nigeria in economic recession for the first time since 1991, investors say they are looking elsewhere on the continent for deals in sectors from consumer goods to healthcare.

"In the short term, in the next 12 to 24 months, east Africa is certainly more appealing than west Africa," says Natalie Kolbe, head of private equity for Actis.

The emerging market-focused group invested hundreds of millions of dollars in Nigerian companies and infrastructure projects in the years before oil prices crashed, in 2014.

Kenya's diversified economy has not been hit by the commodities slump. It is expected to grow above 5 per cent this year. With a population of 160m people, the entire east African region combined has a smaller population than Nigeria. But investors say there are many companies in Kenya ready for relatively red tape-free expansion into markets such as Tanzania and Uganda. "The fastest growing consumer market today is actually Kenya," says Felix Olale, a partner at LeapFrog Investments.

The group has backed finance and healthcare companies on both sides of the continent but currently sees the more diversified economies in the east as riper for investment. "Dollar for dollar . . . Kenya today versus Nigeria, you might end up going to Kenya," said Genevieve Sangudi, a managing director at Carlyle, which closed its first Africa fund, of $700m, in 2014.

Investors say there is now more activity in east Africa, and even a maturing "secondary" market, as private equity groups look to sell their stakes in businesses to other buyout houses. There were 41 disclosed private equity deals in east Africa last year with an average deal size of $38m, according to Kenya-based financial advisory firm I&M Burbidge Capital.

Abraaj, a major private equity investor on the continent, has poured $3.2bn into 80 companies across Africa since 2002 and is sanguine about prospects in Nigeria in the medium to long term.

Mustafa Abdel-Wadood, managing partner and global head of private equity for Abraaj, says the group has been able to navigate "significant headwinds" in Nigeria over the past two years by focusing on "export-driven" businesses.

He cites the purchase of a minority stake for an undisclosed sum in Indorama Corporation, sub-Saharan Africa's largest fertiliser producer, last year.

He also says Abraaj was interested in expanding its investments in healthcare in Nigeria. But he says the approach the company has pursued in east Africa — "of buying into businesses and helping them grow" — could not be replicated in Nigeria, where "significant building of businesses" is still required.

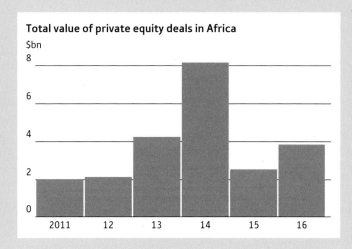

Total value of private equity deals in Africa

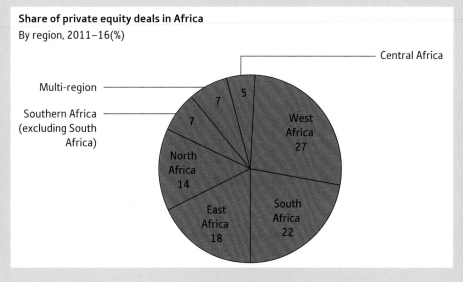

Share of private equity deals in Africa
By region, 2011–16(%)

Business angels (informal venture capitalists)

Business angels are wealthy individuals, generally with substantial business and entrepreneurial experience, who usually invest between £10,000 and £250,000 primarily in start-up, early-stage or expanding firms. About three-quarters of business angel investments are for sums of less than £100,000 and the average investment is £25,000–£30,000. The majority of investments are in the form of equity finance but angels do purchase debt instruments and preference shares. The companies they invest in will be years away from obtaining a quotation or being advanced enough for a sale to other companies or investors, so in becoming a business angel the investor accepts that it may be difficult to dispose of their shares, even if the company is progressing well. They also accept a high degree of risk of complete failure – which happens in about one in three cases. They usually do not have a controlling shareholding and they are willing to invest at an earlier stage than most formal venture capitalists. They often dislike the term business angel, preferring the title informal venture capitalist. They are generally looking for entrepreneurial companies which have high aspirations and potential for growth. A typical business angel makes one or two investments in a three-year period, often in an investment syndicate (with an 'archangel', an experienced investor leading the group). They generally invest in companies within a reasonable travelling distance from their homes because most like to be 'hands-on' investors, playing a significant role in strategy and management – on average angels allocate 10 hours a week to their investments. Most angels take a seat on the board and are actively involved.[9] Business angels are patient investors willing to hold their investment for at least a five-year period.

The main way in which firms and angels find each other is through friends and business associates, although there are a number of formal networks.[10]

Angel network events are organised where entrepreneurs can make a pitch to potential investors, who, if they like what they hear in response to their questions, may put in tens of thousands of pounds. Prior to the event the network organisers (or a member) generally screen the business opportunities to avoid time wasting by the no-hopers. The angel network organisation have an interest in preparing young companies for capital raising and will help with corporation strategy plans, organisation and financial plans, as well as presentation skills (government, 'enterprise support', help is also available)

To be a member of a network investors are expected either to earn at least £100,000 per year or to have a net worth of at least £250,000 (excluding main residence). If an investor has a specialist skill to offer, for example he/she is an experienced company director or chartered accountant, membership may be permitted despite a lower income or net worth. Angel investors often insist on an agreement which maintains their percentage of the voting and economic rights of their shares in later financing rounds.

Entrepreneurs need to be aware that obtaining money from informal venture capitalists is no easy task – the rejection rate runs at over 90%; but following rejection the determined entrepreneur has many other angel networks to try.

Returns to business angel investments are often negative. However, they can be spectacular; the angels who put €2m into Skype multiplied their money by 350 times when the company was sold to eBay for €2.1bn.

Many business angel deals are structured to take advantage of tax breaks such as those through enterprise investment schemes, EIS, which offer income tax relief and capital gains tax deferral (*see* later in this chapter).

Exhibit 10.15 sheds light on the relationship between angel investors and entrepreneurs.

---

9 Nevertheless, many business angels (generally those with investments of £10,000–£20,000) have infrequent contact with the company.

10 A few of the networks in the UK: Angels Den, www.angelsden.com; UK Business Angels Association, www.ukbaa.org; UK Angel Investment Network, www.angelinvestment network.co.uk; London Business Angels, www.angelcapital.co.uk; Northwest Business Angels, www.nwbusinessangels.co.uk; European Business Angels Network (EBAN), www.eban.org, East Midlands Business Angels,

Exhibit 10.15

Business angels that are devils in disguise

By Jonathan Moules

Fundraising is hard, especially if you are running an early-stage venture – which is why business advisers put so much emphasis on finding early-stage investors, known as business angels. But what if your angel turns out to be the devil in disguise?

Hussein Kanji is an angel investor and former venture capitalist at Accel Partners, who moved to the UK from California to get involved in European technology start-ups.

He was recently invited to invest in a UK company, where one of the two original angel investors quit the board just as the business was going into first round of fundraising, seeking $6m. This money was eventually raised – but no thanks to the behaviour of the angel, Kanji says.

Good angel investors are those that offer guidance when needed and wait patiently for results, according to Kanji – and the best ones have already founded companies and sold them on.

'Folks who have done it before tend to be more patient,' he says. 'They also tend to know if what looks like a crisis really is a crisis.'

David Giampaolo, chief executive of Pi Capital, a London-based investor network, sees two common mistakes made by angel investors, as well as company founders seeking investment.

First, some have unrealistic expectations about the performance potential or valuation of the business that they are putting money into.

This may not be purely the fault of the angel, because the entrepreneur may also have unrealistic expectations about his or her potential, Giampaolo explains.

Second, business angels can be either too hands-off or too controlling. 'An angel investor can provide some real value add, but there is a fine line between some advice and mentorship and interference,' Giampaolo says.

But he stresses that problems in angel investing come from both sides of the table.

'I am very critical,' he says. 'I don't only think entrepreneurs need to be more careful about whose money they take, I think investors have to be equally careful to whom they give their money.'

Giampaolo advises entrepreneurs to do due diligence and seek references for potential investors, just as they would expect to be checked out themselves.

'Focus on the calibre of the person rather than the valuation,' he notes. 'I would rather have an £8m valuation for my company with the right partner than a £10m valuation from the wrong partner.'

Alex Hoye, chief executive of Latitude, a London-based digital marketing agency, is both an entrepreneur and an angel investor in internet, media, and consumer businesses.

He says the risk in taking money from angels who have previously had their own businesses is that you get someone who thinks that the way he or she ran their business is the way you should run yours.

'Most successful companies are disruptive by definition, which means they run into unchartered areas,' he points out.

'This means that the way someone else has run their business is unlikely to be the way this business needs to be run.'

According to Hoye, the trick is to be diplomatic about how you receive an angel's advice, adopting the tips on more 'timeless' matters – such as how to find a good sales person or how to launch a product – and politely ignoring the advice on matters specific to the investor's previous forays into business.

However, it is not just founders who can be stung by ill-suited or malevolent angels. Other investors can also fall victim.

Lois Cook had direct experience of this with a group of angels at a technology company she invested in four years ago.

After making her investment, another group of five angels came on board with an offer much larger than the founders had been looking for.

That group then installed their own chairman and finance director in the business and set out a new shareholder agreement that everyone signed up to.

'We didn't want to prevent the company getting another round of funding, so all the angels signed up to it,' Cook recalls. 'That probably wasn't the best thing to do.'

Shortly afterwards, the new chairman put pressure on the company's founders to leave. Again, Cook gave the new angels the benefit of the doubt.

Then the new angels put in a new loan agreement for £50,000 and gave Cook and the original angels an ultimatum either to find the money to match the

▶

Exhibit 10.15 *(continued)*

amount borrowed within 30 days, or face dilution of their combined stake to 10% of its former value.

'We tried hard [to get the money], but we couldn't match it,' Cook says. She consoles herself that she and the other early angels only lost tens of thousands of pounds in the process – known in the industry as 'whitewashing'. But it has made her wary of making any more angel tech industry investments.

Bad angels are a phenomenon that early-stage investing groups would rather not focus on.

Bill Morrow, co-founder of Angels Den – a matching service for investors and entrepreneurs – insists that only a tiny proportion of the deals his organisation facilitates will go bad. But this is little comfort if you are the unlucky one.

For both entrepreneurs and investors, the lesson is that angel relationships should not be entered into lightly. As one entrepreneur puts it: bringing an angel on board is more like a marriage – and should be treated with the same care.

 Financial Times, 10 June 2011, p. 34.

Crowdfunding

There are many websites which connect entrepreneurial firms seeking equity or debt capital with investors in the crowdfunding (also known as (crowd financing or crowd sourced capital) sector. You can look online at a range of companies pitching to raise a few hundred thousand or millions from hundreds of investors putting in amounts ranging upwards from just a few hundred pounds. Examples:

www.crowdcube.com	Crowdcube
www.crowdfunder.co.uk	Crowdfunder
www.fundingcircle.com	Funding Circle
www.kickstarter.com	Kickstarter
www.lendinvest.com	Lendinvest
www.seedrs.com	Seedrs
www.syndicateroom.com	Syndicate Room
www.ratesetter.com	Rate Setter
www.zopa.com	Zopa

The online platforms usually vet the applications from companies. Investors often have voting rights and, in some cases, can participate in strategic decision making. Crowdfunders helped BrewDog to establish itself, but as **Exhibit 10.16** makes clear not all crowd investment turns out so well.

Exhibit 10.16

Small investors risk being lost in the crowd

By Aime Williams

The dream of crowdfunding is to democratise finance — the little guy gets to decide what wins and what loses, not just the seasoned professionals. To its acolytes, it allows businesses in need of fast cash to bypass bankers, private equity and venture capital and go straight to the people, overthrowing the fat cats and making investors a shedload of money along the way.

FT Money readers may not be surprised to hear that's not the whole story, though. High valuations dreamt up by entrepreneurial mavericks is one problem, and

an unorthodox approach to selling debt versus equity is another.

I'll take the example of Scottish independent brewery BrewDog, a favourite among millennial drinkers. It has been phenomenally successful at playing the crowdfunding game. First of all, it realised way back in 2015 that everyone, at heart, just wants to overthrow the ruling elites and came up with a suitable marketing strategy — referring to its investors as "punks", for example.

BrewDog's launch was one of the most successful crowdfunding campaigns of any business, raising £35.5m. But turning the spectre of an idea into a success takes grit and cash.

Lots of businesses that crowdfund fail. The reason is not because they're terrible companies, but because their projected growth rates are based on their wildest dreams.

This failure rate is fine — it's fun, even. Nowhere is investing more thrilling than in the high stakes world of early-stage, high-growth companies.

In reality, things are not so simple. Let's think about the dream from an investor's point of view. You see the potential of a brilliant start-up and you decide to throw them a few quid. How much do you pay for their shares? If it were a listed company, the stock market would decide. In crowdfunding land, the start-up tends to value itself, based on its own projected accounts.

Old private equity hands typically make sure valuations are realistic when they invest, because they understand that in order for them to get their money back, they need to sell their stake for more than they paid. Put another way, the valuation has to rise as they hold it.

Beauhurst, a data company, did some research in 2015 showing that investors on crowdfunding platforms were paying a much higher price for start-up shares than professional investors.

On the valuation front, BrewDog has been an unlikely success story. The company boasted that early investors would have seen the value of their shares increase by 2,800 per cent following a fresh cash injection of £100m by US private equity group TSG Consumer Partners.

The catch is that while BrewDog founders, James Watt and Martin Dickie, have both sold about a third of their personal stakes to the new backer — cashing in ahead of the crowd — other investors have only been able to sell a maximum of 40 shares, earning themselves about £500.

If the company lists, they will, of course, be able to sell shares then, assuming the valuation holds.

Another problem is that about half of BrewDog backers didn't buy shares. They bought debt, and this means they don't get to enjoy the new high valuation of their brewery. If you're a bondholder, the new private equity injection is practically irrelevant. If you're backing a new company with big dreams, whose founders say they can repay by growing very fast, generating lots of new money, then you're taking a fairly big risk. That would be fine, if in exchange for the lower rewards, bond investors took less risk.

In traditional models, bonds are less risky than equities because if the company goes bust, the bondholders are ahead of the equity holders when it comes to being paid back.

The problem is that crowdfunded bonds are usually unsecured: if the start-up goes bust, secured bondholders — usually "fat cats" such as bankers and private equity investors — are ahead in the queue of people wanting their money back.

This is the case with BrewDog. According to filings in Companies House, holders of its bonds would find themselves behind HSBC in the event of a default. HSBC holds around £30m of BrewDog debt, all secured against its assets. This security means the bank's debt is less risky than the unsecured debt offered to retail investors.

Private equity/venture capital

The distinction between venture capital (VC) and private equity (PE) is blurry. Some use private equity to define all unquoted company equity investment; others confine 'private equity' to management buy-outs and the like of companies already well established, leaving 'venture capital' for investment in companies at an early stage of development with high growth potential. Both types are medium- to long-term investment and can consist of a package of debt and equity finance. Venture capitalists often take high risks by investing in the equity of young companies often with a limited (or no) track record. Many of their investments are into little more than a management team with a good idea – which may not have started selling a product or even developed a prototype. It is believed, as a rule of thumb in the venture capital industry, that out of ten investments two will fail completely, two will perform excellently and the remaining six will range from poor to very good.

As we discussed in Chapter 8, high risk goes with high return. Venture capitalists therefore expect to get a return of between five and ten times their initial equity investment in about five to seven years. This means that the firms receiving equity finance are *expected* to produce annual returns of at least 26%, although few achieve this. Alongside the usual drawbacks of equity capital from the investors' viewpoint (last in the queue for income and on liquidation, etc.), investors in small unquoted companies also suffer from a lack of liquidity because the shares are not quoted on a public exchange. There are a number of different forms of non-quoted equity capital (although these days the last five will often be separated from VC and grouped under the title 'private equity' – *see* later in the chapter):

- *Seedcorn* This is financing to allow the development of a business concept. Development may also involve expenditure on the production of prototypes and additional research. Usually involves angel investor funding rather than venture funds.

- *Start-up* A product or idea is further developed and/or initial marketing is carried out. Companies are very young and have not yet sold their product commercially. Usually involves angel investor funding rather than venture funds.

- *Other early-stage or first-round financing* Funds for initial commercial manufacturing and sales. Many companies at this stage will remain unprofitable. Usually involves angel investing rather than venture funds.

- *Expansion (development or growth capital, or possibly 'second-round financing' if it is a further slug of venture money)* Companies at this stage are on to a fast-growth track and need capital to fund increased production capacity, working capital and for the further development of the product or market. The company may be large enough to accept substantial investment from venture funds. If not, then angel investment is more likely.

- *Management buy-outs (MBO)* Here a team of managers makes an offer to its employers to buy a whole business, a subsidiary or a section so that it owns and runs it for itself. Large companies are often willing to sell to these teams, particularly if the business is under-performing and does not fit with the strategic core business. Usually the management team has limited funds of its own and so calls on private equity funds capitalists to provide the bulk of the finance.

- *Management buy-ins (MBI)* A new team of managers from outside an existing business buys a stake, usually backed by a private equity fund providing most of the finance.

- *Leveraged buy-outs (LBO)* The buy-out of an existing company, with the capital raised (and therefore the capital structure for the company afterwards) being between 60% and 90% debt finance. One advantage of this is that interest on debt is tax deductible and therefore less company tax is paid. The major disadvantage is the risk of insolvency with so much debt to be serviced. Private equity groups usually provide the bulk of the equity and perhaps some of the debt or preference share capital, with the rest coming from banks or the financial markets.

- *Secondary purchase* A private equity-backed company is sold to another private equity fund. This is one of the exit strategies, where the first private equity fund can make a capital gain by selling its equity in the company to another private equity fund.

- *Public-to-private (PTP)* The management of a company currently quoted on a stock exchange may return it to unquoted status with the assistance of private equity finance being used to buy the shares.

Private equity firms are less keen on financing seedcorn, start-ups and other early-stage companies than expansions, MBOs, MBIs and PTPs. This is largely due to the very high risk associated with early-stage ventures and the disproportionate time and costs of financing smaller deals. To make it worthwhile for a private equity or venture capital organisation to consider a company the investment must be at least £250,000 – the average investment is about £5m – and it is difficult to find PEs or VCs willing to invest less than £2m.

Because of the greater risks associated with the youngest companies, the PE or VC funds may *expect* returns of the order of 50–80% per annum. For well-established companies with a proven product and battle-hardened and respected management the returns required may drop to the high 20s. These returns may seem exorbitant, especially to the managers set the task of achieving them, but they have to be viewed in the light of the fact that many PE or VC investments will turn out to be failures and so the overall performance of the funds is significantly less than these figures suggest. In fact, the British Private Equity and Venture Capital Association, which represents 'every major source of venture capital in the UK', reports that returns on funds are not excessively high. The overall long-term net returns to investors for funds raised between 1996 and 2012 measured to the end of 2016 was only 4.5% for venture funds and about 12–15% for MBOs. (*See* **Exhibit 10.17**.)

Exhibit 10.17	Returns on UK private equity funds

Average internal rates of return (IRR) to investors since inception of the funds from 1996 to December 2016, net of costs and fees. Only funds raising money 1996–2012.[1]

	Per cent per annum
Venture capital funds	4.5
Small management buy-outs	15.7
Mid management buy-outs	12.3
Large management buy-outs	15.1
Total	13.6
Comparators' returns over 10 years to Dec. 2016	
UK listed shares (FT All-Share index)	5.6
World shares (FTSE World (ex-UK)) index	4.6
European shares (FTSE Europe (ex-UK))	3.3

(Note: Excluding private equity investment trusts and venture capital trusts)

Source: BVCA Private Equity and Venture Capital Performance Measurement Survey 2016 by BVCA, PwC and Capital Dynamics – www.bvca.co.uk

[1] Funds raised from 2013 onwards are not included in the calculation of since-inception returns as these funds are still at the early stage of their life cycle, and their investment return during this period does not provide a meaningful indication of their performance at liquidation.

There are a number of different types of private equity providers, although the boundaries are increasingly blurred as a number of funds now raise money from a variety of sources. The independents can be firms, funds or investment trusts, either quoted or private, which raise capital from more than one source. The main sources are pension and insurance funds, but banks, corporate investors and private individuals also put money into these VC funds. Captives are funds managed on behalf of a parent institution (banks, pension funds, etc.). Semi-captives invest funds on behalf of a parent and also manage independently raised funds.

How an independent private equity fund is established and managed

Private equity usually takes the form of a fund which then invests in a group of companies. Many investments result in total loss and so private equity investment in a single company can be a huge risk. The diversity of private equity funds gives greater opportunities for good overall returns, even if a high proportion of the investee companies turn out bad performances.

The private equity managers that run these funds, looking for and evaluating investment opportunities in companies, are known as the general partners (GPs), while other investors in the funds are called limited partners (LPs); these can be institutions or individuals. The GPs select companies which are deemed suitable for investment using finance provided by their limited partners, and sometimes loans and bank borrowings.

The GPs are paid management fees (usually 1%–2.5% of funds under management) and a share (usually about 20%) in the eventual capital gain, known as carried interest (the carry).

Many private equity funds are established as limited liability partnerships (LLP),[11] raising capital from a group of investors. It is usually stated at the outset that it will be run down after 10 or 12 years and the value in the LLP will be distributed to members. The project is touted to potential investors (e.g. pension funds), often by the investor relations team or by using

11 A partnership in which some or all of the partners have limited liability. Thus each partner is protected from being liable for the misconduct or incompetence of other partners. In the absence of fraud or wrongful trading a partner cannot lose more than the amount invested. As a 'corporate body' it has a life independent of any individual member and so does not have to be dissolved on the death or leaving of a partner.

external placement agents. The investment strategy is set out, e.g. a focus on bio-technology or social media companies. The general partners will state a minimum to be raised to reach 'first close'. When this is achieved the fund comes into existence. There may be a series of 'closes' beyond the minimum to create a much larger fund. The 'final close' is the end of the capital-raising phase.

The investment phase now begins. GPs are given discretion to invest the money; they are usually given a period of up to five years to do so. They are likely to limit exposure to one investment to less than 10% of the fund but might arrange to borrow money to complete individual deals. For the larger investments, particularly MBOs and MBIs, the private equity fund may provide only a fraction of the total funds required. Thus, in a £50m buy-out the LLP might supply (individually or in a syndicate with other private equity funds), say, £15m in the form of share capital (ordinary and preference shares). Another £20m might come from a group of banks in the form of debt finance. The remainder might be supplied as mezzanine debt – high-return high-risk debt – which usually has some rights to share in equity values should the company perform (*see* Chapter 11).

Occasionally the LPs are given the opportunity both to participate in a specific investment via the private equity fund and to invest directly. This is called co-investing.

The fund usually holds on to the investments for three, five or more years to allow it to improve and grow. When the company is in a thriving state, the private equity fund is likely to sell to realise a return on its investment. This is called an exit – the various types of exits are discussed in the next section.

The performance-related return (carried interest) due to the GPs is generally based on the performance of the entire fund rather than on individual deals, although some do give deal-by-deal carried interest. In the first five years the managers are likely to be most dependent on the management fee of 1–2.5% of funds under management rather than carried interest. In the period after five years they are likely to be most motivated by the carried interest on the maturing investments. The various stages are set out in **Exhibit 10.19**.

Exhibit 10.18 describes a private equity fund that raised money to put into Afganistani companies.

Exhibit 10.18

Private equity investors set sights on Afghanistan

By Steve Johnson

Afghanistan would not top many people's lists of the world's most promising investment opportunities. But the first-ever private equity fund focused on the impoverished, war-torn country — where deaths from the conflict between the government and the Taliban continue to surge — has announced its first close.

Admittedly the InFrontier Afghanistan Fund, at $22m, is small, and all of the money has come from two government-backed development finance institutions, CDC of the UK and the Dutch Good Growth Fund. But the money is being invested on commercial terms, and is the latest sign of nascent foreign interest in the opportunities the nation of 33m people can offer.

"We are expecting a commercial return from this. This is not soft money, it's not philanthropy," said Rhyddid Carter, a spokesman for CDC, which provided $15m of the money.

InFrontier, a London and Kabul-based investment house, which will manage the new private equity fund, has made three standalone equity investments in the country, committing a total of $2.5m.

The most high-profile was its acquisition of a stake in the 786 Pharmacy chain last year. This has since expanded from eight to 13 stores and Felix von Schubert, director of InFrontier, said three more were in the process of opening, all in Kabul, although it has plans to expand outside the capital.

"They are doing quite well and we are very pleased with that investment," said Mr von Schubert, who added that 786 had recently conducted a follow-on fundraising at a higher valuation than when InFrontier bought in, although he declined to reveal the valuation for security reasons.

InFrontier has also invested in the marble sector, via a company that seeks to help quarry owners improve their technology and systems in order to create higher value blocks, and in the energy sector.

It has since sold its latter holding, a business that works to replace the burning of wood and rubbish, often for cooking, with lower emission liquefied petroleum gas, for what Mr von Schubert said was a "small profit".

With InFrontier boasting a four-strong team of locals based in Kabul, Mr von Schubert added "we really spend the time and effort inside the companies, we don't spend time in compounds in Kabul".

He believes it was necessary for InFrontier to demonstrate it could seal standalone deals in Afghanistan before launching the private equity fund. Given that the deals completed so far have attracted investment from corporates and wealthy individuals from the UK, Germany, the US and Asia, he is hopeful the fund will attract some commercial investors in time for a putative second close in 2017.

"We thought it was important to show that we could raise money commercially and invest successfully before raising a fund. We have managed to prove it is possible," Mr von Schubert said. Among the sectors InFrontier is looking at are agricultural processing, data centres for Afghanistan's television and mobile phone networks and financial services such as banking, insurance and mobile payments.

"We think we cannot just make a financial return on investments but also make a difference to the people of the country," he added.

Exhibit 10.19   The operation of a private equity fund

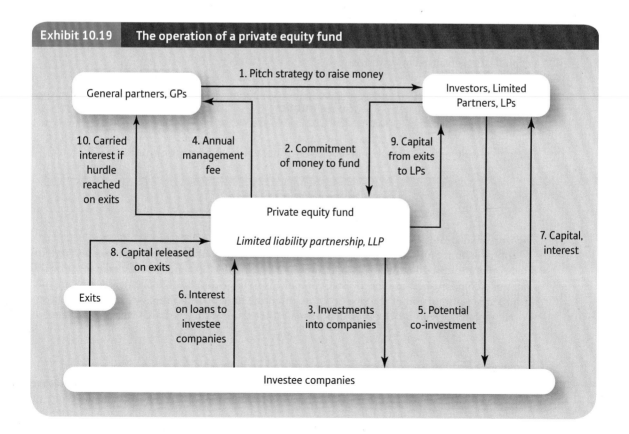

Exits

The exit is when private equity and venture capital investors reap their rewards; this is their goal towards which all efforts have been expended. Before the expiry of the fund (say after ten years), moves will be made to sell the investments. Hopefully the companies within the fund will have prospered or been reorganised enough to make it an attractive proposition for resale or listing on a stock exchange.

Only when the investee company is sold do the private equity or venture capital partners receive any return on their investment, except for the GPs who receive annual fees.[12]

The exit options are:

Repurchase

The company has prospered and the existing management is in a position to purchase the equity in the company, often accompanied by a general recapitalisation of the firm – more debt taken on.

Secondary/Tertiary/Quaternary buy-outs

The equity is sold to another private equity group. This may then be sold on to a third buyer (tertiary buy-out) and, on occasions, a fourth (quaternary buy-out). These are known as 'pass the parcel' deals and can result in an investor paying a performance fee to the fund that is selling, only to end up owning the same assets through the fund that is buying. This happens to pension funds quite a lot because they have money in many PE funds. See **Exhibit 10.20**.

Trade sale

The equity is sold to or merged with another company – usually one in the same industry – and a capital gain is realised for investors.

Going public

The equity is floated on a stock market and a capital gain is realised for investors.

Liquidation

The worst exit strategy – the company goes bust and everyone makes a loss.

Venture capital funds are rarely looking for a controlling shareholding in a company and are often content with a 20 or 30% share. However, MBO/MBI/LBO funds usually take most of the shares of a company because the investee company is so large that the management team can only afford a small proportion of the shares. Quite often the fund provides money by purchasing convertible preference shares or convertible bonds rather than ordinary shares which give rights to

---

12 Limited partners generally accept that their money is locked within the fund for a decade. There is the possibility of selling the rights to receive a return from the fund to other investors before the expiry of the fund, say after three years, but these secondary investors are difficult to find and usually offer low prices. A recent innovation is secondary market 'GP-led' deals, in which the general partners make the effort to find buyers, often though a tender process.

Exhibit 10.20

Core Equity Holdings looks to retain assets for a decade

Private equity group's strategy moves away from industry's 'pass the parcel' model

By Javier Espinoza

Core Equity Holdings, a private equity group is moving away from the "pass the parcel" model implemented by some of its peers as it looks to retain assets for a decade.

Some industry observers believe this might be the beginning of the end of a model whereby a company is sold by one private equity fund to another.

New data by Preqin revealed the private equity industry has grown to $2.9tn, representing eight successive years of growth and a doubling in size since 2006 when global assets stood at $1.16tn.

Core Equity is well on its way to reach its €1.05bn target, with demand for roughly twice the amount it is looking to collect.

The fundraising, which was unusually pursued without a placement agency, is set to become one of the largest buyout funds raised by a first-time group in Europe.

Investors to the fund will pay a "premium" carried interest — the cut of profits that private equity managers share with their investors when deals come to fruition — nearer to 30 per cent. It is typically 20 per cent. The fund will invest between €200m to €500m and will include as key investors university endowments, foundations and family offices.

"The fund's key distinctive feature is that it will move away from the traditional private equity model whereby a group deploys capital for five years, keeps assets for three to five or five to 10 if it is not doing well and then sells on", a person familiar with the strategy said.

Instead, it will look to hold companies for a decade or longer as a "better way to own and manage businesses for the long-term", the person added.

"In 'pass the parcel' deals investors are very pissed off because the transactions end up switching costs, they are disruptive on a business and inefficient," the person said.

The fund will focus on industrials, business services, retail and consumer. The fund will be based in Brussels in light of Brexit. "London is not a very efficient platform to stay close to markets on the Continent and the uncertainty created by Brexit trumps any other benefits London may have provided".

FT   *Financial Times,* 1 February 2017.
All Rights Reserved.

convert these instruments to ordinary shares. If the firm does badly the holders, on liquidation, will have the right to a payout ahead of equity holders, thus lowering risk. In the event that the company performs well the preference shares or bonds will be converted to ordinary shares with a right to participate in the high income flows generated by the firm. The fund may also insist, in an initial investment agreement, on some widespread powers. For instance, the company may need to gain the private equity/venture capitalist's approval for the issue of further securities, and there may be a veto over acquisition of other companies. Even though their equity holding is generally less than 50% the venture capital funds frequently have special rights to appoint a number of directors. If specific negative events happen, such as a poor performance, they may have the right to appoint most of the board of directors and therefore take effective control. More than once the founding entrepreneur has been aggrieved to find him/herself removed from power. (Despite the loss of power, they often have a large shareholding in what has grown to be a multi-million pound company.) They are often sufficiently upset to refer to the fund which separated them from their creation as 'vulture capitalist'. But this is to focus on the dark side. When everything goes well, we have, as they say in the business jargon, 'a win-win-win situation': the company receives vital capital to grow fast, the venture capitalist receives a high return and society gains new products and economic progress.

Private equity categories

As you have gathered by now, as share investment outside stock markets has grown it has become differentiated. The main categories are shown in **Exhibit 10.21**, with private equity as the umbrella term covering the various activities. In this more differentiated setting the term venture capital is generally confined to describing the building of companies from the ground floor, or at least from a very low base.

Management buy-outs and buy-ins of established businesses (already off the ground floor) have become a specialist task, with a number of dedicated funds. Many of these funds are formed as private partnerships by wealthy individuals, a high proportion being American owned.

Small investors can buy shares in listed private equity (LPE) funds which are companies investing in unquoted companies but which have their own shares quoted on a stock exchange. There are about 250 investable listed private equity companies worldwide (*see* www.lpeq.com). They come in two varieties: firstly, those that are straightforward listed companies, and secondly, those that are listed as closed ended funds such as investment trusts, called private equity investment trusts (PEITs). Some PEITs invest in private equity funds ('fund of funds').

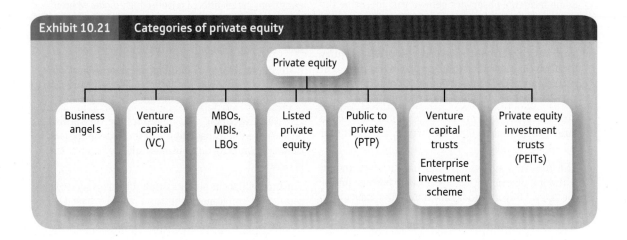

Exhibit 10.21   Categories of private equity

The disadvantage of listed private equity companies is the absence of special tax concessions compared with venture capital trusts and enterprise investment schemes – *see* below. However, investors are able to exit their investments easily by dealing on the stock market.

Venture capital trusts

It is important to distinguish between venture capital funds and venture capital trusts (VCTs), which are investment vehicles with important tax breaks designed to encourage investment in small and fast-growing companies. VCTs are companies whose shares are traded on the London Stock Exchange. The tax breaks for investors putting money into VCTs by buying shares in them include an immediate relief on their current year's income at 30% (by putting £10,000 into a VCT an investor will pay £3,000 less tax on income, so the effective cost is only £7,000). The benefit of this tax relief is only available to investors buying new VCT shares (not VCT shares bought from other investors in the secondary market) who hold the investment for at least five years. Any returns (income and capital gains) on a VCT are exempt from tax. Investors can place up to £200,000 each per year into VCTs. The VCT managers can invest only in companies with gross assets less than £15m and fewer than 250 employees. 'Unquoted' for VCT means not listed on the main list of the London Stock Exchange but can include AIM companies. A maximum of 15% of the VCT fund can be invested in any one company.

These trusts offer investors a way of investing in a broad spread of small firms with high potential, but with greater uncertainty, in a tax-efficient manner. They also offer the possibility of being able to sell the VCT shares in the secondary market (but not before five years have passed if you want to retain the initial tax relief). But beware: many of the funds that have been in operation for a few years have shown low returns due to a combination of poor investment selection and high management charges.

Enterprise investment scheme

Another government initiative to encourage the flow of risk capital to smaller companies is the enterprise investment scheme (EIS). Income tax relief at 30% is available for investments from £500 up to a maximum of £1m made directly (no need for a fund manager as with VCTs) into qualifying company shares. There is also capital gains tax relief, and losses within EISs are allowable against income tax. Investment under EIS means investing when the company issues shares, not the purchase of shares in the secondary market. The tax benefits are lost if the investments are held for less than three years. Investors are not allowed to hold more than 30% of the shares in any EIS company. Certain trading activities are excluded, such as finance, property and agriculture (HMRC gives the definitive list of these exclusions). The company must have fewer than 250 full-time employees. It must not be quoted on LSE's Main Market and the most it can raise under the EIS in any one year is usually £10m. The company must not have gross assets worth more than £15m. Funds which invest in a range of EIS companies are springing up to help investors spread risk. EIS investors are unlikely to be able to regain their investment until the company is sold or floated on a stock market as there is usually no share trading for many years.

There are even better tax breaks for investing in small, early stage companies with fewer than 25 employees and gross assets under £200,000 with the Seed Enterprise Investment Scheme, SEIS. An investor can buy up to £100,000 shares per year and gain 50% tax relief (a £10,000 investment results in £5,000 off income tax). The shares held by one investor must not constitute more than 30% of the company's equity and must be held for three years. No capital gains tax is due on gains made, and any loss can be offset against other income to reduce tax.

Corporate venturing and incubators

Larger companies sometimes foster the development of smaller enterprises. This can take many forms, from joint product development work to an injection of equity finance. The small firm can thereby retain its independence and yet contribute to the large firm: perhaps its greater freedom to innovate will generate new products which the larger firm can exploit to the benefit of both. Intel uses corporate venturing to increase demand for its technology and to make money in technology it hadn't thought of. Shell uses it to promote innovation in energy technology. Nestlé, set up a corporate venturing organisation to provide it with better access to new science, technology and know-how opportunities. Daimler invested in a young company with ambitions in new tech in 2010 called Tesla – I wonder how that is working out.

Incubators are places where a start-up company not only will gain access to finance, but will be able to receive support in many forms. This may include all humdrum operational managerial tasks being taken care of (e.g. accounting, legal, human resources), business planning, the supply of managers for various stages of the company's development, property management, etc. As a result the entrepreneurial team can concentrate on innovation and grow the business, even if they have no prior managerial experience. Royal Bank of Scotland runs 13 accelerators in major cities which encourage entrepreneurship by providing free office space and mentoring.

Government sources

Some local authorities have set up VC-type funds in order to attract and encourage industry. Large organisations with similar aims include the Scottish Enterprise and Finance Wales. Equity, debt and grant finance may be available from these sources. Also the UK government occasionally has initiatives, e.g. The Business Growth Fund is a funding scheme for medium-sized businesses launched by the government together with the British Bankers Association.

Disillusionment and dissatisfaction with quotation

Appendix 10.1 contains a number of newspaper articles about companies which are either dissatisfied with being quoted on a stock exchange or have never been quoted and feel no need to join. A reading of these will provide a wider understanding of the place of stock markets, their importance to some firms and how many companies are able to expand and produce wealth without them.[13] Some of the main points are summarised in **Exhibit 10.22**. The arguments are taken directly from numerous articles (only some of which are reproduced here) and do not necessarily represent reasoned scientific argument.

Exhibit 10.22	Arguments for and against joining a stock exchange

For

- Access to new capital for growth.
- Liquidity for existing shareholders.
- Discipline on management to perform.
- More able to use equity to buy businesses.
- Allows founders to diversify.
- Borrow more easily or cheaply.
- Can attract better management.
- Forces managers to articulate strategy clearly and persuasively.
- Succession planning may be made easier – professional managers rather than family.
- Increased customer recognition.
- Allows local people to buy shares.
- Share incentive schemes are more meaningful.

Against

- Dealing with 'City' folk is time consuming and/or boring.
- City is short-termist.
- City does not understand entrepreneurs.
- Stifles creativity.
- Focus excessively on return on capital.
- Empire building through acquisitions on a stock exchange – growth for its own sake (or for directors) can be the result of a quote.
- The stock market undervalues entrepreneur's shares in the entrepreneur's eyes.
- Loss of control for founding shareholders.
- There are examples of strong family-held companies in Germany, Italy and Asia where stock markets are used less.
- Examples of good strong unquoted companies in UK: JCB (Bamford), Dyson Virgin.
- Press scrutiny is irritating.
- Building market share in an industry (and short-term low profit margins) are more possible off exchange.
- The temptation of over-rapid expansion is avoided off exchange.
- By remaining unquoted, the owners, if they do not wish to put shareholder wealth at the centre of the firm's purpose, don't have to (environment or ethical issues may dominate).
- Costs of maintaining a quote, e.g. SE fees, extra disclosure costs, management time.

Concluding comments

There are many ways of raising finance by selling shares. The advantages and problems associated with each method and type mean that careful thought has to be given to establishing the wisest course of action for a firm, given its specific circumstances. Failure here could mean an unnecessary loss of control, an unbalanced capital structure, an excessive cost of raising funds or some other destructive outcome. But getting the share question right is only one of the key issues involved in financing a firm. The next chapter examines another, that of long-term debt finance.

---

13 You might like to consult the first, second, third, fourth and fifth editions of this book for additional articles.

Key points and concepts

- **Ordinary shareholders** own the company. They have the rights of control, voting, receiving annual reports, etc. They have no rights to income or capital but receive a residual after other claimants have been satisfied. This residual can be very attractive.

- **Debt capital holders** have no formal control but they do have a right to receive interest and capital.

- **Equity** as a way of financing the firm:

Advantages	Disadvantages
1 No obligation to pay dividends – 'shock absorber'.	1 High cost:
	a issue costs;
	b required rate of return.
2 Capital does not have to be repaid – 'shock absorber'.	2 Loss of control.
	3 Dividends not tax deductible.

- **Authorised share** capital is the maximum amount permitted by shareholders to be issued.

- **Issued share** capital is the amount issued (sold) expressed at par value.

- **Share premium** The difference between the sale price and par value of shares.

- **Private companies** Companies termed 'Ltd' are the most common form of limited liability company.

- **Public limited companies** (plcs) can offer their shares to a wider range of investors, but are required to have £50,000 of share capital.

- **Preference shares** offer a fixed rate of return, but without a guarantee. They are part of shareholders' funds but not part of the equity capital.

Advantages to the firm	Disadvantages to the firm
1 Dividend 'optional'.	1 High cost of capital relative to debt.
2 Usually no influence over management.	
3 Extraordinary profits go to ordinary shareholders.	2 Dividends are not tax deductible.
4 Financial gearing considerations.	

- **Types of preference share:** cumulative, participating, redeemable, convertible, variable rate.

- **Ordinary shares** rank higher than **deferred ordinary shares** for dividends, but in a good year the deferred holders (often founders) may receive a large share of the profit. Preferred ordinary shares rank higher than ordinary shares.

- **Golden shares** have extraordinary special powers.

- **To float on London Stock Exchange's Official List with a premium listing** the following are required:

  - a prospectus;
  - an acceptance of new responsibilities (e.g. dividend policy may be influenced by exchange investors; directors' freedom to buy and sell may be restricted);
  - 25% of share capital in public hands;
  - that the company is suitable;
  - usually three years of accounts;
  - competent and broadly based management team;
  - appropriate timing for flotation;
  - a sponsor;
  - a corporate broker;
  - underwriters (usually);
  - accountants' reports;
  - lawyers;
  - registrar.

- **Following flotation on the Main Market:**

  - greater disclosure of information;
  - restrictions on director share dealings;
  - annual fees to LSE;
  - high standards of behaviour.

- **Methods of flotation:**

  - placing;
  - offer for sale;
  - introduction;
  - intermediaries' offer;
  - reverse takeover.

- **Book-building** Investors make bids for shares. Issuers decide price and allocation in light of bids.

- **Stages in a flotation:**

  - pre-launch publicity;
  - decide technicalities, e.g. method, price, underwriting;
  - pathfinder prospectus;
  - launch of public offer – prospectus and price;
  - close of offer;
  - allotment of shares;
  - first trading.

- **The Alternative Investment Market (AIM)** differs from the Main Market in:

  - nominated advisers, not sponsors;
  - lower costs;
  - no minimum capitalisation, trading history or percentage of shares in public hands needed;
  - lower ongoing costs.

▶

- **Costs of new issues:**

  - administrative/transaction costs;
  - the equity cost of capital;
  - market pricing costs.

- **Rights issues** are an invitation to existing shareholders to purchase additional shares.

- **The theoretical ex-rights price** is a weighted average of the price of the existing shares and the new shares.

- The **nil paid rights** can be sold instead of buying new shares.

- **Value of a right on a new share:**

  Theoretical market value of share ex-rights – Subscription price

- **Value of a right on an old share:**

$$\frac{\text{Theoretical market value of share ex-rights} - \text{Subscription price}}{\text{Number of old shares required to purchase one new share}}$$

- **The pre-emption right** can be bypassed in the UK under strict conditions.

- **Placings** New shares sold directly to a group of external investors. If there is a *clawback* provision, so that existing shareholders can buy the shares at the same price instead, the issue is termed an **open offer.**

- **Acquisition for shares** Shares are created and given in exchange for a business.

- **Vendor placing** Shares are given in exchange for a business. The shares can be immediately sold by the business vendors to institutional investors.

- **Scrip issues** Each shareholder is given more shares in proportion to current holding. No new money is raised.

- **Warrants** The holder has the right to subscribe for a specified number of shares at a fixed price at some time in the future. Warrants are sold by the company, which is committed to selling the shares if warrant holders insist.

- **Business angels (informal venture capitalists)** Wealthy individuals investing £10,000 to £250,000 in shares and debt of small, young companies with high growth prospects. Also offer knowledge and skills.

- **Private equity/Venture capital (VC)** Finance for high-growth-potential unquoted firms. Sums: £250,000 minimum, average £5m. Some of the investment categories of VC are:

  - seedcorn;
  - start-up;
  - other early-stage, first-round;
  - expansion, *development or growth capital, 'second-round financing'*;
  - management buy-outs (MBO): existing team buys business from corporation;
  - management buy-ins (MBI): external managers buy a stake in a business and take over management;
  - leveraged buy-out;
  - secondary purchase;
  - Public-to-private (PTP).

- **Rates of return** demanded by VC range from 26% to 80% per annum depending on risk.

- **Exit** ('take-out') is the term used by private equity/venture capitalists to mean the method of selling a holding. A popular method is a trade sale to another organisation. Stock market flotation, own-share repurchase and sale to an institution are other possibilities.

- Venture capitalists often strike **agreements** with entrepreneurs to give the venture capitalists **extraordinary powers** if specific negative events occur, e.g. poor performance.

- **Venture capital trusts (VCTs)** are special tax-efficient vehicles for investing in small unquoted firms through a pooled investment.

- **Enterprise investment scheme (EIS)** Tax benefits are available to investors in small unquoted firms willing to hold the investment for three years.

- **Corporate venturing** Large firms can sometimes be a source of equity finance for small firms. **Incubators** provide finance and business services.

- **Government agencies** can be approached for equity finance.

- **Being quoted has significant disadvantages,** ranging from consumption of senior management time to lack of understanding between the City and directors and the stifling of creativity.

Appendix 10.1: Reasons for and against floating

Exhibit 10.23

Michael Dell: Nerd who remade the gadget business

By Leslie Hook

When Michael Dell drove to his first day of university in 1983, he stashed three computers in the back seat of his BMW. But it was not only the technology of these gadgets that attracted him — it was a way of making money, by upgrading the machines by hand and reselling them for more than he paid. A year later, Mr Dell had dropped out of university and was selling computers full time.

At 19 he used the proceeds from those sales to register his company, and Dell Computer Corporation was born. This week Mr Dell's instinct for the deal has again been on display. His $63bn buyout of storage company EMC is the largest technology acquisition ever. With a mountain of cheap debt, clever financial structuring and a nose for value in an ageing technology that most stock market investors no longer care about, he has shown an undimmed passion for flouting convention.

Mr Dell's re-emergence is testament to a relentless determination and a willingness to follow his own stars. A decade ago he handed control to a professional manager, but took the reins again when the company started to flounder. He has never let his grip slip again.

The perseverance has paid off. Combined with the PC company that bears his name and which he took private two years ago, the 50-year-old Texan will be left with a personal 70 per cent stake in one of the world's largest IT companies.

Mr Dell, whose net worth Forbes puts at $19.5bn, also has a foundation in his and his wife's name that focuses on health and education. Those who know him say Mr Dell's passion has always been business.

His first business model involved selling built-to-order PCs directly to consumers via telephone or fax; once harnessed to the internet in the 1990s, it turned the PC industry upside down. With little inventory and no expensive stores, costs were low and the business generated plenty of cash.

By the time the company was two years old, it was pulling in $60m a year, and Mr Dell was debating whether to go public. He gathered advisers for a strategic retreat.

One of the people he invited was Esther Dyson, a tech investor and journalist. "He was a business nerd," she recalls. "He wasn't trying to write code, he was trying to engineer the business." Even then, she adds, Mr Dell showed "that same doggedness you are certainly seeing played over again now. He doesn't pivot carelessly."

But pivot he has, moving definitively away from the PCs and into corporate IT infrastructure.

In the end, it was a few more years before Mr Dell took his company public — at the age of 23, two years younger than Jobs had been at the time of Apple's initial public offering.

But although his company was a stock market darling of the 1990s, Mr Dell has not always made friends on Wall Street. By the beginning of this decade, he had become a prominent critic of what he regarded as the short-termist ethos of public markets, leading a high-profile fight to take Dell private in 2013.

Only as a private company, he argued, could Dell invest and grow. There was no love lost on either side. Critics, led by the activist investor Carl Icahn, accused him of buying his company back on the cheap. Mr Dell disdained the hassle of being listed. "All the activities required of a public company consume about 20 per cent of a CEO's time and attention," he wrote in a 2014 LinkedIn post. "And frankly it was the most annoying 20 per cent."

Mr Dell still has plenty of fans, however. "He's an entrepreneur of a start-up company; he successfully ran a large company. A lot of people don't make that transition," says Jamie Dimon, head of JPMorgan, who personally helped to pitch the deal to the EMC board.

FT *Financial Times,* 16 October 2015.
All Rights Reserved.

Exhibit 10.24

Facebook puts off IPO until late 2012

By April Dembosky in San Francisco

Facebook is preparing to launch its blockbuster initial public offering in the US towards the end of next year, a later public debut by the social networking site than had been widely anticipated.

The IPO, valuing Facebook at more than $66.5bn, has been expected by the spring with persistent speculation that it could even come this year.

However, people close to the company have told the Financial Times that Mark Zuckerberg, Facebook's chief executive, wants to wait until next September or later in order to keep employees focused on product developments rather than a pay-out.

'There's really no reason to rush a deal,' said Lise Buyer, a consultant who advised Google through its IPO. 'The company doesn't need the money. It is a little easier to focus when you're private. They'll go when they're good and ready, not before.'

'There are so many things you don't have to do until you take public shareholder money,' Ms Buyer said. 'You don't have to take investor phone calls or show up at investor conferences.' Peter Thiel, a prominent Facebook investor, said it was generally desirable for technology companies to defer an IPO for as long as possible. He said Google set a good example by not going public for nearly six years, until it dominated the internet search wars.

'It was a good competitive strategy,' he said. 'And it culturally orientated people toward long-term value and not quarterly numbers.'

According to SEC regulations, once a company accrues more than 500 shareholders, it must file public financial results in the first quarter of the following year. Facebook surpassed 500 shareholders in January when Goldman Sachs became an investor, meaning it will have to publish numbers by April of 2012.

Companies are not obliged to go public after publishing such data but many do so in order to take advantage of market interest and momentum. Some analysts had expected Facebook would go public shortly afterwards after lifting the veil on its financial performance.

Silicon Valley's talent war might also be a factor in the timing of the Facebook IPO. This has made hiring and retaining good employees difficult. While Facebook has been faring relatively well on this front compared to its competitors, some employees are getting keen to cash out in an IPO, a person close to the company said.

Mr Zuckerberg hopes to keep such personnel on staff through next summer in order to complete certain product rollouts, this person said.

Exhibit 10.25

Huawei's founder rejects possibility of stock market listing

By Daniel Thomas

Ren Zhengfei, the founder of Huawei, has described shareholders of public companies as greedy and short-termist, in a forceful rejection of the idea of listing the Chinese telecoms equipment maker.

"In reality, [public] shareholders are greedy and want to squeeze every bit out of a company as soon as possible," he told a gathering of western journalists in London. "People who own this company are not greedy . . . Not listing on the stock market is one of the reasons we have overtaken our peers."

In the rare discussion, Mr Ren said Huawei was already transparent enough in its dealings without a listing, in spite of the concerns raised in the US and Australia about connections to the Chinese state.

The debate has been reversed in recent months after documents from Edward Snowden suggested that the US National Security Agency had itself been hacking into Huawei's corporate servers. Mr Ren said that he had held suspicions that the company was being monitored, but used the Snowden disclosures to emphasise that nothing was being hidden by the Chinese group. "The monitoring behaviour by the United States is within expectations," he said. "I believe that there is no secret around myself. Huawei's approach has [always] been open."

The group was banned from bidding on certain national contracts in Australia, while a US congressional report raised fears about Huawei's links with the Chinese state, although the report presented no evidence of actual wrongdoing.

Mr Ren said there was no need for a public listing to provide greater transparency, instead pointing to dangers of shareholdership. Huawei workers are offered a stake in the company, which Mr Ren said meant there was a "longer-term view". Mr Ren holds the position of chairman and maintains a veto on decisions, even though there are three rotating chief executives under him with operational control. He has never used the right of veto, he said, instead preferring to talk to his senior management.

FT   *Financial Times,* 2 May 2014.

Exhibit 10.26

UK biotech group raises £100m to sell DNA-reading tools in Asia

By Clive Cookson

Oxford Nanopore, one of Britain's fastest growing private technology companies, has raised £100m in new funding to extend its range of portable DNA reading machines. The private share placement brings the total raised so far to £351m.

The funding round announced on Monday morning is led by GT Healthcare, an investment partnership based in Hong Kong and focusing on Asia, which is a new investor in Oxford Nanopore. Existing UK-based shareholders, including Woodford Investment Management and IP Group, also participated.

Gordon Sanghera, chief executive of Oxford Nanopore, said the company would be "using these funds to expand our commercial operations across a range of territories, including Asia".

The quoted IP Group committed a further £14m to Oxford Nanopore in this round. It will have a stake of 19.7 per cent worth £246.3m, which implies a total value for Oxford Nanopore of £1.25bn.

Gordon Sanghera has a grand ambition: to build a new science-based company under British ownership that commands a large global market. The company, founded in 2005 as an Oxford university spinout, has pioneered the development of portable and inexpensive gene-reading machines. It aims to challenge the market leader, Illumina, and other DNA sequencing companies, which produce more powerful but much larger and more expensive kits.

Oxford Nanopore's flagship product, the $1,000 Minion, is the size of a mobile phone and connects to the USB socket of a portable computer. Since its launch last year, Minion has been popular with scientists using it to read the genomes of pathogens in the field, including Ebola in Africa.

Last week, researchers at Oxford university's Wellcome Trust Centre for Human Genetics said that, for the first time, they had used the Minion to read the 3bn biochemical "letters" of the human genome, following an upgrade to the technology.

An even smaller DNA sequencer, called SmidgIon and scheduled for launch late next year, will connect directly to a mobile phone. It could be used by patients at home to carry out DNA tests and send their results to doctors.

Dr Sanghera said the company's goal was to make possible "the analysis of any living thing, by anyone, anywhere". His aim is to build an independent UK technology group.

An IPO is not on the agenda in the short term, he told the FT, but he hopes that Oxford Nanopore will eventually be listed on the London market. It uses a technology based on nanopores, which are microscopic holes within protein molecules. As a strand of DNA passes through an electrically changed nanopore, each of the four "letters" of DNA produces a distinct change in current, which makes it possible to deduce the genetic sequence.

FT   *Financial Times,* 12 December 2016.

Exhibit 10.27

Stannah on the stairway to heaven

By Peter Marsh

Of the potential growth industries of the 21st century, stairlifts may not seem the most obvious.

But for Jon Stannah, the business is full of opportunities. 'We are in a niche where the demographics are helping us considerably. If you are elderly, reasonably well-off and live in a house with more than one storey then there's a fair chance you will at some point be looking for a stairlift.'

Mr Stannah, 44, is a director, part-owner and 'chief spokesman' of Stannah Lifts, one of a handful of companies that are the global leaders in the stairlift industry.

Apart from a division of Germany's ThyssenKrupp, the other large players in the industry – which had total sales last year estimated at £1.3bn – are other

mid-sized businesses including the UK's Acorn, Handicare of Norway and US-based Bruno.

Mr Stannah says his company first spotted the potential of stairlifts when examining how to expand in the Netherlands.

'If you look at a city like Amsterdam, it's full of tall, thin houses which are virtually impossible to adapt to take conventional lifts. It's an ideal place for a company like ours to try to sell to.'

Last year, Stannah, based in Andover, Hampshire, had sales of £180m.

Mr Stannah says his company 'has never given a thought' to going public. 'The fact that I am the fifth generation of the family to be running Stannah gives me a lot of pride. If we were to stop being a family-owned-company, I think we'd lose a lot of our value.'

Exhibit 10.28

JCB chief calls for German approach to manufacturing

By Peter Marsh

Britain should try to emulate Germany by stimulating a cadre of privately owned manufacturers to help re-energise the economy, according to Sir Anthony Bamford, chairman and owner of the JCB excavator business.

While JCB is the biggest family-owned maker of industrial goods in the UK, research by the FT has shown that in Germany, there are 28 privately-owned manufacturers with sales last year that were either the same or larger.

Sir Anthony – who has run JCB since 1975 – said that his company was 'an example' of what the UK was capable of in manufacturing, an area that government ministers are keen to support in efforts

to 'rebalance' the economy away from a dependence on financial services. However, more businesses should be encouraged to follow the JCB pattern. 'We [JCB] haven't gone off the path [of staying private] and that's been an ingredient to our progress.'

The JCB boss believes that – while there is a role for stock market ownership of companies – the UK has created a financial environment that creates too many opportunities for public shareholders to take control of manufacturing businesses, rather than leave them under private ownership. Germany has done better, he says, in establishing a culture that permits private entrepreneurs to build up businesses over decades, rather than expecting quick returns from rapid profits growth, or the large windfalls provided by selling a company.

The result of this culture has been the large pool of so-called Mittelstand family-owned groups, from which can emerge some big companies that remain privately owned. The nature of production businesses means that they often needed years of patient investment, Sir Anthony notes.

'Manufacturing is not [in financial terms] a quick turn,' he points out. 'There is too much short-termism [in Britain], while there isn't in Germany.'

Bernd Venohr, an independent consultant based in Munich who studies Mittelstand businesses, says local banks in Germany provide a form of 'stable support' for many private businesses.

Exhibit 10.29

Managers buy in to buy-outs

By Andrew Hill

In the trophy cabinet at Birds Eye's factory in Lowestoft, a large silver cup has pride of place. It is the 2009 Cash Profit Award – an apt illustration of the venerable frozen food producer's priorities since 2006, when the division was bought from Unilever by Permira, the private equity firm.

'Unilever was a more comfortable place to work,' concedes Craig Hamilton, the enthusiastic Glaswegian who was promoted after the buy-out to run the factory, perched on the easternmost point of the UK. However, he welcomes the discipline of private equity. 'It's a more financially focused business now.'

The common preconception of how private equity operates is that a fierce focus on cost-cutting and determination to pay down acquisition debt comes at the expense of jobs and long-term corporate sustainability.

But managers who once worked for listed groups and have successfully come through the credit crunch say there are also clear benefits to the discipline of private equity ownership.

At the time of the Birds Eye deal, Permira was in the crosshairs of the critics. One union had mounted a stunt by taking a camel to the local church of Damon Buffini, then Permira chairman, in a reference to Jesus's comment that it would be easier for a camel to pass through the eye of a needle than for the wealthy to get to heaven. Union fears seemed to be confirmed when about 850 out of Birds Eye's 5,000 workers lost their jobs in the subsequent closure of its factory in Hull. Those jobs have not returned.

'The objective wasn't to bring a number of jobs back to previous [levels]; the objective was to be as efficient and as competitive as possible,' says Martin Glenn, chief executive of Iglo, which controls the Birds Eye and Iglo brands for Permira.

But Mr Hamilton, is not nostalgic for the comforts of working for a listed multinational. He says staff at the plant were initially nervous about the takeover, but quickly recognised the benefits of becoming more efficient and attracting more volume to Lowestoft's production line.

In fact, he and other executives in the sector are quick to point out the disadvantages of the listed model. William Eccleshare worked for both WPP and Omnicom, the quoted media groups, and is now chief executive of outdoor advertising company Clear Channel International, part of Clear Channel Communications, controlled by Thomas H. Lee Partners and Bain Capital. He says that at the listed companies 'there was always a very short-term pressure to deliver the next quarterly earnings, and never really a great sense of the need to build a long-term strategy'.

John Pearmund, chief executive of Domestic & General, which provides extended electrical appliance warranties, agrees. He ran the company before and after its 2007 buy-out by Advent International.

'With one main investor, all these discussions [about strategy] can be had in a much more open environment – not in one of these presentations to [public company] investors where . . . you get constrained in lots of ways,' he says.

These managers cite four main reasons why they prefer the private equity model. One is the greater proximity between managers and owners. Mr Eccleshare reports to an operating committee of the board, which includes representatives of both TH Lee and Bain Capital. 'We have very intense monthly reviews,' he says, where the questions are more

▶

Exhibit 10.29 (continued)

rigorous and more intelligent than those he used to field when working for listed media companies.

A second reason is the speed with which decisions are taken. Mr Hamilton says that if he can justify capital spending decisions – such as two recent £500,000 investments to produce resealable bags for frozen peas – Iglo is quick to approve them. Previously, he says, getting approval could take longer than the lead time for delivering the machinery.

Third, private equity owners demand focus. "We don't want to over-complicate this business" is a phrase you hear quite often [from the owners],' says Mr Eccleshare.

At D&G, Mr Pearmund was able to drop a diffuse strategy without having to justify the apparent U-turn to critics in the press or investor community. This fourth advantage – privacy – means costly strategic investment or painful restructuring can be done away from public scrutiny. Stepping off the treadmill of quarterly or half-yearly corporate reporting certainly frees up time to manage. Mr Pearmund estimates that he has saved two months in every year that he used to spend briefing analysts and investors.

Unions, however, claim private equity can keep management and investment failures out of the headlines. So does this style of management produce better operational results? Studies of private equity performance carried out for the World Economic Forum two years ago showed that on average, private equity ownership did improve productivity, and that private equity-owned companies demonstrated higher levels of management practice.

But the difference, particularly compared with companies with dispersed shareholders, was small, raising the question of whether the disruption and transaction costs involved in such takeovers is worthwhile. Moreover, during credit bubbles the gains achieved by private equity owners are much lower. 'There is so much easy money to be made by flipping [buying and selling companies in short order] that they don't really do the hard work of adding value,' says Josh Lerner of Harvard Business School, who helped bring together the WEF studies. 'That wouldn't be a problem, except those are the periods where the bulk of money gets invested.'

John Singer, managing partner at Advent International, says: 'The industry did try to do things with arbitrage and leverage, but it's become clear recently that [earnings] growth is the way to add value.'

There may be another, largely unspoken reason why managers prefer private equity to the listed model: the potential payback that buy-out firms offer to those who lead their companies to a profitable exit. By giving such incentives, private equity firms say they align the interests of owners and managers. As Mr Eccleshare says, 'they reward success and they're intolerant of failure'.

This and the operational benefits of managing under private equity ownership help explain why nobody interviewed for this article expressed an urge to return to running a listed company. The prizes for successful management under private equity control still look more valuable.

References and further reading

To keep up to date and reinforce knowledge gained by reading this chapter I can recommend the *Financial Times* and *The Economist*.

Ahmad, W. and Jelic, R. (2014) 'Lockup Agreements and Survival of UK IPOs', *Journal of Business Finance & Accounting,* 41(5) & (6), 717–742, June/July 2014.
    When insiders, such as founder managers, are prevented from selling all or some of their shares in the company for a long period after an IPO the company survives longer.

Armitage, S. (2010) 'Block buying and choice of issue method in UK seasoned equity offers', *Journal of Business Finance & Accounting,* 37(3), (4), pp. 422–48.
    Placings of new shares in already quoted companies more effectively raise money in large blocks for the firm than rights issues.

Armitage, S., Dionysiou, D. and Gonzalez, A. (2014) 'Are the Discounts in Seasoned Equity Offers Due to Inelastic Demand?' *Journal of Business Finance & Accounting,* 41(5) & (6), 743–72, June/July 2014,
    Investigates the large and diverse discounts in UK open offers and placings. Large discounts are a substantial cost to those shareholders who do not buy new shares. Inelastic demand, or illiquidity of the issuer's shares, and financial distress, are key determinants of the discount.

Arnold, G. (2014a) *The Financial Times Guide to Investing* 3rd edition. Harlow: Financial Times Prentice Hall.
    An introduction to financial markets including the new issue market.

Arnold, G. (2012) *Modern Financial Markets and Institutions.* Harlow: FT Prentice Hall.
    A more comprehensive description of the markets, instruments and institutions.

British Private Equity and Venture Capital Association, London (www.bvca.co.uk).
    Variety of paper publications and online material which give an insight into a variety of aspects of venture capital.

Chambers, D. and Dimson, E. (2009) 'IPO underpricing over the very long run', *Journal of Finance,* LXIV(3).
    British IPOs since 1917 have generally been underpriced.

Chemmanur, T.J., Loutskina, E. and Xuan Tian (2014) 'Corporate venture capital, value creation, and innovation', *The Review of Financial Studies,* 27(8), pp. 2433–73.
    Corporate venture backed firms are more innovative, as measured by their patenting outcome, although they are younger, riskier, and less profitable than independent venture backed firms. Greater industry knowledge due to the technological fit between their parent firms and entrepreneurial firms and greater tolerance for failure may explain the results.

Degeorge, F., Martin, J. and Phalippou, L. (2016) 'On secondary buyouts', *Journal of Financial Economics,* 120, pp. 124–45.
    SBOs destroy value for investors when made by buyers under pressure to spend. SBOs made under no pressure to spend perform as well as other buyouts. When buyer and seller have complementary skill sets, SBOs outperform other buyouts. Investors do not pay higher total transaction costs as a result of SBOs, even if they have a stake in both the buying fund and the selling fund.

Demaria, C. (2013) *Introduction to Private Equity: Venture, Growth, LBO and Turnaround Capital,* Chichester: John Wiley and Sons.
    A comprehensive, easy-to-follow description of the private equity industry with a European slant.

Dolvin, S.D. and Jordan, B.D. (2008) 'Underpricing, overhang, and the cost of going public to preexisting shareholders', *Journal of Business Finance & Accounting,* 35(3), (4), pp. 434–58.
    The issue of IPO underpricing is more complicated than it first appears.

EY (annually). Annual Report on the Performance of Portfolio Companies. www.bvca.co.uk.
    Surveys dozens of private equity-backed companies to examine how they are performing with regard to, for example, growth in output, employee salaries.

Fang, L., Ivashina, V. and Lerner, J. (2015) 'The disintermediation of financial markets: Direct investing in private equity', *Journal of Financial Economics*, 116, pp. 160–78.

> Seven large institutions' direct investments in entrepreneurial companies over 20 years are examined. These investments perform better than public market indices, especially buyout investments. Outperformance, relative to private equity fund benchmarks, is limited.

Gompers, P., Kaplan, S. and Mukharlyamov, V. (2015) 'What private equity investors think they do for the companies they buy', *Harvard Business Review*, 18 June.

> They seem to align managerial incentives with shareholder interests, change management and governance structure and stimulate operational improvements.

Gompers, P., Kaplan, S.N. and Mukharlyamov, V. (2016) What do private equity firms say they do? *Journal of Financial Economics*, 121, pp. 449–76.

> A survey of 79 US private equity investors about their practices in firm valuation, capital structure, governance and value creation.

Gregory, A., Guermat, C. and Al-Shawawreh, F. (2010) 'UK IPOs: long run returns, behavioural timing and pseudo timing', *Journal of Business Finance & Accounting*, 37(5), (6), pp. 612–47.

> In the 3–5 years following an IPO these firms generally underperform their peers.

Guo, S., Hotchkiss, E.S. and Song, W. (2011) 'Do buyouts (still) create value?', *Journal of Finance*, 66(2), pp. 479–517.

> Leveraged buy-outs from public to private deals created value.

Haislip, A. (2011) *Essentials of Venture Capital*. Chichester: John Wiley & Sons, Inc.

> An easy-to-read introduction to venture capital, most reference to the USA.

Hellmann, T. and V. Thiele (2015) 'Friends or foes? The interrelationship between angel and venture capital markets', *Journal of Financial Economics*, 115, pp. 639–53.

> Entrepreneurs first receive angel then venture capital funding. The two investor types are 'friends' in that they rely upon each other's investments. However, they are also 'foes', because at the later stage the venture capitalists no longer need the angels.

Invest Europe (www.investeurope.eu).

> Represents the private equity investing community. The website displays various useful publications.

Isenberg, D. and D. Lawton (2014) 'How to finance the scale-up of your company', *Harvard Business Review*, 18 August, pp. 2–4.

> Some simple advice about a wide range of sources of finance.

Kerins, F., Kutsuna, K. and Smith, R. (2007) 'Why are IPOs underpriced? Evidence from Japan's hybrid auction-method offerings', *Journal of Financial Economics*, 85, pp. 637–66.

> Japanese IPO underpricing.

Kerr, W.R., Lerber, J. and Schoar, A. (2014) 'The consequences of entrepreneurial finance: evidence from angel financings', *The Review of Financial Studies*, 27(1), pp. 20–55.

> Ventures funded by two successful angel groups experience superior outcomes to rejected ventures: They have improved survival, exits, employment, patenting, web traffic and financing.

Knauer, A., Lahmann, A., Pflücke, M. and Schwetzler, B. (2014) 'How much do private equity funds benefit from debt-related tax shields?' *Journal of Applied Corporate Finance*, 26(1), Winter, pp. 85–93.

> PE firms get some additional return from the incremental tax shields that result from higher post-LBO leverage.

Larrain, B. and F. Urzúa I. (2013) 'Controlling shareholders and market timing in share issuance', *Journal of Financial Economics*, 109, pp. 661–81.

> Examines market timing in the equity issuance of firms controlled by large shareholders in Chile between 1990 and 2009. Issuance predicts poor future returns and is preceded by high returns, but only when the controlling shareholder's stake is significantly reduced. Consistent with market timing, the results are stronger in the absence of institutional investors and in hot issuance markets.

Lerner, J. (2013) 'Corporate Venturing', *Harvard Business Review*, October, pp. 87–94.

> The case for corporate venturing is made in an easy to read fashion.

Lerner, J., Hardymon, F. and Leamon, A. (2012) *Venture Capital and Private Equity: A Casebook*. 5th edn. Chichester: John Wiley & Sons, Inc.

> This collection of (mostly Harvard) case studies provides thorough insight into the US venture capital and private equity industry with detailed examples.

Lerner, J., Sorensen, M. and Strömberg, P. (2011) 'Private equity and long-run investment: The case of innovation', *Journal of Finance*, 66(2), pp. 445–77.

> Companies subject to a leveraged buy-out continue to produce a high level of patents.

Lerner, J., Sorensen, M. and Stromberg, P. (2013) 'Private equity and investment in innovation: Evidence from patents', *Applied Corporate Finance*, 25(2), Spring, pp. 95–102.

> Private equity investees increase their effectiveness in innovation.

Levis, M. (1990) 'The winner's curse problem, interest costs and the underpricing of initial public offerings', *Economic Journal*, 100, March, pp. 76–89.

Underpricing for some issues is explained by fear on the part of uninformed investors, plus the cost of interest between application for shares and return of cheques in oversubscribed issues.

Loughran, T., Rutter, J.R. and Rydqvist, K. (1994, Updated 2015) 'Initial public offerings: International insights', *Pacific-Basin Finance Journal*, 2, pp. 165–99.
  Evidence from dozens of papers on short and long run share performances of companies going public. Updated to the end of 2013 for 26 of the original 52 countries – see https://site.warrington.ufl.edu/ritter/files/2015/05/Initial-Public-Offerings-International-Insights-2015-05-21.pdf

London Stock Exchange website publications.
  Contain easy-to-read guides to floating a company and other matters.

Loughran, T. and McDonald, B. (2013) 'IPO first-day returns, offer price revisions, volatility, and form S-1 language', *Journal of Financial Economics*, 109, pp. 307–326.
  IPOs with high levels of uncertainty have higher first-day returns, absolute offer price revisions, and subsequent volatility. Our findings provide empirical evidence for the theoretical models of uncertainty, bookbuilding, and prospect theory.

Metrick, A. and Yasuda, A. (2010) *Venture Capital and the Finance of Innovation*. 2nd edn. Chichester: John Wiley & Sons, Inc.
  A useful introduction, but becomes quite theoretical and technical later on.

Mulcahy, D. (2013) 'Six myths about venture capitalists', *Harvard Business Review*, May, pp. 81–83.
  Common misunderstandings about VC corrected.

Mullins, J. (2014) 'VC funding can be bad for your start-up', *Harvard Business Review*, 4 August, pp. 2–4.
  There are many negatives to taking venture capitalist money.

Ngatuni, P., Capstaff, J. and Marshall, A. (2007) 'Long-term performance following rights issues and open offers in the UK', *Journal of Business Finance & Accounting*, 34(1), (2), pp. 33–64.
  Evidence of underperformance of company shares following rights issues in the UK, but positive performance for open offers.

Silva, A. and Bilinski, P. (2015) 'Intended use of proceeds, underwriter quality and the long-run performance of SEOs in the UK', *Journal of Business Finance and Accounting*, 42(9) &(10), November/December, pp. 1282–309.

Share price performance and capital investment levels vary depending on the expressed motive for the fund raising and the choice of underwriter.

Sorensen, M., Neng Wang and Jinqiang Yang (2014) 'Valuing Private Equity', *The Review of Financial Studies*, 27(7), pp. 1977–2021.
  Investigates whether the performance of private equity investments is sufficient to compensate investors for risk, long-term illiquidity, management, and incentive fees charged by the general partner. Management fees, carried interest, and illiquidity are costly, and GPs must generate substantial alpha to compensate LPs for bearing these costs. Debt is cheap and reduces these costs, potentially explaining the high leverage of buyout transactions. Conventional interpretations of PE performance measures appear optimistic. On average, LPs may just break even, net of management fees, carry, risk, and costs of illiquidity.

Stoff, I. and Braun, R. (2014) 'The evolution of private equity fund terms beyond 2 and 20', *The Journal of Corporate Finance*, 26(1), Winter, pp. 65–75.
  There isn't much of a move away from the 2% plus 20% carried interest fee structure, but the fixed fee might drop to 1.5% for very large funds.

Torres, N. (2015) 'What angel investors value most when choosing what to fund', *Harvard Business Review*, 6 August, pp. 2–5.
  Human capital is uniquely important.

Truong X. Duong, R. Singh and Eng-Joo Tan (2015) 'Costly self-insurance of rights offerings', *Journal of Business Finance and Accounting*, 42(9) &(10), November/December, pp. 1251–81.
  A useful survey of rights issues and non-rights SEOs numbers and practices in various countries. It also questions whether self-insurance by offering a deeply discounted issue is truly costless.

Wai-Ming Fong and Kevin C.K. Lam (2014) 'Rights offerings and expropriation by controlling shareholders', *Journal of Business Finance and Accounting*, 41(5) & (6), June/July, pp. 773–90.
  Dominant shareholders can use deep price discounts on rights issues to expropriate value for themselves.

Yi, B., El-Badawi, M.H. and Lin, B. (2008) 'Pre-issue investor optimism and post-issue underperformance', *Financial Analysts Journal*, 64(5), pp. 77–87.
  Underperformance of new issues equity (and debt) over the long run associated with investor optimism prior to the issue.

Case study recommendations

Please see www.pearsoned.co.uk/arnold for case study synopses. Also, another list of useful case studies from the fifth edition can be found there.

- Crowdfunding: concept and economic rationale. Authors: Jayanth R. Varma; Joshy Jacob Indian Institute of Management-Ahmedabad. Available at www.cb.hbsp.harvard.edu

- Angels and crowds. Authors: Jayanth R. Varma; Joshy Jacob, Indian Institute of Management-Ahmedabad. Available at www.cb.hbsp.harvard.edu

- Doctor my eyes: the acquisition of Bausch & Lomb by Warburg Pincus (A) Author: Nori Gerardo Lietz, Harvard Business School. Available at www.cb.hbsp.harvard.edu

- Prada: to IPO or not to IPO: that is the question. Author: Stephen Sapp, Ivey Publishing. Available at www.cb.hbsp.harvard.edu

- Sensegiz: funding a start-up. Authors: Mrinalini Shah; Anuj Kulkarni, Ivey Publishing. Available at www.cb.hbsp.harvard.edu

- Square, Inc.: financing a unicorn. Author: Mark Simonson Harvard Business School. Available at www.cb.hbsp.harvard.edu

- Qalaa Holdings and the Egyptian Refining Company. Authors: Victoria Ivashina; Marc Homsy, Harvard Business School. Available at www.cb.hbsp.harvard.edu

- Narayana Health: the initial public offering decision. Authors: Narendra Nath Kushwaha; Bipin Kumar Dixit; David J. Sharp, Ivey Publishing. Available at www.cb.hbsp.harvard.edu

Websites

Alternative Investment Management Association www.aima.org

Association of Corporate Treasurers www.treasurers.org

Angels Den, www.angelsden.com British Private Equity and Venture Capital Association www.bvca.co.uk

CREST www.euroclear.com

East Midlands Business Angels, www.em-ba.co.uk

Enterprise zone www.enterprisezone.communities.gov.uk

European Business Angels Network (EBAN), www.eban.org, Invest Europe (formerly European Private Equity and Venture Capital Association) www.investeurope.eu

Financial Conduct Authority www.fca.org.uk

Her Majesty's Revenue and Customs www.hmrc.gov.uk

Listed Private Equity www.lpeq.com

London Business Angels, www.angelcapital.co.uk

London Clearing House, LCH. Clearnet www.lch.com

London Stock Exchange www.londonstockexchange.com

National Business Angel Network www.businessangelnetwok.co.uk

Northwest Business Angels, www.nwbusinessangels.co.uk

Private Equity Intelligence www.prequin.com

UK Angel Investment Network, www.angelinvestment network.co.uk

UK Business Angels Association, www.ukbaa.org

United Kingdom Listing Authority www.fca.org.uk/markets/ukla

Video presentations

Chief Executives and finance directors describe their current policy on raising funds on MerchantCantos.com (www.video.merchantcantos.com) – this is free to view.

Self-review questions

1 What is equity capital? Explain the advantages to the firm of raising capital this way. What are the disadvantages?

2 Distinguish between authorised and issued share capital.

3 What is the par value of a share, and what is the share premium?

4 Are all plcs quoted? Describe both terms.

5 What is a preference share and why might a company favour this form of finance?

6 What would be the characteristics of a cumulative redeemable participating convertible preference share?

7 Why are non-voting shares disliked by the City investing institutions?

8 Why does the United Kingdom Listing Authority impose stringent rules on companies floating on LSE's Main Market?

9 Outline the contents of a prospectus in a new issue on LSE's Main Market.

10 How might the working lives of directors change as a result of their company gaining a quotation?

11 What does a sponsor have to do to help a company float?

12 Describe the role of each of the institutions and professional organisations that assist a company in floating on LSE's Main Market.

13 What is an IPO placing and an introduction of a new issue? Which is the cheaper method of flotation?

14 List the differences between a flotation on AIM and LSE's Main Market.

15 What are, and why do the UK authorities insist upon, pre-emption rights?

16 Why are placings of shares for companies already listed on the London Stock Exchange subject to strict rules concerning the extent of price discount?

17 What adjustments need to be made to a balance sheet after a scrip issue?

18 Suggest circumstances when a firm may find the selling of warrants advantageous.

19 What do business angels bring to a firm?

20 What are the following: MBO, MBI, PTP, a venture capital fund, seedcorn?

Questions and problems

Answers to most questions can be found at www.pearsoned.co.uk/arnold.
Answers to questions marked with an asterisk are to be found only in the Lecturer's Guide.

1 (*Examination level*) Bluelamp plc has grown from a company with £10,000 turnover to one with a £17m turnover and £1.8m profit in the last five years. The existing owners have put all their financial resources into the firm to enable it to grow. The directors wish to take advantage of a very exciting market opportunity but would need to find £20m of new equity capital as the balance sheet is already over-geared (i.e. has high debt). The options being discussed, in a rather uninformed way, are flotation on the Main Market of the London Stock Exchange, a flotation on the Alternative Investment Market, and private equity. Write a report to enlighten the board on the merits and disadvantages of each of these three possibilities.

2 In what circumstances would you advise a company to float on the Alternative Investment Market (AIM) in preference to the Main Market of the London Stock Exchange?

3 Checkers plc is considering a flotation on the Main Market of the London Stock Exchange. Outline a timetable of events likely to be encountered which will assist management planning.

4   Describe the three costs associated with gaining a flotation on a stock exchange by selling shares to new shareholders.

5   Discuss the merits and problems of the pre-emption right for UK companies.

6   Explain why failure to carry through a plan to raise capital by floating on the London Stock Exchange Main Market might be highly disruptive to a firm.

7   There are a number of different methods of floating a company on the new issue market of the London Stock Exchange Main Market (e.g. offer for sale and placing). Describe these and comment on the ability of small investors to buy newly issued shares.

8*   Mahogany plc has an ordinary share price of £3 and is quoted on the Alternative Investment Market. It intends to raise £20m through a one-for-three rights issue priced at £2.
     a   What will the ex-rights price be?
     b   How many old ordinary shares were in circulation prior to the rights issue?
     c   Patrick owns 9,000 shares and is unable to find the cash necessary to buy the rights shares. Reassure Patrick that he will not lose value. How much might he receive from the company?
     d   What is the value of a right on one old share?
     e   What do the terms cum-rights and ex-rights mean?
     f   Advise Mahogany on the virtues of a deep-discounted rights issue.

9   Venture capital funds made a low internal rate of return on investments in the ten years up to the end of 2016. Describe the role of venture capitalists in the UK economy and comment on the rates of return they generally intend to achieve.

10   Examine the articles in Appendix 10.1 and write an essay advocating the case for avoiding flotation on a recognised investment exchange.

11   Write an essay advocating the case for flotation on a recognised investment exchange.

12   The shareholders of Yellowhammer plc are to offer a one-for-four rights issue at £1.50 when its shares are trading at £1.90. What is the theoretical ex-rights price and the value of a right per old share?

13   Explain the function of a prospectus in a new share issue.

14   What are the main advantages and disadvantages of raising finance through selling (a) ordinary shares, and (b) preference shares?

15   Discuss the main features of venture capital and explain the dangers to an unwary management.

16   Explain placings and offers for sale for new issues and comment on the reasons for the increased use of placings.

17   If business angels are not connected with divine intervention in business matters, seedcorn capital is not something to do with growing food and a captured fund is not theft, what are they and how might they assist a company?

18   If par values are not something to do with golf, public to private is not something to do with sexual modesty and a pathfinder prospectus is not something to do with scouting, what are they? Explain the context in which these terms are used.

Assignment

Consider the equity base of your company, or one you are familiar with. Write a report outlining the options available should the firm need to raise further equity funds. Also consider if preference share capital should be employed.

Long-term debt finance

LEARNING OUTCOMES

An understanding of the key characteristics of the main categories of debt finance is essential to anyone considering the financing decisions of the firm. At the end of this chapter the reader will be able to:

■ explain the nature and the main types of bonds, their pricing and their valuation;

■ describe the main factors for a firm when borrowing from banks;

■ give a considered view of the role of mezzanine and high-yield bond financing as well as convertible bonds, sale and leaseback, securitisation, project finance and peer to peer lending;

■ demonstrate an understanding of the value of the international debt markets;

■ explain the term structure of interest rates and the reasons for its existence.

Introduction

The concept of borrowing money to invest in real assets within a business is a straightforward one, yet in the sophisticated capital markets of today with their wide variety of financial instruments and forms of debt, the borrowing decision can be bewildering. Should the firm tap the domestic bond market or the Eurobond market? Would bank borrowing be best? If so, on what terms, fixed or floating rate interest, a term loan or a mortgage? And what about syndicated lending, mezzanine finance and high-yield bonds? The variety of methods of borrowing long-term finance is infinite. This chapter will outline the major categories and illustrate some of the fundamental issues a firm may consider when selecting its finance mix. As you can see from the extract from the annual accounts of Unilever (**Exhibit 11.1**) a firm may need knowledge and understanding of a great many different debt instruments. The terms note, bond and commercial paper mentioned in the extract are explained in this chapter. Finance lease and overdrafts are examined in Chapter 12.

Some fundamental features of debt finance

Put at its simplest, debt is something that has to be repaid. Corporate debt repayments have taken the form of interest and capital payments as well as more exotic compensations such as commodities and shares. The usual method is a combination of a regular interest, with capital (principal) repayments either spread over a period or given as a lump sum at the end of the borrowing. Debt finance is less expensive than equity finance, due to the lower rate of return required by finance providers, lower transaction costs of raising the funds (for example, arrangement fees with a bank or the issue costs of a bond) and the tax deductibility of interest. The lower required returns arise because investors recognise that investing in a firm via debt finance is less risky than investing via shares. It is less risky because interest is paid out before dividends are paid so there is greater certainty of receiving a return than there would be for equity holders. Also, if the firm goes into liquidation, the holders of a debt type of financial security are paid back before shareholders receive anything.

Offsetting these plus-points for debt are the facts that lenders do not, generally, share in the value created by an extraordinarily successful business and there is an absence of voting power – although debt holders are able to protect their position to some extent through rigorous lending agreements.

There are dangers associated with raising funds through debt instruments. Creditors are often able to claim some or all of the assets of the firm in the event of non-compliance with the terms of the loan. This may result in liquidation. Institutions which provide debt finance often try to minimise the risk of not receiving interest and their original capital. They do this by first looking to the earning ability of the firm, that is, the pre-interest profits and cash flows in the years over the period of the loan. As a back-up they often require that the loan be secured against assets owned by the business, so that if the firm is unable to pay interest and capital from profits the lender can force the sale of the assets to receive their legal entitlement. The matter of security has to be thought about carefully before a firm borrows capital. It could be very inconvenient for the firm to grant a bank a fixed charge on a specific asset – say a particular building – because the firm is then limiting its future flexibility to use its assets as it wishes. For instance, it will not be able to sell that building, or even rent it without the consent of the bank or the bondholders.

Bonds

A corporate bond is a long-term contract in which the bondholders lend money to a company. In return the company (usually) promises to pay the bond owners predetermined payments (usually a series of coupons) until the bond matures. At maturity the bondholder receives a specified principal sum called the par (face or nominal) value of the bond. This is usually £100, £1,000 or

Exhibit 11.1	Loans and other borrowings for Unilever

Financial liabilities	2016 £m
Preference shares	68
Bank loans and overdrafts	1,146
Bonds and other loans	15,053
Finance lease creditors	143
Derivatives	185
Total	16,595

ANALYSIS OF BOND AND OTHER

LOANS

Unilever N.V.

Floating Rate Notes 2018 (€)	749
1.750% Bonds 2020 (€)	748
0.500% Notes 2022 (€)	743
1.125% Bonds 2028 (€)	692
1.000% Notes 2023 (€)	496
0.500% Notes 2024 (€)	492
0.000% Notes 2020 (€)	299
2.950% Notes 2017 (Renminbi)	41
Commercial paper	819
Total NV	5,079

Unilever PLC

4.750% Bonds 2017 (£)	466
2.000% Notes 2018 (£)	294
Commercial paper	373
Total PLC	1,133

Other group companies

United States

4.250% Notes 2021 (US$)	950
5.900% Bonds 2032 (US$)	942
4.800% Bonds 2019 (US$)	714
2.200% Notes 2019 (US$)	711
2.000% Notes 2026 (US$)	655
0.850% Notes 2017 (US$)	524
1.375% Notes 2021 (US$)	519
2.100% Notes 2020 (US$)	474
3.100% Notes 2025 (US$)	470
7.250% Bonds 2026 (US$)	276
6.625% Bonds 2028 (US$)	216
5.150% Notes 2020 (US$)	149
7.000% Bonds 2017 (US$)	142
5.600% Bonds 2097 (US$)	87
Commercial paper (US$)	1,892
Other countries	120
Total bonds and other loans	15,053

Source: Unilever Annual Report 2016.

£100,000 in the UK, €1,000 or €100,000 in Europe, and $1,000 in the USA.[1] The time to maturity is generally between five and 30 years although a number of firms, for example Disney, IBM and Reliance of India, have issued 100-year bonds.

Bonds may be regarded as merely IOUs (I owe you) with pages of legal clauses expressing the promises made. Many corporate bonds are sufficiently liquid (many transactions, so able to sell/buy at low cost without moving the price) to be *listed* on the London Stock Exchange and other exchanges in Europe, Asia and the Americas but the majority of *trading* occurs in the over-the-counter (OTC) market directly between an investor and a bond dealer. Access to a secondary market means that the investor who originally provided the firm with money does not have to hold on to the bond until the maturity date (the redemption date). However, because so many investors buy and then hold to maturity rather than trade in and out bonds generally have very thin secondary markets compared with shares. The amount the investor receives in the secondary market might be more or less than what he/she paid. For instance, imagine an investor paid £99.80 for a bond which promised to pay a coupon of 9% per year on a par value of £100 and to pay the par value in seven years. If one year after issue interest rates on similar bonds are 20% per annum no one will pay £99.80 for a bond agreement offering £9 per year for a further six years plus £100 on the redemption date. We will look at a method for calculating exactly how much they might be willing to pay later in the chapter.

These negotiable (that is tradable in a secondary market) instruments come in a variety of forms. The most common is the type described above with regular (usually semi-annual or annual) fixed coupons and a specified redemption date. These are known as straight, plain vanilla or bullet bonds. Other bonds are a variation on this. Some pay coupons every three months, some pay no coupons at all (called zero coupon bonds – these are sold at a large discount to the par value and the investor makes a capital gain by holding the bond), some bonds do not pay a fixed coupon but one which varies depending on the level of short-term interest rates (floating-rate or variable-rate bonds), some have interest rates linked to the rate of inflation. In fact, the potential for variety and innovation is almost infinite. Bonds issued in the last few years have linked the interest rates paid or the principal payments to a wide variety of economic events, such as the price of silver, exchange-rate movements, stock market indices, the price of oil, gold, copper – even to the occurrence of an earthquake. These bonds were generally designed to let companies adjust their interest payments to manageable levels in the event of the firm being adversely affected by some economic variable changing. For example, a copper miner pays lower interest on its finance if the copper price falls. Sampdoria, the Italian football club, issued a €3.5m bond that paid a higher rate of return if the club won promotion to the 'Serie A' division, 2.5% if it stayed in Serie B, 7% if it moved to Serie A and if the club rose to the top four in Serie A the coupon would rise to 14%. The John Lewis bond described in **Exhibit 11.2** provides shopping vouchers in addition to coupon payments.

Exhibit 11.2

Companies sweeten offerings to investors

By Mark Wembridge

Dividends, capital gains and the chance to partake in tea and biscuits at the annual meeting are not the only perks offered to shareholders of publicly listed companies.

Many UK companies offer little-publicised sweeteners to encourage retail investors to buy their shares, including discount cards and vouchers.

On Monday John Lewis, the employee-owned department store group, launched its own investor perk by offering discount vouchers to buyers of a £50m ($80.4m) retail bond issue.

The retailer is offering a 6.5% return to investors in the five-year bond, with a 4.5% annual interest rate

---

1 The minimum denominations for bonds to be listed on a European stock market under EU directives without a prospectus is €100,000 or its equivalent in another currency (retail investors are put off a high par value, leaving mostly institutional investors who do not need as much disclosure). The par value on one bond at, say, £100,000, €100,000 or $100,000 is said to have minimum lot or piece. Still, many corporate bonds issue with a par value of £100 or £1,000 or €1,000, which are often tradable by retail investors.

and a further 2% to be paid in vouchers that can be spent at Waitrose, the upmarket grocer it owns.

John Lewis staff and customers will be able to invest lump sums of between £1,000 and £10,000, and investors will receive £32 in cash and £20 in vouchers every year for each £1,000 invested.

 Financial Times, 12 March 2011.
All Rights Reserved.

Debentures and loan stocks

In the UK and a few other countries the most secured type of bond is called a debenture, secured by either a fixed or a floating charge against the firm's assets. A fixed charge means that specific assets (e.g. buildings, machinery) are used as security which, in the event of default, can be sold at the insistence of the debenture bondholder and the proceeds used to repay them. Debentures secured on property may be referred to as mortgage debentures. A floating charge means that the loan is secured by a general charge on all the assets of the corporation (or a class of the firm's assets such as inventory or debtors). In this case the company has a high degree of freedom to use its assets as it wishes, such as sell them or rent them out, until it commits a default which 'crystallises' the floating charge, i.e. the floating charge is converted to a fixed charge over the assets which it covers at that time. If this happens an administrative receiver or administrator will be appointed with powers to manage the business, to either pay the debt through income generation, or dispose of assets and to distribute the proceeds to the creditors, or sell the entire business as a going concern. Even though floating-charge debenture holders can force a liquidation, fixed-charge debenture holders rank above floating-charge debenture holders in the payout after insolvency. Floating-charge holders rank behind preferential creditors who are given priority by statutory law, such as the tax authorities and employees owed wages. Similar collateral charges to the floating charge are the floating lien in the US and a few other places, and the commercial pledge in many European countries.

Virgin Atlantic has come up with an unusual form of collateral, using its rights to fly from Heathrow. These slots can be sold to other airlines should Virgin default on its bonds – *see* **Exhibit 11.3.**

Exhibit 11.3

Virgin Atlantic lands Europe's first bond tied to airport slots

Take-off and landing rights at Heathrow used as collateral to raise £220m for aircraft investment

By Tanya Powley and Gavin Jackson

Virgin Atlantic has become the first European airline to raise money by using its take-off and landing slots at Heathrow as collateral.

The UK carrier raised £220m from the innovative bond, which it plans to use to invest in new aircraft such as the 17 Boeing 787s.

Shai Weiss, chief financial officer, said strengthening the company's financial position was a critical part of its turnround plan. It also represents the first time that Virgin Atlantic has accessed the capital markets. "We've now unleashed the value of these landing and airport slots which we couldn't realise the value of before."

European airlines have long looked at how to use airport access to secure debt. While US airlines have used airport gates as debt collateral for some time, it

▶

Exhibit 11.3 *(continued)*

is a novel practice in Europe, where access is allocated by time slots rather than physical infrastructure.

IAG, parent of British Airways, pulled a similar deal to raise at least £250m three years ago because of its complexity.

Mr Weiss said the deal was made possible by the creation of an airline company — Virgin Atlantic International — which will be on standby to take over the slots if the main airline goes bust.

The parent company, which is the third-largest slot holder at Heathrow, retains the legal title to the slots. In the event of a default it could sell them to repay investors, reducing the risk that they would not get their money back.

Mr Weiss said Virgin Atlantic has spent the past year working on the transaction. "We had to find the right structure that achieves the purpose for both lenders and Virgin Atlantic," he said.

The deal was privately rated by Moody's. Virgin Atlantic said it was not able to reveal the interest rate that it paid but said that it was "very attractive" at a 10-15 year maturity.

Investors included Standard Life Investments and Edmond de Rothschild Asset Management.

Secondary trading of slots at Heathrow has been a reality for some time but the European Commission formally sanctioned the practice in 2012, opening the door for European airlines to diversify their debt funding in this manner.

The terms bond, debenture, loan stock and loan note are often used loosely and interchangeably and the dividing lines between them are fuzzy. As a general rule debentures are secured with collateral and loan stock/notes are unsecured but there are examples which do not fit this classification. If liquidation occurs the unsecured loan stockholders rank beneath the debenture holders and some other categories of creditors such as the tax authorities. In the USA, Canada and some other countries the definitions are somewhat different and this can be confusing. Here a debenture is a long-term *unsecured* bond and so the holders become general creditors who can only claim assets not otherwise pledged. In the USA the secured form of bond is referred to as the mortgage bond and unsecured shorter-dated issues (less than 10 years) are called notes. US subordinated debentures, as well as being unsecured, are further back in the queue for a cash distribution in the event of the company failing to pay its debts than both mortgage bonds/debentures and regular US-style debentures. They carry higher interest rates and are often classified as junk bonds (see later in chapter).

Bonds are often referred to collectively as fixed-interest securities. While this is an accurate description for many bonds, others do not offer *regular* interest payments that are *fixed* amounts. Nevertheless, they are all lumped together as fixed interest to contrast these types of loan instrument with equities that do not carry a promise of a return (Warren Buffett, the financialist, uses the term 'fixed maturity securities').

Trust deeds and covenants

Bond investors are willing to lower the interest they demand if they can be reassured that their money will not be exposed to a high risk. Reassurance is conveyed by placing risk-reducing restrictions on the firm. A trust deed (or bond indenture) sets out the terms of the contract between bondholders and the company. A trustee (if one is appointed) ensures compliance with the contract throughout the life of the bond and has the power to appoint a receiver (to liquidate the firm's assets). If a trustee is not appointed the usual practice is to give each holder an independently exercisable right to take legal action against a delinquent borrower. The loan agreement will contain a number of affirmative covenants. These usually include the requirements to supply regular financial statements, interest and principal payments. The deed may also state the fees due to the lenders and details of what procedures are to be followed in the event of a technical default, for example non-payment of interest.

In addition to these basic covenants are the negative (restrictive) covenants. These restrict the actions and the rights of the borrower until the debt has been repaid in full. Some examples are:

- *Limits on further debt issuance* If lenders provide finance to a firm they do so on certain assumptions concerning the riskiness of the capital structure. They will want to ensure that the loan does not become more risky due to the firm taking on a much greater debt burden relative to its equity base, so they limit the amount and type of further debt issues – particularly debt which is higher ('senior debt') ranking for interest payments and for a liquidation payment. Subordinated debt (junior debt) – with low ranking on liquidation – is more likely to be acceptable.

- *Dividend level* Lenders are opposed to money being taken into the firm by borrowing at one end, while being taken away by shareholders at the other. An excessive withdrawal of shareholder funds may unbalance the financial structure and weaken future cash flows.

- *Limits on the disposal of assets* The retention of certain assets, for example property and land, may be essential to reduce the lenders' risk.

- *Financial ratios* A typical covenant here concerns the interest cover, for example: 'The annual profit will remain four times as great as the overall annual interest charge'. Other restrictions might be placed on working capital ratio levels (the extent to which current assets exceed current liabilities), and the debt to net assets ratio clause may require the firm to limit debt to say 100% of company net worth.

While negative covenants cannot provide completely risk-free lending they can influence the behaviour of the management team so as to reduce the risk of default. The lenders' risk can be further reduced by obtaining guarantees from third parties (for example, guaranteed loan stock). The guarantor is typically the parent company of the issuer.

The trustee, responsible to bond holders, will inform them if the firm has failed to fulfil its obligations under the trust deed and may initiate legal action against the firm. If the firm has to go through a reorganisation of its finances, administration or liquidation, the trustee will continue to act on behalf of the bond holders.

Repayments

The principal on most bonds is paid entirely at maturity. However, some bonds can be repaid before the final redemption date – they have a call provision in the bond agreement that allows the company to buy back the bonds from the holders at pre-determined prices. One way of paying for redemption is to set up a sinking fund, managed by the trustee, that receives regular sums from the firm which will be sufficient, with added interest, to redeem the bonds. Some companies issue bonds with a range of dates for redemption; so a bond dated 2030–2034 would allow a company the flexibility to repay the principal in cash over four years. Another way of redeeming bonds is for the issuing firm to buy the outstanding bonds by offering the holder a sum higher than or equal to the amount originally paid. A firm is also able to purchase bonds on the open market.

Some bonds are described as 'irredeemable' (or 'perpetual') as they have no fixed redemption date. From the investor's viewpoint they may be irredeemable but the firm has the option of repurchase and can effectively redeem the bonds.

Bond variations

Bonds which are sold at well below the par value are called deep discounted bonds, the most extreme form of which is the zero coupon bond. It is easy to calculate the rate of return offered to an investor on this type of bond. For example, if a company issues a bond at a price of £60 which is redeemable at £100 in eight years the annualised rate of return (r) is:

$$60(1 + r)^8 = 100$$

$$r = \sqrt[8]{\frac{100}{60}} - 1 = 0.066 \text{ or } 6.6\%$$

(Mathematical tools of this kind are explained in Appendix 2.1 to Chapter 2.)

These bonds are particularly useful for firms with low cash flows in the near term, for example firms engaged in a major property development which will not mature for many years.

A major market developed during the time of rapid inflation in the 1970s and 1980s called the floating-rate note (FRN) market (also called the variable-rate note market). High and oscillating inflation caused many investors to make large real-term losses on fixed-rate bonds as the interest rate fell below the inflation rate. As a result many lenders became reluctant to lend at fixed rates on a long-term basis. This reluctance led to floaters being cheaper for the issuer because it does not need to offer an interest premium to compensate the investor for being locked into a fixed rate. Secondly, a number of corporations, especially financial institutions, hold assets which give a return that varies with the short-term interest rate level (for example, bank loans and overdrafts) and so prefer to have a similar floating-rate liability. These instruments pay an interest that is linked to a benchmark rate – such as the LIBOR (London Inter-Bank Offered Rate – the rate that top rated banks charge each other for borrowed funds). The issuer will pay, say, 70 basis points (0.7 of a percentage point) over six-month LIBOR. The coupon is set for (say) the first six months at the time of issue, after which it is adjusted every six months; so if LIBOR was 5%, the FRN would pay 5.7% for that particular six months. (There are LIBOR rates for various lengths of time, for example, lending/borrowing between high reputation banks for a few hours (overnight LIBOR), or three months.)

There are many other variations on the basic vanilla bond, two of which will be examined later – high-yield bonds and convertible bonds. We now turn to another major source of long-term debt capital – bank borrowing.

Bank borrowing

An alternative to going to the capital markets to raise money via a public bond issue or a private bond placement is to borrow directly from a bank. In this case a tradable security is not issued. The bank makes the loan from its own resources and over time the borrowing company repays the bank with interest. Borrowing from banks is attractive to companies for the following reasons.

- *Administrative and legal costs are low* Because the loan arises from direct negotiation between borrower and lender there is an avoidance of the marketing, arrangement, regulatory and underwriting expenses involved in a bond issue.
- *Quick* The key provisions of a bank loan can be worked out speedily and the funding facility can be in place within a matter of hours.
- *Flexibility* If the economic circumstances facing the firm should change during the life of the loan banks are generally better equipped – and are more willing – to alter the terms of the lending agreement than bondholders. Negotiating with a single lender in a crisis has distinct advantages. Bank loans are also more flexible in the sense that if the firm does better than originally expected a bank loan can often be repaid without penalty. Contrast this with many bonds with fixed redemption dates, or hire purchase/leasing arrangements with fixed terms.
- *Available to small firms* Bank loans are available to firms of almost any size whereas the bond market is for the big players only.

Factors for a firm to consider

There are a number of issues a firm needs to address when considering bank borrowing.

Costs

The borrower may be required to pay an arrangement fee, say 1% of the loan, at the time of the initial lending, but this is subject to negotiation and may be bargained down.[2] The interest rate can be either

---

2 And indeed the firm should always try, where possible, to negotiate terms each year, or as and when the financial position of the company improves.

fixed or floating. If it is floating then the rate will generally be a certain percentage above the banks' base rate or LIBOR. Because the borrowing corporation is not as safe as a high quality bank taking out the borrowing in the interbank market a corporation will pay say 1% (or 100 basis points) more than LIBOR if it is in a good bargaining position. In the case of base-rate-related lending the interest payable changes immediately the bank announces a change in its base rate. This moves irregularly in response to financial market conditions, which are heavily influenced by the nation's central bank, e.g. The Bank of England, in its attempt to control the economy. For customers in a poorer bargaining position offering a higher-risk proposal the rate could be 5% or more over the base rate or LIBOR. The interest rate will be determined not only by the risk of the undertaking and the bargaining strength of the customer but also by the degree of security for the loan and the size of loan – economies of scale in lending mean that large borrowers pay a lower interest rate. There was a time when it would be more normal to negotiate fixed-rate loans, but most loans today are 'variable rate'.

Floating-rate borrowings have advantages for the firm over fixed-rate borrowings:

● If interest rates fall the cost of the loan falls.

● At the time of arrangement fixed rates are usually above floating rates (to allow for lenders' risk of misforecasting future interest rates).

● Returns on the firm's assets may go up at times of higher interest rates and fall at times of lower interest rates; therefore the risk of higher rates is offset. For example, a bailiff firm may prosper in a high interest rate environment.

However, floating rates have some disadvantages:

● The firm may be caught out by a rise in interest rates if, as with most businesses, its profits do not rise when interest rates rise. Many have failed because of a rise in interest rates at an inopportune time.

● There will be uncertainty about the precise cash outflow impact of the interest. Firms need to plan ahead; in particular, they need to estimate amounts of cash coming in and flowing out, not least so that they can pay bills on time. Fixed rates contribute to greater certainty on cash flows.

Security

When banks are considering the provision of debt finance for a firm they will be concerned about the borrower's competence and honesty. They need to evaluate the proposed project and assess the degree of managerial commitment to its success. The firm will have to explain why the funds are needed and provide detailed cash forecasts covering the period of the loan. Between the bank and the firm stands the classic gulf called 'asymmetric information' in which one party in the negotiation is ignorant of, or cannot observe, some of the information which is essential to the contracting and decision-making process. The bank is unable to assess accurately the ability and determination of the managerial team and will not have a complete understanding of the market environment in which they propose to operate. Companies may overcome bank uncertainty to some degree by providing as much information as possible at the outset and keeping the bank informed of the firm's position as the project progresses.

The finance director and chief executive need to consider both the quantity and quality of information flows to the bank. An improved flow of information can lead to a better and more supportive relationship. Firms with significant bank financing requirements to fund growth will be well advised to cultivate and strengthen understanding and rapport with their bank(s). The time to lay the foundations for subsequent borrowing is when the business does not need the money, so that when loans are required there is a reasonable chance of being able to borrow the amount needed on acceptable terms.

Another way for a bank to reduce its risk is to ensure that the firm offers sufficient collateral for the loan. Collateral provides a means of recovering all or the majority of the bank's investment should the firm fail to repay as promised. If the firm is unable to meet its loan obligations then holders of fixed-charge collateral can seize the specific asset used to back the loan. Also, on liquidation, the proceeds of selling assets will go first to the secured loan holders, including floating-charge bank lenders. Collateral can include stocks, receivables and equipment as well as land, buildings and marketable investments such as shares in other companies. In theory banks often have this strong right to seize assets or begin proceedings to liquidate. In practice they are reluctant to use these powers because the realisation of full value from an asset used as security is sometimes difficult and such draconian action can bring adverse publicity. Banks are careful to create a margin for error in the assignment of sufficient collateral to cover the loan because, in the event of default, assigned assets usually command a much lower price than their value to the company as a going concern. A quick sale at auction produces bargains for the buyers of liquidated assets and usually little for the creditors. Instead of rushing to force a firm to liquidate, banks will often try to reschedule or restructure the finance of the business (e.g. grant a longer period to pay).

Another safety feature applied by banks is the requirement that the firm abide by a number of loan covenants which place restrictions on managerial action in a similar fashion to bond covenants (*see* section on bonds earlier in this chapter). **Exhibit 11.4** discusses EnQuest's net-debt-to-profits ratio covenant.

Exhibit 11.4

EnQuest receives waiver ahead of test on loan covenants

By Nathalie Thomas

Heavily indebted North Sea oil producer EnQuest says it has received a waiver from its banks ahead of a key test of its loan covenants.

Analysts raised questions about the company's liquidity position last month, after it warned production from its new Kraken field in the North Sea had been below expectations. It is relying on its Kraken field to pay off its hefty debt load.

EnQuest was last year forced to secure a $400m debt restructuring and equity raising package so it could complete the $2.4bn Kraken project, which was approved before oil prices crashed in mid-2014.

It now faces covenant tests at the end of each quarter and analysts last month highlighted that it will have to cut its level of net debt to earnings before interest,

tax, depreciation and amortisation [ebitda] by the end of this year. In its half-year results on Thursday, EnQuest said it had applied for, and received, a waiver from its group of banks in advance of the September loan covenant test.

It also indicated it would probably have to seek further breathing space from lenders in future.

Analysts at RBC Capital Markets pointed out the company's net debt to ebitda ratio stood at 3.2 times at the end of the first half and that ratio will have to reach 2.25 times by the end of the year if the company is to meet its December covenant test.

EnQuest hopes to sell part of its 70.5 per cent holding in the Kraken field to help ease its debt burden, which rose slightly to $1.92bn at the end of June compared with $1.91bn at the end of April.

Lenders' risk can be further reduced by obtaining guarantees that the loan will be repaid from third parties. The guarantor is typically the parent company of the borrower. Finally, lenders can turn to the directors of the firm to provide additional security. They might be asked to sign personal guarantees that the firm will not default. Personal assets (such as homes) may be used as collateral. This erodes the principle of limited liability status and is likely to inhibit risk-taking productive activity. However, for many smaller firms it is the only way of securing a loan and at least it demonstrates the commitment of the director to the success of the enterprise.[3]

---

3 Indeed, when the author (Glen Arnold) contacted a number of banks to negotiate a loan for a company he controls, the corporate loan officers were all amazed at his cheek in not accepting a personal guarantee clause – 'but we normally get a personal guarantee, it is just standard practice', they declared. Don't accept this line if you have a strong business plan and strong financial structure.

Repayment

A firm must carefully consider the period of the loan and the repayment schedules in the light of its future cash flows. It could be disastrous, for instance, for a firm engaging in a capital project which involved large outlays for the next five years followed by cash inflows thereafter to have a bank loan which required significant interest and principal payments in the near term. For situations like these repayment holidays or grace periods may be granted, with the majority of the repayment being made once cash flows are sufficiently positive.

It may be possible for a company to arrange a mortgage-style repayment schedule in which monthly payments from the borrower to the lender are constant throughout the term.

A term loan is a business loan with an original maturity of more than one year and a specified schedule of principal and interest payments. It may or may not be secured and has the advantage over the overdraft of not being repayable at the demand of the bank at short notice (*see* Chapter 12). The terms of the loan are usually tailored to the specific needs of the individual borrower and these are capable of wide variation. A proportion of the interest and the principal can be repaid monthly or annually and can be varied to correspond with the borrower's cash flows. It is rare for there to be no repayment of the principal during the life of the loan but it is possible to request that the bulk of the principal is paid in the later years. Banks generally prefer self-amortising term loans with a high proportion of the principal paid off each year. This has the advantage of reducing risk by imposing a programme of debt reduction on the borrowing firm.

The repayment schedule agreed between bank and borrower is capable of infinite variety – four possibilities are shown in **Exhibit 11.5**.

The retail and investment banks are not the only sources of long-term loans. Insurance companies and other specialist institutions such as private equity funds (*see* Chapter 10) will also provide long-term debt finance.

Syndicated loans

For large loans a single bank may not be able or willing to lend the whole amount. To do so would be to expose the bank to an unacceptable risk of failure on the part of one of its borrowers. Bankers like to spread their lending to gain the risk-reducing benefits of diversification. They prefer to participate in a number of syndicated loans in which a few banks each contribute a portion of the overall loan. So, for a large multinational company loan of, say, £500m, a single bank may provide £70m, with perhaps 30 other banks contributing the remainder. The bank originating the loan will usually manage the syndicate and is called the lead manager (there might be one or more lead banks or arranging banks). This bank (or these banks) may invite a handful of other banks to co-manage the loan who then persuade other banks to supply much of the funding. That is, they help the process of forming the syndicate group of banks in the general syndication. The managing bank also underwrites much of the loan while inviting other banks to underwrite the rest – that is, guaranteeing to provide the funds if other banks do not step forward.[4]

Syndicated loans are available at short notice (within one week[5]), can be provided discreetly (helpful if the money is to finance a merger bid, for example), and are usually cheaper to arrange than a bond issue. The loans are generally based on a floating benchmark interest rate, usually LIBOR. Interest payable is adjusted each 'rollover day', usually every three or six months depending on the LIBOR for that period. While they can be a cheap form of borrowing for large well-established firms there will be various fees to pay, from management fees for setting it up (say, 1% of the total, shared among the managing banks) and loan commitment fees (e.g. 0.5% of the undrawn portion) to underwriting fees for guaranteeing the availability of funds and the agent's fee. The agent, usually one of the banks, collects the loan money for transfer to the borrower, and collects interest and other payments from the borrower to transfer to the syndicate banks. It also fixes the LIBOR rate that applies to variable interest rate loans and observes compliance with loan conditions (covenants) including collateral valuation.

---

4 The term 'mandated lead arranger' or MLA is often used for the managing bank(s). Also 'book runner' or 'bookrunner group' indicates those who solicit interest in the loan from lenders and gather offers of support. They gradually 'build a book' – a list of confirmed buyers. They do the syndication.

5 Larger and more complex loans may take three months.

Borrowers can usually draw down portions of the overall loan according to a draw-down schedule. Grace periods of several years are sometimes granted in which no principal is paid. The syndicated market is usually only available for loans of more than £50m. The volume of new international syndicated loans now runs into hundreds of billions of pounds per year.

Exhibit 11.5	Examples of loan repayment arrangements

In all four schemes £10,000 is borrowed, repayable over four years with interest at 10% p.a. (assuming annual payments, not monthly)

(a)	Time period (years)	1	2	3	4
	Payment (£)	3,155	3,155	3,155	3,155
(b)	Time period (years)	1	2	3	4
	Payment (£)	1,000	1,000	1,000	11,000
(c)	Time period (years)	1	2	3	4
	Payment (£)	0	0	0	14,641
(d)	Time period (years)	1	2	3	4
	Payment (£)	0	1,000	6,000	6,831

Credit rating

Firms often pay to have their bonds and other loans rated by specialist credit rating agencies, CRAs. The debt rating depends on the likelihood of payments of interest and/or capital not being paid (that is, default), and on the extent to which the lender is protected in the event of a default (an estimate is made of the likelihood of recouping a proportion of money in the event of insolvency or bankruptcy, the recoverability of the debt)[6]. Government bonds from reputable leading countries have an insignificant risk of default whereas unsecured subordinated corporate loan stock has a much higher risk. We would expect that firms in stable industries and with conservative accounting and financing policies and a risk-averse business strategy would have a low risk of default and therefore a high credit rating. Companies with a high total debt burden, a poor cash flow position, in a worsening market environment causing lower and more volatile earnings, will have a high default risk and a low credit rating. The leading organisations providing credit ratings are Moody's, Standard & Poor's (S&P) and Fitch. The highest rating is AAA or Aaa (triple-A rated). Such a rating indicates very high quality. The capacity to repay interest and principal is extremely strong. Single A indicates a strong capacity to pay interest and capital but there is some degree of susceptibility to impairment as economic events unfold. BBB indicates adequate debt service capacity but vulnerability to adverse economic conditions or changing circumstances. B and C rated debt has predominantly speculative characteristics. The lowest is D which indicates the firm is in default. Ratings of BBB- (or Baa3 for Moody's) or above are regarded as 'investment grade' – this is important because many institutional investors are permitted to invest in investment grade bonds only (*see* **Exhibit 11.6**). The difference in yield (rate of return for the bond holder) between the different grades in the investment grade group can be as little as 30 basis points, but this can rise significantly at times of financial trauma. Bonds rated below BBB- are called high-yield (or junk) bonds. Generally, the specific loan is rated rather than the borrower. If the loan does not have a rating it could be that the borrower has not paid for one, rather than implying anything sinister.

---

6 The rating agencies say that they do not in the strictest sense give an opinion on the likelihood of default, but merely evaluate relative creditworthiness or relative likelihood of default. And because rating scales are relative, default rates (proportion that fail to honour the deal) in particular rating classes fluctuate over time. Thus a group of middle-rated bonds are expected to be consistent in having a lower rate of default than a group of lower-rated bonds, but they will not, year after year, have a default rate of say 2.5%.

| Exhibit 11.6 | | A comparison of Moody's, Standard & Poor's and Fitch's rating scales | |

Standard & Poor's	Moody's	Fitch's	Grades	
AAA	Aaa	AAA	Highest quality, prime, minimal credit risk	
AA+	Aa1	AA+	High grade, high quality, very low credit risk	Investment grade bonds
AA	Aa2	AA		
AA−	Aa3	AA−		
A+	A1	A+	Upper medium grade, low credit risk	
A	A2	A		
A−	A3	A−		
BBB+	Baa1	BBB+	Lower medium grade, moderate credit risk, possessing certain speculative characteristics	
BBB	Baa2	BBB		
BBB−	Baa3	BBB−		
BB+	Ba1	BB+	Speculative elements, subject to significant credit risk	Non-investment grade, speculative grade
BB	Ba2	BB		
BB−	Ba3	BB−		
B+	B1	B+	Speculative, high credit risk	
B	B2	B		
B−	B3	B−		
CCC	Caa1	CCC	Poor standing, substantial credit risk, default a possibility	
	Caa2			
	Caa3			
CC	Ca	CC	Highly speculative. Highly vulnerable, in the near future, to default with some prospect of principal and coupon recovery.	
C	C	C	Near default, or in default with low likelihood of recovery of principal and interest.	
D		D	In default. These trade on the assumed recovery rate following default	

Source: data from credit rating agencies

The rating and re-rating of bonds is followed with great interest by borrowers and lenders and can give rise to some heated argument. Credit ratings are of great concern to the borrowing corporation or government because bonds with lower ratings tend to have higher costs **Exhibit 11.7** describes the impact of a rating change for Noble Group, illustrating the power of the credit rating agencies – the downgrade makes agreeing replacement loans for maturing ones very difficult.

Exhibit 11.7

Noble Group investors brace for heavy losses as bond prices fall

S&P credit rating downgrade adds to pressure on Asian commodities trader

By Robert Smith, Neil Hume and David Sheppard

Noble Group's bond prices fell heavily as investors braced for heavy losses in the event that the Asian commodities trader is unable to get to grips with its debt pile.

▶

Exhibit 11.7 *(continued)*

Two bond investors said the market reaction reflected growing doubts that long-touted white knight Sinochem is still interested in investing in the embattled trader.

Noble's $750m 8.75 per cent 2022 bond plumbed a new low of 42 cents on the dollar, according to Tradeweb data, having been issued at par less than three months ago.

A bond investor saw it marked even lower, being quoted at just 41 cents with one dealer.

A credit rating downgrade from S&P added pressure, with the agency slashing its rating three notches to triple C plus on Monday. The rating remains on a negative outlook.

"The negative outlook on Noble reflects the potential that the company will face distress and a nonpayment of its debt obligations over the next 12 months," S&P said in its downgrade statement.

Traders said the collapse in bond prices reflects increasing pessimism about the recovery value of the debt, given the company's lack of hard assets and the difficulty in independently valuing its portfolio of contracts to source and supply commodities.

One bond investor, who does not hold a position in Noble's debt, said it was very difficult to accurately model the recovery value for the commodity trader's assets.

Noble needs to roll over a $2bn credit facility with banks that help finance its trading activities in the next month.

Over the next year, Noble must then find $1.5bn to repay a $379m bond and a $1.14bn loan.

Bond default rates

Exhibit 11.8 shows the proportion of bonds that have defaulted one, two, three, four, five and ten years after issue over the period 1981–2016. Notice the large differences in default rates between the ratings. After five years only 0.33% of AA bonds defaulted, whereas 18.32% of B bonds defaulted. When examining data on default rates it is important to appreciate that default is a wide-ranging term and could refer to any number of events, from a small missed payment to bankruptcy. For some of these events all is lost from the investor's perspective; for other events a very high percentage, if not all, of the interest and principal is recovered. Hickman (1958) observed that defaulted publicly held and traded bonds tended to sell for 40 cents on the dollar. This average recovery rate rule of thumb seems to have held over time – in approximate terms – with senior secured bonds returning roughly two-thirds of the amount owed and subordinated bonds less than 30%. But the average disguises a wide variety, with many defaulted bonds offering nothing, and others giving a recovery of 80% or more.

Mezzanine finance and high-yield (junk) bonds

Mezzanine debt is a loan offering a high return with a high risk. It may be either unsecured or secured but ranks behind senior loans for payment of interest and capital. This type of debt generally offers interest rates two to nine percentage points more than that on senior debt and frequently gives the lenders some right to a share in equity values should the firm perform well. It is a kind of hybrid finance ranking for payment below straight debt but above equity – it is thus a type of *subordinated* debt, and considered 'low grade'. One of the major attractions of this form of finance for the investor is that it often comes with equity warrants (*see* Chapter 10) or share options (*see* Chapter 21) attached which can be used to obtain shares in the firm – this is known as an 'equity kicker'. Private equity investors might supply mezzanine debt with the right to convert to equity in the event of the firm joining the stock market or default.

Mezzanine financing tends to be used when bank borrowing limits are reached and the firm cannot or will not issue more equity. It is more expensive than bank borrowing, but is cheaper (in terms of required return) than would be available on the equity market; and it allows the owners of a business to raise large sums of money without sacrificing control. It is a form of finance which permits the firm to move beyond what is normally considered acceptable debt:equity ratios (gearing or leverage levels).

A high proportion of mezzanine finance, sometimes called leveraged loans, these days comes from funds established specifically for this purpose. They can structure mezzanine deals, involving a loan with an equity interest, in a variety of ways. For example, a business loan is made where, after a predetermined time, the debt becomes equity. This means that if the company is struggling and having difficulty paying back the loan to the mezzanine fund(s) the lender gets a share of the equity instead allowing the firm to continue until profitability is reached; if it is thriving the mezzanine finance provider benefits from holding the shares. Other mezzanine loans are hybrid forms of capital in the sense that the lender receives a share of profit (rather than shares) of a successful firm as well as interest payments.

Examples of deals include (a) a leveraged management buy-out (MBO) for £100m, or (b) a property purchase for £100m. In either case £65m might be supplied by conventional business loans, with £15m supplied by shareholders and the remaining £20m supplied by a mezzanine fund. The fund insists on both a right to interest on the debt (usually over a 10% annual rate) and a right to gain from profits, perhaps by converting the loan into shares a few years hence for the MBO, or a share of the profit when the property is sold by the property developer.

Exhibit 11.8	Standard and Poors Global Corporate Average Cumulative Default Rates 1981–2016					
Rating	1 year	2 years	3 years	4 years	5 years	10 years
	%	%	%	%	%	%
'AAA'	0	0.03	0.13	0.24	0.35	0.72
'AA'	0.02	0.06	0.13	0.23	0.33	0.77
'A'	0.06	0.15	0.25	0.38	0.53	1.41
'BBB'	0.18	0.51	0.88	1.33	1.78	3.76
'BB'	0.72	2.24	4.02	5.80	7.45	13.33
'B'	3.76	8.56	12.66	15.87	18.32	25.43
'CCC to 'C'	26.78	35.88	40.96	44.06	46.42	51.03
Investment grade	0.10	0.27	0.46	0.71	0.96	2.11
Speculative Grade	3.83	7.48	10.63	13.20	15.29	21.67

Source: Data from Standard and Poors Ratings: 2016 Annual Global Corporate Default Study and Ratings Transitions.

Crucially, unlike most bank loans, which usually involve annual repayments, mezzanine is often like an interest-only mortgage with no capital repayments until the end of the loan. Also mezzanine lenders are usually prepared to lend against the company's prospects in terms of expected cash flows, rather than insisting on security (collateral), as banks tend toward. Mezzanine funds were hit hard by the recession following the 2008 financial crisis, but have bounced back – *see* **Exhibit 11.9**.

Exhibit 11.9

Mezzanine funds poised to take up capital-raising slack

By Eric Platt and Joe Rennison

A string of successful mezzanine fundraisings is poised to boost the market for midsized business financing, as shadow banks and asset managers fill a void created by the retrenchment of traditional lenders.

Three of the 10 largest mezzanine funds have closed [completed a fund raising] over the past three months, with a $4.6bn fund from Crescent Capital lifting last year's overall capital raising near 2008's high water mark.

In all, 36 mezzanine funds raised more than $28bn in 2016, testing 2008's $29bn haul, according to Preqin data and FT calculations. Crescent joins Blackstone's GSO investment division and HPS Investment Partners, the credit investment group spun off from

▶

Exhibit 11.9 *(continued)*

JPMorgan last year, in closing multibillion-dollar mezzanine funds as investors seek out higher returns.

So-called mezzanine debt sits above equity and below bank loans or senior debt in a company's capital structure. The security offers higher returns than more senior debt as it is among the last to be repaid if a company defaults.

Riskier debt far outperformed higher rated obligations last year. Nonetheless, leveraged buyout activity has remained below pre-crisis levels. Crescent has already tapped capital from its latest fund — the seventh largest mezzanine fund ever raised — to invest in leveraged buyouts over the past

year. Its investments include ExamWorks, the medical examinations servicer, and Allied Universal, the security service provider.

Alternative asset managers have taken on roles that were typically left to banks in the past, including direct lending to midsized companies, finding backing from institutional investors seeking out higher income. The Los Angeles-based asset manager, which managed $25bn at the end of last year, counted sovereign wealth funds, pension managers, insurance companies and endowments in its latest fundraising. The mezzanine fund surpassed the group's $3bn target.

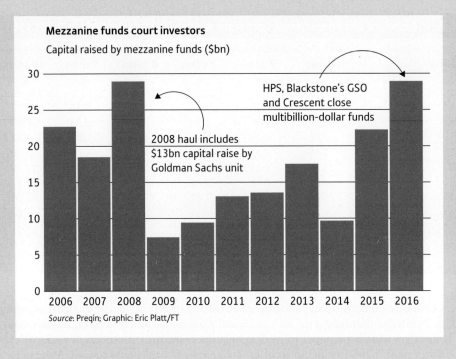

Mezzanine funds court investors

Capital raised by mezzanine funds ($bn)

2008 haul includes $13bn capital raise by Goldman Sachs unit

HPS, Blackstone's GSO and Crescent close multibillion-dollar funds

Source: Preqin; Graphic: Eric Platt/FT

Bonds with high-risk and high-return characteristics are called high-yield (junk) bonds. They are rated below investment grade by rating agencies with ratings of Bs and Cs. Like mezzanine loans, high-yield bonds often come with equity warrants or share options to provide an equity kicker in the form of a right to purchase shares at say £1 each. The bonds may be secured with specific collateral or be unsecured. These may be bonds which started as apparently safe investments but have now become riskier, 'fallen angels' – see **Exhibit 11.10** for examples – or they may be bonds issued specifically to provide higher-risk finance instruments for investors. This latter type began its rise to prominence in the USA in the 1980s and is now a market with over $130bn issued per year. The rise of the US junk bond market meant that no business was safe from the threat of takeover, however large – *see* **Case study 11.1** on Michael Milken.

Historically, high-yield bonds have been much more popular in the US than in Europe, but high yield bonds have grown in popularity in various countries around the world in recent years – see **Exhibit 11.11**. The market started in Europe only in 1997, with the first high-yield bonds denominated in European currencies issued by Geberit, a Swiss/UK manufacturer, raising DM157.5m by selling 10-year bonds offering an interest rate which was 423 basis points (4.23%) higher than the interest rate on a 10-year German government bond. Since then there have been hundreds of issues.

Exhibit 11.10

Bond investors wary of threat from potential 'fallen angels'

Analysts expect more companies to complete slide from investment grade to junk

By Eric Platt

The market now faces an unsettling threat from a potential new wave of fallen angels — companies that first sold debt with investment grade status but have since been downgraded to junk.

More than 55 companies were cut to high-yield, or junk, by rating agency Moody's in the first half of the year, as a tumbling oil price raised questions over the energy sector.

The number of potential fallen angels, or those a downgrade away from junk, climbed to 64 at the end of the second quarter and, at $294bn.

The chances of these potential candidates being cut to junk — and prompting steep and sudden price drops as high-grade debt investors are forced to sell en masse — have been increased by a rapid releveraging by companies.

The list of companies now on the brink of junk includes watchmaker Fossil Group, which suffered a 9 per cent drop in sales in its first quarter, and internet security company Symantec after it agreed to purchase Blue Coat for $4.65bn with $2.8bn of new debt. They join multinationals such as Rémy Cointreau, LG Electronics and miner Goldcorp sitting on the edge of speculative rating territory.

In 1973, fewer than 10 per cent of investment grade companies carried triple B ratings — one of the rungs just above junk. That proportion is now 44 per cent, according to Mr Gootkind.

Chris Barris, deputy chief investment officer of Alcentra: "What are the real benefits to [having an A rating]? When rates are sharply higher and the market is more volatile, there is a benefit to it. But when you have a yield-suppressed market, that incremental 10, 15, 20 basis points might not be as meaningful."

The extra debt companies are taking on, often to fund share buybacks, dividends or mergers and acquisitions, has intensified credit risk, particularly as companies battle a still lacklustre backdrop for global economic growth.

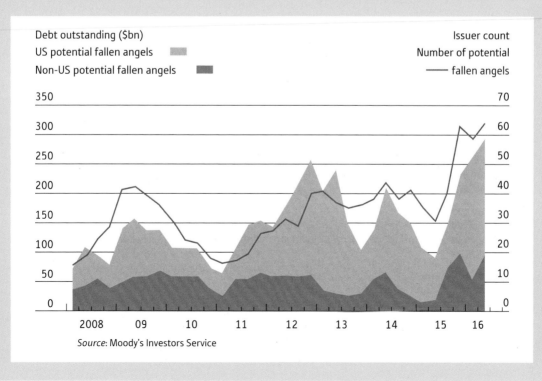

Source: Moody's Investors Service

Exhibit 11.10 *(continued)*

Sliding from investment grade to junk poses a significant threat to portfolio managers, potentially causing a cascade of selling by managers who have mandates to hold only higher-rated bonds. Many investment grade funds were scorched by the downgrades earlier this year, which triggered heavy selling in companies such as Freeport-McMoRan, the US miner. Its bonds maturing in 2022, which traded as low as 41 cents on the dollar after it was downgraded to junk in January, have since more than doubled to 87 cents on the dollar last week.

"Ideally you'd like to hold until you have to sell but many clients say you must sell within 30 to 60 days", says Marc Kremer, a portfolio manager with Franklin Templeton.

Case study 11.1   The junk bond wizard: Michael Milken

While studying at Wharton Business School in the 1970s Michael Milken came to the belief that the gap in interest rates between safe bonds and high-yield bonds was excessive, given the relative risks. This created an opportunity for financial institutions to make an acceptable return from junk bonds, given their risk level. At the investment banking firm Drexel Burnham Lambert, Milken was able to persuade a large body of institutional investors to supply finance to the junk bond market as well as provide a service to corporations wishing to grow through the use of junk bonds. Small firms were able to raise billions of dollars to take over large US corporations. Many of these issuers of junk bonds had debt ratios of 90 per cent and above – for every $1 of share capital $9 was borrowed. These gearing levels concerned many in the financial markets. It was thought that companies were pushing their luck too far and indeed many did collapse under the weight of their debt. The market was dealt a particularly severe blow when Michael Milken was convicted, sent to jail and ordered to pay $600m in fines. Drexel was also convicted, paid $650m in fines and filed for bankruptcy in 1990. The junk bond market was in a sorry state in the early 1990s, with high levels of default and few new issues. However, it did not take long for the market to recover.

Exhibit 11.11

European junk bond market faces September LBO test

By Robert Smith

Bankers are readying a big pipeline of European junk bond sales in September, including large leveraged buyout deals that will test the resilience of the market's strong rally.

The European high-yield market has performed strongly over the past 18 months.

The average yield on Bank of America Merrill Lynch's euro non-financial high-yield index has fallen from 6.5 per cent in February 2016 to just 2.3 per cent today.

Some analysts are wary that it has been a long time since the European junk bond market has had to absorb such an influx of significant fresh supply.

This is because much of this year's volume reflects refinancing transactions that simply recycle old debt. Such refinancings stand in contrast to bonds linked to LBOs and other M&A, which are commonly called "new money" deals because they require fresh funds from investors.

They also require banks to provide hard underwriting agreements, meaning they can incur losses if they cannot sell the bonds within pre-agreed levels.

And that test could now be just around the corner, as bankers prepare to market LBO deals in both high-yield bonds and leveraged loans after the market's customary August shutdown ends.

"September supply looks set to be big — we can see €10bn of loans and a similar amount of bonds," says Michael Marsh, head of leveraged finance Emea at Goldman Sachs. "And a lot of this is new money, so it's not just a big number it's also potentially a material drawdown of funds. That'll be an interesting test for the market."

Cinven and Bain Capital last week agreed the largest leveraged buyout of a European-listed company in four years, having finally managed to corral enough of German generic drugmaker Stada's shareholders to agree to their €4.1bn buyout offer.

While the two private equity sponsors are looking to fund the bulk of the deal in the red-hot leveraged loan market, €825m is earmarked for the high-yield market, split between €485m of secured and €340m of unsecured bonds.

The European high-yield bond market has seen less than €4bn of LBO and private equity driven M&A supply so far this year. Private equity sponsors have been much heavier users of the leveraged loan market instead, which has seen €25bn of such supply year-to-date, its busiest period since 2008.

Sources noted that some riskier LBO and M&A-related deals are looking to eschew the leveraged loan market altogether, in favour of debt packages that only comprise high-yield bonds. This would continue the recent trend of companies with troubled histories in the loan market turning to junk bonds for financing.

A group of banks agreed to underwrite €600m of debt for Spanish retailer Cortefiel last month, for example, with plans to syndicate this in the high-yield bond market after the summer break. Cortefiel has been through several rounds of debt restructuring and its existing loans were still trading at just 80 cents on the euro in June, indicating that its lenders were then expecting steep losses.

These loans are now being repaid at face value as part of the deal, which will also see private equity funds CVC Capital and PAI Partners inject fresh equity.

Discount retail chain Hema's deal has not traded well, however, with its €150m 8.5 per cent unsecured bonds bid at 97 cents.

"It seems very punchy to us," one high-yield banker says of Cortefiel. "There are a bunch of punchier deals coming, but that one stands out."

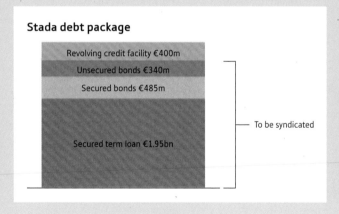

Stada debt package

Revolving credit facility €400m
Unsecured bonds €340m
Secured bonds €485m
Secured term loan €1.95bn
To be syndicated

Mezzanine finance is usually a private form of debt (e.g. loan), rather than a publicly traded bond form of debt. However, mezzanine notes are sometimes issued which are tradable in a secondary market. Mezzanine loans have the advantage over bonds in flexibility on exit. That is, high yield bonds typically have a life of five to seven years, making it expensive to repay early. Mezzanine loans do not carry large penalties for early repayment.

Mezzanine financing and high-yield bonds have been employed by firms 'gearing themselves up' to finance merger activity, and also for leveraged recapitalisations. For instance, a firm might have run into trouble, defaulted, and its assets are now under the control of a group of creditors, including bankers and bondholders. One way to allow the business to continue would be to persuade the creditors to accept alternative financial securities in place of their debt securities to bring the leverage (financial gearing) to a reasonable level. They might be prepared to accept a mixture of shares and mezzanine finance. The mezzanine instruments permit the holders to receive high interest rates in recognition of the riskiness of the firm, and they open up the possibility of an exceptionally high return from warrants or share options should the firm get back to a growth path. The alternative for the lenders may be a return of only a few pence in the pound from the immediate liquidation of the firm's assets.

Mezzanine finance/junk bond borrowing usually leads to high debt levels resulting in a high fixed cost imposition on the firm. This can be a dangerous way of financing expansion and therefore the use of these types of finance has been criticised. On the other hand, some commentators have praised the way in which high gearing and large annual interest payments have focused the minds of managers and engendered extraordinary performance (*see* Chapter 18). Also, without this finance, many takeovers, buyouts and financial restructurings would not take place.

Financing a leveraged buy-out

If the anticipated cash flows are reasonably stable then a highly leveraged buy-out may give an exceptional return to the shareholders. Take the case of Sparrow, a subsidiary of Hawk plc (*see* **Exhibit 11.12**). The managers have agreed a buy-out price of £10m, equal to Sparrow's assets. They are able to raise £1m from their own resources to put into equity capital and have borrowed £9m. The debt pays an interest rate of 14% and the corporate tax rate is 25% (payable one year after year-end). Profits before interest and tax in the first year after the buy-out are expected to be £1.5m and will grow at 25% per annum thereafter. All earnings will be retained within the business to pay off debt.

Exhibit 11.12	Sparrow – Profit and Loss Account and Balance Sheet (£000s)					

			Year			
	1	2	3	4	5	6
Profit before interest and taxes (after depreciation)	1,500	1,875	2,344	2,930	3,662	4,578
Less interest	1,260	1,226	1,144	999	770	433
	240	649	1,200	1,931	2,892	4,145
Tax	0	60	162	300	483	723
Profits available to pay off debt	240	589	1,038	1,631	2,409	3,422

Balance Sheet				Year			
	Opening	1	2	3	4	5	6
Equity	1,000	1,240	1,829	2,867	4,498	6,907	10,329
Debt	9,000	8,760	8,171	7,133	5,502	3,093	0
Assets	10,000	10,000	10,000	10,000	10,000	10,000	10,329

Notes: Past tax liabilities have been accepted by Hawk. Money set aside for depreciation is used to replace assets to maintain £10m of assets throughout. Also depreciation equals capital allowances used for tax purposes.

In the first few years the debt burden absorbs a large proportion of the rapidly increasing profits. However, it only takes six years for the entire debt to be retired. The shareholders then own a business with assets of over £10m, an increase of over tenfold on their original investment. The business is also producing a large annual profit which could make a stock market flotation attractive, in which case the value of the shares held by the management will probably be worth much more than £10m.[7]

---

7 This example is designed to show the effect of leverage. It does lack realism in a number of respects; for example, it is unlikely that profits will continue to rise at 25% per annum without further investment. This can be adjusted for – the time taken to pay off the debt lengthens but the principles behind the example do not alter.

Convertible bonds

Convertible bonds (or convertible loan stocks, or converts, or CBs, or convertible notes) carry a rate of interest in the same way as ordinary bonds, but they also give the holder the right to exchange the bonds at some stage in the future into ordinary shares according to some prearranged formula.[8] The owner of these bonds is not obliged to exercise this right of conversion (normally) and so the bonds may continue until redemption as interest-bearing instruments. The conversion price can vary from as little as 10% to over 65% greater than the share price at the date of bond issuance. So if a £100 bond offered the right to convert to 40 ordinary shares the conversion price would be £2.50 (that is, £100 ÷ 40) which, given the current market price of the shares of, say, £2.20, would be a conversion premium of:

$$\frac{2.50 - 2.20}{2.20} = 0.136 \text{ or } 13.6\%$$

Bayer, the German life science company, sold €4bn of convertibles in November 2016. They each had a principal amount of €100,000 and were issued at par value offering a coupon of 5.625% per annum. They were three-year instruments maturing in November 2019. An unusual feature was the condition that the buyers could be compelled by the company to convert the bonds (actually labelled notes) to shares at the maturity date if the holder had not already converted. The conversion ratio was to be calculated on the basis of the share price on the conversion date with a minimum at €90 and a maximum price set at €108. This represented a maximum conversion premium of 20% over the share price of €90 at the issue date of 22 November 2016.

$$Conversion\ ratio = \frac{Nominal\ (par)\ value\ of\ the\ bond}{Conversion\ price} = \frac{€100,000}{€108} = 925.9\ shares$$

Each bond carries the right to convert to 925.9 shares, which is equivalent to paying €108 for each share at the €100,000 par value of the bond. If the shares rose to be worth, say, €130 each €100,000 bond could be converted to 925.9 shares worth €130 × 925.9 = €120,367.

Convertible bonds usually offer a lower rate of interest (yield) than conventional bonds being sold at a higher price relative to the coupons, due to the added attraction of the option to convert to shares.

Exhibit 11.13　Summary of convertible bond technical jargon

● **Conversion ratio** This gives the number of ordinary shares into which a convertible bond may be converted:

$$Conversion\ ratio = \frac{Nominal\ (par)\ value\ of\ bond}{Conversion\ price}$$

● **Conversion price** This gives the price of each ordinary share obtainable by exchanging a convertible bond:

$$Conversion\ price = \frac{Nominal\ (par)\ value\ of\ bond}{Number\ of\ shares\ into\ which\ bond\ may\ be\ converted}$$

● **Conversion premium** This gives the difference between the conversion price and the market share price, expressed as a percentage:

$$Conversion\ premium = \frac{Conversion\ price - Market\ share\ price}{Market\ share\ price} \times 100$$

The length of time to maturity of the bond affects the conversion premium: the longer it is, the greater likelihood the share will rise above the conversion price and therefore the more the investor will pay for the option to convert.

● **Conversion value** This is the value of a convertible bond if it were converted into ordinary shares at the current share price:

Conversion value = Current share price × Conversion ratio

---

8 Alternatively they may be convertible into preference (preferred) shares.

The value of a convertible bond (a type of 'equity-linked bond') could be analysed as a 'debt portion', which depends on the discounted value of the coupons and principal, and an 'equity portion,' where the right to convert is an equity option. Generally, the value is strongly influenced by the equity option value, which rises or falls with the market value of the ordinary shares, but at a lower percentage rate. Convertibles can therefore be quite volatile. But convertibles with large conversion premiums trade much like ordinary bonds because the option to convert is not a strong feature in their pricing. They are therefore less volatile and offer higher yields.

A convertible bond has two values forming lower bounds through which it should not fall: (1) it must sell for more than its conversion value, otherwise an arbitrageur could buy bonds and immediately convert them to shares, sell the shares and make a quick profit; (2) the value as a straight bond (ignoring the conversion option). When the share price is low, the straight bond value is the effective lower bound, with the conversion option having little impact. When the share price is high, the bond's price is overwhelmingly driven by the conversion value.

If the share price rises above the conversion price the investor may exercise the option to convert if he/she anticipates that the share price will at least be maintained. If the share price rise is seen to be temporary the investor may wish to hold on to the bond.

The right to convert may specify a specific date or several specific dates over, say, a four-year period, or any time between two dates. Most convertible bonds are unsecured but as **Exhibit 11.14** on Greenhills shows, this is not always the case – a good thing for Hunter Ground.

Exhibit 11.14   Secured convertible debentures

Greenhills

The first AIM-traded company to go into receivership was Greenhills, the restaurant operator. A major investor, Hunter Ground, appointed administrative receivers. Hunter Ground held secured convertible debentures from Greenhills worth £506,000.

Source: Investors Chronicle, 20 December 1996, p. 11. Reprinted with kind permission of the Investors Chronicle.

Advantages to the company of convertible bonds

Convertible bonds have the following advantages to the company.

1 *Lower interest than on a comparable straight bond* The firm can ask investors to accept a lower interest on these debt instruments because the investor values the conversion right. This was a valuable feature for many internet companies, such as Amazon, which could pay 5–6% on convertibles – less than half what they would have paid on straight bonds in the early days. In recent years interest rates on convertible bonds have fallen to exceptionally low levels, even to the point where the investor gets less back than what she paid for the bond, a negative interest – *see* **Exhibit 11.15**.

Exhibit 11.15

Making sense of negative yielding convertible bonds

Niche securities occupy place between worlds of debt and equity

By Dan McCrum

This week Safran, the French aerospace group, persuaded investors to pay it for the opportunity to purchase shares at the end of 2020, if the price rises significantly from where it sits now. Helpfully, from the perspective of the company, it gets the money today.

If the share price fails to rise so high by that future date, Safran will give the investors most, but not all, of their cash back, keeping some as commission for the trouble.

Convertible bonds didn't used to work this way. A niche in the investment world, these securities occupy a place somewhere between the worlds of debt and equity. A company would issue a bond, borrowing money with a type of derivative contract written into the terms and conditions. Investors would get both a regular coupon and the chance the bond converts into shares, producing a handsome profit if it does so in the future.

As prices for convertibles reflect an interplay of stock and bond prices, as well as the more complex range of inputs into option prices such as the volatility of the share price in question, they have tended to attract a select group of expert investors.

Institutions such as pension funds give money to these professionals to invest in convertibles on the basis that trading the interplay should be profitable. What has happened illustrates both the strange state of modern finance and inertia in the way institutions decide to invest the money in their care.

As with other parts of the bond world, yields have fallen to zero or gone negative. Where governments and companies used to pay to borrow, now they are paid to look after the money instead.

Safran's €650m convertible was sold at a negative yield of 0.8 per cent, meaning it received €104 for every €100 it will have to pay back in five years if the bond doesn't convert into stock.

Strange prices suggests there are too many specialists chasing too few bonds, and their clients have either failed to notice or don't know what else to do instead.

The negative yield perhaps makes sense because a key Safran shareholder is the French state. It's unlikely a company of strategic importance would be allowed to fail, so it may be a fairly safe place to park cash in a world where such havens are in demand.

The embedded derivative contract does have value, particularly if the stock market becomes more volatile, but (simplifying somewhat), it's really just a way for investors to buy a long dated option on Safran stock.

2   *The interest is tax deductible* Because convertible bonds are a form of debt the coupon payment can be regarded as a cost of the business and can therefore be used to reduce taxable profit.

3   *Self liquidating* When the share price reaches a level at which conversion is worthwhile the bonds will (normally) be exchanged for shares so the company does not have to find cash to pay off the loan principal – it simply issues more shares. This has obvious cash flow benefits. However, the disadvantage is that the other equity holders may experience a reduction in earnings per share and dilution of voting rights.

4   *Fewer restrictive covenants* The directors have greater operating and financial flexibility than they would with a secured debenture. Investors accept that a convertible is a hybrid between debt and equity finance and do not tend to ask for high-level security, impose strong operating restrictions on managerial action or insist on strict financial ratio boundaries – notwithstanding the case of Greenhills. Many tech companies with little more than a website and a brand have used convertibles because of the absence of a need to provide collateral or stick to asset:borrowing ratios.

5   *Underpriced shares* A company which wishes to raise equity finance over the medium term but judges that the stock market is temporarily underpricing its shares may turn to convertible bonds. If the firm does perform as the managers expect and the share price rises, the convertible will be exchanged for equity.

6   *Cheap way to issue shares* Graham and Harvey (2001) found that managers favoured convertibles as an inexpensive way to issue 'delayed' equity. Equity is raised at a later date without the high costs of rights issues etc.

7   *Available finance when straight debt and equity are not available* Some firms locked out of the equity markets (e.g. because of poor recent performance) and the straight debt markets because of high levels of indebtedness may still be able to raise money in the convertible market. Rating agencies treat them as part bond, part equity, usually half and half[9], thus their issue does not impact leverage levels as much as vanilla debt for assessments such as default ratings, making credit downgrades less likely. Firms use convertible debt 'to attract investors unsure about the riskiness of the company' (Graham and Harvey (2001)).

---

9 Except sub-investment grade issuers do not usually qualify for the 50% equity treatment.

Advantages to the investor

The advantages of convertible bonds to the investor are as follows.

1   They are able to wait and see how the share price moves before investing in equity; they may take advantage of the upside.

2   In the near term there is greater security for their principal compared with equity investment, and the annual coupon is usually higher than the dividend yield.

3   For companies that do not pay dividends the investor can gain a regular income stream through a convertible and then (possibly) make a capital gain through conversion.

The bonds sold may not give the right to conversion into shares of the issuer, but shares of another company held by the issuer – *see* the case of Volcan in **Exhibit 11.16**. Note that the term 'exchangeable bond' is probably more appropriate in these cases.

Exhibit 11.16

Volcan/Anglo American: horsing about

Some will wonder if the Indian billionaire spies an opportunity ahead

Lex Column

In the steady breeze, the windmill's sails gently circle. From the hazy horizon, in gallops mining magnate Anil Agarwal, owner of India-focused but London-listed Vedanta Resources. He must have a tilt at Anglo-American. Only he knows why.

Mr Agarwal's holding company Volcan announced this week it will finance the purchase of a 12 per cent stake in Anglo shares with an exchangeable bond.

The market's reaction to his arrival is clear. Anglo's shares jumped 8 per cent on Thursday after the announcement in anticipation that it is a takeover target — not just for Mr Agarwal but any others with interest.

With upturned palms, Mr Agarwal pleads his case for why he wants the stake. He maintains that he simply likes the look of Anglo's assets and thinks them undervalued. Rather than use his own cash he has borrowed the £2bn needed via a special type of bond which will convert into the shares of Anglo, known as a mandatory exchangeable. The bonds offer a coupon of just over 4 per cent.

Should the specialists who take up these Volcan bonds choose to hedge the underlying equity risk by shorting Anglo's shares, Mr Agarwal will happily provide a bid. Together with open market purchases, he expects to amass his stake. His bankers earn a tasty fee.

Financial Times, 16 March 2017.

Valuing bonds

Bonds, particularly those which are traded in secondary markets such as the London Stock Exchange, are priced according to supply and demand. The main influence on the price of a bond will be the general level of interest rates for securities of that risk level and length of time to maturity. If the coupon rate of interest on the par value is less than the current market interest rate the bond will trade at less than the par value of £100 (or €1,000, or €100,000, etc.). Take the case of a £100 irredeemable bond with an annual coupon of 8%. This financial asset offers to any potential purchaser a regular £8 per year for ever (i.e. 8% of the par value of £100). When the bond was issued general interest rates for this risk class may well have been 8% and so the bond may have been sold at £100. However, interest rates change over time and the £8 coupon may not remain sufficient to maintain the bond price at £100.

Suppose that the rate demanded by investors is now 10%. Investors will no longer be willing to pay £100 for an instrument that yields only £8 per year. The market value of the irredeemable bond will fall to £80 (£8/0.10) because this is the maximum amount needed to pay for similar bonds given the current interest rate of 10%. We say that the bond is trading at a 'discount' to its nominal value because it is trading below £100.

If the coupon is more than the current market interest rate the market price of the bond will be greater than the nominal (par) value. Thus if market rates are 6% the irredeemable bond will be priced at £133.33 (£8/0.06). We say that the bond is trading at a 'premium' to its nominal value, i.e. more than £100.

Note that as interest rates fall the price of the bond rises, and vice versa.

The formula relating the price of an irredeemable bond, the coupon and the market rate of interest is:

$$P_D = \frac{i}{k_D}$$

where P_D = price of bond, D stands for debt
         i = nominal annual income (the coupon rate × nominal (par) value of the bond)
         k_D = market discount rate, the annual rate of return required on bonds of similar risk and characteristics

Also:

$$V_D = \frac{I}{k_D}$$

where V_D = total market value of all of the bonds of this type
         I = total annual nominal interest of all the bonds of this type

We may wish to establish the market rate of interest represented by the market price of the bond. For example, if an irredeemable bond offers an annual coupon of 9.5% and is currently trading at £87.50, with the next coupon due in one year, the rate of return is:

$$k_D = \frac{i}{P_D} = \frac{9.5}{87.5} = 0.1086 \text{ or } 10.86\%$$

Redeemable bonds

A purchaser of a redeemable bond buys two types of income promise: first the coupon, second the redemption payment. The amount that an investor will pay depends on the amount these income flows are worth when discounted at the rate of return required on that risk class of debt. The relationships are expressed in the following formulae:

$$P_D = \frac{i_1}{1 + k_D} + \frac{i_2}{(1 + k_D)^2} + \frac{i_3}{(1 + k_D)^3} + \frac{i_4}{(1 + k_D)^4} \cdots \cdots + \frac{i_n}{(1 + k_D)^n} + \frac{R_n}{(1 + k_D)^n}$$

and:

$$V_D = \frac{I_1}{1 + k_D} + \frac{I_2}{(1 + k_D)^2} + \frac{I_3}{(1 + k_D)^3} + \frac{I_4}{(1 + k_D)^4} \cdots \cdots + \frac{I_n}{(1 + k_D)^n} + \frac{R_n^*}{(1 + k_D)^n}$$

where i_1, i_2, i_3 and i_4 = nominal interest per bond in years 1, 2, 3 and 4 up to n years
         I_1, I_2, I_3 and I_3 = total nominal interest in years 1, 2, 3 and 4 up to n years
         R_n and R_n^* = redemption value of a bond, and total redemption of all bonds in year n, the redemption or maturity date

The worked example of Blackaby illustrates the valuation of a bond when the market interest rate is given.

If we need to calculate the rate of return demanded by investors from a particular bond when we know the market price and coupon amounts, we can compute the internal rate of return. For

Worked example 11.1   Blackaby plc

Blackaby plc issued a bond with a par value of £100 in September 2018, redeemable in September 2024 at par. The coupon is 8% payable annually in September – first payment in 2019. The facts available from this are:

- the bond might have a par value of £100 but this may not be what investors will pay for it;
- the annual cash payment will be £8 (8% of par);
- in September 2024, £100 will be handed over to the bondholder (in the absence of default by the issuer).

Question 1

What is the price investors will pay for this bond at the time of issue if the market rate of return for a security in this risk class is 7%?

Answer

$$P_D = \frac{8}{1 + 0.07} + \frac{8}{(1 + 0.07)^2} + \frac{8}{(1 + 0.07)^3} + \dots + \frac{8}{(1 + 0.07)^6} + \frac{100}{(1 + 0.07)^6}$$

$P_D = $ £8 annuity for 6 years @ 7% $= 4.7665 \times 8 = \quad 38.132$

Plus $\dfrac{100}{(1 + 0.07)^6}$ $\qquad = \dfrac{66.634}{£104.766}$

Question 2

It is now three years later. What is the bond's value in the secondary market in September 2021 if interest rates rise by 200 basis points (i.e. for this risk class they are 9%) between 2018 and 2021? (Assume the next coupon payment is in one year.)

Answer

$P_D = $ £8 annuity for 3 years @ 9% $= 2.5313 \times 8 = \quad 20.25$

plus $\dfrac{100}{(1 + 0.09)^3}$ $\qquad = \dfrac{77.22}{£97.47}$

Again, note that as interest rates rise the price of bonds falls.

example, Bluebird plc issued a bond many years ago which is due for redemption at par of £100 in three years. The coupon is 6% and the market price is £91. The rate of return now offered in the market by this bond is found by solving for k_D:

$$P_D = \frac{i_1}{1 + k_D} + \frac{i_2}{(1 + k_D)^2} + \frac{R_n + i_3}{(1 + k_D)^3}$$

$$91 = \frac{6}{1 + k_D} + \frac{6}{(1 + k_D)^2} + \frac{106}{(1 + k_D)^3}$$

To solve this the skills learned in calculating internal rates of return in Chapter 2 are required. First we'll try 9% as this seems roughly right given the capital gain of around 3% per year over the three years (i.e. £9 overall) plus the 6% coupon. At an interest rate (k_D) of 9%, the right side of the equation amounts to £92.41. At an interest rate of 10% the right-hand side of the equation amounts to £90.05. Using linear interpolation:

Interest rate	9%		?	10%
Value of discounted cash flows	£92.41		£91	£90.05

$$k_D = 9\% + \frac{92.41 - 91}{92.41 - 90.05} \times (10 - 9) = 9.6\%$$

This is the yield-to-maturity or YTM discussed in the next section.

An Excel spreadsheet version of this calculation is available at www.pearsoned.com/arnold.

The two types of interest yield

There are two types of yield for fixed interest securities. The income yield (also known as the current yield, flat yield, interest yield and running yield) is the gross (before tax) interest amount divided by the current market price of the bond expressed as a percentage:

$$\frac{\text{Gross interest (coupon)}}{\text{Market price}} \times 100$$

Thus for a holder of Bluebird's bonds the income yield is:

$$\frac{£6}{£91} \times 100 = 6.59\%$$

This is a gross yield. The after-tax yield will be influenced by the investor's tax position.

$$\text{Net interest yield} = \text{Gross yield } (1 - T),$$

where T = the tax rate applicable to the bondholder

The income yield is not the true rate of return available to the investor should he/she buy it because it fails to take into account the capital gain over three years to the expiry of the bond.

At a time when interest rates are higher than 6.59% it is obvious that any potential purchaser of Bluebird bonds in the market will be looking for a return other than from the coupon. That additional return comes in the form of a capital gain over three years of £100−£91 = £9. A rough estimate of this annual gain is (9/91) ÷ 3 = 3.3% per year. When this is added to the interest yield we have an approximation to the second type of yield, the yield to maturity (also called the redemption yield). The yield to maturity of a bond is the discount rate such that the present value of all the cash inflows from the bond (interest plus principal) is equal to the bond's current market price. The rough estimate of 9.89% (6.59% + 3.3%) has not taken into account the precise timing of the investor's income flows. When this is adjusted for, the yield to maturity is 9.6% – the internal rate of return calculated above. Thus the yield to maturity includes both coupon payments and the capital gain or loss on maturity.

In the *Financial Times'* bond tables the column headed 'bid yield' is the yield to maturity given the current bid price (traders quote bid and offer prices; the bid is the price at which market makers will buy from investors; the offer price is what an investor would pay to buy). Examples of these tables are shown later in the chapter, in Exhibit 11.21. It is important to note that many investors sell their bonds before the redemption date. The price received depends on market conditions. If general interest rates have risen over the holding period then a capital loss or a smaller gain than would occur if market interest rates were constant will be experienced, which will have a depressing effect on the rate of return received even though coupons may have been paid during the time the bonds were owned. For example, if an investor bought Bluebird bonds at £91 and sold them one year later when the required rate of return on two-year bonds of this risk level in the market is 10%, instead of receiving the original 9.6% yield to maturity he/she will only achieve a rate of return of 8.86% over the year of holding. This is calculated by allowing for the fact that after one year of holding there are only two cash inflows left: £6 to be received in one year and £106 to be received in two years (£6 coupon plus £100 nominal value).

$$\text{Market value of bond after 1 year} = \frac{6}{1 + 0.1} + \frac{106}{(1 + 0.1)^2} = 93.06$$

Thus the return (r) to our investor is:

$$91 = \frac{93.06 + 6}{1 + r} \quad r = 8.86\%$$

Semi-annual interest

The example of Bluebird given above is based on the assumption of annual interest payments. This makes initial understanding easier and reflects the reality for many types of bond, particularly internationally traded bonds. However, many companies and governments around the world issue bonds with semi-annual interest payments. A bond offering a coupon of 9% will pay £4.50 half-way through the year and the remainder at the end. The rate of return calculation on these bonds is slightly more complicated.

Example

Redwing plc has an 11% bond outstanding which pays interest semi-annually. It will be redeemed in two years at £100 and has a current market price of £96, with the next interest payment due in six months. The yield to maturity on this bond is calculated as follows:

Cash flows

Point in time (years)	0.5	1	1.5	2.0	2.0
Cash flow	£5.5	£5.5	£5.5	£5.5	£100

The nominal interest rate over a six-month period is 5.5% (11%/2):

$$96 = \frac{5.50}{1 + \frac{k_D}{2}} + \frac{5.50}{\left(1 + \frac{k_D}{2}\right)^2} + \frac{5.50}{\left(1 + \frac{k_D}{2}\right)^3} + \frac{105.50}{\left(1 + \frac{k_D}{2}\right)^4}$$

At a rate of 6% for $k_D/2$ the right-hand side equals:

$$5.50 \times 4\text{-period annuity @ 6\%} = 5.50 \times 3.4651 = 19.058$$

$$\text{plus} \quad \frac{100}{(1 + 0.06)^4} \qquad\qquad = \quad \frac{79.209}{£98.267}$$

At a rate of 7% for $k_D/2$ the right-hand side equals:

$$5.50 \times 4\text{-period annuity @ 7\%} = 5.50 \times 3.3872 = 18.630$$

$$\text{plus} \quad \frac{100}{(1 + 0.07)^4} \qquad\qquad = \quad \frac{76.290}{£94.920}$$

The IRR of the cash flow equals:

$$6\% + \frac{98.267 - 96}{98.267 - 94.92} \times (7 - 6) = 6.6773\%$$

The IRR needs to be converted from a half-yearly cash flow basis to an annual basis:

The relationship between semi-annual interest and annual interest is $(1 + s)^2 = (1 + i)$, where s is the semi-annual rate and *i* is the annual rate, i.e. interest received at the half year is compounded. Thus:

$$i = (1 + 0.06677)^2 - 1 = 0.138 \text{ or } 13.80\%$$

International sources of debt finance

Larger and more creditworthy companies have access to a wider array of finance than small firms. These companies can tap the Euromarkets which are informal (unregulated) markets in money held outside the jurisdiction of its country of origin. For example, there is a large market in

Eurodollars. These are dollar credits (loans) and deposits managed by a bank not resident in the USA. This has the distinct advantage of transactions not being subject to supervision and regulation by the authorities in the USA. So, for example, an Italian firm can borrow dollars from a Spanish bank in the UK, and the US regulatory authorities have no control over the transaction. There is a vast quantity of dollars held outside the USA and this money is put to use by borrowers. The same applies to all the major currencies – the money is lent and borrowed outside its home base and therefore is beyond the reach of the domestic regulators. Today it is not unusual to find an individual holding a dollar account at a UK bank – a Eurodeposit account – which pays interest in dollars linked to general dollar rates. This money can be lent to firms wishing to borrow in Eurodollars prepared to pay interest and capital repayments in dollars. There are large markets in Euro Swiss Francs, Eurosterling, Euroyen and many other currencies.[10] The title 'Euro' is misleading as this market is not limited to the European currencies or European banks (and is unconnected with the European single currency, the euro). The title came about because the modern market was started when the former Soviet Union transferred dollars from New York to a Russian-owned bank in Paris at the height of the cold war in 1957. The cable address happened to be EUROBANK. This was long before the currency called the euro was conceived. Nowadays, there is daily Eurosecurities business transacted in all of the major financial centres. To add a little precision: 'Eurocurrency' is short-term (less than one year) deposits and loans outside the jurisdiction of the country in whose currency the deposit/loan is denominated; 'Eurocredit' is used for the market in medium- and long-term loans in the Euromarkets.

The companies which are large enough to use the Eurosecurities markets are able to put themselves at a competitive advantage *vis-à-vis* smaller firms. There are at least four advantages:

● The finance available in these markets can be at a lower cost in both transaction costs and rates of return.

● There are fewer rules and regulations such as needing to obtain official authorisation to issue or needing to queue to issue, leading to speed, innovation and lower costs.

● There may be the ability to hedge foreign currency movements. For example, if a firm has assets denominated in a foreign currency it can be advantageous to also have liabilities in that same currency to reduce the adverse impact of exchange-rate movements (*see* Chapter 22).

● National markets are often not able to provide the same volume of finance. The borrowing needs of some firms are simply too large for their domestic markets to supply. To avoid being hampered in expansion plans large firms can turn to the international market in finance.

For these internationally recognised firms there are three sources of debt finance:

a   the domestic or national market;

b   the financial markets of other countries which make themselves open to foreign firms – the foreign debt market;

c   the Eurosecurities market which is not based in any one country and is not therefore regulated by any country.

Thus, for example, there are three bond markets available to some firms – as shown in **Exhibit 11.17**.

Foreign bonds

A foreign bond is a bond denominated in the currency of the country where it is issued when the issuer is a non-resident. For example, in Japan bonds issued by non-Japanese companies denominated in yen are foreign bonds. (The interest and capital payments will be in yen.) Foreign bonds have been given some interesting names: foreign bonds in Tokyo are known as Samurai bonds, foreign bonds issued in New York and London are called Yankees and Bulldogs respectively. The Netherlands allows foreigners to issue Rembrandt bonds and in Spain Matador bonds are traded.

---

10   Just to confuse everybody traders in this market often refer to all types of Eurocurrency, from Eurosterling to Euroyen as Eurodollars, and do not reserve the term for US dollars.

Exhibit 11.17	The attributes of the different types of bonds			
Type of bond	**Currency of issue**	**Nationality of issuer**	**Place of issue**	**Primary investors**
Domestic bond	Domestic	Domestic	Domestic	Domestic
Foreign bond	Domestic	Foreign	Domestic	Domestic
Eurobond	Eurocurrency, *Euroyen, Eurodollars Eurosterling, etc.*	Any	International	International

Foreign bonds are regulated by the authorities where the bond is issued. These rules can be demanding and an encumbrance to companies needing to act quickly and at low cost. The regulatory authorities in some countries have also been criticised for stifling innovation in the financial markets. The growth of the less restricted Eurobond market has put the once dominant foreign bond market in the shade.

Eurobonds

Eurobonds are bonds sold outside the jurisdiction of the country of the currency in which the bond is denominated. So, for example, the UK financial regulators have little influence over the Eurobonds denominated in sterling issued in Luxembourg, even though the transactions (for example interest and capital payments) are in pounds. Bonds issued in US dollars in Paris are outside the jurisdiction of the US authorities. They are medium- to long-term instruments with standard maturities of three, five, seven and ten years, but there are also long maturities of 15–30 years driven by pension and insurance fund demand for long-dated assets. Because they are issued outside the country of the currency of issue, Eurobonds are not subject to the rules and regulations which are imposed on foreign bonds, such as the requirement to issue a detailed prospectus.[11] More importantly they are not subject to an interest-withholding tax. In most countries the majority of domestic and foreign bonds are subject to a withholding tax by which basic rate income tax is deducted before the investor receives interest. Interest on Eurobonds is paid gross without any tax deducted – which has attractions to investors keen on delaying, avoiding or evading tax. Moreover, Eurobonds are bearer bonds, which means that the holders do not have to disclose their identity – all that is required to receive interest and capital is for the holder to have possession of the bond (originally, this meant physically held bonds, but today many bearer bonds are held in a central depository so that trading and post-trade settlement can take place electronically. The bonds are 'presented' electronically by the trusted depository for coupon payment). In contrast, UK domestic bonds are usually registered, which means that companies and governments are able to identify the owners.

Despite the absence of official regulation, the International Capital Markets Association (ICMA), a self-regulatory body, imposes some restrictions, rules and standardised procedures on Eurobond issue and trading.

Eurobonds are distinct from euro bonds, which are bonds denominated in euros and issued in the eurozone countries. Of course, there have been euro-denominated bonds issued outside the jurisdiction of the authorities in the euro area. These are euro Eurobonds.

The development of the Eurobond market

In the 1960s many countries, companies and individuals held surplus dollars outside the USA. They were reluctant to hold these funds in American banks under US jurisdiction. There were various reasons for this. For example, some countries, particularly the former Soviet Union and

---

11 Although EU rules mean that a prospectus is required if the bond is marketed at retail (non-professional) investors.

other communist bloc countries of the cold war era, thought their interests were best served by using the dollars they had on the international markets, away from the powers of the US authorities to freeze or sequestrate (seize) assets. More recently this sort of logic has applied to countries such as Iran. Also in the 1960s the American authorities had some very off-putting tax laws and created a tough regulatory environment in their domestic financial markets. These encouraged investors and borrowers alike to undertake transactions in dollars outside the USA. London's strength as a financial centre, the UK authorities' more relaxed attitude to business, and its position in the global time zones, made it a natural leader in the Euro markets. The first Eurobond was issued in the early 1960s and the market grew modestly through the 1970s and then at a rapid rate in the 1980s. By then the Eurodollar bonds had been joined by bonds denominated in a wide variety of currencies. The market was stimulated not only by the tax and anonymity benefits, which brought a lower cost of finance than for the domestic bonds, but also by the increasing demand from transnational companies and governments needing large sums in alternative currencies and with the potential for innovatory characteristics. It was further boosted by the recycling of dollars from the oil-exporting countries. Today large American corporations choose not to send home to head office profits earned in other countries because of the high taxes if they do so. Apple, for example, has more than $230bn held offshore; Microsoft has around $120bn held outside the US.

In 1979 less than $20bn worth of bonds were issued in a variety of currencies. The rate of new issuance is now around $2,000bn a year, with a total amount outstanding (bonds issued but not yet repaid) of over $21,000bn. Corporations account for a relatively small proportion of the international bond market, usually around one-quarter to one-half of issuance. The biggest issuers are the banks. The quantity of issues by governments ('sovereign issues') and state agencies in the public sector varies from year to year but is rarely more than 10% of issues. Other issuers are international agencies such as the World Bank, the International Bank for Reconstruction and Development, and the European Investment Bank. The two dominant currencies of issue are the US dollar and the euro. Even though the majority of Eurobond trading takes place through London, sterling is not one of the main currencies, and what is more, it tends to be large US and other foreign banks located in London which dominate the market.

Types of Eurobonds

The Eurobond market is innovative in producing bonds with all sorts of coupon payment and capital repayment arrangements. For example, the currency of the coupon changes half-way through the life of the bond, or the interest rate switches from fixed to floating rate at some point. We cannot go into detail here on the rich variety but merely categorise the bonds into broad types.

1 *Straight fixed-rate bond* The coupon remains the same over the life of the bond. These are usually paid annually, in contrast to domestic bond semi-annual coupons. The redemption of these bonds is usually made with a 'bullet' repayment at the end of the bond's life.

2 *Equity related* These take two forms:

   a *Bonds with warrants attached* Warrants are options which give the holder the right to buy some other asset at a given price in the future. An equity warrant, for example, would give the right, but not the obligation, to purchase shares. There are also warrants for commodities such as gold or oil, and for the right to buy additional bonds from the same issuer at the same price and yield as the host bond. Warrants are detachable from the host bond and are securities in their own right, unlike convertibles.

   b *Convertibles* The bondholder has the right (but not the obligation) to convert the bond into ordinary shares at a preset price.

3 *Floating-rate notes (FRNs)* These have a variable coupon reset on a regular basis, usually every three or six months, in relation to a reference rate, such as LIBOR. The size of the spread over LIBOR reflects the perceived risk of the issuer. The typical term for an FRN is about five to 12 years.

Within these broad categories all kinds of 'bells and whistles' (features) can be attached to the bonds, for example reverse floaters – the coupon declines as the benchmark interest rates, say LIBOR rises; capped bonds – the interest rate cannot rise above a certain level.

Many bonds have 'call back features' under which the issuer may buy the bond back after a period of time has elapsed, say five years, at a price specified when the bond was issued. A 'put' feature gives the bondholder the right, but not the obligation, to sell the bond back to the issuer (usually at par value) on designated dates.

The majority of Eurobonds are rated AAA or AA although some rated below BBB – are issued. Denominations are usually $1,000, $5,000, $10,000, $50,000 or $100,000 (or similar large sums in the currency of issue).

Issuing Eurobonds

With Eurobonds a bank (lead manager or bookrunner or lead underwriter) or group of banks acting for the issuer invite a large number of other banks or other investors to buy some of the bonds.[12] The managing group of banks is responsible for underwriting the issue and it may enlist a number of smaller institutions to use their extensive contacts to sell the bonds (the selling group or syndicate). Exhibit 9.10 in Chapter 9 gave some idea of the relative importance of the Eurobond market to UK-listed firms – in recent years the amount raised on the international market is greater than that raised through domestic debt and equity issues.

Eurobonds are traded on the secondary market through intermediaries acting as market makers. Some bonds are listed on the London, Dublin, Luxembourg or Channel Islands or other stock exchanges. But the market is primarily an over-the-counter one, that is, most transactions take place outside a recognised exchange. Most deals are conducted using the telephone and computers, but there are a number of electronic platforms for trading Eurobonds. The extent to which electronic platforms will replace telephone dealing is as yet unclear. It is not possible to go to a central source for price information. Most issues rarely trade. Those that do are generally private transactions between investor and bond dealer and there is no obligation to inform the public about the deal. **Exhibit 11.18** presents the advantages and disadvantages of Eurobonds.

Exhibit 11.18	Advantages and drawbacks of eurobonds as a source of finance for corporations

Advantage	Drawback
1 Large loans for long periods are available.	1 Only for the largest companies – minimum realistic issue size is about £100m – and only for those with 'good name recognition' (widely regarded as creditworthy).
2 Often cheaper than domestic bonds. The finance provider receives the interest without tax deduction and retains anonymity and therefore supplies cheaper finance. Economies of scale also reduce costs. Also a wider investor base can be tapped than in the domestic market.	2 Because interest and capital are paid in a foreign currency there is a risk that exchange-rate movements mean more of the home currency is required to buy the foreign currency than was anticipated.
3 Ability to hedge interest-rate and exchange-rate risk.	3 The secondary market can be illiquid.
4 The bonds are usually unsecured. The limitations placed on management are less than those for a secure bond.	
5 The lower level of regulation allows greater innovation and tailor-made financial instruments.	
6 Issuance procedures are relatively simple with bonds issued at speed, allowing borrowers to take advantage of an opportunity in a timely way.	

To conclude the discussion of Eurobonds we will consider a few examples and deal with some of the jargon. **Exhibit 11.19** describes the first Eurobond from 40 years ago by Autostrade, a company that continues to make use of this financial market.

The *Financial Times* publishes a table showing a selection of secondary-market bid prices of actively traded international bonds (*see* **Exhibit 11.20**). This gives the reader some idea of current

---

12 Alternatively in a 'bought deal' the lead manager agrees to buy the entire issue at a specific price and yield, then tries to sell it on in the market.

Exhibit 11.19

Autostrade returns to bond market after 40-year gap

By Charles Batchelor and Ivar Simensen

Autostrade, the Italian motorway operator that launched the Eurobond market in 1963, is to return to the bond market this month after a gap of more than 40 years.

The company yesterday revealed plans for a bond issue worth up to E6.5bn (£4.5bn) to pay off bank loans and finance a 10-year investment programme. It would be by far the largest corporate bond offering in Europe this year – ahead of issues by Britain's Network Rail and Telecom Italia.

'We go to the market once every 40 years,' joked Luca Bettonte, who was born in the year the market started and has been finance director of Autostrade since November.

'This will give us a financial structure more adapted to the needs of the group,' he added. Autostrade is expected to issue bonds in both euros and sterling following roadshows in continental Europe, the UK and US.

It was in July 1963 that the motorway group issued a $15m (£9m), 15-year bond, creating a market that was to wrest control of non-US bond issues from the American investment banks and cement London's position as an international financial centre.

European banks had been relegated to an underwriting role by the US banks that managed these issues – and hence earned much lower fees.

Siegmund Warburg, founder of SG Warburg – now part of UBS, the Swiss bank group – led negotiations with regulators in the UK and elsewhere to issue bonds that soaked up the large offshore dollar pool created by recurrent US balance of payments deficits.

The fledgling market received a crucial boost just $21\frac{1}{2}$ weeks after the Autostrade issue when President John F. Kennedy announced an interest equalisation tax.

The president's aim was to improve the US balance of payments but the result was to increase the cost of US borrowing by European issuers.

market conditions and rates of return demanded for bonds of different maturities, currencies and riskiness. The FT has another table, showing similar information for high yield and emerging-market (less financially mature economies, e.g. Argentina) bonds.

Euro medium-term notes and domestic medium-term notes

By issuing a note a company promises to pay the holders a certain sum on the maturity date, and in many cases a coupon interest in the meantime. These instruments are typically unsecured and may carry floating or fixed interest rates. Medium-term notes (MTN) have been sold with a maturity of as little as nine months and as great as 30 years, so the term is a little deceiving, but the period is usually 5–10 years. They can be denominated in the domestic currency of the borrower (MTN) or in a foreign currency outside of the control of the authorities of that currency (Euro MTN). MTNs normally pay an interest rate above LIBOR, usually varying between 0.2% and 3% over LIBOR.

An MTN programme stretching over many years can be established with one set of legal documents. Then, numerous notes can be issued under the programme in future years. A programme allows greater certainty that the firm will be able to issue an MTN when it needs the finance and allows issuers to bypass the costly and time-consuming documentation associated with each stand-alone note/bond. The programme can allow for bonds of various qualities, maturities, currencies or type of interest (fixed or floating). Over the years the market can be tapped at short notice in the most suitable form at that time, e.g. US dollars rather than pounds, or redemption in three years rather than in two. It is possible to sell in small amounts, e.g. $5m, and on a continuous basis, regularly dripping bonds into the market. The banks organising an MTN programme

Exhibit 11.20

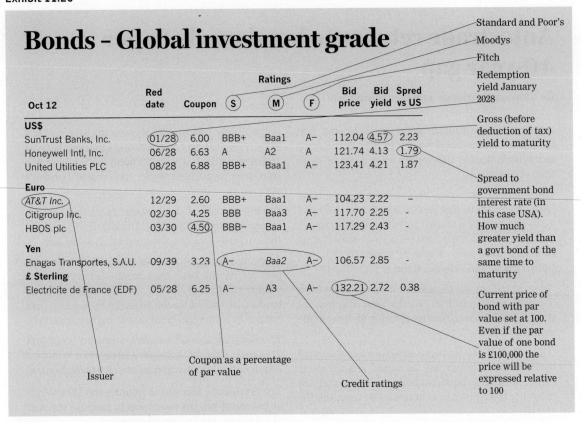

Bonds – Global investment grade

Oct 12	Red date	Coupon	Ratings (S)	Ratings (M)	Ratings (F)	Bid price	Bid yield	Spred vs US
US$								
SunTrust Banks, Inc.	01/28	6.00	BBB+	Baa1	A−	112.04	4.57	2.23
Honeywell Intl, Inc.	06/28	6.63	A	A2	A	121.74	4.13	1.79
United Utilities PLC	08/28	6.88	BBB+	Baa1	A−	123.41	4.21	1.87
Euro								
AT&T Inc.	12/29	2.60	BBB+	Baa1	A−	104.23	2.22	–
Citigroup Inc.	02/30	4.25	BBB	Baa3	A−	117.70	2.25	-
HBOS plc	03/30	4.50	BBB−	Baa1	A−	117.29	2.43	-
Yen								
Enagas Transportes, S.A.U.	09/39	3.23	A−	Baa2	A−	106.57	2.85	-
£ Sterling								
Electricite de France (EDF)	05/28	6.25	A−	A3	A−	132.21	2.72	0.38

Standard and Poor's
Moodys
Fitch
Redemption yield January 2028

Gross (before deduction of tax) yield to maturity

Spread to government bond interest rate (in this case USA). How much greater yield than a govt bond of the same time to maturity

Current price of bond with par value set at 100. Even if the par value of one bond is £100,000 the price will be expressed relative to 100

Issuer

Coupon as a percentage of par value

Credit ratings

charge a 'commitment fee' on available funds authorised by the programme but not used. Management fees will also be payable to the syndication of banks organising the MTN facility.

The success of an MTN programme depends on the efficiency of the lead manager and the flexibility of the issuer to match market appetite for lending in particular currencies or maturities with the issuer's demands for funds. The annual cost of running an MTN programme, excluding credit rating agency fees, can be around £100,000. The cost of setting up an MTN programme is high compared with the cost of a single bond issue (and more expensive than most bank debt, except the very best AAA, AA and some A-rated companies). Many companies are prepared to pay this because they believe that the initial expense is outweighed by the flexibility and cost savings that a programme can provide over time.

Eurocommercial paper and domestic commercial paper[13]

The issue and purchase of commercial paper is one means by which the largest commercial organisations can avoid paying the bank intermediary a middleman fee for linking borrower and lender, because corporations can avoid a bank loan by going directly to the financial market lenders. Commercial paper promises to the holder a sum of money to be paid in a few days. The lender buys these short-term IOUs, with an average life of about 40 days (normal range 30–90 days, but can be up to 270 days in the USA and a year in some countries), and effectively lends money to

---

13 This topic and the previous one do not sit perfectly in a chapter on long-term finance, but they help to give a more complete view of the Euromarkets.

the issuer. Normally these instruments are issued at a discount rather than the borrower being required to pay interest – thus the face value (amount paid on redemption) will be higher than the amount paid for the paper at issuance.[14]

Large corporations with temporary surpluses of cash are able to put that money to use by lending it directly to other commercial firms at a higher rate of effective interest than they might have received by depositing the funds in a bank. Other lenders via the commercial paper market are specialised investment funds, insurance companies, pension funds, governments and banks. This source of finance is usually only available to the most respected corporations with the highest credit ratings, as it is usually unsecured lending. Standard & Poor's and Moody's use a different grading system for short-term instruments (e.g. A–1 or Prime–1, P-1 are the highest ratings). The main buyers, such as money market mutual funds, are often restricted to having the bulk of their portfolios in the form of 'tier-one' rated issues – top ratings from credit rating agencies. Tier-two and tier-three issues do exist, but the demand is very limited.

While any one issue of commercial paper is short term it is possible to use this market as a medium-term source of finance by 'rolling over' issues. That is, as one issue matures another one is launched. A commercial paper programme or note issuance facility (a revolving underwriting facility) can be set up by a bank whereby the bank (or a syndicate of banks) underwrites a speci-fied maximum sum for a period of five to seven years. The borrower then draws on this every few weeks or months by the issue of commercial paper to other lenders. If there are no bids for the paper the underwriting bank(s) buys the paper at a specified price. Eurocommercial paper is issued and placed outside the jurisdiction of the country in whose currency it is denominated.

Project finance

A typical project finance deal is created by a corporation, or number of corporations, providing some equity capital for a separate legal entity (a 'special-purpose vehicle' (SPV)) to be formed to build and operate a project, for example an oil pipeline, an electricity power plant. The project finance borrowings are then provided as bank loans or through bond issues direct to the separate entity. The significant feature is that the loan returns are principally tied to the cash flows and fortunes of a particular project rather than being secured against the parent firm's assets. For most ordinary loans the bank looks at the credit standing of the borrower when deciding terms and conditions. For project finance, while the parent company's (or companies') credit standing is a factor, the main focus is on the financial prospects of the project itself. Many of the small com-panies which develop oil fields and pipelines, for example, would not be able to participate in these industries on the strength of their existing cash flow and balance sheet, but would be able to obtain project finance secured on the oil or pipe fees they would later generate in a SPV.

To make use of project finance the project needs to be easily identifiable and separable from the rest of the company's activities so that its cash flows and assets can offer the lenders some separate security. Project finance has been used across the globe to finance power plants, roads, ports, sewage facilities, telecommunications networks and much more; globally, about $300–400bn is lent annually in this form. A few examples are given in **Exhibit 11.21**.

There is a spectrum of risk sharing in project finance deals. At one extreme there are projects where the parent firm (or firms) accepts the responsibility of guaranteeing that the lenders will be paid in the event of the project producing insufficient cash flows. This is referred to as recourse finance because the lenders are able to seek the 'help' of the parent. At the other extreme, the lenders accept an agreement whereby, if the project is a failure, they will lose money and have no right of recourse to the parent company; if the project's cash flows are insufficient the lenders only have a claim on the assets of the project itself rather than on the sponsors or developers. Between these two extremes there might be deals whereby the borrower takes the risk until the completion of the construction phase (for example, provides a completion guarantee) and the lender takes on the risk once the project is in the operational phase. Alternatively, the commercial firm may take some risks such as the risk of cost overruns and the lender takes others such as the risk of a government expropriating the project's assets.

---

14 A small amount of commercial paper is issued with interest payments, but this is rare.

Exhibit 11.21

Project finance has funded . . .

A liquefied natural gas project in Qatar

The biggest project-financed facility was built in Qatar. Qatargas, the state-controlled energy firm, joined with Exxon and raised $7.6bn from 57 investors to build a gas freezing and storage plant. The gas is now being shipped to the UK in tankers. Not only did forming a separate project with a state-controlled company reduce political risk (see below) but it also opened doors to lenders in the country.

Developing an oil field

Northern Petroleum agreed a £40m project financing facility with Standard Bank to develop a number of onshore oilfields in the Netherlands. Normally a project lender would insist on the sponsoring company or its contractors providing a guarantee that it will be paid back in the event of failure to complete the project construction. However, Standard Bank agreed that Northern Petroleum has the skills to project manage and to forgo the guarantee. In return the bank received options to buy 3 million shares in Northern Petroleum thus taking some extra reward if the company (project) performs well. (An option gives the right to buy shares at a price already agreed – say £3 when the current share price is £2. If the company does well the share might move to, say, £4 in which case the options become worth at least £1 each – Chapter 21 has more on options.)

A telephone infrastructure

Hutchison UK 3G raised £3bn by way of project finance to part-fund the building of its UK's mobile network. This was three-year debt without recourse to shareholders.

The sums and size of projects are usually large and involve a high degree of complexity and this means high transaction and legal costs. Because of the additional risk to the lenders the interest rates charged tend to be higher than for conventional loans. Whereas a well-known highly creditworthy firm might pay 20 basis points (0.20%) over LIBOR for a 'normal' parent company loan, the project company might have to pay 200 basis points (2%) above LIBOR.

Advantages of project finance

Project finance has a number of advantages.

1 *Transfer of risk* By making the project a stand-alone investment with its own financing, the parent can gain if it is successful and is somewhat insulated if it is a failure, in that other assets and cash flows may be protected from the effects of project losses. This may lead to a greater willingness to engage in more risky activities, which may benefit both the firm and society. Of course, this benefit is of limited value if there are strong rights of recourse.

2 *Off-balance-sheet financing* The finance is raised on the project's assets and cash flows and therefore is not recorded as debt in the parent company's balance sheet. This sort of off-balance-sheet financing is seen as a useful 'wheeze' or ploy by some managers – for example, gearing limits can be bypassed. However, experienced lenders and shareholders are not so easily fooled by accounting tricks.

3 *Political risk* If the project is in a country prone to political instability, with a tendency towards an anti-transnational business attitude and acts of appropriation, a more cautious way of proceeding may be to set up an arm's length (separate company) relationship with some risk being borne by the banking community, particularly banks in the host country.

4 *Simplifies the banking relationship* In cases where there are a number of parent companies, it can be easier to arrange finance for a separate project entity than to have to deal with each of the parent companies separately. Also, some of the parents may not be creditworthy enough to take on more debt, whereas the robust contractual framework of the SPV, e.g. regular income from road tolls, can support borrowings.

5   *Managerial incentives* Managers of projects may be given an equity stake in the project if it is set up as a separate enterprise. This can lead to high rewards for exceptional performance.

6   *Combining skills and spreading the risk* It often makes sense to tap into the varied skills and risk appetites of a number of sponsoring companies for high-capital cost projects with long development phases.

Sale and leaseback

If a firm owns buildings, land or equipment it may be possible to sell these to another firm (for example a bank, insurance company or specialised leasing firm) and simultaneously agree to lease the property back for a stated period under specific terms. The seller receives cash immediately but is still able to use the asset. However, the seller has created a regular cash flow liability for itself. For example, KPMG and Lloyds Bank sought sale and leaseback deals in 2017 – *see* **Exhibit 11.22**. In the end KPMG sold for £400m and leased back from a Hong Kong property company, and Lloyds sold and leased back from a Chinese property firm.

Exhibit 11.22

KPMG markets London HQ as office prices hit highs

Accountancy group seeks £400m for building in Canary Wharf in sale-and-leaseback deal

by Judith Evans

The "big four" accountancy group KPMG is marketing its London headquarters in a sale-and-leaseback deal as an influx of overseas capital drives prices for London office buildings to new highs.

The company is seeking about £400m for the 14-storey building at 15 Canada Square in Canary Wharf, London's eastern financial district, according to a person briefed on the potential sale.

The move comes as Lloyds Banking Group also prepares to market its London headquarters at 25 Gresham Street. Like KPMG, Lloyds is seeking to enter into a lease deal with any purchaser rather than moving out of the building.

Philip Davidson, managing partner at KPMG, said: "We are seeing strong demand from investors for prime London assets and we want to capitalise on this rising market. Ownership of property is not core to our business and this move reflects our wider strategy: we lease buildings in 22 locations across the UK, keeping our capital free to invest in our business and facilities."

FT   *Financial Times,* 30 August 2017.

In a number of countries the tax regime propels sale and leaseback transactions. For example, some asset owners are unable to use depreciation and other tax allowances (usually because they do not have sufficient taxable profits). The sale of the asset to an organisation looking to reduce taxable profits through the holding of depreciable assets, such as aircraft or ships, enables both firms to benefit. Furthermore, the original owner's subsequent lease payments are tax deductible.

A further advantage is thought to be the efficiency boost sale and leaseback gives to the firm because managers are made more aware of the value of the assets used in the business. It is thought that when managers see the costs of property ownership in the form of explicit rental payments moving through their profit and loss account, they become more aware of resources tied up in such assets, and therefore control more tightly the proportion of the firm's capital devoted to them.

A sale and leaseback has the drawback that the asset is no longer owned by the firm and therefore any capital appreciation has to be forgone. Also long lease arrangements of this kind usually provide for the rental payments to increase at regular intervals, such as every three or five years. Companies sometimes find that the leaseback arrangement eliminates the flexibility to move to cheaper premises. There are other factors limiting the use of sale and leaseback as a financial tool. Leasing can involve complex documentation and large legal fees, which often make it uneconomic to arrange leases for less than £20m. There is also a degree of inflexibility: for example, unwinding the transaction if, say, the borrower wanted to move out of the property can be expensive. Another disadvantage is that the property is no longer available to be offered as security for loans.

Securitisation

In the strange world of modern finance you sometimes need to ask yourself who ends up with your money when you pay your monthly mortgage, or your credit card bill or the instalment payment on your car. In the old days you would have found that it was the organisation you originally borrowed from and whose name is at the top of the monthly statement. Today you cannot be so sure because there is now a thriving market in repackaged debt. In this market, a mortgage lender, for example, collects together a few thousand mortgage 'claims' it has (the right of the lender to receive regular interest and capital from the borrowers); it then sells those claims in a collective package to other institutions, or participants in the market generally. This permits the replacement of long-term assets with cash (improving liquidity and gearing) which can then be used to generate more mortgages. It may also allow a profit on the difference between the interest on the mortgages and the interest on the bonds. The borrower is often unaware that the mortgage is no longer owned by the original lender and everything appears as it did before, with the mortgage company acting as a collecting agent for the buyer of the mortgages. The mortgage company is usually said to be a seller of asset-backed securities (ABS) to other institutions (the 'assets' are the claim on interest and capital) and so this form of finance is often called asset securitisation. These asset-backed securities may be bonds sold into a market with many players. Rather than selling the bonds in the mortgage company itself a new company is usually established, called a 'special purpose vehicle' (SPV) or 'special purpose entity' (SPE). This new entity is then given the right to collect the cash flows from the mortgages. It has to pay the mortgage company for this. To make this payment it sells bonds secured against the assets of the SPV (e.g. mortgage claims). By creating an SPV there is a separation of the creditworthiness of the assets involved from the general credit of the company.

> Asset backed securitisation involves the pooling and repackaging of relatively small, homogeneous and illiquid financial assets into liquid securities.

The sale of the financial claims can be either 'non-recourse', in which case the buyer of the securities from the mortgage firm or the lender to the SPV (e.g. bond holder) bears the risk of non-payment by the borrowers, or with recourse to the mortgage lender.

Securitisation has even reached the world of rock. Iron Maiden issued a long-dated $30m asset-backed bond securitised on future earnings from royalties. It followed David Bowie's $55m bond securitised on the income from his earlier albums and Rod Stewart's $15.4m securitised loan from Nomura.

Tussauds has securitised ticket and merchandise sales, Keele University has securitised the rental income from student accommodation and Arsenal securitised £260m future ticket sales at the Emirates Stadium. Loans to Hong Kong taxi drivers have been securitised, as have the cash flows from UK funeral fees.

Securitisation is regarded as beneficial to the financial system, because it permits banks and other financial institutions to focus on those aspects of the lending process where they have a competitive edge. Some, for example, have a greater competitive advantage in originating loans than in funding them, so they sell the loans they have created, raising cash to originate more loans. Securitisation was at the heart of the financial crisis when US sub-prime (poor quality) mortgage borrowers failed to repay in substantial numbers. Mortgage-backed bonds of SPVs plummeted in value, the asset-backed bond market froze and the businesses model of lending to households expecting to sell bonds backed with a bunch of mortgages (à la Northern Rock) became untenable as no one would buy the securitised bonds.

Exhibit 11.23 describes the securitisation of Dunkin' Donuts' royalties received from its hundreds of franchises around the world – a steady source of income.

Exhibit 11.23

It's all a question of the right packaging

Richard Beales on fresh ways to isolate a company's income streams and cut its financing costs

In a corporate securitisation, assets and related cash flows are carved out from a business into special purpose entities (SPEs) and repackaged. Debt is then raised against the SPEs alone.

'Securitisation isolates a cash flow and insulates it from extraneous events,' says Ted Yarbrough, head of global securitised products at Citigroup.

Depending on the credit quality and the quantum of borrowing, part or all the debt may be highly rated, and there is sometimes a low-rated or unrated subordinated slice of debt as well.

A financing structured this way can achieve higher credit ratings than the business on its own. This partly reflects the structural aspects – for example, the fact that the SPEs can survive a bankruptcy of the umbrella group – and partly the fact that the securities issued are often 'wrapped', or guaranteed, by highly-rated bond insurers such as Ambac, Figic or MBIA in return for a fee.

This is a complex and costly exercise, but can result in much cheaper debt. Once established, a securitisation can be tapped again later if a business grows.

Sometimes securitisation is best suited to part of a business rather than the whole. When applied to an entire business, as with Dunkin' Brands or Domino's, the new financing typically replaces all traditional debt.

While a securitisation does involve financial constraints, they can be fewer and less onerous than with traditional bank and bond debt. Managers would, for example, have greater flexibility to pay dividends or buy back stock.

This reflects the fact that financiers in a securitisation look only to the specific assets and cash flows held within the SPEs. But Eric Hedman, analyst at Standard & Poor's in New York, notes there can be a trade-off in terms of operational flexibility. 'Prior to the securitisation, Dunkin' was an owner operator. Now, the company is no longer the franchisor, there's an SPE. Any new store agreement is for the benefit of the securitisation.' The company's management also does not have sole discretion over advertising spending, for example.

And the Dunkin' Donuts brand is no longer owned by the company. 'The sign on the wall says "Copyright DD IP Holder LLC". That's a bankruptcy-remote SPE set up for the benefit of noteholders [in the securitisation]', Mr Hedman says.

This kind of shift might not suit all managers. But for some executives – particularly those focused on maximising cash returns to shareholders – such considerations can be outweighed by the financial benefits.

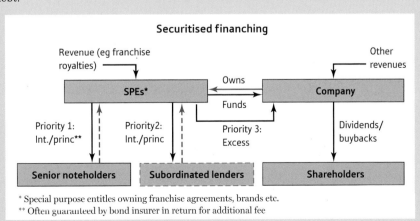

Islamic banking

Under Islamic Sharia (shari'ah) law the payment of *riba*[15] (interest) is prohibited and the receiver of finance must not bear all the risk of failure. Money alone should not create a profit and finance should serve the real economy, not just the financial one. Also investment in alcohol, tobacco, pornography or gambling is not allowed. However, Islam does encourage entrepreneurial activity and the sharing of risk through equity shares. Thus a bank can create profit-sharing products to offer customers. Depositors can be offered a percentage of the bank's profits rather than a set interest rate. Borrowers repay the bank an amount that is related to the profit produced by the project for which the loan was made. One example is **Musharakah,** where a joint enterprise is established by the bank and borrower. Both contribute capital plus management and labour (although some parties, e.g. banks, contribute little other than capital). Profit (loss) is shared in pre-agreed proportions – there is a prohibition against a fixed lump sum for any party. All partners have unlimited liability. For a house purchase the property is purchased by the bank and clients (perhaps 10% of the purchase price). The customer purchases the bank's share gradually, until he is made sole owner after a specified period, usually 25 years. Over the financing period, the bank's share is rented to the customer.

Over 600 banks and financial institutions offer services according to Sharia law. They are most heavily concentrated in the Arabian Gulf countries, Malaysia, Pakistan and Iran. But many conventional banks also offer Sharia products; for example, HSBC and Lloyds have Islamic mortgages available. Growth has been driven by the rising consciousness in Islamic principles over the last 40 years and the rising wealth of Muslim oil states. What is regarded as compliant with Sharia in one part of the world may not be considered by Islamic scholars to be acceptable in another. Malaysia, for example, tends to be more liberal than Saudi Arabia. The UK has introduced tax,[16] legislative and regulatory changes to encourage Islamic financial services in the City. Despite its growth, the worldwide volume of Islamic finance is still only a small fraction of the size of the conventional finance industry.

Islamic bonds (*sukuk*)

Sukuk (the plural form of the Arabic word *sakk* from which the word cheque is derived) are bonds which conform to Sharia law. Whereas conventional bonds are promises to pay interest and principal, *sukuk* represent part *ownership* of tangible assets, businesses or investments, so the returns are generated by some sort of share of the gain (or loss) made, and the risk is shared. They are administered through a special-purpose vehicle (SPV) which issues *sukuk* certificates. These certificates entitle the holder to a rental income or a profit share from the certificate. At maturity, the issuer returns the principal by buying the investor's share in the asset. *Sukuk* may be issued on existing as well as other specific assets that may become available at a future date.

Tesco and Toyota have both issued ringgit *sukuk* in Malaysia. General Electric (GE) has issued *sukuk*. The assets underlying this *sukuk* are GE's interests in aircraft and rental payments from aircraft leasing. In 2014 Goldman Sachs became the third global bank to issue *sukuk* after HSBC and Nomura.

Peer-to-peer lending

The Internet has brought new ways of raising finance directly from savers, e.g. Funding Circle is a platform for individuals and financial institutions to lend to small- and medium-sized businesses; Zopa channels money from individual investors and institutions to individuals and the self-employed; and MarketInvoice allows businesses to sell their unpaid invoices to provide working capital.

---

15 A strict interpretation of the word *riba* is usary or excessive interest.

16 For example, stamp duty on a house sale is not paid twice (when the bank buys and when the customer buys from the bank).

UK peer-to-peer lenders alone have advanced over £3bn (and there are similar websites in other countries), allowing investors to achieve around 6–7%, and enabling companies to borrow at a few percentage points above that. **Exhibit 11.24** describes some peer-to-peer fund raising.

Exhibit 11.24

Small investors lend £1m to manufacturer Mecmesin

By Andrew Bounds

Small investors have lent £1m to a manufacturing business in what is thought to be the largest single peer-to-peer loan to an established company outside the property industry.

Mecmesin, which makes force and torque testing equipment used to measure the quality of products including aircraft brakes, tennis balls and bottle tops, borrowed the money over five years through Money & Co, a crowdfunding platform.

It is a new landmark for the fast-growing lending subsector, which aims to compete with banks as a source of funds for businesses and consumers.

LendInvest, another funding platform, raised £4.1m in short-term finance for a property developer in London in January while Odyssey Airlines, a start up hoping to begin a London to New York service, received £1.9m via the ThinCats platform the same month.

[Mecmesin's] loan has an interest rate of 7.3 per cent. Money & Co takes a 1 per cent fee.

Vashi, a London jeweller, has borrowed £3.7m in five different loans, according to the Peer-to-Peer Finance Association, the industry body.

Mecmesin, based in West Sussex, exports 80 per cent of its products to more than 50 countries. Ms Horlick [of Money & Co] said its asset base and strong record of profits made it a very safe investment.

The family-owned business, founded in 1977, has an annual turnover of more than £10m, makes £1m in annual profit and employs 160.

Robert Oakley, chairman, said he was "frustrated" by the banks. "They want to charge lots of fees. It has been difficult. We have great pedigree and blue-chip customers and the banks want personal guarantees and security. That was the final straw. There is not enough respect for firms like us."

The term structure of interest rates

Until now we have assumed that the annual interest rate on a debt instrument remained the same regardless of the length of time of the loan. So, if the interest rate on a three-year bond is 7% per year it would be 7% on a five-year bond of the same risk and liquidity class. However, it is apparent that lenders in the financial markets demand different interest rates on loans of differing lengths of time to maturity – that is, there is a term structure of the interest rates. Four of these relationships are shown in **Exhibit 11.25** for lending to the UK, Japanese, German (eurozone) and US governments.[17] Note that default risk remains constant along one of the lines; the reason for the different rates is the time to maturity of the bonds. Thus a one-year US government bond

---

17 Using the benchmark yield curves as examples of the term structure of interest rates may offend theoretical purity (because we should be using zero coupon bonds, rather than those with coupons that need to be reinvested before the redemption date without us knowing the reinvestment rate), but they are handy approximate measures and help illustrate this section.

Exhibit 11.25   Yield curves for the UK, USA, eurozone and Japanese government bills and bonds

(the 'Latest' shows the current rates for different maturities. Also shown is a range of rates as calculated one week before and one month before)

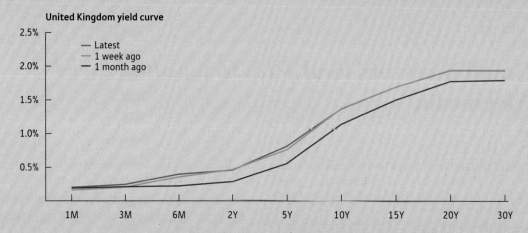

United Kingdom yield curve

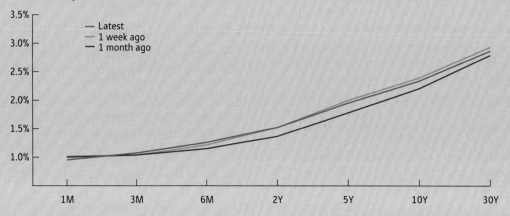

United States yield curve

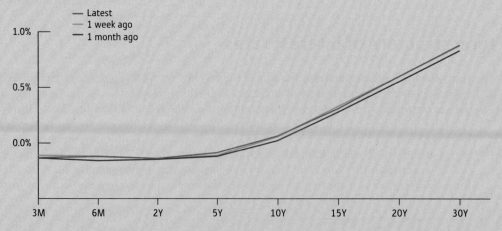

Japan yield curve

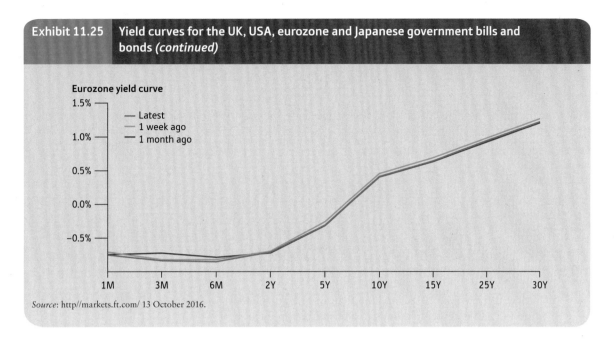

Exhibit 11.25   Yield curves for the UK, USA, eurozone and Japanese government bills and bonds *(continued)*

Eurozone yield curve

Source: http//markets.ft.com/ 13 October 2016.

has to offer 1.39% whereas a 20-year bond offered by the same borrower gives about 2.58%. The German government bond market was distinctly unusual in 2017 because savers would actually pay to lend to the government. If you placed €1,000 with them by buying a two-year bond you would walk away with only €985.25 after compound interest of negative 0.74% per year. Banks and other financial institutions were willing to accept this because they had hundreds or thousands of millions to place somewhere (or were obliged to put it in government bonds by the regulators) and interest rates had been pushed to very low levels by central banks. Negative interest rates occurred in many countries. Note that the yield curve shown for the Eurozone is only for the most creditworthy governments who have adopted the euro; less safe governments have to pay more.

An upward-sloping yield curve occurs in most years but occasionally we have a situation where short-term interest rates (lending for, say, one year) exceed those of long-term interest rates (say, a 20-year bond).

Three main hypotheses have been advanced to explain the shape of the yield curve – all three can operate at the same time to influence the yield curve.

a   the expectation hypothesis;

b   the liquidity-preference hypothesis; and

c   the market-segmentation hypothesis.

The expectations hypothesis

The expectations hypothesis focuses on the changes in interest rates over time. To understand the expectations hypothesis you need to know what is meant by a 'spot rate of interest'. The spot rate is an interest rate fixed today on a loan that is made today. So a corporation, Hype plc, might issue one-year bonds at a spot rate of, say, 8%, two-year bonds at a spot rate of 8.995% and three-year bonds at a spot rate of 9.5%. This yield curve for Hype is shown in **Exhibit 11.26**. The interest rates payable by Hype are bound to be greater than for the UK government across the yield curve because of the additional default risk on these corporate bonds.

Spot rates change over time. The market may have allowed Hype to issue one-year bonds yielding 8% at a point in time in 2018 but a year later (time 2019) the one-year spot rate may have changed to become 10%. If investors expect that one-year spot rates will become 10% at time 2019 they will have a theoretical limit on the yield that they require from a two-year bond when

Exhibit 11.26   The term structure of interest rates for Hype plc at time 2018

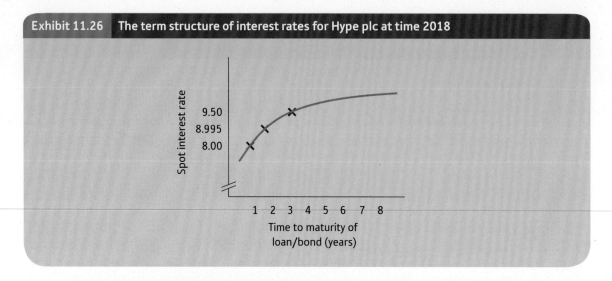

viewed from time 2018. Imagine that an investor (lender) wishes to lend £1,000 for a two-year period and is contemplating two alternative approaches:

1   Buy a one-year bond at a spot rate of 8%; after one year has passed the bond will come to maturity. The released funds can then be invested in another one-year bond at a spot rate of 10%, expected to be the going rate for bonds of this risk class at time 2019.[18]

2   Buy a two-year bond at the spot rate at time 2018.

Under the first option the lender will have a sum of £1,188 at the end of two years:

$$£1,000 \, (1 + 0.08) = £1,080$$
$$\text{followed by } £1,080 \, (1 + 0.1) = £1,188$$

Given the anticipated change in one-year spot rates to 10% the investor will only buy the two-year bond if it gives the same average annual yield over two years as the first option of a series of one-year bonds. The annual interest required will be:

$$£1,000 \, (1 + k)^2 = £1,188$$
$$k = \sqrt{(1,188/1,000)} - 1 = 0.08995 \text{ or } 8.995\%$$

which is the spot rate quoted for a two-year bond in 2018 in the second option.

Thus, it is the expectation of spot interest rates changing which determines the shape of the yield curve according to the expectation hypothesis.

Now consider a downward-sloping yield curve where the spot rate on a one-year instrument is 11% and the expectation is that one year from now one-year spot rates will fall to 8%. An investor considering a two-year investment will obtain an annual yield of 9.49% by investing in a series of one-year bonds, viz:

$$£1,000 \, (1.08) \, (1.11) = £1,198.80$$

$$k = \sqrt{(1,198.8/1,000)} - 1 = 0.0949 \text{ or } 9.49\% \text{ per year}$$

$$\text{or } \sqrt{(1.08)(1.11)} - 1 = 0.0949$$

---

18 I have simplified this to spot rates only. In reality investors in bonds can agree to buy a bond one year (or more years) from now, a **forward.** The price of the forward purchase is agreed now; thus traders can lock-in the interest rate from that point on. This **implied forward rate** can be interpreted as the market's consensus of the spot rates in one year from now.

With this expectation for movements in one-year spot rates, lenders will demand an annual rate of return of 9.49% from two-year bonds of the same risk class.

Thus in circumstances where short-term spot interest rates are expected to fall, the yield curve will be downward sloping.

Worked example 11.2   Spot rates

If the present spot rate for a one-year bond is 5% and for a two-year bond 6.5%, what is the expected one-year spot rate in a year's time?

Answer

If the two-year rate is set to equal the rate on a series of one-year spot rates then:

$$(1 + 0.05)(1 + x) = (1 + 0.065)^2$$

$$x = \frac{(1 + 0.065)^2}{1 + 0.05} - 1 = 0.0802 \text{ or } 8.02\%$$

The liquidity-preference hypothesis

The expectation hypothesis does not adequately explain why the most common shape of the yield curve is upward sloping. The liquidity-preference hypothesis (liquidity premium theory) helps explain the upward slope by pointing out that investors require an extra return for lending on a long-term basis. Lenders demand a premium return on long-term bonds compared with short-term instruments because of the risk of misjudging future interest rates. Putting your money into a ten-year bond on the anticipation of particular levels of interest rates exposes you to the possibility that rates will rise above the rate offered on the bond at some point in its long life. Thus, if five years later interest rates double, say because of a rise in inflation expectations, the market price of the bond will fall substantially, leaving the holder with a large capital loss. On the other hand, by investing in a series of one-year bonds, the investor can take advantage of rising interest rates as they occur. The ten-year bond locks in a fixed rate for the full ten years if held to maturity. Investors prefer short-term bonds so that they can benefit from rising rates and so will accept a lower return on short-dated instruments.

The liquidity-preference theory focuses on a different type of risk attaching to long-dated debt instruments other than default risk – a risk related to uncertainty over future interest rates. A suggested reinforcing factor to the upward slope is that borrowers usually prefer long-term debt because of the fear of having to repay short-term debt at inappropriate moments. Thus borrowers increase the supply of long-term debt instruments, adding to the tendency for long-term rates to be higher than short-term rates.

A further factor is that in many bond markets there is a greater volume of trading for short-dated instruments than longer-dated ones: i.e. there is greater liquidity, an increased speed and ease of sale of an asset. In government bond markets where there is high liquidity for both short- and long-term bonds, the title 'liquidity-preference theory' seems incorrectly used because there is no problem with liquidity for long-term bonds – but it has stuck so we still use it. In the bond markets where liquidity is fairly constant along the yield curve, the premium on long bonds is generally compensation for the extra risk of capital loss; 'term premium' might be a better title for the hypothesis.

The market-segmentation hypothesis

The market segmentation hypothesis argues that the debt market is not one homogeneous whole, that there are, in fact, a number of sub-markets defined by maturity range. The yield curve is therefore created (or at least influenced) by the supply and demand conditions in each of these sub-markets. For example, banks tend to be active in the short-term end of the market and pension funds to be buyers in the long-dated segment. If banks need to borrow large quantities quickly they will sell some of their short-term instruments, increasing the supply on the market and pushing down the price and raising the yield. On the other hand pension funds may be flush with cash and may buy large quantities of 20-year bonds, helping to temporarily move yields downward at the long end of the market. At other times banks, pension funds and the buying and selling pressures of a multitude of other financial institutions will influence the supply and demand position in the opposite direction. The point is that the players in the different parts of the yield curve tend to be different. This hypothesis helps to explain the often lumpy or humped yield curve.

A final thought on the term structure of interest rates

It is sometimes thought that in circumstances of a steeply rising yield curve it would be advantageous to borrow short term rather than long term. However, this can be a dangerous strategy because long-term debt may be trading at a higher rate of interest because of the expected rise in short-term rates and so when the borrower comes to refinance in, say, a year's time, the short-term interest rate is much higher than the long-term rate and this high rate has to be paid out of the second year's cash flows, which may not be convenient.

Concluding comments

So far this book has taken a fairly detailed look at a variety of ways of raising money by selling shares and has examined the main methods of raising funds through long-term debt. The decision to raise equity or debt finance is neither simple nor straightforward. In the next chapter we consider a wider array of financial sources and types, from leasing to factoring. Knowledge of these will enable the finance manager or other executives to select and structure the different forms of finance to maximise the firm's potential. Topics covered later in the book draw on the knowledge gained in Chapters 10, 11 and 12 to permit informed discussion of such crucial questions as: What is the appropriate mixture of debt and equity? How is the cost of various forms of finance calculated? How can the risk of certain forms of finance (for example a floating-interest-rate term loan) be reduced?

Key points and concepts

- **Debt finance has a number of advantages for the company:**

    - it has a lower cost than equity finance:
      a   lower transaction costs;
      b   lower rate of return;
    - debt holders generally do not have votes;
    - interest is tax deductible.

- **Drawbacks of debt:**

    - Committing to repayments and interest can be risky for a firm, ultimately the debt-holders can force liquidation to retrieve payment;
    - the use of secured assets for borrowing may be an onerous constraint on managerial action;
    - covenants may further restrict managerial action.

- A **corporate bond** is a long-term contract in which the bondholders lend money to a company. A

straight 'vanilla' bond pays regular interest plus the capital on the redemption date.

- Debentures are generally more secure than **loan stock** (in the UK).

- A **trust deed** has **affirmative covenants** outlining the nature of the bond contract and **negative (restrictive) covenants** imposing constraints on managerial action to reduce risk for the lenders.

- A **floating rate note (FRN)** is a bond with an interest rate which varies as a benchmark interest rate changes (e.g. LIBOR).

- **Attractive features of bank borrowing:**

    - administrative and legal costs are low;
    - quick;
    - flexibility in troubled times;
    - available to small firms.

- **Factors for a firm to consider with bank borrowing:**

  Costs

  - fixed versus floating;
  - arrangement fees;
  - bargaining on the rate.

  Security

  - asymmetric information;
  - collateral;
  - covenants;
  - personal guarantees.

- **Repayment arrangements**:

  Some possibilities:

  - grace periods;
  - mortgage style;
  - term loan.

- A **syndicated loan** occurs where a number of banks (or other financial institutions) each contribute a portion of a loan.

- A **credit rating** depends on a the likelihood of payments of interest and/or capital not being paid (i.e. default); and b the extent to which the lender is protected in the event of a default.

- **Mezzanine debt** and **high-yield bonds** are forms of debt offering a high return with a high risk. They have been particularly useful in the following:

  - management buyouts (MBOs), especially leveraged management buyouts (LBOs);
  - fast-growing companies;
  - leveraged recapitalisation.

- **Convertible bonds** are issued as debt instruments but they also give the holder the right to exchange the bonds at some time in the future into ordinary shares according to some prearranged formula. Advantages:

  - lower interest than on debentures;
  - interest is tax deductible;
  - self-liquidating;
  - few negative covenants;
  - shares might be temporarily underpriced;
  - cheap way to issue shares;
  - an available form of finance when straight debt and equity are not.

- A bond is **priced** according to general market interest rates for risk class and maturity:

  Irredeemable:

  $$P_D = \frac{i}{k_D}$$

- Redeemable:

  $$P_D = \frac{i_1}{1 + k_D} + \frac{i_2}{(1 + k_D)^2} + \frac{i_3}{(1 + k_D)^3}$$
  $$+ \ \ldots \ + \frac{R_n}{(1 + k_D)^n}$$

- The **interest (flat) yield** on a bond is:

  $$\frac{\text{Gross interest (coupon)}}{\text{Market price}} \times 100$$

- The **yield to maturity** includes both annual coupon returns and capital gains or losses on maturity.

- The **Euromarkets** are informal (unregulated) markets in money held outside the jurisdiction of the country of origin of the currency.

- A **foreign bond** is a bond denominated in the currency of the country where it is issued when the issuer is a non-resident.

- A **Eurobond** is a bond sold outside the jurisdiction of the country of the currency in which the bond is denominated.

- A **project finance** loan is provided as a bank loan or bond finance to an entity set up separately from the parent corporation to undertake a project. The returns to the lender are tied to the fortunes and cash flows of the project.

- **Sale and leaseback** Assets are sold to financial institutions or another company which releases cash. Simultaneously, the original owner agrees to lease the assets back for a stated period under specified terms.

- **Securitisation** Relatively small, homogeneous and liquid financial assets are pooled and repackaged into liquid securities which are then sold on to other investors to generate cash for the original lender.

- Under **Islamic Sharia law** the payment of interest is prohibited. However, a bank may create profit-sharing products, or a bond may be profit sharing.

- The **term structure of interest rates** describes the manner in which the same default risk class of debt securities provides different rates of return depending on the length of time to maturity. There are three hypotheses relating to the term structure of interest rates:

  - the expectations hypothesis;
  - the liquidity-preference hypothesis;
  - the market-segmentation hypothesis.

References and further reading

To keep up to date and reinforce knowledge gained by reading this chapter I can recommend the following publications: *Financial Times, The Economist, Bank of England Quarterly Bulletin, Bank for International Settlements Quarterly Review* (www.bis.org), *The Treasurer* (a monthly journal), and *Finance and Leasing Association* (FLA) *Annual Report* (www.fla.org.uk.)

Arnold, G. (2012a) *Modern Financial Markets and Institutions.* Harlow: FT Prentice Hall.
> Contains more on banking and money markets.

Aslan, H. (2016) 'Do lending relationships affect corporate financial policies?' *Financial Management,* Spring, 45(1), pp. 141–73.
> Evidence on how lending relationships impact firms' financing and investment decisions (leverage ratios, issuance choices, and the investment structures of relationship borrowers).

Baghai, R.P., Servaes, H. and Ane, A. (2014) 'Have rating agencies become more conservative? Implications for capital structure and debt pricing', *Journal of Finance,* 69(5), pp. 1961–2005.
> Rating agencies have become more conservative in assigning corporate credit ratings over the period 1985 to 2009.

Bar-Isaac, H. and Shapiro, J. (2013) 'Rating quality over the business cycle', *Journal of Financial Economics,* 108, pp. 62–78.
> Rating quality is countercyclical; issuing less-accurate ratings when fee-income is high, competition in the market for analysts is tough and securities' defaults probabilities are low.

Berg, T., Saunders, A. and Steffen, S. (2016) 'The total cost of borrowing in the loan market: don't ignore the fees', *Journal of Finance,* June 2016, 71(3), pp. 1357–92.
> In syndicated loans corporate borrowers are effectively sold options, e.g. option to drawdown credit at an optimum time or the option to cancel the loan. Managers need to take into account all fees when evaluating the cost of borrowing.

Bharath, S., Dahiya, S., Saunders, A. and Srinivasan, A. (2007) 'So what do I get? The bank's view of lending relationships', *Journal of Financial Economics,* 85, pp. 368–419.
> Strong relationships with clients raise the probability of banks to sell products and make loans.

Bodie, Z., Kane, A. and Marcus, A.J. (2014) *Investments.* Global Edition. McGraw-Hill.
> More detail on bond markets.

Cerqueiro, G., Ongena, S. and Roszbach, K. (2016) 'Collateralization, bank loan rates, and monitoring', *Journal of Finance,* 71(3), pp. 1295–322.
> An investigation of the importance of collateral in the supply of credit and design of those contracts.

Chava, S. and Roberts, M.R. (2008) 'How does financing impact investment? The role of debt covenants', *Journal of Finance,* LXIII(5), Oct, pp. 2085–121.
> Debt covenants can have a severe impact on borrower company investment after they have been violated.

Chisholm, A.M. (2009) *An Introduction to International Capital Markets.* 2nd edn. Chichester: J. Wiley and Sons.
> Containing four well-written and accessible chapters detailing the bond markets around the world – particularly good on bond valuation calculations.

Eiteman, D.K., Stonehill, A.I. and Moffett, M.H. (2015) *Multinational Business Finance, Global Edition.* 14th edition. Pearson.
> Some useful, easy-to-follow material on international debt markets.

Graham, J.R. and Harvey, C.R. (2001) 'The theory and practice of corporate finance: evidence from the field', *Journal of Financial Economics,* 60(2–3), May, pp. 187–243.
> US survey of corporate use of debt.

Han Xia (2014) 'Can investor-paid credit rating agencies improve the information quality of issuer-paid rating agencies?' *Journal of Financial Economics,* 111, pp. 450–68.
> S&Ps ratings become more responsive to credit risk after Egan-Jones Ratings – a investor-paid organization – starts evaluating a firm and its debt.

Hickman, B.G. (1958) 'Corporate bond quality and investor experience', *National Bureau of Economic Research,* 14, Princeton.
> Early research into the returns and default rates on bonds.

Hicks, J.R. (1946) *Value and Capital: An Inquiry into some Fundamental Principles of Economic Theory.* 2nd edn. Oxford: Oxford University Press.
> Liquidity-preference hypothesis to explain the term structure of interest rates.

Jotikasthira, C., Le, A. and Lundblad, C. (2015) 'Why do term structures in different currencies co-move?' *Journal of Financial Economics,* 115, pp. 58–83.
> Yield curves in different currencies are highly correlated. Macroeconomic shock induces central bank action and investors alter their required compensation for risk.

Lim, J., Minton, B.A. and Weisbach, M.S. (2014) 'Syndicated loan spreads and the composition of the syndicate', *Journal of Financial Economics,* 111, pp. 45–69.
> Increasingly non-bank financial institutions (e.g. hedge funds and private equity funds) take part in syndicated lending. They require a higher interest rate.

Lutz, F.A. and Lutz, V.C. (1951) *The Theory of Investment in the Firm*. Princeton, NJ: Princeton University Press.

Expectations hypothesis of the term structure of interest rates.

Saunders, A. and Cornett, M.M. (2015) *Financial Markets and Institutions*. International edition. 6th edn. Boston, MA: McGraw-Hill.

Contains much more on the US bond markets and on mathematical calculations associated with bond pricing, YTM, etc.

Manso, G. (2013) 'Feedback effects of credit ratings', *Journal of Financial Economics,* 109, pp. 535–48.

Rating downgrades can reduce the probability of firm survival.

Veronesi, P. (2011) *Fixed Income Securities: Valuation, risk and risk management*. New Jersey: John Wiley and Sons.

A much more detailed look at the bond markets, with a focus on the USA.

Case study recommendations

Please see www.pearsoned.co.uk/arnold for case study synopses. Also, another list of useful case studies from the fifth edition can be found there.

- Gilbert Lumber Company. Authors: Steven Rogers; Kenneth Cooper, Harvard Business School. Available at www.cb.hbsp.harvard.edu

- Jones Electrical Distribution (brief case) Authors: Thomas R. Piper; Jeffrey DeVolder, Harvard Business School. Available at www.cb.hbsp.harvard.edu

- Rose Electronics Distributing Company. Authors: Richard S. Ruback; Royce Yudkoff, Harvard Business School. Available at www.cb.hbsp.harvard.edu

- Michael Milken: the junk bond king. Authors: Tom Nicholas; Matthew Preble, Harvard Business School. Available at www.cb.hbsp.harvard.edu

- An introduction to zero-coupon risk-free bonds. Author: Michael J. Schill, Darden School of Business. Available at www.cb.hbsp.harvard.edu

- Cheniere's Lng liquefaction strategy: pushing the boundaries of the project finance debt market. Authors: Paul Tice; Ingo Walter, Harvard Business School. Available at www.cb.hbsp.harvard.edu

- Premier Explosives: finance for organic growth. Authors: Maram Srikanth; Palanisamy Saravanan, Ivey Publishing. Available at www.cb.hbsp.harvard.edu

- Jaguar Land Rover Plc: bond valuation. Author: S. Veena Iyer, Ivey Publishing. Available at www.cb.hbsp.harvard.edu

Websites

Association of Corporate Treasurers www.treasurers.org
Bank for International Settlements www.bis.org
Bank of England www.bankofengland.co.uk
The Economist www.economist.com
Financial Times www.ft.com

Fitch ratings www.fitchratings.com
International Capital Market Association www.icmagroup.org
Moody's www.moodys.com
Standard & Poor's www.standardandpoors.com

Video presentations

Chief executives and financial directors describe their current policy on raising funds www.merchantcantos.com – this is free to view.

Self-review questions

1   What are the relative advantages and drawbacks of debt and equity finance?

2   Explain the following (related to bonds):
    a   Par value.
    b   Trustee.
    c   Debenture.
    d   Zero coupon bond.
    e   Floating-rate note.

3   The inexperienced finance trainee at Mugs-R-Us plc says that he can save the company money on its forthcoming issue of ten-year bonds. 'The rate of return required for bonds of this risk class in the financial markets is 10% and yet I overheard our merchant banking adviser say, "We could issue a bond at a coupon of only 9%." I reckon we could save the company a large sum on the £100m issue.' Do you agree with the trainee's logic?

4   In what circumstances would you recommend borrowing from a bank rather than a capital market bond issue?

5   What are the fundamental considerations to which you would advise a firm to give thought if it were contemplating borrowing from a bank?

6   Is securitisation something to do with anti-criminal precautions? If not, explain what it is and why firms do it.

7   In what ways does the tax regime encourage debt finance rather than equity finance?

8   Why does convertible debt carry a lower coupon than straight debt?

9   What is meant by asymmetric information in the relationship between banker and borrower?

10 What is a syndicated loan and why do banks join so many syndicates?

11 What are the differences between a domestic bond, a Eurobond and a foreign bond?

12 What is the credit rating on a bond and what factors determine it?

13 Why do bond issuers accept restrictive covenants?

14 What are high-yield bonds? What is their role in financing firms?

15 What is a bearer bond?

16 What is a debenture?

17 What is the difference between a fixed-rate and a floating-rate bond?

Questions and problems

Answers to some questions can be found at www.pearsoned.co.uk/arnold.
Answers to questions marked with an asterisk are to be found only in the Lecturer's Guide.

1   Imagine that the market yield to maturity for three-year bonds in a particular risk class is 12%. You buy a bond in that risk class which offers an annual coupon of 10% for the next three years, with the first payment in one year. The bond will be redeemed at par (£100) in three years.
    a   How much would you pay for the bond?
    b   If you paid £105 what yield to maturity would you obtain?

2   A £100 bond with two years to maturity and an annual coupon of 9% is available. (The next coupon is payable in one year.)
    a   If the market requires a yield to maturity of 9% for a bond of this risk class what will be its market price?
    b   If the market price is £98, what yield to maturity does it offer?
    c   If the required yield to maturity on this type of bond changes to 7%, what will the market price change to?

3   a   If the government sold a 10-year gilt with a par value of £100 and an (annual) coupon of 9%, what price can be charged if investors require a 9.5% yield to maturity on such bonds?

      b   If yields to maturity on bonds of this risk class fall to 8.5%, what could the bonds be sold for?

      c   If it were sold for £105, what yield to maturity is the bond offering?

      d   What is the flat yield on this bond if it is selling at £105? An Excel spreadsheet version of these calculations is available at www.pearsoned.com/arnold.

4   The price of a bond issued by C & M plc is 85.50% of par value. The bond will pay an annual 8.5% coupon until maturity (the next coupon will be paid in one year). The bond matures in seven years.

      a   What will be the market price of the bond if yields to maturity for this risk class fall to 7.5%?

      b   What will be the market price of the bond if yields to maturity for this risk class rise to 18%?

5   A zero coupon bond with a par value of £100 matures in five years.

      a   What is the price of the bond if the yield to maturity is 5%?

      b   What is the price of the bond if the yield to maturity is 10%?

6   Bond 1 has an annual coupon rate of 6% and Bond 2 has an annual coupon of 12%. Both bonds mature in one year and have a par value of £100. If the yield to maturity on bonds of this risk class is 10% at what price will the bonds sell? Assume that the next coupons are due in one year's time.

7*   You are considering three alternative investments in bonds. The bonds have different times to maturity, but carry the same default risk. You would like to gain an impression of the extent of price volatility for each given alternative change in future interest rates. The investments are:

      i   A two-year bond with an annual coupon of 6%, par value of £100 and the next coupon payment in one year. The current yield to maturity on this bond is 6.5%.

      ii   A ten-year bond with an annual coupon of 6%, a par value of £100 and the next coupon payable in one year. The current yield to maturity on this bond is 7.2%.

      iii A 20-year bond with an annual coupon of 6%, a par value of £100 and the next coupon due in one year. The current yield to maturity on this bond is 7.7%.

      a   Draw an approximate yield curve.

      b   Calculate the market price of each of the bonds.

      c   Calculate the market price of the bonds on the assumption that yields to maturity rise by 200 basis points for all bonds.

      d   Now calculate the market price of the bonds on the assumption that yields to maturity fall by 200 basis points.

      e   Which bond price is the most volatile in circumstances of changing yields to maturity?

      f   Explain the liquidity-preference theory of the term structure of yields to maturity.

8   What are the factors that explain the difference in yields to maturity between long-term and short-term bonds?

9   Find the current yield to maturity on government securities with maturities of one year, five years and ten years in the *Financial Times*. How has the yield curve changed since 2016 as shown in the chapter? What might account for this shift?

10   If the yield to maturity on a two-year zero coupon bond is 13% and the yield to maturity on a one-year zero coupon bond is 10% what is the expected spot rate of one-year bonds in one year's time assuming the expectations hypothesis is applicable?

11   If the yield to maturity on a one-year bond is 8% and the expected spot rate on a one-year bond, beginning in one year's time, is 7% what will be the yield to maturity on a two-year bond under the expectations hypothesis of the term structure of interest rates?

12   In 2006 the term structure of interest rates for UK government securities was downward sloping whereas in many other years it is upward sloping. Explain how these curves come about with reference to the expectations, liquidity and market-segmentation hypotheses.

13 Iris plc borrows £50m at 9.5% from Westlloyds bank for five years. What cash flows will the firm have to find if the interest and principal are paid in the following ways?

   a   All interest and capital is paid at the end of the period.
   b   Interest only is paid for each of the years (at the year ends); all principal is paid at the end.
   c   £10m of the capital plus annual interest is paid on each anniversary date.

14 What factors should a firm consider when borrowing from a bank?

15 'Convertibles are great because they offer a lower return than straight debt and we just dish out shares rather than having to find cash to redeem the bonds' – executive at Myopic plc. Comment on this statement as though you were a shareholder in Myopic.

16 Lummer plc has issued £60m 15-year 8.5% coupon bonds with a par value of £100. Each bond is convertible into 40 shares of Lummer ordinary shares, which are currently trading at £1.90.

   a   What is the conversion price?
   b   What is the conversion premium?
   c   What is the conversion value of the bond?

17 Explain the following terms and their relevance to debt-finance decision makers:

   a   Negative covenant.
   b   Conversion premium.
   c   Collateral.
   d   Grace periods.

18 Outline the main advantages and disadvantages of fixed and floating interest rates from the borrowing company's perspective.

19 (*Examination level*) Flying High plc plans to expand rapidly over the next five years and is considering the following forms of finance to support that expansion.

   a   A five-year £10m floating-rate term loan from MidBarc Bank plc at an initial annual interest of 9%.
   b   A five-year Eurodollar bond fixed at 8% with a nominal value of US$15m.
   c   A £10m convertible bond offering a yield to redemption of 6% and a conversion premium of 15%.

   As the financial adviser to the board you have been asked to explain each of these forms of finance and point out the relative advantages and drawbacks. Do this in report form.

20 'We avoid debt finance because of the unacceptable constraint placed on managerial actions.' Explain what this executive means and suggest forms of long-term borrowing which have few constraints.

Assignments

1 Review the long-term debt instruments used by a company familiar to you. Consider the merits and drawbacks of these and explain alternative long-term debt strategies.

2 Write a report for the senior management of a company you know well explaining your views on the wisdom of using some of the firm's assets in a sale and leaseback transaction.

Short- and medium-term finance, treasury and working capital management

LEARNING OUTCOMES

This chapter concentrates on a description of the main forms of short- and medium-term finance available, and then explores the appropriate use of these sources in varying circumstances. Once obtained, cash and other short-term assets need to be carefully managed to achieve the appropriate balance of returns and risk. This is one of the key components of treasury management. We then widen the focus to include a variety of practices to achieve good management of working capital.

Specifically, the reader should be able to:

■ describe, compare and contrast bank overdrafts, bank term loans, trade credit, factoring, hire purchase, leasing, bills of exchange and acceptance credits as ways of financing the firm;

■ describe the main roles of a treasury department and discuss how the treasurer might reduce risk and enhance the mix of finance for the firm;

■ discuss the factors influencing the mix of different types of debt in terms of maturity, currency and interest rates;

■ explain the central importance of good working capital management, including debtors (accounts receivable) management, the cash conversion cycle, cash management, inventory management and the investment of temporary surplus funds.

Introduction

Short-term and medium-term finance is presented in this textbook as the third major category of funding. This is not meant to imply that the forms of finance described in this chapter are any less important than the first two (equity and long-term debt finance). Indeed, for many firms, especially smaller ones, a combination of overdrafts and loans, trade credit, leasing and hire purchase make up the greater part of their funding needs. Large companies have access to stock markets, bond markets and syndicated loan facilities, which are often unavailable to the smaller firm, so, in order to achieve their expansion programmes, small and medium-sized enterprises (SMEs) turn to the local banks, finance houses and their suppliers for the funds required to grow. The giants of the corporate world have access to many different types of finance, but they also value the characteristics, cheapness and flexibility of the forms discussed here.

Companies need decision makers who are knowledgeable about the markets and instruments so that they can help to guide the firm in selecting the appropriate balance in sources of finance, and can reduce the risk associated with that finance. As well as dealing with major financial moves treasurers help with many small and short-term finance-related decisions. Despite being individually small and often routine, they are collectively important for the well-being of the firm and the achievement of its goals. This chapter provides a brief overview of the role of the corporate treasurer, but because other chapters cover longer-term issues such as financial gearing or mergers, its main focus is on shorter-term financial concerns.

Working capital decisions are usually handled by line managers, but specialists, such as accountants or treasurers, may assist. An example of the sort of question that needs to be addressed in this area is, what should the organisation do with any temporary surplus cash? Should it merely be deposited in a bank account or should the firm be more adventurous and try to obtain a higher return by placing the funds in the money market? But then, what about the increased risk and loss of liquidity associated with some forms of lending?

The quality of day-to-day interaction with banks and other finance providers is vitally important. Thought and time have to be devoted to cultivating these relationships. Any one encounter with, or information flow to, these backers may be regarded as insignificant, but cumulatively an image of a business is created. Ideally that image needs to be professional and purposeful and to show a sound grasp of the competitive positioning and potential of the firm. A poor image can lead to increased cost of funds, the blocking of expansion and, in extreme cases, the removal of managers.

The treasurer is additionally given the task of managing the risk associated with interest rate and exchange rate change. So a UK firm may sell £1m of goods to a Canadian importer on six months' credit invoiced in Canadian dollars (CAD). What the UK firm does not know is the quantity of sterling (GBP) it will receive when in six months it converts the CAD into GBP. The treasury department will have a range of approaches available to reduce the uncertainty and reassure other managers that the export deal will be a profitable one. Similarly, skilled individuals within the treasury will be able to hedge interest rate risk: that is, make arrangements which reduce the impact of adverse interest rate movements on the firm.

These and many other duties involve short-term decisions in the main, but can make or break a company. *The Economist* described the treasury function as 'the financial engine room of companies',[1] meaning that these decisions do not necessarily have the grandeur and broad sweep of the decisions made in the boardroom of the firm but they are vital to maintaining its progress. This becomes all too tragically apparent when things go wrong and companies fail due to poor working capital management, to running out of cash despite high profits or to losing a fortune on the derivative markets.

Short- and medium-term bank finance

The definitions of short-term and medium-term finance are not clear-cut. Usually finance which is repayable within a year is regarded as short, whereas that due for repayment between one and seven years is taken to be medium. But these cut-offs are not to be taken too seriously. Quite often an overdraft facility, which is due for repayment in, say, six months or one year, is regularly 'rolled over' and so may become relied upon as a medium- or even long-term source of funds.

---

1 *The Economist*, 16 November 1996, p. 131.

Leasing, which is usually classified as a medium-term source, can be used for periods of up to 15 years in some circumstances; in others it is possible to lease assets for a period of only a few weeks, for example, a computer or photocopier.

Bank overdraft

Usually the amount that a depositor can withdraw from a bank account is limited to the amount put in. However, business and other financial activity often requires some flexibility in this principle, and it is useful to make an arrangement to take more money out of a bank account than it contains – this is an overdraft.

An overdraft is an agreement with the bank to overdraw on an account up to a stated limit.

Overdraft facilities are usually arranged for a period of a few months or a year and interest is charged on the overdrawn amount. Overdrafts are popular in Germany and the UK and are frequently used by people and businesses whether by prior arrangement or accidentally (if unauthorised then fees/penalties are charged). In other countries (e.g. France) banks take a very tough line if you try to remove more than you have deposited in an account, unless you have prior authorisation. Unauthorised overdrafts in France incur heavy penalty charges.

Advantages of overdrafts

Overdrafts have the following advantages:

1   *Flexibility* The borrowing firm is not asked to forecast the precise amount and duration of its borrowing at the outset but has the flexibility to borrow up to a stated limit. Also the borrower is assured that the moment the funds are no longer required they can be quickly and easily repaid without suffering a penalty.

2   *Cost* Banks usually charge three to six percentage points over base rate (or LIBOR) depending on the creditworthiness, security offered and bargaining position of the borrower. There may also be an arrangement fee of, say, 1% of the facility applicable when the overdraft is arranged and a renewal fee may be required each time it is renewed.

HSBC Business Banking Fees and Charges as at 29 March 2017 shows the following charges for overdrafts agreed following a formal request:

- *Arrangement fee.* Normally 1.75% of the agreed limit for limits up to and including £30,000 (minimum £25) or 1.50% for limits over £30,000 plus security fees and expenses (if any).

- *Renewal fee.* Normally 1.50% of the agreed limit for limits up to and including £30,000 (minimum £25) or 1.25% for limits over £30,000, plus security fees and expenses (if any).

- *Temporary Overdraft Fees.* A short-term (normally a maximum 31 days) new or increased overdraft limit formally agreed with you in advance. 1% of the new or additional limit (minimum £25).

These charges may seem high but it must be borne in mind that overdrafts are often loans to smaller and riskier firms. Large and well-established borrowers with low gearing and plenty of collateral can borrow on overdraft at lower rates. A major saving comes from the fact that the banks charge interest on only the daily outstanding balance. So, if a firm has a large cash inflow one week it can use this to reduce its overdraft, temporarily lowering the interest payable, while retaining the ability to borrow more another week.

3 *Ease of arranging* An overdraft is usually easy to arrange by a telephone call or visit to the bank. Decisions are taken quickly so companies can get prompt access to funds.

Drawbacks of an overdraft

A major drawback to an overdraft is that they are usually 'repayable on demand'. The bank retains the right to withdraw the facility at short notice.[2] Thus a heavily indebted firm may receive a letter

---

2 This is not always the case. To make themselves more appealing to potential clients some banks offer overdrafts that they cannot withdraw at short notice so long as the borrower is abiding by the terms.

from the bank insisting that its overdraft be repaid within a matter of days. This right to demand immediate repayment lowers the risk to the lender because it can quickly get its money back; this allows it to lower the cost of lending. However, it can be devastating for the borrower and so firms are well advised to think through how they use finance provided by way of an overdraft. It is not usually wise to use the overdraft to buy an asset which cannot be easily liquidated; for example, it could be problematic if an overdraft is used for a bridge-building project which will take three years to come to fruition.

This became a major issue during the aftermath of the 2009 financial crisis – *see* **Exhibit 12.1** when banks, under pressure themselves, asked companies to repay their overdrafts. This caused problems for many companies and in some cases led to companies going into administration.

The risk of a sudden withdrawal of an overdraft facility for most firms used to be slight: banks do not generate goodwill and good publicity by capriciously and lightly cancelling agreed overdrafts. However, following the financial crisis banks have been prepared to demand repayment more readily or will refuse to renew overdrafts when the agreement expires – *see* **Exhibit 12.1**.

Exhibit 12.1

UK lending tougher or non-existent

18 December 2011

By Peter Marsh

When Sue Hunter came to renegotiate her company's £500,000 overdraft with Barclays Bank, she was shocked when the UK bank withdrew the facility completely. The difficulties encountered by Ms Hunter – managing director and part-owner of PSI Global, a maker of filtration equipment in Durham – are becoming more common among UK manufacturers, according to a recent survey by the EEF engineering association. The survey of almost 300 companies said more businesses were reporting a rise in the cost of credit, together with a reduced level of availability of loans, as banks clamped down on lending to reflect tougher economic conditions. In Ms Hunter's case, Barclays switched PSI into a system known as invoice discounting. It put this form of financing into effect early last year, following PSI's weak performance in 2009/10 when it had a loss on sales of £3.5m. Invoice discounting provides companies with a cash "cushion" to offset against future payments by customers – but ties it to specific orders and deliveries. "The good thing about an overdraft is that it comes with no strings attached," says Ms Hunter. "The new system is making us behave more conservatively and spend less than we could have done on areas such as product development and new investment." In the 12 months to next April, PSI expects pre-tax profits of about £360,000 on sales of £4.5m. But in spite of indications of a return to health, Ms Hunter says Barclays is yet to indicate it will give her company a new overdraft.

Another major consideration for the borrower in deciding to lend is the issue of security. Banks usually take a fixed charge (on a specific asset) or a floating charge (over the general assets of the firm) as collateral. Alternatively, or in addition, the bank may require a personal guarantee from the directors or owners of the business placing their private property at risk in the event of a default.

Conditions of lending

A bank will generally examine the following factors before lending to a firm:

1 *Cash flow projections* A healthy set of projected cash flows will be required showing sufficient profitability and liquidity to pay the interest and to pay off the overdraft at the end of the agreed period.

2 *Creditworthiness* This goes beyond examining projected future cash flows and asset backing and considers important factors such as character and talents of the individuals leading the organisation.

3 *The amount that the borrower is prepared to put into the project or activity*, relative to that asked from the bank. If the borrower does not show commitment by putting their own money into a scheme, banks can be reluctant to lend.

4 *Security* The provision of a fixed or floating charge over assets will reassure a lender that it will recover its funds. Bankers look at a firm or a project on two levels. First, they assume that the company is a 'going concern', where cash flows, rather than assets, are more important. Secondly, they might consider a 'liquidation analysis' in which they consider a scenario of business failure when the value of assets available as collateral will be important.

Overdrafts increase and reduce with each cash flow and interest is only charged on the overdrawn amount; therefore overdrafts are particularly useful for seasonal businesses because the daily debit-balance interest charge and the absence of a penalty for early repayment mean that this form of finance can be cheaper than a loan. Take the case of Fruit Growers plc (see Worked example 12.1).

Worked example 12.1   Fruit Growers plc

The management of Fruit Growers plc is trying to decide whether to obtain financing from an overdraft or a loan. The interest on both would be 10% per year or 2.5% per quarter. The cash position for the forthcoming year is represented in **Exhibit 12.2**.

Exhibit 12.2   Monthly cash flow balance for Fruit Growers plc

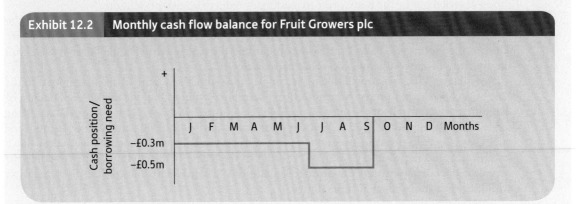

Option 1 A loan for the whole year

A loan for the whole year has the advantage of certainty that the lending facility will be in place throughout the year. A total loan of £500,000 will be needed, and this will be repaid at the end of the year with interest. At the beginning of the year Fruit Growers' account is credited with the full £500,000. For the months when the business does not need the £500,000 the surplus can be invested to receive a return of 2% per quarter.

Interest charged 500,000 × 10%	=	£50,000
Less interest receivable when surplus funds earn 2% per quarter		
January–June 200,000 × 4%	=	£8,000
October–December 500,000 × 2%	=	£10,000
Total cost of borrowing	=	£32,000

Option 2 An overdraft facility for £500,000

An overdraft facility for £500,000 has the drawback that the facility might be withdrawn at any time during the year. However, it is cheaper.

1st quarter (J, F & M) 300,000 × 2.5%		=	£7,500
2nd quarter (A, M & J) 300,000 × 2.5%		=	£7,500
3rd quarter (J, A & S) 500,000 × 2.5%		=	£12,500
4th quarter (O, N & D)		=	£0
Total cost of borrowing		=	£27,500

Note: We will ignore the complications of compounding intra-year interest.

Term loans

A term loan is a loan of a fixed amount for an agreed time which has a specified repayment schedule for principal and interest payments. These loans are normally for a period of between three and seven years, but the period can range from one to 25 years. The interest charged on term loans can be at either fixed or floating rates. A term loan normally requires a rigorous authorisation process carried out by the bank prior to lending to reduce the risk of default.

It may or may not be secured with collateral and has the advantage over the overdraft of not being repayable on demand (provided the borrower complies with the terms of the agreement). The specified terms will include provisions regarding the repayment schedule but may also limit the activities of the company via covenants (see below).

Not all term loans are drawn down in a single lump sum at the time of the agreement. In the case of a construction project which needs to keep borrowing to pay for the different stages of development, an instalment arrangement might be required with, say, 25% of the money being made available immediately, 25% at foundation stage and so on. The lender is not committing large sums secured against an asset not yet created. From the borrower's point of view a drawdown arrangement has the advantage over an overdraft of the lender being committed to providing the finance if the borrower meets pre-arranged conditions, whereas with an overdraft the lender can withdraw the arrangement at short notice.

If the borrower is to apply the funds to a project which will not generate income for a few years it may be possible to arrange a grace period during which only the interest is paid, with the capital being paid off once the project has a sufficiently positive cash flow.

A term loan often has more accompanying documentation than an overdraft because of the lengthy bank commitment. Obligations imposed on the borrowing firm include the requirement to provide regular information to the bank as well as covenants such as specified financial gearing (debt to equity ratio) and liquidity ratio (availability of funds to meet claims) limits. If these financial constraints are breached or interest on capital is not paid on the due dates the company will have breached the terms of the loan and the bank has a right of termination. The bank could decide not to make any more funds available, or, in extreme cases, insist on the repayment of funds already lent. Banks are unlikely to rush into declaring default, seizing assets and liquidating a firm because, even if they take such draconian action, they may not get all of their funds back, and the adverse publicity is a disincentive. Instead they will often try to reschedule or restructure the finance of the business (e.g. grant a longer period to pay). In addition to either a fixed or floating charge over the small firm's assets, banks can insist on guarantees from directors or other third parties.

Revolving credit facility

A revolving credit facility (RCF) provides the borrower with some of the benefits of an overdraft and some of the benefits of a term loan. The RCF is set up by a bank for a fixed period, say five years, during which time the borrower may borrow up to a fixed amount. If the borrower draws the maximum permitted under the agreement for a one-year period, and then repays part of it, the borrower can borrow again up to the maximum at any point before expiry of the agreement without the need to renegotiate with the bank. Interest is only payable on the amount actually drawn. The advantages it has over the term loan are that repayments of principal do not incur a 'break fee' for repaying early, and any monies repaid will be available to be used again (within the period of the facility). Thus, the borrower has a flexible loan, with the lender committed to satisfying the short-term funding needs of the firm. This flexibility does not come for free – the borrower will pay a front end or facility fee for setting up the RCF and a commitment fee (say, 0.5%) to the bank for allowing access to the funds, even if no funds are actually drawn.

Trade credit

Perhaps the simplest and the most important source of short-term finance for many firms is trade credit. Goods or services are delivered to a firm for use in its production but are not paid for immediately, providing a period of credit. These goods and services can then be used to produce income before the supplier invoice has to be paid.

The writer has been involved with a number of small business enterprises, one of which was a small retail business engaged in the selling of crockery and glassware – Crocks. Reproduced as **Exhibit 12.3** is an example of a real invoice (with a few modifications to hide the identity of the supplier). When we first started buying from this supplier we, as a matter of course, applied for

---

Exhibit 12.3   A typical invoice

Supplier XYZ plc
54 West Street, Sussex

Invoice number 501360
Date 29/02/16

Invoice address
Crocks
Melton Mowbray
Leicestershire
LE13 1XH

Branch address
Crocks
Grantham
Lincolnshire

INVOICE

Account	Customer order No.	Sales order	Carrier	AEP	Despatch No.	Due date	Page
TO2251	81535	TO1537		090	000067981	28/03/98	1

Item	Part code	Description	Unit of sale	Quantity despatched	Unit price	%	Amount	VAT code
1	1398973	Long glass	each	12	0.84	0.00	10.08	0
2	12810357	Tumbler	each	12	0.84	0.00	10.08	0
3	1395731	Plate	each	60	1.10	0.00	66.00	0
4	1258732	Bowls	each	30	4.23	0.00	126.90	0
5	1310102	Cup	each	1	4.24	0.00	4.24	0
		VAT 0: 217.30 @ 17.5%						

Note our settlement terms:

$2\frac{1}{2}$% discount may be deducted for payment within 14 days of invoice date; otherwise due 30 days strictly nett.

Nett goods	217.30
Charges	0.00
VAT	38.03
	255.33

trade credit. We received the usual response, that the supplier requires two references vouching for our trustworthiness from other suppliers that have granted us trade credit in the past, plus a reference from our bankers. Once the supplier accepted these confidential references they granted us normal credit terms for retailers of our type of product, that is, 30 days to pay from the date of delivery. One of the things you learn in business is that agreements of this kind are subject to some flexibility. We found that this supplier does not get too upset if you go over the 30 days and pay around day 60: the supplier will still supply to the business on normal credit terms even if you do this on a regular basis.

Each time supplies were delivered by this firm we had to make a decision about when to pay. Option 1 was to pay on the 14th day to receive 2.5% discount (see note at the bottom of the invoice). Option 2 was to take 60 days to pay. (Note: with Option 1 the 2.5% deduction is on the 'nett goods' amount, which is the value of the invoice before value added tax (VAT) is added, that is £217.30.)

Option 1

$$217.30 \times 0.025 = £5.43$$

We could reduce the bill by £5.43 if we paid it within 14 days. This looks good but we need to compare this to the second option.

Option 2

This business had an overdraft, so taking money from the bank account later meant the interest charge would be lower. How much interest could be saved by taking an additional 46 days $(60 - 14)$ to pay this invoice? Assuming the annual percentage rate (APR) charged on the overdraft is 10% the daily interest charge is:

$$(1 + d)^{365} = 1 + i$$

$$d = \sqrt[365]{(1 + i)} - 1$$

$$d = \sqrt[365]{(1 + 0.1)} - 1 = 0.00026116 = 0.026\%$$

Where d = daily interest and i = annual interest interest

Interest charge for 46 days:

$$(1 + 0.00026116)^{46} - 1 = 0.01208 \text{ or } 1.208\%$$

If we go for the early settlement discount and pay on day 14 we would have to pay £255.33 minus the discount of £5.43. As we have an overdraft, over a 46-day period at 10% per annum interest this payment would cost:

$$(255.33 - 5.43) \times 0.01208 = £3.02$$

Thus £3.02 interest is saved by delaying payment to the sixtieth day, compared with a saving of £5.43 on the option of paying early.[3] In this case, taking extended trade credit is not the cheapest source of finance; it is cheaper to pay earlier using the overdraft facility.

This gives the impression that trade credit finance is a free source of funds and therefore the logical course of action is to get as much trade credit as possible. However, a supplier will become tired of dealing with a persistent late payer and may refuse to supply, or will only supply on a basis of cash with order. Another point to be borne in mind is that gaining a bad reputation in the business community may affect relationships with other suppliers. Suppliers, before they

---

3 An alternative approach that is generally sufficiently accurate is:

$$\text{Interest rate for } n \text{ days} = \frac{i}{365} \times (n)$$

give you credit, will normally require two or three trade references from your current suppliers. If they report late payment, you are unlikely to get credit from the new supplier.

Advantages of trade credit

Trade credit has the following advantages.

1 *Convenient/informal/cheap* Trade credit has become a normal part of business in most markets.

2 *Available to companies of any size* Small companies, especially fast-growing ones, often have a very limited range of sources of finance to turn to. Banks frequently restrict overdrafts and loans, so trade credit is important to small companies as a source of funding. However, trade credit is a vital source of finance for the largest companies as well. Tesco reported trade payables of over £9bn at 24 February 2018 and Walmart had $46bn accounts payable at 31 January 2018 (it had only $44bn of inventory). Thus suppliers do not just provide goods and services; they supply much of the money needed for the rest of their customers' operations.

Provision of credit to customers puts small firms under pressure and 'late payment' can cause problems as discussed in **Exhibits 12.4** and **12.5**.

Factors determining the terms of trade credit

Tradition within the industry

Customs have been established in many industries concerning the granting of trade credit. Individual suppliers stepping outside these traditions may lose sales.

Bargaining strength of the two parties

If the supplier has numerous customers wanting to purchase the product, then it may decide not to supply to those firms which demand extended trade credit. On the other hand, if the supplier is selling into a highly competitive market where the buyer has many alternative sources of supply, credit might be used to give a competitive edge.

Exhibit 12.4

Suppliers lend £327bn to businesses in form of late payments

By Norma Cohen

The sums lent to UK businesses by suppliers in the form of late payments are the biggest source of credit in the economy, a study shows. At about £327bn, trade credit between non-financial companies is 20 per cent bigger than outstanding bank credit, according to Charting the Trade Credit Gap, a report by Professor Nick Wilson of the Credit Management Research Centre at Leeds University and Taulia, the credit research group. "We believe this is a serious threat to the UK economy," said Jon Keating, European managing director at Taulia. "Trade credit is being used as a blunt instrument by many companies, with outdated practices poorly adapted to today's new economic environment."

Prof Wilson said although companies often provide goods and services to each other, allowing for a lag between delivery and payment, there are few tools available, particularly to small businesses, when counterparties fail to live up to terms. His study found that the delays between delivery of goods and receipt of payments were widening, despite the economic recovery.

Exhibit 12.5

Mediation and technology focus on scourge of late payments

By Andrew Bounds

The UK government has become the latest to address a bane of many small businesses: late payment. The average small and medium-sized enterprise (SME) in the UK is owed more than £30,000 with some £32bn outstanding in total. "It's enough to force a company into insolvency," Sajid Javid said in his first speech as business minister in May. In 2008, 4,000 UK businesses became insolvent as a direct consequence of late payment, according to the government.

So it is introducing a Small Business Conciliation Service to mediate between creditors and debtors. It is modelled on an Australian system. While SMEs can charge penalties and interest for late payment, they fear losing business from big customers in retaliation. Just 10 per of businesses have considered using late payment legislation: 22 per cent have ended a business relationship with a customer because of continued late payment. While the average declared payment time in the UK is 25 days, in practice it is 44 days, the government says. Some

EU countries are even worse. Spain averages 97 days. Finland is the quickest, with a 27 day turnround.

"The conciliation service will be busy," says Prof Nick Wilson of Leeds University Business School. He is an expert on credit management and says too many British businesses simply survive from month to month. "They have insufficient capital to cope with bad debts and late payment. We need greater bank lending and equity investment."

'John Allan, chairman of the Federation of Small Businesses lobby group, says: "Small businesses often have the law on their side, but find that accessing the legal system is complex, time consuming and expensive. A properly constituted conciliation service should help with this and go some way to addressing the UK's poor payment culture." A third of companies report that they have sought external finance to cover gaps in cash flow caused by late payment. The FSB says that this has led to £180m in debt interest charges.

Product type

Products with a high level of turnover relative to inventory, for example food, are generally sold on short credit terms (say, 10 days rather than 40 days). These products usually sell on a low profit margin and the delay in payment can cause the amount tied up in trade credit to grow to large sums very quickly, having a large impact on the profit margin of the supplier.

Credit standing of individual customers

A less risky customer may be granted long periods to pay. A firm has to consider the trade-off when judging whether to accept trade credit. This is shown in **Exhibit 12.6.**

Factoring

Factoring (or 'invoice finance') companies are financial intermediaries who purchase trade receivables from companies. They provide three services to firms with outstanding debtors (trade receivables), the most important of which, in the context of this chapter, is the immediate transfer of cash from the factor to the company. Cash is provided upfront by the factor on the understanding that when cash is received from customers the proceeds will go to the factor. Factoring is used by companies of all sizes as a way of bringing cash in more quickly to meet cash flow needs. UK Finance which represents about 300 asset based lending and

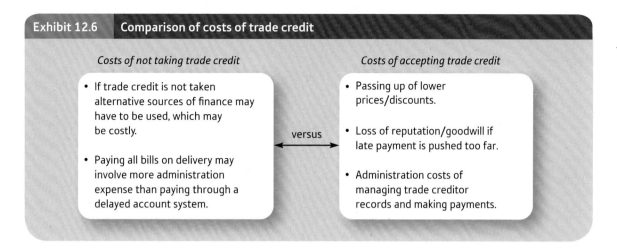

Exhibit 12.6   Comparison of costs of trade credit

Costs of not taking trade credit

- If trade credit is not taken alternative sources of finance may have to be used, which may be costly.

- Paying all bills on delivery may involve more administration expense than paying through a delayed account system.

versus

Costs of accepting trade credit

- Passing up of lower prices/discounts.

- Loss of reputation/goodwill if late payment is pushed too far.

- Administration costs of managing trade creditor records and making payments.

factoring business in the UK and Ireland lists 34 factoring companies of which 11, primarily subsidiaries of the major banks, will lend over £10m (www.uk finance.org.uk).

Three closely related services are offered by factors.

1 The provision of finance

At any time a typical business can have 20% or more of its annual turnover outstanding in trade debts: a firm with an annual turnover of £5m may have a debtor balance of £1m. These large outstanding sums create cash flow difficulties which can put financial pressure on an otherwise healthy business. Factors provide the cash needed to support working capital (buy stock, pay suppliers) and generally aid more profitable trading and growth. The factor provides cash immediately to the company, using the outstanding trade receivables as security. Normally about 80% of the invoice value can be made available to a firm immediately (with some factors this can be as much as 90%). The remaining 20%, less an appropriate % fee, is transferred from the factor when the customer finally pays up. The factor charges a % fee and interest on the money advanced. The cost will vary between clients depending on sales volume, the type of industry, the average value of the invoices and the ease with which the factor considers it can collect. The charge for finance is said by the factoring companies to be comparable with overdraft rates (1.5–3% over base rate). As on an overdraft, the interest is calculated on the daily outstanding balance of the funds that the borrowing firm has received. However, added to this is a service charge that varies between 0.2% and 3% of invoiced sales. The greater the cost of collection and the risk of default, the higher the fees will be.

Exhibit 12.7 shows the stages in a typical factoring transaction. First, goods are delivered to the customer and an invoice is sent. Second, the supplier sells the right to receive the invoice amount to a factor in return for, say, 80% of the face value now. Third, some weeks later the customer pays the sum owing, which goes to the factor and finally, the factor releases the remaining 20% to the supplier less interest and fees.

This form of finance has some advantages over bank borrowing. Factoring can be organised speedily without the long authorisation process required for a loan. The factor does not impose financial ratio covenants or require fixed asset backing. Also the fear of instant withdrawal of a facility (as with an overdraft) is absent as there is usually a notice period. The disadvantages are the raised cost (many potential clients think it is more expensive than an overdraft) and the unavailability of factoring to companies with many small-value transactions. Also, some managers say it removes a safety margin. Instead of spending frugally while waiting for customers to pay, they may be tempted to splurge the advance.

Factors frequently reject clients as unsuitable for their services. The factor looks for 'clean and unencumbered debts' so that it can be reasonably certain of receiving invoice payments. It will also want to understand the company's business and to be satisfied with the competence of its management. **Exhibit 12.8** shows how a factor might calculate the amount to be advanced.

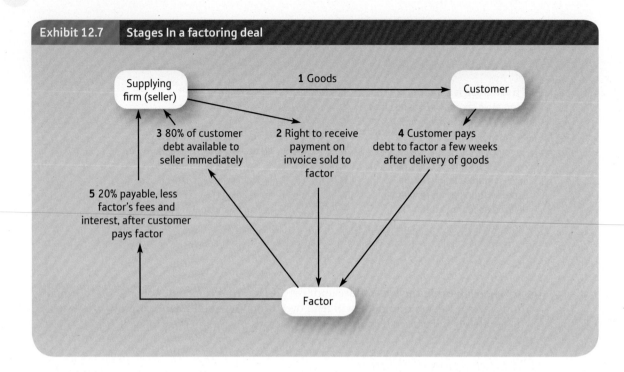

Exhibit 12.7   Stages In a factoring deal

Supplying firm (seller) → **1 Goods** → Customer

3 80% of customer debt available to seller immediately

2 Right to receive payment on invoice sold to factor

4 Customer pays debt to factor a few weeks after delivery of goods

5 20% payable, less factor's fees and interest, after customer pays factor

Factor

Case study 12.1   LG Steelworks

Factoring has been both a blessing and a curse for Lee Gibson's metal fabrication business, LG Steelworks. He signed up to use it as a condition of the recovery of his business, which was put into administration at the end of 2011 after a number of his clients in the construction industry went under themselves. However, he quickly found that he was paying double what he expected to pay because of what he claims were unexpected charges being levied by his provider Bibby Financial Services. "We never knew where we were financially," Mr Gibson said, adding that the charges were double those he was originally led to believe he would be making.

Mr Gibson claims he was lucky because he was able to switch his factoring service to a new provider, without incurring any penalty fees for getting out of his contract with Bibby early. Mr Gibson stresses that the service he now has from his new provider, Partnership Finance, is the opposite of his experience with Bibby. If he had not been able to switch, however, Mr Gibson believes his business could have been back in administration despite having a full order book and a turnover of £600,000. "Factoring is not the problem," he said. "It is the people providing the financing."

A spokesman for Bibby said Mr Gibson was briefed about all the charges associated with its service verbally and in writing in both his agreement and the pack he received when he took on the service. "Some of the charges he disputes related to his decision on numerous occasions to receive overpayments," the spokesman said. "Mr Gibson would have been aware of these charges since he would have had to make a decision to take an overpayment which is greater than the normal amount agreed," the spokesman said.

FT *Financial Times*, 'Alternative funding grows as UK companies struggle for finance' by Jonathan Moules, 19 May 2013.

2 Sales ledger administration

Companies, particularly young and fast-growing ones, often do not want the trouble and expense of setting up a sophisticated system for dealing with the collection of outstanding debts. For a fee (0.75–2.5% of turnover) factors will take over the functions of recording credit sales, checking customers' creditworthiness, sending invoices, chasing late payers and ensuring that debts are paid. The fees might seem high, say £100,000 for a firm with a turnover of £5m, but the company avoids

Exhibit 12.8	Amount available from a factor

A supplying firm has £1,000,000 of outstanding invoices, £40,000 are so old that the factor will not consider them, £60,000 are rejected as poor quality or are export sales and £30,000 are subject to a dispute between the supplier and the customer. The factor is prepared to advance 80% of suitable invoices:

Total invoices		£1,000,000
Less:		
Debts excessively old	£40,000	
Non-approved	£60,000	
In dispute	£30,000	
		(130,000)
		£870,000

The amount the factor is willing to provide to the supplier immediately is 80% of £870,000, or £696,000 (69.6% of total invoices).

the in-house costs of an administrative team and can concentrate attention on the core business. Moreover, factors are experienced professional payment chasers who know all the tricks of the trade (such as 'the cheque is in the post' excuse) and so can obtain payment earlier. With factoring, sales ledger administration and debt collection generally come as part of the package offered by the finance house, unlike with invoice discounting (see below).

3 Credit insurance

The third service available from a factor is the provision of insurance against the possibility that a customer does not pay the amount owed. The charge for this service is generally between 0.3% and 0.5% of the value of the invoices. While not necessary to trade, the availability of trade credit insurance allows suppliers to trade with more confidence. Sometimes suppliers are unwilling to send their goods without insurance that they would get paid. Many companies keep trade credit insurers informed about their financial position and trading strategy, so that they can gain their support. **Exhibit 12.9** indicates the difficulties that can ensue if trade credit insurance is lost.

Exhibit 12.9

Tata's UK steel plants face new threat

By Andrew Bounds and Michael Pooler

Tata's UK steel plants face a new threat after insurance was cancelled, leaving suppliers reluctant to deliver raw materials. The lossmaking business is up for sale but parts of its operations could shut down beforehand because credit insurance that covers suppliers against non-payment has been withdrawn by one big insurer.

One supplier said it could make its final delivery of metals for steelmaking to the Port Talbot plant on Monday. "It is high risk for us to deliver. Even if they paid cash it would go against the debts already accrued, so we would not get paid for that delivery," said a representative of the company, who did not wish to be named.

The person said that Euler Hermes, a subsidiary of German insurer Allianz, had written to clients last week to tell them it was ending cover to all Tata Steel businesses in Europe, including its Dutch plant, on April 25. Credit insurance policies guarantee that clients receive money owed for goods and services supplied.

▶

Exhibit 12.09 *(continued)*

The Association of British Insurers reported in November that its members insured £4.5bn of debts in the steel industry. Steelmakers typically have at least one month's supply of iron ore and coking coal on-site, according to industry figures.

Tata Steel UK had short-term debt — payable within 12 months — of £2.7bn as at March 31 2015, the last available accounts show. Of that, £552m was owed to trade creditors, with the majority to its parent and other group companies.

Insurers say they monitor risks and could restore cover if circumstances change.

Recourse and non-recourse

Most factoring arrangements are made on a non-recourse basis, which means that the factor accepts the risk of non-payment by the customer firm. For accepting this risk, the factor will not only require a higher return but also want control over credit assessment, credit approval and other aspects of managing the sales ledger to ensure payment. Some firms prefer recourse factoring in which they retain the risk of customer default but also continue to maintain the relationship with their customers through the debt collection function without the, sometimes overbearing, intervention of the factor. With confidential factoring the customer is usually unaware that a factor is the ultimate recipient of the money paid over, as the supplier continues to collect debts, acting as an agent for the factor.

Invoice discounting

Firms with an annual turnover under £10m typically use factoring (with sales ledger administration), whereas larger firms tend to use invoice discounting. Here specific invoices are pledged to the finance house in return for an immediate payment of up to 90–95% of the face value. The supplying company guarantees to pay the amount represented on the invoices (recourse) and is responsible for collecting the debt. The customers are generally totally unaware that the invoices have been discounted. When the due date is reached it is to be hoped that the customer has paid in full. Regardless of whether the customer has paid, the supplying firm is committed to handing over the total invoice amount to the finance house and in return receives the remaining 10% less service fees and interest. Note that even invoice discounting is subject to the specific circumstances of the client agreement and is sometimes made on a non-recourse basis.

The finance provider usually only advances money under invoice discounting if the supplier's business is well established and profitable. There must be an effective and professional credit control and sales ledger administration system. Charges are usually lower than for factoring because the sales ledger administration is the responsibility of the supplying company. Fees are 0.2% to 0.8% of company sales plus interest comparable with business overdraft rates. Invoice discounting has the advantage over factoring of maintaining the relationship between customer and supplier without the intervention of a finance house. Thus customer records are kept confidential, the customer does not get nervous about its supplier using a factor – often seen (usually wrongly) as a desperate act, indicating financial troubles – and is not excessively pressurised by a forceful debt collector.

While many companies have been helped by invoice finance, others regard it as relatively expensive, given their financial position – *see* **Exhibit 12.10**.

Hire purchase

With hire purchase (HP) the finance company buys the equipment that the borrowing firm needs. The equipment (plant, machinery, vehicles, medical equipment etc.) belongs to the HP company. However, the finance house allows the 'hirer' to use the equipment in return for a series of

Exhibit 12.10

Alternative funding grows as UK companies struggle for finance

By Jonathan Moules, Enterprise Correspondent

The extreme difficulty some company owners have faced obtaining conventional bank borrowing has proved the making of an alternative funding mechanism in which money is provided in lieu of unpaid invoices. Invoice discounting, as this kind of funding is known, was up 16 per cent year on year at £62.5bn during the final quarter of last year, according to the latest figures from the Asset-Based Finance Association (Abfa), the industry's trade association. This compared with a £2.4bn contraction in net lending recorded by the Bank of England during the same period.

Invoice discounting, while it is increasingly being seen as a cheaper and more accessible option than bank loans, is not for everyone, however. "By the nature of the beast it tends to work for companies that are a bit slicker," says Henry Edjelbaum, managing director of ASC Finance for Business, a broker for commercial loans. "Companies that sell to consumers don't tend to qualify because their customers have more rights to return items and demand repayment." Recruitment firms and haulage companies have traditionally been heavy users of invoice discounting and the similar asset-based funding process of factoring.

Providers usually require borrowers to have quite sophisticated financial management systems to handle payments, Mr Edjelbaum says. "It would not be suitable for a small family business like a guest house. They wouldn't have the systems to deal with it."

The rise of invoice discounting and factoring has been driven in large part by the more lenient regulatory market for these products compared with overdrafts and conventional term loans, say providers. Capital requirements for those providing invoice discounting are much lower and contracts are more lightly regulated because lending against invoices is regarded as short-term, not long-term, funding.

As demand for this kind of funding has grown, so has the number of complaints about the practices of some providers, criticised for excessive charges and in some cases pushing companies that have struggled to settle bills into administration. Brian Moore is running a campaign for regulation of asset-based finance, claiming that a potentially valuable form of funding is being undermined by lenders that impose hidden charges and in extreme cases have put companies into insolvency against their will. "Charges been applied daily simply to wring every penny out of their client for pure profit," Mr Moore says, adding that only regulation of the sector will bring about change.

Abfa is in the process of getting its 30 members, which together provide 95 per cent of all asset-based lending, to sign up to a system of self-regulation, following a code of conduct that was published in February. Kate Sharp, Abfa's chief executive, claims that Mr Moore's campaign is exaggerating the extent of any problems with lenders' practices. "We are talking about probably 100,000 businesses that have used these products over the past three years, of which we have 100 that are complaining," she says.

Ms Sharp has put these points in a written response to Mr Moore's allegations. "I have never said, and could not ever say, that all invoice financiers have always acted perfectly, but the industry I know is full of people seeking to support businesses and do the right thing by their clients, a vast majority of whom are satisfied with their services," she wrote. What is clear is that the demand for asset-based finance is unlikely to subside any time soon.

Last month it received a boost from the BoE, which added factoring corporations to the list of organisations able to tap the Funding for Lending Scheme. This aims to increase the amount of borrowing offered to businesses. Abfa estimates that as many as 250,000 small businesses in the UK operate in markets ideally suited to invoice discounting and factoring. "This is not a fully mature market," Ms Sharp says. "We believe that there is a fairly large, untapped source of funding need out there."

regular payments. These payments are sufficient to cover interest and contribute to paying off the principal. While the monthly instalments are still being made, the HP company has the satisfaction and security of being the legal owner and so can take repossession if the hirer defaults on the payments. After all payments have been made the hirer becomes the owner, either automatically or on payment of an option-to-purchase fee. Nowadays, consumers buying electrical goods or vehicles have become familiar with the attempts of sales assistants to sell an HP agreement also so that the customer pays over an extended period. Sometimes the finance is provided by the same organisation, but more often by a separate finance house. The stages in an HP agreement are as in **Exhibit 12.11**.

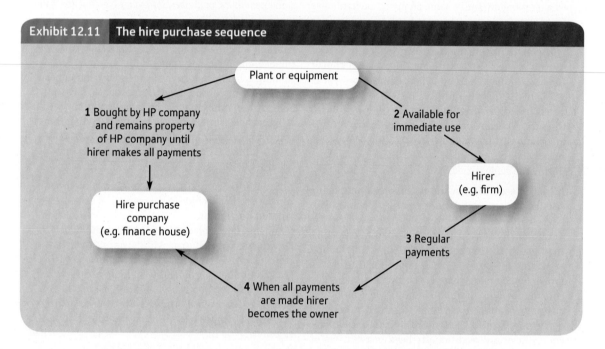

| Exhibit 12.11 | The hire purchase sequence |

The main advantages of this form of finance are as follows:

- *Small initial outlay* The firm does not have to find the full purchase price at the outset. A deposit followed by a series of instalments can be less of a cash flow strain. The funds that the company retains can be used elsewhere in the business for productive investment. Set against this are the relatively high interest charges (high relative to the rates a large firm can borrow at but can be relatively low for a small firm) and the additional costs of maintenance and insurance.

- *Easy and quick to arrange* Usually at point of sale allowing immediate use of the asset.

- *Certainty* This is a medium-term source of finance which cannot be withdrawn provided contractual payments are made, unlike an overdraft. On the other hand the commitment is made for a number of years and it could be costly to terminate the agreement. There are also budgeting advantages to the certainty of a regular cash outflow.

- *HP is often available when other sources of finance are not* For some firms the equity markets are unavailable and banks will no longer lend to them, but HP companies will still provide funds as they have the security of the asset to reassure them.

- *Fixed-rate finance* In most cases the payments are fixed throughout the HP period. While the interest charged is fixed for the duration of the agreement the hirer has to be aware that the HP company will quote an interest rate which is different from the annual percentage rate. The HP company tends to quote the flat rate. On a £9,000 loan repayable in equal instalments of £401.85 over 30 months the flat rate is calculated by using the total payments made, the original £9,000 cost and the number of years. The total paid over the period is £401.85 × 30 = £12,055.50. The flat interest is:

$$\sqrt[2.5]{\left(\frac{12055.50}{9,000}\right)} - 1 = 0.1240 = 12.4\%$$

This would be the annual rate if the entire interest and capital were repaid at the end of the thirtieth month. However, a portion of the capital and interest is repaid each month and therefore the annual percentage rate (APR) is much higher than the flat rate. As a rough rule of thumb the APR is about double the flat rate. To calculate the APR more accurately annuity tables can be used. The present value (PV) is given as £9,000, the regular payments are £401.85 and we need to find the (monthly) interest rate which makes these 30 future inflows, when discounted, the same as the initial outflow.

$$\text{Present value} = \text{annuity} \times \text{annuity factor}$$

$$9,000 = 401.85 \times \text{annuity factor (af)}$$

$$\text{af} = \frac{9,000}{401.85} = 22.3964$$

Using the annuity table (*see* Appendix III) and 30 payment periods, you find the interest rate which corresponds with an annuity factor of 22.3964 − 2% per month.

$$(1 + m)^{12} = 1 - i$$
$$i = (1 + m)^{12} - 1$$
$$i = (1 + 0.02)^{12} - 1$$
$$i = 0.268 \text{ or } 26.8\%$$

An interest rate of 2% per month is equivalent to an annual percentage rate (APR) of 26.8%, over twice the flat rate calculated above. Obtaining the APR from the HP company may not be easy – they tend to talk about the flat rate but the borrower needs to know the APR in order to compare alternative sources of finance.

- *Tax relief* The hirer qualifies for tax relief in two ways:
  - The asset can be subject to a writing-down allowance (WDA) on the capital expenditure. For example, if the type of asset is eligible for a 25% WDA and originally cost £10,000 the using firm can reduce its taxable profits by £2,500 in the year of purchase; in the second year taxable profits will be lowered by £7,500 × 0.25 = £1,875. If tax is levied at 30% on taxable profit the tax bill is reduced by £2,500 × 0.30 = £750 in the first year, and £1,875 × 0.3 = £562.50 in the second year. Note that this relief is available despite the hirer company not being the legal owner of the asset.
  - Interest payments (an element of the monthly instalment) are deductible when calculating taxable profits.

Tax reliefs are valuable only to profitable companies. If the company does not make sufficient profit, then it cannot deduct the tax relief; the WDA has no value for the company. This can make HP an expensive form of finance. An alternative form of finance which circumvents this problem (as well as having other advantages) is leasing.

Leasing

Leasing is similar to HP in that an equipment owner (the lessor) conveys the right to use the equipment in return for regular rental payments by the equipment user (the lessee) over an agreed period of time. The essential difference is that the lessee does not become the owner – the leasing company retains legal title.[4] Subsidiaries of clearing banks dominate the UK leasing market, but many of the world's biggest leasing companies are owned by industrial corporations such as vehicle manufacturers. **Exhibit 12.12** shows that a typical lease transaction involves a firm wanting to make use of an asset approaching a finance house which purchases the asset and rents it to the lessee.

It is important to distinguish between operating leases and finance leases.

---

4 However, with many finance leases, after the asset has been leased for the great majority of its useful life (value), the lessee may have the option to purchase it.

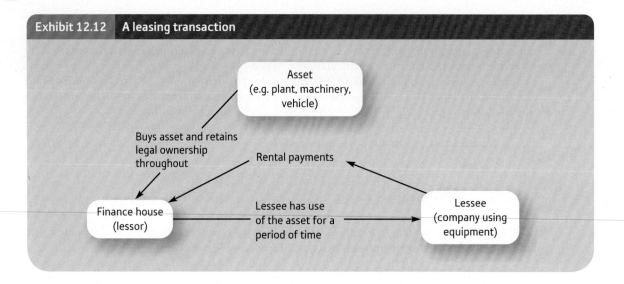

Exhibit 12.12   A leasing transaction

Operating lease

Operating leases commit the lessee to only a short-term contract or one that can be terminated at short notice. These are not expected to last for the entire useful life of the asset and so the finance house has the responsibility of finding an alternative use for the asset when the lessee no longer requires it. Perhaps the asset will be sold in the second-hand market, or it might be leased to another client. Either way the finance house bears the risk of ownership. If the equipment turns out to have become obsolete more quickly than was originally anticipated it is the lessor that loses out. If the equipment is less reliable than expected the owner (the finance house) will have to pay for repairs. Usually, with an operating lease, the lessor retains the obligation for repairs, maintenance and insurance. It is clear why equipment which is subject to rapid obsolescence and frequent breakdown is often leased out on an operating lease. Photocopiers, for example, used by a university department are far better leased so that if they break down the university staff do not have to deal with the problem. In addition the latest model can be quickly installed in the place of an outdated one. The most common form of operating lease is contract hire. These leases are often used for a fleet of vehicles. The leasing company takes some responsibility for the management and maintenance of the vehicles and for disposal of the vehicles at the end of the contract hire period (after 12 to 48 months).

Operating leases are also useful if the business involves a short-term project requiring the use of an asset for a limited period. For example, building firms often use equipment supplied under an operating lease (sometimes called plant hire). Operating leases are not confined to small items of equipment. There is a growing market in leasing aircraft and ships for periods less than the economic life of the asset, thus making these deals operating leases. Many of Boeing's and Airbus's aircraft go to leasing firms – over 6,000 are leased, about one-third of the fleet of commercial aircraft in service. As a result the largest lessors are GE Capital Aviation and International Lease Corporation, rather than the major banks.

Finance lease

Under a finance lease (also called a capital lease or a full payout lease) the finance provider expects to recover the full cost (or almost the full cost) of the equipment, plus interest, over the period of the lease. With this type of lease the lessee usually has no right of cancellation or termination. Despite not legally owning the asset the lessee will have to bear the risks and rewards that normally go with ownership: the lessee will usually be responsible for maintenance, insurance and repairs and suffer the frustrations of demand being below expectations or the equipment becoming obsolete more rapidly than anticipated. Most finance leases contain a primary and a secondary period. It is during the primary period that the lessor receives the capital sum plus interest. In the secondary period the lessee pays a very small 'nominal', rental payment. If the company does not want to continue using the equipment in the secondary period it may be sold second-hand to an unrelated company.

Advantages of leasing

The advantages listed for hire purchase also apply to leasing: small initial outlay, easy to arrange, certainty, available when other finance sources are not, fixed-rate finance and tax relief. There is an additional advantage of operating leases and that is the transfer of obsolescence risk to the finance provider.

The advantage of this being a source of finance when banks are reluctant to lend via conventional loans was brought home to businesses in the aftermath of the financial crisis – *see* **Exhibit 12.13**.

Exhibit 12.13

Expansion in leasing deals

By Jonathan Moules

Use of leasing and hire purchase arrangements to buy or rent new equipment continues to show healthy growth, according to the latest figures by the Finance & Leasing Association, the sector's trade body. The amount of new asset finance business was £1.9bn in November, 29 per cent higher than a year earlier. This was the third largest monthly increase recorded in 2011. In the first 11 months of the year, new business grew by 3 per cent to £18.7bn, but for deals up to £20m, the increase was 9 per cent over the same period.

The growth of asset finance is in contrast to demand for bank debt among small businesses, which has been declining and is set to fall further according to a Bank of England report earlier this month. Around a thousand new asset finance contracts are being signed every day, according to the FLA.

FT *Financial Times,* 13 January 2012.
All Rights Reserved.

The tax advantages for leasing are slightly different from those for HP. The rentals paid on an operating lease are a business expense and so are tax deductible. However, for finance leases the tax treatment is linked to the accounting treatment which requires leased assets and the associated debt to be recognised on the balance sheet. This is designed to prevent some creative accounting which used to allow a company to appear to be in a better gearing (debt/equity ratio) position if it leased rather than purchased its equipment as the company did not have to recognise the debt on its balance sheet. The company could thus lower its apparent gearing ratio and therefore improve its chances of obtaining more borrowed funds. Take the two companies X and Y, which have identical balance sheets initially, as shown in **Exhibit 12.14**.

Company X has a debt/equity ratio of 200% whereas Y has obtained the use of the asset 'off-balance sheet' and so has an apparent gearing ratio of only 100%. A superficial analysis of these two firms by, say, a bank lender, may lead to the conclusion that Y is more capable of taking on more debt. In reality Y has a high level of fixed cash outflow commitments stretching over a number of years under the lease and is in effect highly geared. Under these rules Company Y could also show a higher profit to asset ratio despite the fact that the underlying economic position of each firm is almost identical.

Today finance leases have to be 'capitalised' to bring them on to the balance sheet. The asset is recognised in the balance sheet and the obligations under the lease agreement are stated as a liability. Over subsequent years the asset is depreciated and, as the capital repayments are made to the lessor, the liability is reduced. The profit and loss account is also affected: the depreciation and interest are both deducted as expenses.

Exhibit 12.14	Apparently different gearing levels for Companies X and Y

Initial balance sheet for both X and Y

Shareholders' funds (net assets)	£1,000,000
Debt capital	£1,000,000
Total assets	£2,000,000

Now if X borrows a further £1m to buy equipment, while Y leases £1m of equipment the balance sheets appear strikingly different under the old accounting rules.

	Company X	Company Y
Shareholders' funds (net assets)	1,000,000	1,000,000
Debt capital	2,000,000	1,000,000
Total assets	3,000,000	2,000,000

These rules apply only to finance leases and not to operating leases. A finance lease is defined (usually) as one in which the present value of the lease payments is at least 90% of the asset's fair value (usually its cash price). This has led to some bright sparks engineering leasing deals which could be categorised as operating leases and therefore kept off-balance sheets – some are designed so that 89% of the value is paid by the lessee. However, the authorities are fighting back as **Exhibit 12.15** shows. A new accounting standard (IFRS16) has recently been released which, when it becomes effective on 1 January 2019, removes the different accounting treatments for operating and finance leases (unless the lease term is 12 months or less or the underlying asset has a low value).

Exhibit 12.15

Retailers resist lease obligation plans

By Adam Jones

Plans to force companies to be more transparent about leasing obligations have been some of the most contentious put forward in the dash to converge US accounting standards with those followed in Europe and some other countries.

The proposal that more leases should be placed on the balance sheet could cause assets and liabilities to balloon at some businesses, potentially putting companies in breach of loan agreements.

Retailers and airlines have been particularly hostile to accounting for their leased shops and aircraft in this fashion. New Look, a British clothing retailer, says it would 'require further investment to update our covenant models and legal financing documentation in order to maintain financial covenant headroom'.

Marks and Spencer, a UK high street stalwart, denies that leasing arrangements as they stand are a way of hiding liabilities, arguing that it is often impossible to buy the stores it operates. Coach, a US handbag maker, argues that investors already get enough information from current lease disclosures. Iata, which represents the airline industry, dismisses the plans as too complex, costly and impractical.

Standard-setters will not have been surprised by such opposition to their insistence that the system of operating and finance leases – also known as capital leases – should be replaced with just one accounting model. They say operating leases disguise a company's leverage because the underlying obligations drip through the profit and loss account as a series of rental expenses rather than being capitalised in one highly visible lump.

FT *Financial Times* , 24 February 2011, p. 25.
All Rights Reserved.

A very important tax advantage can accrue to some companies through leasing because of the legal position of the asset not belonging to the lessee. Companies that happen to have sufficient profits can buy assets and then reduce their taxable profits by writing off a proportion of the assets' value (say 18% on a reducing balance) against income each year. However, companies with low profits or those which make a loss are unable to exploit these investment allowances fully and the tax benefit can be wasted. But if the equipment is bought by a finance company with plenty of profits, the asset cost can be used to save on the lessor's tax. This benefit can then be passed on to the customer (the lessee) in the form of lower rental charges. This may be particularly useful to start-up companies and it has also proved of great value to low- or no-profit companies.

To buy or to lease?

A comparison of the relative costs of leasing through a finance lease and purchase through a bank loan is in practice a very complicated calculation. It is necessary to allow for the cost of capital and the tax treatment of alternative sources of finance. These, in turn, depend on the precise circumstances of the company at the time. It is further complicated by the timing of the tax payments and reliefs, by who pays for maintenance and the potential for a residual value of the asset at the end of the primary lease period. Added to all of that is the problem that the tax rules change frequently and so a method of calculation applicable at one time is quickly out of date. The point is that a proper comparison requires highly specialised knowledge and so is beyond the scope of this book. However, if a few simplifying assumptions are made the general principles can be conveyed easily. The simplifying assumptions are:

a Taxation does not exist.

b There is no value in the asset at the end of the lease period.

c The cost of capital applicable to the equipment is the same as the term loan interest rate; this is only valid if investors regard the lease and the bank loan as being perfect substitutes for each other with respect to the capital structure (gearing, etc.) and the riskiness of the cash flows.

Armed with these assumptions we can assess whether it is better for the Quissical Games Company to lease or to buy.

Worked example 12.2   **Quissical Games Company**

The Quissical Games Company needs £10m of equipment to increase its production capacity. A leasing company has offered to purchase the equipment and lease it to Quissical for three annual lease payments of £3.8m, with the first payable immediately, the second at the beginning of the second year and the third at the beginning of the third year. The equipment will have a three-year useful life at the end of which it will have a zero scrap value. A bank has offered to lend £10m on a three-year term loan at a rate of interest of 10% p.a. Which form of finance should Quissical accept?

This problem may be analysed on an incremental cash flow basis, that is, focusing on the differences in the cash flows – as shown in **Exhibit 12.16**.

Exhibit 12.16   **Quissical's lease versus buy decision (£m)**

	Points in time (yearly intervals)		
	0	**1**	**2**
Lease rentals	−3.80	−3.80	−3.80
Cash flows associated with buy option	10.00		
Incremental cash flows (lease vs. buy)	+6.20	−3.80	−3.80
Present value of incremental cash flows at 10%	+6.20	−3.4545	−3.1405
Net present value	−0.395		

The cash flows associated with the lease option have a present value which is £395,000 more than £10m when discounted at 10% and therefore the lease is the more expensive method of finance.

Of course, in reality the tax payments are likely to have a significant impact on the relative merits of a bank loan and leasing finance, but this depends on Quissical's tax position, the time delay in paying tax, the current tax rates, the capital allowance permitted and so on.

Bills of exchange

A bill is a document which sets out a commitment to pay a sum of money at a specified point in time. The simplest example is an ordinary bank cheque which has been dated two weeks hence. The government borrows by selling Treasury bills which commit it to paying a fixed sum in, say, three months. Local authorities issue similar debt instruments, as do commercial organisations in the form of commercial bills (discussed in Chapter 11).

Bills of exchange are mainly used in overseas trade. They have a long history in international trade, particularly in the nineteenth and twentieth centuries. The seller of goods to a customer in another country normally grants the customer a number of months in which to pay. The seller will draw up a bill of exchange (called a 'trade acceptance' in international trade), a legal document showing the indebtedness of the customer. The bill of exchange is then forwarded to, and accepted by the customer, which means that the customer signs a promise to pay the stated amount and currency on the due date. The due date is usually 90 days later but 30, 60 or 180 days bills of exchange are not uncommon. The bill is returned to the seller who then has two choices, either to hold it until maturity, or to sell it to a bank or discount house (the bill is discounted). Under the second option the bank will pay a lower amount than the sum to be received in, say, 90 days from the customer. The difference represents the bank's interest.

For example, if a customer has accepted a bill of exchange which commits it to pay £200,000 in 90 days the bill might be sold by the supplier immediately to a discount house or bank for £194,000. After 90 days the bank will realise a profit of £6,000 on a £194,000 asset, an interest rate of 3.09% ((6,000/194,000) × 100) over 90 days. This gives an approximate annual rate of:

$$(1.0309)^4 - 1 = 0.1294 = 12.94\%$$

Through this arrangement the customer has the benefit of the goods on 90 days credit, the supplier has made a sale and immediately receives cash from the discount house amounting to 97% of the total due. The discounter, if it borrows its funds at less than 12.9%, turns in a healthy profit. The sequence of events is shown in **Exhibit 12.17**.

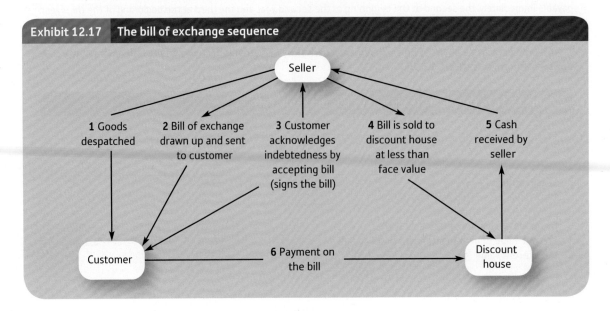

Exhibit 12.17   The bill of exchange sequence

Bills of exchange are normally only used for transactions greater than £75,000. The effective interest rate charged by the discounter is a competitive 1.5% to 4% over interbank lending rates (for example, LIBOR) depending on the creditworthiness of the seller and the customer. The bank that purchased the bill in the discount market has recourse to both of the commercial companies: if the customer does not pay then the seller will be called upon to make good the debt. This overhanging credit risk can sometimes be dealt with by the selling company obtaining credit insurance. Despite the simplification of Exhibit 12.17 many bills of exchange do not remain in the hands of the discounter until maturity but are traded in an active secondary market (the money market). Note also that not all bills of exchange are a form of temporary finance. Some are 'sight drafts', that is, payable on demand without a delay of a few days (as with 'time drafts' or 'term drafts').

Bankers' acceptances (banks bills, acceptance credits)

In the case of bankers' acceptances, the company which is in need of finance requests the drawing up of a document which states that the signatory will pay a sum of money at a set date in the future. This is 'accepted' by a bank rather than by a customer. (Simultaneously the company makes a commitment to pay the accepting bank the relevant sum at the maturity date of the bill.) This bank commitment to pay the holder of the bankers' acceptance can then be sold in the money markets to, say, another bank (a discounter) by the firm to provide for its cash needs. (Alternatively an importing company could give the acceptance credit to its overseas supplier in return for goods – and the supplier can then sell it at a discount if required.) The bankers' acceptance is similar to a bill of exchange between a seller and a buyer, but now the organisation promising to pay is a reputable bank representing a lower credit risk to any subsequent discounter. These instruments therefore normally attract lower discount rates than a trade bill. When the maturity date is reached the company pays the issuing bank the value of the bill, and the bank pays the ultimate holder of the bill its face value.

The company does not have to sell the bankers' acceptance immediately and so can use this instrument to plug finance gaps at opportune times. There are three main costs of bank bill finance.

1   The bank charges acceptance commission for adding its name to the bill.
2   The difference between the discount price and the bankers' acceptance due sum which is the effective interest rate.
3   Dealers take a small cut as they connect firms that want to sell with companies that wish to invest in banker's acceptances.

These costs are relatively low compared with those on overdrafts and there is an ability to plan ahead because of the longer-term commitment of the bank. Bankers 'acceptances are very useful for companies expanding into new markets where their name, and therefore their creditworthiness, is unknown they can take advantage of the superior creditworthiness of the bank issuing the acceptance, which guarantees that payment will be made. Unfortunately this facility is only available in hundreds of thousands of pounds and then only to the most creditworthy of companies. **Exhibit 12.18** summarises the banker's acceptance sequence.

Treasury management

The main areas of treasury and working capital management

Treasurers carry out a wide range of activities, from raising long-term finance to reducing financial risk. **Exhibit 12.19** shows the main issues addressed by treasurers or by line managers dealing with debtors, creditors, inventory and cash resources.

The way in which Treasury is structured and roles assigned to individuals vary tremendously across organisations but the fundamental questions and the need for action remain. These are illustrated in Exhibit 12.19, where the overarching groups of issues to be addressed are shown. The first two, financing and risk management, are usually in the domain of the specialist treasury department, in collaboration with other senior managers, in large multinational firms. The third, working capital and liquidity management, will require some input from the treasury team, especially for the investment of temporary cash, but many of these issues will be examined by line

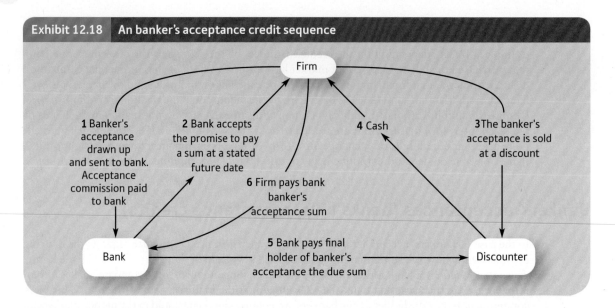

Exhibit 12.18   An banker's acceptance credit sequence

managers with the assistance of the finance and accounting team. The areas of responsibilities covered by either the treasurer or the financial controller (the head of the group concerned more with accounting issues rather than finance) will be unique for every firm, and the list in Exhibit 12.19 is far from exhaustive, but at least it provides a framework for considering the myriad decisions in this area.

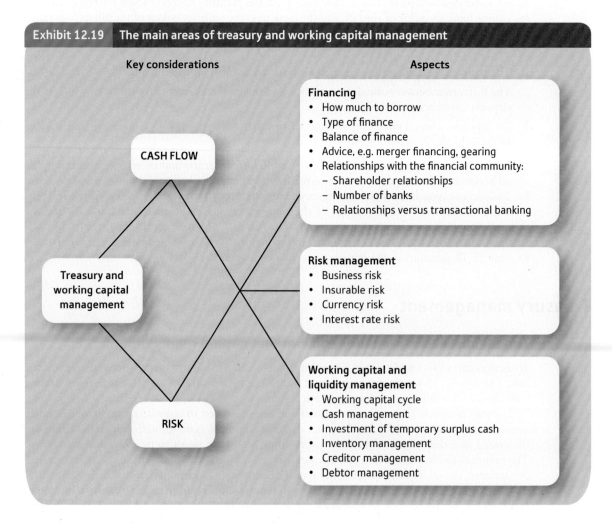

Exhibit 12.19   The main areas of treasury and working capital management

Exhibit 12.19 provides a guide for progress through this chapter but it must be noted that treasurers (leaving to one side the working capital specialists for the moment) must have knowledge of, and contribute towards, a wider range of corporate issues than those in Exhibit 12.19. The Association of Corporate Treasurers regard as key topics those listed in **Exhibit 12.20.**

Exhibit 12.20	Corporate treasury subjects

Capital markets and funding
- Equity financing
- Debt capital markets
- Bank lending
- Trade finance
- Asset & project finance
- Credit ratings

Corporate financial management
- Capital structure
- Corporate strategy
- Business valuation
- Investment appraisal
- Regulation and law
- Accounting and reporting
- Taxation

Treasury operations and controls
- Treasury organisation
- Policy and objectives

- Control and reporting
- Technology and systems
- The treasury professional

Cash and liquidity management
- Cash management
- Short-term liquidity
- Cash-flow forecasting
- Payment and clearing systems

Risk management
- Managing risk
- Business and operational risk
- Foreign exchange risk
- Interest rate risk
- Commodity risk
- Credit risk
- Pensions risk
- Exotic risks

Source: Association of Corporate Treasurers (www.treasurers.org).

Financing

Obtaining the most appropriate mixture of finance is likely to be of great importance to most firms. In this section we first examine the most appropriate forms of borrowing in terms of maturity of that borrowing, for example a short-term overdraft or a 20-year loan, as well as considering the question of the currency of the borrowing and the choice of fixed or floating interest rates; secondly, we look at retained earnings as a source of finance; and thirdly, we consider the more 'strategic' type of financing issues for which a treasurer might be called upon to give advice. There follows a commentary on the importance of maintaining good relationships with the financial community.

Is it better to borrow long or short?

Once a company has decided to raise funds by borrowing, it then has to decide whether to raise the money through (a) short-term debt, (b) medium-term debt, or (c) long-term debt. There are a number of factors to be taken into consideration in making a decision of this nature.

● *Maturity structure* A company will usually try to avoid having all of its debts maturing at or near the same date. It could be disastrous if the firm was required to repay loan capital on a number of different instruments all within, say, a six-month period. Even if the firm is profitable the sudden cash outflow could lead to insolvency.

Most companies include a breakdown of length of time to maturity of their debts in their annual report. The profile for Diageo plc for 2017 is shown in **Exhibit 12.21**.

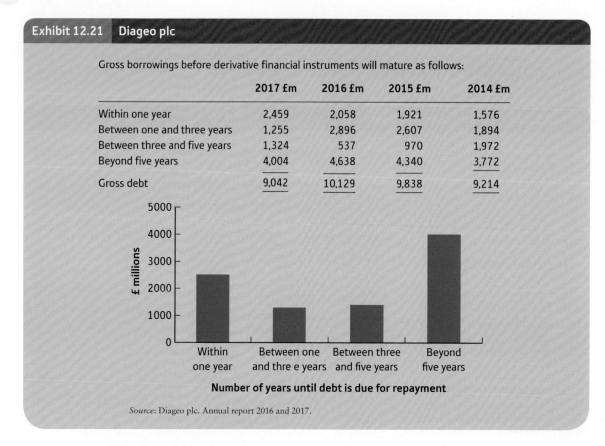

Exhibit 12.21   Diageo plc

Gross borrowings before derivative financial instruments will mature as follows:

	2017 £m	2016 £m	2015 £m	2014 £m
Within one year	2,459	2,058	1,921	1,576
Between one and three years	1,255	2,896	2,607	1,894
Between three and five years	1,324	537	970	1,972
Beyond five years	4,004	4,638	4,340	3,772
Gross debt	9,042	10,129	9,838	9,214

Number of years until debt is due for repayment

Source: Diageo plc. Annual report 2016 and 2017.

Exhibit 12.22 describes the great concern in 2009 when some banks had great difficulty replacing maturing debt.

● *Costs of issue/arrangement* It is usually cheaper to arrange an overdraft and other one-off short-term finance than long-term debt facilities, but this advantage is sometimes outweighed by the fact that if funds are needed over a number of years short-term debt has to be renewed

Exhibit 12.22

Banks face high costs as £7,000bn short-term debt refinancing looms

By Francesco Guerrera and Nicole Bullock in New York

Banks around the world face increases in funding costs that could cut profits and hit their customers as they look to re-finance $7,000bn-plus in short-term debt expiring in the next three years with longer-dated bonds, according to research released today. The flood of expiring debt will hit the US and the UK hard – with $2,000bn of debt coming due by 2012 – and could curb banks' profits or force them to charge individuals and companies more for their services.

The rush to refinance more than $7,000bn of debt by 2012 and a further $3,000bn by 2015 will exacerbate

the divide between winners and losers from the crisis, with healthier banks able to fund themselves at cheaper rates than troubled rivals. Investors said the mountain of maturing debt would increasingly weigh on the cost of bank bonds.

The average maturity of new debt issued by banks has fallen from 7.2 to 4.7 years in the past five years – the shortest average maturity for new debt in 30 years, according to the rating agency Moody's. Average debt maturity in the US sank to 3.2 years in 2009, less than half the long-term average.

more often than long-term debt. So over, say, a 20-year period, the issuing and arrangement costs of short-term debt may be much greater than for a 20-year bond.

- *Flexibility* Short-term debt is more flexible than long-term debt. If a business has fluctuations in its needs for borrowed funds, for example if it is a seasonal business, then for some months it does not need any borrowed funds, whereas at other times it needs large loans. A long-term loan may be inefficient because the firm will be paying interest even if it has surplus cash. True, the surplus cash could be invested but the proceeds are unlikely to be as great as the cost of the loan interest. It is cheaper to take out short-term loans or overdrafts when the need arises which can be paid back when the firm has high cash inflows.

- *The uncertainty of getting future finance* If a firm is investing in a long-term project which requires borrowing for many years it would be risky to finance this project using one-year loans. At the end of each year the firm has to renegotiate the loan or issue a new bond. There may come a time when lenders will not supply the new money. There may, for example, be a change in the bank's policy or a reassessment of the borrower's creditworthiness, a crisis of confidence in the financial markets or an imposition of government restrictions on lending. Whatever the reason, the project is halted and the firm loses money.

  Thus to some extent, the type of project or asset that is acquired determines the type of borrowing. If the project or asset is liquid and short term then short-term finance may be favoured. If it is long term then longer-term borrowing gives more certainty about the availability of finance, and (possibly) the interest rate.

- *The term structure of interest rates* The yield curve is described in Chapter 11. There it is stated that it is usual to find interest rates on short-term borrowing which are lower than on long-term debt. This may encourage managers to borrow on a short-term basis. In many circumstances this makes sense. If a company requires £10m of borrowed funds for a ten-year project and the corporate treasurer expects long-term interest rates to fall over the next year, it is unwise to borrow for the full ten years at the outset, locking in higher interest rates. Instead the firm borrows for one-year initially with the expectation of replacing the loan at the end of the year with a nine-year fixed-rate loan at the then reduced rate.

However, there are circumstances where managers find short-term rates deceptively attractive. For example, they might follow a policy of borrowing at short-term rates while the yield curve is still upward sloping, only switching to long-term borrowing when short-term rates rise above long-term rates. Take the case of Rosa plc, which wishes to borrow money for five years and faces the term structure of interest rates shown in the lower line of **Exhibit 12.23**. If it issued one-year

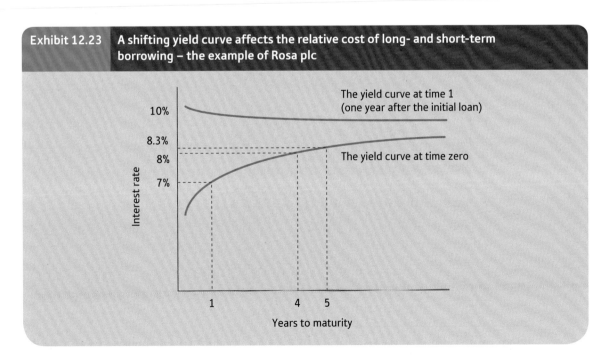

Exhibit 12.23   A shifting yield curve affects the relative cost of long- and short-term borrowing – the example of Rosa plc

bonds the rate of return paid would be 7%. The returns required on four-year and five-year bonds are 8% and 8.3% respectively. The company opts for a one-year bond with the expectation of issuing a four-year bond one year later. However by the time the financing has to be replaced, 365 days after the initial borrowing, the entire yield curve has shifted upwards due to general macroeconomic changes. Now Rosa has to pay an interest rate of 10% for the remaining four years. This is clearly more expensive than arranging a five-year bond at the outset.

The case of Rosa shows that it can be cheaper to borrow long at low points in the interest rate cycle despite the 'headline' interest charge on long-term debt being greater than on short-term loans.[5]

To 'match' or not to 'match'?

Firms usually conclude that there is a need for an appropriate mixture of debt finance with regard to length of time to maturity: some short-term borrowing is desirable alongside some long-term borrowing. The major factors which need to be considered in achieving the right balance are: **a** cost (interest rate, arrangement fee, etc.) and **b** risk (of not being able to renew borrowings, of the yield curve shifting, of not being able to meet a sudden outflow if the maturity is bunched, etc.). Some firms follow the 'matching' principle, in which the maturity structure of the finance matches the maturity of the project or asset. Here fixed assets and those current assets which are needed on a permanent basis (for example cash, minimum inventory or debtor levels) are financed through long-term sources, while current assets whose financing needs vary throughout the year are financed by short-term borrowings. Examples of the latter type of asset might be stocks of fireworks at certain times of the year, or investment in inventories of chocolate Easter eggs in the spring.

Thus there are three types of asset which need to be financed:

- fixed assets;
- permanent current assets;
- fluctuating current assets.

A firm taking the maturity matching approach is considered to be adopting a moderate stance. This is shown in **Exhibit 12.24**, where a rising level of total assets is financed principally through increases in long-term finance applied to fixed assets and permanent current assets. The fluctuating current assets, such as those related to seasonal variations, are financed with short-term funds.

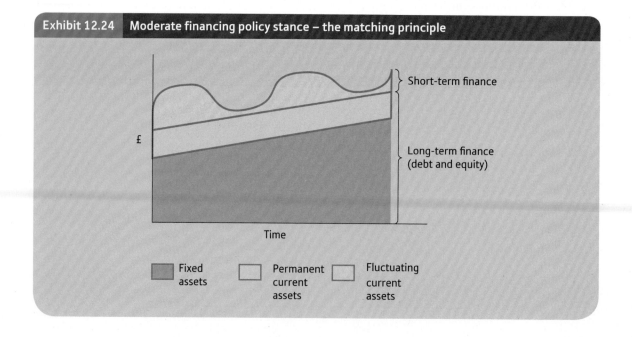

Exhibit 12.24   Moderate financing policy stance – the matching principle

---

5 There are ways of locking in interest rates in years 2, 3, 4 and 5 through the use of derivatives – see Chapter 21.

A more aggressive approach is represented in **Exhibit 12.25**. This entails more risk because of the frequent need to refinance to support permanent current assets as well as fluctuating current assets. If the firm relied on an overdraft for this it would be vulnerable to a rapid withdrawal of that facility. If stocks and cash are reduced to pay back the overdraft the firm may experience severe disruption, loss of sales and output, and additional costs because of a failure to maintain the minimum required working capital to sustain optimum profitability.

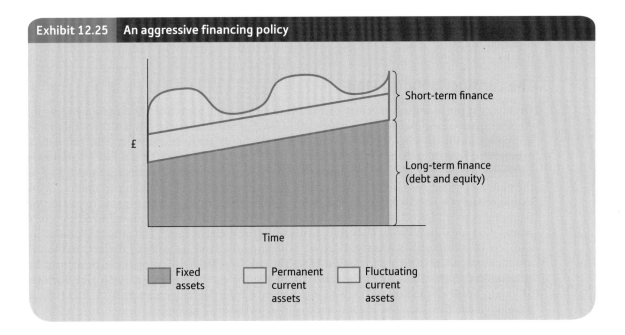

Exhibit 12.25　An aggressive financing policy

The low-risk policy is to make sure that long-term financing covers the total investment in assets. If there are times of the year when surplus cash is available this will be invested in short-term instruments. This type of policy is shown in **Exhibit 12.26**.

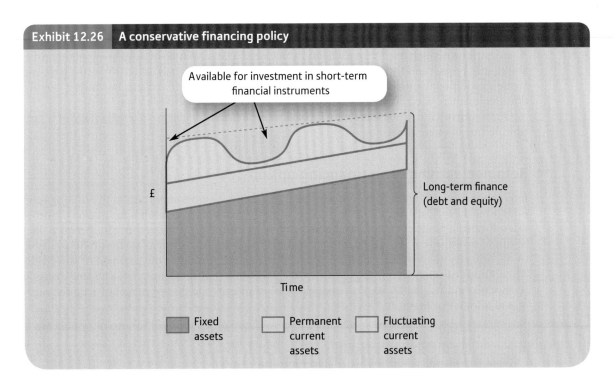

Exhibit 12.26　A conservative financing policy

Many managers feel much happier under the conservative approach because of the lower risk of being unable to pay bills as they arise. However, such a policy may not be in the best interests of the owners of the firm. The surplus cash invested in short-term securities is unlikely to earn a satisfactory return relative to the cost of the long-term funds. In all likelihood shareholders would be better off if the firm reduced its long-term financing, by returning cash to shareholders or paying off some long-term loans.

There is no sound theoretical formula to help decide the balance between long- and short-term finance but many managers seem to follow a policy of matching the maturity of their assets and liabilities, thereby accepting a modest level of risk while avoiding excessive amounts of surplus investible funds.

The currency of borrowing

Deciding on the maturity structure of the firm's debt is one aspect of the financing decision. Another is selecting the currency in which to borrow. For transnational firms it is common to find borrowing in the currency of the country where the funds are to be invested. This can reduce exposure to foreign exchange rate changes. For example, suppose that Union Jack plc borrows £100m to invest in the USA. It exchanges the £100m into $150m at the exchange rate of $1.5 to the pound. The net cash flows in subsequent years are expected to be $30m per annum. If the exchange rate remained constant Union Jack would therefore receive £20m per year to pay for the financing costs and produce a surplus. However, if the rate of exchange moved to $2 for every pound the annual cash inflow in sterling terms would be merely £15m.[6] The project is producing £5m less than originally anticipated despite generating the same quantity of dollars, and this is insufficient as a rate of return for Union Jack. The risk attached to this project can be reduced by ensuring that the liabilities are in the same currency as the income flow. So if Union Jack borrows $150m to invest in the project, even though the exchange rate may move to $2:£1 the project remains viable. Currency risk is considered in more detail in Chapter 22.

The interest rate choice

Another consideration for the debt portfolio is the balance to be struck between fixed and floating interest-rate borrowings. In many circumstances it is thought advisable to have a mixture of the two types of borrowing. If all the borrowings are floating rate then the firm is vulnerable to rising interest rates. This often happens at the most unfortunate times: for example, at the start of recessions interest rates are often high at the same time as sales are in decline.

Industries with high fixed-cost elements, which need a large volume of sales to maintain profitability, may be particularly averse to floating-rate borrowing as this may add to their cost base and create an additional source of risk. Even if they have to pay more for fixed-rate borrowing initially, the directors may sleep better knowing that one element of risk has been eliminated.

On the other hand, if all borrowing is fixed rate the firm is unable to take advantage of a possible decline in interest rates.

Retained earnings as a financing option

Internally generated funds from previous years' profits are the most important source of long-term finance for the typical firm, and yet it is so easily overlooked while attention is focused on the other ways of raising funds in the financial markets. Internal funds typically account for between one-third and two-thirds of the capital invested by UK firms. Retained earnings are the profits available to the ordinary shareholder which are retained within the firm after the payment of dividends. The retained earnings level is the inverse of the decision to pay dividends. The dividend decision is discussed in Chapter 19. We now consider the advantages and disadvantages of retained earnings as a source of finance.

---

6 Assume no hedging in the derivative or money markets.

One significant advantage of retained earnings is that there is no dilution of the existing share-holders' share of corporate control or share of returns. If the alternative of raising long-term funds by selling additional shares to outside shareholders were taken this would reduce the proportionate shareholdings of the existing owners. Even a rights issue might alter the relative position of particular shareholders if some chose not to take up their rights. Secondly, retaining earnings avoids the issuing costs associated with new shares or bonds and the arrangement fees on bank loans. Thirdly, management may value the fact that, in contrast to the position with a new equity or debt issue, they do not have to explain in such detail the use to which the funds will be put. This 'advantage' may not be in the shareholders' best interest, however.

A potential disadvantage of relying on internally generated funds is that they are limited by the firm's profits. Some firms wish to invest and grow at a much faster rate than would be possible through retained earnings. Indeed, some biotechnology firms are not expected to have profits for many years and yet have ambitious growth targets. Also, using retained earnings means reducing the dividend payout. Shareholders, on the whole, like to receive a steadily rising dividend stream. They may not be willing to forgo this simply because the management have a large number of projects in which they wish to invest. Retained earnings also have the drawback of being uncertain as they fluctuate with the ups and downs of the company's fortunes. Depending on this source of finance alone carries the risk of not being able to obtain finance at a vital stage in an investment programme.

Perhaps the most serious problem associated with retained earnings is that many managers regard them as essentially 'free capital'. That is, there is no cost to this capital – no opportunity cost of using these funds. This can encourage firms to invest to a greater extent than can be justified by the availability of positive NPV projects. There can be a resulting diminution of shareholders' wealth as the firm expands beyond a profitable size or diversifies into new areas, or acquires other firms. Forcing firms to raise funds externally subjects them to periodic scrutiny by critically minded investors who ask for a thorough justification. (See Chapters 14 and 15 on shareholder value.)

Retained earnings are not free. Shareholders, by allowing the firm to keep profits within the business, are making a significant sacrifice. They are forgoing dividends which could be invested in other financial securities. These other financial securities, for example shares in other firms of the same risk class, would have given a return. Thus shareholders have an opportunity cost and so the return required on retained earnings is the same as for any equity capital invested at that level of risk.

The treasurer at a strategic level

Treasurers may be asked to advise on matters of great significance to the future direction of the firm. For example, the decision to merge with another firm or to purchase a major business (a trade purchase) will require some assessment of the ability of the organisation to finance such activity. The treasurer will be able to advise on the sources of finance available, the optimum mixture and the willingness of the financial community to support the initiative. In a similar fashion a treasurer could help with disposals of subsidiaries.

Their knowledge of financial markets may permit treasurers to advise on the expected course of interest rates and exchange rates and so may aid vital decisions such as whether to establish a manufacturing facility or begin a marketing campaign in another country (see Chapters 21 and 22). Forecasting interest and exchange rates is notoriously difficult and even the greatest so-called experts frequently predict the future erroneously, and yet the treasurer may be the only person in the company able to make an informed guess.

Another major area of concern is the total amount of borrowing a firm should aim for. If it does not borrow at all then it will be losing the advantage of cheap finance. On the other hand, high levels of borrowing increase the chances of financial distress and the firm could be liquidated. Striking the appropriate balance is important and the treasurer may have some input in this area. Chapter 18 is devoted to the question of how much to borrow.

Relationships with the financial community

Neglecting to engender good relationships with shareholders, banks and other financial institutions can result in difficulties for the firm. The typical treasurer and chief financial officer of a corporation will spend a great deal of time communicating with major finance providers on a weekly, or even a daily basis.

There will be a planned and sustained effort to maintain mutual understanding between shareholders and the organisation. The treasurer might be asked to create a detailed and up-to-date picture of who the shareholders are and then to follow through with a high quality flow of information to enable shareholders to better appreciate the firm and its strategy in order to sustain their commitment. In the absence of informative communication to fill in gaps in their knowledge, shareholders may imagine all kinds of problems. If they are kept informed they are more likely to be supportive when the firm asks for additional finance, or asks for patience in times of difficulty, or appeals for the rejection of a merger bid. The point could be put even more simply: the shareholders own the firm and therefore both desire and deserve comprehensive information about its progress.

We turn now to banking relationships. Most firms make use of the services of more than one bank. A multinational firm may use over 100 banks. For example, Monsanto, the US chemical company, is proud of the fact that it has managed to cut the number down to 150 – it used to have 336. One reason for using so many banks is that large international firms have complex financial issues to deal with and any one bank may not have all the requisite skills and infrastructure to cope with them. Also banks have a tendency to join syndicates to make large loans to firms – an example here is Eurotunnel with 225 banks. In addition, some companies operate in dozens of countries and so may value the local network of the domestic banks in each of those markets.

The relationship between banks and large corporations differs. Some corporate treasurers, in an attempt to cut costs and boost investment returns, insist on banks competing with each other to offer the lowest-cost services. The provision of credit, the arrangement of bonds, notes, loans and commercial paper are put out to tender, as are the foreign exchange and cash management services. This competitive method is called 'transactional banking'. However, there are drawbacks to this mercenary approach. Banks start to view these companies as one-off service takers interested in low cost only, and do not attempt to become knowledgeable about the firms. This leads to complaints from corporations that banks are unable to provide more tailored advice and services which so many of them need. When crises arise firms find banks deserting them and this often poses a threat to their existence. The lack of two-way knowledge means a greater tendency to pull out of a difficult situation rather than help develop imaginative plans for regeneration. Also, maintaining contact with more than 100 bankers can be very costly if the treasury system is not to become chaotic.

More often the emphasis is on 'relationship banking' in which there is much more intimacy, with corporations being open with their banks and attempting to nurture a long-term relationship. As a result the quality of tailored service and the volume of consultancy type advice from banks improves. The banks are frequently willing to supply finance at a low interest rate as a loss leader so that they can pick up fee-based work later. *See* **Exhibit 12.27** for an article illustrating the benefits of relationship banking; the article talks about 'transactions' but implies that this is within a framework of a long-term relationship, which is different to transactional banking

Exhibit 12.27

Talent follows the cash into transaction banking

By Laura Noonan

Managing company money has quietly become a major driver of revenue. Financial institutions are increasingly relying on revenues from cash management and trade finance worldwide. Often obscured by the more glamorous cut and thrust of M&A advisory and equity trading, transaction banking has become the place where investment and corporate banks are increasingly pinning their hopes for the future. The business of managing cash for companies and providing trade finance has been the biggest driver of revenues for global banks since 2011, when it overtook banks' equities and fixed income divisions, according to data compiled for the FT by Coalition, the industry monitor.

In 2016, banks made $209bn from transaction banking, compared with the $172bn made by their trading arms, according to the data, which cover global, regional and local banks. This is almost three times the $77bn that banks made from advising clients on M&A and helping them raise finance.

Transaction services also eclipsed lending revenues for every year since 2011. "There's no question, it is becoming more relevant to the future of Citi, as well as in my view for the [future of the] industry," says Naveed Sultan, global head of treasury and trade solutions at the US bank, whose business boasts revenues of more than $8bn a year across almost 100 countries. Investment in transaction services is at odds with cutbacks in markets and investment banking. Even at Deutsche Bank, where billions of euros of costs and 9,000 jobs are being cut, €1bn has been earmarked for investment in its global transaction banking division.

"At JPMorgan we are number one in investment banking, we are number one in FICC (fixed income, currencies and commodities), we are number two or three in equities," says Takis Georgakopoulos, the bank's global head of treasury services. "The place where we see a lot more upside is the treasury services business." Talent is following the money.

"I've been in transaction banking about 15 years and I'd say we're at a peak when I get a lot of pretty senior investment banking people who are saying they want to move in," says Ather Williams, head of global transaction services at Bank of America Merrill Lynch. "I [recently] had three senior investment bankers come and say to me 'what can I do in your world?'"

Bankers are also attracted by the stability of transaction banking, which gives some respite from the volatility of earnings in investment banking and trading. Coalition data show that the revenue difference between the worst and best years for transaction banking was 11 per cent. For fixed income and equities, the worst year was 23 per cent below its peak. Investment banking's worst year was 19 per cent below its high. At Citi, Mr Sultan says his division has just recorded its 12th consecutive quarter of revenue and profit growth, even though low interest rates have made parts of the business more challenging.

 Financial Times, 6 March 2017.
All Rights Reserved.

Risk management

Running a business naturally entails taking risks – it is what business activity is about. Satisfactory profits rarely emerge from a risk-eliminating strategy; some risk is therefore inevitable. It is up to managers to select those risks the business might take and those which it should avoid. Take a company like GlaxoSmithKline which accepts high risks in its research and development programme. Should it also take a risk with exchange rates when it receives money from sales around the world, or should it try to minimise that particular type of risk? Risk reduction is often costly. For example, insurance premiums may be payable or transaction costs may be incurred in the derivative markets. Given the additional costs, managers have to think carefully about the benefits to be derived from reducing or eliminating risk. There are at least three reasons firms sacrifice some potential profits in order to reduce the impact of adverse events.

- *It helps financial planning* Being able to predict future cash flows, at least within certain boundaries, can be advantageous and can allow the firm to plan and invest with confidence. Imagine trying to organise a business if the future cash flows can vary widely depending on what happens to the currency, the interest rate or the price of a vital raw material input.

- *Reduce the fear of financial distress* Some events can damage a business to the point of threatening its existence. For example, massive claims have been made against firms involved in the production of asbestos. If it had not been for the passing on of this risk to the insurance companies many more of these firms would now be liquidated. A similar logic applies to the insurance of supertankers against an ocean oil spillage. By limiting the potential damage, not only will the managers and shareholders benefit, but other finance providers, such as banks, will have greater confidence in the firm which will lower the cost of capital.

- *Some risks are not rewarded* It is possible to reduce risk in situations where there are no financial rewards for accepting that extra risk. For example, if British Airways contracted to buy a dozen aircraft from Boeing for delivery over the next ten years and had to pay in dollars as each aeroplane was completed it would have to accept the risk of a recession in international flights and numerous other risks, but, in the sophisticated foreign exchange markets of today, at least it can eliminate one risk. It does not have to live with any uncertainty about the cost of the aeroplanes in terms of sterling because it could make an arrangement with a bank at the outset to purchase the required number of dollars for a specified number of pounds at set dates in the future. (This is a forward agreement.) British Airways would then know precisely how many pounds will be needed to buy the dollars to pay Boeing in each year of the next decade (see Chapter 22 for more currency risk-hedging strategies).

There are many different types of risk that a commercial organisation has to deal with. We will discuss the four most important: business risk, insurable risk, currency risk and interest-rate risk.

Business risk

Many of the risks of operating in a competitive business environment have to be accepted by management to a greater or lesser extent. Sales may fall because of, say, recession, or innovative breakthroughs by competitors. Costs may rise because of, say, strong union power or government-imposed tariffs. For some of these risk elements there is little that management can do. However, in many areas management can take positive action to reduce risk. For example, consider a bakery company heavily dependent on buying in wheat. The managers are likely to be worried that the price of wheat may rise over the forthcoming months, thereby making their operations unprofitable. On the other hand farmers may be worried by the possibility of wheat falling in price. Both would value certainty. One way of achieving this is for the baker and farmer to enter into a wheat forward agreement, in which the baker agrees to take delivery of wheat at a later date at a price which is agreed today. Both sides now know exactly how much the wheat will be sold for and so can plan ahead.

There are other ways of reducing business risk. For example, firms are often faced with a choice between two machines. The first is highly specialised to a particular task, for example, turning out a particular component. The second, slightly more expensive machine, can turn out the same component, but can also be used in a more flexible fashion to switch production to other components. The option to use the machine in alternative ways can sometimes have a high value and so it is worthwhile paying the extra initial set-up costs and even higher production costs.

Consider also an electricity generator contemplating the construction of a power plant. The installation of a coal-fired station would be £100m. This would leave the generator dependent on coal price movements for future profitability. An alternative power plant can be switched from coal to gas but costs an additional £30m. The value of the option to switch is then for the management to evaluate and weigh against the extra cost of construction.

Likewise, a car production line may be more expensive if it is to be capable of being used for a number of different models. But the option to use the facility for more than one type of car reduces the firm's risk by making it less dependent on one model. These are examples of real options, which were considered in Chapter 6.

Insurable risk

Many risks encountered by business can be transferred, through the payment of a premium, to insurance companies. These include factory fires, pollution damage and accidental damage to vehicles and machinery. Insurance companies are often better able to bear risk than ordinary commercial firms. The reasons for this are the following:

- experience in estimating probabilities of events and therefore 'pricing' risk more efficiently;
- knowledge of methods of reducing risk. They can pass on this knowledge to the commercial firms which may obtain lower premiums if they take precautionary measures;
- ability to *pool* risks, in other words, to diversify risk. The chance of an accident occurring in one firm is highly uncertain, but the probability of a particular proportion of a portfolio of insurance policies making a claim is fairly predictable.

Insurance can be an expensive option because of the tendency for insurance companies to charge for much more than the probability of having to pay out. For example, if there was a one in a hundred chance of your £10,000 car being stolen in a year and never recovered then for every 100 cars insured the insurance company will expect one £10,000 claim per year. The insurance premium to each owner to cover this specific type of risk would, justifiably, be slightly over £100 (£10,000/100), to allow for a modest profit. However, in reality, the premium may be much more than this. The insurance company is likely to have to bear significant administrative costs in setting up the policy in the first place and then dealing with subsequent claims. Anyone who has had to communicate with an insurance company quickly becomes aware of the mountain of paperwork they generate annually. Insurance companies also have to charge premiums sufficiently high to cover the problems of adverse selection. Put it this way: you may be a sensible car owner, be cautious about where you park your car, never leave the doors unlocked and live in a good part of town, but many of the other purchasers of theft insurance may be less fastidious and fortunate. The grouping together of good and bad risks tends to increase the cost of insurance to relatively good policyholders. This is made worse for the good policyholders by the increased tendency of those in high-risk situations to buy insurance.

The third boost to insurance premiums comes from moral hazard (the encouragement of bad behaviour) which causes holders of insurance to be less careful than they might otherwise be – the 'It's all right, don't worry, it's insured' syndrome. An extreme example of moral hazard has been created with the 'new-for-old' policies for electrical items in which a brand-new HDTV, for example, is provided should the old one suffer accidental damage – some have been tempted to 'accidentally' drop the TV!

These three additional costs may push insurance premiums beyond acceptable levels for a firm. In some cases large corporations have taken the bold decision to bear many insurable risks. They may still pay insurance premiums to safeguard against major events which threaten the continuance of the firm but accept routine risks themselves such as machine breakdown, accidents at work, etc. There seems little point in paying premiums just to receive a regular, but lower, inflow in return. The treasurer may have an important role in deciding which risks to insure and which to accept in-house.

Currency risk

Another major area of responsibility for the corporate treasurer is in the management of risk which arises because exchange rates move. Take the case of Acarus plc which has sold electrical goods to an Australian importer on six months' credit. The importer is sent an invoice requiring payment of AUD20m. The current exchange rate is two Australian dollars to one pound so if currency rates do not change in six months Acarus will receive £10m. If the exchange rate moves to AUD1.80 : £1 then Acarus will receive £11.11m, and will be very pleased with the extra £1.11m of income. However, matters might turn out worse than expected. Say the rate of exchange moved to AUD2.20 : £1, then Acarus would receive only £9.09m. If the management team is risk averse it may say to itself, 'While we like the possibility of making additional profit on the deal this is more than outweighed by the downside risk of making less than £10m'. There are various ways of ensuring that Acarus receives at least £10m and an entire chapter (Chapter 22) is devoted to the subject of exchange-rate risk management. Here we will have just a taster. One of the possibilities is for Acarus to buy an option giving the firm the right but not the obligation to exchange AUD20m for sterling at a rate of AUD2 : £1 in six months. If the dollar appreciates against the pound to AUD1.80 then Acarus would choose not to exercise the option – to let it lapse – and then exchange the AUD20m for £11.11m in the spot market in six months' time. Alternatively, if the dollar falls against sterling Acarus would insist on exercising the option to receive £10m rather than exchanging at the spot rate of AUD2.20 : £1 and therefore achieving a mere £9.09m. By purchasing the option Acarus ensures that the lowest amount it will receive is £10m and the upside potential is unlimited. However, it would need to pay a hefty premium to the option seller for passing on this risk – perhaps 2 to 4% of the amount covered. The difficult part is weighing the cost of risk-reducing action against the benefit.

Interest-rate risk

Future interest rates cannot be predicted with any degree of accuracy. If a company has large amounts of floating-rate debt it could be vulnerable to interest-rate rises. Alternatively, a company with large fixed-rate debt could have to face living with regret, and higher debt costs than necessary, if interest rates fall.

There is a wide variety of financial products which enable a treasurer to reduce the firm's exposure to the volatility of interest rates. Chapter 21 explores a number of them. Here we examine one of the weapons in the treasurer's arsenal – the cap.

Ace plc wishes to borrow £20m to finance a major expansion. It does so at a floating rate of LIBOR plus 150 basis points. LIBOR is currently 5% and therefore Ace pays a rate of 6.5%. This loan is a large sum relative to Ace's capital base and profits, and the management is concerned that if LIBOR rises above 7% the firm will get into serious financial difficulty. To avoid this Ace purchases a cap agreement by which a bank promises to pay any interest charge above a LIBOR of 7%. Thus, if two years later LIBOR rises to 8%, without the cap Ace would pay 9.5%. However, Ace can call upon the bank which made the cap agreement to pay the extra 1%. Ace's effective interest charge cannot go beyond a total of 7% + 1.5% = 8.5%. What is more, Ace can benefit if interest rates fall because rates are linked to a variable LIBOR at any rate below the cap. The premium charged by the bank for this form of interest-rate insurance can be quite substantial but there are ways of offsetting this cost, for example by simultaneously selling a floor, but consideration of this will have to wait until Chapter 21. Suffice to say, the judicious management of interest-rate risk can be an important part of the treasurer's job description.

Exhibit 12.28 highlights the importance of the treasury function in enabling companies to survive the financial turmoil following the financial crisis.

Exhibit 12.28

Crisis alters corporate treasurers' risk outlook

By Richard Milne

Being a corporate treasurer has never been the most high-profile of jobs. Looking after the cash of their companies and managing their financial risks, treasurers have long worked in the background.

But the financial crisis gave companies a new mantra of 'cash is king' and forced treasurers to take a more visible role.

'I had barely been to a board meeting before the crisis. Now when I go, people are paying a lot of attention,' the treasurer of one of Europe's biggest companies says.

As Stuart Siddall, chief executive of the Association of Corporate Treasurers in the UK, says: 'Treasury as a profession has been catapulted into the spotlight by the crisis.'

The crisis put a big strain on companies as they scrambled to gain access to liquidity and to secure funding as loans from banks dried up.

In interviews with the Financial Times, treasurers at some of Europe's largest groups explain how their jobs have changed and how some of their innate conservatism has reaped rewards.

'When the crisis kicked in, I think everybody in the corporate treasury role underestimated the liquidity risk,' the treasurer of one of Germany's most conservative companies says.

That was because of the closure of the commercial paper market, a form of short-term funding frequently used by companies.

'We have become more conservative now as a result,' he says.

Many non-financial companies in Europe are sitting on record levels of cash, giving them strong balance sheets. But rather than feeling it burning a hole in their pockets and splurging on an acquisition or share buy-back, companies are holding on to their cash.

The treasurer of a big European media company says: 'I suspect the M&A market will come back slowly and that, rather than give money back to shareholders, most companies will wait until there is certainty that there is a strong recovery in the economy.'

Another change brought on by the crisis is that many companies have decided to diversify their funding.

A treasurer at a UK company says: 'What should be my short-term and long-term mix? That has changed. Companies have become less reliant on short-term funding. But it is also important that you don't become too dependent on a single source of funding.'

The obvious manifestation of that was in the switch by companies from bank finance to getting funds from the capital markets through bonds.

Take MAN, the German truckmaker. Four years ago, it was entirely bank-financed. Now it does most of its financing through the capital markets.

Many big companies have followed suit. A report by Morgan Stanley shows that for the 162 European groups with an investment-grade credit rating, the funding mix is similar to US groups with 70% bonds and 30% banks.

This has helped push up the use of bond funding. Bonds account for about 35% of all European companies' funding compared with 20–25% before the crisis, according to Morgan Stanley.

But the dependence of small and medium-sized companies on bank funding means the US is way ahead, with about 70% of funding coming from the capital markets.

The finance director of a large European industrial group says: 'In the long run, whatever we can get from capital markets we will do. We won't give up on banks entirely, but the capital markets are more reliable.

'Banks are inclined to say, "Can't we reduce our exposure to you?" You don't get that with the capital markets.'

A UK treasurer says: 'We access the deepest market and then swap it back into the currency we need. So we look at the US public markets, US commercial paper, euro bonds, European commercial paper, sterling bonds, Swiss bonds, anything.'

A prime example is European issuance in Yankee bonds, denominated in US dollars. These account for almost 20% of bond funding this year, the highest proportion for at least a decade.

But this year companies have been more restrained in tapping European bond markets despite low interest rates. This is because many remain well funded after treasurers showed their conservative streak last year by issuing debt at a relatively high cost.

Mr Siddall says: 'A company's view at the time was, if I have to pay a bit too much at the moment it's OK because I've got the funding to secure the group's future. I don't think anyone regrets doing that now.'

 Financial Times, 2 September 2010, p. 31.
All Rights Reserved.

Working capital management

A firm needs to invest in order to thrive. Major long-term investments in a new factory or new machinery are part of that investment. Another necessary element for expansion is additional resources devoted to current assets. Higher levels of output call for extra inventories of raw materials and work in progress (WIP) (partially finished goods). More sales volume often means that additional credit is granted to customers so that the investment in debtors (receivables) increases. Greater sales usually means more inventory held in the form of finished goods. Also, a higher level of general business activity usually requires greater amounts of cash to oil the wheels. Some of the additional investment in inventories, debtors and cash may come from long-term sources of finance but in most cases short-term sources such as trade credit or a bank overdraft will cover much of the increased need.

> Working capital can be defined as the difference between current assets and current liabilities.

Working capital thus means net current assets, or net current liabilities (if current liabilities exceed current assets). It is the investment a company makes in assets which are in continual use and are turned over many times in a year. Working capital encompasses the following:

● Short-term resources:

– inventory;
– debtors (accounts receivable, or receivables);
– investments (marketable securities);
– cash.

Less:

● Short-term liabilities:

– trade creditors (accounts payable, or payables);
– short-term borrowing;
– other creditors repayable within a year.

The working capital cycle

The upper, circular, part of **Exhibit 12.29** shows the working capital cycle for a typical firm. (This chain of events applies to the typical manufacturing firm rather than service businesses, which often miss one or two stages.) It starts with the investment in raw material inventories which are then used in the production process and thereby become partially completed products. Eventually finished goods are produced which are held in inventory until sold. Some of these goods are sold for cash and others are sold on credit, with the customer paying days or weeks later. At each stage of the process expenditure is necessary on labour and other operational inputs. Helping to ease the cash burden of this cycle are suppliers, who provide credit.

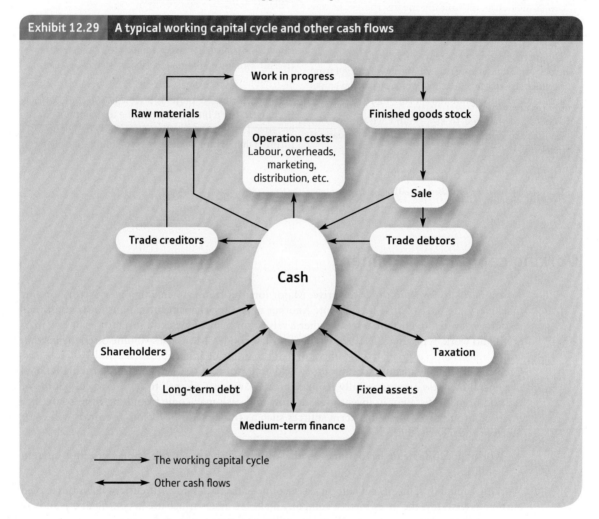

Exhibit 12.29   A typical working capital cycle and other cash flows

The lower half of the diagram in Exhibit 12.29 shows non-working capital cash flows. These are generally infrequent events, involving large sums on each occasion and are of a long-term nature. They will not be considered any further in this chapter.

Money tied up in any stage in the working capital chain has an opportunity cost. In addition there are costs associated with storage and/or administration. The combined costs can be considerable and it is the art of good working capital management to so arrange the affairs of the business as to obtain a balance between the costs and benefits through raising or lowering stocks, cash, debtors and creditors to their optimum levels. **Exhibit 12.30** highlights the enormous sums tied up in 'excess' working capital.

Cash-conversion cycle

The working capital cycle can be expressed in terms of the length of time between the acquisition of raw materials and other inputs and the inflow of cash from the sale of goods. As can be seen from **Exhibit 12.31** this involves a number of intermediate stages.

Exhibit 12.30

Working it out

The Lex Column

Keeping $1,100bn of surplus cash in the bank – about the entire gross domestic product of South Korea – seems like a waste. But that is the amount of excess working capital (which funds a business's day-to-day operations) tied up by the top 1,000 companies in both the US and Europe (compared with best-performing industry peers), according to Ernst & Young.

But, although in theory more efficient working capital management would free up an average of $550m per company that could then be spent elsewhere, progress is not always easy. In many cases, one company's gain is another's loss. Strategies that appear simple, such as demanding customers pay earlier, can cancel each other out if everyone does the same. Last year, for example, the 13% reduction in the working capital requirements of European food producers was due mainly to slower payment to suppliers. The accounts receivables of these suppliers increased commensurately.

Not all working capital efficiency strategies are circular, and the largest companies in the US and Europe have become more adept overall at working capital management. In the past year, European and US companies improved working capital efficiency (working capital as a proportion of revenues) by 4 and 2% respectively. During the past decade, they have become 16 and 13% more efficient respectively.

This year, however, might be different. Ballooning commodity prices in 2010 (particularly for food, metals and oil) will flow through to companies' cost of goods sold in 2011. The extent to which they can pass on these higher prices – and also preserve margins – will determine whether they can maintain the level of working capital efficiency achieved over the past decade. If companies do end up absorbing part of the cost increases themselves, they should be careful in trying to make up the difference by manipulating accounts payable and receivable. Higher funding costs are sometimes an acceptable price to pay to maintain good relations with customers and suppliers.

FT *Financial Times,* 6 June 2011.
All Rights Reserved.

| Exhibit 12.31 | The cash-conversion cycle as part of the working capital cycle |

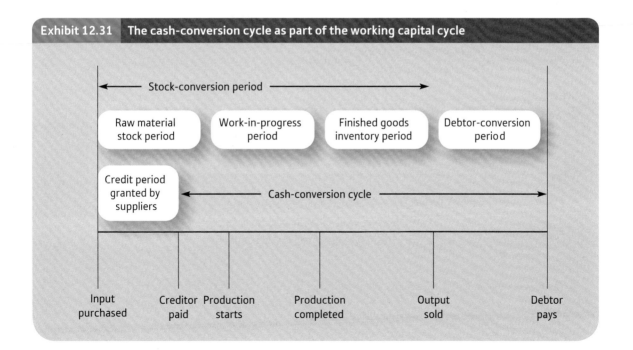

The cash-conversion cycle focuses on the length of time between the company's outlay on inputs and the receipt of money from the sale of goods. For manufacturing firms it is the average time raw materials remain in stock, plus the time taken to produce the company's output, plus the length of time finished goods stay within the company as a form of inventory, plus the time taken for debtors to pay, less the credit period granted by suppliers. The shorter this cycle the fewer resources the company needs to tie up. The cash-conversion cycle can be summarised as the stock-conversion period plus the debtor-conversion period less the credit period granted by suppliers – *see* **Exhibit 12.32**.

Exhibit 12.32	Summary of cash-conversion cycle

Cash-conversion cycle	=	Stock-conversion period	+	Debtor-conversion period	−	Credit period granted by suppliers

The cash-conversion cycle can be calculated approximately using the terms set out in **Exhibit 12.33**.

Exhibit 12.33	Calculation of cash-conversion cycle

● **Raw materials stock period** The average number of days raw materials remain unchanged and in stock:

$$\text{Raw materials stock period} = \frac{\text{Average value of raw materials stock}}{\text{Average usage of raw materials per day}} = X \text{ days}$$

Less

● **Average credit period granted by suppliers** The average length of time between the purchase of inputs and the payment for them:

$$\text{Credit period} = \frac{\text{Average level of creditors}}{\text{Purchases on credit per day}} = X \text{ days}$$

Add

● **Work-in-progress period** The number of days to convert raw materials into finished goods:

$$\text{Work-in-progress period} = \frac{\text{Average value of work in progress}}{\text{Average cost of goods sold per day}} = X \text{ days}$$

Add

● **Finished goods inventory period** The number of days finished goods await delivery to customers:

$$\text{Finished goods inventory period} = \frac{\text{Average value of finished goods in stock}}{\text{Average cost of goods sold per day}} = X \text{ days}$$

Add

● **Debtor-conversion period** The average number of days to convert customer debts into cash:

$$\text{Debtor-conversion period} = \frac{\text{Average value of debtors}}{\text{Average value of sales per day}} = X \text{ days}$$

The cash-conversion cycle can, perhaps, be better understood when some numbers are attached. The figures given in **Exhibit 12.34** can be used to illustrate it.

Exhibit 12.34	Figures invented in order to calculate a cash-conversion cycle			
	20X1	**20X2**	**Mean**	**Per day during 20X2**
Time (year end, as flow for year)	£m	£m	£m	£
Raw materials inventory	22	24	23	
Creditors	12	14	13	
Work-in-progress inventory	10	11	10.5	
Finished goods inventory	9	10	9.5	
Debtors	30	32	31	
Sales (annual)	150	170	–	465,753
Raw material usage (annual)	100	116	–	317,808
Cost of goods sold (annual)	130	146	–	400,000

The cash-conversion cycle is the length of time a pound is tied up in current assets. For the figures given above it is:

$$\text{Raw materials stock period} = \frac{23,000,000}{317,808} = 72 \text{ days}$$

$$\text{Less creditor period*} = \frac{13,000,000}{317,808} = -41 \text{ days}$$

$$\text{Work-in-progress period} = \frac{10,500,000}{400,000} = 26 \text{ days}$$

$$\text{Finished goods inventory period} = \frac{9,500,000}{400,000} = 24 \text{ days}$$

$$\text{Debtor-conversion period} = \frac{31,000,000}{465,753} = 67 \text{ days}$$

$$\text{Cash-conversion cycle} = 148 \text{ days}$$

* This is simplified to the creditor period on a single input, raw materials – there will be other inputs and creditors in most firms.

After observing the length of time money is invested in working capital, the management of the firm tries to think of ways of shortening the cash-conversion cycle – without damaging operations. Debtor (receivables) levels could be cut by changing the conditions of sale or being more forceful in the collection of old debts; inventory levels can be examined to see if overstocking is occurring and whether the production methods can be altered to process and sell goods more quickly; perhaps creditors could be pushed into granting more credit. If these actions can be carried out without any adverse impact on costs or sales, then they should be implemented. The difficult decisions come when reducing the cash-conversion cycle entails costs as well as benefits – then a careful evaluation and balancing of cost and benefits is needed. These will be considered later in the chapter.

Exhibit 12.35 provides a brief overview of the tension with which managers have to cope. If there is too little working capital, it results in inventories, finished goods and customer credit not being available in sufficient quantity. On the other hand, if there are excessive levels of working capital, the firm has unnecessary additional costs: the cost of tying up funds, plus the storage, ordering and handling costs of being overburdened with stock. Running throughout is the risk of being temporarily short of that vital lifeblood of a business – cash (that is, suffering a liquidity risk).

The dynamics of working capital

The level of activity of an organisation is likely to have an impact on the investment needed in working capital. Take a company with annual sales of £10m and the working capital periods set out in **Exhibit 12.36**.

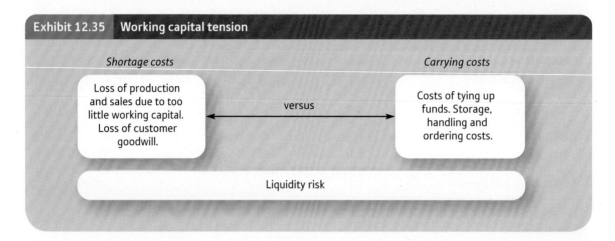

Exhibit 12.35   Working capital tension

Shortage costs   *Carrying costs*

Loss of production and sales due to too little working capital. Loss of customer goodwill.   *versus*   Costs of tying up funds. Storage, handling and ordering costs.

Liquidity risk

Exhibit 12.36   Working capital periods

Stock-conversion period (raw material + WIP + finished goods periods)   2 months
Debtor-conversion period   1.5 months
Creditor period   1 month

Assuming that the input costs are 60% of sales the working capital investment will be £1,750,000:

Stock	60% × £10m	× 2/12	1,000,000
Debtors	£10m	× 1.5/12	1,250,000
Creditors	60% × £10m	× 1/12	−500,000
			£1,750,000

As the level of sales increases there are three possible types of impact on the level of working capital (if we exclude the theoretical fourth possibility of a decline):

1   The investment in working capital increases in proportion to the increase in sales because the conversion periods remain constant.

2   A disproportionate rise in working capital is experienced. The conversion periods may be lengthened because of longer credit granted to customers to increase sales or higher raw materials, WIP and finished goods inventory to support the increased activity. These moves may make logical business sense in order to generate more sales and avoid stock-out costs, or they may be a result of poor working capital management. Much depends on the environment and the economics of the business concerned.

3   Working capital increases at a slower rate than the sales volume.

These three possibilities are shown in **Exhibit 12.37**. What emerges from Exhibit 12.37 is that even though remarkable strides are made in limiting the rise in working capital as a proportion of sales in the third scenario, the firm will still have to find additional finance to invest in this area. If it fails to do so the firm may cease production due to an inability to pay for day-to-day expenses. This is a situation of overtrading, considered later in this chapter.

Working capital policies

Exhibit 12.38 shows three alternative policies for working capital as sales rise. The top line represents a relatively relaxed approach with large cash or near-cash balances, more generous customer credit and/or higher inventories. This may be a suitable policy for a firm operating in a relatively uncertain environment where safety (or buffer) stocks of raw materials, work in progress and finished goods are needed to avoid production stoppages and lost sales due to stock-outs. Customers may demand longer to pay and suppliers are less generous with credit. The aggressive stance is more likely to be taken in an environment of greater certainty over future flows which permits working capital to be kept to relatively low levels. Here the firm would hold minimal safety stocks of cash and inventories and/or would be able to press customers for relatively early settlement while pushing trade creditors to increase the time interval between receipt and payment for inputs. The aggressive policy approach will exhibit a shorter cycle for cash conversion.

Exhibit 12.37	Working capital changes when sales rise by 50%		

Conversion periods	Possibility 1	Possibility 2	Possibility 3
Stock	Constant @ 2 months	Increase to 3 months	Decrease to $1\frac{1}{2}$ months
Debtors	Constant @ $1\frac{1}{2}$ months	Increase to 2 months	Decrease to 1 month
Creditors	Constant @ 1 month	Increase to $1\frac{1}{2}$ months	Decrease to $\frac{1}{2}$ month
	£m	£m	£m
Stock	$60\% \times £15m \times 2/12 =$ 1.5	$60\% \times £15m \times 3/12 =$ 2.25	$60\% \times £15m \times 1\frac{1}{2}/12 =$ 1.125
Debtors	$£15m \times 1\frac{1}{2}/12 =$ 1.875	$£15m \times 2/12 =$ 2.50	$£15m \times 1/12 =$ 1.250
Creditors	$60\% \times £15m \times 1/12 =$ −0.750	$60\% \times £15m \times 1\frac{1}{2}/12 =$ −1.125	$60\% \times £15m \times \frac{1}{2}/12 =$ −0.375
Working capital Investment	2.625	3.625	2.0
Absolute increase	0.875	1.875	0.25
Percentage increase over £1.75m	50%	107%	14%

Exhibit 12.38	Policies for working capital

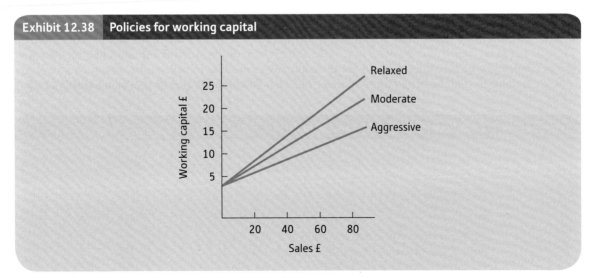

Note: The numbers are illustrative and do not imply a 'normal' relationship between sales and current assets.

Overtrading

A firm operating in a particular business environment and with a given level of activity will have certain levels of working capital needs. For example, a manufacturing firm with a stable level of annual sales will aim to invest an optimum amount in stocks and trade debtors. If sales should rise, by, say, 50%, then it is likely that stocks of raw materials, WIP and finished goods will rise and the money required to support additional debtors will also increase. Perhaps the rise in investment in working capital will need to be more than 50%, or perhaps the economics of the firm means that a lower proportionate rise in working capital is needed for each increase in total activity. Whatever the particular circumstance of each firm it is likely that additional working capital resources will be needed to permit judicious expansion without the fear of overtrading.

> Overtrading occurs when a business has insufficient finance for working capital to sustain its level of trading.

A business is said to be overtrading when it tries to engage in more business than its working capital will allow. It could be that too much money is tied up in stocks and trade debtors, and cash is not coming in quickly enough to meet debts as they fall due. It could be that the firm failed to obtain sufficient equity finance when it was established to support its trading level, or it could be that the managers are particularly bad at managing the working capital resources that they have. The most common cause of overtrading (or under-capitalisation) is a failure to match increases in turnover with appropriate increases in finance for working capital.

It may seem odd that a firm could suffer from an increase in the demand for its products, but in the harsh world of business it is perfectly possible for a firm to double its sales, and its profits, and yet become insolvent. Managers can be sorely tempted by the lure of new sales opportunities and lead the firm to rapid expansion, believing that the additional revenue will more than cover the extra investment needed in working capital to pay day-to-day bills. However, this sometimes does not work out because of the time delays involved in receiving cash from customers and the necessity to make large payments for inventory, labour and other costs.

Thus the firm could find itself unable to pay short-term bills while at the same time anticipating great prosperity in the long run. Take the case of Bits and Rams Ltd which in 2016 had a turnover of £2m and a profit of £200,000:

	£000
Turnover	2,000
Cost of goods sold	1,800
Profit	200

All costs are variable and debtors generally take two and a half months to pay. Inventories for two months' worth of costs of sales are held and trade creditors are paid one and a half months after delivery. In 2017 sales doubled but the company came close to collapse because it could not pay suppliers and the labour force on time. The cash flows for 2017 are as shown in **Exhibit 12.39**.

Exhibit 12.39	Cash flow for Bits and Rams Ltd in 2017

	£000
Turnover	4,000
Cost of goods sold	3,600
Profit	+400
Additional investment in debtors ($2,000 \times 2\frac{1}{2}/12$)	−417
Additional investment in inventories ($1,800 \times 2/12$)	−300
Tax bill from previous year's trading	−67
Increase in trade creditors ($1,800 \times 1\frac{1}{2}/12$)	+225
Cash flow	−159

If Bits and Rams is unable to finance this large increase in working capital it could find itself insolvent. Even if it manages to avoid insolvency, management may have to engage in short-term crisis management to overcome the cash shortage (for example, selling assets, chasing late payers) which is likely to distract them from the more important task of creating long-term shareholder wealth.

In an overtrading situation, if it is not possible to increase the capital base of a firm, by borrowing finance or selling shares, and the management have done all they can to tighten up working capital management (for example, by reducing stock levels) then the only option left open is likely to be to reduce activity. This can be a very painful prescription psychologically for managers as they have to turn down profitable business.

Why is cash important?

Exhibit 12.29 shows the centrality of cash in the operations of firms. Many firms do not have stocks, particularly in the service sector, while others do not have debtors or creditors, but all have to use cash. So what is it about cash which causes all firms to need it? There are three categories of motives ascribed to the holding of cash:

1 *Transaction motive* Cash is needed to pay for wages, buy materials and fixed assets, to pay taxes, service debts and for a host of other day-to-day transactions. This cash is necessary because the daily cash inflows do not match the cash outflows and so cash is needed to act as a buffer to permit activity to continue. This is particularly important in seasonal businesses or where long credit periods are granted to customers.

2 *Precautionary motive* The forecasting of future cash flows is subject to error. The more vulnerable cash flows are to unpredictable shocks the greater the cash balance needed to act as a safety stock. Future cash flows can vary from those originally anticipated for a wide variety of reasons, for example a sales shortfall, a strike or the failure of a supplier.

3 *Speculative motive* This simply means that any unexpected profitable opportunities can be taken immediately, for example to purchase a competitor firm quickly when a fleeting opportunity presents itself.

Operating cash is money held for operating purposes which is earning below-market interest rates because the firm needs quick access to it on a regular basis. So money held in cheque accounts is considered cash even if it is not in the form of the 'foldable stuff', because the interest earned on it is low or nil due to the convenience of account withdrawals. Thus, the firm deliberately makes an interest rate sacrifice to hold cash either in currency or in an easily accessible account.

Exhibit 12.40 shows the trade-off management has to take into account when considering the levels of cash to maintain. (Note that in many firms it is the fluctuations in the overdraft that provide the cash.)

Cash management models

Models have been developed which attempt to set cash levels at a point, or within a range, which strikes the best balance between the costs outlined in Exhibit 12.40. All these models suffer from being over-simplistic and are heavily dependent on the accuracy of the inputs. There is also a danger of managers using them in a mechanical fashion, and neglecting to apply the heavy dose of judgement needed to allow for the less easily quantified variables ignored by the models.

Baumol's cash model

Baumol's model assumes that the firm operates in a steady state environment where it uses cash at a constant rate which is entirely predictable. Take the case of Cypressa plc which pays out £100,000 per week and receives a steady inflow of £80,000. The firm will have a need for additional cash of £20,000 per week. (This may sound like a disastrous pattern at first glance. However, it could be that Cypressa is highly profitable but has these cash flow shortages for the forthcoming months because of large capital expenditure. Eventually there will be a large cash inflow.) If it has a beginning cash balance of £80,000 then the pattern of cash balances over time will be as shown in **Exhibit 12.41**. It takes four weeks for the initial balance to be reduced to zero. At the end of Week 4 the cash balance is topped up to £80,000 by the firm, say, borrowing or selling some of its holdings of securities such as Treasury bills. Both of these actions involve costs. Let us say that the arrangement fees on £80,000 of borrowing or the transaction costs of selling £80,000 of Treasury bills are £500.

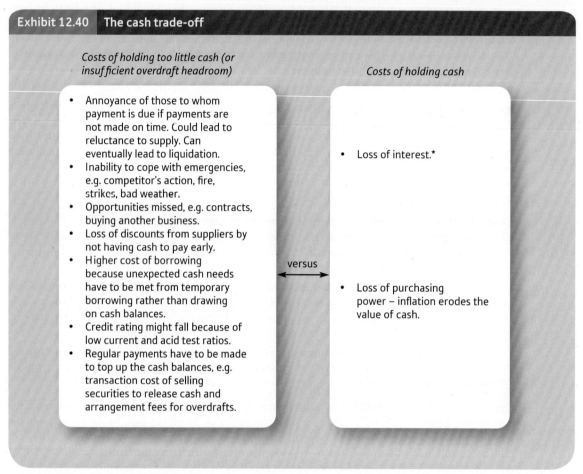

Exhibit 12.40   The cash trade-off

Costs of holding too little cash (or insufficient overdraft headroom)

- Annoyance of those to whom payment is due if payments are not made on time. Could lead to reluctance to supply. Can eventually lead to liquidation.
- Inability to cope with emergencies, e.g. competitor's action, fire, strikes, bad weather.
- Opportunities missed, e.g. contracts, buying another business.
- Loss of discounts from suppliers by not having cash to pay early.
- Higher cost of borrowing because unexpected cash needs have to be met from temporary borrowing rather than drawing on cash balances.
- Credit rating might fall because of low current and acid test ratios.
- Regular payments have to be made to top up the cash balances, e.g. transaction cost of selling securities to release cash and arrangement fees for overdrafts.

versus

Costs of holding cash

- Loss of interest.*

- Loss of purchasing power – inflation erodes the value of cash.

*If an overdraft is used it is the excess cost of borrowing on overdraft as opposed to borrowing elsewhere.

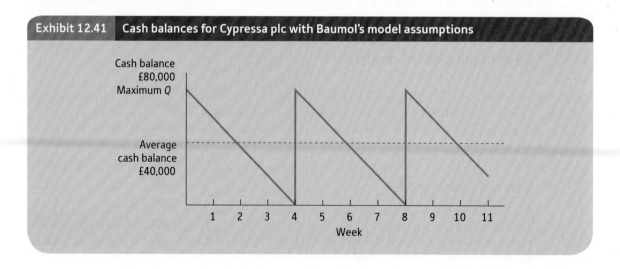

Exhibit 12.41   Cash balances for Cypressa plc with Baumol's model assumptions

Cash balance
£80,000
Maximum Q

Average
cash balance
£40,000

1   2   3   4   5   6   7   8   9   10   11

Week

In **Baumol's cash model** the average amount of cash on hand and therefore earning no interest (an opportunity cost) is half of the maximum cash balance. If we denote the maximum cash balance as Q, the average cash balance is $Q/2 = £40,000$. The firm has the task of deciding on the most appropriate level of Q. For example, instead of £80,000 it could raise the level of the maximum cash balance to £120,000, in which case the average cash balance incurring an opportunity cost of forgoing interest would be £60,000. However, this would also mean a saving on the transaction costs of arranging for a loan or selling securities because this would happen less frequently. Instead of every four weeks new finance would be drawn upon every six weeks. The forgone interest opportunity cost of having large cash holdings has to be compared with the lower transaction costs. This is shown in **Exhibit 12.42**, where, as the amount of cash held is increased, the frequency (and therefore the transaction cost) of selling securities or borrowing declines while the cost of interest forgone rises.

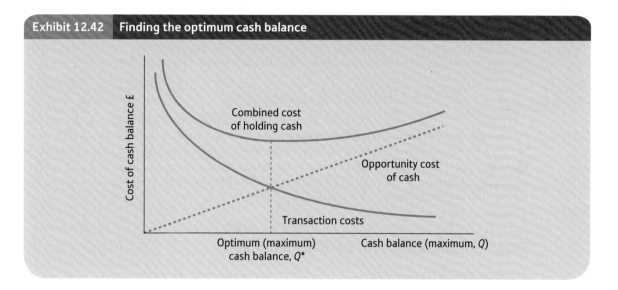

Exhibit 12.42   Finding the optimum cash balance

We have the following factors to help establish the position of Q^* mathematically:

Q = maximum cash balance
$Q/2$ = average cash balance
C = transaction costs for selling securities or arranging a loan
A = total amount of new cash needed for the period under consideration; this is usually one year
K = the holding cost of cash (the opportunity cost equal to the rate of return forgone)

The total cost line consists of the following:

$$\underset{\text{tied up}}{\text{Average amount}} \times \underset{\text{cost}}{\text{Opportunity}} + \underset{\text{transactions}}{\text{Number of}} \times \underset{\text{transaction}}{\text{Cost of each}}$$

$$\frac{Q}{2} \times K + \frac{A}{Q} \times C$$

The optimal cash balance Q^* is found as follows (the mathematics to derive this are beyond the scope of this book – the derivative of the above total cost function is set to zero):

$$Q^* = \sqrt{\frac{2CA}{K}}$$

If we assume the interest rate forgone, K, is 7% then, given that the annual need for cash is (£20,000 × 52) = £1,040,000 for Cypressa, the optimal amount to transfer into cash on each occasion is:

$$Q^* = \sqrt{\frac{2 \times £500 \times £1,040,000}{0.07}} = £121,890$$

Given the assumptions of the model Cypressa should replenish its cash balances when they reach zero to the extent of £121,890.

We can also calculate the number of times replenishment will take place each year:

$$A/Q^* = £1,040,000/£121,890 = 8.5$$

that is, between eight and nine times per year.

Larger firms often find it worthwhile to buy and sell securities to adjust cash balances almost every day of the year. Take the case of a firm with an annual turnover of £2bn which pays £600 transaction costs every time it deals in the money market to, say, purchase Treasury bills. If the annual rate of return on money market instruments is 7%, or 0.0185% per day, then the daily interest on £5.5m (approximately one day's turnover) is £1,018 and it makes sense to lend for one day as the interest received outweighs the transaction costs. Sticking strictly to Baumol's model the firm should deal in £5.86m quantities or 342 times per year – let's say, every day:

$$Q^* = \sqrt{\frac{2 \times £600 \times £2,000,000,000}{0.07}} = £5.86m$$

The basic model demonstrated here could be modified to cope with the need for a safety stock of cash to reduce the probability of cash shortages in a less than certain world. One drawback of the model is its inapplicability when finance is provided by way of an overdraft. If the drawdown of additional cash from an overdraft has no transaction cost, the whole issue boils down to ensuring that the overdraft limit is not exceeded.

Some considerations for cash management

Create a policy framework

It is advisable for frequent and routine decisions to establish a set of policies. This will enable simpler and quicker decisions to be taken at lower levels in the organisation. Such a policy framework needs to retain some flexibility so that exceptional circumstances can bring forth a more detailed consideration. The framework should also be capable of change as the environment changes.

Plan cash flows

Good cash management requires good planning. Management needs to know when cash is likely to be in surplus (so that it can be invested) and when it is necessary to borrow. Cash budgets allow for forward planning. The volume and duration of those surpluses or deficits need to be known in advance so that the best terms and the most appropriate instruments can be used. For example, if £10m is available for investment over three months perhaps a portfolio of commercial and Treasury bills will be purchased; if only £10,000 is available for seven days an interest-bearing bank account might be best. Companies that do not expect a surplus at any time in the forthcoming months but rely on an overdraft facility will still need to plan ahead to ensure that the overdraft limit is not breached. If there is to be an exceptional cash need for a few months perhaps an increased overdraft limit will have to be negotiated.

> The cash budget is an estimate of cash inflows and outflows at fixed intervals over a future period.

Cash budgets may be drawn up on a quarterly, monthly, weekly or daily basis. Generally a monthly budget for the next year plus a more detailed daily budget for the forthcoming month will be drawn up.

Exhibit 12.43 shows the sales for Cedrus plc over the next six months. Cedrus is a manufacturer of nutcrackers and so has a peak in its sales in December. One-third of sales in any month are paid for in the month of delivery, with the remainder paid one month later.

Cedrus maintains a constant level of output through the year and so builds up stocks in the autumn and early winter. During October an old machine tool will be replaced at a cost of

£100,000 payable upon installation. Also, in the November edition of a glossy food and drink magazine the range of nutcrackers will be promoted, costing the firm a further £50,000. In January £150,000 tax will be payable. At the beginning of August the cash balance will be a positive £50,000. Sales on credit outstanding at the end of July are £60,000.

| Exhibit 12.43 | Cedrus plc sales | | |

Sales £000s			
	Total	Paid for in month of delivery	Paid for 1 month later
August	90	30	60
September	90	30	60
October	120	40	80
November	150	50	100
December	600	200	400
January	60	20	40

To calculate the cash budget we can split the problem into three stages:

1 Show the inflows from sales when the cash is actually received rather than when the sale is recorded.
2 List the cash outflows in the month of occurrence.
3 Display the opening cash balance for each month less the cash surplus (or deficit) generated that month to show a closing cash balance (*see* **Exhibit 12.44**).

| Exhibit 12.44 | Cedrus plc cash budget | | | | | |

£000s	Aug	Sep	Oct	Nov	Dec	Jan
Cash inflows						
Sales (delivered and paid for in same month)	30	30	40	50	200	20
Sales (cash received from prior month's sales)	60	60	60	80	100	400
Total inflows	90	90	100	130	300	420
Cash outflows						
Payments for materials	50	50	55	55	55	55
Wages	20	20	22	25	30	22
Rent	10	10	10	10	10	10
Other expenses	10	10	11	9	10	11
New machine			100			
Advertising				50		
Tax						150
Total outflows	90	90	198	149	105	248
Balances						
Opening cash balance for month	50	50	50	(48)	(67)	128
Net cash surplus (deficit) for month (i.e. inflows minus outflows)	0	0	(98)	(19)	195	172
Closing cash balance	50	50	(48)	(67)	128	300

Cedrus is likely to need a borrowing facility to cover its cash shortfall in October and November. For the other four months the management will have to give thought to the best use of surplus cash. Perhaps some will be paid out in the form of dividends, some used to repay long-term debt and some deposited to earn interest. Having considered the projected cash flows the management might also consider ways of boosting net cash inflows by shortening the cash-conversion cycle, for example holding less stock or offering early settlement discount to customers.

Two additional points need to be made about the use of cash budgets in practice. First, the figures represent the most likely outcome and do not allow for the risk of variability from these 'best guesses'. It is more sensible to examine a range of possible outcomes to gain a realistic picture of what might happen and the range of the cash needs. The projection of sales is particularly problematic and yet it has a profound impact on the budget. Secondly, the figures shown are the cash position at the end of each month. It is possible that cash needs or surpluses are much larger than these during some parts of the month.

Control cash flows

Many large firms have operations in a number of regions in one country or in a range of countries. Unilever, for example, manufactures and sells all over the world. To operate effectively Unilever has numerous bank accounts so that some banking transactions can take place near to the point of business. Sales receipts from America will be paid into local banks there; likewise many operating expenses will be paid for with funds drawn from those same banks. The problem for Unilever is that some of those bank accounts will have high inflows and others high outflows, so interest could be payable on one while funds are lying idle or earning a low rate of return in another. Therefore, as well as taking advantage of the benefit of having local banks carry out local transactions, large firms need to set in place a co-ordinated system to ensure that funds are transferred from where there is surplus to where they are needed.

Also, many payments are made centrally, such as dividends, taxes, bond interest, major new investments, and so an efficient mechanism is needed to funnel money to the centre.

Another aspect of good cash management is to try to reduce the level of cash balances needed by ensuring that cash outflows occur at the same time as cash inflows. This is known as **cash flow synchronisation**. For example, some firms insist on customer payment at the end of the month and pay their own suppliers at the same time. The reduced cash balances mean lower bank loans and therefore higher profit.

Managers can make use of the cash budget as a control device by regularly comparing the outcome with the original plan for a period. If there is a substantial deviation then this might prompt enquiries and action to correct any problems.

Management should also consider using the delays in the cheque-clearing system rather than becoming victims of them. There is often a substantial delay between the time that a cheque is written and the time that the ultimate recipient can use the money.

For larger companies, with separate divisions, branches, offices or subsidiaries, each with their own bank accounts and cash inflows and outflows, most banks offer an automated pooling of balances into one master account. This may be done on a purely notional basis (if proper cross-guarantees and set-off agreements are in place). With notional pooling no cash is moved but interest is charged (paid) on the combined balance.

Trade debtor (trade receivables) management

Trade credit is a two-edged sword for businesses. Firms usually benefit from being granted credit by their suppliers but because of the necessity of providing credit to their customers they are burdened with additional costs. So, what considerations does the credit provider have to take into account?

The management of debtors involves a trade-off (*see* **Exhibit 12.45**). On the one hand, the more generous a company is in allowing its customers to delay payment, the greater the sales. Trade credit as well as offering cheap finance to customers, sends a signal of supplier reputation and financial health (Wilson and Summers, 2002). On the other hand, longer credit terms impose costs of financing those goods and services until they are paid for. There may also be a strain on the company's liquidity with a large proportion of the company's assets tied up in debtors. In addition there is the risk of the customer defaulting on the payment and there are also the sometimes considerable costs of administering an effective debtor management system.

Exhibit 12.45	The debtor trade-off

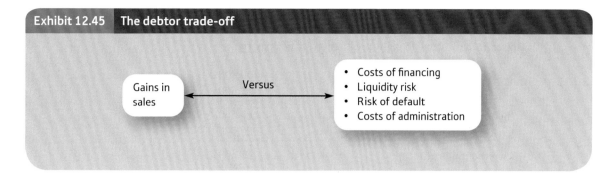

The solution to the debtor trade-off is to compare the incremental returns from a more accommodating credit stance with the incremental costs. The following points are relevant in trade credit management.

Credit (debtor) policy

The first issue in the management of trade debtors is to decide whether to grant credit at all. Credit is not inevitable; many businesses, for example service-based organisations, from hairdressers to vehicle repairers, choose not to offer any credit. If a firm decides that it is in its best interest to allow delayed payment then it needs to set up a system of rules and guidelines which will amount to a debtor policy.

Assessing credit risk

Granting credit is, in effect, the granting of a loan. It is important to assess the probability of either delayed payment or complete failure to pay. Information to make this judgement can come from a variety of sources. First, the customer's accounts could be examined. (All limited liability companies in the UK are required to submit their accounts to Companies House and these are then available for inspection by anyone.) An analysis of the accounts could give some idea of the liquidity and solvency of the customer as well as its trading performance and growth trajectory. Much of this type of public information is now held in electronic form and can be quickly accessed, for example through FAME (Financial Analysis Made Easy). If the credit provider does not wish to become involved in the detail of credit checking it could employ a credit reporting agency (such as Dun and Bradstreet) which uses accounting information combined with knowledge of the problems other companies have had with the customer and special enquiries to rate creditworthiness. In addition to trade references from existing suppliers and bank references the debtor management department could canvass the opinion and impressions of the salespeople. This can be a rich source of anecdotal evidence, as they are the individuals who are most likely to meet the customer in the work environment.

If the customer has been buying from an organisation for some time then it will have a set of records on which to base an assessment of risk. Using this information, and keeping the corporate 'eyes and ears' open in day-to-day dealings for signs of customers experiencing liquidity problems, the supplier can take risk-reducing action early. For example, if a customer has gradually increased the length of time between delivery and payment and the sales team reports that the customer's shops are looking understocked, the firm might move the customer from 30-day credit period terms to payment on delivery ('cash on delivery', COD).

Many companies allocate customers to different risk classes and treat each category differently. Some customers are allowed 60 days, while others are only permitted 10 days. Special discounts are available to some and not to others. Certain small, poorly capitalised companies present particular problems to the supplying firm as it is faced with the difficult choice of whether or not to sell. The first order from a company like this might be valued at only £1,000, the profit on which is only, say, £200. But the supplier has somehow to estimate the lost sales and profits for all future years if it refuses credit on this first purchase. These could mount up to a large present value. In addition, a lost customer will turn to a competitor firm for supplies and assist their expansion. On the other hand, there is a chance that the £1,000 will not be received or may be received months after the due date.

Once customers have been classified into risk categories it is possible to decide whether or not to trade with particular types of firms. For example, suppose that a group of customers has been assessed to have a one in eight probability of not paying:

Sales to these firms	100,000
Less bad debts (1/8 × 100,000)	−12,500
Income from sales	87,500
Costs of production, distribution, etc.	−80,000
Incremental profit	£7,500

Given the present costs of production and creditworthiness of the customers it is worthwhile selling goods on credit to these firms. However, a careful watch will have to be placed on firms of this risk class as their position can deteriorate rapidly.

Assessing credit risk is an area of management which relies less on numerical frameworks than on sound and experienced judgement. There are two rules to bear in mind:

1 *Focus effort on the most risky* Some sales are to large, safe, regular customers with a good reputation for prompt payment. Do not put large resources into monitoring these accounts. Concentrate time and effort on the problematic customers.

2 *Accept some risk: it may lead to greater profit* The minimisation of bad debt is not the key objective. Customers less than perfectly safe may have to be accepted to make sales and generate profit. For example, a relatively risky small customer may be granted credit in the hope that one day it will become large and established.

Agreeing terms

Having decided to sell on credit to a particular firm the supplier has to agree the precise details with the customer. This is going to be heavily influenced by the factors discussed earlier: industry tradition, bargaining strength, product type and credit standing. Firms usually adopt terms which require payment in a number of days from the invoice date or the delivery date (in theory these should be close together). An alternative system requires payment on or before the last day of the month following the date of invoice. Thus goods delivered on 5 August are paid for on 30 September. This approach can lead to almost two months' credit and customers quickly appreciate the advantage of making sure deliveries are made at the start of each month. Payment is usually made electronically directly to the supplier's bank account. Some smaller companies may still pay by cheque. Cheques are still widely used in US and in Germany.

Customers are generally given credit limits, that is, a maximum amount that can be outstanding at any one time. For example, suppose a customer has taken delivery of five consignments of goods over a three-week period from one supplier amounting to £20,000, which is equal to its credit limit with that supplier. That firm will be refused any more deliveries until it has paid off some of its arrears.

Goods are normally sold under a contract whereby the supplier can take repossession should the buyer fail to pay. This has the advantage that the supplier avoids becoming a lowly general creditor of the company and therefore being way down the pecking order in a liquidation. If the goods are perishable the supplier may grant only short credit terms because of the absence of good collateral.

The size of the orders may influence the terms of credit. Customers ordering small quantities are more expensive to manage than those that place large orders and therefore their credit period may be less generous.

Collecting payment

An effective administration system for debtors must be established. The firm needs clearly defined procedures and the customers need to be informed and/or warned that they are expected to conform to certain rules. Some profitable companies go bankrupt because they fail to collect the cash from customers that is vital to sustain production and satisfy their own creditors. The following list sets out some elements of a good system.

- *Be strict with the credit limit* Insist on payment for previous orders before despatching more goods if the credit limit is breached.

- *Send invoices promptly* Ensure that there is no delay between delivery of the goods and dispatch of the invoice, so that the customer is made aware of the due date for payment as early as possible.

- *Systematically review debtors* One measure useful in reviewing debtors is the debtor conversion period described earlier. Another guide to aid decision making and prompt action is the ageing schedule. The total debtor figure is broken down to show how long invoices have been outstanding.

- *Slow payers have to be chased* Any good system will call for a response immediately a debtor has failed to pay on time. This does not mean jumping to court action to recover the debt. There will be a sequence of actions before the drastic involvement of lawyers, such as gentle reminder letters followed by telephone calls and strongly worded letters.

Cash discounts are used as part of the collecting system due to the benefits they give if they stimulate early settlement. Early settlement reduces the cost of carrying the loan. Also, the longer an account remains unpaid the greater the risk of eventual default, the greater the strain on liquidity and the costs of administering the debtors' ledger. The level of discount has to be considered very carefully as the effective cost can be extremely high. Take the case of a firm that normally collects debts after 40 days which introduces a 3% discount for payment on the tenth day. If customers took advantage of this, the cost on an annual basis would be:

Discount over 30 days is: $\dfrac{3}{100 - 3}$ = 0.0309278 or 3.09% for a 30-day period

The number of 30-day periods per year is: $\dfrac{365}{30}$ = 12.167

The annual interest rate is:

$$(1.0309278)^{12.167} - 1 = 44.9\%$$

The effective cost of the discount is very large and has to be compared with the improved cash flow, lowered bad debt risk, lowered liquidity risk, administration costs and increased sales. The use of the cash discount has been further complicated by the fact that some customers abuse the system and take the discount even if they delay payment beyond the specified time.

Another way of encouraging payment at the contracted time is to make it clear that interest will be charged on overdue accounts. Suppliers are often reluctant to use this method as it has the disadvantage of creating resentment and blank refusals to pay the interest.

Firms that grant trade credit need to establish a policy on what to do when an invoice is highly unlikely to be paid, that is, it becomes a bad debt. In many cases there comes a stage when it is better to cease pursuing a debtor than to incur any more expense. The firm will need to work out a set of criteria for deciding when to write off a bad debt.

Integration with other disciplines

There can be conflict between the objectives of the sales team and the finance departments. Sales representatives find new customers and gain large orders from existing clients only to find that the finance function has vetoed the opening of a new account or is enforcing a strict credit limit. The sales personnel often spend years cultivating a relationship which can be seriously damaged by the harsh actions of the debtor collection department, ranging from unpleasant letters to court action. On the other hand, the debtor management department complain that the sales representatives offer the customer generous terms for the customer's risk class in order to meet a monthly sales target. Such conflicts need careful handling. Inter-function communication will help, as will an ethos of shareholder wealth enhancement with rewards and penalties directed at that goal in all departments.

Inventory management

The form of inventory varies from one firm to another. For a construction firm it may consist of bricks, timber and unsold houses, while for a retailer it is goods bought in for sale but as yet unsold. The quantity of inventory held is determined by factors such as the predictability of sales and production (more volatility may call for more safety stocks), the length of time it takes to produce and the nature of the product. On the last point, note that a dairy company is likely to have low stock levels relative to sales because of the danger of deterioration, whereas a jeweller will have large inventories to offer greater choice to the customer. Manufacturers with lengthy production cycles such as shipbuilders will have proportionately higher inventories than, say, a fast food chain.

Firms have the difficult task of balancing the costs of holding inventories against the costs which arise from having low inventory levels. The costs of holding inventories include the lost interest on the money tied up in stocks as well as additional storage costs (for example, rent, secure and temperature-controlled warehousing), insurance costs and the risk of obsolescence. The costs of holding low stock levels fall into two categories. First, a low stock level calls for frequent reordering. Each order involves administration costs (office employees' time, paperwork, etc.) and the physical handling of the goods (warehouse employees' time). Secondly, in a world of uncertainty there is a risk of stock-outs when production is halted for want of raw materials or WIP and/or sales are lost because of inadequate stocks of finished goods. Stock-out costs can be considerable; in the short term sales and profits fall, and in the long run customer goodwill is lost. These costs are shown in **Exhibit 12.46**.

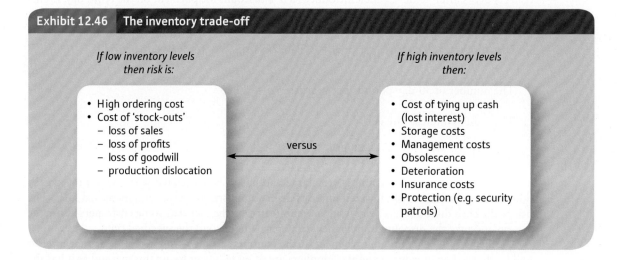

Exhibit 12.46	The inventory trade-off

If low inventory levels then risk is:

- High ordering cost
- Cost of 'stock-outs'
  - loss of sales
  - loss of profits
  - loss of goodwill
  - production dislocation

versus

If high inventory levels then:

- Cost of tying up cash (lost interest)
- Storage costs
- Management costs
- Obsolescence
- Deterioration
- Insurance costs
- Protection (e.g. security patrols)

Investment of temporary surplus funds

Most companies generate occasional cash surpluses which need to be kept within the business to be used at a later date. Action should be taken to generate a return on these funds by following the treasurer's maxim 'never let cash lie idle'. Short-term cash surpluses arise for a number of reasons and for varying periods of time. If a business is seasonal or cyclical there may be a build-up of cash in certain periods. Firms also build up cash reserves to be able to meet large outflow events such as major asset purchases, dividends, tax bills or bond redemptions. In addition, some firms may have sold an asset or raised fresh borrowing but have yet to direct that money to its final use. Alternatively, cash could be in surplus due to good control of working capital. Sometimes cash builds up because the business is highly profitable and the management choose to hold on to it. Apple, Amazon, Facebook, Google and Microsoft between them held USD330 billion of net cash at the end of 2016.

Senior management, in partnership with the treasurer, needs to consider carefully what proportion of surplus cash is permanent and therefore available for dividends or to repay debt and what proportion is really temporary.

The objective

A treasurer wants to maximise the return from temporarily surplus cash, subject to the constraints imposed by risk. One of those risk elements is the possibility of not having cash available at the right time to fund working capital – this is liquidity risk, i.e. not being able to sell the investment and raise cash quickly. There is a requirement to ensure that investments are sufficiently liquid to match anticipated cash flow needs and that there is a reserve (a safety margin) to provide a buffer against unpredictable events. Funds invested in a commercial bill may not be available for a three-month period whereas money placed in a sight bank account can be withdrawn at short notice. There is a price to pay for this degree of flexibility: keeping other factors constant, the rate of return on a more liquid financial asset is less than that on a less liquid one.

Another consideration for the treasurer is the risk of default (credit risk). This is the risk that the borrower will be unable to meet the interest and principal payments. Lending to the UK government (for example, buying Treasury bills) carries a low default risk whereas investment in shares or corporate bonds can carry significant risk of non-payment.

Another risk factor is event risk. This is the probability that some events such as a change in capital structure (leverage) of the borrower will occur which will increase the risk of default. Valuation risk (or price risk or market risk) occurs because of the possibility that when the instrument matures or is sold in the market the amount received is less than anticipated. It could be that interest rates have risen unexpectedly, which will depress bond prices, or the investing firm may have to pay a penalty for early redemption. Inflation risk is the probability of a reduction in purchasing power of a sum of money.

The treasurer has the task of balancing return and acceptable risk when investing temporarily surplus funds, as shown in **Exhibit 12.47**.

Exhibit 12.47	The short-term investment trade-off

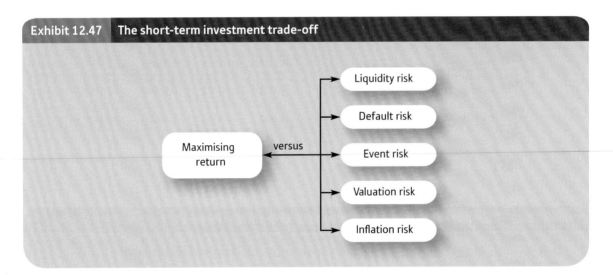

Investment policy

There are three crucial areas in which senior management need to set policy guidelines for treasurers:

1 *Defining the investable funds* How much of the firm's cash to invest is often a difficult decision. Subsidiaries require minimum working capital and so cash has to be allocated to the units by the centre. But subsidiaries often lack the specialised personnel and economies of scale to carry out effective surplus cash investment so this is best done from the centre. It is therefore necessary to have policies and mechanisms for transferring cash between the central treasury and the operating units. The centre will need to provide sufficient cash to the subsidiaries to avoid liquidity risk, that is, a shortage of cash to pay day-to-day bills. This is likely to be uppermost in the minds of subsidiary managers whereas the treasurer will want to keep a tight rein to ensure cash is not being kept idle. This tension needs clever resolution.

2 *Acceptable investment* The treasurer may be permitted to invest in a wide range of investments, from bank deposits to futures and options. Alternatively there may be limits placed on the type

of investment. For example, debt with a 'junk' rating is usually excluded as are foreign investments because of the valuation risk and the risk of exchange rates moving adversely. Investment in derivative instruments is often banned except for the purpose of hedging.

3 *Limits on holdings* Within the acceptable range of instruments it may be necessary to set maximum acceptable holdings. This may be in terms of total monetary amount or as a proportion of the total investable funds. For example, the treasurer may not be permitted to invest more than 30% of funds in Eurobonds.

Investment choice

The range of instruments open to the treasurer is large. Some idea of this can be gained by examining the money market table published daily in the *Financial Times*, one of which is reproduced in **Exhibit 12.48**. Descriptions of the instruments are given in **Exhibit 12.49**.

Exhibit 12.48

INTEREST RATES – MARKET

Jun 11 (Libor: Jun 08)	Over night	Change			One month	Three month	Six month	One year
		Day	Week	Month				
US$ Libor	1.71500	0.001	0.003	0.000	2.04617	2.32631	2.48875	2.74025
Euro Libor	−0.43943	−0.001	−0.001	0.000	−0.40086	−0.35171	−0.30457	−0.22757
£ Libor	0.47259	−0.001	−0.002	0.000	0.49769	0.62721	0.75862	0.93550
Swiss Fr Libor				0.000	−0.79355	−0.73380	−0.64540	−0.52420
Yen Libor				−0.003	−0.07616	−0.03383	0.01795	0.11250
Euro Euribor				0.000	−0.37100	−0.32100	−0.26700	−0.18000
Sterling CDs				0.000	0.50000	0.61000	0.76500	
US$ CDs				0.000	1.92000	2.26000	2.46000	
Euro CDs				0.000	−0.44500	−0.40500	−0.34500	

FT   *Financial Times*, 11 June 2018.
All Rights Reserved.

Exhibit 12.49	**Some of the investments available to a corporate treasurer**
Current account (sight deposit) at a bank	Instant withdrawal – highly liquid but low (no) interest rate.
Deposit account (time deposit) at a bank	Some notice is required to withdraw funds, low interest.
Interbank lending (a) In sterling (b) In foreign currencies	Banks and others with a very high credit rating borrow from each other at these interest rates. LIBOR is the cost of borrowing if you are a top-quality bank borrower. Lenders into the market do not need to be highly rated. Euribor is the interest rate charged to top-quality banks borrowing in euros.
Certificate of deposit (CD) (also, confusingly called 'time deposit')	A company agrees to lock away a sum (e.g. £500,000) in a bank deposit for a period of between seven days and five years (usually three or six months). The bank provides the company with a certificate of deposit stating that the bank will pay interest and the original capital to the holder. This is now a valuable instrument and the company can sell CD to release cash. The buyer of the CD will receive the deposited money on maturity plus interest. Result: the bank has money deposited for a set period and the original lender can obtain cash by selling the CD at any time.

Exhibit 12.49

Treasury bills (e.g. 'US 3m (month) Bills')	Sold by the government at a discount to face value to provide an effective yield. Tradable in the secondary market.
Bank bills (acceptance credits)	A bill accepted by a bank. The bank is committed to pay the amount on the bill at maturity. A company with surplus cash could invest in such a bill.
Local authority deposits or notes	Lending to a local authority (local government).
Money market funds	The firm invests in the money market fund which itself invests in short-term tradable paper, such as Treasury bills or bank bills. The pooling and portfolio effects mean that many market funds can offer good rates, an AAA credit rating and same-day liquidity (able to retrieve money within hours).
Gilts	Purchase of UK government bonds, usually in the secondary market.
Corporate bonds	Secondary-market purchases of bonds issued by other firms.
Eurobonds, FRNs, EMTNs	Lending on an international bond – *see* Chapter 11.
Eurocurrency	Short-term wholesale money market deposits made in a currency outside the jurisdiction of the authorities of that currency.
Commercial paper	Unsecured promissory note: usually 60 days or less to maturity – *see* Chapter 11.
Shares	*See* Chapters 9 and 10.
Derivatives (futures, swaps, options, etc.)	*See* Chapter 22

The extent of marketability (ability to sell in the secondary market) influences the return required by the investor. If you, as an investor, are unable to sell your investment before six months have passed, you are likely to insist on a higher return than if you could sell the financial security at any stage.

The treasurer has not only a range of instruments to choose from but also a range of maturities, from overnight deposits to one-year commitments. It is also necessary to consider carefully the tax implications of each investment decision as well as the foreign exchange risk if non-sterling investments are made. In addition, the treasurer has to consider the administrative complexity and specialist skills needed to understand and use some of the more exotic instruments.

Concluding comments

The modern corporation has an array of alternative sources of funds available to it. Each organisation faces different circumstances so the most appropriate mix of finance will change from one entity to another. Of the forms of finance discussed in this chapter and Chapters 10 and 11 any organisation is unlikely to select more than five or six. However, the knowledge gained by reading these chapters and considering the relative merits of each type will, it is hoped, lead to a more informed choice and contribute to the achievement of the firm's objective.

Considering the complexity of modern finance, it is not surprising that treasury management has become a profession in its own right. The efficient management of short-term assets and liabilities gives the competitive edge needed for a firm to survive and thrive. While this chapter has highlighted the core issues in treasury and working capital management, in all truth, it has only skimmed the surface. One major question left untouched is whether to centralise the treasury function. The oil group, Royal Dutch Shell, has chosen to centralise its treasury functions, so that today, despite Shell businesses operating in 145 countries, its cash and foreign exchange needs are handled by treasury operations in only three centres: London, Rio and Singapore. In 2016 they handled

12 million transactions worth over USD1 trillion in value. They use 2 primary banks and 150 non-primary banks with 2,300 accounts in total. The operating companies that make up Shell are able to use the central treasury for foreign exchange and money market deals. In this way the best rates can be achieved on the market due to economies of scale and netting (combining subsidiary balances and simply dealing with the net amounts), control over risk levels can be exercised, skills can be concentrated and advantage can be taken of the sophisticated computerised treasury management systems. The argument against centralisation is that this can be bureaucratic, inflexible and slow to respond to the immediate needs of the operating managers in far-flung places.

Another fundamental question is whether the treasury should act as a risk minimiser or a profit maximiser. Many companies make use of the derivative markets both to hedge (reduce risk) foreign exchange and interest rates, and for 'trading' purposes to try to make gains. Most firms are adamant that their treasury should not speculate. The danger with instructing the treasury to act as a profit centre is that the managers may be tempted to take excessive risks. There have been some spectacular and well-publicised losses made by members of treasury teams. The embarrassment to ostensibly staid and low-risk firms such as Procter & Gamble (US$100m + lost) can be considerable.

Key points and concepts

- **Overdraft** A permit to overdraw on an account up to a stated limit.

  Advantages: (a) flexibility; (b) cheap. Drawbacks: (a) bank has right to withdraw facility quickly; (b) security is usually required.

- **A bank usually considers the following before lending:**

  - the projected cash flows;
  - creditworthiness;
  - the amount contributed by borrower;
  - security.

- **Term loan** A loan of a fixed amount for an agreed time and on specified terms, usually one to seven years.

- **Trade credit** Goods delivered by suppliers are not paid for immediately.

- The **early settlement discount** means that taking a long time to pay is not cost free.

- **Advantages of trade credit:**

  - convenient, informal and cheap;
  - available to companies of any size.

- **Factors determining the terms of trade credit:**

  - tradition within the industry;
  - bargaining strength of the two parties;
  - product type;
  - credit standing of individual customers.

- **Factoring companies** provide at least three services:

  - providing finance on the security of trade debts;
  - sales ledger administration;
  - credit insurance.

- **Invoice discounting** is the obtaining of money on the security of book debts. Usually confidential and with recourse to the supplying firm. The supplying firm manages the sales ledger.

- **Hire purchase** is an agreement to hire goods for a specified period, with an option or an automatic right to purchase the goods at the end for a nominal or zero final payment.

  The main advantages:

  - small initial outlay;
  - certainty;
  - available when other sources of finance are not;
  - fixed-rate finance;
  - tax relief available.

- **Leasing** The legal owner of an asset gives another person or firm (the lessee) the possession of that asset to use in return for specified rental payments. Note that ownership is not transferred to the lessee.

- **An operating lease** commits the lessee to only a short-term contract, less than the useful life of the asset.

- **A finance lease** commits the lessee to a contract for the substantial part of the useful life of the asset.

  Advantages of leasing:

  - small initial outlay;
  - certainty;
  - available when other finance sources are not;
  - fixed rate of finance;
  - tax relief (operating lease: rental payments are a tax-deductible expense; finance lease: capital value can be written off over a number of years; interest is tax deductible);
  - avoid danger of obsolescence with operating lease.

- **A bill of exchange** is the acknowledgement of a debt to be paid by a customer at a specified time. The legal right to receive this debt can be sold prior to maturity, that is discounted, and thus can provide a source of finance.

- **Banker's acceptance** A financial institution or other reputable organisation accepts the promise to pay a specified sum in the future. The firm in possession of this promise can sell this right, that is discount it, to receive cash from another institution.

- **Working capital** is net current assets or net current liabilities.

- In deciding **whether to borrow long or short** a company might consider the following:

  - maturity structure of debt;
  - cost of issue or arrangement;
  - flexibility;
  - the uncertainty of getting future finance;
  - the term structure of interest rates.

- Firms often strive to **match** the maturity structure of debt with the maturity structure of assets. However, a more **aggressive financing policy** would finance permanent short-term assets with short-term finance. A more **conservative policy** would finance all assets with long-term finance.

- Firms need to consider the currency in which they borrow.

- A balance needs to be struck between fixed and floating interest-rate debt.

- Don't forget **retained earnings** as a financing option:

Advantages	Disadvantages
– No dilution of existing shareholders' returns or control – No issue costs – Managers may not have to explain use of funds (dubious advantage for shareholders)	– Limited by firm's profits – Dividend payment reduced – Subject to uncertainty – Regarded as 'free capital'

- **Treasurers** help decision making at a **strategic level**, e.g. mergers.

- **Good relationships need to be developed with the financial community.**

  This requires effort – often the treasurer makes a major contribution:

  - flow of information;
  - number of banks;
  - transaction banking versus relationship banking.

- Some of the **risks** which can **be reduced or avoided** by a firm:

  - business risk;
  - insurable risk;
  - currency risk;
  - interest-rate risk.

- The **working capital cycle** flows from raw materials, to work in progress, to finished goods stock, to sales, and collection of cash, with creditors used to reduce the cash burden.

- The **cash-conversion cycle** is the length of time between the company's outlay on inputs and the receipt of money from the sale of goods. It equals the stock-conversion period plus the debtor-conversion period minus the credit period granted by suppliers.

- **Working capital tension** Too little working capital leads to loss of production, sales and goodwill. Too much working capital leads to excessive costs of tying up funds, storage, handling and ordering costs.

- **Working capital policies:**

  - relaxed – large proportional increases in working capital as sales rise;
  - aggressive – small proportional increases in working capital as sales rise.

- **Overtrading** occurs when a business has insufficient finance for working capital to sustain its level of trading.

- The **motives for holding cash:**

  - transactional motive;
  - precautionary motive;
  - speculative motive.

- **Baumol's cash management model:**

$$Q^* = \sqrt{\frac{2CA}{K}}$$

- **Some considerations for cash management:**

  - create a policy framework;
  - plan cash flows, e.g. cash budgets;
  - control cash flows.

- **Inventory management** requires a trade-off between the costs of high inventory (interest, storage, management, obsolescence, deterioration, insurance and protection costs) against ordering costs and stock-out costs.

- **Trade debtors (receivables)** are sales made on credit as yet unpaid. The management of debtors requires a trade-off between increased sales and costs of financing, liquidity risk, default risk and administration costs.

▶

- **Debtor management** requires consideration of the following:
    - credit policy;
    - assessing credit risk;
    - agreeing terms;
    - collecting payment;
    - integration with other disciplines.

- When **investing temporary surplus cash:**
    - define the investible funds;
    - decide what are acceptable investments;
    - decide the limits on holding sizes.

References and further reading

Bank of England, www.bankofengland.co.uk.
Numerous useful publications on sources of finance for businesses, e.g. 'Trends in Lending'.

Baumol, W.J. (1952) 'The transactions demand for cash: An inventory theoretic approach', *Quarterly Journal of Economics,* November, 66(4), pp. 545–56.
Cash model is presented.

Bhalla, V.K. (2006) *Working Capital Management.* Anmol Publications Pvt.
A detailed textbook treatment.

Bhattacharya, H. (2009) *Working Capital Management: Strategies and Techniques.* 2nd edn. New Delhi PHI Learning.

Bigelli, M. and Sanchez-Vidal, J. (2012) 'Cash Holdings in Private Firms', *Journal of Banking and Finance,* 36(1), pp. 26–35.
Evidence from a wide sample of Italian private firms shows that cash holdings are significantly related with smaller size, higher risk and lower effective tax rates, therefore supporting predictions from the trade-off model.

Blokdyk, G. (2017) *Treasury management Complete Self-Assessment Guide,* 5STARCooks
This book is for managers, advisors, consultants, specialists, professionals and anyone interested in Treasury management assessment.

Bragg, S.M. (2010) *Treasury Management: The practitioner's guide.* Chichester: John Wiley and Sons.
A short introduction to treasury.

Brigham, E.F. and Ehrhardt, M.C. (2016) *Financial Management: Theory and Practice.* 15th edn. Cengage Learning.
More detailed treatment of working capital issues.

Buckley, A. (2004) *Multinational Finance.* 5th edn. Harlow: FT Prentice Hall.
Contains some easy-to-follow descriptions of types of finance available to firms.

Churchill, N.C. and Mullins J.W. (2001) 'How fast can your company afford to grow?', *Harvard Business Review,* 79(5) pp. 135–43.
An easy-to-read guide to avoid overtrading.

Eiteman, D.K., Stonehill, A.I. and Moffett, M.H. (2015) *Multinational Business Finance.* 14th edn. Pearson.
Discusses many of the additional considerations with regard to working capital, cash and treasury management faced by a multinational enterprise.

Finance and Leasing Association (FLA) Annual Report. London: FLA.
Gives some insight into HP and leasing in the UK, www.fla.org.uk.

Hofmann, E., Maucher, D., Piesker, S. and James, P. R. (2011) *Ways Out of the Working Capital Trap: Empowering Self-Financing Growth,* Springer.
Describes an iterative process to identify and strengthen a company's internal financing.

Irwin, D. and Scott, J.M. (2010) 'Barriers faced by SMEs in raising bank finance', *International Journal of Entrepreneurial Behaviour and Research,* 16, pp. 245–59.
The authors use statistical analysis to investigate barriers to raising bank finance faced by UK SMEs, specifically the impact of personal characteristics (ethnicity, gender and education).

Kelly, S. (2016) 'Making strides with the help of technology', Treasury and Risk Mangement: New York, April.
As treasurers' responsibilities grow, treasury management systems are expanding to meet their needs by enhancing features like analytics and compliance and moving into new areas like supply chain finance.

Miller, M.N. and Orr, D. (1966) 'A model of the demand for money by firms', *Quarterly Journal of Economics,* 80, August, pp. 413–35.
A more sophisticated model than Baumol's.

Tirole, J. (2006) *The Theory of Corporate Finance.* Princeton, NJ: Princeton University Press.
Includes a highly theoretical/algebraic approach to the question of whether to borrow long or short.

The Treasurer (a monthly journal). London: Euromoney. https://www.treasurers.org/thetreasurer
Up-to-date consideration of Treasurer matters.

The Treasurers Wiki, Association of Corporate Treasurers. https://wiki.treasurers.org/wiki/Main_Page

A useful reference work with articles from practitioners.

Van der Wielen, L., W. van Alphen, J. Bergen and P. Lindow (2006) 'International cash management. Riskmatrix.
A practical guide to managing cash flows, liquidity, working capital and short-term financial risks.

Westerman, W. and von Eije, H. (2005) 'Multinational cash management in Europe towards centralisation and disintermediation: the Philips case', *Management Finance*, 31(10), pp. 65–74.
An easy-to-follow description of changes in Philips' cash management across 60 currencies in recent years.

Wilson, N. and Summers, B. (2002) 'Trade credit terms offered by small firms: survey evidence and empirical analysis', *Journal of Business Finance and Accounting*, 29(3) and (4), April/May, pp. 317–51.
Useful UK survey data and discussion.

Zietlow, J.T., Hill, M. and Maness, T.S. (2016) *Short-Term Financial Management*. 5th edn. Cognella Academic Publishing.
A more detailed consideration of many of the issues discussed in this chapter.

Case study recommendations

Please see www.pearsoned.co.uk/arnold for case study synopses. Also, another list of useful case studies from the fifth edition can be found there.

- Shenzhen Jit Technology: accounts receivable management issues. Authors: Dazhi Chu; Li Wang, Ivey Publishing. Available at www.cb.hbsp.harvard.edu

- Reducing delinquent accounts receivable. Author: Jack Boepple, Kellogg School of Management. Available at www.cb.hbsp.harvard.edu

- Wng Capital LLC. Authors: Kenneth Eades; Dorothy C. Kelly; Michael Gangemi, Darden School of Business. Available at www.cb.hbsp.harvard.edu

- Coromandel: enhancement of short-term finance. Authors: Maram Srikanth; Palanisamy Saravanan; Tara Shankar Shaw, Ivey Publishing. Available at www.cb.hbsp.harvard.edu. Page 534

- LP Laboratories Ltd: financing working capital. Author: Jayadev, M., Indian Institute of Management-Bangalore. Available at www.cb.hbsp.harvard.edu

Websites

Association of Corporate Treasurers www.treasurers.org
Bank of England www.bankofengland.co.uk
Better Payments Practice Group www.payontime.co.uk
British Bankers Association www.bba.org.uk
Companies House. www.companieshouse.gov.uk
Department for Business, Innovation and Skills www.bis.gov.uk
Dun and Bradstreet www.dnb.co.uk
Federation of Small Businesses www.fsb.org.uk

Finance and Leasing Association www.fla.org.uk
Financial Times www.ft.com
International Financial Reporting Standards Board www.ifrs.org
National Statistics www.statistics.gov.uk
Treasury Management International www.treasury-management.com
UK Finance www.ukfinance.org.uk

Self-review questions

1 What are the essential differences between an overdraft and a term loan?

2 What do banks take into account when considering the granting of an overdraft or loan?

3 Describe a circumstance in which an overdraft is preferable to a term loan from the borrower's point of view.

4 'Taking a long time to pay suppliers' invoices is always a cheap form of finance.' Consider this statement.

5 What are the main determinants of the extent of trade credit granted?

6 What is hire purchase and what are the advantages of this form of finance?

7 Explain the difference between the flat rate of interest on a hire purchase agreement quoted by a sales representative and the annual percentage rate.

8 How does hire purchase differ from leasing?

9 Explain the terms 'operating lease' and 'finance lease'.

10 How can lease finance be used to create off-balance-sheet debt? How are leases accounted for today?

11 What is a bill of exchange and what does discounting a bill mean?

12 Why do firms hold cash?

13 Why do firms need to make short-term financial investments?

14 Explain what is meant by liquidity risk, event risk and valuation risk.

15 What are the strengths and weaknesses of Baumol's cash management model?

16 Describe the advantages and disadvantages of retained earnings as a source of finance.

17 What are the main considerations when deciding whether to borrow long or short?

18 What are the main areas of risk a treasurer might help to manage?

19 What are relationship banking and transactional banking?

20 Describe the working capital cycle and the cash-conversion cycle.

21 What is overtrading?

22 Why do insurance companies exist?

23 In assessing whether to grant trade credit to a customer what would you take into account and what information sources would you use?

24 Discuss the advantages and disadvantages of offering an early settlement discount on an invoice from the supplier's point of view.

25 What are the main features of a good debtor collection system?

26 What is a certificate of deposit?

27 What is a cash budget?

Questions and problems

Answers to most questions can be found at www.pearsoned.co.uk/arnold.
Answers to questions marked with an asterisk are to be found only in the Lecturer's Guide.

1 Ronsons plc, the jewellery retailer, has a highly seasonal business with peaks in revenue in December and June. One of Ronsons' banks has offered the firm a £200,000 overdraft with interest charged at 10% p.a. (APR) on the daily outstanding balance, with £3,000 payable as an arrangement fee. Another bank has offered a £200,000 loan with a

fixed interest rate of 10% p.a. (APR) and no arrangement fee. Any surplus cash can be deposited to earn 4% APR. The borrowing requirement for the forthcoming year is as follows:

Month	J	F	M	A	M	J	J	A	S	O	N	D
£000s	0	180	150	180	200	0	150	150	180	200	200	0

Which offer should the firm accept?

2 Snowhite plc has taken delivery of 50,000 units of Dwarf moulds for use in its garden ornament business. The supplier has sent an invoice which states the following:

'£50,000 is payable if the purchaser pays in 30 days. However, if payment is within 10 days, a 1% discount may be applied.'

Snowhite has an unused overdraft facility in place, on which interest is payable at 12% annual percentage rate on the daily outstanding balance. If Snowhite paid after 10 days the overdraft facility would have to be used for the entire payment.

a   Calculate whether to pay on the 30th day or on the 10th day, on the basis of the information provided.

b   Despite the 30-day credit limit on the contract Snowhite is aware that it is quite normal in this industry to pay on the 60th day without incurring a penalty legally, financially or in terms of reputation and credit standing. How does this alter your analysis?

3 (*Examination level*) Gordons plc has an annual turnover of £3m and a pre-tax profit of £400,000. It is not quoted on a stock exchange and the family owning all the shares have no intention of permitting the sale of shares to outsiders or providing more finance themselves. Like many small and medium-sized firms, Gordons has used retained earnings and a rolled-over overdraft facility to finance expansion. This is no longer seen as adequate, especially now that the bank manager is pushing the firm to move to a term loan as its main source of external finance.

You, as the recently hired finance director, have been in contact with some financial institutions. The Matey hire purchase company is willing to supply the £1m of additional equipment the firm needs. Gordons will have to pay for this over 25 months at a rate of £50,000 per month with no initial deposit.

The Helpful leasing company is willing to buy the equipment and rent it to Gordons on a finance lease stretching over the four-year useful life of the equipment, with a nominal rent thereafter. The cost of this finance is virtually identical to that for the term loan, that is, 13% annual percentage rate.

Required

Write a report for the board of directors explaining the nature of the four forms of finance which may be used to purchase the new equipment: hire purchase, leasing, bank term loan and overdraft. Point out their relative advantages and disadvantages.

4 The Biscuit company has taken delivery of £10,000 of flour from its long-established supplier. Biscuit is in the habit of paying for flour deliveries 50 days after the invoice/delivery date. However, things are different this time: the supplier has introduced an early settlement discount of 2% if the invoice is paid within 10 days. The rate of interest being charged on Biscuit's overdraft facility is 11% per annum. You may assume no tax to avoid complications.

Required

Calculate whether Biscuit should pay on the 10th day or the 50th day following the invoice date.

5* The Snack company is considering buying £30,000 of new kitchen equipment through a hire purchase agreement stretching over 18 months. £10,000 is paid as a deposit and the hire purchase company will require 18 monthly payments of £1,222.22 each to pay for the £20,000 borrowed, before the ownership of the equipment is transferred to the snack company. The rate of interest the Snack company would pay on an overdraft is 10% per annum.

Required

a   Calculate the annual percentage rate paid on the hire purchase contract.

b   Discuss the relative merits and drawbacks of the two forms of finance mentioned in the question.

6 The Cable Company sells its goods on six months' credit which until now it has financed through term loans and overdrafts. Recently factoring firms have been pestering the managing director, saying that they can offer him immediate cash and the chance to get rid of the hassle of collecting debts. He is very unsure of factoring and has requested a report from you outlining the main features and pointing out the advantages and hazards. Write this report.

7 A small firm is considering the purchase of a photocopier. This will cost £2,000. An alternative to purchase is to enter into a leasing agreement known as an operating lease, in which the agreement can be terminated with only one month's notice. This will cost £60 per month. The firm is charged interest of 12% on its overdraft.

Required

Consider the advantages and disadvantages of each method of obtaining the use of a photocopier.

8 Write an essay with the title: 'Small firms find it more difficult to raise finance than larger firms'.

9 (*Examination level*) A factoring company has offered a one-year agreement with Glub Ltd to both manage its debtors and advance 80% of the value of all its invoices immediately a sale is invoiced. Existing invoices will be eligible for an immediate 80% cash payment.

The annual sales on credit of Glub are £6m spread evenly through the year, and the average delay in payment from the invoice date is at present 80 days. The factoring company is confident of reducing this delay to only 60 days and will pay the remaining 20% of invoice value to Glub immediately on receipt from the customer.

The charge for debtor management will be 1.7% of annual credit turnover payable at the year end. For the advance payment on the invoices a commission of 1% will be charged plus interest applied at 10% per annum on the gross funds advanced.

Glub will be able to save £80,000 during this year in administration costs if the factoring company takes on the debtor management. At the moment it finances its trade credit through an overdraft facility with an interest rate of 11%.

Required

Advise Glub on whether to enter into the agreement. Discuss the relative advantages and disadvantages of overdraft, factoring and term loan financing.   **?**

10 Acorn presently sells on 60 days' credit. Is it financially attractive for a customer to accept a 1.5% discount for payment on the 14th day, given an annual percentage rate of interest of 9%, or continue to take 60 days with no discount?   **?**

11 (*Examination level*) Extracted data from Penguin plc's last accounts are as follows:

	£m
Annual sales	21
Profits before interest and tax	2
Interest	0.5
Shareholder funds	5
Long-term debt	4
Debtors	2.5
Stocks	2
Trade creditors	5
Bank overdraft	4

A major supplier to Penguin offers a discount of 2% on all future supplies if payment is made on the seventh day following delivery rather than the present 70th day. Monthly purchases from this supplier amount to a regular £0.8m. Penguin pays 15% annual percentage rate on its overdraft.

Required

a   Consider what Penguin should do with respect to this supplier.
b   Suggest steps that Penguin could take to improve the balance sheet, profit and loss and cash flow position.

12* (*Examination level*) Oxford Blues plc has standard trade terms requiring its customers to pay after 30 days. The average invoice is actually paid after 90 days. A junior executive has suggested that a 2.5% discount for payment on the 20th day following the invoice date be offered to customers.

It is estimated that 60% of customers will accept this and pay on the 20th day, but 40% will continue to pay, on average, on the 90th day.

Sales are £10m per annum and bad debts are 1% of sales.

The company's overdraft facility costs 14% per annum.

The reduced collection effort will save £50,000 per annum on administration and bad debts will fall to 0.7% of turnover.

Required

a   Should the new credit terms be offered to customers?

b   What are the main considerations you would give thought to in setting up a good credit management system?

13   Tollhouse plc has a large overdraft which is expected to continue. Its annual sales are £10m, spread evenly through the year – the same amount in each week. The interest rate on the overdraft is 11%. The present policy is to pay into the bank the weekly receipts from customers each Friday. However, a new director has raised the question of whether it would be better to pay in on Mondays as well as Fridays especially in the light of the fact that Monday mornings' receipts are three times the level of those of the other days of the working week. No cash is received on Saturdays or Sundays. It costs £35 each time money is paid into the bank account and all daily cash inflows arrive before the regular paying-in time of 3 p.m. Ignore taxation and consider which of the following four policies is the best for Tollhouse:

a   Continue to pay in on Fridays.

b   Pay in on Mondays and Fridays.

c   Pay in every day of the week.

d   Pay in on Mondays and another selected day.

14   As the treasurer of Stokes plc you have been asked to write a report putting forward ideas for the use of temporarily surplus cash. These funds will be available for varying periods – from one week to four months. Describe the main considerations or trade-offs for short-term cash management. Choose any four of the potential investment instruments, describe them and outline their advantages and disadvantages.

15*   Rounded plc, a new retail business, has projected sales as follows:

	£m		£m		£m
Jan.	1.3	May	2.0	Sept.	2.0
Feb.	1.5	June	2.2	Oct.	1.8
March	1.6	July	2.3	Nov.	1.9
April	1.5	Aug.	2.0	Dec.	3.0

One-third of sales are for cash, one-third is received one month after the sale, and one-third is received two months after the sale. The cash balance at the beginning of January is £500,000.

A major investment in new shops will cost £2m in cash in May. Stock (items purchased for sale and sold) costs one-half of sales and is purchased and paid for in the same month it is sold.

Labour and other costs amount to £300,000 per month, paid for as incurred. Assume no tax is payable in this year.

Required

a   Show the monthly cash balance for the first year.

b   Recommend action to be taken based on these cash balances.

16*   Numerical example of treasury investment:

As the treasurer of a firm you anticipate the following cash position which will require either short-term borrowing or investment:

Cash flow forecast for an 11-day period		
Opening balance	£11,000,000	
Day	Net cash flow	Cumulative
1.3.x1	−5,000,000	6,000,000
2.3.x1	−5,000,000	1,000,000
3.3.x1	−6,000,000	−5,000,000
4.3.x1	0	−5,000,000
5.3.x1	+20,000,000	+15,000,000
6.3.x1	−3,000,000	+12,000,000
7.3.x1	−2,000,000	+10,000,000
8.3.x1	+1,000,000	+11,000,000
9.3.x1	0	+11,000,000
10.3.x1	−500,000	+10,500,000
11.3.x1	+2,000,000	+12,500,000

	Borrowing rate	Lending rate
Interbank overnight	5.75%	5.5%
Interbank seven-day	5.88%	5.67%
Time deposit (seven-day)		5%
Sight deposit at bank		4%
Borrowing on overdraft	7%	

Describe how you would manage the firm's money over this 11-day period.
What are the risks inherent in your plan of action?

17 (*Examination level*) You have been asked to prepare a cash budget for Whitborrow plc for the next three months, October, November and December. The managers are concerned that they may not have sufficient cash to pay for a £150,000 investment in equipment in December. The overdraft has reached its limit of £70,000 at the present time – the end of September. Sales during September were a total of £400,000, of which £55,000 was received in cash, £165,000 is expected to be paid in October, with the remainder likely to flow in during November. Sales for the next three months are expected to be:

	Total sales	Cash sales	Credit sales
October	450,000	90,000	360,000
November	550,000	110,000	440,000
December	700,000	140,000	560,000

There is a gross profit margin of 40% on sales. All costs (materials, labour and other) are paid for on receipt. Only 20% of customer sales are expected to be paid for in the month of delivery. A further 70% will be paid after one month and the remainder after two months. Labour and other costs amount to 10% of sales. Debtor levels at the end of September are £400,000 and the investment in stock is £350,000.

Required

a Prepare a cash budget for October, November and December, and state if the firm will be able to purchase the new equipment.

b Recommend action that could be taken to improve the working capital position of Whitborrow.

18* Silk plc invests surplus cash in a range of money-market securities which earn a rate of return of 8% per annum. It tries to hold the smallest cash balances possible while permitting the business to operate. For the next year there will be a need for cash taken from near-cash investments (money market investments) of £40,000 per week. There is a fixed cost of liquidating these securities of £200 regardless of amount (a combination of broker's fees and administration costs). Should Silk draw on these funds every week or at some other interval? Calculate the optimum level of cash balance. **?**

19   It costs £20 in administration expenses and fees every time Davy Ltd pays funds into the bank to reduce its large overdraft on which it is charged 10% annual percentage rate (APR). The company receives net cash from operations of £10,000 per week. How often should Davy pay into the bank? **?**

20   'I run this business the way I want to. Shareholders and bankers are told once a year how we performed but I will not give them details or meet regularly with them. We have a business to run. Bankers should be treated like any supplier – make them compete to provide the lowest cost service and put everything out to tender and let them bid for each scrap of work.'

Consider this statement by a finance director and relate it to the efforts many treasurers and finance directors make in their relationships with finance providers.

21   (*Examination level*) Reraser plc has grown fast and has recently appointed you as its corporate treasurer. You have been asked by the board to write a report pointing out the ways in which the treasurer's department can help the firm to manage its various risks. Write this report.

22   Explain why firms sometimes have temporarily surplus funds. What considerations are relevant when choosing the type of financial instrument to be purchased with these funds?

23   (*Examination level*) 'The treasurer sits up there in his office, earning a salary three times my level, playing with his computer all day. At least I produce something useful for the firm' – a statement by a shopfloor worker.

Try to persuade this worker that the treasurer contributes to the well-being of the firm by illustrating the activities a typical treasurer might undertake (you do not have to justify the relative salary levels).

24   Describe the motives for holding cash. Why is it useful for a firm to draw up cash budgets?

25   (*Examination level*) Describe the cash conversion cycle and suggest ways of making it smaller.

26   'How can we go bankrupt if we have a full order book and sales rising by 100% per year. Don't be ridiculous.' Explain to this incredulous managing director the problem of overtrading and possible solutions to it.

27   Explain the tension managers have to cope with when judging the correct level of working capital. Also describe the alternative approaches to funding business growth.

28   What are the costs of holding too little or too much cash? Describe what is meant by a policy framework for cash management, planning of cash flow and control of cash flow.

29   Companies go bankrupt if they get working capital management badly wrong. Describe two ways in which this might happen.

30* Rubel plc has the following figures:

	£000s	
	20X1	20X2
Year end figures		
Finished goods inventory	50	55
Work-in-progress inventory	40	38
Raw material inventory	100	110
Debtors	300	250
Creditors	150	160
During the year		
Sales (per annum)	1,000	1,200
Cost of goods sold (per annum)	600	650
Raw material purchases and usage (per annum)	500	550

Calculate the cash-conversion cycle during 20X2. **?**

31* (*Examination level*) Sheetly plc has an overdraft of £500,000 which the directors are alarmed about. Their concern is further aroused by the fact that in July a tax demand for £200,000 will be payable. Also the company expects to pay for replacement vehicles at a cost of £150,000 in August. The present time is the beginning of May and the figures in the table are projected for the next six months.

	May £000	June £000	July £000	Aug £000	Sept £000	Oct £000
Anticipated sales	1,100	1,150	900	800	1,300	1,200
Purchases (materials)	800	810	660	600	950	850
Labour	100	110	90	90	110	100
Rent	50	50	50	50	50	50
Other costs	40	50	60	45	50	60

For each month's sales 30% of the cash is received in the month of sale, 40% is received one month later, with the remainder coming in two months after sale. Debtors at the beginning of May are £200,000 and it is expected that of this, £120,000 will be received in May and £80,000 in June.

Suppliers of materials grant one month's credit and at the beginning of May these suppliers were owed £820,000. All other costs are paid for as incurred.

Required

a   Draw up a cash flow forecast for the next six months showing the monthly overdraft if Sheetly continues to rely on this source of finance.

b   Suggest ways in which working capital management policy could be altered to reduce the cash flow strain over the forthcoming months.

c   Consider the following alternatives to the overdraft and describe their advantages vis-à-vis the overdraft:

   – factoring;
   – hire purchase;
   – leasing.

?

Assignments

1   Consider some of the items of equipment that your firm uses and investigate the possibility of alternative methods of financing/obtaining the use of those assets. Write a report outlining the options with their advantages and disadvantages, fully costed (if possible) and make recommendations.

2   Investigate the debtor management policy of a firm with which you are familiar. Write a report contrasting current practice with what you consider to be best practice. Recommend action.

3   If a firm familiar to you is at present heavily reliant on bank finance, consider the relative merits of shifting the current balance from overdraft to term loans. Also consider the greater use of alternative forms of short-term or medium-term finance.

4   Obtain a representative sample of recently paid invoices. Examine the terms and conditions, calculate the benefit of paying early and recommend changes in policy if this seems appropriate.

5   Consider the working capital cycle of a firm you know well. Try to estimate the length of time money is tied up in each stage. Suggest ways of improving the efficiency of working capital management.

6   If your firm does not yet have a designated treasurer write a report pointing out the value of such a role and recommend whether such an appointment should be made or other, less specialised managers should continue to carry out treasury-type functions.

7   Examine the annual reports of six large quoted UK firms and note the role of the treasury by reading the text and between the lines

Stock market efficiency

LEARNING OUTCOMES

By the end of this chapter the reader should be able to:

■ discuss the meaning of the random walk hypothesis and provide a balanced judgement of the usefulness of past price movements to predict future share prices (weak-form efficiency);

■ provide an overview of the evidence for the stock market's ability to take account of all publicly available information including past price movements (semi-strong efficiency);

■ state whether stock markets appear to absorb all relevant (public or private) information (strong-form efficiency);

■ outline some of the behavioural-based arguments leading to a belief in inefficiencies;

■ comment on the implications of the evidence for efficiency for investors and corporate management.

Introduction

The question of whether the stock market is efficient in pricing shares and other securities has fascinated academics, investors and business executives for a long time. This is hardly surprising: even academics are attracted by the thought that by studying in this area they might be able to discover a stock market inefficiency which is sufficiently exploitable to make them very rich, or at least, to make their name in the academic community. In an efficient market systematic undervaluing or overvaluing of shares does not occur, and therefore it is not possible to develop trading rules which will 'beat the market' by, say, buying identifiable underpriced shares, except by chance. However, if the market is inefficient it regularly prices shares incorrectly, allowing a perceptive investor to identify profitable trading opportunities.[1] This is an area of research where millions have been spent trying to find 'nuggets of gold' in the price movements of securities. A small amount of this money has been allocated to university departments, with the vast majority being spent by major securities houses around the world and by people buying investment advice from professional analysts offering to 'pick winners'. Money has also been taken from the computer literati paying for real-time stock market prices and analytical software to be piped into their personal computer, and by the millions of buyers of books which promise riches beyond imagining if the reader follows a few simple stock market trading rules.

They do say that a fool and his money are soon parted – never was this so true as in the world of stock market investment with its fringe of charlatans selling investment potions to cure all financial worries. This chapter may help the reader to discern what investment advice is, and is not, worth paying for. But this is too limited an ambition; the reader should also appreciate the significance of the discovery that for most of the people and for most of the time the stock market in an unbiased way prices shares given the information available (and it is difficult to make more than normal returns). There are profound implications for business leaders and their interaction with the share markets, for professional fund managers, and for small investors.

What is meant by efficiency?

In an efficient capital market, security (for example shares) prices rationally reflect available information.

The efficient market hypothesis (EMH) implies that, if new information is revealed about a firm, it will be incorporated into the share price rapidly and rationally, with respect to the direction of the share price movement and the size of that movement. In an efficient market no trader will be presented with an opportunity for making a return on a share (or other security) that is greater than a fair return for the risk associated with that share, except by chance. The absence of abnormal profit possibilities arises because current and past information is immediately reflected in current prices. It is only new information that causes prices to change. News is by definition unforecastable and therefore future price changes are unforecastable. Stock market efficiency does not mean that investors have perfect powers of prediction; all it means is that the current share price level is an unbiased estimate of its true economic value based on the information revealed.

Market efficiency does not mean that share prices are equal to true value at every point in time. It means that the errors that are made in pricing shares are unbiased; price deviations from true value are random. Fifty per cent of efficiently priced shares turn out to perform better than the market as a whole and 50% perform worse; the efficient price is unbiased in the statistical sense. So if Marks & Spencer's shares are currently priced at £7 it could be, over the next five years, that we discover they were grossly overpriced at £7, or that events show them to be underpriced at £7.

---

1 Even though this discussion of the efficient markets hypothesis is set within the context of the equity markets in this chapter, it must be noted that the efficient pricing of financial and real assets is discussed in many contexts: from whether currencies are efficiently priced vis-à-vis each other to the pricing of commodities, bonds, property and derivative instruments.

Efficiency merely means that there is an equal chance of our being too pessimistic at £7 as being too optimistic. The same logic applies to shares on high or low price-earnings ratios (PERs). That is, shares with low PERs should be no more likely to be overvalued or undervalued than shares with high PERs. Both groups have an equal chance of being wrongly priced given future economic events on both the upside and the downside.

In the major stock markets of the world prices are set by the forces of supply and demand. There are hundreds of analysts and thousands of traders, each receiving new information on a company through electronic and paper media. This may, for example, concern a technological breakthrough, a marketing success or a labour dispute. The individuals who follow the market are interested in making money and it seems reasonable to suppose that they will try to exploit quickly any potentially profitable opportunity. In an efficient market the moment an unexpected, positive piece of information leaks out investors will act and prices will rise rapidly to a level which gives no opportunity to make further profit.

Imagine that BMW announces to the market that it has a prototype electric car which will cost £10,000, has the performance of a petrol-driven car and will run for 500 miles before needing a low-cost recharge. This is something motorists and environmentalists have been demanding for many years. The profit motivated investor will try to assess the value of a share in BMW to see if it is currently underpriced given the new information. The probability that BMW will be able successfully to turn a prototype into a mass market production model will come into the equation. Also the potential reaction of competitors, the state of overall car market demand and a host of other factors have to be weighed to judge the potential of the electric car and the future returns on a BMW share. No analyst or shareholder is able to anticipate perfectly the commercial viability of BMW's technological breakthrough but they are required to think in terms of probabilities and attempt to make a judgement.

If one assumes that the announcement is made on Monday at 10 a.m. and the overwhelming weight of investor opinion is that the electric car will greatly improve BMW's share returns, in an efficient market the share price will move to a higher level within seconds. The new higher price at 10.01 a.m. is efficient but incorporates a different set of information to that incorporated in the price prevailing at 10 a.m. Investors should not be able to buy BMW shares at 10.01 a.m. and make abnormal profits except by chance.

Most investors are too late

Efficiency requires that new information is rapidly assimilated into share prices. In the sophisticated financial markets of today the speedy dissemination of data and information by cheap electronic communication means that there are large numbers of informed investors and advisers. These individuals are often highly intelligent and capable of fast analysis and quick action, and therefore there is reason to believe many stock markets are efficient at pricing securities. However, this belief is far from universal. Thousands of highly paid analysts and advisers maintain that they can analyse better and act more quickly than the rest of the pack and so make abnormally high returns for their clients. There is a well-known story which is used to mock the efficient market theoreticians:

A lecturer was walking along a busy corridor with a student on his way to lecture on the efficient market hypothesis. The student noticed a £20 note lying on the floor and stooped to pick it up. The lecturer stopped him, saying, 'If it was really there, someone would have picked it up by now'.

With such reasoning the arch-advocates of the EMH dismiss any trading system which an investor may believe he has discovered to pick winning shares. If this system truly worked, they say, someone would have exploited it before and the price would have already moved to its efficient level.

This position is opposed by professional analysts: giving investment advice and managing collective funds is a multi-billion pound industry and those employed in it do not like being told that most of them do not beat the market. However, a *few* stock pickers do seem to perform extraordinarily well on a consistent basis over a long period of time. There is strong anecdotal evidence that some people are able to exploit inefficiencies – we will examine some performance records later.

What efficiency does not mean

To provide more clarity on what efficiency is, we need to deal with a few misunderstandings held by people with a little knowledge (a dangerous thing):

● **Efficiency means that prices do not depart from true economic value** This is false. At any one time we would expect most shares to deviate from true value, largely because value depends on the future, which is very uncertain (*see* Chapter 17 on share valuation). However, under the EMH we would expect the deviations to be random.

● **You will not come across an investor beating the market in any single time period** This is false because you would expect, in an efficient market, that approximately one-half of shares bought subsequently outperform. So, many investors, unless they buy such a broad range of shares that their portfolio tracks the market, would outperform. Note that, under the EMH, this is not due to skill, but simply caused by the randomness of price deviations from true economic value.

● **No investor following a particular investment strategy will beat the market in the long term** This is false simply because there are millions of investors. In a completely efficient market, with prices deviating in a random fashion from true value, it is likely that you could find a few investors who have outperformed the market over many years. This can happen because of the laws of probability; even if the probability of your investment approach beating the market is very small, the fact that there are millions of investors means that, purely by chance, a few will beat the market. Unfortunately, it is very difficult to investigate whether a long-term outperformance is luck or evidence against the EMH. We look at the performance of someone who has consistently outperformed for more than 60 years, Warren Buffett, later in the chapter. Some people believe his success is due to luck in an efficient market; others put it down to superior share-picking ability – you will have to make up your own mind.

Types of efficiency

Efficiency is an ambiguous word and we need to establish some clarity before we go on. There are three types of efficiency:

1 *Operational efficiency* This refers to the cost, speed and reliability of transactions in securities on the exchange. It is desirable that the market carries out its operations at as low a cost as possible, speedily and reliably. This may be promoted by creating as much competition between market makers and brokers as possible so that they earn only normal profits and not excessively high profits. It may also be enhanced by competition between exchanges for secondary-market transactions.

2 *Allocational efficiency* Society has a scarcity of resources (that is, they are not infinite) and it is important that we find mechanisms which allocate those resources to where they can be most productive. Those industrial and commercial firms with the greatest potential to use investment funds effectively need a method to channel funds their way. Stock markets help in the process of allocating society's resources between competing real investments. For example, an efficient market provides vast funds for the growth of the electronics, pharmaceuticals and biotechnology industries (through new issues, rights issues, etc.) but allocates only small amounts for slow-growth industries.

3 *Pricing efficiency* It is pricing efficiency that is the focus of this chapter, and the term 'efficient market hypothesis' applies to this form of efficiency only. In a pricing-efficient market the investor can expect to earn merely a risk-adjusted return from an investment as prices move instantaneously and in an unbiased manner to any news.

The black line in **Exhibit 13.1** shows an efficient market response to BMW's (fictional) announcement of an electric car. The share price instantaneously adjusts to the new level. However, there are four other possibilities if we relax the efficiency assumption. First, the market could take a long time to absorb this information (under-reaction) and it could be only after the tenth day that the share price approaches the new efficient level. This is shown in Line 1. Secondly, the market could anticipate the news announcement – perhaps there have been leaks to the press, or senior BMW management has been dropping hints to analysts for the past two weeks. In this case the share price starts to rise before the announcement (Line 2). It is only the unexpected element of the announcement that causes the price to rise further on the announcement day (from point A to point B). A third possibility is that the market overreacts to the new information (Line 3); the 'bubble' deflates over the next few days. Finally, the market may fail to get the pricing right at all and the shares may continue to be underpriced for a considerable period (Line 4).

Exhibit 13.1	New information (an electric car announcement by BMW) and alternative stock market reactions – efficient and inefficient

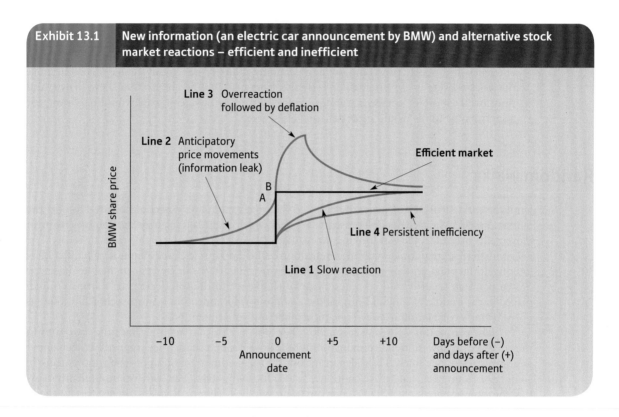

The value of an efficient market

It is important that share markets are efficient for at least three reasons.

1   *To encourage share buying* Accurate pricing is required if individuals are going to be encouraged to invest in private enterprise. If shares are incorrectly priced many savers will refuse to invest because of a fear that when they come to sell the price may be perverse and may not represent the fundamental attractions of the firm. This will seriously reduce the availability of funds to companies and inhibit growth. Investors need to know they are paying a fair price and that they will be able to sell at a fair price – that the market is a 'fair game'.

2   *To give correct signals to company managers* In Chapter 1 it was stated, for the purposes of this book, that the objective of the firm was the maximisation of shareholder wealth. This can be represented by the share price in an efficient market. Sound financial decision making therefore relies on the correct pricing of the company's shares. In implementing a shareholder wealth-enhancing decision the manager will need to be assured that the implication of the decision is accurately signalled to shareholders and to management through a rise in the share price. It is important that managers receive feedback on their decisions from the share market so that they are encouraged to pursue shareholder wealth strategies. If the share market continually gets the pricing wrong, even the most shareholder-orientated manager will find it difficult to know just what is required to raise the wealth of the owners.

In addition share prices signal the rate of return investors demand on securities of a particular risk class. If the market is inefficient the risk–return relationship will be unreliable.

Managers need to know the rate of return they are expected to obtain on projects they undertake. If shares are wrongly priced there is a likelihood that in some cases projects will be erroneously rejected because an excessively high cost of capital (discount rate) is used in project appraisal. In other circumstances, if the share prices are higher than they should be the cost of capital signalled will be lower than it should be and projects will be accepted when they should have been rejected.

Correct pricing is not just a function of the quality of the analysis and speed of reaction of the investment community. There is also an onus placed on managers to disclose information. Shares can only be priced efficiently if all relevant information has been communicated to the market. Managers neglect this issue at their peril.

3 *To help allocate resources* Allocational efficiency requires both operating efficiency and pricing efficiency. If a poorly run company in a declining industry has highly valued shares because the stock market is not pricing correctly then this firm will be able to issue new shares, and thus attract more of society's savings for use within its business. This would be wrong for society as the funds would be better used elsewhere.

Random walks

Until the early 1950s it was generally believed that investment analysis could be used to beat the market. In 1953 Maurice Kendall presented a paper which examined security and commodity price movements over time. He was looking for regular price cycles, but was unable to identify any. The prices of shares, etc. moved in a random fashion – one day's price change cannot be predicted by looking at the previous day's price change. There are no patterns or trends. An analogy has been drawn between security and commodity price changes and the wanderings of a drunken man placed in the middle of a field. Both follow a random walk, or to put it more technically, there is no systematic correlation between one movement and subsequent ones.

To many people this is just unacceptable. They look at a price chart of a share and see patterns; they may see an upward trend running for months or years, or a share price trapped between upper and lower resistance lines. They also point out that sometimes you get persistent movements in shares; for example a share price continues to rise for many days. The statisticians patiently reply that the same apparent pattern or trends can occur purely by chance. Readers can test this for themselves: try tossing a coin several times and recording the result. You will probably discover that there will be periods when you get a string of heads in a row. The apparent patterns in stock market prices are said to be no more significant for predicting the next price movement than the pattern of heads or tails is for predicting what the next toss will produce. That is, they both follow a random walk.

To reinforce this look at **Exhibit 13.2**, which shows two sets of price movements. Many chartists (those who believe future prices can be predicted from past changes) would examine these and say that both display distinct patterns which may enable predictions of future price movements. One of the charts follows the FTSE 100 index each week over a two-year period. The other was generated by the writer's six-year-old son.[2] He was given a coin and asked to toss it 110 times. Starting at a value of 100, if the first toss was a head the 'weekly return' was 4%, if a tail it was –3%. Therefore the 'index' for this imaginary share portfolio has a 50 : 50 chance of ending the first week at either 104 or 97. These rules were applied for each of the imaginary 110 weeks. This chart has a positive drift of 1% per week to imitate the tendency for share indices to rise over time. However, the price movements within that upward drift are random because successive movements are independent.

Dozens of researchers have tested security price data for dependence. They generally calculate correlation coefficients for consecutive share price changes or relationships between share prices at intervals. The results show a serial correlation of very close to zero – sufficiently close to prevent reliable and profitable forecasts being made from past movements.

---

2 He's grown a bit – 16 years later he co-founded Office Pantry, a trendy and very successful supplier of fruit and snacks to offices around the UK.

Exhibit 13.2 Charts showing the movements on the FT 100 share index and a randomly generated index of prices. Which is which?

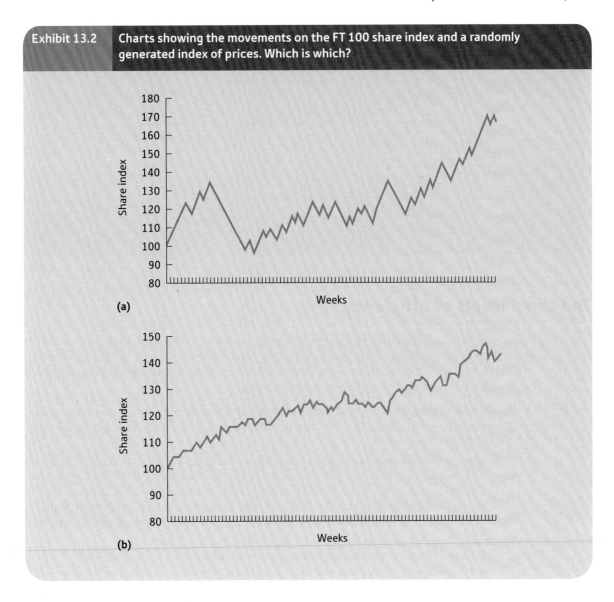

(a)

(b)

Why does the random walk occur?

A random walk occurs because the share price at any one time reflects all available information and it will only change if new information arises. Successive price changes will be independent and prices follow a random walk because the next piece of news (by definition) will be independent of the last piece of news. Shareholders are never sure whether the next item of relevant information is going to be good or bad – as with the heads and tails on a coin there is no relationship between one outcome and the next. Also, there are so many informed market traders that as soon as news is released the share price moves to its new rational and unbiased level.

We can see how an efficient market will not permit abnormal profits by examining **Exhibit 13.3**. Here a chartist at time A has identified a cyclical pattern. The chartist expects that over the next six months the share price will rise along the dotted line and is therefore a 'buy'. However, this chartist is not the only participant in the market and as soon as a pattern is observed it disappears. This happens because investors rush to exploit this 'marvelous' profit opportunity. As a result of the extraordinary buying pressure the price immediately rises to a level which gives only the normal rate of return. The moment a pattern becomes discernible in the market it disappears under the weight of buy or sell orders.

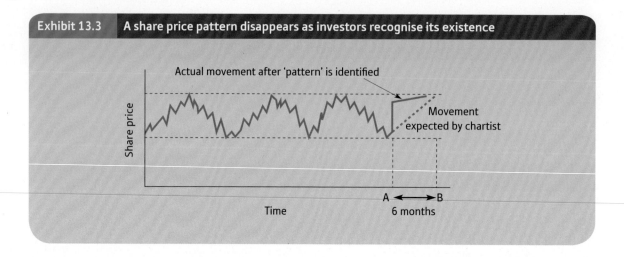

Exhibit 13.3   A share price pattern disappears as investors recognise its existence

The three levels of efficiency

Economists have defined different levels of efficiency according to the type of information which is reflected in prices. Fama (1970) produced a three-level grading system to define the extent to which markets were efficient.[3] These were based on different types of investment approaches which were supposedly designed to produce abnormal returns.

1 *Weak-form efficiency* Share prices fully reflect all information contained in past price movements. It is pointless basing trading rules on share price history as the future cannot be predicted in this way.

2 *Semi-strong form efficiency* Share prices fully reflect all the relevant publicly available information. This includes not only past price movements but also earnings and dividend announcements, rights issues, technological breakthroughs, resignations of directors, and so on. The semi-strong form of efficiency implies that there is no advantage in analysing publicly available information after it has been released, because the market has already absorbed it into the price.

3 *Strong-form efficiency* All relevant information, including that which is privately held, is reflected in the share price. Here the focus is on insider dealing, in which a few privileged individuals (for example directors) are able to trade in shares, as they know more than the normal investor in the market. In a strong-form efficient market even insiders are unable to make abnormal profits – as we shall see the market is acknowledged as being inefficient at this level of definition.

Weak-form tests

If weak-form efficiency is true a naive purchase of a large, broadly based portfolio of shares typically produces returns the same as those purchased by a 'technical analyst' poring over historical share price data and selecting shares on the basis of trading patterns and trends. There will be no mechanical trading rules based on past movements which will generate profits in excess of the average market return (except by chance).

Consider some of the following techniques used by technical analysts (or chartists) to identify patterns in share prices.

---

3 Fama (1991) slightly changed the definitions later but the original versions have the virtues of elegance and simplicity.

A simple price chart

A true chartist is not interested in estimating the intrinsic value of shares. A chartist believes that a chart of the price (and/or volume of trading data) is all that is needed to forecast future price movements. Fundamental information, such as the profit figures or macroeconomic conditions, is merely a distraction from analysing the message in the chart. One of the early chartists, John Magee, was so extreme in trying to exclude any other influences on his 'buy' or 'sell' recommendations that he worked in an office boarded up so that he was not aware of the weather. **Exhibit 13.4** shows one of the best known patterns to which chartists respond – it is called a head and shoulders formation.

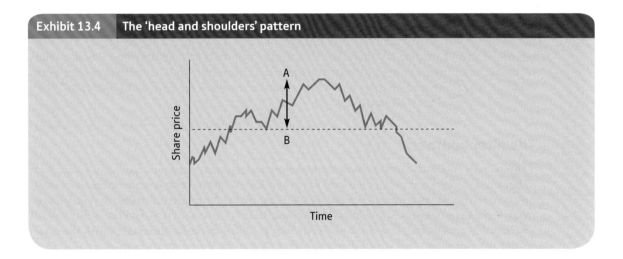

Exhibit 13.4   The 'head and shoulders' pattern

A head and shoulders pattern like the one shown in Exhibit 13.4 is supposed to herald the start of a major price drop. The left shoulder is formed, according to the chartists, by some investors taking profits after a large price rise, causing a minor price drop. The small fall encourages new buyers, hoping for a continuation of the price rally. They keep pushing the shares above the previous high, but prices soon drift down again, often to virtually the same level at which the left shoulder's decline ended. It drops to a support level called the neckline. Finally the right shoulder is formed by another wave of buying (on low volume). This peters out, and when the prices fall below the neckline by, say, 3%, it is time to sell. Some chartists even go so far as to say that they can predict the extent of the fall below the neckline – this is in proportion to the distance AB.

Exhibit 13.5 provides another chart with a pattern, where the share price trades between two trend lines until it achieves 'breakout' through the 'resistance line'. This is a powerful 'bull signal' – that is, the price is expected to rise significantly thereafter.

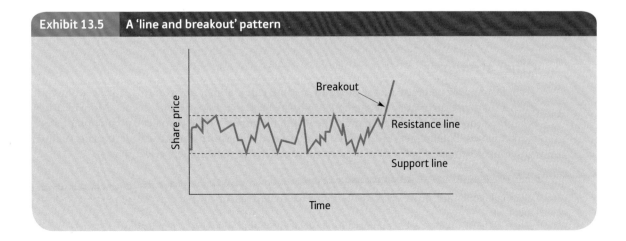

Exhibit 13.5   A 'line and breakout' pattern

Chartists have a very serious problem in that it is often difficult to see a new trend until after it has happened. Many critical voices say that it is impossible for the chartist to act quickly enough on a buy or sell signal because competition among chartists immediately pushes the price to its efficient level. To overcome this, some traders start to anticipate the signal, and buy or sell before a clear breakthrough is established. This leads other traders to act even earlier, to lock themselves into a trade before competition causes a price movement. This, it is argued by EMH proponents, will lead to trends being traded away and prices adjusting to take into account all information regarding past price movements, leading us back to the weak form of stock market efficiency.

In academic studies modern high-powered computers have been used to simulate chartist trades. Researchers were instructed to find the classic patterns chartists respond to, ranging from 'triple tops' and 'triple bottoms' to 'wedges' and 'diamonds'.[4] The general result was that they found that a simple buy and hold strategy of a broadly-based portfolio would have performed just as well as the chartist method, after transaction costs. Dawson and Steeley (2003), for example, found after examining UK share data that 'economic profits arising from the predictive ability of the technical patterns are unlikely to materialise'. However, some academic studies found evidence suggesting trading rules that led to superior returns – see Park and Irwin (2007) for a survey of technical analysis studies.[5]

The filter approach

The filter technique is designed to focus the trader on the long-term trends and to filter out short-term movements. Under this system a filter level has to be adopted – let us say this is 5%. If the share under observation rises by more than 5% from its low point the trader is advised to buy, as it is in an up-trend. If the share has peaked and has fallen by more than 5% it should be sold. Price movements of less than 5% are ignored. In a down-trend, as well as selling the share the trader owns, the trader should also 'sell short', that is, sell shares not yet owned in the anticipation of buying at a later date at a lower price. Again, there has been a considerable amount of academic research of various filter rules, and again the general conclusion goes against the claims of the technical analysts – a simple buy and hold policy performs at least as well after transaction costs. Exceptions to this general conclusion are turning up in the literature – *see* Park and Irwin (2007).

Moving averages

Examining the history of share prices and applying specific simple trading rules will produce abnormal returns according to Brock et al. (1992). They found that if investors (over the period 1897 to 1986) bought the 30 shares in the Dow Jones Industrial Average when the short-term moving average of the index (the average over, say, 50 days) rises above the long-term moving average (the average over, say, 200 days) they would have outperformed the investor who simply bought and held the market portfolio. Investors would also have achieved abnormal performance if they bought when a share 'broke out' from the trading range. 'However, transaction costs should be carefully considered before such strategies can be implemented' (Brock et al., 1992). A number of subsequent studies have found good performances (after transaction costs) from following rules based on moving average price charts (see Park and Irwin, 2007).

Other strategies

Technical analysts employ a vast range of trading rules. Some, for example, advise a purchase when a share rises in price at the same time as an increase in trading volume occurs. More bizarrely, other investors have told us to examine the length of women's dresses to get a prediction of stock market moves. Bull markets are apparently associated with short skirts and bear markets (falling) with longer hemlines! Some even look to sunspot activity to help them select shares.

---

4 For explanations of these terms, the reader is referred to one of the populist 'how to get rich quickly' books.

5 Their earlier working paper contains a lot more detail should you wish to pursue this.

A decade or so ago the conclusion from the academic studies on weak-form efficiency was that overwhelmingly the evidence suggested that stock markets correctly incorporated all past price and volume information into current share prices. That is, it is unlikely that you could achieve an extraordinary high return (for the risk level) by identifying patterns in charts, etc. (However, there were many studies that showed profitable technical trading strategies in the commodity and currency markets.)

This conclusion now needs to be revised in the light of dozens of recent rigorous academic studies into the profitability of 'technical analysis' in shares, as well as further studies into commodities and currency trading. The majority of these indicate that extraordinary high returns are achievable (*see* Park and Irwin, 2007). Note, though, that much of the evidence is disputed. For instance, other academics claim that some of the studies suffer from a number of methodological flaws: data snooping (using the same data to test for a variety of trading strategies and eventually finding one that works in that data set – see **Exhibit 13.6**); selecting the trading rule *after* the period under study; inadequate allowance for extra risk and transaction costs. So this remains a field of intellectual endeavour that is wide open for future enterprising researchers to improve on the research techniques to help us grope towards a conclusion on the profitability of technical trading strategies.

Exhibit 13.6

When use of pseudo-maths adds up to fraud

Many models tweak strategy to fit data or are just statistical flukes

By Stephen Foley

An academic journal called the Notices of the American Mathematical Society may seem an unlikely periodical to have exposed fraud on a massive scale. The investigation, published in the current edition, is certainly not going to sit among the nominees for next year's Pulitzer prizes. But a quartet of mathematicians have just published a piercing article in the public interest and in the nick of time.

In their paper, entitled Pseudo-Mathematics and Financial Charlatanism, they make the case that the vast majority of claims being made for quantitative investment strategies are false.

By calling it fraud, the academics command attention, and investors would be wise to beware. With interest rates about to turn, and a stock market bull run ageing fast, there have never been such temptations to eschew traditional bond and equity investing and to follow the siren sales patter of those who claim to see patterns in the historical data.

The (unnamed) targets of the mathematicians' ire range from individual technical analysts who identify buy and sell signals in a stock chart, all the way up to managed futures funds holding billions of dollars of clients assets. There will be many offenders, too, among investment managers pushing "smart beta" strategies, which aim to construct a portfolio based on signals from history.

There is even a worrying do-it-yourself trend: many electronic trading platforms now have tools encouraging retail investors to back test their own half-baked trading ideas, to see how they would have performed in the past. Twisting strategy to fit data.

The authors' argument is that, by failing to apply mathematical rigour to their methods, many purveyors of quantitative investment strategies are, deliberately or negligently, misleading clients.

It is reasonable to want to test a promising investment strategy to see how it would have performed in the past. The trap comes when one keeps tweaking the strategy until it neatly fits the historical data.

Intuitively, one might think one has finally hit upon the most successful investment strategy; in fact, one is likely to have hit only upon a statistical fluke, a false positive.

This is the problem of "over-fitting", and even checks against it – such as testing in a second, discrete historical data set – will continue to throw up many false positives, the mathematicians argue.

Do not despair. The paper does not conclude that history is bunk, just that backtesting ought to require more statistical thought than investment managers need to display to make a sale to investors.

▶

Exhibit 13.6 *(continued)*

The perennial success of Renaissance Technologies, founded by code-breaking maths genius Jim Simons, suggests that some can separate signal from noise in financial markets.

At least the best quantitative hedge funds are attuned to the problem of overfitting. London's Winton Capital published a paper last year warning that, even if individual researchers are scrupulous about calculating their probabilities, institutions risk "meta-overfitting", because the tendency is to only submit the best fitting strategies for approval to the higher-up management committee.

It seems that finance may need the same overhaul as the pharmaceuticals industry did a decade ago. Amid a furore over the safety of its anti-depressant Paxil in 2004, it was discovered that GlaxoSmithKline had conducted numerous trials that failed to prove the drug was an effective treatment for children.

However, a minority of trials did suggest efficacy, to a statistically significant confidence level, and these were the studies that got published.

It wasn't until scientists added together all the unpublished data that it became clear the drug increased the risk of teen suicides, for no offsetting benefit in treating depression, and it was banned for use by minors. GSK responded by promising to reveal all its trials and to publish all its data, regardless of their outcome, and other large drug companies followed, more or less reluctantly. As a result, we continue to learn that large claims made for blockbuster medicines tend not to stack up over time, Tamiflu being the latest example.

When it comes to quantitative investment strategies claiming to have performed well historically, it is not good enough for managers to stamp "past performance is no guide to future performance" on to a marketing document.

A crucial detail, almost never revealed, is how many discarded tweaks and tests led to the miraculous discovery of the strategy. The authors of the Notices of the AMS paper are upbeat about the chances of banishing pseudo-mathematics from finance. One of their number, Marco Lopez de Prado of Lawrence Berkeley National Laboratory, distributes open source software, at quantresearch.info, which can improve the modelling of mathematical probabilities and limit the risks of overfitting.

Another, David Bailey of the University of California, Davis, suggests that a regulatory body such as Finra could step in to promote best practice in the marketing of mathematical claims, just as the Food and Drug Administration monitors drug advertising.

Together they have created a blog at financial-math. org to debate their ideas. Raising the issue is necessary for raising the bar.

Too many investment managers and advisers, it is claimed, are purveyors of false positives, getting rich on statistical flukes. If their methodologies do not improve in line with the improvements in academic thinking about backtesting and overfitting, then they really will deserve to be called out as frauds.

 Financial Times, 16 April 2014.
All Rights Reserved.

Return reversal

We now turn to a group of studies that seem to indicate that the market might consistently fail to price properly. The first area of research concerns the phenomenon of **return reversal**. That is, shares that have given the highest returns over the previous three to five years (the 'winners') generally go on to underperform the stock market over the subsequent three to five years. Those shares that performed worst over a number of years (the 'losers') then, on average, show returns significantly higher than the market over the next three to five years.

De Bondt and Thaler (1985) selected portfolios of 35 US shares at three-year intervals, between 1933 and 1980. These portfolios contained the shares that had given the worst returns over a three-year period. The performances of these portfolios were then compared with the market as a whole over the subsequent three years. They found that these shares outperformed the market by an average of 19.6% in the next 36 months. Their explanation is that the market had overreacted to the bad news and undervalued the shares. Moreover, when portfolios of shares which had risen the most in the prior three years were constructed and followed for a further three years, they underperformed the market by 5%. De Bondt and Thaler claim: 'Substantial weak form market inefficiencies are discovered', in their analysis. Chopra et al. (1992) carried out a more detailed study and concluded: 'In portfolios formed on the basis of prior five-year returns, extreme prior losers outperform extreme prior winners by 5–10 per cent per year during the subsequent five years'. In a US and Hong Kong study, George and Hwang (2007) found losers outperforming winners by 0.56% per month.

Arnold and Baker (2007) investigated the return reversal phenomenon in UK shares. Our results show a stronger return reversal effect than that displayed in US shares. Every January between 1960 and 1998 we calculated for every share on the London Share Price Data (LSPD) its prior five-year return (capital gains plus dividends). The LSPD contains all the shares listed on the London Stock Exchange for the period 1975 to 2002. Before 1975 it contains share returns for a random one-third sample. Shares were ranked (an average of over 950 companies each January) in order of their five-year performance. They were then split into ten equal sized groups (deciles) with group 1 containing the worst performers ('losers') over the prior five years, group 2 the next worst and so on, to group 10 (the 'winners'). We then imagined buying each of the portfolios of shares and holding them for various periods up to 60 months. Returns, relative to the market index, were recorded. We found that the loser shares (on average, over 39 portfolio formations, 1960–98) outperformed the winner shares by 14% per year when held for five years. Furthermore, the 39 loser portfolios outperformed the market index by an average of 8.9% per year over a five-year holding period.

Exhibit 13.7 shows some of the results. The lines trace the cumulative return for each of the ten portfolios after allowing for the return on the market. The horizontal line at '0' represents the market return re-based to zero throughout. The loser portfolios outperform the market by 53% over five-year holding periods, or 8.9% per year; whereas the winner portfolio, on average over 39 tests, underperforms the market by 47%. Remarkably, all the other portfolios are in the 'right' order: 2 is above 3, 3 above 4, and so on. This lends considerable support to the view that investors overreact to poor news (e.g. declining profits) coming from 'bad' companies and good news coming from the stars, because the greatest extent of return reversal is in the most extreme prior-period return-ranked portfolios. The overreaction hypothesis states that investors push the losers down too far, and push the winners up too much, failing to allow sufficiently for the potential of losers

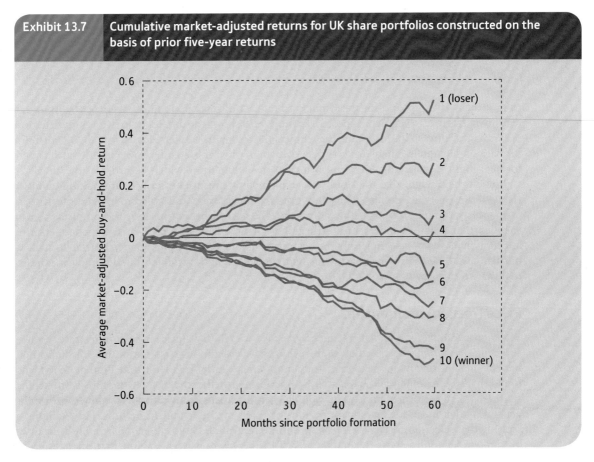

| Exhibit 13.7 | Cumulative market-adjusted returns for UK share portfolios constructed on the basis of prior five-year returns |

A figure of 0.4 should be interpreted as a cumulative return of 40% after allowance for the market return.

Source: Arnold and Baker (2007).

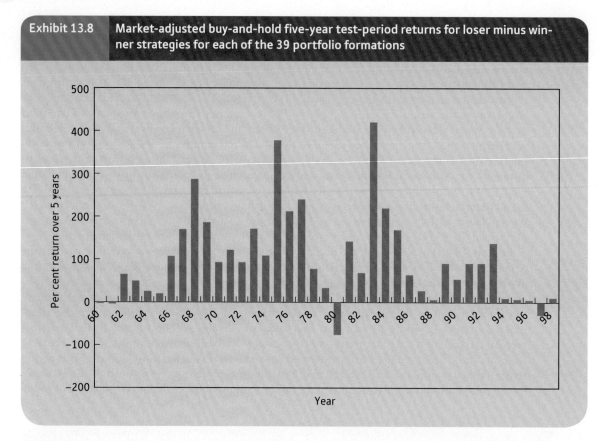

| **Exhibit 13.8** | **Market-adjusted buy-and-hold five-year test-period returns for loser minus winner strategies for each of the 39 portfolio formations** |

The five-year test-period returns for each loser-winner strategy are assigned to the year of formation.

Source: Arnold and Baker (2007).

to pick themselves up, and for the winners to make a mistake and fall off their pedestals, or, at least, to perform less well than expected. **Exhibit 13.8** shows the difference in five-year test-period performance between the losers and the winners (losers minus winners) for each of the 39 portfolio formations separately. There are very few occasions when those companies considered star performers go on to generate better returns for investors than those widely regarded as the 'dogs'.

It might be thought that the results are explained by investors in loser shares taking on more risk than investors in winners. The study tests risk in six ways and failed to explain the outperformance as a result of losers being more risky. The CAPM-beta of losers, for example, is shown to be less than that for winners. In a further study (Arnold and Xiao, 2007) an even better performance was achieved by selecting only those loser companies with strong financial variables such as positive cash flow, improving gearing (using financial strength variables found to indicate abnormal share returns by Piotroski (2000)).

Price (return) momentum

Many professional fund managers and private investors follow a price momentum strategy when choosing shares. That is, they buy shares which have risen in recent months and sell shares that have fallen. The first major academic study in this area was by Jegadeesh and Titman (1993) who found that if you bought US shares that had performed well in the past few months while selling shares that had performed poorly you would generate returns significantly exceeding those on the general market index for investment periods of three, six, nine and 12 months. For example, a strategy that selects shares on their past six-month returns and holds them for six months, realises a compounded return above the market of 12.01% per year on average. Note that these results at first seem diametrically opposed to those of the return reversal, because the best strategy is to buy winners. However, the key to understanding the results and relating it to investor behaviour is to realise that return reversal is a long-term phenomenon stretching over many years, whereas price

| Exhibit 13.9 | Price momentum |

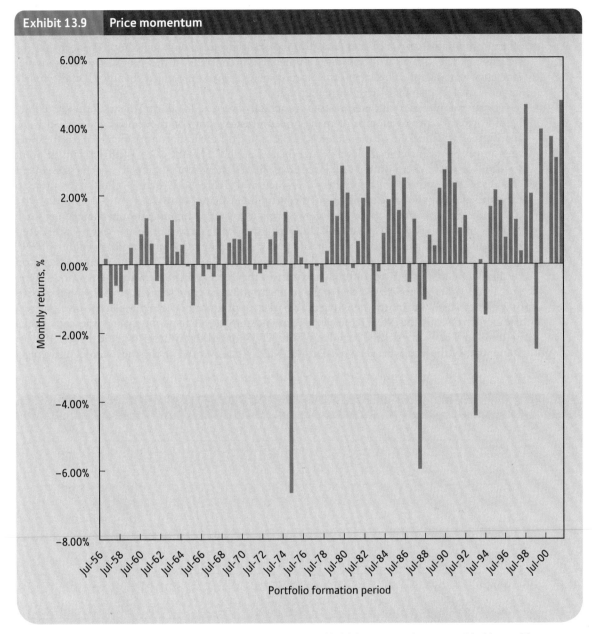

Portfolios are constructed on six-month prior-period returns and held for six months. Buy-and-hold monthly returns over the six months for the winner portfolio minus the loser portfolio. Each portfolio formation is shown separately.

Source: Arnold and Shi (2005).

momentum strategists look only to the returns over the prior three, six, nine or 12 months to select their extreme winners – and they do not hold for more than one year.[6]

Two explanations for price momentum are debated in the literature (apart from the view that the returns are explained by risk differences). The first is that investors underreact to new information. So, if a company has reported large increases in profits over the last six months the share price rises, but it does not rise enough fully to reflect all the new information. The argument runs that investors tend to 'anchor' beliefs about a company and so they are slow to realise that the company has entered an accelerated growth phase. They might, at first, anticipate it fizzling out,

---

6 There are some theoretical explanations for the co-existence of return reversal and momentum, e.g. Barberis et al. (1988), Daniel et al. (1998) and Hong and Stein (1999).

or even that the profit trend will go into reverse. However, as good news accumulates over time, increasing numbers of investors rerate the shares and push up the share price. On the other hand, when examining a stream of bad news from losers, they are at first reluctant to believe that the severity of the bad news will continue and therefore do not sell off the shares as much as market efficiency would imply. This means that as more news arrives they realise that they had previously underreacted, and so the share continues to fall.

The alternative theory is that investors are actually overreacting during the test (after purchase) period. After a series of months of rising prices investors jump on the bandwagon and push the share prices of winners to irrational levels, while selling off the losers unreasonably and so pushing their prices below the efficient level during the test period. The advocates of this argument point to the tendency of these winner and loser portfolios to show return reversal over the subsequent two years or so as proof of temporary overreaction. Perhaps both theories could have a role to play in explaining the price momentum effects found in share returns.

Jegadeesh and Titman's work was followed up with papers examining the phenomenon in stock markets around the world. For example, Rouwenhorst (1998) showed price momentum in 12 developed country stock markets, and then in a number of emerging stock markets (Rouwenhorst, 1999). In the UK Liu et al. (1999) demonstrated the effect for the period 1977–98, but doubt was cast on the likelihood that price momentum is a feature of the UK market at all times by the work of Hon and Tonks (2003), who showed that while momentum was a good strategy to follow in the 1980s and 1990s (which was mostly one long bull market) it produced poor returns in the previous two decades. To discover the extent to which price momentum is a reliable strategy, and whether it works better in bull or bear markets, Arnold and Shi (2005) tested the strategy over the period 1956 to 2001. Some of the results are shown in **Exhibit 13.9**. While over the whole study period, on average,

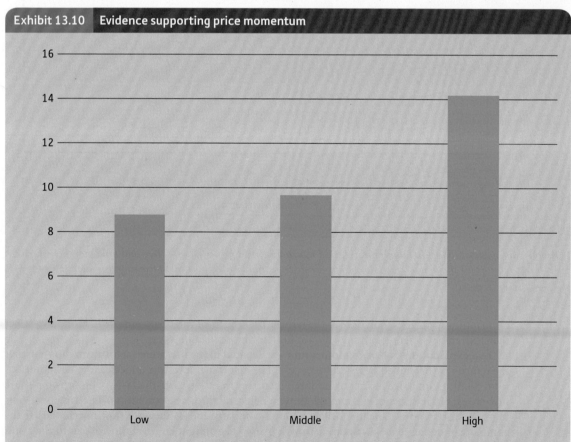

Exhibit 13.10   **Evidence supporting price momentum**

(a) US average annual share returns above the government Treasury bill rate for portfolios defined by past share returns. Percent per year, averaged for one-year holding periods, 1972–2011

Exhibit 13.10   Evidence supporting price momentum *(continued)*

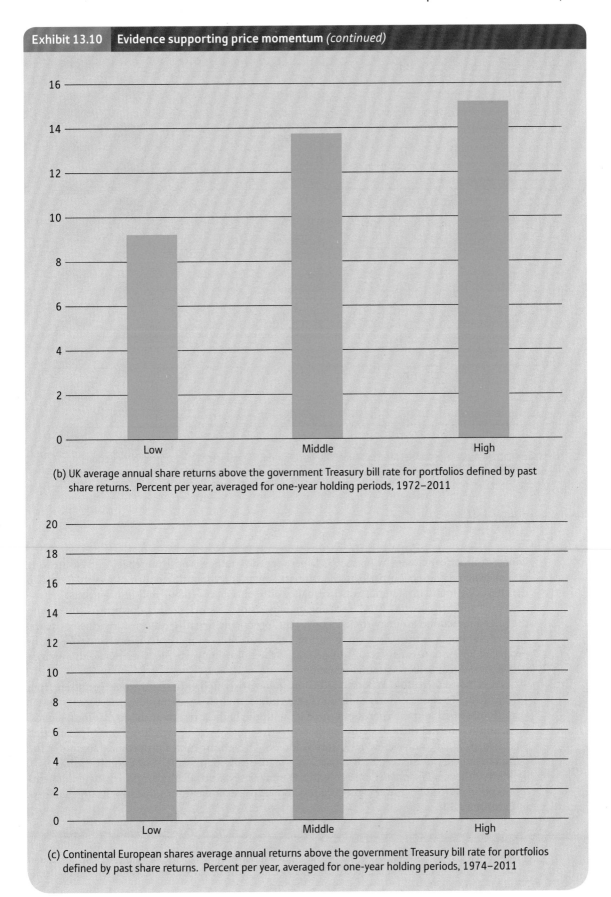

(b) UK average annual share returns above the government Treasury bill rate for portfolios defined by past share returns. Percent per year, averaged for one-year holding periods, 1972–2011

(c) Continental European shares average annual returns above the government Treasury bill rate for portfolios defined by past share returns. Percent per year, averaged for one-year holding periods, 1974–2011

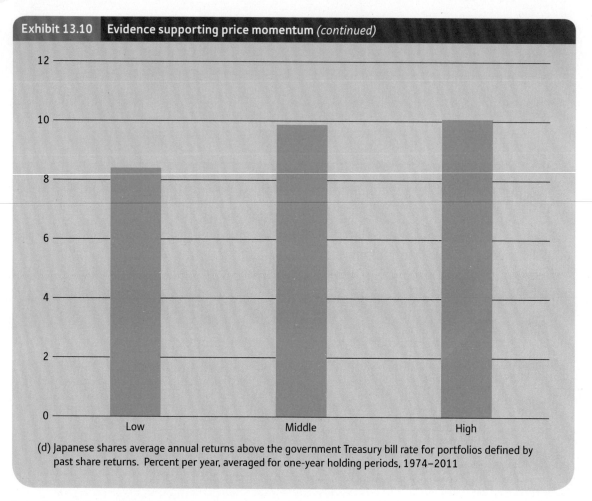

Exhibit 13.10   Evidence supporting price momentum *(continued)*

(d) Japanese shares average annual returns above the government Treasury bill rate for portfolios defined by past share returns. Percent per year, averaged for one-year holding periods, 1974–2011

Source: Asness, Moskowitz and Pedersen (2013).

winners outperform losers by up to 9.92% per year the strategy is fairly unreliable. There are long periods when the losers outperform the winners – an average monthly return of less than zero on the chart. We found no significant performance difference between bull and bear markets.

Daniel and Moskowitz (2016), focusing on periods of US stock market downturns, also found the price momentum strategy to be inconsistent, producing negative returns for strings of years. This is despite, over the whole study period 1927–2013, the winners of the previous 12 months produced an average excess return of 15.3% in the following year; the loser portfolio averaged −2.5% in the year after portfolio formation.

Asness, Moskowitz and Pedersen (2013) examine price momentum in various countries from 1972 to 2011. To classify shares as having Low, Middle or High momentum share returns over one year are observed and the shares put in order with the highest return at the top, second highest next, and so on, and then all shares are allocated to equally-sized portfolios, Low, Middle, High past returns. The results show momentum for US, UK, continental Europe and Japan over the decades studied, but the result for Japan is not statistically significant – see **Exhibit 13.10**.[7]

John Authers, a *Financial Times* columnist summarises the difficulty for price momentum critics (its good performance over eight decades) and for price momentum advocates (its unreliability) in **Exhibit 13.11**.

---

7 Some other papers showing evidence of share price momentum: Sagi and Seasholes (2007), Figelman (2007), Chui et al. (2010) Fama and French (2008), Shu, T. (2013), Barroso and Santa-Clara (2015), Israel and Moskowitz (2013).

Exhibit 13.11

The hard facts about momentum investing

By John Authers

Big Mo is investors' guilty little secret. You can rely on momentum. But it makes many people feel uncomfortable. It is some two decades since academics nailed down a momentum effect in stock markets.

Easily confused with trend following – the tendency for markets to keep going in a particular direction – it refers to the propensity for relative winning stocks to keep winning, and losing stocks to keep losing.

Every so often, momentum reverses. In the past weeks, internet and biotech stocks, after a riotous run, have been clipped back significantly, even as the US stock market remains at record highs.

But when investors set up mechanistic momentum strategies, which hold the winners over a recent period (usually the last six months or the last year) and sell short the losers, and keep rebalancing, they reliably make money.

Academics have documented a momentum effect across the world, and in time periods going back two centuries. In the present, hedge funds use it to make money.

This is discomfiting. Momentum has nothing to do with the fundamentals of a company, and much more to do with the human propensity to extrapolate the flimsiest trends into the future. It feels wrong that money can be made this way.

Further, momentum investing is without redeeming social merit. Invest on the basis of "value" (a strategy of buying stocks when they are too cheap relative to their fundamentals, which has also been proved to beat the market over the long term, and is the virtual opposite of momentum), and you are helping to correct a mispricing. Invest on the basis of momentum, however, and you are deliberately helping a market inefficiency grow even worse.

No wonder that momentum investing seems "politically incorrect". But that should not cloud judgments on whether it works. And so Clifford Asness, founder of the AQR investment group in New York, has taken up the cudgels to defend it. Mr Asness appears to enjoy being politically incorrect, and he argues the case for momentum with characteristic force. A paper he has just published with several colleagues aims to trash 10 "myths" about momentum investing.

Maybe the most important point is that momentum is not particularly volatile. But it is prone to serious setbacks on those occasions when it snaps back and reverses. A prime example came in the spring and summer of 2009, after markets had hit rock bottom and financials, previously the weakest performers, started to lead all others. That momentum reverse is fresh in the memory.

However, the last momentum shock on such a scale had come in 1932. Then, as in 2009, momentum did badly in a fast-rising market. And both came after a period when momentum had fared well (there were great returns from selling short banks in 2008 as they accelerated towards the abyss), and thus provided a useful hedge, at a time when stocks as a whole were selling off.

Value investors, who tended to be heavily weighted in banks, did horribly in 2008 – just as they had done in 1999, at the top of the tech bubble, when momentum fared well.

Further, momentum has been consistent. Using the database of historic US stock returns compiled by Dartmouth University's Kenneth French, Mr Asness and his colleagues show that a "winners minus losers" strategy gained 8.3 per cent per year from 1927 to 2013, compared with the 7.9 per cent by which stocks as a whole outperformed cash, and the 4.7 per cent by which cheap stocks beat expensive ones. This advantage persists even when these returns are adjusted for risk.

It is true that the market has beaten the momentum factor since 1991, a period of turbulence – but value has fared worse.

Complaints that momentum is tax-inefficient (unlikely as it relies more on capital gains than income), and that it incurs excessive trading costs can both be dismissed using data from experience.

Mr Asness and colleagues also trash the notion that momentum works only for small companies and not for larger caps. This is true of value, but not momentum.

Ultimately, his point is well taken.

Stocks show momentum, and it is possible in the real world to design a momentum trading strategy that will show positive returns, even after taxes and trading costs.

He also renders this idea much more palatable by using momentum as a useful hedge to be run alongside value. Both work in the long term, and do not directly cancel each other out, as there are periods when value stocks are beginning to perform and also

▶

Exhibit 13.11 *(continued)*

enjoy momentum. Momentum investing might, then, help make the world safe for value investing.

But many will still feel queasy. Mr Asness has indeed shown that momentum is a strong and robust strategy, and is right to be angry with those who deny it; but he should at least have some sympathy for those who find this fact uncomfortable.

 Financial Times, 11 May 2014.

Semi-strong form tests

The semi-strong form of efficiency has the greatest fascination for most researchers and practitioners. It focuses on the question of whether it is worthwhile expensively acquiring and analysing publicly available information. If semi-strong efficiency is true it undermines the work of millions of fundamental (professional or amateur) analysts whose trading rules cannot be applied to produce abnormal returns because all publicly available information is already reflected in the share price.

Fundamental analysts try to estimate a share's true value based on future business returns. This is then compared with the market price to establish an over- or under-valuation. To estimate the intrinsic value of a share the fundamentalists gather as much relevant information as possible. This may include macroeconomic growth projections, industry conditions, company accounts and announcements, details of the company's personnel, tax rates, technological and social change and so on. The range of potentially important information is vast, but it is all directed at one objective: forecasting future profits and dividends.

There are thousands of professional analysts constantly surveying information in the public domain. Given this volume of highly able individuals examining the smallest piece of news about a firm and its environment, combined with the investigatory and investment activities of millions of shareholders, it would seem eminently reasonable to postulate that the semi-strong form of EMH describes the reality of modern stock markets.

The semi-strong form of EMH is threatening to share analysts, fund managers and others in the financial community because, if true, it means that they are unable to outperform the market average return except by chance or by having inside knowledge.

The great majority of the early evidence (1960s and 1970s) supported the hypothesis, especially if the transaction costs of special trading strategies were accounted for. The onus was placed on those who believed that the market is inefficient and misprices shares to show that they could perform extraordinarily well other than by chance. As **Exhibit 13.12** makes clear most of these professionals who are actively looking for bargains have performed rather poorly. Remember that simply by chance you would expect 50% of them to outperform the market index before fees. In America,

Exhibit 13.12

Active fund managers can add value but price is still too high

By John Authers

What exactly are the arguments for active management? The debate is back in full force after the Standard & Poor's SPIVA service showed last week that 92 per cent of US large-cap mutual funds had failed to match their benchmark over 15 years.

That prompted Capital Group, the biggest active mutual fund manager, to claim that the survey was flawed and that "investors don't need thousands of funds to build a bigger nest egg, just a few good ones".

Indexing creates the potential for distortions and misallocated capital; it makes for weaker price discovery. But while indexing may create broader problems for markets, a paradox is at work. It is still in the interests of investors to gain the best expected return for their money, for a given level of risk, and that means indexing. So what arguments are left?

First, enough investors have beaten the market regularly to suggest it cannot be by chance. Those investors tend to have several facets in common, such as concentrated portfolios [relatively few shares], a willingness to depart from the benchmark, and managers with a substantial stake in their own funds.

Second, there is the contention that index funds will plummet with the market in a downturn, while active funds can take evasive action.

And there is a (reasonable) belief that index funds are dumb. Active funds can wisely avoid bubbles and hot stocks.

So, for an unscientific experiment, let us compare Capital Group's Growth Fund of America, the biggest active fund, with the SPY exchange traded fund, which tracks the S&P 500, and the Fidelity Magellan fund, which for decades was the world's biggest active fund.

Over five years, the Growth Fund of America has returned 88.1 per cent, slightly ahead of SPY and Magellan, on 84.8 and 80.2 per cent, respectively. There was no significant difference in volatility.

But over 24 years, Capital's advantage is impressive. It has compounded at 10.8 per cent per annum, against 9.2 per cent for SPY and 7.9 per cent for Magellan. That works out, with compound interest, at a 344 percentage point advantage over SPY. All of this, however, is thanks to Capital's nimble handling of the late 1990s bull market and the burst dotcom bubble that followed it. For the five years from 1996 to the end of 2000, Growth Fund returned 194 per cent, far ahead of SPY's 128.4 per cent. It did this by loading up on growth stocks as the bubble came to a head, and then shifting into enough of the right stocks that its decline from there was no worse than that of the market.

The hope of great timing like this is why people try an active manager rather than an index tracker. Good timing at critical junctures can lead to years of compounded outperformance. The problem is that timing one market turn does not predict that it will handle the next market turn.

For the five years starting with the S&P's top in October 2007, Growth Fund was flat, while SPY made 4.3 per cent (and Magellan dipped by almost 15 per cent). Since the top in 2007, indeed Growth Fund's performance is almost identical to SPY's. Effectively, they have both given their investors exactly the same thing (SPY is very slightly ahead). It is just that Capital went to much more trouble to come to the same result.

What of the argument that active funds can avoid downturns? There is no evidence for it. From top to bottom after 2000, Growth Fund dropped 46.15 per cent, against 47.5 per cent for SPY.

From top to bottom after 2007, Growth Fund lost 51.7 per cent, versus 55.2 per cent for SPY. (Magellan did much worse both times). These are marginal outperformances, thanks to Growth Fund's small cash holdings. It offered no meaningful drawdown insurance; in both incidents, its investors suffered severe losses.

What of the argument that some managers are indeed skilled? It may well be true, but it is prohibitively hard to find them. Bear in mind that Magellan, an also-ran over the past two decades, had over the previous three decades earned a reputation as the best actively managed fund of all time. And it takes a very long time before we can be sure that outperformance is due to skill rather than randomness and luck.

Victor Haghani of Elm Group offers this illustration. You have two coins, one fair, and one 60 per cent weighted towards heads.

To be 95 per cent sure you know which is the weighted coin, you would need to toss it 143 times.

To spot an active manager who adds significant value on a risk-adjusted basis, compared with others who in the long run merely match the index, could take far longer than a manager's working lifetime.

What of the argument that active managers are smarter at managing risk? Growth Fund holds all the Fang stocks (Facebook, Amazon, Netflix and Google) among its 10 largest holdings. About 15.4 per cent of the fund is in the internet sector.

This shows good recent stock picking, but it is scarcely a recipe to survive the next downturn, unless it is prepared to sell very nimbly. As its stake in Amazon, about 6 per cent of its portfolio, is worth about $8bn, it will be hard to sell in a hurry.

As for asset allocation, it has 93.6 per cent in stocks, 1.5 per cent in cash and a small holding of bonds. In another Lehman-type event, it should beat a tracker fund by a percentage point, but that is about it.

So, active managers can add value, particularly if they time market turns well. But they are prohibitively difficult to identify, and they do not provide drawdown insurance. The rise in indexing does indeed create many reasons for worry — but at present active funds are charging far too much for the public good of market discovery. It is hard to see why investors should be prepared to pay them that price.

FT *Financial Times*, 17 April 2017.

one study reported that only 8% have achieved out-performance after taking their fees – for most other national stock markets the proportion of funds out-performing is rarely above 50%. As a result of disillusionment with those managers trying to beat the market we see increasing amounts of money placed with 'passive funds' (index funds or tracker funds) that aim for low costs by simply buying a portfolio that replicates the market or a segment of it (a 'benchmark').

The fundamental analysts have not lost heart, and have fought back with the assistance of some academic studies which appear to suggest that the market is less than perfectly efficient. There are some anomalies which may be caused by mispricing. For example, small firm shares have performed abnormally well (for certain periods) given their supposed risk class, and 'value investing' seems to produce unexpectedly high returns.

We will now discuss *some* of the evidence for and against semi-strong efficiency.[8]

Seasonal, calendar or cyclical effects

Numerous studies have identified apparent market inefficiencies on specific markets at particular times. One is the weekend effect, in which there appear to be abnormal returns on Fridays and relative falls on Mondays. The January effect refers to the tendency for shares to give excess returns in the first few days of January in the USA. Some researchers have found an hour of the day effect in which shares perform abnormally at particular times in the trading day. For example, the first 15 minutes have given exceptional returns, according to some studies.

The problem for practical investment with placing too much importance on these studies is that the moment they are identified and publicised there is a good chance that they will cease to exist.[9] Investors will buy in anticipation of the January effect and so cause the market already to be at the new higher level on 1 January. They will sell on Friday when the price is high and buy on Monday when the price is low, thus eliminating the weekend effect.

Even if the effects are not eliminated trading strategies based on these findings would be no more profitable than buying and holding a well-diversified portfolio. This is because of the high transaction costs associated with such strategies as, say, buying every Tuesday and selling every Friday. Also the research in this area is particularly vulnerable to the accusation of 'data-snooping'. Sullivan et al. (1999) claim to demonstrate that calendar effects are illusory and findings obtained merely the result of extensive mining of the data until an (apparent) relationship is found:

> Data-snooping need not be the consequence of a particular researcher's efforts. It can result from a subtle survivorship bias operating on the entire universe of technical trading rules that have been considered historically. Suppose that, over time, investors have experimented with technical trading rules drawn from a very wide universe – in principle thousands of parameterizations of a variety of types of rules. As time progresses, the rules that happen to perform well historically receive more attention and are considered 'serious contenders' by the investment community, and unsuccessful trading rules are more likely to be forgotten. After a long sample period, only a small set of trading rules may be left for consideration, and these rules' historical track records will be cited as evidence of their merits. If enough trading rules are considered over time, some rules are bound by pure luck, even in a very large sample, to produce superior performance even if they do not genuinely possess predictive power over asset returns. Of course, inference based solely on the subset of surviving trading rules may be misleading in this context because it does not account for the full set of initial trading rules, most of which are likely to have underperformed.

Small firms

The searchers for inefficiency seemed to be on firmer ground when examining smaller firms. The problem is that the ground only appears to be firm until you start to build. A number of studies in the 1980s found that smaller firms' shares outperformed those of larger firms over a period of

---

8 This is an area with an enormous literature. The References and further reading section at the end of the chapter contains some of the EMH papers.

9 McLean and Pontiff (2016) found that, after publication, the returns on exploiting stock market anomalies decreased by 58%: 'Our findings suggest that investors learn about mispricing from academic publications.'

several decades (the small firm effect, small-capitalisation, or small-cap effects). This was found to be the case in the USA, Canada, Australia, Belgium, Finland, the Netherlands, France, Germany, Japan and Britain.[10] Dimson and Marsh (1986) put the outperformance of small UK firms' shares at just under 6% per year. These studies caused quite a stir in both the academic and the share-investing communities. Some rational explanations for this outperformance were offered: for example, perhaps the researchers had not adequately allowed for the extra risk of small shares – particularly the risk associated with lower liquidity. In most of these studies beta is used as the measure of risk and there are now doubts about its ability to capture all the risk-return relationship (*see* Chapter 8). Besides, the results generally show lower betas for small companies. Some researchers have argued that small firms suffer more in recessions and so can be judged as more risky. Another explanation is that it is proportionately more expensive to trade in small companies' shares: if transaction costs are included, the net return of trading in small company shares comes down (but this does not explain the outperformance of a portfolio bought and held for a long period). There is also the issue of 'institutional neglect', by which analysts fail to spend enough time studying small firms, preferring to concentrate on the larger 100 or so. This may open up opportunities for the private investor who is prepared to conduct a more detailed analysis of those companies to which inadequate professional attention is paid.

The excitement about small companies' shares by investors and their advisers was much greater than in academe, but it was to end in tears. Investors who rushed to exploit this small firm effect in the late 1980s and early 1990s had their fingers burnt. As *The Economist*[11] put it: 'The supposedly inefficient market promptly took its revenge, efficiently parting investors from their money by treating owners of small stocks to seven years of under-performance.' This article refers to the US market but similar underperformance occurred on both the US and UK markets.

UK studies by Dimson, Marsh and Staunton (Dimson and Marsh 1999, Dimson et al., 2001, 2002) showed that smaller companies outperformed large companies by 5.2% per annum between 1955 and 1988 (by 4.5% for small companies and 9.0% for very small (micro) companies). However, in the period 1989 to 1998 the return premium in favour of small companies went into reverse: large companies produced a return 7.0% greater than small companies and 10.5% for micro capitalisation companies The researchers show that this kind of reversal occurred in many different countries in the late 1980s and 1990s. Some people say that what happened was that following the early 1980s' academic studies so many funds were set up to buy small firms' shares that in 1986 and 1987 their prices were pushed up to unsustainable levels (they had 10 years of outperformance pushed into two). In the last two decades small firms have again reasserted themselves as better performers than large firms. The overall result for 90 years to 2015 is that small US firms have produced an average annual return of 12.1% whereas large US companies managed only 9.7%. In the case of the UK over the period 1955–2015 the better performance is even greater at 15.3% compared with 12% – see **Exhibit 13.13**.

Underreaction

Research evidence is building which shows that investors are slow to react to the release of information in some circumstances. This introduces the possibility of abnormal returns following the announcement of certain types of news. The first area of research has been into 'post-earnings-announcement drift'. That is, there is a sluggish response to the announcement of unexpectedly good or unexpectedly bad profit figures. Bernard and Thomas (1989) found that cumulative abnormal returns (CARs) continue to drift up for firms that report unexpectedly good earnings and drift down for firms that report unexpectedly bad figures for up to 60 days after the announcement. (The abnormal return in a period is the return of a portfolio after adjusting for both the market return in that period and risk.) This offers an opportunity to purchase and sell shares after the information has been made public and thereby outperform the market returns. Shares were allocated to 10 categories of standardised unexpected earnings (SUE). The 10% of shares with the highest positive unexpected earnings were placed in category 10. (The worst unexpected return shares were placed

---

10 Key studies in the area are Banz (1981), Reinganum (1981), Keim (1983), Fama and French (1992), Dimson et al. (2002), Israel and Moskowitz (2013), Dimson, et al. (2017) and the annual Hoare Govett Smaller Companies Index reports.

11 *The Economist*, 26 March 1994.

in category 1.) The research results show that after the announcement the shares of companies in category 10 continue to provide positive CARs. Investors did not move the share price sufficiently to incorporate the new information in the earnings announcement on the day of the announcement. Those reporting bad surprises in earnings (the worst of which were in category 1) continued to show a falling return relative to the market in the period after the announcement day. Bernard and Thomas say that a strategy of buying shares in category 10 and selling shares in category 1 on the announcement day and selling (buying) 60 days later would have yielded an estimated abnormal return of approximately 4.2% over 60 days, or about 18% on an annualised basis. Similar results have been reported in studies by Foster et al. (1984), Rendleman et al. (1982), Liu et al. (2003), Lerman et al. (2007), Hirshleifer et al. (2009), Dellavigna and Pollet (2009), Chordia et al. (2009), Kama (2009), Shu, T. (2013) and Caylor et al. (2015). These studies suggest that all the news is not properly priced into the shares at the time of announcement as would be expected under EMH.

The second area of research into underreaction relates to the repurchase of shares. Ikenberry et al. (1995) found that share prices rise on the announcement that the company will repurchase its own shares. This is to be expected as this is generally a positive piece of news. The suggestion of inefficiency arises because after the announcement the shares continue to provide abnormal returns over the next few years. Thirdly, Michaely et al. (1995) and Liu et al. (2008) found evidence of share price drift following dividend initiations and/or omissions. Fourthly, Ikenberry et al. (1996) found share price drift after share split announcements. Fifthly, we have already discussed an underreaction to past price movements (a 'price momentum effect').

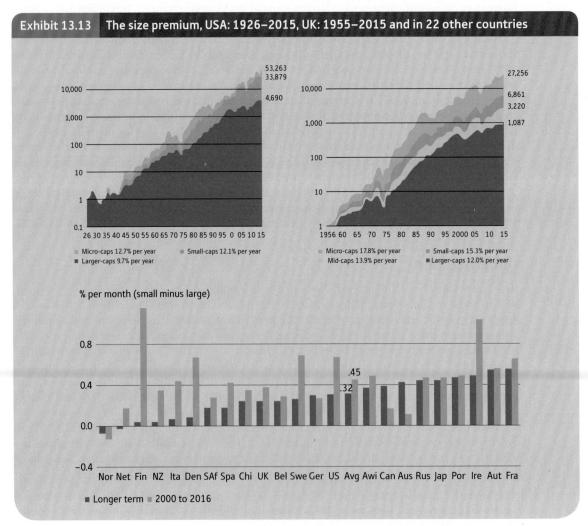

Exhibit 13.13   The size premium, USA: 1926–2015, UK: 1955–2015 and in 22 other countries

Source: Dimson, E., Marsh, P. Staunton, M., R. Kersley and M. O'Sullivan (2017) *Credit Suisse Global Investment Returns Yearbook 2017- slide deck*. London: Credit Suisse.

Value investing

There is a school of thought in investment circles that investors should search for 'value' shares. Different sub-schools emphasise different attributes of an undervalued share but the usual candidates for inclusion are:

- a share with a price which is a low multiple of the earnings per share (low P/E ratios or PERs);
- a share price which is low relative to the balance sheet assets (a market-to-book ratio, or its inverse the book-to-market ratio);
- a share with high dividends relative to the share price (high-yield shares).[12]

We turn first to the purchase of low price-earnings ratio shares as an investment strategy. The evidence generally indicates that these shares generate abnormal returns. Basu (1975, 1977, 1983), Keim (1988) and Lakonishok et al. (1994) have produced evidence which appears to defy the semi-strong EMH, using US data. Mario Levis (1989), Gregory et al. (2001, 2003), Anderson and Brooks (2006) and Li et al. (2009) found exceptional performance of low PER shares in the UK. For Sweden, Hamberg and Novak (2010) and for Japan, Chan et al. (1991) report similar findings. The academic literature tends to agree that low PER shares produce abnormal returns but there is some dispute whether it is the small-size effect that is really being observed; when this factor is removed the PER effect disappears, according to Reinganum (1981) and Banz and Breen (1986). Doubts were raised because small firm shares are often on low PERs and so it is difficult to disentangle the causes of outperformance. Jaffe et al. (1989), based on an extensive study of US shares over the period 1951–86, claimed that there was both a price–earnings ratio effect and a size effect. However, the results were contradicted by Fama and French (1992), who claim that low PER shares offer no extra return but that size and book-to-market ratio are determining factors. On British shares Levis (1989) and Gregory et al. (2001) distinguished between the size and PER effects and concluded that low PERs were a source of excess returns.

One explanation for the low PER anomaly is that investors place too much emphasis on short-term earnings data and fail to recognise sufficiently the ability of many poorly performing firms to improve. Investors seem to put some companies on a very high price relative to their current earnings to reflect a belief in rapid growth of profits, while putting firms with declining profits on unreasonably low prices. The problem is that the market apparently consistently overprices the 'glamour' shares and goes too far in assigning a high PER because of overemphasis on recent performance, while excessively depressing the share prices of companies with low recent earnings. To put it crudely: so much is expected of the 'glamour' shares that the smallest piece of bad news (or news that is less good than was expected) brings the price tumbling. On the other hand, so little is expected of the historically poor performers that good news goes straight into a share price rise. What investors have failed to appreciate is the tendency for extreme profit and growth trends to moderate – 'to revert to the mean'. This was shown in research by Little as early as 1962. He described profit differences from one period to another as higgledy piggledy growth. Fuller et al. (1993) found that portfolios constructed from shares with low PERs showed lower profit growth than portfolios of high PERs shares in each of the eight years after portfolio formation. However, after three to four years the growth rate differences became very small. If investors were buying high PER shares because they expected high earnings growth for decades into the future (thus bidding up the price) they were frequently disappointed. On the other hand, investors buying low PER shares when the price is low because most investors believe the company is locked into low earnings growth found, after three or four years, that the earnings of these companies, on average grew at very nearly the same rate as the glamour shares. Dreman (2007) has written on the tendency for investors to overreact and bid up glamour shares too far – while neglecting other companies.

The efficient market protagonists (e.g. Fama and French) have countered the new evidence of inefficiency by saying that the supposed outperformers are more risky than the average share and therefore an efficient market should permit them to give higher returns. Lakonishok et al. (1994) examined this and found that low PER shares are actually less risky than the average.

---

12 The doyen of the value investing school, Benjamin Graham, regarded the use of a single measure in isolation as a very crude form of value investing. In fact, he would condemn such an approach as not being a value strategy at all. *See Security Analysis* by Graham and Dodd (1934) and *The Intelligent Investor* (1973) by Graham (reprinted 2003).

Before everyone rushes out to buy low PER shares remember the lesson that followed the discovery of a small firm effect in the mid-1980s. Does it still exist?

Shares selling at prices which are a low multiple of the net assets per share (i.e. high book-to-market ratio) seem to produce abnormal returns.[13] Examples of the type of results from studies in this area are shown in **Exhibit 13.14** derived from a 2013 paper by Asness, Moskowitz and Pedersen. For each year the shares were ranked (put in order) based on the ratio of book equity (net asset value from the balance sheet) to market equity (market capitalisation), BE/ME, and then split into three equal groups:

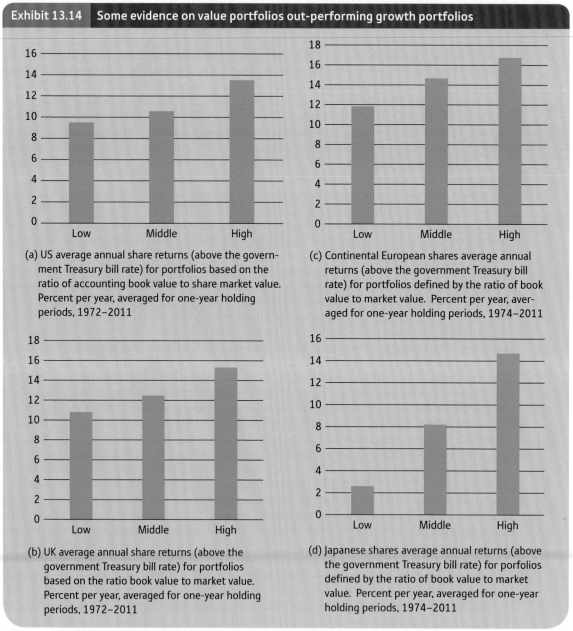

Exhibit 13.14   Some evidence on value portfolios out-performing growth portfolios

(a) US average annual share returns (above the government Treasury bill rate) for portfolios based on the ratio of accounting book value to share market value. Percent per year, averaged for one-year holding periods, 1972–2011

(b) UK average annual share returns (above the government Treasury bill rate) for portfolios based on the ratio book value to market value. Percent per year, averaged for one-year holding periods, 1972–2011

(c) Continental European shares average annual returns (above the government Treasury bill rate) for portfolios defined by the ratio of book value to market value. Percent per year, averaged for one-year holding periods, 1974–2011

(d) Japanese shares average annual returns (above the government Treasury bill rate) for porfolios defined by the ratio of book value to market value. Percent per year, averaged for one-year holding periods, 1974–2011

Source: Asness, Moskowitz and Pedersen (2013) SRC

---

13 For example Lakonishok et al. (1994), Chan et al. (1991), De Bondt and Thaler (1987), Rosenberg et al. (1985), Fama and French (1992, 2006), Capaul et al. (1993), Pontiff and Schall (1998), Reinganum (1988), Gregory et al. (2001, 2003) Dimson et al. (2002), Lewellen (2004), Phalippou (2008), Fama and French (2008), Michou (2009), Shon and Zhou (2010), Asness et al. (2013), Shu, Tao (2013), Israel and Moskowitz (2013). The book-to-market value strategy can be enhanced by selecting only those shares with high gross-profits-to-assets ratios – see Novy-Marx (2013).

- 'Low': the one-third of companies with the lowest BE/ME ratios – glamour shares.
- 'Middle': middling one-third of BE/ME.
- 'High': the one-third of companies with the highest BE/ME ratios – value shares

In America we see that the value portfolios out-performed the growth (glamour) portfolios, giving an average annual return above the Treasury bill rate of 13.2% compared with 9.5%. Value also out-performs growth in the UK sample: 15.3% above the Treasury bill rate, compared with 10.8%. Value shares across Europe gave a 16.7% annual return above Treasury bills compared with 11.8% for glamour shares. In Japan the glamour shares performed quite badly over this period producing only 2.6% per year more than Treasuries. In contrast, the high book equity companies (value) made their investors 14.7% per year.

The out-performance of high book-to-market ratio shares seems odd because (as we discuss in Chapter 17) the main influence on most share prices is the discounted value of their future income flows. Take BSkyB which had a mere £3.8bn of net assets in 2017 and is valued in the stock market at over £16bn. Its assets are largely intangible and not adequately represented in a balance sheet. In other words, there is very little connection between balance sheet asset figures and share price for many shares. The causes of the results of the empirical studies remain largely unexplained. Fama and French (1992, 2006) suggest there may be a systematic difference between companies which have high or low book-to-market value ratios. That is, companies with high book-to-market ratios are more risky. However, company shares have high market price-to-book value for different reasons: for some the nature of their industrial sector means they have few balance sheet recordable assets; for some the share price has risen because of projections of strong earnings growth. It has been suggested that investors underprice some shares in an overreaction to a series of bad news events about the company, while overpricing other shares that have had a series of good news events. Thus, the book-to-market ratio rises as share prices fall in response to an irrational extrapolation of a bad news trend.

Many studies have concluded that shares offering a higher dividend yield tend to outperform the market.[14] Explanations have been offered for this phenomenon ranging from the fact that dividend income is taxed at a higher rate than capital gains and so those investors keen on after-tax income will only purchase high-yielding shares if they offer a higher overall rate of return, to the argument that investors are bad at assessing growth prospects and may underprice shares with a high dividend yield because many have had a poor recent history.

Two other value measures have been examined. The first is the share price to sales; high sales-to-price ratio firms perform better than low sales-to-price firms. Secondly, there is the cash flow (defined as profits after tax plus depreciation and amortisation) to price ratio. Lakonishok et al. (1994) showed a higher return to shares with a high cash flow to price ratio.

The academic papers in the field of semi-form efficiency are widely read in the fund management industry, which spotted a marketing opportunity: if academic researchers report an out-performance to a particular share selection strategy why not simply select a portfolio of shares with that characteristic, e.g. low price earnings ratio or high dividend yield? The fund manager can charge say 1% per year for running the fund on a largely buy and hold basis, making a good income. The saver who buys units or shares in the fund gains exposure to a bunch of shares that should, if the future is like the past, out-perform. There are now hundreds of funds investing based on these 'factors', they are often called 'smart beta' strategies – see **Exhibits 13.15** and **13.16**.

Bubbles

Occasionally financial and other assets go through periods of boom and bust. There are explosive upward movements generating unsustainable prices, which may persist for many years, followed by a crash. These bubbles seem at odds with the theory of efficient markets because prices are not supposed to deviate markedly from fundamental value.

The tulip bulb bubble (tulipmania) in seventeenth-century Holland is an early example in which tulip bulb prices began to rise to absurd levels. The higher the price went the more people considered them good investments. The first investors made lots of money and this encouraged others to sell everything they had to invest in tulips. As each wave of speculators entered the market the prices were pushed higher and higher, eventually reaching the equivalent of £30,000 in today's

---

14 For example, Litzenberger and Ramaswamy (1979), Elton et al. (1983), Levis (1989), Morgan and Thomas (1998), Miles and Timmermann (1996), Dimson et al. (2002) and Lewellen (2004).

Exhibit 13.15

Smart beta: an investment strategy that risks eating itself

The approach based on finding hot new 'factors' runs the risk of repeating time-worn mistakes

By John Authers

To borrow a phrase from Monty Python, smart beta is in danger of getting frightfully silly. The fund management industry's brightest idea of the last few years has opened the real chance to improve returns and reduce costs.

Smart beta is the catch-all phrase for funds that use techniques developed by passive index funds to make active attempts to beat the market. Some take standard stock market indices, which are weighted according to their market value (with the biggest stocks having a proportionately bigger weight), and reweight them according to fundamental characteristics, such as the dividends they pay out, or the sales they make.

Others aim to harness the investment anomalies or "factors" that have been shown by academics to outperform the market in the long term. The most popular include value (stocks that are relatively cheap when they are bought and outperform over time), momentum (winners tend to keep winning while losers keep losing), and size (smaller stocks tend to beat larger stocks).

Like index funds, their costs are low, with lower trading costs and little need to pay for ongoing research. And yet they stand a good chance of beating the market. This makes them an intelligent improvement on traditional actively managed funds, which often traded on these same factors, but in a less systematic way. Smart beta funds are the sales phenomenon of the moment, and companies and advisers are now busily recombining factors into different offerings, and coming up with new factors.

The problem is that as the industry sells smart beta funds, and investors buy them, they are in danger of committing the same mistakes as they ever did. That at least is the thesis of a new paper by a group of researchers for Research Affiliates, a pioneer of smart beta, and it deserves to be taken seriously.

One first issue is data-mining. As the arms race to find new factors continues, historical data are being tortured in new ways. When a factor is publicised, and a fund launched, it tends to have performed very well in the past (even though there were no funds in existence to follow it). In practice, academics have tailored their specifications carefully so that their strategy is shown to have great performance at the point of publication.

It should be no surprise that the team, led by Rob Arnott, found that a factor's performance versus the market roughly halves once it has been published.

Looking at what the returns of eight published factors would have been since 1967, they found an average return in excess of the market of 5.8 per cent per year (a huge number) before publication — and of only 2.6 per cent after publication.

A separate problem is timing. We all want to do it, but we are very bad at it. Over a long period, valuation gives a decent idea as to what might be best to buy at any one moment (even if it gives no help to identifying a top or a bottom).

If a stock or bond is expensive, compared to its own history, it is a good bet that it will perform worse over the following years, and vice versa.

The same applies to factors. Some factors perform well at times when others do not (for example, momentum and value tend to work best at different times). Buying a factor when it is relatively expensive (when the stocks it contains are relatively expensive compared to their historical norm), is as bad an idea as buying a stock when it is expensive. According to Mr Arnott's research, a strategy within US stocks of continuously buying the three most expensive factors would have underperformed the market — while continuously buying the three cheapest would have beaten the market by 3.7 percentage points per year. This looks like a plausible model for funds that could form the backbone for long-term pension savings.

But here comes another endemic problem: performance-chasing. The fund industry revolves around looking for the funds that have performed best recently. It is always a safe thing for an adviser or consultant to recommend.

The logic behind exploiting market anomalies in a systematic way and reducing the costs in the process, remains intact. But such strategies work primarily because they impose a discipline to avoid the endemic errors that we tend to make, both because of our own psychology, and because of the perverse incentives at work on the sales practices of the investment industry. Mr Arnott's research shows there is a real risk that if we are not careful, we will use smart beta funds as a vehicle to make those endemic errors in a new way. That would not be smart.

FT *Financial Times*, 28 September 2016.
All Rights Reserved.

Exhibit 13.16

A clinical test of the 5 most popular Smart Beta factors

If treated like new drugs, most would never be cleared for sale to the public

By John Authers

"Smart Beta" — the attempt to turn investment factors into indices that can be turned into cheap tracker funds or exchange traded funds — has become one of the investment industry's biggest earners. But the rush to identify new anomalies that can be turned into indices, and then lay claim to them in the academic literature, is beginning to resemble the rush to patent new drugs. The total number of "smart beta" factors identified so far comes to 458. If subjected to the same kind of rigorous testing that new drugs go through, most would never be cleared for sale to the public.

Last month the central "smart beta" factors received the investment industry's closest approach to a clinical trial. The trio of British academics Elroy Dimson, Paul Marsh and Mike Staunton have been publishing their Global Investment Returns Yearbook, for many years. Using an enormous database of more than 20 countries' stock markets, going back more than a century, they can test whether elaborate theories would really have worked as claimed over time.

This year they tested the five most popular smart beta factors — value (cheap stocks outperform), size (small stocks beat big), low-risk (also known as "betting against beta" — lower risk, less volatile stocks outperform), momentum (winners keep winning and losers keep losing), and income, known by some as "carry" (the notion that higher income stocks will return more).

These need to be divided into two categories. Size, income and value are reasonably constant over time. You invest in small and cheap companies in the hope that they will eventually become large and expensive, but a portfolio built around these stocks will not need to be reshuffled much. Mr Dimson suggests that these are appropriate for retail funds sold to the public.

The other factors require frequent reshuffling, it becomes vital to minimise trading costs, and they are better left to hedge funds and proprietary trading desks.

Their findings: when it comes to the low-risk anomaly, the great returns come from avoiding the riskiest stocks, rather than seeking out the least risky. Since 1963, when divided into quintiles, the riskiest fifth of stocks returned only 4.1 per cent per year. All others returned at least 10.9 per cent.

A similar study for the UK yielded similar results. The riskiest third of stocks returned only 4.2 per cent per year, while others returned in double digits. Most of this effect was driven by the fallout from the dotcom bust in 2000.

As for momentum, which can be measured in many ways, the team tested a strategy of identifying the best and worst performing quintiles of stocks over six months, waiting a month, and then buying the winners and shorting the losers. This approach was recalculated every six months.

The results showed, as might be expected, that returns were very volatile, but that over time they would have accumulated impressively. (The most powerful winning factor in finance is, of course, compound interest). In the US since 1900 the winners would have beaten the losers by 7.4 percentage points per annum, while in the UK the gap was an enormous 10.4 percentage points. One pound invested in 1900 would have turned into £61 with the losers by now, and more than £5m with the winners. Across 23 countries, the effect proved robust, and has strengthened slightly since it was first demonstrated in 2000 — very different

▶

Exhibit 13.16 *(continued)*

from the experience with other factors. The average global monthly return to winners over losers is now 0.79 per cent, up from 0.71 per cent.

As for the size factor, it endured a long period of failing to outperform as hoped — although the phenomenon that smaller companies behave differently from large ones remains intact.

The value effect, which has had a conspicuously poor time since the 2008 financial crisis, continues to show up, although not universally. The global value premium since 2000 has been 2.5 percentage points (a great return if it is compounded over a few years), but there were four European countries where value has underperformed.

The income factor, a subset of value as a high dividend yield is often regarded as an indicator of cheapness, has performed very well since 2000, but this may be due to the strange yield-hunting conditions that have persisted for much of that time.

In a pleasant surprise, the academics' conclusion is upbeat. All five effects are genuine, in that they tend to cause stocks to perform differently (even if they do not always perform better) and all should be monitored by investors. Their performance will vary greatly over time. If smart beta managers have any sense, they will keep their attentions to these five factors, and resist temptations to over-elaborate.

money for one bulb. But the fundamentals were against the investors and in one month, February 1637, prices collapsed to one-tenth of the peak levels (by 1739 the price had fallen to 1/200th of one per cent of its peak value).

The South Sea Bubble which burst in 1720 was a British share fiasco in which investors threw money at the South Sea Company on a surge of over-optimism only to lose most or all of it. The increase in share prices in the 1920s and before the 1987 crash have also been interpreted as bubbles. The mania for telecoms, media and technology shares in the late 1990s has been identified as leading to a bubble. I wrote in the fourth edition that 'many see property prices in 2007 in many countries as being determined largely by a bubble mentality' – hindsight confirms this (*see* Kindleberger and Aliber (2011), Pastor and Veronesi (2009) and Frehen et al. (2013) for more on bubbles).

One explanation for this seemingly irrational behaviour of markets is what is called noise trading by naive investors. According to this theory there are two classes of traders, the informed and the uninformed. The informed trade shares so as to bring them towards their fundamental value. However, the uninformed can behave irrationally and create 'noise' in share prices and thereby generate bias in share pricing. They may be responding to frenzied expectations of almost instant wealth based on 'a new era' in technology or business innovation, and an extrapolation of recent security (e.g. share) price trends – perhaps they noted from the newspapers that there is an amazing invention drawing-in customers. They may also observe a period where the stock market made investors high returns over a couple of years and so rush to get a piece of the action. This tendency to 'chase the trend' can lead to very poor performance because the dabbler in the markets often buys shares after a sharp rise and sells shares after being shocked by a sharp fall.

To reinforce the power of the uninformed investor to push the market up and up, the informed investor, seeing a bubble developing, often tries to get in on the rise. Despite knowing that it will all end in disaster for some, the informed investor buys in the hope of selling out before the crash. This is based on the idea that the price an investor is willing to pay for a share today is dependent on the price the investor can sell for at some point in the future and not necessarily on fundamental value. Keynes (1936) as far back as the 1930s commented that share prices may not be determined by fundamentals but by investors trying to guess the value other investors will place on shares. He drew the analogy with forecasting the outcome of a beauty contest. If you want to win you are better off concentrating on guessing how the judges will respond to the contestants rather than trying to judge beauty for yourself. George Soros is an example of a very active (informed and successful) investor who is quite prepared to buy into an apparent irrational market move but makes every effort to get out before the uninformed investors. There is evidence that a number of hedge funds rode the technology share bubble in the late 1990s. They did not act as a correcting force returning prices to efficient levels, but reinforced the bubble in a destabilising way (*see* Brunnermeier and Nagel, 2004). Note that the term 'informed investor' does not equal professional investor. There are many professional fund managers and analysts who, on a close examination, fall into the category of ill-informed noise traders (*see* Arnold (2009) for more on the inadequacies of 'professional investors', and Arnold (2011) for an explanation of George Soros' reflexivity theory).

Exhibit 13.17 puts forward the case that the incentives in investing institutions encourage bubbles.

Exhibit 13.17

Individual rationality can mean collective irrationality

By Tony Jackson

Now that even the UK's chief financial regulator has started kicking the theory of efficient markets, the fun has gone out of it somehow. Moderation in all things: and it is worth remarking that just because markets are inefficient, that need not mean investors are irrational.

The point is contentious, and needs defending. As it happens, I have come across an academic paper which does just that. But first, an observation.

Some economists insist that markets must be efficient because they are rational. And if they are not rational, the whole of economic theory collapses.

So be it, we might reply. Better no theory than a dud one. And other theories, based on behaviour rather than rationality, do a better job.

But when it comes to the big stuff, our actions belie that. When we are grappling with the subprime debacle or Chinese economic policy, we ask ourselves what people are up to – not how they behave, but how they are reasoning.

In fact, the theory of rational behaviour is a model – a schematic attempt to portray the big picture. Any such model, in or out of economics, contains anomalies. To dwell on those anomalies, as we all now enjoy doing, risks missing the point. It is only when there are enough of them that the model is more hindrance than help and must be dumped.

So to the paper, by two academics from the London School of Economics – former hedge fund manager Paul Woolley and Professor Dimitri Vayanos. In effect, they argue that markets are inefficient for perfectly rational reasons.

The key lies in the use of agents. Conventional economic theory deals with representative individuals. But in reality, those individuals generally hand their savings to institutions, who hand them on to specialist fund managers.

If those managers underperform the market, it is hard for the investor to know whether they are deliberately avoiding overvalued stocks, or simply messing up. If the situation persists, then investors infer the latter and switch their money.

The germ of the idea came to Dr Woolley a decade ago, he says, when he was running the European end of the US hedge fund GMO. The fund relied on fundamental value during the dotcom boom, when high-tech, telecom and media stocks became grossly overvalued. GMO initially shunned them, thereby underperforming hugely, and by the peak of the frenzy had lost 40% of its funds under management. Until the tide turned, the only way it could stem the flow was to devote part of its funds (and the bulk of its trading) to momentum plays – that is, to the overvalued stuff.

The concept of momentum is important because efficient market theory says it should not exist. If investors decide a stock or sector is worth a price different from the present one, they should move to that price immediately.

In reality, of course, prices overshoot over long periods, then go into reverse. The dotcom example illustrates why.

As investors were bailing out of value funds such as GMO, they were gradually switching more cash into the bubble stocks. Thus those stocks were pushed up and value stocks pushed down. Why gradually? Because it takes time to sack a fund manager and because individual investors capitulate at different levels.

In a sense, this is not new. I myself have banged on for years about how fundamental value is in practice irrelevant, since fund managers who stick to the fundamentals risk losing their jobs.

But I had rather assumed that was because end-investors were behaving irrationally. This thesis suggests otherwise.

The information gap between them and their agents means they are making the best of the knowledge available to them. So it turns out that individually rational actions add up to a collectively irrational outcome. That might seem odd to mainstream economists, but not to the rest of us. Mutually destructive wars have been fought on the same basis.

Financial Times, 31 August 2009, p. 16.

Comment on the semi-strong efficiency evidence

Despite the evidence of some work showing departures from semi-strong efficiency, for most investors most of the time the market may be regarded as efficient. This does not mean the search for anomalies should cease. The evidence for semi-strong efficiency is significant but not so overwhelming that there is no hope of outperformance for the able and dedicated.

While the volume of evidence of pockets of market inefficiencies is impressive, we need to be wary when placing weight on these results. Given the fact that there have been hundreds of researchers examining the data it is not a surprise that some of them find plausible looking statistical relationships indicating excess return opportunities. The research that actually gets published tends to be that which has 'found' an inefficiency. The research that does not show inefficiency receives much less publicity. Furthermore, the excess return strategies may be time specific and may not continue into the future.

On the other hand consider this: suppose that you discover a trading strategy that produces abnormal returns. You could publish it in a respected journal or you could keep it to yourself. Most would select the latter option because publishing may result in the elimination of the inefficiency and with it the chance of high investment returns. So there may be a lot of evidence of inefficiency that remains hidden and is being quietly exploited.

There is a strange paradox in this area of finance: in order for the market to remain efficient there has to be a large body of investors who believe it to be inefficient. If all investors suddenly believed that shares are efficiently priced and no abnormal profits are obtainable they would quite sensibly refuse to pay for data gathering and analysis. At that moment the market starts to drift away from fundamental value. The market needs speculators and long-term investors continually on the prowl for under- or overpriced securities. It is through their buying and selling activities that inefficiencies are minimised and the market is a fair game.

Among academics and their intellectual disciples there was a high degree of faith in the EMH in the 1970s, 1980s and 1990s. Today that faith is slipping. This will have profound implications for investment behaviour and corporate finance.

There are some investors who have rejected the strictures of the EMH and have achieved astonishingly good returns. Here are some of them.[15]

Peter Lynch

From May 1977 to May 1990 Peter Lynch was the portfolio manager of Fidelity's Magellan Fund. Over this 13-year period a $1,000 investment rose to be worth $28,000, a rate of return that is way ahead of the field at 29.2% per annum. Furthermore, the fund's performance was consistent – in only two of those years did it fail to beat the S&P 500. The fund grew from an asset base of $18m to one of more than $14bn. It was not only the best-performing fund in the world; it also became the biggest. There were one million shareholders in 1990, when Lynch quit, at the age of 46, to devote more time to his family. His experiences as a young man gave him a sceptical eye to what was being taught on his MBA course at Wharton:

> It seemed to me that most of what I learned at Wharton, which was supposed to help you succeed in the investment business, could only help you fail . . . Quantitative analysis taught me that the things I saw happening at Fidelity couldn't really be happening. I also found it difficult to integrate the efficient market hypothesis . . . It also was obvious that the Wharton professors who believed in quantum analysis and random walk weren't doing nearly as well as my new colleagues at Fidelity, so between theory and practice, I cast my lot with the practitioners . . . My distrust of theorizers and prognosticators continues to the present day.[16]

John Neff

When John Neff managed the Windsor Fund, his investment philosophy emphasised the importance of a low share price relative to earnings. However, his approach required a share to pass a

---

15 These performances and the underlying investment philosophies are explored more fully in Arnold (2009) and in Arnold (2011).

16 Lynch (1990), pp. 34–5.

number of tests besides the price–earnings criteria. These additional hurdles turn his approach from simple low price–earnings investing to a sophisticated one. John Neff was in charge of the Windsor Fund for 31 years. It beat the market for 25 of those 31 years. He took control in 1964, and retired in 1995. Windsor was the largest equity mutual in the United States when it closed its doors to new investors in 1985. Each dollar invested in 1964 had returned $56 by 1995, compared with $22 for the S&P 500. The total return for Windsor, at 5,546.5%, outpaced the S&P 500 by more than two to one. This was an additional return on the market of 3.15 percentage points a year after expenses. Before expenses the outperformance was 3.5 percentage points.[17] He was always on the lookout for out-of-favour, overlooked or misunderstood stocks. These nuggets of gold always stood on low price–earnings ratios. Not only that; their prospects for earnings growth were good. He believes that the market tends to allow itself to be swept along with fads, fashions and flavours of the month. This leads to overvaluation of those stocks regarded as shooting stars, and to the undervaluation of those which prevailing wisdom deems unexciting, but which are fundamentally good stocks. Investors become caught in the clutch of group-think and en masse ignore solid companies. Bad news tends to weigh more heavily than good news as the investor's malaise deepens. The way Neff saw it, if you could buy a stock where the negatives were largely known, then any good news that comes as a surprise can have a profoundly positive effect on the stock price. On the other hand if you buy into a growth story where great things are expected and built in to the price, the slightest hint of bad news can take the sizzle out of the stock.

Benjamin Graham

Benjamin Graham is regarded as the most influential of investment philosophers. Graham was the leading exponent of the value investing school of thought. Over 20 years (from 1936) the Graham-Newman Corporation achieved an abnormally high performance for its clients: 'The success of Graham-Newman Corporation can be gauged by its average annual distribution. Roughly speaking, if one invested $10,000 in 1936, one received an average of $2,100 a year for the next twenty years and recovered one's original $10,000 at the end.'[18] Graham[19] in 1955 put a slightly different figure on it: 'Over a period of years we have tended to earn about 20 per cent on capital per year'. This is much better than the return available on the market as a whole. For example, Barclays Capital[20] show the annual average real (excluding inflation) rate of return on US stocks with gross income reinvested as 7.4% for those years. Even if we add back average annual inflation of 3.8%[21] to the Barclays' figures to make them comparable, the Graham-Newman figures are much better than the returns received by the average investor. According to Graham, market prices are not determined by any necessarily rational or mathematical relationship to fundamental factors (at least, not in the short run) 'but through the minds and decisions of buyers and sellers';[22] 'The prices of common stock are not carefully thought out computations, but the resultants of a welter of human reactions. The stock market is a voting machine rather than a weighing machine. It responds to factual data not directly, but only as they affect the decisions of buyers and sellers.'[23]

Plainly, he did not believe the efficient markets hypothesis:

> Evidently the processes by which the securities market arrives at its appraisals are frequently illogical and erroneous. These processes . . . are not automatic or mechanical, but psychological for they go on in the minds of people who buy and sell. The mistakes of the market are thus the mistakes of groups of masses of individuals. Most of them can be traced to one or more of three basic causes: exaggeration, oversimplification, or neglect.[24]

---

17 Neff (1999), pp. 62 and 71.
18 Train (1980), p. 98.
19 Reproduced in Lowe (1999), p. 116.
20 Barclays Capital, *Equity Gilt Studies* (published annually).
21 Implicit price deflation for GNP. US Office of Business Economics, *The National Income and Product Accounts of the United States 1929–1965*.
22 Graham and Dodd (1934), p. 12.
23 Graham and Dodd (1934), p. 452.
24 Graham and Dodd (1934), p. 585.

Warren Buffett and Charles Munger

Warren Buffett is the most influential investment thinker of our time; he is also the wealthiest. Charles Munger is Buffett's partner, both intellectually and in the running of one of the world's largest companies. They each started with very little capital. At first, they developed their investment philosophies independently. They were far away from each other, both in their investment approach and geographically (Munger in California and Buffett in Nebraska). Despite the different approaches to stock picking they each created highly successful fund management businesses before coming together. Buffett took managerial control of Berkshire Hathaway in 1965 when the book value per share was $19.46 (as measured at the prior year end 30 September 1964). By year end 2017 the book value, with equity holdings carried at market value, was $211,750 per share. The gain in book value over 53 years came to 19.1% compounded annually. At this rate of return an investment of $100 becomes worth over $1,088,029 over 53 years. There are people who are multimillionaires today because in the 1960s or 1970s they invested a few thousand dollars in Berkshire Hathaway. Warren Buffett owns around 40% of Berkshire Hathaway,[25] a company with a market capitalisation of over $450bn (it was valued at a mere $20m in 1965). **Exhibit 13.18** shows the truly outstanding performance of Berkshire Hathaway. There have been only 13 years in which the rise in book value was less than the return on the S&P 500. It is even better than it looks – the S&P 500 numbers are pre-tax whereas the Berkshire numbers are after-tax!

Berkshire owns shares in publicly traded companies worth $122bn. These holdings include 17.6% of American Express, 9.4% of Coca-Cola, 12.9% of Moody's, 7.4% of Delta Airlines, and 9.9% of Wells Fargo. Some investors have been with Buffett long before he took control of Berkshire. An investor who placed $100 in one of his investment partnerships in the late 1950s, and placed it in Berkshire after the partnership was dissolved, would find that investment worth more than $30m today. In the 13 years of the partnership funds (1957–69) Buffett made annual returns greater than that on Berkshire, at almost 30% per year. The funds managed by the young Buffett outperformed the Dow Jones Industrial Average in every year and made money even when the market was sharply down. If you put the two phases of his career – first the partnership, then Berkshire – together then you have a quite remarkable performance record, one that, to my knowledge, has not been beaten.[26]

Buffett is one of the three richest people in the world. Imagine being one of the lucky people to have trusted Buffett in the early days. It is what investors' dreams are made of. Apparently, the following conversation between two Berkshire shareholders was overheard at the annual meeting in 1996: 'What price did you buy at?' The reply: 'Nineteen,' says the first. 'You mean nineteen hundred?' 'No, nineteen.'[27] These shares are now worth over $280,000 each!

Warren Buffett said:

> I'm convinced that there is much inefficiency in the market . . . When the price of a stock can be influenced by a 'herd' on Wall Street with prices set at the margin by the most emotional person, or the greediest person, or the most depressed person, it is hard to argue that the market always prices rationally. In fact, market prices are frequently nonsensical . . . There seems to be some perverse human characteristic that likes to make easy things difficult. The academic world, if anything, has actually backed away from the teaching of value investing over the last 30 years. It's likely to continue that way. Ships will sail around the world but the Flat Earth Society will flourish.[28]

The question is: are these performances possible through chance? Just to muddy the waters, consider the following situation. You give dice to 100 million investors and ask them each to throw nine sixes in a row. Naturally most will fail, but some will succeed. You follow up the exercise with a series of interviews to find out how the masters of the die did it. Some say it was the lucky cup they use; others point to astrological charts. Of course we all know that it was purely chance that produced success but try telling that to the gurus and their disciples.

---

25 He is gradually reducing his holding to give away his fortune mostly to the Bill & Melinda Gates' charity, assisting developing countries, particularly with medical aid.

26 If you would like to know more about how Buffett made his fortune then you might like to read Arnold (2017) *The Deals of Warren Buffett: Vol. 1, The First $100m.*

27 Urry (1996), p. 1.

28 Warren Buffett (1984).

Exhibit 13.18	Berkshire Hathaway's corporate performance vs. the S&P 500		
	Annual percentage change		
	In per-share book value of Berkshire	In S&P 500 with dividends included	Relative results (1) − (2)
Year	(1)	(2)	
1965	23.8	10.0	13.8
1966	20.3	(11.7)	32.0
1967	11.0	30.9	(19.9)
1968	19.0	11.0	8.0
1969	16.2	(8.4)	24.6
1970	12.0	3.9	8.1
1971	16.4	14.6	1.8
1972	21.7	18.9	2.8
1973	4.7	(14.8)	19.5
1974	5.5	(26.4)	31.9
1975	21.9	37.2	(15.3)
1976	59.3	23.6	35.7
1977	31.9	(7.4)	39.3
1978	24.0	6.4	17.6
1979	35.7	18.2	17.5
1980	19.3	32.3	(13.0)
1981	31.4	(5.0)	36.4
1982	40.0	21.4	18.6
1983	32.3	22.4	9.9
1984	13.6	6.1	7.5
1985	48.2	31.6	16.6
1986	26.1	18.6	7.5
1987	19.5	5.1	14.4
1988	20.1	16.6	3.5
1989	44.4	31.7	12.7
1990	7.4	(3.1)	10.5
1991	39.6	30.5	9.1
1992	20.3	7.6	12.7
1993	14.3	10.1	4.2
1994	13.9	1.3	12.6
1995	43.1	37.6	5.5
1996	31.8	23.0	8.8
1997	34.1	33.4	0.7
1998	48.3	28.6	19.7
1999	0.5	21.0	(20.5)
2000	6.5	(9.1)	15.6
2001	(6.2)	(11.9)	5.7
2002	10.0	(22.1)	32.1
2003	21.0	28.7	(7.7)
2004	10.5	10.9	(0.4)
2005	6.4	4.9	1.5
2006	18.4	15.8	2.6
2007	11.0	5.5	5.5
2008	(9.6)	(37.0)	27.4
2009	19.8	26.5	(6.7)
2010	13.0	15.1	(2.1)
2011	4.6	2.1	2.5
2012	14.4	16.0	(1.6)

Exhibit 13.18 *(continued)*

| | Annual percentage change | | |
| | In per-share book value of Berkshire | In S&P 500 with dividends included | Relative results (1) – (2) |
Year	(1)	(2)	
2013	18.2	32.4	(14.2)
2014	8.3	13.7	(5.4)
2015	6.4	1.4	(5.0)
2016	10.7	12.0	(1.3)
2017	23.0	21.8	1.2
Average annual gain 1965–2016	**19.1%**	**9.9%**	**9.2%**

Source: from Berkshire Hathaway, Annual Report, 2017 (www.berkshirehathaway.com). The material is copyrighted and used with permission of the author.

Warren Buffett has countered this argument – *see* **Exhibit 13.19**. It is very difficult to prove either way whether excellent stock picking performance is due to superior analysis in an inefficient environment or merely good fortune. Ultimately you have to make a subjective judgement given the weight of evidence.

Exhibit 13.19

The superinvestors of Graham-and-Doddsville

By Warren E. Buffett

Many of the professors who write textbooks . . . argue that the stock market is efficient: that is, that stock prices reflect everything that is known about a company's prospects and about the state of the economy. There are no undervalued stocks, these theorists argue, because there are smart security analysts who utilize all available information to ensure unfailingly appropriate prices. Investors who seem to beat the market year after year are just lucky. 'If prices fully reflect available information, this sort of investment adeptness is ruled out,' writes one of today's textbook authors. Well, maybe, but I want to present to you a group of investors who have, year in and year out, beaten the Standard & Poor's 500 stock index. The hypothesis that they do this by pure chance is at least worth examining. Crucial to this examination is the fact that these winners were all well known to me and pre-identified as superior investors, the most recent identification occurring over fifteen years ago. Absent this condition – that is, if I had just recently searched among thousands of records to select a few names for you this morning – I would advise you to stop reading right here. I should add that all these records have been audited. And I should further add that I have known many of those who have invested with these managers, and the checks received by those participants over the years have matched the stated records.

Before we begin this examination, I would like you to imagine a national coin-flipping contest. Let's assume we get 225 million Americans up tomorrow morning and we ask them all to wager a dollar. They go out in the morning at sunrise, and they all call the flip of a coin. If they call correctly, they win a dollar from those who called wrong. Each day the losers drop out, and on the subsequent day the stakes build as all previous winnings are put on the line. After ten flips on ten mornings, there will be approximately 220,000 people in the United States who have correctly called ten flips in a row. They each will have won a little over $1,000.

Now this group will probably start getting a little puffed up about this, human nature being what it is. They may try to be modest, but at cocktail parties they will occasionally admit to attractive members of the opposite sex what their technique is, and what marvellous insights they bring to the field of flipping.

Assuming that the winners are getting the appropriate rewards from the losers, in another ten days we will have 215 people who have successfully called their coin flips 20 times in a row and who each, by this exercise, have turned one dollar into a little over $1 million. $225 million would have been lost; $225 million would have been won.

By then, this group will really lose their heads. They will probably write books on 'How I Turned a Dollar into a Million in Twenty Days Working Thirty Seconds a Morning'. Worse yet, they'll probably start jetting around the country attending seminars on efficient coin-flipping and tackling sceptical professors with, 'If it can't be done, why are there 215 of us?'

But then some business school professor will probably be rude enough to bring up the fact that if 225 million orangutans had engaged in a similar exercise, the results would be much the same – 215 egotistical orangutans with 20 straight winning flips.

I would argue, however, that there *are* some important differences in the examples I am going to present. For one thing, if (a) you had taken 225 million orangutans distributed roughly as the U.S. population is; if (b) 215 winners were left after 20 days; and if (c) you found that 40 came from a particular zoo in Omaha, you would be pretty sure you were on to something. So you would probably go out and ask the zookeeper about what he's feeding them, whether they had special exercises, what books they read, and who knows what else. That is, if you found any really extraordinary concentrations of success, you might want to see if you could identify concentrations of unusual characteristics that might be causal factors.

Scientific inquiry naturally follows such a pattern. If you were trying to analyse possible causes of a rare type of cancer – with, say, 1,500 cases a year in the United States – and you found that 400 of them occurred in some little mining town in Montana, you would get very interested in the water there, or the occupation of those afflicted, or other variables. You know that it's not random chance that 400 come from a small area. You would not necessarily know the causal factors, but you would know where to search.

I submit to you that there are ways of defining an origin other than geography. In addition to geographical origins, there can be what I call an *intellectual* origin. I think you will find that a disproportionate number of successful coin-flippers in the investment world came from a very small intellectual village that could be called Graham-and-Doddsville. A concentration of winners that simply cannot be explained by chance can be traced to this particular intellectual village.

Conditions could exist that would make even that concentration unimportant. Perhaps 100 people were simply imitating the coin-flipping call of some terribly persuasive personality. When he called heads, 100 followers automatically called that coin the same way. If the leader was part of the 215 left at the end, the fact that 100 came from the same intellectual origin would mean nothing. You would simply be identifying one case as a hundred cases. Similarly, let's assume that you lived in a strongly patriarchal society and every family in the United States conveniently consisted of ten members. Further assume that the patriarchal culture was so strong that, when the 225 million people went out the first day, every member of the family identified with the father's call. Now, at the end of the 20-day period, you would have 215 winners, and you would find that they came from only 21.5 families. Some naive types might say that this indicates an enormous hereditary factor as an explanation of successful coin flipping. But, of course, it would have no significance at all because it would simply mean that you didn't have 215 individual winners, but rather 21.5 randomly distributed families who were winners.

In this group of successful investors that I want to consider, there has been a common intellectual patriarch, Ben Graham. But the children who left the house of this intellectual patriarch have called their 'flips' in very different ways. They have gone to different places and bought and sold different stocks and companies, yet they have had a combined record that simply can't be explained by random chance. It certainly cannot be explained by the fact that they are all calling flips identically because a leader is signalling the calls to make. The patriarch has merely set forth the intellectual theory for making coin-calling decisions, but each student has decided on his own manner of applying the theory.

The common intellectual theme of the investors from Graham-and-Doddsville is this: they search for discrepancies between the *value* of a business and the *price* of small pieces of that business in the market. Essentially, they exploit those discrepancies without the efficient market theorist's concern as to whether the stocks are bought on Monday or Thursday, or whether it is January or July, etc. Incidentally, when businessmen buy businesses – which is just what our Graham & Dodd investors are doing through the medium of marketable stocks – I doubt that many are cranking into their purchase decision the day of the week or the month in which the transaction is going to occur. If it doesn't make any difference whether all of a business is being bought on a Monday or a Friday, I am baffled why academicians invest extensive time and effort to see whether it makes a difference when buying small pieces of those same businesses. Our Graham & Dodd investors, needless to say, do not discuss beta, the capital asset pricing model, or covariance in returns among securities. These are not subjects of any interest to them. In fact, most of them would have difficulty defining those terms. The investors simply focus on two variables, price and value.

. . . I think the group that we have identified by a common intellectual home is worthy of study. Incidentally, despite all the academic studies of the influence of such variables as price, volume, seasonality, capitalization size,

▶

Exhibit 13.19 (continued)

etc., upon stock performance, no interest has been evidenced in studying the methods of this unusual concentration of value-oriented winners.

I begin this study of results by going back to a group of four of us who worked at Graham-Newman Corporation from 1954 through 1956. There were only four – I have not selected these names from among thousands. I offered to go to work at Graham-Newman for nothing after I took Ben Graham's class, but he turned me down as over-valued. He took this value stuff very seriously! After much pestering he finally hired me. There were three partners and four of us at the 'peasant' level. All four left between 1955 and 1957 when the firm was wound up, and it's possible to trace the record of three.

The first example is that of Walter Schloss. Walter never went to college, but took a course from Ben Graham at night at the New York Institute of Finance. Walter left Graham-Newman in 1955 and achieved the record shown here over 28 years. [A compound rate of return of 21.3 per cent compared with a market return of 8.4 per cent from 1956 to 1984.]

. . . Walter has diversified enormously, owning well over 100 stocks currently. He knows how to identify securities that sell at considerably less than their value to a private owner. *And that's all he does* . . . He simply says, if a business is worth a dollar and I can buy it for 40 cents, something good may happen to me, and he does it over and over and over again. He owns many more stocks than I do – and is far less interested in the underlying nature of the business; I don't seem to have very much influence on Walter. That's one of his strengths; no one has much influence on him.

The second case is Tom Knapp, who also worked at Graham-Newman with me. Tom was a chemistry major at Princeton before the war; when he came back from the war, he was a beach bum. And then one day he read that Dave Dodd was giving a night course in investments at Columbia. Tom took it on a noncredit basis, and he got so interested in the subject from taking that course that he came up and enrolled at Columbia Business School, where he got the MBA degree. He took Dodd's course again, and took Ben Graham's course. Incidentally, 35 years later I called Tom to ascertain some of the facts involved here and I found him on the beach again. The only difference is that now he owns the beach!

In 1968 Tom Knapp and Ed Anderson, also a Graham disciple, along with one or two other fellows of similar persuasion, formed Tweedy, Browne Partners, and their investment results appear in Table 2 [showing an annual compound rate of return of 20 per cent compared with the market's return of 7 per cent, 1968–83]. Tweedy, Browne built that record with very wide diversification. They occasionally bought control of businesses, but the record of the passive investments is equal to the record of the control investments.

Table 3 describes the third member of the group who formed the Buffett Partnership in 1957. [Table 3, not reproduced here, shows a compound rate of 29.5 per cent against the market rate of 7.4 per cent, 1957–69.] The best thing he did was to quit in 1969. Since then, in a sense, Berkshire Hathaway has been a continuation of the partnership in some respects. There is no single index I can give you that I would feel would be a fair test of investment management at Berkshire. But I think that any way you figure it, it has been satisfactory.

Table 4 shows the record of the Sequoia Fund, which is managed by a man whom I met in 1951 in Ben Graham's class, Bill Ruane. [Table 4, not reproduced here, shows compound annual return of 17.2 per cent against a market return of 10 per cent, 1970–84.] After getting out of Harvard Business School, he went to Wall Street. Then he realized that he needed to get a real business education so he came up to take Ben's course at Columbia, where we met in early 1951. Bill's record from 1951 to 1970, working with relatively small sums, was far better than average. When I wound up Buffett Partnership I asked Bill if he would set up a fund to handle all our partners, so he set up the Sequoia Fund. He set it up at a terrible time, just when I was quitting.

He went right into the two-tier market and all the difficulties that made for comparative performance for value-oriented investors. I am happy to say that my partners, to an amazing degree, not only stayed with him but added money, with the happy result shown.

There's no hindsight involved here. Bill was the only person I recommended to my partners, and I said at the time that if he achieved a four-point-per-annum advantage over the Standard & Poor's, that would be solid performance. Bill has achieved well over that, working with progressively larger sums of money.

. . . I should add that in the records we've looked at so far, throughout this whole period there was practically no duplication in these portfolios. These are men who select securities based on discrepancies between price and value, but they make their selections very differently . . . The overlap among these portfolios has been very, very low. These records do not reflect one guy calling the flip and fifty people yelling out the same thing after him.

. . . A friend of mine who is a Harvard Law graduate . . . set up a major law firm. I ran into him in about 1960 and told him that law was fine as a hobby but he could do better. He set up a partnership quite the opposite of Walter's. His portfolio was concentrated in very few securities and therefore his record was much more volatile but it was based on the same discount-from-value approach [average annual compound rate of return of 19.8 per cent compared with market return of 5 per cent p.a., 1962–75]. He was willing to accept greater peaks and valleys of performance, and he happens to be a fellow whose whole psyche goes toward concentration, with the results shown [not reproduced]. Incidentally, this record belongs to Charlie Munger, my partner for a long time in the operation of Berkshire Hathaway. When he ran his partnership, however, his portfolio holdings were almost completely different from mine and the other fellows mentioned earlier.

Table 6 [not reproduced here] is the record of a fellow who was a pal of Charlie Munger's, another non-business school type – who was a math major at USC. He went to work for IBM after graduation and was an IBM salesman for a while. After I got to Charlie, Charlie got to him. This happens to be the record of Rick Guerin. Rick, from 1965 to 1983, against a compounded gain of 316 percent for the S&P, came off with 22,200 percent which, probably because he lacks a business school education, he regards as statistically significant.

One sidelight here: it is extraordinary to me that the idea of buying dollar bills for 40 cents takes immediately with people or it doesn't take at all. It's like an inoculation. If it doesn't grab a person right away, I find that you can talk to him for years and show him records, and it doesn't make any difference. They just don't seem able to grasp the concept, simple as it is. A fellow like Rick Guerin, who had no formal education in business, understands immediately the value approach to investing and he's applying it five minutes later. I've never seen anyone who became a gradual convert over a ten-year period to this approach. It doesn't seem to be a matter of IQ or academic training. It's instant recognition, or it is nothing.

. . . Stan Perlmeter . . . was a liberal arts major at the University of Michigan who was a partner in the advertising agency of Bozell & Jacobs. We happened to be in the same building in Omaha. In 1965 he figured out I had a better business than he did, so he left advertising. Again, it took five minutes for Stan to embrace the value approach. [Performance: 23 per cent p.a. compared with market return of 7 per cent 1966–83.]

Perlmeter does not own what Walter Schloss owns. He does not own what Bill Ruane owns. These are records made *independently*. But every time Perlmeter buys a stock it's because he's getting more for his money than he's paying. That's the only thing he's thinking about. He's not looking at quarterly earnings projections, he's not looking at next year's earnings, he's not thinking about what day of the week it is, he doesn't care what investment research from any place says, he's not interested in price momentum, volume, or anything. He's simply asking: What is the business worth?

. . . So these are . . . records of 'coin-flippers' from Graham-and-Doddsville. I haven't selected them with hindsight from among thousands. It's not like I am reciting to you the names of a bunch of lottery winners – people I had never heard of before they won the lottery. I selected these men years ago based upon their framework for investment decision-making. I knew what they had been taught and additionally I had some personal knowledge of their intellect, character, and temperament. It's very important to understand that this group has assumed far less risk than average; note their record in years when the general market was weak. While they differ greatly in style, these investors are, mentally, *always buying the business, not buying the stock*. A few of them sometimes buy whole businesses. Far more often they simply buy small pieces of businesses. Their attitude, whether buying all or a tiny piece of a business, is the same. Some of them hold portfolios with dozens of stocks; others concentrate on a handful. But all exploit the difference between the market price of a business and its intrinsic value.

I'm convinced that there is much inefficiency in the market. These Graham-and-Doddsville investors have successfully exploited gaps between price and value.

. . . In conclusion, some of the more commercially minded among you may wonder why I am writing this article. Adding many converts to the value approach will perforce narrow the spreads between price and value, I can only tell you that the secret has been out for 50 years, ever since Ben Graham and Dave Dodd wrote *Security Analysis,* yet I have seen no trend toward value investing in the 35 years that I've practiced it . . . There will continue to be wide discrepancies between price and value in the marketplace, and those who read their Graham and Dodd will continue to prosper.

Source: Warren Buffett (1984), an edited transcript of a talk given at Columbia University in 1984. Reproduced in *Hermes,* magazine of Columbia Business School, Fall 1984 and in both the 1997 and the 2003 reprints of Graham (1973).

Eugene Fama and Kenneth French are perhaps the most well-known advocates of EMH, with a string of quantitative empirical papers to their names. And yet even Fama (winner of a Nobel Prize for Economics in 2013), in this 2002 newspaper interview (**Exhibit 13.20**) shows some doubts.

Exhibit 13.20

Forty years on, Fama holds to his big idea

The Chicago based professor says his theory has stood the test of time

says Simon London

One of the biggest unanswered questions in financial economics is why Eugene Fama has yet to win the Nobel Prize. The University of Chicago business school professor coined the term 'efficient markets' with his 1963 doctoral thesis, pioneered empirical research into the behaviour of capital markets and, in the early 1990s, devised the 'three-factor model' that led to a whole new taxonomy of investment funds.

The passive fund management industry owes its rise to the insight that markets quickly and accurately assimilate new information, and cannot be beaten over the long term without the assumption of additional risk.

So, 40 years on, does Prof Fama believe more or less strongly in the efficiency of capital markets?

'I've never said that markets are totally efficient. I've always said that for most investors, most of the time, markets are efficient. For most corporate managers, markets are efficient – for all practical purposes.'

How, then, does he explain the extraordinary record of Warren Buffet, who has beaten the market with remarkable consistency? 'I think Warren Buffet is great. I am willing to believe that he wins, OK. But what he says is that he can pick an [undervalued] company once every couple of years. And he is the best. He says that for everything else, markets are efficient.

'Remember also that he doesn't just pick companies, he runs them. That is a different activity. No one would argue against the idea that, if you participate in these companies, you might be able to make them better or worse. It doesn't mean that the companies were inefficiently priced to begin with, just that something can be done to make them more attractive. If Warren Buffet can do it only once every couple of years, that is the best thing you can say about market efficiency.'

What about stock market bubbles and crashes? Surely, stocks cannot have been correctly priced on Monday morning if they are worth 30 per cent less by the end of the day? 'I don't know why these things happen so quickly', he concedes. 'We don't know enough about the way in which information gets assimilated into prices. But if you look at crashes,

half of them turn out to be too small and half turn out to be too big.

'The 1987 crash was clearly too big because the market came back so quickly, the '29 crash was too small because the market carried on going down. They are both mistakes, but they are unbiased mistakes.'

In other words, stock market crashes don't have any statistical significance and there is no pattern that can be used as evidence against efficient markets.

Prof Fama's belief in market efficiency has been strengthened by the many inconclusive studies over the years attempting to disprove it: 'Today there are 10,000 finance academics looking for violations of one theory or another, including efficient markets. I think it has stood up very well.'

The fund management industry has a vested interest in undermining the idea that markets are efficient. Fees charged by active managers only make sense if investors believe they have a good chance of beating the market indices.

The snag for active managers is that studies have failed to find real evidence of 'persistency' in the performance of managers who invest on the basis of either fundamental analysis of companies or technical analysis of market trends. 'The thing people can't deal with is that, if you look at the performance of active managers, there is nothing there,' says Prof Fama. According to efficient markets theory, the only way to beat the market over the long term is to accept additional risk. Prof Fama's 'three-factor model,' published with Ken French of Dartmouth College in 1993, says the returns of any portfolio are determined by:

- The market risk of investing in equities rather than less volatile vehicles;
- Whether the stocks in the portfolio have growth or value characteristics;
- Whether the stocks are issued by large medium or small-cap companies.

According to the model, investors in small-cap value stocks should achieve the highest returns over the long term because they are adopting the most risk.

But Prof Fama admits that the nature of these risks remains little understood.

'We don't claim that we totally understand what additional risks you are taking, particularly when it comes to size. But do you think that small firms have the same cost of capital as big firms? No, they have a higher cost of capital. This is the flip side of expected returns: We don't fully understand these mechanisms but we have observed the effect.'

FT *Financial Times*, 3 June 2002, p. 4.
All Rights Reserved.

Strong-form tests

It is well known that it is possible to trade shares on the basis of information not in the public domain and thereby make abnormal profits. The mining engineer who discovers a rich seam of silver may buy the company shares before the market is told of the likely boost to profits. The director who becomes aware of lost orders and declining competitive position may quietly sell shares to 'diversify his interests' or 'pay for school fees', you understand. The investment banker who hears of a colleague assisting one firm to plan a surprise takeover bid for another has been known to purchase shares (or options) in the target firm. Stock markets are not strong-form efficient.

Trading on inside knowledge is thought to be a 'bad thing'. It makes those outside of the charmed circle feel cheated. A breakdown of the fair game perception will leave some investors feeling that the inside traders are making profits at their expense. If they start to believe that the market is less than a fair game they will be more reluctant to invest and society will suffer. To avoid the loss of confidence in the market most stock exchanges attempt to curb insider dealing. It was made a criminal offence in the UK in 1980 where insider dealing is considered to be, besides dealing for oneself, either counselling or procuring another individual to deal in the securities or communicating knowledge to any other person, while being aware that he or she (or someone else) will deal in those securities. The term 'insider' now covers anyone with sensitive information, not just a company director or employee. Most modern economies have rules on insider dealing and the EU has a directive on the subject. Despite the complex legislation and codes of conduct it is hard to believe that insider trading has been reduced significantly in the last three decades. It would appear that the lawyers have great difficulty obtaining successful prosecutions. But the authorities keep trying, for example the Financial Conduct Authority now has the power to fine insiders for 'market abuse' encompassing both insider dealing and attempts to manipulate the market, for example through misleading statements. This is under civil law rather than criminal law and therefore has a lower burden of proof.

Another weapon in the fight against insiders is to raise the level of information disclosure: making companies release price-sensitive information quickly. The London Stock Exchange and the United Kingdom Listing Authority have strict guidelines to encourage companies to make announcements to the market as a whole as early as possible, on such matters as current trading conditions and profit warnings.

A third approach is to completely prohibit certain individuals from dealing in the company's shares for crucial time periods. For example, directors of quoted firms are prevented by the 'Model Code for Director Dealings' from trading shares for a minimum period (two months) before an announcement of regularly recurring information such as annual results. The Code also precludes dealing before the announcement of matters of an exceptional nature involving unpublished information which is potentially price sensitive. These rules apply to other employees in possession of price-sensitive information.

There is a grey area which stands between trading on inside knowledge and trading purely on publicly available information. Some investment analysts, though strictly outsiders, become so knowledgeable about a firm that they have some degree of superior information. Their judgement or guesstimates about future prospects are of a higher order than those of other analysts and certainly beyond anything the average shareholder is capable of. They may make regular visits to the company head office and operating units. They may discuss the opportunities and potential problems for the firm and the industry with the directors and with competitors' employees. Despite the strict rules concerning directors briefing one analyst better than the generality of shareholders it may be possible to 'read between the lines' and gather hints to give an informed edge. The hypothesis that there are some exceptional analysts has limited empirical backing and relies largely on anecdotal evidence and so this point should not be overemphasised. It is clear from previous sections of this chapter that the vast majority of professional analysts are unable to outperform the market.

John Kay, believes that economists need to be much more humble about proclaiming the validity of the EMH – *see* **Exhibit 13.21**.

Exhibit 13.21

Markets after the age of efficiency

By John Kay

Warren Buffett said most of what you need to know about efficient markets. 'Observing correctly that the market was frequently efficient, they [academics, investment professionals and corporate managers] went on to conclude incorrectly that it was always efficient. The difference between the propositions is night and day.'

The difference between these propositions is also the difference between a $50bn fortune and the returns of the average investor. Mr Buffett has made his money not from the part that is frequently efficient, but from the part that is infrequently inefficient.

The efficient market hypothesis has been the bedrock of financial economics for almost 50 years. One of the architects of the theory, Michael Jensen, famously remarked that 'there is no other proposition in economics which has more solid empirical evidence supporting it'. Along with other writers of the time – such as Burton Malkiel, whose A Random Walk down Wall Street is now in its ninth edition – Prof Jensen was anxious to dispel the mystique of the financial services industry. Prices followed a random walk, so paying for active management was a waste of money.

Market efficiency is a hypothesis about the way markets react to information and does not necessarily imply that markets promote economic efficiency in a wider sense. But there is a relationship between the two concepts of efficiency. It has long suited market practitioners and rightwing ideologues to encourage such confusion. Since markets are efficient, they argue, interference in markets is counter-productive and more markets mean more efficiency.

As anyone who has taken Finance 101 knows, there are three versions of the efficient market hypothesis. The strong version claims that everything you might

know about the value of securities is 'in the price'. It is closely bound up with the idea of rational expectations, whose implications have dominated macroeconomics for 30 years. Policy interventions are mostly futile, monetary policy should follow simple rigid rules, market prices are a considered reflection of fundamental values and there can be no such things as asset-price bubbles.

These claims are not just empirically false but contain inherent contradictions. If prices reflect all available information, why would anyone trouble to obtain the information they reflect? If markets are informationally efficient, why is there so much trade between people who take different views of the same future? If the theory were true, the activities it purports to explain would barely exist.

Yet although efficient market theory is not true, it may nevertheless be illuminating. The absurdities of rational expectations come from the physics envy of many economists, who mistake occasional insights for universal truths. Economic models are illustrations and metaphors, and cannot be comprehensive descriptions even of the part of the world they describe. There is plenty to be learnt from the theory if you do not take it too seriously – and, like Mr Buffett, focus on the infrequent inefficiency rather than the frequent efficiency.

The weak efficient market theory tells us that past prices are no guide to what will happen to security prices in future. There is a good deal of evidence for this claim: you would be as well employed studying the patterns on your palm as patterns on charts. But there is also evidence of a tendency for short-term price movements to continue in the same direction – momentum is real. If you know precisely when the short term becomes the long term, this would make you very rich. It is possible to make money – or policy – through reading boom-and-bust cycles. But most participants do not.

The semi-strong version of the theory claims that markets reflect all publicly available information about securities. What is general knowledge will be in the price, so information such as 'General Electric is a well-managed company' or 'Britain has a large budget deficit', although correct, is useless to investors. But inside information, or original analysis, might add value.

The strong version of the efficient market hypothesis is popular because the world it describes is free of extraneous social, political and cultural influences. Yet if reality were shaped by beliefs about the world, not only would we need to investigate how beliefs are formed and influenced – something economists do not want to do – but models and predictions would be contingent on these beliefs. Of course, models and predictions are so contingent, and an understanding of how beliefs form is indispensable. Economics is not so much the queen of the social sciences but the servant, and needs to base itself on anthropology, psychology – and the sociology of ideologies. The future of investing – and economics – lies in that more eclectic vision.

 Financial Times, 7 October 2009, p. 17.

Behavioural finance

There has been a forceful attack on the EMH by finance specialists drawing on a combination of human behavioural literature and their knowledge of markets. At one time, the financial economists, hot on algebra and on modelling the world (or, at least, *a* world), readily dismissed the behaviouralists as lacking robustness in their descriptions of financial decision making. They find it very difficult to be so dismissive now that we have four Noble Prize in Economics winners from the behavioural economics/finance area. The latest was announced in 2017 when Richard Thaler (star of *The Big Short* film, writer of academic papers such as a leading one on the return reversal phenomenon, and inspirer of government 'Nudge' units) who had worked with leading thinker in the field Daniel Kahneman (Noble Prize in 2002 for work on experiments in the psychology of judgement and decision making) joined Robert Shiller (winner in 2013 for work on excessive stock market movements relative to fundamentals, the cyclically adjusted price earnings ratio, the emotional drivers of traders and irrational exuberance). Herb Simon was a pioneer, who won a Noble prize in 1978 for his work on the theory of corporate decision making, bounded rationality, satisficing and preferential attachment.

The EMH rests on the assumption that all investors are rational, or, even if there are some irrational investors, that the actions of rational informed investors will eliminate pricing anomalies through arbitrage. The behavioural finance proponents argue that investors frequently make systematic errors and these errors can push the prices of shares (and other financial securities) away from fundamental value for considerable periods of time.

Behavioural finance models offer plausible reasoning for the phenomena we observe in the pattern of share prices. They offer persuasive explanations for the outperformance of low PER, high dividend yield and low book-to-market ratio shares as well as the poor performance of 'glamour' shares. They can also be drawn on to shed light on both return reversal and momentum effects. In addition, behavioural science has a lot to offer when it comes to understanding stock market bubbles and irrational pessimism.

Many of the investors who made a fortune in the twentieth century have been saying all along that to understand the market you must understand the psychology of investors. In the 1960s, 1970s and even the 1980s, they were denounced as naive at best by the dyed-in-the-wool quantitative financial economist – the economists had 'scientific proof' of the market's efficiency. They insisted that even if investors were generally irrational the market had inherent mechanisms to arrive at the efficient price, leaving no abnormal returns to be had. The successful investors were merely lucky. Worse! They were lucky and had the nerve to go against the scientific 'evidence' and publicly declare that they believed that there are sound investment principles which permit outperformance.

The successful investors continued to believe in the irrationality and exploitability of markets despite the onslaught from many university economists who were characterised as believing that 'It might work in practice, but it'll never work in theory'. Eventually a growing band of respected academics provided theoretical and empirical backing to the behavioural view of financial markets. Now the debate has reached a fascinating point with high-quality modelling and empirical evidence on both sides.

The three lines of defence for EMH

To defend the EMH its adherents have three progressively stronger arguments which have to be surmounted if the behavioural finance advocates are to be able to attack the core.[29]

1   Investors are rational and hence value securities rationally.

2   Even if some investors are not rational, their irrationally inspired trades of securities are random and therefore the effects of their irrational actions cancel each other out without moving prices away from their efficient level.

3   If the majority of investors are irrational in similar ways and therefore have a tendency to push security values away from the efficient level this will be countered by rational arbitrageurs who eliminate the influence of the irrational traders on prices.

Under the first condition all investors examine securities for their fundamental value. That is, they calculate the present value of the future income flow associated with the security using an appropriate discount rate given the risk level (*see* Chapter 17). If any new information comes along which will increase future flows or decrease the discount rate then the price will rise to the new efficient level instantly. Likewise, bad news results in a lower efficient price. This barrier is easy to attack and demolish. It is plain from anecdotal evidence and from empirical study that the majority of share traders do not assess fundamental value – just ask those who are day-traders or those who buy on the basis of a tip from a friend, a newspaper or broker.

The second barrier is more of a challenge. It accepts individual irrational behaviour but the result is collective rationality in pricing because the irrational trades are evenly balanced and so the effect is benign. This may explain the large volume of trades as irrational investors exchange securities with each other, but this does not lead to systematic inefficient pricing away from fundamental value. The key assumption to be attacked here is the absence of correlation in the actions of irrational investors. There is growing evidence that investors do not deviate from rationality randomly but there is a bias to deviate in the same way (that is, there is positive correlation between their deviations) and therefore they lead prices away from fundamental value. The next section of this chapter provides an outline of some of the psychological biases that are being studied to try to explain apparent inefficiencies in pricing.

The third argument says that the actions of rational arbitrageurs are strong enough to restore efficiency even in the presence of numerous investors making cognitive errors. Arbitrage is the act of exploiting price differences on the same security or similar securities by simultaneously selling the overpriced security and buying the underpriced security. If a security did become overpriced because of the combined actions of irrational investors, smart investors would sell this security (or if they did not own it, 'sell it short') and simultaneously purchase other 'similar securities' to hedge their risks. In a perfect arbitrage they can make a profit without any risk at all (and even without money). The arbitrageurs' selling action brings down the security's price to its fundamental value in the EMH. If a security became underpriced arbitrageurs would buy the security and, to hedge risk, would sell short essentially similar securities, lifting the price of the security to its efficient level.

The arbitrage argument is impressive and forms a strong bulwark against the financial behaviourists. However, there are some weaknesses. Shleifer (2000) points out a number of reasons why

---

29   These three arguments are identified by Andrei Shleifer in his excellent book *Inefficient Markets* (2000).

arbitrage does not work well in the real world and therefore prices are not returned to fundamental value. To be effective the arbitrageur needs to be able to purchase or sell a close-substitute security. Some securities, e.g. futures and options, usually have close substitutes, but in many instances there is no close substitute and so locking in a safe profit is not possible. For example, imagine that you, as a rational investor, discover that Unilever's shares are undervalued. What other security (securities) would you sell at the same time as you purchase Unilever's shares to obtain a risk-free return when the price anomaly is detected? If we were talking about the price of a tonne of wheat of the same quality selling on two different markets at different prices we could buy in the low-price market and simultaneously sell in the high-price market and make a profit (guaranteed without risk) even if the price difference was only 10p. But what can you use in arbitrage trade that is the same as a Unilever share? Well, you might consider that Procter & Gamble shares are close enough and so you sell these short.[30] You expect that in six months the pricing anomaly will correct itself and you can close your position in Unilever by selling and close your position in P&G by buying its shares. But this strategy is far from the risk-free arbitrage of economists' ideal. You face the risk of other fundamental factors influencing the shares of Unilever and P&G (e.g. a strike, a product flop). You also face the risk that the irrational investors push irrationality to new heights. That is, the price does not gradually move towards the fundamental value over the next six months, but away from it. If this happens you lose money as a buyer of Unilever shares and have no offsetting gain on P&G shares. There is evidence of the problem of continued movement away from the fundamental value even after an anomaly has been spotted by arbitrageurs (e.g. Froot and Dabora (1999)). For anecdotal evidence we need only remember back to 1999 and the pricing of dotcom stocks where arbitrageurs sold at high prices only to see the price climb higher as thousands of ill-informed investors piled in. This type of risk facing the arbitrageur is called 'noise trader risk' (De Long et al. (1990)) because it is the actions of the poorly informed investors that create noise in the price series; and this can get worse rather than better. So, in the real world 'with a finite risk-bearing capacity of arbitrageurs as a group, their aggregate ability to bring prices of broad groups of securities into line is limited' (Shleifer (2000), p. 14).

Trading in overvalued or undervalued shares and using imperfect substitutes to offset a position is termed 'risk arbitrage' and is a completely different kettle of fish from risk-free arbitrage.[31] Risk arbitrage entails a calculation of the statistical likelihood of the convergence of relative prices and does not deal with certainties.

Shleifer builds a behaviourally based model on the foundation of two observations of real-world markets.

1 Many securities do not have perfect, or even good, substitutes, making arbitrage risky.

2 Even if a good substitute is available arbitrage remains risky because of noise trader risk, and the possibility that prices will not converge to fundamental values quickly enough to suit the arbitrageur's time horizon.

He concludes that market efficiency will only be an extreme special case and financial markets in most scenarios are not expected to be efficient.

---

30 We are assuming that selling shares that you do not own (and therefore have to borrow) is easy and available to a large number of potential investors. However, in reality, borrowing shares is costly, often impossible and open to only a few institutional investors. Also your period of going short is usually only for days, weeks or a few months rather than years.

31 Arbitrageurs face a number of risks.
   a Fundamental risk: they may be wrong about perceived under- or overpricing.
   b Noise trader risk: (i) Horizon risk: prices may revert to a correct level eventually, but the length of time needed may reduce the arbitrageurs' return to very little, e.g. if a 5 per cent underpricing is corrected in one month the annual rate of return is 79.6 per cent. If it takes two years the annual rate of return is under 2.5 per cent. (ii) Margin risk: arbitrageurs often borrow to buy into positions. If the market moves against them the lender may ask for more collateral or, in the derivatives market may ask for more margin (*see* Chapter 21). Arbitrageurs may not be able to meet these requirements and so may be forced to sell their positions at inconvenient times. (iii) Short covering risk: if the arbitrageur has borrowed shares to go short the lender may not be able to continue to supply shares for more than a few days, forcing the arbitrageur to liquidate the position prematurely.

Some cognitive errors made by investors

Investors are subject to a variety of psychological tendencies that do not fit with the economists' 'rational man' model. This, it is argued, can lead to markets being heavily influenced by investor sentiment. The combination of limited arbitrage and investor sentiment pushing the market leads to inefficient pricing. Both elements are necessary. If arbitrage is unlimited then arbitrageurs will offset the herd actions of irrational investors so prices quickly and correctly move to incorporate relevant news. In the absence of investor sentiment prices would not move from fundamental value in the first place. Listed below are some of the psychological tendencies that are thought to impact on investors' buying and selling decisions and thus to create sentiment.

Overconfidence

When you ask drivers how good they are relative to other drivers research has shown that 65–80% will answer that they are above average. Investors are as overconfident about their trading abilities as about their driving abilities. People significantly overestimate the accuracy of their forecasts. So, when investors are asked to estimate the profits for a firm one year from now and to express the figures in terms of a range where they are confident that the actual result has a 95% chance of being within the projected range, they give a range that is far too narrow. Investors make bad bets because they are not sufficiently aware of their informational disadvantage. This line of research may help explain the underreaction effect (Chui et al. 2010). Investors experience unanticipated surprise at, say, earnings announcements because they are overconfident about their earnings predictions. It takes a while for them to respond to new information in the announcement (due to conservatism – *see* below) and so prices adjust slowly. This may contribute to price momentum and earnings momentum.

Overconfidence may be caused, at least in part, by self-attribution bias. That is, investors ascribe success to their own brilliance, but failures in stock picking to bad luck. Overconfidence may be a cause of excessive trading because investors believe they can pick winners and beat the market (Barber and Odean, 1999, 2000; Puetz and Ruenzi (2011)). Inexperienced investors are, apparently, *more* confident that they can beat the market than experienced investors.

Representativeness

Representativeness is the making of judgements based on stereotypes. It is the tendency to see identical situations where none exist. For example, if Michael is an extrovert, the life and soul of the party, highly creative and full of energy, people are more likely to judge that he is an advertising executive rather than a postman. Representativeness can be misleading. Michael is more likely to be a postman than an advertising executive, even though he 'sounds' to be typical of advertising executives: there are far more postmen than advertising executives. People overweight the representative description and underweight the statistical base evidence.

If there is a sharp decline in the stock market, as in 1987, 2001 or 2008, you will read articles pointing out that this is 1929 all over again. These will be backed up by a chart showing the index movement in 1929 and recent index movements. The similarities can be striking, but this does not mean that the Great Depression is about to be repeated, or even that share prices will fall for the next three years. The similarities between the two situations are superficial. The economic fundamentals are very different. Investors tend to give too much weight to representative observation (e.g. share price movements) and underweight numerous other factors.

Representativeness may help explain the return reversal effect. People look for patterns. If a share has suffered a series of poor returns investors assume that this pattern is representative for that company and will continue in the future. They forget that their conclusion could be premature and that a company with three bad years can produce several good profit figures. Similarly investors overreact in being too optimistic about shares that have had a lot of recent success. It may also explain why unit trusts and investment trusts with high past performance attract more of investors' capital even though studies have shown that past performance is a poor predictor of future performance – even poor-quality managers can show high returns purely by chance.

Conservatism

Investors are resistant to changing an opinion, even in the presence of pertinent new information. So, when profits turn out to be unexpectedly high they initially underreact. They do not revise their earnings estimates enough to reflect the new information and so one positive earnings surprise is followed by another positive earnings surprise. This trait may help explain earnings momentum among other market phenomena.

Narrow framing

Investors' perceptions of risk and return are highly influenced by how the decision problems are framed. Many investors 'narrow frame' rather than look at the broader picture. For example, an investor aged under 35 saving for retirement in 30 years pays too much attention to short-term gains and losses on a portfolio. Another investor focuses too much on the price movements of a single share, although it represents only a small proportion of total wealth. This kind of narrow framing can lead to an over-estimation of the risk investors are taking, especially if they are highly risk averse. The more narrow the investor's focus, the more likely he is to see losses. If the investor took a broad frame he would realise that despite short-term market fluctuations and one or two down years the equity market rises in the long term and by the time of retirement a well-diversified portfolio should be worth much more than it is today. Likewise, by viewing the portfolio as a whole the investor does not worry excessively about a few shares that have performed poorly.

Ambiguity aversion

People are excessively fearful when they feel that they do not have very much information. On the other hand they have an excessive preference for the familiar on which they feel they have good information: as a result they are more likely to gamble. For example, ambiguity aversion may explain the avoidance of overseas shares despite the evidence of the benefits of international diversification.

Positive feedback and extrapolative expectations

Stock market bubbles may be, at least partially, explained by the presence of positive-feedback traders who buy shares after prices have risen and sell after prices fall. They develop extrapolative expectations about prices. That is, simply because prices rose (fell) in the past and a trend has been established investors extrapolate the trend and anticipate greater future price appreciation (falls). This tendency has also been found in house prices and in the foreign exchange markets. George Soros describes in his books (1987, 1998, 2008) his exploitation of this trend-chasing behaviour in a variety of financial and real asset markets. Here the informed trader (e.g. Soros) can buy into the trend thus pushing it along, further away from fundamental values, in the expectation that uninformed investors will pile in and allow the informed trader to get out at a profit. Thus the informed trader creates additional instability instead of returning the security to fundamental value through arbitrage.

Regret

Experimental psychologists have observed that people will forgo benefits within reach in order to avoid the small chance of feeling they have failed. They are overly influenced by the fear of feeling regret.

Thus we find investors at certain points in time become overly fearful and therefore risk averse, e.g. in 2009 few people were buying shares because of the financial shock and yet, with hindsight, we see that 2009 was a great time to buy, with returns of over 100% over the next few years. This fear will occur again, investors will go on a buying-strike again – and are likely to do it at the wrong moment, again. People say things like 'I'll just wait until things look a little more certain. If shares fall more I'll just kick myself'. Another example of the feeling of regret leading someone astray: In boom times friends or acquaintances might be making great returns on short-term speculative trades. They recommend a share to you. You're not sure, so you don't buy. Then, in the boom, the share zooms away. You have 'lost out'. You suffer from regret. Next time, to avoid the feeling of regret you'll be less risk averse and buy shares recommended by that friend. But when the tide goes out you'll be caught swimming naked with the rest of them.

Confirmation bias

People desire to find information that agrees with their existing view. Information that conflicts is ignored. For example, in 2007 many people ignored the arguments suggesting property prices might fall. If you are a typical buyer of new cars, afterwards you'll subconsciously look for information that confirms that you made a good choice. Disconfirming evidence is shunned. Thus you'll be drawn to glossy advertisements that make your model look good, but fail to read objective reports that might raise some bad points about your car. Similarly, if you buy shares you'll have a tendency to look for evidence that confirms the wisdom of your choice and ignore opposing data.

Cognitive dissonance

If a belief has been held for a long time people continue to hold it even when such a belief is plainly contradicted by the evidence. People experience mental conflict when presented with evidence that their beliefs or assumptions are wrong, resulting in denial for a considerable period. Charlie Munger put it this way in a Harvard University speech in 1995:

> Well what I'm saying here is that the human mind is a lot like the human egg, and the human egg has a shut-off device. When one sperm gets in, it shuts down so the next one can't get in. The human mind has a big tendency of the same sort. And here again, it doesn't just catch ordinary mortals; it catches the deans of physics. According to Max Planck, the really innovative, important new physics was never really accepted by the old guard. Instead a new guard came along that was less brain-blocked by its previous conclusions. And if Max Planck's crowd had this consistency and commitment tendency that kept their old conclusions intact in spite of disconfirming evidence, you can imagine what the crowd that you and I are part of behaves like.

Availability bias

People may focus excessively on a particular fact or event because it is more visible, fresher in the mind or emotionally charged, at the expense of seeing the bigger picture. The bigger picture may incorporate soundly based probabilities. For example, following a major train crash, people tend to avoid train travel and use their cars more. However, the bigger picture based on the statistical evidence reveals that train travel is far safer than road transport. In financial markets, if some particularly high-profile companies in an industrial sector (e.g. IT) have produced poor results, investors might abandon the whole sector, ignoring the possibility that some excellent companies may be selling at low prices. They overweight the prominent news. In 2018 I and my investment newsletter readers were able to pick up shares in an excellent UK construction company at a time when other investors were abandoning the entire sector after the collapse of Carillion.

Miscalculation of probabilities

Experiments have shown that people attach too low a probability to likely outcomes and too high a probability to quite unlikely ones. Can this explain the low valuations of 'old economy' shares in the late 1990s as the technological revolution was in full swing? Did investors underestimate these companies' prospects for survival and their ability to combine the new technology with their traditional strengths? At the same time did investors overestimate the probability of all those dotcom start-ups surviving and becoming dominant in their segments? Similarly, in 2018 is there too much optimism about Tesla and other pure electric car makers, and not enough optimism about the potential of the older car makers to compete?

Anchoring

When people are forming quantitative assessments their views are influenced by suggestion. So, for example, people valuing shares are swayed by previous prices. They anchor their changes in valuation on the value as suggested in the past. This may contribute to understanding post-earnings-announcement drift as investors make gradual adjustments to historic figures.

There is some meeting of the ways between the rational and the irrational schools of thought, so that investors are viewed as flawed rationalists rather than hopelessly irrational beings. These quasi-rational humans try hard to be rational but are susceptible to repeating the same old mistakes. They have memory limitations, cognitive limitations and emotional limitations.

William Sharpe, the Nobel laureate and developer of the CAPM, believes there is much to be gained by stepping outside economists' models and allowing for human behaviour – *see* **Exhibit 13.22**.

Exhibit 13.22

Life at the Sharpe end of economic modelling

The godfather of index funds says psychology will contribute to the next big breakthrough

Writes Simon London

Prof Sharpe's [Bill Sharpe, the brains behind the Capital Asset Pricing Model] analysis of markets and finance has yet to come to rest and he has several answers as to where financial economics is heading. First, he argues that finance has become too obsessed with mathematics.

'We have got so intent on having elegant solutions to closed-form equations that we have tolerated some really stupid assumptions about people's preferences,' he says.

Linked to this, he wants financial economists to strive for a better understanding of how people really act.

Does that make Prof Sharpe a closet fan of behavioural finance, which tries to explain financial markets by looking at human psychology?

'I'm a fan of good behavioural finance. It is not a question of trying to show that people are irrational or throwing out all the models that involve rationality. The interesting thing is to find out what kinds of decisions people make under conditions of uncertainty if they know what they are doing.'

It is from this marriage of psychology and economics that Prof Sharpe expects the next breakthrough in finance. Fund managers, watch this space.

Financial Times, 29 July 2002, p. 4.
All Rights Reserved.

Richard Thaler discusses the EMH in **Exhibit 13.23**.

Exhibit 13.23

Markets can be wrong and the price is not always right

By Richard Thaler

I recently had the pleasure of reading Justin Fox's new book *The Myth of the Rational Market*. It offers an engaging history of the research that has come to be called the 'efficient market hypothesis'. It is similar in style to the classic by the late Peter

Bernstein, *Against the Gods*. All the quotes in this column are taken from it. The book was mostly written before the financial crisis. However, it is natural to ask if the experiences over the last year should change our view of the EMH.

▶

Exhibit 13.23 *(continued)*

It helps to start with a quick review of rational finance. Modern finance began in the 1950s when many of the great economists of the second half of the 20th century began their careers. The previous generation of economists, such as John Maynard Keynes, were less formal in their writing and less tied to rationality as their underlying tool. This is no accident. As economics began to stress mathematical models, economists found that the simplest models to solve were those that assumed everyone in the economy was rational. This is similar to doing physics without bothering with the messy bits caused by friction. Modern finance followed this trend.

From the starting point of rational investors came the idea of the efficient market hypothesis, a theory first elucidated by my colleague and golfing buddy Gene Fama. The EMH has two components that I call 'The Price is Right' and 'No Free Lunch'. The price is right principle says asset prices will, to use Mr Fama's words, 'fully reflect' available information, and thus 'provide accurate signals for resource allocation'. The no free lunch principle is that market prices are impossible to predict and so it is hard for any investor to beat the market after taking risk into account.

For many years the EMH was 'taken as a fact of life' by economists, as Michael Jensen, a Harvard professor, put it, but the evidence for the price is right component was always hard to assess. Some economists took the fact that prices were unpredictable to infer that prices were in fact 'right'. However, as early as 1984 Robert Shiller, the economist, correctly and boldly called this 'one of the most remarkable errors in the history of economic thought'. The reason this is an error is that prices can be unpredictable and still wrong; the difference between the random walk fluctuations of correct asset prices and the unpredictable wanderings of a drunk are not discernable.

Tests of this component of EMH are made difficult by what Mr Fama calls the 'joint hypothesis problem'. Simply put, it is hard to reject the claim that prices are right unless you have a theory of how prices are supposed to behave.

During the technology bubble violations of this law were observed. When 3Com, the technology company, spun off its Palm unit, only 5 per cent of the Palm shares were sold; the rest went to 3Com shareholders. Each shareholder got 1.5 shares of Palm. It does not take an economist to see that in a rational world the price of 3Com would have to be greater than 1.5 times the share of Palm, but for months this simple bit of

arithmetic was violated. The stock market put a negative value on the shares of 3Com, less its interest in Palm. Really.

Compared to the price is right component, the no free lunch aspect of the EMH has fared better. Mr Jensen's doctoral thesis published in 1968 set the right tone when he found that, as a group, mutual fund managers could not outperform the market. There have been dozens of studies since then, but the basic conclusion is the same. Although there are some anomalies, the market seems hard to beat. That does not prevent people from trying. For years people predicted fees paid to money managers would fall as investors switched to index funds or cheaper passive strategies, but instead assets were directed to hedge funds that charge very high fees.

Now, a year into the crisis, where has it left the advocates of the EMH? First, some good news. If anything, our respect for the no free lunch component should have risen. The reason is related to the joint hypothesis problem. Many investment strategies that seemed to be beating the market were not doing so once the true measure of risk was considered. Even Alan Greenspan, the former Federal Reserve chairman, has admitted that investors were fooled about the risks of mortgage-backed securities.

The bad news for EMH lovers is that the price is right component is in more trouble than ever. Fischer Black (of Black-Scholes fame) once defined a market as efficient if its prices were 'within a factor of two of value' and he opined that by this (rather loose) definition 'almost all markets are efficient almost all the time'. Sadly Black died in 1996 but had he lived to see the technology bubble and the bubbles in housing and mortgages he might have amended his standard to a factor of three. Of course, no one can prove that any of these markets were bubbles. But the price of real estate in places such as Phoenix and Las Vegas seemed like bubbles at the time. This does not mean it was possible to make money from this insight. Lunches are still not free. Shorting internet stocks or Las Vegas real estate two years before the peak was a good recipe for bankruptcy, and no one has yet found a way to predict the end of a bubble.

What lessons should we draw from this? On the free lunch component there are two. The first is that many investments have risks that are more correlated than they appear. The second is that high returns based on high leverage may be a mirage. . . . . but the lure of seemingly high returns is hard to resist. On the price is right, if we include the earlier bubble in Japanese real estate, we have now had three enormous price distortions in recent memory. They led to misallocations of resources measured in the trillions and, in the latest bubble, a global credit meltdown. If asset prices could be relied upon to always be 'right', then these bubbles would not occur. But they have, so what are we to do?

While imperfect, financial markets are still the best way to allocate capital. Even so, knowing that prices can be wrong suggests that governments could usefully adopt automatic stabilising activity, such as linking the down-payment for mortgages to a measure of real estate frothiness or ensuring that bank reserve requirements are set dynamically according to market conditions. After all, the market price is not always right.

Misconceptions about the efficient market hypothesis

There are good grounds for doubting some aspects of the EMH and a reasoned debate can take place with advocates for efficiency and inefficiency stating their cases with rigorous argument and robust empirical methodology. However, the high-quality debate has sometimes been overshadowed by criticism based on one or more misunderstandings of the EMH. There are three classic misconceptions.

1   **Any share portfolio will perform as well as or better than a special trading rule designed to outperform the market** A monkey choosing a portfolio of shares from the *Financial Times* for a buy and hold strategy is nearly, but not quite, what the EMH advocates suggest as a strategy likely to be as rewarding as special inefficiency-hunting approaches. The monkey does not have the financial expertise needed to construct broadly based portfolios which fully diversify away unsystematic risk. A selection of shares in just one or two industrial sectors may expose the investor to excessive risk. So it is wrong to conclude from the EMH evidence that it does not matter what the investor does, and that any portfolio is acceptable. The EMH says that after first eliminating unsystematic risk by holding broadly based portfolios and then adjusting for the residual systematic risk, investors will not achieve abnormal returns.

2   **There should be fewer price fluctuations** If shares are efficiently priced why is it that they move every day even when there is no announcement concerning a particular company? This is what we would expect in an efficient market. Prices move because new information is coming to the market every hour which may have some influence on the performance of a specific company. For example, the governor of the Bank of England may hint at interest rate rises, the latest industrial output figures may be released and so on.

3   **Only a minority of investors are actively trading, most are passive, therefore efficiency cannot be achieved** This too is wrong. It only needs a few trades by informed investors using all the publicly available information to position (through their buying and selling actions) a share at its semi-strong-form efficient price.

Implications of the EMH for investors

If the market is efficient there are a number of implications for investors. Even if it is merely efficient most of the time, for most participants a sensible working assumption is that pricing is based on fundamental values and the following implications apply.

1   **For the vast majority of people public information cannot be used to earn abnormal returns** (This refers to returns above the normal level for that systematic risk class.) The implications are that fundamental analysis is a waste of money and that so long as efficiency is maintained the average investor should simply select a suitably diversified portfolio, thereby avoiding costs of analysis and transaction. This message has struck a chord with millions of investors and thousands of billions of pounds have been placed with fund managers who merely replicate a

stock market index (index funds) rather than try to pick winners in an actively managed fund. It has been found that the active fund managers generally underperform the market indices – so do the 'trackers', but at least they have lower costs.

Another trend has been for small investors to trade shares through execution-only brokers. These brokers do not provide their clients with (nor charge them for) analysis of companies and suggestions for purchases. They merely carry out the client's buy or sell orders in the cheapest manner possible.

2 **Investors need to press for a greater volume of timely information** Semi-strong efficiency depends on the quality and quantity of publicly available information, and so companies should be encouraged by investor pressure, accounting bodies, government rulings and stock market regulation to provide as much as is compatible with the necessity for some secrecy to prevent competitors gaining useful knowledge.

3 **The perception of a fair game market could be improved by more constraints and deterrents placed on insider dealers** Strong-form efficiency does not exist and so insiders can gain an unfair advantage.

Implications of the EMH for companies

The efficient market hypothesis also has a number of implications for companies.

1 **Focus on substance, not on short-term appearance** Some managers behave as though they believe they can fool shareholders. For example creative accounting is used to show a more impressive performance than is justified. Most of the time these tricks are transparent to investors, who are able to interpret the real position, and security prices do not rise artificially.

There are some circumstances when the drive for short-term boosts to reported earnings can be positively harmful to shareholders. For example, one firm might tend to overvalue its inventory to boost short-term profitability; another might not write off bad debts. These actions will result in additional, or at least earlier, taxation payments which will be harmful to shareholder wealth. Managers, aware that analysts often pay a great deal of attention to accounting rate of return, may, when facing a choice between a project with a higher NPV but a poor short-term ARR, or one with a lower NPV but higher short-term ARR, choose the latter. This principle of short-termism can be extended into areas such as research and development or marketing spend. These can be cut to boost profits in the short term but only at a long-term cost to shareholders.

One way to alleviate the short-term/long-term dilemma is for managers to explain why longer-term prospects are better than the current figures suggest. This requires a diligent communications effort.

2 **The timing of security issues does not have to be fine-tuned** Consider a team of managers contemplating a share issue who feel that their shares are currently underpriced because the market is 'low'. They opt to delay the sale, hoping that the market will rise to a more 'normal level'. This defies the logic of the EMH – if the market is efficient the shares are already correctly (unbiasedly) priced and the next move in prices is just as likely to be down as up. The past price movements have nothing to say about future movements.

The situation is somewhat different if the managers have private information that they know is not yet priced into the shares. In this case if the directors have good news then they would be wise to wait until after an announcement and subsequent adjustment to the share price before selling the new shares. Bad news announcements are more tricky – to sell the shares to new investors while withholding bad news will benefit existing shareholders, but will result in loss for the new shareholders. There are rules against withholding price sensitive information.

3 **Large quantities of new shares can be sold without moving the price** A firm wishing to raise equity capital by selling a block of shares may hesitate to price near to the existing share price. Managers may believe that the increase in supply will depress the price of the shares. This is

generally not the case. In empirical studies (e.g. Scholes (1972)), if the market is sufficiently large (for example the London or New York Stock Exchange) and investors are satisfied that the new money will generate a return at least as high as the return on existing funds, the price does not fall. This is as we would expect in an efficient market: investors buy the new shares because of the return offered on them for their level of risk.[32] The fact that some old shares of the same company already exist and that therefore supply has risen does not come into the equation. The key question is: what will the new shares produce for their holders? If they produce as much as an old share they should be priced the same as an old share. If they are not, then someone will spot that they can gain an abnormal return by purchasing these shares (which will push up the price).

4   **Signals from price movements should be taken seriously** If, for instance, the directors announce that the company is to take over another firm and its share price falls dramatically on the day of the announcement this is a clear indication that the merger will be wealth destroying for shareholders – as the majority of mergers are (see Chapter 20). Managers cannot ignore this collective condemnation of their actions. An exception might be allowed if shareholders are dumping the shares in ignorance because the managers have special knowledge of the benefits to be derived from the merger – but then shouldn't the directors explain themselves properly?

Concluding comments

While modern, large and sophisticated stock markets exhibit inefficiencies in some areas, particularly at the strong-form level, it is reasonable to conclude that they are substantially efficient and it is rare that a non-insider can outperform the market. One of the more fruitful avenues of future research is likely to concern the influence of psychology on stock market pricing. We have seen how many of the (suggested) semi-strong inefficiencies, from bubbles to underpricing low PER shares, have at their base a degree of apparent 'non-rationality'.

Another line of enquiry is to question the assumption that all investors respond in a similar manner to the same risk and return factors and that these can be easily identified. Can beta be relied upon to represent all relevant risk? If it cannot, what are the main elements investors want additional compensation for? What about information costs, marketability limits, taxes and the degree of covariability with human capital returns for the investor (e.g. earnings from employment)? These are factors disliked by shareholders and so conceivably a share with many of these attributes will have to offer a high return. For some investors who are less sensitive to these elements the share which gives this high return may seem a bargain. A problem for the researcher in this field is that abnormal returns are calculated after allowance for risk. If the model used employs a risk factor which is not fully representative of all the risk and other attributes disliked by investors then efficiency or inefficiency cannot be established.

One way of 'outperforming' the market might be to select shares the attributes of which you dislike less than the other investors do, because they are likely to be underpriced for you – given your particular circumstances. Another way is through luck – which is often confused with the third way, that of possessing superior analytical skills.

A fourth method is through the discovery of a trading rule which works (but do not tell anybody, because if it becomes widespread knowledge it may stop working, unless it is based on some deep-seated psychological/cognitive error prevalent among investors[33]). A fifth possibility is to be quicker than anyone else in responding to news – George Soros and his teams may fall into this category occasionally. The last, and the most trustworthy method, is to become an insider – the only problem with this method is that you may end up a different kind of insider – in prison.

---

32 Although some studies have shown a decrease in share price when the sale of shares is announced.

33 McLean and Pontiff (2016) found that after publication the returns on exploiting stock market anomalies decreased by 58%: 'Our findings suggest that investors learn about mispricing from academic publications.'

To conclude: the equity markets are generally efficient, but the person with superior analytical ability, knowledge, dedication and creativity can be rewarded with abnormally high returns. However, for people who do not have these four qualities directed effectively at security analysis – the vast majority – it is dangerous to invest or make corporate decisions on the assumption that the share (currency and commodity) markets are inefficient, because most of the time they are efficient. Markets are inefficient in spots. Those spots are first of all difficult to identify, and then, once you think you have identified an area of inefficient pricing it has a tendency to fade away, or additional analysis shows it was not really there in the first place. Playing the game of trying to land yourself in an area of inefficiency is to be played only by the very skilful and knowledgeable. Most corporate managers and fund managers do not qualify.

Key points and concepts

- **In an efficient market security prices rationally reflect available information** New information is **a** rapidly and **b** rationally incorporated into share prices.

- **Types of efficiency:**
  - operational efficiency;
  - allocational efficiency;
  - pricing efficiency.

- **The benefits of an efficient market are:**
  - it encourages share buying;
  - it gives correct signals to company managers;
  - it helps to allocate resources.

- Shares, other financial assets and commodities generally move with a **random walk** – one day's price change cannot be predicted by looking at previous price changes. Security prices respond to news which is random.

- **Weak-form efficiency** Share prices fully reflect all information contained in past price movements.

  Evidence: mostly in support, but there are some important exceptions.

- **Semi-strong form efficiency** Share prices fully reflect all the relevant, publicly available information.

  Evidence: substantially in support but there are some exceptions.

- **Strong-form efficiency** All relevant information, including that which is privately held, is reflected in the share price.

  Evidence: stock markets are strong-form inefficient.

- **Insider dealing** is trading on privileged information. It is profitable and illegal.

- **Behavioural finance studies** offer insight into anomalous share pricing.

- **Implications of the EMH for investors:**
  - for the vast majority of people public information cannot be used to earn abnormal returns;
  - investors need to press for a greater volume of timely information;
  - the perception of a fair game market could be improved by more constraints and deterrents placed on insider dealers.

- **Implications of the EMH for companies:**
  - focus on substance, not on short-term appearances;
  - the timing of security issues does not have to be fine-tuned;
  - large quantities of new shares can be sold without moving the price;
  - signals from price movements should be taken seriously.

References and further reading

Abraham, A. and Ikenberry, D. (1994) 'The individual investor and the weekend effect', *Journal of Financial and Quantitative Analysis*, June.

An examination of a particular form of inefficiency.

Adebambo, B.N. and Yan, X. (2016) 'Momentum, Reversals, and Fund Manager Overconfidence', *Financial Management* (Wiley-Blackwell). Fall 2016, 45(3), pp. 609–39.

Shares held by more overconfident fund managers experience greater momentum profits and stronger return reversals than shares held by less overconfident managers.

Al-Rjoub, S.A.M., Varela, O. and Hassan, M.K. (2005) 'The size reversal in the USA', *Applied Financial Economics,* 15, pp. 1189–97.

> More evidence on the performance of small capitalisation firms vs. large firms.

Ami, E., Kama, I. and Levi, S. (2015) 'Conditional Persistence of Earnings Components and Accounting Anomalies', *Journal of Business Finance & Accounting,* Sep/Oct 2015, 42(7/8), pp. 801–25.

> Provides evidence on US post-earnings announcement drift, post-revenue announcement drift and the accrual anomaly.

Amihud. Y., Hameed, A., Kang, W. and Zhang, H. (2015) 'The illiquidity premium: International evidence', *Journal of Financial Economics,* 117, pp. 350–68.

> Less liquid shares outperform more liquid shares – found across 45 countries.

Anderson, K. and Brooks, C. (2006) 'The long-term price–earnings ratio', *Journal of Business Finance and Accounting,* 33(7) & (8), pp. 1063–86.

> A PER effect with a difference – shows a high return to shares with a low share price relative to the previous eight years of earnings.

Andrikopoulos, P., Daynes, A., Latimer, D. and Pagas, P. (2008) 'Size effect, methodological issues and "risk-to-default": evidence from the UK stock market', *European Journal of Finance,* 14(4) pp. 299–314.

> While a small firm effect is shown it is regarded as 'unreliable'.

Arnold, G. (2009) *The Financial Times Guide to Value Investing: How to become a disciplined investor,* 2nd Edition. London: Financial Times Prentice Hall.

> Brings together the insights from successful investors, finance theory and strategic analysis.

Arnold, G. (2011) *The Great Investors.* Harlow: FT Prentice Hall.

> Explains eight investment philosophies by nine very successful investors, including Warren Buffett and George Soros.

Arnold, G. (2017) *The Deals of Warren Buffett, Vol. 1 The First $100m.* Harriman House, Petersfield, Hampshire.

> The first volume in a series of four covers the first 48 years of Buffett's life with an examination of the rationale behind key investments.

Arnold, G.C. and Baker, R.D. (2007) 'Return reversal in UK shares', Salford Business School Working Paper 107/07.

> Shows evidence supporting the view that investors in shares with the worst recent five-year returns outperform in the subsequent five years (on average).

Arnold, G. and Shi, J. (2005) 'Profitability of momentum strategies in UK bull and bear market conditions', University of Salford Working Papers.

> Momentum effects are present in bull and bear markets.

Arnold, G.C. and Xiao, Y. (2007) 'Financial statement analysis and the return reversal effect'. Salford Business School Working Paper 108/07.

> Shows evidence indicating that portfolios of 'loser' shares (those that give the lowest returns over five years) which also have strong financial variables (e.g. positive cash flow or improving financial gearing) outperform those with poor financial fundamentals.

Asness, C.S., Moskowitz, T. J. and Pedersen, L.H. (2013) 'Value and momentum everywhere', *Journal of Finance,* LXVIII(3), pp. 929–85.

> Evidence for low book-to-market ratio being a differentiator for portfolio performance in US, UK, continental Europe and Japan. Also price momentum is shown for shares in those countries.

Bailey, D.H., Borwein, J.M., López de Prado, M. and Qiji Jim Zhu (2014) 'Pseudo-Mathematics and Financial Charlatanism: The Effects of Backtest Overfitting on Out-of-Sample Performance', *Notices of the American Mathematical Society,* 61(5), pp. 458–71.

> Statisticians fight back against those who present apparent methods of outperforming based on poor analysis.

Ball, R., Gerakos, J., Linnainmaa, J.T. and Nikolaev, V. (2016) 'Accruals, cash flows, and operating profitability in the cross section of stock returns', *Journal of Financial Economics,* 121, pp. 28–45.

> Evidence is shown that by excluding accruals and focusing on cash-based operating profitability outperformance is possible.

Ball, R. and Kothari, S.P. (1989) 'Nonstationary expected returns: Implications for tests of market efficiency and serial correlation in returns', *Journal of Financial Economics,* 25, pp. 51–94.

> Negative serial correlation in relative returns is due largely to changing relative risks and thus changing expected returns.

Ball, R., Kothari, S.P. and Shanken, J. (1995) 'Problems in measuring portfolio performance: An application to contrarian investment strategies', *Journal of Financial Economics,* May, 38, pp. 79–107.

> Performance measurement problems cast doubt on the overreaction study results.

Banz, R. (1981) 'The relationship between return and market value of common stock', *Journal of Financial Economics,* 9, pp. 3–18.

> Important early paper on the small firm effect.

Banz, R.W. and Breen, W.J. (1986) 'Sample-dependent results using accounting and market data: Some evidence', *Journal of Finance,* 41, pp. 779–93.

> A technical article concerned with the problem of bias when using accounting information (earnings). The bias in the data can cause the low PER effect.

Barber, B.M. and Odean, T. (1999) 'The courage of misguided convictions', *Financial Analysts Journal,* 55, November–December, pp. 41–55.
>   Investors who trade frequently perform worse than those who trade little. Support for over-confidence hypothesis.

Barber, B. and Odean, T. (2000) 'Trading is hazardous to your wealth: The common stock investment performance and individual investors', *Journal of Finance,* 55(2), April, pp. 773–806.
>   Investors who trade a lot perform worst.

Barberis, N., Shleifer, A. and Vishny, R.W. (1998) 'A model of investor sentiment', *Journal of Financial Economics,* 49, pp. 307–43.
>   A theoretical model based on behavioural finance ideas in which investors believe at times that the market is trending and at other times it is mean-reverting (draws on representativeness and conservatism).

Barroso P. and Santa-Clara, P. (2015) 'Momentum has its moments', *Journal of Financial Economics,* 116, pp. 111–20.
>   Price momentum has given high returns overall but suffers from bad crashes.

Basu, S. (1975) 'The information content of price-earnings ratios', *Financial Management,* 4, Summer, pp. 53–64.
>   Evidence of a market inefficiency for low PER shares. However transaction costs, search costs and taxation prevent abnormal returns.

Basu, S. (1977) 'Investment performance of common stocks in relation to their price/earnings ratios: A test of the efficient market hypothesis', *Journal of Finance,* 32(3), June, pp. 663–82.
>   Low PER portfolios earn higher absolute and risk-adjusted rates of return than high PER shares. Information was not fully reflected in share prices.

Basu, S. (1983) 'The relationship between earnings' yield, market value and return for NYSE stocks – Further evidence', *Journal of Financial Economics,* June, pp. 129–56.
>   The PER effect subsumes the size effect when both variables are considered jointly.

Benartzi, S. and Thaler, R. (1995) 'Myopic loss aversion and the equity premium puzzle', *Quarterly Journal of Economics,* 110(1), pp. 73–92.
>   Narrow framing leads to unreasonable risk aversity and too little investment in equities.

Bernard, V. (1993) 'Stock price reaction to earnings announcements', in Thaler, R. (ed.) *Advances in Behavioural Finance.* New York: Russell Sage Foundation.
>   Sluggish response.

Bernard, V.L. and Thomas, J.K. (1989) 'Post-earnings-announcement drift: Delayed price response or risk premium?', *Journal of Accounting Research,* 27 (Supplement 1989), pp. 1–36.
>   A study showing slow reaction to unexpected earnings figures indicating inefficiency.

Bernstein, P.L. (1996) *Against the Gods: The Remarkable Story of Risk.* Chichester: John Wiley & Sons, Inc.
>   Chronicles the rise of the tools of modern risk management.

Bessembinder, H. and Zhang, F. (2013) 'Firm characteristics and long-run stock returns after corporate events', *Journal of Financial Economics,* 109, pp. 83–102.
>   Poor research methods used result in apparent anomalies in firms issuing equity in initial public offerings and seasoned equity offerings, firms bidding in mergers, and firms initiating dividends.

Black, F. (1986) 'Noise', *Journal of Finance,* 41(3), July, pp. 529–34.
>   A large number of small events is often a causal factor much more powerful than a small number of large events.

Brock, W., Lakonishok, J. and LeBaron, B. (1992) 'Simple technical trading rules and the stochastic properties of stock returns', *Journal of Finance,* 47, December, pp. 1731–64.
>   Some interesting evidence suggesting weak-form inefficiency.

Brunnermeier, M.K. and Nagel, S. (2004) 'Hedge funds and the technology bubble', *Journal of Finance,* LIX (5), October, pp. 2013–40.
>   Rational investors are not acting as arbitrageurs to return share prices to an efficient level – they reinforce inefficient pricing helping to destabilise.

Brusa, J., Liu, P. and Schulman, C. (2003) 'The weekend and 'reverse" weekend effects: An analysis by month of the year, week of month, and industry', *Journal of Business Finance and Accounting,* 30(5) and (6), June/July, pp. 863–90.
>   Findings: weekend and reverse weekend effects are shown for US share indices.

Buffett, W.E. (1984) 'The superinvestors of Graham-and-Doddsville', an edited transcript of a talk given at Columbia University in 1984.
>   Reproduced in *Hermes,* the magazine of Columbia Business School, Fall 1984 and in the 1997 and 2003 reprints of Graham (1973).

Buffett, W.E. (2000) Letter to shareholders included with the 2000 Annual Report of Berkshire Hathaway Inc: www.berkshirehathaway.com.
>   High-quality thinking and writing from the world's most successful investor.

Caylor, M.L., Christensen, T.E., Johnson, P.M. and Lopez, T.J. (2015) 'Analysts' and Investors' Reactions to Consistent Earnings Signals', *Journal of Business Finance & Accounting,* Nov/Dec 2015, 42(9/10), pp. 1041–74.

Finds that 'analysts underreact more to earnings information revealed by consistent-signal earnings expectation paths than to earnings information communicated by inconsistent-signal expectation paths'.

Capaul, C., Rowley, I. and Sharpe, W.F. (1993) 'International value and growth stock returns', *Financial Analysts Journal*, 49, January–February, pp. 27–36.
Evidence on returns from a book-to-market ratio strategy for France, Germany, Switzerland, the UK and Japan.

Chan, A. and Chen, A.P.L. (1996) 'An empirical re-examination of the cross-section of expected returns: UK evidence', *Journal of Business Finance and Accounting*, 23, pp. 1435–52.
High divided yields associated with high share returns.

Chan, L.K.C. and Lakonishok, J. (2004) 'Value and growth investing: review and update', *Financial Analysts Journal*, January/February, pp. 71–86.
An overview of the value versus growth empirical evidence plus some recent evidence.

Chan, L.K.C., Hamao, Y. and Lakonishok, J. (1991) 'Fundamentals and stock returns in Japan', *Journal of Finance*, 46, pp. 1739–64.
The book-to-market ratio and cash flow yield have influences on the returns. There is a weak size effect and a doubtful PER effect.

Chan, L.K.C. Jegadeesh, N. and Lakonishok, J. (1996) 'Momentum strategies', *Journal of Finance*, 51, December, pp. 1681–713.
Underreaction to both past share returns and earnings surprises.

Chopra, N., Lakonishok, J. and Ritter, J.R. (1992) 'Measuring abnormal performance: Do stocks overact?', *Journal of Financial Economics*, 31, pp. 235–68.
Overreaction effect observed.

Chordia, T., Goyal, A., Sadka, G., Sadka, R. and Shivakumar, L. (2009) 'Liquidity and the post-earnings-announcement drift', *Financial Analysts Journal*, 65(4) pp. 18–32.
Post-earnings-announcement drift occurs mainly in highly liquid shares.

Chordia, T., Subrahmanyam, A. and Tong, Q. (2014) 'Have capital market anomalies attenuated in the recent era of high liquidity and trading activity?' *Journal of Accounting and Economics*, 58: 41–58.
Increased arbitrage activity in financial markets has reduced the returns to stock market anomaly strategies such as size, reversals, momentum, and PEAD, 'Overall, our work indicates that policies to stimulate liquidity and ameliorate trading costs improve capital market efficiency'.

Chui, A.C.W., Titman, S. and Wei, K.C.J. (2010) 'Individualism and momentum around the world', *The Journal of Finance*, LXV(1), Feb. pp. 361–92.

Individualism and self-attribution bias are related to overconfidence, which in turn is related to momentum profits.

Clare, A. and Thomas, S. (1995) 'The overreaction hypothesis and the UK stock market', *Journal of Business Finance and Accounting*, 22(7), October, pp. 961–73.
Overreaction occurs, but it is a manifestation of the small firm effect.

Cronqvist, H., Siegel, S. and Yu, F. (2015) 'Value versus growth investing: Why do different investors have different styles?' *Journal of Financial Economics*, 117, pp. 333–49.
Factors explaining individual investor's value versus growth orientation: 1. A biological basis ingrained from birth; 2. The investor's hedging demands; 3. experiences, both earlier and later in life, are related to investment style.

Cuthbertson, K. (2004) *Quantitative Financial Economics*, 2nd edn. Chichester: Wiley.
Contains a more rigorous mathematical treatment of the issues discussed in this chapter.

Daniel, K. and Moskowitz, T. J. (2016) 'Momentum Crashes', *Journal of Financial Economics*, 122, pp. 221–47.
Momentum strategies experience infrequent but persistent strings of negative returns despite their strong positive returns over the very long term.

Daniel, K. and Titman, S. (1997) 'Evidence on the characteristics of cross-sectional variation in stock returns', *Journal of Finance*, 52(1), March, p. 1–33.
The high returns to high book-to-market ratio shares and small market capitalisation shares are not a result of compensation for risk (opposing Fama and French's view and supporting the behavioural finance view).

Daniel, K., Hirshleifer, D. and Subrahmanyam, A. (1998) 'Investor psychology and security market under- and overreactions', *Journal of Finance*, 53(6), pp. 1839–85.
Behavioural explanation of inefficiencies. Under- and overreactions are due to the psychological biases of investor overconfidence and biased self-attributes.

Davis, J.L., Fama, E.F. and French, K.R. (2009) 'Characteristics, covariances, and average returns: 1929 to 1997', *The Journal of Finance*, LV(1), pp. 389–406.
'The value premium in US stock returns is robust'. Studying book-to-market ratio.

Dawson, E.R. and Steeley, J.M. (2003) 'On the existence of visual technical patterns in the UK stock market', *Journal of Business Finance and Accounting*, 30(1) and (2), January–March, pp. 263–97.
Failure to find profitable trading rules based on technical patterns.

De Bondt, W.F.M. and Thaler, R.H. (1985) 'Does the stock market overreact?', *Journal of Finance*, 40(3), July, pp. 793–805.
An important paper claiming weak-form inefficiency.

De Bondt, W.F.M. and Thaler, R.H. (1987) 'Further evidence on investor overreaction and stock market seasonality', *Journal of Finance,* 42(3), pp. 557–81.
Overreaction effect observed.

Dellavigna, S. and Pollet, J.M. (2009), 'Investor inattention and Friday earnings announcements', *The Journal of Finance,* LXIV(2), pp. 709–49.
Post-earnings-announcement drift is strong for Friday announcements.

De Long, J.B., Shleifer, A., Summers, L.H. and Waldmann, R.J. (1989) 'The size and incidence of the losses from noise trading', *Journal of Finance,* 44(3), July, pp. 681–96.
Noise trading by naive investors can lead to costs for society.

De Long, J.B., Shleifer, A., Summers, L.H. and Waldmann, R.J. (1990) 'Noise trader risk in financial markets', *Journal of Political Economy,* 98, pp. 703–38.
Discussing the risk that irrational ill-informed investors may push prices further away from fundamental value thus throwing the arbitrageurs' trading strategies.

Dimson, E. (ed.) (1988) *Stock Market Anomalies.* Cambridge: Cambridge University Press.
A collection of 19 important articles questioning stock market efficiency.

Dimson, E. and Marsh, P.R. (1986) 'Event study methodologies and the size effect: The case of UK press recommendations', *Journal of Financial Economics,* 17, pp. 113–42.
UK small firm shares outperformed those of larger firms.

Dimson, E. and Marsh P.R. (1999) 'Murphy's law and market anomalies', *Journal of Portfolio Management,* 25(2), pp. 53–69.
Small companies outperformed large companies until the 1980s, then they underperformed.

Dimson, E., Marsh, P.R. and Staunton, M. (2001) *The Millennium Book II: 101 Years of Investment Returns.* London: ABN AMRO and London Business School.
Shows returns on shares and other securities over the twentieth century. The section on small firms shows a reversal of the small-firm effect.

Dimson, E., Marsh, P.R. and Staunton, M. (2002) *The Triumph of the Optimists: 101 Years of Global Investment Returns.* Princeton, NJ: Princeton University Press.
An important study on market returns with a chapter on the small firm effect.

Dimson, E., Marsh, P. and Staunton, M. (2008) *ABN AMRO Global Investment Returns Yearbook 2009.* ABN AMRO, Royal Bank of Scotland and London Business School.
Evidence on price momentum stretching back over 100 years.

Dimson, E., Marsh, P. and Staunton, M. (2017) *Credit Suisse Global Investment Returns Yearbook 2017.* London: Credit Suisse. Available at https://emagazine. credit-suisse.com.
Evidence on the size effect and the value effect.

Dimson, E., Marsh, P., Staunton, M., Kersley, R. and O'Sullivan, M. (2017) *Credit Suisse Global Investment Returns Yearbook 2017- slide deck.* London: Credit Suisse.
A source of charts on securities returns over long periods.

Dissanaike, G. (1997) 'Do stock market investors overreact?', *Journal of Business Finance and Accounting,* 24(1), January, pp. 27–49.
Buying poor-performing shares gives abnormal returns as they are underpriced due to investor overreaction (UK study).

Dreman, D. (2007) *Contrarian Investment Strategies: The psychological edge.* New York: Simon & Schuster.
A sceptic's view on efficiency.

Dreman, D. and Berry, M. (1995) 'Overreaction, underreaction, and the low P/E effect', *Financial Analysts Journal,* 51, July/August, pp. 21–30.
Overreaction and underreaction shown.

Edelena, R.M., Ince, O.S. and Kadlecc, G.B. (2016) 'Institutional investors and stock return anomalies', *Journal of Financial Economics,* 119, pp. 472–88.
'Institutions have a strong tendency to buy stocks classified as overvalued . . . and that these stocks have particularly negative ex post abnormal returns.'

Elton, E.J., Gruber, M.J. and Rentzler, J. (1983) 'A simple examination of the empirical relationship between dividend yields and deviations from the CAPM', *Journal of Banking and Finance,* 7, pp. 135–46.
Complex statistical analysis leads to the conclusion: 'We have found a persistent relationship between dividend yield and excess returns.'

Elton, E.J., Gruber, M.J., Brown, S.J. and Goetzmann, W.N. (2017) *Modern Portfolio Theory and Investment Analysis,* 9th edn. New York: Wiley.
A more technical treatment than that in this chapter.

Fama, E.F. (1965) 'The behaviour of stock market prices', *Journal of Business,* January, pp. 34–106.
Leading early article that first defined market efficiency.

Fama, E.F. (1970) 'Efficient capital markets: A review of theory and empirical work', *Journal of Finance,* May, pp. 383–417.
A review of the early literature and a categorisation of efficiency.

Fama, E.F. (1991) 'Efficient capital markets II', *Journal of Finance,* 46(5), December, pp. 1575–617.
A review of the market efficiency literature with a strong bias in favour of the view that the market is efficient.

Fama, E.F. (1998) 'Market efficiency, long-term returns, and behavioural finance', *Journal of Financial Economics,* 49, September, pp. 283–306.

Anomalies are explained and efficiency is championed.

Fama, E.F. and French, K.R. (1988) 'Permanent and temporary components of stock prices', *Journal of Political Economy,* 96, pp. 246–73.

An interesting paper from EMH proponents.

Fama, E.F. and French, K.R. (1992) 'The cross-section of expected stock returns', *Journal of Finance,* 47, pp. 427–65.

An excellent study casting doubt on beta and showing size of company and book-to-market ratio affecting returns on shares.

Fama, E.F. and French, K.R. (1995) 'Size and book-to-market factors in earnings and returns', *Journal of Finance,* 50(1), pp. 131–55.

Higher returns to smaller companies and those with high book-to-market ratios. These are described as risk factors and so, it is argued, efficiency is maintained.

Fama, E.F. and French, K.R. (1996) 'Multifactor explanations of asset pricing anomalies', *Journal of Finance,* 50(1), March, pp. 55–84.

Efficiency is retained – size and book-to-market are risk factors.

Fama, E.F. and French, K.R. (1998) 'Value versus growth: The international evidence', *Journal of Finance,* 53(6), December, pp. 1975–99.

An average return on global portfolios of high and low book-to-market shares is 7.68 per cent per year. Explanation: additional distress risk.

Fama, E.F. and French, K.R. (2006) 'The value premium and the CAPM', *Journal of Finance,* LXI (5) October, pp. 2163–85.

Value shares (defined by low price-to-earnings ratio or book-to-market ratio) outperform in the USA and in other countries – and they have lower betas.

Fama, E.F. and French, K.R. (2008) 'Average returns, B/M, and share issues', *The Journal of Finance,* LXIII(6), December, pp. 2971–95.

The way in which the book-to-market ratio changed over the previous few years can impact on share returns to reinforce the tendency of value to outperform growth.

Fama, E.F. and French, K.R. (2016) 'Dissecting Anomalies with a Five-Factor Model', *The Review of Financial Studies,* 29(1).

Two more factors are identified as risk factors – profitability of the firm and degree of conservative investment within the firm – in the pricing of shares. Other researchers interpret them as market anomalies (inefficiencies).

Fama, E.F., Fisher, L., Jensen, M.C. and Roll, R. (1969) 'The adjustment of stock prices to new information', *International Economic Review,* 10(1), February, pp. 1–21.

Investigates the adjustment of share prices to the information which is implicit in share splits. Evidence of semi-strong EMH.

Fifield, S.G.M., Power, D.M. and Sinclair, C.D. (2005) 'An analysis of trading strategies in eleven European stock markets', *European Journal of Finance,* 11(6) pp. 531–48.

Investigates weak-form efficiency and finds inefficiency in less developed markets.

Figelman, I. (2007) 'Interaction of stock return momentum with earnings measures', *Financial Analysts Journal,* 63(3), pp. 71–8.

Momentum evidence.

Foster, G., Olsen, C. and Shevlin, T. (1984) 'Earnings releases, anomalies, and the behaviour of security returns', *Accounting Review,* 59(4), October, pp. 574–603.

A delayed response of share prices to earnings surprise news.

Fox, J. (2009) *The Myth of the Rational Market.* London: HarperBusiness.

'Chronicles the rise and fall of the efficient market theory' in a very easy-to-read fashion, bringing to life the key players and their contributions to the debate.

Frazzini, A. (2006) 'The disposition effect and underreaction to news', *Journal of Finance,* LXI (4), August, pp. 2017–46.

Provides a behavioural finance explanation for post-announcement drift.

Frehen, R.G.P., Goetzmann, W.N. and Rouwenhorst, K.G. (2013) 'New evidence on the first financial bubble', *Journal of Financial Economics,* 108, pp. 585–607.

Theories on market bubbles are tested on data from The Mississippi Bubble, South Sea Bubble and the Dutch Windhandel of 1720. 'Our tests suggest that innovation [e.g. global trade and availability of insurance] was a key driver of bubble expectations.'

Froot, K.A. and Dabora, E. (1999) 'How are stock prices affected by the location of trade?', *Journal of Financial Economics,* 53, pp. 189–216.

Evidence of noise trader risk.

Fuller, R.J., Huberts, L.C. and Levinson, M.J. (1993) 'Returns to E/P strategies, higgledy-piggledy growth, analysts' forecast errors, and omitted risk factors', *Journal of Portfolio Management,* Winter, pp. 13–24.

Regression to the mean of earnings growth shown for US companies classified by PER.

George, T.J. and Hwang, C. (2007) 'Long-term return reversals: overreaction or taxes?' *The Journal of Finance,* LXII(6), pp. 2865–96.

A return reversal effect in US shares is found and an explanation provided, based around a capital gains argument.

Graham, B. (1973, revised 2003) *The Intelligent Investor,* revised edition, with commentary by Jason Zweig. New York: Harper Business Essentials.

The classic value investing book.

Graham, B. and Dodd, D. (1934) *Security Analysis.* New York: McGraw-Hill.

The foundation stone for value investors.

Gregory, A., Harris, R.D.F. and Michou, M. (2001) 'An analysis of contrarian investment strategies in the UK', *Journal of Business Finance and Accounting,* 28(9) and (10), November–December, pp. 1193–228.

Value shares outperform the market.

Gregory, A., Harris, R.D.F. and Michou, M. (2003) 'Contrarian investment and macroeconomic risk', *Journal of Business Finance and Accounting,* 30(1) and (2), January–March, pp. 213–55.

Grinblatt, M. and Han, B. (2005) 'Prospect theory, mental accounting and momentum', *Journal of Financial Economics,* 78, pp. 311–39.

Uses behavioural finance models to explain the momentum phenomenon in shares.

Hamberg, M. and Novak, J. (2010) 'Accounting conservatism and transitory earnings in value and growth strategies', *Journal of Business Finance & Accounting,* 37(5), (6), pp. 518–37.

Swedish value shares (earnings-to-price ratio or book-to-market ratio) outperform growth shares.

Harris, A. (1996) 'Wanted: Insiders', *Management Today,* July, pp. 40–1.

A short and thought-provoking article in defence of insider dealing.

Hawawini, G.A. and Michel, P.A. (eds) (1984) *European Equity Markets, Risk, Return and Efficiency.* Garland Publishing.

A collection of articles and empirical work on the behaviour of European equity markets.

Hawawini, G. and Klein, D.B. (1994) 'On the predictability of common stock returns: Worldwide evidence', in Jarrow, R.A., Maksinovic, V. and Ziembas, W.T. (eds) *Finance.* Amsterdam: North-Holland.

More evidence on inefficiency.

Hengelbrock, J., Theissen, E. and Westheide, C. (2013) 'Market Response to Investor Sentiment', *Journal of Business Finance & Accounting,* Aug/Sep 2013, 40(7/8), pp. 901–17.

Analyses the immediate price reaction to the publication of survey-based investor sentiment indicators, finding that the sign of the immediate market response is the same as that of the predictability at intermediate time horizons. The results are consistent with underreaction to cash flow news or with investor sentiment being related to mispricing. It is inconsistent with the alternative explanations of a rational response to cash flow news

or sentiment indicators providing information about future expected returns.

Hillert, A., Jacobs, H. and Müller, S. (2014) 'Media Makes Momentum', *Review of Financial Studies,* Dec, 27(12), pp. 3467–501.

'We find that firms particularly covered by the media exhibit, ceteris paribus, significantly stronger momentum.'

Hirshleifer, D., Lim, S.S. and Teoh, S.H. (2009) 'Driven to distraction: extraneous events and underreaction to earnings news', *The Journal of Finance,* LXIV(5), pp. 2289–325.

Post-earnings-announcement drift is stronger when there are a number of earnings announcements made by other firms on the same day.

Hon, M.T. and Tonks, I. (2003) 'Momentum in the UK stock market', *Journal of Multinational Financial Management,* 13, pp. 43–70.

Momentum of share returns is not present in all periods of stock market history.

Hong, H. and Stein, J.C. (1999) 'A unified theory of underreaction, momentum trading and overreaction in asset markets', *Journal of Finance,* 54(6), pp. 2143–84.

Behavioural explanation of inefficiencies. A model in which information diffuses gradually across the investing population is used to provide an explanation for underreaction and then overreaction.

Ikenberry, D., Lakonishok, J. and Vermaelen, T. (1995) 'Market under reaction to open market share repurchases', *Journal of Financial Economics,* October–November, pp. 181–208.

Share price drift after share repurchase announcements.

Ikenberry, D., Rankine, G. and Stice, E. (1996) 'What do stock splits really signal?', *Journal of Financial and Quantitative Analysis,* 31, pp. 357–75.

Share price drift evidence.

Israel, R. and T. J. Moskowitz (2013) 'The role of shorting, firm size, and time on market anomalies', *Journal of Financial Economics,* 108 pp. 275–301.

A study of the firm size, momentum and value (BE/ME) effects in five countries with a particular emphasis on the influence on shorting in the overall return: it's less than the long position. Value effect most pronounced in smaller companies.

Jaffe, J., Keim, D.B. and Westerfield, R. (1989) 'Earnings yields, market values and stock returns', *Journal of Finance,* 44, pp. 135–48. US data, 1951–86.

Finds significant PER and size effects (January is a special month).

Jegadeesh, N. and Titman, S. (1993) 'Returns to buying winners and selling losers: Implications for stock market efficiency', *Journal of Finance,* 48, March, pp. 65–91.

Holding shares which have performed well in the past generates significant abnormal returns over 3–12-month holding periods.

Jensen, M.C. (1968) 'The performance of mutual funds in the period 1945–64', *Journal of Finance*, 23, May, pp. 389–416.
   Mutual funds were poor at predicting share prices and underperformed the market.

Kahnemann, D. (2012) *Thinking fast and slow*. Penguin.
   A landmark book summarizing a Nobel Laurette's lifetime's work on decision making in the real world. Very easy to read, with profound insights.

Kahnemann, D. and Tversky, A. (2000) *Choices, Values and Frames*. Cambridge: Cambridge University Press.
   An important book on behavioural finance.

Kahneman, D., Slovic, P. and Tversky, A. (1982) *Judgment under Uncertainty: Heuristics and Biases*. Cambridge: Cambridge University Press.
   A collection of classic articles on decision making which have strongly influenced the behavioural finance field.

Kama, I. (2009) 'On the market reaction to revenue and earnings surprises', *Journal of Business Finance & Accounting*, 36(1), (2), pp. 31–50.
   More evidence of post-earnings announcement drift.

Kay, J. (2009) *The Long and Short of It*. London: The Erasmus Press.
   An impressive, easy-to-read book, which while explaining the basics of finance/investment also attacks the current set-up that often does not serve the interests of investors. 'You cannot be an intelligent investor if you believe that markets are always efficient or deny that they are mostly efficient. It is a big mistake to believe that the efficient market hypothesis is true, and a bigger mistake to believe that it is false.'

Keim, D.B. (1983) 'Size-related anomalies and stock return seasonality: Further empirical evidence', *Journal of Financial Economics*, 12, pp. 13–32.
   Small-firm effect.

Keim, D.B. (1988) 'Stock market regularities: A synthesis of the evidence and explanations', in Dimson, E. (ed.) *Stock Market Anomalies,* Cambridge: Cambridge University Press, and in Lofthouse, S. (ed.) (1994) *Readings in Investment*, Chichester: Wiley.
   A non-technical, easy to understand consideration of some evidence of market inefficiencies.

Keim, D.B. and Ziemba, W.T. (eds) (2000) *Security Market Imperfections in World Wide Equity Markets*. Cambridge: Cambridge University Press.
   A collection of empirical articles on the evidence on efficiency.

Kendall, M. (1953) 'The analysis of economic time-series prices', *Journal of the Royal Statistical Society*, 96, pp. 11–25.
   Classic founding article on random walks.

Keynes, J.M. (1936) *The General Theory of Employment, Interest and Money*. London: Harcourt, Brace and World.
   A classic economic text with some lessons for finance.

Kindleberger, C.P. and Aliber, R.Z. (2011) *Manias, Panics and Crashes: A History of Financial Crises*, 6th edn. New York: Macmillan.
   Study of the history of odd market behaviour.

Kothari, S.P., Shanken, J. and Sloan, R.G. (1995) 'Another look at the cross-section of expected stock returns', *Journal of Finance*, 50(1) March, pp. 185–224.
   Apparent excess returns disappear if risk is allowed for.

Lakonishok, J., Shleifer, A. and Vishny, R. (1994) 'Contrarian investment extrapolation and risk', *Journal of Finance*, 49, pp. 1541–78.
   Value share outperformance.

Lamont, O.A. and Thaler, R.H. (2003) 'Can the market add and subtract? Mispricing in tech price equity carve-outs', *Journal of Political Economy*, 111 (2 April), pp. 227–68.
   Examples of odd pricing by the market: e.g. 3Com held a proportion of Palm's shares, yet 3Com was valued by the market at less than the Palm shareholding – a rational market?

La Porta, R. (1996) 'Expectations and the cross-section of stock returns', *Journal of Finance*, 51(5), December, pp. 1715–42.
   'I show that investment strategies that seek to exploit errors in analysts' forecasts earn superior returns.'

La Porta, R., Lakonishok, J., Shleifer, A. and Vishny, R. (1997) 'Good news for value stocks: Further evidence on market efficiency', *Journal of Finance*, 52(2), pp. 859–74.
   Earnings surprises are more positive for value shares: 'The evidence is inconsistent with risk-based explanation for the return differential.'

Lee, D.R. and Verbrugge, J.A. (1996) 'The efficient market theory thrives on criticism', *Journal of Applied Corporate Finance*, 9(1), pp. 3–11.
   An overview of efficiency evidence.

Lerman, A., Livnat, J. and Mendenhall, R.R. (2007) 'Double surprise into higher future returns', *Financial Analysts Journal*, 63(4), pp. 63–71.
   Post-earnings-announcement drift is greater when analysts' forecasts are used rather than historical earnings data to estimate the extent of the surprise.

Levis, M. (1989) 'Stock market anomalies: A reassessment based on UK evidence', *Journal of Banking and Finance*, 13, pp. 675–96.
   Shows that strategies based on dividend yield, PE ratios and share prices appear to be as profitable as (if not more so than) a strategy of concentrating on firm size.

Lewellen, J. (2004) 'Predicting returns with financial ratios', *Journal of Financial Economics*, 74, pp. 209–35.

Evidence that higher returns are attainable by buying high dividend yield shares, high earnings–price ratio shares or high book to market value shares.

Li, X., Brooks, C. and Miffre, J. (2009) 'The value premium and time-varying volatility', *Journal of Business Finance & Accounting*, 36(9), (10), pp. 1252–72.
    Value shares outperforming growth shares. Examines earnings yield, book-to-market and cash flow to price as determining factors.

Li, X. and Wang, S. (2015) 'Post-earnings-announcement drift in global markets: Evidence from an information shock', *Review of Financial Studies*, 28(4), pp. 1242–83.

PEAD has declined when there has been an improvement in firms' financial reporting quality.

Little, I.M.D. (1962) 'Higgledy piggledy growth', *Institute of Statistics Bulletin*, 24(4), pp. 387–412.
    Profit trends for companies are unreliable.

Litzenberger, R.H. and Ramaswamy, K. (1979) 'The effect of personal taxes and dividends on capital asset prices: Theory and empirical evidence', *Journal of Financial Economics*, 7, pp. 163–95.
    Technical paper with the conclusion: 'There is a strong positive relationship between dividend yield and expected return for NYSE stocks.'

Liu, W., Strong, N. and Xu, X. (1999) 'The profitability of momentum investing', *Journal of Business Finance and Accounting*, 26(9) and (10), November–December, pp. 1043–91.
    Following a price momentum strategy was profitable over the period 1977 to 1998.

Liu, W., Strong, N. and Xu, X. (2003) 'Post-earnings-announcement drift in the UK', *European Financial Management*, 9(1), pp. 89–116.
    Post-earnings-announcement drift evident in the UK.

Liu, Y., Szewczyk, S.H. and Zantout, Z. (2008) 'Underreaction to dividend reductions and omissions?' *The Journal of Finance*, LXIII(2), pp. 987–1020.
    'This study reports significantly negative post-earnings announcement long-term abnormal returns' following dividend reductions or omissions.

Lo, A. (2017) *Adaptive Markets: Financial evolution at the speed of thought*. Princeton.
    Humans are not hyper-rational calculating machines. As a result markets are not always efficient. People modify their rules of thumb, if decisions turn out badly, thus they evolve.

Lo, A.W. and Mackinley, A.C. (2001) *A Non-random Walk Down Wall Street*. Princeton, NJ: Princeton University Press.
    A challenge to the random walk hypothesis – they claim some predictability.

Lo, A.W. and Hasanhodzic, J. (2010) *The Evolution of Technical Analysis: Financial Prediction from Babylonian Tablets to Bloomberg Terminals*. New York: John Wiley and Sons.

Explores the fascinating history of technical analysis, tracing where technical analysts failed, how they succeeded, and what it all means for today's traders and investors.

Lowe, J. (1999) *The Rediscovered Benjamin Graham*. New York: John Wiley & Sons.
    Some observations from the most respected practitioner/intellectual, compiled by Janet Lowe.

Lynch, P. (1990) *One Up on Wall Street* (with John Rothchild). New York: Penguin Books. (Originally published by Simon & Schuster, 1989.)
    Fascinating insight into the world of stock picking. Presents sound investment principles.

Lynch, P. (1994) *Beating the Street* (with John Rothchild). New York: Simon & Schuster.
    Revised version of 1993 hardback publication. Fascinating insight into the world of stock picking. Presents sound investment principles.

Malkiel, B.G. (2016) *A Random Walk Down Wall Street*. 11th Revised Edition. New York: W.W. Norton & Co.
    A superb introduction to the theory and reality of stock market behaviour. A witty prose description of the arguments for and against EMH.

Martikainen, T. and Puttonen, V. (1996) 'Finnish days-of-the-week effects', *Journal of Business Finance and Accounting*, 23(7), September, pp. 1019–32.
    There is evidence of a day-of-the-week effect in the cash and derivative markets.

Matti, K., Linnainmaa, J. T. and Nyberg, P. (2016) 'Return seasonalities', *Journal of Finance*, 71(4), pp. 1557–90.
    'Our results suggest that seasonalities are not a distinct class of anomalies that requires an explanation of its own, but rather that they are intertwined with other return anomalies through shared systematic factors.'

McLean, R. D. and Pontiff, J. (2016) 'Does academic research destroy stock return predictability?' *Journal of Finance*, 71(1), pp. 5–32.
    Found that after publication, the returns on exploiting stock market anomalies decreased by 58% 'Our findings suggest that investors learn about mispricing from academic publications'.

Michaely, R., Thaler, R. and Womack, K. (1995) 'Price reaction to dividend initiations and omissions: Overreaction or drift?', *Journal of Finance*, 50, pp. 573–608.
    Share price drift evidence.

Michou, M. (2009) 'Is the value spread a good predictor of stock returns? UK evidence', *Journal of Business Finance & Accounting*, 36(7), (8), pp. 925–50.
    More evidence that the book-to-market ratio can explain high returns to value shares.

Miles, D. and Timmermann, A. (1996) 'Variations in expected stock returns: Evidence on the mispricing of equities from a cross-section of UK companies', *Economica*, 63, pp. 369–82.
    Some interesting evidence and discussion.

Montier, J. (2002) *Behavioural Finance: Insights into Irrational Minds and Markets*. London: John Wiley & Sons.

> A very good overview of the usefulness of developments in the decision-making under uncertainty literature in the real world of fund management. Written by a practising equity strategist.

Montier, J. (2009) *Value Investing: Tools and Techniques for Intelligent Investment*. Chichester: John Wiley & Sons Ltd.

> From the pen of a shrewd observer of markets. A practitioner's insights into the impact of human behavioural traits on market prices. Very definitely not a fan of EMH.

Montier, J. (2010) *The Little Book of Behavioral Investing*. Chichester: John Wiley & Sons, Inc.

> A short book on the impact of human behaviour on market prices, written by a knowledgeable and experienced practitioner.

Morgan, G. and Thomas, S. (1998) 'Taxes, dividend yields and returns in the UK equity market', *Journal of Banking and Finance,* 22, pp. 405–23.

> High dividend yield is correlated with high returns.

Mussweiler, T. and Schneller, K. (2003) '"What goes up must come down" – how charts influence decisions to buy and sell stocks', *The Journal of Behavioral Finance,* 4(3), pp. 121–30.

> Weak for efficiency challenged.

Neff, J. (1999) *John Neff on Investing* (with S.L. Mintz). New York: John Wiley & Sons.

> Decades of investing experience create a very interesting book to guide aspiring investors. Insight into investor/market behaviour.

Novy-Marx, R. (2013) 'The other side of value: The gross profitability premium', *Journal of Financial Economics,* 108, pp. 1–28.

> Firms with higher gross profit-to-assets ratio generate significantly higher returns than unprofitable firms, despite having significantly higher valuation ratios. This metric is shown to enhance the book-to-market ratio effect.

Novy-Marx, R. and Velikov, M. (2016) 'A taxonomy of anomalies and their trading costs', *The Review of Financial Studies,* 29(1), pp. 104–47.

> Deducts trading costs from 23 investing strategies, including PEAD, value and size to reveal that most trading strategies with portfolio turnover less than 50% per month can still generate significant returns.

Park, C-H. and Irwin, S.H. (2007) 'What do we know about the profitability of technical analysis?' *Journal of Economic Surveys,* 21(4), pp. 786–826.

> Examines a great array of literature testing weak form efficiency – the more recent evidence generally supports the technical analyst's view that the share, currency and commodity markets examined are inefficient in many ways.

Pastor, L. and Veronesi, P. (2009) 'Technological revolutions and stock prices', *American Economic Review* 99, 1451–83.

> Growth rates in innovative industries can appear irrational after the event. Share prices for new technology companies rise sharply and then fall as uncertainty about technological innovation is resolved. Looked at US nineteenth-century railroad securities.

Perotti, P. and Wagenhofer, A. (2014) 'Earnings quality measures and excess returns', *Journal of Business Finance & Accounting,* 41(5/6), pp. 545–71.

> Shows that firms with higher earnings quality will be less mispriced than other firms.

Phalippou, L. (2008) 'Where is the value premium?' *Financial Analysts Journal,* 64(2), pp. 41–8.

> The book-to-market ratio effect is concentrated in just 7% of shares.

Piotroski, J.D. (2000) 'Value investing: The use of historical financial statement information to separate winners from losers', *Journal of Accounting Research,* 38, Supplement, pp. 1–51.

> Piotroski uses nine accounting variables (e.g. positive cash flow) to classify high book-to-market ratio shares into different categories of financial strength. He finds evidence that the market does not properly incorporate these financial strength factors because 'strong' company shares significantly outperform 'weak' company shares.

Pontiff, J. and Schall, L.D. (1998) 'Book-to-market ratios as predictors of market returns', *Journal of Financial Economics,* 49, pp. 141–60.

> Book-to-market ratios predict market returns and small-firm excess returns.

Poterba, J.M. and Summers, L.H. (1988) 'Mean reversion in stock prices: Evidence and implications', *Journal of Financial Economics,* 22, pp. 27–59.

> The idea that share returns eventually revert to the average.

Puetz, A. and Ruenzi, S. (2011) 'Overconfidence among professional investors: Evidence from mutual fund managers', *Journal of Business Finance & Accounting,* Jun/Jul, 38(5/6), pp. 684–712.

> 'Consistent with theories of overconfidence, we find that fund managers trade more after good past performance.'

Reinganum, M.R. (1981) 'Misspecification of capital asset pricing: Empirical anomalies based on earnings' yields and market values', *Journal of Financial Economics,* 9, pp. 19–46.

> The PER effect disappears when size is simultaneously considered.

Reinganum, M.R. (1988) 'The anatomy of a stock market winner', *Financial Analysts Journal,* March–April, pp. 272–84.

> More on inefficiencies due to low net assets.

Rendleman, R.J., Jones, C.P. and Latané, H.E. (1982) 'Empirical anomalies based on unexpected earnings and the importance of risk adjustments', *Journal of Financial Economics,* November, pp. 269–87.

Abnormal returns could have been earned by exploiting the slow response to unexpected earnings figures.

Roberts, H.V. (1959) 'Stock market "patterns" and financial analysis: Methodological suggestions', *Journal of Finance,* March, pp. 1–10.

Describes chance-generated price series to cast doubt on technical analysis.

Roll, R. (1981) 'A possible explanation for the small firm effect', *Journal of Finance,* September.

Interesting consideration of the issue.

Roll, R. (1994) 'What every CFO should know about scientific progress in financial economics: What is known and what remains to be resolved', *Financial Management,* 23(2) (Summer), pp. 69–75.

A discussion, in straightforward terms, of Roll's views on the state of play in the efficiency/inefficiency debate.

Rosenberg, B., Reid, K. and Lanstein, R. (1985) 'Persuasive evidence of market inefficiency', *Journal of Portfolio Management,* 11, Spring, pp. 9–16.

Reports the identification of two market inefficiencies.

Rouwenhorst, K.G. (1998) 'International momentum strategies', *Journal of Finance,* 53(1), February, pp. 267–84.

Price momentum evidence for 12 countries.

Rouwenhorst, K.G. (1999) 'Local return factors and turnover in emerging stock markets', *Journal of Finance,* 54(4), pp. 1439–63.

Emerging stock markets exhibit price momentum.

Sagi, J.S. and Seasholes, M.S. (2007) 'Firm-specific attributes and the cross-section of momentum', *Journal of Financial Economics,* 84, pp. 389–434.

A number of firm characteristics drive momentum profits.

Schoenburg, E. (1990) 'Stock price prediction using neural networks', *Neurocomputing,* 2, pp. 17–27.

Some evidence of predictability.

Scholes, M. (1972) 'The market for securities: Substitution versus price pressure effects of information on share prices', *Journal of Business,* April, pp. 179–211.

Evidence that the issue of more shares does not depress share prices.

Shefrin, H. (2000) *Beyond Greed and Fear.* Boston, MA: Harvard Business School Press.

An important book in the field of the application of behavioural finance to inefficiency in the markets.

Shiller, R.J. (1981) 'Do stock prices move too much to be justified by subsequent charges in dividends?', *American Economic Review,* 71, pp. 421–36.

The volatility of US shares is too large to be explained by the volatility of dividends. Taken to be evidence of overreaction and investors' pursuit of fads and the herd.

Shiller, R.J. (2000) *Irrational Exuberance.* Princeton, NJ: Princeton University Press.

Behavioural finance applied to the bubble at the turn of the millennium.

Shivakumar, L. (2006) 'Accruals, cash flows and the post-earnings-announcement drift', *Journal of Business Finance and Accounting,* Jan–Mar, 33(1), pp. 1–25.

Earnings surprises cause post-earnings-announcement drift. However, if earnings are broken down into cash flow and accruals we find cash flows can predict future returns above and beyond that predicted by earnings alone.

Shleifer, A. (2000) *Inefficient Markets: An Introduction to Behavioural Finance.* Oxford: Oxford University Press.

A landmark presentation of the case for the impact of human (irrational) behaviour in financial markets.

Shon, J. and Zhou, P. (2010) 'Do divergent opinions explain the value premium?' *The Journal of Investing,* Summer, pp. 53–62.

More evidence on value shares outperforming growth shares, focusing on book-to-market ratio.

Shu, Tao (2013) 'Institutional investor participation and stock market anomalies', *Journal of Business Finance and Accounting,* 40(5) & (6), pp. 695–718.

Evidence of the presence of the B/M effect in US shares 1980–2005, but 'value premium exists only in stocks with low institutional trading volume and disappears in stocks with high institutional trading volume'. Also found that small firms with low levels of expenditure on corporate investments in plant, machinery and the like outperform firms with high corporate investment commitments; could be due to wasteful empire building by managers. Price momentum also found.

Smith, C. (1986) 'Investment banking and the capital acquisition process', *Journal of Financial Economics,* 15, pp. 3–29.

Lists numerous studies that report a decrease in the share price when a share issue is announced.

Smithers, A. (2009) *Wall Street Revalued: Imperfect markets and inept central bankers.* Chichester: John Wiley & Sons Ltd.

An expert on security valuation and market history provides profound insight into the working of markets, emphasising that markets are neither perfectly efficient nor absurd casinos.

Soros, G. (1987) *The Alchemy of Finance.* New York: John Wiley & Sons. (Reprinted in 1994 with a new preface and a new foreword.)

Provides insight into the investment approach of a highly successful investor.

Soros, G. (1995) *Soros on Soros.* New York: John Wiley & Sons.

Financial theory and personal reminiscence interwoven.

Soros, G. (1998) *The Crisis of Global Capitalism*. New York: Public Affairs.
> More on market irrationality.

Soros, G. (2009) *The Crash of 2008 and What It Means*. New York: Public Affairs.
> The most famous billionaire hedge fund manager explains his reflexivity theory and its impact on market behaviour. Clearly not a believer in EHM.

Sullivan, R., Timmermann, A. and White, H. (1999) 'Data-snooping, technical trading rule performance, and the bootstrap', *Journal of Finance*, 54(5), pp. 1647ff.
> A demonstration of false inferences being drawn from data. Many technical trading rules that had been shown to 'work' in other academic studies are shown to be false when data snooping is eliminated.

Thaler R.H. (2015) *Misbehaving: The making of behavioural economics*. Penguin Random House.
> Behavioural economics/finance explained in an entertaining way

Thaler, R.H. and C.R Sunstein (2009) *Nudge: Improving decisions about health, wealth and happiness*. Penguin.
> A worldwide best-seller drawing on the academic economic decision-making literature. Very influential.

Thaler, R. (ed.) (1993) *Advances in Behavioural Finance*. New York: Russell Sage Foundation.
> An important book in the growth of this developing discipline.

Thaler, R.H. (2005) *Advances in Behavioural Finance*. Volume II. Princeton, NJ: Russell Sage Foundation.
> An important collection of key papers in this young discipline.

Titman, S. J. Wei and Feixue Xie (2004), 'Capital Investments and Stock Returns', *Journal of Financial and Quantitative Analysis*, 39, pp. 677–700.
> Increased investment expenditures can result in negative stock returns. 'If investors fail to appreciate managements' incentive to oversell their firms in these situations, stock returns subsequent to an increase in investment expenditures are likely to be negative. This effect is likely to be especially important for managers who are "empire builders."'

Vayanos, D. and Woolley, P. (2011) 'An institutional theory of momentum and reversal.' London School of Economics Working Paper.
> An attempt to provide a rational explanation for momentum and reversal based on flows between fund managers.

West, K.D. (1988) 'Bubbles, fads and stock price volatility tests: A partial evaluation', *Journal of Finance*, 43(3), pp. 639–56.
> A summary and interpretation of some of the literature on share price volatility. Noise trading by naive investors is discussed.

Xiao, Y. and Arnold, G. (2008) 'Testing Benjamin Graham's Net Current Asset Value Strategy in London', *Journal of Investing*, 17(4), Winter, pp. 11–19.
> Those shares listed on the London Stock Exchange in the period 1981 to 2005 with a net current asset value to market capitalisation ratio greater than 1.5 display significantly positive market-adjusted returns (annualised return up to 19.7 per cent per year) over five holding years. (Net current asset value is total current assets minus all liabilities – long and short liabilities.)

Case study recommendations

Please see www.pearsoned.co.uk/arnold for case study synopses. Also, another list of useful case studies from the fifth edition can be found there.

- Behavioral finance at JP Morgan. Authors: Malcolm P. Baker; Aldo Sesia, Harvard Business School. Available at www.cb.hbsp.harvard.edu

- Note on behavioural finance. Authors: Stephen R. Foerster; Amos Nadler; Michael Lay, Ivey Publishing. Available at www.cb.hbsp.harvard.edu

Self-review questions

1   Explain the three forms of market efficiency.

2   Does the EMH imply perfect forecasting ability?

3   What does 'random walk' mean?

4   Reshape plc has just announced an increase in profit of 50%. The market was expecting profits to double. What will happen to Reshape's share price?

5   Can the market be said to be inefficient because some shares give higher returns than others?

6 What use is inside information in the trading of shares?

7 Why is it important for directors and other managers to communicate to shareholders and potential shareholders as much information as possible about the firm?

8 What are the implications of the EMH for investors?

9 What are the implications of the EMH for managers?

10 What are allocative, operational and pricing efficiency?

11 What are 'technical analysis' and 'fundamental analysis'?

Questions and problems

1 Celtic plc, the quoted football and leisure group, wins the cup and therefore can anticipate greater revenues and profits. Before the win in the final the share price was £1.30.

    a   What will happen to the share price following the final whistle of the winning game?

    b   Which of the following suggests the market is efficient? (Assume that the market as a whole does not move and that the only news is the football match win.)

        (i)   The share price rises slowly over a period of two weeks to reach £1.50.

        (ii)   The share price jumps to £1.80 on the day of the win and then falls back to £1.50 one week later.

        (iii)   The share price moves immediately to £1.50 and does not move further relative to the market.

2 If Marks & Spencer has a 1 for 1 scrip issue when its share price is 550p what would you expect to happen to its share price in theory (no other influences) and in practice?

3 (*Examination level*) 'The paradox of the efficient market hypothesis is that large numbers of investors have to disbelieve the hypothesis in order to maintain efficiency.' Write an essay explaining the EMH and explain this statement.

4 (*Examination level*) 'Of course the market is not efficient. I know lots of people from technical analysts to professional fundamental analysts who have made packets of money on the market.' Describe the terms 'technical' and 'fundamental analyst'. Explain how some individuals might generate a satisfactory return from stock market investment even if it is efficient.

5 (*Examination level*) It could be said that insufficient attention has been paid to psychological factors when explaining stock efficiency anomalies. Outline the efficient stock market hypothesis (EMH) and describe some of the evidence which casts doubts on the semi-strong level of the efficient market hypothesis for which psychological explanations might be useful.

6 (*Examination level*) The efficient market hypothesis, if true, encourages managers to act in shareholder wealth enhancing ways. Discuss this.

7 If the efficient market hypothesis is true an investor might as well select shares by sticking a pin into the *Financial Times*. Explain why this is not quite true.

8 Arcadura plc has been planning a major rights issue to raise £300m. The market has fallen by 10% in the past four days and the investment bank adviser suggests that Arcadura wait another three or four months before trying to sell these new shares. Given that the market is efficient, evaluate the investment banker's suggestion.

9 Chartism and fundamental analysis are traditional methods used by stock market investors to make buy or sell decisions. Explain why modern finance theory has contributed to the growing popularity of share index funds which have a simple strategy of buying and holding a broadly based portfolio.

10 (*Examination level*) 'The world's well developed stock markets are efficient at pricing shares for most of the people most of the time.' Comment on this statement and explain what is meant by stock market efficiency.

11 (*Examination level*) The following statements are extracts from the detailed minutes taken at a Board meeting of Advance plc. This company is discussing the possibility of a new flotation on the main listed market of the London stock market.

Mr Adams (Production Director): 'I have been following the stock market for many years as a private investor. I put great value on patterns of past share prices for predicting future movements. At the moment my charts are telling me that the market is about to rise significantly and therefore we will get a higher price for our shares if we wait a few months. This will benefit our existing shareholders as the new shareholders will not get their shares artificially cheap.'

Mr Cluff: 'I too have been investing in shares for years and quite frankly have concluded that following charts is akin to voodoo magic, and what is more, working hard analysing companies is a waste of effort. The market cannot be predicted. I now put all my money into tracker funds and forget analysis. Delaying our flotation is pointless, the market might just as easily go down.'

Required

Consider the efficient stock markets theory and relate it to Mr Adams' and Mr Cluff's comments.

12 'A number of companies were put off flotation on the London Stock Exchange in 2017 because the market was too low.' Explain the efficient market hypothesis and assess the logic of such postponements.

13 The chief geneticist at Adams Horticultural plc has discovered a method for raising the yield of commercial crops by 20%. The managing director will make an announcement to the Stock Exchange in one week which will result in a sharp rise in the share price. Describe the level of inefficiency this represents. Is the geneticist legally free to try to make money on the share price issue by buying now?

14 Rapid Growth plc has recently changed the methods of accounting for depreciation, stock and research and development, all of which have the effect of improving the reported profit figures. Consider whether the share price will rise as a result of these actions.

15 A famous and well-respected economist announces in a Sunday newspaper that the growth phase of the economy is over and a recessionary trend has begun. He bases his evidence on the results of a dozen surveys which have been conducted and made public by various economic institutes over the past three months. Should you sell all your shares? Explain the logic behind your answer with reference to the efficient market hypothesis.

16 Explain why professional and highly paid fund managers generally produce returns less than those available on a broadly based market index.

17 (*Examination level*) Describe the extent to which the evidence supports the efficient market hypothesis.

Assignment

Consider the actions of the directors of a stock-market quoted company you know well. Do they behave in such a way as to convince you they believe in the efficiency of the stock market? In what ways could they take steps to ensure greater efficiency of stock market pricing of the company's shares?

PART 5

Corporate value

14

Value-based management

LEARNING OUTCOMES

This chapter demonstrates the rationale behind value-based management techniques and the links with corporate strategy. By the end of it the reader should be able to:

■ explain the limitations of accounts-based management (e.g. profits, balance sheet assets, earnings per share and accounting rate of returns) to guide value-maximising decisions;

■ describe the four key drivers of value and five actions that should increase value;

■ explain the ramifications of value-based management;

■ evaluate alternative strategies for the business from a value perspective;

■ map business activities in terms of industry attractiveness, competitive advantage within the industry and life-cycle stage; and

■ make capital allocation choices.

Introduction

Early chapters of this book linked the objective of shareholder wealth maximisation with the acceptance of positive NPV projects, the concepts of the time value of money and the opportunity cost of invested funds. If managers are unable to achieve returns at least as high as those available elsewhere for the same level of risk, then, as agents for investors, they should release cash to the investor to invest elsewhere. If they retain the cash and invest at a lower return, they are destroying value. If a group of investors can earn a return of 14% on an investment, managers who generate lower annual returns, say 10%, are destroying value for those investors if, for the same level of risk, the higher (14%) return is available elsewhere. The extent of this value destruction is summarised in the projected negative NPV figure.

NPV is well-entrenched throughout modern corporations. However, the full potential of the concepts above, which underlie NPV, is now being explored by a few progressive organisations. Applying the idea of opportunity cost of capital and focussing on the cash flow of *new projects* is the start; an increasing number of organisations now examine their *existing* businesses, or parts of their businesses, in terms of the following questions:

● How much money has been (or will be) provided to this business by investors?

● What rate of return is being (or will be) generated for those investors?

● Is this sufficient given the opportunity cost of capital?

These questions can be asked about past performance or future plans. They may be asked about the entire organisation or about a division, strategic business unit (SBU) or product line. If, based on the capital invested, an area of business does not create value by generating a return greater than the minimum required, then management must address this. Ultimately every unit should be contributing to shareholder value.

Identifying the sources of value may not seem particularly remarkable to someone who has absorbed the concepts discussed in Chapters 1 to 8, but to many managers steeped in accounting-based performance measures such as profits, return on investment and earnings per share, this focus on value has revolutionary consequences. The ideas themselves are not revolutionary. It is the application of them, to create a shareholder value-orientated company, that can revolutionise almost everything managers do.

● Instead of plans drawn up in terms of accounting budgets, with their vulnerability to manipulation of 'profit' and 'capital investment', managers **focus on the extent to which their new strategies or initiatives will produce added shareholder value**: a discounted inflow of cash greater than the cash invested.

● Instead of being rewarded for meeting goals set in terms of accounting rates of return and other 'non-value' performance measures, such as earnings per share and turnover, managers are **rewarded by the extent to which they contribute to shareholder value over a long time horizon**. This radically alters incentive systems in most firms.

● Instead of accepting a low cash-flow return on the market value of assets tied up in a poorly performing subsidiary because the accounting profits look satisfactory, managers are forced to consider whether greater wealth would be generated by either closure and selling off the subsidiary's assets or selling the operation to another firm which can make a better return.

● There then follows a second decision: **should the cash released be invested in other company activities or be given back to shareholders to invest elsewhere?** The answers, can be uncomfortable for executives who prefer to expand rather than contract the organisation.

Strategic analysis does not stop at the point of often vague and woolly qualitative analysis, it goes on to further phases of valuation of the strategies and quantitative sensitivity analysis. The decisions on the most appropriate debt levels and the dividend pay-out ratios have, as their core consideration, the impact on shareholder wealth. In a value-based organisation, managers must be motivated and evaluated on the extent to which a return above the cost of capital can be achieved – see **Exhibit 14.1**

Exhibit 14.1

What exactly do we mean by 'shareholder value'? Returns consistently exceed the cost of capital

By Terry Smith

Company managers, fund managers and activist investors often say they are committed to generating or releasing shareholder value without ever spelling out precisely what that means. For me, it is simply determining whether or not a company is creating additional wealth for its ultimate owners, and whether its managers are acting appropriately to achieve this.

I'm not sure this is everyone's definition, though. Latterly I have come to wonder whether this concept has come to be misused, like so many others in finance. Put simply, my definition of value creation is when a company delivers returns that are above the cost of the capital used to generate them. Companies are in essence just like us. If you borrow money at a cost of 10% a year and invest it at a return of 5% a year you will become poorer. If you invest it at a return of 20% a year you will become richer.

Similarly, companies which consistently make returns above their cost of capital become more valuable and vice versa. A company that can sustain a return on capital above its cost of capital creates value for its shareholders, who should want it to retain at least part of its profits to reinvest at these attractive rates of return rather than handing them all over as dividends or using them to buy back shares.

All organisations need a committed workforce; but committed to what? Shareholder value-based management offers an answer but requires managers to communicate, educate and convert all staff to the process of value creation, which may require a shift in culture, systems and procedures as well as additional training.

Value-based management links investors' valuation of shares with the firm's strategy, its organisational capabilities and its finances. It is more than a technique employed by a few individuals 'good with numbers'. The principles behind it must pervade the organisation, touching almost all aspects of organisational life.

Value-based management is a managerial approach in which the primary purpose is long-run shareholder wealth maximisation. The objective of the firm, its systems, strategy, processes, analytical techniques, performance measurements and culture have as their guiding objective shareholder wealth maximisation.

IHG Group (Intercontinental Hotels–Holiday Inn, Crowne Plaza, etc.) has the three key questions identified above at the heart of its value-based management. Directors are focused on creating long-term value for shareholders by generating high returns from every pound employed in the business. They have gradually withdrawn from the business of owning hotel buildings, which requires large amounts of capital for little reward, and have built up a service business of managing hotels, allowing them to release money to give back to shareholders – *see* **Exhibit 14.2**.

Exhibit 14.2

Our strategy for high-quality growth

We are focused on delivering high-quality growth, which for us means delivering consistent, sustained growth in cash flows and profits over the long term, via our portfolio of preferred brands.

Our strategy is unchanged. Through our Winning Model, we focus on value-creation by building preferred brands, delivering a superior owner proposition, leveraging scale and generating revenue through the lowest-cost, direct channels. We concentrate on a Targeted Portfolio that, together with Disciplined Execution of our strategy and a commitment to doing business responsibly, will drive superior shareholder returns.

We measure our performance with a set of carefully selected key performance indicators (KPIs), which monitor our success in achieving our strategy.

(IHG Group – Annual Report 2016)

The focus of IHG strategy is clearly long-run shareholder returns – *see* Exhibit 14.3.

Exhibit 14.3

Superior shareholder returns over the long term

Our proposition to third-party hotel owners is highly competitive and drives superior returns for them. We execute an asset-light strategy with a focus on the most attractive, high-growth markets and industry segments. We take a disciplined approach to capital allocation, investing for the future growth of our brands. This enables us to drive sustainable growth in our profitability and deliver superior shareholder returns over the long term.

(IHG Group – Annual Report 2016)

Other annual reports have emphasised the point even more forcefully stating such things as: a 'key characteristic of the franchised and managed business is that it generates more cash than is required for investment in the business, with a high return on capital employed'.

The shareholder wealth-maximising goal

Why should we feel justified in holding up shareholder wealth maximisation as the primary objective? Isn't growth in sales or market share more worthy? And what about the return to the labour force and to society generally? What follows is a brief recap and extension of some of the comments made in Chapter 1 about the objectives of the firm, in a competitive market environment, that has responsibilities to shareholders.

Shareholders require directors to act in the shareholders' best interests and are increasingly active, using their voting powers to remove directors or to register protest votes. Managers should aim to create as much long-term wealth as possible for the shareholders to satisfy their expectations. Dissatisfied shareholders may sell their shares potentially causing the share price to fall. This fall in share price can make the company an attractive takeover target possibly leading, post-acquisition, to job losses for both management and employees.

Arguably, society will benefit if shareholder-owned firms concentrate on value creation. Scarce capital resources can be directed to their most valuable uses. Maximising the productivity of resources enables high economic growth and higher standards of living.

Confusing objectives

Some managers claim that there are measures of performance that are synonymous with, or good proxies for, shareholder wealth, such as customer satisfaction, market share leadership or lowest-cost producer. These proxies are then set as 'strategic objectives'. In many cases achieving these goals does go hand in hand with shareholder returns but, as Exhibit 14.4 shows, the pursuit of these objectives can be taken too far. There is frequently a trade-off between shareholder value and these proxy goals. Taking market share as an example: it is apparent that for many firms increasing market share will bring greater economies of scale, create barriers to entry for potential competitors and help establish brand loyalty, among other benefits. This sort of situation is demonstrated by moving from A to Z in Exhibit 14.4. High market share is clearly an important factor in many industries, but some firms seem to become trapped in an obsessive quest for market share – see Exhibit 14.5.

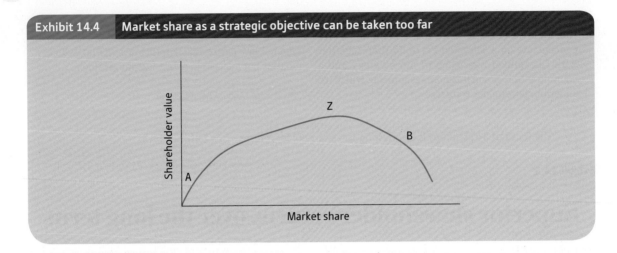

Exhibit 14.4   **Market share as a strategic objective can be taken too far**

Nestlé has recently announced its intention to change its strategy from building market share to improving profit margin. Perhaps they should go further and place long-term shareholder wealth creation above profit margin. Mr Schneider hints at the limits of aiming for high profit margins in terms of shareholder wealth in saying 'If you maximise margins . . . bad things will happen' – *see* Exhibit 14.5.

Exhibit 14.5

Nestlé bows to investor and sector pressures with strategic shift

By Ralph Atkins in Zurich and Scheherazade Daneshkhu in London

Nestlé has for the first time set a target for increasing profit margins, marking a significant shift from its traditional sales-focused model as the Swiss company reacts to competitive pressures facing big consumer goods groups. The world's largest food and drinks company said it would aim for underlying trading operating profit margins of between 17.5% and 18.5% by 2020 — up from 16% last year.

Tuesday's announcement is a strategic switch for Nestlé, which has historically relied on leveraging its size to power sales growth. It was part of a strategy update unveiled in London by Mark Schneider, the former head of German healthcare group Fresenius who became chief executive in January. Mr Schneider, however, also reconfirmed Nestlé's target of

"mid-single digit" like-for-like sales growth by 2020, and said the margin target was unlikely to be raised after 2020. "I've watched this margins arms race in this industry with apprehension. If you maximise margins, you don't have a sustainable business model — bad things will happen," he told investors.

The company said margin improvements could come through cost savings, mainly from manufacturing, procurement and administration. Nestlé was thrown into the spotlight in June when Daniel Loeb, founder and chief executive of Third Point, the US activist hedge fund, disclosed he had taken a 1.25% stake in Nestlé, worth $3.5bn. He called on the group to shake up "its old ways" and proposed a margin target of 18-20% by 2020.

 26 September 2017.
All Rights Reserved.

Three steps of value

There are three steps to creating shareholder value – *see* **Exhibit 14.6**. First, create awareness of, and a genuine commitment to, a shareholder wealth-enhancing mission throughout the organisation. Second, measure whether value is being created, and make sure everyone understands and

Exhibit 14.6	The three steps of value-based management

3 Actively managing to create shareholder value
Identifying and understanding the sources of value, target setting, allocating resources, measuring performance, reward systems, culture.

2 Measuring shareholder value
e.g. for the entire corporation, business unit or investment option.

1 Mission statement
with value for shareholders at its core.

respects the measures adopted. Third, ensure that every aspect of management is committed to the shareholder value objective, from human resource management to research and development; from target setting to the allocation of resources.

It is clearly important to have a management team that both understands and is fully committed to shareholder value. To implement true shareholder wealth maximisation, managers need to know how to measure the wealth-creating potential of their actions.

Traditional measurement techniques

Before turning to appropriate methods of evaluating value creation we will examine some of the popular more traditional measurement techniques used.

Earnings-based management

The *Financial Times's* Lex column expressed a view on the traditional accounting-based performance measure of earnings (profits) per share (eps) and although quite an old comment it is still relevant:

> How do you know a company is doing well? When earnings per share (eps) are growing rapidly, would be the standard reply. Eps is the main valuation yardstick used by investors; it has also become something of a fixation within companies. . . . But eps is not a holy grail in determining how well a company is performing. This is not merely because management still have latitude in deciding what earnings to report; it is because eps growth says little about whether a company is investing shrewdly and managing its assets effectively. It may, for example, be possible to boost eps by stepping up the rate of investment. But unless the return on investment exceeds the cost of capital, a company will be destroying value.[1]

There are many reasons why earnings can mislead in the measurement of value creation, some of which are:[2]

- accounting is subject to distortions and manipulations;
- the investment made is often inadequately represented;
- the time value of money is excluded from the calculation;
- risk is not considered.

---

1 *Financial Times*, 7 May 1996, Lex column.
2 Rappaport (1998) and Cornelius and Davies (1997) go into more detail on these issues.

Accounting numbers

When drawing up financial statements, accountants make judgements and choose accounting policies, trying to match costs and revenues. Unfortunately for the users of the resulting 'bottom line' figures, there can be alternative approaches, which give different results, and yet all follow accounting body guidelines.

Take the example of the start-ups X and Y. In the first three years expected annual profits (before depreciation) are £3m. Both companies invested their initial capital of £10m in plant and machinery. X takes the view that the machinery has a useful life of ten years and that a 25% declining balance depreciation is appropriate. Y is more pessimistic and judges that a seven-year life with straight-line depreciation more truly reflects the economic reality. The first three years' profits are shown in **Exhibit 14.7**.

Exhibit 14.7	Companies X and Y: profits for the first three years		
	Years (£000s)		
	1	**2**	**3**
Company X			
Pre-depreciation profit	3,000	3,000	3,000
Depreciation	2,500	1,875	1,406
Earnings	500	1,125	1,594
Company Y			
Pre-depreciation profit	3,000	3,000	3,000
Depreciation	1,429	1,429	1,429
Earnings	1,571	1,571	1,571

The underlying economic position is the same for both companies, but in the first two years company X appears to be less profitable. Outside observers and management comparing the two companies may gain a distorted view of the quality of stewardship and the potential of the firm.

Investment decisions and incentive schemes based on profit figures can lead to sub-optimal decisions and behaviour. There are several accounting allocations that make comparisons and decisions difficult: goodwill and provisions, one-off items and the treatment of research and development expenditure and other intangibles can vary; these variations occur under normal accounting standards. When companies start using Alternative Performance Measures there is even greater potential for discretion – *see* **Exhibit 14.8**.

Exhibit 14.8

Non-Gaap measures: we're not savages

It is OK to colour outside the lines. Sometimes

"We've got to have rules and obey them. After all, we're not savages." Jack, the nasty lad who urges this in Lord of the Flies, has a point. But companies' GAAP or IFRS results usually come along with metrics that fall outside the lines. It is a bit of a free for all – but a good one, on the whole. Alternative performance measures often present a sort of parallel world – earnings adjusted for one-off gains and losses reflect what management thinks is normal. Ebitda – earnings before interest, taxes, depreciation and amortisation – purports to show the cash flow independent of capital structure. These subjunctive (if not subjective) measures are often a big help. Moody's recently argued that ebitda is useful in signalling rising default risk in today's ocean of covenant-lite corporate debt.

But there are some savages who use APMs too liberally. Groupon's IPO presented adjusted operating income of $60m in 2010. Add back marketing costs – why on earth would one exclude them? – and the loss was $180m. Groupon later abandoned the metric. Valeant presents "adjusted cash flow from operations", a hilariously unhelpful metric. The whole point of cash flow, as opposed to earnings, is that it is not adjusted. But not all problems are obvious. Telecoms companies merrily present ebitda as a proxy for cash profits when capital investment is a constant cash drain.

The danger presented by APMs is no greater than the danger of assuming that any standard set of metrics can fit all companies. "Embedded value" statements present a longer term, more stable picture of insurers than IFRS. APMs have another unique value. Armed with the reconciliations of the standard and non-standard metrics, investors cannot only reach their own conclusions, but also get an important insight into what management thinks is important or irrelevant. Like children given free rein, what executives do with their liberty is very telling.

Ignoring the investment money sacrificed

Examining earnings per share growth as an indicator of success fails to take account of the investment needed to generate that growth. Take the case of companies A and B (*see* **Exhibit 14.9**), both of which have growth in earnings of 10% per year and are therefore equally attractive to an earnings-based analyst or manager.

Exhibit 14.9	Companies A and B: earnings		
	Year (£000s)		
	1	2	3
Earnings of A	1,000	1,100	1,210
Earnings of B	1,000	1,100	1,210

But what additional investment is required to support this growth? The companies may need to offer more generous credit terms to gain sales; therefore investing in receivables, or the less efficient supply chain in company B may mean B needs higher inventories to ensure it can meet customer demand, another additional investment. If A can generate the additional earnings with a lower additional investment than B, then A is generating more value than B from the same level of growth.

When A's and B's accounts are drawn up the additional debtors and inventory are included as an asset in the balance sheet and do not appear as a cost element in the profit and loss account. This results in the costs shown in the profit and loss account understating the cash outflow during a period.

If we examine the cash flow associated with A and B (**Exhibit 14.10**) we can see immediately that A is generating more shareholder value (assuming the pattern continues and all other factors are the same) because it creates more cash for shareholders. Exhibit 14.10 illustrates the conversion from earnings to cash flow figures.

If B also has to invest larger amounts than A in non-current assets for each unit increase in sales, the difference in the relative value created will be even more marked.

Exhibit 14.10	Companies A and B: earnings and cash flow					
	Company A £000s			Company B £000s		
Year	1	2	3	1	2	3
Profit (earnings)	1,000	1,100	1,210	1,000	1,100	1,210
Increase in debtors	0	20	42	0	60	126
Increase in inventory	0	30	63	0	50	105
Cash flow before tax	1,000	1,050	1,105	1,000	990	979
Percentage change		+5%	+5.2%		−1%	−1.1%

Time value of money

Growth in earnings will destroy value if the rate of return earned on the additional investment is less than the required rate. Take the case of a team of managers trying to decide whether to make a dividend payment of £10m. If they retained the money within the business, both earnings and cash flow would rise by £1,113,288 for each of the next ten years. Managers motivated by earnings growth might be tempted to omit the dividend payment. Future earnings would rise and therefore the share price would also rise on the announcement that the dividend would not be paid. Right? Wrong! Investors in this firm are likely to have a higher annual required rate of return on their £10m than the 2% offered by this plan.[3] The share price (in a rational market) will fall and shareholder value will be destroyed. What the managers forgot was that money has a time value and investors value shares on the basis of *discounted* future cash flows.

It seems obvious that a 2% rate of return on invested money is serving shareholders badly. Yet many companies hold millions of pounds in cash rather than giving it back to shareholders to invest elsewhere. These cash mountains give managers a greater sense of security – less risk of liquidation or job losses. This is not effective use of capital; shareholders would prefer this money to be used more effectively. Cash that cannot be used to generate good returns should be returned to shareholders to be invested elsewhere. In recent years activist shareholders have put much more pressure on incumbent managers to use cash effectively or return it to shareholders in dividends or share buy-backs. *See* **Exhibit 14.11** for an example.

Exhibit 14.11

Sotheby's to return overseas capital to US

Auction house scraps dividend and boosts buyback scheme to stave off activist pressure

By Mary Childs in New York

Sotheby's has scrapped its dividend and made plans to bring overseas earnings back to the US to boost its share buyback programme, as the auction house balances pressure from activist investors and intensifying competition in the art market. The New York-based company increased its buyback programme by $200m to $325m, chief executive Tad Smith told analysts on Friday.

---

3 A ten-year annuity of £1,113,288 per year for a £10m investment at time 0 has an effective annual rate of return of about 2%.

The decision to bring back $381m of accumulated overseas earnings will lead to a charge of up to $68m, which will help push the auction house to a loss of between $10m and $19m in the final quarter of 2015, the company said. A staff buyout programme — which has incurred a $37m pre-tax charge — is cutting 5% of its 1,600 employees.

Sotheby's has been in the sights of the Third Point and Marcato hedge funds, which want it to raise profits and return cash to shareholders.

A variation on the theme of growing eps by investing large sums is to acquire other companies. In the case of Vodafone, shareholders have been worried that managers were incentivised to increase eps with insufficient attention being paid to the amount of investment required by shareholders to boost these accounting numbers. The directors and senior executives were granted large share options if eps growth exceeded 15% a year over inflation. Investors were concerned that this could be achieved by acquiring companies on lower price-earnings ratios regardless of the effect of this on shareholder value.

Ignoring risk

Focusing purely on the growth in earnings fails to take account of another aspect of the quality of earnings: risk. Increased profits that are also subject to higher levels of risk require a higher return to finance providers and thus a higher discount rate. Imagine a firm is contemplating two alternative growth options with the same expected earnings, of £100,000 per year to infinity. Each strategy is subject to risk, but S has a wider dispersion of possible outcomes (higher risk) than T – *see* **Exhibit 14.12**.

Exhibit 14.12	Probabilities of annual returns on strategies S and T			
	Strategy S		**Strategy T**	
	Outcome earnings (profits) £	**Probability**	**Outcome earnings (profits) £**	**Probability**
	−100,000	0.10	80,000	0.10
	0	0.20	90,000	0.15
	100,000	0.40	100,000	0.50
	200,000	0.20	110,000	0.15
	300,000	0.10	120,000	0.10
Expected outcome	£100,000		£100,000	

Investors are likely to value strategy T more highly than strategy S – the same expected return but with lower risk. Examining crude profit figures, either historic or projected, fails to adequately reflect risk. In a value-based approach the discount rate would be increased to reflect greater risk, making the projects more comparable – more on this in Chapter 16.

Worked example 14.1	Earnings growth and value

Earnings and earnings per share growth can lead to higher shareholder value in some circumstances. In others it can lead to value destruction. Shareholder value will rise if the return obtainable on new investment is at least as great as the required rate of return for the risk class. Consider EPSOS plc, financed entirely with equity capital and with a required rate of return on that capital of 15% (assume for simplicity that this is the optimal financial gearing level).

▶

Worked example 14.1 *(continued)*

To make the example simple we assume that EPSOS does not need to invest in higher levels of working capital if sales expand. EPSOS pays shareholders its entire earnings after tax every year and is expected to continue doing this indefinitely. Earnings and cash flow amount to £100m per year. (The amount charged as depreciation is just sufficient to pay for investment to maintain sales and profits.) The value of the company given the opportunity cost of shareholders' money of 15% is £100m/0.15 = £666.67m.

	£m
Sales	300.00
Operating expenses	157.14
Pre-tax profit	142.86
Taxes @ 30%	42.86
Profits and cash flow after tax	100.00

Now imagine that EPSOS takes the decision not to pay this year's dividend. Shareholders are made poorer by £100m now. However, because of the additional investment in its operations for the next year and every subsequent year, sales, earnings, eps and cash flows after tax will rise by 20%.

	£m
Sales	360.00
Operating expenses	188.57
Pre-tax profit	171.43
Taxes @ 30%	51.43
Profits and cash flow after tax	120.00

Earnings have grown by 20%. The extra £20m cash flow per annum stretching into the future is worth £20m/0.15 = £133.33m, achieved with a £100m sacrifice now; value has been created. Here a growth in earnings has coincided with an increase in value: £33.33m of value is created.

Now consider a scenario in which sales growth of 20% is achieved by using the £100m to expand the business, but this time the managers, in going for sales growth, push up operating expenses by 32%. Earnings and cash flow increase by a respectable 6.81%, but, crucially, value falls.

	£m
Sales	360.00
Operating expenses (157.14 × 1.32)	207.42
Pre-tax profit	152.58
Taxes @ 30%	45.77
Profits and cash flow after tax	106.81

The incremental perpetual cash flow is worth a present value of £6.81m/0.15 = £45.4m. But the 'cost' of achieving this is the sacrifice of £100m of income now. Therefore, overall shareholder value has been destroyed despite earnings and eps growth. It is surprising how often senior managers make this basic error.

Return on capital employed (ROCE) has failings

Examining profit figures is not enough for good decision making and performance evaluation. The capital invested has to be considered alongside the income earned. This was recognised long before the development of value-based management, as signified by the widespread use of a ratio of profits to assets employed. There are many variations on this theme – return on capital employed (ROCE), return on investment (ROI), return on equity (ROE) and accounting rate of return (ARR) – but they all have the same root. They provide a measure of return as a percentage of resources invested. The major problem with these metrics is that they are still based on accounting data. The profit figure calculations are difficult enough, but when they are combined with balance sheet figures there is the possibility of unacceptable distortion.

One of the problems on the list is the issue of capitalisation. That is the extent to which an item of expenditure is written off against profits as an expense or taken on to the balance sheet and capitalised as an asset. For example, firms differ in their treatment of research and development: companies that spend significant sums on R&D and then have a policy of writing it off immediately are likely to have lower asset value than those that do not write it off against profits in the year of expenditure. Cross-company comparisons of profits/assets can therefore be very misleading.

Focusing on accounting rates of return can lead to short termism. Managers who are judged on this basis may be reluctant to invest in new equipment, as this will raise the denominator in the ratio, producing a poor ARR in the short term. This can destroy value in the long run. Fast-growing companies needing extensive investment in the near term with the expectation of reaping rich rewards in the long term should not be compared with slow-growth and low-investing firms on the basis of ARR.

The superficial highlighting of eps and ARR

One of the most pervasive myths of our time is: 'But our shareholders focus on eps and ARR, don't they?' – and it is easy to see why. Senior executives when talking with institutional shareholders and analysts often find the conversation reverting to a discussion of short-term earnings forecasts. If a merger is announced, directors feel the need to point out in press releases that the result will not be 'earnings dilutive' in the forthcoming year.

This surface noise is deceiving. Intelligent shareholders and analysts are primarily interested in the long-term cash flow returns on shares. The earnings attributable to the next couple of years are usually an insignificant part of the value of a share. Over two-thirds of the value of a typical share is determined by income to be received five or more years hence (*see* Chapter 17 for these calculations). Knowledge of this or next year's earnings is not particularly interesting in itself: it is sought because it sheds light on the medium- and long-term cash flows.

There are hundreds of quoted companies that do not expect to produce any positive earnings at all in the next two to five years and yet these shares are frequently among the most highly valued in the market. There are dozens of tech companies that have tapped shareholders for funds; some have become massive concerns and yet have never made a profit or paid a dividend. **Exhibit 14.13** and **Exhibit 14.14** are articles on eps and ROCE by Terry Smith, a regular FT commentator primarily followed by retail investors.

Exhibit 14.13

AstraZeneca is beginning to look a lot like Tesco

Both companies use similar accounting practices

By Terry Smith

It might be tempting to view last week's fall in the AstraZeneca share price in isolation, related to the disappointing results of the "Mystic" lung cancer drug trial. However, I suspect that AstraZeneca's problems go much deeper than a setback for a single drug. To paraphrase the title of a Christmas song which was a hit for Perry Como in 1951, AstraZeneca is beginning to look a lot like Tesco.

In FT Money nearly two years ago I wrote a column about AstraZeneca's accounting (Why bother cooking the books at all?) in which I highlighted that

AstraZeneca's move to "core" earnings in 2007 had allowed its reported results and most of the investment community to exclude three major costs from its reported profits, namely:

- Restructuring charges
- "Exceptional" legal costs
- Intangible asset amortisation

In other words, major costs were being ignored in the calculation of profits. It is this approach to accounting which is beginning to remind me of Tesco.

▶

Exhibit 14.13 *(continued)*

Historically, Tesco also managed eight changes in the definition of return on capital employed over the period 1998-2011, years when Terry Leahy was chief executive (I examined these in an FT Money column in September 2014, How investors ignored the warning signs at Tesco).

AstraZeneca moved to reporting "core" earnings in 2007. In 2012, it moved to excluding all intangible asset amortisation and impairment charges as opposed to only certain amortisation charges. In a pharmaceutical company, almost all the assets are intangible — namely the drug patents. This change

led to reported "core" earnings in 2012 going up. Quelle surprise.

While this accounting treatment would not fool a decent analyst, who in any event would be looking at cash flows rather than earnings, it certainly seems to have fooled some people. The other way in which AstraZeneca is beginning to resemble Tesco is its vast increase in invested capital at the expense of returns. As you may know, I regard return on capital as the single best measure of financial success for a business (as does Warren Buffett for what it's worth).

Exhibit 14.14

By Terry Smith

I define returns as the "return on capital employed" or Roce. That is fairly easily determined from company accounts; it's basically operating cash flow divided by the sum of shareholders' equity and net debt.

Determining what the cost of capital is for a company is rather more difficult. If you borrow money at a cost of 10 per cent in order to invest, then your cost of capital is fairly clear. A company's cost of debt capital is equally clear and can often be found in, or calculated from, the notes to its accounts. But what about the cost of its equity?

And therein lies one of the problems: a company's cost of capital is not easy to define and can only ever be an estimate. These problems have been compounded more recently because of the financial crisis. This has led some investors to query whether government bonds are truly risk-free, while ultra-low official interest rates, quantitative easing and a lack of inflation have sent bond yields down to record lows and even into negative territory.

Perhaps because cost of capital is not straightforward to define or compute, the most commonly accepted

means of measuring value creation is growth in earnings per share (EPS), which is just the profits net of tax divided by the number of shares in issue. What could be simpler to calculate? Not much — which is probably why so much importance is attached to this simplistic measure of performance and its related valuation metric, the price/earnings ratio. Look through any analyst's research and you'll find dozens of references to them, often on the front page.

Simple they may be, but EPS and p/e ratios suffer from some serious flaws. The most important is that they take no account of the capital employed or the returns made on it. As the Tesco example shows, it is perfectly possible for a company to generate rising EPS at the same time as it is employing increasing amounts of capital at falling and inadequate rates of return. In other words, a company can be busy destroying shareholder value even as it increases its earnings.

So, I'm sticking with Roce as my preferred measure of value creation. But of course neither Roce nor EPS is the same as making the share price go up.

Mr Smith is CEO of Fundsmith LLP which was established in 2010 and which manages £10bn (at 31.12.16) through a range of funds on behalf of wealth managers, private banks, families, charities and pension funds. In Exhibit 14.13 he describes the difference between eps and ROCE before going on, in Exhibit 14.14, to state his preference for ROCE as a performance measure. Mr Smith's definition of ROCE is different from that generally used in that it is cash, not profit based.

Traditional definition ROCE: Operating profit before interest and tax/Capital employed

Mr Smith ROCE: Operating cash flow/Capital employed

The focus on cash flow in the numerator means that Mr Smith's ROCE avoids some of the problems mentioned above with the traditional profit based version ('ROCE has failings' section) as operating cash flow is less likely to be distorted or manipulated. Despite their limitations the traditional performance measures continue to be widely used.

As Mr Smith states 'a company's cost of capital is not easy to define and can only ever be an estimate'. This issue is discussed in full in Chapter 16, 'The cost of capital'.

How a business creates value

Value is created when an investment produces a return greater than the opportunity cost of the capital invested. Shareholder value is driven by the four factors shown in **Exhibit 14.15**.

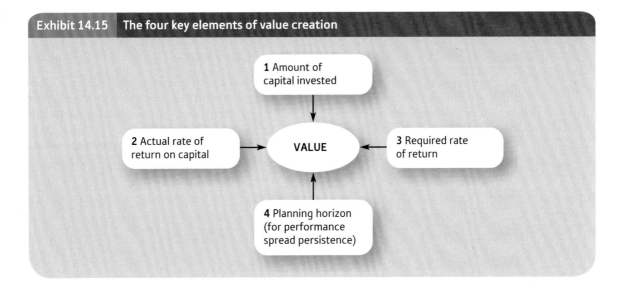

Exhibit 14.15   The four key elements of value creation

The difference between the second and third elements in Exhibit 14.15 is the performance spread. The performance spread is measured as a percentage spread above or below the required rate of return, which is based on the finance provider's opportunity cost of capital. Value is created if the return from the investment is greater than the cost of capital (2 greater than 3) and destroyed if 3 is greater than 2.

The total value generated is determined by the quantity of capital invested multiplied by the performance spread. So, for example, if Black plc has a required rate of return of 14% per annum and produces 17% on an investment base of £1,000,000, it will create £30,000 of value per year:

$$\text{Annual value creation} = \text{Investment} \times (\text{Actual return} - \text{Required return})$$
$$= I\,(r - k)$$
$$= £1,000,000 \times (0.17 - 0.14) = £30,000$$

The fourth element in Exhibit 14.15 needs more explanation. It would be unreasonable to assume that positive or negative return spreads will be maintained for ever. Positive spreads may be as a result of a combination of the attractiveness of the industry and the competitive strength of a firm within that industry. High returns can be earned because of market imperfections. For example, a firm may be able to prevent competitors entering its market segment because of economies of scale, brand strength or legal exclusion through patents. However, most firms will eventually experience increased competition and reduced margins. The higher the initial positive performance spread, the more attractive market entry will be to potential competitors. If return spreads are negative, managers will intervene to prevent continued losses. If they fail to respond shareholders will act through sackings or the acceptance of a merger offer.

In shareholder value analysis it is assumed that returns will, over time, be driven towards the required rate of return. Beyond some point in the future (the planning horizon) any new investment will, on average, earn only the minimum acceptable rate of return. We acknowledge that there are some remarkable businesses that maintain positive performance spreads for decades. Their economic franchises are protected by powerful barriers preventing competitive attack, e.g. Coca-Cola, Proctor & Gamble, Colgate-Palmolive. The financier Warren Buffett calls such companies 'Inevitables' because there is every reason to believe they will be dominating their industries decades from now – *see* Arnold (2009). If we leave Inevitables to one side, we see that for the majority of businesses their value consists of two components, as shown in **Exhibit 14.16**.

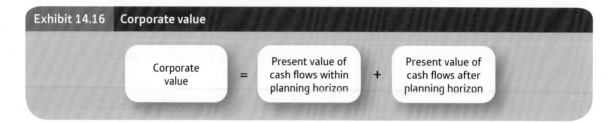

Exhibit 14.16   Corporate value

| Corporate value | = | Present value of cash flows within planning horizon | + | Present value of cash flows after planning horizon |

In the second period (after the planning horizon), even if investment levels are doubled, corporate value will remain constant, as the discounted cash inflows (to time zero) associated with that investment exactly equal the discounted cash outflows (to time zero) – this is discussed further in the next chapter.

If it is assumed that Black plc can maintain its 3% return spread for ten years and pays out all income as dividends, then its future cash flows will look like this:

Years:	$1 \rightarrow 10$	$11 \rightarrow$ infinity
Cash flow:	£170,000	£140,000

The value of the firm is the discounted value of these cash flows.

The discounted cash flow within the planning horizon is:

£170,000 × Annuity factor (10 years, 14%) = £170,000 × 5.2161 = £886,737

plus the discounted cash flow after the planning horizon:

First discounted to time 10: a perpetuity with the first cash flow arising at time 11 gives a value of £140,000/0.14 = £1,000,000.

This is then discounted back ten years to time zero: $\dfrac{1,000,000}{(1 + 0.14)^{10}} = £269,744$

Value of the firm	(£886,737 + £269,744)	£1,156,481
Less initial investment		(£1,000,000)
Value created		£156,481

An alternative approach: the value of the firm is equal to the initial investment in the firm (£1,000,000) plus the present value of all the values created annually.

Investment	+	Value created within planning horizon	+	Value created after planning horizon
£1,000,000	+	£30,000 × 5.2161	+	£1,000,000(0.14 − 0.14)
		£30,000 × Annuity factor (10 years, 14%)		
£1,000,000	+	£156,481	+	0 = **£1,156,481**

The five actions for creating value

Good growth occurs when a business unit or an entire corporation obtains a positive spread on the new investment capital. Bad growth occurs when managers invest in strategies that produce profits but negative return spreads. This can happen if the focus of attention is on sales and earnings growth. To managers, encouraged to believe that their job is to expand the business and improve the bottom line, acceptance of the notion of bad growth in profits is a problem. But, as we have seen, it is perfectly possible to show growing profits on a larger investment base producing an incremental return less than the incremental cost of capital.

Exhibit 14.17 shows the options open to managers. This model can be applied at the corporate, business unit or product line level.

Exhibit 14.17	To expand or not to expand?

	Grow	Shrink
Positive performance spread	Value creation	Value opportunity forgone
Negative performance spread	Value destruction	Value creation

Rob Perrins, CEO of Berkeley, recognises the need to avoid bad growth – *see* **Exhibit 14.18**.

Exhibit 14.18

Berkeley to return £1.7bn to shareholders

By Alistair Gray and Ed Hammond

Berkeley Group has unveiled plans to return about £1.7bn in cash to shareholders over the next decade as the housebuilder cashes in on London's resilient property market.

Shares in Berkeley, which focuses almost exclusively on the capital, jumped 9% on Friday after the FTSE 250 company said it would pay a series of dividends that would amount to £13 a share.

Among the biggest beneficiaries will be chairman Tony Pidgley, who founded Berkeley in 1975. With a 5.1% stake, he should enjoy a pay-out of about £87m.

However, Mr Perrins said the move to pass money back to shareholders also reflected Berkeley's comfort with its size.

'But we don't want to grow the business from here. We are at an optimum size and if you gave us another £1bn in capital we would not be able to make the best use of it,' he added.

The company added it would make changes to its long-term remuneration plan in order to incentivise management 'both to deliver this return and to create value in the ongoing business'.

Earnings per share increased from 58.7p to 70.3p. Shares were trading up 103p at £12.34 in London.

It has been demonstrated above that Black plc produces, at 17%, a satisfactory return on investment. Now assume that the firm consists of two divisions: a clothing factory and a toy import business. Each business is making use of £500,000 of assets (at market value). The clothing division is expected to produce an 11% return per annum over the next ten years whereas the toy division will produce a 23% per annum return over the same period. After the ten-year planning horizon both divisions will produce returns equal to their risk-adjusted required return: for the clothing division this is 13% and for the riskier toy division this is 15%.

The cash flows are:

Year	$1 \rightarrow 10$	$11 \rightarrow$ infinity
Clothing	£55,000	£65,000
Toys	£115,000	£75,000

The annual value creation within the planning horizon is:

$I \times (r - k)$
Clothing £500,000 × (0.11 − 0.13) = −£10,000
Toys   £500,000 × (0.23 − 0.15) = +£40,000

Despite the higher return required in the toy division, it creates value (calculating required rates of return is covered in Chapter 16). For the next ten years a 15% return is achieved plus a shareholder bonus of £40,000. This division could fit into the top left box of Exhibit 14.17. The management team may want to consider further investment in this unit so long as the marginal investment can generate a return greater than 15%. To pass up positive return spread investments would be to sacrifice valuable opportunities and enter the top right box of Exhibit 14.17.

The clothing operation produces negative performance spreads – 11% return versus a 13% cost of capital. Expansion of this unit would be recommended only if the division could transform itself to achieve a positive spread. If this improvement in return is unlikely, then the best option is a scaling down or withdrawal from the market. This will release capital to be more productively invested elsewhere, either within or outside the firm. Such shrinkage would create value by reducing the drag that clothing has on the rest of the firm.

This line of thought can assist managers at all levels to allocate resources. At the corporate level, knowledge of potential good-growth and bad-growth investments will help the selection of a portfolio of businesses. At the business unit level, product and customer groups can be analysed to assess the potential for value contribution. Lower down, products and customers can be ranked in terms of value. A simplified example of corporate-level value analysis is shown in **Exhibit 14.19**.

In Exhibit 14.19, strategic business unit A (SBU_A) is a value destroyer due to its negative return spread. Shareholders would be better served if resources were transferred to other operations. Some managerial teams pay insufficient attention to the amount of capital devoted to an activity: factory space is retained but rarely or lightly used; inventory levels are double what they need to be; expensive offices in town centres are retained when an out-of-town block would be adequate; large cash reserves are held. A positive performance spread may be achievable by reducing the capital used by the SBU. Coca-Cola reduced dramatically the required return charge on capital as it separated and sold off capital-intensive bottling and distribution businesses, releasing capital and allowing it to focus on capital-light elements of the business, such as syrup concentrate. As discussed in Exhibit 14.2, IHG improved its performance by moving out of capital-intensive hotel ownership into capital light hotel management franchises.

SBU_B produces a small positive spread. However, it is only just managing this, and in the uncertain world of business, vigilance is needed to ensure that it continues to produce positive performance spreads. SBU_C produces a lower return spread than SBU_E but manages to create more value because of its higher future investment levels. Some businesses have greater potential than others for growth while maintaining a positive spread. For example, SBU_E might be a niche market player in fine china where greatly expanded activity would reduce the premium paid by customers for the exclusivity of the product – producing negative spread on the marginal production. SBU_C might be in mid-priced tableware competing on design where investment in the design and

Exhibit 14.19   **Value creation and Strategic Business Unit (SBU) performance spreads**

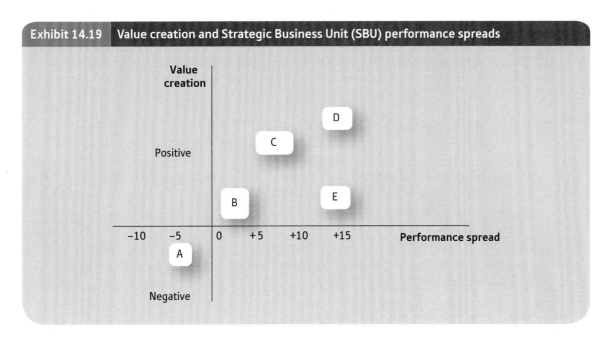

marketing teams might produce positive spread growth. SBU$_D$ is capable of high spreads over a long period, producing the largest overall gain in value. Drugs with lengthy patent rights often produce high positive spreads for many years, leading to high value creation over their lifetimes.

There are five actions available to managers to increase value. These are shown in the value action pentagon (**Exhibit 14.20**).

The five actions in Exhibit 14.20 could be applied to Black plc.

Exhibit 14.20   **The value action pentagon**

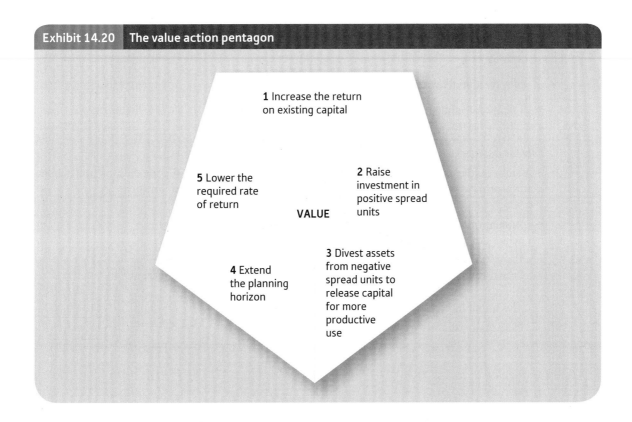

Increase the return on existing capital

The value of Black of £1,000,000 + £156,481 could be increased if the management implemented a plan to improve the efficiency of their existing operations. If the rate of return on investment for the firm over the next ten years is raised to 18% then the firm's value rises to £1,208,644, viz:

Annual value creation	$= I \times (r - k)$	
	$= £1,000,000 \times (0.18 - 0.14)$	
	$= £40,000$	
Present value over ten years	$= £40,000 \times$ Annuity factor (10 years, 14%)	
	$= £40,000 \times 5.2161 =$	£208,644
plus initial investment		£1,000,000
Corporate value		£1,208,644

An increase of £52,163 (£1,208,644 − £1,156,481) in value is available for every 1% improvement in return spread.

Raise investment in positive spread units

If Black could obtain a further £500,000 from investors with a required rate of return of 15% to invest in the toy division to produce a 23% return, the value of the firm would rise to £1,847,242 (of this £500,000 is the new capital invested).

Annual value creation on clothing	=	−£10,000
Annual value creation on toys = £40,000 × 2	=	£80,000
		£70,000

Over ten years
Clothing: −£10,000 × Annuity factor (10 years, 13%)
Toys: £80,000 × Annuity factor (10 years, 15%)

Clothing:	−£10,000 × 5.4262 =	−£54,262
Toys:	£80,000 × 5.0188 =	£401,504
		£347,242
plus the initial investment		£1,500,000
Corporate value		£1,847,242

Divest assets

If Black could close its clothing division, release £500,000 to expand the toy division and achieve returns of 23% on the transferred investment then value increases dramatically:

Annual value creation	$= I \times (r - k)$	
	$= £1,000,000 \times (0.23 - 0.15)$	
	$= £80,000$	
Present value over ten years	$= £80,000 \times$ Annuity factor (10 years, 15%)	
	$= £80,000 \times 5.0188 =$	£401,504
plus initial investment		£1,000,000
Corporate value		£1,401,504

Reckitt Benckiser released £4.2billion by selling its food business, which had produced low returns compared with alternative uses for the money – *see* **Exhibit 14.21**.

Exhibit 14.21

McCormick buys Reckitt Benckiser food business for $4.2bn

By Arash Massoudi in Los Angeles, James Fontanella-Khan and Jessica Dye in New York and Scheherazade Daneshkhu in London

French's Mustard and Frank's RedHot sauces among brands being sold to US group. By selling its foods business, Reckitt can focus on its newly acquired infant nutrition unit.

Reckitt Benckiser cut the mustard on Tuesday by selling its food business that includes French's Mustard and Frank's RedHot sauce for a higher-than-expected price of $4.2bn to McCormick & Company. The US maker of spices, herbs and flavourings beat competition from several strategic bidders, including domestic rival Pinnacle Foods, to secure brands that also include Cattlemen's sauces. The deal will help boost McCormick's net sales to about $5bn a year in 2017. The Schwartz spice maker walked away last year from another UK takeover target it was eyeing,

Premier Foods, the maker of Mr Kipling cakes and Ambrosia custard.

The sale will free up Reckitt to focus on turning around newly acquired Mead Johnson, and reduce the cost of funding $18bn for the infant formula group. Shares in Reckitt rose 1.4%, while shares in McCormick were 5% lower in New York.

Reckitt — which makes products ranging from Durex condoms and Nurofen painkillers to Cillit Bang bathroom cleaners — said in April it had started a "strategic review" of its non-core food business. Rakesh Kapoor, chief executive, hopes to bolster sales growth in the wake of a damaging boycott of Reckitt products in South Korea and the failure of its latest Scholl footcare innovation.

FT *Financial Times,* 19 July 2017.

Extend the planning horizon

Sometimes there are steps that can be taken to exploit a competitive advantage over a longer period than originally expected. For example, perhaps the toy division could negotiate a long-term exclusive import licence with the supplier of an established premium-priced product, thus closing the door on competitors. If we suppose that the toy division will now produce a return spread of 23% for a 15-year period rather than 10 years, the value of the company rises to £1,179,634, viz:

Annual value creation on clothing	=	−£10,000
Annual value creation on toys	=	£40,000
Present value over 10 years (clothing)	=	−£10,000 × Annuity factor (10 years, 13%)
		−£10,000 × 5.4262
	=	−£54,262
Present value over 15 years (toys)	=	£40,000 × Annuity factor (15 years, 15%)
	=	£40,000 × 5.8474 = £233,896
Total value creation	=	£233,896 − £54,262 = £179,634
plus initial investment		£1,000,000
Corporate value		£1,179,634

Lower the required rate of return

It may be possible to lower the required rate of return by adjusting the proportion of debt to equity in the capital structure (examined in Chapters 16 and 18) or by reducing business risk.[4] Suppose that Black can lower its required rate of return by shifting to a higher proportion of debt, so that the overall rate falls to 12%. Then the value of the firm rises to £1,282,510.

Annual value creation	$= I \times (r - k)$	
	$= 1{,}000{,}000 \times (0.17 - 0.12)$	
	$= £50{,}000$	
Present value over ten years	$= £50{,}000 \times$ Annuity factor (10 years, 12%)	
Total value creation	$= £50{,}000 \times 5.6502 =$	£282,510
plus initial investment		£1,000,000
Corporate value		£1,282,510

Many companies finance their businesses almost entirely through equity to reduce the risk of financial distress. This may be due to a desire to serve the interests of shareholders, but more often it is because managers want to avoid financial distress for their own safety. They can become too cautious and forgo the opportunity to reduce the overall cost of capital (discount rate) by not using a higher proportion of cheaper debt finance.

An overview of the application of value principles

The transforming of a corporation from one that is earnings based to one that is focused on value has profound effects on almost all aspects of organisational life. New light is cast on the most appropriate portfolio of businesses making up the firm, and on the strategic thrust of individual business units. Acquisition and divestment strategies may be modified to focus on shareholder wealth creation. Capital structure and dividend pay-out policy are predicated on the optimal approach from the shareholders' point of view, not by 'safety first' or earnings growth consider-ations. Performance measures, target setting and managerial compensation are directly linked to shareholder wealth creation – see **Exhibit 14.22**.

Exhibit 14.22

Where we're going, we don't need profits

By Alexandra Scaggs

Simply put, earnings no longer reliably reflect changes in corporate value and are thus an inadequate driver of investment analysis.

– Profs Feng Gu and Baruch Lev, in a paper for the CFA Institute's Financial Analysts Journal

Well then!

This idea challenges the very heart of traditional equity-market investment analysis. The authors point out that legendary stock-picker Benjamin Graham

spent hundreds of pages of his 1962 book on analysing and predicting earnings and other quarterly metrics. Earnings prediction is still central to most sell-side analysis as well.

But if profits, EBITDA or sales were truly central for corporate valuation, wouldn't markets punish regular loss-makers like Tesla and Amazon more severely? And wouldn't there be a stronger return to predicting profits?

---

4 Business risk can be reduced by, for example, reducing operating gearing (that is, reducing the proportion of costs that are fixed, thus lowering the break-even point; or by encouraging customers (e.g. through advertising) to regard your products as essential rather than discretionary; or by matching assets and liabilities better, in terms of maturity and currency (*see* Chapter 12).

The returns to such predictions have diminished over time, according to the authors of the paper, which might help explain the persistent underperformance by active fund managers. While the professors commit a minor chart crime below by starting the Y-axis at 1.5 per cent, it seems notable that potential gains were lower during the 2009 downturn than during the dot-com bust:

The 30-year pattern of the gains from the earnings growth investment strategy is depicted in Figure 2. Again, the deterioration of gains from perfect growth prediction is evident. Clearly, the problem lies with reported earnings, not in the way investors use them. Simply put, earnings no longer reliably reflect changes in corporate value and are thus an inadequate driver of investment analysis.

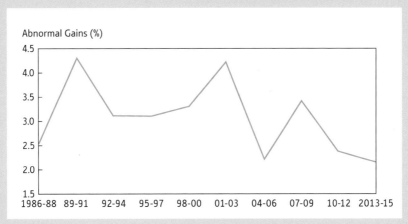

The shrinking gains from the perfect prediction of earnings growth

The decline in profits' importance can be explained by a fundamental change in the way companies create value, they say.

There are lots of names for the change: The information revolution, the rise of the knowledge economy, and so on. No matter what you call it, the idea is that modern production relies less on physical capital and more on intellectual capital.

Accounting and financial analysis methods have failed to adapt to this change, they say. For example, companies are required to expense R&D and sales expenses immediately, while they can amortise expenses from capital investment and acquisitions (including intangibles) over time. They argue those rules penalise the important methods of modern value creation, since R&D costs create lasting returns from new products and SG&A expenses create lasting returns from new customers.

Of course, one person's "internally generated intangibles" can be another's "overpaid salesforce". But the difference in accounting treatment between those costs and acquired intangibles can make it difficult to compare within industries:

Thus, a company pursuing an innovation strategy based on acquisitions will appear more profitable and asset rich than a similar enterprise developing its innovations internally. Consequently, reported earnings, assets, and market multiples (P/E, book-to-market ratio) cannot be compared within industries, and earnings definitely do not reflect intrinsic value creation.

And as far as we can tell, the professors aren't lobbying to start amortising all sales costs and executive compensation. Instead, they say we should stop looking at the *consequences* of corporate value creation — the quarterly reports — and start looking at its *causes*.

They suggest financial analysis based on **strategic assets,** which are **(1)** rare, **(2)** difficult to imitate and **(3)** generate net benefits, like growth in a customer base or sales.

There would be four steps to this type of analysis. From the paper, with our emphasis:

1 **Taking inventory of strategic assets:** Compiling a list of the major strategic assets of the enterprise; distinguishing between operating and dormant assets (e.g., patents under development or licensed out versus abandoned patents), active brands (enabling the charging of a premium product price) and brands in name only, or producing oil and gas properties and those under exploration versus inactive properties. Such inventory taking establishes the foundation—active strategic assets—of the company's competitive advantage.

2 **Enhancing strategic assets:** Without continued investment and replenishment, even highly productive assets will wither on the vine (recall Dell). You should ask, Is the spending on R&D, technology purchases, customer acquisition, brand support, and employee training sufficient to maintain and grow the business? Cutting R&D

▶

Exhibit 14.22 *(continued)*

or employee training to 'make the numbers' clearly bodes ill for future growth.

3 **Defending strategic assets:** These assets are vulnerable to competition (from similar products), infringement, and technological disruption, raising the question of whether the company's assets are adequately protected by continuous innovation, patent defensive walls, and litigation. A continuous loss of market share clearly indicates a failure to protect assets.

4 **Asset deployment and value creation:** Are the strategic assets, along with other company resources, optimally deployed to create value (e.g., retail outlets with increasing same-store sales)? And what is this value? Note that in our analysis, the measurement of the periodic value created is a by-product rather than the focus of the analysis. We prefer to measure value created by cash flows to avoid the multiple managerial estimates embedded in earnings. In contrast to the cash flows generally used by analysts (EBITDA),

however, we add to cash flows the company's investments in value-creating strategic assets, such as R&D, IT, and unusual brand creation expenditures, which are not really operating cash outflows.

Now, if we are living in a period of secular stagnation, this could be seen as an attempt to lower the bar to make up for lacklustre capital investment. (One academic literature review we found on the topic of strategic assets only cites papers from around the time of the dot-com bubble. Fancy that!)

What's more, 'defending strategic assets' can sound a lot like 'maintaining monopoly power', depending on the methods companies use in their defence. So, an investment analysis focused on strategic assets might also require more aggressive anti-trust regulation.

But if you accept the idea that widespread adoption of the internet brought a fundamental and irreversible change in the drivers of growth, there are worse approaches to financial analysis you can take.

To unite the organisation in pursuit of wealth creation raises an enormous educational and motivational challenge. A culture change is often required so that everyone's goals, at all levels, ensure that value is created. Retraining and new reward systems are needed to help lift eyes from the short-term to long-term achievements.

Exhibit 14.23 summarises some of the most important areas where value-based management impacts on the firm. To describe them all fully would require a book as long as this one, so only a short discussion of some of the most important points is undertaken.

Strategic business unit management

A strategic business unit (SBU) is a business unit within the overall corporate entity which is distinguishable from other business units because it serves a defined external market for which management can conduct strategic planning.

Large corporations often have several SBUs which require individual strategic thought and planning. Strategy means selecting which product or market areas to enter/exit and determining how to compete well in those markets. Establishing a good competitive position requires a consideration of issues such as price, service level, quality, product features, methods of distribution, etc., but these issues are secondary to deciding which products to produce and which markets to enter or exit.

It is the local managers of an SBU who are in regular contact with customers in the competitive market environment so it is important that these local managers are closely involved in the development of the SBU strategy which they will be responsible for implementing. Harnessing these managers' local knowledge and encouraging their commitment through a sense of 'ownership' is more likely to result in a successful strategic outcome.

Exhibit 14.23   Value principles influence most aspects of management

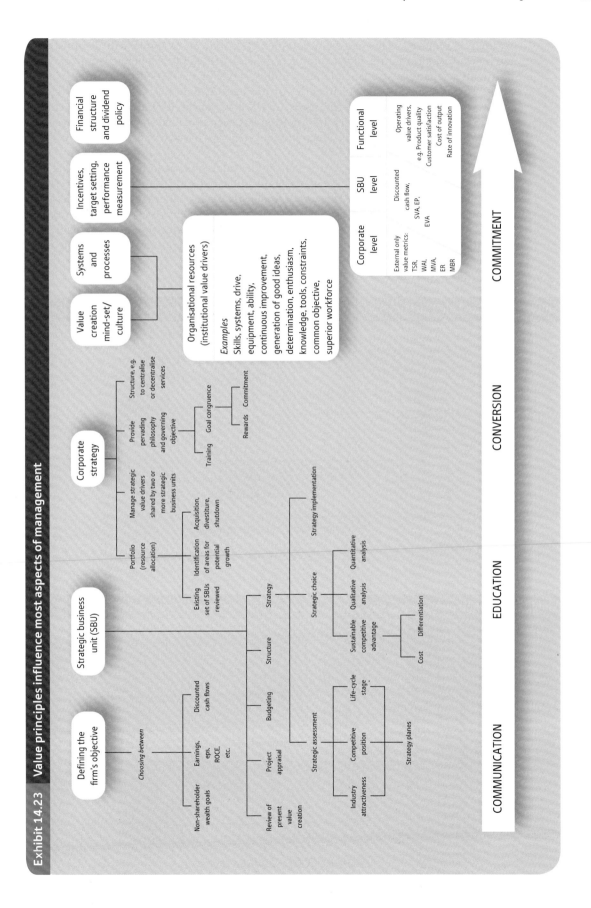

Before the creation of new strategic options a review of the value creation of the present strategy is required. This can be a complex task, but an example will demonstrate one approach. Imagine that the plastic products division of Red plc is a defined strategic business unit with a separable strategic planning ability servicing markets distinct from Red's other SBUs. This division sells three categories of product, A, B and C, to five types of customer: (a) UK consumers, (b) UK industrial users, (c) UK government, (d) European Union consumers and (e) other overseas consumers. Information has been provided showing the value expected to be created from each of the product/market categories based on current strategy. These are shown in **Exhibits 14.24** and **14.25**.

Product line C is expected to destroy shareholder value while absorbing a substantial share of the SBU's resources. Likewise, this analysis has identified sales to UK industry and government as detrimental to the firm's wealth. This sort of finding is not unusual – many businesses have acceptable returns at the aggregate level – but hidden behind these figures are value-destroying areas of activity. The analysis could be made even more revealing by showing the returns available for each product and market category, for example product A in the UK consumer market compared with product A in the European market.

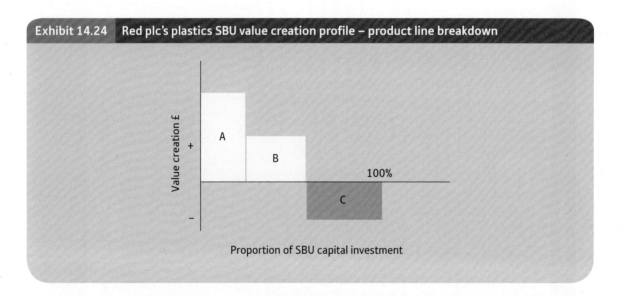

Exhibit 14.24   Red plc's plastics SBU value creation profile – product line breakdown

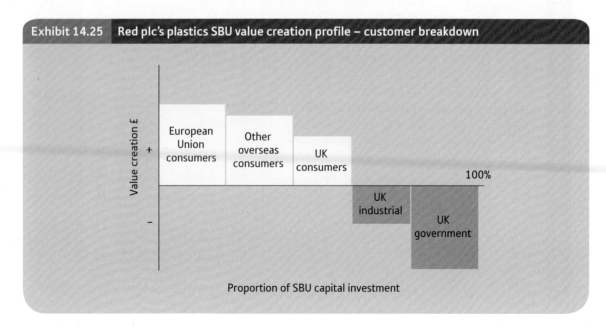

Exhibit 14.25   Red plc's plastics SBU value creation profile – customer breakdown

Warren Buffett, the financier, has made some pithy comments, which are still valid, on the tendency for firms to fail to identify and root out value-destructive activities:

> Many corporations that consistently show good returns both on equity and on overall incremental capital have, indeed, employed a large portion of their retained earnings on an economically unattractive, even disastrous, basis. Their marvellous core businesses, however, whose earnings grow year after year, camouflage repeated failures in capital allocation elsewhere (usually involving high-priced acquisitions of businesses that have inherently mediocre economics). The managers at fault periodically report on the lessons they have learned from the latest disappointment. They then usually seek out future lessons. (Failure seems to go to their heads.)
>
> Source: Berkshire Hathaway 1984 Annual Report.© Warren Buffett. Reproduced with the permission of the author.

To get a clear line of sight from the customer to the shareholder, many businesses need to build an entirely new fact base showing the full economic cost and cash flows associated with customers and product markets. Recognising that some activities are far more valuable than others prepares the ground for a shift of strategic resources. Attention can be directed at restructuring or eliminating value-destructive operations, while building up value-creative aspects of the business

Furthermore, project appraisal, budgeting systems and the organisational structure of each SBU must be in harmony with the principle of value-based management. Project appraisal will be carried out using discounted cash flow techniques. Budgeting will not rely solely on accounting considerations but will have value-based metrics as guides (*see* Chapter 15). The lines of decision-making authority and communication will be the most appropriate, given the market environment, to achieve greatest returns. For example, in a dynamic unpredictable market it is unwise to have a bureaucratic, hierarchical structure with decision making concentrated at the top of long chains of command. Devolved power and responsibility are likely to produce a more flexible response to change in the marketplace, and initiative with self-reliance are to be highly prized and rewarded. In less dynamic or heavily regulated environments, low-cost, close command-and-control management, with an emphasis on continuous improvement, is likely to be most appropriate.

Strategic analysis can be seen as having three parts:

1 *Strategic assessment* – in which the external environment and the internal resources and capability are analysed to form a view on the key influences on the value-creating potential of the organisation.

2 *Strategic choice* – in which strategic options are developed and evaluated.

3 *Strategic implementation* – action will be needed in areas such as changes in organisational structure and systems as well as resource planning, motivation and commitment.

Strategic assessment

There are three primary strategic determinants of value creation.

1 Industry attractiveness

The economics of the market for the product(s) has an enormous influence on the profitability of a firm. In some industries firms have few competitors and there is low customer buying power, low supplier bargaining power and little threat from new entrants or the introduction of substitute products. Here the return to existing firms is likely to be attractive with a positive performance spread.

Other markets are highly competitive with over-capacity, availability of close substitutes, reluctance of participants to quit and little room for growth. These markets are extremely competitive and margins are low. These markets tend to produce negative performance spreads.[5] For example, many of the companies in the car industry have lost money on every car they have sold for most

---

5 For more detail on market attractiveness analysis consult *The Financial Times Guide to Value Investing* (2009: Chapter 9) or *The Financial Times Guide to Investing* (2014a: Chapter 14) both written by Glen Arnold.

of the years of the past decade. Some have survived by owning profitable finance subsidiaries; others have survived with the help of government support or indulgent and over-optimistic shareholders: the directors seem to be able to persuade them that the next round of investment will bring new models that will sweep the board and restore returns.

However, year after year the return on capital for most major car makers is low. As emerging markets have moved into mass car production, competition has intensified. See **Exhibit 14.26** which is an extract from the PwC report on 2017 Automotive trends (www.strategyand.pwc.com/trend/2017-automotive-industry-trends).

Exhibit 14.26

The global auto industry is more challenged than many people realize. On the surface, performance is strong. Worldwide sales reached a record 88 million autos in 2016, up 4.8 percent from a year earlier, and profit margins for suppliers and auto makers (also known as original equipment manufacturers, or OEMs) are at a 10-year high. Nonetheless, viewed through the lens of two critical performance indicators, the industry is in serious trouble.

First, total shareholder return (TSR): Over the last five years, the annual rates of return that the S&P 500 and Dow Jones Industrial Average achieved for investors (including dividends) were 14.8 percent and 10.1 percent, respectively. In that period, average auto maker TSR was only 5.5 percent. Second, return on invested capital: In 2016, the top 10 OEMs returned an anemic 4 percent, about half of the industry's cost of capital. The leading 100 suppliers have done a little better, just beating their costs of capital to enjoy a small positive return, after many years of negative net returns.

These numbers almost outweigh the positive sales and earnings results. They paint a picture of a sector that is a less attractive or less lucrative place to invest than other industries. This assessment suggests that there will be relatively few winners in the auto industry during the next five years and beyond.

To be sure, rates of return on capital have been a problem endemic to the auto industry for years, which is one reason for the many bankruptcies — or near liquidations — among OEMs and suppliers, particularly in the past decade or so. Surviving automotive companies have famously bent over backward to save pennies on every car or component they make. However, the situation is becoming more dire: The cost of capital is unlikely to come down from its already low inflation-adjusted levels, and new capital outlays are rising for advances in, among other areas, connected car and autonomous driving technology.

2 The strength of resources

Value-based companies aim to beat the average rates of return on capital employed within their industries. To beat the averages, companies need something special. That something special comes from the resources that the firm possesses. Most of the resources are ordinary; that is, they give the firm competitive parity. However, the firm may be able to exploit one or two extraordinary resources – those that give a competitive edge. An extraordinary resource is one which, when combined with other (ordinary) resources, gives the firm a competitive advantage and creates new value-generating opportunities. Critical extraordinary resources determine what a firm can do successfully.

Generating value for customers, whether real or perceived, is crucial for superior returns. High returns derive from being able to offer the same benefits to customers , but at a lower price, or being able to offer unique benefits that more than outweigh the associated higher price.

Ordinary resources provide the threshold competence necessary for survival. In the food retail business most firms have a threshold competence in basic activities, such as purchasing, human resource management, accounting and waste control and store layout. However, the large chains have resources that set them apart: they can obtain lower-cost supplies because of their enormous buying power; they can exploit economies of scale in advertising and they have the capital to invest in superior technology.

Despite the large retailers having these advantages it is clear that small stores have survived, and some produce good returns on capital invested. These firms provide value to the customer through their own extraordinary resources: personal friendly service; convenient opening times or locations; delivery services. If the large stores were to imitate they could lose their main competitive advantage – low cost.

The extraordinary resources possessed by the supermarket chains when compared with small shops are not necessarily extraordinary resources in the competitive rivalry *between* the chains. If the focus is shifted to the 'industry' of supermarket chains, factors such as economies of scale may merely give competitive parity – scale is needed for survival. Competitive advantage is achieved through the development of other extraordinary resources, such as the quality of the relationship with suppliers, sophisticated data collection systems and premium locations. However, extraordinary resources will not give superior competitive position for ever. Many of these can be imitated. Long-term competitive advantage depends on the capabilities of the management team to scan the environment for changes in customer needs and to satisfy these before competitors. The extraordinary resource is the distinctive capability of management – the coherence, attitude, intelligence, knowledge and drive to innovate successfully.

Most successful companies see the firm as a collection of resources. The company may expand into apparently unconnected areas, but the connection is the opportunity to exploit their extraordinary resources. Honda has many different product areas: motor boat engines, cars, motor cycles, lawn mowers and electric generators. These are sold through different distribution channels in completely different ways to different customers. The common root is Honda's superior ability to produce engines. Prahalad and Hamel (1990) identified 'core competences' as the foundations of a company's competitiveness. These core competences give access to a range of markets and contribute to product benefits. Being difficult to copy, they provide a barrier to direct competition.

Yang (2015) includes core capabilities and states that: "good organisation culture" and "excellent management team" are the most important "firm fundamentals", which support the successful implementation of core competencies and core capabilities.'

Tallman (2016) goes on to discuss dynamic capabilities stating that in a changing business environment the ability to develop its capabilities is vital: 'The increasing scope and velocity of change in the global business environment make a strong set of dynamic capabilities particularly important for multinational firms.'

The analyst should not be looking for a long list of extraordinary resources in any one firm. If one can be found, that is good – it takes only one to leap ahead of competitors and produce supernormal returns. If two are found, then that is excellent. It is very unusual to come across a company that has three or more extraordinary resources. Coca-Cola is an exception, with an extraordinary brand, a distribution system with connected relationships and managers highly knowledgeable about anti-competitive regulations and how to deal with them.

The TRRACK system

To assist the thorough analysis of a company's extraordinary resource, Glen Arnold has developed the TRRACK system. This classifies extraordinary resources into six categories – *see* **Exhibit 14.27**. Note that most extraordinary resources are intangible; they are qualities that are carried within the individuals who make up organisations, or relate to the interaction between individuals. They are usually developed rather than bought. These qualities are difficult to evaluate to provide objective quantification. Despite our inability to be precise, these people-embodied factors are usually the most important drivers of value creation and we must pay most attention to them.

- *Tangible* Occasionally physical resources provide a sustainable competitive advantage. These are assets that can be physically observed and are often valued (or misvalued) in a balance sheet.

Exhibit 14.27	The TRRACK system

T   Tangible
R   Relationships
R   Reputation
A   Attitude
C   Capabilities
K   Knowledge

They include real estate, materials and production facilities. We also include in this section intangible assets, such as patents and trademarks, which are evidenced by a contract, agreement or licence and are therefore legally enforceable. They can be purchased, but if they were easily purchased they would cease to be extraordinary because all competitors would go out and buy them. There must be some barrier preventing other firms from acquiring the same or similar assets for them to be truly valuable in the long run. Microsoft's ownership of its operating system and other standards within the software industry gives it a competitive edge. McDonald's makes sure that it takes the best locations on the busiest highways, rather than settle for obscure secondary roads. Many smaller businesses have found themselves, or have made smart moves to ensure they are, the owners of valuable real estate adjacent to popular tourist sites. Pharmaceutical companies, such as Merck, own valuable patents giving some protection against rivalry – at least temporarily.

● *Relationships* Over time companies can form valuable business relationships that are difficult or impossible for a potential competitor to emulate. There are contractual relationships negotiated between businesses but the most important are informal or implicit relationships based on a trust that has built up over years. The terms of the implicit contract are enforced by the parties themselves rather than through the court. It is in all the parties' interests to cooperate with integrity because there is the expectation of reciprocation leading to the sharing of collective value created over a long period. A loss of this trust can be immensely damaging.

South African Breweries (SAB) had 80% of the beer market in South Africa in 2016 which was a reduction from its previous almost monopoly position of over 90% It is highly profitable. It had kept out foreign and domestic competitors because of its special relationships with suppliers and customers. Most of South Africa's roads are poor and electricity supplies are intermittent. To distribute its beer SAB has formed some strong relationships. It helps the truck drivers, many of whom are former employees, to set up their small trucking businesses. Shebeens (unlicensed pubs) sell most of the beer. Often, they are tiny, with no more than a few benches. SAB cannot sell directly to the illegal shebeens; instead it maintains an informal relationship via a system of wholesalers. SAB makes sure that distributors have refrigerators and, if necessary, generators. A new entrant to the market would have to develop its own special relationship with truck drivers, wholesalers and retailers. In all likelihood it would have to establish a separate and parallel system of distribution. Even then it would lack the legitimacy that comes with a long-standing relationship. SAB Miller was acquired by Anheuser Busch In-Bev (AB) in 2016 and South African Breweries is now a direct subsidiary of AB. As part of the approval process for the deal, AB agreed with South African authorities that there would be no involuntary job cuts. AB also agreed to invest R1bn ($70m) to continue the SAB support for farmers and the local economy (www.ft.com/content/f4148936-0261-11e6-99cb-83242733f755). However, despite the ongoing support for suppliers and customers, other brewers are starting to make inroads into the lucrative South African beer market with Heineken reaching a 13% market share in 2017 primarily through its investment in Amstel. Culture and employee relationships can give a competitive edge through improved co-operation and creativity. Information is shared, knowledge is developed, innovative activity flows, rapid response to market change is natural, and respect for all pervades. Equally relationships with government can be important to a company; defence contractors invest in cultivating special relationships with governments and work to attract ex-government officials to take up directorships or to head liaison with government. Their contacts and knowledge of the inside workings of purchasing decisions, with the political complications, can be very valuable. A similar logic often applies to heavily regulated industries such as pharmaceutical companies, banks and airlines.

● *Reputation* Reputations are normally made over a long period and, once a good reputation is established, can be a source of high returns. With car hire in a foreign country the consumer is unable to assess quality in advance; therefore certification, often through branding becomes an important selling point. Hertz provides certification for local traders under a franchise arrangement. Without the Hertz certification these firms would not be able to premium price and would therefore have no incentive to provide a better service. Consumers are willing to pay more for the assurance of reliable and efficient car hire, suggested by the Hertz certification. Companies pay a premium to hire well respected firms such as Goldman Sachs when contemplating an issue of securities or a merger. They are willing to pay for 'emotional re-assurance'.[6] The CEO cannot be sure of the outcome of the transaction and, if it were to fail, the penalty would be high – executives might lose bonuses and, perhaps, their jobs, sharehold-ers might lose money. The CEO therefore hires the 'best available' for such transactions. The cost of this hand-holding is of secondary concern. Once an adviser has a history of handling large and complex transactions it can offer an effective 'emotional comfort-blanket'[7] to CEOs than smaller rivals can. This principle applies to all consultants and advisers. Branding is a manifestation of the importance of reputation. A strong brand can be incredibly valuable, especially as companies expand globally.

● *Attitude* Attitude refers to the mentality of the organisation. It is the way in which the organ-isation relates to the world. Terms such as disposition, will and culture are closely connected with attitude. Every sports coach is aware of the importance of attitude. The team may consist of players with the best technique in the business or with a superb knowledge of the game, they may be the fastest and the most skilful, but without a winning attitude they will not suc-ceed. There must be a will to win. A positive attitude can provide a significant competitive edge. Some firms develop a winning mentality based on a culture of innovation; others are determinedly orientated towards customer satisfaction, while some companies are quality driven. 3M has a pervasive attitude of 'having a go'. Testing out wild ideas is encouraged. Employees are given time to follow up a dreamed-up innovation, and they are not criticised for failing. Innovations such as 'Post-it' notes have flowed from this attitude. Canon has the attitude of *Tsushin* – 'heart-to-heart and mind-to-mind communication' between the firm and its customers. In this way trust is developed.

● *Capabilities* Capabilities are derived from the company's ability to undertake a set of tasks. The term 'skill' can be used to refer to a narrow activity or a single task. Capability is used for the combination of a number of skills.[8] For example, a company's capability base could include abilities in narrow areas such as market research, innovative design and efficient manu-facturing that, when combined, result in a superior capability in new product development. A capability is more than the sum of the individual processes – the combination and coordination of individual processes may provide an extraordinary resource. Apple is a company with a few world-class capabilities – understanding the needs of their customers/high design capability – and it uses these to develop a clear identity and to drive value. Microsoft on the other hand is seen as 'ok across the board' and, with a much larger customer base, uses its lucrative assets (software), economies of scale and customer switching costs as key components of its strategy.

● *Knowledge* Knowledge is the awareness of information, and its interpretation, organisation, synthesis and prioritisation, to provide insights and understanding. The retention, exploitation and sharing of knowledge is important in the achievement and maintenance of competitive advantage. All firms in an industry possess basic knowledge. For example, all publishers have some knowledge of market trends, distribution techniques and printing technology. It is not this common knowledge that we are referring to in the context of extraordinary resources. If a publisher builds up data and skills in understanding a particular segment of the market, say investments books, then its superior awareness, interpretation, organisation, synthesis and prioritisation of information can create competitive advantage through extraordinary know-ledge. The company will have greater insight than rivals into this segment of the market. There are two types of organisational knowledge. The first, *explicit* knowledge, can be formalised and passed on in codified form. This is objective knowledge that can be defined and docu-mented. The second, *tacit* knowledge, is ill-defined or undefined. It is subjective, personal and context specific. It is fuzzy and complex. It is hard to formalise and communicate. Examples of explicit knowledge include costing procedures written in company accounting manuals,

---

6 Martin, P. (1998) 'Goldman's goose', *Financial Times*, 11 August, p. 14. Explains why Goldman Sachs can charge a large sum for advice.

7 Ibid.

8 De Wit and Meyer (2015).

formal assessment of market demand, customer complaint data and classification. Explicit knowledge is unlikely to provide competitive advantage: if it is easily defined and codified it is likely to be available to rivals. Tacit knowledge, meanwhile, is difficult to write down and transfer and, in relation to competitive advantage, is difficult for rivals to copy. As industry moves from a manufacturing base into the service sector, knowledge management is a key capability and an essential part of doing business.

If you would like to delve more deeply into competitive resource analysis there are fuller discussions in Arnold (2010: Chapter 10) and Arnold (2014: Chapter 15).

3 Life-cycle stage of value potential

A competitive advantage in an attractive industry will not lead to superior long-term performance unless it provides a *sustainable* competitive advantage and the economics of the industry remain favourable. Rival firms are attracted to industries which provide high returns and competitive advantage is usually whittled away. The longevity of the competitive advantage can be represented in terms of a life-cycle with four stages: development, growth, maturity and decline (*see* **Exhibit 14.28**).

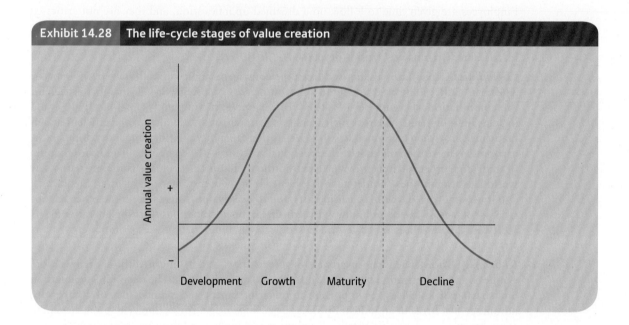

Exhibit 14.28   The life-cycle stages of value creation

In the development phase during which competitive advantage (and often the industry) is established, perhaps through technological or service innovation, the customer base will be small. As demand increases, there is a growth phase in which competitive strength is enhanced by factors such as industry leadership, brand strength and patent rights. A period of competitive advantage and high return can be expected. Eventually others enter the market and the sources of advantage are removed, by competitor imitation, or by customers and suppliers gaining bargaining power. Other possibilities include technological breakthroughs by competitors able to offer a superior product, or poor management leading to a loss of cost control can reduce returns. Whatever the reason for the reduction in the performance spread, the firm now faces a choice of three routes, two of which can lead to a repositioning on the life cycle; the third is to enter a period of negative performance spreads.

The two positive actions are (a) to erect barriers to entry (b) to innovate or improve to stay ahead of potential competition. Barriers prevent outsiders coming into the market and taking market share. Barriers may be real, such as regulations or licensing, or may be perceived. For example, a clear message to the aspiring entrant that they would be subject to retaliatory attack, such as a price war, making it unprofitable to enter. Alternatively, continuous innovation/improvement of the product to reduce cost or premium price is an effective defence. An example of the simultaneous use of those two actions was provided by Microsoft. It was able to dominate the operating software market and the application market because of the high costs for users switching to a competitor's software, the network effect of its Office system being a standard system used throughout the world, and its close working relationships with hardware producers. This made life difficult for potential new entrants. Microsoft was dominant in its industry, its browser, Internet Explorer, holding 95% market share – but competition has now reduced its dominance. Microsoft is no longer the innovator, the one to beat, but it is still producing significant revenue with a healthy 28% margin thanks to the number of customers using its Microsoft Office suite and Windows operating system. It has matured.

Strategy planes

The three elements of strategic assessment can be summarised on a strategy planes chart – see Exhibit 14.29 – for Red plc which, besides the plastics SBU, has a young Internet games division, a coal-mining subsidiary, a publishing group with valuable long-term copyrights on dozens of best sellers, a supermarket chain subject to increasingly intense competition in an over-supplied market, and a small airline company with an insignificant market share. The strategy planes framework can be used at the SBU level or can be redrawn for product/customer segments within SBUs.

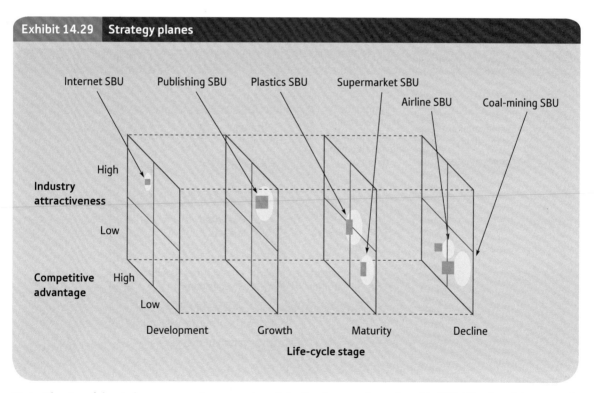

Exhibit 14.29   Strategy planes

Note: The size of the circle represents the proportion of the firm's assets devoted to this SBU. The size of the rectangle represents the current performance spread. If the spread is negative it is shown outside the circle.

Strategic choice

Managers need to consider a wide array of potential strategic options. The process of systematic search for alternative market product entry/exit and competitive approaches within markets is a vital one. The objective of such a search is to find competitive advantage in attractive markets sustainable over an extended period yielding positive performance spreads.

Once a sufficiently wide-ranging search for possible strategic directions has been conducted, the options that come to the fore need to be evaluated. They are usually considered in broad descriptive terms using qualitative analysis with written reports and reflective thought. This qualitative thinking has valuable attributes such as creativity, intuition and judgement in the original formulation of strategic options, the assessment of their merits and the subsequent reiterations of the process. The qualitative strategy evaluation is complemented by a quantitative examination for which accounting terms such as profit, eps, ROCE and balance sheet impact are traditionally used. This has the advantage of presenting the strategic plans in the same format that the directors use to present annual results to shareholders. However, these metrics do not accurately reflect the shareholder value to be generated from alternative strategic plans. The value-based metrics such as economic profit and discounted cash flow described in the next chapter are more appropriate.

Exhibit 14.30 shows the combination of qualitative assessment and quantitative analysis of strategic options. When a shortlist of value-creating strategies has been identified, sensitivity and scenario analysis of the kinds described in Chapter 6 can be applied to discover the vulnerability of the 'most likely' outcome to changes in the input factors such as level of sales or cost of materials. The company also needs to consider whether it has the financial resources necessary to fund the strategy. The issues of finance raising, debt levels and dividend policy come into the equation at this point. Other aspects of feasibility include whether the organisation has the skill base necessary to provide the required quality of product or service, whether it can gain access to the required technology, materials, services and so on.

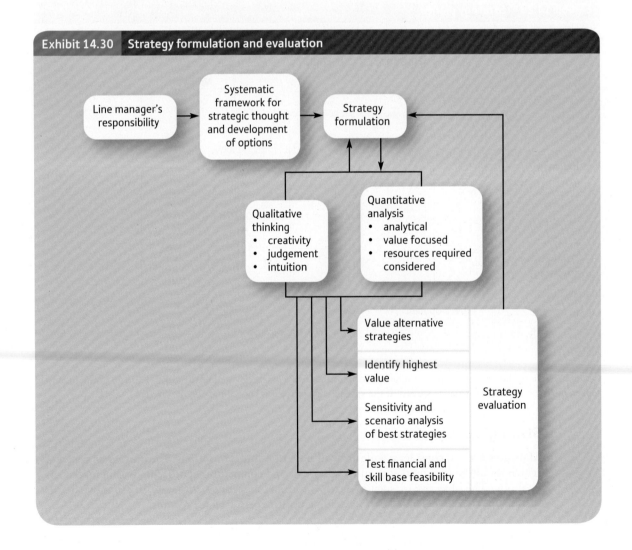

Exhibit 14.30   Strategy formulation and evaluation

Strategy implementation

Making the chosen strategy work requires the allocation of resources and the reorganisation and motivation of people. The firm's switch to value-based principles impacts on these implementation issues. Resources are allocated to units or functions if it can be shown that they will contribute to value creation after taking into account the quantity of resources used. Managers are given responsibilities and targets are set in accordance with value creation.

Corporate strategy

So far, the firm has been described as consisting of a group of strategic business units. So where does the head office fit into this picture if each of these units has a separately identifiable market and is capable of independent strategic action?

We know that companies need to apply value-based principles to all their activities and so this must include the centre. Everything the head office does must create value for shareholders. This means there must be awareness of the quantity of assets used in each task and the return generated by those assets.

In a value-based company the role of the corporate centre (head office) has four main aspects:

1 *Portfolio planning* – allocating resources to those SBUs and product and/or customer areas offering the greatest value creation while withdrawing capital from those destroying value – see **Exhibit 14.31**.

Exhibit 14.31

General Electric steps into an uncertain future. The recent history of the industrial titan holds lessons for all company leaders

When General Electric named John Flannery as its chief executive in June, Jeffrey Immelt listed six of his successor's leadership traits, including "good judgment, resilience, a learner, team builder and a tough-minded individual and competitor". Mr Flannery will need the tough-mindedness and resilience most. On Friday, he promised a thorough "reset" of America's largest industrial group. He aims to redefine the company's culture, run it better, and reduce its complexity. These commitments echo the demands of investors, including activist Nelson Peltz's Trian Partners.

But none of them will be easily achieved at a huge company operating in a capital-intensive, slow-growing, highly competitive set of industries. Mr Flannery has taken astute first steps. GE's third-quarter results on Friday, the first report of his tenure, came in well below analysts' expectations. He called them "completely unacceptable". The grim but resolute tone, and the early speculation about the possibility of a cut to GE's dividend, suggest Mr Flannery has mastered a seventh trait useful to GE leaders since the time of Mr Immelt's predecessor, Jack Welch: expectations management.

Calling out bad news quickly and comprehensively provides room to show improvement later. Indeed, a bit of exaggeration does not hurt. He has also taken a few sacred cows out of the GE herd, reportedly cutting the number of GE research and development centres, deferring part of a headquarters building project, and grounding corporate jets. Mr Flannery is lucky, inasmuch as his predecessor was not. GE's shares fell by more than a third over Mr Immelt's tenure.

He had the unfortunate task of unwinding a huge finance business, cultivated by Mr Welch. After the financial crisis GE Capital's profits proved to be little more than an artefact of a speculative boom. Mr Immelt's acquisitions — particularly in the oil and gas sector — came ahead of a rapid drop in commodity prices. His bets on the industrial "internet of things" have mostly yet to pay off. All this tends to overshadow his rebuilding of the industrial portfolio and the introduction of a less-centralised management approach. Whether or not all of this is down to bad luck, it gives Mr Flannery a low base to build on and a mandate for change. On Friday, he promised that "everything was on the table". Good.

▶

Exhibit 14.31 *(continued)*

Change needs to come quickly, then — but quick improvements are not the goal. The focus has to be on investing for the long term.

The past few decades of leadership at GE has lessons for all companies. Stay focused on areas where you have differentiated skills (engineering, for GE) and avoid trends (financialisaton). Set short-term expectations you can hit, but manage for the long-term. Take hard decisions. And hope for a little bit of good luck.

 Financial Times, 20 October 2017.

2   *Managing strategic value drivers shared by two or more SBUs* – these crucial extraordinary resources, giving the firm competitive advantage, may need to be centrally managed or at least coordinated by the centre to achieve the maximum benefit. An example here could be strong brand management or technological knowledge. The head office needs to ensure adequate funding of these and to achieve full but not over-exploitation.

3   *Providing the pervading philosophy and governing objective* – training, goal setting, employee rewards and the engendering of commitment are all focused on shareholder value. A strong lead from the centre is needed to avoid conflict, drift and vagueness.

4   *The overall structure of the organisation* needs to be appropriate for the market environment and designed to build value. Roles and responsibilities are clearly defined, with clear accountability for value creation.

We can apply the principles of portfolio planning to Red plc. The corporate centre could encourage and work with the plastics division in developing ideas for reducing or eliminating the value losses being made on some of its products and markets – recall (from Exhibits 14.24 and 14.25 earlier in this chapter) that it is destroying value in product line C and in sales to UK industrial customers and the UK government. Once these have been fully evaluated, head office could ensure that resources and other services are provided effectively to implement the chosen strategy. For example, if the highest value-creating option is gradually to withdraw capital from product line C and to apply the funds saved to product line A, the management team at C are likely to become demotivated as they reduce the resources under their command and experience lower sales (and profit) rather than, the more natural predisposition of managers, a rising trend. The centre can help this process by focusing the targets and incentives of these managers away from growth and empire building towards shareholder value.

On the level of corporate-wide resource allocation, the directors of Red plc have a great deal of work to do. The publishing division is already creating high value from its existing activities and yet it is still in the early growth phase. The subsidiary management team believe that significant benefits would flow from buying rights to other novels and children's stories. By combining these with its present 'stable' it could enter more forcefully into negotiations with book retailers, television production companies wishing to make screen versions of its stories, and merchandising companies intending to put the image of some of the famous characters on articles ranging from T-shirts to drink cans. This strategy will involve the purchase of rights from individual authors as well as the acquisition of firms quoted on the stock exchange. It will be costly and require a substantial shift of resources within the firm. But, as can be seen from **Exhibit 14.32**, the value created makes the change attractive.

The Internet division has been put on a tight rein in terms of financial resources for its first three years because of the high risk attached to businesses involved in speculative innovation in this market. However, the energetic and able managers have created a proven line of services with a technological lead over competitors, a high market share and substantial barriers to entry in the form of copyrights and patents. The directors decide to expand this area.

The plastics division as a whole is in a mature market with positive but gradually declining performance spreads. Here the strategic approach is to reduce the number of product lines competing on cost and transfer resources to those niche markets where product differentiation allows a premium price to be charged. The intention is to move gradually to a higher competitive

Exhibit 14.32	**Using strategy plane analysis. Red plc's shifting strategic plan**

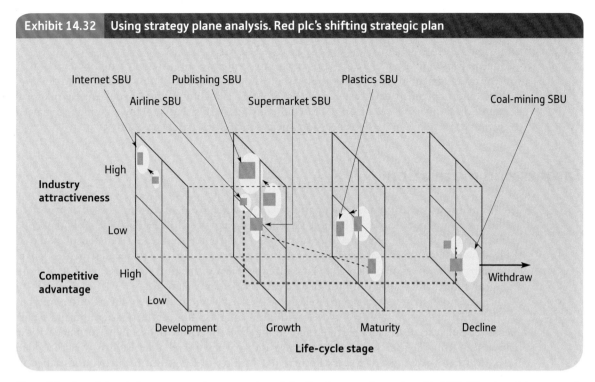

Note: The size of the circle represents the proportion of the firm's assets devoted to this SBU. The size of the rectangle represents the current performance spread. If the spread is negative it is shown outside the circle.

advantage overall but accept that industry attractiveness will decline. Overall resources dedicated to this division will remain approximately constant, but the directors will be watching for deterioration greater than that anticipated in the current plan.

The supermarket division is producing a positive performance spread but a prolonged price war is forecast for the industry, to be followed by a shake-out, leading to a withdrawal of many of the current firms. Some directors are in favour of supporting this division vigorously through the troublesome times ahead in the expectation that when many of the weaker players have left the field, margins will rise to abnormally high levels – producing large performance spreads and high value in the long run. In terms of the value-creating life cycle this SBU would be shifted from the maturity strategy plane to the growth plane (shown in Exhibit 14.32). Other directors are not willing to take the risk that their firm will not be one of the survivors from the battle for market share. Furthermore, they argue that even if they do win, the enormous resources required, over the next five years, will produce a value return less than that on the publishing or Internet SBUs. Therefore, if financial resources are to be constrained, they should put money into these 'star' divisions.

The coal-mining division is haemorrhaging money. The industry is in terminal decline because of the high cost of coal extraction and the increasing tendency for the electricity-generating companies to source their coal needs from abroad. Moreover, Red is a relatively small player in this market and lacks the economies of scale to compete effectively. To add insult to injury a large proportion of the corporation's capital is tied up in the coal stockpiles required by the electricity firms. The decision is taken to withdraw from this industry and the best approach to achieve this is investigated – sale to a competitor or liquidation.

The airline operation has never made a satisfactory return and is resented by the managers in other divisions as a drain on the value they create. However, the recent deregulation of air travel and especially the opening up of landing slots at major European airports has presented an important new opportunity. Despite being one of the smallest operators and therefore unable to compete on price, it provides a level of service which has gained it a high reputation with business travellers. This, combined with its other major value driver, the strength of its marketing team, leads the divisional managers and the once sceptical directors to conclude that a sufficiently high premium ticket price can be charged to produce a positive performance spread. The new European rules enable the division to be placed on the growth plane as the spread is thought to be sustainable for some time.

The analysis in Exhibit 14.32 of Red's corporate strategy is an extremely simplified version of strategy development in large corporations where thousands of staff-hours are needed to develop, evaluate and implement new strategic plans. Strategy is a complex and wide-ranging practical academic discipline and we can only scratch the surface in this chapter. However, managers need to ensure that finance discussions/decisions always include the strategic context.

Targets and motivation

The remaining aspects of management affected by a switch from an earnings-based approach to a value-based approach shown in Exhibit 14.23 have already been touched on and, given the scope of this book, will not be explained any further here. The interested reader can consult some of the leading writers in this area (see References and further reading). The financial structure debate concerning the proportion of debt in the overall capital mix of the firm is discussed in Chapters 16 and 18 and the dividend pay-out ratio debate is described in Chapter 19.

One final point to note with regard to Exhibit 14.23 is the importance of having different types of value-creating targets at different levels within the organisation. At the board room and senior executive level, it seems reasonable that there should be a concern with overall performance of the firm as seen from the shareholders' perspective and so Total Shareholder Return, Wealth Added Index, Market Value Added, Excess Return and Market to Book Ratio (metrics described in Chapter 15) would be important guides to performance, and incentive schemes would be (at least partially) based upon them. Economic Profit, Economic Value Added, Discounted Cash Flow and Shareholder Value Analysis are also useful guides for senior managers. These metrics are described and critically assessed in the next chapter.

Moving down the organisation, target setting and rewards need to be linked to the level of control and responsibility over outcomes. SBU performance needs to be expressed in terms of value metrics such as Discounted Cash Flow, Economic Profit and Economic Value Added. Outcomes here are usually under the control of divisional and other middle-ranking managers and so the reward system might be expressed in terms of achieving targets expressed in these metrics. At the operating level where a particular function contributes to value creation but the managers in that function have no control over the larger value centre itself, perhaps the emphasis should shift to rewarding high performance in particular operational value drivers such as throughput of customers, reduced staff turnover, cost of production, faster debtor turnover, etc. *See* **Case study 14.1**.

| **Case study 14.1** | **Strategy, planning and budgeting at Lloyds TSB[9]** |

Although business units are responsible for their own strategy development, the Lloyds TSB group provides guidelines on how strategy should be developed. These unit plans are then consolidated into an aggregate plan for the value centre. The process undertaken is then subjected to scrutiny by the centre. The strategic planning process consists of five stages:

1 *Position assessment* Business units are required to perform a value-based assessment of the economics of the market in which the business operates and of the relative competitive position of the business within that market. Market attractiveness and competitive position must include a numerical rather than a purely qualitative assessment.

2 *Generate alternative strategies* Business units are required to develop a number of realistic and viable alternatives.

---

9 Lloyds TSB separated into two banks Lloyds Bank and TSB in 2013 but both remained part of the Lloyds Banking Group until TSB was floated in 2014. TSB was then taken over by Sabadell, a Spanish bank, in 2015.

3   *Evaluate alternative strategies* Business units are required to perform shareholder value calculations in order to prioritise alternatives. Even if a potential strategy has a high positive net present value, this does not necessarily mean that it will be accepted. An assessment of project risk or do-ability is overlaid across the net present value calculations.

4   *Agree chosen strategy with the centre* While it is perceived to be vital that the managers who best understand their business are given sufficient authority to develop strategies which they consider to be most appropriate, it is nevertheless considered equally important that there is a challenge mechanism at the centre to ensure that appropriate analyses have been performed and assumptions made are credible.

5   *The chosen strategy becomes a contract* Once the preferred strategy has been agreed with the centre, resource allocation and milestones are agreed. Budgetary performance targets are derived from the projections included within the strategic plan. Beyond this, however, business unit managers are free to choose whatever structures and performance indicators are considered to be relevant and appropriate.

Source: M. Davies (2000), 'Lessons from practice: VBM at Lloyds TSB', in G. Arnold and M. Davies (eds), *Value-Based Management*. Chichester: John Wiley & Sons.

> *Key rule: All managers should agree to both short- and long-term targets.* This counters the natural tendency in all of us to focus on short-term goals that might not be optimal in the long run.

Concluding comments

The switch from management by accounting metrics to management using concepts such as value, the time value of money and opportunity cost is not widespread. Some highly successful firms have introduced value-based management systems which integrate management strategy and financial control. This has required a re-examination of all aspects of management, ranging from performance measurement systems and strategic planning to motivational schemes and training programmes. A commercial organisation that adopts value principles is one that has an important additional source of strength. The rigorous thought process involved in the robust application of these principles helps managers to understand their value drivers and having reviewed systems and product and market strategies ensure a contribution to shareholder value from all parts of the company.

The rest of this part of the book builds on the basic principles behind value-based management discussed in this chapter.

Key points and concepts

- **Value-based management** is a managerial approach in which the primacy of purpose is long-run shareholder-wealth maximisation. The objective of the firm, its systems, strategy, processes, analytical techniques, performance measurement and culture have as their guiding objective shareholder-wealth maximisation.

- **Shareholder-wealth maximisation** is the superior objective in most commercial organisations operating in a competitive market for many reasons. For example:
  - owners of the business have a right to demand this objective;
  - managers who do not satisfy shareholders may lose their roles (e.g. via a merger);
  - society's scarce resources can thereby be better allocated.

- **Non-shareholder wealth-maximising goals** may go hand in hand with shareholder value. Loyal customers, motivated employees and reliable suppliers are all important elements in value creation But sometimes the two are contradictory and then shareholder wealth becomes paramount.

- **Earnings- (profit)-based management is flawed:**
  - profit figures are drawn up following subjective allocations and calculations relying on judgement rather than science;
  - profit figures are open to manipulation and distortion;

▶

- – the investment required to produce earnings growth is not made explicit;
- – the time value of money is ignored;
- – the riskiness of earnings is ignored.

● **Bad growth** is when the return on the marginal investment is less than the required rate of return, given the finance providers' opportunity cost of funds. This can occur even when earnings-based figures are favourable.

● **Using accounting rates of return** (ROCE, ROI, ROE, etc.) is an attempt to solve some of the problems associated with earnings or earnings per share metrics, especially with regard to the investment levels used to generate the earnings figures. However, balance sheet figures are often too crude to reflect capital employed. Using ARRs can also lead to short termism.

● **That shareholders are interested solely in short-term earnings and eps is a myth.** These figures are interesting only to the extent that they cast light on the quality of stewardship over fund providers' money by management and therefore give an indication of long-term cash flows. Evidence:

- – most of the value of a share is determined by income to be received five or more years hence;
- – hundreds of quoted firms producing zero or negative profits have high market values;
- – earnings changes are not correlated with share price changes; for example, earnings can fall due to a rise in R&D spending and yet share prices may rise;
- – the window-dressing of accounts (creative accounting) does not, in most cases, influence share prices.

● **Value is created** when investment produces a rate of return greater than that required for the risk class of investment.

● **Four key elements drive shareholder value:**

1 Amount of capital invested.
2 Required rate of return.
3 Actual rate of return on capital.
4 Planning horizon (for performance spread persistence).

● **Performance spread**

Actual rate of return on capital – required return, $r - k$

● **Corporate value**

$$= \boxed{\begin{array}{c}\text{Present value of}\\\text{cash flows within}\\\text{planning horizon}\end{array}} + \boxed{\begin{array}{c}\text{Present value of}\\\text{cash flows after}\\\text{planning horizon}\end{array}}$$

● **To expand or not to expand?**

	Grow	Shrink
Positive performance spread	Value creation	Value opportunity forgone
Negative performance spread	Value destruction	Value creation

- **The value action pentagon** shows five sources of increased value:

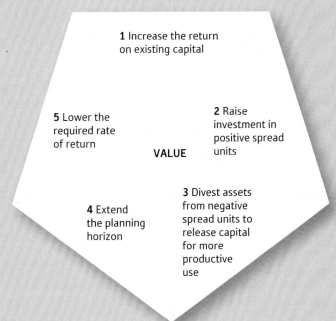

1 Increase the return on existing capital

5 Lower the required rate of return

VALUE

2 Raise investment in positive spread units

4 Extend the planning horizon

3 Divest assets from negative spread units to release capital for more productive use

- **Switching to value-based management principles affects many aspects of the organisation.** These include:

  - strategic business unit strategy and structure;
  - corporate strategy;
  - culture;
  - systems and processes;
  - incentives and performance measurement;
  - financial policies.

- **A strategic business unit (SBU)** is a business unit within the overall corporate entity which is distinguishable from other business units because it serves a defined external market in which management can conduct strategic planning in relation to products and markets.

- **Strategy** means selecting which product or market areas to enter/exit and how to ensure a good competitive position in those markets or products.

- **SBU managers** should be involved in strategy development because (a) they usually have great knowledge to contribute and (b) they will have greater 'ownership' of the subsequently chosen strategy.

- **A review of current SBU** activities using **value-creation profile charts** may reveal particular product or customer categories that destroy wealth.

- **Strategic analysis** has three stages:

  - strategic assessment;
  - strategic choice;
  - strategic implementation.

- **Strategic assessment** focuses on the three determinants of value creation:

  - industry attractiveness;
  - competitive resources;
  - life-cycle stage of value potential.

▶

- **Competitive resource analysis** can be conducted using the **TRRACK system**:

  - Tangible
  - Relationships
  - Reputation
  - Attitude
  - Capabilities
  - Knowledge

- A company's SBU positions with regard to the three value-creation factors could be represented in a **strategy planes diagram.** The product and/or market segment within SBUs can also be shown on strategy planes.

- To make good **strategic choices,** a wide search for alternatives needs to be encouraged.

- In the **evaluation of strategic options** both qualitative judgement and quantitative valuation are important. The shortlisted options can be tested in sensitivity and scenario analysis as well as for financial and skill-base feasibility.

- **Strategy implementation** is making the chosen strategy work through the planned allocation of resources and the reorganisation and motivation of people.

- The **corporate centre** has four main roles in a value-based firm:

  - portfolio planning;
  - managing strategic value drivers shared by SBUs;
  - providing and inculcating the pervading philosophy and governing objective;
  - structuring the organisation so that rules and responsibilities are clearly defined, with clear accountability for value creation.

- **Targets, incentives and rewards** should be based on metrics appropriate to the level of management within the firm, as shown in **Exhibit 14.33**.

Exhibit 14.33

Senior management	External value metrics: TSR, WAI, MVA, ER, MBR
SBU management	Discounted cash flow, SVA, EP, EVA
Operational functions	Operating value drivers: e.g. cost of output, customer satisfaction

References and further reading

Arnold, G. (2014a) *The Financial Times Guide to Value Investing.* 3rd edn. London: Financial Times Prentice Hall.

An investment book that considers corporate strategy and the potential for value creation.

Arnold, G.C. (2011) *The Financial Times Guide to Investing.* 2nd edn. London: Financial Times Prentice Hall.

Contains chapters on strategic evaluation of companies.

Arnold, G.C. and Davies, M. (eds) (2000) *Value-Based Management*. London: John Wiley & Sons.

A collection of research monographs focuses on this emerging field.

Bouwens, J. and Lent, L.V. (2007) 'Assessing the performance of business unit managers', *Journal of Accounting Research*, 45(4), pp. 667–97.

Using a sample of 140 managers, this paper investigates the use of various performance metrics in determining the assessment, bonus decisions, and career paths of business unit managers. The results suggest separate and distinct roles for different types of performance measures.

Buffett, W. (1984) *Berkshire Hathaway Annual Report*. Omaha, NE: Berkshire Hathaway.

As with all reports by Buffett, this one is full of profound and witty insight. www.berkshirehathaway.com

Burkert, M. and Lueg, R. (2013) 'Differences in the sophistication of Value-based management – The role of top executives', *Management Accounting Research*, 24(1), 3–22.

This paper examines how the characteristics of CEOs and CFOs as well as perceived environmental uncertainty (PEU) of the top management team (TMT) affect the sophistication of value-based management (VBM).

Collis, D.J. and Montgomery, C.A. (2005) *Corporate Strategy: A resource-based approach*. 2nd edn. New York: McGraw-Hill.

A very important and easy-to-read book on the subject of resources of companies.

Cornelius, I. and Davies, M. (1997) *Shareholder Value*. London: Financial Times: Financial Publishing.

A good account of value-based management and the metrics used.

Davies, M. (2000) 'Lessons from practice: VBM at Lloyds TSB', in G.C. Arnold and M. Davies (eds) *Value-Based Management*. Chichester: John Wiley & Sons.

Insights into a company making use of VBM principles.

Davies, M., Arnold, G.C., Cornelius, I. and Walmsey, S. (2000) *Managing for Shareholder Value*. London: Informa Publishing Group.

An introductory overview of VBM.

Dekker, H. C., Groot, T., Schoute, M. and Wiersma, E. (2012) 'Determinants of the use of value-based performance measures for managerial performance evaluation', *Journal of Business Finance & Accounting*, 39(9), 1214–39. doi:10.1111/jbfa.12004

This paper investigates the use of value-based performance measures including firms' cost of capital and finds that their use for performance evaluation is less extensive than their benefits would suggest.

De Wit, B. and Meyer, R. (2015) *Strategy: Process, Content, Context*. 5th edn. Andover: Cengage.

Some interesting sections in a very long book.

Elgharbawy, A. and Abdel-Kader, M. (2013) Enterprise governance and value-based management: A theoretical contingency framework. *Journal of Management & Governance,* 17(1), 99–129.

The provides a framework to link a performance management system, i.e. VBM, to the Enterprise Governance framework aiming to bridge the gap between management accounting, corporate governance and entrepreneurship.

Johnson, G. and Scholes, K. (2017) *Exploring Corporate Strategy*. 11th edn. Harlow: Pearson Education.

A well-regarded introductory textbook to the strategic management of firms.

Kay, J. (1993) *Foundations of Corporate Success*. New York: Oxford University Press.

A book using strategic and economic analysis to explain firm success.

Lueg, R. and Schäffer, U.J. Betriebswirtsch (2010) 'Assessing empirical research on value-based management: Guidelines for improved hypothesis testing', *Journal für Betriebswirtschaft,* 60: 1.

This paper investigates the claims that value-based management (VBM) increases corporate performance. It suggests that even though many studies have been conducted, the evidence on whether users outperform non-users is inconsistent.

McKinsey and Company (Koller, T., Goedhart, M. and Wessel, D.) (2015) *Valuation*. 6th edn. New York: John Wiley & Sons.

The management of value-based organisations and the principles behind the techniques are explained.

McKinsey (Koller, T., Goedhart, M. and Wessel, D.) (2011) *Value: The four cornerstones of corporate finance*. New York: John Wiley & Sons.

A short guide to value principles by consultants.

McTaggart, J.M., Kontes, P.W. and Mankins, M.C. (1994) *The Value Imperative*. New York: Free Press.

A very good book showing the application of value-based techniques to strategy and other disciplines.

Pitman, B. (2003) 'Leading for value', *Harvard Business Review,* April, pp. 41–6.

The former CEO and chairman describes clearly and succinctly the evolution of Lloyds Bank from a company without a clear objective to a focus on shareholder value, using return on equity relative to cost of equity to evaluate company operations and reward managers. The logic of a value focus led to 'we had to accept that it was all right to get smaller, to stay close to home, to focus on unglamorous products . . . getting rid of unprofitable customers, getting out of unprofitable markets'.

Porter, M.E. (1980) *Competitive Strategy*. New York: Free Press.

One of the most important books on strategy ever written.

Porter, M.E. (1985) *Competitive Advantage*. New York: Free Press.

   More valuable insight into strategic analysis.

Prahalad, C.K. and Hamel, G. (1990) 'The core competence of the corporation', *Harvard Business Review,* 68(3), May–June, pp. 79–91.

   A paper that led to increased interest in seeing the corporation as a collection of resources, some of which are extraordinary.

Rapp, M.S., Schellong, D., Schmidt, M. and Wolff, M. (2011) 'Considering the shareholder perspective: Value-based management systems and stock market performance', *Review of Managerial Science,* 5(2–3), pp. 171–94.

   The paper studies value-based management systems in listed German firms and examines implications for firms' stock market performance. In 2008, 42% of their sample firms had implemented a VBM system and the analysis found that firms implementing value-based management systems earn abnormal stock market returns.

Rappaport, A. (1998) *Creating Shareholder Value.* (Revised and updated version.) New York: Free Press.

   A landmark book. Presents an important value metric – shareholders' value analysis (SVA).

Rappaport, A. (2011). *Saving Capitalism from Short-termism: How to build long-term value and take back our financial future* (1st edn). New York: McGraw-Hill.

   Rappaport investigates the problem of short termism and concludes that it is primarily due to compensation schemes. In the second half of the book, he considers potential solutions.

Reimann, B.C. (1989) *Managing for Value*. Oxford: Basil Blackwell.

   Useful because it brings together strategy and value.

Ryan, H.E. and Trahan, E.A. (2007) 'Corporate financial control mechanisms and firm performance: The case of value-based management systems', *Journal of Business Finance & Accounting,* 34(1–2), 111–138. doi:10.1111/j.1468-5957.2006.00660.x

   Having examined 84 firms, the paper concluded that VBM improves economic performance and efficient use of capital

Stewart, G.B. (1991) *The Quest for Value.* New York: HarperBusiness.

   Written by a founding partner in Stern Stewart and Co., the US consultancy which has so successfully promoted MVA and EVA. Some useful insights.

Stewart, G.B. (2001) 'Market myths', in *The New Corporate Finance.* 3rd edn. Edited by Donald H. Chew, New York: McGraw-Hill/Irwin.

   An easy-to-read discussion of the difficulties with accounting metrics and the triumphing of value principles.

Tallman, S. (2016) 'Capabilities and capability development', *Wiley Encyclopaedia of Management,* 6(1–3).

   Discusses the role of capabilities in supporting competitive advantage.

Yang, C.C. (2015) 'The Integrated Model of Core Competence and Capability', *Total Quality Management and Business Excellence,* 26(1–2).

   Discusses the importance of 'good organisation culture' and 'excellent management team' as the most important 'firm fundamentals', which support the successful implementation of core competences and core capabilities.

Video presentations

Chief executives and finance directors describe their current thinking on the strategy they are pursuing (you can check on previous year's video presentation to see how consistent they are) at www.merchantcantos.com – free to view.

Case study recommendations

Please see www.pearsoned.co.uk/arnold for case study synopses. Also, another list of useful case studies from the fifth edition can be found there.

- Rosewood Hotels and Resorts: branding to increase customer profitability and lifetime value. Author: Chekitan S. Dev; Laure Mougeot Stroock, Harvard

Business School. Available at www.cb.hbsp.harvard.edu

- Ludhiana City Bus Services Limited: pricing for profits. Author: Neeraj Pandey; Gaganpreet Singh, Darden School of Business. Available at www.cb.hbsp.harvard.edu

Self-review questions

1   In what ways are accounting-based performance measures inadequate for guiding managerial decisions?

2   Define value-based management.

3   What are the four key drivers of shareholder value creation?

4   What are the five actions available to increase value?

5   Describe at least three arguments for managers putting shareholder-wealth maximisation as the firm's objective.

6   Invent a mission statement and strategic objectives that comply with value-based management principles.

7   Outline the evidence against the popular view that shareholders judge managerial performance on the basis of short-term earnings figures.

8   What is 'good growth' and what is 'bad growth'?

9   In what circumstances would you reduce investment in a strategic business unit even if its profits are on a rising trend?

10 List the main areas in which value principles have an impact on the managerial process. Write a sentence explaining each one.

11 What is an SBU and how can a value-creation profile chart be used to improve on an SBU's performance?

12 List the three stages of strategic analysis and briefly describe the application of value-based management ideas to each one.

13 Invent a company and show how the strategy planes diagram can be used to enhance shareholder wealth. Explain each dimension of the planes as you do so.

14 Briefly describe the main roles of the corporate centre in a value-led organisation.

Questions and problems

Answers to most questions can be found at www.pearsoned.co.uk/arnold.
Answers to questions marked with an asterisk are to be found only in the Lecturer's Guide.

1   (*Examination level*) 'Fifty years ago we measured the success of our divisional managers on the basis of market share growth, sales and profits. In the late 1970s we switched to return on capital employed because the old system did not take account of the amount of capital invested to achieve growth targets. Now you are telling me that we have to change again to value-based performance metrics. Why?' Explain in the form of an essay to this chief executive what advantages value-based management has over other approaches.

2   Describe three of the ways in which accounts can be manipulated and distorted.

3   Gather some more data on Intercontinental Hotel Group from newspapers, industry sources, annual reports, etc. and give a more detailed account than that given in this chapter of the ways in which value was created or destroyed.

4   Shareholder value management has been described as a 'weird Anglo-American concept'. Describe this philosophy and consider whether it has applicability outside the Anglo-American world.

5   Do you feel comfortable with the notion that commercial organisations acting in a competitive environment should put shareholders' wealth creation as their first priority? If not, why not? Explain your reasoning.

6   'eps (earnings per share) is not a holy grail in determining how well a company is performing': Lex column of the *Financial Times*, 7 May 1996. Describe and explain the reasons for dissatisfaction with eps for target setting and increasing performance.

7* Which of the following two companies creates more value, assuming that they are making the same initial investment?

Company A's projected profits

Year	Profit (£000s)
Last year	1,000
1 (forthcoming year)	1,000
2	1,100
3	1,200
4	1,400
5	1,600
6 and all subsequent years	1,800

Company B's projected profits

Year	Profit (£000s)
Last year	1,000
1 (forthcoming year)	1,000
2	1,080
3	1,160
4	1,350
5	1,500
6 and all subsequent years	1,700

Profits for both companies are 20% of sales in each year. With company A, for every £1 increase in sales 7p has to be devoted to additional debtors because of the generous credit terms granted to customers. For B, only 1p is needed for additional investment in debtors for every £1 increase in sales. Higher sales also mean greater inventory levels at each firm. This is 6p and 2p for every extra £1 in sales for A and B respectively.

Apart from the debtor and inventory adjustments, the profit figures of both firms reflect their cash flows. The cost of capital for both firms is 14%. **?**

8 Ready plc is financed entirely by equity capital with a required return of 13%. Ready's business is such that as sales increase, working capital does not change. Ready currently has £10m in cash not needed for business operations that could be used to pay a dividend immediately. Under current policy, post-tax earnings (and free cash flow) of £10m per year are expected to continue indefinitely. All earnings in future years are expected to be paid out as dividends in the year of occurrence.

Calculate

a   The value of the company before the current dividend is paid from the £10m of cash.
b   The value of the company if the current dividend (time 0) is missed and the retained earnings are put into investments (with the same risk as the current set of projects) yielding an extra £2m per year to infinity in addition to the current policy's earnings. What happens to earnings and cash flow? Is this good or bad investment?
c   The value of the company if half of the current dividend is missed and the retained earnings are put into investment yielding £0.5m per year to infinity. What happens to earnings and cash flows? Is this good or bad investment? **?**

9 What is the annual value creation of Sheaf plc which has an investment level of £300,000 and produces a rate of return of 19% per annum compared with a required rate of return of 13%? What is the performance spread?
Assuming that the planning horizon for Sheaf plc is 12 years, calculate the value of the firm. (Assume the investment level is constant throughout.) **?**

10* Busy plc, an all equity-financed firm, has three strategic business units. The polythene division has capital of £8m and is expected to produce returns of 11% for the next five years. Thereafter it will produce returns equal to the required rate of return for this risk level of 14%. The paper division has an investment level of £12m and a planning horizon of ten years. During the planning horizon it will produce a return of 22% compared with a risk-adjusted required rate of return of 15%. The cotton division uses £2m of capital, has a planning horizon of seven years and a required rate of return of 16% compared with the anticipated actual rate of 17% over the first seven years.

    a   Calculate the value of the firm.

    b   Draw a value-creation and strategic business unit performance spread chart.

    c   Develop five ideas for increasing the value of the firm. State your assumptions.

11 (*Examination level*) Imagine you are an expert on finance and strategy and have been asked by a large company with subsidiaries operating in a variety of industrial sectors to explain how the organisation might be changed by the adoption of value principles. Write a report to convince the managerial team that the difficulties and expense of transformation will be worth it.

12 In the form of an essay, discuss the links between strategy and finance with reference to value-based management principles.

13 Payne plc has six SBUs engaged in different industrial sectors:

		Proportion of firm's capital	Annual value creation (£m)
1	Glass production	0.20	3
2	Bicycles retailing	0.15	10
3	Forestry	0.06	2
4	Electrical goods manufacture	0.20	5
5	Car retailing	0.25	−1
6	Road surfacing	0.14	−10

Make assumptions (and explain them) about the industry attractiveness and competitive position of Payne and its stage in the life cycle of value potential. Place the SBUs on a strategy planes diagram. Explain and show how you would alter the portfolio of the company.

14 'The corporate centre in most firms is an expensive drag on the rest of the organisation.' Explain to this sceptical head of an SBU how the corporate centre can contribute to value creation.

Assignments

1 Apply the four key elements of value creation, the 'expand or not to expand?' model and the value action pentagon to a firm you are familiar with. Write a report for senior executives.

2 Identify an SBU in a company you know well. Conduct a value-based analysis and write a report showing the current position and your recommendations for change. Include in the analysis value-creation profile charts, strategy planes diagrams, sources of competitive advantage (value drivers) and qualitative evaluation of strategies.

Value-creation metrics

LEARNING OUTCOMES

The previous chapter outlined the principles of value-based management. This chapter examines metrics developed by practitioners and consultants to measure and guide the creation of value. By the end of this chapter the reader should be able to explain the following value metrics, evaluating their advantages and the problems in practical use:

- discounted cash flow;
- shareholder value analysis;
- economic profit (economic value added);
- total shareholder return;
- wealth added index;
- market value added;
- excess return;
- market-to-book ratio.

Introduction

Managers need reliable measures of value to help them choose between alternative plans and monitor performance against plan. The aim is to make sure every member of staff understands what value is, and that each person becomes fully committed to creating it; staff understand how much finance has been invested in a plan and are clear on the required rate of return. Everyone knows that extra rewards flow to those who help achieve returns above the required rate of return. Targets are set, and, as milestones are reached, incentive schemes can bestow a share of the value created on those responsible. The first three metrics discussed in this chapter are useful for these purposes; by quantifying the plan, targets and incentives they can be used to judge the performance of the entire firm or just part of it – an SBU, a product line, a project. The amount of cash invested is known and the return on that cash is monitored.

The chapter moves on to describe five 'market-based' measures of value performance. The feature that runs through all these measures is the focus on the stock market's valuation of the company.

- **Total Shareholder Return (TSR)**, measures the rise or fall in the capital value of a company's shares combined with any cash payment, e.g. dividends, received by shareholders over time, be it one year, three years or ten years. This gets to the heart of the issue for owners of companies – what return do I get on my shares from the activities of the managers hired to steward the resources entrusted to them?

- **The Wealth Added Index (WAI)**[1] examines the change in share values (capital gains plus dividends) after allowance for the required rate of return over the period examined.

- **The Market Value Added (MVA)**[2] and **the Market to Book Ratio (MBR)** examine the current market value of the company. These metrics relate the current market values of equity and debt to the amount of capital put into the business, by shareholders and lenders, since its foundation. If the company's strategic and operational actions have generated shareholder value, the current market value of the equity and debt should be significantly greater than the amount invested (equity and debt). If, however, the market currently values the shares and the debt at less than the value of finance provided, then value has been destroyed.

The observation of a positive difference between current valuation and amount injected may or may not mean value has been generated. This depends on whether the investment made by shareholders and debt holders produced a sufficient *rate* of return given the period over which the money was held in the stewardship of the directors. So, for example, if a firm founded 15 years ago with £1m of shareholder capital and £1m of debt which paid out no dividends and received no more funds from finance providers is now valued at £3.54m for its shares and £1m for its debt, we need to know the required rate of return on equity for this risk class given the shareholders' opportunity cost to judge whether the annual rate of return of around 8.8% is sufficient. Excess Return (ER) is a modified MVA, allowing for this opportunity cost of capital over the period.

The five market-based metrics can only be used for 'entire firm' assessment for companies with a stock market price quotation. They cannot be used for analysis of parts of the business as there is no share price for a section of a company. But, in every country, only a fraction of companies pay for a share quotation on a regulated market. For example, there are only around 2,000 UK companies quoted on either the Main Market of the London Stock Exchange or its Alternative Investment Market compared with about 4m incorporated companies in the UK.

On the other hand, the first three metrics discussed can be used both for entire firm or disaggregated analysis, whereas market-based metrics can only be used for entire firm analysis. These eight metrics are not mutually exclusive; they are complementary if calculated and viewed with sufficient informed thought.

Using cash flow to measure value

Consultants push a variety of metrics for managers seeking to create value. However, they all agree that the measure that lies at the theoretical heart of all the others is discounted cash flow.

---

1 Wealth Added Index and WAI are both registered trademarks of the consulting firm Stern Stewart and Co.
2 Market Value Added and MVA are both registered trademarks of the consulting firm Stern Stewart and Co.

Note: to understand this chapter the reader needs the concepts and tools developed in Chapter 2 and its appendix. You may want to refresh your knowledge of basic discounted cash flow analysis before proceeding.

In Chapter 2 the value of an investment is described as the sum of the discounted cash flows (NPV). An investment with a positive net present value, discounted at the company's cost of capital, adds value. If the investment produces a rate of return greater than the finance provider's opportunity cost of capital it is wealth enhancing. The same logic can be applied to a range of different categories of business decisions, including:

- resource allocation;
- business unit strategies;
- corporate-level strategy;
- motivation, rewards and incentives.

Consider the figures for Gold plc in **Exhibit 15.1**. These could refer to the entire company, a strategic business unit (SBU) or a product line. In Exhibit 15.1 we start with forecast profit figures and then make adjustments to arrive at cash flows. In most businesses, plans are in the form of accounting budgets rather than cash flows, and managers need to know how to work from the accounting numbers to cash flows rather than predicting cash flows from scratch.

Profit figures are calculated after several deductions, such as depreciation, that do not affect the company's cash flow for the year. Depreciation is the recognition of the use of an asset to generate profit. Depreciation is an expense which reduces profit; it is not however a cash outflow. It is only when capital items are paid for that cash flows out. To move from profit to cash flow we therefore add back depreciation and any other non-cash expenses that were deducted in calculating the profit figures. Instead of depreciation, we deduct the cost of investment in capital equipment such as factories, machinery and vehicles when the cash flow occurs.

In drawing up the profit figures the accountant does not recognise the investment of funds when inventory (e.g. raw materials stock) or debtors (granting credit to customers) are increased. The accountant observes one asset (cash in hand) being replaced by another (inventory money owed by customers) and so there is no expense to deduct. However, the cash is being used to increase these items as the business grows, and so adjustment to the profit figures is required to get to cash flows.

Similarly, if cash is tied up in cash floats to run the business (e.g. cash in the tills) the fact that this cash is no longer available to shareholders needs to be recognised. If shareholders had to supply extra cash floats in a period, this is deducted from the profit numbers when trying to get at cash flow.

Whether suppliers send input goods and services to this firm for payment on 'cash on delivery terms' or 'credit terms' the accountant, rightly, records the value of these as an expense, and deducts this from the profit and loss account, in the year of delivery and use. The cash flow analyst needs to make an adjustment here because the full amount of the expense may not yet have flowed out in cash. So, if creditor balances increase we need to recognise that the profit and loss account has overstated the outflow of cash. We need then to add back the extent to which the creditor amount outstanding has increased from the beginning of the year to the end to arrive at the cash flow figure.

We also add back the interest charged to profit because the 12% discount rate already includes an allowance for the required return to lenders. To include a deduction for interest in calculating cash flow would be to double-count this element.

The cash flow figures at the bottom of the columns are sometimes referred to as free cash flow. That is, they represent the amount that is free to be paid out to the firm's investors (shareholders and lenders). These amounts could be paid out without affecting future operating cash flows because the necessary investment for future growth in the form of fixed capital items and working capital (inventory, debtor, cash floats less trade credit) is already allowed for.

The total of the discounted cash flows provides us with a value of the SBU (or firm, etc.) after considering all the cash inflows/outflows and discounting those distant cash flows to present value by the required rate of return (the opportunity cost of capital). This discount rate is based on a blend of the required return to shareholders' capital and the required return to debt holders' capital. Chapter 16 describes the logic behind the derivation of the discount rate, which is a weighted average of the required returns to equity and debt – the weighted average cost of capital or WACC.

Exhibit 15.1   Gold plc forecast cash flows

Required rate of return = 12% per annum

Year	1	2	3	4	5	6	7	8 and subsequent years
	£	£	£	£	£	£	£	£
Forecast profits	1,000	1,100	1,100	1,200	1,300	1,450	1,600	1,600
Add book depreciation and other non-cash items (e.g. amortisation of goodwill)	500	600	800	800	800	800	800	800
Less fixed capital investment	−500	−3,000	−600	−600	−300	−600	−800	−800
Less additional investment in working capital*								
Inventory	50	−100	−70	−80	−50	−50	−50	0
Debtors	−20	−20	−20	−20	−20	−20	−20	0
Creditors	10	20	10	10	20	20	30	0
Cash	−10	−10	−10	−10	−10	−10	−10	0
Add interest previously charged to profit and loss account	100	150	200	200	200	200	200	200
Taxes	−300	−310	−310	−420	−450	−470	−550	−550
Cash flow	830	−1,570	1,100	1,080	1,490	1,320	1,200	1,250

$$\text{Discounted cash flow} \quad \frac{830}{1.12} - \frac{1,570}{(1.12)^2} + \frac{1,100}{(1.12)^3} + \frac{1,080}{(1.12)^4} + \frac{1,490}{(1.12)^5} + \frac{1,320}{(1.12)^6} + \frac{1,200}{(1.12)^7} + \frac{1,250}{0.12} \times \frac{1}{(1.12)^7}$$

	741	−1,252	783	686	845	669	543	4,712

Note: * A positive figure for inventory, debtors and cash floats indicates cash released from these forms of investment. A negative figure indicates additional cash devoted to these areas. For creditors a positive figure indicates higher credit granted by suppliers and therefore a boost to cash flows. An Excel spreadsheet version of this calculation is available at www.pearsoned.co.uk/arnold.

By examining the discounted cash flow management can assess the value contribution. The management team putting forward these projected cash flows can then be judged and rewarded on the basis of performance targets expressed in cash flow terms.

The planning horizon[3] is seven years and so the present value of the future cash flows is:

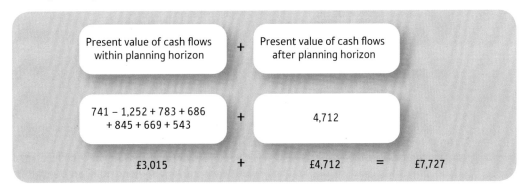

3 Discussed in Chapter 14.

In analysis of this kind it is not unusual to find that most of the value arises after the planning horizon. However, bear in mind that it is the actions (strategic positioning, etc.) and the investments made within the planning horizon that creates the platform for these high post-planning-horizon free cash flows.

Note that in Exhibit 15.1 we have not shown a large initial cash outflow, as was seen in Chapter 2. As with any present value calculation we only want to include future cash flows. Any historic costs such as initial set-up costs are sunk costs and so are not relevant for decisions about the future.

The value shown in Exhibit 15.1 is based on one particular plan. The outcome can be compared with alternative plans to identify which provides the highest value. Sensitivity and scenario analysis (*see* Chapter 6) can be used to highlight areas of concern allowing managers to identify and focus on key success factors and thus reduce the probability of poor outcomes.

Corporate value

If the firm or SBU that we are valuing has other assets that are not used in the creation of operational free cash flow and those assets have a market value, then we add this to the total of the discounted operational cash flow to arrive at the total firm or SBU value. For example, many firms hold portfolios of shares or bonds as investments with no connection to the firm's operations. The market value of these financial assets adds to the value of the firm derived from the operational free cash flow. Likewise, if a company owns an empty and unused factory which could be sold its value can be added to the total.

Corporate value (enterprise value)	=	Present value of free cash flow from operations	+	Value of non-operating assets

Shareholder value from operations and total shareholder value

If the value of debt is deducted from the total present value from operations, we derive the value belonging to shareholders from operations. So, if we assume that this SBU has £3,000 of debt the shareholder value before taking account of non-operating assets is £4,727.

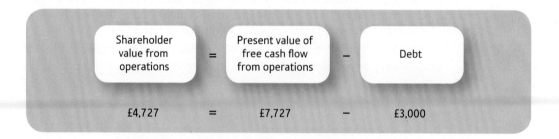

Shareholder value from operations	=	Present value of free cash flow from operations	−	Debt
£4,727	=	£7,727	−	£3,000

The term 'debt' here extends beyond interest-bearing debt to finance lease obligations, under-funded pension plans and contingent liabilities.

If we now assume that this SBU has £800 of government bonds held as investments separate from operations and £600 of equity investment total shareholder value amounts to £6,127:

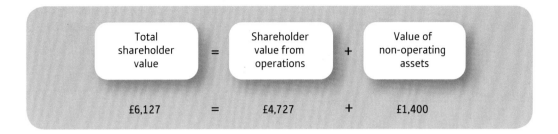

Comparing the discounted free cash flows with alternatives

The figure of £4,727 is the shareholder value of all the future operating cash flows. An alternative course of action is to sell off the SBU's assets, either piecemeal or as a whole. We should compare these alternatives with the present value of continuing to own and run the business. The opportunity cost of following the strategy is the value of the best forgone alternative.

Real management is not about precise numbers – it's about what lies behind the numbers

By embarking on analysis (cash-based analysis or shareholder value analysis or economic profit analysis or economic value-added analysis) the decision maker is forced to investigate and understand the underlying business. This means a knowledge of the competitive environment and the extraordinary resources that the firm possesses to produce high returns in its chosen industry(ies) – see Chapter 14. The decision maker needs to investigate the key 'value drivers' in the company and the industry. Only by thorough understanding of the business, is the analyst going to put realistic numbers into future projections.

However, there is a trap here. A manager lacking the intellectual tools, theoretical frameworks and facts to carry out high-quality strategic analysis will produce simplistic and misleading input numbers to the cash flow forecasts: GIGO – garbage in/garbage out.

Value-based management is not a mechanical discipline. It is not about inputting a few numbers to a computer programme and then waiting until *the* answer pops out. It is a process requiring judgement every step of the way; it requires careful reflection on the results and their sensitivity to the input numbers. Deep thought is required to appreciate the impact of making different judgements on the input variables and in assessing the probabilities of variations occurring. Value-based management is a decision-making-under-uncertainty discipline. How can it be otherwise if it is to be useful in the real world of unpredictability and vagueness? But it gives us a framework and the tools for navigating the best-judged route given these circumstances.

A premium is paid for people who can exercise good judgment despite the imprecision – uncertainty does not paralyse them. These people search for more data to try to see through the haze of the future. More data leads to thought and action designed to reduce the range of probable outcomes.

Investment after the planning horizon

After the planning horizon annual cash flows may well differ from the figure of £1,250 (Exhibit 15.1) due to additional investment in fixed and working capital but this will make no difference to present value as any new investment made (when discounted) will be the same as the discounted value of the future cash inflows from that investment. In other words, the company can earn merely the required rate of return from Year 8 onwards, so no new investment can create value. For example, suppose that Gold raised additional funds of £1,000 and at time 9 (nine years from the present time) invested this in a project generating a perpetual annual net cash inflow of £120 starting at time 10. When these figures are discounted to time 0 the NPV is zero:

Present value of cash outflow $\dfrac{-£1,000}{(1.12)^9} = -360.61$

Present value of cash inflows $\dfrac{£120/0.12}{(1.12)^9} = +360.61$

Thus, incremental investment beyond the planning horizon generates no incremental value and so can be ignored for value calculations.

The connection with stock market valuation

The discounted cash flow analysis illustrated in Exhibit 15.1 is used by financial institutions to value shares. Interest paid to lenders is subtracted to determine the cash flow attributable to equity shareholders which is then discounted at the required return for shares of that risk class. (They do not use a weighted average cost of capital including the return to debt holders – *see* Chapter 17.) Given the emphasis by the owners of the firm on cash-flow generation it makes sense for managers, when evaluating strategies, projects, product lines and customers, to use a similar method.

Shareholder value analysis

Alfred Rappaport (1998) took the basic concept of cash flow discounting and developed a simplified method of analysis. In the example of Gold plc (*see* Exhibit 15.1) the component elements of the cash flow did not change in a regular pattern. For example, fixed capital investment was ten times as great in Year 2 as in Year 5. Rappaport's shareholder value analysis assumes relatively smooth change in the various cash flow elements from one year to the next as they are all taken to be related to the sales level. Rappaport's seven key factors that determine value are as set out in **Exhibit 15.2**.

Rappaport calls the seven key factors value drivers. This can be confusing given that other writers describe a value driver as a factor that provides some degree of competitive advantage. To distinguish the two types of value driver the quantitative seven listed in Exhibit 15.2 will be referred to as Rappaport's value drivers. To estimate future cash flows Rappaport assumes a constant percentage rate of growth in sales. The operating profit margin is a constant percentage of sales. Profit here is defined as profit before deduction of interest and tax, PBIT. The tax rate is a constant percentage of the operating profit. Fixed capital and working capital investment are related to the *increase* in sales.

Exhibit 15.2	Rappaport's value drivers
	1 Sales growth rate
	2 Operating profit margin
	3 Tax rate
	4 Fixed capital investment
	5 Working capital investment
	6 The planning horizon (forecast period)
	7 The required rate of return

So, if sales for the most recent year amount to £1,000,000 and are expected to continue to rise by 12% per year, the operating profit margin on sales[4] is 9%, taxes are 31% of operating profit, the incremental investment in fixed capital items is 14% of the *change* in sales, and the incremental working capital investment is 10% of the *change* in sales, the cash flow for the next year will be as set out in **Exhibit 15.3**.

Exhibit 15.3	Silver plc: Sales, operating profit and cash outflows for next year		
Sales in year 1 = Sales in prior year × (1 + Sales growth rate)			
	= 1,000,000 × 1.12		
			1,120,000
Operating profit = Sales × Operating profit margin			
	= 1,120,000 × 0.09		
			100,800
Taxes = Operating profit × 31%			
	= 100,800 × 0.31		
			−31,248
Incremental investment in fixed capital = Increase in sales × Incremental fixed capital investment rate			
	= 120,000 × 0.14		
			−16,800
Incremental investment in working capital = Increase in sales × Working capital investment rate			
	= 120,000 × 0.10		
			−12,000
Operating free cash flow			£40,752

Using shareholder value analysis to value an entire company

Corporate value is the combined value of the debt portion and equity portion of the overall capital structure:

Corporate value = Debt + Shareholder value

The debt is the market value of debt, such as long-term loans and overdrafts, plus the market value of quasi-debt liabilities, such as preference shares. In practice, the balance sheet book value of debt is often used as a reasonable approximation to the market value.

The above equation can be rearranged to derive shareholder value:

Shareholder value = Corporate value − Debt

Rappaport's corporate value has three elements, due to his separation of the discounted cash flow value of marketable securities – these are assets not needed in operations to generate the business's cash flows – from the cash flows from operations (see **Exhibit 15.4**). The value of the marketable securities is expressed as their current market price.

---

4 Operating profit margin on sales is sales revenue *less* cost of sales and all selling and administrative expenses before deduction of tax and interest.

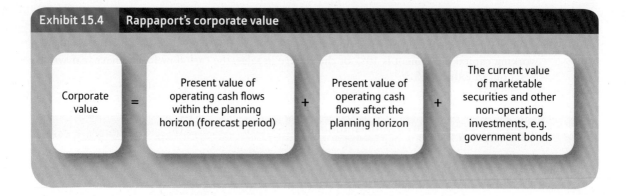

Exhibit 15.4   Rappaport's corporate value

Corporate value = Present value of operating cash flows within the planning horizon (forecast period) + Present value of operating cash flows after the planning horizon + The current value of marketable securities and other non-operating investments, e.g. government bonds

A *closer look at depreciation and investment in fixed capital*

Investment in plant, machinery, vehicles, buildings, etc. consists of two parts:

- **Type 1.** Annual investment to replace worn-out equipment and so on, leaving the overall level of assets constant.
- **Type 2.** Investment that adds to assets, presumably with the intention of permitting growth in productive capacity. This is called incremental fixed-capital investment.

A simplifying assumption often employed in shareholder value analysis is that the 'depreciation' figure in the profit and loss account is equal to the type 1 investment. This avoids the necessity of first adding back depreciation to operating profit figures and then deducting type 1 capital investment. It is only necessary to account for that extra cash outflow associated with incremental fixed capital investment.

Thus, free cash flow is the operating cash flow after fixed and working capital investment; that which comes from the *operations* of the business. It excludes cash flows arising from, say, the sale of shares by the company or bond issue. It also excludes payments of interest or dividends (*see* **Exhibit 15.5**).

Illustration

We can calculate the shareholder value of Silver plc by using Rappaport's seven value drivers if we assume a planning horizon of eight years and a required rate of return of 15% (*see* **Exhibits 15.6** and **15.7**).

The company also has £60,000 of investments in foreign and domestic shares and £50,000 in long-term fixed interest rate securities. These are assets not required to produce operating profit and can be sold off with the proceeds given to their owners, i.e. the shareholders.

Corporate value is as set out in **Exhibit 15.8**.

The required rate of return used in shareholder value analysis is the weighted average required return on debt and equity capital (the WACC) which allows for a return demanded by the debt holders and shareholders in proportion to their provision of capital (see Chapter 16 for the WACC calculation). This explains why cash flows before deduction of interest are discounted rather than just those attributable to shareholders: some of those cash flows will go to debt holders. The discounted cash flows derived in this way are then summed to give corporate value (sometimes called enterprise value). When debt, in this case £200,000, is deducted, shareholder value is obtained.

Shareholder value = Corporate value − Debt

Shareholder value = £705,000 − £200,000 = £505,000

Again, this kind of analysis can be used at different levels:

- whole business;
- division/SBU;
- operating unit;
- project;
- product line or customer.

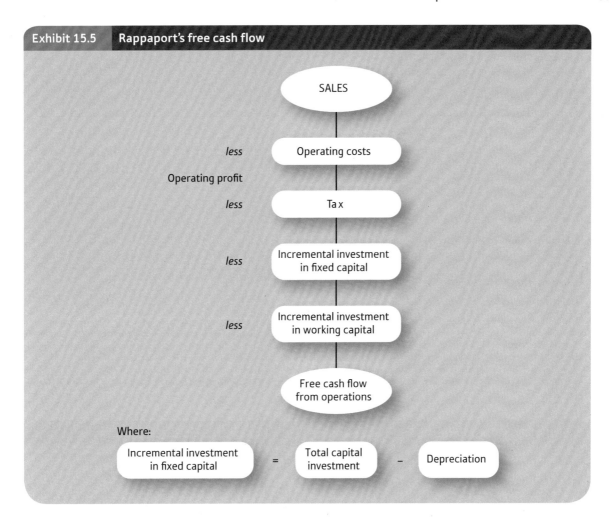

Exhibit 15.5   Rappaport's free cash flow

SALES

less   Operating costs

Operating profit

less   Tax

less   Incremental investment in fixed capital

less   Incremental investment in working capital

Free cash flow from operations

Where:

| Incremental investment in fixed capital | = | Total capital investment | − | Depreciation |

Exhibit 15.6   Rappaport's value drivers applied to Silver plc

1	Sales growth	12% per year
2	Operating profit margin	9% of sales
3	Taxes	31% of operating profit
4	Incremental fixed capital investment	14% of the change in sales
5	Incremental working capital investment	10% of the change in sales
6	The planning horizon (forecast period)	8 years
7	The required rate of return	15% per year

Strategy valuation using shareholder value analysis

The quantitative evaluation of alternative strategies in terms of value creation can assist strategic choice. It is advisable when applying shareholder value analysis to a business unit or corporate-level strategy formulation and evaluation to consider at least four alternative strategic moves:

● a continuation of the current strategy – the 'base-case' strategy;
● liquidation;

Exhibit 15.7	An example of shareholder value analysis – cash flow calculation									

Year	0	1	2	3	4	5	6	7	8	9 and subsequent years
£000s										
Sales	1,000	1,120	1,254	1,405	1,574	1,762	1,974	2,210	2,476	2,476
Operating profits		101	113	126	142	159	178	199	223	223
Less taxes		−31	−35	−39	−44	−49	−55	−62	−69	−69
Less incremental investment in fixed capital		−17	−19	−21	−24	−26	−30	−33	−37	0
Less incremental working capital investment		−12	−13	−15	−17	−19	−21	−24	−27	0
Operating free cash flow		41	46	51	57	65	72	80	90	154

Note: All figures are rounded to whole numbers. There is no additional investment in fixed assets and working capital after year 8 shown. This indicates that the perpetual cash flow of £154,000 can be produced without expanding the physical capacity of the firm (no new factories, etc.). However, investment in the form of replacement of existing facilities subject to wear and tear is taking place, equal to the depreciation amount deducted before the figure for operating profits is input to the analysis. Investment beyond this replacement investment may take place, but it has no impact on the value calculation because investment after the planning horizon generates a return equal to the required rate of return, i.e. there is no performance spread for these assets, and so such investment is ignored for the calculation of firm value. An Excel spreadsheet showing the calculations from Exhibits 15.7 and 15.8 is available at www.pearsoned.co.uk/arnold.

Exhibit 15.8	Corporate value

Present value of operating cash flows within the planning horizon (forecast period)

$$\frac{41}{1.15} + \frac{46}{(1.15)^2} + \frac{51}{(1.15)^3} + \frac{57}{(1.15)^4}$$

$$+ \frac{65}{(1.15)^2} + \frac{72}{(1.15)^2} + \frac{80}{(1.15)^7} + \frac{90}{(1.15)^8} = 259$$

+

Present value of operating cash flows after the planning horizon

$$\frac{154}{0.15} = 1,027$$

then discount result by eight years $\frac{1,027}{(1.15)^8}$ = 336

+

The current value of marketable securities and other non-operating investments

$60 + 50$ = 110

Corporate value = 705

or £705,000

- a trade sale (selling the entire business to another firm or selling a business unit, while perhaps retaining a stake) or a spin-off (creating two separate companies owned by the same shareholders);
- a new operating strategy.

Imagine that Silver plc is involved in the production of plastic guttering for houses and the shareholder value figure of £505,000 represents the base-case strategy, consisting of relatively low levels of incremental investment and sales growing at a slow rate.

Alternatives

- The company has recently been approached by a property developer interested in purchasing the company's depot and offices for the sum of £400,000. Other assets (vehicles, inventory, machinery) could be sold to raise a further £220,000 and the marketable securities could be sold for £110,000. This liquidation would result in shareholders receiving £530,000 (£400,000 + £220,000 + £110,000 − £200,000). This liquidation option produces slightly more than the base-case strategy.

- The third possibility is a trade sale or spin-off. Companies can sell separable businesses to other firms or float off strategic business units or groups of SBUs on the stock market. Following a strategic review carried out in Q4 2017 under its new CEO, GlaxoSmithKline plc announced plants to 'scrap products not bringing in enough value'. GSK will divest non-core nutrition products such as Horlicks. In the case of the fictional guttering firm, it is too small to obtain a separate quotation for component parts, and its operations are too well integrated to allow a trade sale of particular sections. However, in the past shareholders have been approached by larger competitors to discuss the possibility of a takeover. The three or four major industry players are trying to build up market share with the stated aim of achieving 'economies of scale and critical mass' and there is the distinct impression that they are being over-generous to selling shareholders in smaller firms – they are paying 'silly prices'. The management judge that if they could get a bidding war going between these domineering larger firms they could achieve a price of about £650,000 for shareholders.

- The fourth possibility involves an expansion into a new product area of multi-coloured guttering. This will require large-scale investment but should result in rapidly rising sales and higher operating margins. The expected Rappaport value drivers are as set out in **Exhibit 15.9**. Note the increased investment in capital items. Also note the higher risk of this strategy compared with the base-case is reflected in the increased discount rate from 15% to 16%.

Exhibit 15.9	Rappaport's value drivers applied to an expansion of Silver plc
1 Sales growth	25% per year
2 Operating profit margin	11% of sales
3 Taxes	31% of operating profit
4 Incremental fixed capital investment	15% of the change in sales
5 Incremental working capital investment	10% of the change in sales
6 The planning horizon (forecast period)	8 years
7 The required rate of return	16% per year

The guttering firm's shareholder value under the new strategy is set out in **Exhibit 15.10**. This shows that there are lower cash flows in the first three years with this strategy compared with the base-case strategy because of the increased investment; yet the overall expected shareholder value rises from £505,000 to £1,069,000.

Sensitivity and scenario analysis

(These comments apply to cash flow analysis as well.)
To make a more informed choice the directors may wish to carry out sensitivity and scenario analysis (see Chapter 6). A worst-case and a best-case scenario could be constructed and the sensitivity to changes in certain variables could be scrutinised. For example, alternative discount rates and incremental investment in fixed capital rates could be examined for the multi-coloured product strategy as shown in **Exhibit 15.11**.

Exhibit 15.10	The guttering firm's shareholder value under the new strategy

Year	0	1	2	3	4	5	6	7	8	9 and subsequent years
£000s										
Sales	1,000	1,250	1,563	1,953	2,441	3,052	3,815	4,768	5,960	5,960
Operating profits		138	172	215	269	336	420	524	656	656
Less taxes		−43	−53	−67	−84	−104	−130	−162	−203	203
Less incremental investment in fixed capital		−38	−47	−59	−73	−92	−114	−143	−179	0
Less incremental working capital investment		−25	−31	−39	−49	−61	−76	−95	−119	0
Operating free cash flow		32	41	50	63	79	100	124	155	453

Discounted cash flows within planning horizon
$$\frac{32}{1.16} + \frac{41}{(1.16)^2} + \frac{50}{(1.16)^3} + \frac{63}{(1.16)^4} + \frac{79}{(1.16)^5} + \frac{100}{(1.16)^6} + \frac{124}{(1.16)^7} + \frac{155}{(1.16)^8} = 295$$

Discounted cash flow beyond planning horizon $\frac{453}{0.16} = 2{,}831$, then $\frac{2{,}831}{(1.16)^8}$ $= 864$

Marketable securities $= 110$

Corporate value $1{,}269$

Shareholder value = Corporate value − Debt
= £1,269,000 − £200,000
= £1,069,000

Exhibit 15.11	Shareholder value for the guttering firm under different discount and capital investment rates

£000s		Discount rate		
		15%	16%	17%
Incremental fixed capital investment rates	15%	1,205	1,069	951
	20%	1,086	955	843

One observation that may be made from Exhibit 15.11 is that even if the amount of incremental capital investment required rises to 20% of the increase in sales and the discount rate moves to 17% this strategy produces the highest value of all the four options considered. The management team may wish to consider the consequences and the likelihood of other variables changing from the original expected levels.

Targets, rewards and alignment of managerial effort

Following an initial shareholder value analysis, it can be useful to break down each of the seven Rappaport value drivers into more detail. So, for example, if the operating profit margin is 20% you could investigate what proportion of the 80% of income from sales flows out in the form of wages, or material costs, or overheads, etc. This will permit focus of managerial attention and allows performance measures and targets to be more detailed. Thus, the production manager can be set targets in terms of raw material wastage and shop floor employee efficiency. These operating targets can then feed into the goal to improve the operating margin and the goal of shareholder wealth maximisation. Similarly, managers with responsibility for fixed and working capital investment can agree targets that are aligned with those of all the other managers in terms of being focused on value.

Another use of this analytical method: the value drivers (and their component parts) can be used to benchmark the company against competitors. So, if, for example, you find that your firm has the highest level of work-in-progress inventory per unit of sales you may want to see if there are efficiency gains to be made.

Problems with shareholder value analysis

There are some disadvantages to the use of shareholder value analysis:

- Constant percentage increases in value drivers lack realism in some circumstances; in others it is a reasonable simplification.

- It can be misused in target setting; for example if managers are given a specific cash flow objective for a 12-month period they may be dissuaded from necessary value-enhancing investment (i.e. using cash) to achieve the short-term cash flow target. Alleviate this problem by setting both short- and long-term targets. The short-term ones may show negative cash flows.

- Data availability – many firms' accounting systems are not equipped to provide the necessary input data. The installation of a new cash flow-orientated system may be costly.

Alfred Rappaport discussed some of the stated 'flaws' in Shareholder Value Analysis in an article for the *Financial Times* in 2016 – see **Exhibit 15.12**.

Exhibit 15.12

What managers misunderstand about shareholder value. The reasoning over short-term orientations is deeply flawed

By Alfred Rappaport

Why do companies obsess over quarterly earnings and fail to invest adequately in long-term growth? And why would a company such as Volkswagen lie to its customers and government emission testers? Conventional wisdom places the blame squarely on the pursuit of shareholder value which, it is claimed, has fuelled pernicious short-term thinking and irresponsible behaviour.

That is wrong. The culprit is not shareholder value but rather corporate executives, investment managers and the business press who incorrectly believe that the governing objective of shareholder value is to boost a company's near-term stock price by meeting the market's quarterly earnings expectations. This misguided thinking has hijacked

the good name of "shareholder value". Consequently, companies commonly "talk" shareholder value but "walk" quarterly earnings in their everyday operations.

Let us be clear what managing for shareholder value really means. It means focusing on cash flow, not earnings. It means managing for the long-term, not the short-term. And it means that managers must take risk into account in their capital allocation decisions. Properly implemented, there is no better cure for short-termism than managing for shareholder value with its long-term orientation.

Critics also contend that shareholder value encourages the exploitation of other stakeholders. Quite the opposite is true. Shareholder value

▶

Exhibit 15.12 *(continued)*

companies recognise that their long-term success depends on a solid relationship with each of their stakeholders. Customers expect high-quality products and services at competitive prices. Companies that charge too much will lose customers. Those that charge too little will have happy customers today but will find it difficult to fund the investments needed to provide better products and services tomorrow. The challenge is to find the price that adds value for both customers and shareholders.

Likewise, employees seek competitive remuneration and a satisfying work environment. Paying employees too little ensures that a company will have a substandard workforce. Paying too much, as the US car industry discovered, damages a company's ability to remain competitive. Companies risk their viability if any one stakeholder gets too much or too little for an extended period.

The shareholder value concept also draws fire from critics who claim that it fails to address social issues such as the environment, global warming, poverty, and public health. Everybody wins when investments in socially responsible projects create shareholder value as well. But when companies invest in social initiatives at the expense of shareholder value, shareholders bear the cost through lower returns. The cost is ultimately borne by consumers through

higher prices and employees via lower wages and fewer jobs.

Companies can prioritise the interests of stakeholders or the public rather than those of their shareholders. However, to honour their fiduciary duty to their investors they should disclose the circumstances under which they would invest in social initiatives that are expected to yield returns below the minimum return required to create value.

Finally, many executives claim they have no choice but to adopt a short-term orientation given that the average holding period for shares in managed funds is only about one year. They do not feel compelled to consider the interests of long-term shareholders because there are none. This reasoning is deeply flawed. What should matter is not portfolio turnover but the time horizons of the beneficiaries, typically individuals who are saving to meet long-term needs.

Because companies have not done shareholder value right, critics have concluded that it is flawed. Such thinking is backward. Shareholder value has not failed management. Management has failed the true principles of shareholder value.

The writer is professor emeritus at the Kellogg School of Management and author of 'Creating Shareholder Value'.

Economic profit

Economic profit, EP (also called **residual income**), has an advantage over shareholder value analysis because it uses the existing accounting and reporting systems of firms by focusing on profit rather than cash flow information. Metrics that can use existing information without the need to overhaul data-collection and reporting procedures are attractive to management, especially when they use the familiar concept of profit. Managers used to 'bottom line' figures are more likely to understand and accept this metric than one based on cash flow information.

> Economic profit for a period is the amount earned by a business after deducting all operating expenses and a charge for the opportunity cost of the capital[5] employed.

A business only produces an economic profit if it generates a return greater than that demanded by the finance providers given the risk class of investment. There are two versions of economic profit.

---

5 The meaning of 'capital' here is different from its meaning in accounting. 'Capital' in accounting is a part of the shareholders' equity of the company ('capital issued', 'paid-in capital', etc.). 'Capital' in the present context means the sum of shareholders' equity (and of the borrowings of the company in the first version of EP), only some of which may be recognised in a balance sheet (see p. 677 for a discussion on 'invested capital').

1 The entity approach to EP

One version of EP is based on profit after tax but before interest is deducted. There are two ways to calculate this EP.

a   *The profit less capital charge method* Here a charge for the use of capital equal to the invested capital multiplied by the return required by the share and debt holders (which is a weighted average cost of the debt and the equity, WACC) is deducted from the operating profits after tax:

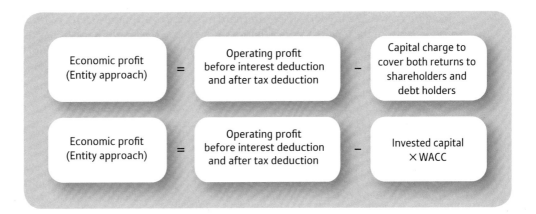

b   *The 'performance spread' method* The difference between the return achieved on invested capital and the weighted average cost of capital (WACC), i.e. the required rate of return, is the performance spread. This percentage figure is then multiplied by the quantity of invested capital to obtain EP:

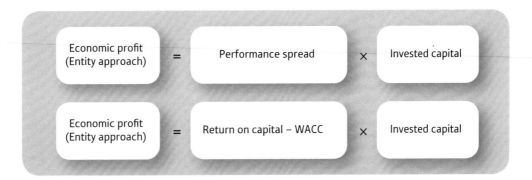

The WACC allows for an appropriate risk-adjusted return to each type of finance provider, debt as well as equity. As can be seen from the following illustration either method leads to the same EP.

Illustration

EoPs plc has a weighted average cost of capital (required rate of return) of 12% and has used £1,000,000 of invested capital (share and debt) to produce an operating profit before interest deduction and after tax of £180,000 during the past year.

Profit less capital charge approach

$$\text{EP} = \text{Operating profits before interest and after tax} - (\text{Invested capital} \times \text{WACC})$$
$$= £180{,}000 - (£1{,}000{,}000 \times 0.12)$$
$$= £60{,}000$$

Performance spread approach

$$EP = (\text{Return on capital} - WACC) \times \text{Invested capital}$$
$$= (18\% - 12\%) \times £1,000,000$$
$$= £60,000$$

2 The equity approach to EP

The entity EP approach (described above), based on operating profit before the deduction of interest, calculates the surplus above the return to *all* the finance providers to the business entity including the debt holders. The alternative is the 'equity approach'. With this, interest is deducted from the profit after tax figure, so we obtain the profit that belongs to the shareholders. The required return is the return demanded on the equity capital only. So, EP is the profit attributable to shareholders after a deduction for the implicit cost of employing shareholders' capital.

| Economic profit (Equity approach) | = | Operating profit after deduction of interest and tax | − | Invested equity capital | × | Required return on equity |

| Economic profit (Equity approach) | = | Return on equity − Required return on equity | × | Invested equity capital |

Illustration

In the case of EoPs let us assume that one half of the £1,000,000 of capital is equity and the other half debt. The equity required rate of return is 15% and the debt required rate of return is 9% (i.e. £45,000 per year), therefore the weighted average cost of capital (WACC) is 12% (that is, $(15\% \times 0.5) + (9\% \times 0.5) = 12\%$).

Profit less capital charge approach

Deducting £45,000 of interest from the operating profit figure we have £135,000.

$$EP(\text{equity}) = \text{Operating profits after interest and tax} - (\text{Invested equity capital} \times \text{Required return on equity})$$
$$= £135,000 - (£500,000 \times 0.15)$$
$$= £60,000$$

Performance spread approach

$$EP\ (\text{equity}) = (\text{Return on equity} - \text{Required return on equity}) \times \text{Invested equity capital}$$
$$= (27\% - 15\%) \times £500,000$$
$$= £60,000$$

The return on equity[6] is 27% (£135,000/£500,000).

---

6 See Appendix 15.1 for an understanding of how the entity EP equity value may differ from the equity EP equity value, and the care that is needed when making these calculations.

A short history of economic profit

The principles behind economic profit have a long antecedence. Economists are aware of the need to recognise the minimum return to be provided to the finance provider as a 'cost' of operating a business. Enlightened chief executives have taken account of the amount of capital used by divisional managers when setting targets and measuring performance, with some sort of implicit, or explicit, cost being applied. David Solomons (1965) formalised the switch from return on capital employed (ROCE) and other accounting rates of return measures to 'the excess of net earnings over the cost of capital as the measure of managerial success'. But even he drew on practical innovation that had taken place in a number of large companies.

Usefulness of economic profit

- A focus on EP rather than the traditional accounting profit has the advantage that every manager down the line is encouraged (rewarded) for paying close attention to the cost associated with using capital in a business unit, project, product line or the entire corporation. The introduction of EP targets has resulted in reductions in money tied up wastefully in assets such as raw material stocks, and to reductions in requests for major fixed capital expenditure. Managers who are judged on profits may not be as keen to reduce capital employed as those judged on EP.

- Economic profit can be used to evaluate strategic options that produce returns over several years. For example, Spoe plc is considering the investment of £2,000,000 in a new division that is expected to produce a consistent operating profit after tax of £300,000 per year to infinity without the need for any further investment in fixed capital or working capital in subsequent years. The company has a required rate of return on capital of 13%. The extra 'value' created on top of the initial investment of £2m is:

$$\text{Economic profit (entity) per year} = (\text{Return on capital} - \text{WACC}) \times \text{Invested capital}$$
$$= (15\% - 13\%) \times £2,000,000$$
$$= £40,000$$

The present value of this perpetuity is:

$$£40,000/0.13 = £307,692$$

This £307,692 is the additional value, in present terms, of economic profit. Of course, we can only call this value if we make the bold assumption that profit numbers bear a close resemblance to cash flow numbers (an assumption too frequently and too glibly made by consultant writers in this area) and there are challenges to this assumption. To obtain the total value of this division we add to this the initial investment:

$$\text{Value of new division} = \text{Present value of economic profit} + \text{Initial investment}$$
$$= £307,692 + £2,000,000 = £2,307,692$$

Having expressed the new strategy in terms of EP, EP targets are set annually and rewards for achieving (exceeding) those targets can be made.

- Economic profit has an advantage over shareholder value analysis in that it can be used to look back at how the firm (unit) has performed relative to the amount of capital used each year as well as creating future targets in terms of EP. Shareholder value analysis is generally used only in forward-looking mode. Once shareholder value analysis estimates have been made for a strategy it is possible to set interim targets, which, as time passes, are monitored so, in this sense, it can be used in backward-looking mode, i.e. within a plan. With EP, however, it is possible to go to a firm and examine past performance from scratch, without the need for pre-established plans.

- Economic profit per unit can be calculated: for example, economic profit per square foot or economic profit per unit of output. Economic profit sends a more powerful signal because it is expressed in absolute amounts of money generated for shareholders above the minimum required, e.g. £1.20 EP per unit sold, rather than a percentage, e.g. a profit margin of 14%. Profit margin metrics fail to allow for the size of the capital commitment.

The use of economic profit is becoming more widespread

Major US firms, including Walt Disney, PepsiCo and AT&T, have used economic profit as a performance measurement. The focus of economic profit on the productive use of capital can have profound consequences. Roberto Goizueta, CEO of Coca-Cola, put the basic philosophy this way: 'We raise capital to make concentrate, and sell it at an operating profit. Then we pay the cost of that capital. Shareholders pocket the difference.'[7] When Xerox adopted Six Sigma, an approach to problem solving developed by General Electric that emphasises small teams, measurement and economic return, it found a significant improvement. 'Six Sigma is very rigid and disciplined . . . Every project is managed with economic profit metrics. There is none of the squishy stuff . . . The learning process begins with taking out waste, working out where value gets added and where it does not,' says Xerox manager Anne Mulcahy.[8]

Barclays Bank adopted the technique in 2000 declaring their aim to double economic profit every four years. 'Economic profit comprises profit after tax and non-controlling interests, less a capital charge (average shareholders' equity . . . multiplied by Barclays cost of capital)' (2010 annual report). Barclays believed that economic profit encouraged both profitable growth and the efficient use of capital. For the next eight years it did rather well at generating economic profit. For example, the 2008 report stated that it produced economic profit of £1.76bn. It used the equity method with 'average shareholders' equity for economic profit purposes'. In 2008 this was £27,400m and the cost of equity was 10.5%. The capital charge was £2,876m. It also set four-year performance goals for the period 2008 to 2011. The primary goal was to achieve compound annual growth in economic profit in the range of 5% to 10% (£9.3bn to £10.6bn of cumulative economic profit) over the 2008 to 2011 goal period.

The financial crisis then intervened. Barclays made economic losses rather than profits. In its 2010 report it stated: 'The Group cost of capital has been applied at a uniform rate of 12.5%. From 1st January 2011 the Group's cost of capital has changed from 12.5% to 11.5%. Economic loss for the Group increased to £2,488m (2009: £1,890m) reflecting an increase of £916m profit for economic purposes more than offset by a £1,514m increase in the economic capital charge, due to a significant rise in average shareholders' equity' (it had increased the amount of share capital in the business).

It reported the following numbers:

	2010 £m	2009 £m
Profit for economic profit purposes (profit after tax and some technical adjustments)	3,892	2,976
Capital charge at 12.5% of average shareholders' equity for economic profit purposes	(6,380)	(4,866)
Economic loss	(2,488)	(1,890)

Because of the poor economic profit performance, the rewards to senior executives were greatly reduced in these years. Later annual reports do not discuss economic profit as a key metric.

---

7 Quoted in Tully, S. (1993) 'The real key to creating wealth', *Fortune Education Collection*, September 1993, p. 93.

8 *Financial Times,* 23 September 2005, p. 13.

Difficulties with economic profit

There are some disadvantages to the use of economic profit.

1 *The balance sheet does not reflect invested capital* Balance sheets are not designed to provide information on the present economic value of assets being used in a business. Assets are generally recorded at historic cost less depreciation, amortisation (reduction in intangibles) and depletion (e.g. reduction in oil reserves). With or without inflation, it does not take many years for these balance sheet values to deviate dramatically from the theoretically correct capital employed figures for most firms. Generally, balance sheets significantly understate the amount of capital employed, and this understatement therefore causes EP to appear high. Moreover, many businesses invest in assets that never find their way to a balance sheet. For example, some firms invest in building brands, developing intellectual property or customer relationships, with the pay-off arising years later. Accounting convention insists on such expenditures being written off against profits, as their value cannot be reliably measured, rather than being taken into the balance sheet as investments in assets. This means that both operating profit and capital invested are understated and so impact on the EP calculation. As the knowledge economy expands where intellectual property, customer relationships and brand are increasingly important, this problem grows with financial statements only reflecting part of the total invested. The early theorists in value measurement suggested using current values of assets. Depending on the circumstances, either (a) the sum of the resale value of individual assets, or (b) the replacement cost could be used. Much depends on the objective of the analysis:

- If the objective is to monitor past performance, examining the efficiency with which money invested was used, the historic amount seems relevant as the 'capital' figure. However, there will be many circumstances where the capital figure derived from a balance sheet does not reflect asset value, e.g. when assets were acquired decades before the current period.

- If you are monitoring current performance the replacement value or the sum of the resale value of individual assets may be most useful. The resale value may be very low when the assets are highly specific with little secondary market. In such a case relying on the resale value alone would give an artificially low asset value. In other circumstances the replacement value is above the level at which any manager would replace and so a more informed decision can be made by using the sum of resale values as this figure represents the opportunity cost of using the assets this year.

- If the asset value is needed to make future-oriented decisions then the resale value of the assets would be most useful because this would capture the opportunity cost – the firm could sell off these assets as an alternative. The sunk costs associated with past investment are not relevant in such a decision and so balance sheet values are not very useful.

- If the decision concerns obtaining new assets to implement a project/strategy, then the purchase cost is relevant.

Note that we use the 'sum of the resale value of individual assets' rather than the current market value of all-the-assets-when-welded-together-as-a-coherent-whole for the corporation/SBU because to use the latter would eliminate any value. For example, if a firm starts up with £1m of capital and a brilliant idea, immediately the strategy is put in place to exploit the idea the resale value of the firm as an operating entity rises to, say, £10m. That is, the resale value of the firm is equal to the initial capital plus the present value of the future cash flows or EPs. The £10m current market value of all-the-assets-when-welded-together-as-a-coherent-whole includes £9m of value, but the value of the sum of the individual assets is in the region of £1m.

2 *Manipulation and arbitrariness* Accounting data is open to manipulation and a degree of subjectivity. For example, if a business has sold goods on credit, some customers may fail to pay on the due date. The problem is to decide when particular debts will never be paid: is it after three months, six months or a year? Until they are declared 'bad debts' they are recorded as assets. At each balance sheet date judgement is required to establish an estimate of the value of the debtor balance to the firm. Similar flexibility and potential for manipulation is possible with the estimate of the length of life of an asset (which influences annual depreciation), and with R&D expenditure or inventory valuation.

Having a wide range of choices of treatment of key inputs to the financial statements makes comparability over time, and between companies, difficult.

3 ***High economic profit and negative NPV *can* go together*** Imagine a firm uses economic profit and divisional managers are judged on annual economic profit. Their bonuses and promotion prospects rest on good performance spreads over the next 12 months. This may prompt managers to accept projects with a positive EP over the short term whether or not they have positive life-time NPVs. Projects that produce poor or negative EPs in the first few years, for example biotechnology investments, will be rejected even if they will enhance shareholder wealth in the long term.

Another potential problem is that, during the life of a project, managers may be given specific EP targets for a particular year. To ensure the EP target is met, managers may cut down on expenditures such as training, marketing and maintenance. The target will be achieved but long-term damage may be inflicted. The CEO of Siemens, Klaus Kleinfield, was quoted in the *Financial Times*[9] saying that 'management pay is based on the "economic value added" each division provides against each year's budget. But a former senior director says this has led to a lack of investment in some parts of the business as managers look to earn as much as possible.'

A third value-destroying use of EP occurs when managers are demotivated by being set EP targets. For example, if managers have no control over the capital employed in their part of the business, they may become resentful of and cynical about value-based management if they are told nevertheless to achieve certain EP targets.

When examining the EP (or EVA) to judge performance, particularly in annual league tables, observers must be mindful of where the company is in its developmental cycle. Misleading impressions can occur where firms that are on a high value-creating path may have years where EP is low (or nil). Equally, there are firms on a value-destructive path which report high current-year EP. It is only possible to judge performance over several years. When EP is used internally to monitor performance against plan, however, it does make sense to produce annual (or even six-monthly) EP figures to see if the value-creation strategy is on target. Within the plan there will probably be periods of negative EP (e.g. in the start-up phase), as well as periods of high surpluses over the cost of capital.

4 ***Difficult to allocate revenues, costs and capital to business units, products, etc.*** To carry out EP analysis at the sub-firm level it is necessary to measure profit and capital invested separately for each area of the business. Many costs and capital assets are shared between business units, product lines and customers. It can be difficult to identify the proportion of the cost, debt or asset that is attributable to each activity. It can also be an expensive exercise.

Economic value added (EVA®)

Economic value added (EVA), developed and trademarked by the US consultants Stern Stewart & Co (now Stern Value Management), is a variant of EP. As a commercial product, significant resources were invested in the dissemination and marketing of EVA which is now recognised as a useful performance management tool, particularly in developed economies.

EVA = Adjusted invested capital × (Adjusted return on capital − WACC)

or

EVA = Adjusted operating profits after tax − (Adjusted invested capital × WACC)

EVA recognises that many of the investments made by a company in training, in marketing, in brand development which are written off as expenses in traditional financial statements, are in fact investments and EVA adjusts both profit and capital to reflect this view. The adjustments to profit and capital figures are meant to refine the basic EP.[10] Stern Stewart suggested that up to

9   6 November 2006, p. 24.

10 Notice that EVA is derived from the entity EP rather than equity EP because the WACC contains an allowance for a return to all finance providers including debt holders. Therefore, the 'adjusted invested capital' is equity plus debt capital.

164 adjustments to the accounting data may be needed. For example, spending on marketing and R&D helps build value and so if expenditure on these has been deducted in past years it is added back to the balance sheet as an asset (and amortised over the period expected to benefit from the expenditure). Goodwill on acquisitions previously written off is also returned and is expressed as an asset, thus boosting both profits and the balance sheet.

There are several difficulties with these adjustments – they are complex and require subjective decisions opening EVA up to opportunities for manipulation. For example, over what period should these reconstituted 'assets' be amortised? After all they are not expected to be valuable forever; they often gradually (or suddenly) fail to maintain their contributions to the firm, but we usually find it difficult to guess the period over which the deterioration happens.

EVA, like the generic EP, has the virtue of being based on familiar accounting concepts and it is arguably more accurate than taking ordinary accounting figures; but, the adjustments can be time consuming and costly, and many are subjective.

EVA provides a framework for executive compensation tying management reward into improved shareholder value. However, poorly implemented EVA reward systems can produce results that satisfy targets for EVA, but which produce poor decisions with regard to NPV. Furthermore, the problem of allocating revenue, costs and capital to business units and products is not solved by EVA.

The Stern Stewart definition of capital is 'the sum of all the cash that has been invested in a company's net assets over its life' (Stewart, 1991, p. 86). Imagine the difficulties in establishing this given that most invested cash put in will be in the form of many years of retained earnings. Added to this problem is the issue of accepting this capital figure as relevant for many decisions. For example, in judging future strategic plans perhaps the opportunity cost of those assets (the sum of the individual resale values) would be more relevant than what was paid for them, much of which may have become a sunk cost years ago (see Chapter 3). What is relevant is the opportunity cost of capital – the value of those assets in their best alternative use today not the money invested historically. Likewise, if you are monitoring managers' performance this year the historic cost of assets may be irrelevant to the analysis of their efficiency, whereas the money that they could have raised through the alternative of selling off the assets rather than operating them, might be of interest, as this may be the best alternative use.

Despite the outstanding problems companies see benefits from using EVA. Recent EVA results reported by companies show that like all other measures the context is critical. EVA numbers have been rising recently because, post financial crisis, companies have enjoyed lower than normal cost of capital due to low interest rates. This has allowed EVA to grow. Rises in costs and interest rates may cause EVA to fall. Then management will need to focus on driving sales to add value which may be difficult if consumer confidence is lacking.

When EVA was introduced, the positive approach to dissemination from Stern Stewart and the search by companies for better metrics produced a lot of interest in EVA. However, some of the issues raised above, not least the complexity of the adjustments required, have limited its widespread adoption. Recent concerns about executive pay and the need for it to be linked more directly to shareholder value, may reawaken interest in the method.

Exhibit 15.13 describes the performance of the engineering company IMI, which switched to EVA for the business and for managerial pay.

Exhibit 15.13

IMI's fairytale transformation

Martin Lamb has the perfect riposte to 'the UK can't do manufacturing'

By Alistair Blair

Fifty years ago IMI was a division of ICI, the once huge chemical conglomerate that disappeared from the stock market in 2007. IMI has been independent since 1978 but never seemed much more than a ▶

Exhibit 15.13 *(continued)*

doughty Midlands metal basher. Headquartered in a fortress-like edifice on the Birmingham site where it had been founded in 1862, it produced an awful lot of copper. Aspirational diversifications into pipes, valves and bar-top drinks dispensers added sales but not a lot of value.

This leopard has convincingly changed its spots via a textbook remodelling. The process started in January 2001 when Martin Lamb, then 40 and boss of the drinks dispenser division, was appointed chief executive. Mr Lamb set out a low-key manifesto in his first annual report, explaining that there would be changes to the composition of the group and earmarked £40m for immediate restructuring costs, including moving 1,200 jobs to emerging economies in Mexico, Eastern Europe and China.

Soon after, he indicated that Polypipe would go and IMI would focus on five global niche markets each worth at least £1bn a year, growing by at least 5%

annually and where after-sale support was at least as critical as product supply.

Many new chief executives start off with such aspirations, but find it hard to fulfil them. However, IMI has delivered in spades. In addition to the strategic initiatives, Mr Lamb adopted the doctrine of economic value added (EVA) as the group's key financial measure. EVA measures profit after charging for the capital involved in making the profit. Thus whereas a company that emphasises pure traditional accounting profit might boast higher profits without reference to a self-defeating expansion of its capital employed, an EVA system is more inclined to keep managers honest. IMI's share reward schemes, which have made Martin Lamb a very considerable fortune, are based on EVA.

EVA profit was £164m.

Shareholders are delighted. The shares moved from 200p to 600p.

Source: https://www.investorschronicle.co.uk/2011/09/08/comment/no-free-lunch/imi-s-fairytale-transformation-61gXT1obsCFjVNrgM1GCeI/article.html

Total shareholder return (TSR)

Shareholders are interested in the total return earned on their investment relative to general inflation, a peer group of firms, and the market. Total return includes dividends and share price changes over a specified period. For one-period TSR:

$$TSR = \frac{\text{Dividend per share} + (\text{Share price at end of period} - \text{Initial share price})}{\text{Initial share price}} \times 100$$

Consider a share that rises in price over a period of a year from £1 to £1.10 with a 5p dividend paid at the end of the year. The TSR is 15%.

$$TSR = \frac{d_1 + (P_1 - P_0)}{P_0} \times 100$$

$$TSR = \frac{0.05 + (1.10 - 1.00)}{1.00} \times 100 = 15\%$$

When dealing with multi-period TSRs we need to account for all the dividends received over the period. The TSR can be expressed either as a total return over the period or as an annualised rate.

For example, if a share had an initial price of £1, paid annual dividends at the end of each of the next three years of 9p, 10p and 11p and had a closing price of £1.30, the total average annual return (assuming dividends are reinvested in the company's shares immediately on receipt) is calculated via the internal rate of return (see Chapter 2 for IRR):

Time	0	1	2	3
Price/cash flow (p)	−100	9	10	11 + 130

$$-100 + \frac{9}{1 + r} + \frac{10}{(1 + r)^2} + \frac{141}{(1 + r)^3} = 0$$

At:

$r = 19\%: -1.7037$

$r = 18\%: 0.6259$

$$\text{The internal rate of return} = 18 + \frac{0.6259}{0.6259 + 1.7037} = 18.27\%$$

The annualised TSR is 18.27%.

The total shareholder return over the 3 years $= (1 + 0.1827)^3 - 1 = 65.4\%$.

In **Exhibit 15.14** the TSRs of the ten largest UK companies are shown for one year and for five years. Some perform better over one year relative to the others in the group; others perform better over five years. The 'dividend yield plus capital gain' metric needs to be used in conjunction with a benchmark to filter out economy-wide or industry-wide factors. So, it would make sense to compare the TSR for Unilever with the TSR for the household goods sector to be able to judge whether a particular performance is due to factors lifting the entire sector or is attributable to good management in the firm.

Exhibit 15.14	TSRs for the ten largest UK quoted companies over one year and five years to January 2018	
	TSR – 1 year %	TSR – 5 years %
HSBC	36	72
BP	58	49
Vodafone	−1	46
Royal Dutch Shell	60	23
GlaxoSmithKline	21	37
Unilever	20	76
Prudential	15	197
Tesco	45	−45
Lloyds	−5	167
Legal and General	2	227

Source: Data on share prices and dividends collected from a range of sources including London Stock Exchange, Hargreaves Lansdown and company websites.

TSR is a common long-term performance measure and is often used in director incentive schemes. For example, incentive payments to top executives at BP rest on TSR relative to the TSR of other major oil companies (the executives thus shared the pain after the 2010 Deepwater Horizon oil spill).

See the total return calculator under the share price information page at http://investors.baesystems.com.

Thoughtful use of the TSR

There are four issues to be borne in mind when making use of the TSR:

1 *Relate return to risk class* Two firms may have identical TSRs and yet one may be subject to more risk due to the greater volatility of earnings. The risk differential must be allowed for in any comparison. This may be particularly relevant in the setting of incentive schemes for executives. Managers may try to achieve higher TSRs by taking greater risk.

2 *Reliance on TSR means the user is assuming efficient share pricing* It is difficult to assess the extent to which a high share return is due to management performance and how much is due

to exaggerated/optimistic/pessimistic expectations of investors at the start and end of the period being measured. If the market is not efficient in pricing shares and is capable of being swayed by irrational optimism or pessimism, then TSR can be an unreliable guide to managerial performance. Even an efficient market often prices shares away from true economic value – it just does so in an unbiased manner.

3   *TSR is dependent on the period chosen* A TSR over a three-year period can look very different from a TSR measured over a one-year or ten-year period. Consider the annual TSRs for company W in **Exhibit 15.15**. Measured over the last two years the TSR of company W is very good. However, over five years a £1,000,000 investment grows to only £1,029,600, an annual rate of return of 0.6%.

4   *TSR cannot be used for companies not quoted on a stock market (over 99% of firms)*

Like all metrics, TSR must be used with caution. Incentive schemes allied to TSR can distort management behaviour by encouraging them to take more risk to improve the overall return or to reduce investment to improve cash flow and thus allow them to pay higher dividends or drive the share price higher. Performance bonuses dependent on one-year TSRs may result in managers being rewarded for general stock market movements beyond their control. Even worse would be the encouragement of the selective release of information to boost short-term TSR so that managers can trigger higher bonuses – see **Exhibit 15.16**.

Exhibit 15.15	Annual TSRs for company w	
	Annual TSR	**Value of £1m investment made at the end of 20X2**
20X3	+10%	£1,100,000
20X4	−20%	£880,000
20X5	−40%	£528,000
20X6	+30%	£686,400
20X7	+50%	£1,029,600

Exhibit 15.16

LEX, Cable & Wireless

Bashing fat cats is all the rage. So it is only fair to note when big pay incentives deliver results. Governance watchdogs bayed three years ago when Richard Lapthorne, chairman of Cable & Wireless, unveiled a private-equity style scheme to reward top managers working on a turnaround at the UK's second-biggest phone company. Love the scheme or hate it, the operator has delivered for shareholders – many of whom were initially against the incentive plan.

Including dividends, C&W returned 44.5 per cent to investors in the three years to the end of March. Total returns on the FTSE 100, meanwhile, were minus 27 per cent for the same period. C&W has beaten the UK benchmark by nearly 6 per cent since the collapse of Lehman Brothers. Investors should therefore not feel too aggrieved as managers pocket their first pay-outs. This year's planned windfall, of £32m, is a relatively small price to pay for the £1.4bn of market value added to the company since the scheme took effect.

Still, the 10 per cent fall in C&W's share price following its full-year results on Thursday suggests investors are antsy. Much of that comes down to disappointing sales growth and concern about earnings targets, rather than governance. But the fact that management felt compelled to respond to investor jitters about routine executive share sales during the earnings call suggests incentives remain a concern.

Now that C&W's incentive scheme has started to pay out, extra care is required to ensure that management's incentives remain broadly in line with those of shareholders. The link between future pay-outs and share price performance above a certain hurdle rate will keep them in line for now. As the rest of the plan unfolds, an increase in turnover among top executives, or excessive risk-taking, would be two signs that the incentives have come unstuck.

Financial Times, 21 May 2009.

Wealth Added Index (WAI)

The Wealth Added Index, promoted by consultant firm originally developed by Stern Stewart & Co, measures the increase in shareholders' wealth through dividends received and share capital gains (or losses) over time, say five years, after deducting the 'cost of equity', defined as the return required for shares of that risk class. It thus addresses one of the key criticisms of TSR by checking whether an increase in market capitalisation has produced a return greater than the investors' opportunity cost given the length of time over which the growth is measured.

To calculate the WAI:

- observe the rise in market capitalisation (the market value of all the shares) over, say, five years.

- deduct the rise that is due to the firm obtaining more money from shareholders in this period, for example from a rights issue.

- add back cash returned to shareholders in the form of dividends and share buy-backs.

- deduct the required return on the money shareholders committed to the company for the relevant period – this is the equity opportunity cost (*see* Chapter 16 for a discussion of opportunity cost of capital).

Under WAI analysis those companies whose share values grow by more than the return required by investors create value. Those that return less than the required return destroy value. Take the case of Vone plc over the five years to September 2017 (see **Case study 15.1**).

Case study 15.1   **Vone's wealth added index**

Vone plc had a market capitalisation of £61,685m on 18 September 2012. By 18 September 2017 this had grown to £88,291m. This seems an impressive rise, but to evaluate whether it is a good enough return we need to know whether shareholders put more money into the company in the intervening five years and whether the company paid out dividends or made share buy-backs. We want to judge whether the gain is more than or less than the required rate of return for shares of this risk class. The WAI takes these factors into account.

To calculate the WAI, we could consult the annual reports to establish the amount contributed to the company by shareholders in new share issues. This is £802m over the five years. We could also examine the accounts to find the amounts paid to shareholders in dividends and share buy-backs. Buy-backs were £20,628m and dividends were £10,650m, a total paid out of £31,278m.

The consultants use CAPM to calculate the cost of equity – see Chapter 8 for discussion of CAPM. The ten-year UK government bond yield in September 2012 was 1.6% – this is our risk-free rate of return (see Chapter 16 for a discussion on this). Beta is trickier because we ideally need to know the beta in 2012. We could search for a database which had historic betas, but we'll simply take 1.0 as the value. The equity risk premium can be taken as 5% – see Chapter 8 for a discussion on this. Thus, the required rate of return is

Over one year: $r_i = r_f + \beta(RP) = 1.6 + 1(5) = 6.6\%$

Over five years: $(1 + 0.066)^5 - 1 = 0.38$ or 38%.

▶

Case study 15.1 *(continued)*

	£m
Change in market capitalisation over five years (88,291 − 61,685)	26,606
Less the rise due to additional money injected by shareholders[11]	−802
Plus dividends, share buy-backs, etc.	31,278
Less required rate of return over five years £61,685 × 0.38	−23,440
Wealth Added Index	33,642

Thus, Vone added wealth to shareholders above their required rates during this five-year period. However, to put this into perspective the total return (dividends + capital gains) on the FTSE All Share index in the five years to 2017 was 63%. (FTSE Russell Fact Sheet – 29 December 2017)

Points to consider when using the WAI

- Stern Stewart relies on the CAPM to calculate the required return on share capital. There are serious problems with CAPM – *see* Chapter 8.

- There is an assumption that stock markets price shares correctly given company prospects at both the start and end dates. The experience of the tech bubble around the turn of the millennium and the crash of 2008 should have raised doubts here, let alone the evidence of share mispricing in the academic literature (*see* Chapter 13). So, one has to be sceptical as to whether outperformance is due to managerial skill or market movements. Volatile markets can turn an apparent 'wealth creator' into a 'wealth destroyer' which may have little to do with managerial performance.

- Critics say that the WAI, in most circumstances, is no better than the use of an appropriately benchmarked TSR (i.e. benchmarked against a group of peers). Certainly, in a period of declining share prices (e.g. 2000–3, or 2008) you will find that the clear majority of companies show depressingly negative WAI because the deduction of CAPM-required returns remains so high (usually between 6% and 10% per year). Comparing total return performance against peers (e.g. industry group) may be quicker, more informative and more just to the managers. At the heart of the problem is the artificiality of requiring companies to achieve increases in market capitalisation above a theoretical minimum rate in all market conditions and regardless of whether all similar companies are experiencing an industry or market-wide shock.

- Because the WAI measures in cash terms rather than percentages the biggest companies appear at the top (and bottom) of the league tables, pushing out smaller companies with higher percentage rates of return on shareholders' capital.

Market Value Added (MVA)

Stern Stewart has also developed the concept of Market Value Added (MVA). This looks at the difference between the total amount of capital put into the business by finance providers (debt and equity) and the current market value of the company's shares and debt. It provides a measure of how executives have performed with the capital entrusted to them. A positive MVA is supposed to indicate that value has been created. A negative MVA supposedly indicates value has been destroyed.

---

11 To follow Stern Stewart's recommendation strictly we should recognise that any new funds raised from shareholders over the period require a rate of return. Thus, the cost of equity capital should be applied to the new funds from shareholders from the date that the money was raised to the end date – thus there should be a further deduction which is not shown to keep the example reasonably simple.

$$\text{MVA} = \text{Market value} - \text{Invested capital}$$

where:

Market value   =   Current value of debt, preference shares and ordinary shares.

Invested capital   =   All the cash raised from finance providers or retained from earnings to finance new investment in the business, since the company was founded. In practice, balance asset values (with a few adjustments) are used.

Managers can push up the conventional yardstick, total market value of the business, simply by investing more capital. The MVA, by subtracting capital injected or retained from the calculation, measures net value generated for shareholders.

Worked example 15.1   Illustration of MVA

MerVA plc was founded 20 years ago with £15m of equity finance. It has no debt or preference shares. All earnings have been paid out as dividends. The shares in the company are now valued at £40m. The MVA of MerVA is therefore £25m:

$$\text{MVA} = \text{Market value} - \text{Capital}$$
$$\text{MVA} = £40m - £15m = £25m$$

If the company now has a rights issue raising £5m from shareholders the market value of the firm must rise to at least £45m for shareholder wealth to be maintained. If the market value of the shares rose to only £44m because shareholders are doubtful about the returns to be earned when the rights issue money is applied within the business (that is, a negative NPV project) shareholders will lose £1m of value. This is summarised in the table below.

	Before rights issue	After rights issue
Market value	£40m	£44m
Capital	£15m	£20m
MVA	£25m	£24m

According to Stern Stewart if a company pays a dividend both the 'market value' and the 'capital' parts of the equation are reduced by the same amount, and MVA is unaffected. Imagine an all-equity financed company with an equity market value of £50m at the start of the year, which increased to £55m by the end of the year after generating £10m of post-tax profit in the year and the payment of a £6m dividend. The capital put into the firm by shareholders over the company's life by purchasing shares and retained earnings amounted to £20m at the start of the year, as shown in the table below.

	At start of year		At end of year
Market value	£50m		£55m
Capital	£20m	£20m	
	plus earnings	£10m	
	less dividend	−£6m	
			£24m
MVA	£30m		£31m

If the company had not paid the dividend then, according to Stern Stewart, both the market value and the capital rise by £6m and the MVA would remain at £31m, as shown in the next table.

▶

Worked example 15.1 *(continued)*

	At start of year	At end of year
Market value	£50m	£61m
Capital	£20m	£30m
MVA	£30m	£31m

This dividend policy irrelevance argument is challenged in Chapter 19, where it is shown that increasing or decreasing the dividend may add value. The point to take from this section is that profits produced by the business are just as much part of the ownership capital as money raised through the sale of shares to owners at the foundation of the business or in later years. If £1 is to be retained rather than paid out to shareholders, then market capitalisation should rise by £1 to avoid loss of shareholder value. If it does not, then that £1 can be put to a better use outside the firm.

A short cut

In the practical application of MVA analysis it is often assumed that the market value of debt and preference shares equals the book value of debt and preference shares. This permits the following version of the MVA, cutting out the necessity to obtain data for the debt levels (market value or balance sheet value) or the preference share values:

MVA = Market value of ordinary shares − Capital supplied by ordinary shareholders

Judging managerial performance by an MVA

The absolute level of MVA is perhaps less useful for judging performance than the change in MVA over a period. Alistair Blair, writing in *Management Today*,[12] was quite scathing about crude MVA numbers:

> An MVA includes years old and now irrelevant gains and losses aggregated on a pound-for-pound basis with last year's results and today's hope or despair, as expressed in the share price. Surely, what we are interested in is current performance, or if we're going to be determinedly historic, performance since the current top management team got its hands on the controls.

Although from 1997, these concerns remain relevant today. Alistair Blair is questioning the usefulness of a 'lifetime' performance measure when what we want to do is isolate the value-creating contribution of the current leadership.

Points to consider when using an MVA

There are several issues to be borne in mind when using MVA.

● **Estimating the amount of cash invested** Measuring the amount of capital put into and retained within a business after it has been trading for a few years is fraught with problems. For example, does R&D expenditure produce an asset (i.e. become part of shareholders' funds) or is it an expense to be written off the profit and loss account? How do you treat goodwill on acquisitions? The accountants' balance sheet is not designed for measuring capital supplied by finance providers, but at least it is a starting point. Stern Stewart make use of a proxy measure called 'economic book value'. This is based on the balance sheet capital employed figure, subject to a number of adjustments. Critics have pointed out that these adjustments are rather arbitrary and complex, making it difficult to claim that economic book value equals the theoretically correct 'capital' in most cases.

---

12 Alistair Blair, *Management Today,* January 1997, p. 44.

- **When was the value created?** The fact that a positive MVA is produced is often of limited use when it comes to evaluating the quality of the current managers. For a company that is a few decades old the value drivers may have been put in place by a previous generation of directors and senior managers. The MVA measure can be considered crude in that it measures value created over the entire life of the firm but fails to pinpoint when it was created. Nor does it indicate whether value creation has stopped, and the firm is living off accumulated fat in terms of strong market positions, patents, etc. Ideally, we need to know whether new value-creating positions are being constructed rather than old ones being eroded.

- **Is the rate of return high enough?** It is difficult to know whether the amount of MVA generated is sufficiently in excess of capital used to provide a satisfactory return relative to the risk-adjusted time value of money. Positive MVA companies can produce poor rates of return. Take company B in Worked example 15.2. Firm B has a much lower rate of return on capital than A and yet it has the same MVA.

Worked example 15.2

	A	B
MVA	£50m	£50m
Market value	£100m	£100m
Capital	£50m	£50m
Age of firm	3 years	30 years

Both firms have paid out profits each year as dividends; therefore the capital figure is the starting equity capital.

- **Inflation distorts the MVA** If the capital element in the equation is based on a balance sheet figure then during times of inflation the value of capital employed may be understated. If capital is artificially lowered by inflation vis-à-vis current market value for companies where investment took place a long time ago, then the MVA will appear to be superior to that for a similar firm with recently purchased assets.

- **Trusting that the stock market prices shares correctly at all times.**

- **The MVA is an absolute measure** Judging companies based on absolute amounts of pounds means that companies with larger capital bases will tend to be at the top (and bottom) of the league tables of MVA performance. Size can have a more significant impact on the MVA than efficiency. This makes comparison between firms of different sizes difficult. The market to book ratio, MBR, described below, is designed to alleviate this problem.

- Two companies showing the same MVA can produce different levels of real wealth for shareholders – *see* the example of AVerseM in the next section.

Excess return (ER)

Two of the major drawbacks of the MVA are illustrated in the case of AVerseM. This company was established five years ago with £10m of equity capital (assume no debt throughout the example). At that time equity at this level of risk was required to produce a return of 10% per year. The company made after-tax profits of £1m in its second year and £1m in its third year (zero in the other years). These profits were paid out as dividends in the year of occurrence. AVerseM now has a market capitalisation of £11m and is therefore showing a MVA of £1m.

MVA = Market value − Invested capital
Invested capital = Original capital + Retained earnings = £10m + £0m
MVA = £11 − £10m = £1m

[Stern Stewart defines capital as 'essentially a company's net assets (total assets less non-interest-bearing current liabilities)' (Stewart, 1991, p. 744) rather than strictly the amount of money put into the business by investors. They make three major groups of adjustments to the raw balance sheet numbers, such as adding the capital value of leases and adding back R&D expenses previously written off, to try to get closer to the amount put into the business by investors, but using balance sheet numbers for a firm that has operated for a number of years must be considered crude.]

If the original £10m put into AVerseM had been invested elsewhere to yield its required rate of return for the same risk, 10%, today shareholders would hold an investment worth £16.1m:

$$10 (1 + 0.1)^5 = £16.1m$$

Determining whether AVerseM has achieved shareholder wealth creation is far from clear with the MVA, even if we had a precise 'invested capital' figure. Notice how the MVA has ignored the value of dividends. If there was another company that also started with £10m of capital and has a current market capitalisation of £11m, but has made no profits and paid no dividends over the five years, it would also show an MVA of £1m, despite the fact that it has not generated as much wealth for shareholders as AVerseM.

Also notice that the time value of money is not allowed for (the third problem listed for the MVA). To cope with these two problems, we could use **excess return, ER**.[13] This metric examines the amount of capital invested in previous years and then charges the company for its use over the years. It also credits companies for the returns shareholders can make from the money paid to them (e.g. as dividends) when re-invested in the market.

Excess return expressed in present value terms	=	Actual wealth expressed in present value terms	−	Expected wealth expressed in present value terms

Expected wealth is calculated as the value of the initial investment in present value terms if it had achieved the required rate of return over the time it has been invested in the business. So, for AVerseM this is £16.1m. (Of course, if AVerseM had raised more money from shareholders, in, say, the fourth year, through a rights issue, we would include that here too.)

Actual wealth is the present values of cash flows received by shareholders, plus the current market value of the shares. Each cash flow received in past years needs to be compounded up to the present.

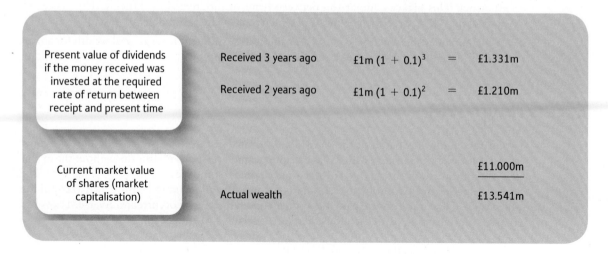

Present value of dividends if the money received was invested at the required rate of return between receipt and present time	Received 3 years ago	$£1m (1 + 0.1)^3$	=	£1.331m
	Received 2 years ago	$£1m (1 + 0.1)^2$	=	£1.210m
Current market value of shares (market capitalisation)				£11.000m
	Actual wealth			£13.541m

---

13 This method is promoted by Young and O'Byrne (2001) in their book.

Excess return = Actual wealth − Expected wealth
Excess return = £13.541 − £16.1m = −£2.559m

Value has been destroyed as the return achieved is less than 10% per year.

Expected return suffers from many of the other drawbacks associated with the MVA, such as finding the figure for the capital injected by shareholders for a company that has traded for many years, faith that the market will price the shares correctly and the fact that because it is an absolute measure rather than a percentage it favours larger firms when making comparisons. There is also the difficulty of selecting the required rate of return (*see* Chapters 8 and 16).

Also, if inflation turned out to be much higher than anticipated when the bulk of the capital was invested, ER will be distorted as nominal returns on the stock market rise, lifting the current market value of shares.

Market to book ratio (MBR)

Rather than using the arithmetical difference between the capital raised and the current value, as in the MVA, the MBR is the market value divided by the capital invested. If the market value of debt can be taken to be the same as the book value of debt, then a version of the MBR is the ratio of the market value of the company's ordinary shares to the amount of capital provided by ordinary shareholders (if preference share capital can be regarded as debt for value-based management).

There is, of course, the problem of estimating the amount of capital supplied, as this is usually dependent on adjusted balance sheet net asset figures. For example, goodwill write-offs and other negative reserves are reinstated, as in the MVA. It is also suggested that asset values be expressed at replacement cost so that the MBR is not too heavily distorted by the effects of inflation on historic asset figures.

Worked example 15.3 **Illustration of the MBR**

MaBaR plc has an equity market value of £50m, its book debt is equal to the market value of debt, and the capital contributed by ordinary shareholders amounts to £16m.

Market value	£50m
Capital	£16m
MVA	£34m
MBR £50m/£16m	= 3.125

MaBaR has turned every pound put into the firm into £3.125 (if the capital figure is money put into the firm).

The rankings provided by the MBR and the MVA differ sharply. The largest companies dominating the MVA ranks generally have lower positions when ordered in terms of MBR. The MBR suffers from the problems listed for the MVA, except for the issue of measuring in absolute amounts of money. An additional problem for the MBR is that care must be taken when using the MBR for performance measurement and target setting because if it is wrongly applied it is possible for positive NPV projects to be rejected in order for MBR to be at a higher level. Take the case of a company with an MBR of 1.75 considering fundraising to make an investment of £10m in a project estimated to produce a positive NPV of £4m. Its MBR will fall even though the project is shareholder wealth enhancing (*see* Worked example 15.4).

Worked example 15.4				
		Before project		**After project acceptance**
Value of firm		£70m	(70 + 10 + 4)	£84m
Capital		£40m		£50m
MVA		£30m		£34m
MBR	70/40 =	1.75	84/50 =	1.68

The new project has an incremental MBR of 1.4 (14/10 = 1.4). This is less than the firm's original overall MBR of 1.75, which is therefore dragged down by the acceptance of the project. This effect should be ignored by managers motivated by shareholder wealth enhancement. They will focus on NPV.

The techniques reviewed are summarised below – *see* **Exhibit 15.17**.

Exhibit 15.17	Summary table of market-based performance metrics

	Merits	Problems
TSR	• Very easy to understand and calculate.	• Vulnerable to distortion by the selection of period over which it is measured.
	• Not affected by the problems of having to rely on accounting balance sheet values.	• Need to express the TSR relative to a peer group to compare performance.
	• Subjective and complex adjustments are avoided.	• It fails to relate risk to the TSR.
	• Not affected by relative size of firms.	• Assumes stock market perfection in share pricing.
	• Better able to identify when value is created than are the MVA and the MBR.	• Useless for firms without a quotation.
WAI	• Relates return to risk class by allowing for opportunity cost of capital.	• There are doubts about the CAPM as a method of calculating the required rate of return.
	• No need to make a (dubious) estimation of the amount of capital injected into a business from its balance sheet.	• The assumption of stock market pricing efficiency can be challenged.
	• Better able to identify when value is created than the MVA and the MBR.	• In bear markets most companies show negative WAI for years, despite the management performing well against their sector or the market.
		• Cannot be used for unquoted companies.
		• Affected by relative size of firms – favours large firms.
MVA	• Assesses wealth generated over entire business life.	• Many doubts about the validity of the capital invested figure used.
	• Managers judged on the MVA have less incentive to invest in negative NPV projects than those judged on earnings growth.	• Excessive faith in the correct pricing of shares by stock markets.
	• Measures in absolute amounts of money.	• Size of business not allowed for in inter-firm comparisons.
		• Do not know in which part of the firm's history the value was created.
		• Inflation can distort the MVA.
		• Do not know if rate of return obtained is higher or lower than the required rate or return given the opportunity cost of capital.

Exhibit 15.17	Summary table of market-based performance metrics

	Merits	Problems
MVA		• Do not know if rate of return obtained is higher or lower than the required rate of return given the opportunity cost of capital. • Two firms with the same MVA may have generated different levels of wealth for shareholders because the MVA fails to allow properly for dividends paid in previous years.
ER	• Allows for the time value of money on shareholder funds put into the business. • Gives credit for dividends received by shareholders. • Assesses wealth generated over the entire life of the firm. • Managers judged on an ER have less incentive to invest in negative NPV projects than those judged on earnings growth. • Measures in absolute amounts of money.	• Size of business not allowed for in inter-firm comparisons. Larger companies tend to produce the better ERs. • Excessive faith in the correct pricing of shares by stock markets. • There is difficulty in selecting the appropriate required rate of return, especially if inflation has varied considerably. • Useless for firms without a quotation for their shares.
MBR	• Assesses wealth generated over entire business life. • Measures in percentage terms and therefore allows comparison between firms of all sizes.	• Same problems as the MVA except it is not an absolute measure and therefore does not favour larger firms. • Over-reliance on the MBR for performance measurement and incentive schemes can lead to bad investment decisions. • Useless for those firms without a market quote for their shares.

A final article – see **Exhibit 15.18** – reviewing some of the metrics discussed in this chapter underlines the difficulties faced in implementing these in practice and the ongoing and unresolved debate about which metrics are most appropriate.

Exhibit 15.18

Tesco fiasco fuels fears executive pay metrics can skew priorities

Critics say a range of other factors must also be used to assess managerial performance

By Steve Johnson

The latest fiasco at Tesco – where four executives were suspended after the discovery of a £250m black hole in its accounts, sending the shares spinning to an 11-year low – came out of the blue. But some canny investors had long steered clear of the UK's largest retailer. Terry Smith, the plain-speaking chief executive of investment house Fundsmith, for instance, said in the FT earlier this month that

▶

Exhibit 15.18 *(continued)*

investors had long ignored warning signs. Mr Smith showed that Tesco's return on capital employed (ROCE) had fallen sharply between 1998 and 2011. Yet during this period the retailer was lauded because its earnings per share (EPS), on which analysts and investors are far more fixated, rose fourfold.

This in turn raised questions, among some FT readers at least, about the metrics Tesco uses to calculate executive remuneration, and whether this might have led bosses to prioritise EPS over ROCE. As it happens, both measures are used to calculate executives' long-term bonuses, with Tesco saying "the best way to deliver value is to increase earnings over the long term while maintaining a sustainable level of return on capital employed". This is unlikely to make the issue disappear.

Deloitte's annual review of FTSE 100 directors' pay packets, published this month, found total shareholder return (TSR) is a determinant (either solely or in conjunction with other measures) of 75 per cent of FTSE directors' long-term incentive plans, while EPS is "one of the primary measures" in 55 per cent of plans. This pattern holds despite the Pension Fund Investors, an industry grouping arguing there has been an "over emphasis on measures such as EPS or TSR". In contrast, "return measures", which include return on equity (ROE) – which has its own critics – as- well as return on capital, are a factor in only 30 per cent of plans, Deloitte found, most commonly in the retail and services sectors.

Mr Smith is not the only one to question this. As he points out, Warren Buffett said way back in 1979: "The primary test of managerial economic performance is the achievement of a high earnings rate on equity capital employed [without undue leverage, accounting gimmickry etc.] and not the achievement of consistent gains in earnings per share."

APG Asset Management, which runs €374bn on behalf of 4.5m Dutch pension scheme members, is exercised about the widespread use of TSR, which encompasses share price appreciation and dividend pay-outs. As with EPS, there is a view that managers can game this measure by prioritising share buybacks. The use of these measures may also deter managers from making long-term investments that may be highly profitable in the fullness of time.

"In theory and at first glance [TSR] is a good way of aligning shareholders' interests, but it creates an incentive to manage earnings and even the share price, through buybacks, rather than invest in a project that creates value over 35 years," says Herman Bots, head of fundamental equities at APG. Leon Kamhi, a director at Hermes Equity Ownership

Services, which advises more than 30 institutional investors in 10 countries with combined assets of £109bn, concurs, saying remuneration metrics should not encourage a pharmaceutical company to cut back on research and development, or a consumer goods group to slash marketing expenditure.

APG, which has just issued its first remuneration guidelines for the companies it invests in, says it is "concerned about overly complex incentives or incentives that seem vulnerable to the risk of manipulation of corporate activity to improve pay-outs. "In the most basic terms, we believe that long-term value creation to shareholders is the added economic value over and above the cost of capital. We believe pay policies should be set to reflect and support this."

The head of executive compensation at one professional services firm, who declined to be named, says the use of ROCE as a determinant of executive pay is more commonplace at American companies, or non-US businesses that have a significant US shareholder base, than in the UK. This reflects its greater use in fundamental stock analysis in the US. Yet even this measure has its critics. Mr Kamhi says it has a "downside", in that a narrow focus on maximising ROCE can produce "a very profitable business, but a very small business". For instance, if a company has a ROCE of 30 per cent, this figure will fall if it embarks on a project with an estimated ROCE of 20 per cent. A ROCE maximiser would therefore shun this investment. Yet if the company's cost of capital is 10 per cent, taking on this project would still increase its profitability. Mr Kamhi instead suggests ROCE should be used in combination with a measure of profit, such as economic value added or economic profit. He also says industry-specific factors should be built into the remuneration equation, such as for retailers, sales per square foot.

APG is in favour of the additional use of non-financial factors, such as customer satisfaction, human capital, health and safety and sustainability performance, in determining pay, alongside consideration of pay differentials across the company. The Deloitte report suggests companies are increasingly using a matrix of factors to determine long-term incentive plans.

Whereas 10-15 years ago TSR or EPS were typically used in isolation, only 15 per cent of FTSE 100 companies now base share awards on a single metric. Measures of cash flow and revenues or sales are becoming more commonplace, while 10 blue-chip UK companies now use non-financial measures as well, although Deloitte cautions "there is not a lot of detail disclosed" about them. This in turn creates a new conundrum. Most investors are calling for a wider range of factors to be fed into the calculation of executive pay, yet most investors also insist that the methodology used should be clear and transparent. Satisfying both of these demands may be less than straightforward.

The metrics used to calculate remuneration

Earnings per share (EPS) A company's net income divided by the number of shares in issuance. Can potentially be gamed by using excess leverage (thereby increasing risk and weakening companies' capital bases) to increase net income, or through excessive use of buybacks to reduce the number of shares in issue. Can also act as a disincentive to long-term investment.

Total shareholder return (TSR) A combination of share price appreciation (or depreciation) and dividend pay-outs over a period of time. Can be gamed in the same manner as EPS.

Return on equity (ROE) The amount of net income returned as a percentage of shareholders' equity. It ignores the quantum of debt deployed, and as a result its use in determining executive pay has been blamed for encouraging excessive leverage, particularly in the banking sector before the financial crisis.

Return on capital employed (ROCE) As above, except that it encompasses debt as well as equity. A potential downside is that it can deter profitable investments that may nevertheless reduce a company's ROCE.

Concluding comments

This chapter has described several value-based metrics. The foundation for all of them is discounted cash flow allowing for a suitable return on the funds invested.

Rather than selecting one value metric, many companies, for both strategic investment discussion and performance targeting and measurement, will use both cash flow and economic profit targets. This counters some of the problems raised by using each separately and helps to alleviate short-termism; the tendency of managers to focus on short-term targets at the expense of long-term wealth. However, managers must remain aware of the drawbacks of each approach so that they do not use these metrics inappropriately. The five market-based measures should also be used in a complementary way. Relying on one indicator is unnecessarily restrictive. It is possible to use several measures simultaneously and thereby overcome many of the individual weaknesses.

Key points and concepts

- **Discounted cash flow** is the bedrock method underlying value management metrics. It requires the calculation of future annual free cash flows attributable to both shareholders and debt holders, then discounting these cash flows at the weighted average cost of capital.

- **Corporate value (Enterprise value)** equals present value of free cash flows from operations plus the value of non-operating assets.

- **Shareholder value from operations** equals present value of free cash flows from operations minus debt.

- **Total shareholder value** equals shareholder value of free cash flows from operations plus the value of non-operating assets.

- **Investment after the planning horizon does not increase value.**

- **Shareholder value analysis** simplifies discounted cash flow analysis by employing **(Rappaport's) seven value drivers,** the first five of which change in a consistent fashion from one year to the next.

▶

- **Rappaport's seven value drivers:**

  1 Sales growth rate.
  2 Operating profit margin.
  3 Tax rate.
  4 Fixed capital investment.
  5 Working capital investment.
  6 The planning horizon.
  7 The required rate of return.

- **At least four strategic options should be considered** for a SBU or product and/or market segment:

  - base-case strategy;
  - liquidation;
  - trade sale or spin-off;
  - new operating strategy.

- **Merits of shareholder value analysis:**

  - easy to understand and apply;
  - consistent with share valuation;
  - makes value drivers explicit;
  - able to benchmark.

- **Problems with shareholder value analysis:**

  - constant percentages unrealistic;
  - can lead to poor decisions if misused;
  - data often unavailable.

- **Economic profit (EP)** is the amount earned after deducting all operating expenses and a charge for the opportunity cost of the capital employed. A major advantage over shareholder value analysis is that it uses accounting data.

- **The entity approach to EP**

  a The profit less capital charge method

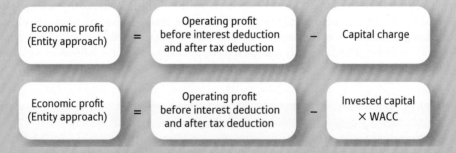

  b The 'performance spread' method

● **The equity approach to EP**

| Economic profit (Equity approach) | = | Operating profit after deduction of interest and tax | − | Invested equity capital | × | Required return on equity |

| Economic profit (Equity approach) | = | Return on equity − Required return on equity | × | Invested equity capital |

● **Usefulness of economic profit:**

  ● Managers become aware of the value of the investment in an SBU, product line or entire business.
  ● Can be used to evaluate strategic options.
  ● Can be used to look back at past performance.
  ● Economic profit per unit can be calculated.

● **Difficulties in using EP:**

  ● the balance sheet does not reflect invested capital;
  ● open to manipulation and arbitrariness;
  ● high economic profit and negative NPV can go together;
  ● problem with allocating revenues, costs and capital to business units.

● **Economic value added (EVA®)** is an attempt to overcome some of the accounting problems of standard EP.

  $$\text{EVA} = \text{Adjusted invested capital} \times (\text{Adjusted return on capital} - \text{WACC})$$

  or

  $$\text{EVA} = \text{Adjusted operating profit after tax} - (\text{Adjusted invested capital} \times \text{WACC})$$

● **Total shareholder returns (TSR)**

  Single period:

  $$\text{TSR} = \frac{\text{Dividend per share} + (\text{Share price at end of period} - \text{Initial share price})}{\text{Initial share price}}$$

  Multi-period:

  Allow for intermediate dividends in an internal rate of return calculation.

● **Wealth Added Index (WAI)**

  $$\text{WAI} = \text{Change in market capitalisation over a number of years}$$

  Less net additional money put into business by investors after allowance for money returned to investors by dividends, etc.

  Less required rate of return

● **Market Value Added (MVA)**

  $$\text{MVA} = \text{Market value} - \text{Invested capital}$$

  or, if the market value of debt (and preference shares) equals the book value of debt (and preference shares):

  $$\text{Equity MVA} = \text{Ordinary shares' market value} - \text{Capital supplied by ordinary shareholders}$$

▶

- **Excess return (ER)**

Excess return expressed in present value terms	=	Actual wealth expressed in present value terms	−	Expected wealth expressed in present value terms

Expected wealth is calculated as the value of the initial investment (plus any other monies placed in the business by shareholders) in present value terms if it had achieved the required rate of return over the time it has been invested in the business. Actual wealth is the present values of cash flows received by shareholders, plus the current market value of the shares. Each cash flow received in past years needs to be compounded up to the present:

Actual wealth	=	Present value of dividends if the money received was invested at the required rate of return between receipt and present time	+	Current market value of shares (market capitalisation)

- **Market to book ratio (MBR)**

$$MBR = \frac{Market\ value}{Capital\ invested}$$

An alternative is the equity MBR:

$$MBR = \frac{Market\ value\ of\ ordinary\ shares}{Amount\ of\ capital\ invested\ by\ ordinary\ shareholders}$$

References and further reading

Abdeen, A.M. and Haight, T. (2011) 'A fresh look at economic value added: Empirical study of the fortune five-hundred companies', *Journal of Applied Business Research*, 18(2).

This article focuses on the uses, benefits and limitations of economic value added (EVA) as a value creation measure

Aggarwal, R. (2001) 'Using economic profit to assess performance: A metric for modern firms', *Business Horizons,* Jan/Feb, pp. 55–60.

A brief overview of the issues raised by implementing an EP-based programme.

Anderson, A.M., Bey, R.P. and Weaver, S.C. (2005) 'Economic Value Added® adjustments: Much ado about nothing?' Working Paper. Bethlehem, PA: Lehigh University.

Casts doubt on the usefulness of moving away from EP. EVA's adjustments from accounting income and capital do not make much difference to residual income.

Arnold, G.C. and Davies, M. (eds) (2000) *Value-Based Management*. London: John Wiley & Sons.

A collection of research monographs.

Barker, R. (2001) *Determining Value: Valuation models and financial statements*. Harlow: Financial Times Prentice Hall.

Provides a detailed discussion of economic profit, EVA and shareholder value analysis and CFROI. Good if you are keen on model proofs and theoretical linkages between the metrics.

Bergman, J. and Van Cieaf, M, (2012) 'Total Shareholder Return (TSR) and management performance: A performance metric appropriately used, or mostly abused?', *Rotman International Journal of Pension Management*, 5(2), pp. 26–33.

This article identifies the complex issues associated with the use of total shareholder return (TSR) as a metric to represent the gains (or otherwise) in shareholder wealth.

Cheremushkin, V.S. (2008). What's wrong with the Economic Value Added?. [Online] Available: http://ssrn.com/abstract=1120917.

This paper looks at how the capital charge used in EVA is and should be calculated.

Davies, M. (2000) 'Lessons from practice: VBM at Lloyds TSB', in Arnold, G.C. and Davies, M. (eds) *Value-Based Management*. London: John Wiley & Sons.

Insights into a company making use of VBM principles.

Davies, M., Arnold, C., Cornelius, I. and Walmsley, S. (2001) *Managing for Shareholder Value*. London: Informa.

An overview of shareholder value management for practitioners.

Fernández, P. (2001) 'EVA and cash value added do NOT measure shareholder value creation', available at http://papers.ssrn.com/sol3/papers.cfm?abstract_id=270799

Empirical evidence casting doubt on the connection between high EVA and high returns to shareholders.

Fernández, P. (2002) *Valuation and Shareholder Value*. San Diego, CA: Academic Press. Available electronically at Amazon.co.uk (free).

A thought-provoking book on value.

Fernández, P. (2008) 'Three residual income valuation methods and discounted cash flow valuation', available at http://papers.ssrn.com/sol3/papers.cfm?abstract_id=296945

A theoretical paper to prove the links between various value metrics in a simplified world.

Fernández, P., Aguirreamalloa, J. and Corres, L. (2010) 'Shareholder value creators in the S&P 500: 1991–2010', available at www.ssrn.com

A paper that uses a measure very similar to excess return to calculate value created by each of the 500 companies.

Martin, J.D. and Petty, J.W. (2000) *Value Based Management: Corporate response to the shareholder revolution*. Boston, MA: Harvard Business School Press.

There are good chapters on free cash flow and CFROI.

McClatchey, Christine. (2011) 'Using EVA as a decision metric in capital budgeting', . *Journal of Applied Business Research*, 20(4).

This paper measures the usefulness of EVA as a metric in making capital budgeting decisions.

McKinsey and company (Koller, T., Goedhart, M. and Wessel, D.) (2015) *Valuation*. 6th edn. New York: John Wiley & Sons.

The management of value-based organisations and the principles behind the techniques are explained.

McKinsey (Koller, T., Goedhart, M. and Wessel, D.) (2011) *Value: The four cornerstones of corporate finance*. New York: John Wiley & Sons.

A short guide to value principles by consultants.

Raiyani, J.R. and Joshi, N.K. (2011) 'EVA based performance measurement: A case study of SBI, HFDC Bank', *Management Insight*, 7(1), June, pp. 31–43.

The report examines EVA as an appropriate way of evaluating the performance of Indian banks and finds out which Indian banks have been able to create (or destroy) shareholders.

Rappaport, A. (1998) *Creating Shareholder Value*. Revised and updated edition. New York: Free Press.

A landmark book. Presents an important value metric – shareholder value analysis.

Rappaport, A. and Mauboussin, M.J. (2002) 'Valuation matters', *Harvard Business Review,* 1 March.

A straightforward guide to value calculations.

Rappaport, A. (2006) 'Ten ways to create shareholder value', *Harvard Business Review,* 1 September.

A leading advocate of shareholder value emphasises the need to focus on long-term value.

Sabol, A. and Sverer, F. (2017) A Review of the Economic Value added Literature and Application. Special issue, *UTMS Journal of Economics,* 8(1): 19–27.

Reviews the role of the concept of EVA in the process of value and performance management, as well as strategic management.

Sharma, A.K. and Kumar, S. (2010) 'Economic value added: Literature review and relevant issues', *International Journal of Economics and Finance,* 2(2), May, pp. 200–20.

This paper presents a literature review of 112 papers published on the EVA from 1994 to 2008. It identifies the gaps in existing literature and suggests the direction for future research.

Solomons, D. (1965) *Divisional Performance: Measurement and control*. Reproduced 1983. Connecticut: M. Wiener Publishing.

An early formulation of residual income (economic profit).

Stern, J.M., Stewart, G.B. and Chew, D.H. (2001) 'The EVA® financial management system', in Chew, D.H. (ed.) *The New Corporate Finance*. New York: McGraw-Hill/Irwin.

The case for the use of EVA for motivating operating heads is presented in an easy-to-read fashion.

Stewart, G.B. (1991) *The Quest for Value*. New York: HarperBusiness.

Written by a founding partner in Stern Stewart & Co., the US consultancy, which has so successfully promoted MVA and EVA. Some useful insights.

Stewart, G.B. (2001) 'Market myths', in Chew, D.H. (ed.) *The New Corporate Finance*. 3rd edn. New York: McGraw-Hill/Irwin.

Advocating the value approach.

Stewart, G.B. (2014) 'The role of the cost of capital in EVA and in corporate value-based management', in Pratt, S.P. and Grabowski, R.J. (eds) *Cost of Capital: Applications and Examples,* John Wiley & Sons, Inc., Hoboken, New Jersey.

Updated arguments from the author on the usefulness of EVA.

Weaver, S.C. (2001) 'Measuring Economic Value Added®: A survey of the practices of EVA® proponents', *Journal of Applied Finance,* Fall/Winter, pp. 7–17.

Evidence that EVA is implemented in a variety of ways (different 'adjustments', different 'WACC' calculations).

Young, S.D. and O'Byrne, S.F. (2001) *EVA® and Value-based Management: A practical guide to implementation,* New York: McGraw-Hill.

An easy-to-follow description of EVA with a critical edge.

Zaima J.K. (2008) 'Portfolio investing with EVA', *The Journal of Portfolio Management,* Spring, pp. 34–40.

Some evidence on the relationship between EVA and share returns.

Case study recommendations

Please see www.pearsoned.co.uk/arnold for case study synopses. Also, another list of useful case studies from the fifth edition can be found there.

● Lloyds TSB Group (A): business portfolio restructuring and development. Authors: Laurence Capron; Mark Hunter; Fares Boulos, INSEAD. Available at www. cb.hbsp.harvard.edu

● TTK Prestige: economic value added analysis. Authors: Varun Dawar; Rakesh Arrawatia; Arit Chaudhury, Ivey Publishing. Available at www. cb.hbsp.harvard.edu

● Valjibhai Stones. Author: Debashis Sanyal; Smita Mazumdar, Ivey Publishing. Available at www. cb.hbsp.harvard.edu

Websites

Stern Value Management sternvaluemanagement.com/
Stern Stewart and Co. www.sternstewart.com
Economic Value Added www.eva.com/

Self-review questions

1 List the stages in the conversion of profit and loss accounts to cash flow figures.

2 What is shareholder value analysis and what are the seven value drivers as described by Rappaport?

3 What is economic profit (EP)? Describe the alternative ways of measuring it.

4 Describe the relative merits and problems of shareholder value analysis and EP.

5 What are the alternatives when trying to establish a figure for the amount of capital devoted to a business?

6 What is the total shareholder return (TSR) and what are its advantages and problems as a metric of shareholder wealth creation?

7 Compare the metrics total shareholder return (TSR) and wealth added index (WAI).

8 Describe the metric market value added (MVA) and note the problems in its practical use.

9 Outline the market to book ratio (MBR) and state why it is superior to the MVA for some purposes.

10 Compare the value metrics market value added (MVA) and excess return (ER).

Questions and problems

Answers to most questions can be found at www.pearsoned.co.uk/arnold.
Answers to questions marked with an asterisk are to be found only in the Lecturer's Guide.

1 Blue plc is a relatively small company with only one SBU. It manufactures wire grilles for the consumer market for cooker manufacturers and for export. Following a thorough investigation by the finance department and the heads of the customer lines some facts emerged about the returns expected in each of the customer sectors. The consumer sector uses £1m of the firm's capital and is expected to produce a return of 18% on this capital, for the next five years, after which it will return the same as its risk-adjusted cost of capital (WACC), 15%.

The cooker sales sector uses £2m of capital and will return 14% per annum for seven years when its planning horizon ends. Its WACC is 16%.

The export sector has a positive performance spread of 2% over WACC for the next six years. The required rate of return is 17%. From Year 7 the performance spread becomes zero. This division uses £1.5m of capital.

Required

a Calculate the annual (entity version) economic profit of each sector.
b What is the total value creation from each if you assume profit numbers equate to cash flow numbers?
c Display a value-creation profile chart and suggest possible action.

2* Apply shareholder value analysis to an all-equity firm with the following Rappaport value drivers, assuming that the last reported annual sales were £25m.

Sales growth rate	13%
Operating profit margin before tax	10%
Tax rate	31%
Incremental fixed capital investment (IFCI)	11% of the change in sales
Incremental working capital investment (IWCI)	8% of the change in sales
Planning horizon	4 years
Required rate of return	15%

Marketable securities amount to £5m and depreciation can be taken to be equal to the investment needed to replace worn-out equipment.

(*An Excel spreadsheet version of the answers to this question is available in the lecturer's section of the website www.pearsoned.co.uk/arnold.*)

3* Regarding the answer obtained in Question 2 as the 'base-case' strategy, make a judgement on the best strategic option given the following:

- If the firm were liquidated the operating assets could be sold, net of the repayment of liabilities, for a total of £20m.
- If the firm separated its A division from its B division then A could be sold for £10m and the B division would have the following Rappaport value drivers:

Sales	15%
Operating profit margin before tax	12%
Tax rate	31%
Incremental fixed capital investment (IFCI)	13% of change in sales
Incremental working capital investment (IWCI)	10% of change in sales
Planning horizon	6 years
Required rate of return	14%

The B division had sales in the last year of £15m.

- If both divisions are retained and a new product differentiation strategy is attempted then the following Rappaport value drivers will apply:

Sales	18%
Operating profit margin before tax	12%
Tax rate	31%
Incremental fixed capital investment (IFCI)	15%
Incremental working capital investment (IWCI)	9%
Planning horizon	5 years
Required rate of return	17%

4* a Conduct sensitivity analysis on the shareholder value analysis of Question 2, changing the required rate of return to 14% and 16%, and changing the planning horizon to Year 5 and Year 6. Present the results in a table and comment on them briefly.

   b Discuss the advantages and disadvantages of using shareholder value analysis.

5 Last year Tops plc (a firm financed entirely by equity) produced an accounting operating profit after tax of £5m. Its equity cost of capital is 14% and the firm has £50m of capital. What was the economic profit?

6 Buit plc is trying to estimate its value under the current strategy. The managerial team have forecast the following profits for the next five years:

Year	1	2	3	4	5
	£m	£m	£m	£m	£m
Forecast profit	12	14	15	16	16

Depreciation of fixed capital items in each of the first two years is £2m. In each of the following three years it is £3m. This has been deducted before arriving at the profit figures shown above. In years 1, 2 and 3 capital expenditure will be £5m per year which both replaces worn-out assets and pays for fresh investment to grow the business. In the fourth and fifth year capital expenditure will be £3m.

The planning horizon is four years. Additional working capital will be needed in each of the next four years. This will be £1m in year 1, £1.2m in year 2, £1.5m in year 3 and £1.8m in year 4.

The company is partially financed by debt – it owes £20m – and partially by equity capital. The required rate of return (WACC) is 10%.

The forecast profit figures include a deduction for interest of £1.2m per year, but do not include a deduction for tax, which is levied at 30% of forecasted profits, payable in the year profits are made.

The company also owns a number of empty factories that are not required for business operations. The current market value of these is £16m.

Required

a   Calculate the future cash flows for the company to an infinite horizon – assume year 5 cash flows apply to each year thereafter. Discount the cash flows and calculate the present value of all the cash flows.

b   Calculate corporate value and shareholder value.

7   Mythier plc, in its first year, produced profits after deduction of tax but before deduction of interest of £1m. The amount invested by debt holders was £4m. Equity holders also invested £4m. Interest paid during the year was £0.24m and the weighted average cost of capital is 8%, while the cost of equity capital is 10%.

a   Calculate economic profit using the entity approach.

b   Calculate economic profit using the equity approach.

c   Describe the advantages of using economic profit in the modern corporation.

d   Explain the difficulties with economic profit.

8   Explain and contrast economic profit and shareholder value analysis.

9   a   Tear plc has not paid a dividend for 20 years. The current share price is 580p and the current share market index level is 3,100. Calculate total shareholder returns for the past three years, the past five years and the past ten years, given the following data:

Time before present	Share price (pence)	Share index
1 year	560	3,000
2 years	550	2,400
3 years	600	2,500
4 years	500	2,000
5 years	450	1,850
6 years	400	1,700
7 years	250	1,300
8 years	170	1,500
9 years	130	1,300
10 years	125	1,000

b   Comment on the problems of total shareholders' returns as a metric for judging managerial performance.

c   Calculate the wealth added index for ten and five years for Tear plc given the following assumptions:

● The required rate of return on shares of the same risk class as Tear plc, over both ten and five years, was 9% per year.

● The company had 10 million shares in issue throughout the entire period.

d   Discuss the advantages of the wealth added index compared with the total shareholder return. What are the difficulties in the practical use of the wealth added index?

10   Sity plc has paid out all earnings as dividends since it was founded with £15m of equity finance 25 years ago. Today its shares are valued on the stock market at £90m and its long-term debt has a market value and book value of £20m.

a   How much market value added (MVA) has Sity produced?

b   What is Sity's market to book ratio (MBR)?

c   Given that another company, Pity plc, was founded with £15m of equity capital five years ago and has paid out all earnings since its foundation and is now worth (equity and debt) £110m (£90m equity, £20m debt), discuss the problems of using the MVA and the MBR for inter-firm comparison.

d Calculate the excess return (ER) for both Sity and Pity given that the required rate of return for Sity is 8% per year and the required rate of return is 10% per year for Pity. Sity has paid only two dividends: £2m was paid five years ago and £3m was paid three years ago. Pity has paid £2m in dividends at the end of every year since its foundation.

e Discuss the advantages and disadvantages in using the MVA and ER to judge managerial performance.

Assignments

1 Conduct a value-based analysis and write a report for a company you know well. Show the current position and your recommendations for change. Include in the analysis value-creation profile charts, strategy planes diagrams, sources of competitive advantage (value drivers), qualitative evaluation of strategies, cash flow analysis, shareholder value analysis and EP.

2 Using data on a company you know well try to calculate the TSR, WAI, MVA, ER and MBR. Point out the difficult judgements you have had to make to calculate these figures.

Appendix 15.1

Further consideration of the entity and equity EP

The entity EP and the equity EP give the same annual EP figures but can give different equity values if calculated with a WACC determined by the initial proportions of debt and equity (i.e. those amounts put into the business by shareholders and debt holders). This is apparent in the following illustration. (To be read after absorbing the fundamentals of the WACC in Chapter 16.) Valucrazee plc is set up with £50m from shareholders and £50m of debt capital. Equity at this risk level requires a rate of return of 20%, while debt requires 10%; therefore the WACC (based on initial proportions of debt and equity) = 15%. The company is expected to produce cash flow available for all the finance providers (i.e. before deduction of interest but after tax) of £25m per year to infinity.

Value under the entity approach

> Annual EP = Profit after tax before interest − Capital × Required rate of return
> Annual EP = £25m − (£100m × 15%) = £10m
> Corporate value = Initial total capital + Present value of annual economic profit
> Corporate value = £100m + £10m/0.15 = £166.67m
> Equity value = Corporate value − Debt value = £166.67m − £50m = £116.67m

Value under the equity approach

> Annual EP = Profit after tax and interest − Equity capital × Required rate of return
> Annual EP = (£25m − £5m) − (£50m × 20%) = £10m
> Equity value = Initial equity + Present value of annual equity economic profit
> Equity value = £50m + £10m/0.20 = £100m

The reason for the £16.67m difference is that the surplus cash flow above the minimum required is discounted at different rates. In the first case the £10m surplus cash flow (which must all be attributable to shareholders as the debt holders are satisfied with the 'required rate of return' deduction) is discounted at 15%, whereas in the second case it is discounted at 20%.

To make the two equity values equal we need to follow the rule when calculating the WACC of using market value weights for debt and equity (i.e. what the total value of the shares in the company is after going ahead) rather than original book (balance sheet) values. The market value of debt remains the same if a value-enhancing project is accepted – that is, £50m. However, the market value of the equity is significantly higher than the amount first put in by the shareholders.

The annual cash flow to equity of £20m when discounted at 20% is £100m. Therefore, the weights used to calculate the WACC are:

Debt	£50m	Weight: £50m/£150m = 0.333
Equity	£100m	Weight: £100m/£150m = 0.667
Total capital	£150m	

$$\text{WACC} = k_E W_E + k_D W_D = 0.2 \times 0.667 + 0.1 \times 0.333 = 16.67\%$$

This changes the valuation under the entity approach:

Annual EP = Profit after tax before interest − Capital × Required rate of return
Annual EP = £25m − (£100m × 16.67%) = £8.33m
Corporate value = Initial total capital + Present value of annual economic profit
Corporate value = £100m + £8.33m/0.1667 = £150m
Equity value = Corporate value − Debt value = £150m − £50m = £100m
(the same as under the equity approach)

Under the WACC-adjusted-for-market-value-of-equity approach we observe a fall in the annual EP when using the entity approach from £10m to £8.33m because we, correctly, require 20% return on two-thirds (£100m) of capital employed out of a total of £150m (at market values).

What is the practical manager to do? In theory you should be using the market value proportions of debt and equity that are optimal for your firm for all projects and SBUs and for valuing the entire firm. That is, the firm should have target levels of debt relative to the equity base that produces the lowest WACC (see Chapter 16).

The reality in most firms is that the optimum mix of debt and equity is unlikely to be known with any precision as the factors determining the optimum, at base, can only be quantified through subjective probability estimates, e.g. the chance of financial distress (see Chapter 18). So, it is reasonable to think of the optimum proportions of debt and equity as a range rather than a pinpoint percentage. For most firms the reasonable range is quite large. It could easily run from 50:50 gearing to 33:66 gearing. The advice to think in terms of a range for the WACC is reinforced by the many difficulties in other inputs to the WACC calculation, from the cost of equity (what is the risk premium? Is beta the appropriate adjustment for risk?) to the risk-free rate of return – see Chapters 8 and 16.

Given the complications with the WACC under the entity approach many analysts would simply plump for the equity approach in the first place.

CHAPTER 16

The cost of capital

LEARNING OUTCOMES

By the end of this chapter the reader should be able to:

- calculate and explain the cost of debt capital, both before and after tax considerations;

- describe the difficulties in estimating the equity cost of capital and explain the key elements that require informed judgement;

- calculate the weighted average cost of capital (WACC) for a company and explain the meaning of the number produced;

- describe the evidence concerning how companies actually calculate the WACC;

- explain the outstanding difficulties in this area of finance.

Introduction

Until this point a cost of capital (required rate of return) has been assumed for, say, a project or a business unit strategy, but we have not gone into much detail about how an appropriate cost of capital is calculated. This vital issue is now addressed.

The objective set for management in a value-based organisation is the maximisation of long-term shareholder wealth. This means achieving a return on invested money that is greater than shareholders could obtain elsewhere for the same level of risk. Shareholders (and other finance providers) have an opportunity cost associated with putting money into your firm. They could withdraw the money placed with you and invest it in a comparable company's securities. If, for the same risk, the alternative investment offers a higher return than your firm's shares, then as a management team you are destroying shareholder wealth.

The cost of capital is the rate of return that a company has to offer finance providers to induce them to buy and hold a financial security. This rate is determined by the returns offered on alternative securities with the same risk.

Using the correct cost of capital as a discount rate is important. If it is too high investment will be constrained, firms will not grow as they should and shareholders will miss out on value-enhancing opportunities. There can be a knock-on effect to the macroeconomy and this causes worry for politicians. For example, the one-time President of the Board of Trade, Michael Heseltine, complained:

Businesses are not investing enough because of their excessive expectations of investment returns . . . The CBI tells me that the majority of firms continue to require rates of return above 20 per cent. A senior banker last week told me his bank habitually asked for 30 per cent returns on capital.[1]

This chapter focuses on the question of how to measure the returns available on a variety of financial securities at different risk levels. This will be developed into an overall cost of capital for the firm and provide a method for calculating the benchmark rate for the firm, SBUs and projects.

A word of warning

Too often, academics and consultants give the impression of scientific precision in calculating a firm's cost of capital. The reality is that behind any final number generated lies an enormous amount of subjective assessment or, worse, opinion. Choices have to be made between competing judgements on a range of issues, including the appropriate risk premium, financial gearing level and risk measure. Good decision making comes from knowing the limitations of the input variables to the decision. Knowing where informed judgement has been employed in the cost of capital calculation is required to make value-enhancing decisions and thus assist the art of management. In short, the final number for the required rate of return is less important than knowledge of the factors behind the calculation and the likely size of the margin of error. Precision is less important than knowledge of what is a reasonable range.

The required rate of return

The capital provided to large firms comes in many forms. The main forms are equity and debt capital, but there are a number of hybrids, such as convertible bonds. When a finance provider chooses to supply funds in the form of debt finance, there is a deliberate attempt to reduce risk, e.g. by imposing covenants or requiring collateral. However, a lender to a corporation cannot expect to eliminate all risk and so the required rate of return is going to be above that of lending to a reputable state such as the USA or the UK. Placing your savings with the UK government by

---

1 Quoted in Philip Coggan and Paul Cheeseright, *Financial Times*, 8 November, 1994.

buying its bonds in return for the promise of regular interest and the payment of a capital sum in a future year is the closest you are going to get to risk-free lending. The rate of return offered on government bonds and Treasury bills is the bedrock rate that is used to benchmark other interest rates. It is called the risk-free rate of return, given the symbol r_f.

A stable well-established company with a relatively low level of borrowing and low-risk operations might have to pay a slightly higher rate of return on debt capital than the UK government. Such a company, if it issued a corporate bond with a high credit rating, would pay, say, an extra 100 basis points per year. This is described as the risk premium (RP) on top of the risk-free rate:

Then, the cost of debt capital, k_D, is:

$$k_D = r_f + RP$$

If the current risk-free rate is 4%, then $k_D = 5\%$.

If the firm has a high level of debt it may need to offer, say, 300 basis points above the risk-free rate. So the required return might be 7%.

$$k_D = r_f + RP = 4 + 3 = 7\%$$

If the form of finance provided is equity capital then the investor is accepting a fairly high probability of receiving no return at all on the investment. On the other hand, if the firm performs well very high returns can be expected. It is the expectation of high returns that causes ordinary shareholders to accept high risk.

Different equities have different levels of risk, and therefore returns. A shareholder in Marks & Spencer is likely to be content with a lower return than a shareholder in, say, an internet start-up, or a company quoted on the Russian stock exchange. Thus we have a range of financial securities with a variety of risk and associated return (*see* **Exhibit 16.1**).

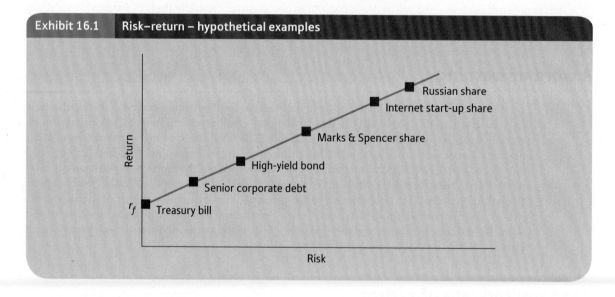

Exhibit 16.1   Risk–return – hypothetical examples

Two sides of the same coin

The issues of the cost of capital for managerial use within the business and the value placed on a share (or other financial security) are two sides of the same coin. They both depend on the level of return (*see* **Exhibit 16.2**). The holders of shares make a valuation on the basis of the returns they estimate they will receive. Likewise, from the firm's perspective, it estimates the cost of raising money through selling shares (or retaining earnings) as the return that the firm will have to pay to shareholders to induce them to buy and hold the shares. The same considerations apply to bondholders, preference shareholders and so on. If the future cash flowing from the form of finance is anticipated to fall from a previously assumed level then the selling price of the share,

Exhibit 16.2	Two sides of the same coin

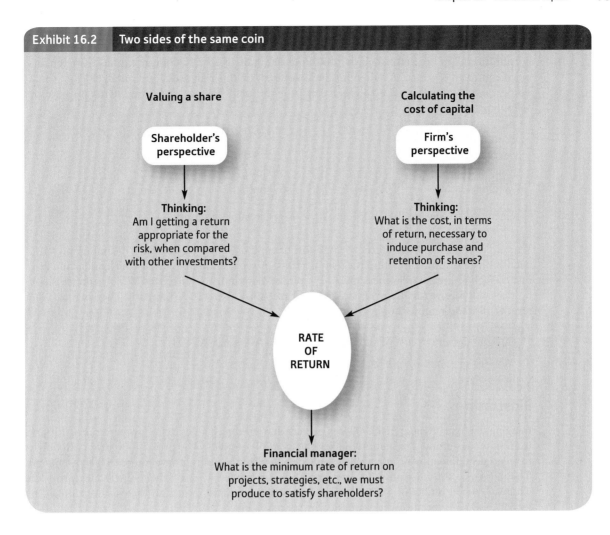

bond, etc. goes down until the return is at the level dictated by the returns on financial securities of a similar type and risk. If a company fails to achieve returns that at least compensate finance providers for their opportunity cost it is unlikely to survive for long.

The weighted average cost of capital (WACC)

We have established that firms need to offer returns to finance providers commensurate with the risk they are undertaking. The amount of return is determined by what those investors could get elsewhere at that risk level (e.g. by investing in other companies). If we take a firm that is financed entirely by share capital (and this is the optimal capital structure – *see* Chapter 18), then the required rate of return to be used in value analysis, e.g. a project or SBU appraisal, is the required return demanded by investors on the company's shares. However, this is only true if the new project (or division) has the same level of systematic risk as the existing set of projects.

The stock market prices shares on the basis of the current riskiness of the firm. This is determined by the activities it undertakes. A company can be seen as merely a bundle of projects from the perspective of ordinary shareholders. If these projects are, on average, of high risk then the required return will be high. If the proposed project (or division) under examination has the same risk as the weighted average of the current set then the required return on the company's equity capital is the rate appropriate for this project (if the company received all its capital from shareholders and none from lenders). If the new project has a lower risk, the company-wide cost of capital needs to be adjusted down for application to this project.

If, however, we are dealing with a company that has some finance in the form of debt and some in the form of equity the situation becomes a little more complicated. Imagine that a corporation is to be established by obtaining one-half of its £1,000m of capital from lenders, who require an 8% rate of return for an investment of this risk class, and one-half from shareholders, who require a 12% rate of return for the risk they are accepting. Thus we have the following facts:

Cost of debt			$k_D = 8\%$
Cost of equity			$k_E = 12\%$
Weight of debt	$V_D/(V_D + V_E)$	£500m/£1bn	$W_D = 0.5$
Weight of equity	$V_E/(V_D + V_E)$	£500m/£1bn	$W_E = 0.5$

Where V_D = Market value of debt, V_E = Market value of equity

We need to calculate the **weighted average cost of capital (WACC)** to establish the minimum return needed on an investment within the firm that will produce enough to satisfy the lenders and leave just enough to give shareholders their 12% return. Anything less than this WACC and the shareholders will receive less than 12%. They will recognise that 12% is available elsewhere for that level of risk and remove money from the firm.

Weighted average cost of capital, $\text{WACC} = k_E W_E + k_D W_D$

$\text{WACC} = (12 \times 0.5) + (8 \times 0.5) = 10\%$

Illustration

Imagine the firm invested £100,000 in a project that produced a net cash flow per year of £10,000 to infinity (assuming a perpetuity makes the example simple). The first call on that cash flow is from the debt holders, who effectively supplied £50,000 of the funds. They require £4,000 per annum. That leaves £6,000 for equity holders – an annual return of 12% on the £50,000 they provided. Thus an overall return of 10% (the WACC) provides an 8% return on the capital supplied by lenders and 12% on the capital supplied by shareholders.

If things go well and a return of £11,000 (i.e. 11%) is generated then debt holders still receive the contracted amount of £4,000, but the equity holders get a return significantly above the minimum they require, a 14% return: £7,000 is left to pay out to shareholders on their £50,000 capital input to this project.

Of course, this example assumes that all new projects use the same proportions of debt and equity finance as the firm as a whole, that is 50% of its capital comes from debt. The issue of whether you should use different types (or weights) of finance for different projects (say, borrow all the £100,000 for this particular project at 8%) rather than use the 50 : 50 mixture (for this firm) is discussed later.

Lowering the WACC and increasing shareholder returns

Examining the WACC formula we see an apparently simple way of reducing the required rate of return, and thus raising the value of a project, division or the entire firm: change the weights in the formula in favour of debt. In other words, alter the capital structure of the firm by having a higher proportion of its capital in the form of cheaper debt – the jargon referring to levels of debt relative to equity capital is 'financial gearing' or 'leverage'.[2]

For example, if the company is expected to produce £100m cash flow per year (to infinity), and its WACC is 10%, its total corporate value ('enterprise value', that is, the value of the debt and equity) is:

£100m/0.10 = £1,000m

Let us try to lower the WACC.

---

2 More details of gearing definitions and types of gearing can be found in Chapter 18.

Imagine that instead of the firm being established with 50% debt in its overall capital it is set up with 70% debt. The proportion of total capital in the form of equity is therefore 30%. *If* (a big if) the equity holders remain content with a 12% return while the debt holders accept an 8% annual return the WACC will fall, and the value of the firm will rise.

$$\text{WACC} = k_E\,W_E + k_D\,W_D$$
$$\text{WACC} = (12 \times 0.3) + (8 \times 0.7) = 9.2\%$$
$$\text{Firm value} = £100\text{m}/0.092 = £1,086.96\text{m}$$

Why don't all management teams increase the proportion of debt in the capital structure and 'magic up' some shareholder value? The fly in the ointment for many firms is that equity investors are unlikely to be content with 12% returns when their shares have become more risky due to the additional financial gearing. The key question is: how much extra return do they demand? The financial economists and Nobel laureates Franco Modigliani and Merton Miller (MM) presented the case that in a perfect capital market (in which all participants such as shareholders and managers have all relevant information, all can borrow at the same rate of interest, etc.) the increase in k_E would exactly offset the benefit from the increase in the debt proportion; this would leave the WACC constant, so increasing the debt proportion does not add to shareholder value; the only factor that can add value is the improvement in the underlying performance of the business, i.e. its cash flows. According to this view (that there is no optimal capital structure that will maximise shareholder wealth) there is no point in adjusting the debt or equity proportions.

In this stylised world k_D remains at 8%, but k_E moves to 14.67%, leaving the WACC, firm value and shareholder value constant.

$$\text{WACC} = k_E\,W_E + k_D\,W_D$$
$$\text{WACC} = (14.67 \times 0.3) + (8 \times 0.7) = 10\%$$

However, there is hope for managers trying to improve shareholder wealth by adjusting the capital structure because in constructing a perfect world Modigliani and Miller left out at least two important factors: tax and financial distress.[3]

The benefit of tax

The first consideration is tax. A benefit of financing through debt is that the annual interest can be used to reduce taxable profit thus lowering the cash that flows out to the tax authorities. In contrast, the annual payout on equity (dividends) cannot be used to reduce the amount of profit that is taxed. The benefits gained from being able to lower the tax burden through financing with debt reduces the effective cost of this form of finance. (Note this reduction is only valid if the company is profitable and paying corporation tax.)

To illustrate: Firm A is a company in a country that does not permit interest to be deducted from taxable profit. Firm B is in a country that does permit interest to be deducted. In both companies the interest is 8% on £500m. Observe the effect on the amount of profit left for distribution to shareholders in the table below.

	Firm A *£m*	*Firm B* *£m*
Profits before interest and tax	100	100
Interest		−40
Taxable profit	100	60
Amount taxed @ 30%	−30	−18
Interest	−40	
Amount available for distribution shareholders	30	42

---

3 Modigliani and Miller did not ignore tax and financial distress in their work, but did downplay them in the formulation of their early model.

The extra £12m for Firm B reduces the effective cost of debt from 8% to only 8 (1 − T), where T = the corporation tax rate, 30%. The cost of debt capital falls to 8 (1−0.3) = 5.6, or £28m on £500m of debt. The taxman, by taking £12m less from the company purely because the tax rules allow the deductibility of interest from taxable profit, lowers the effective cost of the debt.

So including the tax shield effect, we find a reduction in the WACC that leads to an increase in the amount available for shareholders. In our example, if we assume tax on corporate profits at 30% then the effective cost of debt falls to 5.6%. This results in the WACC becoming 8.8%.

k_{DBT} = Cost of debt before tax benefit = 8%
k_{DAT} = Cost of debt after tax benefit = 8 (1 − T) = 8 (1 − 0.30) = 5.6%

If we assume a 50 : 50 capital structure the WACC is:

$$\text{WACC} = k_E\,W_E + k_{DAT}\,W_D$$
$$\text{WACC} = (12 \times 0.5) + (5.6 \times 0.5) = 8.8\%$$

Investment project cash flows discounted at this lower rate will have a higher present value than if discounted at 10%. Given that the debt holders receive only their contractual interest and no more, this extra value flows to shareholders.

Financial distress constrains gearing

The introduction of the tax benefit strongly pushes the bias towards very high gearing levels to obtain a lower WACC and higher value. However, we do not observe such extreme gearing very often in real-world companies. There are a number of reasons for this, the most important of which is the increasing risk to the finance providers (particularly equity capital holders) of financial distress and, ultimately, liquidation. (*See* Chapter 18 for more reasons and a more detailed discussion of capital structure.)

As gearing rises so does the probability of equity investors receiving a poor (no) return. So they demand higher expected returns to compensate. At first, the risk premium rises slowly, but at high gearing levels it rises so fast that it more than offsets the benefit of increasing debt in the capital structure. This is demonstrated in **Exhibit 16.3**, in which the WACC at lower levels of debt is primarily influenced by the increasing debt proportion in the capital structure, and at higher levels by the rising cost of equity (and eventually debt).

The conclusion drawn from the capital structure literature is that there is an optimal gearing level that achieves the lowest WACC and highest firm value. When companies are calculating their

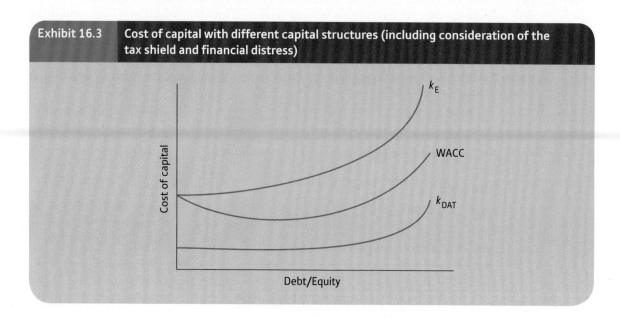

Exhibit 16.3   Cost of capital with different capital structures (including consideration of the tax shield and financial distress)

WACC they should use this target gearing ratio and not a gearing ratio they happen to have at the time of calculation.

So, if in our example the required return on equity rises from 12% to 13% when the proportion of the debt in the capital structure rises to 65% from 50%, and the effective rate of return payable on debt is 5.6% after the tax shield benefit (i.e. remaining at 8% before the tax benefit) then the WACC falls and the value available for shareholders rises.

$$\text{WACC} = k_E \, W_E + k_{DAT} \, W_D$$
$$\text{WACC} = (13 \times 0.35) + (5.6 \times 0.65) = 8.19\%$$

Taking financial gearing too far

For this particular company we will assume that 65% gearing is the optimum debt/equity ratio. If we go to 80% debt we find this reduces shareholder wealth because the firm's projects (in aggregate) are now discounted at a higher rate of return (WACC), reducing their present value. The main reason the discount rate rises significantly is that the required return on shares rises to, say, 30% as investors fear massive potential loss due to the large commitment of the firm to pay out interest whether or not the firm is doing well. The debt holders are also worried about increased financial distress risk – i.e. they might not receive their capital or interest – and so they increase their required rate of return to 10% before the tax shield benefit, which is an effective cost to the firm of 7% after allowing for the tax shield benefit.

$$\text{WACC} = k_E \, W_E + k_{DAT} \, W_D$$
$$\text{WACC} = (30 \times 0.2) + (7 \times 0.8) = 11.6\%$$

Worked example 16.1	Poise plc

The rate of return offered to debt holders of Poise plc before considering the benefit to shareholders of the tax shield, k_{DBT}, is 10 per cent, whereas the required return on equity is 20%. The total amount of capital in use (equity + debt), V, is £2m. Of that, £1.4m represents the market value of its equity, V_E, and £600,000 equals the market value of its debt, V_D. These are the optimum proportions of debt and equity.

Thus:

$$k_{DBT} = 10\%$$
$$k_E = 20\%$$
$$V = £2m$$
$$V_E = £1.4m$$
$$V_D = £0.6m$$

The weight for equity capital is:

$$W_E = \frac{V_E}{V} = \frac{1.4}{2.0} = 0.7$$

The weight for debt is:

$$W_D = \frac{V_D}{V} = \frac{0.6}{2.0} = 0.3$$

The corporate tax rate is 30% and therefore the after-tax cost of debt is:

$$k_{DAT} = k_{DBT} (1 - T)$$
$$k_{DAT} = 10 (1 - 0.30) = 7\%$$

The weighted average cost of capital for Poise is:

$$\begin{aligned} \text{WACC} &= k_E W_E + k_{DAT} W_D \\ &= 20\% \times 0.7 + 7\% \times 0.3 \\ &= 16.1\% \end{aligned}$$

▶

Worked example 16.1 *(continued)*

This is the rate of return Poise needs to achieve on new business projects if they are of the same risk as the average risk of the current set of projects. If the new projects are of higher or lower risk an adjustment needs to be made to the discount rate used – this is discussed in more detail later in the chapter.

If Poise is considering a project that requires an investment of £1m at Time 0 and then produces after-tax annual cash flows before interest payments of £161,000 as a perpetuity (i.e. it achieves a 16.1% rate of return) then the net cost of satisfying the debt holders after the tax shield benefit is £21,000. (The debt holders supplied 30% of the £1m invested, i.e. £300,000; and the cost to the firm of satisfying them is £300,000 × 7% = £21,000.)

The remainder of the annual cash flows go to the shareholders; so they receive £140,000 per year, which is a 20% return on the £700,000 they supplied.

If the project produces a much lower annual cash flow of £100,000 (a rate of return of 10%) then the debt holders still receive £21,000, leaving only £79,000 for the shareholders. These investors could have achieved a return of 20% by investing in other companies at this level of risk. An annual return of £79,000 represents a mere 11.3% return (£79,000/£700,000). Thus shareholders suffer a loss of wealth relative to the forgone opportunity.

An Excel spreadsheet version of these calculations is available at www.pearsoned.co.uk/arnold.

The *Financial Times* article in **Exhibit 16.4** makes use of the cost of capital concept. (We'll turn a blind eye to the reference to return on invested capital, ROIC. This is operating *profit* divided by the total capital for a year rather than the more correct consideration of all discounted *cash flows*. It would be a half blind eye if we accept that, in this particular case, operating profit is a close substitute for cash flow.)

Exhibit 16.4

Lex column – SHIRE: DETAILS MATTER

Announcing its $5.2bn purchase of NPS Pharma, Shire said it "expects that the transaction will deliver return on invested capital in excess of its weighted average cost of capital". One might hope this would go without saying.

So — an analyst asks on the conference call — what is your cost of capital? Shire declined to be specific. The number moves around.

Typically high single-digits, it offered, and no, we will not estimate when ROIC will pass WACC. The details are going to matter because Shire has paid up. The 51 per cent premium to NPS's undisturbed price amounts to $1.8bn. How to get that back?

Those with the bad luck to have studied finance know that when ROIC is below WACC, the buyer becomes worse off. Even after Shire has told investors that it is not trying to make them poorer, then, detail is welcome.

If one opens a spreadsheet and adds 2017 estimates for Shire's earnings to what analysts expect NPS to earn (backing out cost savings and financing costs) the deal looks nicely additive to Shire's earnings per share.

This does not imply that ROIC will exceed WACC, but does reflect analysts' optimism about NPS's growth.

Financial Times, JANUARY 12, 2015

The cost of equity capital

A shareholder has in mind a minimum rate of return determined by the returns available on other shares of the same risk class. Managers, in order to maximise shareholder wealth, must obtain this level of return for shareholders from the firm's activities. If a company does not achieve the rate of return to match the investor's opportunity cost it will find it difficult to attract new funds and will become vulnerable to takeover or liquidation.

With debt finance there is generally a specific rate payable for the use of capital. In contrast, ordinary shareholders are not explicitly offered payments. However, there is an implicit rate of return that has to be offered to attract investors. It is the expectation of high returns that causes ordinary shareholders to accept high risk.

Investors in shares require a return that provides for two elements. First, they need a return equal to the risk-free rate (usually taken to be that on government securities). Secondly, there is the risk premium, which rises with the degree of systematic risk:

$$\text{Rate of return on shares} = \text{Risk-free rate} + \text{Risk premium}$$
$$k_E = r_f + RP$$

The risk-free rate gives a return sufficient to compensate for both impatience to consume and inflation (*see* Chapter 2).[4] To estimate the relevant risk premium on a firm's equity we generally take two steps.

- Stage one is to estimate the average extra return demanded by investors above the risk-free return to induce them to buy a portfolio of average-risk-level shares. We usually look back at the returns shareholders have *actually* received on average-risk shares above the risk-free return in the past and make the assumption that this is what they also demanded before the event, *ex ante* in the jargon,[5] and then make the further assumption that this is the extra rate that they demand on shares today. The average annual risk premium actually obtained by shareholders can only be calculated over an extended period of time (many decades) as short-term returns on shares can be distorted (they are often negative for a year or a decade, for example). The risk premium is expressed as the difference between the market return, r_m, and the risk-free return, r_f, that is $(r_m - r_f)$.

- The second stage is to adjust the risk premium for a typical (average-risk-level) share to suit the risk level for the particular company's shares under consideration. If the share is more risky than the average then $(r_m - r_f)$ is multiplied by a systematic risk factor greater than 1. If it is less risky it may be multiplied by a systematic risk factor of less than 1, say 0.8, to reduce the premium.

The Capital Asset Pricing Model (CAPM)

In the forty years following the development of the CAPM, in practical cost of capital calculations, the risk premium was generally adjusted by a beta based on the extent to which a share had moved when a market index moved (its covariance with the market), say month by month over a five-year period:

$$k_E = r_f + \beta \, (r_m - r_f)$$

There are some fairly obvious problems with this approach; for example, does historic co-movement with the market index reflect future risk accurately? (*See* Chapter 8 for more problems.) But at least we have some anchor points for equity cost calculations. We have general acceptance that it is only systematic risk that is compensated for in the required returns. We also have an approximate figure for the historic risk premium on the average-risk share and thus, given a certain risk-free rate, we know roughly what rate of return is required for an average share – with rates

---

4 This is assuming that future inflation is included in the projected cash flows. That is, we are using nominal cash flows and a nominal interest rate. An alternative method is to use real cash flows and a real discount rate (i.e. with inflation removed).

5 An alternative is the 'forward looking approach' in which the analyst tries to obtain estimates of what extra future annual return investors require at this time for investing in an averagely risky share. There are some serious doubts about the subjective nature of the inputs to these calculations – the Gordon growth model, explained in the next section, is one such method.

on government securities at say 3% this would be around 7–9%. Despite this progress we are still left with some uncertainty over how to adjust the average risk premium for specific shares – beta is less than perfect (see Chapter 8).

The Gordon growth model method for estimating the cost of equity capital

The most influential model for calculating the cost of equity in the early 1960s (and one which is still used in a few firms today) was created by Gordon and Shapiro (1956), and further developed by Gordon (1962). Suppose a company's shares priced at P produce earnings of E per share and pay a dividend of d per share. The company has a policy of retaining a fraction, b, of its earnings each year to use for internal investments. If the rate of return (discount or capitalisation rate) required on shares of this risk class is k_E then, under certain restrictive conditions, it can be shown that earnings, dividends and reinvestment will all grow continuously, at a rate of $g = br$, where r is the rate of return on the reinvestment of earnings, and we have:

$$P = \frac{d_1}{k_E - g}$$

(There is more on this formula in Chapter 17.)

Solving for k_E we have:

$$k_E = \frac{d_1}{P} + g$$

where d_1 is the dividend to be received next year.

That is, the rate of return investors require on a share is equal to the prospective dividend yield (d_1/P) *plus* the rate at which the dividend stream is expected to grow (g).

Gordon and Shapiro said that there are other approaches to the estimation of future dividends than the extrapolation of the current dividend on the basis of the growth rate explicit in b and r, so we can derive g in other ways and still the k_E formula remains valid. So if we estimate that a particular company's earnings and dividends will grow in real terms (no inflation) by 2.5% per year for ever (a reasonable estimate for the average company in an economy that has real GDP growth of 2.5%) and the current dividend yield is 3.5% (roughly what it is in the UK in 2018), then the real required rate of return on equity is 6%. If we allow for future inflation of 2% then the nominal return could be estimated at 8%.

A major problem in the practical employment of this model is obtaining a trustworthy estimate of the future growth rate of dividends to an infinite horizon. Gordon and Shapiro (1956) told us to derive this figure from known data in an objective manner, using common sense and with reference to the past rate of growth in a corporation's dividend. In other words a large dose of judgement is required. The cost of equity capital under this model is very sensitive to the figure put in for g, and yet there is no reliable method of estimating it for the *future*; all we can do is make reasoned estimates and so the resulting k_E is based merely on an informed guess. Using past growth rates is one approach, but it means that it is assumed that the future growth of the company's earnings and dividends will be exactly the same as in the past – often an erroneous supposition. Professional analysts' forecasts could be examined, but their record of predicting the future is generally a poor one – especially for more than two years ahead (remember this model requires us to estimate g for all future years, to an infinite horizon).

Choosing a cost of equity can create great tensions – see **Exhibit 16.5**. Selecting 6.7% rather than 7.5% can making quite a difference to the price that National Grid can charge its customers.

Exhibit 16.5

Power behind the throne

By Jonathan Guthrie

Have at ye! National Grid is so furious with Ofgem's price control plans that it will retaliate with a . . . webinar. If that sounds limp, it reflects the reality that regulators have the whip hand over heavily regulated businesses.

Ofgem wants National Grid to put up £22bn to upgrade the UK's electricity and gas distribution network by 2021. The spat is over the return that Ofgem will permit the company to earn from higher charges met indirectly by consumers. The Grid pitched for a cost of equity of 7.5 per cent. Ofgem has come back with an offer of 7 per cent on electricity transmission, 6.8 per cent on gas transmission and 6.7 per cent on gas distribution.

This was below the expectations of City analysts. Ofgem was expected to be more generous, partly because it agreed a 7 per cent cost of equity for an upgrade of Caledonian power pipes with Scottish and Southern. It still may. A new bidding system was meant to reduce haggling. But the relatively sanguine response of National Grid's shares to Monday's bad news suggests a compromise is still likely.

The energy company is firmly under Ofgem's thumb – it can hardly rip up the power cables and decamp abroad. But investors are more mobile. It is a point that government and its agencies need to understand if they expect the private sector to finance a larger share of infrastructure spending.

The cost of retained earnings

The most important source of long-term finance for most corporations is retained earnings. There are many large companies that rarely, if ever, go to their shareholders to raise new money, but rely on previous years' profits. There is a temptation to regard retained earnings as 'costless' because it was not necessary for the management to go out and persuade investors to invest by offering a rate of return.

However, retained earnings should be seen as belonging to the shareholders. They are part of the equity of the firm. Shareholders could make good use of these funds by investing in other firms and obtaining a return. These funds therefore have an opportunity cost. We should regard the cost of retained earnings as equal to the expected returns required by shareholders buying new shares in a firm. There is a slight modification to this principle in practice because new share issues involve costs of issuance and therefore are required to give a marginally higher return to cover the costs of selling the shares.

The cost of debt capital

The cost of debt is generally determined by the following factors:

- the prevailing interest rates for corporations more generally;
- the risk of default (and expected rate of recovery of money lent in the event of default);
- the benefit derived from interest being tax deductible.

There are two types of debt capital. The first is debt that is traded, that is, bought and sold in a security market. The second is debt that is not traded.

Traded debt

In the UK bonds are often issued by companies to lenders with a nominal value of £100. Vanilla bonds carry an annual coupon rate until the bonds reach maturity when the nominal or par value of £100 is paid to the lender (*see* Chapter 11 for more details). The rate of return required by the firm's creditors, k_D, is represented by the interest rate in the following equation which causes the future discounted cash flows payable to the lenders to equal the current market price of the bond P_D. We know the current price P_D of the bond in the market, the annual cash flow that will go to the lenders in the form of interest, i, and we know the cash to be received, R_n, when the bond is redeemed at the end of its life. The only number we don't yet have is the rate of return, k_D. This is found in the same way as the internal rate of return is found:

$$P_D = \sum_{t=1}^{t=n} \frac{i}{(1 + k_D)^t} + \frac{R_n}{(1 + k_D)^n}$$

where:

i = annual nominal interest (coupon payment) receivable from year 1 to year n;
R_n = amount payable upon redemption;
k_D = cost of debt capital (before the tax benefit).

$\sum_{t=1}^{t=n}$ means add up the results of all the $\frac{i}{(1 + k_D)^t}$ from next year (year 1) to the t number of years of the bond's life.

For example, Elm plc issued £100m of bonds six years ago carrying an annual coupon rate of 8%. They are due to be redeemed in four years for the nominal value of £100 each. The next coupon is payable in one year and the current market price of a bond is £93. The cost of this redeemable debt can be calculated by obtaining the internal rate of return, imagining that a new identical set of cash flows is being offered to the lenders from a new (four-year) bond being issued today. The lenders would pay £93 for such a bond (in the same risk class) and receive £8 per year for four years plus £100 at the end of the bond's life. Thus, the cash flows from the firm's perspective are:

Year	0	1	2	3	4
Cash flow	+£93	−£8	−£8	−£8	−£108

Thus the rate of return being offered is calculated from:

$$93 = \frac{8}{1 + k_D} + \frac{8}{(1 + k_D)^2} + \frac{8}{(1 + k_D)^3} + \frac{108}{(1 + k_D)^4}$$

With k_D at 11% the discounted cash flow on the right hand side = 90.69.
With k_D at 10% the discounted cash flow on the right hand side = 93.66.
Using linear interpolation the IRR can be found:

$$k_D = 10\% + \frac{93.66 - 93.00}{93.66 - 90.69}(11 - 10) = 10.22\%$$

Even though the bonds were once worth a total of £100m in the market, this is no longer their value because they are now selling at £93 each. The total market value of the bonds today, V_D, is calculated as follows:

$$V_D = £100m \times \frac{£93}{£100} = £93m$$

We are concerned with finding the cost to a company of the various types of capital it might use to finance its investment projects, strategic plans, etc. It would be wrong to use the coupon rate of 8% on the bond for the cost of debt. This was the required rate of return six years ago (assuming the bond was sold for £100). A rate of 10.22% is appropriate because this is the rate of return bond investors are demanding in the market today. The cost of capital is the best available return elsewhere for the bondholders for the same level of risk. Managers are charged with using the money under their command to produce a return at least equal to the opportunity cost. If the cash flows attributable to these lenders for a project or SBU are discounted at 8% then a comparison of the resulting net present value of the investment with the return available by taking the alternative of investing the cash in the capital markets at the same risk is not being made. However, by using 10.22% for the bond cost of capital we can compare the alternatives available to the lenders in the financial markets.

In the calculation for Elm plc taxation has been ignored and so the above calculation of 10.22% should be properly defined as the cost of debt before tax, k_{DBT}. An adjustment is necessary to establish the true cost of the bond capital to the firm.

If T is the rate of corporate tax, 30%, then the cost of debt after tax, k_{DAT}, is:

$$k_{DAT} = k_{DBT} (1 - T)$$
$$k_{DAT} = 10.22 (1 - 0.30) = 7.15\%$$

A short cut

We have calculated the yield to redemption on a very simple bond from first principles, to illustrate the key elements. In reality, most bonds offer coupon payments every six months – this complicates the type of analysis shown above (*see* Chapter 11). However, yields to redemption on bonds of different risk classes are easily available, which avoids effort. The *Financial Times,* for example, displays the yields ('bid yield') offered on a range of frequently traded bonds of various risk classes (see the tables, 'Global Investment Grade' and 'High Yield and Emerging Market Bonds'). Many websites display bond yields. These sources may not be able to provide the yield to redemption for the particular bond that interests you, but you can discover the rates payable for bonds of different credit ratings. So if you know or can estimate the credit rating of the company under examination you can obtain an approximate rate of return (before the tax shield benefit K_{DBT}).

Untraded debt

Most debt capital, such as bank loans, is not traded and repriced regularly on a financial market making it more difficult to establish its cost. We need to find the rate of interest that is the opportunity cost of lenders' funds – the current 'going rate' of interest for the risk class. In some circumstances you can look at the rate being offered on similar tradable debt securities to make the estimate. In other cases, the company often states in its annual reports the rate it is paying banks, or this can be estimated by using knowledge of the ball-park interest rate charged by banks to companies in those circumstances, e.g. a company with low financial gearing or with substantial property assets available for collateral.

Floating-rate debt

Most companies have variable-rate debt in the form of either bonds or bank loans. Usually the interest payable is set at a margin over a benchmark rate such as bank base rate or LIBOR. For practical purposes the current interest payable can be taken as the before-tax rate of return (k_{DBT}) because these rates are the market rates. There is a rational argument against this simple approach based on the difference between short- and long-term interest rates. For example, it may be that a firm rolls over a series of short-term loans and so in effect will be using this as long-term finance. In this case the theoretically correct approach is to use the long-term interest rate and not the current short-term rate because the former more accurately reflects what is likely to be required to be paid over the life of the loan.

The cost of preference share capital

Preference shares have some characteristics in common with debt capital (e.g. a specified annual payout of higher ranking than ordinary share dividends) and some characteristics in common with equity (dividends may be missed in some circumstances, and the dividend is not tax deductible)

– see Chapter 10 for more details. If the holders of preference shares receive a fixed annual dividend and the shares are irredeemable the perpetuity formula may be used to value the security:

$$P_p = \frac{d_1}{k_p}$$

where P_p is the price of preference shares, d_1 is the annual preference dividend, k_p is the investors' required rate of return.

Therefore, the cost of this type of preference share is given by:

$$k_p = \frac{d_1}{P_p}$$

Hybrid securities

Hybrid securities can have a wide variety of features – e.g. a convertible bond is a combination of a straight bond offering regular coupons and an option to convert the bond to shares in the company. It is usually necessary to calculate the cost of capital for each of the component elements separately. This can be complex, involving option values, and is beyond the scope of this chapter.

Calculating the weights

Book (balance sheet) values for debt and equity should not be used in calculating the weighted average cost of capital. Market values should be used. For example, a company might have raised £100m by selling £100 perpetual bonds, which promised annual coupons of £5 each without a definite cease date, when interest rates were 5%. However, if general interest rates rise to, say, 10% for this risk class bonds offering £5 per year will not be attractive at £100 each; therefore the price will fall to £50 until they yield the required 10% return. It is the £50m current market value figure that should be used in the weightings. The rationale for using market values is that we need to generate a return for the finance providers on the basis of their current contribution to the capital of the firm and in relation to the current opportunity cost – accounting values have little relevance to this. Investors in bonds right now are facing an opportunity cost of £50m (i.e. they could sell the bonds and release £50m of cash) so this is the figure that managers should see as the amount sacrificed by these finance providers, not the £100m the bonds once traded at.

With equity capital it is correct to use the market capitalization figure (current share price multiplied by number of shares issued to investors). This is the amount that current investors are sacrificing to invest in this company today – the shares could be sold in the marketplace at that value. The balance sheet value for equity shareholders' funds is not relevant. This is likely to be very different from the market capitalisation. Balance sheets consist of a series of historic accounting entries that bear little relation to the value placed on the shares by investors. Most financial websites provide market capitalization figures, e.g. www.londonstockexchange.com.

The WACC with three or more types of finance

The formula becomes longer, but not fundamentally more difficult, when there are three (or more) types of finance. For example, if a firm has preference share capital as well as debt and equity the formula becomes:

$$\text{WACC} = k_E W_E + k_{DAT} W_D + k_P W_P$$

where W_P is the weight for preference shares and,

$$W_E = \frac{V_E}{V_E + V_D + V_P} \qquad W_D = \frac{V_D}{V_E + V_D + V_P} \qquad W_P = \frac{V_P}{V_E + V_D + V_P}$$

The weight for each type of capital is proportional to market values – and, of course, $W_E + W_D + W_P$ totals to 1.0.

Classic error

Managers are sometimes tempted to use the cost of the latest capital raised to discount projects, SBUs, etc. This is wrong. Also they must not use the cost of the capital they might be about to raise to finance the project.

The latest capital raised by a company might have been equity at, say, 12%, or debt at a cost of, say, 8%. If the firm is trying to decide whether to go ahead with a project that will produce an IRR of 10.5% the project will be rejected if the latest capital-raising exercise was for equity and the discount rate used was 12%. On the other hand the project will be accepted if, by chance, the latest funds raised happen to be debt with a cost of 8%. The WACC should be used for all projects – at least, for all those of the same risk class as the existing set of projects. The reason is that a firm cannot move too far away from its optimum debt-to-equity ratio level. If it does its WACC will rise. So, although it may seem attractive for a subsidiary manager to promote a favoured project by saying that it can be financed with borrowed funds and therefore it needs only to achieve a rate of return in low single figures it must be borne in mind that the next capital-raising exercise after that will have to be for equity to maintain an appropriate financial gearing level.

What about short-term debt?

Short-term debt should be included as part of the overall debt of the firm when calculating the WACC. The lenders of this money will require a return. However, to the extent that this debt is temporary or offset by cash and marketable securities held by the firm it may be excluded.

Finance and operating leases usually require fixed regular payments over lengthy periods of time incorporating an interest rate. These commitments are similar to bank loan obligations and so the capitalised value of the leases should be regarded as adding to the debt of the firm.

Applying the WACC to projects and SBUs

The overall return generated on the finance provided to a firm is determined by the portfolio of current projects. Likewise the risk (systematic) of the firm is determined by the collection of projects to which it is currently committed. If a firm made an additional capital investment that has a much higher degree of risk than the average in the existing set then it is intuitively obvious that a higher return than the normal rate for this company will be required. On the other hand if an extraordinarily low-risk activity is contemplated this should require a lower rate of return than usual.

Many multidivisional firms make the mistake of demanding that all divisions achieve the same rate of return. For example, the Association for Financial Professionals (2011) found that 32% of US companies did not adjust the rate they used for project risk. In the case of German, Austrian and Swiss companies, 60% did not vary the cost of capital on the basis of individual 'cash generating units' – see KPMG (2016). Demanding the companywide rate of return on all investments means that low-risk projects are rejected when they should be accepted and high-risk projects are accepted when they should be rejected.

Exhibit 16.6 is drawn up for an all-equity financed firm, but the principle demonstrated applies to firms financed by a mixture of types of capital. Given the firm's normal risk level the market demands a return of 11%. If another project is started with a similar level of risk then it would be reasonable to calculate NPV on the basis of a discount rate of 11%. This is the opportunity cost of capital for the shareholders – they could obtain 11% by investing their money in shares of other firms in a similar risk class. If, however, the firm invested in project A with a risk twice the normal level management would be doing their shareholders a disservice if they sought a mere 11% rate of return. At this risk level shareholders can get 16% on their money elsewhere. This sort of economic decision making will result in projects being accepted when they should have been rejected. Conversely project B if discounted at the standard rate of 11% will be rejected when it should have been accepted. It produces a return of 8.5% when all that is required is a return of 7.5% for this risk class. It is clear that this firm should accept any project lying on or above the sloping line and reject any project lying below this line.

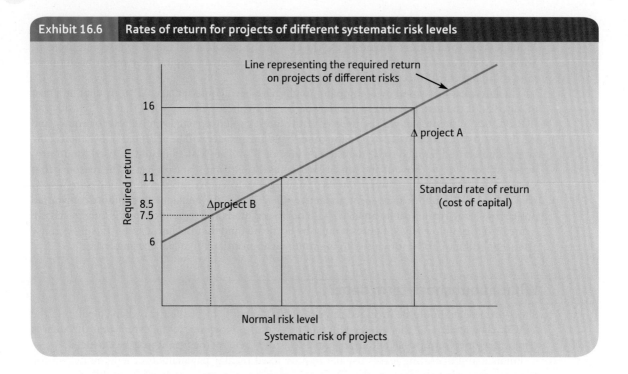

Exhibit 16.6   Rates of return for projects of different systematic risk levels

The rule discussed earlier (that a firm should accept any project that gives a return greater than the opportunity cost of capital) now has to be refined. This rule can only be applied if the marginal project has the same systematic risk level as the existing set of projects. Projects with different systematic risk levels require different levels of return.

Just how high the discount rate has to be is as much a matter for managerial judgement as one based on the measures of risk and return developed by theorists. The CAPM provides a starting point, a framework for thinking about risk premiums, but judging the viability of a project or division is still largely an art which requires experience and perceptive thought, not least because it is very difficult to quantify the likely risk of, say, an internet business. It may be possible to classify projects into broad categories, say, high, medium and low, but precise categorisation is difficult. What is clear is that the firm should not use a single discount rate for all its activities.

Some firms approach the problem of adjusting for project/business systematic risk by allowing for the three elements of 'fundamental beta' discussed in Chapter 8 – see page 308. Firstly, adjust for the type of business with reference to the sensitivity of cash flow in that business area to the ups and downs of the economy – if the cash flows are strongly related to the business cycle then we are probably dealing with a high beta project, e.g. in luxury items, cars, machine tools. Second, if operational gearing is high (large fixed operating costs with low variable costs) then an additional element of systematic risk is introduced and therefore a higher expected return required. The third element, financial gearing, should already be allowed for within the standard WACC calculation by an increase in the equity cost of capital as the debt-to-equity ratio rises. But special attention is often needed here to ensure that the decision maker has adequately allowed for this extra risk in the cost of equity (and debt).

UBS was ridiculed in the *Financial Times* for making this mistake of not properly varying the required return: 'UBS . . . allocated capital to divisions using the group cost of capital rather than adjusting for that division's risk. It is hard to imagine a serious industrial company being this primitive' (*Financial Times*, 22 April 2008, p. 20).

Empirical evidence of corporate practice

Academic literature promotes forcefully the use of the WACC. But to what extent have companies adopted the recommended methods? In 1983 Richard Pike expressed a poor opinion of the techniques used by business people to select the cost of capital: 'the methods commonly applied in setting hurdle rates are a strange mixture of folk-lore, experience, theory and intuition.' In 1976 Westwick and Shohet reported that less than 10% of the firms used a WACC. The position has changed significantly. Arnold and Hatzopoulos (2000), in a study of 96 UK firms, found that the majority calculate a WACC – *see* **Exhibit 16.7** – and Jagannathan *et al.* (2016) report that three out of four US large companies calculate a WACC. The American Association for Financial Professionals (2011) found a similar proportion for US firms.

Exhibit 16.7	Replies to the question: How does your company derive the discount rate used in the appraisal of major capital investments? (percentage of respondents)			
	Category of company			
Method used	**Small (%)**	**Medium (%)**	**Large (%)**	**Composite (%)**
WACC	41	63	61	54
The cost of equity derived from the Capital Asset Pricing Model	0	8	16	8
Interest payable on debt capital	23	8	1	11
An arbitrarily chosen figure	12	4	3	6
Dividend yield on shares plus estimated growth in capital value of share	0	0	3	1
Earnings yield on shares	3	0	0	1
Other	12	8	11	10
Blank	9	8	5	7

Source: Arnold and Hatzopoulos (2000).

Despite years of academic expounding on the virtues of the WACC and extensive managerial education, a significant minority of firms do not calculate a WACC for use in capital investment appraisal. Furthermore, as **Exhibits 16.8** and **16.9** show, many firms that calculate a WACC do not follow the prescribed methods.[6] Further evidence of a light grasp of textbook procedure was demonstrated in some of the statements made by respondents: 'Above is a minimum [WACC].

Exhibit 16.8	Method of calculating the weighted average cost of capital (percentage of respondents that use the WACC)			
	Category of company			
Method	**Small (%)**	**Medium (%)**	**Large (%)**	**Composite (%)**
Using the Capital Asset Pricing Model for equity and the market rate of return on debt capital	50	68	79	70
Cost of the equity calculated other than through the Capital Asset Pricing Model with the cost of debt derived from current market interest rates	50	32	18	29
Other	0	0	3	1

Source: Arnold and Hatzopoulos (2000).

6 Brounen *et al.* (2004) report similar numbers for UK, Netherlands and French firms.

Exhibit 16.9	If the weighted average cost of capital is used, then how are the weights defined? (percentage of respondents)			
	Category of company			
Method of defining weights	Small (%)	Medium (%)	Large (%)	Composite (%)
A long-term target debt and equity ratio	19	26	39	30
The present market values of debt and equity	44	47	42	44
Balance sheet ratios of debt and equity	37	26	19	26

Source: Arnold and Hatzopoulos (2000).

A hurdle rate is also used which is the mid-point of the above [WACC] and the lowest rate of return required by venture capitalists' 'WACC + safety margin'. Gregory and Rutterford (1999) and Rutterford (2000) carried out a series of in-depth interviews with 18 FTSE 100 company finance directors or heads of corporate finance in 1996. All 18 estimated their weighted average cost of capital. They found that 14 of the companies made use of the capital asset pricing model to estimate the equity cost of capital, five used the dividend yield plus growth method (Gordon's growth model), four used the historic real rate of return on equity and five used more than one method.

The American Association for Financial Professionals (2011) reported a higher proportion using CAPM at 87%. Their survey showed similar diversity to the UK regarding the methods used to weight debt and equity:

● 28% used a target debt-to-equity ratio;

● 23% used present market values of debt and equity;

● 30% used a current book debt-to-equity ratio;

● 19% used a current book debt-to-current market equity ratio.

Smaller US companies (under $1bn revenue) and those privately held are more likely to use current book debt-to-equity ratio (35%), while larger companies tend more toward the present market debt-to-equity ratio (27%) than smaller firms.

In the case of German, Austrian and Swiss companies we find the following weights (KPMG, 2016):

● 11% used a target debt-to-equity ratio at market values;

● 20% used the present market values of debt and equity;

● 61% derived the capital structure and cost of debt from a peer group;

● 12% Other.

Risk-free rate and betas used

In terms of the risk-free rate, Gregory and Rutterford (1999) found most UK firms used the yield on UK government bonds – they generally chose a bond with a maturity of between seven and 20 years. The remainder used a real (excluding inflation) rate of interest. None used the Treasury bill rate.

The American Association for Financial Professionals (2011) study showed almost half (46%) used the 10-year US government Treasury note to estimate the risk-free rate. Other choices were the 5-year Treasury note rate (12% of firms), the one-year Treasury rate (5%) and the 20- or 30-year US government Treasury bond was used by 15%. But only 12% used the Treasury bill rate (90-day bills).

The German, Austrian and Swiss study (KPMG, 2016) explained that companies generally regard themselves as a 'going concern' and have an 'infinite timeframe of a corporate valuation' and therefore the 'longest-term interest rate is preferred'. Thus, the government bond rate with a maturity date of at least 30 years is used in the case of 45% of the 196 companies in the study. Another one-third use the rate on bonds with between 10 and 30 years to maturity.

Betas are now widely available on financial websites, but the way in which those betas are calculated varies tremendously. The American Association for Financial Professionals (2011) study found that 29% of companies use a beta measured by looking at share returns data over one year; 13% measure beta over two years; 15% use three years; and 41% use five years. After selecting the period, companies/databases then need to decide whether to use weekly, biweekly or monthly returns during that span of time. Most select monthly returns, but a significant minority use weekly returns (31%) with only 3% using biweekly returns. On top of this room for discretion we discover about half of US companies arbitrarily 'adjust' the beta to make it closer to a value of one (they are motivated by some evidence in the literature indicating that betas tend to revert to the mean over time).

The German, Austrian and Swiss study suggested a more disaggregated approach with particular 'CGUs' (cash generating units) within the parent company having their own betas estimated in the case of 93% of the companies. Naturally, these business units within the larger organisation do not have shares traded on the markets, so betas cannot be calculated from market returns data. Instead, they estimate betas by obtaining 'peer group beta' based on the average betas in the industry, derived from returns of companies in those industries with a share quotation. But there is a problem: 'Due to the increasing convergence of industries, it is becoming ever more difficult to obtain a suitable peer group that reflects the operative risk of the CGU' (KPMG, 2016, p. 29). In other words, there are just not enough quoted share prices for companies that are purely in one industry. Even if you had a lot of companies in an industry we must remain suspicious that they may not adequately represent systematic risk for the strategic business unit under consideration. For example, take the retail sector: is the beta of Asos representative alongside fellow 'industry' constituents AA, Morrison and Dignity funeral directors? Are we justified in simply averaging the beta? If we did average through, would we then be correct to apply the derived beta to a project to open a dozen shops selling DIY products?

Risk premiums used

A few years ago it was common for academics to estimate an equity risk premium based on long-term studies of share and bond returns such as the Barclays Capital Equity Gilt Study or the Credit Suisse Global Investment Returns Yearbook. In the 1990s, after a long period of high returns on equities and low returns on bonds, researchers would often derive an equity risk premium of over 7% from these sorts of databases. Some companies also picked up from these reports an equity risk premium of 7% or more. The leading corporate finance textbooks of that period reinforced this kind of premium.

But practitioners are a sceptical and practical lot; they were worried about using such a high equity risk premium. Even the 1990s surveys showed that they most frequently plumped for a figure in the 4.5% to 6% range. The firms admitted that their estimates were a 'gut feel' choice 'that came from our planning manager. He's an MBA and a lot of his MBA work was on the cost of capital. 5% is a figure he's plucked out of the air based on his experience and knowledge' (Company O: Gregory and Rutterford, 1999, p. 43). Alternatively, managers tended to rely on advice from their bankers that the current equity risk premium was lower than at any time in the past. This intuitive approach has been borne out by the downward revision of historic risk premiums in empirical studies.

The remarkably high returns on government bonds in the first two decades of the twenty-first century and the poor performance of shares in Europe and North America have dragged down average equity risk premiums when measured over a period of a hundred years or so. This has led to a general consensus that a more acceptable equity risk premium is significantly below 7%. Dimson et al. (2011, 2017) indicate a risk premium for most countries in the range of 3–4%. The recent debate and analysis have strengthened the view of managers that they should use a moderate premium. This is reflected in the American Association for Financial Professionals (2011) study which shows the following equity risk premiums:

- 11% of companies use less than 3%;
- 23% of companies use 3–4%;
- 49% of companies use 5–6%;
- 17% of companies use 7% or greater.

After examining the responses from German, Austrian and Swiss companies KPMG (2016) stated: 'The average market risk premium applied in the period from 2007/2008 to 2011/2012 ranged between 5.0% and 5.2%. As a result of the economic and financial crisis it increased . . . to 6.3% . . . Only 1% each of the German study participants applied a market risk premium of below 5% or above 7.5% in determining their costs of capital' (pp. 26–7).

Cost of debt

When estimating the cost of their debt UK firms use the cost of long-term debt. Many base this on the cost of government debt and either take this as the cost of debt or add a credit risk premium. Others take the yield on their own outstanding bonds or choose a long-term bond yield 'based on experience'. 'We do not put in our real cost of debt. There are certain, for example tax driven, vehicles which give us actually quite a low cost of debt . . . So we tend to ignore those. That does build up a nice margin of safety within the target (cost of capital) of course' (Company C: Gregory and Rutterford, 1999, p. 46).

In the American Association for Financial Professionals (2011) study 37% of companies use the rate of return they observe on the company's existing debt; 34% forecasted the rate for new debt issuance; 22% used the average rate on outstanding debt over a defined period in the recent past, and 7% use the historical rate on outstanding debt.

The studies of UK companies found that they generally allow for the corporate tax rate to reduce the effective cost. Similarly, the American Association for Financial Professionals (2011) showed tax deductibility being taken into account: 64% use the effective tax rate they pay to reduce the cost of debt; 29% use the marginal tax rate on each additional dollar of earnings; and 7% use a target tax rate.

In 2016 German, Austrian and Swiss companies on average used a cost of debt of 3.4%. Considering that investment grade corporate bonds in 2016 in Germany yielded only 1.1%, in Austria 2.1%, and in Switzerland near to zero, we have an indication that companies regarded those market rates as abnormally low (caused by central bank intervention to lower interest rates), and so they used, not the market rate of 2016, but what they regarded as a more normal rate, i.e. somewhere between 3% and 4%.

Hurdle rates

Corporations seem to make a distinction between the WACC and the hurdle rate. Gregory and Rutterford found that the average *base hurdle rate* was 0.93% higher than the average WACC. The base hurdle rate is defined as the rate for standard projects, before any adjustments for divisional differences in operating risk, financial risk or currency risk. Most of the firms had a range of hurdle rates, depending on the project or the risk factors. There was a general impression of sophistication in attaining the WACC in the first place, followed by a rule-of-thumb-type approach when making risk adjustments: 'The comment I make in terms of the hurdle rates for investment purposes is that we do it relatively simplistically in terms of low risk, high risk, country-specific risk' (Company P: Gregory and Rutterford, 1999, p. 53). Methods range from adding two percentage point increments, to having two possible hurdle rates, say, 15% and 20%. Fifteen firms had premiums of between 0% to 8% over the base hurdle rate, while three firms added more than 10 percentage points for the highest-risk projects.

Jagannathan et al. (2016) showed that US chief financial officers typically use a discount rate far above their calculated WACC: the average used for project appraisal is 15%, while the average WACC is 8%. It is thought that this increased rate acts as a form of capital rationing when the company is short of skilled workers, managerial time or organisational capability. The consequence is that not all positive NPV projects are undertaken. But, offsetting that, the policy provides a mechanism for coping with the natural limitations of humans in a growing company; the authors write the following: 'More than half of our survey respondents agree somewhat (40.0%) or strongly (15.3%) with the statement "We cannot take all profitable projects due to limited resources in the form of limited qualified management and manpower". . . Firms that report their project selection to be limited by operational constraints use higher discount rates than other firms.'

Another factor pushing up the discount rate used above its 'proper' WACC is to make allowance for extra risks that the WACC ignores because it usually assumes use of the CAPM in conditions of perfect diversification. In reality, many managers see that their shareholders are not fully diversified and therefore face some unsystematic risk. On top of that, the raised rate 'could also reflect an undiversified manager's private interest in safer projects. Using a greater safety margin to select projects can protect the manager from poor corporate performance that could endanger his or her reputation and job security' (Jagannathan et al., 2016).

A further factor is the opportunity to build up cash reserves ready to deploy to take advantage of expected better investment opportunities in the near future. A cash pile derived from rejecting projects on discount rates between 8% (the average WACC) and 15% (the average discount rate actually applied) lowers the cost of access to cash in a hurry and the risk of being refused it: 'such firms also tend to hoard cash to avoid the cost and time of raising external funds . . . holding cash assures that they have the financial flexibility to exploit their growth options at short notice without incurring excessive costs' (Jagannathan et al., 2016).

Duke University's Fuqua School of Business and *CFO* magazine regularly conduct surveys of CFOs and report results in their Global Business Outlook (www.cfosurvey.org). They corroborate the evidence of Jagannathan et al. (2016). In their third quarter 2017 survey they asked whether managers require that proposed projects earn a higher expected return (e.g. set a higher hurdle rate) because of a shortage of management time or expertise, and found that a fifth did insist on a higher rate – *see* **Exhibit 16.10**. The average WACC reported is 9.2% (across the entire survey sample), but the average hurdle rate used is 13.5%.

More than half said they do not invest in all positive NPV projects – *see* **Exhibit 16.11** – with the given reasons mostly relating to operational constraints, such as shortage of management time and expertise, of employees, of production capacities, or that the supply chain cannot accommodate the project.

The Duke survey (www.cfosurvey.org) of European companies showed an average hurdle rate used to evaluate investment projects at 12.67%, whereas the companies' own estimates of their WACC average 8.67%. The discount rate is set at a higher level because of the shortage of management time or expertise in 63.7% of European firms, resulting in more than half of companies not pursuing all positive NPV projects.

Exhibit 16.10	Does your firm require that proposed projects earn a higher expected return (e.g., set a higher hurdle rate) because of a shortage of management time or expertise?		
		Number of companies	**Percentage**
	YES	73	20.0%
	NO	272	74.5%
	DON'T KNOW	20	5.5%
	Total	365	100.0%

Source: Duke CFO magazine Global Business Outlook survey – U.S. – Third Quarter, 2017, www.cfosurvey.org/

Exhibit 16.11	Responses of those who indicated a shortage of management time or expertise prevents their firm from pursuing some NPV > 0 projects that they would otherwise pursue		
		Number of companies	**Percentage**
	YES	46	32.2%
	NO	90	62.9%
	DON'T KNOW	7	4.9%
	Total	143	100.0%

Source: Duke CFO magazine Global Business Outlook survey – U.S. – Third Quarter, 2017 www.cfosurvey.org/

Some way to go yet

Even when the textbook model is accepted a range of WACCs can be estimated for the same firm: 'for example, altering the choice of target debt/equity ratio or equity risk premium can have an impact of 2 per cent or more on the resulting WACC figure. Furthermore, little work has yet been done to extend the complex analysis for the firm's WACC to the divisional level' (Rutterford, 2000, p. 149). This lack of sophistication was confirmed in another study, carried out by Francis and Minchington (2000) which discovered that 24% of firms (of varied sizes) used a divisional cost of capital that reflected the cost of debt capital only, thus significantly underestimating the cost of capital. Furthermore, 69% did not use a different rate for different divisions to reflect levels of risk.[7] As though all the above problems were not enough, Bernstein, the wealth manager, points out that a very low interest rate environment causes the majority of value creation from a project or SBU to arise in the distant horizon – *see* **Exhibit 16.12**.

Exhibit 16.12

Bernstein questions foundation of finance. Again.

By David Keohane

Bernstein . . . has now set itself against DCF models in a zero rate world. Thing is though, this low rate world of ours is maybe messing everything up.

As Bernstein's Inigo Fraser-Jenkins and team put it, if it is not possible to put a "price on time" then there is a genuinely intellectually painful environment where model structure is called into question:

The problem is that [DCF models] were invented and historically used in a world where risk free rates averaged 5% or more. In a world where the risk free rate is close to zero then the errors in such models explode.

Specifically, if the overall discount rate (WACC) falls from 10% to 5% in a very simple DCF then the proportion of the net present value accounted for by cash flows more than 5 years in the future rises from 70% to 95%. How far in the future can any analyst forecast?

We would suggest that any human's ability to forecast financial variables more than about 5 years in the future is limited at best. At the very least small errors at that forecasting horizon become very significant.

As Bernstein admit, it has always been known that DCF models put a larger than ideal weight on uncertain cash flows that run far into the future. It's just that the problem is now more intense.

And that "any framework that ascribes anything approaching 90% of current value to cash flows that are necessarily unknowable far in the future has to be flawed. We have never had discount rates at such low levels as we have today and hence have never had this problem before."

The solution to all of this? Well, er, hmmm, they don't really have one:

---

7 The method used throughout the book is the 'post-tax approach' in which the cost of equity is calculated as a return required after tax deductions on returns and the cost of debt is after the tax shield effect. This is to be used when the cash flows of the project or company to be discounted are calculated after tax has been deducted. Alternatively the 'pre-tax approach' could be used in which the cost of equity is 'grossed up' by $1 - T$ (T = corporation tax rate).

$$k_{\text{E pre-tax}} = \frac{k_{\text{E post-tax}}}{1 - T}$$

Then Post-tax WACC = Pre-tax WACC $(1 - T)$.

This pre-tax WACC can be used for cash flows before a deduction for tax is made. Regulators, such as those for energy supply (Ofgem), often use a third WACC. This is called 'vanilla WACC'. The required return is set equal to a weighted average of post-tax cost of equity (e.g. normal CAPM calculation shown in this chapter) and pre-tax cost of debt. Tax is estimated and allowed for separately in a similar way as other elements of operating expenditure.

What should investors do? We cannot reject discounting and there is no choice but to use it anyway. So we will keep using DCFs. We just have to be aware that a by-product of the low rate world is a

scale of forecast error that is outside the bounds of what has been previously seen and it is likely that those forecast errors may swamp any other differences between stocks.

How large is the equity risk premium?

To understand the controversy over the equity risk premium we need to appreciate that it can only ever be a subjective estimate. The reason for this is that we are trying to figure out how much additional annual return investors in an averagely risky share require above the risk-free rate today. When deciding this, investors are looking at the future, not the past. Each investor is likely to have a different assessment of the appropriate extra return compared with the risk-free investment. We need to assess the weighted average of investors' attitudes.

Using historical returns to see the size of the premium actually received may be a good starting point, but we must be aware that we are making a leap of faith to then assume that the past equity risk premium is relevant for today's analysis with its future focus. In using historic data we are making at least two more implicit assumptions:

● There has been no systematic change in the risk aversion of investors over time.

● The index being used as a benchmark has had an average riskiness that has not altered in a systematic way over time.

What is clear is that obtaining the risk premium is not as scientific as some would pretend. The range of plausible estimates is wide and the choosing of 2% rather than 4.4%, or even 7.5%, can have a significant effect on the acceptance or rejection of capital investment projects within the firm, or the calculation of value performance metrics. One of the respondents to the Arnold and Hatzopoulos survey expressed the frustration of practitioners by pointing out that precision in the WACC method is less important than to have reliable basic data: 'The real issue is one of risk premium on equity. Is it 2% or 8%?!'

The importance of and the difficulties of estimating the equity risk premium are considered by the economist John Kay in **Exhibit 16.13**.

The three article excerpts in **Exhibit 16.14** show how WACC calculations make an enormous difference to consumers and managers of regulated industries. Note that the WACC numbers

Exhibit 16.13

The past is a poor guide to future share earnings

By John Kay

In the 20th century, returns on equities substantially exceeded returns on safer assets. The size of the difference depends on the time period, the country and the method of calculation. But estimates of the average long-run value of the equity premium are mostly in the range of 3 per cent to 8 per cent.

Equity investment is riskier than cash or bonds. But not that much riskier. If the average return were even 3 per cent higher, medium to long-term

investment in equities would be almost certain to yield more: the risk would become negligible. In countries such as Britain and the US with large equity markets, 5 per cent or more of national income is needed to compensate people for worrying about the value of their stocks.

So why is the historic equity premium figure so high and will be as high in the future? Estimates of the prospective equity premium determine the cost of

▶

Exhibit 16.13 *(continued)*

capital to business. Such estimates are central to every long-term economic decisions – how to fund pensions, whether to build nuclear power stations, what to do about climate change.

Some explanations of historic levels of the equity premium imply that it will continue to be high in future. Perhaps there are many people who really need to be richly compensated to invest in equities. Even a small probability of large loss causes them great distress, or puts their job at risk. They invest a lot of emotional energy in turning nervously every morning to the share price pages of the Financial Times. They twitch over their BlackBerries in the airport lounge. They pay fees and commissions to financial advisers in generally unsuccessful pursuit of better returns.

If these are indeed the explanations, then the moral is to discipline yourself to avoid these traps. Accept that there are more important things to worry about than a falling stock market, recognise that daily share price movements are meaningless noise, restrict yourself to reviewing your portfolio only once a year. Stick with a few good stocks and take a cynical view of the claims of financial advisers. You will then gain most of the additional return from equity investment for little of the added cost.

But other explanations of the high equity premium offer less reassurance: they imply that the future cannot be like the past. If you examine figures at the higher end of estimates of the historic premium, you realise that they are arithmetically unsustainable: within a few decades, profits and dividends would absorb the whole of national income.

Perhaps the past century was just a very good time for equity investors. It was the age of inflation, in which real assets did better than nominal assets: the age of the large public corporation, in which big, professionally managed companies came into being and a regulatory framework was put in place that enabled small savers to trust business people with their money. Shareholders benefited from changes in the economic environment that will not happen again.

All historic analysis of investment performance suffers from survivor bias. Returns on the successful investments of the past are generally higher than you can expect on similar investments in the future. Investment managers advertise their best funds, not their dogs; unsuccessful hedge funds close. The equity markets of western Europe and the US are the bourses that remain open. People who put their money a century ago in Russian bonds, Chinese equities and Argentinian tramways lost most of it and there are today no analysts of these markets to tell the sorry tale.

Since none of these explanations is wholly convincing, the most plausible account of the equity premium paradox is that there is a bit of truth in all of them. That would imply that a future premium would be much lower than a historic premium, but still surprisingly high. But with real returns on indexed bonds below 2 per cent around the world and much lower in the UK, an equity premium at the low end of estimates of the historic range would offer a prospective real return on stocks below 5 per cent. That is a lot less than most people expect and many are counting on.

Exhibit 16.14

The Practical use of the WACC

Scratch the surface and PFI resemblance goes

By Oliver Ralph

A group of investors agrees to build a piece of public infrastructure. In return for funding the building costs up front, they receive regular payments from the users over a number of years. Anyone looking at the broad structure of the Thames Tideway Tunnel deal would conclude it bears a strong resemblance to a classic Private Finance Initiative project.

But dig a little deeper, and the project begins to look very different. Start with the cost. At £4.2bn, the tunnel is far bigger than a regular PFI scheme. A classic PFI project — a hospital, say, or a school — might cost somewhere in the tens or hundreds of millions. It is the size of the project that drove its structure.

The tunnel was always likely to have been too big for Thames Water to finance alone. Compare the building cost with Thames's regulatory capital value (a regulator-set measure of the value of Thames's assets), which is £11.8bn. Few water companies have to consider projects that are such a large chunk of RCV.

Thames has more debt than other water companies — its net debt is 80 per cent of RCV, against 61 per cent for Severn Trent, for example. But even if Thames's debt ratio had been as low as Severn Trent's, it would have struggled to finance the project.

In a regular PFI deal, the public sector is the client — it contracts the investors to build the infrastructure, and pays them over several years. But here the role of the government is not quite so direct. It has offered several guarantees — it has agreed to meet insurance costs that cannot be covered by the market, for example, while it has also agreed to fund any "exceptionally large" cost overrun. That support, together with low interest rates, has helped keep the cost down.

The return investors have demanded for building the tunnel — the weighted average cost of capital, in the industry jargon, — has not been disclosed, but several investors expect it to be much lower than the water industry's overall WACC of 3.7 per cent. That is partly because, as a new company, Thames Tideway Tunnel will be able to borrow more cheaply than the water companies were when they put their debt in place.

But it is also because of the government support, which removes some of the risk from the project. The final oddity is the position of the public. Thames Water customers will see their bills rise by up to £80 a year to pay for the tunnel.

FT *Financial Times*, 26 July 2015.

Exhibit 16.14 *(continued)*

Water operators hit by Ofwat's demands

By *Michael Kavanagh*

Ofwat has turned the screw on water industry operators across England and Wales by demanding they accept lower rates of return on equity and capital in the next five-year regulatory period that runs to 2020.

The regulator confirmed on Monday that companies should expect their weighted average cost of capital (WACC) – a blended measure of the return on the mix of debt and equity needed to underpin investment and spending plans – should be pegged to no more than 3.85 per cent.

The statement by Ofwat follows complaints from lobby group Consumer Council for Water that plans put forward by companies in December, demanding returns averaging 4.3 per cent, could offer too much reward to investors at the expense of customers. All but two of 19 water and sewage service operators governed by Ofwat put in pricing proposals that will see bills held or reduced in real terms in the five years from 2015.

In spite of the prospect of static or lower bills in real terms for most UK households, Ofwat said on Monday that business plans assuming an average cost of capital of 4.3 per cent across the sector for the period were too generous. The regulator has instead concluded that an acceptable cost of debt to companies is in the range of 2.2 to 2.8 per cent for the period.

It also set an acceptable average cost of equity at nearly one percentage point below companies' average claim of 6.6 per cent, stating "current total equity return expectations should be below historical evidence on returns".

Sonia Brown, head of regulation at Ofwat, said the overall guidance took account of an anticipated increase in gearing for most companies compared with the past, which would allow operators to benefit still more from access to historically low levels of interest rates.

Guidelines on Monday suggested that an increase of half a percentage point in WACC – close to the spread between Ofwat's guidance of 3.85 per cent and average companies' assumption of 4.3 per cent – equated to a notional increase in annual bills of about £10.

Water UK, the body that represents operators, suggested it could be some time before companies made clear whether they accepted the calls for accepting lower returns and keener prices. "Ofwat has published significant information and companies will take time to understand fully the implications," it said.

▶

FT *Financial Times*, 27 January 2014.

Exhibit 16.14 *(continued)*

Broadband price blow for BT

By Andrew Parker

BT suffered a setback as the telecoms regulator Ofcom proposed cuts in the price of its wholesale products.

Ofcom wants BT to reduce the price of its wholesale broadband products in order to improve internet access in rural areas.

The regulator also outlined a lower-than-expected estimate of BT's cost of capital – the assumption of what it costs BT to fund its business. UBS analysts said that could cut BT's earnings by up to 8 per cent. Shares in the telecoms company fell 2.7p to close at 176.6p.

Ofcom's calculations of its price controls for BT are partly based on its estimate of the company's cost of capital.

It proposed a lower cost of capital for BT Openreach, the subsidiary that provides the company's rivals with access to its fixed-line connections running to homes and offices.

The regulator reduced BT Openreach's weighted cost of capital from 10.1 per cent in May 2009 to 8.6 per cent in January 2011, partly to reflect lower interest rates. Analysts said this would in turn cut the price of the subsidiary's wholesale products across the country.

TalkTalk, and other companies that use BT Openreach's products, could pass on any reduction in its wholesale charges to their customers. In these circumstances, BT Retail might feel obliged to make a similar move. If it did, group revenue could be cut by £150m in 2013-14. Earnings could decline by 8 per cent.

BT said Ofcom's proposed cost of capital for BT Openreach could reduce annual wholesale revenue by 'low tens of millions' of pounds. It added that the regulator's price controls for its wholesale broadband products should 'strike the right balance between control and incentives to invest in rural areas'.

FT *Financial Times,* 21 January 2011.
All Rights Reserved.

discussed in the Press are often 'real', that is, inflation has been removed (unlike the calculations we did above). You need to add two percentage points or so inflation allowance to arrive at the 'post-tax nominal WACC' comparable with the method we have used in this chapter. Note also that the regulators are assuming a quite high level of borrowing with full tax shields, which brings down the WACC. (The detailed rationale for these calculations is set out in reports posted on the websites of the regulators – well worth a read if you are pursuing this topic in depth.)

Some thoughts on the cost of capital

Progress

There have been a number of significant advances in theory and in practice over the last forty years. No longer do most firms simply use the current interest rate, or adjust for risk in an entirely arbitrary manner. There is now a theoretical base to build on, both to determine a cost of capital for a firm, and to understand the limitations (or qualities) of the input data and economic modelling.

It is generally accepted that a weighted average of the costs of all the sources of finance is to be used. It is also accepted that the weights are to be based on market values (rather than book values), as market values relate more closely to the opportunity cost of the finance providers. Furthermore, it is possible that the WACC may be lowered and shareholder value raised by shifting the debt/equity ratio.

Even before the development of modern finance it was obvious that projects (or collections of projects, as firms are) that had a risk higher than that of investing in government securities require a higher rate of return. A risk premium must be added to the risk-free rate to determine the required return. However, modern portfolio theory has refined the definition of risk, so the analyst need only consider compensation (additional return) for systematic risk.

Outstanding issues

Despite the progress, considerable difficulties remain. Practitioners need to be aware of both the triumphs of modern financial theory as well as its gaps. The area of greatest controversy is the calculation of the cost of equity capital. In determining the cost of equity capital we start with the following facts.

● The current risk-free rate is the bedrock. It is acceptable to use the rate on a government bond with the same maturity as the project, SBU, etc.

● The return should be increased to allow for the risk of a share with average systematic risk. (Add a risk premium to the risk-free rate return.) As a guide, investors have received a risk premium of around 3–5% for accepting the risk level equivalent to that on the average ordinary share over the past 100 years or so.

● A particular company's shares do not carry average equity risk; therefore the risk premium should be increased or decreased depending on the company's systematic risk level.

So, if the project or SBU under examination has a systematic risk which is lower than that on the average share it would seem sensible that the returns attributable to shareholders on this project should be somewhere between the risk-free rate and the risk-free rate plus, say, 5%. If the project has a systematic risk greater than that exhibited by shares generally then the returns required for shareholders will be more than the risk-free rate plus, say, 5%.

There is a major difficulty calculating the systematic risk level. In the heyday of the CAPM this was simple: beta was all you needed. Today we have to allow for the possibility that investors want compensation for a multiplicity of systematic risk factors. Not unnaturally many business people are unwilling to adopt such a burdensome approach and fall back on their 'judgement' to adjust for the risk of a project. In practice it is extremely difficult to state precisely the risk of a project – we are dealing with future uncertainties about cash flows from day-to-day business operations subject to sudden and unforeseen shocks. The pragmatic approach is to avoid precision and simply place each proposed project into one of three risk categories: low, medium or high. This neatly bypasses the complexities laid out by the theorists and also reflects the fact that decisions made in the real world are made with less than complete knowledge: mechanical decision making within the firm based on over-simplistic academic models is often a poor substitute for judgement that recognises the imperfections and difficulties of real-world business.

One thing is certain: if anyone ever tells you that they can unequivocally state a firm's cost of capital to within a tenth of a percentage point, you know you are talking to someone who has not quite grasped the complexity of the issue.

Concluding comments

A firm that asks an unreasonably high rate of return will be denying its shareholders wealth-enhancing opportunities and ceding valuable markets to competitors. One that employs an irrationally low cost of capital will be wasting resources, setting managers targets that are unduly easy to reach and destroying wealth.

This chapter has described the academic foundations for calculating a company's cost of capital. It has also pointed out the practical difficulties of calculating real-world discount rates. The difficulties are severe, but please don't throw your hands up and conclude that the economists and finance theorists have taken us on a long, arduous road back to where we started. We are not at square one. We have a set of rules to provide a key management number. We now know that judgement is required at many stages in the process and where those particular points are. This allows us to view any number produced by our own calculations, or those of the finance team, with the required amount of reasoned scepticism. And, in making decisions on whether to invest in that new factory or close down a division, we have some grasp of the degree to which there is room for error in the value calculation. This part of the book reinforces again that in this uncertain world we should think in terms of a range of possible outcomes, with all too imprecise subjective probabilities, not in terms of cut-and-dried pinpoint precision. The arguments in this chapter should, I hope, allow you to estimate the boundaries for the range of values you feel comfortable with. Returns falling below the acceptable range can be easily rejected, those with a good margin above are simple to make a decision about. Management at these extremes is survivable even for the humdrum executive. It is those projects that give returns lying in the middle that require insightful judgement that is the art of management: they call for leaders.

Key points and concepts

- **The cost of capital** is the rate of return that a company has to offer finance providers to induce them to buy and hold a financial security.

- **The weighted average cost of capital (WACC)** is calculated by weighting the cost of debt and equity in proportion to their contribution to the total capital of the firm:

  $$\text{WACC} = k_E W_E + k_{DAT} W_D$$

- **The WACC can be lowered** (or raised) by altering the proportion of debt in the capital structure.

- **Investors in shares** require a return, k_E, which provides for two elements:

  - a return equal to the risk-free rate; plus
  - a risk premium.

  The most popular method for calculating the risk premium has two stages:

  - estimate the average risk premium for shares $(r_m - r_f)$; and:
  - adjust the average premium to suit the risk on a particular share.

  The CAPM using a beta based on the relative co-movement of a share with the market has been used for the second stage but other risk factors appear to be relevant.

- An alternative method for calculating the required rate of return on equity is to use the **Gordon growth model:**

  $$k_E = \frac{d_1}{P} + g$$

- The **cost of retained earnings** is equal to the expected returns required by shareholders buying new shares in a firm.

- The **cost of debt capital**, k_D, is the current market rate of return for a risk class of debt. The cost to the firm is reduced to the extent that interest can be deducted from taxable profits:

  $$k_{DAT} = k_{DBT}(1 - T)$$

- The cost of **irredeemable constant dividend preference share** capital is:

  $$k_p = \frac{d_1}{P_P}$$

- The **weights in the WACC are based on market values,** not balance sheet values.

- For projects, etc. with similar risk to that of the existing set, use the WACC, which is based on the target debt to equity ratio. **Do not use the cost of the latest capital raised.**

- For projects, SBUs, etc. of a **different systematic risk level from that of the firm,** raise or lower the discount rate in proportion to the risk.

- Companies use a mixture of theoretically correct techniques with rules of thumb to calculate hurdle rates of return.

- Calculating a cost of capital relies a great deal on judgement rather than scientific precision. But there is a theoretical framework to guide that judgement.

References and further reading

Al-Ali, J. and Arkwright, T. (2000) 'An investigation of UK companies' practice in the determination, interpretation and usage of the cost of capital', *Journal of Interdisciplinary Economics*, 11, pp. 303–19.
Some interesting survey results.

Ap Gwilym, O., Seaton, J., Suddason, K. and Thomas, S. (2006) 'International evidence on the payout ratio, earnings, dividends and returns', *Financial Analysts Journal*, 62(1) pp. 36–53.
'In short, substantial reinvestment of retained earnings does not lead to faster future real earnings growth.' Quite a challenge to the Gordon growth model.

Arnold, G.C. and Davies, M. (eds) (2000) *Value-Based Management*. London: John Wiley & Sons.
A collection of research monographs making use of the cost of capital concept.

Arnold, G.C. and Hatzopoulos, P.D. (2000) 'The theory practice gap in capital budgeting: Evidence from the United Kingdom', *Journal of Business Finance and Accounting*, 27(5) and (6), June/July, pp. 603–26.
Evidence on what UK companies do.

Arnott, R.D. and Asness, C.S. (2003) 'Surprise! Higher dividends = higher growth', *Financial Analysts Journal,* January, 59, pp. 71–87.

The evidence that future earnings growth is faster for high dividend payout ratio companies is a challenge to the Gordon growth model.

Association for Finance Professionals (2011) 'Current trends in estimating and applying the cost of capital', www.afponline.org.

An interesting survey of practice in the USA.

Barclays Capital, *Equity Gilt Studies.* London: Barclays. Annual publications which are an important source of data on historic returns.

Blanco, B., Garcia Lara, J.M. and Tribo, J. A. (2015) 'Segment disclosure and cost of capital', *Journal of Business Finance & Accounting,* Apr/May, Vol. 42, pp. 367–411.

Managers giving investors more information about different segments of the business results in a lower cost of equity and lower WACC.

Brounen, D., de Jong, A. and Koedijk, K. (2004) 'Corporate finance theory in Europe: Confronting theory with practice', *Financial Management.* Winter, pp. 71–101.

A survey of managerial practice in various European countries.

Chen, Y., C. Truong and M. Veeraraghavan, (2015) 'CEO risk-taking incentives and the cost of equity capital', *Journal of Business Finance & Accounting,* Sep/Oct, 42(7/8), pp. 915–46.

The more sensitively executive's wealth goes up and down with changes in the company's share prices the lower the cost of equity capital.

Damodaran, A. (2012) 3rd edn. *Investment Valuation.* New York: John Wiley & Sons.

Chapters 7 and 8 have some good material on the elements required to calculate the WACC.

Damodaran, A. (2014) *Applied Corporate Finance: A User's Manual.* 4th edn. New York: John Wiley & Sons.

A book prepared to deal with the difficult practical issues of WACC calculation and employment.

Dimson, E., Marsh, P. and Staunton, M. (2001) *The Millennium Book II: 101 Years of Investment Returns.* London: London Business School and ABN AMRO.

Fascinating new evidence on risk premiums.

Dimson, E., Marsh, P. and Staunton, M. (2002) *Triumph of the Optimists: 101 Years of Global Investment Returns.* Princeton, NJ: Princeton University Press.

Fascinating evidence on risk premiums.

Dimson, E., Marsh, P. and Staunton, M. (2006) The Cap Worldwide Equity Premium: A smaller puzzle. Social Science Research Network (www.ssrn.com).

Provides an alternative view on how to calculate the equity risk premium. Arrives at a figure of 3 to 3.5% (geometric mean) for the world index.

Dimson, E., Marsh, P. and Staunton, M (2011) 'Equity risk premia around the world', Available at SRN: https://ssrn.com/abstract=1940165 or http://dx.doi.org/10.2139/ssrn.1940165

'For our 19-country World index, over the entire 111 years, geometric mean real returns were an annualized 5.5%; the equity premium relative to Treasury bills was an annualized 4.5%; and the equity premium relative to long-term government bonds was an annualized 3.8%. The expected equity premium is lower, around 3% to $3\frac{1}{2}$% on an annualized basis.'

Dimson, E., Marsh, P. and Staunton, M (2017) Credit Suisse Global Investment Returns Yearbook 2017. Credit Suisse.

Returns on shares and other securities are presented and discussed.

Duc Hung Tran (2014) 'Multiple corporate governance attributes and the cost of capital – Evidence from Germany', *The British Accounting Review,* 46, pp. 179–97.

Evidence suggesting that firms with high levels of financial transparency and bonus compensations face lower cost of equity. In addition, block ownership is negatively related to firms' cost of equity when the blockholders are other firms, managers or founding-family members. Creditors demand lower cost of debt from large firms with block ownerships held by corporations or banks.

Duke University's Fuqua School of Business and *CFO* magazine CFOs and report results in their Global Business Outlook (www.cfosurvey.org)

Regular surveys of US corporate practice.

Fernández, F. (2002) 'Valuation methods and shareholder value creation'. Available as download from www.sciencedirect.com/science/book/9780122538414 or http://books.google.co.uk/.

A detailed consideration of valuation issues.

Fernández, F. (2003) '80 common and uncommon errors in company valuation', a paper available on SSRN http://papers.ssrn.com/.

A professor of finance describes mistakes made by practitioners and academics is using valuation tools.

Fernández, F. (2010) 'WACC: definition, misconceptions and errors', a paper available on SSRN http://papers.ssrn.com/sol3/papers.cfm?abstract_id=1620871.

A technical discussion of some of the issues raised when practitioners/academics simplify in order to obtain a workable WACC.

Francis, G. and Minchington, C. (2000) 'Value-based Metrics as Divisional Performance Measures', in Arnold, G.C. and Davies, M. (eds) *Value-Based Management.* Chichester: John Wiley & Sons.

Empirical evidence and discussion.

Gordon, M.J. (1962) *The Investment, Financing and Valuation of the Corporation.* Homewood, IL: Irwin.

Dividend growth model.

Gordon, M.J. and Shapiro, E. (1956) 'Capital equipment analysis: The required rate of profit', *Management Science,* III, pp. 102–10.

Dividend growth model.

Graham, J.R. and Harvey, C.R. (2001) 'The theory and practice of corporate finance: Evidence from the field', *Journal of Financial Economics,* 60(2–3), May, pp. 187–243.

A survey of US corporations: includes a section on how they calculate the WACC and its components.

Gregory, A. and Rutterford, J. (1999) 'The cost of capital in the UK: A comparison of industry and the city'. CIMA monograph, May.

Evidence on UK practice.

Hann, R.N., Ogneva, M. and Ozbas, O. (2013) 'Corporate diversification and the cost of capital', *Journal of Finance,* October, 68(5), pp. 1961–99.

'We find that diversified firms have, on average, a lower cost of capital than comparable portfolios of stand-alone firms. In addition, diversified firms with less correlated segment cash flows have a lower cost of capital, consistent with a coinsurance effect.'

Jacobs, M.T. and Shivdasani, A. (2012) 'Do you know your cost of capital?' *Harvard Business Review,* July–August, pp. 118–24.

A short easy-to-read run through of theory combined with the evidence of the variety of practices of US corporations.

Jagannathan, R., Matsaa, D.A., Meier, I. and Tarhan, V. (2016) 'Why do firms use high discount rates?' *Journal of Financial Economics,* 120, pp. 445–63.

A survey of chief financial officers shows evidence consistent with business operational constraints leading firms to use high discount rates that average twice the firms' cost of financial capital. Firms with abundant access to capital but limited qualified management or manpower appear to forgo profitable projects in preparation for more profitable future investment opportunities.

KPMG (2016) Cost of Capital Survey 2016. KPMG London (https://assets.kpmg.com/content/dam/kpmg/ch/pdf/cost-of-capital-study-2016-en.pdf)

A survey of practice in Germany, Austria and Switzerland.

Krüger, P., A. Landier and D. Thesmar (2015) 'The WACC fallacy: The real effects of using a unique discount rate', *Journal of Finance.* June, 70(3), pp. 1253–85.

Evidence that US conglomerates inadequately adjust for different risk levels (CAPM-beta) when estimating WACCs for different divisions.

Li, X (2015) 'Accounting conservatism and the cost of capital: An international analysis', *Journal of Business Finance & Accounting.* June, 42(5/6), pp. 555–82.

The more conservative a country's accounting system the lower the cost of equity and debt capital, but only in countries with strong legal enforcement, and where accounting covenants are widely used.

Lister R. (2005) 'Cost of capital: The case for the prosecution', *Investment Management and Financial Innovations,* 2, pp. 142–57.

Argues that the conventional method of calculating the WACC (as described in this chapter) is fundamentally flawed.

Lister, R. (2006) 'Cost of capital is beyond our reach', *Accountancy,* December, pp. 42–3.

Points out the difficulties in calculating the WACC and is sceptical about our ability to overcome them.

McLaney, E., Pointon, J., Thomas, M. and Tucker, J. (2004) 'Practitioners' perspectives on the UK cost of capital', *European Journal of Finance,* 10, April, pp. 123–38.

A survey of finance directors in 1997 provides some additional insight into how managers go about calculating the WACC.

Ofcom UK (telecommunications and media regulator) (www.ofcom.org.uk).

This website posts numerous reports that carefully take the reader through the background finance theory and practical difficulties of calculating a WACC.

Ofgem (UK energy regulator) (www.ofgem.gov.uk).

This website posts numerous reports that describe the key elements making up the WACC calculations used for some regulated companies.

Ofwat (UK water regulator) www.ofwat.

Website has many reports discussing WACC calculations to be used to set prices for water supply.

Pike, R.H. (1983) 'A review of recent trends in formal capital budgeting processes', *Accounting and Business Research,* Summer, pp. 201–8.

Evidence of practitioner approaches.

Rutterford, J. (2000) 'The cost of capital and shareholder value', in Arnold, G.C. and Davies, M. (eds) *Value-Based Management.* Chichester: John Wiley & Sons.

Some fascinating evidence of UK practice.

Westwick, C.A. and Shohet, P.S.D. (1976) 'Investment Appraisal and Inflation', ICAEW Research Committee, Occasional Paper, No. 7.

Early evidence of techniques used in practice.

Wright, S., Mason, R., Satchell, S., Hari, K. and Baskaya, M. (2006) Smither's and Co.'s report on the cost of capital provided to Ofgem (www.ofgem.gov.uk).

Considers a number of the practical difficulties in estimating a WACC. It is remarkable how many 'judgements' need to be made along the way.

Case study recommendations

Please see www.pearsoned.co.uk/arnold for case study synopses. Also, there is another list of useful case studies in the fifth edition

- H. J. Heinz: estimating the cost of capital in uncertain times. Author: Marc Lipson, Darden School of Business. Available at www.cb.hbsp.harvard.edu
- Flash Memory, Inc. (brief case). Authors: William E. Fruhan; Craig Stephenson. Harvard Business School. Available at www.cb.hbsp.harvard.edu
- Midland Energy Resources, Inc.: cost of capital (brief case). Authors: Timothy A. Luehrman; Joel L.

Heilprin, Harvard Business School. Available at www. cb.hbsp.harvard.edu
- Mercury Athletic: valuing the opportunity. Authors: Timothy A. Luehrman; Joel L. Heilprin, Harvard Business School. Available at www.cb.hbsp .harvard.edu
- Royal Mail Plc: cost of capital. Author: Michael J. Schill, Darden School of Business. Available at www.cb.hbsp.harvard.edu
- Nextel Peru: emerging market cost of capital. Authors: Luis M. Viceira; Joel L. Heilprin, Harvard Business School. Available at www.cb.hbsp .harvard.edu

Websites

Competition and Market Authority, www.gov.uk/ government/organisations/ competition-and-markets-authority
Investors Chronicle www.investorschronicle.co.uk
Ofcom www.ofcom.org.uk

Ofgem www.ofgem.gov.uk
Ofwat www.ofwat.gov.uk
London Stock Exchange www.londonstockexchange.com

Video presentations

Chief executives and finance directors discuss various financial issues on MerchantCantos (www.merchantcantos.com) – this is free to view.

Self-review questions

1 Explain the term 'the cost of capital'.

2 Explain how you might calculate the cost of equity capital.

3 Why can we not always take the coupon rate on a bond issued years ago as the cost of bond capital?

4 Describe the weighted average cost of capital and explain why a project SBU or product line should not

be evaluated using the cost of finance associated with the latest portion of capital raised.

5 Should the WACC be used in all circumstances?

6 Explain two of the practical difficulties in calculating a firm's cost of capital.

Questions and problems

Answers to most questions can be found at www.pearsoned.co.uk/arnold.
Answers to questions marked with an asterisk are to be found only in the Lecturer's Guide.

1* (*Examination level*) Burgundy plc is financed through bonds and ordinary shares. The bonds were issued five years ago at a par value of £100 (total funds raised £5m). They carry an annual coupon of 10%, are due to be redeemed in four years and are currently trading at £105.

   The company's shares have a market value of £4m, the return on risk-free government securities is 8% and the risk premium for an average-risk share has been 5%. Burgundy's shares have a lower than average risk and its historic beta as measured by the co-movement of its shares and the market index correctly reflects the risk adjustment necessary to the average risk premium – this is 0.85. The corporate tax rate is 30%. Burgundy has a net asset figure of £3.5m showing in its balance sheet.

Required

a   Calculate the cost of debt capital.
b   Calculate the cost of equity capital.
c   Calculate the weighted average cost of capital.
d   Should Burgundy use the WACC for all future projects and SBUs? Explain your answer.

2 (*Examination level*) Petalt plc wishes to carry out a shareholder value analysis for which it has gathered the information shown in the table below:

   The managers do not yet know the cost of capital but do have the following information. The capital is in three forms:

1   A floating-rate bank loan for £1m at 2% over bank base rate. Base rates are currently 9%.
2   A 25-year vanilla bond issued 20 years ago at par (£100) raising £1m. The bond has an annual coupon of 5% and is currently trading at £80. The next coupon is due in one year.
3   Equity capital with a market value of £2m.

Latest annual sales	£1m
Sales growth rate	10%
Operating profit margin before tax	10%
Tax rate on corporate profits	31%
Incremental fixed capital investment	17% of sales change
Incremental working capital investment	6% of sales change
Planning horizon	5 years

   The rate of return available by purchasing long-term government securities is currently 6% and the average risk premium for shares over the risk-free rate has averaged 5%. Petalt's shares have an above-average risk and its historic beta as measured by the co-movement of its shares and the market index correctly reflects the risk adjustment necessary to the average risk premium – this is 1.3.

Required

a   Calculate the cost of bond finance.
b   Calculate the cost of equity finance.
c   Calculate the weighted average cost of capital.
d   Calculate shareholder value using Rappaport's method.
e   Conduct sensitivity analysis on the calculated shareholder value by altering the operating profit margin and the number of years in the planning horizon. Show a table containing alternative profit margin assumptions and planning horizon assumptions.

(*An Excel spreadsheet version of these calculations is available at www.pearsoned.co.uk/arnold.*)

3   (*Examination level*) Diversified plc is trying to introduce an improved method of assessing investment projects using discounted cash flow techniques. For this it has to obtain a cost of capital to use as a discount rate.

The finance department has assembled the following information:

  – The company has an equity beta of 1.50, which may be taken as the appropriate adjustment to the average risk premium. The yield on risk-free government securities is 7% and the historic premium above the risk-free rate is estimated at 5% for shares.
  – The market value of the firm's equity is twice the value of its debt.
  – The cost of borrowed money to the company is estimated at 12% (before tax shield benefits).
  – Corporation tax is 30%.

Assume: No inflation.

Required

  a   Estimate the equity cost of capital using the capital asset pricing model (CAPM). Create an estimate of the weighted average cost of capital (WACC).
  b   Comment on the appropriateness of using this technique for estimating the cost of capital for project appraisal purposes for a company with many subsidiaries in different markets.
  c   Given the difficulties in the calculation of WACC are companies justified in using rules of thumb rather than theoretically precise methods? Explain the difficulties and describe the approximations used by business people. **(?)**

4   The projected cash flows for a company to be established are £1m per year for ever. The company will require £9m in capital to be viable and produce the £1m annual cash flows. The prospective directors suggest that they raise £2m by borrowing from a bank at a fixed rate of 6% per year. The remaining £7m will come from an issue of shares. Shares with a similar systematic risk are currently offering an expected return of 11%. This cautious level of borrowing suits the directors because their livelihood depends on the survival of the firm. The corporation tax rate is 30%.

Required

  a   Calculate the WACC and the value of the enterprise (debt + equity value)
  b   If a higher level of financial gearing is targeted such that £5m of the capital comes from lenders and £4m comes from shareholders the required rates of return change. The debt holders now require 7% per annum, whereas the equity holders expect a return of 16% per year. Does this capital structure raise or lower the WACC and value of the firm?

(An Excel spreadsheet version of these calculations is available at pearsoned.co.uk/arnold.)

5   Triglass plc has three types of capital. The market capitalisation of its equity is £20m. These ordinary shares have a beta of 0.9, as measured over the past five years of monthly returns which may be taken as the appropriate adjustment to the average risk premium. The current risk-free rate on government bonds is 4.5%. The historic equity risk premium is 5% per year. The market value of its irredeemable non-participating non-convertible preference shares is £5m and the rate of return being offered is 7.5% per year. The debt of the firm amounts to £15m and costs 6.5% per year before allowing for tax shield benefits. The corporation tax rate is 30%. Calculate the WACC for Triglass plc.

(An Excel spreadsheet version of these calculations is available at www.pearsoned.co.uk/arnold.)

Assignment

Calculate the weighted average cost of capital for a company or SBU of a company you know well. Explain those areas where you have made difficult judgements in deciding which numbers to use.

Valuing shares

LEARNING OUTCOMES

By the end of this chapter the reader should be able to:

■ describe the principal determinants of share prices and estimate share value using a variety of approaches;

■ demonstrate awareness of the most important input factors and appreciate that they are difficult to quantify;

■ use valuation models to estimate the value of shares when managerial control is achieved.

Introduction

Knowledge of the main influences on share prices is important from the perspective of two groups. The first group is managers, who, if they are to be given the responsibility of maximising the wealth of shareholders, need to know the factors influencing that wealth, as reflected in the share price of their own company. Without this understanding they will be unable to determine the most important consequence of their actions – the impact on share value. Managers need to appreciate share price derivation because their company's share price is one of the key factors by which they are judged. It is also useful for them to know how share prices are set if the firm plans to gain a flotation on a stock exchange, or when it is selling a division to another firm. In mergers an acquirer needs good valuation skills so as not to pay more than necessary, and a seller needs to ensure that the price is fair.

The second constituency for whom the ideas and models presented in this chapter will be of practical use is investors, who risk their savings by buying shares.

This chapter describes the main methods of valuing shares: net asset value, dividend valuation models, price-earnings ratio models and cash flow models. There is an important subsection in the chapter which shows that the valuation of shares is somewhat different when the size of the shareholding is large enough to give managerial control over the firm compared with the valuation when there is only a small holding providing a small minority stake.

Two skills are needed to be able to value shares. The first is analytical ability, to be able to understand and use mathematical valuation models. Second, and most importantly, good judgement is needed, because most of the inputs to the mathematical calculations are factors, the precise nature of which cannot be defined with absolute certainty, so great skill is required to produce reasonably accurate results. The main problem is that the determinants of value occur in the future, for example future cash flows, dividends or earnings.

The monetary value of an asset is what someone is prepared to pay for it. Assets such as cars and houses are difficult enough to value with any degree of accuracy. At least corporate bonds generally have a regular cash flow (coupon) and an anticipated capital repayment. This contrasts with the uncertainties associated with shares, for which there is no guaranteed annual payment and no promise of capital repayment.

The difficulties of share valuation are amply represented by the case of Amazon.com.

Case study 17.1   Amazon.com

Amazon floated in 1997 and it failed to make any profit at all for six years. For example, it lost over $700m in 1999 and offered little prospect of profits in the near term. So, if you were an investor in early 2000 what value would you give to a company of this calibre? Anything at all? Amazingly, investors valued Amazon at over $30bn in early 2000 (more than all the traditional book retailers put together). The share price had gained 6,000% in 30 months. The brand was well established and the numbers joining the online community rose by thousands every day. Investors were confident that Amazon would continue to attract customers and produce a rapid rate of growth in revenue. Eventually, it was thought, this revenue growth would translate into profits and high dividends. When investors had calmed down after taking account of the potential for rivalrous competition in this business and the fact that by 2001 Amazon was still not producing profits they reassessed the value of Amazon's likely future dividends. In mid-2001, they judged the company to be worth only $4bn – it had run up losses of $1.4bn in 2000, indicating that profits and dividends were still a long way off. However, in 2016 the company generated earnings of $2.4bn. It has broadened its offering beyond books. By the end of 2017 the market valued its shares at $570bn, which was over 220 times earnings. This was taking a lot of future growth on trust.

In 2017 the market's value of Tesla surpassed that of Ford despite selling only a fraction of the vehicles and losing over $1bn per year – *see* **Exhibit 17.1**. Snap made losses of over $500m but was still valued at over $30bn, that is, 70 times the previous year's sales – *see* **Exhibit 17.2**. Is there a rational base for share valuations? Answering this question is what this chapter is all about.

Exhibit 17.1

Tesla overtakes Ford as investors bet on electric dream

Concerns rise about traditional industry running out of steam after weak sales figures

By Patti Waldmeir and Richard Waters

Tesla, the upstart electric carmaker, surpassed US motor pioneer Ford in market value on Monday, as investors look to a future beyond the internal combustion engine.

Shares of Tesla, founded in 2003, rose 7.3 per cent to a market capitalisation of $48.7bn, gliding past the 100-year-old Ford, whose shares fell 1.7 per cent after disappointing March sales results to a market value of $45.3bn.

While it is symbolic for a Silicon Valley start-up to surpass the valuation of a company that helped make motor cars ubiquitous in early 20th century America, car market analysts point out that Tesla achieved the feat based on global deliveries of only 76,000 cars last year, compared with Ford's global sales in 2016 of 6.6m.

"The stock market has always treated Ford like an industrial stock while Tesla has been considered a tech stock," said Michelle Krebs of Autotrader.com. "Let's remember: Ford earns money, lots of it. Tesla does not."

The real test for Tesla comes when it launches the Model 3, the high-volume, mainstream-priced electric vehicle that is supposed to help the company achieve profitability. Investors appear to be betting that Tesla's Model 3 can do for electric cars what Henry Ford's Model T did for traditionally powered cars a century ago: make them cheap and convenient.

Exhibit 17.2

Why Wall Street embraced the Snapchat owner IPO

Blockbuster debut reflects booming stock market and demand for tech listings

Nicole Bullock

A tell-tale sign of a booming equity market is a hot technology listing, and the blockbuster debut by Snap duly summoned memories of the dotcom era. Shares in the parent of the popular messaging app surged more than 40 per cent in their New York Stock Exchange debut on Thursday where the fresh-faced co-founders rang the opening bell to cheers from the trading floor. On Friday, they added another 11 per cent to $27.09.

While the company lost more than $500m last year and faces questions over its corporate governance as well as heightened competition from rival Facebook,

it has effortlessly achieved a market valuation of more than $30bn.

That puts Snap ahead of the likes of the century-old Kellogg's, but at a fraction of Facebook and Google at nearly $400bn and just under $600bn, respectively.

Three factors help explain why Snap is a hit on Wall Street and raised $3.4bn in capital from investors — starting with a compelling sense of timing.

Investors have consistently pushed US equity benchmarks into record territory in recent months, prompting talk of a return of "animal spirits", a reference to the buying enthusiasm associated with increased risk-taking on Wall Street.

Mounting confidence in the US economy and a sustained recovery in earnings growth in the backdraught of a pro-business agenda from the Trump administration remains the main driver of bullish equity market sentiment, providing fertile ground for an initial public offering. "It is easier to IPO when markets are at all-time highs," said Matthew Kennedy, an analyst at Renaissance Capital, "Snap's successful debut also reflects the absence of a big tech IPO since Alibaba, when the Chinese ecommerce giant went public with a record $25bn deal in September 2014.

Against that backdrop, investors were hungry for a growth company such as Snap which saw a near sevenfold increase in revenue last year to $405m — albeit yet to turn a profit.

Many of the fast-growing tech companies, including Uber and Airbnb, have opted to stay private, raising billions of dollars through private fundraising at high valuations and creating a herd of so-called unicorns, or tech companies that have achieved valuations of $1bn or more without going public. Snap's performance bodes well for other unicorns planning to make their way to Wall Street.

The other key element at play was a fear among investors of missing out on a hot investment opportunity that — despite all the doubts about Snap's long-term prospects — may ultimately emulate the performance of Facebook, Netflix and Amazon.

Multiple investors who took part in Snap's roadshow, or marketing campaign, said they were struck by how many people had attended the events, with a lunch at the swanky Mandarin Oriental hotel in New York attracting some 500 prospective buyers.

 Financial Times, 3 March 2017.

Valuation using net asset value (NAV)

The balance sheet seems an obvious place to start when faced with the task of valuation. In this method the company is viewed as being worth the sum of the value of its net assets. The balance sheet is regarded as providing objective facts concerning the company's ownership of assets and obligations to creditors. Here non-current assets (fixed assets) are recorded along with inventories, receivables (debtors), cash and other liquid assets. With the deduction of long-term and short-term creditors from the total asset figure we arrive at the net asset value (NAV).

An example of this type of calculation is shown in **Exhibit 17.3** for Unilever.

Exhibit 17.3	Unilever plc abridged balance sheet as at 31 December 2016

	€m
Non-current assets (fixed assets)	42,545
Current assets	13,884
Non-current liabilities	(18,893)
Current liabilities	(20,556)
Net assets	16,980

Source: Unilever plc, Annual Report 2016.

Unilever's NAV of £17bn compares with a market value placed on all the issued shares when totalled of £45bn. This great difference makes it clear that the shareholders of Unilever are not rating the firm on the basis of balance sheet net asset figures. This point is emphasised by an examination of **Exhibit 17.4**.

Some of the firms listed in Exhibit 17.4 have a very small balance sheet value in comparison with their total market capitalisation. Vodafone and Bloomsbury, the exceptions, boosted their balance sheets by including a lot of intangible assets in the form of goodwill following acquisitions (goodwill is an amount placed on the balance sheet as the difference between the amount

Exhibit 17.4	Net asset values and total capitalisation of some firms	
Company (Accounts year)	**NAV**	**Total capitalisation (market value of company's shares)**
AstraZeneca (2016)	$16.7bn	$80bn
Sky (2017)	£4bn	£16bn
Bloomsbury (2017)	£139m	£137m
Marks & Spencer (2017)	£3.2bn	£4.9bn
WPP (2016)	£8bn	£16bn
Vodafone (2017)	€72.2bn	€68bn

Source: Annual reports and accounts.

paid for the target and the fair value of the assets acquired). Analysts may adjust values shown on balance sheets to replacement cost or realisable values, e.g. a property asset bought five years ago and valued on the balance sheet at cost may be adjusted to its current market value. However, even with many alterations of this kind for most companies market value will remain a long way from NAV.

For most companies, investors look to the income flow to be derived from a holding. This flow is generated when the balance sheet assets are combined with assets impossible to quantify: these include the unique skills of the workforce, the relationships with customers and suppliers, the value of brands, the reservoir of experience within the management team, and the competitive positioning of the firm's products. Thus assets, in the crude sense of balance sheet values, are only one dimension of overall value – *see* **Exhibit 17.5**. Investors in the market generally value intangible, unmeasurable assets more highly than those which can be identified and recorded by accountants.

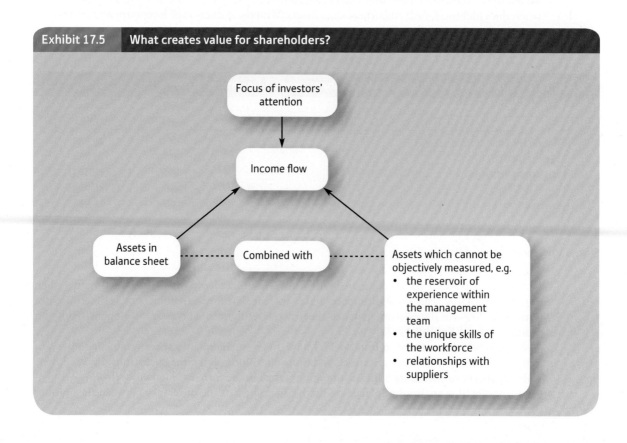

Exhibit 17.5   What creates value for shareholders?

Criticising accountants for not producing balance sheets which reflect the true value of a business is unfair. Accounts are not usually designed to record up-to-date market values. Land and buildings are frequently shown at cost rather than market value; thus the balance sheet can provide a significant over- or under-valuation of the assets' current value. Plant and machinery is shown at the purchase price less a depreciation amount. Inventory is valued at the lower of cost or net realisable value – this can lead to a significant underestimate, as the market value can appreciate to a figure far higher than either of these. The list of balance sheet entries vulnerable to subjective estimation, arbitrary method and even cynical manipulation is a long one: goodwill, provisions, merger accounting, receivables, intangible brand values and so on.

When asset values are particularly useful

The balance sheet approach to share value is fraught with problems but there are circumstances in which asset backing is given more attention.

Firms in financial difficulty

Shareholders of firms in financial difficulty may pay a great deal of attention to the asset backing of the firm. They may weigh up the potential for asset sales or asset-backed borrowing. In extreme circumstances they may try to assess the break-up value. Here the liquidation value is key: what could be realised by selling the assets and paying off all liabilities. Liquidation value may or may not be close to NAV.

Takeover bids

In a takeover bid shareholders will be reluctant to sell at less than NAV even if the prospect for income growth is poor. A standard defensive tactic in a takeover battle is to revalue balance sheet assets to encourage a higher price.

When discounted income flow techniques are difficult to apply

For some types of company there is no straightforward way of employing income-flow-based methods:

1 *Property investment companies* are primarily valued on the basis of their assets. It is generally possible to put a fairly realistic up-to-date price on the buildings owned by such a company. These market values have a close link to future cash flows. That is, the future rents payable by tenants, when discounted, determine the value of property assets and thus the company. If higher rent levels are expected than were previously anticipated, chartered surveyors will place a higher value on the asset, and the NAV in the balance sheet will rise, forcing up the share price. For such companies, future income, asset values and share values are all linked.

2 *Investment trusts* The future income of investment trusts comes from the individual shareholdings. The shareholder in a trust would find it extremely difficult to calculate the future income to be received from each of the dozens or hundreds of shares held. An easier approach is simply to take the current share price of each holding as representing the future discounted income. The share values are aggregated to derive the trust's NAV and this has a strong bearing on the price at which the trust shares are traded.

3 *Resource-based companies* For oil companies, mineral extractors, mining houses and so on, the proven or probable reserves have a significant influence on the share price.

Valuation using income-flow methods

The value of a share is usually determined by the income flows that investors expect to receive in the future from its ownership. Information about the past is only of relevance to the extent that it contributes to an understanding of expected future performance. Income flows will occur at different points in the future and so they have to be discounted. There are three classes of income valuation model:

● dividend-based models;
● earnings-based models;
● cash-flow-based models.

Dividend valuation models

The dividend valuation models (DVMs) are based on the premise that *the market value of ordinary shares represents the sum of the expected future dividend flows, to infinity, discounted to present value.*

The only cash flows that investors ever receive from a company are dividends. This holds true if we include a 'liquidation dividend' upon the sale of the firm or on formal liquidation, and any share repurchases can be treated as dividends. Of course, an individual shareholder is not planning to hold a share forever to gain the dividend returns to an infinite horizon. An individual holder of shares will expect two types of return:

a   income from dividends, and

b   a capital gain resulting from the appreciation of the share and its sale to another investor.

The fact that the individual investor is looking for capital gains as well as dividends to give a return does not invalidate the model. The reason for this is that when a share is sold, the purchaser is buying a future stream of dividends, therefore the price paid is determined by future dividend expectations.

To illustrate this, consider the following: a shareholder intends to hold a share for one year. A single dividend will be paid at the end of the holding period, d_1 and the share will be sold at price P_1 in one year.

To derive the value of a share at time 0 to this investor (P_0), the future cash flows, d_1 and P_1, need to be discounted at a rate which includes an allowance for the risk class of the share, k_E.

$$P_0 = \frac{d_1}{1 + k_E} + \frac{P_1}{1 + k_E}$$

Worked example 17.1

An investor is considering the purchase of some shares in Willow plc. At the end of one year a dividend of 22p will be paid and the shares are expected to be sold for £2.43. How much should be paid if the investor judges that the rate of return required on a financial security of this risk class is 20%?

Answer

$$P_0 = \frac{d_1}{1 + k_E} + \frac{P_1}{1 + k_E}$$

$$P_0 = \frac{22}{1 + 0.2} + \frac{243}{1 + 0.2} = 221p$$

The dividend valuation model to infinity

The relevant question to ask in order to understand DVMs is: where does P_1 come from? The buyer at time 1 estimates the value of the share based on the present value of future income given the required rate of return for the risk class. So if the second investor expects to hold the share for a further year and sell at time 2 for P_2, the price P_1 will be:

$$P_1 = \frac{d_2}{1 + k_E} + \frac{P_2}{1 + k_E}$$

Returning to the P_0 equation we are able to substitute discounted d_2 and P_2 for P_1. Thus:

$$P_0 = \frac{d_1}{1 + k_E} + \frac{P_1}{1 + k_E}$$

$$P_0 = \frac{d_1}{1 + k_E} + \frac{d_2}{(1 + k_E)^2} + \frac{P_2}{(1 + k_E)^2}$$

If a series of one-year investors bought this share, and we in turn solved for P_2, P_3, P_4, etc., we would find:

$$P_0 = \frac{d_1}{1 + k_E} + \frac{d_2}{(1 + k_E)^2} + \frac{d_3}{(1 + k_E)^3} + \ldots + \frac{d_n}{(1 + k_E)^n}$$

Even a short-term investor has to consider events beyond his or her time horizon because the selling price is determined by the willingness of a buyer to purchase a future dividend stream. If this year's dividends are boosted by short-termist policies such as cutting out R&D and brand-support marketing the investor may well lose more on capital value changes (as other investors push down the share price when their forecasts for future dividends are lowered) than the gains in dividend income.

Worked example 17.2

If a firm is expected to pay dividends of 20p per year to infinity and the rate of return required on a share of this risk class is 12% then:

$$P_0 = \frac{20}{1 + 0.12} + \frac{20}{(1 + 0.12)^2} + \frac{20}{(1 + 0.12)^3} + \ldots + \frac{20}{(1 + 0.12)^n}$$

$$p_0 = 17.86 + 15.94 + 14.24 + \ldots + \ldots +$$

Given this is a perpetuity there is a simpler approach:

$$P_0 = \frac{d_1}{k_E} = \frac{20}{0.12} = 166.67p$$

The dividend growth model

In contrast to the situation in the above example, for most companies dividends are expected to grow from one year to the next. To make DVM analysis manageable simplifying assumptions are usually made about the patterns of growth in dividends. Most managers attempt to make dividends grow more or less in line with the firm's long-term earnings growth rate. They often bend over backwards to smooth out fluctuations, maintaining a high dividend even in years of poor profits or losses. In years of very high profits they are often reluctant to increase the dividend by a large percentage for fear that it might have to be cut back in a downturn.[1] So, given management propensity to make dividend payments grow in an incremental or stepped fashion it seems that a reasonable model could be based on the assumption of a constant growth rate. (Year to year deviations around this expected growth path will not materially alter the analysis.) See Worked examples 17.3 and 17.4 for the use of the constant dividend growth model.

Worked example 17.3   A constant dividend growth valuation: Shhh plc

If the last dividend paid was d_0 and the next is due in one year, d_1, then this will amount to $d_0 (1 + g)$ where g is the growth rate of dividends.

For example, if Shhh plc has just paid a dividend of 10p and the growth rate is 7% then:

d_1 will equal $d_0 (1 + g) = 10 (1 + 0.07) = 10.7p$

and

d_2 will be $d_0 (1 + g)^2 = 10 (1 + 0.07)^2 = 11.45p$

▶

---

1 For a discussion on the propensity for directors to keep to a steadily rising dividend policy see Chapter 19.

Worked example 17.3 *(continued)*

The value of a share in Shhh will be all the future dividends discounted at the risk-adjusted discount rate of 11%:

$$P_0 = \frac{d_0(1+g)}{(1+k_E)} + \frac{d_0(1+g)^2}{(1+k_E)^2} + \frac{d_0(1+g)^3}{(1+k_E)^3} + \ldots + \frac{d_0(1+g)^n}{(1+k_E)^n}$$

$$P_0 = \frac{10(1+0.07)}{1+0.11} + \frac{10(1+0.07)^2}{(1+0.11)^2} + \frac{10(1+0.07)^3}{(1+0.11)^3} + \ldots + \frac{10(1+0.07)^n}{(1+0.11)^n}$$

Using the above formula could require a lot of time. Fortunately it is mathematically equivalent to the following formula which is much easier to employ. (This is called the Gordon growth model – discussed in Chapter 16.)

$$P_0 = \frac{d_1}{k_E - g} = \frac{d_0(1+g)}{k_E - g} = \frac{10.7}{0.11 - 0.07} = 267.50p$$

Note that, even though the shortened formula only includes next year's dividend all the future dividends are represented. In using the model you are assuming the inclusion of all dividends stretching to an infinite horizon growing at a constant rate of *g*.

A further illustration is provided by the example of Pearson plc.

Worked example 17.4   Pearson plc

Pearson plc, the publishing, media and education group, has the following dividend history.

Year	dividend per share (p)
2001	22.3
2002	23.4
2003	24.2
2004	25.4
2005	27.0
2006	29.3
2007	31.6
2008	33.8
2009	35.5
2010	38.7
2011	42.0
2012	45.0
2013	48.0
2014	51.0
2015	52.0
2016	52.0

The average annual growth rate, *g*, over this period has been:

$$g = \sqrt[15]{\frac{52.0}{22.3}} - 1 = 0.058 \; or \; 5.8\%$$

If it is assumed that this historic growth rate will continue into the future (a big *if*) and 10% is taken as the required rate of return, the value of a share can be calculated.

$$P_0 = \frac{d_1}{k_E - g} = \frac{52(1+0.058)}{0.10 - 0.058} = 1,310p$$

In 2016 Pearson's shares ranged from as high as £10 to as low as £7. So there were times when investors were a little more pessimistic than we have been in the above analysis, and times when they were a lot more pessimistic. Perhaps they were anticipating a slower rate of growth in future than in the past or even a fall in profits and dividend. Or they judged the risk to be greater, thus raising k_E.

Their pessimism concerning the likelihood of past profits and dividend trends continuing was borne out by the profit warning in January 2017 caused by poor performance in its core markets in digital education and books. Its shares plunged 29% in a day, to £5.74. The *Financial Times* (which Pearson used to own, but swapped for some cash in 2015) commented that it 'expects to slash the dividend'. In August 2017 it announced another 3,000 job cuts on top of the 7,000 already lost, and said it would cut its interim dividend to 5p (from 18p for the same period in 2016). It was expected that only 10p would be paid in the second half, making 15p for the year, a dramatic change from the historical trend. This case illustrates the importance of understanding the drivers of profits and dividends rather than simply extrapolating from the past. Sometimes a continuation of trend makes sense; other times (indeed, most times) a more nuanced analysis is needed given the qualitative drivers of future profits (see section 'Determinants of growth' later in the chapter).

Non-constant growth

Firms tend to go through different phases of growth. If they have a strong competitive advantage in an attractive market they might enjoy super-normal growth for a while. Eventually, however, most firms come under competitive pressure and growth becomes normal. Ultimately, many firms fail to keep pace with the market environmental change in which they operate and growth falls to below that for the average company.

To analyse companies which will go through different phases of growth a two-, three- or four-stage model may be used. In the simplest case of two-stage growth the share price calculation requires the following:

1   Calculate each of the forecast annual dividends in the first period.

2   Estimate the share price at the point at which the dividend growth shifts to the new permanent rate.

3   Discount each of the dividends in the first period and the share price given in 2. Add all the discounted numbers to obtain the current value.

Worked example 17.5   Use of the two-stage growth model – Noruce plc

You are given the following information about Noruce plc.

The company has just paid an annual dividend of 15p per share and the next is due in one year. For the next three years dividends are expected to grow at 12% per year. This rapid rate is caused by a number of favourable factors: for example an economic upturn, the fast acceleration stage of newly developed products and a large contract with a government department.

After the third year the dividend will grow at only 7% per annum, because the main boosts to growth will, by then, be absent.

Shares in other companies with a similar level of systematic risk to Noruce produce an expected return of 16% per annum.

What is the value of one share in Noruce plc?

Answer

Stage 1 Calculate dividends for the super-normal growth phase.

$$d_1 = 15\,(1 + 0.12) = 16.8$$
$$d_2 = 15\,(1 + 0.12)^2 = 18.8$$
$$d_3 = 15\,(1 + 0.12)^3 = 21.1$$

Stage 2 Calculate share price at time 3 when the dividend growth rate shifts to the new permanent rate.

$$P_3 = \frac{d_4}{k_E - g} = \frac{d_3\,(1 + g)}{k_E - g} = \frac{21.1(1 + 0.07)}{0.16 - 0.07} = 250.9$$

▶

Worked example 17.5 *(continued)*

Stage 3 Discount and sum the amounts calculated in Stages 1 and 2.

$$\frac{d_1}{1 + k_E} = \frac{16.8}{1 + 0.16} = 14.5$$

$$+ \frac{d_2}{(1 + k_E)^2} = \frac{18.8}{(1 + 0.16)^2} = 14.0$$

$$+ \frac{d_3}{(1 + k_E)^3} = \frac{21.1}{(1 + 0.16)^3} = 13.5$$

$$+ \frac{P_3}{(1 + k_E)^3} = \frac{250.9}{(1 + 0.16)^3} = \underline{160.7}$$
$$\underline{202.7\text{p}}$$

An Excel spreadsheet version of this calculation for Noruce is available at www.pearsoned.co.uk/arnold.

What is a normal growth rate?

Growth rates will be different for each company but for corporations taken as a whole dividend growth will not be significantly different from the growth in nominal gross national product (real GNP plus inflation) over the long run. If dividends did grow in a long-term trend above this rate then they would take an increasing proportion of national income – ultimately squeezing out the consumption and government sectors. This is, of course, ridiculous. Thus in an economy with inflation of 2% per annum and growth of 2.5% we might expect the long-term growth in dividends to be about 4.5%. Also, it is unreasonable to suppose that a firm can grow its earnings and dividends forever at a rate significantly greater than that for the economy as a whole. To do so is to assume that the firm eventually becomes larger than the economy. There will be years, even decades, when average corporate dividends do grow faster than the economy as a whole and there will always be companies with much higher projected growth rates than the average for periods of time. Nevertheless the real GNP + inflation growth relationship provides a useful benchmark.

Companies that do not pay dividends

Some companies, for example Alphabet (parent company of Google) and Warren Buffett's Berkshire Hathaway, do not pay dividends. This is a deliberate policy as there is often a well-founded belief that the funds are better used within the firms than they would be if the money was given to shareholders. Alphabet, for example, is investing in driverless cars, smart contact lenses, the android mobile operating system and a high-altitude balloon with internet connectivity. It also needs cash for acquisitions having purchased more than 150 companies, including YouTube.

The absence of a dividend presents an apparent problem for the DVM but the formulae can still be applied because it is reasonable to suppose that one day these companies will start to pay dividends. Perhaps this will take the form of a final break-up payment, or perhaps when the founder is approaching retirement he/she will start to distribute the accumulated resources. At some point dividends must be paid; otherwise there would be no attraction in holding the shares. Microsoft is an example of a company that did not pay a dividend for 28 years. However, in 2003 it decided it would start the process of paying out some of its enormous cash pile and paid a dividend. Apple did not pay a dividend until 2012, but now pays the largest amount in the world, over $13bn a year.

Some companies do not pay dividends for many years due to regular losses. Often what gives value to this type of share is the optimism that the company will recover and that dividends will be paid in the distant future.

Problems with dividend valuation models

Dividend valuation models present the following problems.

1   They are highly sensitive to the assumptions. Take the case of Pearson above. If we change the growth assumption to 8% and reduce the required rate of return to 9.5%, the value of the share leaps to 3,744p.

$$P_0 = \frac{d_1}{k_E - g} = \frac{52\,(1 + 0.08)}{0.095 - 0.08} = 3,744\text{p}$$

So, a little more investor optimism on the perceived risk of Pearson's shares (lowering the k_E) and a little more optimism on the projected growth of dividends lead to a more than doubled estimate of value.

2   The quality of input data is often poor. The problems of calculating an appropriate required rate of return on equity were discussed in Chapter 8. Added to this is great uncertainty about the future growth rate, g, discussed below.

3   If g exceeds k_E a nonsensical result occurs. This is a problem for those who would use the model in a mechanical way by simply using the historic growth rate for g. However, in intelligent use of the model we replace the short-term super-normal growth rate plus the lower rate after the super-normal period with a g which is some weighted average growth rate reflecting the return expected over the long run. This is unlikely to result in a g more than one or two percentage points greater than the growth rate for the economy as a whole (if the largest weight is given to the near term non-supernormal growth period, we may allow a growth rate slightly higher than the economy.) Alternatively, for those periods when g is greater than k, one may calculate the specific dividend amounts and discount them as in the non-constant growth model (e.g. the two-stage model). For the years after the super-normal growth occurs, the usual growth formula may be used – as we did for Noruce plc in Worked example 17.5.

The difficulties in using the DVMs are real and yet the methods are to be favoured, less for the derivation of a single number than for the understanding of the principles behind the value of financial assets that the exercise provides. They demand a disciplined thought process that makes the analyst's assumptions (about earnings and dividend growth, about reasonable required rates of return, etc.) explicit, thus allowing him or her to question the validity of any final number produced. The analyst is also made aware of the possibility of a range of values, which depend on varying the assumptions made.

Forecasting dividend growth rates – *g*

The most influential variable, and the one subject to most uncertainty, on the value of shares is the growth rate expected in dividends. Accuracy here is a much sought-after virtue. While this book cannot provide readers with perfect crystal balls for seeing future dividend growth rates, it can provide a few pointers.

Determinants of growth

There are four factors which influence the rate of dividend growth.

1   *The quantity of resources retained and reinvested within the business* This relates to the percentage of earnings not paid out as dividends. In general, the more a firm invests the greater its potential for growth. (But, as you'll find in real-world investing, many directors invest in industries and projects they are familiar with regardless of whether a positive return is generated – very irrational, but it can be observed over and over again[2]).

---

2 Some examples are explained in the Deep Value Shares newsletters on ADVFN.com by Glen Arnold.

2 *The rate of return earned on those retained resources* The efficiency with which retained earnings are used will influence value.

3 *Rate of return earned on existing assets* This concerns the amount earned on the existing baseline set of assets, that is, those assets available before reinvestment of profits. This category may be affected by a sudden increase or decrease in profitability. If the firm, for example, is engaged in oil exploration and production, and there is a worldwide increase in the price of oil, profitability will rise on existing assets. Another example would be if a major competitor is liquidated, enabling increased returns on the same asset base due to higher margins because of an improved market position.

4 *Additional finance* In addition to using retained earnings, investment funds can be raised and future value can be boosted just so long as the firm has positive net present value projects. The new shareholders and debt holders will not take all the additional value (usually) and so returns to existing shareholders can be raised.

There is a vast range of influences on the future return from shares. One way of dealing with the myriad variables is to group them into two categories: at the firm and the economy level.

Focus on the firm

A dedicated analyst would want to examine numerous aspects of the firm, and its management, to help develop an informed estimate of its growth potential. These will include the following.

1 *Strategic analysis* The most important factor in assessing the value of a firm is its strategic position. The analyst needs to consider the attractiveness of the industry, the competitive position of the firm within the industry and the firm's position on the life cycle of value creation to appreciate the potential for increased dividends (*see* Chapter 14 and, for a fuller discussion, see Arnold (2009) or Arnold (2011). For up-to-date examples see Deep Value Shares newsletter on ADVFN.com by Glen Arnold).

2 *Evaluation of management* Running a close second in importance for the determination of a firm's value is the quality of its management. A starting point for analysis might be to collect factual information such as the age of the key managers and their level of experience (particularly longevity with the company) and of education. But this has to be combined with far more important evaluatory variables which are unquantifiable, such as judgement, and even gut feeling about issues such as competence, integrity, intelligence and so on. Having honest managers with a focus on increasing the wealth of shareholders is at least as important for valuing shares as the factor of managerial competence. Investors downgrade the shares of companies run by the most brilliant managers if there is any doubt about their integrity – highly competent crooks can destroy shareholder wealth far more quickly than any competitive action. (For a fuller discussion of the impact of managerial competence and integrity on share values *see* Arnold (2009).)

3 *Using the historical growth rate of dividends* If a company demonstrated an annual growth rate of 6% over the past ten years it might be reasonable to use this as a starting point for evaluating its future potential. This figure will probably have to be adjusted for new information such as new strategies, management or products – that is the tricky part.

4 *Financial statement evaluation and ratio analysis* An assessment of the firm's profitability, efficiency and risk through an analysis of accounting data can be enlightening. However, adjustments to the published figures are likely to be necessary to view the past clearly, let alone provide a guide to the future. Warren Buffett comments:

> When managers want to get across the facts of the business to you, it can be done within the rules of accounting. Unfortunately when they want to play games, at least in some industries, it can also be done within the rules of accounting. If you can't recognise the differences, you shouldn't be in the equity-picking business.[3]

Accounts are valuable sources of information but they have three drawbacks: **a** they are based in the past when it is the future which is of interest, **b** the fundamental value-creating processes

---

3 Warren Buffett seminar held at Columbia University Business School, 'Investing in equity markets', 13 March 1985, transcript, p. 23. Reproduced in Janet Lowe (1997).

within the firm are not identified and measured in conventional accounts, and **c** they are frequently based on guesses, estimates and judgements, and are open to manipulation.

Armed with a questioning frame of mind the analyst can adjust accounts to provide a truer and fairer view of a company. The analyst may wish to calculate three groups of ratios to enable comparisons:

a   Internal liquidity ratios permit some judgement about the ability of the firm to cope with short-term financial obligations – quick ratios, current ratios, etc.

b   Operating performance ratios may indicate the efficiency of the management in the operations of the business – asset turnover ratio, profit margins, debtor turnover, etc.

c   Risk analysis concerns the uncertainty of income flows – sales variability over the economic cycle, operational gearing (fixed costs as a proportion of total), financial gearing (ratio of debt to equity), cash flow ratios, etc.

Ratios examined in isolation are meaningless. It is usually necessary to compare with the industry, or the industry sub-group comprising the firm's competitors. Knowledge of changes in ratios over time can also be useful.

Focus on the economy

All firms, to a greater or lesser extent, are influenced by macroeconomic changes. The prospects for a particular firm can be affected by sudden changes in government fiscal policy, the central bank's monetary policy, changes in exchange rates, etc. Forecasts of macroeconomic variables such as GNP are easy to find. Finding a forecaster who is reliable over the long term is much more difficult. Perhaps the best approach is to obtain a number of projections and through informed judgement develop a view about the medium-term future. Alternatively, the analyst could recognise that there are many different potential futures and then develop analyses based on a range of possible scenarios – probabilities could be assigned and sensitivity analysis used to provide a broader picture.

It is notable that the great investors (e.g. Benjamin Graham, Philip Fisher, Warren Buffett and Charles Munger) pay little attention to macroeconomic forecasts when valuing companies. The reason for this is that value is determined by income flows to the shareholder over many economic cycles stretching over decades, so the economists' projection (even if accurate) for this or that economic number for the next year is of little significance.

Another approach to estimating *g*

Some analysts use the following logic for estimating g: first, they assume that the only source of growth in earnings comes from using additional capital from retained earnings. In other words, g cannot rise due to changes in industry conditions, e.g. government changing permitted price levels, price of oil rising (the third point on p. 746). Nor can it rise due to more external finance being available (the fourth point on p. 746).

Second, assume that the historical return on equity capital (labelled r_E) as shown in the accounts is going to continue for every additional £1 of extra equity capital (retained from profits) for every future year. That is every extra pound, whether the 10,000th pound or the 10 millionth pound, generates the same return.

Third, assume a constant retention ratio (labelled *b*) for all future years, i.e.:

$$\frac{Earnings - Dividends}{Earnings}$$

then,

$$g = br_E$$

So, for example, if Slightly Unrealistic plc retains three-quarters of its earnings, $b = 0.75$. Over the past five years it has obtained a return on equity, given its equity capital base, of 10%, and this will continue for any expansion of the business operations.

The growth estimate is $g = br_E = 0.75 \times 0.10 = 7.5\%$ per year.

The assumptions made may be challenges to your perception of the real world – you are right to be suspicious. However, this approach at least provides a starting point for estimating g – after all, some firms are able to invest in similar operations with each annual increment of retained earnings and produce similar rates of return to those achieved in the past. But it would be wrong to generalise from that.

You still need to make a judgement on the likely reasonable range of values for future bs and r_Es given the specific circumstances of the firm under consideration. Note that many (most?) companies cannot, year after year, simply open yet another factory or another retail outlet with their retained earnings and expect to obtain the same return on equity capital on the additional investment as they do on the existing assets.

The price-earnings ratio (PER) model

The most popular approach to valuing a share is to use the price-to-earnings ratio (PER). The historic PER compares a firm's share price with its latest earnings (profits) per share. Investors estimate a share's value as the amount they are willing to pay for each unit of earnings. If a company produced earnings per share of 10p in its latest accounts and investors are prepared to pay 20 times historic earnings for this type of share it will be valued at £2.00. The historic PER is calculated as follows:

$$\text{Historic PER} = \frac{\text{Current market price of share}}{\text{Last year's earnings per share}} = \frac{200\text{p}}{10\text{p}} = 20$$

So, the retailer Next which reported earnings per share of 429.6p for the 12 months to end July 2017 with a share price of £43 in November 2017 had a PER of 10. PERs of other retailers are shown in **Exhibit 17.6**.

Investors are willing to buy Next shares at 10 times last year's earnings compared with only 5.7 times last year's earnings for Debenhams. One explanation for the difference in PERs is that companies with higher PERs are expected to show faster growth in earnings in the future. Next may appear expensive relative to Debenhams based on historical profit figures but the differential may be justified when forecasts of earnings are made. If a PER is high investors expect profits to rise. This does not necessarily mean that all companies with high PERs are expected to perform to a high standard, merely that they are expected to do significantly better than in the past. Few people would argue that Marks & Spencer has performed, or will perform, well in comparison with Next over the past two years and yet it stands at a higher historic PER, reflecting the market's belief that M&S has more growth potential from its low base than Next.

So, using the historic PER can be confusing because a company can have a high PER because it is usually a high-growth company or because it has recently had a reduction of profits from which it is expected soon to recover.

PERs are also influenced by the uncertainty of the future earnings growth. So, perhaps, Morrisons and Moss Bros might have the same expected growth rate but the growth at Morrisons is subject to more risk and therefore the market assigns a lower earnings multiple. **Exhibit 17.7** discusses the PER of Just Eat

PERs over time

There have been great changes over the years in the market's view of what is a reasonable multiple of earnings to place on share prices. What is excessive in one year is acceptable in another. This is illustrated in **Exhibit 17.8**, which looks at the average PER for the 250 largest UK companies outside of the FTSE100 index.

Exhibit 17.6	PERs for retailers

Retailer	PER
Debenhams	5.7
Dunelm	19.4
Halfords	12.1
JD Sports	17.9
Kingfisher	12.1
Laura Ashley	3.6
Marks & Spencer	26.3
Morrisons	14.1
Moss Bros	15.8
Next	10.0

Source: *Financial Times*, 28 November 2017.

Exhibit 17.7

Curry in a hurry as Just Eat delivers

As the takeaway website's earnings improve, its valuation looks less rich

MATTHEW VINCENT

What value can be put on a technology that has revolutionised the way we interact with people, music, video and information? How much is the artificial intelligence that makes driverless cars a reality worth? And what price an app that makes ordering a chicken tikka masala, saag aloo and a plain naan marginally easier than phoning up The Star of India and simply explaining what you'd like?

Helpfully, the stock market makes these assessments for us: it currently values iPhone maker Apple on 16.7 times earnings, algorithm developer Google on 29.9 times, and takeaway food app Just Eat on 96.7 times.

Sometimes, it seems tech company multiples are more about growth rates than great leaps. This would certainly appear to be the case with Just Eat. Its full-year results suggest that there remains huge scope for connecting people.

Even after a 52 per cent rise in annual sales, to £376m, the group still has the 51 per cent of orders placed by telephone and notepad to go after. In the UK, this takeaway food market is now worth £6.1bn, having grown 10 per cent in the past year.

But is this enough to justify a valuation like that of a pizza-munching app developer? Arguably not — but then Just Eat now differs from an app developer in several ways. It keeps beating profit forecasts — underlying earnings were 4 per cent ahead of consensus estimates.

Its cash generation is strong — net operating cash flow was up 31 per cent to £97m last year.

It is improving its profit margin even as it expands geographically — based on underlying earnings before interest, tax, depreciation and amortisation, its margin last year rose 700 basis points.

It is not buying sales — the UK business saw marketing costs dip as a percentage of revenue, as reordering rates increased. And it appears to have technology that is easy to use, even with one hand on a deep fat fryer — more than 50 per cent of UK orders were processed in kitchens using its tablet-based platform.

However, the risk factors will smell all too familiar to tech investors. It is about to lose the chief executive who drove its growth, pre- and post-flotation.

One analyst described David Buttress as "one of the UK's standout entrepreneurs of the last decade", and no successor has yet been found. Its like-for-like order growth has also slowed for a second consecutive year.

▶

Exhibit 17.7 *(continued)*

As Just Eat's earnings improve, though, its valuation looks less rich: 33 times 2017's earnings, 24 times 2018's. It may not be delivering a technological revolution. But it has perhaps worked out the iPhone's — and the driverless car's — ultimate function.

FT   *Financial Times,* 7 March 2017.

| **Exhibit 17.8** | **PERs for the UK stock market's FTSE 250 index, 1994–2017** |

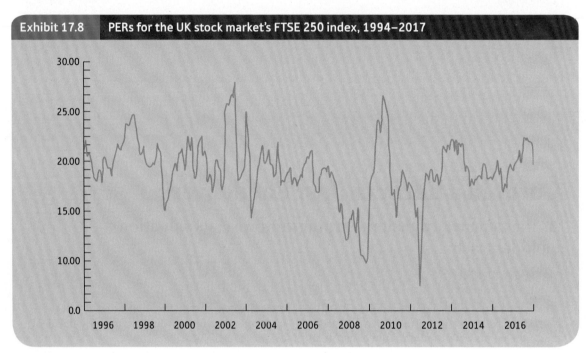

Source: The Financial Times, https://markets.ft.com/data/indices/tearsheet/charts?s=MCX.P:FSI

The crude and the sophisticated use of the PER model

Some analysts use the **historical PER** (P_0/E_0), to make comparisons between firms without making explicit the considerations hidden in the analysis. They have a view of an appropriate PER based on current prevailing PERs for other firms in the same industry. So, for example, in 2017 Barclays with a PER of 15.8 may be judged to be priced correctly relative to similar firms – HSBC had a PER of 35.3, Lloyds 15.2, and Virgin Money 8.4. Analysing through comparisons lacks intellectual rigour. First, the assumption that the 'comparable' companies are correctly priced is a bold one. It is easy to see how the market could be pulled up (or down) by its own bootstraps and lose touch with fundamental considerations by this kind of thinking. Good examples of this are the rise of telecommunication shares in the 1998–2000 bubble or social media companies in 2017. Secondly, it fails to provide a framework for the analyst to test the important implicit input assumptions – for example, the growth rate expected in earnings in each of the companies, or the difference in required rate of return given the different risk level of each. These elements are probably in the mind of the analyst, but there are benefits in making these explicit. This can be done with the more complete PER model which is forward looking and recognises both risk levels and growth projections.

The infinite dividend growth model can be used to develop the more complete PER model because they are both dependent on the key variables of growth, g (in dividends or earnings), and the required rate of return, k_E. The dividend growth model is:

$$P_0 = \frac{d_1}{k_E - g}$$

If both sides of the dividend growth model are divided by the expected earnings for the next year, E_1, then:

$$\frac{P_0}{E_1} = \frac{d_1/E_1}{k_E - g}$$

Note this is a *prospective* PER because it uses next year's earnings, rather than a historic PER, which uses E_0.

In this more complete model the appropriate multiple of earnings for a share rises as the growth rate, g, goes up; and falls as the required rate of return, k_E, increases. The relationship with the ratio d_1/E_1 is more complicated. If this payout ratio is raised it will not necessarily increase the PER because of the impact on g – if more of the earnings are paid out less financial resource is being invested in projects within the business, and therefore future growth may decline.

Worked example 17.6   Ridge plc

Ridge plc is anticipated to maintain a payout ratio of 48% of earnings. The appropriate discount rate for a share for this risk class is 14% and the expected growth rate in earnings and dividends is 6%.

$$\frac{P_0}{E_1} = \frac{d_1/E_1}{k_E - g}$$

$$\frac{P_0}{E_1} = \frac{0.48}{0.14 - 0.06} = 6$$

The spread between k_E and g is the main influence on an acceptable PER. A small change can have a large impact. If we now assume a k_E of 12% and g of 8% the PER doubles.

$$\frac{P_0}{E_1} = \frac{0.48}{0.12 - 0.08} = 12$$

If k_E becomes 16% and g 4% then the PER reduces to two-thirds of its former value:

$$\frac{P_0}{E_1} = \frac{0.48}{0.16 - 0.04} = 4$$

Worked example 17.7   Whizz plc

You are interested in purchasing shares in Whizz plc. This company produces high-technology products and has shown strong earnings growth for a number of years. For the past five years earnings per share have grown, on average, by 10% per annum.

Despite this performance and analysts' assurances that this growth rate will continue for the foreseeable future you are put off by the exceptionally high prospective price earnings ratio (PER) of 25.

In the light of the more complete forward-looking PER method, should you buy the shares or place your money elsewhere?

Whizz has a beta of 1.8 which may be taken as the most appropriate systematic risk adjustment to the risk premium for the average share.

The risk premium for equities over government bills has been 5% over the past few decades, and the current risk-free rate of return is 7%.

Whizz pays out 50% of its earnings as dividends.

Answer
Stage 1 Calculate the appropriate cost of equity.

$$k_E = r_f + \beta(r_m - r_f)$$
$$k_E = 7 + 1.8\,(5) = 16\%$$

▶

Worked example 17.7 (*continued*)

Stage 2 Use the more complete PER model.

$$k_E = r_f + \beta(r_m - r_f)$$

$$k_E = 7 + 1.8\,(5) = 16\%$$

$$\frac{P_0}{E_1} = \frac{d_1/E_1}{k_E - g} = \frac{0.5}{0.16 - 0.10} = 8.33$$

The maximum multiple of next year's earnings you would be willing to pay is 8.33. This is a third of the amount you are being asked to pay; therefore you will refuse to buy the share.

Prospective PER varies with g and k_E

If an assumption is made concerning the payout ratio, then a table can be drawn up to show how PERs vary with k_E and g – *see* **Exhibit 17.9**.

Exhibit 17.9	Prospective PERs for various risk classes and dividend growth rates

Assumed payout ratio $= \dfrac{d_1}{E_1} = 0.5$

		Discount rate, k_E			
Growth rate, g		8	9	10	12
	0	6.3	5.6	5.0	4.2
	4	12.5	10.0	8.3	6.3
	5	16.7	12.5	10.0	7.1
	6	25.0	16.7	12.5	8.3
	8	–	50.0	25.0	12.5

A payout ratio of 40–50% of after-tax earnings is normal for UK shares.

We can draw out the implicit elements hidden in the crude PER model by using the more complete model – *see* **Exhibit 17.10**.

The more complete model can help explain the apparently perverse behaviour of stock markets. If there is 'good' economic news such as a rise in industrial output or a fall in unemployment the stock market often falls. The market likes the increase in earnings that such news implies, but this effect is often outweighed by the effects of the next stage. An economy growing at a fast pace is vulnerable to rises in inflation and the market will anticipate rises in interest rates to reflect this. Thus the r_f and the rest of the SML are pushed upward. The return required on shares, k_E, will rise, and this will have a depressing effect on share prices.

Cyclically adjusted price/earnings ratio (CAPE)

A good way of gaining perspective on the current market price of a single company's share (or the market as a whole) is to compare it with the average earnings over the past ten years. This is the cyclically adjusted price/earnings ratio, CAPE. The idea is that the CAPE takes into account earnings from years with a variety of economic circumstance, ranging from booms to recessions. Simply using last year's earnings or an estimate of next year's earnings may give a

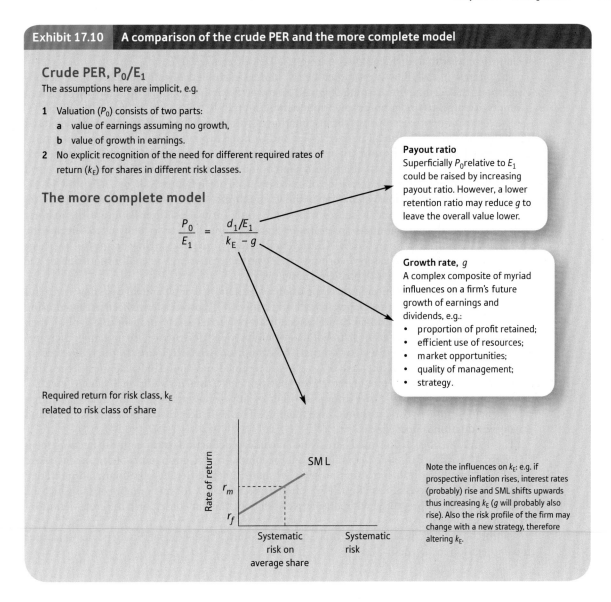

Exhibit 17.10   A comparison of the crude PER and the more complete model

Crude PER, P_0/E_1

The assumptions here are implicit, e.g.

1 Valuation (P_0) consists of two parts:
   a value of earnings assuming no growth,
   b value of growth in earnings.
2 No explicit recognition of the need for different required rates of return (k_E) for shares in different risk classes.

The more complete model

$$\frac{P_0}{E_1} = \frac{d_1/E_1}{k_E - g}$$

Payout ratio
Superficially P_0 relative to E_1 could be raised by increasing payout ratio. However, a lower retention ratio may reduce g to leave the overall value lower.

Growth rate, g
A complex composite of myriad influences on a firm's future growth of earnings and dividends, e.g.:
• proportion of profit retained;
• efficient use of resources;
• market opportunities;
• quality of management;
• strategy.

Required return for risk class, k_E related to risk class of share

Rate of return

r_m

r_f

SML

Systematic risk on average share

Systematic risk

Note the influences on k_E: e.g. if prospective inflation rises, interest rates (probably) rise and SML shifts upwards thus increasing k_E (g will probably also rise). Also the risk profile of the firm may change with a new strategy, therefore altering k_E.

distorted view of fundamental value if the current period happens to be a boom time or an economic downturn.

The main way in which CAPE is used is to calculate it year-after-year over many decades and plot the extent to which the CAPE is above or below its long-term average. In 2000 CAPEs for many equity markets were at record highs (even higher than in 1929) which was sending a clear signal of over valuation relative to earnings power over a ten-year period. In 2017 market-wide CAPEs in Europe are generally at their long-run averages, whereas the US CAPE is at 30, significantly above its long-term average. (The other years when it has been this high are 1929 and 2000. Spot a pattern?) Charts of CAPEs can be viewed on various websites.

Valuation using cash flow

The third and most important income-based valuation method is cash flow. In business it is often said that 'cash is king'. From the shareholders' perspective the cash flow relating to a share is crucial – they hand over cash and are interested in the ability of the business to return cash to them. John Allday, head of valuation at Ernst and Young, says that discounted cash flow 'is the purest way. I would prefer to adopt it if the information is there'.[4] Investment banks valuing companies prior to initial public offerings mainly use discounted cash flows, which are also found to be more accurate than dividend discounting (*see* Deloof et al., 2009).

The interest in cash flow is promoted by the limited usefulness of published accounts. Scepticism about the accuracy of earnings figures, given the flexibility available in their construction, prompts attempts to find a purer valuation method than PER.

The cash flow approach involves the discounting of future cash flows, that is, the cash generated by the business after investment in fixed assets and working capital to fully maintain its long-term competitive position and its unit volume, and to make investment in all new value-creating projects. To derive the cash flow attributable to shareholders, any interest paid in a particular period is deducted. The process of the derivation of cash flow from profit figures is shown in **Exhibit 17.11**.

An example of a cash flow calculation is shown in **Exhibit 17.12**. Note that these numbers are forward projections. A buyer of shares will receive only future cash flows and not the historic flows. However, the past numbers are useful background information to allow us to forecast the cash flows. The earnings figures for 20X2 are very different from the cash flow because of the large capital investment in fixed assets – earnings are positive because only a small proportion of the cost of the new fixed assets is depreciated in that year.

There is a subtle assumption in this type of analysis. This is that all annual cash flows are paid out to shareholders rather than reinvested. If all positive NPV projects have been accepted using the money allocated to additional capital expenditures on fixed assets and working capital, then to withhold further money from shareholders would be value destructive because any other projects would have negative NPVs. An alternative assumption, which amounts to the same effect in terms of share value, is that any cash flows that are retained and reinvested generate a return that merely equals the required rate of return for that risk class; thus no additional value is created. Of course, if the company either knows of other positive-value projects at the outset or comes across them in future years, it should take them up. This will alter the numbers in the table and so a new valuation is needed.

The definition of cash flow used here (which includes a deduction of expenditure on investment in fixed and working capital to maintain long-term competitive position, unit volume, and to make investment in all new value-creating projects) is significantly different from many accountants' and analysts' definitions of cash flow. They often neglect to allow for one or more of these factors. Be careful if you are presented with alternative cash flow numbers based on a different definition of cash flow.

Exhibit 17.13 describes the importance of the discounted cash flow method, and demonstrates the imprecision involved.

Valuation using owner earnings

A simplified version of cash flow analysis is owner earnings.[5] For shares, intrinsic value is the discounted value of the owner earnings that can be taken out of a business during its remaining life. These correspond with standard cash flow analysis shown in the last section except that we calculate a sustainable level of owner earnings for a typical year (subject to a steady growth) rather than unique cash flows for the future years. Future owner earnings are determined by the strength and durability of the economic franchise (attractiveness of the industry plus competitive position of the firm in the industry), the quality of management and the financial strength of the business. In the following analysis we make use of Warren Buffett's definition of owner earnings, but with the additional factor in c and d of 'investment in all new value-creating projects'. Owner earnings are defined as:

a   earnings after tax and interest; *plus*

b   depreciation, depletion (e.g. of oil reserves), amortisation and certain other non-cash charges; *less*

---

4 Quoted by Robert Outram (1997), p. 70.

5 This form of analysis is set out in Arnold (2009).

Exhibit 17.11	Cash flow approach: from projected profit figures

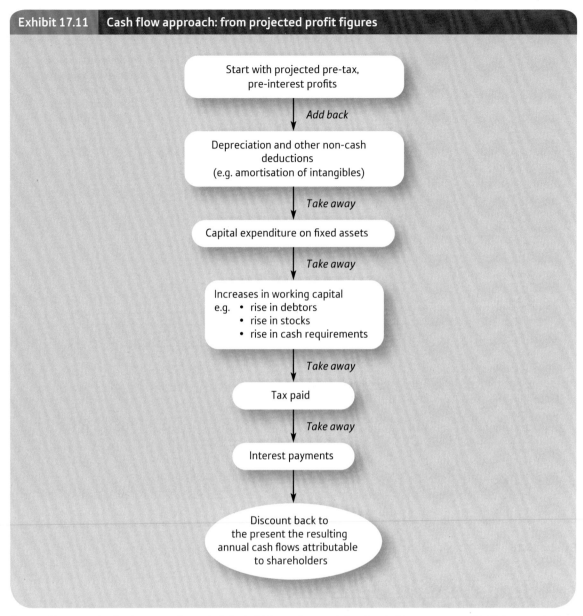

Footnote: We are assuming that there are no changes in the level of debt, e.g. that no cash flowed out in debt repayments, or, if it did, it was matched by new debt capital raising to produce offsetting cash inflows. We also assume that any receipt of cash from the sale of fixed assets is deducted from the 'capital expenditure on fixed assets' figure.

c   the amount of expenditures for plant and machinery, etc. that a business requires to fully maintain its long-term competitive position and its unit volume and to make investment in all new value-creating projects; *less*

d   any extra amount for working capital that is needed to maintain the firm's long-term competitive position and unit volume and to make investment in all new value-creating projects.

Note that there are two types of investment. First, that which is needed to permit the firm to continue to maintain its existing competitive position at the current level of output. Secondly, investment in value-creating growth opportunities beyond the current position.

So, for example, Cotillo plc has reported earnings after tax for the most recent year of £16.3m. In drawing up the income (profit and loss) account deductions of £7.4m were made for

Exhibit 17.12   Cash flow-based share valuation

£m	20X1	20X2	20X3	20X4	20X5	Estimated average annual cash flow for period beyond planning horizon 20X6–infinity
Forecast pre-tax, pre-interest profits	+11.0	+15.0	+15.0	+16.0	+17.0	
Add non-cash items: depreciation, amortisation, etc.	+1.0	+2.5	+5.5	+4.5	+4.0	
Working capital increase (−) decrease (+)	+1.0	−0.5	0.0	+1.0	+1.0	
Tax (paid in year)	−3.3	−5.0	−5.0	−5.4	−5.8	
Interest on debt capital	−0.5	−0.5	−0.5	−0.6	−0.7	
Fixed capital investment	−1.0	−16.0	0.0	−1.2	−1.8	
Cash flow	+8.2	−4.5	+15.0	+14.3	+13.7	+14.0
Cash flow per share (assuming 100m shares)	8.2p	−4.5p	15p	14.3p	13.7p	14p

$$\text{Discounted cash flow} \quad k_E = 14\% \qquad \frac{8.2}{1.14} - \frac{4.5}{(1.14)^2} + \frac{15}{(1.14)^3} + \frac{14.3}{(1.14)^4} + \frac{13.7}{(1.14)^5} + \frac{14}{0.14} \times \frac{1}{(1.14)^5}$$

| Share value = | 7.20 | −3.5 | +10.1 | +8.5 | +7.1 | +51.9 | = 81.3p |

An Excel spreadsheet version of this is available at www.pearsoned.co.uk/arnold.

Exhibit 17.13

A ding-dong in Delaware

A dispute brought by Dell investors shows that valuations should be more than academic

By Sujeet Indap

In New York, mergers and acquisitions are the province of investment bankers with slicked-back hair and polished wingtips. But, if a deal price does not meet with universal cheers, the battlefield often shifts from a Manhattan conference room to a Delaware courtroom because US companies are domiciled in that state.

There, the focus suddenly shifts to egghead professors sporting pocket protectors who offer competing, and often different, calculations of how much a company is worth.

In one closely watched case decided two weeks ago, the focus was on the technology company, Dell, which was taken private by founder Michael Dell in 2013. Some investors believed they had been short-changed, so they challenged the price in what has become known as an "appraisal" case.

Once an obscure quirk of Delaware law, appraisal has become a key remedy for shareholders and a tool for opportunistic hedge funds. When a company is sold for cash, unhappy stockholders can exercise so-called "dissenters" rights and ask a judge to assign a new value for their shares. This court-determined price can be higher than the deal price or lower.

But, in many cases, it turns out to be the same because judges opt to defer to the deal.

It can be reached in a less rounded way, however.

When bankers advise company boards about what would constitute an acceptable buyout price, they often present a series of different calculations on a grid. A premiums analysis shows how much recent deals exceeded market trading prices. A "capitalised" earnings calculation applies a multiplication factor to an earnings forecast. Another approach involves adding up future cash flows and discounting them to reach a fair value today. For bankers, valuation is the painting of an intricate mosaic.

Alas, the Delaware court is often less nuanced. Although the appraisal statute has been interpreted to allow judges to choose whatever valuation method(s) they deem appropriate, in virtually all recent cases — including Dell — the court has relied solely on discounted cash flow.

"The DCF valuation methodology has featured prominently [because it] merits the greatest confidence within the financial community," the court has said. DCF also happens to be the favoured approach of scholars because of its theoretical elegance: an asset's value should strictly be equal to the net cash it generates.

In the Dell dispute, the company's expert witness was noted Columbia Business School economist Glenn Hubbard, best known for advising Republican politicians.

Dell's shareholders, seeking a higher price, retained Bradford Cornell of Caltech, the university that is home to Nasa's rocket laboratory.

They are among around a dozen valuation experts who can bill $1,000 per hour for their services, and work as affiliates of litigation consultancies — the best known being Analysis Group, Charles River Associates, Compass Lexecon and NERA. They are not formal employees but get to use the firms' resources — notably an army of spreadsheet jockeys to do the supporting maths.

Despite the Delaware court's confidence in DCF, the Dell expert's use of it proved contentious. Dr Hubbard's DCF, for the Dell side, computed that the company was worth $12.68 per share, suggesting that the $13.75 per share buyout price was a magnificent win for shareholders.

Mr. Cornell, for the dissenters, concluded Dell was worth a wild $28.61 per share.

As the judge wryly noted, this implied a $28bn aggregate valuation difference on a buyout worth only $25bn. Still, the judge thought the differences on their inputs to the calculations — profits, debt and equity levels, discount rates, cash adjustments — were all arrived at in good faith. So he cherry-picked the bits of each professor's work that he found most defensible, to reach a valuation of $17.62 per share.

It seems the court is aware of the peril in this approach, writing in an earlier case: "The value of a corporation is not a point on a line, but a range of reasonable values, and the judge's task is to assign one particular value within this range as the most reasonable value in light of all the relevant evidence and based on considerations of fairness."

Still, such humility looks hollow when expert witnesses and judges use a single, fraught, technique. Bankers with their more circumspect, holistic approach to valuation offer a lesson to the professors and the courts who rely upon them.

$/share

- Dell Expert Witness
- Actual Buyout Price
- Delaware judge
- Dissenters Expert Witness

0   10   20   30

depreciation and £152,000 for the amortisation of intangible assets, and £713,000 of goodwill was written off. It is estimated that an annual expenditure of £8.6m on plant, machinery, etc. will be required for the company to maintain its long-term competitive position and unit volume. For the sake of simplicity we will assume that no further monies will be needed for extra working capital to maintain long-term competitive position and unit volume. Also, Cotillo has no new value-creating projects.

The trading record of Cotillo plc has been remarkably stable in the past and is unlikely to alter in the future. It is therefore reasonable to use the above figures for all the future years. (Note, while we look to past figures to gain information, the numbers that go into the calculation are forecasts of the future.) This would result in estimated annual owner earnings of £15.965m (*see* **Exhibit 17.14**).

Exhibit 17.14	Cotillo plc, owner earnings	
		£000s
a	Reported earnings after tax	16,300
	Plus	
b	Depreciation, depletion, amortisation and other non-cash charges (7,400 + 152 + 713)	8,265
		24,565
	Less	
c and d	Expenditure on plant, equipment, working capital, etc. required to maintain long-term competitive position, unit volume and investment in new projects	8,600
		15,965

The discounted value of this perpetuity = £159.65m, if we take the discount rate to be 10%:

$$\text{Intrinsic value} = \frac{£15.965\text{m}}{0.10} = £159.65\text{m}$$

Intrinsic value is determined by the owner earnings that can be *taken out* of the business during its remaining life. Logically the management of Cotillo should pay out the full £15.965m each year to shareholders if the managers do not have investment projects within the firm that will generate returns of 10% or more because shareholders can get 10% return elsewhere for the same level of risk as holding a share in Cotillo. If the managers come across another project that promises a return of exactly 10% shareholder wealth will be unchanged whether the company invests in this or chooses to ignore the project and continues with the payment of all owner earnings each year. If the management discover, in a future year, a value-creating project that will produce, say, a 15% rate of return (for the same level of risk as the existing projects) then shareholders will welcome a reduction in dividends during the years of additional investment. The total value of discounted future owner earnings will rise and intrinsic value will be greater than £159.65m if such a project is undertaken.

Now let us assume that Cotillo has a series of new value-creating projects (i.e. generating returns greater than 10%) in which it can invest. By investing in these projects owner earnings will rise by 5% year on year (on the one hand owner earnings are decreased by the need for additional investment under **c** and **d**, but, on the other hand reported earnings are boosted under **a**, to produce a net 5% growth). The intrinsic value becomes £335.26m, viz:

$$\text{Next year's owner earnings} = £15.965\text{m} (1 + g) = £15.965\text{m} (1 + 0.05) = £16.763\text{m}$$

$$\text{Intrinsic value} = \text{next year's owner earnings}/(k_E - g) = \frac{16.763}{0.10 - 0.05} = £335.26\text{m}$$

It is legitimate to discount owner earnings because they amount to that which can be paid out to shareholders after all value-creating projects are financed and payments have been made for the investment to maintain the firm's competitive position and unit volume. It would not be legitimate to discount conventional accounting earnings. These are much larger than dividends because part of these earnings is ploughed back into the business for capital items and working capital. Owner earnings are much smaller than conventional earnings, and are in general closer to the dividend level than the conventional earnings figure, much of which could not be paid out to shareholders without jeopardising the future income flows of the business.

It is important to realise that the use of only one year of Cotillo's cash inflows and outgoings is presented to simplify the initial explanation. It is recommended that when applying the technique to real-world companies you calculate at least five past years of owner earnings before estimating the likely future annual owner earnings and intrinsic value. Having five to ten years of owner earnings in front of you will allow some perspective on the sustainability of the forecast numbers. One year in isolation may have freakishly good or freakishly bad numbers due to, say, managerial poor luck, recession or a drop in raw material prices. The case of Henton plc in Worked example 17.8 shows five years of historical numbers to estimate future owner earnings.

Worked example 17.8   Henton plc. Owner earnings and intrinsic value estimation

Henton plc is a company that is not quoted on a stock market. However, the directors have approached you to help them value it, with a view to floating on the Alternative Investment Market later in the year. They have asked you to use the owner earnings method of valuation. The following information has been taken from Henton's accounts.

	Four years ago £m	Three years ago £m	Two years ago £m	Last year £m	Recently reported £m
Pre-tax profits	10.0	12.0	11.0	13.0	14.0
Corporation tax	3.0	3.6	3.3	4.0	4.3
Amortisation of intangible assets	1.0	1.2	1.2	1.4	1.4
Fixed capital expenditure	1.2	1.3	1.4	1.2	1.2
Decrease/(increase) in inventories in year	0.5	(0.6)	0.3	(0.7)	(0.4)
Decrease/(increase) in receivables in year	(0.2)	(0.3)	(0.3)	(0.4)	(0.4)
Increase/(decrease) in payables	0.7	0.5	0.6	0.7	0.8
Dividends paid	1.0	1.1	1.2	1.3	1.4
Depreciation	1.2	1.2	1.2	1.2	1.2
Number of ordinary shares in issue(millions)	100	100	100	100	100

The required rate of return on shares carrying the same amount of systematic risk as Henton is 10% per year.

Calculate the value of the company today by forecasting future owner earnings (a) under the assumption of zero future growth of owner earnings, and (b) under the assumption that they grow at the same rate as in the past five years.

Solution
Past owner earnings:

	Four years ago £m	Three years ago £m	Two years ago £m	Last year £m	Recently reported £m
Pre-tax profits	10.0	12.0	11.0	13.0	14.0
Less tax	−3.0	−3.6	−3.3	−4.0	−4.3
Plus amortisation of intangible assets	1.0	1.2	1.2	1.4	1.4
Plus depreciation	1.2	1.2	1.2	1.2	1.2
	9.2	10.8	10.1	11.6	12.3
Fixed capital expenditure	−1.2	−1.3	−1.4	−1.2	−1.2
Inventories	0.5	−0.6	0.3	−0.7	−0.4
Receivables	−0.2	−0.3	−0.3	−0.4	−0.4
Payables	0.7	0.5	0.6	0.7	0.8
OWNER EARNINGS	9.0	9.1	9.3	10.0	11.1

▶

Worked example 17.8 *(continued)*

Growth in owner earnings over five years:

$$\sqrt[4]{\frac{11.1}{9.0}} - 1 = 0.054 \text{ } or \text{ } 5.4\% \text{ per annum}$$

(a) Zero growth: *Value of Henton* $= \dfrac{d}{k_E} = \dfrac{11.1}{0.1} = £111m$

(b) Growth at 5.4% p.a.: *Value of Henton* $= \dfrac{d_1}{k_E - g} = \dfrac{11.1(1.054)}{0.1 - 0.054} = £254m$

Of course it will be necessary to adjust the numbers if a past event had a major impact, e.g. Henton taking over another company, followed by the consolidation of the accounts leading to a very large increase in working capital items as the two component company amounts are added together; or the firm sold off a subsidiary reducing fixed capital and working capital needs.

Given that you are estimating the future sustainable OE you are encouraged to think of alternative growth assumptions rather than simply extrapolating the past. In reality, you would need to consider the qualitative factors such as strategic position and managerial ability and integrity to estimate how much cash will flow to shareholders in the future (see Arnold (2009)). Also bear in mind the benchmark of economy-wide company earnings growing at roughly the same rate as nominal national output (GDP). Thus when dealing with a company showing past five-year earnings growth of, say, 30% per year, be aware that it is unrealistic to project such a growth rate into

Case study 17.2   N Brown – owner earnings analysis

(Taken from newsletter posted by Glen Arnold on ADVFN 29.11.17 www.newsletters.advfn.com/deepvalueshares/)

Yesterday's newsletter explained that, at a market capitalisation of £795m (share price £2.80) N Brown does not look like a bargain for a value investor on the basis of its 11-year cyclically adjusted price earnings ratio.

However, I will not give up on it yet. Today I'll value it using the owner earnings method as recommended by Warren Buffett.

Brief description of the company

N Brown is a collection of fashion brands. It mostly sells online (72%), but still sells quite a lot using paper catalogues. It has around a dozen specialised niches, with a reputation for serving larger people and older people.

Some of its brands are well-known, e.g. *Simply Be* is advertised on TV a lot at the moment, *Tall & Mighty* is well-known to larger men. Others are more niche, e.g. *Julipa* for corsetry.

It sells over £600m of clothing and other merchandise per year, but also makes a significant amount of money from supplying finance to its 4 million regular customers – revenue (interest and fees) in its finance division is over £260m.

What is owner earnings?

With owner earnings we are trying to obtain the earnings that, in future, would be left for shareholders after the managers' use of the cash generated to pay for items of expenditure to maintain the strength of the economic franchise (e.g. additional capital items, additional working capital, marketing spend, R&D and staff training) and to maintain unit volume and to invest in all value-generating projects available.

Depending on circumstances, the owner earnings figure may be the same for every future year or on a steadily rising (or falling) trend.

Naturally, owner earnings are impossible to obtain with any degree of precision because many of the input numbers are merely educated guesses about the future. Despite this imprecision it remains an important method for thinking through valuations.

Owner earnings analysis is about future cash available for shareholders to take out of the business. But the only evidence we have available is past data. We start with that, and then use qualitative analysis to judge whether to simply project forward the past pattern or modify the previous trend for future orientated thinking.

In the following we use what the company *actually* invested in new working capital, WC, items and in new fixed capital items, and what they spent on marketing, R&D and staff training etc. already deducted from the P&L.

What the analysis really requires is the amount *necessary* to maintain the quality of the economic franchise, unit volume and invest in value generating projects. To start with we make the bold assumption that what was spent by the managers was also the necessary amount.

When we move to forward-looking analysis to value the firm we need to make another bold assumption on the real amount needed to invest in new WC, fixed capital items, etc., in the future. The historical analysis helps us make that judgment.

£m YEAR	2013	2014	2015
Profit after interest and tax deduction (before exceptional items)	79	76	59
Add back **non-cash items such as depreciation, goodwill and other amortisation**	19	20	23
Totals to: **Amount available for distribution to shareholders before considering the need to spend on fixed capital items and working capital items to maintain the company's economic franchise, unit volume and invest in value generating projects.**	98	96	82
Deduct **fixed capital and working capital investment. (The figures shown are actual expenditures and are therefore a rough proxy for the 'needed' expenditures to maintain franchise, etc.)**	−41	−88	−69
Owner earnings	57	8	13

£m YEAR	2016	2017	1st half 2018 times 2
Profit after interest and tax deduction (excluding gains on property)	68	65	42
Add back **non-cash items such as depreciation, goodwill and other amortisation**	25	28	26
Totals to: **Amount available for distribution to shareholders before considering the need to spend on fixed capital items and working capital items to maintain the company's economic franchise, unit volume and invest in value generating projects.**	93	93	68
Deduct **fixed capital and working capital investment. (The figures shown are actual expenditures and are therefore a rough proxy for the 'needed' expenditures to maintain franchise, etc.)**	−76	−68	−41
Owner earnings	17	25	27

Before I accept the historical numbers I need to make allowance for the exceptional items that these managers like to write off. Here is a summary (after tax) – only those years with exceptional items.

£m	2015	2016	2017	2018
Mis-selling PPI 2006–14 (mostly stopped by end 2011)	0	0	18	36
Closing shops	0	6	0	11
Tax dispute with HMRC	5	2	2	1
Strategy costs, e.g. reorganisation and outsourcing	5	6	0	0

Most of the PPI mis-selling occurred before 2013 and therefore I'll ignore this element when looking at owner earnings for the more recent years.

▶

Case study 17.2 *(continued)*

Store closures, tax dispute and strategy costs should, ideally, be allocated to the year they apply. I am not privy to that information so I'll knock £6m off the owner earnings for each of the years under analysis – arbitrary, but the best I can do. My thinking is: they might incur these sorts of expenses in future years.

The average 'owner earnings' over six years is £25m before deduction of exceptionals. If £6m is removed from this we have £19m.

Intrinsic value

Intrinsic value is the discounted value of all future owner earnings. We have one estimate of future owner earnings, i.e. £19m per year available to hand out to shareholders if the past level of expenditure on new property, machinery, inventory, receivables, etc. is continued, and the owner earnings does not rise.

Then intrinsic value = annual owner earnings divided by the discount rate.

A rate of return on shares of this risk class of around 8% per year could be argued with intellectual rigour.

Then intrinsic value = £19m/0.08 = £238m, significantly lower than the market capitalisation at £795m.

A more optimistic estimate

We can see from the table that the company 'uses up' tangible and intangible fixed assets, represented by depreciation and amortisation, at a rate of around £19m – £28m in a year.

But in the last six years it has poured money into new property, machinery, inventory, receivables, etc. at a rate of between £41m and £88m. In particular it has spent £100.4m on an IT system to serve its clothing brands in the modern age of eCommerce.

Note that in four out of the six years the managers spent more on WC and capex than the amount generated in post-tax profits.

Arguably, the accumulation of all this additional fixed capital and working capital items will, one day, produce a decent amount of growth in the owner earnings numbers.

Even if it does not produce an improvement in earnings, the act of stopping further expenditure on these future projects and reverting to a 'maintenance only' mode would change our view of likely future earnings because the WC and capex spending can be slashed.

There are two ways of allowing for the past extraordinary investment when it comes to our estimates for the future:

1 *Growth will occur.* Owner earnings will grow from the current level, at a rate of slightly above nominal GDP growth rate, say 5% per year. This implies a continued pumping in of money to WC and capex at very high levels year after year.

   Intrinsic value = £19m/(0.08 − 0.05) = £633m

2 *WC and capex expenditure will fall to match the average depreciation and amortisation over the last six years.* This means owner earnings will jump next year. The average depreciation plus amortisation of intangibles for a year has been £23m.

However, the average WC and Capex expenditure has been £64m.

Arguably, N Brown has been over-spending by £64m minus £23m per year, on average = £41m.

If there is no growth in revenue and profits why spend so much on additional inventories, receivables, property and IT systems?

Thus when thinking about future owner earnings assume a no growth strategy with WC and capex expenditure purely on a replacement basis.

So, we could add the extra £41m to the £19m historical number to arrive at £60m perpetuity of owner earnings flowing to shareholders (no growth because no additional property, plant, equipment, inventory or receivables).

Intrinsic value = £60m/0.08 = £750m.

An optimistic scenario

If the WC and capex investment of the last six years creates a platform for rapid international and product line expansion (which is clearly what the directors anticipate) and the amount spent on these items can fall to a level of say £35m (still allowing some growth in the business) then next year's owner earnings might be £53m. (The average income before deducting investment items is £88m over six years, then deduct £35m.)

And owner earnings might grow on that £53m base at a rate of 5% per year. Then intrinsic value is:

£53m/(0.08 − 0.05) = £1,767, double the current level.

The 2017 Annual report stated, 'Looking forward, we are on track to complete the final stages of our systems programme by Summer 2018, which will enable even faster growth… We have significantly grown the number of third party brands we stock on our websites… We are also partnering with other retailers, selling capsule collections of our ranges through their sites or stores.'

With an investment of £100.1m in the new IT system combined with the managers' experience in running a complex online service this company can present a barrier to entry to other firms. Other barriers include:

● knowledge of niche markets;

● experience of managing a customer loan book;

● balance sheet strength; and

● authorisation to run a financial service company (from the FCA).

(See earlier Newsletters dated 4–12 May 2017, 30 June 2017 for the qualitative analysis of N Brown.)

Despite all these positive aspects I have to admit that this last scenario puts a lot of trust in the directors to deliver the growth, placing a lot of value on hope. After all, the fashion business is very competitive. This does not have enough margin of safety for me, so I can't see that at a share price of £2.80 it can be bought.

The next Newsletter will examine N Brown using return on net tangible assets metric.

the future. Perhaps you need to use a two-stage growth model as described for Noruce plc in Worked example 17.5 (modified to OE rather than dividends).

EBITDA

EBITDA is classified by some commentators as a cash flow measure of value. EBITDA means earnings before (deduction of) interest, taxation, depreciation and amortisation. Many financiers and press reporters use EBITDA in a ratio with enterprise value, EV (market value of equity + market value of debt − cash in the business). It is compared to EV, rather than equity value, because it includes the interest element.

$$\frac{EV}{EBITDA} = \frac{\text{Market value of equity} + \text{market value of debt} - \text{cash}}{EBITDA}$$

The common use is to compare the EV/EBITDA multiple of the company the commentator is examining with the multiples currently shown for comparable companies. For instance, when one company attempts to take over another the press often look at the EV/EBITDA multiple the acquirer is offering in the light of the multiples paid for other recently acquired companies in that sector, and in the light of the current multiples for comparable stock market quoted firms, e.g. those at roughly the same risk level.

There are a number of benefits claimed for the use of EBITDA (pronounced e-bit-dah) in valuation:

- **EBITDA is close to cash flow.** We cannot say this. It does not take account of tax payments or the need to invest in working capital, for example. It is still vulnerable to a wide range of accrual accounting adjustments, e.g. the valuation of receivables.

- **Because the estimation of depreciation, amortisation and other non-cash items is vulnerable to judgement error we can be presented with a distorted profit number in conventional valuations; by focusing on profit before these elements are deducted we can get at a truer estimation of cash flow.** When making comparisons between firms and discovering a wide variety of depreciation methods being employed (leading to poor comparability) this argument does have some validity: to remove all depreciation, amortisation etc. may allow us to compare the relative performances more clearly. However, this line of reasoning can take us too far away from accrual accounting. If we accept the need for accruals accounting to provide us with more useful earnings numbers, then we simply cannot dispose of major accrual items when it suits us. By using EBITDA we distort the comparison anyway, because high capital expenditure firms are favoured by the removal of their non-cash item deductions.

- **If we are focused on future income from the firm's operations we need not allow for the depreciation and amortisation because this is based on historical investment in fixed assets that has little relationship with the expected future capital expenditure.** While alighting on a truth, the substitution of EBITDA for conventional profit (or for proper cash flow numbers) is wrong because it fails to take into account the need for investment in fixed capital items (and working capital). In the real world directors (and valuers) cannot ignore (however much they would want to) the cost of using up and wearing out equipment and other assets or the fact that interest and tax need to be paid. Warren Buffett made the comment: 'References to EBITDA make us shudder – does management think the tooth fairy pays for capital expenditures?'[6]

- **EBITDA is more useful for valuing companies that do not currently make profits, thus enlarging the number of companies that can be analysed.** But note that all the methods described in this chapter can be used for companies that are currently loss-making – we simply forecast future cash flows, dividends or earnings. EBITDA does not really have an edge over the others in this regard.

- **When comparing firms with different levels of borrowing EBITDA is best because it does not deduct interest.** It is true that EBITDA increases comparability of companies with markedly different financial gearing, but it is also true that the less distortionary EBIT (earnings before interest and tax deduction) can do the same without the exclusion of depreciation or amortisation.

There will be no promoting of EBITDA as a useful measure of valuation in this book, because it can lead to some very distorted thinking. EBITDA became a very popular measure of a company's performance in the late 1990s. It was especially popular with managers of firms that failed to make a profit. Managers liked to emphasise this measure in their communications to shareholders because large positive numbers could be shown. Some cynics have renamed it, 'Earnings Before I Tricked the Dumb Auditor'.

If you run an internet company that makes a £100m loss and the future looks pretty dim unless you can persuade investors and bankers to continue their support, perhaps you would want to add back all the interest (say £50m), depreciation on assets that are wearing out or becoming obsolete (say £40m), and the declining value of intangible assets, such as software licences and goodwill amortisation of, say, £65m, so that you could show a healthy positive number on EBITDA of £55m. And if your loss seems to get worse from one year to the next as your acquisition strategy fails to pay off it is wonderfully convenient to report and emphasise a stable or rising EBITDA.

The use of EBITDA by company directors can make political spin doctors look amateurs by comparison. EBITDA is not covered by any accounting standards so companies are entitled to use a variety of methods – whatever shows the company in the best light, I guess.

Another ratio that is calculated is market capitalisation divided by EBITDA. The problem here is that the numerator is an equity measure whereas the denominator relates to income flowing to both debt and equity holders. Those companies with very high debt burdens will look reasonably priced on this measure, when in fact they might be overpriced.

Having listed the drawbacks of the use of EBITDA in valuation it is important to point out its role in another area. That is, in judging the financial stability and liquidity of the firm. A key

---

6 Warren Buffett, a letter to shareholders attached to the *Annual Report of Berkshire Hathaway Inc* (2000). Reprinted with kind permission of Warren Buffett. © Warren Buffett.

measure is the EBITDA to interest ratio. That is how many times greater are the 'earnings' of the company than the gross annual interest bill.

$$\text{EBITDA interest coverage} = \frac{\text{EBITDA}}{\text{Gross interest}}$$

This is used to judge short-term ability to pay interest if the firm could stop paying out for fixed capital items. But there might still be taxes to pay above and beyond this. Also note that while capital item expenditure may be stopped in the short-run, if the company wants to maintain competitive position it will need to keep up with rivals.

Regular users of EBITDA are the private equity firms, particularly when trying to sell their shares in a company that they have been running for a while. Long-term capital expenditure to maintain the firm's competitive position, unit volume and investing in positive NPV projects may not be their highest priority when preparing a company for sale (they might also be skimping on R + D, customer relations and marketing) – so remember *caveat emptor*.

Valuing unquoted shares

The principles of valuation are the same for companies with a quoted share price on an exchange and for unquoted firms. The methods of valuation discussed above in relation to shares quoted on an exchange may be employed, but there may be some additional factors to consider in relation to unquoted firms' shares.

1 *There may be a lower quality and quantity of information* The reporting statements tend to be less revealing for unquoted firms. There may also be a managerial reluctance to release information – or managers may release information selectively so as to influence price, for example, in merger discussions.

2 *These shares may be subject to more risk* Firms at an early stage in their life cycle are often more susceptible to failure than are established firms.

3 *The absence of a quotation usually means the shares are less liquid,* that is, there is a reduced ability to sell quickly without moving the price. This lack of marketability can be a severe drawback and often investors in unquoted firms, such as venture capitalists, insist on there being a plan to provide an exit route within, say, five years, perhaps through a stock market float. But that still leaves a problem for the investor within the five years should a sale be required.

4 *Cost of tying in management* When a substantial stake is purchased in an unquoted firm, in order for the existing key managers to be encouraged to stay they may be offered financial incentives such as 'golden handcuffs' which may influence value. Or the previous owner-managers may agree an 'earn-out' clause in which they receive a return over the years following a sale of their shares (the returns paid to these individuals will be dependent on performance over a specified future period).

5 *Owner/director compensation* When considering a takeover price for an unquoted company the reported figures need to be examined carefully because it is often the case that the owner-directors have been over-paying themselves from company coffers. Therefore an upward adjustment is needed to the profit/cashflow numbers. On the other hand, owner-directors may have under-paid themselves and a takeover would mean their replacements would need to be paid considerably more.

Unquoted firms' shares tend to sell at significantly lower prices than those of quoted firms. The BDO Stoy Hayward Private Company Price Index (www.bdo.co.uk) shows that generally unquoted firms are sold at an average PER of under two-thirds that for quoted shares.

Unusual companies

Obtaining information to achieve accuracy with discounted income flow methods is problematic for most shares. But in industries subject to rapid technological innovation it is extraordinarily difficult. While discounted income flow remains the ultimate method of valuation some analysts use more immediate proxies to estimate value. (A less scientific-sounding description is 'rules of thumb'.) For example, Gerry Stephens and Justin Funnell, media and telecoms analysts at Nat-West Markets, describe the approach often adopted in their sector:[7]

> Rather than DCF (discounted cash flow), people are often more comfortable valuing telemedia project companies using benchmarks that have evolved from actual market prices paid for similar assets, being based on a comparative measure or scale such as per line, per subscriber, per home or per pop (member of population). For example, an analyst might draw conclusions from the per-pop price that Vodaphone [sic] trades at to put a price on the float of Telecom Italia Mobile. The benchmark prices will actually have originated from DCF analysis and the price paid can give an element of objective validation to the implied subjective DCF.

This sort of logic has been employed in the valuation of internet companies. In their attempt to value future profits that were far from certain 'analysts' become more and more extreme in clutching at straws to value internet companies – they focus on the number of 'unique users' (number of people who visited the sites) and 'page views' (number of pages users clicked on). This approach is demonstrated with the $1bn valuation of Twitter, which was based on volume of users rather than revenue and profits (this was in 2009, before it had its first substantive revenues and only 100 employees). In 2015 Delivery Hero's valuation was compared with Just Eat on the basis of multiple of sales, 32 times for Delivery Hero and 17 times for Just Eat (Delivery Hero was growing its sales at double the percentage rate). Snap was valued based on the growth of the number of snaps per day, by its 'daily active users', when it floated in 2017 – up to 166m in the middle of 2017.

Other sectors difficult to value directly on the basis of income flow include: advertising agencies, where a percentage of annual billings is often used as a proxy; mobile phone operators, where ARPU (average revenue per user) is used; fund managers, where value of funds under management is used; hotels, where star ratings may be combined with number of rooms and other factors such as revenue per room; cement companies, where multiples of annual production capacity (or sales) in metric tons is used; car parking lots, where a multiple of the number of parking spaces is used, and; insurance companies, where multiples of annual premiums are used.

Managerial control and valuation

The value of a share can change depending on whether the purchaser gains a controlling interest in the firm. The purchase of a single share brings a stream of future dividends without any real influence over the level of those dividends. However, control of a firm by, say, purchasing 50% or more of the shares, permits the possibility of changing the future operations of the firm and thus enhancing returns. A merger may allow economies of scale and other synergies, or future earnings may be boosted by the application of superior management skills.

The difference in value between a share without management control and one with it helps to explain why we often witness a share price rise of 30–50% in a takeover bid battle. There are two appraisals of the value of the firm, both of which may be valid depending on the assumption concerning managerial control. **Exhibit 17.15** shows that extra value can be created by merging the operations of two firms.

Exhibit 17.15 is not meant to imply that the acquiring firm will pay a bid premium equal to the estimated merger benefits. The price paid is subject to negotiation. The acquirer is likely to try to offer significantly less than the combined amount of the target firm's value 'as is' and the merger benefits. This will enable it to retain as much as possible of the increased value for itself rather than pass value on to the target shareholders. (*See* Chapter 20 for more detail.)

Valuation models and managerial control

The merger of Anheuser-Busch InBev with SABMiller provides an illustration of a possible use of the income flow model when managerial control is obtained. In 2015 AB InBev, when it announced the bid, claimed that by buying SABMiller they could cut costs by at least $1.4bn per year starting four years after taking control. These cost reductions were to come mostly from job cuts, particularly through integrating corporate and regional headquarters, and from savings in

---

7 Stephens and Funnell (1995), p. 20.

Exhibit 17.15   Value creation through merger

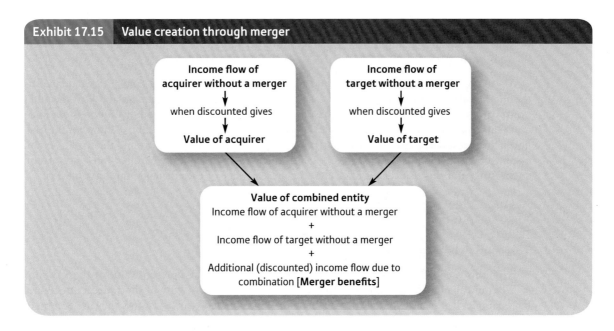

procurement, brewing operations and distribution. In addition to the cost savings AB InBev was thought to be eyeing some strengthening of market power, particularly increasing its grip on the Latin American market. The combined firm could also more effectively expand in the rising markets of Africa. It would supply one in four beers globally.

However, to complete the takeover it paid around £1.5bn in fees to banks, other financial institutions and lawyers, as well as $475m in stamp duty – we'll round those costs up to a total of $2bn.

In the absence of a takeover the value of a share in either company is the discounted value of all future dividends:

$$P_0 = \frac{d_1}{k_E - g}$$

This is where d_1 and g are generated by the existing structure and strategy.

Alternatively, we could examine the entire cash flow of the company (available to be paid out to shareholders after maintaining the firm's competitive position and unit volume and investing in all value-generating projects) rather than a single share.

$$V_E = \frac{C_1}{k_E - g_c}$$

where:

V_E = value of the entire share capital of the firm;

C_1 = total cash flows at time 1 expected to continue growing at a constant rate of g_c in future years.

If there is a new strategy the values in the equations change:

$$P_0 = \frac{d_1^*}{k_E - g^*}$$

or, for the entire cash flow:

$$V_E = \frac{C_1^*}{k_E - g_c^*}$$

d_1^*, C_1^*, g^*, g_c^* allow for the following:

● synergy;

● cutting out costs;

● tax benefits;

- superior management;
- other benefits (for example, lower finance costs, greater public profile, market power) less any additional costs.

Alternatively, a marginal approach could be adopted in which $C_1{}^*$, $d_1{}^*$, g^* and $g_c{}^*$ are redefined as the *additional* cash flows and growth in cash flows due to changes in ownership and V_E is the additional equity value. For example, let us assume that the annual earnings gain of $1.4bn is obtained four years from now but does not increase thereafter. Let us add another $1.2bn to allow for the cash flow gains derived from increased market power, e.g. in local monopolies around the world. Again, assume no growth in this sum, so $g = 0$. Let us further assume that the required rate of return on an investment of this risk class is 8%. Thus the present value of the efficiency gains at time 3 is:

$$V_E = \frac{C_1^*}{k_E - g_c^*} = \frac{\$2.6bn}{0.08 - 0} = \$32.5bn$$

This needs to be discounted to time zero: $\dfrac{\$32.5bn}{(1 + 0.08)^3} = \$25.8bn$

From this we need to deduct the $2bn upfront cost to arrive at a present value of the $23.8bn.

We could change the assumptions to gain insight into the sensitivity of the added value figure. For example, if it is anticipated that the benefits will rise each year by 2% (so they are $2.6bn in Year 4, but $2.65bn in Year 5 and $2.71m in Year 6, etc.) then the maximum bid premium will rise.

First, the value at time 3:

$$V_E = \frac{C_1^*}{k_E - g_c^*} = \frac{\$2.6bn}{0.08 - 0.02} = \$43.3bn$$

This needs to be discounted to time zero: $\dfrac{\$43.3bn}{(1 + 0.08)^3} = \$34.4bn$

From this we need to deduct the $2bn upfront cost to arrive at a present value of the $32.4bn.

Prior to the bid SABMiller's total market capitalization was $50bn. AB InBev initially offered $44 per share, or a total of $75bn. In October 2016, after much wrangling, SABMiller shareholders accepted an offer of $79bn, a premium of $29bn on the market value in the month before the first bid.

It might be the case that we've been over-impressed by the potential for cost savings and market power gains, meaning our $2.6bn annual gain is far too optimistic. Given the well-known difficulties of integrating two large businesses and the possibility for a culture clash and resentment we might actually witness negative incremental cash flows in future years. (*See* Chapter 20 for a discussion on the problems of post-merger integration, and hubris as a driver of merger activity.)

Allowing for real option values

The expected income flows to be received by shareholders are the foundation for share valuation. But what about companies that have no projected income flows? Take an oil company that has fallen on hard times. It has shut down all of its oil wells because the cost of extraction is greater than the current market price of oil. In fact the oil price would have to double to make it worthwhile reopening the wells. So there is little that the analyst can put into, say, a discounted cash flow calculation because the chances are that the company will never produce income again. However, this is not to say that there is no value. The company has the right but not the obligation to start taking oil from its wells when it wants to. This can be worth a lot of money, if an event happens, e.g. the price of oil triples.

The same logic applies to parts of a firm. There may be little prospect of the asset producing an income flow for the shareholders and yet there is value because of the existence of an option someday to implement the project should circumstances change. Thus to the value of identifiable income flows we should add the value of the collection of options that the firm may be holding, ranging from expansion options, delaying options to the option to quit. This area of finance is known as contingent claim valuation: cash flows are to some extent contingent on the occurrence or non-occurrence of some event and therefore the asset being valued is greater than the present value of the expected cash flows. BT owns thousands of patents some of which may be worth millions, if not billions, when the time is ripe. Indeed, we may discover at some point in the future that one or two of the inventions and innovations produced in the labs and currently hidden away in the vaults are worth more than all the currently projected cash flows on its existing business. We will not know until the contingent event happens (e.g. a complementary technological break-through) and the new business is created. Another example: if you were a song writer in the 1970s and you were smart you would have held on to the rights to use your music in any form. Even though you could not at that time value those rights for use in devices you could not even imagine (mobile phones, iPads, YouTube, etc.) you did figure out that circumstances change and options to do something can suddenly become amazingly valuable.

Knowing that real options are important is one thing; valuing them is quite another. Most are very difficult to value. Be cautious: people can come up with very suspect numbers vulnerable to bias. Chapter 6 discusses real options.

Worked example 17.9   Thingamees

Big plc has made it clear to the widget industry that it is willing to sell its subsidiary, Little plc, a manufacturer of thingamees. You are a member of the strategy management team at Thingamees International plc, the largest produc-ers of thingamees in the UK. Your firm is interested in acquiring Little and as a first step has obtained some information for the most recent years from Big plc.

Little plc Balance Sheet	20x7	£m	Trading record Year	Total earnings, £m (owner earnings)
Fixed assets		10	20x7	1.86
Current assets			20x6	1.70
Cash	0.5		20x5	1.65
Stock	1.5		20x4	1.59
Debtors	3.0		20x3	1.20
		5	20x2	1.14
Current liabilities		(6)	20x1	1.01
Bank loan		(4)		
Net assets		5		

Additional information

By combining the logistics departments you estimate that transport costs could be lowered by £100,000 per annum, and two secretarial posts eliminated, saving £28,000 p.a.

The closure of Little's head office would save £400,000 p.a. in staffing and running costs, but would also mean an additional £250,000 of administration costs at Thingamees plc to undertake some crucial tasks. The office building is situated in a good location and would raise a net £5m if sold immediately. A potential liability not displayed in Little's balance sheet is a possible legal claim of £3m relating to an earlier disposal of an asset. The plaintiff and Little's board have not yet reached agreement (Little's board is adamant that there is no liability).

Your appraisal of Little's management team is that it is a mixed bunch – some good, some very bad. Profits could be raised by £500,000 per year if you could impose your will quickly and remove poor managers. However, if you have to take a more gradual 'easing out' approach, operating profits will rise by only £300,000 per year.

The problems connected with a quick transition are: **a** sacking left, right and centre may cause disaffection among the good managers, encouraging hostility, departures and **a** profits collapse, and **b** Big plc is keen that you provide a commitment to avoid large-scale redundancies.

Big, Little and Thingamees International all have a beta of 1.5, which is representative of the appropriate adjustment to the risk premium on the average share given the systematic risk. The risk-free rate of return is 8% and the historical risk premium of share portfolios over safe securities has been 5%.

The increased market power available to Thingamees International after purchasing Little would improve margins in Thingamees International's existing business to provide an additional £100,000 per annum.

Assume that tax is irrelevant.

Required

a   Calculate the value of Little plc in its present form, assuming a continuation of its historic growth rate.

b   Calculate the value of Little plc if you took it over but were unable to push for maximum management redundan-cies and Little continued with its historical growth rate for its profits (that is, the profits before merger benefits). Include the annual merger benefits assuming they are constant for all future years to an infinite horizon: that is, there is no growth in these.

▶

Worked example 17.9 *(continued)*

c   Calculate the value of Little plc on the assumption that you are able to push through the rapid management changes and the pre-acquisition earnings continue on their historic growth path. (Add on the annual merger savings assuming these are the same for every future year.)

d   Discuss the steps you would take to get around the obstacles to shareholder wealth maximisation.

Answers

a   First calculate the required rate of return:

$$k_E = r_f + \beta(r_m - r_f)$$
$$= 8 + 1.5\ (5) = 15.5\%$$

Then calculate growth rate of cash flows:

$$g = \sqrt[6]{\frac{1.86}{1.01}} - 1 = 10.71\%$$

Then calculate the value of Little plc:

$$V_E = \frac{C_1}{k_E - g} = \frac{1.86(1 + 0.1071)}{0.155 - 0.1071} = \pounds42.990m$$

The value of Little to its shareholders under its present strategy and managers is £42.990m.

b   Calculate the present value of the future cash flows. These come in three forms.

   i   Those cash flows available immediately from selling assets, etc., less the amount due on a legal claim (taking the most conservative view):

Time 0 cash flows	
Sale of head office	£5m
less legal claim	£3m
	£2m

   ii   Merger benefit cash flow – constant for all future years:

	£m
Transport	0.100
Secretaries	0.028
Head office	0.150
Managerial efficiency	0.300
Market power	0.100
Boost to cash flow	0.678

   This is a perpetuity which has a present value of:

   $$\frac{0.678}{0.155} = \pounds4.374m$$

   iii   The present value of Little under its existing strategy, £42.990m.

   Add these values together:

i	£2.000m
ii	£4.374m
iii	£42.990m
Total value	£49.364m

c Value of business in existing form   £42.990m

    plus value of annual savings and benefits

$$\frac{678{,}000 \,+\, 200{,}000}{0.155}$$ £5.665m

    plus Time 0 cash flows   £2.000m

    Total value   £50.655m

Thingamees International now has a bargaining range for the purchase of Little. Below £42.99m the existing shareholders will be reluctant to sell. Above £50.665m, Thingamees may destroy value for its own shareholders even if all poor managers can be removed.

d Some ideas: one possible step to reduce risk is to insist that Big plc accepts all liability relating to the legal claim.

Another issue to be addressed in the negotiation phase is to avoid being hamstrung by redundancy commitments.

Also plan the process of merger integration. In the period before the merger explain your intentions to Little's employees. After the transfer do not alienate the managers and other employees by being capricious and secretive – be straight and honest. If pain is to be inflicted for the good of the firm, be quick, rational and fair, communicate and explain. (*See* Chapter 20 for more detail.)

Exhibit 17.16 discusses some of the practical difficulties in valuation.

Exhibit 17.16

The black art of valuation is fraught with dangers

By Tony Jackson

In formal terms, at least, DCF lies at the root of all investment decisions – whether to buy a share, acquire a company or build a factory. It is a simple three-step process: determine the sum of future cash flows, reduce them to present value through a discount rate, and compare the result with today's price.

Warren Buffett has argued repeatedly that DCF is not just the main, but the only valuation tool. Price/earnings ratios, dividend yields and even growth rates are irrelevant, except insofar as they help clarify the scale and timing of future cash flows.

But Mr Buffett is a special case. What if, for the rest of us, DCF is a fantasy?

One thoughtful if jaundiced observer of the scene, James Montier of Société Générale, effectively argues just that.

First, he says, analysts are hopeless at forecasting. And the further out they go, the more hopeless they get.

I have some sympathy with that.

As a novice analyst some three decades ago, I was aghast at the notion of five or 10-year forecasts. Mere 12-month projections of earnings, balance sheets and cash flows seemed daunting enough.

Second, the discount rate used by analysts is essentially subjective.

Spurred on by financial theory, they use at least three components: the risk-free rate (usually the Treasury bond yield), the equity risk premium and the stock's beta.

The first seems fair enough. The second is a notional figure which can be calculated all sorts of ways – by sector, by market, ex post or ex ante and so on.

More to the point, the figure arrived at is typically 3 to 4 per cent – which, given the huge risks and uncertainties in the forecast itself, is bogus precision.

The stock's beta, meanwhile, is arguably a red herring, as we shall see in a moment. But first, what would Mr Buffett say to all that?

'Even an experienced and intelligent analyst,' he wrote some years ago, 'can go wrong in estimating future cash flows.

▶

Exhibit 17.16 *(continued)*

'The answer is to stick to businesses which are relatively simple and stable in character.'

Mr Buffett explicitly rules out businesses or industries that are new, unstable or subject to rapid change, such as investment banking or technology.

Without wishing to put words into the great man's mouth, this seems to include most of the market.

Taken as a simple syllogism, this is rather daunting. It says that 1) the only rational valuation method is DCF; 2) DCF is not applicable to most businesses, and therefore 3) most businesses cannot be rationally valued.

And yet business people go on making valuation decisions every day. How come?

Part of the answer, I suspect, is that executives proceed much more cautiously than analysts. Their cash-flow projections are lower, their discount rates higher. This makes sense.

If a fund manager buys a stock on false assumptions, he can dump it. If an executive builds a plant on the same basis, he is stuck.

The other part of the answer is that the market works as a kind of blundering average. The point is not that it is setting the right price, but that it is setting a price at all.

This is what Mr Buffett means when he says 'Mr Market' is there to serve you, not to guide you. It is also why he rejects the use of beta. Suppose a stock that normally tracks the market suddenly collapses for no good reason. Should you not buy it, just because its beta has gone up?

Alas, for the average fund manager the answer is normally yes. If the market says a stock is risky, so it is. And if DCF says a stock is cheap but its market price is falling, end of story.

Concluding comments

There are two points about valuation worth noting. First, going through a rigorous process of valuation is more important than arriving at *an* answer. It is the understanding of the assumptions and an appreciation of the nature of the inputs to the process which give insight, not a single number at the end. It is the recognition of the qualitative, and even subjective, nature of key variables in a superficially quantitative analysis that leads to knowledge about values. We cannot escape the uncertainty inherent in the valuation of a share – what someone is willing to pay depends on what will happen in the future – and yet this is no excuse for rejecting the models as unrealistic and impractical. They are better than the alternatives: guessing, or merely comparing one share with another with no theoretical base to anchor either valuation. At least the models presented in this chapter have the virtue of forcing the analyst to make explicit the fundamental considerations concerning the value of a share. As the sage of finance, Warren Buffett, says, 'Valuing a business is part art and part science'.[8]

The second point leads on from the first. It makes sense to treat the various valuation methods as complementary rather than rivals. Obtain a range of values in full knowledge of the weaknesses of each approach and apply informed judgement to provide an idea of the value region.

Key points and concepts

- **Knowledge of the influences on share value** is needed by:

  a managers seeking actions to increase that value;
  b investors interested in allocating savings.

- **Share valuation requires a combination of two skills:**

  a analytical ability using mathematical models;
  b good judgement.

- The **net asset value (NAV)** approach to valuation focuses on balance sheet values. These may be adjusted to reflect current market or replacement values.

  Advantage: 'objectivity'.

  Disadvantages: – excludes many non-quantifiable assets;

  – less objective than is often supposed.

---

8 Quoted by Adam Smith, 'The modest billionaire', *Esquire,* October 1988, p. 103. Reprinted in Janet Lowe (1997), p. 100.

- **Asset values are given more attention in some situations:**

  - firms in financial difficulty;
  - takeover bids;
  - when discounted income flow techniques are difficult to apply, for example in property investment companies, investment trusts, resource-based firms.

- **Income flow valuation methods** focus on the future flows attributable to the shareholder. The past is only useful to the extent that it sheds light on the future.

- **The dividend valuation models (DVM)** are based on the premise that the market value of ordinary shares represents the sum of the expected future dividend flows to infinity, discounted to a present value.

- **A constant dividend valuation model:**

$$P_0 = \frac{d_1}{k_E}$$

- **The dividend growth model:**

$$P_0 = \frac{d_1}{k_E - g}$$

  This assumes constant growth in future dividends to infinity.

- **Problems with dividend valuation models:**

  - highly sensitive to the assumptions;
  - the quality of input data is often poor;
  - If g exceeded k_E a nonsensical result would occur, but then, on a long-term view, g would not exceed k_E.

- **Factors determining the growth rate of dividends:**

  - the quantity of resources retained and reinvested;
  - the rate of return earned on retained resources;
  - the rate of return earned on existing assets;
  - the use of additional finance.

- **How to calculate g, some pointers:**

  a Focus on the firm:

  - evaluate strategy;
  - evaluate the management;
  - extrapolate historic dividend growth;
  - financial statement evaluation and ratio analysis.

  b Focus on the economy.

- **The historic price-earnings ratio (PER)** compared with PERs of peer firms is a crude method of valuation (it is also very popular):

$$\text{Historic PER} = \frac{\text{Current market price of share}}{\text{Last year's earnings per share}}$$

- **Historic PERs may be high for two reasons:**

  - the company is fast growing;
  - the company has been performing poorly, has low historic earnings, but is expected to improve.

  The linking factor is the anticipation of high future growth in earnings. Risk is also reflected in differences between PERs.

- **The more complete PER model:**

$$\frac{P_0}{E_1} = \frac{d_1/E_1}{k_E - g}$$

  This is a prospective PER model because it focuses on next year's dividend and earnings.

- **The discounted cash flow method:**

$$P_0 = \sum_{t=1}^{t=n} (C/(1 + k_E)^t)$$

  For constant cash flow growth:

$$P_0 = \frac{C_1}{k_E - g_c}$$

- **The owner earnings model** requires the discounting of the company's future owner earnings which are standard expected earnings after tax and interest deduction plus non-cash charges less the amount of expenditure on plant, machinery and working capital needed for the firm to maintain its long-term competitive position and its unit volume and to make investment in all new value-creating projects.

- **EBITDA** is earnings before (deduction of) interest, tax, depreciations and amortisation. It is a very flawed measure of value.

- Additional factors to consider when **valuing unquoted shares:**

  - lower quality and quantity of information;
  - more risk;
  - less marketable;
  - may involve 'golden hand-cuffs' or 'earn-outs';
  - adjustment for over- or under-paying of director-owners.

- Some companies are extraordinarily **difficult to value**; therefore **proxies are used for projected cash flow**, such as:

  - telemedia valuations: multiply the number of lines, homes served or doors passed;

▶

- advertising agencies: annual billings;
- fund managers: funds under control;
- hotels: star ratings and bedrooms.

● **Control over a firm** permits the possibility of changing the future cash flows. Therefore a share may be more highly valued if control is achieved.

● **A target company could be valued on the basis of its discounted future cash flows**, e.g.:

$$V_E = \frac{C_1^*}{k_E - g_c^*}$$

● Alternatively the **incremental flows** expected to flow from the company under new management could be discounted to estimate the bid premium (d_1^*, C_1^* and g^* are redefined to be incremental factors only):

$$P_0 = \frac{d_1^*}{k_E - g^*} \quad \text{or} \quad V_E = \frac{C_1^*}{k_E - g_c^*}$$

● **Real options** or **contingent claim values** may add considerably to a share's value.

References and further reading

Alexander, G.J., Bailey, J.V. and Sharpe, W.F. (2008) *Investments*. 6th edn. Upper Saddle River, NJ: Prentice-Hall.

    A wider range of valuation issues is discussed in an accessible introductory style.

Arnold, G. (2009) *The Financial Times Guide to Value Investing: How to become a disciplined investor*. 2nd edn. London: Financial Times Prentice Hall.

    An integration of strategic analysis with equity market investment principles.

Arnold, G. (2014a) *The Financial Times Guide to Investing*. 3rd edn. Pearson.

    An introduction to share valuation including guidance on industry and competitive position analysis.

Arnold, G. (on-going) Deep Value Shares newsletter. http://newsletters.advfn.com

    Three or four newsletter posts per week analysing companies or discussing investment ideas/philosophies.

Bodie, Z., Kane, A. and Marcus, A.J. (2017) *Investments*. 11th edn. New York: McGraw-Hill.

    Contains a well-written chapter on valuation models – easy to follow.

Damodaran, A. (2012) *Investment Valuation*. 3rd edn. New York: John Wiley & Sons.

    Covers many aspects of share and company valuation at introductory and intermediate level.

Damodaran, A. (2014) *Applied Corporate Finance: A User's Manual*. 4th edn. New York: John Wiley & Sons.

    A good chapter on share valuation.

Deloof, M., De Maeseneire, W. and Inghelbrecht, K. (2009) 'How do investment banks value initial public offerings (IPOs)?' *Journal of Business Finance and Accounting*, 36(1), (2) pp. 130–60.

    In IPOs several valuation methods are used. Discounted free cash flow is the most popular and produces unbiased estimates (dividend valuation methods produce underestimates).

Duke, L.K. and Upadhyay, A. (2006) 'Drivers of investment and marketing performance: Implications for mutual fund management', *Journal of Investing*, 15(2), pp. 107–11.

    A survey reveals that analysts in financial institutions value shares using a variety of approaches, but the most popular is forecast PER (looking forward only 1–2 years) rather than discounted cash flow.

Feldman S.J. (2005) *Principles of Private Firm Valuation*. New Jersey: John Wiley & Sons.

    An introduction to valuation with particular focus on unquoted firms.

Fernández, P. (2001) 'Valuation using multiples: How do analysts reach their conclusions?' Available at SSRN: http://papers.ssrn.com/sol3/papers.cfm?abstract_id=274972.

    Argues that valuations based on multiples, such as PER and EBITDA, are highly debatable.

Fernández, P. (2004) 'Discounted cash flow valuation methods: Examples of perpetuities, constant growth and general case.' Available at SSRN: http://papers.ssrn.com/sol3/papers.cfm?abstract_id=743229.

    A theoretical consideration of discounted cash flow valuation methods.

Fernández, P. (2007a) 'Company valuation methods: The most common errors in valuations.' IESE Working Paper No. 449.

    An examination in easy-to-read form of the main valuation methods.

Fernández, P. (2007b) 'Valuing companies by cash flow discounting: Ten methods and nine theories', *Managerial Finance*, 33(11), pp. 853–76.

    A wide variety of discounted cash flow valuation methods is described and shown to be related (under certain theoretical assumptions).

Fernández, P. (2008a) 'Valuation of brands and intellectual capital.' Available at SSRN: http://papers.ssrn.com/sol3/papers.cfm?abstract_id=270688.

The tricky issue of valuing these intangibles is critically assessed through an examination of the most popular techniques.

Fernández, P. (2008b) 'Cash flow is fact. Net income is just an opinion.' Available at SSRN: http://papers.ssrn.com/sol3/papers.cfm?abstract_id=330540.

A theoretical discussion of the links between different definitions of cash flow and net income.

Gordon, M.J. (1962) *The Investment, Financing and Valuation of the Corporation.* Homewood, IL: Irwin.

An early statement of a dividend growth model.

Gordon, M.J. and Shapiro, E. (1956) 'Capital equipment analysis: The required rate of profit', *Management Science*, III, pp. 102–10.

Dividend growth model presented.

Hoffmann, N. (2013) 'Discounted cash flow valuation for small cap M&A integration', *Journal of Applied Corporate Finance*, Spring, 25(2), pp. 116–21.

An examination of 145 valuations conducted for companies being acquired by Landmark Inc. DCF was used with a ten-year forecast horizon. 'The justification for DCF analysis . . . was not that it produced superior valuations compared with those of historic cash flow multiples. Instead, the exercise was valued for its requirement that management carefully evaluate the economic drivers of the business, the opportunities to control costs, the rationality of forecasted growth rates, and the probability of competition and market forces affecting short- and long-term results.' However, DCF can lead 'investors astray, supporting the assertion that contemporary DCF valuation in megamergers is used more to justify irrational transaction premiums than to define a firm's intrinsic value.'

Lowe, J. (1997) *Warren Buffett Speaks.* New York: John Wiley & Sons.

A knowledgeable, witty and wise financier's comments are collected and presented. An excellent antidote to theoretical purism.

McKinsey and Company (Koller, T., Goedhart, M. and Wessel, D.) (2015). *Valuation.* 6th edn. New York: John Wiley & Sons.

Some valuation issues are presented in an accessible style.

Outram, R. (1997) 'For what it's worth', *Management Today,* May, pp. 70–1.

Rappaport, A. (1999) *Creating Shareholder Value.* New York: Free Press. Revised and updated.

Describes cash flow valuation models clearly.

Solomon, E. (1963) *The Theory of Financial Management.* New York: Columbia University Press.

An early discussion of the Gordon and Shapiro dividend growth model.

Stephens, G. and Funnell, J. (1995) 'Take your partners . . .', *Corporate Finance,* London: Euromoney monthly journal, July.

Discusses the difficult issue of valuation of telemedia companies.

Case study recommendations

Please see www.pearsoned.co.uk/arnold for case study synopses. Also, another list of useful case studies from the fifth edition can be found there.

- Federal Bank: dividend discount valuation. Author: Debasish Maitra; Varun Dawar Harvard Business School Available at www.cb.hbsp.harvard.edu

- The valuation and financing of Lady M Confections. Authors: Mihir A. Desai; Elizabeth A. Meyer, Harvard Business School. Available at www.cb.hbsp.harvard.edu

- Jumbo Group: initial public offering. Authors: Ruth S.K. Tan; Zsuzsa R. Huszar; Weina Zhang, Ivey Publishing. Available at www.cb.hbsp.harvard.edu

- Tiger Airways: buyout offer from Singapore International Airlines. Authors: Ruth S.K. Tan; Zsuzsa R. Huszar; Weina, Ivey Publishing. Available at www.cb.hbsp.harvard.edu

- Teuer Furniture (A): discounted cash flow valuation. Author: Mitchell A. Petersen, Kellogg School of Management. Available at www.cb.hbsp.harvard.edu

- Valuing Wal-Mart 2010. Authors: James E. Hatch; Cyrus Zahedi, Ivey Publishing. Available at www.cb.hbsp.harvard.edu

- Valuation of Airthread Connections. Authors: Erik Stafford; Joel L. Heilprin, Harvard Business School. Available at www.cb.hbsp.harvard.edu

- Rosetta Stone: pricing the 2009 IPO Authors: Michael J. Schill; Suprajj Papireddy, Darden School of Business. Available at www.cb.hbsp.harvard.edu

- Subscription businesses are booming. here's how to value them. Authors: Daniel McCarthy; Peter Fader, Harvard Business School. Available at www.cb.hbsp.harvard.edu

- Altagas Ltd: acquisition of Decker Energy International. Authors: Craig Dunbar; Cherise Nielsen; Ken Mark, Ivey Publishing. Available at www.cb.hbsp.harvard.edu

- Primer on multiples valuation and its use in private equity industry. Authors: Victoria Ivashina; Henrik Boe, Harvard Business School. Available at www.cb.hbsp.harvard.edu

- Cemex and the Rinker Acquisition (A). Author: Michael Moffett, Thunderbird School of Global Management. Available at www.cb.hbsp.harvard.edu

- Price or relationship: Securenow's dilemma. Authors: Ripsy Bondia; Ashutosh Dash, Ivey Publishing. Available at www.cb.hbsp.harvard.edu

- Ferrari: the 2015 initial public offering. Authors: Michael J. Schill; Jenny Craddock, Harvard Business School. Available at www.cb.hbsp.harvard.edu

- Applied Mobile Labs: valuation of a start-up. Authors: Jaslene Kaur Bawa; Vinay Goyal; S.K. Mitra, Ivey Publishing. Available at www.cb.hbsp.harvard.edu

Websites

The Society of Share and Business Valuers www.ssbv.org
The Institute of Chartered Accountants www.icaew.co.uk
The Chartered Institute of Taxation www.tax.org.uk
American Society of Appraisers www.appraisers.org
Canadian Institute of Chartered Business Valuators www.cicbv.ca.

Self-review questions

1 What are the problems of relying on NAV as a valuation method? In what circumstances is it particularly useful?

2 Why do analysts obtain historical information on a company for valuation purposes?

3 Name the three types of future income flows which may be examined to value shares.

4 Explain why the dividend valuation model discounts all dividends to infinity and yet individual investors hold shares for a shorter period, making capital gains (and losses).

5 The dividend growth model takes the form:

$$P_0 = \frac{d_1}{k_E - g}$$

Does this mean that we are only valuing next year's dividend? Explain your answer.

6 What are the main investigatory routes you would pursue to try to establish the likely range of future growth rates for a firm?

7 What are the differences between the crude PER model and the more complete PER model?

8 Why do PERs vary over time, and between firms in the same industry?

9 What additional factors might you consider when valuing an unquoted share rather than one listed on a stock exchange?

10 Why might a share have a different value to someone who was able to exercise control over the organisation than to someone who had a small, almost powerless, stake?

Questions and problems

Answers to most questions can be found at www.pearsoned.co.uk/arnold.
Answers to questions marked with an asterisk are to be found only in the Lecturer's Guide.

1 'Valuing shares is either a simple exercise of plugging numbers into mathematical formulae or making comparisons with shares in the same sector.' Explain the problems with this statement.

2 'Some companies do not pay dividends, in others the growth rate is higher than the required rate of return, therefore the dividend valuation models are useless.' Explain your reasons for agreeing or disagreeing with this statement.

3 Shades plc has the following dividend history:

Year	Dividend per share
Recently paid	21p
Last year	19p
Two years ago	18p
Three years ago	16p
Four years ago	14p
Five years ago	12p

The rate of return required on a share of this risk class is 13%. Assuming that this dividend growth rate is unsustainable and Shades will halve its past rate in the future, what is the value of one share? **?**

4 ElecWat is a regulated supplier of electricity and water. It is expected to pay a dividend of 24p per share per year forever. Calculate the value of one share if a company of this risk class is required to return 10% per year. **?**

5 Tented plc has developed a new tent which has had rave reviews in the camping press. The company paid a dividend of 11p per share recently and the next is due in one year. Dividends are expected to rise by 25% per year for the next five years while the company exploits its technological and marketing lead. After this period, however, the growth rate will revert to only 5% per year.

The rate of return on risk-free securities is 7% and the risk premium on the average share has been 5%. Tented is in a systematic risk class which means that the average risk premium should be adjusted by a beta factor of 1.5.

Calculate the value of one share in Tented plc. **?**

6 (*Examination level*) The current share price of Blueberry plc is 205p. It recently reported earnings per share of 14p and has a policy of paying out 50% of earnings in dividends each year. The earnings history of the firm is as follows:

Last reported	14p
One year ago	13p
Two years ago	12p
Three years ago	11p
Four years ago	10p
Five years ago	9p

The rate of growth in earnings and dividends shown in the past is expected to continue into the future.

The risk-free rate of return is 6.5% and the risk premium on the average share has been 5% for decades. Blueberry is in a higher systematic risk class than the average share and therefore the risk premium needs to be adjusted by a beta factor of 1.2.

Required

a Calculate the historical price-earnings ratio.
b Calculate the future growth rate of dividends and earnings.
c Calculate the required rate of return on a share of this risk class.
d Use the more complete PER model to decide whether the shares at 205p are over- or under-priced.
e Describe and explain the problems of using the crude historical PER as an analytical tool.
f What additional factors would you need to allow for when valuing an unquoted share rather than one listed on a stock exchange? **?**

7   (*Examination level*) The following figures are extracted from Tes plc's Annual Report and Accounts.

Balance sheet	
	£m
Fixed assets	
Tangible assets	5,466
Investments	19
	5,485
Current assets	
Inventories	559
Receivables	80
Investments	54
Cash at bank and in hand	38
	731
Creditors: falling due within one year	(2,002)
Creditors: falling due after more than one year	(598)
Provisions for liabilities and charges	(22)
	3,594
Capital and reserves	
Called-up share capital	108
Share premium account	1,383
Other reserves	40
Profit and loss account	2,057
Equity shareholders' funds	3,588
Minority equity interests	6
	3,594

Dividend and earnings history	*Dividends per share*	*Earnings per share*
16 years ago	0.82p	3.51p
Most recent	9.60p	21.9p

The average risk premium over risk-free securities is 5%. The risk-free rate of return is 6.25% and Tes's beta of 0.77 represents the appropriate adjustment to the average risk premium.

Required

a   Calculate a revised net asset value (NAV) for the Tes Group assuming the following:
 – buildings are overvalued in the balance sheet by £100m;
 – 20% of the receivables figure will never be collected;
 – the inventories figure includes £30m of unsaleable stock;
 – 'Current investments' now have a market value of £205m.

b   The total market capitalisation of Tes at the present time is £8bn. Provide some plausible possibilities for the great difference between the value that the market placed on Tes and the NAV.

c   For what type of company and in what circumstances does NAV provide a good estimate of value?

d   If you assume that the dividend growth rate over the past 16 years is unsustainable, and that in the future the rate of growth will average half the rate of the past, at what would you value one share using the dividend growth model?

e   Give some potential explanatory reasons for the difference between the value given in (d) and the value placed on a share in the London Stock Market of 355p.

f   Given the answer in (d) for share price, what is the *prospective* price-earnings ratio (PER) if future earnings grow at the same rate as future dividends?

g   What would be the PER if, (i) $k = 14$, $g = 12$; (ii) $k = 15$, $g = 11$ and next year's dividend and earnings are the same as calculated in (d) and (f) and the payout ratio is the same for all future years?

h   If you assumed for the sake of simplicity that all the long-term debt in the balance sheet is a debenture issued six years ago which is due for redemption three years from now at par value of £100, what is the weighted average cost of capital for this firm?

Other information

- The debenture pays a coupon of 9% on par value.
- The coupons are payable annually – the next is due in 12 months.
- The debenture is currently trading at 105.50.
- The balance sheet shows the nominal value, not the market value.
- Tax is payable at 30% (relevant to question (h) only).
- Use the capitalisation figure given in b for the equity weight.
- You can ignore short-term debt.

8* Lanes plc, the retail butchers, is considering the purchase of ten shops from Roberts plc, the conglomerate. The information gathered on the ten shops trading as a separate subsidiary company is as follows:

Balance sheet		
		£m
Fixed assets		2
Current assets		
Cash	0.1	
Stock	0.6	
Debtors	0.1	
		0.8
Current liabilities		(0.5)
Long-term loan		(1.0)
Net assets		1.3

Trading history	
Year	Earnings (£m)
Last year	1.4
1 year ago	1.3
2 years ago	1.1
3 years ago	1.2
4 years ago	1.0
5 years ago	1.0

If the shops remain part of Roberts, earnings growth is expected to continue at the average historical rate to infinity. The rate of return required on a business of this risk class is 13% per annum.

Required

a Calculate the value of the shops to Roberts' shareholders.
b Lanes' management believes that the ten shops will be a perfect fit with its own. There are no towns in which they both trade, and economies of scale can be obtained. Suppliers will grant quantity discounts which will save £1m per annum. Combined transportation costs will fall by £200,000 per year and administration costs can be cut by £150,000 per year. These savings will remain constant for all future years. In addition, the distribution depot used by the ten shops could be closed and sold for £1.8m with no adverse impact on trading. Calculate the value of the ten shops to Lanes' shareholders on the assumption that the required return remains at 13% and underlying growth continues at its past rate.

9 (*Examination level*) Green plc is a conglomerate quoted on the main London market. The latest set of accounts has just been published. The balance sheet is summarised below.

Green plc	Balance sheet	1 June 20X8
		£m
Fixed assets		
Tangible fixed assets		140
Investments		40
		180
Current assets		
Inventories	180	
Receivables	120	
Cash	30	
		330
Creditors (amounts falling due within one year)		(200)
Creditors (amounts falling due after more than one year)		(100)
Net assets		210

Other information

Dividend history								
(dividend per share)	20X0	20X1	20X2	20X3	20X4	20X5	20X6	20X7	20X8
	5p	5.3	6	6.2	7	7.5	8	8.5	9.2p

Green plc has demonstrated an equity beta of 1.3 over the past five years (and this can be taken as an appropriate adjustment factor to the average risk premium for shares over risk-free securities). The risk-free return is currently 6.5% and the risk premium for equities over risk-free securities has averaged 5% per annum.

Shares in issue: 300 million (constant for the last ten years).

Required

a Calculate a net asset value for each of Green's shares after adjusting the balance sheet for the following:

- tangible assets are worth £50m more than shown in the balance sheet;
- one-half of the receivables figure will never be collected; and
- in your judgement Green's directors have overestimated the inventory value by £30m.

b Comment on some of the problems associated with valuing a share or a corporation using net asset value. For what type of company is net asset value particularly useful?

c Use a dividend valuation model to calculate the value of one share in Green plc. Assume that future dividend growth will be the same as the average rate for recent years.

d Calculate the weighted average cost of capital (WACC) for Green plc on the assumptions that the share price calculated in question c is the market share price and the entry 'Creditors (amounts falling due after more than one year)' consists entirely of a debenture issued at a total par value of £100m five years ago and this is the only liability relevant to the WACC calculation. The debenture will pay a coupon of 8% in one year, followed by a similar coupon in two years from now. A final coupon will be paid in three years upon redemption of the debenture at par value. The debenture is currently trading in the secondary market at £103 per £100 nominal.

For the purpose of calculating the weighted average cost of capital the tax rate may be assumed to be 30%.

10* (*Examination level*) You have been asked to carry out a valuation of Dela plc, a listed company on the main London market.

At the last year end Dela's summarised balance sheet is as shown in Table 1.

Table 1 Dela plc summarised balance sheet.

		£m
Fixed assets		300
Current assets		
Inventories	70	
Receivables	120	
Cash at bank	90	280
Liabilities		
Creditors: trade creditors falling due within one year		(400)
Creditors falling due after more than one year		(50)
Shareholders' funds (Net assets)		130

Table 2 Dela plc trading history

Year-end	Earnings per share (pence)	Dividend per share (pence)
20X8	20	10
20X7	18	9.5
20X6	17	9
20X5	16	8
20X4	13	7
20X3	12	6
20X2	10	5.5
20X1	10	5

Datastream has calculated a beta for Dela of 1.2 and this may be used as the appropriate adjustment to the risk premium on the average share. The risk-free rate of return on UK Treasury bills is 6.5% and the latest study shows an annual equity risk premium over the yield on UK government bonds of 5% for the past 100 years.

The impressive average annual growth in Dela's earnings and dividends over the last few years is likely to persist.

Additional information

- You have obtained an independent valuation of Dela's fixed assets at £350m.
- You believe that Dela has overstated the value of inventories by £30m and one-quarter of its receivables are likely to be uncollectable.
- There have been no new issues of shares in the past eight years.
- Dela has 1,000 million shares in issue.

Required

a   Value Dela using the net asset value (NAV) method.
b   Briefly explain why balance sheets generally have limited usefulness for estimating the value of a firm.
c   Briefly describe two circumstances where balance sheet net asset values become very important for corporate valuation.
d   Value one of Dela's shares using the dividend valuation model. (Assume the dividend of 10p has just been paid and the next dividend is due in one year.)
e   What is the prospective price to earnings ratio (P/E ratio) given the share price in d?
f   Calculate a weighted average cost of capital given that the balance sheet entry 'Creditors falling due after more than one year' consists entirely of the nominal value of a debenture issue and this is the only form of debt you need to consider for a WACC calculation. The debenture will be redeemed at par in three years, it carries an annual coupon of 8% (the next payment will be in one year) and it is presently trading in the market at 96.50 per £100 nominal. The total nominal value is £50m.

Assume for the purpose of (f) that the shares are valued at your valuation in (d) and that Dela is taxed at a rate of 30%.

Assignments

1   Estimate the value of a share in your company (or one you know well) using the following approaches:

- net asset value;
- dividend valuation model;
- crude price-earnings ratio – comparing with peer firms;
- more complete price-earnings ratio model;
- cash flow model;
- owner earnings model.

In a report make clear your awareness of the sensitivity of the results to your assumptions.

2   If your company has recently acquired a business or is considering such a purchase obtain as much data as you can to calculate a possible bargain range. The upper boundary of this is fixed by the value of the business to your firm, given the implementation of a plan to change the future cash flows. The lower boundary is fixed by the value to the present owner.

Capital structure

LEARNING OUTCOMES

Capital structure refers to the firm's mix of debt and equity. The level of debt relative to ordinary share capital is, for most firms, of secondary consideration behind strategic and operational decisions. However, if the value of the firm can be increased by getting the right mix of debt and equity, managers need to understand the key influences. By the end of the chapter the reader should be able to:

■ discuss the effect of gearing;

■ explain business and financial risk;

■ describe the underlying assumptions, rationale and conclusions of Modigliani and Miller's models, in worlds with and without tax;

■ describe other key relevant theories on capital structure;

■ incorporate evidence from the real world into their thinking about capital structure;

■ explain the relevance of some important, but often non-quantifiable, influences on the optimal gearing level question.

Introduction

If future company cash flows are assumed to be constant, can managers, by altering the proportion of debt in the total capital structure, increase the value of the firm and thus increase shareholder value? If it is possible to increase shareholder wealth by changing the debt to equity ratio, then surely managers have a duty to move the firm towards the optimal debt proportion.

Debt is generally considered to be of lower risk than equity and therefore debt holders require a lower rate of return than equity providers; this means debt is cheaper. The traditional view was that it would be beneficial to increase gearing (the debt to equity ratio) because the firm would then be financed by cheaper borrowed funds, reducing the weighted average cost of capital (WACC). The discounting of future cash flows at this lower WACC would produce a higher present value and so shareholder wealth would be enhanced.

However, as debt levels rise the firm's earnings attributable to shareholders, which is the profit after interest and tax, become increasingly volatile due to the requirement to pay large amounts of interest. The large interest charge reduces the earnings available to pay dividends. If profits fall or interest rates rise, the burden of a large interest bill can lead the firm to become financially distressed and, in extreme circumstances, to liquidation.

The traditional answer to the question of whether there was an optimal gearing level was 'yes'. If the gearing level is too low, shareholder value opportunities are foregone by not substituting 'cheap' debt for equity. If it is too high, the additional risk leads to a loss in shareholder value through a higher discount rate being applied to the future cash flows attributable to ordinary shareholders. This is because of the higher risk and, at very high gearing, the real possibility of complete business failure.

Other ideas

In 1958 Franco Modigliani and Merton Miller developed a theory which said that capital structure had no impact on corporate value. They concluded that it did not matter whether the firm had a gearing level of 90% debt or 2% debt – the overall value of the firm would be constant and shareholder wealth could not be enhanced by altering the gearing. This conclusion was based on assumptions of perfect markets requiring a perfect world of perfect knowledge in which individual shareholders could borrow and lend at the same rate as giant corporations, and in which taxation and cost of financial distress did not exist.

In 1963 Modigliani and Miller (MM) modified the no-taxation assumption. This led to a different conclusion. As the interest on debt is treated as a business expense and is tax deductible the use of debt provides a tax shield which reduces the cost of debt and thus increases the value of the firm. Under MM 1963, the best capital structure for a firm interested in shareholder wealth maximisation is to increase debt as far as possible. Their conclusion was that the value of a geared company was the value of the ungeared company plus the present value of the tax shield. This was an astonishing result; it meant that a company financed with £99m of debt and £1m of equity serves its shareholders better than one funded by £50m of debt and £50m of equity. More importantly, this was evidently not what was happening in the real world. Companies were taking on debt, but none operated at such high debt levels.

Within academic circles thousands of hours of thinking and research time have been spent over the past five decades building on the MM foundations, and millions of hours of undergraduates' and postgraduates' precious time have been spent learning the intricacies of the algebraic proofs lying behind MM conclusions. However, this chapter will not dwell on algebra (the interested reader is referred to some more advanced reading at the end of the chapter). Emphasis will be given to explanations which have been advanced to explain actual real-world gearing levels. A conclusion will be drawn which fits neither the MM first conclusion, that there is not an optimal gearing level, nor their modified theory with taxes, in which there is an optimum at the most extreme level of debt.

Empirical evidence shows that directors, analysts and financial commentators believe that there is an optimal gearing range which helps to maximise shareholder wealth which lies at neither 100% equity nor 100% debt. **Exhibit 18.1** provides an example of a capital structure review.

Exhibit 18.1

Noble Group reviews capital structure

By Neil Hume, Commodities Editor

Noble Group, one of Asia's biggest commodities trading companies, has launched a review of its financial structure that could pave the way for capital to be returned to shareholders.

Speaking after the release of third quarter figures, Noble chief executive Yusuf Alireza said the company was looking for ways to deploy the $1.5bn of proceeds from the sale of a majority stake in its agricultural business to Cofco, the Chinese state-owned grain trader. However, if Noble could not find suitable investment opportunities that met its return criteria, Mr. Alireza said the company would not keep excess cash on its balance sheet.

"We are reviewing all aspects of capital structure, which includes our leverage, how much equity we have, how much equity we need, our dividend policy all of those things," he said. "We have the strongest balance sheet in our history."

Analysts at Barclays said Noble's net debt could decline from $5.4bn to $2bn by the end of the year once the entire proceeds of the Cofco deal – including a debt repayment of $1.9bn – are received. "While debt reduction will strengthen its balance sheet, the company could practically be debt free excluding the liquid inventories," said analyst Ephrem Ravi.

Debt finance is cheaper and riskier (for the company)

Financing a business through borrowing is cheaper than using equity. This is because lenders consider debt to be a less risky investment than equity and therefore they require a lower rate of return than ordinary shareholders. Debt presents a lower risk than shares for the finance providers because debt holders have prior claims on annual income and, in the event of liquidation, have prior claims on repayment. In addition, security is often demanded and covenants imposed, both of which lower the risk of the finance provider not being able to recoup their lending.

Debt interest is treated as a business expense and is normally tax deductible. This means the interest cost can be deducted from pre-tax profits before the calculation of the corporation tax bill. The tax liability is calculated as taxable profits multiplied by the tax rate so lower taxable profits (due to the interest charge) reduce the tax paid. The cost to the company of the debt interest is the post-tax cost.

Finally, issuing and transaction costs associated with raising and servicing debt are generally less than for ordinary shares.

Although there are valuable benefits from financing a firm with debt, firms tend to avoid very high gearing levels. The main reason is financial distress risk. Debt interest must be paid regardless of the cash flow of the business. If the firm hits a rough patch in its business, it may have trouble paying its bondholders, bankers and other creditors. If the company does not pay its interest it is 'in default' and this can mean that it is charged a higher interest rate or has to repay its borrowing immediately. If it cannot pay, it may end up in liquidation. **Exhibit 18.2** shows that, as gearing increases, the risk of financial failure grows.

Note the crucial assumption in Exhibit 18.2 – if the returns to equity are constant, or do not rise much, as new cheaper debt is introduced the overall cost of finance (WACC) declines. However as more debt continues to be added, shareholders will not be so relaxed and as the risk of financial distress rises ordinary shareholders are likely to demand higher returns. At this point the WACC will start to rise again. This is an important issue and we will return to it after a discussion of some basic concepts about gearing.

Exhibit 18.2	At low gearing levels the risk of financial distress is low, but the cost of capital is high; this reverses at high gearing levels

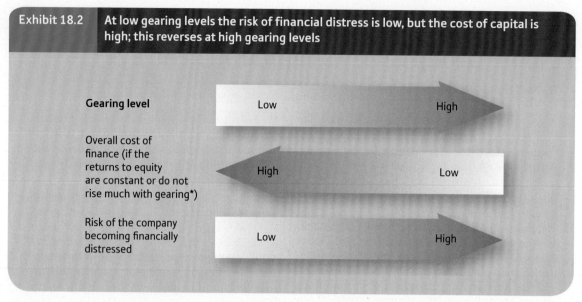

Note: *This assumption is considered in the text.

What do we mean by 'gearing'?

First, we should make a distinction between financial gearing and operating gearing.

Financial gearing is the focus of this chapter and concerns the proportion of debt in the capital structure.

Operating gearing is not directly related to the financing of the firm. It impacts on the earnings available to ordinary shareholders. Operating gearing refers to the extent to which the firm's costs are fixed. The earnings of firms with high operating gearing – a high proportion of fixed costs – such as car or steel manufacturers, are sensitive to changes in the level of sales. Firms with high operating gearing have high break-even points. The break-even point is the sales level at which variable and fixed costs are fully covered. At the break-even point profit is nil but, for every sale thereafter, the full contribution per unit (selling price – variable cost) is added to profit. Equally, however, when sales fall, the impact on the bottom line is significant, due to the high fixed costs.

In firms with high financial gearing and thus high finance costs, the earnings available to the ordinary shareholder is sensitive to changes in operating profit because the fixed finance cost, where there is no change in the level or cost of the debt, represents a larger percentage of the reduced operating profit. This means that the earnings available to the ordinary shareholder are reduced by a greater percentage than the operating profit reduction. See Worked example 18.1 below. The units sold, selling at £10 per unit (variable cost of £5) drop from 11,000 to 10,000. A 9% reduction in revenue results in a 33% reduction in earnings available for distribution to the ordinary shareholder.

Worked example 18.1	Impact on earnings of reduction in sales volume

	£000	£000	Reduction %
Sales (11,000 × £10/10,000 × £10)	110	100	−9%
Variable costs (11,000 × £5/10,000 × £5)	55	50	
Contribution	55	50	−9%
Fixed costs	30	30	
Operating profit	25	20	−20%
Finance costs	10	10	
Profit before tax	15	10	−33%
Tax at 20%	3	2	
Profit for the year – available to the ordinary shareholder	12	8	−33%

The terms 'gearing' and 'leverage' are used interchangeably by most practitioners, although leverage is used more in America. There are different ways of calculating financial gearing (to be called simply 'gearing' throughout this chapter). Gearing may be measured by reference to balance sheet (book) figures, but most finance theory concentrates on the market values of debt and equity. Both book and market approaches are useful, depending on the purpose of the analysis. You must make it clear in any analysis you carry out whether you are using book or market values for debt and equity.

There are two ways of putting into perspective the levels of debt that a firm carries – see **Exhibit 18.3**. Capital gearing focuses on the extent to which a firm's total capital is in the form of debt. Income gearing is concerned with the proportion of the annual income stream (that is, the pre-interest profits) which is devoted to the prior claims of debt holders: in other words, what proportion of profits is taken by interest charges?

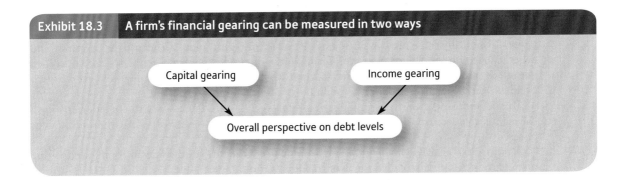

Exhibit 18.3	A firm's financial gearing can be measured in two ways

Capital gearing

There are alternative measures of capital gearing. One popular approach is the ratio of long-term debt to shareholders' funds (the debt to equity ratio). The long-term debt is usually taken as the balance sheet item 'amounts falling due after more than one year', and shareholders' funds is the net asset (or net worth) figure in the balance sheet.[1] Net assets is total assets less total liabilities.

$$\text{Capital gearing (1)} = \frac{\text{Long-term debt}}{\text{Shareholders' funds}}$$

This ratio is of interest because it may give some indication of the firm's ability to sell assets to repay debts. For example, if the ratio stood at 0.3, or 30%, lenders and shareholders might feel relatively comfortable as there would be, apparently, over three times as many net assets as long-term debt. So, if the worst came to the worst, the company could (probably) sell assets to pay its long-term lenders.

There is a major problem with relying on this measure of gearing. The book value of assets can be quite different from the saleable value. This may be because the assets have been recorded at historical purchase value (perhaps less depreciation) and have not been revalued over time. It may also be because companies forced to sell assets to satisfy creditors often have to do so at greatly reduced prices if they are in a hurry.[2] Secondly, this measure of gearing can have a range of values from zero to infinity and this makes inter-firm comparisons difficult.

---

1 Some analysts substitute total liabilities for long-term debt.
2 These problems also apply to capital gearing measures (2) and (3).

The measure shown below puts gearing within a range of zero to 100% as debt is expressed as a fraction of all long-term capital.[3]

$$\text{Capital gearing (2)} = \frac{\text{Long-term debt}}{\text{Long-term debt} + \text{Shareholders' funds}}$$

These ratios could be further modified by the inclusion of 'provisions', that is, sums set aside in the accounts for anticipated loss or expenditure, for example a bad debt or costs of merger integration. Deferred tax likewise may be included as an expected future liability. A modification of this is total liabilities/total assets.

The third capital gearing measure, in addition to allowing for long-term debt, includes short-term borrowing.

$$\text{Capital gearing (3)} = \frac{\text{All borrowing}}{\text{All borrowing} + \text{Shareholders' funds}}$$

Many firms rely on overdraft facilities and other short-term borrowing, for example commercial paper. Technically these are classified as short term. In reality, many firms use the overdraft and other short-term borrowing as a long-term source of funds. Furthermore, if we are concerned about the potential for financial distress, then we must recognise that an inability to repay an overdraft can be just as serious as an inability to service a long-term bond.

To add sophistication to capital gearing analysis it is often necessary to consider any cash (or marketable securities) holdings in the firm as these can be used to offset the threat that debt poses.

A measure of gearing which is gaining prominence is the ratio of debt to the total market value of the firm's equity (also called the debt to equity ratio (market value)).

$$\text{Capital gearing (4)} = \frac{\text{Long-term debt}}{\text{Total market capitalisation}}$$

This has the advantage of being closer to the market-value-based gearing measures (assuming book long-term debt is similar to the market value of the debt). It gives some indication of the relative share of the company's total value belonging to debt holders and shareholders.

There is a variety of capital gearing measures and it is important to know which measure people are using – it can be very easy to find yourself talking at cross-purposes.

Most of the capital gearing measures rely on the appropriate valuation of net assets either in the balance sheet or in a revaluation exercise. This is a difficult task; try valuing a machine on a factory floor or a crate of raw material. Also, the capital gearing measures focus on a worst-case scenario: 'What could we sell the business assets for, if we had to, in order to pay creditors?'

Income gearing

It may be erroneous to focus exclusively on assets when trying to judge a company's ability to repay debts. A successful advertising agency may have limited saleable assets, and yet it can borrow because it can generate cash to make interest payments. Thus, quite often, a more appropriate measure of a firm's ability to repay debt is one concerned with the level of a firm's income relative to its interest commitments:

$$\text{Interest cover} = \frac{\text{Profit before interest and tax}}{\text{Interest charges}} \text{ or } \frac{\text{Operating cash flow}}{\text{Interest charges}}$$

The lower the interest cover ratio the greater the chance of interest payment default and potential liquidation. The inverse of interest cover measures the proportion of profits (or cash flow) paid

---

3 To make this discussion easier to follow it will be assumed that there are only two types of finance: debt and ordinary shares. However, the introduction of other types of finance does not fundamentally alter the analysis.

out in interest – this is called income gearing. Another popular ratio is operating cash flow to total debt, which shows a company's ability to service its debt from annual cash flow.

Net debt to EBITDA (earnings before interest, tax, depreciation and amortisation) is another common measure of credit worthiness. While EBITDA has serious drawbacks as a measure for share valuation (*see* Chapter 17) it has much more acceptability as an income gearing metric because it provides a gauge of the size of the cash flow, before allowing for investment in new and replacement fixed capital items such as machinery and paying tax bills, relative to the total amount of debt that needs to be serviced. So, if net debt is kept below, say, three times EBITDA and interest rates on that debt are reasonably low then the firm should have only a low probability of failing to pay the interest.

The ratios considered above are now calculated for Rolls-Royce. The data in **Exhibit 18.4** and in the following calculations are taken from the Annual Report 2016.

Exhibit 18.4	Rolls-Royce balance sheet and profit figures

Consolidated Balance Sheet at 31 December

	2016 £m	2015 £m
Assets		
Non-current assets	12680	10208
Current assets – see breakdown below	12858	12116
Total assets	**25538**	**22324**
Liabilities		
Current liabilities– see breakdown below	(9534)	(8173)
Non-current liabilities– see breakdown below	(14140)	(9135)
Total liabilities	**(23674)**	**(17308)**
Net assets	**1864**	**5016**
Equity attributable to ordinary shareholders	1862	5014
Non-controlling interests	2	2
Total equity	**1864**	**5016**
Profit before interest and taxation	41	1501
Interest payable[1]	(77)	(71)
Market capitalisation (1838 million 20p shares)	13601	10569
Current assets		
Inventories	3086	2637
Trade and other receivables	6956	6244
Cash and cash equivalents	2771	3176
Other assets – tax, financial assets, assets held for sale	45	59
	12858	12116
Current liabilities		
Borrowing	172	419
Other financial liabilities	651	331
Trade and other payables	7957	6923
Other financial liabilities – deferred tax and provisions	754	500
	9534	8173
Non-current liabilities		
Borrowings	3185	2883
Other financial liabilities	5129	1651
Trade and other payables	3459	2317
Post-retirement scheme deficits	1375	1140
Other financial liabilities – deferred tax and provisions	992	1144
	14140	9135

Source: Rolls-Royce Annual Report 2016.

1 "Finance costs" per P/L includes net fair value losses on currency contracts and other items which are not relevant here

We now calculate some ratios using the data in Exhibit 18.4. As previously indicated, there are alternative measures which could be used and in discussions of gearing you should ensure you clearly specify or understand which ratio definition is being used.

$$\text{Capital gearing (1)} = \frac{\text{Long-term debt}}{\text{Shareholders' funds}} \times 100$$

	2016	2015
Long-term debt – borrowings	3,185	2,883
Shareholders' funds	1,864	5,016
Capital gearing (1)	171%	57%

Rolls Royce made a loss of £4032 million for 2016 which markedly reduced its shareholders' funds. This loss was partly due to a drop of £229 million in gross profit due to a lower gross margin of 20% (2015 −24%) and to one-off costs of nearly £1000 million, included in "commercial and administrative costs" due to regulatory fines and restricting of the UK pension fund.

The sharp increase in the capital gearing (1) ratio is primarily due to the reduction in shareholders' funds. The above debt shows only non-current liabilities. If current borrowings, due to be repaid within one year, were included the total debt would be £3357 million for 2016 and £3302 million for 2015, an increase of only 1.7%.

$$\text{Capital gearing (2)} = \frac{\text{Long-term debt}}{\text{Long-term debt } + \text{ Shareholders' funds}} \times 100$$

	2016	2015
Long-term debt – borrowings	3,185	2,883
Shareholders' funds	1,864	5,016
Total capital provided	5,049	7,899
Capital gearing (2)	63%	36%

$$\text{Capital gearing (3)} = \frac{\text{All borrowing}}{\text{All borrowing } + \text{ Shareholders' funds}} \times 100$$

	2016	2015
Long-term debt – borrowings	3,185	2,883
Current borrowing	172	419
All borrowing	3,357	3,302
Shareholders' funds	1,864	5,016
Total capital provided (3)	5,221	8,318
Capital gearing (3)	64%	40%

Note that although long term borrowing has increased by 10%, when you include current borrowing as well the overall increase is reduced to 1.7%. This underlines the importance of defining clearly what you are including in your gearing ratio.

$$\text{Capital gearing (4)} = \frac{\text{Long-term debt}}{\text{Market capitalisatation}} \times 100$$

	2016	2015
Long-term debt – borrowings	3,185	2,883
Market value per share at year end (GBP)	6.68	5.75
Market capitalisation (1,838 million 20p shares)	12,645	10,569
Capital gearing (4)	25%	27%

$$\text{Interest cover} = \frac{\text{Profit before interest and tax}}{\text{Interest charges}}$$

	2016	2015
Profit before interest and taxation	41	1,501
Interest payable	(77)	(71)
Interest cover	0.53	21 times

$$\text{Interest gearing} = \frac{\text{Interest charges}}{\text{Profit before interest and tax}} \times 100$$

	2016	2015
Interest payable	(77)	(71)
Profit before interest and taxation	41	1,501
Interest gearing	187%	5%

It is obvious that the company's financial position is not as strong as in prior years. In 2016, Rolls Royce had several market and other issues, resulting in a loss of £4,302 million which distorts some of the ratios. The Board of Directors, in their 'Going Concern' statement in the Annual Report 2016 page 53, state that they are confident that they can continue to operate for the foreseeable future and that they are viable over the next five years, the medium-term forecast period.

Managers became more cautious with borrowing levels following the 2008 crisis – *see* **Exhibit 18.5** which describes the 'de-leveraging' mood. Whereas net debt as a proportion of shareholders' funds averaged 30% over 20 years, directors, frightened of the economic slowdown, pushed average gearing much lower.

Exhibit 18.5

Gearing levels set to fall dramatically

By Jeremy Grant

When Stuart Siddall was corporate treasurer of Amec four years ago, analysts were critical when the engineering group swung from having substantial net debt on its balance sheet to sitting on a huge cash pile after completing disposals.

'The analysts were saying "this is inefficient balance sheet management",' says Mr Siddall.

Companies back then were expected to be highly geared, with net debt to shareholders' funds at historically high levels.

How times have changed. With a wave of rights issues and other equity issuance now expected from the UK's non-financial companies – and with funds from these being used to pay down debt – the pendulum is rapidly swinging back in favour of more conservative balance sheet management. Gearing levels are set to fall dramatically, analysts say.

'There is going to be an appreciable and material drop in gearing, by about a quarter or a third over the

▶

Exhibit 18.5 *(continued)*

next three years,' predicts Mr Siddall, now chief executive of the Association of Corporate Treasurers.

Historically, gearing levels – as measured by net debt as a proportion of shareholders' funds – have run at an average of about 30% over the past 20 years.

Peak levels were reached in the past few years as companies took advantage of cheap credit. Current predictions see it coming down to about 20% – and staying there for a good while to come.

One of the most immediate concerns to heavily indebted companies is whether, in a recessionary environment, they will be able to generate the profit and cash flows to service their debts.

But the standard gearing denominator – shareholders' funds – does not reflect earnings potential or the current market value of the company, for that matter. A more meaningful measure of a company's leverage compares its net debt to earnings before interest, tax, depreciation and amortisation.

Predicting where leverage by this measure will end up is tricky, because of uncertainty over the outlook for corporate earnings. That was underscored last week when Unilever, the UK consumer goods group, and GlaxoSmithKline, the drugs group, scrapped their financial targets for the current year. Adrian Cattley, European equity strategist at Citi, says: 'One of the challenges will be for companies not just to get gearing down but [to ensure] that people are comfortable with the level of gearing when profits are down.'

Analysts say that for a typical industrial company banks are likely in future to make debt covenants stricter, so that net debt cannot exceed two-and-a-half to three times ebitda, compared with a current average of three to four times.

Gearing levels vary from sector to sector as well. Oil companies prefer low levels given their exposure to the volatility of oil prices. BP's net debt-shareholders' funds ratio of 21% is at the low end of a 20–30% range it considers prudent.

Miners' gearing is on a clear downward trend already. Xstrata, the mining group, stressed last month that its £4.1bn rights issue would cut gearing from 40% to less than 30%. A week later, BHP said its $13bn of first-half cash flows had cut gearing to less than 10%. Rio, which had gearing of 130% at the last count in August 2008, is desperately trying to cut it by raising fresh equity.

Utilities tend to be highly geared because they can afford to borrow more against their typically reliable cash flows. But even here the trend is downwards.

Severn Trent, the UK water group, says its appropriate long-term gearing level is 60%. But 'given ongoing uncertainties . . . it is prudent in the near term to retain as much liquidity and flexibility as possible'. It does not expect to pursue that target until credit markets improve.

FT *Financial Times,* 11 February 2009, p. 19.
All Rights Reserved.

The effect of gearing

The introduction of interest-bearing debt 'gears up' the returns to shareholders. Compared with those of the ungeared firm, the geared firm's returns to its owners are subject to greater variation than underlying earnings. If profits are high, the geared firm's shareholders will experience a more than proportional boost in their returns compared to the ungeared firm's shareholders. On the other hand, if profits turn out to be low the geared firm's shareholders will find their returns declining by more than the reduction in profit before interest.

The effect of gearing can best be explained through an example. Harby plc is shortly to be established. The prospective directors are considering three different capital structures which will all result in £10m of capital being raised.

1   All equity – 10 million shares sold at a nominal value of £1.

2   £3m debt (carrying 10% interest) and £7m equity.

3   £5m debt (carrying 10% interest) and £5m equity.

To simplify their analysis the directors have assigned probabilities to three potential future performance levels (*see* **Exhibit 18.6**).

Exhibit 18.6	Probabilities of performance levels	
Customer response to firm's products	**Income before interest[*]**	**Probability (%)**
Modest success	£0.5m	20
Good response	£3.0m	60
Run-away success	£4.0m	20

[*]Taxes are to be ignored.

We can now examine what will happen to shareholder returns for each of the gearing levels.

Exhibit 18.7 shows what happens as gearing increases: the changes in earnings attributable to shareholders are magnified. For example, when earnings before interest rise by 500% from £0.5m to £3.0m the returns on the 30% geared structure rises by 1,200% from 3% to 39%. This magnification effect works in both positive and negative directions – if earnings before interest are only £0.5m the all-equity structure gives shareholders some return, but with the 50% geared firm they will receive nothing. Harby's shareholders would be taking a substantial risk that they would have no profits if they opted for a high level of gearing.

Exhibit 18.7	The effect of gearing		
Customer response	**Modest**	**Good**	**Run-away**
Earnings before interest	£0.5m	£3.0m	£4.0m
All-equity structure			
Debt interest at 10%	0.0	0.0	0.0
Earnings available for shareholders	£0.5m	£3.0m	£4.0m
Return on shares	$\dfrac{£0.5m}{£10m} = 5\%$	$\dfrac{£3.0m}{£10m} = 30\%$	$\dfrac{£4.0m}{£10m} = 40\%$
30% gearing (£3m debt, £7m equity)			
Debt interest at 10%	£0.3m	£0.3m	£0.3m
Earnings available for shareholders	£0.2m	£2.7m	£3.7m
Return on shares	$\dfrac{£0.2m}{£7m} = 3\%$	$\dfrac{£2.7m}{£7m} = 39\%$	$\dfrac{£3.7m}{£7m} = 53\%$
50% gearing (£5m debt, £5m equity)			
Debt interest at 10%	£0.5m	£0.5m	£0.5m
Earnings available for shareholders	0.0	£2.5m	£3.5m
Returns on shares	$\dfrac{£0.0m}{£5m} = 0\%$	$\dfrac{£2.5}{£5m} = 50\%$	$\dfrac{£3.5m}{£5m} = 70\%$

The data for the ungeared and the 50% geared capital structure are displayed in **Exhibit 18.8**. The direction of the effect of gearing depends on the level of earnings before interest. If this is greater than £1m, the return to shareholders is increased by gearing. If it is less than £1m, the return is reduced by gearing. Note that the return on the firm's overall assets at this pivot point is 10% (£1m/£10m). If a return of more than 10% (debt cost of capital) on assets is achieved, shareholders' returns are enhanced by gearing.

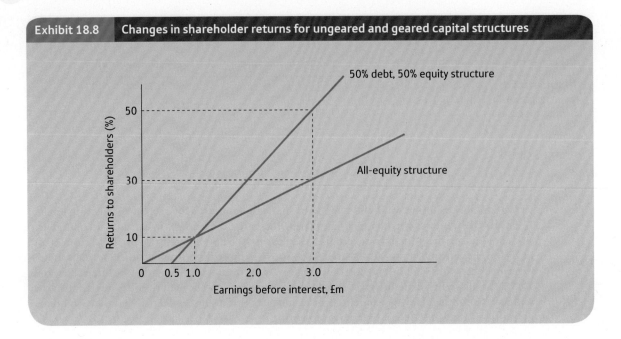

Exhibit 18.8 Changes in shareholder returns for ungeared and geared capital structures

Expected returns and standard deviations for Harby plc

It makes intuitive sense to say that year-to-year variations in income will be greater for a more highly geared firm as it experiences good and bad trading years. Interest has to be paid to debt providers irrespective of the level of operating profit achieved. At lower profit levels it is possible that the earnings will be zero or negative.

Exhibit 18.9 shows the calculations of standard deviation (a measure of risk) of the return to shareholders under the three gearing levels. As Exhibit 18.9 indicates, as the gearing levels rise, the expected return for shareholders also rises (from 27% to 34.6% to 44%), but this is accompanied by a rising level of risk. Management must weigh up the relative importance of the 'good' resulting from the increase in expected returns and the 'bad' from the wider dispersion of returns attributable to shareholders.

Exhibit 18.9 Expected returns and standard deviations of return to shareholders in Harby plc

All equity

Return, R (%)	Probability, p_i	Return × probability
5	0.2	1
30	0.6	18
40	0.2	8
		$\overline{27}$

Expected return, $\overline{R} = 27\%$

Return, R (%)	Expected return, $\overline{R}$	Probability	$(\overline{R} - R)^2 p_i$
5	27	0.2	96.8
30	27	0.6	5.4
40	27	0.2	33.8

Variance $\sigma^2 = \underline{136.0}$

Standard deviation $\sigma = 11.7\%$

30% gearing

Return, R (%)	Probability, p_i	Return $\times$ probability	
3	0.2	0.6	
39	0.6	23.4	
53	0.2	10.6	
		34.6	Expected return, $\bar{R} = 34.6\%$

Return, R (%)	Expected return, $\bar{R}$	Probability	$(\bar{R} - R)^2 p_i$
3	34.6	0.2	199.71
39	34.6	0.6	11.62
53	34.6	0.2	67.71
		Variance $\sigma^2 =$	279.04
		Standard deviation $\sigma =$	16.7%

50% gearing

Return, R (%)	Probability, p_i	Return $\times$ probability	
0	0.2	0	
50	0.6	30	
70	0.2	14	
		44	Expected return, $\bar{R} = 44\%$

Return, R (%)	Expected return, $\bar{R}$	Probability	$(\bar{R} - R)^2 p_i$
0	44	0.2	387.2
50	44	0.6	21.6
70	44	0.2	135.2
		Variance $\sigma^2 =$	544.0
		Standard deviation $\sigma =$	23.3%

Business risk and financial risk

Business risk is the variability of the firm's operating income, that is, the income before interest. In the case of Harby this is found by examining the dispersion of returns for the all-equity capital structure. Business-related factors, such as the characteristics of the industry and the competitive advantage possessed by the firm within that industry, cause this dispersion. This risk is influenced by factors such as the variability of sales volumes, prices, input costs, the degree of market power and the level of growth.

The business risk of a monopoly supplier of electricity, gas or water is significantly less than that for, say, an entrepreneurial company trying to gain a toehold in the fintech market. The range of possible demand levels and prices is likely to be narrower for the utilities than for the high-tech firm. Business risk is determined by general business and economic conditions and is not related to the firm's financial structure.

Financial risk is the additional variability in returns to shareholders and the increased probability of insolvency that arises because the financial structure contains debt. In **Exhibit 18.10** the standard deviation gives a measure of total risk. If a 50% geared structure is selected the returns to shareholders would have a high dispersion, that is, a standard deviation of 23.3%. Of this overall risk, roughly half is caused by underlying business risk and half by financial risk. The increasing proportion of debt raises the firm's fixed financial costs. At high gearing levels there is an increased probability of the firm not only failing to make a return to shareholders, but also failing to meet the interest cost obligation, and thus raising the likelihood of insolvency.

| Exhibit 18.10 | Business and financial risk | | | |

Gearing (%)	Expected return to shareholders (%)	Standard deviation (total risk) (%)	Business risk (%)	Remaining total risk due to financial risk* (%)
0 (all-equity)	27	11.7	11.7	0
30	34.6	16.7	11.7	5
50	44	23.3	11.7	11.6

*This is a simplified representation of the relationship between total risk, financial risk and business risk. It should be: Variance of total risk = (Business risk standard deviation)^2 + (Financial risk standard deviation)^2. To be even more strict: we should be considering systematic risk rather than standard deviation.

Firms with low business risk can take on relatively high levels of financial risk without exposing their shareholders to excessive total risk. The increased expected return more than compensates for the higher variability resulting in climbing share prices.

It is appropriate at this point to remember that, until now we have focused primarily on accounting values for debt and equity – book debt, net assets in the balance sheet, etc. In the models which follow, the correct bases of analysis are the market values of debt and equity. This is because we are interested in the effect of the capital structure decision on share values in the marketplace, not on accounting entries.

By 2011, three years after the start of the recession, companies were so cautious that they had built up large cash piles. This reluctance to use their strong balance sheets to invest and grow by spending cash and borrowing some more was a major contributor to the lengthening of the downturn in the world economy, and greatly concerned politicians – *see* **Exhibit 18.11** ('net debt' is after allowing for cash to offset debt).

Exhibit 18.11

Rivers of riches

By Richard Milne and Anousha Sakoui

Feike Sijbesma has a dilemma. But – in common with many chief executives today – it is a pleasant one. DSM, the Dutch life sciences group he runs, has at least €2bn of cash on its balance sheet. 'We are sitting on cash – and cash we need to spend,' he says. 'The market isn't pressuring us but we need to act in a certain time frame, yes. We want to do acquisitions.'

How companies spend their cash will be crucial to the way in which the global economy recovers. Given western governments' huge indebtedness, if the private sector continues to save it will act as a big brake on economic growth.

But executives, investors and bankers all suggest that a return to pre-crisis levels of exuberance is unlikely any time soon. Groups will be more cautious, scarred by the crisis and wary about the strength of the upturn. 'Companies, albeit with some exceptions, will be more conservative in the future. They will

want to keep a bigger cash buffer than they had going into the crisis,' says Rodolfo De Benedetti, chief executive of CIR, the energy-to-media conglomerate.

Colleen Denzler of Janus Capital Management, a large US fund manager, agrees that companies will hold on to more cash as they seek to learn the lessons of the financial crisis. 'It is all about confidence. Put yourself in the shoes of a CFO in 2008. They had been increasing leverage, had an underfunded pension fund and so went into the crisis in a tenuous position,' she says. 'You will never put your company back into that situation. So, you have been amassing a pile of cash.'

The firepower available to companies is extraordinary. Balance sheets are as healthy as they have ever been, with leverage – the proportion of debt to equity – at its lowest in at least 20 years, according to analysts at the UK's HSBC. If leverage

Debt and deals

Leverage in non-financial businesses globally
(Net debt as a % of shareholder equity)

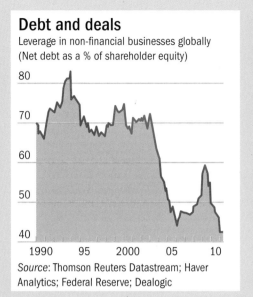

Source: Thomson Reuters Datastream; Haver
Analytics; Federal Reserve; Dealogic

returned only to the average level of the past decade, they estimate, companies would have an extra $2,700bn to spend.

Cash represents the biggest proportion of total assets in the US than at any time in the past half century. On top of this, official interest rates in the US and UK are at or close to record lows, meaning the returns on

cash are close to zero, providing a powerful incentive to use that money.

Mr Sijbesma thinks companies will delve into their war chests but will be careful not to load up on too much debt. Like many companies, DSM has become attached to its credit rating – in its case single-A – and any acquisitions would have not to threaten it. 'The level of leverage we had before isn't coming back: first of all, in the financial sector, but more importantly also in the corporate sector. That doesn't mean that everyone can sit on cash. Now the crisis is over, people can't say cash is king. We have to spend it,' he says.

Nick Gartside, a chief investment officer at JPMorgan Asset Management, says: 'There is future uncertainty. If you look at growth in the developed world, forecasts keep on coming down. If you are a corporate treasurer are you going to invest or are you going to wait and see?'

'Today, many big companies are more cautious than in the past, after having directly experienced market volatility and funding difficulties during the most acute phase of the crisis,' says Mr De Benedetti. 'Having cash in hand in this kind of market context is a bit like having an insurance policy against the risk of financial tension.'

However, in subsequent years, with interest rates at all-time lows and suggestions that they may be about to start rising, many companies have started to reissue corporate debt to take advantage of investors' interest in 'safe debt' and to lock in the low rates (see **Exhibit 18.12**).

Exhibit 18.12

US company debt sales power ahead as borrowing costs drop

Host of companies including Apple, IBM, Home Depot and Visa tap investors for funding

By Eric Platt and Nicole Bullock in New York

Sales of high-grade US corporate bonds for 2017 surged past the $1tn mark this week, surpassing the level faster than ever before as the lowest interest rates for companies this year enticed the likes of Apple, IBM, Home Depot and Visa.

The average yield on investment grade US corporate debt fell to 3.05 per cent this week, matching the

lowest level since last November, according to Bank of America Merrill Lynch.

"Corporate treasurers are going to take advantage of those lower rates while they can and build up liquidity," said Michael Cuggino, president and portfolio manager of the Permanent Portfolio Family of Funds. "We have seen companies over

▶

Exhibit 18.12 *(continued)*

the past few years doing that and it has just continued."

Helping companies tap debt markets has been a surge of money into bond funds as investors seek paper sold by highly rated companies. Investors across the globe have piled into US fixed income in search of higher income, as trillions of dollars of Japanese and European government bonds trade with yields below zero. Strategists with Wells Fargo, who cite EPFR data, note more than $218bn has been added to funds that can invest in high-grade US corporate bonds this year.

Companies borrowed more than $40bn this week via US debt markets and deals have lifted overall bond sales by investment-grade companies and banks in the US for 2017 to more than $1tn, according to Dealogic.

Top-rated companies have already been able to lock in rates below 3 per cent on new 10-year bonds, with Apple drumming up strong investor demand as it borrowed $5bn this week. The iPhone maker priced its new 10-year bonds with a yield of 2.913 per cent, or 85 basis points above the yield on a Treasury that matures in a decade. That was marginally above the yield investors demanded to hold its existing 10-year notes.

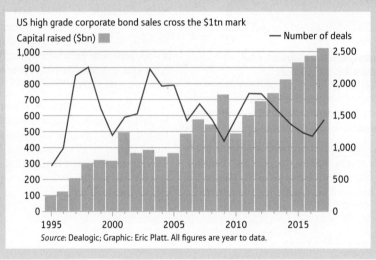

US high grade corporate bond sales cross the $1tn mark

Source: Dealogic; Graphic: Eric Platt. All figures are year to data.

The value of the firm and the cost of capital

Recall from Chapters 16 and 17 that the value of the firm is calculated by estimating its future cash flows and then discounting these at the cost of capital. For the sake of simplification, we will assume, in the following theoretical discussion, that the future cash flows are constant and perpetual (at annual intervals to an infinite horizon) and thus the value of the firm is:

$$V = \frac{C_1}{\text{WACC}}$$

where:

V = value of the firm;
C_1 = cash flows to be received one year hence;
WACC = the weighted average cost of capital.

The same logic can be applied to cash flows which are increasing at a constant rate, or which vary in an irregular fashion. The crucial point is this: if the cash flows are assumed to be at a set level then the value of the firm depends on the rate used to discount those cash flows. If the cost of capital is lowered the value of the firm is raised.

What is meant by the value of the firm, V, is the combination of the market value of equity capital, V_E (total capitalisation of ordinary shares), plus the market value of debt capital, V_D.

$$V = V_E + V_D$$

Does the cost of capital (WACC) decrease with higher debt levels?

The question of whether the cost of capital decreases with higher debt levels is obviously crucial to the capital structure debate. If the WACC is diminished by increasing (or decreasing) the proportion of debt in the financial structure of the firm, then company value will rise and shareholders' wealth will increase.

The firm's cost of capital depends on both the return needed to satisfy the ordinary shareholders given their opportunity cost of capital, k_E, and the return needed to satisfy lenders given their opportunity cost of capital k_D. (We will ignore taxes for now.)

$$\text{WACC} = k_E\,W_E + k_D\,W_D$$

where:

W_E = proportion of equity finance to total finance;
W_D = proportion of debt finance to total finance.

If some numbers are now put into this equation, conclusions might be possible about the optimal debt level and therefore the value of the firm. If it is assumed that the cost of equity capital is 20%, the cost of debt capital is 10%, and the equity and debt weights are both 50%, the overall cost of capital is 15%.

$$\text{WACC} = (20\% \times 0.5) + (10\% \times 0.5) = 15\%$$

If it is further assumed that the firm is expected to generate a perpetual annual cash flow of £1m, then the total value of the firm is:

$$V = \frac{C_1}{\text{WACC}} = \frac{£1m}{0.15} = £6.667m$$

This whole area of finance revolves around what happens when the proportion of debt is increased. So, let us assume that the debt ratio is increased to 70% through the substitution of debt for equity. We will consider four possible consequences.

Scenario 1: The cost of equity capital remains at 20%

If shareholders remain content with a 20% return, irrespective of the level of debt, the WACC decreases:

$$\text{WACC} = k_E\,W_E + k_D\,W_D$$
$$\text{WACC} = (20\% \times 0.3) + (10\% \times 0.7) = 13\%$$

If the cost of capital decreases, the value of the firm (and shareholder wealth) increases:

$$V = \frac{C_1}{\text{WACC}} = \frac{£1m}{0.13} = £7.69m$$

Under this scenario the debt proportion could be increased until it was virtually 100% of the capital. The WACC would then approach 10% (assuming that the cost of debt capital remains at 10%).

Scenario 2: The cost of equity capital rises due to the increased financial risk to exactly offset the effect of the lower cost of debt

In this case the WACC and the firm's value remain constant.

$$\text{WACC} = k_E\,W_E + k_D\,W_D$$
$$\text{WACC} = (26.67\% \times 0.3) + (10\% \times 0.7) = 15\%$$

Scenario 3: The cost of equity capital rises, but this does not completely offset all the benefits of the lower cost of debt capital

Let us assume that equity holders demand an increased return of 22% at a 70% gearing level:

$$\text{WACC} = k_E\,W_E + k_D\,W_D$$
$$\text{WACC} = (22\% \times 0.3) + (10\% \times 0.7) = 13.6\%$$

In this case the firm, by increasing the proportion of its finance which is in the form of debt, manages to reduce the overall cost of capital and thus to increase the value of the firm and shareholder wealth.

$$V = \frac{C_1}{\text{WACC}} = \frac{£1m}{0.136} = £7.35m$$

Scenario 4: The cost of equity rises to more than offset the effect of the lower cost of debt

Here the equity holders are demanding much higher returns as compensation for the additional volatility and risk of liquidation. Let us assume that shareholders require a return of 40%.

$$\text{WACC} = k_E\,W_E + k_D\,W_D$$
$$\text{WACC} = (40\% \times 0.3) + (10\% \times 0.7) = 19\%$$

$$V = \frac{C_1}{\text{WACC}} = \frac{£1m}{0.19} = £5.26m$$

The first of the four scenarios presented above is unrealistic and is rarely seen in the real world. If the amount of debt that a firm has to service is increased, the riskiness of the shares will presumably rise and therefore the shareholders will demand a higher return. Thus, we are left with the three other scenarios. It is around these three possibilities that the capital structure debate rumbles.

Modigliani and Miller's argument in a world with no taxes

The capital structure decision was first tackled in a rigorous theoretical analysis by the financial economists Modigliani and Miller (MM) in 1958. MM created a simplified model of the world by making some assumptions (see below). Given these assumptions they concluded that the value of a firm remains constant regardless of the debt level. As the proportion of debt is increased, the cost of equity will rise just enough to leave the WACC constant. If the WACC is constant then the only factor which can influence the value of the firm is its cash flow generated from operations. Capital structure is irrelevant. Thus, according to MM, firms can only increase the wealth of shareholders by making good investment decisions. This brings us to MM's first proposition.

Proposition 1

The total market value of any company is independent of its capital structure

The total market value of the firm is the net present value of the income stream. For a firm with a constant perpetual income stream:

$$V = \frac{C_1}{\text{WACC}}$$

The WACC is constant because the cost of equity capital rises to exactly offset the effect of cheaper debt and therefore shareholder wealth is neither enhanced nor destroyed by changing the gearing level.

The assumptions

The assumptions upon which this conclusion is reached include:

1   There are perfect capital markets, with perfect information available to all economic agents and no transaction costs.

2   There is no taxation.

3   There are no costs of financial distress and liquidation (if a firm is liquidated, shareholders will receive the same as the market value of their shares prior to liquidation).

4   Firms can be classified into distinct risk classes.

5   Individuals can borrow as cheaply as corporations.

Clearly, some of these assumptions are unrealistic. For now, it is necessary to suspend disbelief so that the consequences of the MM model can be demonstrated. Many of the assumptions will be modified later in the chapter.

An example to illustrate the MM no-tax capital structure argument

In the following example it is assumed that the WACC remains constant at 15% regardless of the debt to equity ratio.

A company is shortly to be formed, called Pivot plc. It needs £1m capital to buy machines, plant and buildings. The business generated by the investment has a given systematic risk and the required return on that level of systematic risk for an all-equity firm is 15%.

The expected annual cash flow is a constant £150,000 in perpetuity. This cash flow will be paid out each year to the suppliers of capital. The prospective directors are considering three different finance structures.

● **Structure 1** All-equity (1,000,000 shares selling at £1 each).

● **Structure 2** £500,000 of debt capital giving a return of 10% per annum. Plus £500,000 of equity capital (500,000 shares at £1 each).

● **Structure 3** £700,000 of debt capital giving a return of 10% per annum. Plus £300,000 of equity capital (300,000 shares at £1 each).

Exhibit 18.13 shows that the returns to equity holders, in this MM world with no tax, rise as gearing increases so as to leave the WACC and the total value of the company constant. Investors purchasing a share receive higher returns per share for a more highly geared firm but the discount rate also rises because of the greater risk, to leave the value of each share at £1.

Exhibit 18.13	Pivot plc capital structure and returns to shareholders		
	Structure 1 £	**Structure 2 £**	**Structure 3 £**
Annual cash flows	150,000	150,000	150,000
less interest payments	0	50,000	70,000
Dividend payments	150,000	100,000	80,000
Return on debt, k_D	0	50,000/500,000 = 10%	70,000/700,000 = 10%
Return on equity, k_E	150,000/1m = 15%	100,000/500,000 = 20%	80,000/300,000 = 26.7%
Price of each share, $\dfrac{d_1}{k_E}$	$\dfrac{15p}{0.15} = 100p$	$\dfrac{20p}{0.20} = 100p$	$\dfrac{26.7p}{0.267} = 100p$
WACC $(k_E W_E + k_D W_D)$	$(15 \times 1.0) + 0 = 15\%$	$(20 \times 0.5) + (10 \times 0.5) = 15\%$	$(26.7 \times 0.3) +$ $(10 \times 0.7) = 15\%$
Total market value of debt, V_D	0	500,000	700,000

▶

Exhibit 18.13	Pivot plc capital structure and returns to shareholders *(continued)*		

| Total market value of equity, V_E | $\dfrac{150,000}{0.15} = 1m$ | $\dfrac{100,000}{0.2} = 0.5m$ | $\dfrac{80,000}{0.267} = 0.3m$ |
| Total value of the firm, $V = V_D + V_E$ | £1,000,000 | £1,000,000 | £1,000,000 |

The relationship given in the tabulation in Exhibit 18.13 can be plotted as a graph (*see* **Exhibit 18.14**). Under the MM model the cost of debt remains constant at 10%,[4] and the cost of equity capital rises just enough to leave the overall cost of capital constant.

Exhibit 18.14	The cost of debt, equity and WACC under the MM no-tax model

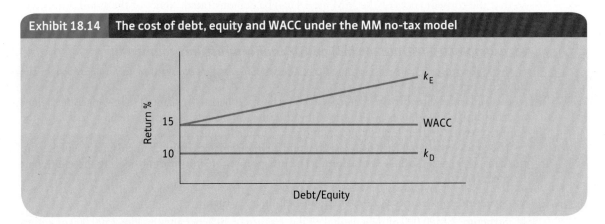

If the WACC is constant and cash flows do not change, then the total value of the firm is constant:

$$V = V_E + V_D = £1m$$

$$V = \frac{C_1}{\text{WACC}} = \frac{£150,000}{0.15} = £1m$$

This is presented in **Exhibit 18.15**.

Exhibit 18.15	Value of the firm under the MM no-tax model

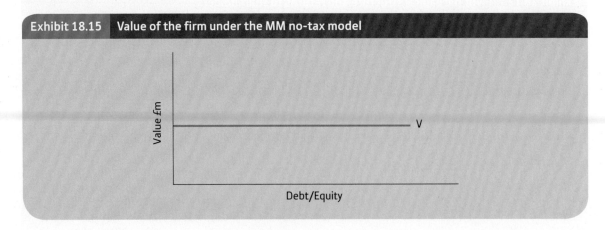

Pivot also illustrates the second and third propositions put forward by MM.

---

4 An alternative scenario is also discussed in the MM 1958 paper in which the cost of debt rises at high gearing levels and the cost of equity declines at high gearing levels.

Proposition 2

The expected rate of return on equity increases proportionately with the gearing ratio

As shareholders see the risk of their investment increase because the firm is taking on increasing debt levels they demand a higher level of return. The geared firm pays a risk premium for financial risk. The increase in the cost of equity exactly offsets the benefit to the WACC of 'cheaper' debt.

Proposition 3

The cut-off rate of return for new projects is equal to the weighted average cost of capital – which is constant regardless of gearing

MM expressed Proposition 3 differently: 'the cut-off point for investment in the firm will in all cases be ρ_k and will be completely unaffected by the type of security used to finance the investment. Equivalently, we may say that, regardless of the financing used, the marginal cost of capital to a firm is equal to the average cost of capital, which is in turn equal to the capitalisation rate for an unlevered stream in the class to which the firm belongs' (MM (1958), p. 288).

Worked example 18.2	Cost of equity capital for a geared firm that becomes an all-equity financed firm in a world with no taxes

Assume that the world is as described by MM, with no taxes, to answer the following.

What would the cost of equity capital be if the firm described below is transformed into being all-equity financed rather than geared?

$$\frac{\text{Market value of debt}}{\text{Market value of debt} + \text{Market value of equity}} = 0.40$$

$k_D = 9\%$ regardless of gearing ratio.
At a gearing level of 40%, $k_E = 22\%$.

Answer

Calculate the weighted average cost of capital at the gearing level of 40%.

$$\text{WACC} = k_E\,W_E + k_D\,W_D$$
$$\text{WACC} = (22 \times 0.6) + (9 \times 0.4) = 16.8\%$$

Under the MM no-tax model the WACC is constant at all gearing levels; therefore, at zero debt the required return to equity holders will be 16.8%.

The capital structure decision in a world with tax

The real world is somewhat different from that created for the purposes of MM's original 1958 model. One of the most significant differences is that individuals and companies *do* have to pay taxes. MM corrected for this assumption in their 1963 version of the model – this changed their analysis dramatically.

Most tax regimes permit companies to offset the interest paid on debt against taxable profit. The effect of this is a tax saving which reduces the effective cost of debt capital.[5] The cost to the company of the debt is the after-tax cost of interest. (*See* Chapter 16 for a discussion of this.)

---

5 Note that the required rate of return on debt is not lowered; rather, the cash outflow to the tax authorities is less, resulting in more being available for equity investors, thus the effective cost of debt is less.

In the previous no-tax analysis the advantage of gearing up (a lower cost of debt capital) was exactly matched by the disadvantage (the increased risk for equity holders and therefore an increased k_E). The introduction of taxation brings an additional advantage to using debt capital: it reduces the tax bill. Now value rises as debt is substituted for equity in the capital structure because of the tax benefits (or tax shield). The WACC declines for each unit increase in debt so long as the firm has taxable profits. This argument can be taken to its logical extreme, such that the WACC is at its lowest and corporate value at its highest when the capital of the company is almost entirely made up of debt.

In **Exhibit 18.16** the cost of equity rises but the extent of the rise is insufficient to exactly offset the cheaper debt. Thus, the overall WACC falls throughout the range of gearing. In a 30% corporate tax environment a profitable firm's cost of debt falls from a pre-tax 10% to only 7% after the tax benefit (assuming continued firm profitability):

$$10\%(1 - T) = 10\%(1 - 0.30) = 7\%$$

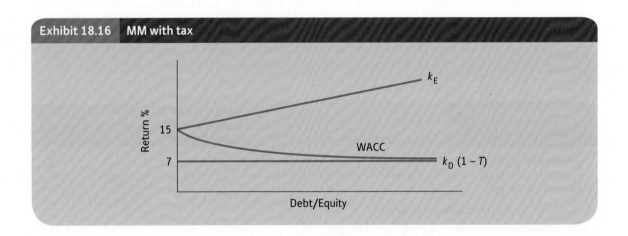

Exhibit 18.16   MM with tax

For a perpetual income firm, the value is $V = C_1/\text{WACC}$. As the WACC falls, the value of the company rises, benefiting ordinary shareholders. *See* **Exhibit 18.17**.

The conclusion from this stage of the analysis, after adjusting for one real-world factor, is that companies should be as highly geared as possible.

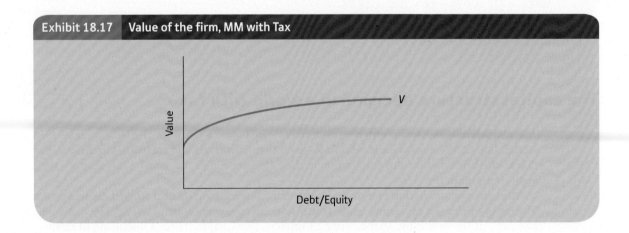

Exhibit 18.17   Value of the firm, MM with Tax

The article reproduced in **Exhibit 18.18** shows a company that did structure itself so that it could take on an extreme capital structure – Glas Cymru was financed entirely by debt. It is a single purpose company which owns, finances and manages Welsh Water and is a private company limited by guarantee which has no shareholders. It is funded by bonds and retained financial surpluses. Note that this structure was initially possible only because the risk of financial distress had been substantially reduced. The bond offerings were eagerly taken up by lenders.

Exhibit 18.18

Glas Cymru launches bond campaign

Water marketing drive in plan to raise £2bn for purchase of Dwr Cymru

By Aline van Duyn and Andrew Taylor

Glas Cymru, the self-styled 'Welsh people's company' which has agreed to buy the principality's water supplier, will today launch a £2bn bond marketing campaign to turn the company into the UK's first fully debt-financed water utility.

The bond issues, if successful, will reduce Glas Cymru's cost of capital to between 4 and 4.5%, compared with a 6.5% industry threshold set by the regulator.

Glas Cymru, a non-profit making company led by Lord Burns, former permanent secretary at the Treasury, will buy Dwr Cymru (Welsh Water) in return for taking on debts of £1.8bn. It will be fully debt financed and switch from shareholder ownership . . .

Bond investors in the water sector have seen prices on their holdings fall after rating downgrades following the regulatory price cuts and concern over diversification strategies.

The Glas Cymru deal aims to address these concerns by giving bondholders full control and ensuring that they are exposed purely to the water sector, which is a monopoly business with stable cash flows.

Most of the bonds will be denominated in sterling, although euro and dollar tranches are also being considered. About £1bn worth of bonds will have a Triple A rating, the highest rating category, due to a guarantee from an insurance company.

Just under £700m worth will be rated A minus. About £250m is rated Triple B, with £100m worth of unrated bonds also sold.

The Glas Cymru structure is possible because the assets are bought for less than their regulatory asset value, giving a £150m cushion. Between now and the next regulatory price review in 2004–2005, Glas Cymru can lock in a lower cost of capital and accumulate the excess, boosting its reserves to £350m. It expects to tap the markets for £100m–£150m a year.

 Financial Times, 9 April 2001, p. 26.
All Rights Reserved.

Many commentators criticise the disparity in the tax treatment of debt and equity, which sees interest on debt treated as business expenses and therefore tax deductible whereas dividends are treated as distributions from post-tax earnings. Arguments state that this can lead to excess borrowings to the point where companies do not have enough of a safety buffer of equity ('redundancy' in the capital structure). High debt leaves firms vulnerable to shocks such as sharp rises in interest rates or a deep recession as was clearly seen during the global financial crisis.

Additional considerations

In the real world companies do not, generally, raise gearing to very high levels. This suggests that the models described so far are not yet sufficient to explain capital structure decisions. There are some important influences on capital structure not yet considered. As Stewart Myers[6] wrote, 'Our theories don't seem to explain actual financing behaviour, and it seems presumptuous to advise firms on optimal structure when we are so far from explaining actual decisions'.

We now turn to some additional factors which have a bearing on the gearing level.

Financial distress

A major disadvantage for a firm taking on higher levels of debt is that it increases the risk of financial distress, and ultimately liquidation. This may have a detrimental effect on both the equity holders and the debt holders.

> Financial distress: where obligations to creditors are not met or are met with difficulty.

The risk of incurring the costs of financial distress has a negative effect on a firm's value which offsets the value of tax relief of increasing debt levels. These costs become considerable with very high gearing. Even if a firm manages to avoid liquidation its relationships with suppliers, customers, employees and creditors may be seriously damaged.

Suppliers providing goods and services on credit are likely to reduce the generosity of their terms, or even stop supplying altogether, if they believe that there is an increased chance of the firm not being in existence in a few months' time. EMI's financial troubles caused by high borrowing resulted in many of the key suppliers, various artists, refusing to sign up – *see* **Exhibit 18.19**.

Exhibit 18.19

EMI's battle with banks over debt makes artists wary of signing up

By Andrew Edgecliffe-Johnson in New York and Salamander Davoudi in London

Uncertainty over EMI's financial future is deterring some leading music industry managers and lawyers from signing artists to its record label as its parent company battles with its bankers over the debt burden of its 2007 buy-out.

Terra Firma, the private equity firm run by Guy Hands, has won over one vocal early critic of its buy-out of EMI: Tim Clark, the manager of singer Robbie Williams. Two years ago, Mr Clark accused Mr Hands of acting like a plantation owner but he has told the Financial Times he was 'incredibly pleased' with EMI's handling of his client's latest album.

However, a clear majority of managers, music lawyers, consultants and financiers interviewed by the FT, most of whom asked not to be named, said

artists were wary of signing with EMI Music, the group's recorded music arm, because of the parent company's debt load.

'It would be very difficult to say to your client you should sign to EMI,' Jonathan Shalit, manager of Jamelia and Myleene Klass, told the FT.

Another manager, who asked not to be named, said: 'In terms of artists talking to EMI, I have pulled back. I have held off because of the uncertainty.'

Managers and lawyers said EMI had been at pains to persuade artists that concern about its capital structure had not affected its ability to generate hits. There has been little sign of managers' concerns affecting its chart performance. EMI Music has signed about 200 artists in the past 18 months.

The situation may be similar with customers. Many customers expect to develop long-term relationships with their suppliers, and plan their own production on the assumption of a continuance of that relationship. If there is any doubt about the longevity of a firm it will not be able to secure high-quality contracts. In the consumer markets customers often need assurance that firms

---

6 Myers (1984), p. 575.

are sufficiently stable to deliver on promises, for example package holiday companies taking bookings six months in advance.

Employees may become demotivated in a struggling firm as they sense increased job insecurity and few prospects for advancement. The best staff will start to move to posts in safer companies.

Bankers and other lenders will tend to look upon a request for further finance from a financially distressed company carefully – taking a safety-first approach – and this can continue for many years after the crisis has passed. Bankers may also insist that managerial freedom to act be constrained through covenants. For example, limiting the amount of capital expenditure or dividend payments.

Management finds that much of their time is spent 'fire-fighting' – dealing with day-to-day liquidity problems – and focusing on short-term cash flow rather than long-term shareholder wealth. Companies are often forced to sell off profitable operations to raise cash. For instance, Toys "R" Us was considering selling off brand assets to help it to reduce its debt – *see* **Exhibit 18.20**. Unfortunately, it ended up filing for Chapter 11 bankruptcy on September 18, 2017 – *see* **Exhibit 18.21**.

Exhibit 18.20

S&P pushes Toys R Us deeper into junk amid reports retailer has hired advisers

By Mamta Badkar

Ratings agency S&P Global on Thursday pushed Toys R Us deeper into junk territory after it cut its corporate credit rating by one notch to 'CCC+' from 'B–' and placed all ratings on CreditWatch with negative implications, leaving it at risk of a further downgrade.

The agency said that its decision reflects the view that there is an "increased possibility" the private equity-owned US toy chain could address some of its debt due to mature in 2018 "at less than par or engage in a broader restructuring". The downgrade comes a day after reports that the New Jersey-based retailer has tapped lawyers to advise on restructuring its debt load and that bankruptcy could be one possible outcome.

Toys R US — which was taken private in a $6.6bn deal in 2005 by Bain Capital, Kohlberg Kravis Roberts and Vornado Realty Trust — has roughly $400m of secured and unsecured debt maturing in May and October 2018, and "significantly more in 2019", according to S&P.

"Our previous concerns over capital market access for leveraged retailers such as Toys R Us has been sharpened by the very negative bond price reaction to these media reports," S&P said. And while the rating agency does not expect a broader restructuring,

it does argue that the incentive for a timely refinancing of its debt maturities at par next year is now lower, given the drop in the price of unsecured debt due in 2018.

S&P said: "We still view existing liquidity as sufficient for the upcoming holiday season and note that market prices for most other debt issues did not appear to decline even after the recent news. Still, with 2019 maturities looming and a lack of clear prospects for improving operating performance, we believe Toys' capital structure may be unsustainable in the long term."

Aggressive discounting by competitors alongside the rise of e-commerce juggernaut Amazon and big box retailers like Target and Walmart have hurt the once-dominant retailer. It has seen same-store sales — a closely watched measure of sales in stores that have been open at least 12 months — fall for three consecutive quarters.

Reports of a possible Toys R Us bankruptcy come as more than 20 retailers have already filed for bankruptcy in the first six months of the year — including Gymboree, Payless, BCBG — with the accumulated liabilities of all retailers that filed for bankruptcy rising to over $5bn in aggregate, according to accountancy firm BDO.

Exhibit 18.21

Toys R Us files for bankruptcy protection

By Anna Nicolaou, James Fontanella-Khan and Eric Platt in New York

Toys R Us filed for bankruptcy protection late on Monday as the storied US toy retail chain, which has been wrestling with a heavy debt load, grapples with a shift towards online shopping. The company said it secured $3bn of debtor-in-possession financing to keep its 1,600 stores operating "as usual" during the restructuring of $5bn of long-term debt. The filing is the latest in a grim year for traditional retailers ravaged by the rising popularity of ecommerce, particularly among companies that took on large debts in the years leading up to the financial crisis.

Toys R Us, founded during the post-second world war baby boom of the 1950s, became the dominant American toy store but has failed to keep up with the shift to online and stiff competition from big box retailers such as Walmart.

Bain Capital, KKR and Vornado Realty Trust took Toys R Us private in 2005 in a $6.6bn leveraged buyout. "Today marks the dawn of a new era," said Dave Brandon, chief executive of Toys R Us, adding that "the financial constraints that have held us back will be addressed in a lasting and effective way".

The New Jersey-based company, faced with $400m of secured and unsecured debt maturing in 2018, had hired law firm Kirkland & Ellis to help with restructuring. Sales at Toys R Us have slipped on a same-store basis for three consecutive quarters, with the company in June reporting a quarterly net loss of $164m on sales of $2.2bn.

Vendors in turn have become cautious, limiting shipments of inventory to Toys R Us, according to people familiar with the matter. The difficulties have come in the run-up to the all-important holiday shopping season, during which Toys R Us makes about 40 per cent of its more than $11bn in annual sales.

The grim year for retailers has led to an uptick in bankruptcies this year. Last week Aerosoles, the women's footwear company, filed for bankruptcy, adding to the 24 US retailers that filed for Chapter 11 protection this year, compared with 18 for all of 2016, according to data from S&P Global Market Intelligence.

Bonds sold by Toys R Us slid rapidly as news of a possible bankruptcy filing was reported. Debt that matures in October 2018 declined to 18 cents on the dollar on Monday afternoon, more than halving in value from the close of trading on Friday, according to Finra. The bonds were marked at roughly 97 cents on the dollar at the start of September.

The company was hit with twin downgrades from rating agencies S&P Global and Fitch earlier on Monday. Fitch warned that the evolution of the toy industry would "make it attractive" for competitors to continue to gain market share from Toys R Us, and lowered its rating on the company deeper into distress territory. Monica Aggarwal, an analyst with Fitch, called the company's capital structure "unsustainable in the long term".

 Financial Times, 19 September 2017.
All Rights Reserved.

The indirect costs associated with financial distress can be much more significant than the more obvious direct costs such as paying for lawyers and accountants and for refinancing programmes. Some of these indirect and direct costs are shown in **Exhibit 18.22**.

| Exhibit 18.22 | Costs of financial distress |

Indirect examples

- Uncertainties in customers' minds about dealing with this firm – lost sales, lost profits, lost goodwill.
- Uncertainties in suppliers' minds – lost inputs, more expensive trading terms.
- If assets have to be sold quickly the price may be very low.
- Delays, legal impositions, and the tangles of financial reorganisation may place restrictions on management action, interfering with the efficient running of the business.

Direct examples

- Lawyers' fees.
- Accountants' fees.
- Court fees.
- Management time.

● Management may give excessive emphasis to short-term liquidity, e.g. cut R&D and training, lower credit terms are offered to customers, which impacts on the marketing effort.
● Temptation to sell healthy businesses as this will raise the most cash.
● Loss of staff morale, tendency to examine possible alternative employment, difficulty in recruiting talented people.

As the risk of financial distress rises with the gearing ratio shareholders (and lenders) demand an increasing return in compensation. The important issue is at what point does the probability of financial distress so increase the cost of equity and debt that it outweighs the benefit of the tax relief on debt? **Exhibit 18.23** shows that there is an optimal level of gearing. At low levels of debt shareholders do not perceive a significant increase in risk from the addition of debt so they do not ask for a significant increase in return; the major influence on the overall cost of capital is the cheaper after-tax cost of debt so WACC reduces. As gearing rises investors become more concerned about the risk of financial distress and therefore their required rates of return rise and the rise is greater than the reduction from the lower cost debt. As a result, WACC starts to increase. The concern about financial distress overrides the impact of the cheaper debt. As further debt gets added, all finance providers – equity and debt – perceive greater risk and so WACC increases significantly. The fear of insolvency becomes of overriding importance at high gearing levels.

Exhibit 18.23	The cost of capital and the value of the firm with taxes and financial distress, as gearing increases

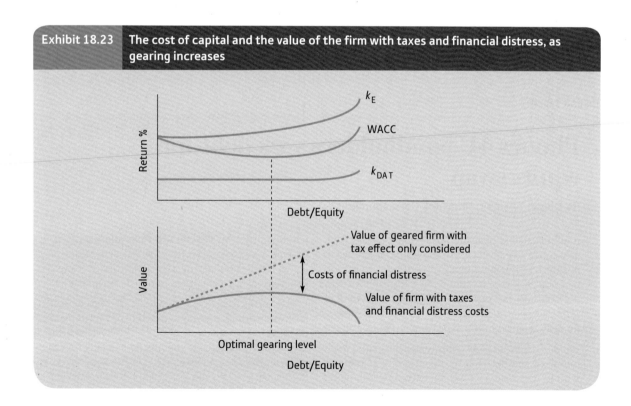

In the literature on capital structure the balancing of the benefits of debt, such as the tax shield, with the costs of debt, such as distress costs, to achieve an optimal debt to equity ratio, is known as the **trade-off model**.

Resolving Insolvency

Following the global financial crisis, banks and other lenders were slow to liquidate a company as a solution to retrieving cash from distressed companies due to the reduced valuation of assets. Different jurisdictions offer different ways to deal with insolvency.

Chapter 11

In the US companies have the option of Chapter 11 protection intended to allow the company to continue in operation while they attempt to negotiate with lenders and suppliers to restructure their finances. While under 'protection' management continues to run the company but all decisions must be approved by a court. The company can stop paying its debt payments which allows it to invest its cash in the business and hopefully return to profit exiting from Chapter 11 on a stronger sustainable basis. It must negotiate with creditors, bondholders and shareholders to reach agreement on a new financial structure which is fair to all finance providers. There is not a direct equivalent in the UK. Companies can enter into a 'Creditors Voluntary Arrangement' but this is not as widely used as Chapter 11. France has a system called 'Judicial Composition'. Companies entering into Chapter 11 can still ultimately end up in liquidation.

Administration

Administration is a court administered process for companies facing insolvency which protects the company from creditors while a court appointed administrator works with management to supervise an orderly process to negotiate new funding, find a buyer for the company or its assets or to wind it down.

As reported by PwC on 15 September 2014: 'Robert Jonathan Hunt, Ian David Green and Robert John Moran of PwC have today been appointed as administrators to Phones 4u Limited (P4U), a leading independent mobile phone retailer with an annual turnover of £1 billion, operating from more than 700 outlets with 5,596 employees.' (*See* **Exhibit 18.24**).

Exhibit 18.24

Phones 4U bondholders seek debt-for-equity swap

By Daniel Thomas, Telecoms Correspondent

Bondholders in Phones 4U have proposed plans for a debt-for-equity swap that would keep the retailer in business as the administrator continues to talk to potential buyers of its stores. Most of the £760m debt in Phones 4U will be almost wiped out, according to rating agencies, which is likely to lead to heavy losses for investors backing the failed mobile phone retailer.

Phones 4U went into administration this week following the decision by EE, its only remaining mobile network partner, to withdraw following similar moves by Vodafone and O2. Facing heavy losses in the administration process, holders of the £430m senior secured notes – which rank after a £125m credit facility likely to be paid – have discussed a restructuring deal, according to one person familiar with the situation. This could involve offering a debt-for-equity swap to allow the business to continue to trade, while also giving the flexibility to renew negotiations with operators to return as partners.

Louise Verrill, partner at Brown Rudnick, who is acting for a large group of senior secured bondholders, said that they would take "a significant write-down on their debt which would make the business commercially viable and lay foundations for the 5,596 jobs to be saved". She added: "Our bondholder group has been working hard to ensure that the company's cost structure can be adjusted to meet the commercial terms that EE and Vodafone put to the previous owners. "So, we have proposed a restructure of the business that means the capital structure will no longer be an impediment to achieving the commercial outcome which allows the company to continue as a going concern. We look forward to meaningful engagement with PwC, Vodafone and EE, collectively, to save the jobs and maximise returns to creditors and other stakeholders."

PwC, the administrator for Phones 4U, said on a call with bondholders this week that it would create "a private forum of creditors where we can discuss strategy". Another call is scheduled at 3pm on Thursday. However, owners of the debt will need support from mobile operators, whose withdrawal hastened the end of the retailer this week. EE and Vodafone have separately been in talks with PwC about buying parts of the business, which would protect some of the 6,000 jobs at risk.

At least 800 jobs have been salvaged already, however, after Dixons Carphone confirmed on Wednesday that it had struck a deal with the administrators to employ staff that had worked in 160 Phones 4U

concessions in its stores. But the debt holders still stand to be hard hit by the collapse.

Standard & Poor's said that it expected the "low end" of its estimate that between 10-30 per cent of the largest slice of secure debt would probably be paid out. Exact ownership of the bonds is difficult to gauge given they are traded frequently, although Bloomberg data shows that owners have included some of the world's biggest fund managers such as Fidelity and BlackRock.

Brown Rudnick, a US law firm, represents the senior secured bondholders. Standard & Poor's said: "We believe that secured debt holders should be able to recover value from the group's receivables and inventories sufficient to provide at least 10 per cent recovery for note holders." Owners of £430m in senior secured notes would still see a higher recovery rate than the £205m payment-in-kind (PIK) toggle notes, which could be worthless according to rating agencies.

The UK government 'Insolvency Service' reports 4,152 insolvencies between April and July 2017 (an increase of 14.5% over the same period in 2016) of which 3,087 were creditors' voluntary arrangements (www.gov.uk/government/statistics/insolvency-statistics-april-to-june-2017).

The World Bank (www.doingbusiness.org/data/exploretopics/resolving-insolvency) reports on the outcome of resolving insolvency in different jurisdictions (June 2016). Interestingly although many practitioners would like to see Chapter 11 procedures being available in the UK, the UK recovers more, more quickly and at a lower cost than the US. The top performers are Finland and Japan. Some countries such as United Arab Emirates (UAE) do not have a straight forward process – *see* **Exhibit 18.25**.

	Recovery rate Cents on dollar	Time to resolve Years	Cost % of estate
United States	78.6	1.5	10%
United Kingdom	88.6	1.0	6%
Finland	90.3	0.9	3.5%
Japan	92.1	0.6	4.2%

Exhibit 18.25

UAE's bankruptcy laws: unworkable

By Simeon Kerr

The UAE's insolvency laws have been in force since 1993 but lawyers are hard pressed to come up with a single example of their being used to wind down a

struggling company. Untested and widely regarded as unworkable, they are in bad need of replacement. The juddering impact of the global financial crisis

Exhibit 18.25 *(continued)*

has persuaded the government to draft a new set of regulations, which will hopefully allow companies to conduct orderly wind-downs through the courts.

It won't be easy. Bankruptcy carries a heavy stigma anywhere but especially in the Gulf, where owners of small businesses can bear personal responsibility and, when businesses fail, often flee the country rather than face public humiliation or, worse, imprisonment. Even then, with nobody seeking the courts' protection, it takes on average more than five years to wind a company down under the current framework.

When Dubai World went bust in 2009 a special decree – Number 57 – was enacted to bypass the local laws and prevent angry creditors from sidestepping the UAE's courts and taking legal action overseas. Even decree 57 was never enforced but it did succeed in underpinning negotiations that within nine months had secured 90 per cent creditor support for the $25bn restructuring of the sprawling conglomerate, which had amassed liabilities of $60bn.

The five years it takes to wind down a company compares with an average of about three years for the Middle East and north Africa. And after a long, costly process, the recovery rate averages just 11 per cent, according to Nasser Saidi, executive director Hawkamah, a corporate governance institute, citing World Bank statistics. The World Bank's Ease of Business survey ranks the UAE 33rd overall out of 180 global economies, but the federation comes in at a dismal 151st in terms of resolving insolvency.

Ironically, the grey area surrounding insolvency has kept many UAE companies afloat through the financial crisis. Large indebted companies that have gained finance without recourse to personal guarantees can hobble along by not paying their debts. The lengthy, expensive and uncertain process of enforcing contracts on such debts often persuades creditors to enter into restructuring agreements. Small enterprises, however, are generally less lucky. Only 20 per cent of the Middle East's companies have access to bank credit – understandable given that personal guarantees often underpin loans. In the absence of workable insolvency laws, entrepreneurs face the threat of prison if they default on their guarantees.

Financial Times, 13 December 2011.
All Rights Reserved.

Some factors influencing the risk of financial distress costs

The susceptibility to financial distress varies from company to company. The shareholders are concerned with earnings and the company's ability to pay dividends; the debt holders are concerned about payment of interest and repayment of principal. Where these are put at risk, the finance providers will demand a higher return. Here are some influences:

1 *The sensitivity of the company's revenues to the general level of economic activity* If a company's revenues are highly responsive to the ups and downs in the economy, shareholders and lenders may perceive a greater risk of liquidation and/or distress and demand a higher return as when revenues fall there is a danger that the companies may not be able to meet interest or dividend payments.

2 *The proportion of fixed to variable costs* A firm which is highly operationally geared – has high fixed costs – and which also takes on high borrowing, may find that equity and debt holders demand a high return for the increased risk.

3 *The liquidity and marketability of the firm's assets* Some firms hold assets which can be easily sold at a reasonably high and certain value should the firm go into liquidation. This collateral reassures finance providers and so they may not demand such a high-risk premium. A hotel chain, for example, should it suffer a decline in profitability, can usually sell hotels in a reasonably active property market. On the other hand, an advertising agency, with few saleable assets, would struggle to raise cash quickly by selling assets and so investors would be less relaxed about rises in gearing.

4 *The cash-generative ability of the business* Some firms produce a high regular flow of cash and so can reasonably accept a higher gearing level than a firm with lumpy, uncertain cash inflows.

Exhibit 18.26 illustrates that the optimal gearing level for two example firms shifts depending on key characteristics of the underlying business.

Exhibit 18.26	The characteristics of the underlying business influences the risk of liquidation/ distress, and therefore WACC, and the optimal gearing level	
Characteristic	**Food retailer**	**Steel producer**
Sensitivity to economic activity	Relatively insensitive to economic fluctuations	Dependent on general economic prosperity
Operational gearing	Most costs are variable	Most costs are fixed
Asset liquidity	Shops, stock, etc., easily sold	Assets have few/no alternative uses. Thin second-hand market
Cash-generative ability	High or stable cash flow	Irregular cash flow
Likely acceptable gearing ratio	**HIGH**	**LOW**

Agency costs

Another restraining influence on the decision to take on high debt is the agency cost of doing so. Agency costs arise out of what is known as the 'principal–agent' problem. In most large firms the finance providers (principals) do not actively manage the firm. They employ 'agents' (managers) and it is possible for these agents to act in ways which are not always in the best interests of the equity or debt holders.

Agency costs are the direct and indirect costs of attempting to ensure that agents act in the best interest of principals as well as the loss resulting from failure to get them to act in this way.

If management is acting for the maximisation of shareholder wealth debt holders may have reason to fear agency problems, because there may be actions which potentially benefit the owners at the expense of lenders. It is possible for lenders to be fooled or misled by managers. For example, management might raise money from bondholders, saying that this is low-risk lending (and therefore paying a low interest rate) because the firm has low gearing and the funds will be used for a low-risk project. In the event the managers invest in high-risk ventures, and the firm becomes more highly geared by borrowing more. As a result, the original lenders do not receive a return sufficient for the level of risk and the firm has the benefit of low-interest financing.

Alternatively, consider a firm already in financial distress. From the shareholders' point of view there is little to lose from taking an enormous gamble by accepting very high-risk projects. If the gamble pays off the shareholders will win but the debt holders will gain no more than the obligatory fixed interest. If it fails, the shareholders are no worse off but the lenders experience default on their securities. Another temptation is for the shareholders to take large amounts out of a business through the payment of dividends when the managers become aware of a high chance of liquidation, leaving the debt holders with little to salvage.

The problem boils down to one of *information asymmetry* – that is, the managers are in possession of knowledge unavailable to the debt providers. The lenders will require a premium on the debt interest to compensate for this additional cost. One solution is to spend money on monitoring. Also, restrictions (covenants) are usually built into a lending agreement. Covenants may be positive – you must maintain your current ratio at 2:1 – or negative – you cannot sell this asset without our permission. For example, there may be limits on the level of dividends so that shareholders do not strip the company of cash, limits placed on the overall level of indebtedness, with precise capital and income-gearing ratios or managers may be restricted in the disposal of major assets or constrained in the type of activity they may engage in.

Covenants imposed by lenders can be costly for shareholders because they reduce the firm's operating freedom and investment flexibility. Projects with a high NPV may be foregone because of the cautiousness of lenders. The opportunity costs can be especially frustrating for firms with high growth potential.

Agency costs include monitoring costs passed on as higher interest rates and the loss of value caused by the inhibition of managerial freedom to act. These increase with gearing, raising the implicit cost of debt and lowering the firm's value.[7]

There may also be a psychological element related to agency costs; managers generally do not like restrictions placed on their freedom of action. They try to limit constraints by not raising a large proportion of capital from lenders. This may help to explain why, in practice, we find companies generally have modest gearing levels.

Borrowing capacity

Borrowing capacity has a close connection with agency costs. Lenders prefer secured lending, which sets an upper limit on gearing. Lenders like to have security so that if the worst happened and the firm was unable to meet its interest or repayment obligations the lenders could seize assets to sell off to recover their cash. Thus, high levels of gearing are unusual because companies run out of suitable assets to offer as security against loans. So, the gearing level may not be determined by a theoretical, informed and considered management decision, but by the limits to total borrowing imposed by lenders.

Firms with assets which have an active second-hand market, and which do not tend to depreciate, such as property, are likely to have a higher borrowing capacity than firms that invest in assets with few alternative uses.

Managerial preferences

This is another agency cost. Liquidation affects not only shareholders, but managers and other employees. Indeed, the impact on these people can be far greater than the impact on well-diversified investors. It may be argued that managers have a natural tendency to be cautious about borrowing.

On the other hand, there are two motives for managers to increase gearing levels. First, they often receive bonuses based on earnings per share. These can be raised by substituting equity in the capital structure with debt. Second, more debt can raise the bargaining position of the firm relative to the workers. Low debt encourages the workers, through their unions, to raise their wage demands. However, a firm with high cash outflows to pay interest can more forcefully argue that it cannot afford to be generous to workers (Matsa (2010) found evidence for this in the USA).

Pecking order

Research and empirical studies have suggested that there is a 'pecking order' for financing – firstly retained earnings, then debt, and less commonly equity. Pecking order theory was first put forward by Donaldson in 1961 and was revisited in 1984 by Myers and Majluf. The proposition was that firms prefer to finance with internally generated funds. If a firm has potentially profitable investments it will try to finance the investments by using retained profits. If still more funds are needed, firms will go to the capital markets, calling firstly on the debt market, and only as a last resort will companies raise equity finance. The pecking order of financing is in sharp contrast to the MM plus financial distress analysis (the 'trade-off model'), in which an optimal capital structure is targeted. Myers (1984, p. 581) puts it this way: 'In this story, there is no well-defined target debt–equity mix, because there are two kinds of equity, internal and external, one at the top of the pecking order and one at the bottom.'

One reason for placing new issues of equity at the bottom is supposedly that the stock markets perceive an equity issue as a sign of problems – an act of desperation. Myers and Majluf (1984) provide a theoretical explanation of why an equity issue might be bad news – managers will only issue shares when they believe the firm's shares are overpriced. In the capital structure literature, the term 'adverse selection problem' is used to convey the idea that managers are likely to act on their informational advantage over investors and so there is an extra degree of risk for equity investors because usually only those managers observing overpricing of their shares relative to the company's prospects would elect for a new share issue. Companies with under-priced shares would generally raise debt capital. This means that equity has 'an adverse selection premium' – a raised level of return required – making newly raised equity an expensive form of finance, thus only the desperate raise funds by selling shares. Stewart G.B. (1990, p. 391) puts it differently: 'Raising equity

---

7 On the other hand, Jensen (1986) has argued that if managers have less free cash flow they are less likely to invest in negative NPV projects, and this restraint is better for shareholders.

conveys doubt. Investors suspect that management is attempting to shore up the firm's financial resources for rough times ahead by selling over-valued shares.' Some theorists have taken the argument a step further: managers will want to issue debt even if their shares are currently over-valued. The logic is as follows: investors are aware that managers have an incentive to sell shares when they are over-priced and therefore take an equity issue as a bad signal. So, if management go ahead with the share sale the equity price will fall. To avoid this, managers choose to issue debt.

There is an argument that firms do not try to reach the 'correct' capital structure as dictated by theory, because managers are following a line of least resistance. Internal funds are the first choice because using retained earnings does not involve contact with outside investors. This avoids the discipline involved in trying to extract investors' money. For example, the communication process required to raise equity finance is usually time consuming and onerous, with a formal prospectus, etc., and investors will scrutinise the detailed justifications advanced for the need to raise additional finance. It seems reasonable to suppose that managers will feel more comfortable using funds they already have in their hands. However, if they do have to obtain external financing then debt is next in the line of least resistance. This is because the degree of questioning and publicity associated with a bank loan or bond issue is usually significantly less than that associated with a share issue.

Another reason for a pecking order is that ordinary shares are more expensive to issue (in terms of administrative costs) than debt capital, which in turn is more expensive than simply applying previously generated profits. The costs of new issues and rights issues of shares can be very expensive, whereas retained earnings are available without transaction costs.

The pecking order idea helps to explain why the most profitable companies often borrow very little. It is not that they have a low target debt ratio, but because they do not need outside finance. If they are highly profitable they will use these profits for growth opportunities and so end up with very little debt and no need to issue shares.

Less profitable firms with many positive NPV projects to fund issue debt because they do not have internal funds sufficient for their capital investment programme and because debt is first in the pecking order of externally raised finance.

Market timing

A counter argument to the reluctance to issue equity under the pecking order theory is the 'market timing theory' (see Baker and Wurgler, 2002). Here gearing decreases when firms can issue shares at a high price ('over-priced'), for example because the share or the stock market generally is at a high level. When stock values are low firms can buy-back their own shares at low values and thus gearing increases (remember that gearing is measured by market values of debt and equity not balance sheet values). Thus, gearing varies in response to opportunities to issue or buy shares not according to a trade-off theory rationale; and movement away from optimal gearing levels persists into the long term. In Baker and Wurgler's view there is no attempt at an optimal capital structure; market timing decisions just accumulate into a capital structure.

However, Alti (2006) shows that despite advantage being taken of high share prices the gearing ratio effect of this completely vanishes within two years (this study examined 'hot' initial public offerings): 'the results are consistent with the modified version of the traditional trade-off view of capital structure, one that includes market timing as a short-term factor' (Alti, p. 1684). Also, Leary and Roberts (2005) show that Baker and Wurgler's market timing effects of gearing are more likely to be due to the high cost of regularly changing debt or equity levels (issue or redemption costs). Firms do move back towards the target debt–equity range (see Kayhan and Titman (2007)) but the high cost of issuance of debt and so on means that this is gradual. Furthermore, Graham and Harvey's (2001) survey confirmed that most firms have debt–equity ratio targets. Bancel and Mittoo (2011) report in their survey of managers that practice varies from financial theory. Some support for the trade-off and pecking order theories exists but the two dominant factors in managers' decision making are financial flexibility and earnings per share dilution.

Financial flexibility (financial slack)

Operating and strategic decisions are generally the prime determinants of company value, not the financing decision. Being able to respond to opportunities as they appear is important. If a firm is already highly geared it may find it difficult to gain access to more funds quickly as the need arises. Financial flexibility (slack) means having cash (or near-cash) and/or spare debt capacity.

This flexibility (slack) can be extremely valuable and firms may restrict debt levels below that of the 'optimal' gearing level in order that the risk of missing profitable investments is reduced (see Almazan et al., 2010). Graham and Harvey (2001) show that 59% of US companies deliberately restrict debt 'so we have enough internal funds available to pursue new projects when they come along'. This was the most important factor determining the debt levels of these firms, out-ranking tax deductibility of debt and risk of distress.

Financial flexibility (slack) is also valuable for meeting unforeseen circumstances. Managers may wish to be cautious and have a reserve of cash or spare borrowing capacity to cope with a 'rainy day'.

An interesting example of this is described by the treasurer of Pfizer, Richard Passov, who argued in a *Harvard Business Review* article (2003) that the reason Pfizer, Intel and other firms with high levels of investment in intangible assets have cash on their balance sheets and no borrowing is because they are subject to high business risk through their risky R&D programmes. This means that they cannot take the chance of having any financial risk at all. They have billions in cash as cushions to meet unforeseen shocks and allow the continuance of investment in potential winners, many of which may not be providing cash inflows for five years or more. They are concerned about the potential for financial distress either to halt promising investment or to force the hurried sale of expensive equity (i.e. selling a chunk of the company too cheaply) at a time of crisis.

It is interesting to note the size of the cash piles of leading hi-tech firms. In 2016 five hi-tech companies – Apple, Microsoft, Alphabet (Google), Cisco and Oracle – held over $500 billion dollars in cash (see **Exhibit 18.27**). Some of this was due to cash being kept out of the USA because of high tax, but much of it was due to a deliberate policy of running a 'conservative balance sheet' in the face of economic uncertainty, the rising cost of innovation to stay one step ahead of rivals and the potential to grow through acquisitions.

If managers have been through tough times before they are more risk-averse and like to maintain financial flexibility (*see* **Exhibit 18.28**). The global financial crisis of 2007/2008 when banks' attitudes to lending hardened significantly taught another generation to be more cautious of excessive gearing and the years since have seen substantial deleveraging – some voluntary and some imposed by lenders who refused to renew borrowing facilities (*see* **Exhibit 18.29**).

Exhibit 18.27

US companies' cash pile hits $1.7tn

By Eric Platt

Five US tech giants are hoarding more than half a trillion dollars, a record sum that underscores how cash has become increasingly concentrated at a handful of groups seeking to avoid a tax hit.

Apple, Microsoft, Alphabet, Cisco and Oracle had amassed $504bn of cash by the end of 2015, nearly a third of the total $1.7tn held on the balance sheets of US non-financial companies, according to a new report from rating agency Moody's. The top 50 holders accounted for $1.1tn of that amount.

US multinationals have left roughly $1.2tn of their earnings overseas in an effort to skirt the tax charge of moving profits back to US shores under the country's complex tax code.

It is the first time the top five cash hoarders have been made up exclusively of tech groups, an industry that generates more of its sales abroad than any other sector and one that has been embroiled in tax disputes in both the US and Europe.

The ever increasing amount of cash also highlights how US boardrooms are reticent to invest in their businesses, choosing instead to increase dividends, in a sign of the continued anxiety that economic activity could still slow at home or in China.

The report showed the first annual dip in capital spending since the US emerged from recession. Expenditures on things like new equipment slipped 3 per cent to $885bn as energy and mining groups retrenched in the face of sharply lower commodity prices.

"Companies are hoarding cash," said Jack Ablin, chief investment officer at BMO Private Bank.

Apple accounted for more than a tenth of the total cash reserves, holding $216bn, 93 per cent of which is overseas. The top-five list included the addition of Oracle, which ousted Pfizer after the pharmaceuticals group completed its $17bn takeover of Hospira.

The iPhone maker is currently under investigation by the European Commission for its overseas tax practices, with Brussels questioning whether its huge cash pile was compiled by sweetheart tax deals in Ireland. A decision in the case, which could include a multibillion-dollar fine, is expected within the next two months.

Despite the mounting pressure, Moody's analysts expect companies to leave cash abroad as the US election looms. Groups are instead expected to deepen their reliance on debt, issuing bonds to finance shareholder returns and mergers and acquisitions.

"At this stage in the political cycle and given strong differences on both sides of the aisle in Washington, we do not expect tax law reform that would prompt overseas cash repatriation," said Moody's Richard Lane.

The failure of companies to invest their cash pile has frustrated investors who say companies are not ploughing enough back into their underlying businesses, in research and development, to reinvigorate sales.

"If you look at the most recent GDP report. . . investment was down at an annualised rate of well over 5 per cent, a dramatic drop," said Mr Ablin.

But the rising cash piles mask a rapid increase in debt. For the first time since 2012, cash, short-term investments and liquid long-term investments slipped below debt maturities due over the next five years, Moody's found.

At this stage in the political cycle . . . we do not expect tax law reform that would prompt overseas cash repatriation

Moody's Richard Lane

Total debts rose nearly $850bn last year to $6.6tn, a separate report from S&P showed, which put overall cash levels in the US at a slightly higher $1.8tn. While cash had increased by about $600bn over the past five years, obligations surged by $2.8tn.

The increased leverage has been concentrated in smaller and lower quality groups that took advantage of record-low borrowing costs spurred by stimulative monetary policy.

While the top 25 cash hoarders hold cash in excess of their obligations, the cash-to-debt ratio fell to 12 per cent for low-rated junk companies. In 2010, that figure stood above 20 per cent.

"Companies aren't exactly flush with cash," S&P analyst Andrew Chung added. "As the credit cycle ages, rates rise and macroeconomic growth slows, that's when companies in the bottom 99 per cent who levered up [could have] funding issues."

The increased leverage has not deterred investors from hoovering up large US debt sales, which topped $400bn earlier this week as bankers completed billion-dollar plus transactions for Dell, CVS Health, Southern Co and Boeing.

Investors have pointed to the drop in sovereign debt yields as they buy up corporate bonds, with nearly $10tn of debt trading with a negative yield.

Exhibit 18.28

Great Portland Estates sells largest development ahead of expected downturn

By Nicholas Megaw

Great Portland Estates has announced the sale of its largest ever development project at a discount to its most recent valuation, as the West End property developer steels itself for an expected dip in the London property market.

A company owned by German investment fund Deka has agreed to purchase the Rathbone Square development in Fitzrovia – the future London home of Facebook – for a headline price of £435m, a four

per cent discount to its valuation from last September. The sale brings Great Portland's total capital return for the development project to £110m, which it expects to return to shareholders through a special dividend.

Great Portland said it would retain the remainder of the proceeds to provide it with more "financial flexibility" as it prepares for "a continued period of market uncertainty".

Exhibit 18.29

BHP takes steps to protect balance sheet amid downturn

By Mamta Badkar

BHP Billiton signalled its determination to protect its balance sheet during the commodities downturn, hinting at the potential for a change to its long-standing progressive dividend policy.

Announcing production figures for the six months to the end of December, the Anglo-Australian miner said it wanted financial flexibility to be able to take advantage of the mid-term recovery in copper and oil, potentially by snapping up cheap assets, writes James Wilson in London.

BHP said its iron ore output this financial year to the end of June was likely to be 10m tonnes lower than previously guided, reflecting the suspension of mining at the Samarco operation in Brazil after a fatal dam accident in November. BHP also said its underlying attributable profit for the half-year would include additional charges of between $300m and $450m. The charges relate to redundancy costs, inventory write-downs after the commodity price slump, and royalty and tax charges, including potential litigation.

The miner is widely expected to consider a change in its commitment to maintain or increase its dividend when it reveals financial results next month. Tumbling oil prices – which led to a write-down of more than $7bn pre-tax on US shale assets this month – have added to the pressure exerted by falling iron ore and copper prices.

In a statement Andrew Mackenzie, chief executive, said: Commodity prices fell substantially in the first half of the 2016 financial year putting pressure on the whole resources sector. We continue to cut costs and remain focused on safely improving our operational performance to enhance the resilience of our business. In this environment, we are also committed to protecting our strong balance sheet so we have the financial flexibility to manage further volatility and take advantage of the expected recovery in copper and oil over the medium term.

Signalling

Managers and other employees have a powerful incentive to ensure the continuance of the business as they are the people who suffer most should it become insolvent. It is argued that, because of this, managers will generally increase the gearing level only if they are confident about future cash flows being sufficient.

Shareholders, who have limited access to company information, use management actions to obtain information about the company's prospects, and changes in financing become a signal of management's assessment of future returns. Ross (1977) suggests that an increase in gearing should lead to a rise in share price as managers are signalling their optimism. Managers, therefore, need to consider the signal transmitted to the market concerning future income whenever they announce major gearing changes.

Control

The source of finance chosen may be determined by the effect on the control of the organisation. Shareholders own the company and have voting rights. If shares are issued by a rights issue and all shareholders take up their full rights, then each shareholder's holding in the company remains the same. However, if a shareholder is unable to pay for more shares in a rights issue, he or she may be reluctant to allow the company to raise funds in this way, as someone else will buy the new shares and the shareholder's ownership % will be reduced – this is called dilution of control.

This limits the range of sources of finance available and may lead to a rise in debt levels. Brav (2009) found that UK firms not quoted on stock exchanges – private companies – rely almost exclusively on debt financing and have higher gearing ratios. He shows these companies are reluctant to cede control by selling voting shares: 'the larger the desire to retain control over the firm . . . the larger is the reluctance of the firm to visit the external equity capital markets' (page 305).

Tax exhaustion

As previously discussed debt interest is tax deductible, but this is only useful if you have sufficient profits to use the tax deduction. If operating profit is lower than the interest charge, then the excess interest charge cannot be used to reduce taxable profit. Some companies' profits are not high enough to benefit from the tax shield and therefore they restrict the level of debt.

Interestingly, Faulkender and Smith (2016) report that multinational groups use higher debt and lower interest cover ratios in high tax jurisdictions. The high tax makes the tax shield more valuable.

Industry group gearing

Suppose you are a financial manager trying to decide on an appropriate gearing ratio and have absorbed all the above theories, ideas and models. You have concluded that there is no precise formula to establish the *optimal gearing*. It depends on so many specific, and often difficult to measure, factors; the tax position of the firm, the likelihood of financial distress, the type of business the firm is in, the saleability of its assets, the level of business risk and the attitude of the market.

Given all these difficulties about establishing the theoretically 'correct' gearing level to maximise shareholder wealth, managers may be tempted to follow the crowd, to look at what similar firms in their industry are doing, to find out what the financial markets seem to regard as reasonable, and to do the same.

Some further thoughts on debt finance

There are some intriguing ideas advanced to promote the greater use of debt in firms' capital structure. Three of them will be considered here.

Motivation

High debt will motivate managers to perform better and in the interests of shareholders. Consider this thought: if an entrepreneur (an owner-manager) wishes to raise finance for expansion purposes, debt finance is regarded as the better choice from the perspective of entrepreneurs and society. The logic works like this: if new shares are sold to outside investors, this will dilute the entrepreneur's control and thus the level of interest of the entrepreneur in the success of the business. The entrepreneur would now be more inclined to take rewards in the form of salary, perks and leisure rather than concentrating purely on returns to shareholders. The firm will be run less efficiently because the key player is less focused on the shareholder's interest.

Or consider this argument: Bennett Stewart believes that in firms without a dominant shareholder and with a diffuse shareholder base, a recapitalisation which substitutes debt for equity can result in the concentration of the shares in the hands of a smaller, more proactive group. These shareholders have a greater incentive to monitor the firm. (If managers are made part of this shareholder owning group there is likely to be a greater alignment of shareholders' and managers' interests.) Large quoted firms often have tens of thousands of shareholders, any one of whom has little incentive to go to the expense of opposing managerial action detrimental to shareholders' interests – the costs of rallying and co-ordinating investors often outweigh the benefits to the individuals involved. However, if the shareholder base was shrunk through the substitution of debt for equity, assuming the debt finance was used to buy back shares and reduce the number of shareholders, the remaining shareholders would have greater incentive to act against mismanagement.

An extreme form of this switch to concentration of shareholders is when a management team purchases a company through a leveraged buy-out or buy-in. Here a dispersed, divided and effectively powerless group of shareholders is replaced with a focused and knowledgeable small team, capable of rapid action and highly motivated to ensure the firm's success.

Reinvestment risk

High debt forces the firm to make regular payments to debt holders, thereby denying 'spare' cash to the managers. In this way the firm avoids placing a temptation in the manager's path which might lead to investment in negative NPV projects and to making destructive acquisitions. Deliberately keeping managers short of cash avoids the problem that shareholders' funds may be applied to projects with little thought to returns. If funds are needed, instead of drawing on a large pot held within the firm, managers have to ask debt and equity finance providers. This will help to ensure that their plans are subject to the scrutiny and discipline of the market.

The problem of managers over-supplied with money, given the limited profitable investment opportunities open to them, seems to be widespread, but specific examples are only clearly seen with hindsight. For example, in the 1990s GEC was a cash-rich company under Arnold Weinstock. New managers changed the name to Marconi and spent billions buying high-technology communication infrastructure companies working at the cutting edge, but with little in the way of certainty over the likely future demand for the services/goods they offered. Hope of a glorious future was all that was needed for the spending of the large pot of money (as well as additional borrowings). When demand projections were shown to be absurdly optimistic the company barely survived – shareholder value was destroyed on a massive scale.

The danger of poor investment decisions is at its worst in firms that are highly profitable but which have few growth opportunities. The annual surplus cash flow is often squandered on increasingly marginal projects within existing SBUs or wasted in a diversification effort looking to buy growth opportunities: unfortunately, these often cost more than they are worth (*see* the evidence on merger failure in Chapter 20). It is far better, say Stewart (1990), Hart (1995a), Jensen (1986) and others, that managers are forced to justify the use of funds by having to ask for it at regular intervals. This process can be assisted by having high debt levels which absorb surplus cash through interest and principal payments and deposit it out of the reach of empire-building, perk-promoting managers.

High debt can also bring with it covenants and monitoring that restrict managerial activities to reduce the risk of over-investment for both debt and equity-holders. Evidence for this benefit was found in emerging financial markets by Harvey *et al*. (2004). **Exhibit 18.30** provides an example of reinvestment risk.

Exhibit 18.30

Centrica strategy fails to inspire

By Bryce Elder

Centrica missed out on a London market rally yesterday on worries that it would turn to acquisitions to restore growth. The decision by Centrica this week to exit the UK's nuclear reactor building programme suggested that the British Gas owner will look to prioritise investment in North America over the UK, said analysts.

Centrica is due to give a strategy update with full-year results on February 27. "Centrica may have already used most of its investor-pleasing arsenal, and reinvestment risk could now dominate," said Merrill Lynch. "Against a backdrop of pedestrian organic earnings growth, we think it will be difficult to inspire investors to award further multiple expansion for a plan likely to be centred on acquisitions."

Operating and strategic efficiency

'Equity is soft; debt is hard. Equity is forgiving; debt is insistent. Equity is a pillow; debt is a dagger.' This statement by Bennett Stewart (1990, p. 580) emphasises that operating and strategic problems and inefficiencies are less likely to be attended to and corrected with a primarily equity base. The geared firm, it is argued, simply cannot afford to have any value-destructive activities (SBUs or product lines). Managers are spurred on by the pressing need to make regular payments, to reform, dispose or close – and quickly.

These are some of the arguments put forward in support of high debt. In America there was an era of massive leveraged buyouts (LBOs), junk bonds and share repurchase programmes (in the 1980s and 1990s), and in 2006–7 private equity firms took over well-known companies and geared up their capital structures. John Plender discusses the poor capital structure decisions in the past in **Exhibit 18.31**. He was prescient; a large number of companies did add excessive debt in the low interest rate era to leave then vulnerable to financial distress by 2018. Far from acting counter-cyclically on leverage they built up debt when the sun shone, leaving them over-exposed for the rainy days of business downturns and interest rises.

Exhibit 18.31

A good time to think again about capital structures

By John Plender

Remember balance sheet efficiency? This was one of the countless virtues, much trumpeted in business schools, that private equity was supposed to bring to the quoted corporate sector. It turned out to be largely claptrap, as the debris from numerous leveraged buy-outs bears witness. The academics were doing a splendid job in softening up business on private equity's behalf, but performing a singular disservice to the wider community in peddling their intellectually toxic wares.

As financial nostrums go – and it has pretty much gone now – the concept of the efficient balance sheet was not entirely loopy. It had its roots in the celebrated theorem of Franco Modigliani and Merton Miller, which asserts that capital structure is an irrelevance. Whether the business is financed by debt or equity should not, according to the M&M theorem, affect its market value.

But those who put it into practice ignored authorial caveats. Modigliani and Miller were saying only that capital structure was irrelevant in the absence of taxes, bankruptcy costs and information asymmetry, and assuming that markets worked efficiently.

These strictures were ignored by many managers, lulled into a false sense of security by what economists dubbed 'the great moderation'. Confronting the pressures of competition in the midst of a credit bubble, they raised seemingly cheap debt to transform unexciting returns on assets into exciting returns on equity. Nowhere more so than in banking, where leverage was taken to extremes to which even the most red-blooded hedge funds did not aspire.

For their part, institutional investors egged on management to gear up balance sheets by paying special dividends or conducting share buybacks when shares were overvalued in the bull market. Some thought, not always unreasonably, that it was their right as shareholders to allocate a company's surplus capital as they saw fit, rather than leaving it with companies that were short of investment opportunities. Others were simply engaging in short-termism in the hope of improving quarterly performance numbers. Individual shareholder activists – you know, the usual suspects – were pursuing a fast buck before leaving the wasted corporate carcass for dead.

The resulting leverage was, of course, incurred without giving too much thought to risk. To make matters worse, fair value accounting had increased the cyclicality of corporate reporting, thereby increasing vulnerability to breaches of covenant. Deficits in the defined benefit pension scheme – as much a leveraged off-balance sheet entity as any conduit or structured investment vehicle – added to the sponsoring company's leverage. Embedded leverage implicit in the structure of hedging

▶

Exhibit 18.31 *(continued)*

instruments such as swaps and options gave a further twist to the risk spiral.

We are in an interregnum where investors are circumspect about leverage. Even in very stable businesses such as utilities, they have become more averse to high levels of debt. Private equity, with little access to leverage, no longer poses a predatory threat to quoted companies that run 'inefficient' balance sheets. There is time for companies to think again about capital structures.

AA plc, the roadside emergency company, was one of those taken over by private equity and it has been fighting to reduce its debt burden ever since. Having to cover significant interest payments meant the company was starved of cash to invest in operations – *see* **Exhibit 18.32**.

Exhibit 18.32

AA to raise £935m to cut annual interest costs

By Andy Sharman, Motor Industry Correspondent

The AA has unveiled plans to raise almost £1bn in equity and debt as part of refinancing measures that will allow the roadside assistance group to cut its annual interest costs. The Hampshire-based company, which turns 110 this year, listed in June following a management buy-in of the group led by Bob Mackenzie, now executive chairman. The new leadership team is trying to overhaul the motoring organisation after years of under-investment, while paying down expensive debt inherited from the previous owners.

As part of the refinancing, unveiled on Wednesday, the AA will raise £200m of equity through a placing and open offer and issue £735m in bonds. The measures were accompanied by strategic changes, including plans to invest in IT systems and the company's digital services, as well as increase spending on marketing and attracting new members.

Up until the summer, the AA was owned by private equity groups Charterhouse, CVC and Permira, who in 2007 merged the motoring organisation with over-50s insurance company Saga in a £6bn deal. Under a July 2013 refinancing arrangement, the AA was left carrying about £3bn in net debt as part of plans to separate the company from Saga, which is now also separately listed.

A subsequent refinancing at the AA saw it issue £350m of high-yield payment-in-kind notes, financial instruments that pay a high level of interest or dividends in debt rather than cash. Half of those notes were paid off in December, using proceeds from the initial public offering, and Wednesday's refinancing will allow the company to redeem the remainder. It will also refinance £655m of bonds that, like the Pik notes, were paying 9.5 per cent interest, almost double the average interest rate on the company's borrowings.

As a result of the latest refinancing plan, the AA's £190m annual interest costs will fall by £45m and it said the moves would allow it to start paying dividends worth "no less than £50m" for the year to the end of January 2016. The company unveiled the measures alongside preliminary results for the year to the end of January. Revenues were broadly flat at £983.5m, while operating profit fell by about 13 per cent to £326m, which the company blamed on costs related to the IPO and other restructuring measures. Net debt stood at just under £3bn at the end of January, versus £3.2bn a year ago. "This company can support very high levels of debt," said Mr. Mackenzie. AA shares fell 1.8 per cent to 419p on Wednesday morning, valuing the company's equity at £2.3bn. The shares have risen around 80 per cent since the June flotation.

Concluding comments

The proportion of debt in the total capital of a firm can influence the overall cost of capital and therefore the value of the firm and the wealth of shareholders. It is generally observed, at least initially, that as gearing increases the WACC declines because of the lower cost of debt and the tax relief available on debt capital. If, as a result of increasing the gearing ratio, it is possible to lower the weighted average cost of capital, then all the future net cash flows will be discounted at a lower rate, resulting in a higher present value of the shares.

Exhibit 18.33   The WACC is U-shaped and value can be altered by changing the gearing level

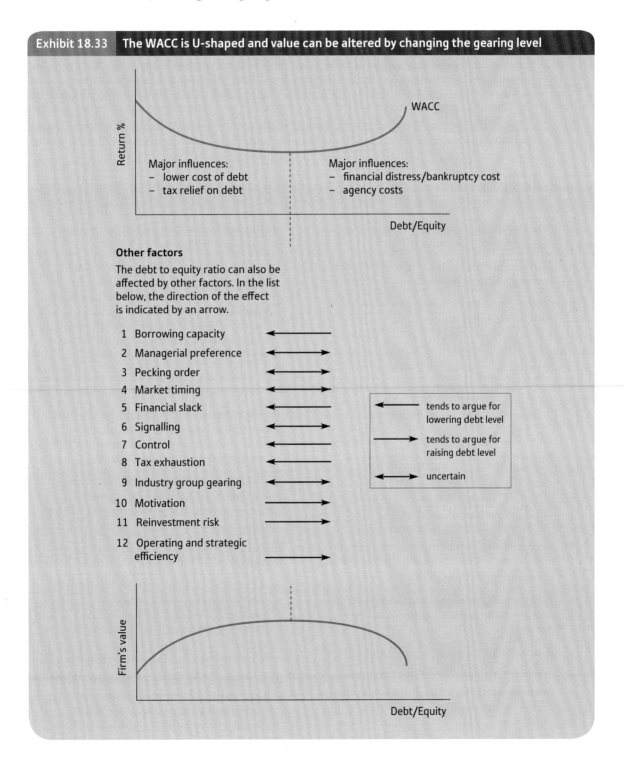

However, as gearing rises the risk of financial distress causes shareholders (and eventually debt holders) to demand a greater return. This eventually rises to such an extent that it outweighs the benefit of the lower cost of debt, and the WACC starts to rise. This risk factor is difficult, if not impossible, to quantify and therefore the exact position and shape of the WACC curve for each firm remain largely unknown. Nevertheless, it seems reasonable to postulate there is a U-shaped relationship like that shown in **Exhibit 18.33**.

We cannot establish with precision an optimal gearing ratio. There are many complicating factors which determine the actual capital structure adopted by firms, so that, while we accept that the WACC is probably U-shaped for firms generally, we cannot calculate, with any certainty, an optimal gearing level. This explains why there is such a variation in gearing levels.

Variations derive from both internal and external factors. Internal factors include the profitability and stability of the company's cash flow, the company's borrowing capacity which may be restricted by availability of assets as security. Emotions and opinions also influence behaviour including the personalities involved, management self-belief, shareholder attitude. External factors include the economic environment, the norms in the industry, the volatility of the market or the availability of credit.

So, to the question of whether a firm can obtain a level of gearing which will maximise shareholder wealth the answer is 'yes'. The problem is finding this level in such a multifaceted analysis.

Key points and concepts

- **Financial gearing** concerns the proportion of debt in the capital structure.

- **Operating gearing** refers to the extent to which the firm's total costs are fixed.

- **Capital gearing** can be measured in a number of ways. For example:

  $$1 \quad \frac{\text{Long-term debt}}{\text{Shareholders' funds}}$$

  $$2 \quad \frac{\text{Long-term debt}}{\text{Long-term debt + Shareholders' funds}}$$

  $$3 \quad \frac{\text{All borrowing}}{\text{All borrowing + Shareholders' funds}}$$

  $$4 \quad \frac{\text{Long-term debt}}{\text{Total market capitalisation}}$$

- **Income gearing** is concerned with the proportion of the annual income stream which is devoted to the prior claims of debt holders.

- The **effect of financial gearing** is to magnify the volatility of a firm's profit available to ordinary shareholders.

- **Business risk** is the variability of the firm's operating income (before interest).

- **Financial risk** is the additional variability in returns to shareholders due to debt in the financial structure.

- In **Modigliani and Miller's perfect no-tax world** three propositions hold true:

  1 The total market value of any company is independent of its capital structure.
  2 The expected rate of return on equity increases proportionately with the gearing ratio.
  3 The cut-off rate of return for new projects is equal to the weighted average cost of capital – which is constant regardless of gearing.

- In an **MM world with tax** the optimal gearing level is the highest possible.

- The **risk of financial distress** is one factor which causes firms to moderate their gearing levels. Financial distress is where obligations to creditors are not met, or are met with difficulty.

- The **indirect costs of financial distress**, such as deterioration in relationships with suppliers, customers and employees, can be more significant than the direct costs, such as legal fees.

- **Financial distress risk is influenced by the following:**

  - the sensitivity of the company's revenues to the general level of economic activity;
  - the proportion of fixed to variable costs;
  - the liquidity and marketability of the firm's assets;
  - the cash-generative ability of the business.

- **Agency costs** are the direct and indirect costs of ensuring that agents (e.g. managers) act in the best interests of principals (e.g. shareholders, lenders), for example monitoring costs, restrictive covenants, loss of managerial freedom of action and opportunities foregone.

- **Financial distress and agency costs eventually outweigh the lower cost of debt** as gearing rises causing the WACC to rise and the firm's value to fall. (the '**trade-off**' theory).

- **Borrowing capacity** is determined by the assets available as collateral – this restricts borrowing.

- There can be a **managerial preference** for a lower risk stance on gearing. Alternatively, the managers might prefer greater debt to boost earnings per share or to bargain with unionists.

- **The pecking order** of finance:

  1 internally generated funds;
  2 borrowings;
  3 new issue of equity.

  The reasons for the pecking order:

  - equity issue perceived as 'bad news' by the markets;
  - line of least resistance;
  - transaction costs.

- **Market timing theory** is founded on the observation that firms tend to issue shares when their share price is high and repurchase shares when it is low. This leads to the idea of an absence of a movement towards an optimal capital structure in the short or long term. However, the evidence suggests that in the medium or long term firms do move towards a target optimal debt/equity ratio.

- **Financial flexibility (slack)** means having cash (or near-cash) and/or spare debt capacity so that opportunities can be exploited quickly (and trouble avoided) as they arise in an unpredictable world and to provide a contingency reserve – it tends to reduce borrowing levels.

- **Signalling** An increased gearing level is taken as a positive sign by the financial markets because managers would only take the risk of financial distress if they were confident about future cash flows.

- The source of finance chosen may be determined by the effect on the **control** of the organisation.

- **Tax exhaustion** (profit insufficient to take advantage of debt's tax shield benefit) may be a factor limiting debt levels.

- Managers may be tempted to adopt the **industry group gearing** level.

- It is suggested that high gearing **motivates** managers to perform if they have a stake in the business, or if a smaller group of shareholders are given the incentive to monitor and control managers.

- High gearing **diminishes reinvestment risk.**

- It is argued that **operating and strategic efficiency** can be pushed further by high gearing.

Appendix 18.1: Asset beta

The assets of a business contain only business systematic risk. However, the equity of a geared company has to bear both (**a**) business systematic risk, and (**b**) financial systematic risk due to the additional variability caused by borrowing. The business systematic risk remains constant regardless of gearing level. The equity systematic risk, however, rises with higher gearing

In the CAPM the beta of the equity (β_E) rises as the firm takes on higher gearing. Debt can also have a beta. That is, the returns to the lenders have a co-variability greater than zero with the market portfolio's returns. Both types of finance providers, debt and equity, bear risk – it is just that the shareholders bear a greater risk.

Imagine that an individual owned all the equity and all the debt of a firm. This person therefore bears all the risks. If these two holdings form this person's entire portfolio then the overall systematic risk is a weighted average of the two component betas (ignoring taxes).

$$\beta_{\text{portfolio}} = W_E \beta_E + W_D \beta_D = \beta_A$$

where

β_D = beta of debt
β_A = asset beta
W_E = proportion of total finance that is equity
W_D = proportion of total finance that is debt

So, if debt has a beta of 0.3 and equity a beta of 1.3 in a company with equal amounts of capital from debt and equity the overall beta for the firm, the asset beta, β_A, is:

$$\beta_A = (0.5 \times 1.3) + (0.5 \times 0.3) = 0.8$$

The asset beta is a weighted average of the beta values of the debt and equity that financed the assets. To be more accurate, the asset beta determines the equity beta and debt beta. Asset beta remains constant regardless of the gearing level because it is determined by the business systematic risk, which does not change with the debt level. So, if in the example above the company lowered its gearing from the position where debt accounts for half of the capital to the point where it accounts for only 25% the systematic risk on both the equity and debt would decrease. Assuming that the debt beta falls to 0.2 we can work out the new equity beta:

$$\beta_A = 0.8 = W_E\beta_E + W_D\beta_D$$
$$0.8 = 0.75\beta_E + (0.25 \times 0.2)$$
$$\beta_E = 1$$

Note that both the debt and equity betas fall as a result of lower gearing but the asset beta remains the same.

If the borrowing is eliminated the asset beta equals the equity beta:

$$\beta_A = 0.8 = 1 \times \beta_E + 0$$
$$\beta_A = \beta_E = 0.8$$

Asset beta is the equity beta of the ungeared company given its underlying business systematic risk.

It is often assumed that the beta of debt is zero. This makes usable the following formulae:

$$\beta_A = \beta_E \times W_E$$

and

$$\beta_E = \beta_A \times 1/W_E$$

or

$$\beta_E = \beta_A(1 + D/E)$$

where D = amount of borrowing
E = amount of equity finance

In this case equity beta rises in direct proportion to the gearing level.

If we now switch to a world where there are taxes, then (keeping the assumption of debt beta of zero) the tax shield on debt results in the following relationship:

$$\beta_E = \beta_A[1 + (1 - T)(D/E)]$$

where T = corporation tax rate.

The equity beta is reduced because the tax relief (shield) on debt capital effectively lowers the financial risk borne by the equity holders at all gearing levels.

Users of this formula should never forget the major assumption that the lenders bear no systematic risk (debt beta is zero). There is also the assumption that the CAPM is the right model for risk. If it is not the betas estimated may not reflect the true market risk exposure for the equity. In addition, the model excludes the possibility that β_E might rise in a non-linear fashion with gearing. (CAPM is discussed further in Chapter 8.)

Perhaps the most useful point to make about asset beta analysis is that it is good to be aware that the beta obtained from commercial sources is an equity beta dependent on the gearing levels for the firms at the time that the beta was estimated. This gearing level may not be the gearing level applicable to WACC calculations and so some adjustment is needed. If, after reading Chapter 8, you still want to use CAPM-beta then the equity beta can be *ungeared* by using the above formulae, and then calculated for a variety of gearing levels (if a few bold assumptions are made).

Appendix 18.2: Adjusted present value (APV)

In the adjusted present value approach, the value of financial gearing is separated from the value of the firm (project) without debt. The APV is equal to the value of the firm or project at zero debt (the NPV) plus the present value of the benefits (costs) of debt financing.

> APV = NPV + PV of effects of gearing.

Or,

> APV = value with all equity financing + PV of the effects of gearing.

Start by calculating the NPV of a project (or firm) as though it was to be financed entirely by equity. For example, a project is being considered that will produce annual cash flows of £1m for every future year to infinity. The project's business risk is such that the appropriate discount rate for this all-equity financed project is 10%. The initial investment required is £10.5m.

> NPV = −£10.5m + £1m/0.1 = −£0.5m

Under this all-equity capital structure, the project produces a negative NPV and the managers would be inclined to reject it.

Now consider the same project in the circumstances where one half of the firm's (and project's) finance is debt and one half is equity. The debt finance carries with it a tax shield due to the ability to reduce taxable profit, and therefore the amount of tax paid, by the amount of interest. In other words, interest payments on debt are tax deductible, while cash flows on equity have to be paid out of after-tax cash flows.

If we make a few assumptions we can value the tax shield. If the interest rate on the £5.25m of debt is 6%, and the tax rate, T, on income is 30%, the annual tax savings from being able to deduct interest from taxable profits are:

> Annual interest on the debt = $k_D \times D$
>
> $\qquad$ = 0.06 × £5.25m = £315,000
>
> Annual tax savings due to interest payments = $T \times k_D \times D$
>
> $\qquad\qquad$ = 0.3 × 0.06 × £5.25m = £94,500

If we make the following four assumptions we can calculate the present value of all the future tax savings due to interest payments:

- The debt remains at the same level forever; therefore the tax savings are a perpetuity.
- The discount rate to be used to obtain the present value of all the future tax savings is the interest rate on debt (because it reflects the riskiness of debt).
- The tax rate will be the same for all future periods.
- The company will always be in a tax-paying position. There are always annual taxable profits that can be decreased by the payment of interest.

In these circumstances the present value of the savings is:

> Present value of tax savings due to debt $= \dfrac{T k_D D}{k_D} = TD$
>
> $\qquad$ = 0.3 × £5.25m
>
> $\qquad$ = £1.575m

Thus, the tax rate multiplied by the amount of debt gives us the present value of the effects of gearing in this simple case where there is only one effect of gearing: the tax shield benefit. We will introduce other effects later.

We can now add together the value of the project in the all-equity case and the value of the tax shield.

APV = value with all-equity finance + PV of the effects of gearing

= −£0.5m + £1.575m = £1.075m

As a result of changing the financing structure the project generates positive value and should be accepted.

In separating the value of gearing the APV approach has the suggested advantage that we can more easily calculate overall value at a variety of debt levels than by using the WACC. For example, in a leveraged buy out where there is rapid pay-down of the debt, so that the ratio changes from year to year, the APV provides a computationally easier way of calculating value than the WACC.

However, some caution is needed when employing the APV. It assumes, for instance, that the firm can fully benefit from the tax shield at all debt levels. In reality tax shields will often be unused and therefore not adding value because the firm is not paying taxes. There may be periods of the future when the company is not making profits. Also, very high debt levels need very high taxable income to gain all the benefit from the deductibility of interest. The tax shield value may be much less than that calculated using the simple formula above.

In addition, to use the APV you need to be able to predict debt ratio levels for each of the future years with some considerable accuracy.

Most importantly, the APV formula used so far has ignored the disadvantages of higher debt. It implicitly assumes that the benefits of debt increase as the gearing level rises (as in MM's world with tax model). The logical extreme outcome of this would be to select a capital structure that was virtually all debt. In reality, there are some drawbacks of higher debt, the most important of which are financial distress, agency costs and loss of financial slack. So, the APV formula needs to be modified to allow for the disadvantages of debt:

$$
\text{APV} = \begin{array}{c} \text{Value with} \\ \text{all-equity} \\ \text{financing} \end{array} + \begin{array}{c} \text{PV of tax} \\ \text{benefits of} \\ \text{debt} \end{array} - \begin{array}{c} \text{PV of expected} \\ \text{disadvantages} \\ \text{of debt} \end{array}
$$

At low levels of debt, the tax benefits will outweigh the disadvantages, but at high gearing it will be the other way round and the APV will fall with an increasing proportion of debt.

In this more realistic model the valuation of the financially geared company at different debt levels is far more complex, not least because it is very difficult to put numerical values on the disadvantages. To add to the complexity, there are a number of other factors we should allow for: for example, the benefit of higher debt leading to more highly motivated managers, the benefit of government loan subsidies, the transaction costs of issuing debt.

References and further reading

Almazan, A., De Motta, A., Titman, S. and Uysal, V. (2010) 'Financial structure, acquisition opportunities and firm locations', *The Journal of Finance,* LXV (2), pp. 529–58.

'We develop a model where being located within an industry cluster increases opportunities to make acquisitions, and to facilitate those acquisitions, firms within clusters maintain more financial slack.' They find the empirical evidence fits the model, particularly in hi-tech clusters of firms.

Alti, A. (2006) 'How persistent is the impact of market timing on capital structure?' *Journal of Finance,* 61(4), August, pp. 1681–710.

Evidence from the US that 'market timing' of equity issues does affect gearing (because if shares are easy to sell in large volume firms take advantage of that fact – the firms studied are 'hot' IPO stocks). However, the effect is short-lived – 'at the end of the second year following the IPO, the impact of market timing on leverage completely vanishes'.

Anderson, R.C., Mansi, S.A. and Reeb, D.M. (2003) 'Founding family ownership and the agency cost of debt', *Journal of Financial Economics,* 68, pp. 263–85.

Evidence is presented that suggests that debt holders' agency worries are less in companies with family ownership of shares. Interest rates are less because the founding family better protects debt holders' interests, it is posited.

Andrade, G. and Kaplan, S. (1998) 'How costly is financial (not economic) distress? Evidence from highly leveraged transactions that became distressed', *Journal of Finance*, 53, pp. 1443–93.

This paper studies thirty-one highly leveraged transactions HLTs that become financially distressed

Baker, A. and Wurgler, J. (2002) 'Market timing and capital structure', *Journal of Finance*, 62(1), February, pp. 1–32.

Firms tend to issue equity when market values are high, and repurchase shares when market values are low. These actions influence the debt to equity ratio in the short run and, more surprisingly, over the long run. Thus 'capital structure is largely the cumulative outcome of past attempts to time the equity market. In this theory, there is no optimum capital structure, so market timing decisions just accumulate over time into the capital structure outcome.'

Bancel, F. and Mittoo, U. (2004) Cross-country determinants of capital structure choice: A survey of European firms, *Financial Management*, 33, pp. 103–32.

The paper surveyed managers in 16 European countries to determine what the primary concerns of managers were in determining capital structure.

Bancel F. and Mittoo, U. (2011) 'Survey evidence on financing decisions and cost of capital'. In H.K. Baker and Martin, G. (Eds.), *Capital Structure and Corporate Financing Decisions – Theory, Evidence, and Practice* (pp. 229–48). Hoboken, New Jersey: John Wiley, Ch. 13.

Traditional empirical studies are based on large samples of financial data. This chapter focuses on surveys of how managers make decisions on the capital structure and other financial issues.

Banerjee, S., Dasgupta, S. and Kim, Y. (2008) 'Buyer–supplier relationships and the stakeholder theory of capital structure', *The Journal of Finance*, LXIII (5), pp. 2507–52.

If a supplier firm is dependent on a customer for a major part of its sales, the supplier may lower its leverage to reduce the risk of financial distress, and may prefer the principal customer to become less levered.

Bevan, A.A. and Danbolt, J. (2004) 'Testing for inconsistencies in the estimation of UK capital structure determinants', *Applied Financial Economics*, 14, pp. 55–66.

UK empirical evidence showing debt (relative to asset base) rises with company size, perhaps because larger firms have less financial distress and agency cost risk. Also, more profitable companies have lower debt levels (pecking order theory support?). And companies with more tangible assets carry more debt (adverse selection and moral hazard lead lenders to demand collateral).

Booth, L., Aivazian, V., Demirgue-Kunt, A. and Maksimovic, V. (2001) 'Capital structures in developing countries', *Journal of Finance,* 61(1), February, pp. 87–130.

The same decision variables influence capital structure in developing and developed countries. This is especially true of pecking order factors, e.g. the more profitable the firm the lower the debt.

Brav, O. (2009) 'Access to capital, capital structure, and the funding of the firm', *The Journal of Finance,* LXIV (1).

Examining UK private and public firms Brav discovers that unquoted companies rely almost exclusively on debt financing to grow and have higher leverage ratios. Private equity is more costly than public equity and there is the desire for owners to maintain voting control.

Brierley, P. and Bunn, P. (2005) 'The determination of UK corporate capital gearing', *Bank of England Quarterly Bulletin,* Autumn, pp. 356–66.

Empirical evidence that UK companies' gearing is positively related to company size and negatively correlated with growth opportunities and the importance of intangible assets. Until 1995 highly profitable firms had low gearing but this changed after 1995.

Brounen, D., de Jong, A. and Koedijk, K. (2004) 'Corporate finance in Europe: Confronting theory with practice', *Financial Management,* pp. 71–101.

A survey of European practice, 'financial flexibility appears to be the most important factor in determining the amount of corporate debt'.

Bulan, L. and Yan, Z. (2009) 'The pecking order theory and the firm's life cycle', *Banking and Finance Letters,* 1(3), pp. 129–140.

The paper examines the predictions of the pecking order theory of financing among firms in two life cycle stages, growth and maturity.

Bulan, L. and Yan, Z. (2011) 'Firm maturity and the pecking order theory', *International Journal of Business and Economics,* 9(3), pp. 179–200.

The paper identifies firms according to two life cycle stages, growth and maturity, and tests the pecking order theory.

Bunn, R. and Young, G. (2004) Corporate capital structure in the United Kingdom: Determinants and adjustment. Bank of England Working Paper 226 (www.bankofengland.co.uk/wp/index.html).

Evidence that UK companies comply with the trade-off model by borrowing to take advantage of the tax benefits of debt, which they set against possible costs of over-indebtedness. Also, companies adjust gearing through dividend payments, new equity issues and to a lesser extent lowering or raising capital investment.

Damodaran, A. (2014) *Applied Corporate Finance*. 4th edn. New York: John Wiley & Sons.
> An accessible introduction to the practical estimation of optimum capital structure.

Danis, A., Daniel, A.R. and Whited, T.M. (2014) 'Refinancing, profitability, and capital structure', *Journal of Financial Economics,* 114, pp. 424–43.
> The paper considers whether leverage is correlated with positive or negative performance.

Donaldson, G. (1961) *Corporate Debt Policy and the Determination of Corporate Debt Capacity*. Boston: Harvard Graduate School of Business Administration.
> A study of the financing practices of large corporations: discussion of pecking order theory. Proposes a measure of debt capacity based on distressed cashflow.

Donaldson, G. (1969) *Strategy for Financial Mobility*. Boston: Harvard University.
> An early discussion of financial slack.

Fama, E.G. (1978) 'The effects of a firm's investment and financing decisions', *American Economic Review,* 68(3), June, pp. 272–84.
> A development of the economic modelling approach.

Fama, E.F. and French, K.R. (2005) 'Financing decisions: Who issues stocks?', *Journal of Financial Economics,* 76, pp. 549–82.
> Evidence against the pecking order theory prediction that firms rarely issue equity.

Faulkender M. and Smith J.M. (2016) 'Taxes and leverage at multinational corporations', *Journal of Financial Economics,* 122(1), pp. 1–20.
> Firms do have higher leverage ratios and lower interest coverage ratios when they operate in countries with higher tax rates, as the theory predicts.

Fernández, P. (2001) 'Optimal capital structure: problems with the Harvard and Damodaran Approaches', IESE Business School Working Paper.
> A theoretical critique of optimal capital structure models.

Fischer, E., Heinkel, R. and Zechner, J. (1989) 'Dynamic capital structure choice', *Journal of Finance,* 44, 19–40.
> This paper develops a model of dynamic capital structure choice in the presence of recapitalization costs and finds that even small recapitalization costs lead to wide swings in a firm's debt ratio over time

Flannery, M.J. and Rangan, K.P. (2006) 'Partial adjustment toward target capital structures', *Journal of Financial Economics,* 79, pp. 469–506.
> Provides evidence that US companies have target ratios of debt/equity and try to (rapidly) move towards them – thus supporting the trade-off theory. The evidence provides only weak support for the pecking order theory or the idea that firms decrease gearing when their share price is high by issuing more shares (the 'market-timing theory').

Frank, M.Z. and Goyal, V.K. (2003) 'Testing the pecking order theory of capital structure', *Journal of Financial Economics,* 67, pp. 217–48.
> Evidence contradictory to the pecking order model.

Graham, J.R. and Harvey, C.R. (2001) 'The theory and practice of corporate finance: Evidence from the field', *Journal of Financial Economics,* 60(2–3), pp. 187–243.
> Empirical evidence on capital structure decisions.

Graham, J. and Leary, M. (2011) 'A review of empirical capital structure research and directions for the future', *Annual Review of Financial Economics,* 3, 309–345.
> This article reviews empirical capital structure research, concentrating on papers published since 2005. They document three dimensions of capital structure variation: cross firm, cross industry, and within firm through time and summarise how well the traditional trade-off and pecking order approaches explain these sources of variation and highlight their empirical shortcomings.

Harris, M. and Raviv, A. (1991) 'The theory of capital structure', *Journal of Finance,* 46, pp. 297–355.
> A helpful review of the subject.

Hart, O.D. (1995) *Firms, Contracts and Financial Structure*. Oxford: Oxford University Press.
> High debt helps to align the interests of owners and managers.

Harvey, C.R., Lins, K.V. and Roper, A.H. (2004) 'The effect of capital structure when expected agency costs are extreme', *Journal of Financial Economics,* 74, pp. 3–30.
> Evidence that the issuance of debt (e.g. syndicated term loans, international bonds and Yankee bonds) that comes with restrictive operational covenants and monitoring of firms reduces agency costs and information problems. In particular, overinvestment is reduced. The more intensive monitoring and the constraints serve shareholders well.

Hovakimian, A., Kayhan, A. and Titman, S. (2012) 'Are corporate default probabilities consistent with the static trade-off theory?' *Review of Financial Studies,* 25, pp. 315–34.
> Default probability plays a central role in the static trade-off theory of capital structure. This paper tests this theory by regressing the probability of default on proxies for costs and benefits of debt.

Jensen, M.C. (1986) 'Agency costs of free cashflow, corporate finance and takeovers', *American Economic Review,* 26 May, p. 323.
> Discusses the problem of encouraging managers to pay to shareholders cash above that needed for all positive NPV projects.

Jensen, M.C. (1989) 'Eclipse of the public corporation', *Harvard Business Review,* September–October, pp. 61–74.
High debt levels impose a discipline on managers. In particular they are forced to distribute cash, reducing the potential waste of free cash flow investment. Also in LBOs managers are incentivised by becoming owners.

Journal of Economic Perspectives (1988) Fall.
A collection of review articles on MM propositions.

Kayhan, A. and Titman, S. (2007) 'Firms' histories and their capital structures', *Journal of Financial Economics,* 83, pp. 1–32.
Cash flows, investment expenditures and share price histories have a substantial influence on changes in capital structure, 'capital structures tend to move towards target debt ratios that are consistent with the trade-off theories of capital structure'.

Kisgen, D.J. (2006) 'Credit ratings and capital structure', *Journal of Finance,* 61(3), June, pp. 1035–72.
US firms' capital structure decisions are influenced by credit ratings.

Korajczyk, R.A. and Levy, A. (2003) 'Capital structure choice: Macroeconomic conditions and financial constraints', *Journal of Financial Economics,* 68, pp. 75–109.
Macroeconomic conditions affect capital structure.

Kraus, A. and Litzenberger, R. (1973) 'A state-preference model of optimal financial leverage', *Journal of Finance,* 28, pp. 911–22.

Leary, M.T. (2009) 'Bank loan supply, lender choice, and corporate capital structure', *The Journal of Finance,* LXIV (3), pp. 1143–85.
Bank funding constraints influence firms' capital structures.

Leary, M.T. and Roberts, M.R. (2005) 'Do firms rebalance their capital structures?', *Journal of Finance,* 60(6), December, pp. 2575–619.
Findings: 'We find that firms actively rebalance their leverage to stay within an optimal range. Our evidence suggests that the persistent effect of shocks on leverage observed in previous studies is more likely due to adjustment costs than indifference toward capital structure'.

Luehrman, T.A. (1997) 'Using APV: A better tool for valuing operations', *Harvard Business Review,* 75 (May–June), pp. 145–54.
An easy-to-read introduction to adjusted present value.

Marsh, P. (1982) 'The choice between equity and debt: An empirical study', *Journal of Finance,* 37, March, pp. 121–44.
Evidence that companies appear to have target debt levels. These targets are a function of company size, bankruptcy risk and asset composition.

Matsa, D.A. (2010) 'Capital structure as a strategic variable: Evidence from collective bargaining', *Journal of Finance,* 65(3), pp. 1197–232.
High debt helps with negotiating with organised labour – a US study.

Merton, R.C. (2005) 'You have more capital than you think', *Harvard Business Review,* November, pp. 1–10.
Argues that modern large firms can use derivatives to lower risk thus allowing a reduction in equity capital.

Miller, M.H. (1977) 'Debt and taxes', *Journal of Finance,* 32, May, pp. 261–75.
A further contribution to the theoretical debate – technical and US focused.

Miller, M.H. (1988) 'The Modigliani–Miller propositions after thirty years', *Journal of Economic Perspectives* (Fall). Also reproduced in Chew, D.H. (ed.) (2001) *The New Corporate Finance.* New York: McGraw-Hill. 3rd edn.
Miller muses on the original propositions and the debate over 30 years. He acknowledges the departure of real-world practice from the artificial world constructed for the models.

Miller, M.H. (1991) 'Leverage', *Journal of Finance,* 46, pp. 479–88.
An interesting article by a leader in the field.

Modigliani, F. and Miller, M.H. (1958) 'The cost of capital, corporation finance and the theory of investment', *American Economic Review,* 48, June, pp. 261–97.
The classic original economic modelling approach to this subject.

Modigliani, F. and Miller, M.H. (1963) 'Corporate income taxes and the cost of capital: A correction', *American Economic Review,* 53, June, pp. 433–43.
A technical account of the important correction to the 1958 article – allows for taxes.

Modigliani, F. and Miller, M.H. (1969) 'Reply to Heins and Sprenkle', *American Economic Review,* 59, September, pp. 592–5.
More on the economic model approach.

Myers, S.C. (1974) 'Interaction of corporate financing and investment decisions – implications for capital budgeting', *Journal of Finance,* 29 (March), pp. 1–25.
The adjusted present value method is developed in this article.

Myers, S.C. (1984) 'The capital structure puzzle', *Journal of Finance,* 39, July, pp. 575–82.
Easy-to-read consideration of capital structure theory – particularly of pecking order theory.

Myers, S. and Majluf, N. (1984) 'Corporate financing and investment decisions when firms have information investors do not have', *Journal of Financial Economics,* June, pp. 187–221.

Pecking order theory is advanced as an explanation for capital structure in practice.

Passov, R. (2003) 'How much cash does your company need?' *Harvard Business Review,* November, pp. 1–8.

Knowledge-based companies need low debt or net cash to allow ongoing investment without resort to the financial market where finance can be exorbitantly expensive or simply unavailable.

Ross, S. (1977) 'The determination of financial structure: The incentive-signalling approach', *Bell Journal of Economics,* 8, pp. 23–40.

The signalling hypothesis of debt increases is advanced.

Shyam-Sunder, L. and Myers, S.C. (1999) 'Testing static trade off against pecking order models of capital structure', *Journal of Financial Economics,* 51, pp. 219–44.

Supporting evidence for the pecking order model.

Solomon, E. (1963) *The Theory of Financial Management*. New York: Columbia University Press.

An early discussion of the WACC.

Stern, J. (1998) 'The capital structure puzzle', *Journal of Applied Corporate Finance,* II(I), Spring, pp. 8–23.

A round-table discussion between Joel Stern, Stewart Myers and other capital structure specialists. It focuses particularly on managerial performance and incentives. There is also a discussion of financial slack by the Treasurer of Sears – very interesting.

Stewart, G.B. (1991) *The Quest for Value*. New York: Harper Business.

Chapter 13 is written in praise of capital structures with high debt levels.

Tirole J. (2006) *The Theory of Corporate Finance*. Princeton, NJ: Princeton University Press.

An algebraic/theoretical approach to the borrowing question.

Watson, R. and Wilson, N. (2002) 'Small and medium size enterprise financing: A note of some empirical implications of a pecking order', *Journal of Business Finance and Accounting,* 29(3) and (4) April/May, pp. 557–78.

A testing of the pecking order model in UK shares. Evidence found in support.

Welch, I. (2004) 'Capital structure and stock returns', *Journal of Political Economy,* 112(1), pp. 106–31.

A major influence on the gearing level is fluctuations in the equity market capitalisation raising or lowering the equity figure in the debt/equity ratio. Firms are slow to raise or pay off finance to counteract market capitalisation fluctuations. This is an 'inertia' explanation of capital structure.

Welch, I. (2011) 'Two common problems in capital structure research: The financial debt-to-asset ratio and issuing activity versus leverage changes', *International Review of Finance,* 11, 1–17.

The paper discusses two common problems in capital structure research.

Case study recommendations

Please see www.pearsoned.co.uk/arnold for case study synopses. Also, another list of useful case studies from the fifth edition can be found there.

- A new financial policy at Swedish Match. Authors: Bo Becker; Michael Norris, Harvard Business School. Available at www.cb.hbsp.harvard.edu

- Blaine Kitchenware, Inc.: capital structure (brief case). Authors: Joel L. Heilprin; Timothy A. Luehrman,

Harvard Business School. Available at www.cb.hbsp. harvard.edu

- Asahi India Glass Limited: leverage, a double-edged sword. Authors: Sanjay Dhamija; David J. Sharp, Ivey Publishing. Available at www.cb.hbsp.harvard.edu

Video presentations

Chief executives and finance directors describe their current policy on capital structure on Cantos.com (https://www.merchantcantos.com/) – this is free to view.

Self-review questions

1 What was the traditional (pre-MM) view on optimal gearing levels?

2 Explain how debt finance is 'cheaper and riskier' for the firm.

3 Explain the terms operating gearing, financial gearing, capital gearing, income gearing.

4 What are business risk and financial risk?

5 Modigliani and Miller's original model resulted in three propositions. Describe them. Also, what are the major assumptions on which the model was built?

6 Describe how MM analysis changes if taxes are allowed into the model.

7 What is financial distress and how does it affect the gearing decision?

8 What are agency costs and how do they affect the gearing decision?

9 Describe the following ideas which are advanced to explain the low levels of gearing in some companies:
   a   Borrowing capacity.
   b   Managerial preferences.
   c   Pecking order.
   d   Financial flexibility (slack).
   e   Control.

10 Some writers advocate the increased use of debt because of its beneficial effect on (**a**) managerial motivation, (**b**) reinvestment risk and (**c**) operating and strategic efficiency. Explain these ideas.

Questions and problems

Answers to most questions can be found at www.pearsoned.co.uk/arnold.
Answers to questions marked with an asterisk are to be found only in the Lecturer's Guide.

1* Calculate and comment upon some gearing ratios for Vopod plc.

Extracts from Vopod plc Balance sheet and profit and loss account, 20X1

	£m	£m
Non-current assets		96,804
Current assets:		
Inventory	288	
Trade and other receivables	5,023	
Taxation recoverable	21	
Cash and cash equivalents	7,481	
		12,813
Current liabilities of which:		(18,946)
Short term borrowings	4,817	
Long term borrowings		(17,798)
Other Non-current liabilities		(5,580)
Net assets		67,293
Profit before interest and taxation (ignoring goodwill impairment)		9,200
Interest payable		(1,612)
Market capitalisation		93,300

Note: Assume net assets equal shareholder funds.

2 (*Examination level*) Eastwell is to be established and the founders are considering their options with regard to capital structure. A total of £1m will be needed to establish the business and the three ways of raising these funds being considered are:

a   Selling 500,000 shares at £2.00.
b   Selling 300,000 shares at £2.00 and borrowing £400,000 with an interest rate of 12%.
c   Selling 100,000 shares at £2.00 and borrowing £800,000 at an interest rate of 13%.

There are three possible outcomes for the future annual cash flows before interest:

Success of product	Cash flow before interest	Probability
Poor	£60,000	0.25
Good	£160,000	0.50
Excellent	£300,000	0.25

Note: Taxes may be ignored.

Required

a   Calculate the expected annual return to shareholders under each of the capital structures.
b   Calculate the standard deviation of the expected annual return under each of the capital structures.
c   Explain the terms 'business risk' and 'financial risk'.
d   Some writers have advocated the high use of debt because of the positive effect on managerial actions. Describe these ideas and consider some counter-arguments.   **?**

3 a (*Examination level*) Hose plc presently has a capital structure which is 30% debt and 70% equity. The cost of debt (i.e. borrowings) before tax shield benefits is 9% and that for equity is 15%. The firm's future cash flows, after tax but before interest, are expected to be a perpetuity of £750,000. The tax rate is 30%.
Calculate the WACC and the value of the firm.

   b The directors are considering the partial replacement of equity finance with borrowings so that the borrowings make up 60% of the total capital. Director A believes that the cost of equity capital will remain constant at 15%; Director B believes that shareholders will demand a rate of return of 23.7%; Director C believes that shareholders will demand a rate of return of 17% and Director D believes the equity rate of return will shift to 28%. Assuming that the cost of borrowings before income taxes remains at 9%, what will the WACC and the value of the firm be under each of the directors' estimates?

   c Relate the results in question 3b to the capital structure debate. In particular draw on Modigliani and Miller's theory, financial distress and agency theory.   **?**

4 (*Examination level*) 'It is in management's interest to keep the financial gearing level as low as possible, while it is in shareholders' interests to keep it at a high level.' Discuss this statement.

5 (*Examination level*) In 1984 Stewart Myers wrote, 'our theories do not seem to explain actual financing behaviour', when referring to the capital structure debate. In what ways do the main MM economic models of gearing fail? Discuss some alternative explanations for the actual gearing levels of companies.

6 a (*Examination level*) Hickling plc has estimated the cost of debt and equity for various financial gearing levels:

Proportion of debt	Required rate of return	
$\dfrac{V_D}{(V_D + V_E)}$	Debt k_{DAT} %	Equity, k_E %
0.80	9.0	35.0
0.70	7.5	28.0
0.60	6.8	21.0
0.50	6.4	17.0
0.40	6.1	14.5
0.30	6.0	13.5
0.20	6.0	13.2
0.10	6.0	13.1
0.00	–	13.0

What is the optimal capital structure?

b   Describe and explain the factors which might lead to a rise in the overall cost of capital for Hickling.

7   (*Examination level*) The managing director of your firm is thinking aloud about an appropriate gearing level for the company:

> 'The consultants I spoke to yesterday explained that some academic theorists advance the idea that, if your object-ive is the maximisation of shareholder wealth, the debt to equity ratio does not matter. However, they did com-ment that this conclusion held in a world of no taxes. Even more strangely, these theorists say that in a world with tax it is best to "gear-up" a company as high as possible. Now I may not know much about academic theories but I do know that there are limits to the debt level which is desirable. After listening to these consultants, I am more confused than ever.'

You step forward and offer to write a report for the managing director both outlining the theoretical arguments and explaining the real-world influences on the gearing levels of firms.

8   (*Examination level*) Within a given industry, wide variations in the degree of financial gearing of firms are observed. What might explain this?

9   Given the following facts about Company X, what would the equity cost of capital be if it was transformed from its current gearing to having no debt, if Modigliani and Miller's model with no tax applied?

$$k_E = 30\%$$
$$k_D = 9\%$$
$$\frac{V_D}{(V_D + V_E)} = 0.6$$

Assignments

1   Obtain accounting and other information on a com-pany of interest to you and calculate gearing ratios. Point out in a report the difficulties involved in this process.

2   Analyse a company you know well in the light of the various ideas, theories and models regarding capital structure. Write up your findings in a report, and include implications and recommendations for action.

Dividend policy

LEARNING OUTCOMES

This area of finance has no neat over-arching theoretical model to provide a simple answer. However, there are some important arguments which should inform the debate within firms. By the end of this chapter the reader should be able to:

■ explain the rationale and conclusion of Miller and Modigliani's dividend irrelevancy hypothesis, as well as the concept of dividends as a residual;

■ describe the influence of particular dividend policies attracting different 'clients' as shareholders, the effect of taxation and the importance of dividends as a signalling device;

■ outline the hypothesis that dividends received now, or in the near future, have much more value than those in the far future because of the resolution of uncertainty and the exceptionally high discount rate applied to more distant dividends;

■ discuss the impact of agency theory on the dividend decision;

■ discuss the role of scrip dividends and share repurchase (buy-back).

'Dividend policy is often reported to shareholders, but seldom explained. A company will say something like, "Our goal is to pay out 40 per cent to 50 per cent of earnings and to increase dividends at a rate at least equal to the rise in the CPI."[1] And that's it – no analysis will be supplied as to why that particular policy is best for the owners of the business. Yet, allocation of capital is crucial to business and investment management. Because it is, we believe managers and owners should think hard about the circumstances under which earnings should be retained and under which they should be distributed.'

Source: Warren Buffett, a letter to shareholders attached to the *Annual Report of Berkshire Hathaway Inc* (1984). Reprinted with kind permission of Warren Buffett. © Warren Buffett.

Introduction

Dividends are distributions to shareholders. When a company has made a profit, it can distribute that profit, or part of it, to shareholders. The directors recommend the appropriate dividend and it is then approved, or not, by shareholders at the AGM. The question is – how much to pay out as a dividend.

As we saw in Chapter 12, retained profit is one of the most important sources of funds for firms and the more that is distributed as dividend the less there will be available as retained earnings for reinvestment. Directors have to determine a dividend policy which satisfies the needs of the business for reinvestment and the wishes of the shareholders.

No one has more right to speak on dividend policy than Warren Buffett, who has become a multi-billionaire by investing through the company he runs, Berkshire Hathaway. Mr Buffett invests in companies that pay out dividends but his own company, Berkshire Hathaway, does not pay out dividends. This is because Buffett believes that the company can use the cash more wisely by reinvesting it in new acquisitions or in share repurchases.

Buffett notes a need for a clear, consistent and rational dividend policy but this is not always available. On the issue of whether to retain profits, or distribute them to shareholders, there can be vagueness and confusion.

This chapter will review the major influences on the level of the dividend. Some company policies are fully 'rational' in the sense of the economist's model; others are less quantifiable, and stem more from the field of psychology.

Directors have to weigh up a range of forces – do they pay out a consistently high or low proportion of earnings? Do they provide a stable and consistent dividend, or do they vary the dividend? These are, of course, merely the forces influencing managers who are fully committed to shareholder wealth maximisation and thinking 'hard about the circumstances under which earnings should be retained'. If we recognise that some managers have other goals, the possible outcomes on the dividend level can range widely.

Defining the problem

Dividend policy is the determination of the proportion of profits to be paid out to shareholders – usually periodically. The issue to be addressed is whether shareholder wealth can be enhanced by altering the *pattern* of dividends not the *size* of dividends overall. Naturally, if dividends over the lifetime of a firm are larger, value will be greater. So, in the following analysis we will assume that:

a   the underlying investment opportunities and returns on business investment are constant; and

b   the extra value that may be created by changing the capital structure (the debt to equity ratio) is constant.

Therefore, only the pattern of dividend payments may add or subtract value. For example, perhaps a pattern of high pay-outs in the immediate future, with a consequential reduction in dividend growth thereafter, may be superior to a policy of zero or small dividends now followed by more rapid growth over time.

---

1 The CPI, consumer price index, is the main US measure of inflation.

Another aspect of the pattern question is whether a steady, stable dividend growth rate is better than a volatile one which varies from year to year depending on the firm's internal need for funds.

Some background

UK-quoted companies usually pay dividends every six months. In each financial year there is an interim dividend related to the first half-year's trading, followed by the final dividend after the financial year end. The board of directors recommend the dividend level but it is a right of shareholders as a body to vote at the annual general meeting on whether or not it should be paid. Not all companies follow the typical cycle of two dividends per year: a few pay dividends quarterly and others choose not to pay a dividend at all.

Dividends may only be paid out of accumulated distributable profits and not out of capital. This means that companies which have loss-making years may still pay dividends, but only up to the point that they have retained profits from previous years.[2] This rule is designed to provide protection to creditors by putting a barrier in the way of shareholders removing funds from the firm, and thereby withdrawing the cushion of capital. Further restrictions may be placed on the firm's freedom of action by constraints on dividend pay-outs contained in bond, preference share and bank-loan agreements.

The proportion of after-tax earnings paid as dividends varies greatly between firms, from zero to more than 100%. The average for European companies is usually around 40–50% – *see* **Exhibit 19.1**.

Exhibit 19.1

European pay-outs rise by more than 10%

Banks lead the way as dividends from Eurofirst 300 companies hit €187bn

By Alison Smith and Patrick Mathurin in London

Europe's largest companies have increased shareholder pay-outs by the highest annual amount since the financial crisis, largely driven by greater contributions from the banks.

Regular dividends from the Eurofirst 300 companies totalled €187.3bn in 2014, up more than 10% on the €169bn paid in 2013, according to analysis from Markit. However, the data provider forecast a more modest rise of nearly 7% to €200bn for 2015. The rise in shareholder pay-outs – which is higher than the increase in earnings – should help allay investor concerns that tougher regulatory requirements were making banks less attractive as investments.

Spain's Banco Santander paid out the biggest dividend of €7.72bn while Swiss consumer group Nestlé made the second-highest payment of €6.62bn.

Within the 2014 total, banks accounted for more than 16% of the overall amount, against 13.5% in 2013. It is their highest proportion since before 2010. US companies have also been increasing their dividends to shareholders. Total pay-outs for 2014 were 12% higher compared with the previous year. Markit forecasts dividend payments at US companies will increase a further 9% this year.

Despite European banks lagging behind their US rivals, their dividend growth was twice the level of the US. In Europe, bank pay-outs grew 32% while in the US they increased 17%. US banks contributed 6% to the total dividends, while in Europe the figure was 16%. The **average pay-out ratio in Europe in 2014 was 53%** – 9 percentage points higher than the 44% reported in 2010. More than half the relevant

---

2 A company cannot pay a dividend, even in a profitable year, if there are accumulated losses brought forward from earlier years that remain uncovered by previous years' retained profits in the balance sheet.

Eurofirst 300 companies raised their pay-out ratios last year while just one-quarter reduced them.

French carmaker Renault was among the groups cutting its pay-out ratio sharply. At a sectoral level, utilities were still the industry with the highest pay-out ratio, at 73%. However, this was down from 85% in 2013. Thomas Matheson, an analyst at Markit, said the 2014 reduction was partly the result of a big payment by Veolia in 2013 that was not repeated the following year. After utilities, the next biggest sector was telecoms at 65%. The largest proportionate increase in 2014 came from oil and gas companies, which increased their pay-out ratios by more than one-fifth to 62%, though the collapse in oil prices is putting pressure on dividend payments in 2015.

 Financial Times, 29 March 2015.
All Rights Reserved.

Miller and Modigliani's dividend irrelevancy proposition

According to a 1961 paper by Miller and Modigliani (MM), dividend policy is irrelevant to share value. MM stated that the determinant of value is the availability of projects with positive NPVs; and the pattern of dividends makes no difference. The share price would not move if the firm declared either a zero-dividend policy or a policy of high near-term dividends. The assumptions underlying their proposition included:

1   There are no taxes.

2   There are no transaction costs; for example:

    a   investors face no brokerage costs when buying or selling shares;

    b   companies can issue shares with no transaction costs.

3   All investors can borrow and lend at the same interest rate.

4   All investors have free access to all relevant information.

5   Investors are indifferent between dividends and capital gains.

Given these assumptions, dividend policy can become irrelevant. A firm which has plenty of positive NPV projects but nevertheless paid all profits each year as dividends would not necessarily be destroying shareholder wealth because, in this ideal world, any money paid out could quickly be replaced by having a new issue of shares.[3] The investors in these new shares, having access to all relevant information, would willingly pay a fair price. The shares can be issued by the firm without costs of underwriting or investment banks' fees, etc., and bought by the shareholders without brokers' fees or costs associated with the time spent filling in forms, etc. That is, there are no transaction costs.

    If a company chose not to pay dividends and shareholders required an income, this could be achieved while leaving the firm's value intact. 'Homemade dividends' can be created by shareholders selling a portion of their shares to other investors. With no transaction costs and no taxation, the effect is identical to the receipt of cash in the form of an ordinary dividend from the firm.

    Take the example of Belvoir plc, an all-equity company which has a policy of paying out all annual net cash flow as dividend. The company is expected to generate a net annual cash flow of £1m, and thus a dividend of £1m, forever. If the cost of equity capital is 12% we can calculate the value of this firm using the dividend valuation model including the £1m of dividend due to be paid immediately d_0 and the £1 perpetuity (with zero growth – *see* Chapter 17 for details).

$$P_0 = d_0 + \frac{d_1}{k_E} = £1m + \frac{£1m}{0.12} = £9.33m$$

---

3   The complicating effect of capital structure on firms' value is usually eliminated by concentrating on all-equity firms.

Now suppose that the management have identified a new investment opportunity, requiring a £1m investment now, which will produce additional cash flows of £180,000 per year starting in one year. There are two ways in which this investment could be funded. First, the managers could skip the present dividend and retain £1m. Alternatively, the company could maintain its dividend policy for this year and pay out £1m, but simultaneously launch a new issue of shares, say a rights issue, to gain the necessary £1m.

It will now be demonstrated that in this perfect world, with no transaction costs, shareholder value will be the same whichever dividend policy is adopted; what *will* increase shareholder value is the NPV of the project.

$$\text{NPV} = -£1\text{m} + \frac{£180,000}{0.12} = £500,000$$

The value of the firm is raised by £500,000, by the acceptance of the project and not because of the dividend policy. If the project is financed through the sacrifice of the present dividend the effect on shareholder wealth is:

Year	0	1	2	3, etc.
Cash flow to shareholders	0	1,180,000	1,180,000	1,180,000

$$\text{Shareholder's wealth} = \frac{1,180,000}{0.12} = £9.833\text{m}$$

Thus, shareholders' wealth is increased by £500,000.

If the project is financed through a rights issue while leaving the dividend pattern intact the effect on shareholder wealth is the same – an increase of £500,000.

Year	0	1	2	3, etc.
Cash flow to shareholders				
Receipt of dividend	+£1,000,000			
Rights issue	−£1,000,000			
	0	1,180,000	1,180,000	1,180,000

$$\text{Shareholder's wealth} = \frac{1,180,000}{0.12} = £9.833\text{m}$$

Shareholders' wealth is enhanced because £1m of shareholders' money is invested in a project which yields more than 12%. If the incremental cash inflows amounted to only £100,000 then the wealth of shareholders would fall, because a 10% return is insufficient given the opportunity cost of shareholders' money:

$$\frac{£1,100,000}{0.12} = £9.167\text{m}$$

If the new investment produces a 12% return shareholders will experience no loss or gain in wealth. The critical point is that in this hypothetical, perfect world the pattern of dividend makes no difference to shareholders' wealth which is determined purely by the investment returns.

If a firm chose to miss a dividend for a year, because it had numerous high-yielding projects to invest in, this would not decrease share values, because the perfectly well-informed investors would be aware that any cash retained will be going into positive NPV projects which will generate future dividend increases for shareholders. If a shareholder needs income, he/she can sell a proportion of shares held to create a 'homemade dividend' confident in the knowledge that a fair price would be obtained in this perfect world, which takes into account the additional value from the project.

Dividends as a residual

Imagine that the raising of external finance (for example rights issues) is so expensive that the only realistic source of finance for additional investment is earnings. Returning to the example of Belvoir, paying this year's dividend will reduce potential shareholder value by £500,000 because the new project will have to be abandoned.

In this 'retained earnings as funding' world, shareholders should only receive a dividend once the firm has financed all positive NPV projects. Investors are then given 'what's left' – the residual. They should receive this cash because they can use it to invest in other firms of the same risk class which provide an expected return at least as great as the required return on equity capital, k_E.

In these circumstances dividend policy becomes an important determinant of shareholder wealth:

1 If cash flow is retained and invested within the firm at less than k_E, shareholder wealth is destroyed; therefore, it is better to raise the dividend pay-out rate.

2 If retained earnings are insufficient to fund all positive NPV projects shareholder value is lost, and it would be beneficial to lower the dividend.

What about the world in which we live?

We have discussed two extreme positions so far and have reached opposing conclusions. In a perfect world the dividend pattern is irrelevant; the firm can always fund positive NPV projects costlessly and shareholders can costlessly generate 'homemade dividends' by selling some of their shares. In a world with no external finance the pattern of dividends becomes crucial to shareholder wealth, as an excessive pay-out reduces the ability to invest in positive NPV projects; and an unduly low pay-out means value destruction because investors miss out on investment opportunities elsewhere in the financial securities market.

In the real world there are transaction costs. If a firm pays a dividend to meet its dividend policy and then, in order to fund projects, needs to raise new funds through a rights issue, this is not frictionless: there are costs. The expenses include the legal and administrative costs of organising the issue of shares, the cost of a prospectus and advertising costs. Underwriting fees are normally about 2% of the amount raised but can be as much as 4%. Tax liabilities, which will be different for each individual shareholder, further complicate the issue.

Dividend policy makes a difference to the funds available for reinvestment in the company. This may explain why many young rapidly growing firms with a need for investment have a very low/zero dividend pay-out, whereas mature 'cash cow' firms can offer a high pay-out rate. In 2011 Sir Stelios thought that EasyJet had moved from being a fast-growing firm to one that should pay out large amounts in dividends – *see* **Exhibit 19.2**. A few months later it paid out £190m in dividends.

Exhibit 19.2

Founder demands special EasyJet pay-out

By Mark Odell

Sir Stelios Haji-Ioannou, the founder of EasyJet, has taken another pot-shot at the management of the UK low-cost airline by demanding a special dividend.

The airline had £1.44bn ($2.35bn) of gross cash at the end of March, falling to £220m when bank loans and aircraft lease obligations are netted off.

'The company's balance sheet is too lazy as a result of the previous absurd policy of zero dividends for 11 years after the IPO,' said Sir Stelios, the biggest single shareholder with control over a 38% stake.

Sir Stelios, who stepped down as chairman in November 2002, said the airline had £600m more in cash than the mandated board policy.

▶

Exhibit 19.2 *(continued)*

'I think shareholders would be better off if the board returned this surplus cash to them, so they can invest it in other businesses.'

Last May he quit the board and won a campaign to get the company to start paying regular dividends – the maiden pay-out will be announced at the full-year results this year.

Carolyn McCall, EasyJet's chief executive, said she planned to speak to shareholders over the next week and would 'keep the balance sheet under review', adding that it was 'too early to consider a request for a special dividend'.

The relationship between investment opportunity and dividend policy is a far from perfect one and there are several other forces pulling on management to select a particular policy. These will be considered after some more down-to-earth arguments from Warren Buffett (*see* **Exhibit 19.3** – sell-off policy means shareholders selling some shares to create homemade dividends).

| **Exhibit 19.3** | **Buffett on dividends** |

Dividends

A number of Berkshire shareholders – including some of my good friends – would like Berkshire to pay a cash dividend. It puzzles them that we relish the dividends we receive from most of the stocks that Berkshire owns, but pay out nothing ourselves. So, let's examine when dividends do and don't make sense for shareholders.

A profitable company can allocate its earnings in various ways (which are not mutually exclusive). A company's management should first examine reinvestment possibilities offered by its current business – projects to become more efficient, expand territorially, extend and improve product lines or to otherwise widen the economic moat separating the company from its competitors.

I ask the managers of our subsidiaries to unendingly focus on moat-widening opportunities, and they find many that make economic sense. But sometimes our managers misfire. The usual cause of failure is that they start with the answer they want and then work backwards to find a supporting rationale. Of course, the process is subconscious; that's what makes it so dangerous.

Your chairman has not been free of this sin. In Berkshire's 1986 annual report, I described how twenty years of management effort and capital improvements in our original textile business were an exercise in futility. I wanted the business to succeed and wished my way into a series of bad decisions. (I even bought another New England textile company.) But wishing makes dreams come true only in Disney movies; it's poison in business.

Despite such past miscues, our first priority with available funds will always be to examine whether they can be intelligently deployed in our various businesses. Our record $12.1 billion of fixed-asset investments and bolt-on acquisitions in 2012 demonstrate that this is a fertile field for capital allocation at Berkshire. And here we have an advantage: Because we operate in so many areas of the economy, we enjoy a range of choices far wider than that open to most corporations. In deciding what to do, we can water the flowers and skip over the weeds.

Even after we deploy hefty amounts of capital in our current operations, Berkshire will regularly generate a lot of additional cash. Our next step, therefore, is to search for acquisitions unrelated to our current businesses. Here our test is simple: Do Charlie and I think we can effect a transaction that is likely to leave our shareholders wealthier on a per-share basis than they were prior to the acquisition?

I have made plenty of mistakes in acquisitions and will make more. Overall, however, our record is satisfactory, which means that our shareholders are far wealthier today than they would be if the funds we used for acquisitions had instead been devoted to share repurchases or dividends.

But, to use the standard disclaimer, past performance is no guarantee of future results. That's particularly true at Berkshire: Because of our present size, making acquisitions that are both meaningful and sensible is now more difficult than it has been during most of our years.

Nevertheless, a large deal still offers us possibilities to add materially to per-share intrinsic value. BNSF is a case in point: It is now worth considerably more than our carrying value. Had we instead allocated the funds required for this purchase to dividends or repurchases, you and I would have been worse off. Though large transactions of the BNSF kind will be rare, there are still some whales in the ocean.

The third use of funds – repurchases – is sensible for a company when its shares sell at a meaningful discount to conservatively calculated intrinsic value. Indeed, disciplined repurchases are the surest way to use funds intelligently: It's hard to go wrong when you're buying dollar bills for 80¢ or less. We explained our criteria for repurchases in last year's report and, if the opportunity presents itself, we will buy large quantities of our stock. We originally said we would not pay more than 110% of book value, but that proved unrealistic. Therefore, we increased the limit to 120% in December when a large block became available at about 116% of book value.

But never forget: In repurchase decisions, price is all-important. Value is destroyed when purchases are made above intrinsic value. The directors and I believe that continuing shareholders are benefitted in a meaningful way by purchases up to our 120% limit.

And that brings us to dividends. Here we have to make a few assumptions and use some math. The numbers will require careful reading, but they are essential to understanding the case for and against dividends.

Aside from the favorable math, there are two further – and important – arguments for a sell-off policy. First, dividends impose a specific cash-out policy upon all shareholders. If, say, 40% of earnings is the policy, those who wish 30% or 50% will be thwarted. Our 600,000 shareholders cover the waterfront in their desires for cash. It is safe to say, however, that a great many of them – perhaps even most of them – are in a net-savings mode and logically should prefer no payment at all.

The sell-off alternative, on the other hand, lets each shareholder make his own choice between cash receipts and capital build-up. One shareholder can elect to cash out, say, 60% of annual earnings while other shareholders elect 20% or nothing at all. Of course, a shareholder in our dividend-paying scenario could turn around and use his dividends to purchase more shares. But he would take a beating in doing so: He would both incur taxes and also pay a 25% premium to get his dividend reinvested. (Keep remembering, open-market purchases of the stock take place at 125% of book value.)

The second disadvantage of the dividend approach is of equal importance: The tax consequences for all taxpaying shareholders are inferior – usually far inferior – to those under the sell-off program. Under the dividend program, all of the cash received by shareholders each year is taxed whereas the sell-off program results in tax on only the gain portion of the cash receipts.

Above all, dividend policy should always be clear, consistent and rational. A capricious policy will confuse owners and drive away would-be investors. Phil Fisher put it wonderfully 54 years ago in Chapter 7 of his Common Stocks and Uncommon Profits, a book that ranks behind only The Intelligent Investor and the 1940 edition of Security Analysis in the all-time-best list for the serious investor. Phil explained that you can successfully run a restaurant that serves hamburgers or, alternatively, one that features Chinese food. But you can't switch capriciously between the two and retain the fans of either.

Most companies pay consistent dividends, generally trying to increase them annually and cutting them very reluctantly. Our 'Big Four' portfolio companies follow this sensible and understandable approach and, in certain cases, also repurchase shares quite aggressively.

We applaud their actions and hope they continue on their present paths. We like increased dividends, and we love repurchases at appropriate prices.

At Berkshire, however, we have consistently followed a different approach that we know has been sensible and that we hope has been made understandable by the paragraphs you have just read. We will stick with this policy as long as we believe our assumptions about the book-value **build-up** and the market-price premium seem reasonable. If the prospects for either factor change materially for the worse, we will **re-examine** our actions.

Source: Warren Buffett, A letter to shareholders attached to the *Annual Report of Berkshire Hathaway Inc* (2013). Reprinted with kind permission of Warren Buffett. © Warren Buffett.

Clientele effects

Total return on shares is made up of two elements – dividends and capital growth. Some shareholders prefer income; others prefer greater capital growth. There may be natural clienteles for shares which pay out a high proportion of earnings, and another clientele for shares which have a low pay-out rate.

Retired people, living off their private investments, may prefer a steady income, so they would tend to be attracted to firms with a high and stable dividend yield. Likewise, pension funds need regular cash receipts to meet payments to pensioners. Shareholders who need a steady flow of income could generate a cash flow stream by selling off a proportion of their shares on a regular basis, but this approach will result in transaction costs (brokerage, market makers' spread and loss of interest while waiting for cash after sale). Also, it is time consuming and inconvenient to sell off blocks of shares regularly; it is much easier to receive a series of dividend cheques.

Furthermore, people often acknowledge self-control problems and so make rules for themselves, such as 'we will live off the income but never touch the capital' (Shefrin and Statman, 1984). They are afraid of selling off a proportion of shares each year in case they are tempted to over-indulge. Thus, shares with high dividends are attractive because they give income without the need to dig into capital.

Another type of clientele are not interested in receiving high dividends; they prefer to invest in companies with good growth potential; companies which pay low dividends and use the retained money to invest in projects with positive NPVs within the firm. Capital gains (a rising share price) will be the main way in which the shareholder receives a return. An example of such a clientele group might be wealthy middle-aged people who have more than enough income from their paid employment for their consumption needs. Equally those saving for University fees or for pensions want long-term growth not current dividends. If these people did receive large dividends now they would probably only reinvest it in the stock market. A cycle of receiving dividends followed by reinvestment is inefficient due to tax and transaction costs.

A significant proportion of shareholders choose to purchase shares in particular companies because the dividend policy suits them. This puts pressure on the management to maintain a stable and consistent dividend policy to satisfy these investors. Inconsistency would result in the client group selling their shares and would depress the share price. Management therefore, to some extent, attracts a particular clientele.[4]

The clientele force acting on dividend policy at first glance seems to be the opposite of the residual approach. With the clientele argument, stability and consistency are required to attract a particular type of clientele, whereas with the residual argument, dividends depend on the opportunities for reinvestment – the volume of which may vary in a random fashion from year to year, resulting in fluctuating retentions and dividends. Most firms seem to 'square this circle' by having a consistent dividend policy based on a medium- or long-term view of earnings and investment capital needs. The shortfalls and surpluses in particular years are adjusted through other sources of finance: for example, borrowing or raising equity through a rights issue in years when retained earnings are insufficient; paying off debt or storing up cash when retentions are greater than investment needs. There are costs associated with such a policy, for example the costs of rights issues, and these have to be weighed against the benefit of stability.

Exhibit 19.4 hints at strong clientele effects.

---

4 The following researchers present evidence on the clientele effect: Pettit (1977), Lewellen, Stanley, Lease and Schlarbaum (1978), Litzenberger and Ramaswamy (1982), Shefrin and Statman (1984), Crossland, Dempsey and Moizer (1991), Graham and Kumar (2006), Dhanani (2005) and Becker et al. (2011).

Exhibit 19.4

Telstra's first dividend cut for 20 years sends shares tumbling

Group's defensive move at odds with Australia's income-focused investing culture

By Jennifer Hughes in Hong Kong and Jamie Smyth in Sydney

Telstra shares plunged as much as 12 per cent after Australia's biggest telecoms group warned it would cut its dividend for the first time in 20 years – upending a central tenet of Australian stock investing. The company reported a one-third fall in actual full-year net profit as the benefits of a one-off sale last year disappeared. Based on continuing operations, profits rose 1 per cent. But investors reacted with horror to the dividend cut after Telstra said it would lower its pay-out for the next financial year by 29 per cent and direct the saved cash to investments.

"It is the magnitude of the cut and the abruptness of the cut in spite of a strong balance sheet that has shocked investors," said Brian Han, analyst at Morningstar. "I expected Telstra to cut gradually to 25 cents per share by fiscal 2021. But they have cut straight away to 22 cents per share. This came as a real shock to the market." Telstra's shares closed down 10.6 per cent at A$3.87 for the company's worst day in seven years. So far, this year, its shares are the second-worst performer in the ASX 100, down 24 per cent.

Australian investors prize dividends, as the country's franking system generates valuable tax credits for shareholders and offsets the double taxation of dividends common elsewhere. Critics of the system have, however, warned the pay-out culture risks incentivising shareholder returns over investment in expansion, a factor that has made some Australian companies risk-averse.

Big Australian companies are among the most generous in the world in paying dividends, with a pay-out ratio averaging 80 per cent, according to Bloomberg. That ranks them second just behind the UK's FTSE 350 and far ahead of S&P 500 companies, which average 50 per cent. Telstra typically pays out about 90 per cent of its profits but will cut that ratio to between 75 per cent and 90 per cent from next year to reinvest the cash in its business.

The company said: "We have consulted extensively with shareholders and other stakeholders during this review and the overwhelming and consistent feedback has been that planning for the longer term and retaining financial flexibility is a priority." Its decision is, however, one of only a handful of occasions where Australia's biggest dividend payers have cut pay-outs when not coming under extreme financial pressure. The country's biggest banks pared pay-outs after the financial crisis as they built reserves and, more recently, miners BHP Billiton and Rio Tinto slashed payments as commodity prices slumped. Like Telstra, both groups are staples of investor portfolios.

The telecoms group's decision comes as it faces significant challenges from rising competition and the rollout of competing technologies. For example, the government has established a National Broadband Network, which will result in the migration of Telstra's fixed-line customers to the new state-backed network – a move that will eat into its earnings. David Kaynes, analyst at Citi, which had warned a dividend cut was looming, welcomed Telstra's move but said it would not suit everyone. "Shareholders will need to adjust to the new dividend and capital policies and, in our view, yield-focused investors are likely to be disappointed with the new trajectory for dividends," he added.

The next factor we will examine, taxation, often reinforces the clientele effect.

Taxation

The taxation of dividends and capital gains on shares influences the preference of shareholders for receiving cash either in the form of a regular payment from the company (a dividend) or by selling shares (in the market to create homemade dividends or in a share buy-back – see later in the chapter). If shareholders are taxed more heavily on dividends than on capital gains they are more likely to favour shares which pay lower dividends. In the past, UK and US dividends were taxed at a significantly higher rate than that which applied to the capital gains made on the sale of shares. However, in recent years, the difference has narrowed significantly.

Dividends are taxed as income in the period in which they are received. The tax rates for 2017/2018 are 7.5% for basic rate taxpayers and 32.5% for higher rate taxpayers. In the UK capital gains are now taxed at 18–28% (depending on total taxable income). Investors can make annual capital gains of £11,300 (for 2017/2018) tax free. Furthermore, they only pay tax when the shares are sold. Therefore, they can delay payment by continuing to hold the shares or sell them in portions to take advantage of more than one year's capital allowance.

Dividends as conveyors of information

Dividends appear to act as important conveyors of information about companies. A dividend is regarded as a sign of how the directors view the prospects of the firm. An unusually large increase in the dividend is often taken to indicate an optimistic view about future profitability. A declining dividend often signals that the directors view the future with some pessimism.

The importance of the dividend as an information-transferring device occurs because of a significant market imperfection – information asymmetry. That is, managers know far more about the firm's prospects than do the finance providers. Investors are continually trying to piece together information about a firm. Dividends are one source that the investor can draw upon. They are used as an indicator of a firm's sustainable level of income. Managers choose a target dividend pay-out ratio based on the sustainable long-term earnings trend.[5]

It is the increase or decrease over the *expected* level of dividends that leads to a rise or fall in share price. This phenomenon is illustrated almost daily in the *Financial Times* as companies report falling profits but the market reacts by raising the share price because the company also signals confidence by raising the dividend by an unexpectedly large amount. **Exhibit 19.5** illustrates how the share price can rise despite a cut in dividend.

Exhibit 19.5

Severn Trent dividend cut invites marauders

By Neil Collins

When you have softened up the market to expect a 10 per cent cut in the dividend, a mere 5 per cent cut is considered a result. Which is why Severn Trent shares rose this week, as the last of the big water companies capitulated to the demands of the regulator, along with the usual blather about a fair balance between the interests of the shareholders and the customers.

The dividend, in the deathless prose of such setbacks, is to be "rebased", and look, we are hoping to raise it in line with the Retail Prices Index every year for the next five. How's that for sustainability? Of course, the five-year cycle of water regulation does make life harder for the companies than, say, running a bath, but dividend sustainability is measured in decades. Us shareholders like dependable divis.

"Rebasing" does serious damage to the idea that the income stream can be relied upon. Had Severn been under the cosh to protect its all-important credit

---

5 Lintner (1956) observed this. It was also recorded in a 3i (1993) survey, in which 93% of finance directors agreed with the statement that 'dividend policy should follow a long-term trend in earnings'. Baker, Powell and Veit (2002) found that more than 90% of Nasdaq company managers surveyed agreed that a firm should avoid increasing its regular dividend if it expected to reverse the decision in a year or so and the firm should strive to maintain an uninterrupted record of dividend payments. Brav et al. (2005) say that 'managers express a strong desire to avoid dividend cuts'.

rating, the cut would be understandable, even sensible. But the company is actually making its capital position worse by launching a £100m share buyback programme. The £10m a year saved from cutting the dividend looks hardly relevant by comparison.

The company bangs on about capital efficiency, and the difference between the balance sheet and the profit and loss account, but cash is cash is cash, and paying a dividend has (almost) exactly the same effect on the company finances as a share buyback. The clear winners from this move are the brokers who will handle the trades. There is no mention of

price. The intention is to keep buying (prudently, of course) until the money runs out.

Severn Trent is among the best-run water companies and two years ago it fought off a takeover approach at £22 a share, 25 per cent above its previous peak. A combination of good performance and plunging debt costs has finally closed that gap, but the Canadian pension fund that led the charge last time will also have adjusted its target returns to today's flatlining interest rates. This ill-judged cut to the dividend may be just what the marauders need to renew their assault.

Character Group raised its dividends to send a signal of confidence despite falling profits. However, the shares still fell due to underlying problems – *see* **Exhibit 19.6**.

Exhibit 19.6

Confidence call by Character

By Tom Burgis

Character Group raised its dividend on Tuesday in spite of a fall in profits, in a move designed to signal confidence that the toymaker was on the road to recovery following a product recall and a bleak Christmas.

Pre-tax profit tumbled to £3.25m for the six months to the end of February, against £7m last time, on revenue of £48.6m (£56.2m).

The shares fell 7p to 110p. A slump to a low of $68\frac{1}{2}$p last year knocked about £170m off its market

capitalisation and followed a recall of the Bindeez beads range after they were found to contain a chemical that acted similarly to a dangerous date-rape drug when ingested, and a pre-Christmas warning that festive sales would be disappointing.

Richard King, executive chairman, said cash of £10m and no debt justified the pay-out increase of 10% to 2.2p.

Generally, company earnings fluctuate to a far greater extent than dividends. This smoothing of the dividend flow is illustrated in **Exhibit 19.7** where Pearson has shown a rise and a fall in earnings per share but a steadily rising dividend for the 20 years to 2016. With an average of 64%, the dividend pay-out ratio has ranged from 46% to 99%.

In 2015, Pearson reported that, in response to challenging conditions, the Board planned to hold its dividend at this 2015 – 52p – level until 2020 while it 'rebuilt cover', reflecting the Board's confidence in the medium-term outlook. This was achieved for 2016 but Pearson then had to announce a 're-basing' of the dividend from 2017 onwards. First-half trading in 2017 saw the interim dividend reduced to 5p (2016 – 18p) alongside job losses and restructuring. As reported in **Exhibit 19.8** the final dividend of 10p is expected, reducing the total dividend sharply to 15p for 2017.

Exhibit 19.7	Pearson plc earnings and dividends, twenty-year record (pence per share)

Year	Earnings	Dividends
1997	31.2	17.4
1998	37.5	18.8
1999	43.3	20.1
2000	31.9	21.4
2001	22.5	22.3
2002	30.3	23.4
2003	27.6	24.2
2004	27.5	25.4
2005	34.1	27.0
2006	43.1	29.3
2007	46.7	31.6
2008	57.7	33.8
2009	65.4	35.5
2010	77.5	38.7
2011	86.5	42.0
2012	84.2	45.0
2013	70.1	48.0
2014	66.7	51.0
2015	70.3	52.0
2016	58.8	52.0

Source: Pearson website. Reprinted with permission.

Exhibit 19.8

Pearson to cut another 3,000 jobs and slash dividend. Education group seeks to restore investor confidence as losses narrow

By David Bond, Media Correspondent

Pearson is to cut 3,000 jobs as it pushes ahead with a £300m restructuring programme in an attempt to restore investor confidence after a series of profit warnings and record losses last year. The latest redundancies announced on Friday follow a cost-cutting drive that started in 2013 that resulted in 7,000 workers losing their job. By 2020, the education group and publisher aims to have reduced its workforce by 10,000, saving a total of £1bn.

The company also confirmed it would cut its interim dividend to 5p for the six months to the end of June,

from 18p for the same period in 2016. Finance chief Coram Williams said he anticipated the company would maintain its "one-third, two-thirds" dividend policy, meaning investors could expect a 10p dividend in the second half of the year.

The job losses are part of a long-term plan to make the company "leaner and more efficient", according to chief executive John Fallon, as Pearson attempts to transition from an "analogue" publishing business to a digital education company.

A reduction in earnings is usually not followed by a reduction in dividends, unless the earnings fall is perceived as likely to persist for a long time. Researchers, ever since Lintner's (1956) survey on managers' attitudes to dividend policy in the 1950s, have shown that directors are aware that the market reacts badly to dividend downturns and they make strenuous efforts to avoid a decline. By continuing the income stream to shareholders, management signals that a decline in earnings is temporary.

Equally, when times are good and profits are high directors tend to be cautious about large dividend rises. To increase dividends in good years risks having to reduce dividends should profits fall and damages the predictability and stability of dividends that are cherished by shareholders.

Signals are funny things. A number of the large US technology companies started paying dividends for the first time in the years 2000–4. In many cases the share price fell. The reason: investors took the dividends as a signal that the companies had run out of growth opportunities. A similar question was asked of Starbucks in 2010 – *see* **Exhibit 19.9**.

Exhibit 19.9

Dividend theory

The Lex Column

Nowhere do actions speak louder than words than in business. One of the best ways to understand whether a company is being run efficiently and in the best interests of shareholders is to watch what it does with its cash. What to make, therefore, of Starbucks' announcement last week that it intends to pay a dividend for the first time since it went public?

Assuming tax neutrality, investors in theory should not care whether companies pay a dividend or not.

All other things being equal too, companies should be indifferent as to whether they hoard cash or raise equity. What matters, therefore, is opportunity cost. Would the internal rate of return generated for shareholders be larger if cash was put to work by management or paid out?

Timing is everything. Forget the hogwash that rising dividends are a positive signal. Sometimes they are, sometimes they aren't. If a company has been growing rapidly with low pay-out ratios and suddenly increases its dividend, investors should question whether management is running short of investment ideas. This is what should be asked of Starbucks – now targeting a 35–40% pay-out ratio – although management swears it still has plenty of cash for investment.

There is nothing wrong with a company going ex-growth provided it recognises the fact by running its businesses for cash and, if it wishes, paying it out. There are two classic management mistakes to watch out for, however. First is a growing company upping dividends and buy-backs while not reinvesting enough in its business. Here investors should make sure capital expenditure-to-sales ratios do not start falling. The second, more common, mistake is mature or declining companies deluding themselves that they are still growth stocks. Starbucks appears to have avoided both extremes. Beware companies that do not.

 Financial Times, 5 April 2010, p. 16.
All Rights Reserved.

Resolution of uncertainty

Myron Gordon (1963) argued that investors perceive that a company, by retaining and reinvesting a part of its current cash flow, is replacing a certain dividend flow to shareholders now with an uncertain more distant flow in the future. Because the returns from any reinvested funds will occur in the far future they are therefore subject to more risk and investors apply a higher discount rate than they would to near-term dividends. Thus, the market places a greater value on shares offering higher near-term dividends. Investors are showing a preference for the early resolution of uncertainty. Under this model investors use a set of discount rates which rise through time to calculate share values; therefore, the dividend valuation model becomes:

$$P_0 = \frac{d_1}{1 + k_{E1}} + \frac{d_2}{(1 + k_{E2})^2} + \dots + \frac{d_n}{(1 + k_{En})^n} + \dots$$

where:

$$k_{E1} < k_{E2} < k_{E3} \dots$$

The dividends received in Years 2, 3 or 4 are of lower risk than those received seven, eight or nine years hence.

The crucial factor here may not be actual differences in risk between the near and far future, but *perceived* risk. It may be that immediate dividends are valued more highly because the investors' perception of risk is not perfect. They overestimate the risk of distant dividends and thus undervalue them. However, whether the extra risk attached to more distant dividends is real or not, the effect is the same – investors prefer a higher dividend in the near term than they otherwise would and shareholder value can be raised by altering the dividend policy to suit this preference – or so the argument goes.

There have been some impressive counter-attacks on what is described as the 'bird-in-the-hand fallacy'. The riskiness of a firm's dividend derives from the risk associated with the underlying business and this risk is already allowed for through the risk-adjusted discount rate, k_E. To discount future income even further would be excessive. Take a company expected to produce a dividend per share of £1 in two years and £2 in ten years. The discount rate of, say, 15% ensures that the £2 dividend is worth, in present value terms, less than the dividend received in two years, and much of this discount rate is a compensation for risk.

$$\text{Present value of £1 dividend} = \frac{£1}{(1.15)^2} = 75.6\text{p}$$

$$\text{Present value of £2 dividend} = \frac{£2}{(1.15)^{10}} = 49.4\text{p}$$

Alternatively, take a company which pays out all its earnings in the hope of raising its share price because shareholders have supposedly had resolution of uncertainty. Now, what is the next move? We have a company in need of investment finance and shareholders wishing to invest in company shares – as most do with dividend income. The firm has a rights issue. In the prospectus the firm explains what will happen to the funds raised: they will be used to generate dividends in the future. Thus, shareholders buy shares on the promise of future dividends; they discount these dividends at a risk-adjusted discount rate determined by the rate of return available on alternative, equally risky investments, say, 15% (applicable to *all* the future years). To discount at a higher rate would be to undervalue the shares and pass up an opportunity of a good investment.

Owner control (agency theory)

Many people take the view that firms pay out an excessive proportion of their earnings as dividends. The argument then runs that this stifles investment because of the lower retention rate.

However, set alongside this concern should go the observation that many firms seem to have a policy of paying high dividends, and then, shortly afterwards, issuing new shares to raise cash for investment. This is a perplexing phenomenon. The cost of issuing shares can be burdensome and shareholders generally pay tax on the receipt of dividends. One possible answer is that it is the signalling (information) value of dividends that drives this policy. But the costs are so high that it cannot always be explained by this. A second potential explanation lies with agency cost.

Managers (the agents) may not always act in the best interests of the owners. One way for the owners to regain some control over the use of their money is to insist on relatively high pay-out ratios. Then, if managers need funds for investment they have to ask. A firm that wishes to raise external capital will have its plans for investment scrutinised by a number of experts, including:

- investment bankers who advise on the issue;
- underwriters who, like investment bankers, will wish to examine the firm and its plans as they are attaching their good names to the issue;
- analysts at credit-rating agencies;
- analysts at stockbroking houses who advise shareholders and potential shareholders;
- shareholders and fund managers.

In ordinary circumstances the firm's investors can only influence managerial action by voting at a general meeting (which is usually ineffective due to apathy and the use of proxy votes by the board), or by selling their shares. When a company has to ask for fresh capital investors can tease out more information and can examine managerial action and proposed actions. They can exercise some control over their savings by refusing to buy the firm's securities if they are at all suspicious of managerial behaviour. Of particular concern might be the problem of investment in projects with negative NPV for the sake of building a larger managerial empire (Easterbrook, 1984; Jensen 1986).

A more generous view, from the field of behavioural finance, is that managers are merely over-optimistic and over-confident about their ability to invest the money wisely.

From the viewpoint of lenders there is also an agency problem. Managers may pay out excessive dividends to shareholders to keep the money out of the reach of the lenders – particularly in the case of a company likely to fail. Thus, lenders' agreements often restrict dividend payments.

Exhibit 19.10 discusses an implicit bargain in which companies return to investors capital they do not need, on the understanding that it will be returned to the company when it is needed.

Exhibit 19.10

Lurid acquisitions lose their edge as the retro dividend makes a comeback

Shareholders are pushing companies to return surplus cash instead of pursuing the vagaries of capital appreciation

writes Henry Tricks

There was a fashion statement buried deep in French Connection's interim results yesterday that had nothing to do with fcuk, and everything to do with the dowdy world of dividends.

In an era of bare midriffs, the UK corporate sector is revisiting a fashion that dates back to a time when City gents wore bowler hats and bow ties.

After a long spell in the cold, the dividend is making a comeback. Bankers say there is such pressure on companies to hand back cash to shareholders that some are forsaking the lurid world of acquisitions as a result.

Yesterday, French Connection, the fashion retailer, showed its commitment to the dividend with a 20% half-year increase – double the rate of earnings growth – in spite of headwinds in the UK high streets. Redrow, the housebuilder, also raised its dividend 20%, pledging to do the same for the next three years even if the housing market cooled.

Merrill Lynch, meanwhile, said yesterday that for the second month running its monthly survey of 290 global fund managers showed more preferred companies to return cash than increase capital spending or improve balance sheets.

▶

Exhibit 19.10 *(continued)*

This represented a significant change from 2002 and 2003, which is as far back as Merrill's survey goes.

'It's a story that's still gathering momentum,' said David Bowers, Merrill's chief global investment strategist. 'The economy isn't strong enough to justify increased capex, but it isn't really weak enough to persuade companies to rebuild their balance sheets.'

The watershed for dividend payments started across the Atlantic this summer when Microsoft risked its established rating as a growth company by agreeing to pay $32bn in a special dividend this year, and $44bn in buy-backs and an enhanced dividend over the next four years . . .

Michael Tory, head of UK investment banking at Morgan Stanley, said the UK was far ahead of its continental European counterparts in getting the message.

The backdrop, he said, was the period of balance sheet repair that went on after the dotcom collapse, which had put much of corporate Britain on a

sounder fiscal footing. However, the uncertain economic outlook, together with a more disciplined and selective approach towards mergers and acquisitions, meant companies had more surplus cash. This combination had intensified investor pressure to return cash, he said.

'The implicit bargain is that companies that are well managed and return capital they don't immediately need will be supplied if they do change their minds and need the capital back,' Mr Tory said.

In boardrooms, the debate about what to do with cash on the balance sheet is often tense. Returning it to shareholders is not the virile growth sport executives are used to. Often, non-executive directors will have to fight the shareholders' corner.

It is also feared that returning too much cash to shareholders can carry risks, however. Companies should not liquidate their cash balances to please investors if that jeopardises their ability to compete on the global stage . . .

Scrip dividends

A scrip dividend gives shareholders an opportunity to receive additional shares in proportion to their existing holding instead of a cash dividend. The shareholders can then either keep the shares or sell them for cash. From the company's point of view scrip dividends have the advantage that *cash does not leave the company.* This may be important for companies going through difficult trading periods or as a way of adjusting the gearing (debt to equity) ratio. Shareholders may welcome a scrip dividend because they can increase their holdings without brokerage costs and other dealing costs.

An enhanced scrip dividend is one where the shares offered are worth substantially more than the alternative cash pay-out. Such an offer is designed to encourage the take-up of shares and is like a mini-rights issue.

Share buy-backs and special dividends

An alternative way to return money, held within the company, to the owners is to repurchase issued shares. For the 12 months to March 2017, S&P500 companies spent $508 billion on share repurchases (2016 – £589 bn, a drop of 14%).

Buy-backs are a useful alternative when the company is unsure about the sustainability of an increase in the normal cash dividend. A stable policy on dividends is retained and when surplus cash arises, shares are repurchased. This two-track approach avoids sending an over-optimistic signal about future growth.

A second approach to returning funds, without signalling that all future dividends will be raised abnormally, is to pay a special dividend. This is the same as a normal dividend but usually bigger and paid on a one-off basis. A special dividend must be offered to all shareholders.

Share repurchases are permitted under UK law, subject to the requirement that the firm gain the permission of shareholders as well as warrant holders, option holders or convertible holders. The rules of the London Stock Exchange (and especially the Takeover Panel) must also be obeyed. These are generally aimed at avoiding the creation of an artificial market in the company's shares.

However, a share repurchase may not always be open to all shareholders as it can be accomplished in one of three ways:

a   purchasing shares in the stock market;

b   all shareholders are invited to sell some, or all, of their shares;

c   an arrangement with particular shareholders.

Share buy-backs have the advantage over special dividends by giving shareholders a choice – they can retain their shares or sell their shares back to the company for cash. The individual shareholder's tax position may mean that they prefer to hold on to their shares anticipating rising share prices. After the share buy-back there will be fewer shares in issue; therefore, if earnings can be maintained despite the cash out-flow, the earnings per share and share price should increase.

A buy-back is often seen as a signal that the managerial team is not holding on to cash to empire build for their own glory. However, there is always the danger that buy-backs are conducted to provide short-term boosts to the share price and earnings per share rather than for rational long-term shareholder wealth enhancement. The fashion for high borrowings in the mid-2000s led to many buy-backs at a high share price, say, £5 followed by a desperate attempt to raise equity after 2008 by selling shares for, say, £1 per share. A similar pattern is emerging in 2017–18. Existing shareholders are not pleased when outsiders buy a portion of the company at such low values.

Buy-backs and special dividends vary in popularity. Sometimes the market responds positively but they are not always regarded as 'good news'. Investors' response to share buy-backs may depend on why companies announce repurchase programmes. Are repurchases made from the residual cash flow after investment spending or do companies repurchase shares instead of investing, thus potentially missing opportunities for longer term growth? – *see* **Exhibit 19.11**, **Exhibit 19.12** and **Exhibit 19.13**.

A round-up of the arguments

There are two questions at the core of the dividend policy debate.

- *Question 1* Can shareholder wealth be increased by changing the pattern of dividends over a period of years?

- *Question 2* Is a steady, stable dividend growth rate better than one which varies from year to year depending on the firm's internal need for funds?

Exhibit 19.11

Diageo hits record after share buy-back announcement

By Mehreen Khan

Diageo shares are sitting pretty at the top of the FTSE 100 this morning after the world's largest distiller announced a £1.5bn share buy-back programme. The company behind Smirnoff vodka and Johnnie Walker scotch also raised its margin forecast from 100bps to 175bps for the full year as it announced a rise in organic sales and profits in 2016/17.

Shares are up 5.5 per cent at publication time to a fresh record of £23.90. Phil Carroll, analyst at Shore Capital, said: "There are still challenges in a number of markets but the group as a whole is looking to have strong momentum, and notably enough for management to launch a surprise buyback which given recent acquisition activity is somewhat of a surprise and upgrade margin guidance."

Exhibit 19.12

Why big and small groups love to buy back shares

But companies must be able to prove it is the best use of cash for investors

By Kate Burgess

It is not just vast companies settling into their mature years that retire stock. Thousands of companies from the multinational Unilever to the tiniest companies are buying their own shares. About the titchiest company in the UK to buy back shares this year is IndigoVision, the video security designer with a market capitalisation of £18m. And just last week the smallish Domino's Pizza in the UK announced it would spend £15m on repurchasing its shares.

US companies have spent more than $2.2tn on buy backs in the past six years, according to Société Générale, although they began to abate last year. Bankers, traders and executives, not to mention Warren Buffett, love a good share buy-back, it seems.

In general, say fans, it makes sense to convert expensive equity into cheaper debt when interest rates are low. Buy backs are tax efficient and lift earnings per share and share prices. That in turn raises portfolio valuations. Then there is the gratifying effect on bosses' bonuses linked to earnings per share. WH Smith, the ex-growth stationer, is proof of how companies can shrink to raise returns on investment to record levels.

Domino's Pizza, though, aspires to being "the number one pizza company in the world". Recent same-store sales growth slowed to 2 per cent in the first half of the year. But overall revenues rose 10 per cent. Using valuable resources to shrink the capital base seems counter-intuitive, if not risky, for a business that is still relatively small and bent on expansion — like sticking a "not-wanted-on-voyage" label on a ship's ballast.

However, the group operates through franchises. It has a capital light model, pays a dividend, plans to spend £60m on capital projects in 2017 and says debt will not exceed 1.25 times its earnings before interest, tax and other financial nasties. And its shares are trading at about 18 times earnings forecasts for 2018.

The buyback announced by Trinity Mirror, the newspaper group, last year arguably makes more sense. Its pension deficit is many times its market capitalisation. But it has been reducing debt, contributing into the pension pot, paying a dividend and £10m isn't a lot, say apologists.

Still, some analysts see repurchasing stock as a market heresy. They believe repurchasing programmes are a kind of sleight of hand, transferring value from those who hold on to shares to those wanting an exit. Rises in share prices and earnings per share are fleeting, they say. There is little positive effect on long-term returns, particularly if groups use debt to pay for shares. McKinsey consultants say companies would do better to pay off borrowings, increase dividends or invest in other ways.

Recent research from Andrew Lapthorne, analyst at Société Générale, shows most businesses that buy back shares are "weak" and "negatively correlated" to fast-growing companies with strong balance sheets and higher levels of profitability. That will chime with the cynics who say executives start buying in shares when they have run out of ideas, knowing that they will not be fired for returning cash to shareholders but they might be fired for poorly executed M&A.

Buybacks are widely misunderstood, counters the cerebral Lord Wolfson of Aspley Guise, boss of retailer Next. They do not work as share support schemes but they do deliver value, because they increase profits per share. However, the maths work for Next, which has been buying in shares since 1999, because Lord Wolfson has a formula to ensure that Next earns more by buying its own shares than, say, opening new shops or investing in a new business. And Next only buys in shares after it has paid a dividend. "We have never allowed our share buyback programme to threaten our investment-grade status," Lord Wolfson says.

Other bosses show less self-control. The argument will rage on. Boards will continue to succumb to the perceived advantages. But if they want to sidestep accusations of market heresy, they should follow the Wolfson rule book. A vague plan to reward shareholders for their patience will not do. They must be able to prove it is the best use of shareholders' cash. And they need to be sure it is the right time to tell investors to take their money elsewhere.

Exhibit 19.13

Buyback trade' fizzles as stock repurchases slow

The rewards to companies that buy back shares have declined along with the practice

By Robin Wigglesworth, US markets editor

The lucrative "buyback trade", that rewarded investors who bought shares in US companies actively repurchasing their own stock, has fizzled this year, even as the market has marched to record highs. Corporate share buybacks have been the single biggest source of demand for US equities since the financial crisis, as companies largely shunned business investment plans in favour of ploughing their earnings – and, increasingly, borrowed money – into their own stock. But the buyback spree began to abate last year and companies have sharply reduced the purchases of their own shares in 2017, while the market rewards for generous buyback programmes have faded.

Low rates benefited investors more than ordinary Americans This year the S&P 500 Buyback index – which consists of 100 large US companies repurchasing the greatest proportion of their shares – has returned 9.6 per cent including dividends, while the broader stock market index has returned 13.3 per cent. That is a reversal of relative fortune. Between the start of 2009 and the end of 2016, the buyback index gained 266 per cent, compared to the broader market's 145 per cent gain. "In the

short run buybacks can help with window-dressing [improving a company's earnings per share] but in the longer run what is rewarded more is dividends, and we are seeing them come to the fore again," said Kristina Hooper, global market strategist at Invesco.

For the 12 months ending June 2017, S&P 500 companies spent just over $500bn on buybacks, according to S&P Dow Jones, down 14.5 per cent from the preceding 12 months. Ms Hooper said that downward shift was probably caused by elevated equity valuations and rising scepticism around what the Trump administration could achieve on tax reform and economic growth. "There could be some policy uncertainty coming to the fore, with the reality setting in about what we can actually expect to see from the administration," she said.

Apple, Charter Communications, JPMorgan Chase, Home Depot and Boeing were the biggest repurchasers of their own stock in the second quarter. Apple's buybacks alone were almost equivalent to the next three biggest combined, even though the iPhone maker trimmed the size of its programme modestly.

The answer to the first question is 'yes'. The accumulated evidence suggests that shareholders for one reason or another value patterns of dividends across time. However, there is no neat, straightforward formula into which we can plug numbers to calculate the best pattern. It depends on numerous factors, many of which are unquantifiable, ranging from the type of clientele shareholder the firm is trying to attract to changes in the taxation system.

Taking the residual theory alone the answer to Question 2 is that the dividend will vary from year to year because the dividend paid out is what is left over after the firm has retained funds for investment in all available projects with positive NPVs. Dividends will be larger in years of high cash flow and few investment opportunities, and will be reduced when the need for reinvestment is high relative to internally generated cash flow. However, in practice, shareholders appear to prefer stable, consistent dividend growth rates. Many of them rely on a predictable stream of dividends to meet (or contribute to) their consumption needs. They would find an erratic dividend flow inconvenient. Investors also use dividend policy changes as an information signal of a firm's prospects. A reduced dividend could send an incorrect signal and depress the share price.

So many factors influence dividend policy that it is very difficult to imagine that someone could develop a universally applicable model which would allow firms to identify an optimal pay-out ratio. **Exhibit 19.14** shows the range of forces pulling managers towards a high pay-out rate, and

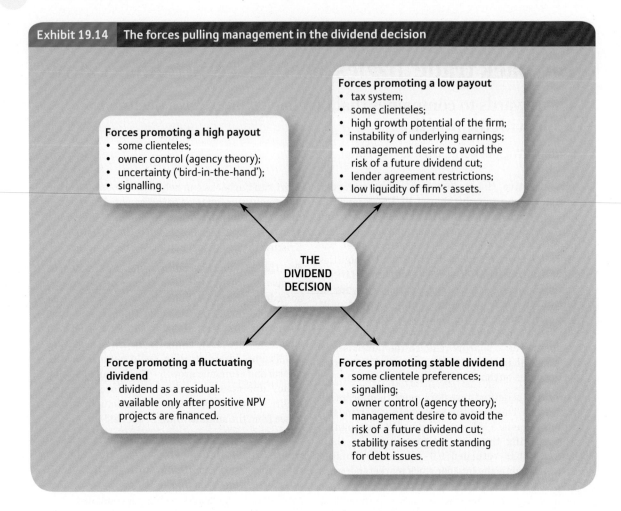

Exhibit 19.14   The forces pulling management in the dividend decision

Forces promoting a high payout
- some clienteles;
- owner control (agency theory);
- uncertainty ('bird-in-the-hand');
- signalling.

Forces promoting a low payout
- tax system;
- some clienteles;
- high growth potential of the firm;
- instability of underlying earnings;
- management desire to avoid the risk of a future dividend cut;
- lender agreement restrictions;
- low liquidity of firm's assets.

THE DIVIDEND DECISION

Force promoting a fluctuating dividend
- dividend as a residual: available only after positive NPV projects are financed.

Forces promoting stable dividend
- some clientele preferences;
- signalling;
- owner control (agency theory);
- management desire to avoid the risk of a future dividend cut;
- stability raises credit standing for debt issues.

other forces pulling towards a low pay-out rate. Simultaneously, there are forces encouraging a fluctuating dividend and other factors promoting a stable dividend.

Most of the factors in Exhibit 19.14 have already been explained, but there are two which need a comment here: liquidity and credit standing. Dividends require an outflow of cash from firms; therefore, companies with plenty of liquid assets, such as cash and marketable securities, are more able to pay a dividend. Other firms, despite being highly profitable, may have very few liquid assets. For example, a rapidly growing firm may have a large proportion of its funds absorbed by fixed assets, inventory and debtors. Thus, some firms may have greater difficulty paying cash dividends than others.

Lenders generally prefer to entrust their money to stable rather than erratic firms, as this reduces risk. A consistent dividend flow suggests stability and therefore helps to raise the credit standing of the firm, lowering the interest rates payable. Creditors suffer from information asymmetry as much as shareholders and therefore look to the dividend decision for an indication of managerial confidence about the firm's prospects.

Concluding comments

This section considers a possible practical dividend policy, considering the various arguments presented in the chapter.

Most large firms forecast their financial position for a few years ahead. Their forecasts will include projections for fixed capital expenditure and additional investment in working capital as well as sales, profits, etc. This information, combined with a specified target debt to equity ratio, allows an estimation of medium- to long-term cash flows.

These companies can then determine a sustainable dividend level that will leave sufficient retained earnings to meet the financing needs of their investment projects without having to resort to selling shares. (Not only does issuing shares involve costs of issue but, as described in Chapter 18, investors sometimes view share issues as a negative signal.) Thus, a maintainable regular dividend on a growth path is generally established, providing some certainty to a particular clientele group and reducing the likelihood of sending misleading signals. At the same time the residual theory conclusions have been recognised, and (over, say, a five-year period) dividends are intended to be roughly the same as surplus cash flows after financing all investment in projects with a positive NPV. Agency costs are alleviated to the extent that managers do not, over the long run, store up (and misapply) cash flows greater than those necessary to finance high-return projects.

The future is uncertain and so companies may consider their financial projections under various scenarios. They may focus particularly on the negative possibilities. Dividends may be set at a level low enough that, if poorer trading conditions do occur, the firm is not forced to cut the dividend. Thus, a margin for error is introduced by lowering the pay-out rate.

Companies that are especially vulnerable to macroeconomic volatility, such as those in cyclical industries, are likely to be tempted to set a relatively low maintainable regular dividend to avoid the dreaded consequences of a reduced dividend in a particularly bad year. In years of plenty directors can pay out surplus cash in the form of special dividends or share repurchases. This policy of low regular pay-outs supplemented with irregular bonuses allows shareholders to recognise that the pay-outs in good years might not be maintained at the extraordinary level. Therefore, they do not interpret them as a signal that profits growth will persist at this high level.

If a change in dividend policy becomes necessary, then firms are advised to make a gradual adjustment, as a sudden break with a trend can send an erroneous signal about the firms' prospects. And, of course, the more information shareholders are given concerning the reasons behind a change in policy, the less likelihood there is of a serious misinterpretation.

Firms in different circumstances are likely to exhibit different pay-out ratios. Those with plentiful investment opportunities will, in general, opt for a relatively low dividend rate as compared with that exhibited by companies with few such opportunities. Each type of firm is likely to attract a clientele favouring its dividend policy. For example, investors in fast-growth, high-investment firms are prepared to accept low (no) near-term dividends in return for the prospect of higher capital gains.

A suggested action plan

A suggested action plan for a dividend policy is as follows.

1 Forecast the 'surplus' cash flow resulting from the subtraction of the cash needed for investment projects from that generated by the firm's operations over the medium to long term.

2 Pay a sustainable regular dividend based on this forecast. This may be biased on the conservative side to allow for uncertainty about future cash flows.

3 If cash flows are greater than projected for a particular year, keep the maintainable regular dividend constant (hopefully with stable growth), but pay a special dividend or initiate a share repurchase programme. If the change in cash flows is permanent, gradually shift the maintainable regular dividend while providing as much information to investors as possible about the reasons for the change in policy.

Key points and concepts

- **Dividend policy** concerns the pattern of dividends over time and the extent to which they fluctuate from year to year.

- UK-quoted companies generally pay dividends every six months – an **interim** and a **final**. They may only be paid out of distributable profits.

- **Miller and Modigliani** proposed that, in a perfect world, the policy on dividends is irrelevant to shareholder wealth. Firms can **finance investments** from retained earnings or new share sales at the same cost (with no transaction costs). Investors are able to manufacture '**homemade dividends**' by selling a portion of their shareholding.

- In a world with **no external finance dividend policy should be residual.**

- In a world with some transaction costs associated with issuing dividends and obtaining investment finance through the sale of new shares, dividend policy will be influenced by, but not exclusively determined by, the 'dividends as a residual approach' to dividend policy.

- The **clientele effect** is the concept that shareholders are attracted to firms that follow dividend policies consistent with their objectives. The clientele effect encourages stability in dividend policy.

- **Taxation** can influence the investors' preference for the receipt of high dividends or capital gains from their shares.

- **Dividends can convey information.** An unexpected change in dividends is regarded as a **signal** of how directors view the prospects of the firm.

- It has been argued (e.g. by Myron Gordon) that **investors perceive more distant dividends as subject to more risk;** therefore they prefer a higher near-term dividend – a 'bird in the hand'. This **'resolution of uncertainty'** argument has been attacked because it implies an extra risk premium on the rate used to discount cash flows.

- The **owner control** argument says that firms are encouraged to distribute a high proportion of earnings so that investors can reduce the **principal–agent problem** and achieve greater goal congruence. Managers have to ask for investment funds; this subjects their plans to scrutiny.

- A **scrip dividend** gives the shareholders an opportunity to receive additional shares in proportion to their existing holding instead of the normal cash dividend.

- A **share repurchase** is when the company buys a proportion of its own shares from investors.

- A **special dividend** is similar to a normal dividend but is usually bigger and paid on a one-off basis.

References and further reading

Alzahrani, M. and Laffer, M. (2012) 'Investor protection, taxation, and dividends', *Journal of Corporate Finance,* 18, pp. 745–62.

Firms in strong investor protection countries pay lower cash dividends than in weak protection countries when the classical tax system is implemented, but they repurchase more shares to maximise their shareholders' after-tax returns. In weak protection countries, cash dividends and repurchases are low and less responsive to taxes.

Baker, H.K., Powell, G.E. and Veit E.T. (2002) 'Revisiting managerial perspectives on dividend policy', *Journal of Economics and Finance,* 26(3), pp. 267–83.

Evidence for avoidance of dividend cuts and the maintenance of dividend continuity.

Baker, M. and Wurgler, J. (2004) 'A catering theory of dividends', *Journal of Finance,* 59(3), June, pp. 1125–65.

'Managers give investors what they currently want.'

Becker, B., Ivković, Z. and Weisbenner, S. (2011) 'Local dividend clienteles', *Journal of Finance,* 66(2), pp. 655–83.

Older investors prefer dividend paying shares.

Black, F. (1976) 'The dividend puzzle', *Journal of Portfolio Management,* 2, pp. 5–8.

A consideration of the issue by a leading writer in the field.

Brav, A., Graham, J.R., Harvey, C.R. and Michaely, R. (2005) 'Pay-out policy in the 21st century', *Journal of Financial Economics,* 77, pp. 483–527.

A survey of US executives. Confirms Lintner's (1956) observation that perceived stability of future earnings affects dividend policy. Signalling is asymmetric; therefore, firms are reluctant to cut dividend.

Brennan, M. (1971) 'A note on dividend irrelevance and the Gordon valuation model', *Journal of Finance,* December, pp. 1115–21.

A technical discussion of the opposing theories of MM and Gordon.

Breuer, W., Rieger, M.O. and Soypak, K.C. (2014) 'The behavioural foundations of corporate dividend policy: A cross-country approach', *Journal of Banking and Finance,* 42, pp. 247–65.

A panel analysis across 29 countries and over 43,000 firm-years demonstrates that their model studying the relation between dividends and patience, loss aversion, and ambiguity aversion can be verified empirically.

Crossland, M., Dempsey, M. and Moizer, P. (1991) 'The effect of cum- to ex-dividend changes on UK share prices', *Accounting and Business Research,* 22(85), pp. 47–50.

'Our statistical analysis provides evidence of the clientele effect in the UK stock market' – shareholders in the high-income, low capital gains tax bracket hold shares in high-growth companies and shareholders with low income and in the high capital gains tax bracket hold shares in low-growth companies.

Damodaran, A. (2014) *Applied Corporate Finance.* 4th edition. New York: Wiley.

Chapters 10 and 11 consider dividend policy and cash returned to shareholders in a practical exposition.

Desai, M. and Jin, L. (2011) 'Institutional tax clienteles and pay-out policy', *Journal of Financial Economics,* 100, pp. 68–84.

A survey of UK managers. Signalling and clienteles (with the influence of tax) are apparent.

The tax preferences of institutional shareholders and firm pay-out policy may reflect dividend-averse institutions gravitating towards low dividend paying firms or managers adapting their pay-out policies to the interests of their institutional shareholders. Evidence shows that both effects are operative.

Dhanani, A. (2005) 'Corporate dividend policy: The views of British financial managers', *Journal of Business Finance and Accounting,* 32(7) and (8), Sept/Oct, pp. 1625–72.

A survey of UK managers. Signalling and clienteles (with the influence of tax) are apparent.

Drobetz, W., Grüninger, M. and Hirschvogl, S. (2010) 'Information asymmetry and the value of cash', *Journal of Banking and Finance,* 34, pp. 2168–84.

Considers the pecking order theory and the free cash flow theory in relation to the market value of a marginal dollar of cash. The results support the free cash flow theory and indicate that the value of corporate cash holdings is lower in states with a higher degree of information asymmetry.

Easterbrook, F.H. (1984) 'Two *agency-cost* explanations of dividends', *American Economic Review,* 74(4), September pp. 650–60.

Managers may act in their own self-interest. Agency cost explanation of dividends.

Ferris, S.P., Noronha, G. and Unlu, E. (2010) 'The more, merrier: An international analysis of the frequency of dividend payment', *Journal of Business Finance and Accounting,* 37(1), (2) pp. 148–70.

Investors receive a higher utility when a given level of dividends is paid more frequently – firm value rises with greater frequency.

Floyd E., Li, N. and Skinner D. (2015) 'Pay-out policy through the financial crisis: The growth of repurchases and the resilience of dividends', *Journal of Financial Economics,* 118(2) pp. 299–316.

Banks use dividends to indicate financial strength.

Gordon, M.J. (1959) 'Dividends, earnings and stock prices', *Review of Economics and Statistics,* 41, May, pp. 99–105.

Discusses the relationship between dividends, earnings and share prices.

Gordon, M.J. (1963) 'Optimal investment and financing policy', *Journal of Finance,* May.

A refutation of the MM dividend irrelevancy theory based on the early resolution of uncertainty idea.

Graham, J.R. and Kumar, A. (2006) 'Do dividend clienteles exist? Evidence on dividend preferences of retail investors', *Journal of Finance* 61(3), June, pp. 1305–36.

Evidence for clienteles (e.g. older investors prefer high dividend yields). Also, tax influences preferences of clienteles.

Grullon, G. and Michaely, R. (2002) 'Dividends, share repurchases, and the substitution hypothesis', *Journal of Finance,* 57(4), pp. 1649–84.

US companies have increasingly substituted share repurchases for dividends – tax considerations were a major reason.

Gustavo, G. and Roni, M. (2004) 'The information content of share repurchase programs', *Journal of Finance,* April, 59(2), pp. 651–80.

Finds evidence consistent with free cash flow hypothesis of dividend policy.

Jagannathan, M., Stephens, C.P. and Weisbach, M.S. (2000) 'Financial flexibility and the choice between dividends and stock repurchases', *Journal of Financial Economics,* 57(3), September, pp. 355–84.

US study. Repurchases are pro-cyclical, dividends are steady. Repurchases used to distribute high temporary cash flows.

Jensen, M.C. (1986) 'Agency costs of free cash flow, corporate finance and takeovers', *American Economic Review,* 76, pp. 323–9.

Managers act in their own interests; therefore increased dividends increase the value of mature cash-generating companies.

Keane, S. (1974) 'Dividends and the resolution of uncertainty', *Journal of Business Finance and Accountancy,* Autumn.

Discusses the 'bird-in-the-hand' theory of dividend policy.

Koch, A.S. and Sun, A.X. (2004) 'Dividend changes and the persistence of past earnings changes', *Journal of Finance,* 59(5), October, pp. 2093–116.

'Results confirm the hypothesis that changes in dividends cause investors to revise their expectations about the persistence of past earnings changes', thus dividend changes act as a signalling device.

Lewellen, W.G., Stanley, K.L., Lease, R.C. and Schlarbaum, G.G. (1978) 'Some direct evidence of the dividend clientele phenomenon', *Journal of Finance,* December, pp. 1385–99.

An investigation of the clientele effect.

Lintner, J. (1956) 'Distribution of income of corporations among dividends, retained earnings and taxes', *American Economic Review,* 46, May, pp. 97–113.

An empirical study and theoretical model of dividend policy practices.

Litzenberger, R. and Ramaswamy, K. (1982) 'The effects of dividends on common stock prices: Tax effects or information effects?', *Journal of Finance,* May, pp. 429–43.

A technical paper which presents 'evidence consistent with the Tax-Clientele CAPM'.

Miller, M.H. and Modigliani, F. (1961) 'Dividend policy, growth and the valuation of shares', *Journal of Business,* 34, October, pp. 411–33.

In an ideal economy dividend policy is irrelevant – algebraic proofs.

Mougoué, M. and Rao, R.P. (2003) 'The information signalling hypothesis of dividends: Evidence from cointegration and causality tests', *Journal of Business Finance and Accounting*, 30(3) and (4), April/May, pp. 441–78.

Evidence consistent with the information-signalling hypothesis.

Nissim, D. and Ziv, A. (2001) 'Dividend changes and future profitability', *Journal of Finance*, 56(6), pp. 2111–33.

Strong support for the information content of dividends hypothesis.

Oded, J. and Michel, A. (2008) 'Stock repurchases and the EPS enhancement fallacy', *Financial Analysts Journal*, 64(4), pp. 62–75.

Evidence that share repurchases often result in lower earnings per share.

Pettit, R.R. (1977) 'Taxes, transaction costs and clientele effects of dividends', *Journal of Financial Economics*, December.

Discusses the clientele effect.

Tse, C-B, (2005) 'Use dividends to signal or not: An examination of the UK dividend pay-out patterns', *Managerial Finance*, 31(4), pp. 12–33.

'Some firms need to use dividends to signal but some do not need to. For example, a firm that has built up reputational capital can communicate directly with shareholders'.

Case study recommendations

Please see www.pearsoned.co.uk/arnold for case study synopses. Also, another list of useful case studies from the fifth edition can be found there.

- Dividend policy at Linear Technology. Authors: Malcolm P. Baker; Alison Berkley Wagonfeld Harvard Business School. Available at www.cb.hbsp.harvard.edu

- Dividend policy at SRF Limited: buyback of shares. Authors: Kulbir Singh; David J. Sharp; S. Ramanna

Vishwanath, Ivey Publishing. Available at www.cb.hbsp.harvard.edu

- Rockboro Machine Tools Corporation. Author: Kenneth Eades, Darden School of Business. Available at www.cb.hbsp.harvard.edu

- Dividend policy at Fuyao Glass. Authors: Hugh Thomas; Joyce L. Wang; Yuhui Wu, Ivey Publishing. Available at www.cb.hbsp.harvard.edu

Video presentations

Chief executives and finance directors talk about company results including dividend policy at videos.merchantcantos.com – this is free to view.

Self-review questions

1 What are the two fundamental questions in dividend policy?

2 Explain the main elements of MM's dividend irrelevancy hypothesis.

3 Explain the idea that dividends should be treated as a residual.

4 How might clientele effects influence dividend policy?

5 What is the effect of taxation on dividend pay-out rates?

6 What is meant by 'asymmetry of information' and 'dividends as signals'?

7 Explain the 'resolution of uncertainty' argument supporting high dividend pay-out rates. What is the counter-argument?

8 In what ways does agency theory influence the dividend debate?

9 When are share repurchases and special dividends particularly useful?

10 Outline a dividend policy for a typical fast-growth and high-investment firm.

Questions and problems

Answers to most questions can be found at www.pearsoned.co.uk/arnold.

1 (*Examination level*) 'These days we discuss the dividend level for about an hour a year at board meetings. It changes very little from one year to the next – and it is just as well if you consider what happened to some of the other firms on the stock exchange which reduced their dividend' – director of a large company.

   Explain, with reference to dividend theory, how this firm may have settled into this comfortable routine. Describe any problems that might arise with this approach.

2 (*Examination level*) 'We believe managers and owners should think hard about the circumstances under which earnings should be retained and under which they should be distributed.'

   Use the above sentence together with the following one written in the same letter to shareholders by Warren Buffett (1984), plus dividend policy theory, to explain why this is an important issue: 'Nothing in this discussion is intended to argue for dividends that bounce around from quarter to quarter with each wiggle in earnings or in investment opportunities.'

3 (*Examination level*) Sendine plc has maintained a growth path for dividends per share of 5% per year for the past seven years. This was the maintainable regular dividend. However, the company has developed a new product range which will require major investment in the next 12 months. The amount needed is roughly equivalent to the proposed dividend for this year. The project will not provide a positive net cash flow for three to four years but will give a positive NPV overall.

Required

Consider the argument for and against a dividend cut this year and suggest a course of action.

4 (*Examination level*) Vale plc has the following profit-after-tax history and dividend-per-share history:

Year		Profit after tax £	Dividend per share
This year	(t_0)	10,800,000	5.4
Last year	($t - 1$)	8,900,000	4.92
2 years ago	($t - 2$)	6,300,000	4.48
3 years ago	($t - 3$)	5,500,000	4.083
4 years ago	($t - 4$)	3,500,000	3.71
5 years ago	($t - 5$)	2,600,000	3.38

Two years ago the number of issued ordinary shares was increased by 30% (at the beginning of the financial year $t - 1$). Four years ago a rights issue doubled the number of shares (at the beginning of financial year $t - 3$). Today there are 100 million ordinary shares in issue with a total market value of £190m. Vale is quoted on the Alternative Investment Market. Vale's directors are committed to shareholder wealth maximisation.

Required

a Explain the following dividend theories and models and relate them to Vale's policy:
   i   dividends as a residual;
   ii   signalling;
   iii clientele preferences.

b The risk-free return on government securities is currently 6.5%, the risk premium for shares above the risk-free rate of return has been 5% per annum and Vale is in a risk class of shares which suggests that the average risk premium of 5 should be adjusted by a factor of 0.9. The company's profits after tax per share are expected to continue their historic growth path, and dividends will remain at the same proportion of earnings as this year.

   Use the dividend valuation model and state whether Vale's shares are a good buying opportunity for a stock market investor.

5   (*Examination level*) Tesford plc has estimated net cash flows from operations (after interest and taxation) for the next five years as follows:

Year	Net cash flows £
1	3,000,000
2	12,000,000
3	5,000,000
4	6,000,000
5	5,000,000

The cash flows have been calculated before the deduction of additional investment in fixed capital and working capital. This amounts to £2m in each of the first two years and £3m for each year thereafter. The firm currently has a cash balance of £500,000 which it intends to maintain to cope with unexpected events. There are 24 million shares in issue. The directors are committed to shareholder wealth maximisation.

Required

a   Calculate the annual cash flows available for dividend payments and the dividend per share if the residual dividend policy was strictly adhered to.

b   If the directors chose to have a smooth dividend policy based on the maintainable regular dividend what would you suggest the dividends in each year should be? Include in your consideration the possibility of a special dividend or share repurchase.

c   Explain why companies tend to follow the policy in b rather than a.

6   (*Examination level*) The retailers Elec Co. and Lighting are competitors in the electrical goods market. They are similar firms in many respects: profits per share have been very similar over the past 10 years, and are projected to be the same in the future; they both have (and have had) a 50% debt to equity ratio; and they have similar investment needs, now and in the future. However, they do differ in their dividend policies. Elec Co. pays out 50% of earnings as dividends, whereas Lighting has adopted a stable dividend policy. This is demonstrated in the table.

The managing director of Elec Co. has asked you to conduct a thorough review of dividend policy and to try to explain why it is that Lighting has a market value much greater than Elec Co. (Both companies have, and have had, the same number of shares in issue.)

Write a report detailing the factors that influence dividend policy and recommend a dividend policy for Elec Co. based on your arguments.

Year	Elec Co.		Lighting	
	Earnings per share	Dividend per share	Earnings per share	Dividend per share
20 × 1	11p	5.5p	11p	5.5p
20 × 2	16p	8.0p	17p	6.25p
20 × 3	13p	6.5p	11p	7.11p
20 × 4	20p	10.0p	21p	8.1p
20 × 5	10p	5.0p	9p	9.2p
20 × 6	0	0	0	10.5p
20 × 7	15p	7.5p	17p	11.9p
20 × 8	25p	12.5p	24p	13.5p
20 × 9	30p	15.0p	31p	15.4p
20 × 10	35p	17.5p	35p	17.5p

7   (*Examination level*) Guff plc, an all-equity firm, has the following earnings per share and dividend history (paid annually).

Year	Earnings per share	Dividend per share
This year	21p	8p
Last year	18p	7.5p
2 years ago	16p	7p
3 years ago	13p	6.5p
4 years ago	14p	6p

This year's dividend has just been paid and the next is due in one year. Guff has an opportunity to invest in a new product, Stuff, during the next two years. The directors are considering cutting the dividend to 4p for each of the next two years to fund the project. However, the dividend in three years can be raised to 10p and will grow by 9% per annum thereafter due to the benefits from the investment. The company is focused on shareholder wealth maximisation and requires a rate of return of 13% for its owners.

Required

a   If the directors chose to ignore the investment opportunity and dividends continued to grow at the historical rate what would be the value of one share using the dividend valuation model?

b   If the investment is accepted, and therefore dividends are cut for the next two years, what will be the value of one share?

c   What are the dangers associated with dividend cuts and how might the firm alleviate them?

Assignments

1   Consider the dividend policy of your firm or one you know well. Write a report detailing the factors contributing to the selection of this policy. Make recommendations on the decision-making process, range of influences considered and how a change in policy could be executed.

2   Write a report which relates the dividend frameworks and theories discussed in this chapter to the evidence provided by the following UK companies.

Year	Marks & Spencer		Vodafone		Astra Zeneca	
	Earnings	Dividends	Earnings	Dividends	Earnings	Dividends
2012	32.5	17.0	13.74	9.52	499	280
2013	29.2	17.0	0.87	10.19	204	280
2014	32.5	17.0	223.84	11.00	98	280
2015	29.7	18.0	(21.75)	11.22	223	280
2016	24.9	18.7	(−15.08)	11.45	277	280
2017	7.2	18.7	(−22.51)	14.77	237	280
2018	1.6	18.7	8.78	15.07	n/a	n/a

Note: figures in brackets indicate a loss.

Mergers

LEARNING OUTCOMES

The study of mergers is a subject worthy of a textbook in its own right. This chapter provides an overview of the subject and raises the most important issues. By the end of the chapter the reader should be able to:

■ describe the rich array of motives for a merger;

■ express the advantages and disadvantages of alternative methods of financing mergers;

■ describe the merger process and the main regulatory constraints;

■ comment on the question: 'Who benefits from mergers?';

■ discuss some of the reasons for merger failure and some of the practices promoting success.

Introduction

The topic of mergers is one of those areas of finance which attracts interest from the general public as well as finance specialists and managers. There is nothing like an acrimonious bid battle to excite the press, where one side is portrayed as 'David' fighting the bullying 'Goliath', or where one national champion threatens the pride of another country by taking over a key industry. Each twist and turn of the campaign is reported on radio and television news broadcasts, and, finally, there is a victor and a victim. So many people have so much hanging on the outcome of the conflict that it is not surprising that a great deal of attention is given by local communities, national government, employees and trade unionists. The whole process can become emotional and overhyped to the point where rational analysis is pushed to the side.

This chapter examines the reasons for mergers and the ways in which they are financed. Then the merger process itself is described, along with the rules and regulations designed to prevent unfairness. A major question to be addressed is: Who gains from mergers? Is it shareholders, managers, advisers, society, etc.? Evidence is presented which suggests that in less than one half of corporate mergers do the shareholders of the acquiring firm benefit. To help the reader understand the causes of this level of failure the various managerial tasks involved in achieving a successful (that is, a shareholder wealth enhancing) merger, including the 'soft' science issues, such as attending to the need to enlist the commitment of the newly acquired workforce, are discussed.

The merger decision

Expanding the activities of the firm through acquisition involves significant uncertainties. Very often the acquiring management seriously underestimates the complexities involved in merger and post-merger integration.

Theoretically the acquisition of other companies should be evaluated on essentially the same criteria as any other investment decision, i.e. using NPV; adding shareholder value is the focus.

In practice, the myriad collection of motivations for expansion through merger, and the diverse range of issues such an action raises, means that mergers are usually extremely difficult to evaluate using discounted cash flow techniques. Consider these two complicating factors.

1 The benefits from mergers are often difficult to quantify. The motivation may be to 'apply superior managerial skills' or to 'obtain unique technical capabilities' or to 'enter a new market'. The fruits of these labours may be real, and directors may judge that the strategic benefits far outweigh the cost, and yet these are difficult to express in numerical form.

2 Acquiring companies often do not know what they are buying. If a firm expands by building a factory here, or buying in machinery there, it knows what it is getting for its money. With a merger information is often sparse – especially if it is a hostile bid in which the target company's managers are opposed to the merger. In Chapter 17 it was stated that most of the value of many firms is in the form of assets which cannot be expressed on a balance sheet, for example the reservoir of experience within the management team, the reputation with suppliers and customers, competitive position and so on. These attributes are extremely difficult to value, especially from a distance, and when there is a reluctance to release information. Even the quantifiable elements of value, such as stock, buildings and free cash flow, can be miscalculated by an 'outsider'.

Definitions and semantics

Throughout this book the word merger is used to mean the *combining of two business entities under common ownership.*

Many people, for various reasons, differentiate between the terms merger, acquisition and takeover – for example, for accounting and legal purposes. However, most commentators use the three terms interchangeably, and with good reason. It is sometimes very difficult to decide whether a particular unification of two companies is more like a merger, in the sense of being the coming together of roughly equal sized firms on roughly equal terms and in which the shareholders remain as joint owners, or whether the act of union is closer to what some people would say is an **acquisition** or **takeover** – a purchase of one firm by another with the associated implication of financial and managerial domination. In reality it is often impossible to classify the relationships within the combined entity as a merger or a takeover. The literature is full of cases of so called mergers of equals which turn out to be a takeover of managerial control by one set of managers at the expense of the other.[1] Jürgen Schrempp, the chairman of DaimlerChrysler, shocked the financial world with his honesty on this point. At the time of the union of Chrysler with Daimler Benz in 1998 it was described as a merger of equals. However, in 2000 Schrempp said, 'The structure we have now with Chrysler [as a standalone division] was always the structure I wanted. We had to go a roundabout way but it had to be done for psychological reasons. If I had gone and said Chrysler would be a division, everybody on their side would have said: "There is no way we'll do a deal."'[2] Jack Welch, the well-respected industrialist, supports Schrempp: 'This was a buyout of Chrysler by Daimler. Trying to run it as a merger of equals creates all kinds of problems . . . There is no such thing as a merger of equals . . . There has to be one way forward and clear rules.'[3] Lord Browne, chief executive of BP, following the mergers with Amoco and Arco, expressed strong views on this subject: 'There is a big cultural problem with mergers of equals . . . in the end there has to be a controlling strain from the two companies.'[4] This book uses the terms merger, acquisition and takeover interchangeably.

Economic and/or strategic definitions of mergers

Mergers have been classified into three categories: horizontal, vertical and conglomerate.

1   *Horizontal* In a **horizontal merger** two companies which are engaged in similar lines of activity are combined. Recent examples include the merger of fund managers Standard Life and Aberdeen Asset Management, and mining houses Glencore and Xstrata. One of the motives advanced for horizontal mergers is that economies of scale can be achieved. But not all horizontal mergers demonstrate such gains. Another major motive is the enhancement of market power resulting from the reduction in competition. Horizontal mergers often attract the attention of government competition (antitrust) agencies such as the Competition and Markets Authority, CMA, in the UK.

2   *Vertical* **Vertical mergers** occur when firms from different stages of the production chain amalgamate. So, for instance, if a manufacturer of footwear merges with a retailer of shoes this would be a (downstream) vertical merger. If the manufacturer then bought a leather producer (an upstream vertical merger) there would be an even greater degree of vertical integration. The major players in the oil industry tend to be highly vertically integrated. They have exploration subsidiaries, drilling and production companies, refineries, distribution companies and petrol stations. Vertical integration often has the attraction of increased certainty of supply or market outlet. It also reduces costs of search, contracting, payment collection, advertising, communication and coordination of production. An increase in market power may also be a motivation: this is discussed later.

3   *Conglomerate* A **conglomerate merger** is the combining of two firms which operate in unrelated business areas. For example, GE ought companies in areas as diverse as jet engines, medical imaging and oil production equipment.

    Some conglomerate mergers are motivated by risk reduction through diversification; some by the opportunity for cost reduction and improved efficiency. Others have more complex driving motivations – many of which will be discussed later.

---

1   For example, see Cartwright and Cooper (1992); Buono and Bowditch (2003).
2   Tim Burt and Richard Lambert, 'The Schrempp Gambit . . .', *Financial Times*, 30 October 2000, p. 26.
3   Tim Burt, 'Steering with his foot to the floor', *Financial Times*, 26 February 2001, p. 12.
4   David Buchan and Tobias Buck, 'Refining BP's management', *Financial Times*, 1 August 2002, p. 21.

Merger statistics

The figures in **Exhibit 20.1** show that merger activity has occurred in waves, with peaks in the early 1970s, late 1980s and late 1990s and 2007 – periods of rising stock market prices. The vast majority (over 95%) of these mergers was agreed ('friendly'), rather than opposed by the target (acquired) firm's management ('hostile'). Only a small, but often noisy, fraction enter into a bid battle stage. The phenomenon of merger activity rising to very high levels for a few years and then subsiding to more pedestrian levels for a long time has been observed in many countries. Peaks in merger activity tend to occur at peaks in economic activity following a sustained period of growth, which is usually accompanied by stock market exuberance, e.g. 1929, 1971–2, 1988–9 and 2000. In the USA, for example, there were bursts of activity in the following periods: 1890–1905 (creating monopoly power from oligopolistic and near-competitive industries); 1920–9 (oligopoly power sought); 1965–71 (rapid growth, many conglomerates, shift towards greater diversification); 1986–90 (restructuring to core businesses – 'focus strategy' – away from conglomerate structures; assistance from leveraged finance); 1997–2000 (focus strategy on core extraordinary resources, dot.com, telecoms and media mania, globalisation, consolidation of fragmented industries); 2014–17 (economies of scale, market power, private equity deals, protection against industry disrupters such as Facebook, Amazon, Netflix and Google, e.g. shopping mall owners combining, Disney and Fox).

Exhibit 20.1	UK merger activity, 1970–2016 (UK firms merging with UK firms)

	Number of UK companies acquired	Expenditure (£m)
2011	276	8,089
2012	216	3,413
2013	175	7,665
2014	150	8,032
2015	194	6,920
2016	na	24,688

	Preference shares and loans (%)	Ordinary shares (%)	Cash (%)
2011	3.5	9.5	87
2012	8	10	82
2013	2.5	6	91.5
2014	0.5	28	71.5
2015	4	15.5	80.5
2016	3	45	52

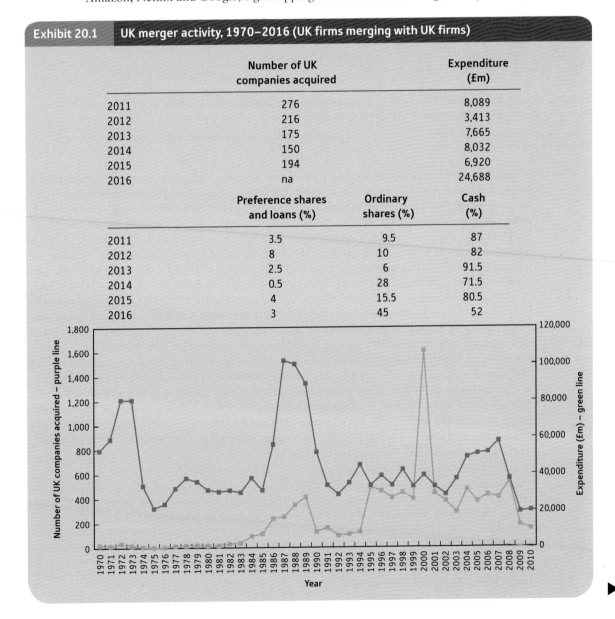

▶

| Exhibit 20.1 | UK merger activity, 1970–2016 (UK firms merging with UK firms) (continued) |

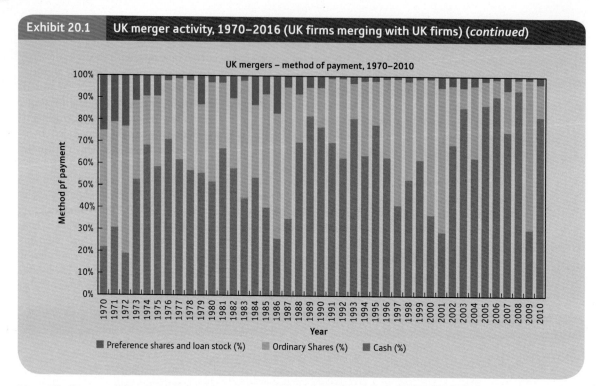

Note: *The figures include all industrial and commercial companies (and financial institutions for 1995), quoted or unquoted, which reported the merger to the press (small private mergers are excluded).*

Source: Office for National Statistics, *Financial Statistics*. © Crown Copyright. Reproduced by the permission of the Controller of HMSO and the Queen's Printer for Scotland.

In the stock market boom of the late 1990s shares became a significant means of payment in UK mergers. Rhodes-Kropf et al. (2005) suggest that higher share market valuations make equity-financed mergers more attractive to both acquirers and targets. However, for most years cash is the dominant form of consideration. The advantages of different types of payment are discussed later.

Worldwide, mergers exceeded $3,000bn in each of the four years 2014–17. The new big players in mergers come from China, which accounts for about the same value of deals within its borders as within Europe. China also accounts for a significant proportion of cross-border deals. By far the most active market in companies is the North American one, at over $1,500bn per year – *see* **Exhibit 20.2**.

Merger waves may occur because merger enthusiasm strikes a particular industry (e.g. new technology changes the most efficient scale). This drive for mergers may be managerial behavioural phenomena (e.g. managers see a number of mergers in their industry and so rush to merge before they are acquired). Alternatively, managers and investors become very optimistic about the value-generating potential of mergers during periods of economic and stock market growth. Those that have experienced success in the recent past continue to expand via acquisition believing in the power of their talent to improve target companies – much of this is hubris, as revealed in the economic downturn that follows boom. Another reason for merger waves is that suppliers of finance suffer bouts of irrational exuberance in economic and market booms too, supplying plentiful cheap finance and going easy on things like debt covenants, financial gearing and interest cover ratios.[5]

---

5 Maksimovic, et al. (2013) found access to cheaper finance a driver of merger waves and overvaluation in the stock market relative to fundamentals is associated with more transactions. Harford (2005) found waves occur in part because it is easier to raise low cost money when the economy is improving. Rhodes-Kropf et al. (2005) found that mis-valuation may explain why mergers cluster over time, that managers may suffer from ill-informed optimism regarding potential synergies and are more likely to buy when given positive signals from the stock market. Duchin and Schmidt (2013) found that at times of high merger activity there tends to be poorer quality of analysts' forecasts, greater uncertainty and lower penalties for managers initiating inefficient mergers.

Exhibit 20.2

Global M&A exceeds $3tn for fourth straight year

By Arash Massoudi, James Fontanella-Khan and Don Weinland

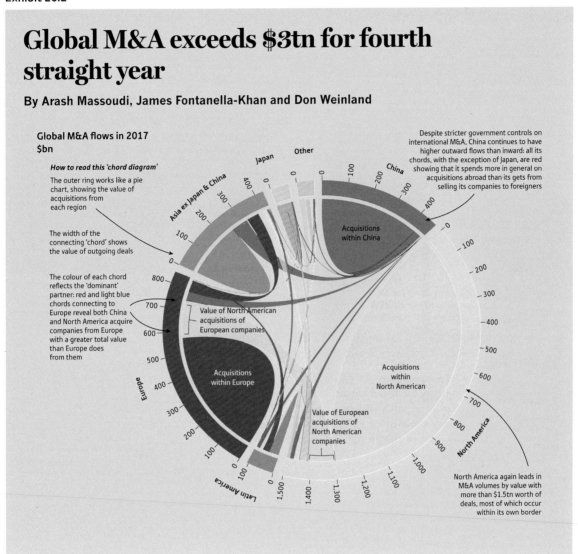

Global M&A flows in 2017
$bn

How to read this 'chord diagram'

The outer ring works like a pie chart, showing the value of acquisitions from each region

The width of the connecting 'chord' shows the value of outgoing deals

The colour of each chord reflects the 'dominant' partner: red and light blue chords connecting to Europe reveal both China and North America acquire companies from Europe with a greater total value than Europe does from them

Value of North American acquisitions of European companies

Acquisitions within Europe

Europe

Latin America

Japan   Other

Asia ex Japan & China

China

Despite stricter government controls on international M&A, China continues to have higher outward flows than inward: all its chords, with the exception of Japan, are red showing that it spends more in general on acquisitions abroad than its gets from selling its companies to foreigners

Acquisitions within China

Acquisitions within North American

Value of European acquisitions of North American companies

North America

North America again leads in M&A volumes by value with more than $1.5tn worth of deals, most of which occur within its own border

Merger motives

Firms decide to merge with other firms for a variety of reasons. **Exhibit 20.3** identifies four classes of merger motives. This may not be complete but at least it helps us to focus.

Synergy

In the first column of Exhibit 20.3 we have the classic word associated with merger announcements – synergy. The idea underlying this is that the combined entity will have a value greater than the sum of its parts. The increased value comes about because of boosts to revenue and/or the cost base. Perhaps complementary skills or complementary market outlets enable the combined firms to sell more goods, as when BT, the broadband, TV and fixed-line supplier merged with EE, the mobile phone company to offer 'quadplay' packages in 2016. Sometimes the ability to share sources of supply or production facilities improves the competitive position of the firm. In the case of Sainsbury and Argos' 2016 merger £120m cost saving and revenue synergies are

Exhibit 20.3   Merger motives

Synergy	Superior management	Managerial motives	Third party motives
The two firms together are worth more than the value of the firms apart. • $PV_{AB} = PV_A + PV_B + gains$ • Market power • Economies of scale • Internalisation of transactions • Entry to new markets and industries • Tax advantages • Risk diversification.	Target can be purchased at a price below the present value of the target's future cash flow when in the hands of new management. • Elimination of inefficient and misguided management • Conglomerate's advantages in allocating capital and in using extraordinary resources • Under-valued shares: strong form or semi-strong form of stock market inefficiency.	• Empire building • Status • Power • Remuneration • Hubris • Survival: speedy growth strategy to reduce probability of being takeover target • Free cash flow: management prefer to use free cash flow in acquisitions rather than return it to shareholders.	• Advisers • At the insistence of customers or suppliers.

envisaged as Argos shops are shut and replaced with in-store Sainsbury's outlets. Some of the origins of synergy are listed in the first column of the exhibit. Before discussing these we will look at the concept of synergy in more detail.

If two firms, A and B, are to be combined a gain may result from synergistic benefits to provide a value above that of the present value of the two independent cash flows:

$$PV_{AB} = PV_A + PV_B + gains$$

where:

PV_A = discounted cash flows of company A;
PV_B = discounted cash flows of company B;
PV_{AB} = discounted cash flows of the merged firm.

Synergy is colloquially expressed in the form $2 + 2 = 5$.

Value is created from a merger when the gain is greater than the transaction costs. These usually comprise advisers' fees, underwriters' fees, legal and accounting costs, stock exchange fees, public relations bills and so on. So if we assume that A and B as separate entities have present values of £20m and £10m respectively, the transaction costs total £2m and the value of the merged firms is £40m (£42m before paying transaction costs), then the net (after costs) gain from merger is £10m:

£40m = £20m + £10m + gain

But who is going to receive this extra value? The incremental value may be available for the acquirer or the target, or be split between the two. If company A is the acquirer, it might pay a price for B which is equal to the PV of B's cash flows (£10m), in which case all of the gain from the merger will accrue to A. However, this is highly unlikely. Usually an acquiring firm has to pay a price significantly above the pre-bid value of the target company to gain control – this is called the acquisition premium, bid premium or control premium.

If it is assumed that before the bid B was valued correctly on the basis of its expected future cash flows to shareholders then the bid premium represents the transferring of some of the gains to be derived from the created synergy. For example, if A paid £15m for B then B's shareholders receive £5m of the gain. If A has to pay £20m to acquire B then A receives no gain.

Wood Group expected to make £110m of annual synergies from combining with Amec Foster Wheeler – *see* **Exhibit 20.4**.

Exhibit 20.4

Wood Group/Amec: going with the grain

LEX column

Pagans have always venerated trees: stolid, slow-growing symbols of nature's strength. Touching trees to ward off evil probably led to the superstition of knocking on wood for good luck. Think of UK oil services specialist Wood Group in the same way, strong and steady no matter what commodity storm blows by.

More than just good fortune has kept it in business over the years. The Aberdeen group prides itself on avoiding big risks. Its £2.2bn all-share acquisition of UK peer Amec Foster Wheeler, however, means Wood is branching out.

By taking on Amec Foster Wheeler, Wood diversifies its business too. Once just a deepwater oil services engineer, Wood still sources 85 per cent of its revenues from oil and gas.

Adding Amec, with its spread of services including renewables and mining, should mean hydrocarbons exploration and production accounts for about 60 per cent. However, Wood has also taken on a group in transition, to put things mildly.

Amec's chief executive Jon Lewis, recently parachuted in from US-listed Halliburton, was midway through his own root and branch restructuring.

A poorly timed £2bn purchase of Foster Wheeler just as oil prices collapsed in 2014 did the company no favours. Its balance sheet still bends under net debt of over £1bn, more than three times earnings before interest, tax, depreciation and amortisation.

Amec had planned a £500m rights issue. Instead, Wood will bail it out. Given promises of £110m in annual cost cuts, this deal works. Taxed and capitalised, these savings, even with one-off costs, amount to £422m, which easily covers the premium paid. The combined company should generate enough free cash flow to pay down debt. No wonder both acquirer and target share prices rallied.

Amec's top executives, based in expensive London, may well suffer the brunt of the Wood cutters' axes. About 30 per cent of expected reductions will come from the C-suite. This deal looks a sensible one for Wood.

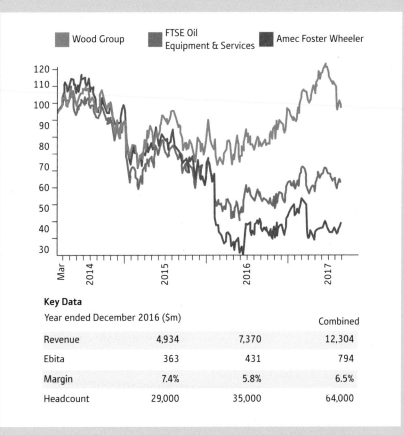

Key Data

Year ended December 2016 ($m)

			Combined
Revenue	4,934	7,370	12,304
Ebita	363	431	794
Margin	7.4%	5.8%	6.5%
Headcount	29,000	35,000	64,000

Note another possibility known as the 'winner's curse' – the acquirer pays a price higher than the combined present value of the target and the potential gain. The winner's curse is illustrated in **Exhibit 20.5**.

Exhibit 20.5

HBOS collapse shows danger of the winner's curse

BY JOHN KAY

British regulators have finally published their report into HBOS, the bank formed from the merger of Halifax with Bank of Scotland, more than seven years after its collapse. The 600-odd pages contain much detail on events and personalities. But there are general lessons for all businesses. Avoid the diversifier's fallacy. Beware the winner's curse. Fear adverse selection.

The diversifier's fallacy is a generalisation of the Peter Principle: individuals rise within an organisation until they are given a job they are not competent to do. Companies diversify until they are engaged in businesses in which they have a competitive disadvantage relative to incumbents. This seems particularly common among financial companies. Most of the institutions hit in the crisis — most strikingly troubled insurer AIG — were crippled by losses in areas far from their principal business.

HBOS enjoyed market leading positions in UK mortgage lending and retail banking within Scotland. But these markets did not offer sufficient growth to meet the aspirations of HBOS executives. Since these expectations could not be met by things the bank knew how to do well, they were fulfilled by increasing market share in areas it did not know well: corporate banking in the UK and retail banking in Ireland and Australia.

While mortgage losses increased after the 2008 crisis, the core lending activity of Halifax remained not only viable but profitable. While the problems that became a crisis in October 2008 manifested themselves as a crisis of liquidity born of over dependence on wholesale funding, the underlying issue was one of solvency. Losses from diversification into corporate banking and international operations proved more than sufficient to wipe out shareholders equity.

When similar individuals or businesses are contenders for an object whose true value is uncertain, the winner will usually be the bidder who offers to pay too much. First observed in auctions of offshore oil blocks, the winner's curse explains why mobile phone licence auctions raised so much more than governments expected.

HBOS's rival, Royal Bank of Scotland, experienced the curse when it outbid Barclays for ABN Amro, a contest whose outcome was likely to bankrupt whichever bank "won". What the corporate banking division of HBOS described as "innovative lending" was lending on more aggressive terms than any other bank. The same principle underpinned expansion in Western Australia, a far away country of which Edinburgh knew nothing, and in Ireland, a market already crowded with foolish lenders.

In Ireland, the winner's curse was aggravated by adverse selection: when HBOS rolled out a new branch network after 2005, the borrowers who came through its doors inevitably included many whom better established banks had turned away. In credit markets, you can earn profits by doing better credit assessment than your rivals, or gain sales by doing worse credit assessment than your rivals. HBOS chose the latter.

Much is made, and rightly, of the failures of risk control in HBOS. The underlying issue is more fundamental. The sustainable rate of profitable growth in any business is determined by the strength of its competitive advantage and the scope of the application of that advantage. It is always a mistake to set growth targets to meet the expectations of ambitious executives or analysts rather than to derive them from a realistic assessment of the competitive position of the business. The result is to drive the organisation towards the diversifier's fallacy, the winner's curse and adverse selection. For HBOS, that meant strategy and risk control would inevitably come into conflict, and strategy would win. Until everyone, and everything, lost.

The writer was a director of Halifax from 1991–2000

Market power

One of the most important forces driving mergers is the attempt to increase market power. This is the ability to exercise some control over the price of the product. It can be achieved through either (a) monopoly, oligopoly or dominant producer positions, etc., or (b) collusion or de facto cooperation (where there is no formal agreement but signals are sent to competitors to avoid price competitions).

If a firm has a large share of a market it often has some degree of control over price. It may be able to push up the price of goods sold because customers have few alternative sources of supply. Even if the firm does not control the entire market, a reduction in the number of participating firms to a handful makes collusion easier. Whether openly or not, the firms in a concentrated market may agree among themselves to charge customers higher prices and not to undercut each other. The regulatory authorities are watching out for such socially damaging activities and have fined a number of firms for such practices, for example in the cement, vitamins and chemicals industries – **Exhibit 20.6** discusses a measure of increased market power leading to high returns for shareholders.

Exhibit 20.6

Modern robber barons ride wave of M&A deals

Not concerned about industry concentration? You should be, says Steve Johnson

In the unlikely event of ever being asked to name an economist on the TV quiz show Pointless, one could do worse than nominate either of the wonderfully obscure Orris Herfindahl or Albert Hirschman.

Given the events of the past week or so, maybe it is time for investors, politicians, regulators (at least outside the US) and consumer groups to dust off their A-Zs of economic theory and get up to speed with the duo's largely overlooked contribution to the subject.

In recent days, AT&T, the US telecoms group, has bid $85bn for Time Warner, the media conglomerate, and British American Tobacco offered $47bn for the shares it does not already own of its US peer, Reynolds American.

In the more important agribusiness sector, three potential deals are awaiting regulatory approval: ChemChina's $44bn offer for Swiss peer Syngenta, Bayer's $66bn deal for Monsanto and a proposed $130bn tie-up between Dow Chemical and DuPont.

If these three deals are all given the green light, nearly two-thirds of the global seed and chemical supply chain will be in the hands of just three companies. This matters, and the largely forgotten work of our unsung economic heroes gives us a framework to measure just how much.

The Herfindahl-Hirschman index, calculated by summing the squares of the market shares of the participants in a given market, is used by the US Department of Justice to measure industry concentration.

It is also used, uniquely it would seem, by the European equities team at BNP Paribas Investment Partners to attempt to make money. And, spoiler alert, it seems to work.

The French bank's asset management team, led by chief investment officer Andrew King, uses the HH index to find industries that are becoming either more concentrated, often as a result of mergers and acquisitions, or more fragmented. They are often minded to invest in the former and steer clear of the latter.

That a concentrated sector allows scope for a cabal of powerful oligopolists to gouge prices and bank excess profit was a truism fully grasped by the robber barons of the late 19th century. That more than a century of antitrust legislation has failed to eradicate the problem is perhaps more disturbing.

Mr King wields an impressive array of charts to demonstrate. In Colombia's highly concentrated beer industry, for example, the HHI is almost 10,000 and earnings before interest and tax are 42 per cent of revenues. In the hyper-competitive German beer market, where the HHI is in the low hundreds, the Ebit margin is just 10 per cent. Across a wide array of countries, there is a clear relationship between lack of competition and profitability.

On a global basis, the HHI of the beer industry had risen from around 170 in the mid-1990s to more than 900 in 2014, as a result of constant consolidation. This was even before industry leader AB InBev's takeover of

▶

Exhibit 20.6 (continued)

SABMiller, the number-two player by sales, which is likely to send it spiralling to around 1400. Over the same period, the average operating margin of the four largest brewers has risen relentlessly from 8 per cent to 20 per cent, the Paris-based asset manager's figures show.

Similarly, the UK mortgage market was competitive before the global financial crisis, with a HHI of around 900 and a mortgage spread (over the cost of funding) of around 0.35 percentage points in 2007. As the likes of the Icelandic and Irish banks retreated after the crisis, and Santander hoovered up a host of lenders, the HHI jumped to 1500 by 2010, and mortgage spreads ballooned to 2.8 percentage points.

The same can be seen in Spain, where the number of lenders has fallen from 52 to 13, but not in Germany or Italy, where the market remains fragmented and profitability is poor.

This focus on what Mr King refers to as "well-structured industries" has helped his Parvest Equity Best Selection Europe fund to outperform the MSCI Europe index by 28 percentage points since 2008, admittedly before fees.

The upshot is that regulators and their political overlords need to start fighting harder to prevent industries becoming overly concentrated. Although the resultant elevated profit margins could be driven by greater efficiency in part, the bulk is likely to spring from price gouging.

Moreover, if industries generally are becoming more concentrated, this could be a contributory factor in the widely observed, and lamented, trend for a rising share of income to flow to corporates and a declining share to labour.

Mr King is unconvinced about the latter, arguing that excess profit pools act like a "red flag to a bull" in drawing entrants into a market, such as the UK food retail sector, where a cosy oligopoly was upended by cut-price insurgents Aldi and Lidl.

Competition is less likely to be reinvigorated where barriers to entry are high, however, suggesting politicians and regulators should strive to keep these to a minimum.

Mr King cites the tobacco sector, where advertising bans mean entrants could never get off the ground, and profit margins may be as high as 80 per cent in the UK. Politicians might not care much about smokers nowadays, but consumers in general deserve better protection from the profiteers.

FT   *Financial Times*, 30 October 2016.

Market power is a motivator in vertical as well as horizontal mergers. Downstream mergers are often formed in order to ensure a market for the acquirer's product and to shut out competing firms. Upstream mergers often lead to the raising or creating of barriers to entry or are designed to place competitors at a cost disadvantage.

Even conglomerate mergers can enhance market power. For example, a conglomerate may force suppliers to buy products from its different divisions under the threat that it will stop buying from them if they do not comply. It can also support each division in turn as it engages in predatory pricing designed to eliminate competitors. Or it may insist that customers buy products from one division if they want products from another.

Or it can raise prices across the board if the customer has few/no alternatives. Suppliers to Boeing and Airbus have been merging to increase their power over the aircraft assemblers, e.g. United Technologies combined its engine making division, Pratt and Whitney, with the avionics company Rockwell Collins by buying it for $30bn in 2017. There have been a number of similar mergers resulting in better profits for the suppliers. In the two years to 2017 their profit margins were between 14% and 17%, compared with 9% for the planemakers (*The Economist*, 2017). The suppliers now often control the production of the most complex parts of the aircraft, e.g. Rolls-Royce supplies engines, but makes half its sales and all its profits from servicing the engines – *it* holds that expertise, rather than the assemblers. In response to the power shift, the planemakers are trying to make more in-house. But the game goes on, with the biggest suppliers engaging in more mergers to give them more clout with customers and suppliers.

Economies of scale

An important contributor to synergy is the ability to exploit economies of scale. Larger size often leads to lower cost per unit of output (or may lead to increased sales efficiency). Rationalising and consolidating manufacturing capacity at fewer, larger sites can lead to economies of production utilising larger machines. Economies in marketing can arise through the use of common distribution channels or joint advertising. There are also economies in administration, research and development and purchasing. AB InBev, selling one in four beers worldwide anticipates economies of scale from merging with SAB Miller – see **Exhibit 20.7**.

Exhibit 20.7

Hard work on AB InBev mega deal begins now

Takeover of SABMiller involves major integration challenges

Scheherazade Daneshkhu

Anheuser-Busch InBev will wake up to the reality of its "Dream Big" mantra on Monday when the Stella Artois brewer's £79bn takeover of smaller rival SABMiller completes, and the hard graft of delivering the returns promised to shareholders begins.

Though AB InBev's purchase of Britain's SAB is sizeable — it ranks as the largest takeover of a British company, and the third largest acquisition ever — it is just the latest in a long series of deals by the Belgian brewer over the past 27 years. These deals have transformed AB InBev from a domestic Brazilian drinks maker once called Brahma into the world's biggest brewer, now selling one in four beers around the world and taking 45 per cent of the industry's profits.

AB InBev can point to a successful record of integrating the companies it has bought, and extracting large-scale cost-savings. This has helped to raise the company's profit margins to the highest in the industry. At the level of earnings before interest, tax, depreciation and amortisation, the company's margins have risen from 26 per cent in 2004 to 38.6 per cent last year, according to analysts at Jefferies.

Over the past decade the company's total shareholder return has been 492 per cent, outflanked in the brewing and spirits industry only by SAB itself, which has returned 508 per cent,

SAB is the most complex business AB InBev has bought so far, with operations spread across 70 countries, mostly in emerging markets. AB InBev operates in 26 countries, with just two — Brazil and the US — accounting for almost half its sales. Its previous targets have tended to be regionally focused, which has made them easier to integrate, such as Anheuser Busch, the Budweiser brewer in the US, and Modelo the Corona brewer in Mexico.

Despite the challenges, most analysts and investors expect AB InBev to surpass the $1.4bn of annual savings that it has promised from the SAB takeover in four years, at a one-off cost of $900m. This $1.4bn target equates to 13 per cent of SAB's net sales (after taking into account the disposal of SAB assets, including Peroni and Grolsch beers). It is at the lower end of a range of 12 to 21 per cent that AB InBev has achieved in previous deals.

As part of the cost-cutting drive, 5,500 jobs will be lost — or 3 per cent of the combined workforce. AB InBev expects 30 per cent of the cost savings to come from shutting overlapping regional offices, 25 per cent from using its increased clout to drive down the price of raw materials and packaging, and the rest, broadly, from higher brewing and distribution efficiencies, and productivity improvements.

Even with mergers of the conglomerate type managers claim achievable economies of scale. They identify savings from the sharing of central services such as administrative activities and accounting. Also the development of executives might be better at a large firm with a structured programme of training and access to a wider range of knowledgeable and experienced colleagues. Financial economies, such as being able to raise funds more cheaply in bulk, are also alluded to.

Many businesses possess assets such as buildings, machinery or people's skills which are not used to their full limits. For example, banks own high street sites. In most cases neither the buildings nor the employees are being used as intensively as they could be. Hence we have one of the motivating forces behind bank mergers. Once a merger is completed, a number of branches can be closed, to leave one rather than two in a particular location. Thus the customer flow to the remaining branch will be, say, doubled, with the consequent saving on property and labour costs.

Another synergistic reason for financial service industry mergers is the ability to market successful products developed by one firm to the customers of the other. Also when two medium size banks become large, funds borrowed on the capital market are provided at a lower cost per unit of transaction and at lower interest rates.

Economies of scope arise when costs are spread over an increased range of products or services (or sales benefit from offering an increased range of products). For example, the unit delivery costs (trucks, etc.) of tinned soup can be reduced if the truck also carries baked beans. On the sales side Kraft took over first Cadbury and, in 2015, merged with Heinz partly in order to gain access to valuable distribution channels in many countries.

Occasionally firms present themselves to financial backers as 'industry consolidators', meaning that they perceive their industry as having too many companies with too much capacity chasing too little business. The logical actions are to reduce the output of the industry thus permitting prices to rise and/or to reduce the number of production sites to gain economies of scale. Industry returns on capital employed will rise to or above the required rates of return. A further boost comes from the selling off of assets, e.g. closed warehouses might become trendy apartments, or a factory is sold to a company in another industry. Nestlé pursues a policy of buying confectionery companies around the world, combining manufacturing, distribution and marketing, selling off surplus assets and gaining market power and economies of scale. The hunt for scale, and the increased customer recognition and loyalty that it brings, has motivated mergers in the hotel management business – *see* **Exhibit 20.8**.

It is sometimes very difficult for regulators to weigh up the social benefit from a merger. On the one hand economies of scale or scope create lower costs, but on the other these savings may not be passed on to consumers due to the increased market power created by the merger – *see* **Exhibit 20.9** for a description of this dilemma in mobile phones. In the end, the EU blocked the merger on competition grounds.

Exhibit 20.8

Accor and Hyatt to the fore as hotels join deals rush

Property owners scramble to adapt to world of WeWork and Airbnb

By Malcolm Moore and Anna Nicolaou

Global hotel room count

Hilton	Marriott	IHG Intercontinental Hotels Group	WYNDHAM WORLDWIDE	CHOICE HOTELS
735,788	731,436	701,146	667,095	506,062

ACCOR HOTELS	starwood	Best Western	CARLSON	HYATT
494,932	356,329	303,749	172,367	158,418

Source: 2015 STR Global

After sitting on the sidelines, some of the world's best-known hotel brands are finally joining the current dealmaking boom as they look to boost profits and race to add hotel rooms.

Accor, the French hotel group is closing in on a $3bn deal to buy FRHI Hotels & Resorts, which owns luxury hotel brands Fairmont, Raffles and Swissôtel. Meanwhile Starwood, whose brands include St Regis, Sheraton and the W chains, sold its timeshare business to Interval Leisure Group for about $1.5bn and then became a target for Hyatt Hotels.

The rush to consolidate comes as occupancy and room rates reach record highs, especially in the US.

In the past, growing a hotel company required enormous capital investment, but over the past two decades, many hotel groups have expanded by adopting an "asset-light" model of managing, rather than owning, properties.

This strategy has allowed companies to focus on the less-capital intensive business of operating properties for fees, leaving third parties to pick up other hefty costs.

InterContinental Hotels Group, which owns the Holiday Inn and Crowne Plaza brands, now generates 95 per cent of its profits through its fee business.

Investors have welcomed the asset-light approach. But it has also locked hotel groups like Accor into a race to secure the largest number of properties under their management. "The issue is growth," said Mr Hearn [of Amaris Hospitality]. "When you are asset light, it is a flag race: how many flags can you get." Lukas Hartwich, analyst at Green Street Advisors, says the hunt for scale has lured companies towards deals, especially for Starwood, which has trailed rivals Hilton and Marriott in adding hotel rooms. "Really in the end of all this we will have a few very large players . . . the bigger you are, the more people know you and will stay at your hotel."

The global hotel industry is still fragmented; the top five hotel operators manage or franchise only just over a fifth of the world's hotel rooms.

For some groups, acquisitions would help expand their geographical footprint. Hilton, Marriott and IHG have 83 per cent, 81 per cent and 65 per cent of their rooms in the Americas. A merger between Hyatt and Starwood would create a company with the leading estate, in terms of size, in Asia.

Such a combination would also offer significant benefits in combining loyalty programmes and marketing operations.

The enlarged hotel companies would also have more clout to take on Expedia and Priceline, who control 61 per cent of the global travel booking market, and negotiated lower commissions. "If customers are being lured to online travel agents rather than hotel brands as a first stop then that puts pressure on the biggest holders of brands," said Mr Hearn.

FT   *Financial Times,* 6 November 2015.
All Rights Reserved.

Exhibit 20.9

In the telecoms industry, the consumer comes first

Margrethe Vestager shows little patience for flaky anti-competitive arguments

Nobody applies to be European antitrust chief if they do not relish a fight. Much time is spent in running battles with companies such as Gazprom, Microsoft and Google — not the sort to roll over easily. A steely ruthlessness is what is required. So it is good to see these words used to describe Margrethe Vestager, the Danish politician who now holds the portfolio.

She will need a stern resolve to keep Europe's telecoms market competitive. Merger activity is building.

In the UK, mobile providers O2 and Three hope to combine, which would create a firm of 32m customers with just two domestic competitors. Other mergers in France, Germany and Austria look likely to have a similar effect in their home markets.

It is no mystery why such firms are so eager to consolidate. Cost savings and a lessening of competitive pressure both boost margins, delighting the shareholder. The effect on the customer is less

▶

Exhibit 20.9 (*continued*)

clear and often highly deleterious. As a result, to build the public case for a merger these firms claim that a little extra pricing power encourages great investment, improving the network for customers and the wider economy.

To a political ear this makes curtailing competition sound rather attractive. More investment means more jobs for Europeans; investment in telecoms is even better, enhancing the still fragmented digital single market. Leading politicians, including Angela Merkel, chancellor of Germany, and Jean-Claude Juncker, president of the European Commission, sound convinced. They look enviously upon the US, where capital expenditure in telecoms is growing at a much faster pace.

As a result Ms Vestager faces a fight not just against the continent's telecoms groups but also much of its political establishment. Under the same pressure, her predecessor Joaquín Almunia resisted for a while but eventually waved through a number of mergers in exchange for assurances about keeping spectrum available for "virtual operators".

Ms Vestager plans to be more robust, defending what has been a significant European success story. Declining revenues are in this case a sign that the market is working. Roaming charges have fallen through the floor, cutting €8bn off customers' bills.

Returns on invested capital may have fallen too but remain well above US levels. Other measures of quality, like download speeds, are as good or better in the EU. The weakness of the case against competition is demonstrated by how it is buried in euphemism. Politicians talk not of undermining the consumer but of building national champions. Rather than acknowledge that he is calling for less competition within national markets, Mr Juncker spoke of "applying EU competition law with a continental spirit". Coy about calling for higher prices, telecoms bosses ask for "greater financial security and a more stable environment". Ms Vestager's steelier approach is right. Virtual competitors do not nip as fiercely at the heels of incumbents as the more tangible sort. Competition could just as easily encourage as dissuade investment — no firm wants to be left behind as rivals build out a superior network. The higher investment that is meant to be encouraged by lesser competition is difficult to detect. Steeper consumer prices in places such as Austria are a clear fact. Ms Vestager faces a patchwork landscape of national markets and overlapping services that include broadband, television and wireless. Disentangling innovative from predatory behaviour will never be easy. But her unambiguous defence of the consumer is an excellent place to start.

Financial Times, 10 March 2015.
All Rights Reserved.

Internalisation of transactions

By bringing together two firms at different stages of the production chain an acquirer may achieve more efficient coordination of the different levels. The focus here is on the costs of communication, the costs of bargaining, the costs of monitoring contract compliance and the costs of contract enforcement. Vertical integration reduces the uncertainty of supply or the prospect of finding an outlet, as well as having the potential to deny competitors' access to supply or customers. It also avoids the problems of having to deal with a supplier or customer in a strong bargaining position. Naturally, the savings have to be compared with the extra costs which may be generated because of the loss of competition between suppliers – managers of units may become complacent and inefficient because they are assured of a buyer for their output.

Entry to new markets and industries

If a firm has chosen to enter a particular market but lacks the right knowhow, the quickest way of establishing itself may be through the purchase of an existing player in that product or geographical market. To grow into the market organically, that is, by developing the required skills and market strength through internal efforts alone, may mean that the firm, for many years, will not have the necessary critical size to become an effective competitor. During the growth period losses may well be incurred. Furthermore, creating a new participant in a market may generate oversupply and excessive competition, producing the danger of a price war and thus eliminating profits. An example of a market entry type of merger is Unilever's 2017 merger with Sundial Brands, a US skincare company whose customers are mainly African-American. This follows a string of other small company acquisitions designed to obtain on-trend products, ecommerce savvy or exposure to local markets.

Many small firms are acquired by large ones because they possess particular technical skills. The small firm may have a unique product developed through the genius of a small team of enthusiasts, but the team may lack the interest and the skills to produce the product on a large scale, or to market it effectively. The purchaser might be aware that its present range of products is facing a declining market or is rapidly becoming obsolescent. It sees the chance of applying its general managerial skills and experience to a cutting-edge technology through a deal with the technologically literate enthusiasts. Thus the two firms are worth more together than apart because each gains something it does not already have. The large pharmaceutical companies frequently team up with biotechnology firms so that they can each draw on the strengths of the other, e.g. the innovative drive of the smaller company and the resources to pay for clinical trials and initial marketing of the larger firm.

Another reason for acquiring a company at the forefront of technology might be to apply the talent, knowledge and techniques to the parent company's existing and future product lines, and vice versa, to give the group a competitive edge through technological synergy.[6] Many Chinese companies have this in mind when they buy Western firms.

Tax advantages

In some countries, if a firm makes a loss in a particular year these losses can be used to reduce taxable profit in a future year. More significantly, for this discussion about mergers, not only can past losses be offset against current profits within one firm in one line of business, past losses of an acquired subsidiary can be used to reduce present taxable profits of the parent company and thus lower tax bills. Thus there is an incentive to buy firms which have accumulated tax losses.

In the UK the rules are more strict. The losses incurred by the acquired firm before it becomes part of the group cannot be offset against the profits of another member of the group. The losses can only be set against the future profits of the acquired company. Also that company has to continue operating in the same line of business.

Risk diversification

One of the primary reasons advanced for conglomerate mergers is that the overall income stream of the holding company will be less volatile if the cash flows come from a wide variety of products and markets. At first glance the pooling of unrelated income streams would seem to improve the position of shareholders. They obtain a reduction in risk without a decrease in return.

The problem with this argument is that investors can obtain the same risk reduction in an easier and cheaper way. They could simply buy a range of shares in the separately quoted firms. In addition, it is said that conglomerates lack focus – with managerial attention and resources being dissipated.

A justification which is on more solid theoretical grounds runs as follows. A greater stability of earnings will appeal to lenders, thus encouraging lower interest rates and greater willingness to lend. Because of the reduced earnings volatility there is less likelihood of the firm producing negative returns and so it should avoid defaulting on interest or principal payments. The other group that may benefit from diversification is individuals who have most of their income eggs in one basket – that is, the directors, founding family and employees.

Superior management

The first column of Exhibit 20.3 deals with the potential gains available through the combining of two firms' trading operations. The second column shows benefits which might be available to

---

6 Bena and Li (2014) found evidence that synergies obtained by combining innovation capabilities are an important impetus for many corporate acquisitions.

an acquiring company which has a management team with superior ability, either at running a target's operations, or at identifying undervalued firms which can be bought at bargain prices.

Inefficient management

If the management of firm X is more efficient than the management of firm Y then a gain could be produced by a merger if X's management is dominant after the unification. Inefficient management may be able to survive in the short run but eventually the owners will attempt to remove them by, say, dismissing the senior directors and management team through a boardroom coup. Alternatively the shareholders might invite other management teams to make a bid for the firm, or simply accept an offer from another firm which is looking for an outlet for its perceived surplus managerial talent.

A variation on the theme is where the target firm does have talented management but they are directing their efforts in their own interests and not in the interests of shareholders. In this case the takeover threat can serve as a control mechanism limiting the degree of divergence from shareholder wealth maximisation.

A conglomerate's superior efficiency in allocating capital and in using an extraordinary resource

In less well developed markets, where banking, stock markets, accounting and legal infrastructures are weak, investors are wary of providing capital to young companies for growth. Conglomerates can often step in here as they are able to allocate capital to businesses better than individual businesses seeking capital in the external markets (banks, bonds and equity). Internal assessment and monitoring will suffer from fewer information asymmetry problems, leading to a lower cost of capital than if external finance is used. Also internal finance might be able to take a longer-term perspective.

Some companies possess an extraordinary resource that allows them to outperform competitors. Often, this resource is under utilised. By merging with another company the resource can be shared with little additional cost to the parent. For example, film studios buy theme parks and allow the parks to make use of their film characters to develop rides and in marketing. Or a brand is extended into another product line through merger, e.g. Virgin Group moves into TV or banking.

Undervalued shares

Many people believe that stock markets occasionally underestimate the value of a share. This could be because the market is excessively concerned by short-term problems facing the company and does not allow sufficiently for bounce-back due to, say, improved management or better industry conditions. Always on the prowl are private equity firms (among others) looking for undervalued targets with potential to generate higher cash flows, often after a reorganisation or by combining with other industry firms owned by the private firm. These types of mergers are instigated by what is termed a financial bidder, as opposed to a strategic bidder, which is a company in a related field of business, such as a competitor, supplier or customer which looks for targets offering long-term operational synergies. Financial bidders are usually looking for an exit by selling the business after a period of say 5–10 years, whereas strategic bidders look to buy and hold.

Even if the potential target firm is being operated in the most efficient manner possible and productivity could not be raised even if the most able managerial team in the world took over it might be lowly valued by the stock market because the management are not very aware of the importance of a good stock market image. Perhaps they provide little information beyond the statutory minimum and in this way engender suspicion and uncertainty. Investors hate uncertainty and will tend to avoid such a firm. On the other hand, the acquiring firm might be very conscious of its stock market image and put considerable effort into cultivating good relationships with the investment community.

This line of thinking does not automatically reject semi-strong form efficiency. This requires that share prices fully reflect all publicly available information. In many of these situations the acquiring firm has knowledge that goes beyond that which is available to the general public. It may be intimately acquainted with the product markets, or the technology, of the target firm and so can value the target more accurately than most investors. Or it may simply be that the acquirer puts more resources into information searching than anyone else. Alternatively the acquirer may be an insider, using private information, and may buy shares illegally.

Managerial motives

The reasons for merger described in this section are often just as rational as the ones which have gone before, except, this time, the rational objective may not be shareholder wealth maximisation.

One group which seems to do well out of merger activity is the management team of the acquiring firm. When all the dust has settled after a merger they end up controlling a larger enterprise. And, of course, having responsibility for a larger business means that the managers *have* to be paid a lot more money. Not only must they have higher monthly pay to induce them to give of their best, they must also have enhanced pension contributions and myriad perks. Being in charge of a larger business and receiving a higher salary also brings increased status. Some feel more successful and important, and the people they rub shoulders with tend to be in a more influential class.

As if these incentives to grow rapidly through mergers were not enough, some people simply enjoy putting together an empire – creating something grand and imposing gives a sense of achievement and satisfaction. To have control over ever larger numbers of individuals appeals to basic instincts: some measure their social position and their stature by counting the number of employees under them. Warren Buffett comments, 'The acquisition problem is often compounded by a biological bias: many CEOs attain their positions in part because they possess an abundance of animal spirits and ego. If an executive is heavily endowed with these qualities – which, it should be acknowledged, sometimes have their advantages – they won't disappear when he reaches the top. When such a CEO is encouraged by his advisors to make deals, he responds much as would a teenage boy who is encouraged by his father to have a normal sex life. It's not a push he needs.'[7]

John Kay points out that many managers enjoy the excitement of the merger process itself:

> For the modern manager, only acquisition reproduces the thrill of the chase, the adventures of military strategy. There is the buzz that comes from the late night meetings in merchant banks, the morning conference calls with advisers to plan your strategy. Nothing else puts your picture and your pronouncements on the front page, nothing else offers so easy a way to expand your empire and emphasise your role.[8]

These first four managerial motives for merger – empire building, status, power and remuneration – can be powerful forces impelling takeover activity. But, of course, they are rarely expressed openly, and certainly not shouted about during a takeover battle.

Hubris

The fifth reason, hubris, is also very important in explaining merger activity. It may help particularly to explain why mergers tend to occur in greatest numbers when the economy and companies generally have had a few good years of growth, and management are feeling rather pleased with themselves.

Richard Roll in 1986 spelt out his hubris hypothesis for merger activity. Hubris means overweening self-confidence or, less kindly, arrogance. Managers commit errors of over-optimism in evaluating merger opportunities due to excessive pride or faith in their own abilities. The suggestion is that some acquirers do not learn from their mistakes and may be convinced that they can see an undervalued firm when others cannot. They may also think that they have the talent, experience and entrepreneurial flair to shake up a business and generate improved profit performance (*see* **Exhibit 20.10**).

7 Warren Buffett, Berkshire *Hathaway Annual Report* 1984.

8 John Kay, 'Poor odds on the takeover lottery', *Financial Times*, 26 January 1996.

Exhibit 20.10

Warren Buffett on hubris

On toads and princesses

'Many managements apparently were overexposed in impressionable childhood years to the story in which the imprisoned, handsome prince is released from the toad's body by a kiss from the beautiful princess. Consequently, they are certain that the managerial kiss will do wonders for the profitability of Company T(arget). Such optimism is essential. Absent that rosy view, why else should the shareholders of Company A(cquisitor) want to own an interest in T at the 2X takeover cost rather than at the X market price they would pay if they made direct purchases on their own? In other words, investors can always buy toads at the going price for toads. If investors instead bankroll princesses who wish to pay double for the right to kiss a toad, those kisses had better pack some real dynamite. We've observed many kisses, but very few miracles. Nevertheless, many managerial princesses remain serenely confident about the future potency of their kisses – even after their corporate backyards are kneedeep in unresponsive toads.'

Source: Warren Buffett, *Berkshire Hathaway Annual Report 1981*. Reprinted by kind permission of Warren Buffett. © Warren Buffett.

Note that the hubris hypothesis does not require the conscious pursuit of self-interest by managers. They may have worthy intentions but can make mistakes in judgement.

Survival

It has been noticed by both casual observers and empiricists that mergers tend to take place with a large acquirer and a smaller target. Potential target managements may come to believe that the best way to avoid being taken over, and then sacked or dominated, is to grow large themselves, and to do so quickly. Thus, mergers can have a self-reinforcing mechanism or positive feedback loop – the more mergers there are in an industry the more vulnerable management feel and the more they are inclined to carry out mergers – *see* **Exhibit 20.11**. Firms may merge for the survival of the management team and not primarily for the benefit of shareholders.[9] **Exhibit 20.12** discusses the 'eat or be eaten' mentality in the pharmaceutical sector.

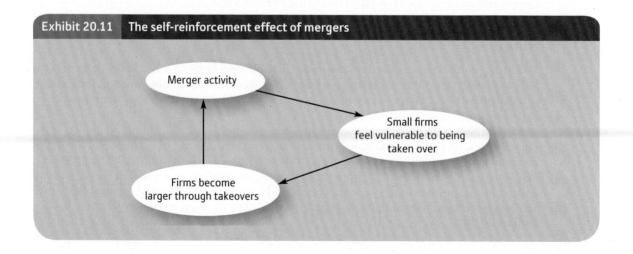

| **Exhibit 20.11** | **The self-reinforcement effect of mergers** |

9 *See* Louis (2004b) for an example in banking and Gorton et al. (2009) for the more general case.

Exhibit 20.12

Healthcare sector leads feverish M&A activity

By Arash Massoudi and James Fontanella-Khan

On March 2, the chief executives of Johnson & Johnson, Pfizer and AbbVie all rushed to California to make one last pitch to Pharmacyclics, a cancer drugmaker with just one product to its name.

All three were bidding to buy the company and, two days later, AbbVie prevailed in a fiercely contested auction, splashing $21bn on a cash-and-shares deal. It valued Pharmacyclics at a 60 per cent premium to its share price in early February — and exemplified the competition for pharmaceuticals assets that has driven global dealmaking.

In the first three months of 2015, the total value of healthcare deals reached $95.3bn,

This feverish M&A activity has been led by drugmakers seeking new treatments that can replace the billions of dollars in sales they will lose when their existing patents expire.

Analysts say the 'eat or be eaten' mindset will drive further deal activity in the coming months, as smaller drug companies such as Endo Pharmaceuticals and Mallinckrodt look to challenge their larger rivals for other assets.

Free cash flow

Free cash flow is defined as cash flow in excess of the amount needed to fund all projects that have positive NPVs. In theory firms should retain money within the firm to invest in any project which will produce a return greater than the investors' opportunity cost of capital. Any cash flow surplus to this should be returned to shareholders (*see* Chapter 19).

However, Jensen (1986) suggests that managers are not always keen on simply handing back the cash which is under their control. This would reduce their power. Also, if they needed to raise more funds the capital markets will require justification concerning the use of such money. So instead of giving shareholders free cash flow the managers use it to buy other firms. Peter Lynch is more blunt: '[I] believe in the bladder theory of corporate finance, as propounded by Hugh Liedtke of Pennzoil: The more cash that builds up in the treasury, the greater the pressure to piss it away.'[10]

Third party motives

Advisers

There are many highly paid individuals who benefit greatly from merger activity. Advisers charge fees to the bidding company to advise on such matters as identifying targets, the rules of the take-over game, regulations, monopoly references, finance, bidding tactics, stock market announcements and so on. Typical fees are between 0.3% and 1.5% of the value of the target company for advisory work, often amounting to tens of millions of pounds – *see* **Exhibit 20.13**. Fees for helping to raise finance to pay for the merger, e.g. underwriting a rights issue, could be 3–4% of the amount raised. Advisers are also appointed to the target firms. Other groups with a keen eye on the merger market include accountants and lawyers; their fees can be at the same level as the investment bankers' advisory fee.

There is also the press, ranging from tabloids to specialist publications. Even a cursory examination of them gives the distinct impression that they tend to have a statistical bias of articles which

---

10 Lynch (1990), p. 204.

emphasise the positive aspects of mergers. It is difficult to find negative articles, especially at the time of a takeover. They like the excitement of the merger event and rarely follow up with a considered assessment of the outcome. Also the press reports generally portray acquirers as dynamic, forward-looking and entrepreneurial.

It seems reasonable to suppose that professionals engaged in the merger market might try to encourage or cajole firms to contemplate a merger and thus generate turnover in the market. Some provide unsolicited reports on potential targets to try and tempt prospective clients into becoming

Exhibit 20.13

Goldman Sachs dominates the league table that matters: deal fees

By Sujeet Indap

In the post-financial crisis era, the most powerful US M&A advisors can be divided into two groups. At the top, the traditionally dominant investment banks, Goldman Sachs and Morgan Stanley. Below them, a coterie of much smaller, boutique firms who have exploited the turmoil at the large universal banks to poach talent and who are winning an increasingly large share of deals.

An FT analysis of deal fees paid between 2014 and 2016 confirms that broad picture, but it exposes some

stark realities that are not picked up in the traditional M&A league tables, which typically rank advisers based on the size of the deal, rather than the metric that really matters: fees.

The first is that Goldman is even more dominant than usually recognised. Over the three years to 2016, it earned nearly $2bn as an adviser on the sellside of deals involving US public companies valued at greater than $500m, implying a fee share of greater than 20%.

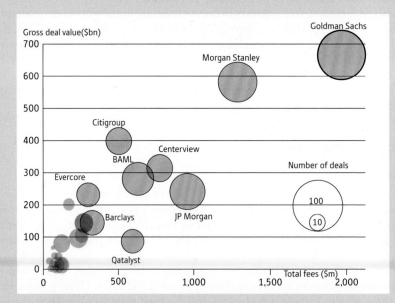

Typically, sellside deal fees are set as a percentage of the company's equity or enterprise value. The fee rate typically decreases as transaction sizes grow. For example, the average total fee in the FT study for

transactions valued at between $1bn and $5bn was 0.92 per cent; for transactions between $10bn and $25bn, the average rate was 0.29 per cent.

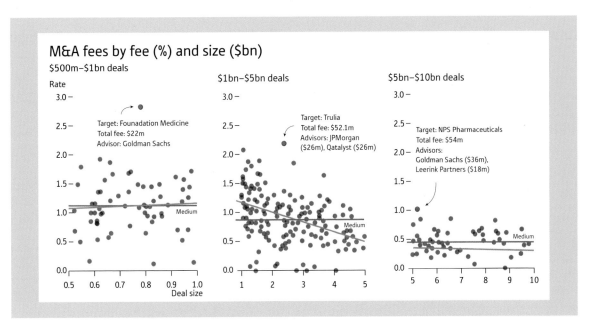

M&A fees by fee (%) and size ($bn)

$500m–$1bn deals

Rate

Target: Founadation Medicine
Total fee: $22m
Advisor: Goldman Sachs

Medium

Deal size

$1bn–$5bn deals

Target: Trulia
Total fee: $52.1m
Advisors: JPMorgan
($26m), Qatalyst ($26m)

Medium

$5bn–$10bn deals

Target: NPS Pharmaceuticals
Total fee: $54m
Advisors:
Goldman Sachs ($36m),
Leerink Partners ($18m)

Medium

acquirers. Of course, the author would never suggest that such esteemed and dignified organisations would ever stoop to promote mergers for the sake of increasing fee levels alone. You may think that, but I could not possibly comment.

Suppliers and customers

The Coca-Cola business model splits the ownership of the brand and concentrate from the capital-intensive bottling and logistics, most of which is handled by independent franchises. At one time there were over 270 bottlers. But recently Coca-Cola executives saw a way of making the bottlers more efficient, which, in turn, would allow Coca-Cola to charge them more for supplying concentrate: encourage them to merge into fewer larger operators. Many combinations followed, for example, the merger of eight Spanish and Portuguese bottlers and four in Japan. In 2015 three of Coca-Cola's European bottlers agreed to unite in a $27bn deal. Then in 2017 Coca-Cola East Japan joined with Coca-Cola West Japan forming a group with 90% of the domestic market. Car producers are intent on reducing the number of car parts suppliers and on putting more and more responsibility on the few remaining suppliers. Instead of buying-in small mechanical parts from dozens of suppliers and assembling them themselves into, say, a braking system, the assemblers want to buy the complete unit. This pressure has resulted in numerous mergers already and is expected to prompt many more. An example of suppliers promoting mergers is at the other end of the car production chain. Motor dealers in the UK were sent a clear message from the manufacturers that a higher degree of professionalism and service backup was required. This prompted a flurry of merger activity as the franchisees sought to meet the new standards.

Exhibit 20.3 provided a long list of potential merger motives. This list is by no means complete. Examining the reasons for merger is far from straightforward. There is a great deal of complexity, and in any one takeover, perhaps half a dozen or more of the motives discussed are at play.

Financing mergers

Exhibit 20.1 showed the relative importance of alternative methods of paying for the purchase of shares in another company over five decades. The popularity of each method has varied considerably over the years but in most years cash is the most attractive option, followed by shares, and finally the third category, comprising mostly debentures, loan stocks, convertibles and preference shares.

The chart tends to give a slightly distorted view of the financial behaviour of acquiring firms. In many cases where cash is offered to the target shareholders the acquirer does not borrow that cash or use cash reserves. Rather, it raises fresh funds through a rights issue of shares before the takeover bid.

The chart may also be misleading in the sense that a substantial proportion of mergers do not fall neatly into the payment categories. Many are mixed bids, providing shareholders of the target firms with a variety of financial securities or offering them a choice in the consideration they wish to receive, for example cash or shares, shares or loan stock. This is designed to appeal to the widest range of potential sellers. When George Lucas sold Lucasfilm Group to Disney in 2012 he was paid $2.2bn in cash and 37.1m Disney shares worth at that time $1.9bn; therefore total deal value was $4.1bn (the Disney shares doubled within five years).

Cash

One of the advantages of using cash for payment is that the acquirer's shareholders retain the same level of control over their company. That is, new shareholders from the target have not suddenly taken possession of a proportion of the acquiring firm's voting rights, as they would if the target shareholders were offered shares in the acquirer. Sometimes it is very important to shareholders that they maintain control over a company by owning a certain proportion of the firm's shares. Someone who has a 50.1% stake may resist attempts to dilute that holding to 25% even though the company may more than double in size.

The second major advantage of using cash is that its simplicity and preciseness give a greater chance of success. The alternative methods carry with them some uncertainty about their true worth. Cash has an obvious value and is therefore preferred by vendors, especially when markets are volatile.

From the point of view of the target's shareholders, cash has the advantage – in addition to being more certain in its value – that it also allows the recipients to spread their investments through the purchase of a wide-ranging portfolio. The receipt of shares or other securities means that the target shareholder either keeps the investment or, if diversification is required, has to incur transaction costs associated with selling the shares.

A disadvantage of cash to the target shareholders is that they may be liable for capital gains tax (CGT). This is payable when a gain is 'realised'. If the target shareholders receive cash for shares which have risen in value they may pay CGT. If, on the other hand, the target shareholders receive shares in the acquiring firm then their investment gain is not regarded as being realised and therefore no capital gains tax is payable at that time. The tax payment will be deferred until the time of the sale of the new shares – assuming an overall capital gain is made. (Note that some investment funds, e.g. pension funds, do not pay CGT and so this problem does not arise. Also, CGT can be reduced by tax-free allowances, and capital losses on other investments and so many shareholders will not consider CGT a burden.)

Offering cash may put a strain on the acquiring company's cash flow. Also any risk of misvaluing the target rests wholly with the acquirer – if shares in the acquirer are accepted by the target shareholders then they take some of the mis-valuation risk.

In certain circumstances the Takeover Panel insists on a cash offer or a cash alternative to an all-share offer.

One further consideration: borrowing cash that is then paid out for the target's shares may be a way of adjusting the financial gearing (debt to equity ratio) of the firm. On the other hand, the firm may already have high borrowings and be close to breaching loan covenants and so is reluctant to borrow more.

Shares

There are two main advantages for target shareholders of receiving shares in the acquirer rather than cash. First, capital gains tax can be postponed because the investment gain is not realised. Secondly, they maintain an interest in the combined entity. If the merger offers genuine benefits the target shareholders may wish to own part of the combined entity; e.g. in December 2017 the

Murdoch family agreed to sell their stake in 21st Century Fox to Disney for shares. They will hold 5% of the new entertainment giant.

To the acquirer, an advantage of offering shares is that there is no immediate outflow of cash. In the short run this form of payment puts less pressure on cash flow. However, the firm may consider the effect on the capital structure of the firm and the dilution of existing shareholders' positions.

Another reason for the acquirer to use shares as the consideration is that the price-earnings ratio (PER) game can be played. Through this companies can increase their earnings per share (eps) by acquiring firms with lower PERs than their own. The share price can rise (under certain conditions) despite there being no economic value created from the merger.

Imagine two firms, Crafty plc and Sloth plc. Both earned £1m last year and had the same number of shares. Earnings per share on an historic basis are therefore identical. The difference between the two companies is the stock market's perception of earnings growth. Because Crafty is judged to be a dynamic go-ahead sort of firm with management determined to improve earnings per share by large percentages in future years it is valued at a high PER of 20.

Sloth, on the other hand, is not seen by investors as a fast-moving firm. It is considered to be rather sleepy. The market multiplies last year's earnings per share by only a factor of 10 to determine the share price – *see* **Exhibit 20.14**.

Exhibit 20.14	Illustration of the price to earnings ratio game – Crafty and Sloth	
	Crafty	**Sloth**
Current earnings	£1m	£1m
Number of shares	10m	10m
Earnings per share	10p	10p
Price to earnings ratio	20	10
Share price	£2	£1

Because Crafty's shares sell at a price exactly double that of Sloth's it would be possible for Crafty to exchange one of its shares for two of Sloth's. (This is based on the assumption that there is no bid premium, but the argument that follows works just as well even if a reasonable bid premium is paid.)

Crafty's share capital rises by 50%, from 10 million shares to 15 million shares. However, eps are one-third higher. If the stock market still puts a high PER on Crafty's earnings, perhaps because investors believe that Crafty will liven up Sloth and produce high eps growth because of their more dynamic management, then the market capitalisation of Crafty increases and Crafty's shareholders are satisfied.

Each old shareholder in Crafty has experienced an increase in earnings per share and a share price rise of 33%. Also, previously Sloth's shareholders owned £10m of shares in Sloth; now they own £13.33m of shares (*see* **Exhibit 20.15**).

Exhibit 20.15	Crafty after an all-share merger with Sloth
	Crafty
Earnings	£2m
Number of shares	15m
Earnings per share	13.33p
Price to earnings ratio	20
Share price	267p

This all *seems* rational and good, but shareholders are basing their valuations on the assumption that managers will deliver on their promise of higher earnings growth through operational efficiencies, etc. Managers of companies with a high PER may see an easier way of increasing eps and boosting share price. Imagine you are managing a company which enjoys a high PER. Investors in your firm are expecting you to produce high earnings growth. You could try to achieve this through real entrepreneurial and/or managerial excellence, for example by product improvement, achieving economies of scale, increased operating efficiency, etc. Alternatively you could buy firms with low PERs and not bother to change operational efficiency. In the long run you know that your company will produce lower earnings because you are not adding any value to the firms that you acquire, you are probably paying an excessive bid premium to buy the present earnings and you probably have little expertise in the new areas of activity.

However, in the short run, eps can increase dramatically. The problem with this strategy is that in order to keep the earnings on a rising trend you must continue to keep fooling investors. You have to keep expanding at the same rate to receive regular boosts. One day expansion will stop; it will be revealed that the underlying economics of the firms bought have not improved (they may even have worsened as a result of neglect), and the share price will fall rapidly. Here is another reason to avoid placing too much emphasis on short-term eps figures. The Americans call this the bootstrap game. It can be very lucrative for some managers who play it skillfully. However, there can be many losers – society, shareholders, employees.

There are some significant dangers in paying shares for an aquisition, as Buffett makes clear in **Exhibit 20.16**.

Exhibit 20.16

Wealth for shareholders from mergers: the view of Warren Buffett

Our share issuances follow a simple basic rule: we will not issue shares unless we receive as much intrinsic business value as we give. Such a policy might seem axiomatic. Why, you might ask, would anyone issue dollar bills in exchange for fifty cent pieces? Unfortunately, many corporate managers have been willing to do just that.

The first choice of these managers in making acquisitions may be to use cash or debt. But frequently the CEO's cravings outpace cash and credit resources (certainly mine always have). Frequently, also, these cravings occur when his own stock [shares] is selling far below intrinsic business value. This state of affairs produces a moment of truth. At that point, as Yogi Berra has said, 'You can observe a lot just by watching.' For shareholders then will find which objective the management truly prefers – expansion of domain or maintenance of owners' wealth.

The need to choose between these objectives occurs for some simple reasons. Companies often sell in the stock market below their intrinsic business value. But when a company wishes to sell out completely, in a negotiated transaction, it inevitably wants to – and usually can – receive full business value in whatever kind of currency the value is to be delivered. If cash is to be used in payment, the seller's calculation of value received couldn't be easier. If stock [shares] of the buyer is to be currency, the seller's calculation is still relatively easy: just figure the market value in cash of what is to be received in stock.

Meanwhile, the buyer wishing to use his own stock as currency for the purchase has no problems if the stock is selling in the market at full intrinsic value.

But suppose it is selling at only half intrinsic value. In that case, the buyer is faced with the unhappy prospect of using a substantially undervalued currency to make its purchase.

Ironically, were the buyer to instead be a seller of its entire business, it too could negotiate for, and probably get, full intrinsic business value. But when the buyer makes a partial sale of itself – *and that is what the issuance of shares to make an acquisition amounts to* – it can customarily get no higher value set on its shares than the market chooses to grant it.

The acquirer who nevertheless barges ahead ends up using an undervalued (market value) currency to pay for a fully valued (negotiated value) property. In effect, the acquirer must give up $2 of value to receive $1 of value. Under such circumstances, a marvelous business purchased at a fair sales price becomes a terrible buy. For gold valued as gold cannot be purchased intelligently through the utilization of gold – or even silver – valued as lead.

If, however, the thirst for size and action is strong enough, the acquirer's manager will find ample rationalizations for such a value destroying issuance of stock. Friendly investment bankers will reassure him as to the soundness of his actions. (Don't ask the barber whether you need a haircut.)

A few favorite rationalizations employed by stock issuing managements follow:

(a) 'The company we're buying is going to be worth a lot more in the future.' (Presumably so is the interest in the old business that is being traded away; future prospects are implicit in the business valuation process. If 2X is issued for X, the imbalance still exists when both parts double in business value.)

(b) 'We have to grow.' (Who, it might be asked, is the 'We'? For present shareholders, the reality is that all existing businesses shrink when shares are issued. Were Berkshire to issue shares tomorrow for an acquisition, Berkshire would own everything that it now owns plus the new business, but *your* interest in such hard-to-match businesses as See's Candy Shops, National Indemnity, etc. would automatically be reduced. If (1) your family owns a 120 acre farm and (2) you invite a neighbor with 60 acres of comparable land to merge his farm into an equal partnership – with you to be managing partner, then (3) your managerial domain will have grown to 180 acres but you will have permanently shrunk by 25 per cent your family's ownership interest in both acreage and crops. Managers who want to expand their domain at the expense of owners might better consider a career in government.) . . .

There are three ways to avoid destruction of value for old owners when shares are issued for acquisitions. One is to have a true business-value-for-business-value merger, . . . Such a merger attempts to be fair to shareholders of *both* parties, with each receiving just as much as it gives in terms of intrinsic business value . . . It's not that acquirers wish to avoid such deals, it's just that they are very hard to do . . .

The second route presents itself when the acquirer's stock sells at or above its intrinsic business value. In that situation, the use of stock as currency actually may enhance the wealth of the acquiring company's owners . . .

The third solution is for the acquirer to go ahead with the acquisition, but then subsequently repurchase a quantity of shares equal to the number issued in the merger. In this manner, what originally was a stock-for-stock merger can be converted, effectively, into a cash-for-stock acquisition. Repurchases of this kind are damage repair moves. Regular readers will correctly guess that we much prefer repurchases that directly enhance the wealth of owners instead of repurchases that merely repair previous damage. Scoring touchdowns is more exhilarating than recovering one's fumbles.

The language utilized in mergers tends to confuse the issues and encourage irrational actions by managers. For example, 'dilution' is usually carefully calculated on a pro forma basis for both book value and current earnings per share. Particular emphasis is given to the latter item. When that calculation is negative (dilutive) from the acquiring company's standpoint, a justifying explanation will be made (internally, if not elsewhere) that the lines will cross favorably at some point in the future. (While deals often fail in practice, they never fail in projections – if the CEO is visibly panting over a prospective acquisition, subordinates and consultants will supply the requisite projections to rationalize any price.) Should the calculation produce numbers that are immediately positive – that is, antidilutive – for the acquirer, no comment is thought to be necessary.

The attention given this form of dilution is overdone: current earnings per share (or even earnings per share of the next few years) are an important variable in most business valuations, but far from all powerful.

There have been plenty of mergers, non-dilutive in this limited sense, that were instantly value-destroying for the acquirer. And some mergers that have diluted current and near term earnings per share have in fact been value enhancing. What really counts is whether a merger is dilutive or antidilutive in terms of intrinsic business value (a judgment involving consideration of many variables). We believe calculation of dilution from this viewpoint to be all-important (and too seldom made).

A second language problem relates to the equation of exchange. If Company A announces that it will issue shares to merge with Company B, the process is customarily described as 'Company A to Acquire Company B', or 'B Sells to A'. Clearer thinking about the matter would result if a more awkward, but more accurate description were used: 'Part of A sold to acquire B' or 'Owners of B to receive part of A in exchange for their properties'. In a trade, what you are giving is just as important as what you are getting . . .

Managers and directors might sharpen their thinking by asking themselves if they would sell 100% of their business on the same basis they are being asked to sell part of it. And if it isn't smart to sell all on such a basis, they should ask themselves why it is smart to sell a portion. A cumulation of small managerial stupidities will produce a major stupidity – not a major triumph. (Las Vegas has been built upon the wealth transfers that occur when people engage in seemingly small disadvantageous capital transactions.) . . .

Finally, a word should be said about the 'double whammy' effect upon owners of the acquiring company when value diluting stock issuances occur. Under such circumstances, the first blow is the loss of intrinsic business value that occurs through the merger itself. The second is the downward revision in market valuation that, quite rationally, is given to that now diluted business value. For current and prospective owners understandably will not pay as much for assets lodged in the hands of a management that has a record of wealth destruction through unintelligent share issuances as they will pay for assets entrusted to a management with precisely equal operating talents, but a known distaste for anti-owner actions. Once management shows itself insensitive to the interests of owners, shareholders will suffer a long time from the price/value ratio afforded their stock (relative to other stocks), no matter what assurances management gives that the value diluting action taken was a one-of-a-kind event.

Source: Warren Buffett's letter to Shareholders in the *Berkshire Hathaway Annual Report 1982*. Reprinted with permission. © Warren E. Buffett and Berkshire Hathaway Inc.

An obvious disadvantage of using shares is when the acquirer is not quoted on a stock exchange – the target shareholders are unable to see a market price for the shares they receive. Also they will be unable to sell easily in a secondary market should they wish to do so.

Even a stock market quoted acquirer might have great difficulty persuading target shareholders to accept its shares if they have doubts about the sustainability of high equity market valuations. This problem stymied a lot of mergers in the 2017/18 US stock market boom, when the proportion of deals that were all-share offers fell to record lows (10.6%). While some acquirers were able to fall back on their access to borrowed funds to complete their deals they would have preferred to issue shares if they could. But target shareholders were (a) concerned about the acquirers' share prices falling dramatically during a merger process, meaning that the final bid could be significantly lower than the original proposal, and (b) fearful about the longer-term prospects for the shares generally. Rockwell Automation, for example, rejected a $29bn offer from Emerson Electric partly due to 'the risks associated with Emerson's stock-based currency'.

Other types of finance

Alternative forms of consideration including debentures, loan stock, convertibles and preference shares are unpopular, largely because of the difficulty of establishing a rate of return on these securities which will be attractive to target shareholders. Also, these securities often lack marketability and voting rights over the newly merged company.

Deferred payment

Deferred payment, in which the total to be paid over the next few years depends on performance targets being achieved, is a useful way of tying in key personnel to the combined company (they might be offered an 'earnout' deal). Another advantage of deferring payment is the reduced cash flow strain.

The merger process

The regulatory bodies

The City Panel on Takeovers and Mergers provides the main governing rules for companies engaged in merger activity in the UK. It is often referred to as 'The Takeover Panel' or simply the 'Panel'. Its rules are expressed in the City Code on Takeovers and Mergers (the 'Takeover Code' or 'Code').

The Takeover Panel was originally set up by City institutions, bankers, accountants, the London Stock Exchange, and the Bank of England as a self-regulatory non-statutory organisation in 1968. It was viewed as a model of self-regulation around the world because it could be very quick in making decisions and enforcing them. Also, because it was run by very knowledgeable practitioners from the City, it could maintain a high degree of flexibility, e.g. it could quickly change the rules to meet new challenges – especially when clever financiers thought they had found a way around the restrictions. It could also maintain a degree of informality in providing companies with guidance on what is acceptable and what is not – a 'word-in-the-ear' or a 'raised eyebrow' could prevent many actions that would have been against the spirit of the Panel's rules. The alternative approach (adopted in many countries), one based on statute and lawyers, was seen as bureaucratic, expensive and slow.

Somehow the Panel has managed to hold on to its old speed, flexibility and informality despite it now having statutory backing (under the Companies Act 2006 and the EU's Directive on Takeover Bids). It has some strong legal powers, such as the right to insist on receiving information from anyone involved in a bid. Panel decisions are legally enforceable. However, it still operates with a high degree of self-regulation and independence of the state; for example, it can amend its own rules.

It also still relies on an informal relationship with the regulated community, and uses subtle power and influence, rather than a rigid set of statutory rules subject to constant challenge in the courts. Even now it very rarely goes to court to enforce or defend a decision – the courtroom is seen very much as a last resort. The litigation culture that bedevils a lot of other countries is something the City and the government have tried to avoid.

Thus, we still have a 'light-touch' regulatory system, with an emphasis on the spirit of the rules and the Panel seen as approachable for consultation, guidance and negotiation, rather than a heavy-handed rule enforcer.

The sanctions it employs are largely the same as those used before it received statutory backing. These range from private or public reprimands (embarrassing and potentially commercially damaging to bidder, target or adviser) to the shunning of those who defy the Code by regulated City institutions – the Financial Conduct Authority, FCA, demands that no regulated firm (such as a bank, broker or adviser) act for a client firm that seriously breaks the Panel's rules ('cold shouldering'). Practitioners in breach of the Code may be judged not fit and proper persons to carry on investment business by the FCA, so there is considerable leverage over City institutions that might otherwise be tempted to assist a rule-breaker. The Panel may give a ruling restraining a person from acting in breach of its rules. It may also insist on compensation being paid. The FCA can also take legal action under market abuse legislation – e.g. when there is share price manipulation. In rare cases the Panel may temporarily remove voting rights from particular shareholders.

Note, however, that the Panel does not offer a view on either the commercial merit of the bid nor on competition or other public policy issues that might arise.

As well as having regulatory power over companies quoted on public markets, the Panel can regulate the behaviour of all other public limited companies.

The fundamental objective of the Takeover Panel regulation is to ensure fair and equal treatment for all shareholders. The main areas of concern are:

- shareholders being treated differently, for example large shareholders getting a special deal;
- insider dealing (control over this is assisted by statutory rules);
- target management action contrary to its shareholders' best interests; for example, the advice to accept or reject a bid must be in the shareholders' best interests, not that of the management;
- lack of adequate and timely information released to shareholders;
- artificial manipulation of share prices; for example an acquirer offering shares cannot make the offer more attractive by getting friends to push up its share price;
- the bid process dragging on and thus distracting management from their proper tasks.

The Competition and Markets Authority, CMA, also takes a keen interest in mergers to ensure that mergers do not produce 'a substantial lessening of competition'. It has the power to clear a merger on competition grounds. A small minority of proposed mergers may, after an initial screening, be followed by a thorough investigation. Following which the FCA may insist on major changes to the merged entity. For example, in 2017 Euro Car Parts was forced to sell nine car part branches out of the 102 branches acquired with Andrew Page, in those towns where the two companies were close competitors and the merger could significantly reduce competition for local customers. A FCA inquiry may take several months to complete, during which time the merger bid is put on hold. Another hurdle in the path of large intra-European Union mergers is their scrutiny by the European Commission in Brussels.

Pre-bid

Exhibit 20.17 shows the main stages of a merger. The acquiring firm usually employs advisers to help make a takeover bid. Most firms carry out mergers infrequently and so have little expertise in-house. The identification of suitable targets may be one of the first tasks of the advisers. Once these are identified there would be a period of appraising the target. The strategic fit would be considered and there would be a detailed analysis of what would be purchased. The product markets and types of customers could be investigated and there would be a financial analysis showing sales, profit and rates of return history. The assets and liabilities would be assessed, as would assets that are truly valuable but are never recorded on a balance sheet, e.g. employees' extraordinary abilities when working as a team.

Exhibit 20.17 **The merger process**

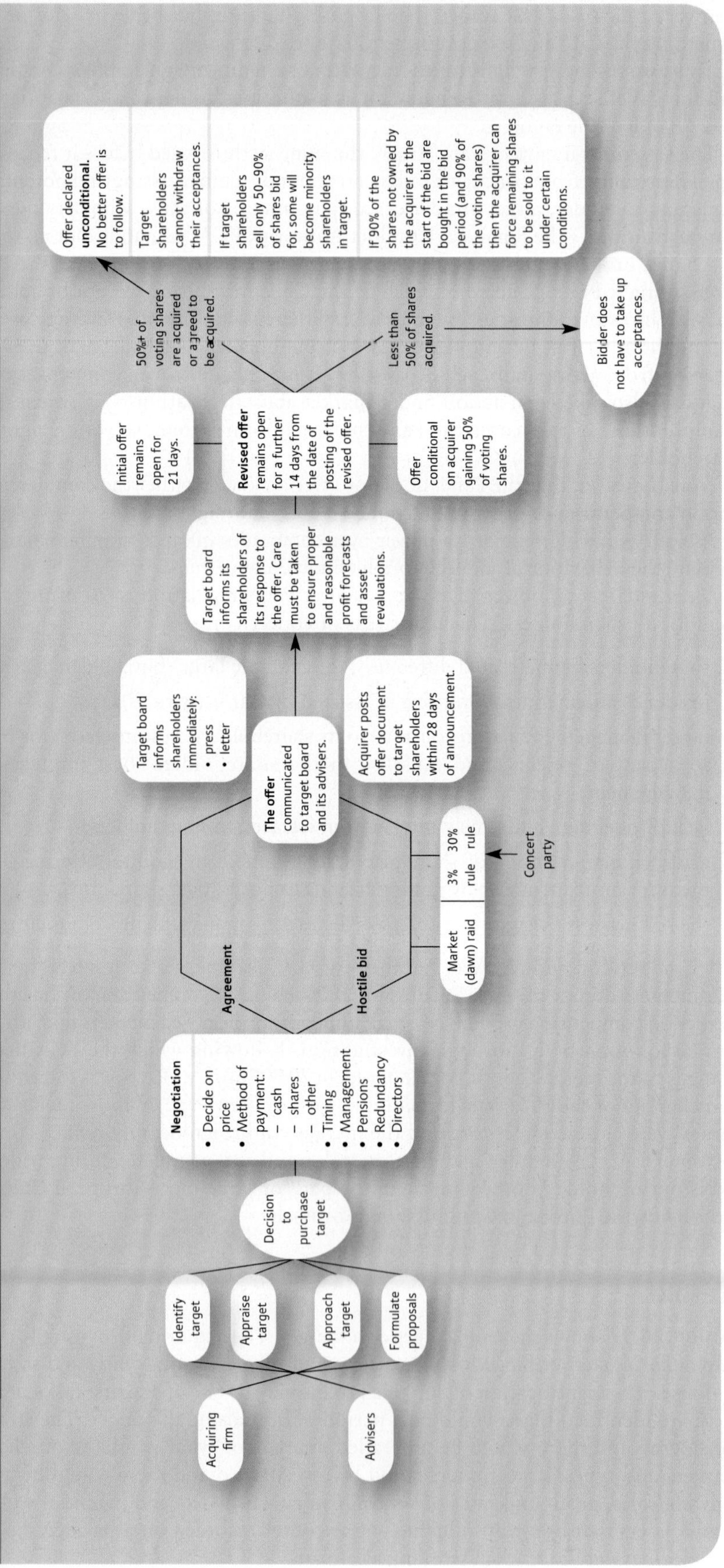

Negotiation
- Decide on price
- Method of payment:
  - cash
  - shares
  - other
- Timing
- Management
- Pensions
- Redundancy
- Directors

Decision to purchase target

Identify target

Appraise target

Approach target

Formulate proposals

Acquiring firm

Advisers

Agreement

Hostile bid

Market (dawn) raid

3% rule | 30% rule

Concert party

The offer communicated to target board and its advisers.

Target board informs shareholders immediately:
- press
- letter

Acquirer posts offer document to target shareholders within 28 days of announcement.

Target board informs its shareholders of its response to the offer. Care must be taken to ensure proper and reasonable profit forecasts and asset revaluations.

Initial offer remains open for 21 days.

Revised offer remains open for a further 14 days from the date of posting of the revised offer.

Offer conditional on acquirer gaining 50% of voting shares.

50%+ of voting shares are acquired or agreed to be acquired.

Less than 50% of shares acquired.

Bidder does not have to take up acceptances.

Offer declared **unconditional**. No better offer is to follow.

Target shareholders cannot withdraw their acceptances.

If target shareholders sell only 50–90% of shares bid for, some will become minority shareholders in target.

If 90% of the shares not owned by the acquirer at the start of the bid are bought in the bid period (and 90% of the voting shares) then the acquirer can force remaining shares to be sold to it under certain conditions.

If the appraisal stage is satisfactory the firm may approach the target. Because it is often cheaper to acquire a firm with the agreement of the target management, and because the managers and employees have to work together after the merger, in the majority of cases discussions take place which are designed to produce a set of proposals acceptable to both groups of shareholders and managers.

During the negotiation phase the price and form of payment (e.g. cash) have to be decided upon. In most cases the acquirer has to offer a bid premium. This tends to be in the range of 20%–100% of the pre-bid price. The average is about 30–50%. The timing of payment is also considered. For example, some mergers involve 'earn-outs' in which the selling shareholders (usually the same individuals as the directors) receive payment over a period of time dependent on the level of post-merger profits. The issue of how the newly merged entity will be managed will also be discussed: who will be chief executive? Which managers will take particular positions? Also the pension rights of the target firm's employees and ex-employees have to be considered, as does the issue of redundancy, especially the removal of directors – what payoffs are to be made available?

If agreement is reached then the acquirer formally communicates the offer to the target's board and shareholders. This will be followed by a recommendation from the target's board to its shareholders to accept the offer.

If, however, agreement cannot be reached and the acquirer still wishes to proceed, the interesting situation of a hostile bid battle is created. One of the first stages might be a 'dawn raid'. This is where the acquirer acts with such speed in buying the shares of the target company that the raider achieves the objective of obtaining a substantial stake in the target before the target's management have time to react. The acquirer usually offers investors and market makers a price which is significantly higher than the closing price on the previous day. This high price is only offered to those close to the market and able to act quickly.

An important trigger point for disclosure of shareholdings in a company, whether the subject of a merger or not, is the 3% holding level. If a 3% stake is owned then this has to be publicly declared to the company. Following the formal notice the information is posted on free financial websites. This disclosure rule is designed to allow the target company to know who is buying its shares and to give it advance warning of a possible takeover raid. The management can then prepare a defence and present information to shareholders should the need arise. The 3% rule also applies to holdings via derivatives of shares.

If a person or company builds up a stake of 30% or more the Takeover Panel rules usually oblige it to make a cash bid for all of the target company's shares (or a share offer with a cash alternative) at the highest price paid in the previous 12 months (a 'mandatory bid'). A 30% stake often gives the owner a substantial amount of power. It is thought the shareholders need to be given the opportunity to decide if they want to continue to hold shares in a company with a dominant shareholder. It is very difficult for anyone else to bid successfully for the firm when someone already has 30%. It is surprising how often one reads in the financial press that a company or individual has bought a 29.9% holding so that they have as large a stake as possible without triggering a mandatory bid.

Sometimes, in the past, if a company wanted to take over another it would, to avoid declaring at the 3% level (or 5% as it was then), or to avoid bidding at the 30% level, sneak up on the target firm's management and shareholders. It would form a 'concert party' by persuading its friends, other firms and individuals to buy stakes in the target. Each of these holdings would be below the threshold levels. When the acquirer was ready to pounce it would already have under its control a significant, if not a majority, controlling interest. Today all concert party holdings are lumped together for the purposes of disclosure and trigger points. The very strict concert party rules were perceived as reducing the potential for shareholders to work together to correct a bad management or bad strategy. These rules have now been relaxed for non-bid situations – *see* **Exhibit 20.18**.

Once a company becomes a bid target any dealings in the target's shares by the bidder (or an associate) must be publicly disclosed no later than 12 noon on the business day following the transaction. Furthermore, once an offer is under way, any holder of 1% or more of either the bidder or the target must publicly disclose dealings by midday of the next business day. An investor holding 1% must disclose any dealings in the bidder's or target's shares, warrants, convertibles, contracts for difference, options, other derivatives and all other securities in the company.

Exhibit 20.18

FSA clarifies position on activist investors

By Brooke Masters and Kate Burgess

Investors can work actively together to oust a chief executive or change corporate strategy without falling foul of European Union and UK rules against market abuse and acting in concert, the Financial Services Authority [fore-runner of the FCA] said.

But such alliances must be based on specific corporate issues rather than a long-term agreement to vote together, and the investors cannot trade on information they may glean while working together, the City watchdog added.

Some investors have said they were reluctant to work together for fear of falling foul of 2007 guidance from the FSA that warned activist investors not to collude. Sally Dewar, FSA managing director for wholesale markets, wrote: 'We do not believe that our regulatory requirements prevent collective engagement by institutional shareholders designed to raise legitimate concerns on particular corporate issues, events or matters of governance with the management of investee companies.'

 Financial Times, 20 August 2009, p. 17.

A tactic that has become common is for a potential bidder to announce that it is thinking of making a bid rather than actually doing it – it makes an 'indicative offer' (dubbed a 'virtual bid'), saying it might bid but not committing itself to the expense and strict timetable of a formal offer. Shareholders in targets may gain from having potential bidders announce an interest in buying their shares and are in favour of allowing time for the bid to be put together. On the other hand, it is not in the shareholders' interest for the management continually to feel under siege. The Takeover Panel permits indicative offers, but within 28 days of an approach to the target, or target confirmation that discussions are taking place, a formal bid must be brought (a 'put up or shut up' rule) or the company must confirm that it does not intend to make an offer (they cannot return with a bid for another six months without the target board's consent).

Traps for bidders to avoid

If the bidder purchases shares carrying 10% or more of the voting rights in the offer period or in the previous 12 months before a bid, the offer must include a cash alternative at the highest price paid by the bidder. A potential bidder, therefore, should be careful not to buy any shares at a price higher than a fair value.

If the bidder buys shares in the target at a price above the offer price during a bid the offer must be increased to that level. So, the bidder should be careful of topping up acceptances by offering a high price to a few shareholders.

The bid

In both a friendly and a hostile bid the acquirer is required to give notice to the target's board and its advisers that a bid is to be made. The press/financial websites and the Stock Exchange are also informed. The target management must immediately inform their shareholders (and the Takeover Panel). This is done through an announcement to the Stock Exchange and a press notice (disseminated on numerous free financial websites), which must be quickly followed by a letter explaining the situation.[11] In a hostile bid the target management tends to use phrases like 'derisory

---

11 Even if the target company has merely been politely approached for discussions about a bid, if the company is the subject of rumour and speculation or there is an untoward movement in the share price then an announcement is required. De La Rue got into trouble with the regulators when it received an indicative offer but did not disclose this to the market for several days.

'offer' or 'wholly unacceptable'. The target is now in an 'offer period'. Being in an offer period restricts the firm's actions such as not being able to issue new shares to make a merger more difficult.

Within 28 days of the initial notice of an intention to make an offer the offer document has to be posted to each of the target's shareholders. Details of the offer, the acquirer and its plans will be explained. The sending of the offer document starts the 'bid clock'. If the acquisition would increase the total value of the acquirer's assets by more than 15% the acquirer's shareholders need to be informed about the bid. If the asset increase is more than 25% then shareholders must vote in favour of the bid proceeding. They are also entitled to vote on any increase in authorised share capital.

The target management have 14 days from the dispatch of the offer document in which to respond to the offer by writing to all its shareholders ('defence document'). Assuming that they recommend rejection, they will attack the rationale of the merger and the price being offered. They may also highlight the virtues of the present management and reinforce this with revised profit forecasts and asset revaluations. There follows a period of attack and counterattack through press releases and other means of communication. Public relations consultants may be brought in to provide advice and to plan tactics.

The offer remains open for target shareholders to accept for 21 days from the date of posting the offer document. If the offer is revised it must be kept open for a further 14 days from the posting date of the revision.[12] However, to prevent bids from dragging on endlessly the Panel insists that the maximum period for a bid is 60 days from the offer document date (posting day). The final revision of offer day is day 46, which allows 14 days for acceptances. There are exceptions: if another bidder emerges, then it has 60 days, and its sixtieth day becomes the final date for both bidders; if the Board of the target agrees to an extension; if the bid is referred to the Competition and Markets Authority the Panel can 'stop the clock', allowing it to proceed only after it has been approved. If the acquirer fails to gain control within 60 days then it is forbidden to make another offer for a year, to prevent continual harassment.

Exhibit 20.19 lists some of the ways of defending yourself from a takeover attack.

Exhibit 20.19	Defence tactics

Roughly one-half of UK hostile bids are unsuccessful. Here are a few of the tactics employed by target managers to prevent a successful bid or to reduce the chances of a bid occurring.

Before bidding starts

- *Eternal vigilance* Be the most effective management team and educate shareholders about your abilities and the firm's potential. Cultivate good relationships with unions, workforce and politicians. Polish social image.
- *Defensive investments* Your firm buys a substantial proportion of the shares in a friendly firm, and it has a substantial holding of your shares.
- *Forewarned is forearmed* Keep a watch on the share register for the accumulation of shares by a potential bidder.

After bidding has started

- *Attack the logic of the bid* Also attack the quality of the bidder's management.
- *Improve the image of the firm* Use revaluation, profit projections, dividend promises, public relations consultants.
- *Attack the value creating (destroying) record of the bidder.*
- *Try to get a Competition and Market Authority inquiry.*
- *Encourage unions, the local community, politicians, customers and suppliers to lobby on your behalf.*
- *White Knight* Invite a second bid from a friendly company.

▶

---

12 If an offer is revised all shareholders who accepted an earlier offer are entitled to the increased payment.

Exhibit 20.19	Defence tactics (*continued*)

- *Lobby your major shareholders.*
- *Buy another business to make the firm too big or incompatible with the bidder.*
- *Arrange a management buyout of your company.*
- *Begin litigation against the bidder* Bidders sometimes step over the legal boundary in their enthusiasm – e.g. making false statements, gaining private information by going through dustbins – a court case could be embarrassing.
- *Employee share ownership plans (ESOPs)* These can be used to buy a substantial stake in the firm and may make it more difficult for a bidder to take it over.
- *Share repurchase* Reduces the number of shares available in the market for bidders.
- *Grey Knight* A new bidder who is a rival to the hostile bidder launches a bid. The rivalry may produce a higher takeover price.

The following tactics are likely to be frowned upon or banned by the Takeover Panel in the UK, but are used in the USA and in a number of continental European countries.

- *Poison pills* Make yourself unpalatable to the bidder by ensuring additional costs should it win – for example, target shareholders are allowed to buy shares in the target or acquirer at a large discount should a bid be successful. 'Shareholder rights plans' trigger the issuance of new shares or allow investors to sell at a premium.
- *Crown jewels defence* Sell off the most attractive parts of the business.
- *Pac-Man defence* Make a counterbid for the bidder.
- *Asset lock-up* A friendly buyer purchases those parts of the business most attractive to the bidder.
- *Stock lock-up* (*White squire*) Target shares are issued to a friendly company or individual(s).
- *Golden parachutes* Managers get massive payoffs if the firm is taken over.
- *Give in to greenmail* Key shareholders try to obtain a reward (for example, the repurchase of their shares at premium) from the company for not selling to a hostile bidder or for not becoming a bidder themselves. (Green refers to the colour of a US dollar.)
- *Limit voting rights* In some European states the management has the ability to limit voting rights to say a maximum of 15% regardless of the actual shareholding.
- *Sell shares* carrying multiple voting rights to friendly parties, e.g. employees.
- *Change of control covenant* This, in effect, forces a company to default on its debts because of the takeover managers do not approve of.

Postbid

Usually an offer becomes unconditional when the acquirer has bought, or has agreed to buy, between 50 and 90% of the target's shares. Prior to the declaration of the offer as unconditional the bidding firm would have said in the offer documents that the offer is conditional on the acquirer gaining (usually) 90% of the voting shares (or whatever figure they select above 50%). This allows the bidding firm to receive acceptances from the target shareholders without the obligation to buy.[13] Once the bid is declared unconditional the acquirer is making a firm offer for the shares which it does not already have, and indicating that no better offer is to follow. Before the announcement of unconditionality those target shareholders who accepted the offer are entitled to withdraw their acceptance. After it, they are forbidden to do so.

Usually in the days following unconditionality the target shareholders who have not already accepted quickly do so. The alternative is to remain a minority shareholder – still receiving dividends (if management and majority shareholders decide to pay dividends) but with power concentrated in the hands of a majority shareholder. There is a rule to avoid the frustration of having a small group of shareholders stubbornly refusing to sell. If the acquirer has bought nine-tenths of the shares (and 90% of voting shares) it bid for, it can, within three to six months of the last date on which the offer can be accepted, insist that the remaining shareholders sell at the final offer price.

---

13 If 90% of the target shares are offered, the bidder must proceed (unless there has been a material adverse change of circumstances). At lower levels of acceptance, it has a choice of whether to declare unconditionality.

If the bid has lapsed or not been declared unconditional the bidder cannot bid again for a 12-month period. However, the bidder is allowed to bid again if a bid is made by another company or the bidder's renewed offered is recommended by the target management.

A scheme of arrangement is an alternative way of taking over another company – *see* Exhibit 20.20.

Exhibit 20.20

Bid tactics

By Martin Dickson

Are conventional takeover bids an endangered species? You might think so, judging by recent trends. Yesterday New Look, the fashion chain, received a buyout bid, to be carried out via a scheme of arrangement – the same mechanism Wm Morrison is using for its takeover of Safeway, approved by shareholders on Wednesday.

A scheme is an increasingly popular bid mechanism that involves a target company convening an extraordinary meeting where the takeover is voted on. Approval requires 75 per cent of the shares voted and the courts then sanction the deal. It is an alternative to the more traditional route, whereby a bidder offers to buy a target's shares and wins once it has got acceptances for more than 50 per cent.

A scheme has three big advantages over a traditional bid. It often can be completed much faster; it can be cheaper, since it is not subject to stamp duty; and private equity bidders – which account for a large proportion of takeovers – like it.

This is because they automatically end up with 100 per cent of the company. Under a conventional bid, they can only force out minority shareholders if 90 per cent of investors have accepted the offer – and there have been several recent cases of large fund managers blocking this.

However, schemes are not as flexible as conventional bids and put control of the process in the hands of the target company, which calls the EGM. So it is not appropriate for a hostile offer, where the target is fighting to the death . . .

 Financial Times, 14 February 2004, p. M2.
All Rights Reserved.

The impact of mergers

There has been a significant amount of empirical research into mergers and their impact. Some of the questions asked and answered will be considered in this section.

Are target firms poor performers?

One of the proclaimed benefits of mergers is that they can be a spur to increased efficiency. Surely, it is argued, the most inefficient managers will be removed through a takeover by more efficient managers, won't they? Some evidence suggests that those firms which become targets are no less profitable than those which do not. Singh (1971) provided some evidence on the best way to avoid becoming a takeover victim. It has little to do with performance and more to do with size. Singh concluded that once firms reach an average profitability there is no incentive to increase profits further in order to avoid being taken over. His rules to avoid being taken over are:

- For *small firms with low profitability* – increase profitability to just above average (note: satisficing not maximising).
- For *medium and large firms* – increase size rather than the rate of profit.

Other researchers who have identified larger size as a factor that decreases the likelihood of being taken over include Hasbrouck (1985), Palepu (1986), Ambrose and Megginson (1992), Levine and Aaronovitch (1981), Powell and Thomas (1994) and Louis (2004b). This evidence suggests that the threat of takeovers, rather than inducing profit maximisation, encourages firms to grow bigger and faster.

Franks and Mayer (1996) found that hostile bids in the UK do not appear to be directed at poorly performing firms. Bhide's (1993) research, on the other hand, showed that US target firms generally had poor, or at best mediocre, performance records. Targets of friendly mergers were more likely to be well managed.

Does society benefit from mergers?

One way in which society could benefit from a merger is if the resulting combination could produce goods at a lower cost as a result of economies of scale or improved management. However, set alongside this is the fact that mergers may also result in social costs in the form of monopoly power. Investigators have attempted to weigh up these two offsetting outcomes of mergers in general. Singh (1971), Firth (1980), Lev (1992), Fee and Thomas (2004) and Shahrur (2005) show customers and suppliers gain from the greater efficiency flowing from mergers through increased buying power and economies of scale (not completely offset by exploitation of increased market power). Maksimovic et al. (2013) found that productivity rose. Sheen (2014) found when two competitors in a product market merge, the quality of goods was unchanged but the consumer price fell relative to the competition, 'consistent with the existence of synergies and scale economies. If two manufacturing plans are reduced to one, firms can cut costs and lower prices'. Lel and Miller (2015) found that the relaxation of takeover laws to encourage more mergers leads to greater managerial discipline, greater efficiency replacement of poorly performing CEOs.

Do the shareholders of acquirers gain from mergers?

Some of the evidence on the effects of acquisitions on the shareholders of the bidding firm is that in slightly over half of the cases shareholders benefit. However, most studies show that acquiring firms give their shareholders poorer returns on average than firms that are not acquirers. Even studies which show a gain to acquiring shareholders tend to produce very small average gains – *see* **Exhibit 20.21**.

Exhibit 20.21	Summary of some of the evidence on merger performance from the acquiring shareholders' perspective	
Study	**Country of evidence**	**Comment**
Franks and Harris (1989)	UK and USA	Share returns are poor for acquirers on average for the two years under one measurement technique, but better than the market as a whole when the CAPM is used as a benchmark.
Sudarsanam, Holl and Salami (1996)	UK	Poor return performance relative to the market for highly-rated (judged by price to earnings ratio) acquirers taking over low-rated targets. However, some firms do well when there is a complementary fit in terms of liquidity, slack and investment opportunities.
Manson, Stark and Thomas (1994)	UK	Cash flow improves after merger, suggesting operating performance is given a boost.
Gregory (1997)	UK	Share return performance is poor relative to the market for up to two years post-merger, particularly for equity-financed bids and single (as opposed to regular) bidders.
Loughran and Vijh (1997)	US	In the five post-merger years firms that offer shares as payment show negative returns relative to the market. Those that offer cash show positive market-adjusted returns.
Rau and Vermaelen (1998)	US	Acquirers underperform post-merger. This is due to over-optimism by investors leading to overpricing of some acquirers regarded as glamour stocks at the time of the merger.

Study	Country of evidence	Comment
Sudarsanam and Mahate (2003)	UK	Generally acquirers underperform. Cash acquirers generate higher returns than equity payment acquirers. High price to earnings ratio (and low book to market ratio) acquirers do not perform as well as low PER acquirers (and low book to market ratio acquirers).
Goergen and Renneboog (2004)	Europe wide study	On average bidder performance is roughly the same as the market during the four months around the merger announcement date. Bids financed by equity produce better announcement period returns than those financed by cash.
Conn, Cosh, Guest, and Hughes (2005)	UK	Quoted companies acquiring UK companies results in poor returns around the announcement date and over the subsequent three years on average (-22%). UK acquirers in cross-border mergers of quoted companies also produce poor performers. However, non-quoted UK acquirers tend to produce zero post-acquisition returns on average.
Gregory (2005)	UK	Acquirers underperform the market by 19.9% over 60 months. Acquirers with a high level of free cash flow perform better than acquirers with low free cash flow in the five years following merger as measured by total return.
Moeller, Schlingemann and Stulz (2005)	US	On average acquirer shareholders experience a poor return in the few days around acquisition announcement – particularly in 1998–2001 (hi-tech boom period).
Cosh, Guest, and Hughes (2006)	UK	The larger the holding of shares in the company by the chief executive the better the post-merger long-term share returns.
Powell and Stark (2005)	UK	Takeovers result in modest improvements in operating performance of acquirers.
Antoniou, Petmezas and Zhao (2007)	UK	In the short-run bidders break even when acquiring public targets and gain significantly when buying private and subsidiary targets. In the long-run acquirers' shareholders lose regardless of the target type (markets are over-optimistic in the short-run).
Savor and Lu (2009)	US	Overvalued firms create value for shareholders by using their equity as currency.
Duchin and Schmidt (2013)	US	Average long-term performance of acquisitions initiated in merger waves is significantly worse.
Fu, Lu and Officer (2013)	US	Shareholders of overvalued acquirers would actually benefit if their firms had not pursued the acquisitions as there are 'substantial declines in the value of the acquirer's stock over the bid period and negative long-run abnormal stock returns'.

Much of the recent research has drawn attention to differences in post-acquisition performance of acquirers that are highly rated by investors at the time of the bid ('glamour shares') and the post-acquisition performance of low rated acquirers ('value shares'), e.g. with low price–earnings ratios or low share price relative to balance sheet net asset value. This overvaluation of glamorous shares seems to be at least a partial explanation for subsequent underperformance. Over time investors reassess the price premium placed on the glamour shares, bringing their prices down – whether they are acquirers or not.

Do target shareholders gain from mergers?

Acquirers usually have to pay a substantial premium over the pre-bid share price to persuade target shareholders to sell. The empirical evidence in this area is overwhelming – target shareholders gain from mergers.

Do the employees gain?

In the aftermath of a merger it sometimes happens that large areas of the target firm's oper-ations are closed down with a consequent loss of jobs. Often operating units of the two firms are fused and overlapping functions are eliminated, resulting in the shedding of staff. However, sometimes the increased competitive strength of the combined entity saves jobs and creates many more.

Do the directors of the acquirer gain?

The directors of the acquirers often gain increased status and power. They also generally receive increased remuneration packages.

Do the directors of the target gain?

We do not have a definitive answer as to whether the directors of the target gain. In the press they are often unfairly described as the failed managers and therefore out of a job. They are the losers in the 'market in managerial control'. In reality they often receive large payoffs on their lengthy employ-ment contracts and then take on another highly paid directorship. Another possibility is that they stay within the merged company, having been offered an attractive remuneration package.[14]

Do the financial institutions gain?

The financial institutions benefit greatly from merger activity. They usually receive large fees, regardless of whether they are on the winning side in a bid battle.

Warren Buffett sums up the evidence on the winners from mergers:

> They are a bonanza for the shareholders of the acquiree; they increase the income and status of the acquirer's management; and they are a honey pot for the investment bankers and other professionals on both sides. But, alas, they usually reduce the wealth of the acquirer's shareholders, often to a substantial extent.[15]

Jonathan Guthrie, an FT columnist calls for greater shareholder questioning of managers when they pursue mergers in **Exhibit 20.22**.

Exhibit 20.22

If acquisitions are worthwhile, they are worth discussing openly

If the argument for a deal is strong, debate will endorse it

Lombard column by JONATHAN GUTHRIE

The protruding nail will be knocked flat. Dermot Desmond, campaigner against Ladbrokes' £2.2bn merger with Gala Coral, was lucky to avoid the same fate as fellow investors rushed to vote in favour of the deal. The real wonder is that so few shareholders resist takeovers as the Irish billionaire did. It is a glaring failure of stewardship.

Academic studies suggest takeovers that destroy value for acquirers outnumber those that create it. Peter Clark, at University College London, says the ratio is 2:1, rising to more than 4:1 at the peak of the M&A cycle. Costly deals such as Pfizer's purchase of Allergan and AB InBev's absorption of SABMiller signal that summit is in sight.

---

14 There is some evidence that when the acquirer's managers have strong social ties with the target's man-agers prior to the merger the returns to shareholders are diminished, 'Moreover, acquirer-target social ties significantly increase the likelihood that the target firm's chief executive officer (CEO) and a larger frac-tion of the target firm's pre-acquisition board of directors remain on the board of the combined firm after the merger' (Ishii and Xuan, 2014).

15 Letter to shareholders in the Berkshire Hathaway Annual Report 1995.

Mr Clark and his ilk tend to measure value creation reductively by whether estimated cost synergies outweigh premiums. Acquirers may have good strategic reasons for purchases. Struggling bookie Ladbrokes needs to strengthen its online side, for example.

However, human incentives are stacked so heavily in favour of dealmaking that the intelligent cynic is forced to assume much of it benefits agents more than principals. Acquisitive bosses get pay rises for running expanded businesses. Their M&A advisers, a ferociously smart and opportunistic breed, make fat fees on each side of the transaction.

Why do investors so rarely object? In fairness, big shareholders kill off some riskier deals in private discussions with companies they own. Many others get through, as illustrated by Premier Foods' 2006 purchase of RHM.

Shareholders tend to see public discussion as disloyal to management. They shouldn't. If the argument for a deal is strong, debate will endorse it. Shell should therefore welcome a recent intervention from Ian McVeigh of Jupiter Asset Management. He has articulated a growing view that the oil major is overpaying for gas group BG.

There are plenty of counter arguments. Shell needs to fatten its supply base. Two-thirds of the consideration of £38bn would be paid in Shell shares, which have dropped in tandem with the oil price. Many big investors hold roughly the same percentage stake in BG as in Shell, reducing their price exposure.

The objections of Mr Desmond to Ladbrokes' tie-in with Gala Coral look more convincing. It will create a group still heavily dependent on the betting shops that are fast fading from fashion with punters. Both men should be congratulated for letting some air into the stuffy rooms where takeovers are negotiated. If rationales for bids were tested more rigorously, fewer bad deals would go through on the nod. "Opposition is true friendship", as the great cockney poet William Blake put it.

Financial Times, 24 November 2015.

Managing mergers

Many mergers fail to produce shareholder wealth and yet there are companies that pursue a highly successful strategy of expansion through mergers. This section highlights some of the reasons for failure and some of the requirements for success.

The three stages of mergers

There are three phases in merger management. It is surprising how often the first and third are neglected while the second is given great amounts of managerial attention. The three stages are:

- preparation;
- negotiation and transaction;
- integration.

In the preparation stage strategic planning predominates. A subset of the strategic thrust of the business might be mergers. Targets need to be searched for and selected with a clear purpose – shareholder wealth maximisation in the long term. There must be a thorough analysis of the potential value to flow from the combination and tremendous effort devoted to the plan of action which will lead to the successful integration of the target.

The negotiation and transaction stage has two crucial aspects to it.

1 **Financial analysis and target evaluation** This evaluation needs to go beyond mere quantitative analysis into fields such as human resources and competitive positioning.

2 **Negotiating strategy and tactics** It is in the area of negotiating strategy and tactics that the specialist advisers are particularly useful. However, the acquiring firm's management must keep a tight rein and remain in charge.

The integration stage is where so many mergers come apart. It is in this stage that the management need to consider the organisational and cultural similarities and differences between the firms. They also need to create a plan of action to obtain the best post-merger integration.

The key elements of these stages are shown in **Exhibit 20.23.**

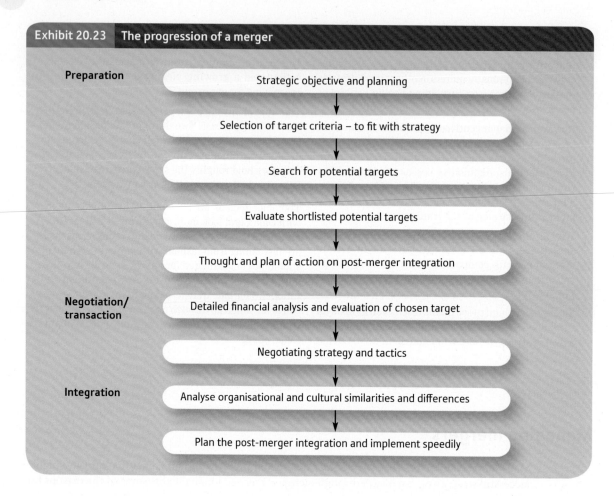

Exhibit 20.23   The progression of a merger

Preparation

Strategic objective and planning

↓

Selection of target criteria – to fit with strategy

↓

Search for potential targets

↓

Evaluate shortlisted potential targets

↓

Thought and plan of action on post-merger integration

↓

Negotiation/ transaction

Detailed financial analysis and evaluation of chosen target

↓

Negotiating strategy and tactics

↓

Integration

Analyse organisational and cultural similarities and differences

↓

Plan the post-merger integration and implement speedily

Too often the emphasis in managing mergers is firmly on the 'hard' world of identifiable and quantifiable data. Here economics, finance and accounting come to the fore. There is a worrying tendency to see the merger process as a series of logical and mechanical steps, each with an obvious rationale and a clear and describable set of costs and benefits. This approach all but ignores the potential for problems caused by non-quantifiable elements, for instance, human reactions and inter-relationships. Matters such as potential conflict, discord, alienation and disloyalty are given little attention. There is also a failure to make clear that the nature of decision making in this area relies as much on informed guesses, best estimates and hunches as on cold facts and figures.

The organisational process approach

The organisational process approach takes into account the 'soft' aspects of merger implementation and integration. Here the acquisition process, from initial strategic formulations to final complete integration, is perceived as a complex, multifaceted programme with the potential for a range of problems arising from the interplay of many different hard and soft factors. Each merger stage requires imaginative and skilled management for the corporate objective to be maximised. (Sudarsanam (2010) is a good guide.)

Problem areas in merger management

We now examine some of the areas where complications may arise.

The strategy, search and screening stage

The main complicating element at the stage of strategy, search and screening is generated by the multitude of perspectives regarding a particular target candidate. Each discipline within a management team may have a narrow competence and focus, and thus there is potential for a fragmented approach to the evaluation of targets. For example, the marketing team may focus exclusively on the potential for marketing economies and other benefits, the research and development team on the technological aspects and so on. Communication between disparate teams of managers can become complicated and the tendency will be to concentrate the communication effort on those elements which can be translated into the main communicating channel of business, that is, quantifiable features with 'bottom lines' attached. This kind of one dimensional communication can, however, all too easily fail to convey the full nature of both the opportunities and the problems. The more subtle aspects of the merger are likely to be given inadequate attention.

Another problem arises when senior managers conduct merger analysis in isolation from managers at the operating level. Not only may these 'coalface' managers be the best informed about the target, its industry and the potential for post-merger integration problems; their commitment is often vital to the integration programme.

There is an obvious need to maximise the information flow effort both to obtain a balanced, more complete view of the target, and to inform, involve and empower key players in the successful implementation of a merger strategy.

The bidding stage

Once a merger bid is under way a strange psychology often takes over. Managers seem to feel compelled to complete a deal. To walk away would seem like an anticlimax, with vast amounts of money spent on advisers and nothing to show for it. Also they may feel that the investment community will perceive this management as being one unable to implement its avowed strategic plans. It may be seen as 'unexciting' and 'going nowhere' if it has to retreat to concentrate on its original business after all the excitement and promises surrounding a takeover bid.

Managers also often enjoy the thrill of the chase and develop a determination to 'win'. Pay, status and career prospects may hinge on rapid growth. Additionally, acquirers may be impelled to close the deal quickly by the fear of a counterbid by a competitor, which, if successful, would have an adverse impact on the competitive position of the firm.

Thus mergers can take on a momentum which is difficult to stop. This is often nurtured by financial advisers keen on completing a transaction.

These phenomena may help to explain the heavy emphasis given to the merger transaction to the detriment of the preparation and integration stages. They may also go some way to explaining merger failure – in particular, failure to enhance shareholder value as a result of the winner's curse.

Expectations of the acquiring firm's operational managers regarding the post-merger integration stage

Clarity and planning are needed to avoid conflict and disappointment among managers. For example, the integration strategy may outline a number of different tasks to be undertaken in the 12–24 months following an acquisition. These may range from disposal of assets and combining operating facilities to new product development and financial reconstruction. Each of these actions may be led by a different manager. Their expectations regarding the speed of implementation and the order in which each of these actions will be taken may be different. A clear and rational resource-planning and allocation mechanism will reduce ambiguity and improve the coordination of decision making.

Aiming for the wrong type of integration

There are different degrees of integration when two firms come together under one leadership. At the one extreme is the complete absorption of the target firm and the concomitant fusing of two cultures, two operational procedures and two corporate organisations. At the other extreme is the holding company, preservation or portfolio approach where the degree of change of the acquired subsidiary may amount merely to a change in some financial control procedures, but otherwise the target firm's management may continue with their own systems, unintegrated operations and culture.

The complete integration approach is usually appropriate in situations where production and other operational costs can be reduced through economies of scale and other synergies, or revenues can be enhanced through, say, combined marketing and distribution. The preservation approach is most suitable when it is recognised that the dis-benefits of forcing organisations together outweigh the advantages, for example when the products and markets are completely different and the cultures are such that a fusion would cause an explosive clash. These arm's length mergers are typical of the acquisitive conglomerates. In such mergers general management skills are transferred along with strict financial performance yardsticks and demanding incentive schemes, but little else is changed.

With symbiosis-based mergers there is a need to keep a large degree of difference, at least initially, in culture, organisation and operating style, but at the same time to permit communication and cross-fertilisation of ideas. There may also be a need to transfer skills from one part of the combined organisation to another, whether through training and teaching or by personnel reassignment. An example might be where a book publisher acquires an online publisher; each is engaged in a separate market but there is potential for profitable cooperation in some areas. As well as being aware of the need for mutual assistance each organisation may be jealous of its own way of doing things and does not want its *esprit de corps* disrupted by excessive integration.

Exhibit 20.24 expresses the failure of some acquirers to plan a merger properly or to allow adequately for the complicating human factor.

Exhibit 20.24

How to make a corporate marriage work

The tendency to relax after the deal has been done must be resisted – this is the make or break period for a takeover

says Stefan Stern

The deal has been signed, the analysts have been charmed and the press conference is over. But before placing an extra order for tomorrow's newspapers, the wise chief executive will remember that the hardest part of a merger or acquisition is just about to start.

Bringing two companies together is an enormous task, as executives at Proctor & Gamble and Gillette, the consumer goods giants that announced a deal last month, will now be discovering. There are grand, big-picture questions that need to be resolved, such as the new group's strategy and direction. There are also administrative, logistical and technical challenges. Will new contracts of employment be required? Where should the headquarters of the combined operations be located? How can the companies' information technology systems be integrated?

'It takes a certain humility to make a merger work,' says Charles Hampden-Turner, co-author of *Building Cross-cultural Competence*. 'It doesn't follow that your company is a better one simply because it has taken another company over. It just means that you've got more money and have been prepared to pay,' he says. 'You should be ready to sit down and learn from the acquired business. There may be expertise there that needs to be respected.'

Work on bringing the partners together should start well before the deal becomes public knowledge.

Ravi Chanmugam, a partner at Accenture, the management consultancy, says: 'In essence, there should not be separate M&A and post-merger integration processes, but a holistic approach to the deal, from strategy to target identification and valuation to integration.'

Speed is of the essence. Roger Pudney of the UK's Ashridge business school says: 'There is often a tendency for companies to relax once the deal is signed, but this is precisely the point at which speed of implementation becomes crucial. Successful M&A companies stress the importance of quick wins as a way of demonstrating that the new combination is already producing added value.'

Managers will inevitably be occupied with practical, administrative changes, such as establishing new terms and conditions and pushing through any redundancies. Yet dealing with the cultural issues in a merger is more subtle and challenging. And when things go wrong in this context they can go wrong very quickly. Witnesses to board meetings of the newly merged Carnaud Metal Box in 1989, for instance, recalled that French and British directors at times refused even to speak to each other.

Michelle Bligh, a professor at Claremont Graduate University, California, has suggested measures leaders should take to avoid the worst consequences of mergers. After studying a merger of health organisations in the US, Prof Bligh advised leaders to avoid taking a dictatorial, top-down approach or micromanaging the transition. They need to respond as the new situation demands, she says, and must 'help followers negotiate, modify and even manipulate cultural similarities and differences in the post-merger environment.'

Prof Bligh identifies a few simple ground rules. Managers should recognise cultural differences between the companies, for example, by learning about the history of the new partner. They should give employees reasons why change is necessary, and find practical ways of communicating. As one manager told her: 'When you sit down and start showing employees the nitty-gritty, you get buy-in a lot quicker.'

Symbolism matters too. 'Instead of making great speeches,' Dr Hampden-Turner suggests, 'why not start acting differently and providing a lead that way? Words are too easy, but actions will be noticed.'

Even apparently mundane gestures can count. Discussing employees' new working conditions and being visible on the 'shop floor', for example, may reassure staff that management has an interest in their wellbeing. One manager in Prof Bligh's study said: 'We have to start with the little things: they really matter to people.'

Nevertheless, the post-merger period can be a draining, emotionally charged time for staff. Reflecting on her experience of the healthcare merger, a nurse said: 'The emotions were so strong, I would rather have my skin peeled off than go through that again.' Counselling services or an employee assistance programme can provide a useful outlet for tensions among staff.

Marriages succeed or fail in the years following the wedding. Even before the hangover has worn off, the hard work has to begin.

Next steps in making that merger work

- Should you be starting from here? Are there compelling strategic reasons for this deal? Or is the company under pressure from investors and the media? Is the chief executive looking for a last hurrah before moving on?
- Get your integration plan right. Set target dates for major decisions on structure
- Define key functions in the new entity – including finance, HR, IT, legal – as soon as you can
- Plan to resolve cultural differences; this will largely happen through good communication
- Be careful to give customers priority during the transition; employees will not be the only stakeholder feeling unsettled

Financial Times, 7 February 2005, p. 10.

Why do mergers fail to generate value for acquiring shareholders?

A definitive answer as to why mergers fail to generate value for acquiring shareholders cannot be provided, because mergers fail for a host of reasons. However, there do appear to be some recurring themes.

The strategy is misguided

History is littered with strategic plans which turned out to be value destroying rather than value creating. Major British banks went on a shopping spree in 2006–8 only to find that they ran into dis-economies of scale – too many activities and people to manage – following over-paying for some appallingly bad businesses and assets. Dozens of banks only escaped complete failure because government stepped in to rescue them with massive injections of taxpayers' money. At the turn of the millennium TimeWarner thought it needed to pay a very high price ($163bn) to merge with AOL (giving away half of its shares) so that it could take a leading part in the convergence of media and information/communication technology. The plan was to distribute media content via the Internet. It didn't work. Nine years later AOL was spun off valued at only $3.44bn. Rio Tinto, the mining company, was forced to write off $10bn in 2013 related to its disastrous $38bn purchase of Canada's Alcan, largely a manufacturer, in 2007. In the same year it wrote off £3.7bn related to its Mozambiquan coal mines purchased only two years before. One top-20 shareholder was quoted in the *Financial Times* as saying 'I think there is a recognition that it was a mistake to try to create value by acquisitions.'[16] Rio Tinto's growth now comes from carefully considered organic building of low-cost assets (the costs of digging and moving ore from ground to customer).

Fashion also seems to play its part, as with the conglomerate mergers of the 1960s, the cross-border European mergers of the early 1990s prompted by the development of the single market and the dot.com merger frenzy around the turn of the millennium.

Overoptimism

Acquiring managers have to cope with uncertainty about the future potential of their acquisition. It is possible for them to be overoptimistic about the market economics, the competitive position and the operating synergies available. They may underestimate the costs associated with the resistance to change they may encounter, or the reaction of competitors. Merger fever, the excitement of the battle, may lead to an openness to persuasion that the target is worth more than it really is (see **Exhibit 20.25**). A common mistake is the underestimation of the investment required to make a merger work, particularly in terms of managerial time.

Exhibit 20.25

On masquerading skimmed milk, lame horses and sexy deals

We believe most deals do damage to the shareholders of the acquiring company. Too often, the words from HMS Pinafore apply: 'Things are seldom what they seem, skim milk masquerades as cream.' Specifically, sellers and their representatives invariably present financial projections having more entertainment value than educational value. In the production of rosy scenarios, Wall Street can hold its own against Washington.

In any case, why potential buyers even look at projections prepared by sellers baffles me. Charlie and I never give them a glance, but instead keep in mind the story of the man with an ailing horse. Visiting the vet, he said: 'Can you help me? Sometimes my horse walks just fine and sometimes he limps.' The Vet's reply was pointed: 'No problem – when he's walking fine, sell him.' . . .

Talking to *Time Magazine* a few years back, Peter Drucker got to the heart of things: 'I will tell you a secret: Dealmaking beats working. Dealmaking is exciting and fun, and working is grubby. Running anything is primarily an enormous amount of grubby detail work . . . dealmaking is romantic, sexy. That's why you have deals that make no sense.'

. . . I can't resist repeating a tale told me last year by a corporate executive. The business he grew up in was a fine one, with a long-time record of leadership in its industry. Its main product, however, was distressingly glamorless. So several decades ago, the company hired a management consultant who – naturally – advised diversification, the then current fad. ('Focus' was not yet in style.) Before long, the company acquired a number of businesses, each after the consulting firm had gone through a long – and expensive – acquisition study. And the outcome? Said the executive sadly: 'When we started we were getting 100% of our earnings from the original business. After ten years, we were getting 150%.'

Source: Warren Buffett. letter to shareholders, *Berkshire Hathaway Annual Report 1995*. Reprinted with permission © Warren E. Buffett and Berkshire Hathaway Inc.

Exhibit 20.26 illustrates the overoptimism problem.

Exhibit 20.26

Empire builders fall prey to their vanity

By Luke Johnson

Just as confidence is vital to success, so overconfidence typically leads to downfall. And nowhere is such hubris more prevalent than when boardrooms suffer from acquisition mania.

A stunning recent example was the purchase by Cisco of Pure Digital, the parent company for the bestselling camcorder, Flip, in 2009 for $590m. Having owned the business for less than two years, Cisco

---

16 Neil Hume, Helen Thomas and David Oakley, 'Albanese steps down as Rio Tinto chief following $14bn writedown', *Financial Times*, 18 January 2013.

announced last month that it was shutting it down – in spite of Flip's enduring popularity. Now John Chambers, Cisco's chief executive, might argue that he has grown the group from revenue of $1.2bn in 1995 to $40bn this year, and hence a write-off on the scale of the Flip debacle makes little difference to his overall achievements.

Nevertheless, such an extraordinarily rapid and absolute destruction of value takes some doing – especially since Cisco has delivered much of its expansion via acquisitions. Yet the stock market appeared to approve of Cisco's high profile exit from consumer products. All public companies must dance to the whims of institutional investors, and these gyrations distort their M&A behaviour, because too often they are bullied to buy at the top and sell at the bottom.

However, there have been many, very much bigger mistakes than Flip. Recall the catastrophic purchase by Daimler of Chrysler for $38bn, or indeed the series of terrible deals done by Ford Motor in the 1990s, including Volvo for $6.5bn, Jaguar for $2.4bn, and Kwik-Fit for $1.6bn. At the time, Ford was embracing the idea of diversifying into a services organisation. Their stagnant core business was still throwing off lots of cash, which enabled the group to squander many billions in ill-advised purchases. Kwik-Fit was subsequently almost given away to private equity

house CVC for a third of its original cost, just three years after its purchase. Typically, the architect of the strategy, Jacques Nasser, then departed and new management felt less shame in taking the loss and moving on. Ford refocused, and has just delivered record first-quarter net income of $2.6bn.

I was on the other side in a similar situation. We sold a restaurant business called My Kinda Town for about £56m in cash to Capital Radio in the 1990s. As a seller, I was baffled as to why a radio company was interested in our casual dining chain but I had not led the negotiations and assumed they knew what they were doing. Shockingly, the cheerleader for this curious diversification left the broadcaster within months. It soon became apparent that the acquirer could not manage its new division. Within a few years, it had broken the business up and sold off the pieces for a fraction of the purchase price. The rationale for the merger was flawed – the compelling synergy between entertainment and eating was an illusion.

It is scary how often deals are done for reasons of ego or narcissism. Making attractive returns from acquisitions is extremely difficult, yet momentum, vanity and impatience too often play a big part in the process, especially in bidding wars and contested takeovers. And even veteran buyers can get carried away when the desire to possess an asset becomes overwhelming.

FT *Financial Times,* 4 May 2011, p. 12.
All Rights Reserved.

Failure of integration management

One problem is the over-rigid adherence to prepared integration plans. Usually plans require dynamic modification in the light of experience and altered circumstances. The integration programme may have been based on incomplete information and may need post-merger adaptation to the new perception of reality.

Common management goals and the engendering of commitment to those goals is essential. The morale of the workforce can be badly damaged at the time of a merger. The natural uncertainty and anxiety has to be handled with understanding, tact, integrity and sympathy. Communication and clarity of purpose are essential as well as rapid implementation of change. Cultural differences need to be tackled with sensitivity and trust established. According to a former Safeway executive, Morrisons was very insensitive when it took over: 'When they marched into Safeway, there were lots of capable, competent people. I know Martin Ackroyd's [finance director of Morrison] opening words when he arrived were "don't think this is a merger, this is a take-over" . . . Overnight everyone was disaffected and wanted to leave as quickly as they could'.[17] As a result of the mass of resignations Morrisons struggled to understand and use Safeway's accounting system and failed in many other managerial areas. Morrisons' share price plummeted.

Lord Browne, formerly of BP, advises quick integration: 'It's very important to mix the cultures early on. If the entities that existed previously still exist, then there is great reluctance to change anything.' He also suggests using a third party to help select the best managers. Following the merger with Amoco BP sent 400 top executives to an independent recruitment agency for assessment. 'When you merge with a company, you basically play with half a deck [of cards] because

17 *Financial Times,* 24 March 2005, p. 23.

you know all your people, and they know all theirs. So how do you find a way of actually knowing everything about everyone – the answer is get a third party in.'[18]

The absence of senior management commitment to the task of successful integration severely dents the confidence of target and acquired managers.

Coopers & Lybrand, the international business advisers, conducted 'in-depth interviews with senior executives of the UK's top 100 companies covering 50 deals'. There emerged some factors which seem to contribute to failure, and others which are critical for raising the chances of success. These are shown in **Exhibit 20.27**.

Exhibit 20.27   Survey on the reasons for merger failure and success – Coopers & Lybrand

The most commonly cited causes of failure include:		The most commonly cited reasons for success include:	
Target management attitudes and cultural differences	85%	Detailed post-acquisition plans and speed of implementation	76%
Little or no post-acquisition planning	80%	A clear purpose for making acquisitions	76%
Lack of knowledge of industry or target	45%	Good cultural fit	59%
Poor management and poor management practices in the acquired company	45%	High degree of management co-operation	47%
Little or no experience of acquisitions	30%	In-depth knowledge of the acquiree and his industry	41%

The ten rules listed in **Exhibit 20.28** are *not* recommended for shareholder-wealth-orientated managers.

Exhibit 20.28   Arnold's ten golden rules for alienating 'acquired' employees

1 Sack people in an apparently arbitrary fashion.

2 Insist (as crudely as possible) that your culture is superior. Attack long-held beliefs, attitudes, systems, norms, etc.

3 Don't bother to find out the strengths and weaknesses of the new employees.

4 Lie to people – some of the old favourites are:
   – 'there will not be any redundancies';
   – 'this is a true merger of equals'.

5 Fail to communicate your integration strategy:
   – don't say why the pain and sacrifice is necessary, just impose it;
   – don't provide a sense of purpose.

6 Encourage the best employees to leave by generating as much uncertainty as possible.

7 Create stress, loss of morale and commitment, and a general sense of hopelessness by being indifferent and insensitive to employees' needs for information.

8 Make sure you let everyone know that you are superior – after all, you won the merger battle.

9 Sack all the senior executives immediately – their knowledge and experience and the loyalty of their subordinates are cheap.

10 Insist that your senior management appear uninterested in the boring job of nuts-and-bolts integration management. After all, knighthoods and peerages depend upon the next high-public-profile acquisition.

---

18 Lord Browne quoted in David Buchan and Tobias Buck, 'Refining BP's management', *Financial Times*, 1 August 2002, p. 21. Reprinted with permission.

Kraft has managed to alienate many Cadbury veterans post-merger – see **Exhibit 20.29**.

Exhibit 20.29

Cadbury people still chewing on Kraft culture

By Louise Lucas

A posse of high-profile departures, about 100 rank-and-file job losses and falling quarterly sales in key markets: one year on, Cadbury under Kraft Foods – like the 20g smaller Dairy Milk bars coming out next month – looks rather lighter than it did this time last year.

True, the UK confectionery maker is in better shape than many predicted.

At the height of the battle over the £11.7bn takeover – which was agreed a year ago next week – Lord Mandelson (then business secretary) and others raised the spectre of Britain itself being sold down the river. Jobs and taxes would divert to Zurich, doomsayers moaned; our chocolate would taste like plastic and the benign capitalism fostered by the Quaker-founded company would become a distant memory.

But the real loser, according to some analysts, is Kraft. 'Cadbury had a cutting edge understanding of the shopper and its retail customers,' says one former Cadbury employee. 'We spent years building that at Cadbury, and that's been lost.'

Kraft disagrees. Trevor Bond, who ran Cadbury's in the UK and now has an expanded Europe-wide portfolio at Kraft, says that Cadbury sales have gone 'incredibly well' in the UK, and promises many product launches under the Cadbury name. And in spite of departures post-takeover of former Cadbury employees such as Ignasi Ricou, who ran European sales and the gum and candy business, the group is gung-ho on its future.

'The culture of the two organisations is so similar it's been easy to get Kraft and Cadbury to mingle and get together,' says Mike Clarke, Kraft's head of Europe.

Mr Bond says he finds it personally insulting to speak of a 'brain drain'. Kraft calculates about one-third of its 400 top executives are former Cadbury staff, adding that most of the departures were due to personal reasons.

But insiders retort that Kraft's propensity for lengthy meetings, and a desire to include top-level executives on every decision, made the new jobs less compelling in any case.

'Put simply, Gorilla would never have got done under Kraft,' says one, referring to the ground-breaking TV ads.

Another says there is much grumbling about 'the number of layers and amount of people that have to be involved to make things happen . . . Forget the brand manager having a voice in anything.'

Sir Roger Carr, who as chairman of Cadbury mounted a robust defence, says: 'Cadbury had successfully converted to a pure-play confectionery model, with all the benefits of clarity and identity that flow from focus.'

'So a return to a conglomerate ownership was always going to be challenging from the perspective of morale, motivation and momentum.'

More than one former employee points to the 'Orwellian' feel of Cadbury under Kraft. The US foods group launched its internal website under the slogan 'more delicious than ever' and – say staff – failed to see the irony of typing in these words to discover your redundancy package.

Staff feedback was encouraged on the site but, since anonymity was not, comment was circumspect. Months further out, workers grumble that audiences with Irene Rosenfeld, Kraft chief executive, are similarly staged: questions must be submitted in advance.

Jennie Formby, national officer at the Unite union, says: 'People say she is very remote: she talks at them not to them.'

Ms Rosenfeld did not attend the Commons select committee meeting in March about the deal, drawing more censure from critics. Kraft will not say if she will attend the upcoming select committee meeting.

This has left workers feeling nervous. The decision to close Kraft's UK business in Cheltenham – staff will have the choice to switch to Cadbury's offices at the end of this year – means, according to one, that Kraft employees, too, are losing morale. 'They felt as the ones doing the takeover they should be dominant, but they are the ones having to move or lose their jobs.'

Factory workers, in the meantime, are fretting about their future. The union won a two year guarantee on jobs, but that expires in another year. 'Kraft is highly leveraged and has got to pay down that debt somehow. It's clear there are opportunities to "rationalise", as companies put it,' says Ms Formby.

Exhibit 20.30 has comments from pharmaceutical industry veterans on what has worked for them following mergers – and what did not.

Exhibit 20.30

Pharma split on nature of mergers as kill or cure

By Andrew Jack

There are two kinds of senior executive in the pharmaceuticals sector: those who are against megamergers, and those who have recently completed or are actively considering doing one.

After a decade of big deals up to the mid-1990s in which many of the world's biggest medicine manufacturers were created – such as GlaxoSmithKline (GSK), AstraZeneca and Sanofi-Aventis – there was a period of four quiet years, before the onset of a new wave of consolidation this year.

At least in part, this has been set off by the downturn as valuations have fallen and any structural issues such as pricing have been accentuated.

Even Roche, which had long championed an arm's length model of ownership and management for its leading subsidiaries in Japan and the US, has changed tack. It concluded a peace treaty in the same month with biotech company Genentech in San Francisco, and bought out its minority shareholders for $47bn after a protracted hostile bid.

Many pharmaceutical sector employees, investors, analysts – and even investment bankers until they became particularly hungry for fees in recent months – say mega-mergers have delivered little long-term benefit. Yet others – including some not involved in the latest round of restructuring – believe there is value to be gained if the target is chosen effectively and the combination is well handled.

'I have not seen value creation through pharmaceutical mergers in the past 10 years,' says Steve Arlington, head of the pharma R&D practice at PwC, the professional services firm. 'The industry has suffered from disruption through mergers, post-merger activity. Can big pharma become too big? You see a loss of leadership. The internal machine becomes very complex, and compliance overtakes leadership.'

But Daniel Vasella, chairman and chief executive of Novartis, who had an active role in the Swiss company's creation through the merger of Ciba-Geigy and Sandoz in 1996, as well as several big

takeovers since, is more positive. He argues that some companies might have been in a far worse shape if they had not combined. 'An industry which has mounting pressure has a tendency to consolidate,' he says. 'It's a normal process. We have not yet reached the point of lethal size which is destructive.'

For deals to be successful, one lesson that veterans of such big initiatives cite is the need to move quickly in putting in place a new organisational structure in order to avoid protracted demoralisation. 'You have to be aggressive, demanding and fast, or people start to retract and you lose a lot of energy and value-creating activities,' says Mr Vasella.

'You have to move quickly,' agrees Martin Mackay, head of research at Pfizer. As a longtime company executive who experienced the absorption of Warner Lambert and Pharmacia, he has taken a pivotal role in the latest acquisition, unveiling in April a new structure that includes several divisions to be headed by his counterparts from Wyeth.

Bill Burns, chief executive of Roche's pharmaceutical arm, agrees on the need for decisiveness, while adding a second piece of advice: 'You can never communicate enough,' he says, emphasising the great uncertainty that pertains just after a takeover.

Even more speedily than Pfizer, Roche unveiled a new organisational structure within weeks of its agreement with Genentech. It emphasised that Genentech would retain its brand in the US, while Art Levinson, a key architect of its success, would join the main corporate board in Switzerland. Even so, his replacement as Genentech's longstanding chief executive by a Roche manager has raised concerns among investors and Genentech employees alike over their continued success.

A third lesson in making acquisitions work is the need to be radical. Tachi Yamada, who ran GSK's research and development operations for six years after its merger in 2000, says: 'The most important lesson when you do a merger is to be really bold in creating change. Otherwise you will create an organisation that is twice as big, and just as unsuccessful. People are very entrenched in their practices in R&D. They think they know the answers and identify for a long time as being from company X or company Y and not part of company Z.'

A fourth lesson is the need to embrace change in both the combined businesses, in spite of an imbalance in power. The chief executives of target and acquirer companies alike may have briefly shared the stage when announcing the latest deals, but there was no doubt who was in charge. 'The name of the new company is Pfizer,' was the blunt announcement of Jeff Kindler, Pfizer's chief executive, as he sat alongside Bernard Poussot, the outgoing head of Wyeth.

Yet Mr Vasella at Novartis cautions: 'Even if you say it's a pure acquisition, the acquirer and acquired are not the same any more. It's a big mistake if you don't use a large transaction to build a new entity.' He too enjoys the benefit of hindsight when he says that when Novartis was created, it did not move quickly enough to create new, combined IT systems – a mistake it was later forced to correct.

In spite of all the talk of radical change and renewed innovation, however, one common theme of big acquisitions has only intensified in the latest round: the promise of short-term returns from cost cutting. Whatever the longer-term hopes for fresh productivity from combined teams and pipeline projects, all have stressed the rapidity with which their takeovers will prove beneficial to earnings.

That creates a significant pitfall. As Andrew Witty, the chief executive at GSK appointed one year ago, argues, big takeovers can act as a brake on progress because of the many inevitable distractions. 'A merger of equals would be significantly distracting for R&D. We have been building sustainable revenue by buying good businesses, but we will not buy companies just to take out costs. That distracts people.'

His view is shared by several of his peers, including John Lechleiter at Eli Lilly and David Brennan at AstraZeneca, who have dismissed the idea of participating in big acquisitions. Yet others, at a different stage in the cycle of patent expiries, drug development pipelines and cost cutting, remain more ambivalent.

Chris Viehbacher, who took over Sanofi-Aventis late last year, says: 'Big acquisitions? You would never say never. Some deals are just about getting bigger and doing the same thing, without putting your company on the growth track. But while today it may not look like they make an awful lot of sense, why shut the door?'

In spite of the pitfalls, today's market conditions and varied corporate circumstances may yet turn some of the critics of past takeovers into advocates of future consolidation.

FT *Financial Times,* 2 June 2009.
All Rights Reserved.

Concluding comments

At a minimum this chapter should have made it clear that following a successful merger strategy is much more than simply 'doing the deal'. Preparation and integration are usually of greater significance to the creation of value than the negotiation and transaction stage. And yet, too often, it is towards this middle stage that most attention is directed.

Doubts have been raised about the purity of the motives for mergers but we should restrain ourselves from being too cynical as many mergers do create wealth for shareholders and society. Industries with a shifting technological or market base may need fewer larger firms to supply goods at a lower cost. The savings from superior managerial talent are genuine and to be praised in many cases. Restructuring, the sharing of facilities, talent and ideas, and the savings from the internalisation of transactions are all positive outcomes and often outweigh the negative effects.

Like many tools in the armoury of management, growth through mergers can be used to create or destroy.

Key points and concepts

- **Mergers are a form of investment** and should, theoretically at least, be evaluated on essentially the same criteria as other investment decisions, for example using NPV. However there are complicating factors:

  - the benefits from mergers are difficult to quantify;
  - acquiring companies often do not know what they are buying.

- **A merger is the combining of two business entities under common ownership.** It is difficult for many practical purposes to draw a distinction between merger, acquisition and takeover.

- A **horizontal** merger is when the two firms are engaged in similar lines of activity.

- A **vertical** merger is when the two firms are at different stages of the production chain.

- A **conglomerate** merger is when the two firms operate in unrelated business areas.

- **Merger** activity has occurred in waves. **Cash** is the most common method of payment except at the peaks of the cycle when **shares** are a more popular form of consideration.

- **Synergistic merger motives**:

  - market power;
  - economies of scale;
  - internalisation of transactions;
  - entry to new markets and industries;
  - tax advantages;
  - risk diversification.

- **Superior management merger motives**:

  - elimination of inefficient and misguided management;
  - conglomerate advantages in allocating capital and in using extraordinary resources;
  - undervalued shares.

- **Managerial merger motives**:

  - empire building;
  - status;
  - power;
  - remuneration;
  - hubris;
  - survival;
  - free cash flow.

- **Third-party merger motives**:

  - advisers;
  - at the insistence of customers or suppliers.

- **Value is created from a merger** when the gain is greater than the transaction cost.

  $$PV_{AB} = PV_A + PV_B + gain$$

  The gain may go to A's shareholders, or B's, or be shared between the two.

- The **winner's curse** is when the acquirer pays a price higher than the combined present value of the target and the potential gain.

- **Cash as a means of payment**

  For the acquirer

Advantages	Disadvantages
— Acquirers' shareholders retain control of their firm. — Greater chance of early success.	— Cash flow strain.

  For the target shareholders

Advantages	Disadvantages
— Certain value. — Able to spread investments.	— May produce capital gain tax liability

- **Shares as a means of payment**

  For the acquirer

Advantages	Disadvantages
— No cash outflow. — The PER game can be played.	— Dilution of existing shareholders' control — Greater risk of overpaying. — Unquoted acquirers may not be able to do this.

  For the target shareholders

Advantages	Disadvantages
— Postponement of capital gains tax liability. — Target shareholders maintain an interest in the combined entity.	— Uncertain value. — Not able to spread in the investment without higher transaction costs.

- The **City Code on Takeovers and Mergers** provides the main governing rules. It applies to quoted and unlisted public companies. It has statutory backup but still behaves like a self-regulatory organisation, using subtle power and being approachable for consultation, guidance and negotiation. Its objective is to ensure fair and equal treatment for all shareholders.

- The **Competition and Markets Authority, CMA,** investigate potential cases of competition constraints.

- **Prebid**
  - advisers appointed;
  - targets identified;
  - appraisal;
  - approach target;
  - negotiate.

- A **'dawn raid'** is where a substantial stake is acquired with great rapidity.

- Shareholdings of **3%** or more must be notified to the company.

- A stake of **30%** usually triggers a bid.

- **Concert parties,** where a group of shareholders act as one, but each remains below the 3% or 30% trigger levels, are now treated as one large holding for the key trigger levels.

- **The bid**
  - notice to target's board;
  - offer document sent within 28 days;
  - target management respond to offer document within 14 days;
  - offer open for 21 days, but can be frequently revised and thereby kept open for up to 60 days (or longer if another bidder enters the fray).

- **Postbid**
  - When a bid becomes unconditional (usually at 50–90% acceptances), the acquirer is making a firm offer and no better offer is to follow.

- **Target firms are not on average poor performers** relative to others in their industry.

- **Society sometimes benefits** from mergers **but some studies suggest a loss,** often through the exploitation of monopoly power.

- The **shareholders of acquirers tend to receive returns lower than the market** as a whole after the merger. However many acquirers do create value for shareholders.

- **Target shareholders, directors of acquirers and advisers gain significantly** from mergers. For the **directors of targets and other employees** the evidence is mixed.

- **There are three stages of mergers.** Most attention should be directed at the first and third, but this does not seem to happen. These stages are:
  - preparation;
  - negotiation and transaction;
  - integration.

- **Non-quantifiable,** 'soft', human elements often determine the success or otherwise of mergers.

- **Mergers fail for three principal reasons:**
  - the strategy is misguided;
  - over-optimism;
  - failure of integration management.

References and further reading

Acemoglu, D., Johnson, S. and Mitton, T. (2009) 'Determinants of vertical integration: financial development and contracting costs', *Journal of Finance,* LXIV(3), pp. 1251–90.
   Find greater vertical integration in countries that have both greater contracting cost and greater financial development

Ahern, K.R. and J. Harford (2014) 'The Importance of Industry Links in Merger Waves', *Journal of Finance,* 69(2), pp. 527–76.
   Stronger product market connections lead to a greater incidence of cross-industry mergers. Mergers propagate in waves across the network through customer-supplier links. Merger activity transmits to close industries quickly and to distant industries with a delay. The network of real economic transactions helps to explain the formation and propagation of merger waves.

Aktas, N., de Bodt, E. and Roll, R. (2013) 'Learning from repetitive acquisitions: Evidence from the time between deals', *Journal of Financial Economics,* 108, pp. 99 117.
   Knowledge gleaned from previous acquisitions may confer valuation expertise and other benefits. But numerous acquisitions also entail costs, due to

problems of incorporating diverse units into an ever larger firm. [We find] evidence of learning gains through repetitive acquisitions.

Ambrose, B.W. and Megginson, W.L. (1992) 'The role of asset structure, ownership structure, and takeover defences in determining acquisition likelihood', *Journal of Financial and Quantitative Analysis,* 27(4), pp. 575–89.
> Larger company size decreases the chance of being taken over.

Antoniou, A., Petmezas, D. and Zhao, H. (2007) 'Bidder gains and losses of firms involved in many acquisitions', *Journal of Business Finance and Accounting,* 34(7), (8), pp. 1221–44.
> In the short run bidders break even when acquiring public targets and gain significantly when buying private and subsidiary targets. However, over the long run acquirers are losers.

Arikan, A.M. and Stulz (2016) 'Corporate acquisitions, diversification, and the firm's life cycle', *Journal of Finance,* 71(1), pp. 139–94.
> 'While younger firms make more related and diversifying acquisitions than mature firms, the acquisition rate follows a U-shape over firms' life cycle. Consistent with neoclassical theories, we show that acquiring firms have better performance and growth opportunities and create wealth through acquisitions of nonpublic firms throughout their life. Consistent with agency theories, older firms experience negative stock price reactions for acquisitions of public firms.'

Bena, J. and Li, K. (2014) 'Corporate innovations and mergers and acquisitions', *Journal of Finance,* October, 69(5), pp. 1923–60.
> Companies with large patent portfolios and low R&D expenses are acquirers, while companies with high R&D expenses and slow growth in patent output are targets. Further, technological overlap between firm pairs has a positive effect on transaction incidence, and this effect is reduced for firm pairs that overlap in product markets. Synergies obtained from combining innovation capabilities are important drivers of acquisitions.

Bhattacharyya, S. and Nain, A. (2011) 'Horizontal acquisitions and buying power: A product market analysis', *Journal of Financial Economics,* 99, 97–115
> Horizontal mergers exert price pressure on dependent suppliers and adversely affect their performance.

Bhide, A. (1993) 'The causes and consequences of hostile takeovers', in Chew, Jr, D.H. (ed.), *The New Finance: Where Theory Meets Practice.* New York: McGrawHill.
> Target firms are poor performers.

Botsari, A. and Meeks, G. (2008) 'Do acquirers manage earnings prior to a share for share bid?' *Journal of Business Finance and Accounting,* 35(5), (6), pp. 633–70.
> Earnings management/manipulation by acquirers ahead of share for share bids may affect whether a bid succeeds, and hence which management team controls

the target assets and the distribution of gains between the target and acquiring shareholders – UK study.

Buffett, W. (1982) Letter to Shareholders accompanying the Berkshire Hathaway Annual Report. Omaha, NE. www.berkshirehathaway.com.
> Words of wit and wisdom forged by business experience.

Buffett, W. (1995) Letter to Shareholders accompanying the Berkshire Hathaway Annual Report. Omaha, NE. www.berkshirehathaway.com.
> Words of wit and wisdom forged by business experience.

Buono, A. and Bowditch, J. (2003) *The Human Side of Mergers and Acquisitions.* Beard Books, US.
> Explains the importance of the management of people during and after merger.

Cartwright, S. and Cooper, C. (2005) *Mergers and Acquisitions: The Human Factor.* Jaico Publishing House.
> Cultural and other 'soft' issues of mergers are discussed.

Conn, R.L., Cosh, A., Guest, P.M. and Hughes, A. (2005) 'The impact on UK acquirers of domestic, cross-border, public and private acquisitions', *Journal of Business Finance & Accounting,* 32(5) and (6), June/July.
> UK quoted companies acquiring UK companies results in relatively poor returns around the announcement date and over the subsequent three years on average (−22%). UK acquirers in cross-border mergers of quoted companies are also poor performers. However, private UK (not on stock market) acquirers tend to produce zero post-acquisition returns on average.

Coopers & Lybrand and OC & C (1993) *A Review of The Acquisition Experience of Major Uk Companies.* London: Coopers & Lybrand.
> An interesting survey of the top 100 firms' reasons for difficulties and triumphs in post-merger management.

Cosh, A., Guest, P.M. and Hughes, A. (2006) 'Board share ownership and takeover performance', *Journal of Business Finance & Accounting,* 33(3/4), Apr/May pp. 459–510.
> UK study. The larger the holding of shares in the company by the chief executive the better the post-merger long-term share returns.

Cowling, K., Stoneman, P. and Cubbin, J. et al. (1980) *Mergers and Economic Performance.* Cambridge: Cambridge University Press.
> Discusses the societal costs and benefits of mergers.

Duchin, R. and B. Schmidt (2013) 'Riding the merger wave', *Journal of Financial Economics,* 107, pp. 69–88.
> At times of high merger activity there tends to be poorer quality of analysts' forecasts, greater uncertainty and lower penalties for managers initiating inefficient mergers. Average long-term performance of acquisitions initiated in merger waves is significantly worse.

Epstein, M.J. (2005) 'The determinants and evaluation of merger success', *Business Horizons,* 48, pp. 37–46.

Offers six key factors needed for merger success; US case study incorporated.

Faelten, A., M. Gietzmann and Vitkova, V. (2014) 'Naked M&A Transactions: How the lack of local expertise in cross-border deals can negatively affect acquirer performance – and how informed institutional investors can mitigate this effect', *Journal of Business Finance & Accounting.* 41(3/4), pp. 469–506.
Having local expertise leads to better outcomes for shareholders.

Fee, C.E. and Thomas, S. (2004) 'Sources of gains in horizontal mergers: Evidence from customer, supplier, and rival firms', *Journal of Financial Economics,* 74(3), Dec., pp. 423–60.
Improved productivity and buying power as a result of merger.

Firth, M. (1980) 'Takeovers, shareholders' returns and the theory of the firm', *Quarterly Journal of Economics,* 94, March, pp. 235–60.
UK study. Results: **a** The target shareholders benefit; **b** the acquiring shareholders lose; **c** the acquiring firm's management increases utility; **d** the economic gains to society are, at best, zero.

Firth, M. (1991) 'Corporate takeovers, stockholder returns and executive rewards', *Managerial and Decision Economics,* 12, pp. 421–8.
Mergers leading to increased size of firm result in higher managerial remuneration.

Franks, J. and Harris, R. (1989) 'Shareholder wealth effects of corporate takeovers: The UK experience 1955–85', *Journal of Financial Economics,* 23, pp. 225–49.
Study of 1,800 UK takeovers. Gains of 25–30% for targets. Zero or modest gains for acquirers. Overall there is value created for shareholders.

Franks, J. and Mayer, C. (1996) 'Hostile takeovers and correction of managerial failure', *Journal of Financial Economics,* 40, pp. 163–81.

Fu, F., Lu, L. and Officer, M.S. (2013) 'Acquisitions driven by stock overvaluation: Are they good deals?' *Journal of Financial Economics,* 109, pp. 24–39.
Overvalued acquirers significantly overpay for their targets. These acquisitions do not, in turn, lead to synergy gains. Moreover, these acquisitions seem to be concentrated among acquirers with the largest governance problems. CEO compensation, not shareholder value creation, appears to be the main motive.

Ghosh, A. (2004) 'Increasing market share as a rationale for corporate acquisitions', *Journal of Business Finance & Accounting,* 31(1) & (2), January/March, pp. 209–47.
US study of 2,000 acquisitions. Increasing market share following merger is correlated with positive acquirer abnormal returns and operating performance.

Goergen, M. and Renneboog, L. (2004) 'Shareholder wealth effects of European domestic and cross-border takeover bids', *European Financial Management,* 10(1), pp. 9–45.

Europe-wide study. On average bidder performance is roughly the same as the market during the four months around the merger announcement date. Bids financed by equity produce better announcement period returns than those financed by cash.

Gorbenko, A.S. and Malenko, A. (2014) 'Strategic and financial bidders in takeover auctions', *Journal of Finance,* 69(6), pp. 2513–55.
A typical target is valued higher by strategic bidders than financial bidders, but 22.4% of targets are valued higher by financial bidders. These are mature, poorly performing companies. The results suggest that different targets appeal to different types of bidders, rather than that strategic bidders always value targets more because of synergies.

Gorton, G., Kahl, M. and Rosen, R.J. (2009) 'Eat or be eaten: A theory of mergers and firm size', *Journal of Finance,* LXIV(3), pp. 1291–344.
Mostly theoretical but the empirical evidence supports the belief that managers buy other firms to avoid being taken over.

Gregory, A. (1997) 'An examination of the long-run performance of UK acquiring firms', *Journal of Business Finance and Accounting,* 24(7–8), Sept., pp. 971–1002.
More evidence on the poor performance of acquirers.

Gregory, A. (2005) 'The long run abnormal performance of UK acquirers and the free cash flow hypothesis', *Journal of Business Finance & Accounting,* 32(5) & (6), June/July, pp. 777–814.
UK acquirers underperform the market by 19.9% over 60 months 1984–92. Acquirers with a high level of free cash flow perform better than acquirers with low free cash flow in the five years following merger as measured by total return.

Hampden-Turner, C. and Trompenaars, F. (2000) *Building Crosscultural Competence.* Self-published.
A focus on the difficulties of getting merged organisations and cultures to work together.

Harding, D., Rovit, S. and Corbett, A. (2005) 'Three steps to avoiding merger meltdown', *Harvard Management Update,* March, pp. 1–5.
A short article offering post-merger integration advice.

Harford, J. (2005) 'What drives merger waves', *Journal of Financial Economics,* 77(3), pp. 529–60.
Economic, regulatory and technological shocks drive industry merger waves.

Hasbrouck, J. (1985) 'The characteristics of takeover targets: q and other measures', *Journal of Banking and Finance,* 9, pp. 351–62.

Haspeslagh, P. and Jemison, D. (1991) *Managing Acquisitions.* New York: Free Press.
A thorough and well-written guide to the management of firms that engage in mergers.

Hodgkinson, L. and Partington, G.H. (2008) 'The motivation for takeovers in the UK', *Journal of Business Finance and Accounting,* 35(1), (2), pp. 102–26.

Evidence of bids motivated by synergy, hubris and agency elements.

Hoffmann, N. (2013) 'Discounted cash flow valuation for small cap M&A integration', *Journal of Applied Corporate Finance,* Spring, 25(2), pp. 116–21.

A case study a successful strategy of buying up dozens of small companies and integrating them well.

Ishii, J. and Xuan, Y. (2014) 'Acquirer-target social ties and merger outcomes', *Journal of Financial Economics,* 112, pp. 344–63.

'The extent of cross-firm social connection between directors and senior executives at the acquiring and the target firms has a significantly negative effect on the abnormal returns to the acquirer and to the combined entity upon merger announcement. . . . our results suggest that social ties between the acquirer and the target lead to poorer decision making and lower value creation for shareholders overall.'

Jensen, M.C. (1986) 'Agency costs of free cashflow, corporate finance and takeovers', *American Economic Review,* May, p. 323.

Dividend payouts reduce managers' resources and lead to greater monitoring if they go to the capital markets for funds. Internal funding is thus preferred and surplus cash flow leads to value destroying mergers. Easy to read.

Jensen, M.C. and Meckling, W.H. (1976) 'Theory of the firm: Managerial behavior, agency cost and ownership structure', *Journal of Financial Economics,* October, pp. 305–60.

An important paper on agency theory.

Lel, U. and Miller, D.P. (2015) 'Does takeover activity cause managerial discipline? Evidence from international M&A laws', *Review of Financial Studies,* 28(6), pp. 1588–622.

The passage of takeover laws results in poorly performing firms experiencing more frequent takeovers; the propensity to replace poorly performing CEOs increases, especially in countries with weak investor protection; and directors of targeted firms are more likely to lose board seats following corporate-control events.

Lev, B. (1992) 'Observations on the merger phenomenon and a review of the evidence'. Reprinted in J.M. Stern and D. Chew (eds), *The Revolution in Corporate Finance.* 2nd edn. Oxford: Blackwell.

Merger motives, and who wins from mergers, are discussed in an introductory style.

Levine, P. and Aaronovitch, S. (1981) 'The financial characteristics of firms and theories of merger activity', *Journal of Industrial Economics.* 30, pp. 149–72.

Liu, B. and McConnell, J.J. (2015) 'CEOs, abandoned acquisitions, and the media', *Journal of Applied Corporate Finance,* 27(3), Summer, pp. 113–20.

Managers will reverse a bad decision to try to acquire if the stock market sees it as value reducing and media attacks the idea, thus reducing the CEO's 'reputational capital'.

Loughran, J. and Vijh, A.M. (1997) 'Do long term shareholders benefit from corporate acquisitions?', *Journal of Finance,* 52(5), pp. 1765–90.

Empirical evidence on post-merger performance.

Louis, H. (2004a) 'Earnings management and the market performance of acquiring firms' *Journal of Financial Economics,* 74(1), Oct., pp. 121–48.

Evidence suggesting that acquiring firms overstate earnings in the quarter before acquiring – linked to poor post-merger performance.

Louis, H. (2004b) 'The cost of using bank mergers as defensive mechanisms against takeover threats' *Journal of Business,* 77(2) pt.1, pp. 295–310.

Evidence to show that by acquiring other banks managers can avoid being taken over.

Lynch, P. (1990) *One Up on Wall Street.* New York: Penguin.

One of the greatest investors comments on companies and managers in a witty fashion.

Maksimovic, V., Phillips, G. and Yang, L. (2013) 'Public and private merger waves', *Journal of Finance,* LXVIII(5), October, pp. 2177–216.

Evidence that merger waves are associated with high stock markets and easy credit markets. Post-merger productivity improves at all points on the merger cycle.

Manson, S., Stark, A. and Thomas, H.M. (1994) 'A cash flow analysis of the operational gains from takeovers', *Research Report 35.* London: Chartered Association of Certified Accountants.

Post-merger and premerger consolidated operating performance measures are compared. Operational gains are produced on average. A study of 38 companies.

Mitchell, M.L. and Lehn, K. (1990) 'Do bad bidders become good targets?', *Journal of Political Economy,* 98(2), pp. 372–98.

'Hostile bust-up takeovers often promote economic efficiency by reallocating the targets' assets to higher valued uses . . . In aggregate, we find that the returns to acquiring firms are approximately zero; the aggregate data obscure the fact that the market discriminates between "bad" bidders which are more likely to become takeover targets, and "good" bidders, which are less likely to become targets.'

Moeller, S.B., Schlingemann, F.P. and Stulz, R.M. (2004) 'Firm size and the gains from acquisitions', *Journal of Financial Economics,* 73, pp. 201–28.

US study. Acquiring firm announcement period abnormal return is on average slightly positive for small firms but negative for large firms. Given that larger firms offer larger acquisition premiums and enter acquisitions with negative dollar synergy gains 'the evidence is consistent with managerial hubris playing more of a role in the decisions of large firms'.

Moeller, S.B., Schlingemann, F.P. and Stulz, R.M. (2005) 'Wealth destruction on a massive scale? A study of acquiring firm returns in the recent merger wave', *The Journal of Finance*, LX(2), April, pp. 757–82.

US study. On average acquirer shareholders experience a poor return in the few days around acquisition announcement – particularly so in the period 1998–2001 (hitech boom period).

Morosini, P. and Steger, U. (eds) (2004) Managing Complex Mergers: Real world lessons in implementing successful cross cultural M&As. Harlow: Financial Times Prentice Hall.

Provides an accessible overview of thinking on the issue of merger failure and merger management.

Palepu, K.G. (1986) 'Predicting takeover targets: A methodological and empirical analysis', *Journal of Accounting and Finance*, 8, pp. 3–35.

The Panel on Takeovers and Mergers, *The City Code* www.thetakeoverpanel.org.uk The complex set of rules are laid out in reasonably easy-to-follow fashion. Updated regularly.

Powell, R.G. and Stark, A.W. (2005) 'Does operating performance increase post takeover for UK takeovers? A comparison of performance measures and benchmarks', *Journal of Corporate Finance*, 11(1 & 2), March, p. 293–317.

Powell, R.G. and Thomas, H.M. (1994) 'Corporate control and takeover prediction', Working paper 94/07 (Department of Accounting and Financial Management, University of Essex).

Rappaport, A. (1998) *Creating Shareholder Value*. New York: Free Press.

Revised and updated. Chapter 8 provides a shareholder value perspective on mergers.

Rau, P.R. and Vermaelen, T. (1998) 'Glamour, value and the post-acquisition performance of acquiring firms', *Journal of Financial Economics*, 49(2), pp. 223–53.

Ravenscraft, D. and Scherer, F. (1987) *Mergers, Sell-Offs and Economic Efficiency*. Washington, DC: Brookings Institution.

An overview of mergers: rationale, activity, profitability, economics. US based.

Rhodes-Kropf, M., Robinson, D.T. and Viswanathan, S. (2005) 'Valuation waves and merger activity: The empirical evidence', *Journal of Financial Economics*, 77(3), pp. 561–603.

'Misvaluation drives mergers. . . affects who buys whom, as well as method of payment, and combines with neoclassical explanations to explain aggregate merger activity.'"

Rhodes-Kropf, M. and Viswanathan, S. (2005) 'Market valuation and merger waves', *Journal of Finance*, 59, pp. 2685–718.

Mis-valuation can lead to merger waves.

Roll, R. (1986) 'The hubris hypothesis of corporate takeovers', *Journal of Business*, 59(2), pt. 1, April, pp. 197–216. Also reproduced in R. Thaler (ed.) (1993) *Advances in Behavioral Finance*. New York: Russell Sage Foundation.

'Bidding firms infected by hubris simply pay too much for their targets.'

Savor, P.G. and Lu, Q. (2009) 'Do stock mergers create value for acquirers?' *Journal of Finance*, LXIV(3), pp. 1061–97.

Overvalued shares create value for long-term shareholders by using their equity as currency.

Serdar, D.I. and Erel, I. (2013) 'Economic nationalism in mergers and acquisitions', *Journal of Finance*, Dec., 68(6), pp. 2471–514.

In the EU there is widespread economic nationalism in which the government prefers that target companies remain domestically owned rather than foreign-owned, deterring foreign companies from bidding for companies.

Shahrur, H. (2005) 'Industry structure and horizontal takeovers: Analysis of wealth effects on rivals, suppliers, and corporate customers', *Journal of Financial Economics*, 76, pp. 61–98.

'Inconsistent with the collusion and buyer power motives, we find significant positive abnormal returns to rivals, suppliers, and corporate customers for the subsample of takeovers with positive combined wealth effect to target and bidder shareholders. Overall, our findings suggest that the average takeover in our sample is driven by efficiency considerations.'

Sheen, A. (2014) 'The real product market impact of mergers', *The Journal of Finance* 69(6), August 2014.

Singh, A. (1971) *Takeovers*. Cambridge: Cambridge University Press.

Provides evidence on the type of firms which become targets.

Sirower, M.L. (2008) *The Synergy Trap: How Companies Lose the Acquisition Game*. New York: Free Press.

A practical, easy to read guide to mergers and the reasons for the failure to create value.

Sudarsanam, S. (2010) *Creating Value from Mergers and Acquisitions: The challenge*. 2nd edn. Harlow: Financial Times Prentice Hall.

An easy-to-read comprehensive guide to all aspects of mergers – well worth reading.

Sudarsanam, S. and Mahate, A. (2003) 'Glamour acquirers, methods of payment and postacquisition performance: The UK evidence', *Journal of Business Finance and Accounting*, 30(1 & 2), pp. 299–341.

Sudarsanam, S., Holl, P. and Salami, A. (1996) 'Shareholder wealth gains in mergers: Effect of synergy and ownership structure', *Journal of Business Finance and Accounting,* July, pp. 673–98.

> Financial synergy dominates operational synergy in UK mergers. A marriage between companies with a complementary fit in terms of liquidity slack and surplus investment opportunities is value creating for both groups of shareholders. But high-rated acquirers taking over low rated firms lose value.

Weston, J.F., Mitchell, M.L. and Mulherin, J.H. (2013) *Takeovers, Restructuring, and Corporate Governance.* Pearson.

> A US textbook covering the field of mergers.

Xiao, G.B. and Gregory, A. (2011) 'Stock market driven acquisitions versus the Q theory of takeovers: The UK evidence', *Journal of Business Finance and Accounting,* 38(5), (6), pp. 628–56.

> UK mergers study shows that equity overvaluation plays an important role in determining the financing method.

Case study recommendations

Please see www.pearsoned.co.uk/arnold for case study synopses. Also, another list of useful case studies from the fifth edition can be found there.

- 3 ways M&A is different when you're acquiring a digital company. Author: Arnaud Leroi, Harvard Business School. Available at www.cb.hbsp.harvard.edu

- Neptune Orient Lines: valuation and capital structure. Authors: Ruth S.K. Tan; Zsuzsa R. Huszar; Weina Zhang, Ivey Publishing. Available at www.cb.hbsp.harvard.edu

- FNAC-Darty merger: from bidding wars to entity integration. Authors: Wiboon Kittilaksanawong; Hanna Tayeb, Ivey Publishing. Available at www.cb.hbsp.harvard.edu

- H. J. Heinz M&A. Authors: David P. Stowell; Nicholas Kawar, Kellogg School of Management. Available atwww.cb.hbsp.harvard.edu

- Stanley Black & Decker, Inc. Author: William E. Fruhan, Harvard Business School. Available at www.cb.hbsp.harvard.edu

- Monmouth, Inc. (brief case). Authors: Thomas R. Piper; Heide Abelli, Harvard Business School. Available atwww.cb.hbsp.harvard.edu

- Roche's acquisition of Genentech. Authors: Carliss Y. Baldwin; Bo Becker; Vincent Dessain Harvard Business School. Available at www.cb.hbsp.harvard.edu

- What does whole foods get from Amazon? Alexa, for starters. Author: Benjamin Gomes-Casseres, Harvard Business School. Available at www.cb.hbsp.harvard.edu

- Beam Suntory: striving for optimal post-acquisition integration. Authors: Wiboon Kittilaksanawong; Kendall Marin Wyckoff, Ivey Publishing. Available at www.cb.hbsp.harvard.edu

Websites

www.berkshirehathaway.com
www.ft.com
www.home.kpmg.com
www.londonstockexchange.com

www.thetakeoverpanel.org.uk
www.gov.uk/government/organisations/competition-and-markets-authority

Video presentations

Chief executives and finance directors discuss their recent mergers (e.g. motives, people problems, and financial success) on MerchantCantos.com (www.merchantcantos.com) – this is free to view.

Self-review questions

1 List as many motives for mergers as you can.

2 Briefly describe the alternative methods of payment for target firms and comment on their advantages and disadvantages.

3 Explain the significance of the following for the merger process:
   – a concert party;
   – the 3% rule;
   – the 30% rule;
   – the Takeover Panel;
   – the Competition and Markets Authority;
   – a dawn raid.

4 List the potential beneficiaries from mergers and briefly explain whether, on average, they do gain from mergers.

5 What are the three stages of a merger?

6 List some actions which might assist a successful post-merger integration.

7 Explain the following in the context of mergers:
   – synergy;
   – the internalisation of transactions;
   – bargain buying;
   – hubris;
   – the survival motive;
   – the free cash flow merger motive.

8 How do mergers differ from other investment decisions?

9 Explain the terms horizontal mergers, vertical mergers and conglomerate mergers.

10 What is the winner's curse?

11 What does it mean when an offer goes 'unconditional'?

Questions and problems

Answers to most questions can be found at www.pearsoned.co.uk/arnold.
Answers to questions marked with an asterisk are to be found only in the Lecturer's Guide.

1* Large plc is considering the takeover of Small plc. Large is currently valued at £60m on the stock market while Small is valued at £30m. The economies of scale and other benefits of the merger are expected to produce a market value for the combined firm of £110m. A bid premium of £20m is expected to be needed to secure Small. Transaction costs (advisers' fees, etc.) are estimated at £3m. Large has 30 million shares in issue and Small has 45 million. Assume the managers are shareholder-wealth maximisers.

   Required
   a Does this merger create value for Large plc?
   b If the purchase is made with cash what will be the price offered for each of Small's shares?
   c What would be the value of each of Large's shares after this merger?

2 Which of the following mergers is horizontal, vertical or conglomerate?
   a Marks & Spencer and Next.
   b Premier Foods and Sainsbury.
   c Harriman House Publishers and Waterstones bookstores.
   d Rolls Royce and Electrolux.
   e Ford and Microsoft.

3* Box plc is considering the acquisition of Circle plc. The former is valued at £100m and the latter at £50m by the market. Economies of scale will result in savings of £2.5m annually in perpetuity. The required rate of return on both firms and the combination is 11%. The transaction costs will amount to £1m.

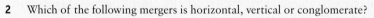

Required

a   What is the present value of the gain from the merger?

b   If a cash offer of £70m is accepted by Circle's shareholders what is the value created for Box's shareholders?

c   If shares are offered in such a way that Circle's shareholders would possess one-third of the merged entity, what is the value created for Box's shareholders?
?

4*   High plc has an historic PER of 22 and Low plc has an historic PER of 12. Both companies have 100 million shares in issue and produced earnings of £20m in the last financial year. High has offered three of its shares for every five held by Low's shareholders.

Required

a   If you held 1,000 shares in Low and accepted the offer from High, by how much would your wealth increase assuming High's shares remain at the pre-bid price?

b   What is the bid premium being offered?

c   If High was able to increase the rate of growth of Low's earnings to the same as High's and therefore place them on the same PER as High, what would High's share price move to?

d   If High makes no changes to Low's operations and so earnings growth continues at its present rate what will the intrinsic value of a share in High be, assuming the current PERs reflect accurately future growth in earnings?

e   Explain the PER game and how High could continue to acquire firms, make no changes to underlying earnings and yet show a rising earnings per share trend.
?

5*   Consider the following companies:

	A	B
Earnings per share (recent)	50p	10p
Dividends per share (recent)	25p	5p
Number of shares	5m	3m
Share price	£9.00	75p

The cost of equity capital for both firms is 12%. B is expected to produce a growth in dividends of 5% per annum to infinity with its current strategy and management. However if A acquired B and applied superior management and gained benefits from economies of scale the growth rate would rise to 8% on the same capital base. The transaction costs of the merger would amount to £400,000.

Required

a   What value could be created from a merger?

b   If A paid £1.20 cash for each of B's shares what value created by the merger would be available for each group of shareholders?

c   If A gave one of its shares for seven of B's what value created by the merger would be available for each group of shareholders?

d   If none of the merger benefits is realised, because of problems of integration, what is the loss or gain in value to A and B shareholders under both the cash offer and the shares offer?
?

6   White plc and Black plc have made separate all-share bids for Blue plc.

	White	Black	Blue	White + Blue	Black + Blue	Blue
Pre-merger share price	£4	£3	£1			
Number of shares issued	1m	2m	1.5m			
Market capitalisation	£4m	£6m	£1.5m	£6.8m	£8.0m	

Assume no transaction costs.

Required

a   If you were the managing director of White what is the maximum number of White shares you would offer for every 10 Blue shares? (Fractions of shares may be used.)

b   If you were the managing director of Black, what is the maximum number of Black shares you would offer for every 10 Blue shares? (Fractions of shares may be used.)

c   Some mergers produce increased returns for the acquirer's shareholders, whereas others do not. Discuss the reasons for merger failure from the acquirer's shareholders' perspective.   **?**

7   (*Examination level*) Some of the motives for mergers lead to benefits for society, some to shareholders, some to the management of the acquirer and others result in benefits to more than one group. Describe these in the form of an essay.

8   (*Examination level*) The directors of Trajectory plc have decided to expand rapidly through mergers. You have been asked to explain the process itself, from appointing an adviser to the offer going unconditional. Do this in the form of an essay.

9   (*Examination level*) Mergers fail to produce value for the shareholders of acquirers in many cases. Describe and explain some reasons for merger failure.

Assignment

Obtain as much information as you can on a recent merger. Relate the elements discussed in this chapter (merger motives, process, planning and integration) to the merger under examination. Write a report and make recommendations for improvement should any future mergers be contemplated.

PART 6

Managing risk

Derivatives

LEARNING OUTCOMES

This chapter describes the main types of derivatives. Continued innovation means that the range of instruments broadens every year but the new developments are generally variations or combinations of the characteristics of derivatives discussed here. At the end of this chapter the reader should be able to:

■ explain the nature of options and the distinction between different kinds of options, and demonstrate their application in a wide variety of areas;

■ show the value of forwards, futures, FRAs, swaps, caps and floors markets by demonstrating transactions which manage and transfer risk.

Introduction

A derivative instrument is an asset whose performance is based on (derived from) the behaviour of the value of an underlying asset (usually referred to simply as the 'underlying'). The most common underlyings include commodities (for example, tea or pork bellies), shares, bonds, share indices, currencies and interest rates. Derivatives are contracts which give the right, and sometimes the obligation, to buy or sell a quantity of the underlying, or benefit in another way from a rise or fall in the value of the underlying. It is the legal *right* that becomes an asset, with its own value, and it is the right that is purchased or sold. Derivative instruments include the following: futures, options, swaps, forward rate agreements (FRAs), forwards.

The derivatives markets have received an enormous amount of attention from the press in recent years. This is hardly surprising as spectacular losses have been made and a number of companies brought to the point of collapse through the employment of derivative instruments. Some examples of the unfortunate use of derivatives are:

- Barings, Britain's oldest merchant bank, which lost over £800m on Nikkei Index (the Japanese share index) contracts on the Singapore and Osaka derivatives exchanges, leading to the bank's demise in 1995.

- Long-Term Capital Management, which attempted to exploit the 'mispricing' of financial instruments, by making use of option pricing theory. In 1998 the firm collapsed and the Federal Reserve Bank of New York cajoled 14 banks and brokerage houses to put up $3.6bn to save LTCM and thereby prevent a financial system breakdown.

- Financial institutions were destroyed in 2008 by buying derivatives whose value depended on US mortgage borrowers continuing to be able to pay their mortgages. When a proportion could not pay their debts, the derivatives (of asset-backed securitised bonds) became either valueless or very difficult/impossible to value. The uncertainty surrounding the value of these derivatives led to a freezing of the short-term debt markets for months, which in turn led to financial distress for financial institutions that had no connection with the US mortgage market or the related derivatives, e.g. Northern Rock.

- UBS lost $2.3bn in 2011 as a result of derivative trades undertaken by a single young trader who took bets on equity index futures including the S&P 500, DAX and Euro Stoxx.

In many of the financial scandals derivatives have been used (or misused) to speculate rather than to reduce risk. This chapter examines both of these applications of derivatives but places particular emphasis on the hedging (risk-mitigating) facility they provide. These are powerful tools and managers can abuse that power either through ignorance or through deliberate acceptance of greater risk in the anticipation of greater reward. However, there is nothing inherently wrong with the tools themselves. If employed properly they can be remarkably effective at limiting risk.

A long history

Derivative instruments have been employed for more than two thousand years. Olive growers in ancient Greece unwilling to accept the risk of a low price for their crop when harvested months later would enter into forward agreements whereby a price was agreed for delivery at a specific time. This reduced uncertainty for both the grower and the purchaser of the olives. In the Middle Ages forward contracts were traded in a kind of secondary market, particularly for wheat in Europe. A futures market was established in Osaka's rice market in Japan in the seventeenth century. Tulip bulb options were traded in seventeenth-century Amsterdam.

Commodity futures trading really began to take off in the nineteenth century with the Chicago Board of Trade regulating the trading of grains and other futures and options, and the London Metal Exchange dominating metal trading.

So derivatives are not new. What is different today is the size and importance of the derivatives markets. The last quarter of the twentieth century witnessed an explosive growth of volumes of trade, variety of derivatives products, and the number and range of users and uses.

In the thirty years to 2017 the face value of outstanding derivatives contracts rose dramatically to stand at about US$540 trillion (US$540,000,000,000,000). Compare that with a UK annual GDP of £2 trillion.

Options

An option is a contract giving one party the right, but not the obligation, to buy or sell a financial instrument, commodity or some other underlying asset at a given price, at or before a specified date. The purchaser of the option can either exercise the right or let it lapse – the choice is theirs.

A very simple option would be where a firm pays the owner of land a non-returnable premium (say £10,000) for an option to buy the land at an agreed price because the firm is considering the development of a retail park within the next five years. The property developer may pay a number of option premiums to owners of land in different parts of the country. If planning permission is eventually granted on a particular plot the option to purchase may be exercised. In other words the developer pays the price agreed with the farmer at the time that the option contract was arranged, say £1,000,000, to purchase the land. Options on other plots may be allowed to lapse and will have no value. By using an option the property developer has 'kept the options open' with regard to which site to buy and develop and, indeed, whether to enter the retail park business at all.

Options can also be *traded*. Perhaps the option to buy could be sold to another company keener to develop a particular site than the original option purchaser. It may be sold for much more than the original £10,000 option premium, even before planning permission has been granted.

Once planning permission has been granted the greenfield site may be worth £1,500,000. If there is an option to buy at £1,000,000 the option right has an intrinsic value of £500,000, representing a 4,900% return on £10,000.

From this comparison we can see the gearing effect of options: very large sums can be gained in a short period of time for a small initial cash outlay.

Share options

Share options have been traded for centuries but their use expanded dramatically with the creation of traded option markets in Chicago, Amsterdam and, in 1978, the London Traded Options Market, now incorporated into ICE Futures Europe.

A share call option gives the purchaser the right, but not the obligation, to *buy* a fixed number of shares at a specified price at some time in the future. In the case of traded options on ICE Futures Europe, one option contract relates to a quantity of 1,000 shares. The seller of the option, who receives the premium, is referred to as the writer. The writer of a call option is obligated to sell the agreed quantity of shares at the agreed price some time in the future. American-style options can be exercised by the buyer at any time up to the expiry date, whereas European-style options can only be exercised on a predetermined future date. Just to confuse everybody, the distinction has nothing to do with geography: most options traded in Europe are American-style options.

Call option holder (call option buyers)

Now let us examine the call options available on an underlying share – Unilever on 1 August 2017. There are a number of different options available for this share, many of which are not reported in the table presented in the *Financial Times*.[1] A section of this table is reproduced as **Exhibit 21.1**.

---

1 See www.ft.com, or the original source, https://www.theice.com/products.

Exhibit 21.1	Call options on Unilever shares, 1 August 2017		
	Call option prices (premiums) pence		
Exercise price	September	December	March
2500p	72.5	87.5	101.5
2600p	13.5	36.5	51.0
Share price on 1 August 2017 = 2567p			

Source: *Financial Times*. Reprinted with permission.

So, what do the figures mean? If, on 1 August 2017, you wished to obtain the right to buy 1,000 shares on or before late December 2017, at an exercise price of 2600p, you would pay a premium of £365 (1,000 × 36.5p). If you wished to keep your option to purchase open for another three months you could select the March call. But this right to insist that the writer sells the shares at the fixed price of 2600p on or before a date in late March[2] will cost another £145 (the total premium payable on one option contract = £510 rather than £365). This extra £145 represents additional time value. Time value arises because of the potential for the market price of the underlying to change in a way that creates intrinsic value.

The intrinsic value of an option is the pay-off that would be received if the underlying were at its current level when the option expires. In this case, there is currently (1 August 2017) no intrinsic value because the right to buy is at 2600p whereas the share price is 2567p. However, if you look at a call option with an exercise price of 2500p then the right to buy at £25 has intrinsic value because if you purchased at 2500p by exercising the option, thereby obtaining 1,000 shares, you could immediately sell at 2567p in the share market: intrinsic value = 67p per share, or £670 for 1,000 shares. The longer the time over which the option is exercisable the greater the chance that the price will move to give intrinsic value – this explains the higher premiums on more distant expiry options. Time value is the amount by which the option premium exceeds the intrinsic value.

The two exercise price (also called strike price) levels presented in Exhibit 21.1 illustrate an in-the-money option (the 2500 call option) and an out-of-the-money option (the 2600 call option). The underlying share price is above the strike price of 2500 and so this call option has an intrinsic value of 67p and is therefore in-the-money. The right to buy at 2600p is out-of-the-money because the share price is below the option exercise price and therefore has no intrinsic value. The holder of a 2600p option would not exercise this right to buy at 2600p because the shares can be bought on the stock exchange for 2567p. (It is sometimes possible to buy an at-the-money option, which is one where the market share price is equal to the option exercise price.)

To emphasise the key points: the option premiums vary in proportion to the length of time over which the option is exercisable (e.g. they are higher for a March option than for a December option). Also, call options with lower exercise prices will have higher premiums.

An illustration

Suppose, on 1 August, you are confident that Unilever shares are going to rise significantly over the next eight months to £30 and you purchase a March 2500 call at 101.5 pence.[3] The cost of this right to purchase 1,000 shares is £1015 (101.5p × 1,000 shares). If the share rises as expected then you could exercise the right to purchase the shares for a total of £25,000 and then sell these in the market for £30,000. A profit of £5,000 less £1,015 = £3,985 is made before transaction costs (the brokers' fees, etc. would be in the region of £20–£50). This represents a massive 393% rise before costs (£3,985/£1,015).

---

2 The expiry date (last trading day) is the third Friday of the expiry month.

3 For this example we will assume that the option is held to expiry and not traded before then. However, in many cases this option will be sold on to another trader long before the expiry date approaches (probably at a profit or loss).

However, the future is uncertain and the share price may not rise as expected. Let us consider two other possibilities. First, the share may remain at 2567p throughout the life of the option. Secondly, the stock market may have a severe downturn and Unilever shares may fall to 2000p. These possibilities are shown in **Exhibit 21.2**.

Exhibit 21.2	Profits and losses on the March 2018 call option following purchase on 1 August 2017		
	Assumptions on share price in March at expiry		
	3000p	**2567p**	**2000p**
Cost of purchasing shares by exercising the option	£25,000	£25,000	£25,000
Value of shares bought	£30,000	£25,670	£20,000
Profit from exercise of option and sale of shares in the market	£5,000	£670	Not exercised
Less option premium paid	£1,015	£1,015	£1,015
Profit (loss) before transaction costs	£3985	−£345	−£1,015
Percentage return over 3 months	393%	−34%	−100%

In the case of a standstill in the share price the option gradually loses its time value over the three months until, at expiry, only the intrinsic value of 67p per share remains. The fall in the share price to 2000p illustrates one of the advantages of purchasing options over some other derivatives: the holder has a right to abandon the option and is not forced to buy the underlying share at the option exercise price – this saves £5,000. It would have added insult to injury to have to buy at £25,000 and sell at £20,000 after having already lost £1,015 on the premium for the purchase of the option.

A comparison of **Exhibits 21.3** and **21.4** shows the extent to which the purchase of an option gears up the return from share price movements: a wider dispersion of returns is experienced. On 1 August 2017, 1,000 shares could be bought for £25,670. If the price rose to £30,000, a 17% return would be made, compared with a 393% return if options are bought. We would all like the higher positive return on the option than the lower one available on the underlying – but would we all accept the downside risk associated with this option? Consider the following possibilities:

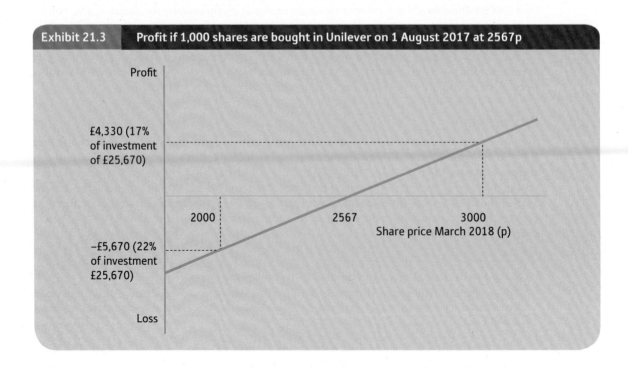

Exhibit 21.3   Profit if 1,000 shares are bought in Unilever on 1 August 2017 at 2567p

Exhibit 21.4	Profit if one March 2500 call option contract (for 1,000 shares) in Unilever is purchased on 1 August 2017 and held to maturity

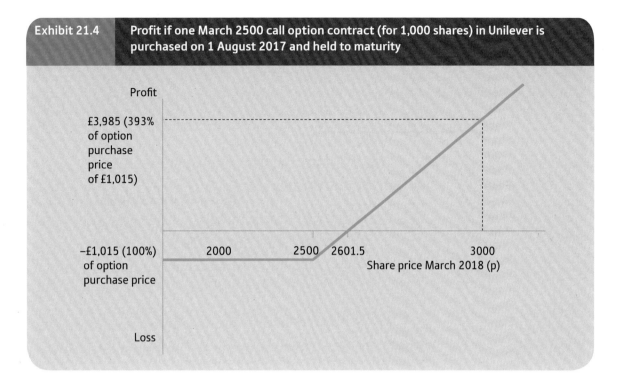

- If share price remains at 2567p:

  - Return if shares are bought: 0%
  - Return if one 2500 March call option is bought: −34% (paid £1,015 for the option which declines to its intrinsic value of only £670)[4]

- If share price falls to 2000p:

  - Return if shares are bought: −22%
  - Return if one 2500 March call option is bought: −100% (the option is worth nothing)

The holder of the call option will not exercise unless the share price is at least 2500p: at a lower price it will be cheaper to buy the 1,000 shares on the stock market. Break-even does not occur until a price of 2601.5p because of the need to cover the cost of the premium (2500p + 101.5p). However, at higher prices the option value increases, penny for penny, with the share price. Also the downside risk is limited to the size of the option premium.

Call option writers

The returns position for the writer of a 2500 March call option in Unilever can also be presented in a diagram (*see* **Exhibit 21.5**). With all these examples note that there is an assumption that the position is held to expiry.

If the market price is less than the exercise price (2500p) in March the option will not be exercised and the call writer profits to the extent of the option premium (101.5p per share). A market price greater than the exercise price will result in the option being exercised and the writer will be forced to deliver 1,000 shares for a price of 2500p. This may mean buying shares on the stock market to supply to the option holder. As the share price rises this becomes increasingly onerous and losses mount.

Note that in the sophisticated traded option markets of today very few option positions are held to expiry. In most cases the option holder sells the option in the market to make a cash profit or loss. Option writers often cancel out their exposure before expiry – for example they could purchase an option to buy the same quantity of shares at the same price and expiry date.

---

4 £670 is the intrinsic value at expiry (2567p − 2500p) × 1,000 = £670.

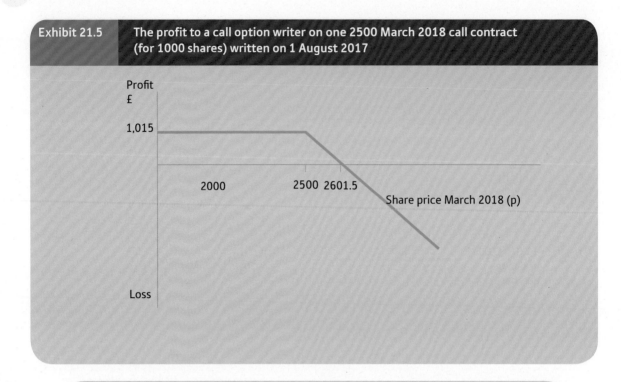

Exhibit 21.5 The profit to a call option writer on one 2500 March 2018 call contract (for 1000 shares) written on 1 August 2017

An example of an option-writing strategy

Joe has a portfolio of shares worth £100,000 and is confident that while the market will go up steadily over time it will not rise over the next few months. He has a strategy of writing out-of-the-money (i.e. no intrinsic value) call options and pocketing premiums on a regular basis. Today (1 August 2017) Joe has written one option on March calls in Unilever for an exercise price of 2600p (current share price 2567p). In other words, Joe is committed to delivering (selling) 1,000 shares at any time between 1 August 2017 and the third Friday in March 2018 for a price of 2600p at the insistence of the person who bought the call. This could be very unpleasant for Joe if the market price rises to, say, 3500p. Then the option holder will require Joe to sell shares worth £35,000 to him/her for only £26,000. However, Joe is prepared to take this risk for two reasons. First he receives the premium of 51p per share up front – this is 2% of each share's value. This £510 will cushion any feeling of future regret at his actions. Secondly, Joe holds 1,000 Unilever shares in his portfolio and so would not need to go into the market to buy the shares to then sell them to the option holder if the price did rise significantly. Joe has written a **covered call option** – so called because he has backing in the form of the underlying shares. Joe only loses out if the share price on the day the option is exercised is greater than the strike price (2600p) plus the premium (51p). He is prepared to risk losing some of the potential upside (above 2600p + 51p = 2651p) to gain the premium. He also reduces his loss on the downside: if the shares in his portfolio fall he has the premium as a cushion.

Some speculators engage in **uncovered (naked) option writing.** It is possible to lose a multiple of your current resources if you write many option contracts and the price moves against you. Imagine that Joe had only £10,000 in savings and entered the options market by writing 40 Unilever March 2600 calls receiving a premium of 0.51 × 40 × 1,000 = £20,400.[5] If the price moves to 2800p Joe has to buy shares for £28 and then sell them to the option holders for £26, a loss of £2 per share: £2 × 40 × 1,000 = £80,000. Despite receiving the premiums Joe has wiped out his savings.

LIFFE share options

The *Financial Times* lists over fifty companies' shares in which options are traded (*see* **Exhibit 21.6**).

---

5 This is simplified. In reality Joe would have to provide margin of cash or shares to reassure the clearing house that he could pay up if the market moved against him. So it could be that all of the premium received would be tied up in margin held by the clearing house (the role of a clearing house is explained later in the chapter).

Exhibit 21.6

EQUITY OPTIONS

Option		Calls Aug	Sep	Oct	Puts Aug	Sep	Oct
AstraZeneca (*4338.5)	4200	154	216	260	33	124	169.5
	4300	83.5	–	–	76	–	–
Aviva (*493.7)	480	19.25	23.75	26.25	5.5	9.75	15.25
	490	13	17.5	20.25	9.25	13.5	20
BAE Systems (*426.1)	420	9.75	14.75	17.75	3.5	8.25	11.25
	430	4.25	9.25	12.75	8	13	16.25
Barclays (*224.25)	220	6.5	10.25	12.25	3.25	6.75	8.75
	225	3.75	7.75	9.75	5.5	9.25	11.25
BG Group (*1208.5)	1150	62.5	72	81	6	20.5	29.5
	1200	24.5	41.5	51.5	21	41	50
BHP Billiton (*2011.5)	1950	79	96.5	105	17	56	71
	2000	46	66.5	77.5	34.5	80	95.5
BP (*482.950)	470	13.5	15.75	18	3.5	8.25	10.25
	480	6	10	12.5	7.75	12.5	14.75
BAT (*3443.5)	3400	75	90.5	107.5	31	84.5	105.5
	3500	24.5	43.5	63.5	80	143	163.5
BT Group (*381.8)	370	13	14.5	16.25	3.5	8.25	10.5
	380	6.25	8.25	10.75	8.75	12.75	15.5
Diageo (*1778)	1750	39	48	60.5	26	45.5	60
	1800	12.5	25	36	58.5	75.5	86
GlaxoSmKl (*1416.5)	1350	67	68.5	72.5	4.5	15.5	22
	1400	22.5	33	41	19.5	34.5	42
HSBC (*629.3)	600	31.25	32.25	34.5	1.75	6.25	9.75
	620	15.25	18	21.25	6	13.5	17
ICA (*338.2)	340	11	18	22	12.75	19.75	23.5
	350	6.75	13.5	17.5	18.5	22.25	29
Kingfisher (*290)	300	5	10	12.5	4.25	9	13.75
	310	1.5	6	8.25	10.75	15.25	20
Land Sec Gp (*1036)	1050	6.75	15.75	22.25	20.5	35	42
	1100	0.25	3.5	8	64.25	73.75	78.25
Legal & Gen (*232.1)	230	4.25	6.5	7.5	2.25	6.25	7.5
	235	1.75	4	5	4.75	9	10.25
Lloyds Blg (*73.330)	72	2	3	3.75	1	2	2.5
	74	1.25	2.25	2.75	2	3	3.5
Man Group (*116.8)	115	4.25	5.5	7.75	3.5	5.25	7.5
	120	2.25	3	5.5	6.75	8	10.25
Marks & S (*427.5)	430	6.75	13	17.75	9	15.25	20
	440	3.25	8.75	13.5	15.75	21	25.5

Option		Calls Aug	Sep	Oct	Puts Aug	Sep	Oct
Morrison (Wm) (*169.4)	165	5.75	8	9	1.25	3.5	7
	170	2.5	5.75	6.5	3	6.25	10
Natl Grid (*840)	820	24	30.25	–	3.75	9.75	–
	840	9.5	17.75	23.25	9.25	17.25	22.25
Rio Tinto (*3354.5)	3400	49	85	113	134.5	179.5	206.5
	3500	20	53	77.5	212.5	248.5	271.5
Royal Bk Scot (*350)	340	15	19.75	22.5	4.75	9.5	12
	350	8.75	13.75	17	8.75	13.5	16.5
Rl Dch Shell 'B' (*2529)	2400	131	135	141	5	21.5	31
	2500	44.5	59.5	73	29	53	67
RSA Ins GP (*451.7)	450	9	14	17.25	7.25	12	15
	460	4.75	9.25	12.25	13	17.25	20.25
Sainsbury (*310.9)	300	12.75	16.75	19.5	1.75	5.75	8.25
	310	5.75	10.75	13.75	4.75	9.5	12.5
Shire (*4871)	4600	291	367.5	482.5	19	85	204
	4800	129.5	206.5	362.5	57.5	134.5	284
Std Chartd (*1222)	1200	34	42	50	20.5	33.5	42
	1250	10	20	26.5	51	62.5	68.5
Tesco (*253.6)	240	14.5	16.75	18.25	1	3	6
	250	6.5	10	11.5	3	6.25	10
Vodafone (*196.450)	190	7.5	9.75	10.75	1	3	4
	195	3.75	6.5	7.75	2.25	5	6
Xstrata (*356.150)	328	35	–	–	10	–	–
	393	6.5	–	–	46.5	–	–

Option		Calls Sep	Dec	Mar	Puts Sep	Dec	Mar
3i Group (*373.2)	373	11.5	18.75	25.75	11	19.5	26.75
	380	8.25	–	–	15	–	–
Carnival (*2146)	2000	157.5	191	208	20	65	91.5
	2100	82.5	129.5	–	48.5	105	–
Compass (*957)	925	37.25	47.5	–	5	14.75	–
	965	10.25	23.5	–	18	31	–
Experian (*1009)	980	44	–	–	14.5	–	–
	1000	31.5	56	69	22	45	61.75
Impl Tobacco (*2537)	2400	162	202.5	213.5	23.5	60.5	121.5
	2500	93.5	–	–	54.5	–	–
IntCont Hotels (*2375)	2312	126.5	–	–	76	–	–
	2412	74	138	166	124	185.5	227.5

Option		Calls Sep	Dec	Mar	Puts Sep	Dec	Mar
ITV (*205.6)	200	9.5	14.5	18.5	3.75	9.75	13.25
	205	6.75	–	–	6	–	–
Lon Stk Exchg (*1903)	1900	68.5	109.5	139.5	64	110	138.75
	1950	46.25	–	–	92	–	–
Next (*6715)	6600	260.5	–	–	141	–	–
	6696	206	319	427	182.5	319.5	422
Pearson (*1137)	1100	44.75	65.25	82.5	20.75	43	58
	1150	17.75	–	–	46.75	–	–
Reckitt Benck (*5215)	5200	74.5	128.5	160	111.5	170	199.5
	5400	23.5	68.5	91	267.5	310	331
Reed Elsevier (*947)	920	36	50.5	66.25	12.25	25.5	38.5
	940	23.5	–	–	20	–	–
Rentokil Init (*116.1)	110	7.25	8.75	11.25	1.5	3.25	5.25
	115	4	–	–	3.5	–	–
Rolls-Royce H (*1040)	1000	55.5	77	91.5	14.75	41.75	55.25
	1050	26.75	–	–	36.25	–	–
SAB Miller (*3204)	3100	126.5	–	–	65	–	–
	3200	72	148	198.5	113	197	245
Sage Group (*366)	360	13	20.75	24.5	6.75	14	22.25
	370	7.75	–	–	11.5	–	–
Sm & Nephew (*1065)	1000	80	99.75	112	14.25	38.25	49.25
	1050	51.5	–	–	35.75	–	–
SSE (*1438)	1400	64.5	86	98.5	25.5	45	73
	1450	35	–	–	46	–	–
Standard Life (*365.5)	360	12.5	18.5	25	9.75	17.25	23.25
	370	7.25	–	–	15.5	–	–
Unilever (*2567)	2500	72.5	87.5	101.5	17.5	39.5	52.5
	2600	13.5	36.5	51	66.5	88.5	102
Utd Utilities (*856)	840	31	46	51.75	14.5	34.25	43
	860	20.75	–	–	24.25	–	–
Whitbread (*4273)	4000	299.5	347.5	391	23.5	83	125.5
	4200	154.5	–	–	78.5	–	–
Wolseley (*3087)	3000	157.5	197.5	241	68.5	147	190.5
	3100	97	–	–	108	–	–
WPP (*1180)	1150	54	–	–	23.25	–	–
	1200	25.75	50	70.25	45	79	97.5

Put options

A **put option** gives the holder the right, but not the obligation, to sell a specific quantity of shares on or before a specified date at a fixed exercise price.

Imagine you are pessimistic about the prospects for Sainsbury on 1 August 2017. You could purchase, for a premium of 5.75p per share (£57.5 in total), the right to sell 1,000 shares in or before late September 2017 at 300p (*see* Exhibit 21.6). If a fall in price subsequently takes place, to, say, 250p, you can insist on exercising the right to sell at 300p. The writer of the put option is obliged to purchase shares at 300p while being aware that the put holder is able to buy shares at 250p on the stock exchange. The option holder makes a profit of $300 - 250 - 5.75 = 44.25$p per share, a 770% return (before costs).

For the put option holder, if the market price exceeds the exercise price, it will not be wise to exercise as shares can be sold for a higher price on the stock exchange. Therefore the maximum loss, equal to the premium paid, is incurred. The option writer gains the premium if the share price remains above the exercise price, but may incur a large loss if the market price falls significantly (*see* **Exhibits 21.7** and **21.8**).

As with calls, in most cases the option holder would take profits by selling the option on to another investor via ICE Futures Europe rather than waiting to exercise at expiry.

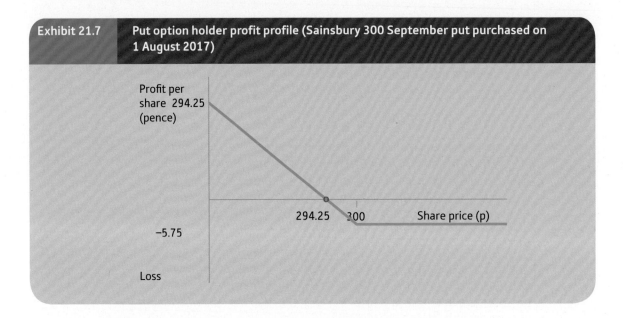

| Exhibit 21.7 | Put option holder profit profile (Sainsbury 300 September put purchased on 1 August 2017) |

Using share options to reduce risk: hedging

Hedging with options is especially attractive because they can give protection against unfavourable movements in the underlying while permitting the possibility of benefiting from favourable movements. Suppose you hold 1,000 shares in Sainsbury on 1 August 2017. Your shareholding is worth £3,109 (see price in brackets beneath the share name in Exhibit 21.6). There are rumours flying around the market that the company may become the target of a takeover bid. If this materialises the share price will rocket; if it does not the market will be disappointed and the price will fall dramatically. What are you to do? One way to avoid the downside risk is to sell the shares. The problem is that you may regret this action if the bid does subsequently occur and you have forgone the opportunity of a large profit. An alternative approach is to retain the shares and buy a put option. This will rise in value as the share price falls. If the share price rises you gain from your underlying share holding.

Assume a 300 October put is purchased for a premium of £82.50 (*see* Exhibit 21.6). If the share price falls to 250p in late October you lose on your underlying shares by £609 ((310.9p − 250p) × 1,000).

Exhibit 21.8	Put option writer profit profile (Sainsbury 300 September put sold 1 August 2017)

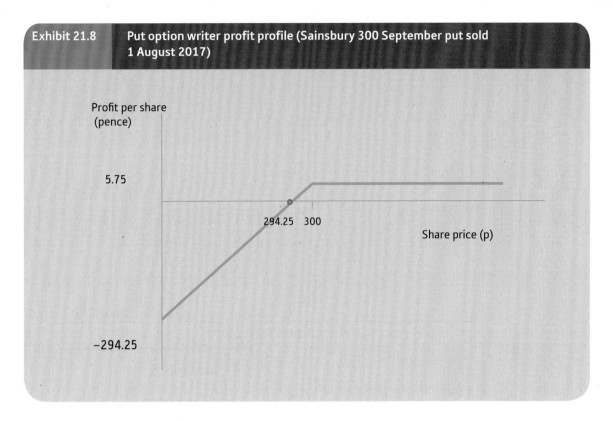

However, the put option will have an intrinsic value of £500 ((300p − 250p) × 1,000), thus reducing the loss and limiting the downside risk. Below 300p, for every 1p lost in a share price, 1p is gained on the put option, so the maximum loss is £191.5 (£109 intrinsic value + £82.5 option premium). The size of the gain should the share price rise is limitless, as is shown in **Exhibit 21.9**.

This hedging reduces the dispersion of possible outcomes. There is a floor below which losses cannot be increased, while on the upside the benefit from any rise in share price is reduced.

If the share price stands still at 310.9p, however, you may feel that the premium you paid to insure against an adverse movement at 8.25p or 2.7% of the share price was excessive. If you keep buying this type of 'insurance' through the year it can reduce your portfolio returns substantially.

A simpler example of risk reduction occurs when an investor is fairly sure that a share will rise in price but is not so confident as to discount the possibility of a fall. Suppose that the investor wished to buy 10,000 shares in Diageo, currently priced at 1778p (on 1 August 2017) – *see* Exhibit 21.6. This can be achieved either by a direct purchase of shares in the market or through the purchase of an option. If the share price does fall significantly, the size of the loss is greater with the share purchase – the option loss is limited to the premium paid.

Suppose that ten September 1750 call options are purchased at a cost of £4,800 (48p × 1,000 × 10).**Exhibit 21.10** shows that the option is less risky because of the ability to abandon the right to buy at 1750p.

Writing a put option can be a very risky thing to do, as General Motors found out to its cost – see **Exhibit 21.11**.

Mexico uses put options on oil to gain certainty over the income it receives from exports – *see* **Exhibit 21.12**.

Mike Ashley arranged for the company he founded, Sports Direct, to write put options on Tesco – *see* **Exhibit 21.13**. There are two potential payoffs (a) premium received (if the shares don't fall significantly), (b) some influence in negotiations if the Tesco shares are bought.

Exhibit 21.9   Profit profile for a put option and shares

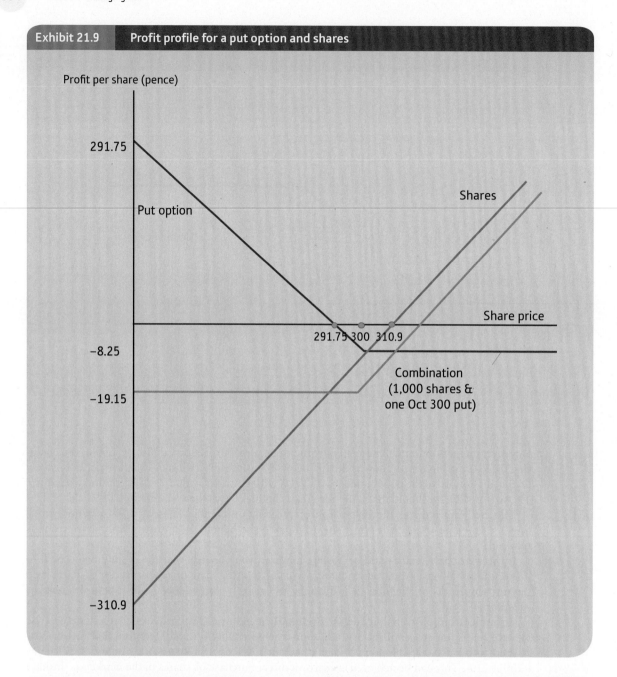

Exhibit 21.10   Losses on alternative buying strategies

Diageo share price falls to:	Loss on 10,000 shares	Loss on 10 call options
1700p	£7,800	£4,800
1650p	£12,800	£4,800
1600p	£17,800	£4,800
1550p	£22,800	£4,800
1500p	£27,800	£4,800

Exhibit 21.11

GM pays Fiat €1.55bn to end joint ventures

By Adrian Michaels and Bernard Simon

General Motors and Fiat ended threats of legal action yesterday when the US industrial group agreed to pay €1.55bn (£1.07bn) to terminate the companies' joint venture agreements and forestall attempts to force it to take over the Italian company's lossmaking car division.

GM is paying a heavy price to cancel an agreement it signed with Fiat in headier days for both companies five years ago. In 2000 GM took a 20% stake in Fiat Auto, subsequently reduced to 10%, and agreed to a 'put' arrangement that gave Fiat the option to sell the rest of its car unit to GM.

Neither company dreamed the put would become an issue but both have stumbled badly. GM was keen to avoid taking over Fiat Auto and argued that the Italian company invalidated the put by restructuring.

About two-thirds of GM's €1.55bn payment will go towards settling the put option. The remaining third will pay for GM's stake in the Polish diesel engine plant and for technology currently held by Fiat on two diesel engines installed in GM vehicles.

Exhibit 21.12

Mexico's Pemex spends $134m in first-ever oil hedging programme

By Jude Webber

Pemex, Mexico's state oil company, has spent $133.5m on a hedging programme, the first in its history, to protect its balance sheet from falling crude prices. Since 2005, Mexico's finance ministry has conducted an annual hedging programme. It is the market's largest such oil trade and usually shrouded in secrecy. Pemex's programme was not expected to change that.

"The two things have nothing to do with one another," a spokeswoman said, indicating that the ministry hedge would go ahead as usual.

"The finance ministry's hedge is to protect direct government income and this hedge is directly to protect our income in order to meet the financial balance goal," he said.

The size of the two operations is also wildly different. The government has spent an average of about $1bn a year on its oil hedge for the past decade, and last year netted $2.65bn from the programme.

The Pemex hedge covers a maximum of 409,000 barrels per day for the May to December period at a price of $42 per barrel – that being the target price

established in the budget for 2017. "The hedge provides protection for Pemex if the average monthly price of the Mexican mix is between $42 and $37 per barrel. The investment was $133.5m," the company said. The price of the Mexican export mix was $42.45 yesterday.

"As such, for the first time in 11 years, Pemex has its own hedging programme, which will favour its ability to meet operating and investment commitments and will give more certainty over its income in the face of the possible fall in hydrocarbons prices," the statement added.

Pemex said such operations were common among oil majors worldwide

The federal government's 2016 hedging scheme consisted of a put option on 212m barrels of oil at $49 per barrel.

The 2017 programme covers 250m barrels and hedged the oil price at $42 per barrel via a put option at $38 per barrel and the $4 per barrel balance covered by 18.62bn pesos set aside in the [government's] budget fund.

Exhibit 21.13

Sports Direct's Mike Ashley takes bet on Tesco with options deal

Sportswear chain agrees 'put' option over supermarkets group

By Andrea Felsted

Mike Ashley's Sports Direct has made a dramatic intervention in the turmoil surrounding Tesco, taking a bet that shares in Britain's biggest retailer will rally. The sportswear chain controlled by the billionaire owner of Newcastle United football club said that it had agreed a deal with Goldman Sachs that will see it benefit from any rise in Tesco's share price from its current decade lows.

Under the arrangement, Sports Direct sold a put option in Tesco. This gives Goldman the right to sell 23m Tesco shares to Sports Direct if they fall below a certain undisclosed exercise price, or receive an equivalent payment.

If the shares are trading above the agreed price on the contract's expiry, Sports Direct receives an undisclosed premium from Goldman.

The deal means Sports Direct in effect has a "long" exposure to Tesco shares, which the company said runs to a maximum of £43m.

People close to the situation said investing in this way, rather than simply buying the shares, meant Sports Direct had potentially obtained access to a sizeable stake, and tied up a smaller proportion of its balance sheet until the option matured.

They said Sports Direct was interested in taking surplus space in Tesco stores and selling its sporting goods through Tesco stores and its online platform.

Sports Direct has already taken space in Tesco stores in central Europe and Malaysia. The Financial Times reported last year that Sports Direct was in talks with Tesco to take surplus space in some of its big UK stores, although a deal has yet to come to fruition.

The Tesco bet marks the second time this year that Mr Ashley has used derivatives to insert himself into the affairs of a struggling retailer. In January, he sold a similar put on Debenhams shares, even as he pressured them to work more closely with Sports Direct. On Thursday, Sports Direct said in its announcement that the derivative "reflects Sports Direct's growing relationship with Tesco and belief in Tesco's long-term future".

Sports Direct has since begun a trial selling its goods in two Debenhams stores. Goldman is the counterparty to both the Debenhams and the Tesco deals.

| Exhibit 21.14 | Aunt Agathas and derivatives |

Millions of ordinary small investors (Aunt Agathas in the City jargon) have their money applied to the derivatives markets even though they may remain blissfully unaware that such 'exotic' transactions are being conducted on their behalf. Take the case of equity-linked bonds. Investors nervous of investing in the stock market for fear of downward swings are promised a guarantee that they will receive at least the return of their original capital, even if the stock market falls. If it rises they will receive a return linked to the rise (say the capital gain element – excluding dividends). The bulk of the capital invested in these equity-linked bonds may be placed in safe fixed-interest investments, with the stock-market-linked return created through the use of options and other derivatives.

Corporate uses of options

There are a number of corporate uses of options.

1 *Share option schemes* Many companies now grant (or sell to) employees share options (calls) as a means of achieving commitment and greater goal congruence between agents and principals. Employees are offered the right to buy shares at a fixed price some time in the future. They then have the incentive over the intervening years to perform well and push up the share price so as to realise a large gain when the options may be exercised.

2 **Warrants** A share warrant is an option issued by a company which gives the owner the right, but not the obligation, to purchase a specified number of shares at a specified price over a given period of time. Note that it is the company that writes the option rather than speculators or hedgers.

3 **Convertible bonds** A convertible bond can be viewed as a bundle of two sets of rights. First, there are the usual rights associated with a bond, for example interest and principal payments, and secondly, there is the right, but not the obligation, to exercise a call option and purchase shares using the bond itself as the payment for those shares.

4 **Rights issues** In a rights issue shareholders are granted the right, but not the obligation, to purchase additional shares in the company. This right has value and can be sold to other investors.

5 **Share underwriting** Effectively when an underwriter agrees to purchase securities, if investors do not purchase the whole issue, a put option has been bought with the underwriting fee, and the company has the right to insist that the underwriter buys at the price agreed.

6 **Commodities** Many firms are exposed to commodity risk. Firms selling commodities, or buying for production purposes, may be interested in hedging against price fluctuations in these markets. Examples of such firms are airlines, food processors, car manufacturers, chocolate manufacturers, which may hedge oil, metals, cocoa, sugar, etc.

7 **Taking control of a company** An interesting use of options occurred in 2003 when the family that founded the retail chain Monsoon sold put options to shareholders owning 19.5% of Monsoon's shares. The holders of the put bought a right to sell their shares at 140p. If the share price on the stock market remains below 140p many holders will exercise the option. The founding family controlled 72.5% of the company and saw the use of put options as a cheap way of raising their stake to 92.5%, cheaper than a full takeover bid. However, the plan did not work as put holders thought the business worth more than 140p per share and did not exercise their options.

8 **Protecting the company from foreign exchange rate losses** This topic is covered in Chapter 22.

9 **Real options** These are options that arise from business operations. *See* Chapter 6.

Forwards

Imagine you are responsible for purchasing potatoes to make crisps for your firm, a snack food producer. In the free market for potatoes the price rises or falls depending on the balance between buyers and sellers. These movements can be dramatic. Obviously you would like to acquire potatoes at a price which was as low as possible, while the potato producer wishes to sell for a price that is as high as possible. However, both parties may have a similar interest in reducing the uncertainty of price. This will assist both to plan production and budget effectively. One way in which this could be done is to reach an agreement with the producer(s) to purchase a quantity of potatoes at a price agreed today to be delivered and paid for at a specified time in the future. Crisp producers buy 80% of their potatoes up to two years forward. Once the forward agreements have been signed and sealed they may later be somewhat regretful if the spot price (price for immediate delivery) subsequently falls below the price agreed months earlier. Unlike option contracts, forwards commit both parties to complete the deal. However, the crisp makers are obviously content to live with this potential for regret in order to remove the risk associated with such an important raw material.

> A **forward contract** is an agreement between two parties to undertake an exchange at an agreed future date at a price agreed now.

The party buying at the future date is said to be taking a long position. The counterparty which will deliver at the future date is said to be taking a short position.

There are forward markets in a wide range of commodities but the most important forward markets today are for foreign exchange, in which hundreds of billions of dollars worth of currency are traded every working day – this will be considered in Chapter 22.

Forward contracts are tailor-made to meet the requirements of the parties. This gives flexibility on the amounts and delivery dates. Forwards are not traded on an exchange but are 'over-the-counter instruments' – private agreements outside the regulation of an exchange. This makes them different from futures, which are standardised contracts traded on exchanges. A forward agreement exposes the counterparties to the risk of default – the failure by the other to deliver on the agreement. The risk grows in proportion to the extent to which the spot price diverges from the forward price as the incentive to renege increases.

Forward contracts are difficult to cancel, as agreement from each counterparty is needed. Also to close the contract early may result in a penalty being charged. Despite these drawbacks forward markets continue to flourish – an example of which you can see in **Exhibit 21.15**.

Exhibit 21.15

Reading the corn time-spreads

The spot and forward differentials suggest higher prices next spring

By Javier Blas in London

Forget about the drop in near-term corn prices. The real action is the sharp swing in the spread between spot and forward contract prices.

When the cost of corn rallied to an all-time high of $8.43³/₄ a bushel in August on the back of the worst drought in the US in half a century, the cost of spot corn surged to a hefty premium to forward months. The argument was that the shortage was so intense that corn for immediate delivery should be more expensive.

But the market is starting to realise that the real shortage would not happen now, as the ongoing harvest means an abundance of grain in the near term. Thus, spot prices have fallen back to $7.44 a

bushel, the lowest since mid-July. At the same time, forward prices are stubbornly high as fears of a shortage in early 2013 grow by the day.

Spot corn prices are suffering relative to forward prices in part because of a front-loaded harvest. Ironically, the drought means that corn supplies in the US are running ahead of their usual pace as the crop matured earlier due to high temperatures, allowing farmers to harvest their fields ahead of normal schedules. Agriculture analysts estimate US farmers last week have already harvested 40 per cent of their fields, double the previous record of 20 per cent at this time of the year in 2010.

Futures

Futures contracts are in many ways similar to forward contracts. They are agreements between two parties to undertake a transaction at an agreed price on a specified future date. However, they differ from forwards in some important respects. Futures contracts are exchange-based instruments traded on a regulated exchange. The buyer and the seller of a contract do not transact with each other directly. The clearing house becomes the formal counterparty to every transaction. This reduces the risk of non-compliance with the contract significantly for the buyer or seller of a future, as it is highly unlikely that the clearing house will be unable to fulfil its obligation.

In contrast to buying options, which give you the choice to walk away from the deal, with futures you are committed and are unable to back away. This is a very important difference. In purchasing an option the maximum you can lose is the premium paid whereas you can lose multiples of the amount you employ in taking a futures position.

A simple example will demonstrate this. Imagine a farmer wishes to lock in a price for his wheat, which will be harvested in six months. You agree to purchase the wheat from the farmer six months hence at a price of £60 per tonne. You are hoping that by the time the wheat is delivered the price has risen and you can sell at a profit. The farmer is worried that all he has from you is the promise to pay £60 per tonne in six months, and if the market price falls you will walk away from the deal. To reassure him you are asked to put money into what the farmer calls a margin account. He asks for, and you agree to deposit, £6 for each tonne you have agreed to buy. If you fail to complete the bargain the farmer will be able to draw on the money from the margin account and then sell the wheat as it is harvested at the going rate for immediate ('spot') delivery. So, as far as the farmer is concerned, the price of wheat for delivery at harvest time could fall to £54 and he is still going to get £60 for each tonne: £6 from what you paid into the margin account and £54 from selling at the spot price.

But what if the price falls below £54? The farmer is exposed to risk – something he had tried to avoid by entering a futures deal. It is for this reason that the farmer asks you to top up your margin account on a daily basis so that there is always a buffer. He sets a maintenance margin level of £6 per tonne. This means you have to maintain at least £6 per tonne in the margin account. So, if the day after you buy the future, the harvest time price in the futures market falls to £57 you have only £3 per tonne left in the margin account as a buffer for the farmer. You agreed to buy at £60 but the going rate is only £57. To bring the margin account up to a £6 buffer you will be required to put in another £3 per tonne. If the price the next day falls to £50 you will be required to put up another £7 per tonne. You agreed to buy at £60, with the market price at £50 you have put a total of £6 + £3 + £7 = £16 into the margin account. By putting in top-ups as the price moves against you, you will always ensure there is at least £6 per tonne, providing security for the farmer. Even if you go bankrupt or simply renege on the deal he will receive at least £60 per tonne, either from the spot market or from a combination of a lower market price plus money from the margin account. As the price fell to £50 you have a £10 per tonne incentive to walk away from the deal except for the fact that you have put £16 into an account that the farmer can draw on should you be so stupid or unfortunate. If the price is £50 per tonne at expiry of the contract and you have put £16 in the margin account you are entitled to the spare £6 per tonne of margin.

It is in the margin account that we have the source of multiple losses in the futures markets. Say your life savings amount to £10 and you are convinced there will be a drought and shortage of wheat following the next harvest. In your view the price will rise to £95 per tonne. So, to cash in on your forecast you agree to buy a future for one tonne of wheat. You have agreed with the farmer that in six months you will pay £60 for the wheat, which you expect to then sell for £95. (The farmer is obviously less convinced than you that prices are destined to rise.)

To gain this right (and obligation) to buy at £60 you need only have £6 for the initial margin. The other £4 might be useful to meet day-to-day margin calls should the wheat price fall from £60 (temporarily, in your view). If the price does rise to £95 you will make a £35 profit, having laid out only £6 (plus some other cash temporarily). This is a very high return of 583% over six months. But what if the price at harvest time is £40? You have agreed to pay £60; therefore the loss of £20 wipes out your savings and you are made bankrupt. You lose over three times your initial margin. That is the downside to the gearing effect of futures.

The above example demonstrates the essential features of futures market trading, but in reality participants in the market do not transact directly with each other, but go through a regulated exchange. Your opposite number, called a *counterparty*, is not a farmer but an organisation that acts as counterparty to all futures traders, buyers or sellers, called the central counterparty at the clearing house.

In the example we have assumed that the maintenance margin level is set at the same level as the initial margin. In reality it is often set at 70 to 80% of the initial margin level.

An exchange provides standardised legal agreements traded in highly liquid markets. The contracts cannot be tailor-made e.g. for 77 tonnes of wheat or coffee delivered in 37 days from now. The fact that the agreements are standardised allows a wide market appeal because buyers and sellers know what is being traded: the contracts are for a specific quality of the underlying, in specific amounts with specific delivery dates. For example, for white sugar traded on NYSE Liffe/ ICE Futures Europe (*see* **Exhibit 21.16**) one contract is for a specified grade of sugar and each contract is for a standard 50 tonnes with fixed delivery days in late March, May, August, October and December.

In examining the table in Exhibit 21.16, it is important to remember that it is the contracts themselves that are a form of security bought and sold in the market. Thus the March future priced at $332.20 per tonne is a derivative of sugar and is not the same thing as sugar. To buy this future is to enter into an agreement with rights and obligations. It is these that are being bought and sold and not the commodity. When exercise takes place then sugar is bought.[6] However, as with most derivatives, usually futures positions are cancelled by an offsetting transaction before exercise.

---

6 Note that some future contracts have cash delivery rather than physical delivery (*see* later).

Exhibit 21.16

Some of the commodity futures prices shown in the Financial Times, 12 January 2018.

PRECIOUS METALS

	Sett price	Day's chge	High	Low	Vol 000s	Open interest, 000s
■ GOLD						
COMEX (100 Troy oz; $/troy oz)						
Jul	1251.6	8.3	1259.9	1253.7	0.00	0.18
Aug	1253.5	4.6	1262.4	1253.3	145.68	322.63
Total					**157.15**	**494.85**
■ PLATINUM						
NYMEX (50 Troy oz; $/troy oz)						
Jul	841.8	29.0	844.0	796.9	0.06	0.43
Aug	841.8	28.8	842.4	802.9	0.03	0.11
Total					**8.86**	**83.63**
■ PALLADIUM						
NYMEX (100 Troy oz; $/troy oz)						
Jul	945.4	0.0	0.0	0.0	0.00	0.00
Aug	946.0	0.0	0.0	0.0	0.00	0.00
Total					**1.02**	**21.98**
■ SILVER						
COMEX (5,000 Troy oz; $/troy oz)						
Jul	16.0	0.0	16.1	16.0	0.02	1.47
Aug	16.0	0.1	16.1	16.0	0.03	1.10
Total					**32.50**	**205.74**

SOFTS

	Sett price	Day's chge	High	Low	Vol 000s	Open interest, 000s
■ COCOA						
NYSE LIFFE (10 tonnes; $/tonne)						
Jul	1860	−10	1860	1849	2.13	28.08
Sep	1798	−1	1798	1787	3.37	54.40
Dec	1808	0	1808	1796	1.15	63.83
Mar	1790	3	1791	1778	1.04	53.78
May	1784	0	1784	1772	0.37	24.92
Jul	1777	4	1777	1767	0.23	11.48
Total					**8.78**	**251.86**
■ COCOA						
NYBOT (10 tonnes; $/tonne)						
Jul	2418	−80	2385	2385	0.00	0.16
Sep	2454	−48	2543	2437	18.37	93.25
Dec	2477	−42	2557	2461	6.68	73.72
Mar	2486	−37	2559	2470	3.11	47.75
May	2493	−37	2559	2480	1.23	16.22
Jul	2499	−43	2547	2485	0.39	6.00
Total					**30.20**	**252.47**
■ COFFEE						
NYSE LIFFE (10 tonnes; $/tonne)						
Jul	1739	10	1752	1745	0.01	7.50
Sep	1689	7	1695	1684	2.62	63.56
Total					**4.89**	**118.34**

	Sett price	Day's chge	High	Low	Vol 000s	Open interest, 000s
■ COFFEE 'C'						
NYBOT (37,500lbs; cent/lbs)						
Jul	108	4	110	108	0.00	0.06
Sep	112	0	113	112	22.40	162.64
Dec	115	0	116	115	7.84	65.23
Mar	119	0	120	119	4.24	25.29
May	121	0	122	121	2.15	17.09
Jul	124	0	125	123	0.81	5.62
Total					**38.08**	**287.18**
■ WHITE SUGAR						
NYSE LIFFE (50 tonnes; $/tonne)						
Aug	341.1	4.4	342.9	337.8	4.06	25.21
Oct	331.6	3.1	333.2	329.6	3.20	37.11
Dec	328.8	1.8	329.9	328.1	0.65	13.25
Mar	332.2	2.3	334.1	332.0	0.21	10.74
May	336.2	2.7	338.2	336.3	0.08	5.54
Aug	340.5	2.1	341.3	340.9	0.01	4.25
Total					**8.30**	**98.53**
■ SUGAR '11'						
NYBOT (112,000lbs; cents/lbs)						
Oct	11.39	−0.15	11.69	11.24	80.13	520.68
Mar	12.12	−0.18	12.43	12.01	29.48	259.09
May	12.21	−0.21	12.55	12.13	9.79	65.87
Jul	12.33	−0.21	12.67	12.26	5.60	43.05
Oct	12.55	−0.21	12.86	12.47	2.06	37.86
Total					**128.64**	**946.40**
■ COTTON						
NYBOT (50,000lbs; cents/lbs)						
Jul	84.54	−0.06	84.44	84.44	0.01	0.15
Oct	83.80	0.28	84.18	83.50	0.01	0.13
Dec	82.81	−0.12	83.66	82.60	16.51	177.52
Mar	82.48	−0.33	83.37	82.39	4.16	45.87
May	82.62	−0.14	83.42	82.55	0.62	6.75
Total					**22.10**	**254.62**
■ ORANGE JUICE						
NYCE (15,000lbs; cents/lbs)						
Jul	166.50	−6.60	162.25	162.25	0.31	0.52
Sep	167.70	1.25	169.30	165.75	0.55	10.79
Nov	167.45	1.35	168.85	165.55	0.13	2.23
Jan	168.05	0.75	168.35	167.45	0.01	0.45
Mar	168.25	−0.45	167.55	167.55	0.00	0.06
Total					**1.01**	**14.05**
■ RAPESEED						
NYSE LIFFE (8,000kilos; €/kilo)						
Aug	361.75	1.75	362.50	359.25	3.39	25.92
Nov	368.00	1.75	368.75	365.50	3.94	38.44
Total					**8.40**	**75.69**

Marking to market and margins

With the clearing house being the formal counterparty for every buyer or seller of a futures contract, an enormous potential for credit risk is imposed on the organisation given the volume of futures traded and the size of the underlying they represent. (ICE Futures Europe has an average daily volume of around 5 million contracts worth hundreds of billions of pounds.) If only a small fraction of market participants fail to deliver this could run into hundreds of millions of pounds. To protect itself the clearing house operates a margining system by which the futures buyer or seller has to provide, usually in cash, an initial margin. The amount required depends on the futures market, the level of volatility of the underlying and the potential for default; however it is likely to be in the region of 0.1% to 15% of the value of the underlying. The initial margin is not a 'down payment' for the underlying: the funds do not flow to a buyer or seller of the underlying but stay with the clearing house. It is merely a way of guaranteeing that the buyer or seller will pay up should the price of the underlying move against them. It is refunded when the futures position is closed (if the market has not moved adversely).

The clearing house also operates a system of daily marking to market. At the end of every trading day the counterparties' profits or losses created as a result of that day's price change are calculated. The counterparty that made a loss has his/her member's margin account debited. The following morning the losing counterparty must inject more cash to cover the loss if the amount in the account has fallen below a threshold level (the *maintenance margin*). An inability to pay a daily loss causes default and the contract is closed, thus protecting the clearing house from the possibility that the counterparty might accumulate further daily losses without providing cash to cover them. The margin account of the counterparty that makes a daily gain is credited. This may be withdrawn the next day. The daily credits and debits to members' margin accounts are known as the variation margin.

Worked example 21.1 illustrates the effect of leverage in futures contracts.

Worked example 21.1   **Margins**

Imagine a buyer and seller of a future on Monday with an underlying value of £50,000 are each required to provide an initial margin of 10%, or £5,000. The buyer will make profits if the price rises while the seller will make profits if the price falls. In the following table (see **Exhibit 21.17**) it is assumed that counterparties have to keep all of the initial margin permanently as a buffer.[7] (In reality this may be relaxed by an exchange.)

Exhibit 21.17   **Example of initial margin and marking to market**

£			Day		
	Monday	Tuesday	Wednesday	Thursday	Friday
Value of future (based on daily closing price)	50,000	49,000	44,000	50,000	55,000
Buyers' position					
Initial margin	5,000				
Variation margin (+ credited)	0	−1,000	−5,000	+6,000	+5,000
(− debited)					
Accumulated profit (loss)	0	−1,000	−6,000	0	+5,000
Sellers' position					
Initial margin	5,000				
Variation margin (+ credited)	0	+1,000	+5,000	−6,000	−5,000
(− debited)					
Accumulated profit (loss)	0	+1,000	+6,000	0	−5,000

---

7 Initial margin is the same as maintenance margin in this case.

At the end of Tuesday the buyer of the contract has £1,000 debited from his/her member's account. This will have to be paid over the following day or the exchange will automatically close the member's position and crystallise the loss. If the buyer does provide the variation margin and the position is kept open until Friday the account will have an accumulated credit of £5,000. The buyer has the right to buy at £50,000 but can sell at £55,000. If the buyer and the seller closed their positions on Friday the buyer would be entitled to receive the initial margin plus the accumulated profit, £5,000 + £5,000 = £10,000, whereas the seller would receive nothing (£5,000 initial margin minus losses of £5,000).

The initial margin payments are small relative to the value of the underlying. When the underlying changes by a small percentage the effect is magnified for the future, and large percentage gains and losses are made on the amount committed to the transaction:

$$\text{Underlying change (Monday–Friday)} \frac{55,000 - 50,000}{50,000} \times 100 = 10\%$$

$$\text{Percentage return to buyer of future} \frac{5,000}{5,000} \times 100 = 100\%$$

$$\text{Percentage return to seller of future} \frac{-5,000}{5,000} \times 100 = -100\%$$

To lose all the money committed to a financial transaction may seem disappointing but it is nothing compared with the losses that can be made on futures. It is possible to lose a multiple of the amount set down as an initial margin. For example, if the future rose to £70,000 the seller would have to provide a £20,000 variation margin – four times the amount committed in the first place. Clearly playing the futures market can seriously damage your wealth. This was proved with a vengeance by Nick Leeson of Barings Bank. He bought futures in the Nikkei 225 Index – the main Japanese share index – in both the Osaka and the Singapore derivative exchanges. He was betting that the market would rise as he committed the bank to buying the index at a particular price. When the index fell margin payments had to be made. Leeson took a double or quits attitude, 'I mean a lot of futures traders when thve market is against them will double up'.[8] He continued to buy futures. To generate some cash, to make variation margin payments, he wrote combinations of call and put options ('straddles'). This compounded the problem when the Nikkei 225 Index continued to fall. The put options became an increasingly expensive commitment to bear – counterparties had the right to sell the index to Barings at a price much higher than the prevailing price. Over £800m was lost.

Settlement

Historically the futures markets developed on the basis of the physical delivery of the underlying. So if you had contracted to buy 40,000 lb. of lean hogs you would receive the meat as settlement.[9] However, in most futures markets today (including that for lean hogs) only a small proportion of contracts result in physical delivery. The majority are closed out before the expiry of the contract and all that changes hands is cash, either as a profit or as a loss. Speculators certainly do not want to end up with ten tonnes of coffee or 15,000 lb. of orange juice and so will reverse their trade before the contract expires; for example, if they originally bought a contract for 50 tonnes of white sugar they later sell a contract for 50 tonnes of white sugar.

Hedgers, say confectionery manufacturers, may sometimes take delivery from the exchange but in most cases will have established purchasing channels for sugar, cocoa, etc. In these cases

---

8 Initial margin is the same as maintenance margin in this case.

9 If a seller of a future which is about to expire wishes to deliver the underlying (say cocoa, coffee or zinc) it gives the exchange notice of intention to deliver a few days before the expiry of the futures contract. Then the underlying is transported to a delivery point at the seller's expense – the exchange usually maintains warehouses. The buyer who wishes to take physical delivery notifies the exchange when the contract expires. The exchange will decide which buyers may take away which warehoused underlying.

they may use the futures markets not as a way of obtaining goods but as a way of offsetting the risk of the prices of goods moving adversely. So a confectionery manufacturer may still plan to buy, say, sugar, at the spot price from its longstanding supplier in six months and simultaneously, to hedge the risk of the price rising, will buy six-month futures in sugar. This position will then be closed before expiry. If the price of the underlying has risen the manufacturer pays more to the supplier but has a compensating gain on the future. If the price falls the supplier is paid less and so a gain is made here, but, under a perfect hedge, the future has lost an equal value.

As the futures markets developed it became clear that most participants did not want the complications of physical delivery and this led to the development of futures contracts where cash settlement takes place. This permitted a wider range of futures contracts to be created. Futures contracts based on intangibles such as a share index or a rate of interest are now extremely important financial instruments. With these, no physical delivery takes place and if the contract is held to the maturity date one party will hand over cash to the other (via the clearing house system).

Equity index futures

Equity index futures are an example of a cash settlement market. The underlyings here are collections of shares, for example 225 Japanese shares for the Nikkei 225. Hedgers and speculators do not want 225 different shares to be delivered say one month from now. They are quite content to receive or hand over the profit or loss made by buying and then selling (or the other way around) a future of the index.

The equity index futures table (**Exhibit 21.18**) from FT.com shows futures in indices from stock markets around the world for 22 September 2014. These are notional futures contracts. If not closed out before expiry (by the holder of a future doing the reverse transaction to their first – so if they bought the future first, selling will close the position) they are settled in cash based on the average level of the relevant index (say the FTSE 100) between stated times on the last day of the contract. This table is very much a cut-down version of the futures available to traders. As well as the December delivery future shown traders are offered the possibility of buying or selling futures that 'deliver' in March, June and September. Delivery dates are the third Friday of the month.

Exhibit 21.18

Equity

EQUITY INDEX FUTURES

Sep 22		Open	Sett	Change	High	Low	Est. Vol.	Open int.
DJIA	DEC4	–	17099.00	–	–	–	79	5,206
DJ Euro Stoxx‡	DEC4	3248.00	3244.00	−20.00	3263.00	3231.00	623,103	2,976,624
S&P 500	DEC4	2002.10	1986.30	−17.50	2002.90	1983.00	2,055	120,854
Nasdaq 100	DEC4	4091.00	4052.75	−40.25	4091.75	4036.50	1,258	3,308
DAX	DEC4	9762.50	9753.50	−69.00	9817.00	9723.50	83,214	127,036
FTSE 100	DEC4	6819.00	6747.50	−67.00	6820.00	6733.00	80,584	600,035
Hang Seng	SEP4	23998.00	23991.00	−301.00	24012.00	23874.00	2,423	119,624
Nikkei 225†	DEC4	16160.00	16160.00	−60.00	16210.00	16090.00	16,744	301,952

The table shows the first price traded at the beginning of the day (Open), the settlement price, 'Sett', used to mark to market (usually the last traded price), the change from the previous day's settlement price, the highest and lowest prices during the day's settlement price, the number of contracts traded that day (Est. vol.) and the total number of open contracts (these are trading contracts opened over the last few months that have not yet been closed by an equal and opposite futures transaction).

Each point on the UK's FTSE 100 share index future is worth £10, by convention. So if the future rises from 6,500 to 6,550 and you bought a future at 6,500 you have made $50 \times £10 = £500$ if you were to now sell at 6,550.

Traders in futures may be asked to inject money into their margin accounts every day the position is open so they cannot buy/sell a future and then ignore the markets (unless they leave plenty of cash with the broker to meet margin calls). Market prices are available online; *see* for example, www.theice.com/futures-europe.

Worked example 21.2   Hedging with a share index future

It is 22 September 2014 and the FTSE 100 is at 6774. A fund manager wishes to hedge a £13,000,000 fund against a decline in the market. A December FTSE 100 future is available at 6747.5 – see Exhibit 21.18. The investor retains the shares in the portfolio and *sells* 193 index futures contracts. Each futures contract is worth £67,475 (6,747.5 × £10). So 193 contracts are needed to cover £13,000,000 (that is £13,000,000/(£10 × 6,747.5) = 193).

Outcome on third Friday in December

For the sake of argument assume that the index falls by 10% to 6,097, leaving the portfolio value at £11,700,000 (assuming the portfolio moves exactly in line with the FTSE 100 index). The closing of the futures position largely offsets this £1,300,000 loss by buying 193 futures at 6,097 to close the position producing a profit[10] of:

Able to sell at 6,747.5 × 193 × £10	=	£13,022,675
Able to buy at 6,097 × 193 × £10	=	−£11,767,210
		£1,255,465

These contracts are cash settled so £1,255,465 will be paid. Furthermore, the investor receives back the margin laid down, less broker's fees.

Case study 21.1   Protecting a portfolio against a major market fall

In December 2017 Glen Arnold, who now invests more or less full time, was concerned about the impact of a major US equity market fall on his share portfolio, and so bought index put options on the Dow Jones Industrial Average. He explained his reasoning to his newsletter subscribers (http://newsletters.advfn.com/deepvalueshares) as follows:

Insurance through shorting the Dow

I'm quite content to continue holding the portfolio of shares I have; British shares, as a whole, are not over-priced, being at roughly their historical average using most valuation measures. Besides which, I don't buy the market, I buy shares that are neglected, unloved and cheap. So I'll carry on doing that. However, I think the world of finance at the global level is going through one of those weird, losing-touch-with-reality periods.

People speculating on cryptocurrency is but the most extreme expression of this. These bits of nothingness are supposedly worth $300bn. When the people who mortgaged their houses and maxed credit cards to buy these pieces of air discover that there is no greater fool to pass the parcel onto there will be much wailing and gnashing of teeth – they'll find out that they are the greater fools. Many financial institutions backing the scams will come a cropper, and there will be domino effects through the system, ending up who knows where. Oh well, at least we'll be able to add a chapter to a book that already contains Tulipmania and the South Sea Bubble – Bitcoin has elements of both.

▶

---

10 Assuming that the futures price is equal to the spot price of the FTSE 100. This would occur close to the expiry date of the future.

Case study 21.1 *(continued)*

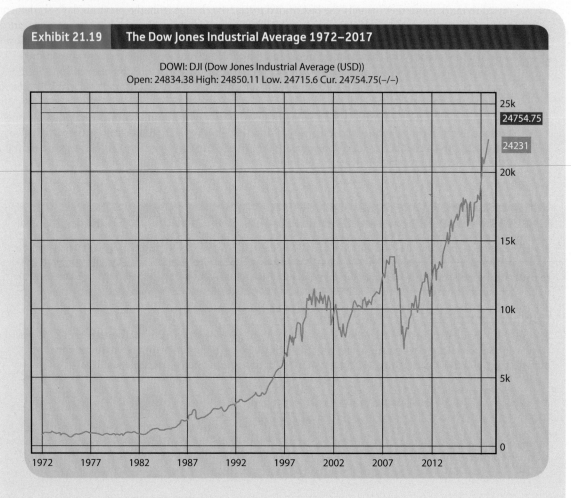

Exhibit 21.19   The Dow Jones Industrial Average 1972–2017

DOWI: DJI (Dow Jones Industrial Average (USD))
Open: 24834.38 High: 24850.11 Low. 24715.6 Cur. 24754.75(–/–)

What could go wrong?

There are so many things. In a number of June Newsletters I examined (with statistical evidence) the indebtedness of the Americans and Chinese. If their creditors ever took fright the consequences could be almost as dire as the sub-prime crash. A loss of confidence in things like Chinese property, Chinese giant companies, US growth projections, the low interest rate paradigm, could provoke a shock response in which money is suddenly taken off the table, asset prices fall, begetting greater loss of confidence, begetting more money withdrawal and a general hunkering down.

And then we have political risk. Here are a few:

- What happens if the Trump stimulus is nothing but hot air?

- What if the Trump stimulus works really well, and US unemployment is pushed to 2–3%, leading to inflation and interest rates rising to 5%? A lot of capital losses for bond investors? A boom followed rather quickly by recession? Even without a recession interest rates at 5% could bring down the equity markets because bonds then offer higher yields.

- What if war breaks out in Korea, or Iran?

- What if Chinese political leaders clamp down on the shadow banks stopping the flow of money to companies, property developers and local authorities, polluting firms and the scandal of the politically-connected getting massive loans?

- What if Chinese buying of assets from Vancouver and Auckland, from New York to London stops?

Vulnerability

All of these risks and many more can be absorbed in a financial system that has low expectations, i.e. low asset prices relative to the likely income flow. But right now we have some of the most extreme pricing ever.

Many markets are priced for a perfect future, e.g. we have interest rates on 'junk bonds' at only 4–5%. If the perfect future arrives these investors will be very pleased with themselves. But what are the odds?

Another example is house prices in prime locations; the average London home price is 13 times average income – similar multiples are seen from Sydney to Toronto.

US shares

When it comes to looking at shares around the world, we find some expensive markets, some cheap, and some in-between.

The most respected measure of value is the cyclically adjusted price earnings ratio which divides the current price by the average earnings over the last 10 years, thought to be a period long enough to cover years of economic growth and those of recession.

I wrote in July that, at a ratio of 30, the CAPE had never been this high except in two years, 1929 and 1999. Since then the market has climbed further. Now at 32.5 it even surpasses the level of 1929 (i.e. an earnings yield of 3%). There is plenty of academic research showing that very high CAPEs generally result in very low equity returns over the next five or ten years – admittedly, they do not necessarily point to a crash though.

Insurance

If you buy insurance to cover the risk of your house burning down and it does not, are you disappointed that you 'lost' say £500 on the insurance premium? Of course, you'd rather keep paying the premium year after year and prefer it if you never have to call on the insurance company to make a claim.

It is similar with the 'insurance' I bought through put options on the Dow Jones Industrial Average, giving the right but not the obligation to 'sell' the Dow.

I bought a put option that expires Friday 21 September 2018 – so I now have nine months of insurance cover. I bought options giving me the right but not the obligation to sell the Dow at an index level of 17,500. With the Dow currently over 24,700 this instrument is an extreme form of an 'out of the money' option.

If the market stays above 17,500 my options will expire worthless and the $119 per contract I paid as a premium to buy the right to sell at 17,500 will have been 'wasted'.

If however the Dow goes to 16,000 each of my options has an intrinsic value of 15 points x $100 = $1,500. That is a $1,381 profit, an increase of 11.6 times.

How the Dow options work

The 'underlying' for index options is not the straightforward Dow average, say 23,000 or 18,000. Rather, it is one-hundredth of the true Dow. Thus the option 'strike price' of 230 or 180 represents the Dow at 23,000 or 18,000. Likewise the premiums you pay to say buy or sell at 20,000 (a '200 call') are expressed in one-hundredths of what you actually pay.

My option

The strike price is expressed as a 'September 175 put' at a price of $1.19 per contract. But because of the convention of 100 points on the Dow being worth 1 point in options, I actually paid $119 per contract. I have the right to sell the market at any time up to 21 September 2018 at a price of 175 (which is really 17,500).

If the underlying moved to a Dow of 17,400, in option terms that would be 174. This is one point below the 175 at which my option can be 'exercised' through the exchange or sold to another option buyer. In reality the options are not truly exercised in the sense that I can insist the option writer hands over shares in 30 US companies. Instead the exchange 'cash settles' – in this case hands over $100 of intrinsic value (the writer of the 175 option will receive a bill for the same amount from the exchange).

If the Dow moves to 17,300 this will be 173 in option terms and thus 2 points are made, each worth $100. I have the right to sell at 175, but can purchase at 173.

▶

Case study 21.1 *(continued)*

Value at the final expiry date

I don't have to sell the option within the nine months (nor do I have to buy the 30 shares of the Dow). I could just let the time go all the way to the third Friday in September and receive a cash difference between the option strike price and the underlying from the exchange (if it has intrinsic value) at the expiry date. It is most likely that I will simply hold the option for the full nine months. If the Dow is below 175 the exchange will automatically cash settle – my broker account will be credited – *see* Exhibit 21.20.

The cost of the insurance as a percentage of the current Dow is $119/$24,700 = 0.5%.

Exhibit 21.20	Some scenarios for Dow put option payoffs	
Dow Jones	**Number of intrinsic value points on the 175 put option**	**What I receive in September on one option (% return)**
17,500 or above	Zero	Zero (−100%)
17,000	5	$500 (320%)
16,000	15	$1,500 (1,160%)
15,000	25	$2,500 (2,000%)

The insurance does not pay out if the Dow falls less than 29% (from 24,700 to 17,500), which is analogous to having a large 'excess' on a car insurance policy. I'll have to take these smaller loses on the chin if they manifest in my UK shares.

I've bought a sufficient number of Dow put options so that I do not need to worry about a major upset in US markets and the ricochet effects around the world – what I'll lose on my UK shares I'll, roughly, make on the option.

Short-term interest rate futures

Trillions of pounds, dollars and euros of trading takes place every year in the short-term interest rate futures markets. These are notional fixed-term deposits, usually for three-month periods starting at a specific time in the future. The buyer of one contract is buying the (theoretical) right to deposit money at a particular rate of interest for three months.

So if the current time is August you could arrange a futures contract for you to 'deposit' and 'receive interest' on, say £1,000,000, with the deposit starting next December and ending in March. The rate of interest you will 'receive' over the three months is agreed in August. (This is a notional receipt of interest, as these contracts are cash settled rather than actual deposits being made and interest received – see below for an example.) So you now own the right to deposit £1m and receive x% interest for three months (at least in notional terms).

Short-term interest rate futures will be illustrated using the three-month sterling market, that is, deposits of pounds receiving notional interest for three months starting at some point in the future. Note, however, that there are many other three-month deposits you could make. For example, you could 'deposit' euros for three months, the interest rate on which is calculated with reference to 'Euribor 3m', which is the interest rate highly rated banks pay to other banks. Other three-month deposits, often for money held outside the jurisdiction of the currency's country of origin (i.e. 'Euro' currencies, in the sense of being international money and not the currency in the Eurozone) include Swiss francs deposited in London (Euroswiss), Eurodollars and Euroyens – see **Exhibit 21.21**. (Eurocurrency is discussed in Chapter 11.)

The unit of trading for a three-month sterling time deposit is £500,000. Cash delivery by closing out the futures position is the means of settlement, so the buyer would not actually require the seller of the future to accept the £500,000 on deposit for three months at the interest rate indicated by the futures price. Although the term 'delivery' no longer has significance for the underlying it does define the date and time of the expiry of the contract. This occurs in late September,

December, March and June and the nearest three consecutive months. (See www.theice.com/products for precise definitions and delivery dates.)

Short-term interest contracts are quoted on an index basis rather than on the basis of the interest rate itself. The price is defined as:

$$P = 100 - i$$

where:

P = price index;
i = the future interest rate in percentage terms.

Thus, on 1 August 2017 the settlement price for a December three-month sterling future was 99.22, which implies an interest rate of $100 - 99.22 = 0.78\%$ for the period December to March – *see* Exhibit 21.21. Similarly the March quote implies an interest rate of $100 - 99.00 = 1.00\%$ for the three months March to June 2018.

In both cases the implied interest rate refers to a rate applicable for a notional deposit of £500,000 for three months on expiry of the contract – the March futures contract expires in March (i.e. the right to 'deposit' in March through to June expires in March) and the December future expires in December. The 0.78% rate for three-month money starting from December 2017 is the annualised rate of interest even though the deal is for a deposit of only one-quarter of a year.

Exhibit 21.21

Interest rates – futures

INTEREST RATES – FUTURES

Aug 1		Open	Sett	Change	High	Low	Est. vol.	Open int.
Euribor 3m*	Sep	99.79	99.79	–	99.80	99.79	24,868	483,512
Euribor 3m*	Dec	99.80	99.80	–	99.81	99.80	21,279	426,773
Euribor 3m*	MAR5	99.81	99.81	+0.01	99.82	99.81	22,235	389,540
Euribor 3m*	JUN5	99.81	99.81	+0.01	99.82	99.80	15,484	321,964
Euroswiss 3m*	Sep	99.99	100.00	+0.01	100.00	99.99	1,790	54,187
Euroswiss 3m*	Dec	100.01	100.02	+0.01	100.02	100.00	2,997	46,548
Euroswiss 3m*	MAR5	100.03	100.04	+0.01	100.04	100.02	3,831	47,290
Sterling 3m*	Sep	99.38	99.39	+0.01	99.39	99.37	35,044	376,708
Sterling 3m*	Dec	99.20	99.22	+0.03	99.22	99.19	55,831	447,127
Sterling 3m*	MAR5	98.96	99.00	+0.04	99.00	98.95	62,292	359,658
Sterling 3m*	JUN5	98.73	98.77	+0.05	98.77	98.71	54,531	252,667
Eurodollar 3m †	Sep	99.760	99.76	–	99.765	99.755	200	843,416
Eurodollar 3m †	Dec	99.715	99.73	+0.005	99.735	99.710	216,888	907,982
Eurodollar 3m †	MAR5	99.595	99.63	+0.030	99.635	99.585	343,580	1,122,558
Eurodollar 3m †	JUN5	99.390	99.44	+0.055	99.455	99.375	360.056	975.044
Fed Fnds 30d ‡	Aug	0.000	99.91	0.00	0.000	0.000	–	–
Fed Fnds 30d ‡	Sep	0.000	99.90	−0.01	0.000	0.000	–	–
Fed Fnds 30d ‡	Oct	0.000	99.90	–	0.000	0.000	–	–
Euroyen 3m ‡‡	Sep	99.795	99.795	–	99.795	99.795	4,006	79,258
Euroyen 3m ‡‡	Dec	99.800	99.805	–	99.805	99.800	2,887	39,735
Euroyen 3m ‡‡	MAR5	99.810	99.810	−0.005	99.815	99.810	1,414	37,593
Euroyen 3m ‡‡	JUN5	99.820	99.815	−0.005	99.820	99.815	3,205	45,995

The price of 99.22 is not a price in the usual sense – it does not mean £99.22. It is used to maintain the standard inverse relationship between prices and interest rates. For example, if traders in this market one week later, on 8 August 2017, adjusted supply and demand conditions because they expect generally raised inflation and raised interest rates by the winter 2017/18, they would push up the interest rates for three-month deposits starting in December 2017 to, say, 1.1%. Then the price of the future would fall to 98.90. Thus, a rise in interest rates for a three-month deposit of money results in a fall in the price of the contract – analogous to the inverse relationship between interest rates offered on long-term bonds and the price of those bonds.

In relation to short-term interest rate futures it is this inverse change in capital value when interest rates change that it is of crucial importance to grasp. Understanding this is more important than trying to envisage deposits of £500,000 being placed some time in the future.

Forward rate agreements (FRAs)

FRAs are useful devices for hedging future interest rate risk. They are agreements about the future level of interest rates. The rate of interest at some point in the future is compared with the level agreed when the FRA was established and compensation is paid by one party to the other based on the difference.

Worked example 21.3 — Hedging three-month deposits

An example of these short-term interest rate futures derivatives in use may help with gaining an understanding of their hedging qualities. Imagine the treasurer of a large company anticipates the receipt of £100m in late March 2018, almost 8 months hence. She expects that the money will be needed for production purposes in July 2018 but for the three months following late March it can be placed on deposit. There is a risk that interest rates will fall between now (early August 2017) and March 2018 from their present level of 1.00% per annum for three-month deposits starting in late March. (The Sterling 3m March future in Exhibit 21.21 shows a price of 99.00, indicating an interest rate of 1.00.)

The treasurer does not want to take a passive approach and simply wait for the inflow of money and deposit it at whatever rate is then prevailing without taking some steps to ensure a good return.

To achieve certainty in March 2018 the treasurer buys, in August 2017, March 2018 expiry three-month sterling interest rate futures at a price of 99.00. Each future has a notional value of £500,000 and therefore she has to buy 200 to hedge the £100m inflow.

Suppose in March 2018 that three-month interest rates have fallen to 0.7%. Following the actual receipt of the £100m the treasurer can place it on deposit and receive a return over the next three months of £100m $\times$ 0.007 $\times$ $^3/_{12}$ = £175,000. This is significantly less than if March 2018 three-month deposit interest rates had remained at 1.00% throughout the 8-month waiting period.

Return at 1.00% (£100m $\times$ 0.01 $\times$ $^3/_{12}$)	= £250,000
Return at 0.7% (£100m $\times$ 0.007 $\times$ $^3/_{12}$)	= £175,000
Loss	£75,000

However, the caution of the treasurer pays off because the futures have risen in value as the interest rates have fallen.

The 200 futures contracts were bought at 99.00. With interest rates at 0.7% for three-month deposits starting in March the futures in March have a value of 100 − 0.7 = 99.30. The treasurer in March can close the futures position by selling the futures for 99.30. Thus, a purchase was made in August 2017 at 99.00 and a sale in March 2018 at 99.30; therefore the gain amounts to 99.3 − 99.0 = 0.30.

This is where a **tick** needs to be introduced. A tick is the minimum price movement on a future. On a three-month sterling interest rate contract a tick is a movement of 0.01% on a trading unit of £500,000.

One-hundredth of 1% of £500,000 is equal to £50, but this is not the value of one tick. A further complication is that the price of a future is based on annual interest rates whereas the contract is for three months. Therefore £50/4 = £12.50 is the value of a tick movement in a three-month sterling interest rate futures contract. In this case we have a gain of 30 ticks with an overall value of 30 $\times$ £12.50 = £375 per contract, or £75,000 for

200 contracts. The profit on the futures exactly offsets the loss of anticipated interest when the £100m is put on deposit for three months in March.

Note that the deal struck in August was not to enter into a contract to actually deposit £100m with the counterparty on the market. The £100m is deposited in March with any one of hundreds of banks with no connection to the futures contract that the treasurer entered into. The actual deposit and the notional deposit are two separate transactions. However, the transactions are cleverly arranged so that the value movements on these two exactly offset each other. All that is received from ICE Futures Europe is the tick difference, based on the price change between buying and selling prices of the futures contracts – no interest is received.

Worked example 21.4　Hedging a loan

In August 2017 Holwell plc plans to borrow £5m for three months at a later date. This will begin in June 2018. Worried that short-term interest rates will rise Holwell hedges by *selling* ten three-month sterling interest rate futures contracts with June expiry. The price of each futures contract is 98.77, so Holwell has locked into an annual interest rate of 1.23% or 0.3075% for three months. The cost of borrowing is therefore:

£5m × 0.003075 = £15,375

Suppose that interest rates rise to annual rates of 2%, or 0.5% per quarter. The cost of borrowing for Holwell will be:

£5m × 0.005 = £25,000

However, Holwell is able to *buy* ten futures contracts to close the position on the exchange. Each contract has fallen in value from 98.77 to 98.0; this is 77 ticks. The profit credited to Holwell's margin account on ICE Futures Europe will now stand at:

Bought at 98.00, sold at 98.77:
77 ticks × £12.50 × 10 contracts = £9,625

Holwell pays interest to its lender for the three months June to September at 2% annual rate. The extra interest is £9,625 (£25,000 − £15,375) compared with the rate in the market for June to September deposits when Holwell was looking at the issue back in August. However, the derivative profit offsets the extra interest cost on the loan Holwell takes out in June.

Note that if interest rates fall Holwell will gain by being charged lower interest on the actual loan, but this will be offset by the loss of the futures. Holwell sacrifices the benefits of potential favourable movements in rates to reduce risk.

For example, a company needs to borrow £6m in six months' time for a period of a year. It arranges this with bank X at a variable rate of interest. The current rate of interest is 7% but the company does not know what it will be in six months. (For the sake of argument assume that this is the LIBOR rate for borrowing starting in six months and lasting one year, and that this company can borrow at LIBOR.) The company is concerned that by the time the loan is drawn down interest rates will be higher than 7%, increasing the cost of borrowing.

The company enters into a separate agreement with another bank (Y) – an FRA. It 'purchases' an FRA at an interest rate of 7%. This is to take effect six months from now and relates to a 12-month loan. Bank Y will never lend any money to the company but it has committed itself to paying compensation should interest rates (LIBOR) rise above 7%.

Suppose that in six months spot one-year interest rates are 8.5%. The company will be obliged to pay Bank X this rate: £6m × 0.085 = £510,000; this is £90,000 more than if the interest rates were 7%. However, the FRA with Bank Y entitles the company to claim compensation equal to the difference between the rate agreed in the FRA and the spot rate. This is (0.085 − 0.07) × £6m = £90,000. So any increase in interest cost above 7% is exactly matched by a compensating payment provided by the counterparty to the FRA.[11] However, if rates fall below 7% the company makes payments to Bank Y. For example, if the spot rate in six months is 5% the company benefits because of the lower

---

11 All figures are slightly simplified because we are ignoring the fact that the compensation is received in six months whereas interest to Bank X is payable in 18 months.

rate charged by Bank X, but suffers an equal offsetting compensation payment to Bank Y of $(0.07 - 0.05) \times £6m = £120,000$. The company has generated certainty over the effective interest cost of borrowing in the future. Whichever way the interest rates move it will pay £420,000.

This example is a gross simplification. In reality FRAs are generally agreed for three-month periods. So this company could have four separate FRAs for the year. It would agree different rates for each three-month period. If three-month LIBOR turns out to be higher than the agreed rate, Bank Y will pay the difference to the company. If it is lower the company pays Bank Y the difference.

The 'sale' of an FRA by a company protects it against a fall in interest rates. For example, if £10m is expected to be available for putting into a one-year bank deposit in three months from now the company could lock into a rate now by selling an FRA to a bank. Suppose the agreed rate is 6.5% and the spot rate in three months is 6%, then the depositor will receive 6% from the bank into which the money is placed plus $\frac{1}{2}$% from the FRA counterparty bank.

These two examples are described as 6 against 18 (or 6×18) and 3 against 15 (or 3×15). The first is a 12-month contract starting in six months, the second is a 12-month contract starting in three months. Typically sums of £5m–£100m are hedged in single deals in this market. Companies do not need to have an underlying lending or borrowing transaction – they could enter into an FRA in isolation and make or receive compensating payments only.

There is more on FRAs in Appendix 21.2.

A comparison of options, futures, forwards and FRAs

We have covered a great deal of ground in the field of derivatives. It is time to summarise the main advantages and disadvantages of the derivatives discussed so far – *see* **Exhibit 21.22**.

Exhibit 21.22	A comparison of options, futures, forwards and forward rate agreements	
Options	**Futures**	**Forwards and FRAS**
Advantages		
Downside risk is limited but the buyer is able to participate in favourable movements in the underlying.	Can create certainty: specific rates are locked in.	Can create certainty: specific rates are locked in.
Available on or off exchanges. Exchange regulation and clearing house reduce counterparty default risk for those options traded on exchanges.	Exchange trading only. Exchange regulation and clearing house reduce counterparty default risk.	Tailor-made, off-exchange. Not standardised as to size, duration and terms. Good for companies with non-standard risk exposures.
	No premium is payable. (However margin payments are required.)	No margins or premiums payable.[12] (Occasionally a good faith performance margin is required by one or more parties in a forward. Also credit limits may be imposed.)
For many options there are highly liquid markets resulting in keen option premium pricing and ability to reverse a position quickly at low cost. For others trading is thin and so premiums payable may become distorted and offsetting transactions costly and difficult.	Very liquid markets. Able to reverse transactions quickly and cheaply.	
Disadvantages		
Premium payable reduces returns when market movements are advantageous.	No right to let the contract lapse. Benefits from favourable movements in underlying are forgone.	No right to let the contract lapse. Benefits from favourable movements in underlying are forgone.

Options	Futures	Forwards and FRAS
	In a hedge position if the underlying transaction does not materialise the future position owner can experience a switch from a covered to an uncovered position; the potential loss is unlimited.	In a hedge position if the underlying transaction does not materialise the forward/FRA position owner can experience a switch from a covered to an uncovered position, the potential loss is unlimited.
Margin required when writing options.	Many exchange restrictions – on size of contract, duration (e.g. only certain months of the year), trading times (e.g. when ICE Futures Europe is open).	Greater risk of counterparty default – not exchange traded therefore counterparty is not the clearing house. However, this may change for many OTC derivatives as they move to exchanges.
		Generally the minimum contract size is for millions rather than a few thousand (as on the futures or options markets).
	Margin calls require daily work for 'back office'.	More difficult to liquidate position (than with exchange-traded instruments) by creating an offsetting transaction that cancels position.

Caps

An interest rate cap is a contract that gives the purchaser the right effectively to set a maximum level for interest rates payable. Compensation is paid to the purchaser of a cap if interest rates rise above an agreed level. This is a hedging technique used to cover interest rate risk on longer-term borrowing (usually two to five years). Under these arrangements a company borrowing money can benefit from interest rate falls but can place a limit to the amount paid in interest should interest rates rise.

Worked example 21.5   Interest rate cap

Oakham plc wishes to borrow £20m for five years. It arranges this with bank A at a variable rate based on LIBOR plus 1.5%. The interest rate is reset every quarter based on three-month LIBOR. Currently this stands at an annual rate of 3%. The firm is concerned that over a five-year period the interest rate could rise to a dangerous extent.

Oakham buys an interest rate cap set at LIBOR of 4.5% from bank B. For the sake of argument we will assume that this costs 2.3% of the principal amount, or £20m × 0.023 = £460,000 payable immediately to the cap seller. If over the subsequent five years LIBOR rises above 4.5% in any three-month period Oakham will receive sufficient compensation from the cap seller to offset exactly any extra interest above 4.5%. So if for the whole of the third year LIBOR rose to 5.5% Oakham would pay interest at 5.5% plus 1.5% to bank A but would also receive 1% compensation from the cap seller (a quarter every three months), thus capping the interest payable. If interest rates fall Oakham benefits by paying bank A less.

The premium (£460,000) payable up front covers the buyer for the entire five years, with no further payment due.

---

12 Regulators around the world are currently moving towards insistence that many over-the-counter derivatives be cleared through a formal system with a central counterparty (a clearing house) reducing risk for each participant. This will mean margin payments are required.

Caps are usually arranged for amounts of £5m or more, but can be for underlyings of only $1m – but when they are this low it may be difficult to obtain competing cost quotes from the banks. It is up to the client to select the strike rate and whether the rollover frequency (when LIBOR is compared with the strike) will be, say, three months or six months. They are available in all the main currencies.

The size of the cap premium[13] depends on the difference between current interest rates and the level at which the cap becomes effective; the length of time covered and the expected volatility of interest rates. The cap seller does not need to assess the creditworthiness of the purchaser because it receives payment of the premium in advance. Thus a cap is particularly suitable for highly geared firms, such as leveraged buyouts.

Floors and collars

Buyers of interest rate caps are sometimes keen to reduce the large cash payment at the outset. They can do this by simultaneously selling a floor, which results in a counterparty paying a premium. With a floor, if the interest rate falls below an agreed level, the seller (the floor writer) makes compensatory payments to the floor buyer. These payments are determined by the difference between the prevailing rates and the floor rate.

Returning to Oakham, the treasurer could buy a cap set at 4.5% LIBOR for a premium of £460,000 and sell a floor at 2% LIBOR receiving, say, £200,000. In any three-month period over the five-year life of the loan, if LIBOR rose above 4.5% the cap seller would pay compensation to Oakham; if LIBOR fell below 2% Oakham would save on the amount paid to bank A but will have to make payments to the floor buyer, thus restricting the benefits from falls in LIBOR. Oakham, for a net premium of £260,000, has ensured that its effective interest payments will not diverge from the range 2% + 1.5% = 3.5% at the lower end, to 4.5% + 1.5% = 6% at the upper end.

The combination of selling a floor at a low strike rate and buying a cap at a higher strike rate is called a collar.

Swaps

A swap is an exchange of a series of future cash payment obligations. An interest rate swap is where one company arranges with a counterparty to exchange interest rate payments. For example, the first company may be paying fixed-rate interest but prefers to pay floating rates. The second company may be paying floating rates of interest, which go up and down with LIBOR, but would benefit from a switch to a fixed obligation. For example, imagine that firm S has a £200m ten-year loan paying a fixed rate of interest of 8%, and firm T has a £200m ten-year loan on which interest is reset every six months with reference to LIBOR, at LIBOR plus 2%. Under a swap arrangement S would agree to pay T's floating-rate interest on each due date over the next ten years, and T would be obligated to pay S's 8% interest.

One motive for entering into a swap arrangement is to reduce or eliminate exposure to rises in interest rates. Over the short run, futures, options and FRAs could be used to hedge interest rate exposure. However, for longer-term loans (more than two years) swaps are usually more suitable because they can run for the entire lifetime of the loan. So if a treasurer of a company with a large floating-rate loan forecasts that interest rates will rise over the next four years, he/she could arrange to swap interest payments with a fixed-rate interest payer for those four years.

Another reason for using swaps is to take advantage of market imperfections. Sometimes the interest rate risk premium charged in the fixed-rate borrowing market differs from that in the floating-rate market for a particular borrower. See **Worked example 21.6.**

---

13 The word 'premium' gives a clue as to the underlying nature of these instruments: they are a series of options for the buyer to decide at, say, three-monthly intervals whether to exercise the option to insist that the difference between the agreed fixed rate of interest and the current LIBOR will be paid over. Thus on each three-month rollover day throughout the five years the cap holder will compare the strike on his cap (4.5% for Oakham) with the three-month LIBOR fixing that morning (fixed by asking the safest banks what interest they would have to pay that morning to borrow for three months in the inter-bank market) and exercise the cover if it makes sense to do so.

Worked example 21.6   Swaps

Take the two companies, Cat plc and Dog plc, both of which want to borrow £150m for eight years. Cat would like to borrow on a fixed-rate basis because this would better match its asset position. Dog prefers to borrow at floating rates because of optimism about future interest rate falls. The treasurers of each firm have obtained quotations from banks operating in the markets for both fixed- and floating-rate eight-year debt. Cat could obtain fixed-rate borrowing at 10% and floating-rate at LIBOR +2%. Dog is able to borrow at 8% fixed and LIBOR +1% floating:

	Fixed	Floating
Cat can borrow at	10%	LIBOR +2%
Dog can borrow at	8%	LIBOR +1%

In the absence of a swap market Cat would probably borrow at 10% and Dog would pay LIBOR +1%. However, with a swap arrangement both firms can achieve lower interest rates.

Notice that because of Dog's higher credit rating it can borrow at a lower rate than Cat in both the fixed- and the floating-rate market – it has an absolute advantage in both. However the risk premium charged in the two markets is not consistent. Cat has to pay an extra 1% in the floating-rate market, but an extra 2% in the fixed-rate market. Cat has an absolute disadvantage for both, but has a comparative advantage in the floating-rate market.

To achieve lower interest rates each firm should borrow in the market where it has comparative advantage and then swap interest obligations. So Cat borrows floating-rate funds, paying LIBOR +2%, and Dog borrows fixed-rate debt, paying 8%.

Then they agree to swap interest payments at rates which lead to benefits for both firms in terms of: **a** achieving the most appropriate interest pattern (fixed or floating), and **b** the interest rate that is payable, which is lower than if Cat had borrowed at fixed and Dog had borrowed at floating rates. *One* way of achieving this is to arrange the swap on the following basis:

- Cat pays to Dog fixed interest of 9.5%;
- Dog pays to Cat LIBOR +2%.

This is illustrated in **Exhibit 21.23**.

Exhibit 21.23   An interest rate swap

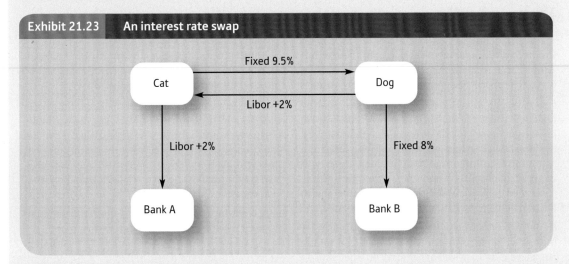

Now let us examine the position for each firm.

Cat pays LIBOR +2% to a bank but also receives LIBOR +2% from Dog and so these two cancel out. Cat also pays 9.5% fixed to Dog. This is 50 basis points (0.5%) lower than if Cat had borrowed at fixed rate directly from the bank. On £150m this is worth £750,000 per year.

Cat:

Pays	LIBOR +2%
Receives	LIBOR +2%
Pays	Fixed 9.5%
Net payment	Fixed 9.5%

Worked example 21.6 *(continued)*

Dog takes on the obligation of paying a bank fixed interest at 8% while receiving 9.5% fixed from Cat on the regular payment days. The net effect is 1.5% receivable less the LIBOR +2% payment to Cat – a floating-rate liability of LIBOR +0.5%.

Dog:

Pays	Fixed 8%
Receives	Fixed 9.5%
Pays	LIBOR +2%
Net payment	LIBOR +0.5%

Again there is a saving of 50 basis points or £750,000 per year.[14] The net annual £1.5m saving is before transaction costs.

Prior to the widespread development of highly liquid swap markets each counterparty incurred considerable expense in making the contracts watertight. Even then, the risk of one of the counterparties failing to fulfil its obligations was a potential problem. Today intermediaries (usually banks) take counterparty positions in swaps and this reduces risk and avoids the necessity for one corporation to search for another with a corresponding swap preference. The intermediary generally finds an opposite counterparty for the swap at a later date. Furthermore, standardised contracts reduce the time and effort to arrange a swap and have permitted the development of a thriving secondary market, and this has assisted liquidity.

A practical use of a swap arrangement by an individual is shown in **Exhibit 21.24**. The mortgage holder starts by paying base rate plus 1% to the mortgage company (5.5% + 1%) but agrees a swap whereby he pays 6.2 fixed rate and receives base rate.

Exhibit 21.24

Rate rise is music to the ears of 'swappers'

Unlike many home owners, those who have taken out interest rate swaps will be hoping that the Bank of England raises interest rates sooner rather than later.

One client of Stonehenge, which advises wealthy families, recently arranged an interest rate swap on his £5m mortgage for three years. Due to the size of the loan he had to take out a variable mortgage at a rate of 6.5%. Convinced that interest rates will increase significantly over the next three years he was concerned that his variable rate left him vulnerable to the possibility of large and changeable repayments.

He decided to take out a swap, which effectively takes the cost of his mortgage to 7.2%. This meant taking out a 3 year swap priced at 6.2%, 0.7 of a percentage point above current base rates of 5.5%.

If base rates go above his swap rate of 6.2%, the bank will pay him the difference between his fixed rate and the interest rate, effectively insuring him against further interest rate hikes. If base rates stay below this level he pays out the difference.

The benefits come if the Bank of England raises rates higher. If rates rise to 6.5%, say, his variable mortgage would jump to 7.5% and each year he would need to pay £375,000. While rising interest rates will push up his variable rate, they will also push up the amount he receives back from his bank on his swap.

In this case he would get back the difference between his swap rate of 6.2% and the interest rate of 6.5%. He can then use this 0.3% payment of 7.5%, keeping his payments at a fixed rate of 7.2%.

But by using an interest rate swap, he has ensured that his payments never exceed 7.2% – or £360,000 per year.

 Financial Times, 30 June 2007, Money p. 2. All Rights Reserved.

---

14 Under a swap arrangement the principal amount (in this case £150m) is usually not swapped and Cat retains the obligation to pay the principal to bank A. Neither of the banks is involved in the swap and may not be aware that it has taken place. The swap focuses entirely on the three-monthly or six-monthly interest payments.

There are many variations on the swaps theme. For example, a 'swaption' is an option to have a swap at a later date. With a straight currency swap a borrower takes up a loan offer in a currency, say euros. However, the borrower prefers to have money and exposure to sterling-based borrowing. It arranges a swap with a swap dealer (usually a bank) whereby the borrower agrees to immediately swap the euros received for sterling. It also agrees to pay periodic (say three-month intervals) interest in sterling to the dealer. The dealer in return will pay regular euro interest (that way the borrower can satisfy its euro creditor). The final element of the swap occurs at the maturity of the loan: the borrower now swaps back the sterling principal amount to the swap dealer in return for the euros. The borrower can then use these euros to pay off the debt. The currency swap might be motivated by potentially lower overall interest rates and/or hedging of interest rate positions and/or hedging of foreign exchange risk. Note that, unlike interest rate swaps, currency swaps involve the exchange of principal. An example of such an arrangement is shown in **Exhibit 21.25**.

Exhibit 21.25

Yankees ride to rescue of EU credit

Big US companies turn to euro debt markets for low borrowing costs

By Ralph Atkins

Bankers make poor wordsmiths. When foreign companies issue bonds in New York, they are known as "Yankee bonds". So what name is chosen when the trend is the opposite, and US companies issue in euros? "Reverse Yankees", of course.

The nomenclature is inelegant but it rolls off bankers' lips these days. Euro-denominated issuance by US companies and financial institutions in 2015 has already exceeded €33bn — three times as much as in the same period last year, according to Dealogic. Big-name issuers include Coca-Cola, Warren Buffett's Berkshire Hathaway investment vehicle and, this week, Kinder Morgan, America's largest energy infrastructure company.

The "reverse Yankee" surge is a fillip for Europe's corporate debt markets at a time when policy makers are keen to boost alternatives to bank financing. It also says a lot about the post-2007 crises world in which big international companies tap funding where the terms are most advantageous but, crucially, also diversify investor bases and hedge against currency turmoil.

"The dollar, euro and sterling markets — sometimes you can add in Swiss francs — have become the playground of international companies," says Demetrio Salorio, global head of debt capital markets at Société Générale. Not just US companies are raising funds in euros. Mainland China-based companies have shunned "dim sum" bonds, or offshore renminbi debt, and sold almost as much euro-denominated debt as in the whole of 2014.

The big attraction is that the cost of borrowing in euros is at historic lows and is cheap relative to dollar funding.

Until recently, the imbalance between dollar and euro markets had meant a US company could issue in euros, arrange a currency swap deal to convert into dollars — and still pay significantly less than it would have paid to raise the same sum originally in dollars.

If US companies offer a few extra basis points of yield to get a deal done, that is good news for yield-starved European investors. It enables portfolio managers restricted to investing in euros to buy into US companies.

But the bigger story is also about something easier than a reverse Yankee for the ordinary person to understand: the globalisation of finance. If they expect the euro to keep falling, it makes sense for foreigners to issue debt in the single currency. Meanwhile, tapping different markets widens a company's investor base. That not only allows finance directors to take advantage of changing financial conditions, it reduces the risk of being caught out in the next crisis.

With commodity price swaps each counterparty agrees to make regular payments to the other where one of the payments is determined by the varying price of a commodity or an index of commodities. Thus an airline vulnerable to a rise in the price of oil, might agree to pay regular fixed amounts to a swap dealer over several years in return for the swap dealer paying – on the same dates – a sum based on the price of an oil index. So if the price of oil rises the airline will pay more in the oil marketplace, but will receive more from the swap dealer than it pays the swap dealer.

There is more on swaps in Appendix 21.2.

Derivatives users

There are three types of user of the derivatives markets: hedgers, speculators and arbitrageurs.

Hedgers

To hedge is to enter into transactions which protect a business or assets against changes in some underlying. The instruments bought as a hedge tend to have the opposite-value movements to the underlying. Financial and commodity markets are used to transfer risk from an individual or corporation to another more willing and/or able to bear that risk.

Consider a firm which discovers a rich deposit of platinum in Kenya. The management is afraid to develop the site because it is uncertain about the revenues that will actually be realised. Some of the sources of uncertainty are that: **a** the price of platinum could fall, **b** the floating-rate loan taken out to develop the site could become expensive if interest rates rise and **c** the value of the currencies could move adversely. The senior managers have more or less decided that they will apply the firm's funds to a less risky venture. A recent graduate steps forward and suggests that this would be a pity, saying: 'The company is passing up a great opportunity, and Kenya and the world economy will be poorer as a result. Besides, the company does not have to bear all of these risks given the sophistication of modern financial markets. The risks can be hedged, to limit the downside. For example, the platinum could be sold on the futures market, which will provide a firm price. The interest-rate liability can be capped or swapped into a fixed-rate loan. Other possibilities include using the FRA and the interest futures markets. The currency risk can be controlled by using currency forwards or options.' The board decides to press ahead with development of the mine and thus show that derivatives can be used to promote economic well-being by transferring risk.

The US oil and gas shale fracking industry is greatly assisted by the producers' ability to use futures and options to hedge against low prices for their commodities by selling future production. The reduced risk makes it easier to secure finance to raise production.

Speculators

Speculators take a position in financial instruments and other assets with a view to obtaining a profit on changes in price. Speculators accept high risk in anticipation of high reward. The gearing effect of derivatives makes speculations in these instruments particularly profitable, or particularly ruinous. Speculators are also attracted to derivatives markets because they are often more liquid than the underlying markets. In addition the speculator is able to sell before buying (to 'short' the market) in order to profit from a fall. More complex trading strategies are also possible.

The term speculator in popular parlance is often used in a somewhat critical fashion. This is generally unwarranted. Speculators are needed by financial markets to help create trading liquidity. Many people argue that prices are more, not less, likely to be stable as a result of speculative activity. Usually speculators have dissimilar views regarding future market movements and this provides two-way liquidity which allows other market participants, such as hedgers, to carry out a transaction quickly without moving the price. Imagine if only hedgers with an underlying were permitted to buy or sell derivatives. Very few trades would take place each day. If a firm wished to make a large hedge this would be noticed in the market and the price of the derivative would be greatly affected. Speculators also provide a kind of insurance for hedgers – they accept risk in return for a premium.

Speculators are also quick to spot new opportunities and to shift capital to new areas of economic output. For example, if a speculator foresees a massive rise in the demand for cobalt because of its use in batteries they will start to buy futures in the commodity, pushing up the price. This will alert the mining companies to go in search of more cobalt deposits around the world and pump money into those countries that have it, such as Congo. The speculator has to examine the underlying economic messages emanating from the world economy and respond to them in a truthful manner – dumping the currency of a badly run country or selling bond derivatives in banks, for example. Those on the receiving end of those messages often resent having the truth revealed when they have tried to conceal it for so long and hoped to go on doing so.

Arbitrageurs

The act of arbitrage is to exploit price differences on the same instrument or similar assets. The arbitrageur buys at the lower price and immediately resells at the higher price. So, for example, Nick Leeson claimed that he was arbitraging Nikkei 225 Index futures. The same future is traded in both Osaka and Singapore. Theoretically the price should be identical on both markets, but in reality this is not always the case, and it is possible simultaneously to buy the future in one market and sell the future in the other and thereby make a risk-free profit. An arbitrageur waits for these opportunities to exploit a market inefficiency. The problem for Barings Bank was that Nick Leeson obtained funds to put down as margin payments on arbitrage trades but then bought futures in both markets – surreptitiously switching from an arbitrage activity to a highly risky, speculative activity. True arbitrageurs help to ensure pricing efficiency – their acts of buying or selling tend to reduce pricing anomalies.

Over-the-counter (OTC) and exchange-traded derivatives

An OTC derivative is a tailor-made, individual arrangement between counterparties, usually a company and its bank. Standardised contracts (exchange-traded derivatives) are available on dozens of derivatives around the world, for example the CME Group (includes Chicago Board of Trade, CBOT, the old Chicago Mercantile Exchange, CME, and the New York Mercantile Exchange, NYMEX), ICE Futures Europe, and the Eurex in Germany and Switzerland. Roughly one-half of outstanding derivatives contracts are traded on exchanges.

Many derivatives markets are predominantly, if not exclusively, OTC: FRAs, swaps, caps, collars, floors, currency forwards and currency swaps. **Exhibit 21.26** compares OTC and exchange-traded derivatives.

Exhibit 21.26   OTC and exchange-traded derivatives

OTC derivative

Advantages
- Contracts can be tailor-made, which allows perfect hedging and permits hedges of more unusual underlyings. It also permits contracts of very long maturities.
- Companies with a longstanding relationship with a bank can often arrange derivative deals with it, without the need to find any specific margin or deposit. The bank is willing to accept the counterparty risk of its customer reneging on the deal because it regards this possibility as very low risk, given its longstanding knowledge of the firm.

Disadvantages
- It might be difficult to find a counterparty willing to take the opposite position for a very specific contract that suits you, e.g. to buy 250 tonnes of orange juice exactly 290 days from now. Even if the counterparty can be found the deal might be at a disadvantageous price to you because of the limited choice of counterparties you have available.
- There is a risk that the counterparty will fail to honour the transaction; therefore close attention is paid to the creditworthiness of participants – those with less than high quality reputations may not be able to transact in OTC derivatives (unless secured by a great deal of collateral). Many OTC derivative markets now have a central organisation that is counterparty to both the long holder and the short holder.

▶

Exhibit 21.6 *(continued)*

- Low level of market regulation with resultant loss of transparency (e.g. what deals have taken place?) and price dissemination (private deals are not usually made public).
- Often difficult to reverse a hedge once the agreement has been made. It is sometimes difficult to find a counterparty willing to do exactly the opposite transaction to your first position. Even if you find one, you then have two counterparty risks, and often the maturity dates of the two contracts do not exactly match, leaving some unhedged exposure.
- Higher transaction costs. Because they are tailor-made both sides need to scrutinise the deal (e.g. using expensive lawyers) and monitor counterparties subsequently. This extra cost is not worth it for small deals and so forward contracts are usually counted in millions of pounds, euros etc., whereas futures are usually in tens or hundreds of thousands.
- Transactions may not be settled promptly at the agreed time – whereas the clearing house on an exchange will insist on prompt settlement.

Exchange-traded derivative

Advantages
- Counterparty risk is reduced because the clearing house is counterparty.
- High regulation encourages transparency and openness on the price of recent trades.
- Liquidity is usually much higher than for OTC – large orders can be cleared quickly due to high daily volume of trade.
- Positions can be reversed by closing quickly – an equal and opposite transaction is completed in minutes.

Disadvantages
- Standardisation may be restrictive, e.g. standardised terms for quality of underlying, quantity, delivery dates. Small companies, with say a £100,000 share portfolio to hedge or a €400,000 loan to hedge, find the standard quantities cumbersome. For example, short-term interest rate futures for euros are in €1,000,000 multiples only.
- The limited trading hours and margin requirements may be inconvenient.

Concluding comments

From a small base in the 1970s derivatives have grown to be of enormous importance. Almost all medium and large industrial and commercial firms use derivatives, usually to manage risk, but occasionally to speculate and arbitrage. Banks are usually at the centre of derivatives trading, dealing on behalf of clients, as market makers or trading on their own account. Other financial institutions are increasingly employing these instruments to lay off risk or to speculate. They can be used across the globe, and traded night and day.

The trend suggests that derivatives will continue their relentless rise in significance. They can no longer be dismissed as peripheral to the workings of the financial and economic systems. The implications for investors, corporate institutions, financial institutions, regulators and governments are profound. These are incredibly powerful tools, and, like all powerful tools, they can be used for good or ill. Ignorance of the nature of the risks being transferred, combined with greed, has already led to some very unfortunate consequences (the pain that followed the sub-prime mortgage meltdown is but one example. Many traders were given power to gain derivative exposure without anyone in the organisation really understanding the nature of the risks they were taking on).[15] However, on a day-to-day basis, and away from the newspaper headlines, the ability of firms to quietly tap the markets and hedge risk encourages wealth creation and promotes general economic well-being.

---

15 *See* Chapter 16 of *Modern Financial Markets and Institutions* (2012) by Arnold for an account of the courses of the crisis.

Key points and concepts

- **A derivative instrument** is an asset whose performance is based on the behaviour of an underlying asset (the underlying).

- **An option** is a contract giving one party the right, but not the obligation, to buy (call option) or sell (put option) a financial instrument, commodity or some other underlying asset, at a given price, at or before a specified date.

- The **writer of a call option** is obligated to sell the agreed quantity of the underlying at some time in the future at the insistence of the option purchaser (holder). A **writer of a put** is obligated to purchase.

- **American-style options** can be exercised at any time up to the expiry date whereas **European-style options** can only be exercised on a predetermined future date.

- **Intrinsic** value on an option: the pay-off that would be received if the underlying is at its current level when the option expires. For a call option this is determined by how much the current market price is above the exercise price. For a put it is the extent to which the current price of the underlying is below the exercise price.

- An **out-of-the-money option** is one that has no intrinsic value.

- An **in-the-money option** has intrinsic value.

- **Time value** arises because of the potential for the market price of the underlying, over the time to expiry of the option, to change in a way that creates intrinsic value.

- **Share options** can be used for hedging or speculating on shares.

- **Corporate uses of options include**:
  - share options schemes;
  - warrants;
  - convertible bonds;
  - rights issues;
  - share underwriting;
  - commodity options;
  - taking control of a company;
  - protecting the company from foreign exchange losses;
  - real options.

- A **forward contract** is an agreement between two parties to undertake an exchange at an agreed future date at a price agreed now. Forwards are tailor-made, allowing flexibility.

- **Futures** are agreements between two parties to undertake a transaction at an agreed price on a specified future date. They are exchange-traded instruments with a clearing house acting as counterparty to every transaction standardised as to:
  - quality of underlying;
  - quantity of underlying;
  - legal agreement details;
  - delivery dates;
  - trading times;
  - margins.

- For futures, **initial margin** (0.1% to 15%) is required from each buyer or seller. Each day profit or losses are established through **marking to market**, and **variation margin** is payable by the holder of the future who makes a loss (to avoid going below the maintenance margin).

- The majority of futures contracts are **closed** (by undertaking an equal and opposite transaction) **before expiry** and so **cash losses or profits** are made rather than settlement by delivery of the underlying. Some futures are **settled by cash** only – there is no **physical delivery.**

- **Short-term interest-rate futures** can be used to hedge against rises and falls in interest rates at some point in the future. The price for a £500,000 notional three-month contract is expressed as an index:

$$P = 100 - i$$

As interest rates rise the value of the index falls.

- **Forward rate agreements** (FRAs) are arrangements whereby one party pays the other should interest rates at some point in the future differ from an agreed rate.

- An interest rate **cap** is a contract that gives the purchaser the right effectively to set a maximum interest rate payable through the entitlement to receive compensation from the cap seller should market interest rates rise above an agreed level. The cap seller and the lender are not necessarily the same.

- A **floor** entitles the purchaser to payments from the floor seller should interest rates fall below an agreed level. A **collar** is a combination of a cap and a floor.

- A **swap** is an exchange of cash payment obligations. An interest rate swap is where interest obligations are exchanged. In a currency swap the two sets of interest payments are in different currencies.

- Some **motives for swaps**:
  - to reduce or eliminate exposure to rising interest rates;
  - to match interest rate liabilities with assets;

▶

- to exploit market imperfections and achieve lower interest rates.

● **Hedgers** enter into transactions to protect a business or assets against changes in some underlying.

● **Speculators** accept high risk by taking a position in financial instruments and other assets with a view to obtaining a profit on changes in value.

● **Arbitrageurs** exploit price differences on the same or similar assets.

● **Over-the-counter (OTC)** derivatives are tailor-made and available on a wide range of underlyings. They allow perfect hedging and the possibility of avoiding margin or deposit. However, they suffer from counterparty risk (if they are not traded on recently introduced systems with an OTC central counterparty), poor transparency, poor price dissemination, low regulation, frequent inability to reverse a hedge and higher transaction cost.

● **Exchange-traded** derivatives have lower credit (counterparty) risk, greater regulation, higher liquidity and greater ability to reverse positions than OTC derivatives. However, standardisation can be restrictive.

Appendix 21.1: Option pricing

This appendix describes the factors that influence the market value of a call option on a share. The principles apply to the pricing of other options. The complex mathematics associated with option pricing will be avoided because of their unsuitability for an introductory text. Interested readers are referred to the References and further reading list later in this chapter.

Notation to be used:

C = value of call option
S = current market price of share
X = exercise price
r_f = risk-free interest rate (per annum)
t = time to expiry (in years)
σ = standard deviation of the share price
e = mathematical fixed constant: 2.718 . . .

The factors affecting option value

1 *Options have a minimum value of zero*

$$C \geq 0$$

Even if the share price falls significantly below the exercise price of the option the worst that can happen to the option holder is that the option becomes worth nothing – no further loss is created.

2 *The market value of an option will be greater than the intrinsic value at any time prior to expiry* This is because there is a chance that if the option is not exercised immediately it will become more valuable due to the movement of the underlying – it will become (or will move deeper) in-the-money. *An option has time value* that increases, the longer the time to expiry.

$$\text{Market value} = \text{Intrinsic value} + \text{Time value}$$

3 *Intrinsic value $(S - X)$ rises as share price increases or exercise price falls* However this simple relationship needs to be made a little more sophisticated because $S - X$ is based on the assumption of immediate exercise when the option is about to expire. However if the option is not about to expire there is some value in not having to pay the exercise price until the future exercise date. (Instead of buying the share a call option could be purchased and

the remainder invested in a risk-free asset until the exercise date.) So intrinsic value is given a boost by discounting the exercise price by the risk-free rate of return:

$$\text{Intrinsic value} = S - \frac{X}{(1 + r_f)^t}$$

4 **The higher the risk-free rate of return the higher will be intrinsic value** because the money saved by buying an option rather than the underlying security can be invested in a riskless rate of return until the option expires.

5 **The maximum value of an option is the price of the share**

$$C \leq S$$

6 **A major influence boosting the time value is the volatility of the underlying share price** A share which has a stable, placid history is less likely to have a significant upward shift in value during the option's lifetime than one which has been highly variable. In option pricing models this factor is measured by the variance (σ^2) or standard deviation (σ) of the share price.

Black and Scholes' option pricing model

Black and Scholes' option pricing model (BSOPM) was published in 1973 and is still widely employed today despite the more recent modifications to the original model and the development of different option-pricing models. The BSOPM is as follows:

$$C = SN(d_1) - Xe^{-rf^t} N(d_2)$$

where:

N = cumulative normal distribution function of d_1 and d_2

$$d_1 = \frac{\ln(S/X) + (r_f + \sigma^2/2)t}{\sigma\sqrt{t}}$$

$\ln$ = natural log

$$d_2 = d_1 - \sigma\sqrt{t}$$

Appendix 21.2: The relationship between FRAs and swaps

If a corporation buys (or sells) a sequence of LIBOR-based FRAs stretching over, say, two years, in which each of the three-month periods making up that two years is covered by an FRA then we have an arrangement very similar to a two-year swap. The company has made a series of commitments to pay or receive differences between the FRA agreed rate and the prevailing spot rate at three-month intervals.

For example, Colston plc has a loan for £100m. This is a floating-rate liability. Interest is set at three-month LIBOR every three months over its two-year life. So, every three months, whatever the rate that London banks are charging for three-month loans to each other is to be charged to Colston. (This rate can be observed in the *Financial Times*. It changes daily, once agreed it is fixed for the three months.)

Thus the company is vulnerable to interest rate rises. The current time is June 20X1 and spot LIBOR rate is set at 5.09%. This is the annualised rate that Colston will pay for the next three months (it will pay one-quarter of this for three-month borrowing). To lock in a rate for the next rollover date, i.e. in September, the company could buy (in June) an FRA set at LIBOR for the three months starting in September and ending in December (a 3 × 6 forward rate agreement). This FRA is priced at 5.71%. The amount covered can be exactly £100m because FRA arrangements are flexible to suit the client, being an over-the-counter market. The £100m is known as the notional amount.

The FRA buyer (Colston) has technically agreed to deliver to the FRA seller 5.71%. In return the FRA seller will pay Colston whatever is the spot rate for LIBOR in September. Of course, it would be inefficient to have these two payments made when only one payment (set as the difference between these rates) is needed. So, if LIBOR is 5.71% in September no payment is made by either side.

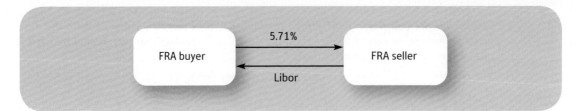

However, if LIBOR in September resets at 6.2% Colston will receive a settlement cash flow of 0.49%, or 49 basis points, on £100m for the three-month period. Thus a payment of £122,500 is received (£100m × 0.0049 × 3/12) from the FRA seller.[16]

If, however, the spot LIBOR in September is 5.5%, Colston will pay a settlement cash flow of 21 basis points: £100m × 0.0021 × 3/12 = £52,500.

FRAs are priced at-the-money, i.e. the current rate in the market for future LIBOR. In the case of Colston in June this is 5.71% for September three-month FRA. The participants in this market consider that the market rate has zero initial value to both parties. However, as rates change the contract gains value for one or other of the contractors.

Colston has locked in the interest rate it will pay for the three months September to December, but what about the other months of the two-year loan commitment? It could enter a series of FRAs for each of the remaining rollover dates. The rates that would be set are shown in **Exhibit 21.27**.

Exhibit 21.27	FRA prices for the next two years

Time	LIBOR rate quoted in June 20X1 for three-month periods starting at various dates over next two years
June 20X1 (Spot)	5.09
Sept. 20X1	5.71
Dec. 20X1	6.05
Mar. 20X2	6.42
June 20X2	6.70
Sept. 20X2	6.98
Dec. 20X2	7.06
Mar. 20X3	7.18

By executing seven FRAs at these rates Colston would pay its lender 5.09% (annualised rate) for the first three months. Thereafter, regardless of how LIBOR moves, the effective cost of the loan is 5.71% for the second three months, 6.05% for the third, and so on. Each one of these FRA deals is like a mini swap, with Colston committed to delivering the rate shown in the exhibit and the FRA seller committed to delivering LIBOR to Colston. Or, rather, net payments on the difference between the FRA rate and LIBOR are made. So, to illustrate for the first four payments:

Using FRAs in this way Colston knows how much it has to pay out over the next two years and so is not vulnerable to unexpected changes in LIBOR. But note that the interest rates are different from one three-month period to another. An alternative open to Colston is to buy a contract with the same rate payable in each of the eight quarters. This rate would be an approximate average of

---

16 This is the amount payable in December for the September FRA. If the agreement is for payment to be made in September the amount will be reduced (discounted) at the annualised rate of 6.2%.

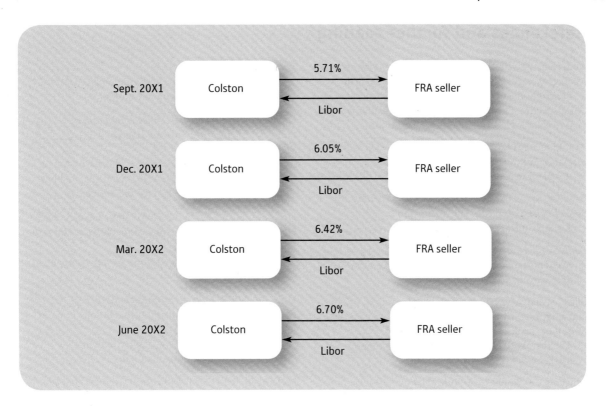

the FRA rates stretching over the two years. This is called a swap. A rough average of the eight LIBOR rates payable in Exhibit 21.25 is 6.39%. The interest rate swap arrangement is shown in **Exhibit 21.28**. For each three-month period Colston pays the counterparty the swap rate (6.39%) and receives LIBOR. If interest rates rise above 6.39% Colston would benefit from the swap arrangement because it receives payments from the swap counterparty, which amount to the difference between 6.39% and LIBOR. This enables Colston to accept any increase in LIBOR with equanimity, as the effective cost of the loan is constant at 6.39% regardless of how much is paid to the lender.

The swap rates quoted by banks in the financial markets are largely determined by the average of the forward rates to create one fixed rate for all quarterly settlements. The banks act as market makers quoting prices both for those who want to make fixed payments (as in the case of Colston) and those who wish to pay LIBOR and receive the swap rate – say, 6.39%. In reality the market maker will charge slightly different rates (a bid/ask spread) depending on whether the company wants to receive the fixed rate or pay the fixed rate. This can be as little as two basis points but is sufficient to provide the market maker with a profit.

Exhibit 21.28	Colston's payouts and receipts under a swap

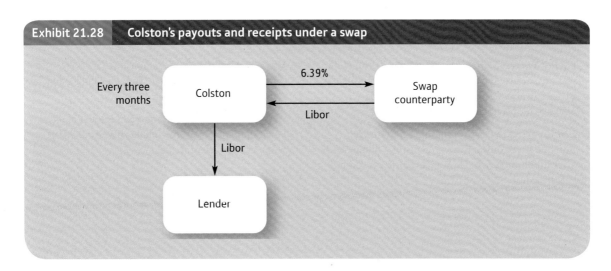

References and further reading

Andersen, T.J. (2006) *Global Derivatives: A Strategic Management Perspective*. Harlow: FT Prentice Hall.
  Describes the use of derivatives from a corporate perspective. Easy to read and takes the reader from an introductory level to an intermediate level.

Arnold, G. (2014a) *The Financial Times Guide to Investing*. 3rd edn. Harlow: FT Prentice Hall.
  A wider range of derivative instruments is discussed.

Baltazar, M. (2008) *The Beginners Guide to Financial Spread Betting*, 2nd edn. Harriman House.
  A simple introductory guide.

Bank of England Quarterly Bulletins.
  An important and easily digestible source of up-to-date information.

Black, F. and Scholes, M. (1973) 'The pricing of options and corporate liabilities', *Journal of Political Economy*, May/June, pp. 637–59.
  The first useful option pricing model – complex mathematics.

Chisholm, A.M. (2009) *An Introduction to International Capital Markets*. 2nd edn. Chichester: John Wiley.
  Deals with a number of more technical aspects clearly.

Choudhry, M., Joannas, D., Landuyt, G., Periera, R. and Pienaar, R. (2010) *Capital Market Instruments: Analysis and valuation*, 3rd edn. London: Palgrave Macmillan.
  A textbook-style book written by practitioners. Some basic material but mostly higher level with plenty of mathematics.

The Economist.
  Valuable reading for anyone interested in finance (and world affairs, politics, economics, science etc.).

Financial Times.
  An important source for understanding the latest developments in this dynamic market.

Galitz, L. (2012) *Financial Times Handbook of Financial Engineering*. 3rd edn. London: FT Prentice Hall.
  A clearly written and sophisticated book on use of derivatives. Aimed at a professional readership but some sections are excellent for the novice.

Headley, J.S. and Tufano, P. (2001) 'Why manage risk?' Harvard Business School Note. Available from Harvard Business Online.
  A short easy-to-read description of why companies hedge risk.

Hull, J.C. (2017) *Option, Futures and Other Derivatives, Global Edition*. 9th edn. Harlow: Pearson Education.
  A relatively easy-to-follow description but also contains some high-level material.

McDonald, R.L. (2013) *Derivatives Markets*. 3nd edn. Harlow: Pearson.
  A more technical/theoretical approach.

Miller, M.H. (1997) *Merton Miller on Derivatives*. New York: Wiley.
  An accessible (no maths) account of the advantages and disadvantages of derivatives to companies, society and the financial system.

Taylor, F. (2010) *Mastering Derivatives Markets*. 4th edn. London: FT Prentice Hall.
  A good introduction to derivative instruments and markets.

Case study recommendations

Please see www.pearsoned.co.uk/arnold for case study synopses. Also, another list of useful case studies from the fifth edition can be found there.

- Interest-rate swap offered by Sumitomo-Mitsui Bank: was this for hedging or speculation? Author: Mitsuru Misawa, University of Hong Kong. Available at www.cb.hbsp.harvard.edu

- Exotic interest rate swaps: snowballs in Portugal. Authors: Boris Vallee; Patrick Augustin; Philippe Rich, Harvard Business School. Available at www.cb.hbsp.harvard.edu

- Hedging at Porsche. Author: Stefan Nagel, WDI Publishing at the University of Michigan. Available at www.cb.hbsp.harvard.edu

- Has Libor lost its stature in derivatives markets? Authors: Walid Busaba; Ken Mark Ivey Publishing, Available at www.cb.hbsp.harvard.edu

- Julia Reka: analyzing put options. Authors: Hubert Pun; Siddharth Aiyar, Ivey Publishing. Available at www.cb.hbsp.harvard.edu

Websites

www.advfn.com	ADVFN
www.money.cnn.com	CNN Financial News
www.bloomberg.com	Bloomberg
www.uk.reuters.com	Reuters
www.theice.com	ICE Futures
www.theice.com/futures-europe	ICE Futures Europe
www.fia.org	Futures Industry Association
www.cmegroup.com	CME group
www.wsj.com	*Wall Street Journal*
www.ft.com	*Financial Times*
www.globalinvestorgroup.com	*Futures and Options World* and *ISF*
www.cboe.com	Chicago Board Options Exchange
www.nyse.com	New York Stock Exchange
www.eurexchange.com	Eurex, the European Derivative Exchange
www.isda.org	International Swaps and Derivatives Association

Self-review questions

1 What are derivatives and why do they have value?

2 Why can vast sums be made or lost in a short space of time speculating with derivatives?

3 Describe the following:
- traded option
- call option
- put option
- in-the-money option
- out-of-the-money option
- intrinsic value
- time value
- index option
- option writer

4 Compare the hedging characteristics of options and futures.

5 Distinguish between delivery of the underlying and cash settlement.

6 List and briefly describe the application of options to industrial and commercial organisations.

7 Explain the advantages of entering into a forward contract.

8 How do futures differ from forwards?

9 Describe the following:
- clearing house
- initial margin
- marking to market
- variation margin

10 Explain forward rate agreements, caps, floors and collars.

11 Describe what is meant by a swap agreement and explain why some of the arrangements are entered into.

12 Distinguish between a hedger, a speculator and an arbitrageur.

13 Why do the over-the-counter markets in derivatives and the exchange-based derivatives markets coexist?

Questions and problems

Answers to most questions can be found at www.pearsoned.co.uk/arnold.
Answers to questions marked with an asterisk are to be found only in the Lecturer's Guide.

1   You hold 20,000 shares in ABC plc which are currently priced at 500p. ABC has developed a revolutionary flying machine. If trials prove successful the share price will rise significantly. If the government bans the use of the machine, following a trial failure, the share price will collapse.

Required

a   Explain and illustrate how you could use the traded options market to hedge your position.
Further information
Current time: 30 January.
Traded option quotes on ABC plc on 30 January:

	Option	Calls			Puts		
		March	June	Sept.	March	June	Sept.
ABC plc	450	62	88	99	11	19	27
	500	30	50	70	30	42	57
	550	9	20	33	70	85	93

b   What is meant by intrinsic value, time value, in-the-money, at-the-money and out-of-the-money? Use the above table to illustrate.

2   Palm's share price stands at £4.80. You purchase one March 500p put on Palm's shares for 52p. What is your profit or loss on the option if you hold the option to maturity under each of the following share prices?

a   550p
b   448p
c   420p

3   What is the intrinsic and time value on each of the following options given a share price of 732p?

Exercise price	Calls Feb.	Puts Feb.
700	$55\frac{1}{2}$	$17\frac{1}{2}$
750	28	40

Which options are in-the-money and which are out-of-the-money?

4   Adam, a speculator, is convinced that the stock market will fall significantly in the forthcoming months. The current market index (14 August) level is 4997 (FTSE 100). He is investigating a strategy to exploit this market fall:

Sell five FTSE 100 Index futures with a December expiry, current price 5086.
Extracts from the Financial Times

FTSE 100 Index Futures £10 per full index point

	Open	Sett.price
Sept.	5069	5020
Dec.	5218	5086

Assume: No transaction costs.

Required

i   What would the profit (loss) be if the index rose to 5500 in December under the strategy?
ii   What would the profit (loss) be if the index fell to 4500 in December under the strategy?
iii   Discuss the relative merits of using traded options rather than futures for speculation.

5   On 14 August British Biotech traded options were quoted as follows:

	Option	Calls			Puts		
		Sept.	Dec.	March	Sept.	Dec.	March
British Biotech	160	$30\frac{1}{2}$	40	53	$7\frac{1}{2}$	$16\frac{1}{2}$	$23\frac{1}{2}$
(current share price: $177\frac{1}{2}$)	180	$20\frac{1}{2}$	31	$45\frac{1}{2}$	$16\frac{1}{2}$	27	$34\frac{1}{2}$

Assume: No transaction costs.

Required

a   Imagine you write a December 180 put on 14 August. Draw a graph showing your profit and loss at share prices ranging from 100p to 250p.
b   Add to the graph the profit or loss on the purchase of 1,000 shares in British Biotech held until late December at share prices between 100p and 250p.
c   Show the profit or loss of the combination of a and b on the graph.

6*   A manager controlling a broadly based portfolio of UK large shares wishes to hedge against a possible fall in the market. It is October and the portfolio stands at £30m with the FTSE 100 Index at 5020. The March futures price is 5035 (£10 per Index point).

Required

a   Describe a way in which the manager could hedge against a falling market. Show the number of derivatives.
b   What are the profits/losses if the FTSE 100 Index moves to 4000 or 6000 in March?
c   Draw a profit/loss diagram for the strategy. Show the value of the underlying portfolio at different index levels, the value of the derivative and the combined value of the underlying and the derivative.

7   (*Examination level*) A buyer of a futures contract in Imaginationum with an underlying value of £400,000 on 1 August is required to deliver an initial margin of 5% to the clearing house. This margin must be maintained as each day the counterparties in the futures are marked to market.

Required

a   Display a table showing the variation margin required to be paid by this buyer and the accumulated profit/loss balance on her margin account in the eight days following the purchase of the future. (Assume that the maintenance margin is the same as the initial margin.)

Day	1	2	3	4	5	6	7	8
Value of Imaginationum (£000s)	390	410	370	450	420	400	360	410

b   Explain what is meant by 'gearing returns' with reference to this example.
c   Compare forwards and futures markets and explain the mutual coexistence of these two.

8* A corporate treasurer expects to receive £20m in late September, six months hence. The money will be needed for expansion purposes the following December. However in the intervening three months it can be deposited to earn interest. The treasurer is concerned that interest rates will fall from the present level of 8% over the next six months, resulting in a poorer return on the deposited money.

   A forward rate agreement (FRA) is available at 8%.
   Three-month sterling interest futures starting in late September are available, priced at 92.00.
   Assume: No transaction costs and that a perfect hedge is possible.

   Required

   a Describe two hedging transactions that the treasurer could employ.
   b Show the profit/loss on the underlying and the derivative under each strategy if market interest rates fall to 7%, and if they rise to 9%.   **?**

9* a Black plc has a £50m ten-year floating-rate loan from Bank A at LIBOR + 150 basis points. The treasurer is worried that interest rates will rise to a level that will put the firm in a dangerous position. White plc is willing to swap its fixed-interest commitment for the next ten years. White currently pays 9% to Bank B. LIBOR is currently 8%. Show the interest-rate payment flows in a diagram under a swap arrangement in which each firm pays the other's interest payments.
   b What are the drawbacks of this swap arrangement for Black?
   c Black can buy a ten-year interest rate cap set at a LIBOR of 8.5%. This will cost 4% of the amount covered. Show the annual payment flows if in the fourth year LIBOR rises to 10%.
   d Describe a 'floor' and show how it can be used to alleviate the cost of a cap.   **?**

10 Three-month sterling interest rate futures are quoted as follows on 30 August:

	£500,000, points of 100% Settlement price
September	91.50
December	91.70
March	91.90

   Red Wheel plc expects to need to borrow £15m at floating rate in late December for three months and is concerned that interest rates will rise between August and December.
   Assume: No transaction costs.

   Required

   a Show a hedging strategy that Red Wheel could employ to reduce uncertainty.
   b What is the effective rate of interest payable by Red Wheel after taking account of the derivative transaction if three-month spot rates are 10% in December? Show the gain on the derivative.
   c What is the effective rate of interest after taking account of the derivative transaction if three-month spot rates are 7% in December? Show the loss on the derivative.
   d Compare short-term interest rate futures and FRAs as alternative hedging techniques for a situation such as Red Wheel's.   **?**

11 'The derivatives markets destroy wealth rather than help create it; they should be made illegal.' Explain your reasons for agreeing or disagreeing with this speaker.

12 Invent examples to demonstrate the different hedging qualities of options, futures and forwards.

13 Speculators, hedgers and arbitrageurs are all desirable participants in the derivatives markets. Explain the role of each.

Assignments

1   Describe as many uses of options by a firm you know well as you can. These can include exchange-traded options, currency options, other OTC options, corporate uses of options (for example, underwriting) and operational and strategic decision options.

2   Investigate the extent of derivatives use by the treasury department of a firm you know well. Explain the purpose of derivatives use and consider alternative instruments to those used in the past.

Managing

exchange-rate risk

LEARNING OUTCOMES

By the end of this chapter the reader should be able to:

■ explain the role and importance of the foreign exchange markets;

■ describe hedging techniques to reduce the risk associated with transactions entered into in another currency;

■ consider methods of dealing with the risk that assets, income and liabilities denominated in another currency, when translated into home-currency terms, are distorted;

■ describe techniques for reducing the impact of foreign exchange changes on the competitive position of the firm;

■ outline the theories designed to explain the reasons for currency changes.

Introduction

Changes in exchange rates increase uncertainty about income from operations in foreign countries or from trading with foreign firms. Shifts in foreign exchange rates have the potential to undermine the competitive position of the firm and destroy profits. This chapter describes some of the techniques used to reduce the risk associated with business dealings outside the home base.

Case study 22.1

What a difference a few percentage point moves on the exchange rate make

Until autumn 1992, sterling was a member of the European exchange rate mechanism (ERM), which meant the extent it could move vis-à-vis other European currencies was severely limited. Then came 'Black Wednesday' when the pound fell out of the ERM, the government gave up the fight to retain the high level of sterling and the pound fell by around 20%. George Soros was one of the speculators who recognised economic gravity when he saw it, and bet the equivalent of $10bn against sterling by buying other currencies. After the fall of the pound, the money held in other currencies could be converted back to make $1bn profit in just a few days.

When sterling was highly valued against other currencies exporters found life very difficult because, to the foreign buyer, British goods appeared expensive – every unit of their currency bought few pounds. However, in the four years following 'Black Wednesday' UK exporters had a terrific boost and helped pull the economy out of recession as overseas customers bought more goods. Then things turned around. Between 1996 and 2001 the pound rose against most currencies. Looked at from the German importers' viewpoint, UK goods relative to domestic goods rose in price by between 30 and 40%. UK firms lined up to speak of the enormous impact the high pound was having on profits, jobs were lost.

James Dyson, the technology entrepreneur, announced he was planning to build a factory in East Asia rather than Britain because of the strength of the pound. Toyota, Honda and Nissan, which had established plants in Britain, complained bitterly about the high level of the pound. Their factories were set up to export cars. They were hurt by having to reduce prices and also by their commitment to buy 70% of components from UK suppliers (continental European suppliers benefited from a 30–40% price advantage because of the high pound).

Then things turned around again. European companies had an increasingly hard time trying to export, particularly into the US and UK markets, because, between 2002 and 2010, the euro rose by around 50%, making European goods 50% more expensive in the eyes of US and UK consumers. Worse, US exporters could compete against their European rivals more effectively when selling to countries in Asia and elsewhere because of the rise in the euro. Heineken, exporting beer to the USA, to maintain profits *should* have raised its export prices by 50%, but found competition meant it could only raise them 2–3% per year.

Also complaining were the UK companies that buy goods and services and borrow money abroad, because their margins were being squeezed as they paid more to obtain euros. The high street retailer, Next, sources most of its goods from overseas manufacturers; the low pound against the dollar as well as the euro meant that they had to pay more in pound terms for the same items. The housebuilder Taylor Wimpey suffered because most of their debt was in dollars, which now needed more pounds for each unit of dollar interest. Worse, for cheese lovers: Branston Pickle (Premier Foods) prices rose in part because the falling pound pushed up the cost of many of its (imported) raw materials.

Those benefiting from the weak pound included pharmaceutical companies which make a large share of their revenues overseas but report their results in pounds. And, of course, exporters, from engineers to English hoteliers, received a boost when their products or services became more competitive in the eyes of the overseas buyer.

The pound gradually rose through 2015 and into 2016, making life difficult for exporters but better for importers. Then the Brexit vote happened – the pound fell by 18% giving UK exporters a boost when they approached customers with lower prices in their currencies. This kept the economy above water during the period of maximum uncertainty of Brexit negotiations. But there was a price to pay for the low pound as the cost of imported items shot up, hurting retailers and others, from petrol stations to builder's merchants, who obtain most of their goods or components from abroad.

Foreign exchange shifts and the management of the associated risks are not issues to be separated and put into a box marked 'for the attention of the finance specialists only'. The profound implications for jobs, competitiveness, national economic growth and firms' survival mean that all managers need to be aware of the consequences of foreign exchange rate movements and of how to prepare the firm to cope with them. Fluctuating exchange rates create currency risk and badly managed risk can lead to a loss of shareholder wealth.

The effects of exchange-rate changes

Shifts in the value of foreign exchange, from now on to be referred to as simply 'forex' (FOReign EXchange) or FX, can impact on various aspects of a firm's activities:

- *Income to be received from abroad* If a UK firm has exported goods to Canada on six months' credit terms, payable in Canadian dollars (C$ or CAD), the UK company is uncertain as to the number of pounds it will actually receive because the exchange rate for the Canadian dollar is very likely to move in the intervening period.

- *The amount actually paid for imports at some future date* A Japanese firm, importing wood from the USA, has a liability to pay dollars a few months later. The quantity of yen (¥) it will have to use to exchange for the dollars at that point in the future is uncertain at the time the deal is struck. Puma profits fell 42% for 2015 due to currency fluctuations increasing apparel costs – *see* **Exhibit 22.1**. The fall in the pound post Brexit has made overseas goods more expensive for UK consumers – *see* **Exhibit 22.2**.

Exhibit 22.1

Strong dollar drags Puma full-year profits down 42%

By James Shotter Herzogenaurach

Puma, the German sports brand that sponsors Jamaican sprinter Usain Bolt, said that its net profit slumped 42 per cent last year due to the surge in the value of the US dollar. Puma, which is seeking to make up lost ground after losing market share to local rival Adidas and US sports giant Nike in recent years, posted net profit of €37.1m — or €2.48 per share — in 2015, down from €64.1m the year before. Analysts had expected €39.4m, according to a Reuter's poll.

Stripping out currency fluctuations, Puma posted its fastest growth in the Americas, where sales were up 8.8 per cent. In Asia and the Pacific region, they were up 7.6 per cent, while in Europe they climbed 3.6 per cent. Bjørn Gulden, who has been working to turn Puma's fortunes around since becoming chief executive in 2013, said that the group knew "we still have a lot to improve". He added that the company had bolstered its brand and products in 2015, as well as reinforcing co-operation with its retail partners. "Unfortunately the strengthening of the US dollar versus nearly all other currencies has had a significant impact on both our gross profit margin and our operating expenses, and therefore also on our operating profits and net earnings," he said.

Despite the currency impact — Puma sources a lot of its products in Asia via contracts denominated in US dollars, but has significant revenues in euros — Mr Gulden struck an upbeat note on the group's prospects.

Exhibit 22.2

Brexit costs to hit UK consumers' pockets

Bills set to increase after sterling drops but electricity predicted to be cheaper

FT reporters

Petrol: expect higher prices at the pumps UK motorists will face higher petrol costs in the wake of the Brexit vote if concerns about the economic outlook lead to sterling falling faster than the oil price. Brent crude, the dollar-priced international oil benchmark, has fallen more than 7 per cent since Thursday as selling by investors hit equities and commodities. But when looking at Brent priced in sterling over the same period, the price of crude has risen by 5 per cent.

David Sheppard

Retail: weaker pound will force stores to raise prices The tumbling value of the pound will also affect costs on the high street, as companies that import goods from abroad pass on higher prices to consumers. This is unlikely to happen immediately, analysts say, because most retailers put in place "hedges" for several months' worth of their foreign exchange needs. As those hedges expire, however, shops face a choice to either increase prices and risk losing the custom of recession-wary Brits, or accept lower margins on the items they sell.

Lord Wolfson, the Conservative peer and chief executive of Next, who was a prominent Vote Leave supporter, indicated that clothing prices could rise from next year. "Most retailers will have covered forward the balance of this year so [the fall in sterling] will not be reflected in prices this year," he said. "Next has covered 60 per cent of its requirement of dollars and euros for spring/summer next year and I imagine the rest of the industry will be in a similar position. So

the volatility in currency markets will have no effect until the spring, maybe the summer of next year."

Analysts said the weaker pound would be most noticeable on more expensive goods. "If we're going to have a consumer recession, the companies that are going to be squeezed are the ones selling big-ticket items," said Tony Shiret, an analyst at Haitong Securities. "People are going to get much more price-sensitive about things like widescreen televisions. It won't make so much difference if you're selling socks and jumpers."

Paul McClean, Mark Vandevelde

Travel: groups braced for holiday booking decline The fall in sterling means foreign currency is more expensive, and spending money will not go as far as it did last week. On Thursday, £300 would have bought you $450 — today it will get you just $395. Analysts say this will reduce demand for holidays, at least in the short term.

Paul McClean

Energy: cheaper household prices, but more uncertainty over trade deals One rare area where consumers could potentially benefit is electricity prices, which could fall if the price of oil and gas tumbles again. That would make the UK's heavy energy users more competitive with companies overseas and aiding consumers.

Gill Plimmer

- *The valuation of foreign assets and liabilities* In today's globalised marketplace, many firms own assets abroad and incur liabilities in foreign currencies. The value of these, in home currency terms, changes when the exchange rate changes. The fall in the value of the Rouble in 2015 meant that Russian companies with debt denominated in US dollars had to find more roubles to clear their liability – *see* **Exhibit 22.3**. The Brexit vote in June 2016 impacted Sterling – *see* **Exhibit 22.4**.

- *The long-term viability of foreign operations* The long-term future returns of subsidiaries located overseas can be enhanced by a favourable forex change or destroyed by an adverse change.

Exhibit 22.3

Rouble decline stokes fears of Russian credit crunch

Oil price swings and knock-on effects on currency heighten concerns about foreign debt pile

By Kathrin Hille in Moscow

Late last year, a sharp fall in the price of crude cut deeply into the foreign exchange revenues on which Russia's corporate sector relies heavily. Together with sanctions, which almost entirely barred Russian banks and companies from raising fresh funds in western capital markets, this stoked fears that some might struggle to repay foreign creditors on which they previously depended.

Those concerns receded after the rouble strengthened back to 49 to the dollar this May and the central bank stepped in to offer foreign currency loans. But since then the rouble resumed its slide to about 65, a 23 per cent decline in value, making Russia's total $410bn in external debt more expensive to service, according to central bank statistics.

Banks and non-financial companies are due to repay $61bn, including interest, between now and the end of the year. Most of this is concentrated in two massive redemption peaks this month and in December.

According to three bankers interviewed by the Financial Times, the largest external debt coming up for redemption includes a $950m loan to Gazprombank, the country's third-largest bank, a $680m loan to TNK-BP, the oil company, and a $330m loan to Sberbank, Russia's largest bank, in September. Bonds coming due the same month include $750m at Evraz, the steelmaker, $400m at VTB, the state bank, and $350m at Otkritie, Russia's largest privately owned bank.

Large redemptions later in the year include $1.7bn at Gazprom, the state gas monopolist, $1.5bn at Sberbank and more debt maturing at Evraz and Otkritie.

Exhibit 22.4

Pound tumbles to 30-year low as Britain votes Brexit

Sterling tumbles below $1.33 as Leave camp wins

By Roger Blitz in London and Leo Lewis in Tokyo

The pound slumped to the lowest level in 30 years on Friday, tumbling as much as 13 per cent, as investors took fright at Britain's shock decision to leave the EU. In a morning of financial and political turmoil, sterling sank as low as $1.3224 and racked up significant declines against the euro and the yen.

A stunning slide in sterling at 3.40am London time saw the currency plummet below $1.40, and 20 minutes later it had breached $1.35 to levels last plumbed 31 years ago in the Thatcher-Reagan era.

An hour later, the pound had found a new low at $1.3224 before coming off that level by 8am. Sterling's gyrations added up to a record 13 per cent intraday range for the pound, smashing the 6.5 per cent from October at the height of the 2008 financial crash and the 4.9 per cent range on Black Wednesday in 1992.

Kit Juckes, FX strategist at Société Générale, said that despite the scale of sterling's fall "there is a grave danger of further weakness in the weeks ahead. Indeed, the view of policymakers will be that a weaker pound is a vital economic shock absorber".

The vote to leave will sharpen focus on the UK's problematic current account and budget deficits, they said. Concerns about the UK's trade agreements with the EU would make it harder for the UK to finance these deficits, and sterling would act as "the adjustment mechanism", HSBC predicted.

- *The acceptability, or otherwise, of an overseas investment project* When evaluating the value-creating potential of major new investments, future currency changes will have a significant effect on estimated NPV. However, future currency movements are difficult to predict.

Volatility in foreign exchange

Exhibits 22.5 to **22.7** show the extent to which forex rates can move even over a period as short as a few weeks – 5 or 10% point shifts are fairly common. In October 2016, following the uncertainty surrounding the pound due to Brexit, there was a 'flash crash' on the Asian markets and the value of the pound dropped 6% against the US dollar in less than 2 minutes and 9% overall. The Bank of International Settlements (BIS) investigated, reporting in January 2017 that there was no one cause but rather a mix of the time of day, meaning less experienced traders were in place, stop-loss orders, a more risk averse attitude in Asia and a lack of liquidity. They did however note that these events were becoming more common in faster electronic markets. In a report on the sterling flash crash issued on 13 January 2017 by the Bank for International Settlements Markets Committee, they quoted Mark Carney, governor of the Bank of England (www.bis.org/press/p170113.htm) stating that:

It is vital. . . that we learn the lessons of this flash event and similar episodes in other financial markets, as orderly market functioning underpins market confidence. It is also important that firms have adequate governance, systems and controls and give due consideration to the potential impact of their activity on market functioning.

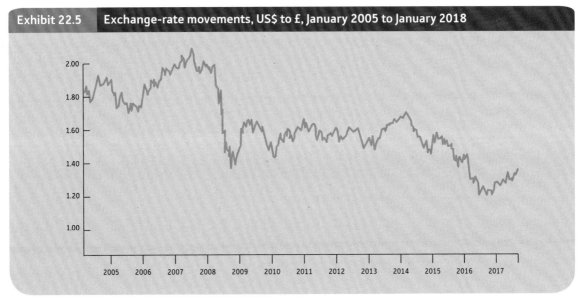

Exhibit 22.5   Exchange-rate movements, US$ to £, January 2005 to January 2018

https://markets.ft.com/data/currencies/tearsheet/summary?s=GBPUSD

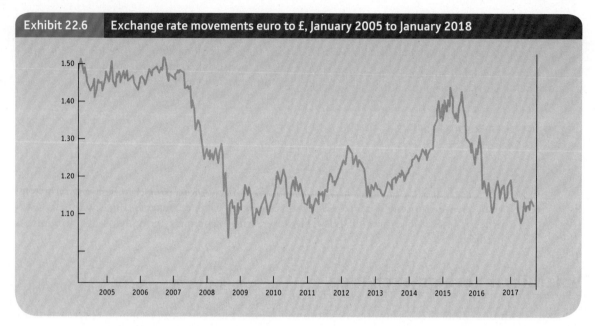

Exhibit 22.6   Exchange rate movements euro to £, January 2005 to January 2018

https://markets.ft.com/data/currencies/tearsheet/summary?s=GBPEUR.

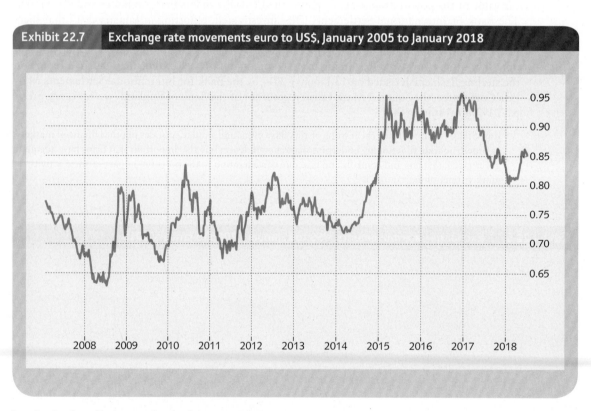

Exhibit 22.7   Exchange rate movements euro to US$, January 2005 to January 2018

https://markets.ft.com/data/currencies/tearsheet/summary?s=USDEUR

In the mid-1970s a regime of (generally) floating exchange rates replaced the fixed exchange-rate system which had been in place since the 1940s. Today most currencies fluctuate against each other, at least to some extent. The movement in exchange rates is primarily dictated by the market and by supply of and demand for the currencies

If a UK firm holds dollars or assets denominated in dollars and the value of the dollar rises against the pound a forex profit is made. Conversely, should the pound rise relative to the dollar, a forex loss will be incurred. These potential gains or losses can be very large.

For example, between between the end of October 2017 ($1.3291/£) and October 2018 ($1.2768/£) the dollar appreciated by 4% against the pound. Exchanging £1,000 at the end of October 2017 would have given you $1,329; holding the dollars for the year and exchanging the same $1,329 US dollars back into pounds in May 2018 you would have received £1,041, a gain of £41 for doing nothing more than holding onto the dollars; even before the money was put to use, say, earning interest. Fluctuating forex rates may bring gains or losses from a project, an export deal or a portfolio investment in addition to the actual profits or losses from the underlying transactions.

Political and economic events in 2016/7 significantly moved markets – the Brexit vote, the election of Donald Trump, the fragility of the Eurozone. The pound ($1.20) and the euro (€1.05) started 2017 in weak positions against the dollar but improved steadily during 2017 to finish the year at $1.35/£ and $1.20/€. Despite a strengthening of both currencies against the dollar in early 2018, by the end of May 2018 they had fallen back to $1.2877/£ and $1.167/€.

The foreign exchange markets

The function of the currency (forex) market is to facilitate the exchange of one currency into another. Conducted every three years, the Bank for International Settlements (BIS) Triennial Bank Survey provides information on the size and structure of the global forex market. The survey from April 2016 indicated daily activity of US$5,100 billion. The forex market has grown dramatically, although the growth in trading, particularly in spot transactions, slowed in 2016.

$bn	2001	2004	2007	2010	2013	2016
Forex	1381	1884	3123	3665	4915	5088
Growth		36%	66%	17%	34%	4%

Source: BIS Triennial Survey (April 2016). Turnover at April 2016 exchange rates.

London is the biggest currency trading centre, with a 37% share, followed by the USA (19%). Asian trading centres have grown and now represent 20% of forex trading. Singapore has expanded to 8% moving ahead of Japan and Hong Kong both at 6%. The US$ continues to be the dominant currency representing US$4,458 billion (88%) of all trades. The Euro accounts for 32%, Japanese Yen 22% and Sterling 13%. The rise of the Renminbi or Chinese Yuan is noteworthy, having increased to 4% in 2016 (2013 – 2%). Note: the total is 200% as there are two currencies involved in each trade.

Who is trading?

The BIS Triennial Survey 2016 separates the share of trading by trading parties as shown:

- Reporting dealers (42% of trades)
  - Large commercial and investment banks and securities houses trading electronically via the inter-dealer market on their own account and for large customers.
- Other financial institutions (51% of trades)
  - Smaller banks, pension funds, insurance companies, hedge funds, central banks, sovereign wealth funds.

- Non-financial customers (7% of trades)
  - Any other trader, primarily trading via online trading portals or by telephone and would include tourists, investors in real or financial assets overseas.

The big players are the large commercial banks and speculators, such as hedge funds. In addition to dealing on behalf of customers, or acting as market makers, the banks carry out proprietary transactions of their own in an attempt to make a profit by taking a position in the market – that is, speculating on future movements – although this has been heavily curtailed by regulators after the financial crisis – *see* **Exhibit 22.8**. Companies and individuals usually obtain their foreign currencies from the banks.

Exhibit 22.8

UK-based banks still active in proprietary trading

Data show 26 managers are responsible for such activity despite regulatory crackdown

By Laura Noonan

UK-based banks still employ 26 people to oversee their proprietary trading businesses, despite an extended regulatory crackdown that has made it progressively more expensive for banks to trade on their own behalf. New data obtained by recruitment firm DHR International under the Freedom of Information Act show that the 26 managers are listed as responsible for proprietary trading under the Financial Conduct Authority's Senior Managers Regime. The number, as of the end of June, is down from the 32 people with proprietary trading responsibilities when the SMR was launched in March 2016 to hold bankers more personally accountable for activities on their watch.

Proprietary trading has been out of favour with regulators since the financial crisis, when banks took heavy losses after betting some of their own capital on future market moves. US banks are particularly constrained under the Volcker rule, which prohibits them from trading on their own account, beyond a small number of exceptions. The activity is still possible in Europe, but post-crisis capital rules make it expensive and curbed banks' enthusiasm for what was once a lucrative earner.

US banks could theoretically get some reprieve on their restrictions if Donald Trump's deregulation push extends to the Volcker rule. Most of them say that they do not want to pile into proprietary trading again, but that they would welcome respite from the heavy compliance burden of proving that they are compliant.

The challenge arises because banks are still able to act as 'market makers', maintaining an inventory so that they can buy and sell from clients who cannot find other investors who want to take opposite positions. The area between market making and proprietary trading can become blurry — for market making, banks must be able to demonstrate that their positions are to satisfy "the reasonably expected near-term demand of clients, customers, or counterparties", which is not an exact science. All banks operating in the US must also prove they have adequate systems and controls in place to ensure that market making needs the Volcker definitions guidelines — Deutsche Bank became the first institution to fall foul of that requirement last year, resulting in a $157m penalty from the Federal Reserve.

Foreign exchange interbank brokers act as intermediaries between large buyers and sellers. They allow banks to trade anonymously, thus ensuring that the price does not move simply because of the revelation of the name of a bank in a transaction.

The market has changed significantly in the twenty-first century. According to statistics from Aite Group LLC, a Boston based research and consulting firm, electronic forex dealing, which represented 20% of transactions in 2001, had increased to 66% of all trades by 2013. The expectation is that 80% of trades will be conducted electronically by 2018. Traders deal alongside banks on a number of electronic platforms where computers match deals automatically, e.g. Electronic Broking Services (EBS) or Thomson Reuters. Customer demand for price transparency and lower transaction charges is driving the shift to electronic trading. Banks are also keen to reduce the risk from human involvement, after the fixing scandals[1] of recent years, despite the reduced margins available from electronic trading. Electronic platforms allow smaller banks to access the best prices and provide them with the opportunity to deal alongside the large banks on an even basis because of the transparency of the systems.

Transactions

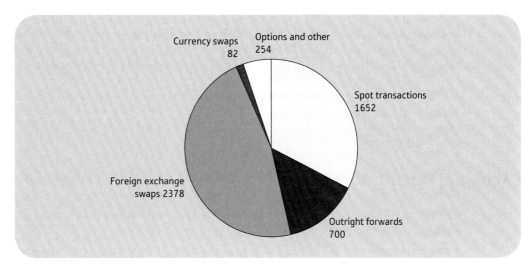

Source: BIS Triennial Survey 2016

Spot and forwards

Spot market transactions are transactions involving the exchange of two currencies at a rate agreed on the date of the contract for delivery within two business days. Forwards contracts involve the exchange of two currencies at a specified future date at a rate agreed at the date of the contract.

Foreign exchange swap (FX swap)

A single deal with two parts to it. First, there is the actual exchange of two currencies on a specific date at a rate agreed at the time of the conclusion of the contract – this is usually a spot exchange but it can be a forward. Secondly, there is a reverse exchange of the same two currencies at a date further in the future at a rate agreed at the time of the contract. The rates of exchange are usually different in the two parts. These FX swaps take place all the time between professional players based in banks as they try to balance out their currency positions, reduce their risk exposure or speculate to gain higher returns.

---

1 It is difficult to establish the rate for a currency; to help businesses establish a rate, a daily exchange rate fix is held. Reuters calculate a 'fix rate' based on transactions in the 30 seconds immediately before and after 1600 GMT. The forex market is so big it was thought impossible to manipulate the benchmark but in November 2014, regulators accused traders in some of the large banks of fixing the rate to make profit. The scandal has led to prosecutions with banks paying billions in fines and regulations being tightened.

Twenty-four hour trading

Dealing takes place on a 24-hour basis, with trading concentration moving as one major financial centre closes and the next opens. Most trading occurs when both the European and New York markets are open – this is when it is afternoon in Frankfurt, Zurich and London and morning on the east coast of the Americas. Later the bulk of the trade passes to San Francisco and Los Angeles, followed by Sydney, Tokyo, Hong Kong and Singapore. There are at least 40 other trading centres around the world in addition to these main ones.

The vast sums of money traded every working day across the world mean that banks are exposed to settlement risk: the risk that they may irrevocably pay over currency to a counterparty before they receive another currency in return because settlement systems are operating in different time zones. This is also known as **Herstatt risk** after a German bank that failed in 1974. It had received currency in Europe but had not yet paid the dollars that it owed when it failed. Its failure caused panic and gridlock in the forex market, which took weeks to unravel. Following this disaster, the major banks formed a new means of settlement, **Continuous Linked Settlement (CLS)**, which began operating in 2002. Owned by the world's leading banks, **CLS Bank International**, allows both legs of the trade to be paid simultaneously, eliminating the risk that one bank might fail in midstream. Under CLS net payments are made by banks to an orderly schedule in a five-hour slot the day after the deal. If a trade is not matched, it is returned to its originator, so there is no possibility of one party to the trade suffering loss due to the other party's failure to settle. A second major advantage of this system is that the net values of the trades are settled rather than the gross amount of trades. So if a bank sold $1 billion, but also bought $900 million the settlement is for only $100 million.

Exchange rates

We now look more closely at exchange rates. We start with some terms used in forex markets. First, we provide a definition of an **exchange rate**:

> An exchange rate is the price of one currency (the base currency) expressed in terms of another (the secondary, counter or quote currency).

Therefore if the exchange rate between the US dollar and the pound is US$1.40 = £1.00 this means that £1.00 will cost US$1.40. Taking the reciprocal, US$1.00 will cost 71.4p. The standardised forms of expression are:

US$/£ : 1.40
or
US$1.40/£
or
GBPUSD 1.40£

As foreign exchange trading is now primarily digital, you will regularly see the ISO-4217 codes which are used in digital trading such as GBP, USD, EUR, YEN. In digital trading the quote is provided as for example GBPUSD where the first currency, GBP, is the base currency which is always equal to 1 and the second currency, USD, is the **counter currency**. The counter is variable, i.e. it moves.

Most currencies are quoted to four decimal places and the smallest variation used in trading is called a **pip** which is one ten-thousandth of one unit of currency (e.g. $1) or 0.0001. So for the US$/£ exchange rate early in the day on 13 January 2018 the rate for exchanging GBP for USD is:

US$/£   1.3733 or   GBPUSD   1.3733

However, this is still not completely accurate because currency exchange rates are not expressed in terms of a single 'middle rate' as above, but are given as two rates – the bid rate at which the dealer will buy the variable currency or the offer rate at which the dealer will sell the variable currency. As this is a trade, if the dealer is buying, then you are selling; so the dealer's offer rate is your bid rate – the rate at which you can buy the counter currency (USD) and your offer rate at which you can sell the counter currency (USD). Data reported in the press is normally shown from the public viewpoint and so will show the bid-offer spread at which you can buy or sell.

In the case of the US$/£ exchange rate the market rates later in the day on 13 January 2018 were: US$1.37325/£ 'middle rate'

YOU	*Your bid rate*	*Your offer rate*
	You can buy dollars from a bank or broker at this rate.	You can sell dollars to a bank or a broker at this rate.
US$/£	1.3731	1.3734
DEALER	*Dealer offer rate* The dealer will sell dollars to you at this rate	*Dealer bid rate* The dealer will buy dollars from you at this rate

The difference (the spread) between bid and offer is 3 pips.

So if you wished to purchase and sell US$1m the transaction outcomes would be:

	USD ($)	Rate	GBP (£)
You buy	1,000,000	1.3731	728,279
You sell	1,000,000	1.3734	728,120
		0.0003	£159

The foreign exchange dealers are transacting with numerous buyers and sellers every day and they make a profit on the difference between the bid price and offer price (the bid/offer spread). In the above example if a dealer sold US$1m and bought US$1m with a bid/offer spread of 0.03 of a cent a profit of £728,279 − £728,120 = £159 is made.

Worked example 22.1   Forex

The basic elements of forex are so important for the rest of the chapter that it is worthwhile to pause and consolidate understanding of the quoted rates through some exercises.

Answer the following questions on the basis that the EURUSD or $/€ exchange rate was 1.2114–1.2116. Here the Euro is the base currency and the US dollar is the counter or variable currency. You can give Euros and buy US dollars at 1.2114 and you can sell US dollars and get Euros at 1.2116. The spread is 0.0002.

1 What is the cost of buying €200,000?
2 How much would it cost to purchase US$4m?
3 How many dollars would be received from selling €800,000?
4 How many euros would be received from selling US$240,000?

Answers

	Euros	Rate	Dollars
Buy Euros/paying in dollars	200,000	1.2116	242,320
Paying in Euros/buy dollars	3,301,965	1.2114	4,000,000
Selling Euros/receiving dollars	800,000	1.2114	969,120
Receiving Euros/selling dollars	198,085	1.2116	240,000

Currencies are divided into three categories – major, minor and exotic. There are seven major currencies: the US dollar (USD), the Euro (EUR), sterling (GBP), the Australian and Canadian dollars (AUD/ CAD), the Swiss Franc (CHF) and the Japanese Yen (JPY). Major currency pairs all contain the USD on one side of the trade. The EURUSD is the most highly traded pair representing 23% (BIS2016) of the total market.

The spot and forward exchange markets

There are two main forex markets.

- In the spot market transactions are officially for 'immediate delivery' but in practice this usually takes place two business days after the deal is struck.

- In the forward market a deal is arranged to exchange currencies at some future date at a price agreed now. The periods of time are generally one, three or six months, but it is possible to arrange an exchange of currencies at a predetermined rate many years from now. The BIS Triennial Survey reports that outright forward trading volume was $700 billion per day in 2016 (2013 – $679 bn) with only $17 billion of that trading being for forward contracts of more than one year.

You can arrange a forward contract in all the major currencies but there are currencies for which forward quotes are difficult to obtain. Exotic currencies, for which there is little trading demand, generally do not have forward rates quoted by dealers.

The *Financial Times* reports the previous day's trading in the forex market. The figures shown in **Exhibit 22.9** relate to dealing on 11 January 2018. Of course, by the time a newspaper reader receives the information in this table the rates have changed as the 24-hour markets follow the sun around the world. However, FT.com and other websites provide much more current detailed information.

Exhibit 22.9	Currencies						
		DOLLAR		**EURO**		**POUND**	
Jan 11	Currency	Closing Mid	Day's Change	Closing Mid	Day's Change	Closing Mid	Day's Change
Argentina	Argentine Peso	18.6550	−0.0900	22.4718	0.0125	25.2487	−0.1160
Australia	Australian Dollar	1.2701	−0.0040	1.5299	0.0033	1.7190	−0.0051
Bahrain	Bahrainin Dinar	0.3770	–	0.4541	0.0024	0.5103	0.0001
Bolivia	Bolivian Boliviano	6.9100	–	8.3238	0.0446	9.3524	0.0022
Brazil	Brazilian Real	3.2234	−0.0175	3.8829	−0.0001	4.3627	−0.0226
Canada	Canadian Dollar	1.2537	0.0055	1.5102	0.0147	1.6968	0.0078
Chile	Chilean Peso	606.4250	−4.1150	730.5005	−1.0180	820.7688	−5.3794
China	Chinese Yuan	6.5085	−0.0083	7.8401	0.0320	8.8090	−0.0092
Colombia	Colombian Peso	2862.2950	−32.9750	3447.9251	−21.0437	3873.9870	−43.7285
Costa Rica	Costa Rican Colon	569.9600	0.0700	686.5747	3.7610	771.4151	0.2722
Czech Republic	Czech Koruna	21.1909	−0.1449	25.5265	−0.0370	28.6809	−0.1895
Denmark	Danish Krone	6.1825	−0.0328	7.4475	0.0006	8.3678	−0.0425
Egypt	Egyptian Pound	17.7067	0.0197	21.3295	0.1378	23.9652	0.0322
Hong Kong	Hong Kong Dollar	7.8228	0.0012	9.4234	0.0520	10.5879	0.0041
Hungary	Hungarian Forint	256.5292	−1.6689	309.0154	−0.3446	347.2006	−2.1785
India	Indian Rupee	63.6625	0.0563	76.6879	0.4781	86.1643	0.0959
Indonesia	Indonesian Rupiah	13399.5000	−35.0000	16141.0600	44.5064	18135.6218	−43.1886
Israel	Israeli Shekel	3.4188	−0.0067	4.1182	0.0140	4.6271	−0.0081
Japan	Japanese Yen	111.4050	0.0500	134.1986	0.7786	150.7816	0.1023
..One Month		111.4048	0.0496	134.1987	0.7787	150.7815	0.1022

Jan 11	Currency	DOLLAR		EURO		POUND	
		Closing Mid	Day's Change	Closing Mid	Day's Change	Closing Mid	Day's Change
..Three Month		111.4044	0.0489	134.1987	0.7788	150.7813	0.1018
..One Year		111.4024	0.0448	134.1989	0.7792	150.7815	0.1008
Kenya	Kenyan Shilling	103.1000	–	124.1944	0.6652	139.5412	0.0321
Kuwait	Kuwaiti Dinar	0.3016	0.0001	0.3633	0.0020	0.4082	0.0002
Malaysia	Malaysian Ringgit	3.9875	−0.0170	4.8033	0.0054	5.3969	−0.0218
Mexico	Mexican Peson	19.3300	0.0771	23.2849	0.2171	26.1623	0.1103
New Zealand	New Zealand Dollar	1.3813	−0.0074	1.6639	0.0001	1.8695	−0.0096
Nigeria	Nigerian Naira	360.0000	–	433.6566	2.3225	487.2437	0.1121
Norway	Norwegian Krone	8.0193	−0.0397	9.6600	0.0042	10.8537	−0.0512
Pakistan	Pakistani Rupee	110.5050	–	133.1145	0.7129	149.5635	0.0344
Peru	Peruvian Nuevo Sol	3.2173	−0.0042	3.8755	0.0157	4.3544	−0.0047
Philippines	Philippine Peso	50.3925	0.0075	60.7029	0.3341	68.2040	0.0258
Poland	Polish Zloty	3.4641	−0.0216	4.1728	−0.0036	4.6884	−0.0282
Romania	Romanian Leu	3.8534	−0.0186	4.6418	0.0025	5.2153	−0.0240
Russia	Russian Ruble	56.6757	−0.2675	68.2716	0.0451	76.7079	−0.3443
Saudi Arabia	Saudi Riyal	3.7504	0.0001	4.5177	0.0243	5.0760	0.0013
Singapore	Singapore Dollar	1.3294	−0.0043	1.6014	0.0034	1.7993	−0.0054
South Africa	South African Rand	12.4338	−0.0100	14.9777	0.0682	16.8285	−0.0097
South Korea	South Korean Won	1072.0500	0.2500	1291.3932	7.2159	1450.9711	0.6719
Sweden	Swedish Krona	8.1346	−0.0474	9.7990	−0.0043	11.0099	−0.0615
Switzerland	Swiss Franc	0.9749	−0.0018	1.1744	0.0041	1.3196	−0.0021
Taiwan	New Taiwan Dollar	29.6045	0.0080	35.6616	0.2006	40.0683	0.0200
Thailand	Thai Baht	32.0000	−0.1400	38.5473	0.0387	43.3106	−0.1795
Tunisia	Tunisian Dinar	2.4833	0.0206	2.9914	0.0406	3.3610	0.0286
Turkey	Turkish Lira	3.7811	−0.0216	4.5547	−0.0015	5.1175	−0.0281
United Arab Emirates	UAE Dirham	3.6729	−0.0002	4.4244	0.0235	4.9711	0.0009
United Kingdom	Pound Sterling	0.7388	−0.0002	0.8900	0.0046	–	–
..One Month		0.7390	−0.0002	0.8899	0.0046	–	–
..Three Month		0.7393	−0.0002	0.8898	0.0046	–	–
..One Year		0.7408	−0.0002	0.8890	0.0046	–	–
United States	United States Dollar	–	–	1.2046	0.0065	1.3535	0.0003
..One Month		–	–	1.2044	−0.1485	1.3536	0.0003
..Three Month		–	–	1.2039	−0.1486	1.3539	0.0003
..One Year		–	–	1.2014	−0.1485	1.3554	0.0003
Venezuela	Venezuelan Bolivar Fuerte	10.4007	0.4307	12.5286	0.5831	14.0768	0.5860

▶

Exhibit 22.9 *(continued)*

Jan 11	Currency	DOLLAR		EURO		POUND	
		Closing Mid	Day's Change	Closing Mid	Day's Change	Closing Mid	Day's Change
Vietnam	Vietnamese Dong	22708.5000	−1.0000	27354.7667	145.3631	30734.9967	5.7612
European Union	Euro	0.8301	−0.0045	–	–	1.1236	−0.0058
..One Month		0.8299	−0.0045	–	–	1.1235	−0.0058
..Three Month		0.8295	−0.0045	–	–	1.1233	−0.0058
..One Year		0.8270	−0.0045	–	–	1.1225	−0.0058

The prices shown under the pound columns in Exhibit 22.9 are the middle price of the foreign currency in terms of £1 in London the previous afternoon.[2] So, for instance, the midprice of £1 for immediate delivery is 1.7190 Australian dollars. For the dollar columns the rate shown is the number of units of the other currency per US$1 – for example, 1.2537 Canadian dollars per US dollar. For the euro columns the rate shown is the number of units of the other currency per euro – for example the spot midrate against the pound is 89 pence per euro.

On Mondays the FT publishes a much more comprehensive list of exchange rates for over 200 countries, again with their values set against the dollar, euro, pound and yen.

Forward prices for the pound, dollar and euro are also given in the table. The first forward price (middle price) is given as the 'One month' rate. So you could commit yourself to the sale of a quantity of dollars for delivery in one month at a rate that is fixed at about US$1.3536 per pound. In this case you will need more US dollars to buy £1 in one month's time compared with the spot rate of exchange; therefore the dollar is at a *discount* on the one-month forward rate.

The forward rate for one month shows a different relationship with the spot rate for the euro against the US dollar. Here fewer dollars are required ($1.2044) to purchase a euro in one month's time compared with an 'immediate' spot purchase ($1.2046); therefore the dollar on one-month forward delivery is at a *premium* to the euro.

The *Financial Times* table lists quotations up to one year, but, as this is an over-the-counter market (*see* Chapter 21), you can go as far forward in time as you wish – provided you can find a counterparty. The use of forwards markets is widespread. For example, airline companies expecting to purchase planes many years hence may use this distant forward market to purchase the foreign currency they need to pay the manufacturer so that they know with certainty the quantity of their home currency they are required to find when the planes are delivered.

The table in Exhibit 22.9 displays standard periods of time for forward rates. These are instantly available and are frequently traded. However, forward rates are not confined to these particular days in the future. It is possible to obtain rates for any day in the future, say, 74 or 36 days hence, but this would require a specific quotation from a bank. One of the big advantages of forward contracts is that they are customisable.

---

2 The *Financial Times* (or rather, WM/Reuters) takes a representative sample of rates from major dealers in London at 4 pm.

Covering in the forward market

Suppose that on 11 January 2018 a UK exporter sells goods to a customer in France invoiced at €5,000,000. Payment is due three months later. With the spot rate of exchange at €1.1236/£ (*see* Exhibit 22.9) the exporter, in deciding to sell the goods, has in mind a sales price of:

Euros (EUR)	Rate (GBPEUR)	Sterling (GBP)
5,000,000	1.1236	4,449,982

The UK firm bases its decision on the profitability of the deal on this amount expressed in pounds.

However, the rate of exchange may vary between January and April: the size and direction of the move is uncertain. If sterling strengthens against the euro, and the rate is €1.20/£ the UK exporter makes a currency loss by waiting three months and exchanging the euro received into sterling at spot rates in April. The exporter will receive only £4,166,667, a loss of £283,315:

Euros	*Rate*	*Sterling*
5,000,000	1.1236	4,449,982
5,000,000	1.2000	4,166,667
Loss = 283,315		

If sterling weakens to, say, €1.00/£ a currency gain is made. £5 million is received in April, if the euros are exchanged at the April spot rate, a gain of £550,018.

Euros	*Rate*	*Sterling*
5,000,000	1.1236	4,449,982
5,000,000	1.0000	5,000,000
Gain = 550,018		

Rather than run the risk of a possible loss on the currency side of the deal the exporter may decide to cover in the forward market. Under this arrangement the exporter promises to sell €5,000,000 against sterling in three months (the agreement is made on 11 January 2018 for delivery of currency in April 2018). The forward rate available[3] on 11 January is 1.1233/£ (*see* Exhibit 22.9). This forward contract fixes the amount the exporter will receive (£4,451,171) in April regardless of the way in which spot exchange rates move over the three months.

In April the transactions shown in **Exhibit 22.10** take place.

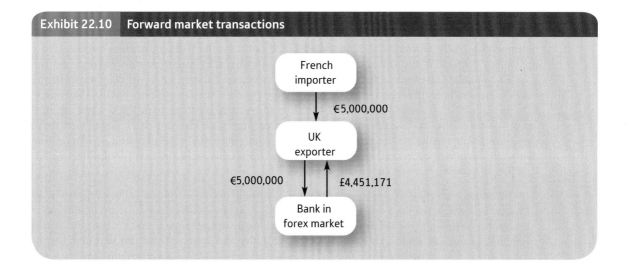

Exhibit 22.10   Forward market transactions

---

3 If we ignore the market makers' bid/offer spread and transaction costs.

From the outset (in January) the exporter fixed the amount to be received in April (assuming away counterparty risk). It might, with hindsight, have been better not to use the forward market but to exchange the euro in April at a more favourable spot rate of, say, €1/£. This would have resulted in a larger income for the firm, but, when the transaction occurred in January, there was uncertainty about the spot rate in April. If the spot rate in April had turned out to be €1.2/£ the exporter would have made much less. Covering in the forward market fixes the amount to be received which leads to greater certainty – and certainty has value. For many companies it is vital that they have this certainty about income and expenditure; they cannot afford to leave things and hope they will turn out satisfactorily.

Types of foreign-exchange risk

There are three types of currency risk for firms operating in an international marketplace:

- transaction risk;
- translation risk;
- economic risk.

Transaction risk

Transaction risk is the risk that cash flows from transactions already entered into, or for which the firm is likely to have a commitment in a foreign currency, will be different from expected in the home currency because of exchange-rate movements.

Transaction risk is primarily associated with imports or exports. If a company imports or exports goods on credit the amount it will pay out or receive in home-currency terms is uncertain due to changes in the exchange rate.

Transaction risk also arises when firms invest abroad, say, opening a new office or manufacturing plant. If the costs of construction are paid for over time, the firm may be exchanging home currency for foreign currency to make the payments. The amounts of the home currency required are uncertain – the amounts will change as the exchange rate changes. The cash inflows back to the parent are also subject to exchange-rate risk.

In addition, when companies borrow in a foreign currency, committing themselves to regular interest and principal payments in the foreign currency, they are exposed to forex risk.

Translation risk

Translation risk arises because financial data denominated in one currency are then reported in another currency. Between two accounting dates the figures can be affected by exchange-rate movements, greatly distorting comparability. The financial statements of overseas business units are usually translated into the home currency in order that they might be consolidated into the group's financial statements. Income, expenses, assets and liabilities have to be restated in the home currency. Note that this is purely a paper-based exercise; it is translation and not the conversion of real money from one currency to another. If exchange rates were stable, comparing subsidiary performance and asset position would be straightforward. However, if exchange rates move significantly the results can be severely distorted. When the Euro crisis occurred in 2012, many companies were very concerned about the possibility of the collapse of the Euro. *See* **Exhibit 22.11**.

There are two elements to translation risk.

1 *The balance sheet effect* Assets and liabilities denominated in a foreign currency fluctuate in value in home-currency terms with forex-market changes. For example, if a UK company acquires A$1,000,000 of assets in Australia when the rate of exchange is A$1.8/£ this can go into the UK group's accounts at a value of £555,556. If, over the course of the next year, the Australian dollar falls against sterling to A$2.0/£, when the consolidated accounts are drawn up and the asset is translated at the exchange rate at the end of the year it is valued at only £500,000 (1,000,000/2.0), a 'loss' of £55,556. And yet the asset has not changed in value in A$ terms. These 'losses' are unrealised or paper losses and are normally dealt with through balance sheet reserves.

Exhibit 22.11

Currencies: Companies make plans in case the euro collapses

By Andrea Felsted

Businesses trading internationally have long had to deal with currency fluctuations. But with the crisis in the eurozone, concern has moved from the impact of currency movements to what would happen if the single currency itself were to collapse. Companies including Diageo, the drinks maker, Tesco, the world's third-biggest supermarket chain by sales, Schroders, the UK fund manager and Siemens, the German engineering group, have all been making contingency plans.

At the end of last year, Tesco said it was holding off entering long-term contracts or placing big orders until there was more certainty in the zone. "Any business has to take seriously the disruption in the eurozone," Laurie McIlwee, Tesco's finance director said in December, when fears were particularly acute. Car manufacturers, energy groups, consumer goods companies and other multinationals have also taken actions to minimise risk, placing cash reserves in safe places and controlling non-essential expenditure. Siemens even established its own bank in order to deposit funds with the European Central Bank.

Vivian Pereira, a banking and capital markets partner at Deloitte, the consultancy, says companies tend to protect themselves against "transaction risk", where they have entered into a contract and there is a risk of exchange rates moving unfavourably before the final amount is settled. Companies also protect themselves against "translation risk", whereby exchange rate movements could adversely affect the financial statements of foreign subsidiaries when they are translated at group level. Typically, derivative contracts are used to provide this type of protection.

2 *The profit and loss account effect* Currency changes can have an adverse impact on the group's profits because of the translation of foreign subsidiaries' profits. This often occurs even though the subsidiaries' managers are performing well and increasing profit in terms of the currency in which they operate. As reported by Puma in Exhibit 22.1 local sales in regions grew at between 8% and 14% but profit reported in home currency fell by 42%, primarily due to currency movements.

Economic risk

A company's economic value may decline as a result of forex movements causing a loss in competitive strength. The worth of a company is the discounted cash flows payable to the owners. It is possible that a shift in exchange rates can reduce the cash flows of foreign subsidiaries and home-based production far into the future (and not just affect the near future cash flows as in transaction exposure). There are two ways in which competitive position can be undermined by forex changes:

● *Directly* If your firm's home currency strengthens then foreign competitors can gain sales and profits at your expense because your products are more expensive (or you have reduced margins) in the eyes of customers both abroad and at home.

● *Indirectly* Even if your home currency does not move adversely vis-à-vis your customer's currency you can lose competitive position. For example, suppose a South African firm is selling into Hong Kong and its main competitor is a New Zealand firm. If the New Zealand dollar weakens against the Hong Kong dollar the South African firm has lost some competitive position. Swiss watch manufacturers are hoping for a boost to sales from a weaker Swiss franc – *see* **Exhibit 22.12**.

Exhibit 22.12

Swiss franc's fall buoys embattled watchmakers

By Ralph Atkins

For Swiss watchmakers, the timing has been perfect. Just when support was needed for a nascent recovery in the watches and jewellery sector, it arrived — in the form of a weaker Swiss franc. The currency's recent depreciation — from 1.08 against the euro in mid-June to 1.14 at the end of August — has boosted hopes that sales of Swiss-made timepieces will catch up with the broader recovery in the global luxury goods industry.

"The franc's weakness has been only against the euro — so it's a Europe story," says René Weber, analyst at private bank Vontobel in Zurich. "But Europe is an important market, accounting for about a third of Swiss watch exports, and the weaker currency will boost profit margins."

Signs of a turnround in luxury watches have gathered since earlier this year. Always among the most optimistic in the sector, Nick Hayek, chief executive of the Swatch Group, told the Financial Times in July that his factories were running at "maximum capacity", with the "most aggressive growth" in the group's high-end luxury brands such as Omega and Blancpain. Swiss rival Richemont, the group behind brands such as Cartier and Montblanc, has remained cautious. Johann Rupert, the group's wealthy founder, said in May that "volatility and uncertainty" were "likely to prevail". But figures published by the Federation of the Swiss Watch Industry showed exports increased year-on-year for a third consecutive month in July, when they were 3.6 per cent higher than in July 2016.

The highlight this year has been the strong improvement in exports to mainland China — which were 22 per cent higher in seven months to July than a year earlier. That has reinforced the view among analysts that Chinese consumer spending will determine long-term growth trends in the sector. In contrast, the US has remained a difficult market — exports there were down 4.8 per cent over the same period, probably reflecting the impact of smartwatches, especially on sales of lower-end mechanical timepieces.

A weaker Swiss franc should give further support to a turnround, following sharp falls in sales in recent years. On top of sluggish global economic growth, a glut of unsold stock in Hong Kong shops and a clampdown on Chinese "gifting", Switzerland's watchmakers have in the past few years suffered from the country's role as a haven for investors at times of financial turmoil.

In January 2015, the Swiss National Bank gave up trying to cap the franc's value against the euro. The currency's sudden appreciation against the euro and dollar made Swiss watches much more expensive to produce and buy. Back then, Mr Hayek warned the SNB's action had created "a tsunami for the export industry". The Swiss franc weakened a little subsequently, but remained a significant drag on sales.

Since July, however, the currency's decline against the euro has accelerated, falling to levels not seen since January 2015. The reason is mounting expectations that the European Central Bank will soon start withdrawing its exceptional stimulus measures to boost eurozone economic growth and ward off deflation threats. As the euro strengthens, the price of Swiss watches should become more attractive to consumers in other countries. Some 69 per cent of exported Swiss watches are paid for in francs, according to calculations by Credit Suisse, based on 2015 data. Still, Swiss watchmakers remain cautious. The process of European monetary policy "normalisation" is likely to be slow. Even at the current rate, the Swiss franc "remains clearly and strongly overvalued, at a totally exaggerated level", a Swatch Group spokesman says.

While the franc's weakness against the euro was good news for Swatch and Richemont, given much of their fixed cost base was priced in francs, "it remains well above historical levels, in particular levels seen during the watch industry boom of 2003 to 2007," says Thomas Chauvet, analyst at Citigroup. Mr Chauvet adds: "As far as the US dollar is concerned, which is particularly relevant to Hong Kong and Asian markets, it has actually depreciated against the Swiss franc year-to-date and is back to year-ago levels."

Swiss watch sales are less responsive to currency movements than other products — they are sold on quality rather than price. What could be more significant in driving sales growth is the spending power of Chinese consumers. Growth of nearly 10 per cent in arrivals of Chinese tourists in Switzerland so far this year was "more important" than the franc's weakness, says Mr Weber. "Maybe four or five years ago, they would buy four or five watches. Nowadays, because of border controls, they buy only one, which they wear on their wrist — but a year ago, Chinese tourist arrivals were down sharply."

Another indirect effect occurs even for firms which are entirely domestically oriented. For example, the cafés and shops surrounding a large export-oriented manufacturing plant may be severely affected by the closure of the factory due to an adverse forex movement.

Transaction risk strategies

This section illustrates a number of strategies available to deal with transaction risk by focusing on the alternatives open to an exporter selling goods on credit.

Suppose a UK company exports £1,290,000 of goods to a Canadian firm when the spot rate of exchange is C$1.7054/£, a payable of C$2,200,000 is created. The Canadian firm is given three months to pay, and naturally the spot rate in three months is unknown at the time of the shipment of goods. The UK firm does not know how much it will actually receive in £. What can the firm do?

Invoice the customer in the home currency

One easy way to bypass exchange-rate risk is to insist that all transactions are in your home currency: foreign customers pay in your home currency and your firm pays all suppliers in your home currency. In this example, the Canadian importer will be required to pay £1m in three months.

However, the exchange rate risk has not gone away; it has just been passed on to the customer. This policy has an obvious drawback: your customer may dislike it, the marketability of your products is reduced and your customers look elsewhere for supplies. If you are a monopoly supplier you might get away with the policy but for most firms this is a not possible due to competition.

Do nothing

Under this policy the UK firm invoices the Canadian firm for C$2.2m, waits three months and then exchanges into sterling at whatever spot rate is available then. Perhaps an exchange-rate gain will be made; perhaps a loss will be made. Many firms adopt this policy and take a 'win some, lose some' attitude. Given the fees and other transaction costs of some hedging strategies this can make sense.

There are two considerations for managers here. The first is their degree of risk aversion to higher cash flow variability, coupled with the sensitivity of shareholders to reported fluctuations of earnings due to foreign exchange gains and losses. The second, which is related to the first point, is the size of the transaction. If £1.29 m is a large proportion of annual turnover, and greater than profit, then the managers may be more worried about forex risk. If, however, £1.29 m is a small fraction of turnover and profit, and the firm has numerous forex transactions, it may choose to save on hedging costs. There is an argument that it would be acceptable to do nothing if it was anticipated that the Canadian dollar will appreciate over the three months. Be careful. Predicting exchange rates is a dangerous game and more than one 'expert' has made serious errors of judgement.

Netting

Multinational companies often have subsidiaries in different countries selling to other members of the group. Netting is where the subsidiaries settle intra-group currency debts for the net amount owed in a currency rather than the gross amount. For example, if a UK parent owned a subsidiary in Canada and sold C$2.2m of goods to the subsidiary on credit while the Canadian subsidiary is owed C$1.5m by the UK company, instead of transferring a total of C$3.7m the intra-group transfer is the net amount of C$700,000 (*see* **Exhibit 22.13**).

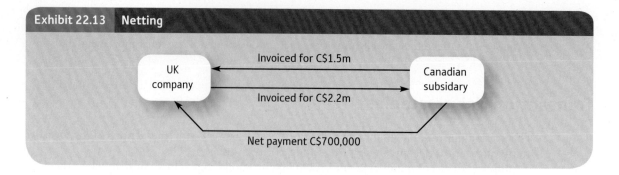

Exhibit 22.13   Netting

UK company → Invoiced for C$1.5m → Canadian subsidary
UK company → Invoiced for C$2.2m → Canadian subsidary
Net payment C$700,000

The reduction in the size of the currency flows by offsetting inflows and outflows in the same currency diminishes the net exposure to currency risk which may have to be hedged. It also reduces the transaction costs of currency transfers in terms of fees and commissions.

This type of netting, involving two companies within a group, is referred to as bilateral netting, and is simple to operate without the intervention of a central treasury. However, for organisations with a matrix of currency liabilities between numerous subsidiaries in different parts of the world, multilateral netting is required. A central treasury is usually needed so that there is knowledge at any particular time of the overall exposure of the firm and its component parts. Subsidiaries will be required to inform the central group treasury about their overseas dealings and the central group treasury then co-ordinates payments after netting out intra-company debts. The savings on transfer costs levied by banks can be considerable.

Matching

Netting only applies to transfers within a group of companies. Matching can be used for both intra-group transactions and those involving third parties. The company matches the inflows and outflows in different currencies caused by trade, etc., so that it is only necessary to deal on the forex markets for the unmatched portion of the total transactions.

So if, say, the Canadian importer is not a group company and the UK firm also imported a raw material from another Canadian company to the value of C$2m it is necessary only to hedge the balance of C$200,000 (*see* **Exhibit 22.14**).

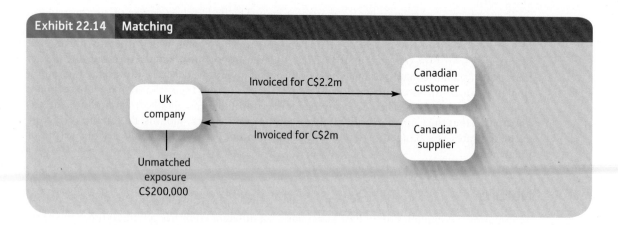

Exhibit 22.14   Matching

UK company → Invoiced for C$2.2m → Canadian customer
UK company ← Invoiced for C$2m ← Canadian supplier
Unmatched exposure C$200,000

Naturally, to net and match properly, the timing of the expected receipts and payments would have to be the same.

Leading and lagging

Leading is paying early: bringing forward, from the original due date, the payment of a debt. Lagging is the postponement of a payment beyond the due date. This speeding up or delaying of payments is particularly useful if you are convinced exchange rates will shift significantly between now and the due date. However, it is very difficult to accurately predict exchange rate movements.

If the UK exporter, which has invoiced a Canadian company for C$2.2m on three months' credit, expects that the Canadian dollar will fall over the forthcoming three months, it may try to obtain payment immediately and then exchange for sterling at the spot rate. Naturally the Canadian firm will need an incentive to pay early and this may be achieved by offering a discount for immediate settlement.

An importer of goods with an obligation to pay in a currency which is anticipated to fall in value may attempt to delay payment as long as possible. This may be achieved either by agreement or by exceeding credit terms.

Forward market hedge

Although other forms of exchange-risk management are available, forward cover represents the most frequently employed method of hedging. A contract is agreed, usually with a bank, to exchange two currencies at a fixed time in the future at a predetermined rate. The exchange rate is now fixed and so the risk of forex variation is removed.

So if the three-month forward rate is C$1.7084/£ the UK exporter could lock in the receipt of £ 1,287,755 in three months by selling forward C$2.2m.

CAD	Rate	GBP
2,200,000	1.7084	1,287,755

No foreign exchange-rate risk now exists because the dollars to be received from the importer are matched by the funds to be exchanged for sterling. (There does remain the risk of the importer not paying, at all or on time, and the risk of the counterparty in the forex market not fulfilling its obligations.)

Sterling had been weak since the Brexit vote in June 2016. A strengthening of the pound, in autumn 2017, saw some companies taking out forward contracts to lock in the higher sterling rates. As Brexit negotiations continued, further volatility in the value of the pound was expected – *see* **Exhibit 22.15**.

Exhibit 22.15

Firmer pound sparks greater demand for hedging

Retailers and food companies among those buying insurance against sterling's moves

By Roger Blitz

A rebound in the pound has spurred a rush among businesses, funds and individuals to buy insurance against a future bout of weakness in the currency as uncertainty clouds Brexit negotiations. Currency advisers are reporting a sharp take-up in hedging demand for the US dollar, euro and Poland's zloty against the pound from clients, taking advantage of recent strength in sterling.

The pound has been buoyed as the Bank of England has stepped up warnings about the possibility of interest rate rises and sits near $1.36, its firmest level since the June 2016 EU referendum. For importers, the ever-present danger since Brexit has been how to cope with rising costs, which invariably forces them to consider increasing prices. The rebound in sterling since June therefore opens the

▶

Exhibit 22.15 *(continued)*

opportunity of shoring up companies' revenues by locking in the pound's exchange rate over a chosen period of time.

"We are seeing people really getting their act together quite quickly," said James Stretton of forex risk manager JCRA, naming general retailers, food companies and importers among those taking out insurance against sterling moves for durations averaging 12 months. He noted a preference for sterling hedges versus the dollar, the euro and zloty.

Sterling remains near recent peaks, but the currency came under pressure at the end of last week when Moody's lowered the UK's credit rating. James Wood-Collins, at Record Currency Management, said the uptick in strategic hedging in recent weeks has "more to do with sterling's performance during the past few months reminding unhedged investors of the risks they face by not hedging their currency exposure". When they balance all the factors of where sterling might go, they conclude that it's better than it was and may be as good as it's going to get.

James Stretton at JCRA Moneycorp, the forex operator, said the pound's rise was coinciding with the expiry of businesses' pre-referendum hedges, which was forcing them to confront the effect of sterling's devaluation on the cost of their imports. This combination "has prompted many businesses to take out forward contracts before they budget for the year ahead", said Mark Horgan, chief executive of Moneycorp. In the week ending September 15, clients bought the dollar at close to five times the amount purchased in the same week last year, while euro buying was nearly 60% higher. "We've seen particularly high activity off the back of the sterling-dollar rate and some businesses are committing to longer timeframes to lock in this value over an extended period," said Mr Horgan.

Given the rebound in the UK currency, some euro-denominated funds with plans to sell UK assets are taking out hedges ahead of those exits, said JCRA's Mr Stretton, while others are considering whether now is the time to bring forward those proposed asset sales. "When they balance all the factors of where sterling might go, they conclude that it's better than it was and may be as good as it's going to get," Mr Stretton said.

Money market hedge

Money market hedging involves borrowing and investing in the money markets. If your company has a future foreign asset (a receivable) due in three months, you create a future foreign liability in the money markets to match to it. You borrow today in the foreign currency; the amount borrowed today is calculated to match (principal and interest) the receivable due in three months. The borrowed foreign currency is exchanged into the home currency today at the known spot rate and then invested at home at a today's known home interest rate for three months, i.e. until the foreign receivable arrives. The spot rate and the home interest rate are all known today, so you know today how much this will be worth in three months in the home currency. When the foreign receivable arrives, you use the foreign receivable to clear the foreign liability. Your company can then keep the invested home currency. The uncertainty is removed; you know today how much home currency you are going to have in three months, thus forex risk is removed.

If the interest rate charged over three months is 2% then the appropriate size of the loan is:

	Borrow today CAD	Interest rate	Receivable in 3 months CAD
Company has receivable in 3 months			2,200,000
Company creates liability today which will equate to receivable value at end of 3 months	2,156,863	2% for 3 months 2200000/1.02	2,200,000

Thus the exporter has created a liability (borrowed funds) which matches the asset (receivable from Canadian firm).

The borrowed dollars are then converted to sterling on the spot market for the exporter to receive £1,264,725 immediately:

Exchange transaction

Canadian funds borrowed	CAD 2,156,863
Exchange rate	GBPCAD 1.7054
UK funds now available	GBP 1,264,725

The exporter has removed forex risk because it now holds cash in sterling. It can use this cash now, or it can invest that cash in the UK and receive interest. The company may not want to spend the money yet in case the customer does not pay their debt and the UK funds are needed to clear the Canadian borrowing. Equally the company could pay down UK loans, thus saving interest, or could invest in company projects and get a return greater than WACC.

Three months later C$2.2m is received from the importer and this exactly matches the outstanding Canadian debt:

Amount borrowed + Interest = Debt owed at end of period

CAD 2,156,863 + (CAD 2,156,863 × 0.02) = CAD 2.2m

The receipt of £1,264,725 is £25,275 less than the GBP1,290,000 (CAD2.2m/1.7054) originally anticipated. However, it is received three months earlier and can earn interest, giving GBP 1,283,696

	Invest today *GBP*	*Interest rate* *1.5%*	*Available in 3* *months GBP*
Company has asset in GBP	GBP 1,264,725	1,264,725 × 1.015	1,283,696

Note that if the funds are invested for three months the sterling funds at three months are very similar whether a forward contract or a money market hedge is used – this is due to the link between forward rates and interest rates which will be discussed further later in this chapter.

The steps in the money market hedge are as follows:

1   Invoice Canadian customer for CAD2.2m.

2   Borrow CAD2,156,863.

3   Sell CAD2,156,863 at spot to receive pounds now – can be invested to earn interest.

4   In three months receive CAD2.2m from customer.

5   Clear total liability (principal and interest) by paying lender CAD2.2m.

An importer could also use a money market hedge. A Swiss company importing Japanese cars for payment in yen in three months has a future foreign liability. The Swiss company creates a future foreign asset (an investment in yen) to match and clear this future foreign liability. The Swiss company borrows in Swiss francs now, converts the funds at the spot rate into yen and invests these. The yen is deposited to earn interest so that, after three months, the principal plus interest invested in yen equals the yen liability – the invoice amount. By investing today, using Swiss francs, the company has fixed how much it will pay in Swiss francs and so has no further forex risk.

Futures hedge

A foreign currency futures contract is an agreement to exchange a specific amount of a currency for another at a fixed future date for a predetermined price. Futures are similar to forwards in many ways. They are, however, standardised contracts traded on regulated exchanges. Forwards are normally contracts with a bank, although they can be negotiated with other counterparties, and can be tailor-made in a wide range of currencies as to quantity of currency and delivery date. Futures are standardised and are exchange traded and so are only available in the limited, but rapidly growing, range of currencies offered by the exchange and for specified forward time periods. The vast majority of futures market trading in currencies is through the CME Group (CME) and the Intercontinental Exchange (ICE) group.

A single futures contract is for a fixed amount of currency. For example, a sterling contract is for £62,500; a euro contract for €125,000. It is not possible to transact in quantities other than whole-number multiples of these contract sizes. E-micro forex futures contracts are exchange-traded currency futures contracts that are one-tenth the size of the traditional currency futures contracts. All futures are to swap the currency of the futures contract for US dollars and the futures are priced in dollars.

To buy a sterling futures contract is to make a commitment to deliver a quantity of US dollars and receive in return £62,500.

On 22 December 2014 the CME and New York Board Of Trade (NYBOT) quoted contracts (www.ft.com) for delivery in March and June 2015 (and for no months in between)[4] – *see* **Exhibit 22.16**. For example, the June contract for euros and US$ was priced at 1.2241 at the end of the trading day. The 'Open' column indicates the rate at the start of trading on, the 'Sett' column indicates closing prices. This means that if you *buy* one contract you are committed to delivering US$1.2241 for every euro of the €125,000 you will receive in late June, which is US$153,013. If you *sold* one contract at 1.2241 you would deliver €125,000 and receive US$153,013.

Exhibit 22.16	Currency futures							
Dec 22		**Open**	**Sett**	**Change**	**High**	**Low**	**Est. vol**	**Open int**
$-Can$†	MAR5	0.8597	0.8573	−0.0029	0.8621	0.8571	28,917	90,756
$-Euro€†	MAR5	1.2231	1.2230	−0.0005	1.2281	1.2226	93,918	370,678
$-Euro€†	JUN5	1.2242	1.2241	−0.0005	1.2291	1.2238	112	2,482
$-Sw Franc†	MAR5	1.0175	1.0172	−0.0004	1.0214	1.0169	21,867	53,636
$-Yen†	MAR5	0.8372	0.8342	−0.0031	0.8387	0.8331	63,173	223,169
$-Yen†	JUN5	0.8386	0.8351	−0.0031	0.8395	0.8348	24	1,970
$-Ster-ling†	JUN5	1.5603	1.5572	−0.0040	1.5639	1.5555	1	160
$-Aust$†	MAR5	0.8085	0.8088	−0.0007	0.8124	0.8079	34,428	116,175
$-Mex Peso†	MAR5	68150	68060	−90.000	68,380	67,850	16,761	132,384

Sources: *NYBOT; Sterling €100,000 and Yen: €100,000. †CME: Australian $: A$100,000, Canadian $: C$100,000, Euro: €125,000; Mexican Peso: 500,000, Swiss Franc: SFr125,000; Yen: ¥12,5m ($ per ¥100); Sterling: £62,500. CME volume, high & low for pit & electronic trading at settlement. Contracts shown are based on the volumes traded in 2004.

Hedging with futures is a parallel transaction to the underlying operational cash flow and the company will hope to make a profit in the futures market to counteract any loss in the operational world. One of the downsides of futures is that the company also has to accept the opposite impact – that any gain made in the operational world may be offset by a loss on the futures contract. However many financial officers are prepared to accept this limitation on upside in return for the downside protection.

A firm hedging with currency futures will usually attempt to have a futures position that has an equal and opposite profit profile to the underlying transaction. Frequently the futures position

---

4 The CME and NYBOT trade other months than those shown by the *Financial Times,* but these are usually at three-month intervals. Delivery for traditional futures contracts is on the third Wednesday of the delivery month.

will be closed before delivery is due, to give a cash profit or loss to offset the spot market profit or loss (for more details on futures *see* Chapter 21) – although physical delivery of the currency is possible. The company 'closes out' before expiry of the future by making an equal but opposite transaction to the original transaction so, if it bought 10 Euro futures contracts originally, it would sell 10 Euro futures contracts to close out and leave the market.

If a US firm exported €125,000 worth of goods to a German firm on 22 December 2014 on credit for payment in late March and the spot exchange rate at that date was US$1.2258/€ there is a foreign exchange risk. If the March future was trading at a price of US$1.2230 per euro the exporter's position could be hedged by selling one euro futures contract on CME.

If in March the dollar strengthens against the euro to US$1.0644/€ the calculation is:

Value of €125,000 received from customer when converted to $ at spot in March (€125,000 × 1.0644)	US$133,050
Amount if exchange rate was constant at US$1.2258/€	US$153,225
Forex loss	US$20,175

However, an offsetting gain is made on the futures contract:

Sold at US$1.2230/€ (€125,000 × 1.2230)	US$152,875
Bought in March to close position at US$1.0644/€ (€125,000 × 1.0644)	US$133,050
Futures gain	US$19,825

Alternatively the exporter could simply deliver the €125,000 received from the importer to CME in return for US$152,875.

(Note that the futures contract rate of exchange in March converges with the spot rate at the date of expiry, in late March, i.e. US$1.0644/€.)

In the above example a perfect hedge was not achieved because the gain on the futures contract did not exactly offset the loss on the underlying position. Perfect hedging is frequently unobtainable with futures because of their standardised nature. Perhaps the amount needed to be hedged is not equal to a whole number of contracts, for example €125,000, or the underlying transaction takes place in a month when no future is available.

Currency option hedge

The final possible course of action to reduce forex transaction risk to be discussed in this chapter is to make use of the currency option market.

A currency option is a contract giving the buyer (that is, the holder) the right, but not the obligation, to buy or sell a specific amount of currency at a specific exchange rate (the strike price), on or before a specified future date.[5]

A **call** option gives the right to **buy** a particular currency.
A **put** option gives the right to **sell** a particular currency.

The option writer (usually a bank) guarantees, if the option buyer chooses to exercise the right, to exchange the currency at the predetermined rate. Because the writer is accepting risk the buyer must pay a premium to the writer – normally within two business days of the option purchase. An option is more like an insurance product where you pay a premium and only use the option if the market moves against you. (For more details on options *see* Chapter 21.)

Currency options premiums are shown for the currency rates between the US$ and the UK pound in **Exhibit 22.17**. This data is taken from the website of the CME on 15 January 2018 as trading is taking place. For the US$/UK£ or GBPUSD call options the purchaser has the right but not the obligation to purchase pounds for dollars. The potential call option buyer has a number

---

5 With some currency options the exercise can take place at any time up to the expiry date, rather than only on the expiry date.

| Exhibit 22.17 | Options on British Pound Futures (Underlying Future – March 2018), quoted on 15 January 2018 |

Premium-Quoted European Option Expiring March 2018

	Calls			Puts	
Volume	Last (premium)	Strike price	Last (premium)	Volume
0		13600	0.0073	177
16	0.0230	13650	0.0091	54
49	0.0197	13700	0.0099	5
5	0.0185	13750		0
50	0.0169	13800		0
121	0.0141	13850	0.0163	21
65	0.0119	13900	0.0195	8
28	0.0079	13950		0
45	0.0070	14000		0

of possible rates of exchange open to him/herself. The exhibit shows strike prices of $1.36/£ to $1.40/£ in the central column. The premium payable, shown for calls in the second column and for puts in in the fourth column, are quoted as US dollars per pound and are paid, in dollars, when the contract is entered into. One contract is for £62,500, and only whole numbers of contracts can be purchased on the exchange. If you purchased a 13850 call option, the highest volume strike price, for expiry in March you would pay a premium of $0.0141 per £ or 1.41US cents per UK pound (the total premium payable would be $0.0141 × 62,500 = $881.25) giving you the right to buy pounds with dollars in March 2018 at a rate of $1.3850/£. Note that a less favourable exchange rate, e.g. 14000 ($1.4000/£) – you are always going to get £62,500 but you will need to pay more dollars to get those pounds – commands a lower premium, only 0.7 cents per pound under the contract.

The purchase of a put option gives you the right but not the obligation to sell pounds and receive dollars. Again, the quantity of a contract is for £62,500. From the volume columns you can see which options are being traded more regularly – puts at 13600 and calls at 13850. The underlying March 2018 future was trading at 1.3801. Companies often have to balance the protection from the option with the cost of the upfront premium.

The crucial advantage an option has over a forward is the absence of an obligation to buy or sell. It is the option buyer's decision whether to insist on exchange at the strike rate or to let the option lapse. This means the buyer gets protection from the downside risk but is able to take advantage of a favourable exchange rate movement.

With a forward contract you have entered into a contract and so you are locked in. There is a hedge against both a favourable and an unfavourable movement in forex rates but you have to deliver against the contract. This means that if the exchange rate happens to move in your favour after you are committed to a forward contract you cannot take any advantage of that movement. We saw above that if the forward rate was C$1.7084/£ the exporter would receive £1,287,755 in three months. If the spot exchange rate had moved to, say, C$1.65/£ over the three months the exporter would have liked to abandon the agreement to sell the dollars at C$1.7084/£, as the company would receive more money in the spot market, but is unable to do so because of the legal commitment. By abandoning the deal and exchanging at spot when the Canadian firm pays the exporter would receive an income of £1,333,333 a difference of £45,578.

CAD	Rate	GBP
2,200,000	1.7084	1,287,755
2,200,000	1.65	1,333,333
Difference		45,578

An option permits both:

– hedging against unfavourable currency movement; and

– profit from favourable currency movement.

Option contracts are generally for sums greater than US$1,000,000 on the OTC (over-the-counter) market (direct deals with banks) whereas one sterling contract on the CME exchange is for £62,500. The drawback with exchange-based derivatives is the smaller range of currencies available and the inability to tailor-make a hedging position. You can only hedge in multiples of the contract size. However they do reduce counterparty risk and have lower transaction costs than over-the-counter transactions.

It can be very difficult to determine the correct hedging strategy – as the case of Air Products illustrates in **Exhibit 22.18**.

Worked example 22.2   Currency option contract

The treasurer of the UK firm hedges by buying an over-the-counter three-month sterling call option giving the right but not the obligation to deliver Canadian dollars in exchange for pounds with a strike price of C$1.71/£ when the goods are delivered to the Canadian firm. To induce a bank to make the commitment to exchange at the option holder's behest a premium will need to be paid up front. Assume this is 2% of the amount covered, that is, a non-refundable 0.02 × C$2,200,000 = C$44,000 is payable two business days after the option deal is struck.[6]

Three months later

The dollars are delivered by the importer on the due date. The treasurer now has to decide whether or not to exercise the right to exchange those dollars for sterling at C$1.71/£. Let us consider two scenarios.

Scenario 1

The dollar has strengthened against the pound to C$1.69/£. If the treasurer exercises the right to exchange at C$1.71/£ the UK firm will receive £1,286,549. If the treasurer takes the alternative and lets the option lapse – 'abandons it' – and exchanges the dollars in the spot market, the amount received will be £1,301,775 – see the table below.

CAD	Rate	GBP
2,200,000	1.71	1,286,549
2,200,000	1.69	1,301,775
Benefit of allowing option to lapse		15,226

Clearly in this case the best course of action would be not to exercise the option, but to allow the option to lapse and exchange at the spot rate. Note that the benefit of this action is somewhat reduced by the earlier payment of C$44,000 for the premium, although that is a sunk cost and would not affect today's decision as to whether to exercise or allow the option to lapse.

Scenario 2

Now assume that the dollar has weakened against sterling to C$1.75/£. If the treasurer contacts the bank (the option writer) to confirm that the exporter wishes to exercise the option the treasurer will arrange delivery of C$2,200,000 to the bank and will receive the amount guaranteed under the option of £1,286,549 in return. The alternative, to abandon the option and sell the C$2.2m in the spot forex market, is unattractive as fewer pounds would be received.

With the option, the worst that could happen is that the exporter receives £1,286,549, less the premium. However the upside potential is unconstrained.

CAD	Rate	GBP
2,200,000	1.71	1,286,549
2,200,000	1.75	1,257,143
Advantage of exercising		29,406

(*Note*: It is possible to elect for cash settlement (i.e. profit if the market value is greater than exercise value) on the option rather than the physical exchange of the currencies.)

---

6 We are assuming in this example that over-the-counter options are written by a bank rather than exchange-based options on, say, the CME.

Exhibit 22.18

Choose the correct path for a viable deal

James Politi evaluates the options available to those implementing currency hedging strategies

In May 2002, Air Products & Chemicals came out with a sobering announcement. Because of opposition from regulators at the US Federal Trade Commission, the Pennsylvania-based industrials group would drop an $11.2bn deal to buy British rival BOC that it had sealed with France's Air Liquide a year earlier.

In addition to being forced to abandon a crucial strategic move, there was another reason for Air Products and its investors to be gloomy. A strong fluctuation in the dollar/pound exchange rate in previous months meant Air Products would have to take a charge of nearly $300m, mostly from losses on the currency hedge that the company had put in place for the BOC deal in January 2000.

The Air Products case illustrates the challenges facing corporate chiefs and investment banks as they study ways to manage foreign exchange risk during M&A deals. A tricky balance has to be struck between properly managing currency exposure, and not hedging so much that it underlines the economics of a deal.

Paul Huck, chief financial officer of Air Products, grappled with these issues. Speaking to the FT today, he believes his company had little choice but to put a hedge in place once it expected the BOC takeover to be approved.

'We still feel we did the right thing in hedging the transaction,' says Mr Huck. 'When you do M&A you worry about having the economics of a deal change because of currency movements, and we're not in the business of making currency bets.'

The trouble with the hedge put in place by Air Products – a mix of options and forward contracts – is that its structure may have been too optimistic. While forwards are less expensive than options because they carry no fee, they leave the company heavily exposed to a currency shift in the wrong direction if the deal does not close. Options, on the other hand, can be expensive, carrying hefty up-front fees.

However, if the currency moves in the wrong direction and the deal does not close, the company can simply let the options expire.

'If I had been willing to do this [use more options and less forwards] and pay higher premiums, it would have been very expensive, and might have hurt the deal [if the FTC had approved it],' says Mr Huck.

Hedging currency risk in M&A deals has become an increasingly popular product in the universe of risk management.

As global M&A volumes have grown, the markets for derivatives – the primary hedging instruments – have become increasingly liquid, banks have been able to match supply and demand on foreign exchange risk with a series of customised hedging packages (see above).

FX Option

A foreign exchange option gives the buyer of the option the right to purchase the currency at a specific price. The client would buy a call option to protect itself against a rising currency and would pay a premium for the option – typically in the range of 50–200 basis points (depending on the maturity and price of the strike). The most money one can lose on an option is the premium that one pays for it, which makes it a particularly good strategy for cross-border M&A. With an option you will always know how much you will spend on your hedge, which makes budgeting for the hedge relatively easy. An option is also a marketable asset and could be sold in the free market in the event the hedge needs to be liquidated. The only disadvantage of an option is its upfront cost.

Do Nothing

'Clients may adopt this strategy, particularly early in the M&A process, as the uncertainty surrounding deal completion can be significant,' says Leo Civitillo and Steve Zannetos at Morgan Stanley.

'When the deal progresses and the probability of completion increases, execution of a currency hedge is typically warranted. However, there may also be other considerations that drive a decision not to hedge, including a view on the market, the implied costs of hedging, and accounting considerations.

'The risk of remaining unhedged is that the currency could significantly move against the company and adversely affect the economics of the acquisition.'

Natural Hedge

'A natural hedge would essentially be issuing the debt for the acquisition in the target's local currency, which would negate the need for foreign exchange hedge', says Courtney McLaughlin, head of the foreign exchange capital markets group in the investment banking division at Credit Suisse, the Swiss bank.

'If the deal is signed and the currency appreciates, the acquirer will pay more for the business in dollar terms, but because they are issuing debt in the local currency market they are getting more (in dollar terms) for the debt they are issuing, thereby creating the natural hedge.'

FX Forward

'FX forwards are simply an obligation to exchange one currency or another at a specified rate on a future date,' say Mr Civitillo and Mr Zannetos at Morgan Stanley.

'We typically do not recommend that clients employ vanilla FX forwards to hedge the currency risk embedded in a cross-border transaction until we are absolutely certain that the deal will close. The reason is that the potential breakage or unwind cost

of an FX forward can be significant, if the underlying transaction does not close as expected. However, assuming that all of the deal risks have passed, forward contracts can be a very efficient and cost effective way to lock-in the price of a foreign asset.'

Deal-Contingent FWD

A deal-contingent forward is similar to a vanilla forward with two key differences: the ability of the client to walk away from the contract if the deal is not consummated, and its price. A deal-contingent forward allows a client to exchange one currency for another at a specified rate on a future date. The client would define contingencies that, if met, would allow the client to walk away from the forward with no cost or obligation. Typical contingencies are: material adverse change clauses, shareholder approvals and regulatory approvals. A deal-contingent forward has an implicit cost that is paid for by striking the forward rate slightly off market. It allows the client to enjoy the efficiency of a forward without the out-of-pocket cost of an option.

FT   *Financial Times,* 25 January 2007, p. 2.
All Rights Reserved.

Managing translation risk

The effect of translation risk on the balance sheet can be lessened by matching the currency of assets and liabilities. For example, Graft plc has decided to go ahead with a US$135m project in the USA. One way of financing this is to borrow £100m and exchange this for dollars at the current exchange rate of US$1.35/£. Thus at the beginning of the year the additional entries into the consolidated accounts are as shown in Worked example 22.3.

Worked example 22.3	Translation risk

Opening balance sheet

	Liabilities			Assets	
Loan		£100m	US assets		£100m

The US$135m of US assets are translated at US$1.35/£ so all figures are expressed in the parent company's currency.

Now imagine that over the course of the next year the dollar depreciates against sterling to US$1.50/£. In the consolidated group accounts there is still a £100m loan but the asset bought with that loan, while still worth US$135m,[7] is valued at only £90m (US$135/1.50) when translated into sterling. In the parent company's currency terms, £10m needs to be written off:

▶

7 Assuming, for the sake of simplicity, no diminution of asset value in dollar terms.

Worked Example 22.3 *(continued)*

Year-end balance sheet

Liabilities		Assets	
Loan	£100m	US assets	£90m
	£100m		£90m
Forex loss	£10m		

Alternatively Graft plc could finance its dollar assets by obtaining a US$135m loan. Thus, when the dollar depreciates, both the asset value and the liability value in translated sterling terms reduce.

Opening balance sheet

Liabilities		Assets	
Loan	£100m	US assets	£100m

If forex rates move to US$1.50/£:

Year-end balance sheet

Liabilities		Assets	
Loan	£90m	US assets	£90m

There is no currency loss to deal with.

One constraint on the solution set out in Worked example 22.3 is that some governments insist that a proportion of assets acquired within their countries is financed by the parent firm. Another constraint is that the financial markets in some countries are insufficiently developed to permit large-scale borrowing.

Many economists and corporate managers believe that translation hedging is unnecessary because, on average over a period of time, gains and losses from forex movements will even out to be zero.

Managing economic risk

Economic exposure is concerned with the long-term effects of forex movements on the firm's ability to compete and add value. These effects are very difficult to estimate in advance, given their long-term nature, and therefore the hedging techniques described for transaction risk are of limited use. The forwards markets may be used to a certain extent, but these only extend for a short period for most currencies. Also the matching principle could be employed, whereby overseas assets are matched as far as possible by overseas liabilities.

The main method of insulating the firm from economic risk is to position the company in such a way as to maintain maximum flexibility – to be able to react to changes in forex rates which may be causing damage to the firm. Firms which are internationally diversified may have a greater degree of flexibility than those based in one or two markets. For example, a company with production facilities in numerous countries can shift output to those plants where the exchange rate change has been favourable. The international car assemblers have an advantage here over the purely domestic producer.

Forex changes can impact on the costs of raw materials and other inputs. By maintaining flexibility in sourcing supplies a firm could achieve a competitive advantage by deliberately planning its affairs so that it can switch suppliers quickly and cheaply.

An aware multinational could allow for forex changes when deciding in which countries to launch an advertising campaign. For example, it may be pointless increasing marketing spend in a country whose currency has depreciated rapidly recently, making the domestically produced competing product relatively cheap. It might be sensible to plan in advance the company's response to a forex movement with regard to the pricing of goods so that action can be rapid. For example, a UK company exporting to Norway at a time when sterling is on a rising trend can either keep the product at the same price in sterling terms to maintain profits and face the consequential potential loss of market share, or reduce the sterling price to maintain a constant price in kroner and thereby keep its market share. Being prepared may avert an erroneous knee-jerk decision.

The principle of contingency planning, to permit a quick reaction to forex changes, applies to many areas of the business operations, from production through marketing and raw material sourcing. This idea links with the notion of the real option described in Chapter 6. The option to switch sources of supply and output, or to change marketing focus, may have a high value. Despite the cost of creating an adaptable organisation, rather than a dedicated fixed one, the option to switch may be worth far more in an uncertain world.

Exhibit 22.19 describes the moves made by Weir to reduce their economic risk exposure.

Exhibit 22.19

Engineer Weir considers moving production to UK after Brexit

By Michael Pooler

Weir, the engineer, is examining whether to move production of some equipment from overseas to the UK to benefit from the weaker pound.

The UK company's Todmorden foundry in West Yorkshire casts metal components for heavy-duty pumps found in mines in countries including Chile, Finland and Russia, as well as in Canada's tar sands.

Before the UK's EU referendum, the site in the Calder Valley had already benefited from its status as one of the most cost-effective facilities run by the FTSE 250 group, with a significant manufacturing workload transferred there this year.

Jon Stanton, chief executive, said the lower exchange rate following the vote for Brexit would figure in calculations about whether more should follow.

"At the moment, it is all about how the demand profile develops from a European and global perspective. That will dictate how we potentially move some production there," he told the *Financial Times*.

"The weakening of sterling makes [the Todmorden] facility potentially more competitive and that will be a consideration as we think about production allocation."

Weir, which also makes pumps and valves for the energy industry, operates foundries in Australia, Brazil, Chile Malaysia and South Africa as well as the UK.

The prospect of manufacturing being "reshored" to Britain would be a boost from Brexit. While the pound's devaluation — it is down 10.5 per cent against a basket of trade-weighted currencies since the referendum result — should make British goods more competitive, so far the impact on the sector appears mixed.

Factory order books were at their most full for 20 months in the three months to December, according to a survey by the CBI employers' organisation. But the Office for National Statistics said there was only limited evidence that currency depreciation had boosted exports.

Mr Stanton said a sustained weaker pound would make Britain a "relatively more attractive" place to invest, balanced against any possible trade tariffs under a final Brexit settlement.

But he stressed this was not immediately shaping Weir's decisions: "At the moment I'm not saying I need to put more capital into the UK relative to anywhere else".

In his first formal interview since taking the helm in October after six years as finance director, he said his strategy would be one of "evolution rather than revolution".

This suggests a continuation of the path set out by Keith Cochrane, his predecessor who continued the company's expansion in part through a series of acquisitions.

After benefiting from the boom in global energy and mining production, the Scotland-based group has grappled with a downturn in both of its main markets in the past few years, as customers have slashed investment in response to the collapse in commodity prices.

▶

Worked Example 22.19 *(continued)*

This is particularly pronounced in Weir's oil and gas division, which is the largest provider of frac pumps to the North American shale industry. Group sales fell by more than a fifth in 2015 to £1.92bn, and the company recently warned profits would be lower than previously expected this year.

The downturn has also hit UK-listed peers such as IMI, Smiths Group and Rotork, which also supply the oil and gas sector.

Even so, Weir's management has been credited by analysts for navigating the storm with harsh cost-cutting measures, such as reducing its workforce by more than 10 per cent and closing plants.

Mr Stanton said there were "signs of recovery" in Weir's markets. The US oil rig count has risen, crude prices were "more supportive" and miners' profit margins had increased with the rebound in commodity prices, he said.

Investors seem to be pricing in an eventual upturn. Weir's share price has rallied 87 per cent this year, placing it among the top 10 performing stocks in the mid-cap index. But, trading at around £19, the shares remain below a peak of £28 before the crude price crash in 2014.

Some City analysts have queried whether the company's collection of businesses needs refining. Weir's third and smallest division provides flow control systems such as valves for industry.

Harry Phillips, analyst at Peel Hunt, said: "Can a portfolio contain two businesses [minerals and oil and gas] with such incredibly different cyclical profiles in an efficient manner? People would like to see. . . that core assumption retested".

Weir said it was on track to meet a target of £100m from disposals this year. Asked whether there would be further sales next year, Mr Stanton said he did not "see anything in the wings".

Exchange-rate determination

A number of factors influence the rate of exchange between currencies. This section briefly considers some of them.

Purchasing power parity

The theory of purchasing power parity (PPP) is based on the 'law of one price' – the idea that a basket of goods should cost the same regardless of the currency in which it is sold. For example, if a basket of goods sold for £10,000 in the UK and an identical 'basket' sold for US$15,000 in the USA then the rate of exchange should be US$1.50/£. Imagine what would happen if this were not the case; say, for example, the rate of exchange was US$3.00/£. Now British consumers can buy a basket of goods in the US market for half the price they would pay in the UK market (£5,000 can be exchanged for US$15,000). Naturally the demand for dollars would rise as UK consumers rushed out of sterling to buy dollars. This would cause the forex rates to change – the dollar would rise in value until the purchasing power of each currency was brought to an equilibrium, that is, where there is no incentive to exchange currencies to take advantage of lower prices abroad because of a misaligned exchange rate.

The definition of PPP is:

> Exchange rates will be in equilibrium when their domestic purchasing powers at that rate of exchange are equivalent.

So, for example:

Price of a basket of goods in UK in sterling	×	US$/£ exchange rate	=	Price of a basket of goods in USA in dollars
£10,000	×	1.50	=	US$15,000

The PPP theory becomes more interesting if relationships over a period of time are examined. Inflation in each country will affect the price of a basket of goods in domestic currency terms. This in turn will influence the exchange rate between currencies with different domestic inflation rates.

Let us suppose that sterling and the US dollar are at PPP equilibrium at the start of the year with rates at US$1.50/£. Then over the year the inflation rate in the UK is 5% so the same basket costs £10,500 at the end of the year. If during the same period US prices rose by 3% the US domestic cost of a basket will be US$15,450. If the exchange rate remains at US$1.50/£, the US basket would equate to £10,300; there will be a disequilibrium and PPP is not achieved. A UK consumer is faced with a choice of either buying £10,500 of UK-produced goods or exchanging £10,500 into dollars and buying US goods. The consumer's £10,500 will buy US$15,750 at US$1.50/£. This is more than one basket; therefore the better option is to the buy goods in America. The buying pressure on the dollar will shift exchange rates to a new equilibrium in which a basket costs the same price in both countries. To find this new equilibrium we use the following formula:

$$\frac{1 + I_{US}}{1 + I_{UK}} = \frac{US\$/£_1}{US\$/£_0}$$

$$\frac{1 + 0.03}{1 + 0.05} = \frac{US\$/£_1}{1.50}$$

$$US\$/£_1 = \frac{1.03}{1.05} \times 1.50 = 1.4714 \ \$/£$$

where:

I_{US} = US inflation rate;

I_{UK} = UK inflation rate;

$US\$/£_1$ = the spot rate of exchange at the end of the period;

$US\$/£_0$ = the spot rate of exchange at the beginning of the period.

The US dollar appreciates against sterling (you need fewer US$ to buy £1) because inflation is lower in the USA over the period.

At this new exchange rate a basket of goods costing US$15,450 in the USA has a sterling cost of 15,450/1.4714 = £10,500 and thus PPP is maintained.

The pure PPP concludes that the country with the higher inflation rate will be subject to a depreciation of its currency, and the extent of that depreciation is proportional to the relative difference in the two countries' inflation rates. However, the theory is most valid for countries which are geographically close. The PPP theory has some serious problems when applied in practice:

● It only applies to goods freely traded internationally at no cost of trade

Many goods and services do not enter international trade and so their relative prices are not taken into account in the determination of currency rates. Medical services, haircuts, building and live entertainment, to name but a few, are rarely imported; therefore they are not subject to PPP. The theory also has limited applicability to goods with a high transportation cost relative to their value, for example, road stone or cement. The PPP disequilibrium would have to be very large to make it worthwhile importing products of this kind. There may also be barriers inhibiting trade, for example regulations, tariffs, quotas, cultural resistance.

● It works in the long run, but that may be years away

Customers may be slow to recognise the incentive to purchase from another country when there is a PPP disequilibrium. There is usually some inertia due to buying habits that have become routine. Furthermore, governments may manage exchange rates for a considerable period, thus defying the forces pressing toward PPP. In addition, in the short term there are other elements at play such as balance of payments disequilibria, capital transactions (purchase of assets such as factories, businesses or shares by foreigners) and speculation.

The evidence is that relative inflation is one influence on exchange rates, but it is not the only factor. There have been large deviations from PPP for substantial periods.

Exhibit 22.20

Economic focus: Beefed-up burgernomics

The Organisation for Economic Co-operation and Development (OECD) uses its resources to produce continuously updated statistics indicating what the exchange should be for a representative basket of goods to cost 100 units of domestic currency. Another set of statistics and a far simpler indicator of currency discrepancies based on PPP is the 'Big Mac Index', initiated by *The Economist,* which compares the price of a Big Mac in different countries or the Starbucks index which compares the price of a coffee.

Interest rate parity

While PPP is concerned with differences in spot rates at different points in time and relating these to inflation rates, the interest rate parity (IRP) theory concerns the relationship between spot rates and forward rates, and links differences between these to the nominal interest rates available in each of the two currencies.

> The interest rate parity theory holds true when the difference between spot and forward exchange rates is equal to the differential between interest rates available in the two currencies.

The theory behind IRP predicts that if you place your money in a currency with a high interest rate you will be no better off when you convert the sum back into your home currency via a prearranged forward transaction than you would have been if you had simply invested in an interest-bearing investment carrying a similar risk, at home. What you gain on the extra interest you lose on the difference between spot and forward exchange rates.

For example, suppose a UK investor is attracted by the 8% interest rate being offered on one-year US government bonds. This compares well with the similarly very low risk one-year UK government bond offering 6% interest. The IRP theory says that this investor will not achieve an extra return by investing abroad rather than at home because the one-year forward rate of exchange will cause the US$ to be at a discount relative to the present spot rate. Thus, when the investment matures and the dollars are converted to sterling the investor will have achieved the same as if the money had been invested in UK government bonds.

Consider these steps:

1   *Beginning of year*

   a   Exchange £1m for US$1.5m at the spot rate of US$1.5/£.

   b   Buy US$1.5m government bonds yielding 8%.

   c   Arrange a one-year forward transaction at US$1.5283/£ to sell dollars.

2   *End of year*

Exchange US$1.62m (US$1.5m × 1.08) with the bank which agreed the forward exchange at the beginning of the year at the rate 1.5283 to produce 1.62 ÷ 1.5283 = £1.06m. This is equal to the amount that would have been received by investing in UK government bonds, 6% over the year. The differential between the spot and forward rates exactly offsets the difference in interest rates.

The formula which links together the spot, forward and interest rate differences is:

$$\frac{1 + r_{US}}{1 + r_{UK}} = \frac{US\$/\pounds_F}{US\$/\pounds_S}$$

where:

r_{US} = interest rate available in the USA;

r_{UK} = interest rate available in the UK (for the same risk)

$US\$/\pounds_F$ = the forward exchange rate;

$US\$/\pounds_S$ = the spot exchange rate

To test this relationship consider the case where both the spot rate and the forward rate are at US$1.50/£. Here the investor can prearrange to convert the dollar investment back into sterling through a forward agreement and obtain an extra 2% by investing in the USA. However, the investor will not be alone in recognising this remarkable opportunity. Companies, forex dealers and fund managers will turn to this type of trading. They would sell UK bonds, buy dollars spot, buy US bonds and sell dollars forward. However, this would quickly lead us away from disequilibrium as the pressure of these transactions would lower UK bond prices and therefore raise interest rates, cause a rise in the value of the spot dollar against sterling, a rise in the price of US bonds and therefore a fall in interest rates being offered and a fall in the dollar forward rate. These adjustments will eliminate the investment return differences and re-establish IRP equilibrium.

The IRP insists that the relationship between exchange and interest rates is:

- *High nominal interest rate currency* Currency trades at a discount on the forward rate compared with spot rate.

- *Low nominal interest rate currency* Currency trades at a premium on the forward rate compared with spot rate.

The IRP theory *generally* holds true in practice. However, there are deviations caused by factors such as taxation (which alters the rate of return earned on investments), or government controls on capital flows, controls on currency trading and intervention in foreign exchange markets interfering with the attainment of equilibrium through arbitrage.

Levich (2011), studying the impact of the financial crisis, compared deviations from IRP for the EUR/USD and found that for several years pre-crisis the prices of all spot and 3 month swaps were within 25 basis points of parity, with 90% being within 10 basis points. However, post the collapse of Lehman Brothers in September 2008, the deviations increased to 200 basis points and remained above 100 basis points for the next 3 months.

Expectations theory

> The expectations theory states that the current forward exchange rate is an unbiased predictor of the spot rate at that point in the future.

Note that the theory does not say that the forward rate predicts precisely what spot rates will be in the future; it is merely an unbiased predictor or provides the statistical expectation. The forward rate will frequently under or over-estimate the actual future spot rate. On (a statistical) average, however, it predicts the future spot rate because it neither consistently under- nor consistently over-estimates.

Traders in foreign currency nudge the market towards the fulfilment of the expectations theory. If a trader takes a view that the forward rate is lower than the expected future spot price there is an incentive to buy forward. Then when the forward matures and the trader's view on the spot rate turns out to be correct the trader is able to buy at a low price and immediately sell at spot to make a profit. The buying pressure on the forward raises the price until equilibrium occurs, in which the forward price equals the market consensus view on the future spot price, which is an unbiased predictor.

The general conclusions from the empirical studies investigating the truthfulness of the expectations theory is that for the more widely traded currencies it generally works well. However, there may be numerous periods when relative interest rates (under IRP theory) are the dominant influence. For the corporate manager and treasurer the forward rate can be taken to be unbiased as a predictor of the future spot rate. That is, it has an equal chance of being below, or of being above, the actual spot rate. However, it is a poor predictor – sometimes it is wide of the mark in one direction and sometimes wide of the mark in the other.

This knowledge may be useful to a corporate manager or treasurer when contemplating whether to hedge through using forward rates, with the attendant transaction costs, on a regular basis or whether to adopt a 'do nothing' policy, accepting that sometimes one loses on forex and sometimes one wins. For a firm with numerous transactions, the future spot rate will average the same as the forward rate, and so the 'do nothing' policy may be the cheaper and more attractive option.

The influence of a current-account deficit and capital flows

Another influence on exchange rate movements is the presence or otherwise of an unsustainable balance of payments. If an economy is importing more goods and services than it is exporting it is said to have a current account deficit. The exchange rate will move (in theory) so as to achieve current-account balance. So, an overvalued exchange rate makes exporting difficult and encourages consumers to buy goods produced in other countries. If the exchange rate then declines exporters can sell more abroad and consumers are more likely to purchase the domestically produced version of a product as it becomes cheaper relative to imported goods. The trade deficit is eventually eliminated through this mechanism. The Fundamental Equilibrium Exchange Rate (FEER) is the exchange rate that results in a sustainable current-account balance. Any movement away from the FEER is a disequilibrium that sets in train forces that tend to bring the exchange rate back to equilibrium. That is the theory. In reality, there are many factors other than the trade balance causing forex rates to move.

Only around 1% of all forex transactions are related to imports and exports of goods and services. Exchange rates can diverge from FEER for many years if foreign investors are willing to continue to finance a current account deficit. They do this by buying assets (bonds, shares, companies, property, etc.) in the country with the negative balance of payments. The main influence on these capital transfers of money (and therefore demand for the deficit country's currency) is investors' expectations regarding the returns available on financial assets. If investors believe that the economy with a current account deficit nevertheless offers good future returns on the bond market or the equity market, say, they will still bid up the value of its currency as they buy it to invest.

In the period 2000–4 the USA ran a very large current-account deficit and yet the currency did not fall in value. Foreign investors thought that the returns offered on US financial assets, particularly shares, were attractive and so continued to support the dollar as they pumped money into the economy. While the American people went on a spending spree (with expenditure higher than take-home pay), in the process buying mountains of foreign-produced goods, money flowed in as financial assets were bought, thus allowing the dollar to remain high. In the later stages of this unsustainable deficit the major buyers of US assets were Asian central banks. Countries such as China and Japan bought US Treasury bills and bonds to inject demand for dollars so that their exporters did not suffer from a rising currency against the dollar. Of course, it was widely recognised that the dollar could plummet should overseas investors ever start to believe that the US economic miracle is over (or that it was not really a productivity miracle after all) if they were to sell US financial assets, sell the dollar and move funds to somewhere else in the world offering more exciting (or safer) returns. This is what happened in 2004–7. But it was halted by the financial crisis. The US was seen as a 'safe haven', and so investors around the world bought dollars to invest in US assets in the eight years following the 2008 crisis. Ironic, really, as it was the US mortgage market and Wall Street shenanigans that caused the crisis.

2017 has seen a change in attitude which some are predicting may continue. Both the pound, weakened post the Brexit vote and Europe, damaged by the Euro crisis, started 2017 at low levels against the dollar but they have strengthened throughout the year. At the start of the Trump presidency with the talk of tax cuts and huge infrastructure expenditure it was expected that investment would flow into the US to take advantage of growth opportunities and thus the dollar would strengthen. However, the unpredictability of President Trump's actions and the delays in implementing policies appear to have scared investors – see **Exhibit 22.21**.

Exhibit 22.21

Donald Trump compounds dollar's woes

Failure to make progress on economic stimulus package takes toll on currency

By Dan McCrum

Donald Trump has become the soft-dollar president, with the US currency hitting the lowest level in more than a year on Thursday, measured against a basket of foreign alternatives. The dollar has lost a tenth of its value on that basis since early January, largely because of a surge in the European single currency.

To attempt to answer the question of where the dollar goes from here requires coming up with an explanation for the drop so far, however, and a few reasons present themselves. The most obvious might be monetary policy. Thursday's fall followed a statement from the Federal Reserve that suggested the US central bank has been surprised by the continued weakness of inflation. Less need to fight inflation ultimately means less chance of higher bond yields and the capital inflows they attract. Yet expectations for a third interest rate rise this year are little changed from January, with money market prices implying a roughly 50-50 chance.

A rival explanation for a weaker dollar, however, is politics: the failure of Mr Trump's party to enact his legislative priorities, with the latest attempt to deliver on a campaign promise to repeal Obamacare foundering. Mihir Kapadia, head of Sun Global Investments, says: "The American healthcare reform bill is effectively dead in its current form, casting a cloud on President Donald Trump's broader economic revitalisation and reform agenda."

Anticipation of the boost such policies would bring had powered markets after Republicans gained full control of government in November's election. Mr Gallo says a diminished set of tax reforms could yet weaken the dollar. Some of the more ambitious changes considered early this year, such as a move to encourage repatriation of offshore corporate profits, or a border adjustment tax, might have boosted the US currency. The world's reserve currency hit a 14-month low after the Fed's statement on monetary policy this week Simple tax cuts that expand the deficit are likely to have the reverse effect, he says, and he predicts the dollar will fall another 4 per cent to 5 over the next year.

The efficiency of the currency markets

Whether the forex markets are efficient at pricing spot and forward currency rates is hotly debated. If they are efficient then speculators on average should not be able to make abnormal returns by using information to take positions. In an efficient market the best prediction of tomorrow's price is the price today, because prices move in a random walk fashion, depending on the arrival of new information. Prices adjust quickly to new information, but it is impossible to state in advance the direction of future movements because, by its nature, news is unpredictable (it might be 'bad' or it might be 'good').

If the market is efficient, forecasting by corporate treasurers is a pointless exercise because any information the treasurer might use to predict the future will have already been processed by the market participants and be reflected in the price.

There are three levels of market efficiency:

- **Weak form** Historic prices and volume information are fully reflected in current prices, and therefore a trader cannot make abnormal profits by observing past price changes and trying to predict the future.

- **Semi-strong form** All publicly available information is fully reflected in prices, and therefore abnormal profits are not available by acting on information once it is made public.

● *Strong form* Public and private (that is, available to insiders, for example those working for a central bank) information is reflected in prices.

Much empirical research has been conducted into currency market efficiency and the overall conclusion is that the question remains open. Some strategies, on some occasions, have produced handsome profits. On the other hand, many studies show a high degree of efficiency with little opportunity for abnormal reward. Most of the studies examine the major trading currencies of the world – perhaps there is more potential for the discovery of inefficiency in the more exotic currencies. Central bank intervention in foreign exchange markets also seems to be a cause of inefficiency.

As far as ordinary humble corporate treasurers are concerned, trying to outwit the market can be exciting, but it can also be dangerous. Alan Greenspan, former chairman of the US Federal Reserve, said, 'To my knowledge no model projecting movements in exchange rates is superior to tossing a coin.'[8]

Concluding comments

Managers need to be aware of, and to assess, the risk to which their firms are exposed. The risk that arises because exchange rates move over time is one of the most important for managers to consider. Once the extent of the exposure is known managers then need to judge what, if anything, is to be done about it. Sometimes the threat to the firm and to the returns to shareholders are so great as to call for robust risk-reducing action. In other circumstances the cost of hedging outweighs the benefit. Analysing and appraising the extent of the problem and weighing up alternative responses are where managerial judgement comes to the fore. Knowledge of derivatives markets and money markets, and of the need for flexible manufacturing, marketing and financing structures, is useful background, but the key managerial skill required is discernment in positioning the company to cope with forex risk. The ability sometimes to stand back from the fray, objectively assess the cost of each risk-reducing option and say, 'No, this risk is to be taken on the chin because in my judgement the costs of managing the risk reduce shareholder wealth with little to show for it,' is sometimes required.

Key points and concepts

● An **exchange rate** is the price of one currency expressed in terms of another.

● **Exchange rates are quoted** with a bid rate (the rate at which you can buy) and an offer rate (the rate at which you can sell).

● **Forex shifts can affect:**

  – income received from abroad;
  – amounts paid for imports;
  – the valuation of foreign assets and liabilities;
  – the long-term viability of foreign operations;
  – the acceptability of an overseas project.

● The **foreign exchange market** grew dramatically over the last quarter of the twentieth century. Over US$5,100bn is now traded on an average day. Most of this trading is between banks rather than for underlying (for example, import/export) reasons.

● **Spot market** transactions take place which are to be settled quickly (usually one or two days later). In the **forward market** a deal is arranged to exchange currencies at some future date at a price agreed now.

● **Transaction risk** is the risk that transactions already entered into, or for which the firm is likely to have a commitment in a foreign currency, will have a variable value.

● **Translation risk** arises because financial data denominated in one currency then expressed in terms of another are affected by exchange-rate movements.

● **Economic risk** Forex movements cause a decline in economic value because of a loss of competitive strength.

---

8 Quoted in Samuel Brittan, 'The dollar needs benign neglect', *Financial Times,* 30 January 2004, p. 21.

- **Transaction risk strategies:**

    - invoice customer in home currency;
    - do nothing;
    - netting;
    - matching;
    - leading and lagging;
    - forward market hedge;
    - money market hedge;
    - futures hedge;
    - currency option hedge.

- One way of **managing translation risk** is to try to match foreign assets and liabilities.

- The **management of economic exposure** requires the maintenance of flexibility with regard to manufacturing (for example, location of sources of supply), marketing (for example, advertising campaign, pricing) and finance (currency).

- The **purchasing power parity (PPP) theory** states that exchange rates will be in equilibrium when their domestic purchasing powers at that rate are equivalent. In an inflationary environment the relationship between two countries' inflation rates and the spot exchange rates between two

points in time is (with the USA and the UK as examples):

$$\frac{1 + I_{US}}{1 + I_{UK}} = \frac{US\$/£_1}{US\$/£_0}$$

- The **interest rate parity (IRP) theory** holds true when the difference between spot and forward exchange rates is equal to the differential between the interest rates available in the two currencies. Using the USA and the UK currencies as examples:

$$\frac{1 + I_{US}}{1 + I_{UK}} = \frac{US\$/£_F}{US\$/£_S}$$

- The **expectations theory** states that the current forward exchange rate is an unbiased predictor of the spot rate at that point in the future.

- The **Fundamental Equilibrium Exchange Rate (FEER)** is the exchange rate that results in a sustainable current account balance.

- **Flows of money for investment** in financial assets across national borders can be an important influence on forex rates.

- The currency markets are generally **efficient**, but there is evidence suggesting pockets of inefficiency.

References and further reading

To keep up to date and reinforce knowledge gained by reading this chapter we recommend the following publications: *Financial Times, The Economist, Bank of England Quarterly Bulletin, Bank for International Settlements Quarterly Review* (www.bis.org), and *The Treasurer* (a monthly journal).

Baba, N. and Packer, F. (2009) 'Interpreting deviations from covered interest parity during the financial market turmoil of 2007-08', *Journal of Banking and Finance*, 33, pp. 1953–62.

Covered interest parity states that interest rate differentials between currencies should be reflected in the FX forward discount rates because, otherwise, an arbitrageur could transact in interest and exchange markets to make a risk-free profit. This paper investigates the effects of turbulence in the money markets in 2007–08 on the short-term covered interest parity (CIP) condition between the US dollar and the euro. From August 2007, the spread between the FX swap implied dollar rate and the actual dollar LIBOR rate widened which could suggest that the CIP condition did not hold. Baba et al. argue that this was

primarily due to dollar funding shortages and was not linked to the CIP condition.

Bank for International Settlements (2016) *Triennial Central Bank Survey of Foreign Exchange and OTC derivatives markets in 2016*. Available at https://www.bis.org/publ/rpfx16.htm

An excellent source of data and comment.

Bonini, S., Dallocchio, M., Raimbourg, P. and Salvi, A. (2016) 'Do firms hedge translation risks?', *Journal of Financial Management*, Markets and Institutions, 4(2), 155–78.

Investigates the translation hedging risk strategy of MNCs and finds that a significant percentage (47%) do manage this risk.

Burnside, C., Eichenbaum, M., Kleschelski, I. and Rebelo, S. (2006) 'The returns to currency speculation', NBER Working Paper No. 12489. Available at www.nber.org/papers/w12489.

'Currencies that are at a forward premium tend to depreciate. This "forward-premium puzzle" represents an egregious deviation from uncovered interest parity.'

Coffey, N., Hrung, W.B. and Sarkar, A. (2009) 'Capital constraints, counterparty risk, and deviations from covered interest rate parity', Federal Reserve Bank of New York Staff Reports, no. 393 (September).

The paper investigated deviations from the Covered Interest Parity (CIP) relationship since August 2007 (the financial crisis) and found a breakdown of arbitrage transactions in the international capital markets during the crisis that stemmed partly from lack of funding and partly from heightened counterparty credit risk

Desai, M.A. (2004) 'Foreign exchange markets and transactions', Harvard Business School note. (Available at Harvard Business School website.)

A very easy-to-follow introduction to the basics of forex markets.

Eiteman, D.K., Stonehill, A.I. and Moffett, M.H. (2015) Multinational Business Finance, 14th edn. Reading, MA: Pearson/Addison Wesley.

A good introduction to many financial aspects of running a multinational business. Easy to read. Useful case studies.

Levich, Richard M (2011) 'Evidence of financial globalisation and crises: interest rate parity', In The Encyclopedia of Financial Globalization. Edited by Gerard Caprio. Amsterdam: Elsevier Publishing.

This paper looks at the IRP relationship.

Madura, J. (2018) International Financial Management, 13th edn. London: Thompson.

A well-written, easy-to-follow introduction to forex markets. European focus.

Mancini-Griffoli, T. and Ranaldo, A, (2011) 'Limits to Arbitrage During the Crisis: Funding Liquidity Constraints and Covered Interest Parity.' Available at SSRN: https://ssrn.com/abstract=1569504 or http://dx.doi.org/10.2139/ssrn.1569504

Arbitrage normally ensures that covered interest parity (CIP) holds. Until recently, excess profits, if any, were documented to last merely seconds and reach a few pips. Instead, this paper finds that following the Lehman bankruptcy, these were large and persisted for months.

McBrady, M.J., Mortal, S. and Schill, M.J. (2010) 'Do Firms Believe in Interest Rate Parity?'. Review of Finance, 14(4), (October), pp. 695–726.

Using a broad sample of international corporate bond offerings, the paper presents evidence that corporate borrowers make opportunistic currency choices, in that they denominate the currency of their bonds in a manner that is inconsistent with a belief in either covered or uncovered interest rate parity.

Pilbeam, K. (2018) Finance and Financial Markets, 4th edn. London: Palgrave.

Contains an accessible chapter with more on the economic theories of exchange rate determination (PPP, IRP theories, etc.).

Pukthuanthong-Le, K., Levich, R.M. and Thomas III, L.R. (2007) 'Do foreign exchange markets still trend?', The Journal of Portfolio Management, Fall, pp. 114–52.

In the early years of floating exchange rates (1970s and 1980s) the major currencies showed trends that were exploitable by speculators, thus defying the weak-form efficiency hypothesis. But this came to an end some time ago. However, exotic currencies have shown trending more recently.

Pukthuanthong-Le, K. and Thomas III, L.R. (2008) 'Weak-form efficiency in currency markets', Financial Analysts Journal, 64(3), pp. 31–52.

Following a trend in major currency rates used to work for speculators, but profits from this strategy have been negligible since 2000, supporting the assertion that forex markets have become weak-form efficient. However, for some other currencies, following a trend can be profitable.

Taylor, F. (2011) Mastering Derivatives Markets, 4th edn. Harlow: FT Prentice Hall.

Contains a useful chapter on currency options and swaps.

Wei, K.D. and Starks, L.T. 'Foreign exchange exposure, elasticity and financial distress', Financial Management (Wiley Blackwell), Winter 2013, 2(4), pp. 709–35.

Firms with a greater likelihood and higher costs of financial distress exhibit greater abnormal returns in response to large exchange rate shocks.

Case study recommendations

Please see www.pearsoned.co.uk/arnold for case study synopses. Also, another list of useful case studies from the fifth edition can be found there.

- Foreign exchange hedging strategies at General Motors: competitive exposures. Authors: Mihir A. Desai; Mark F. Veblen, Harvard Business School. Available at www.cb.hbsp.harvard.edu

- Foreign exchange hedging strategies at General Motors: transactional and translational exposures. Authors: Mihir A. Desai; Mark F. Veblen, Harvard Business School. Available at www.cb.hbsp.harvard.edu

- F. Mayer Imports: hedging foreign currency risk. Author: Wallace Fan, Ivey Publishing. Available at www.cb.hbsp.harvard.edu

Websites

www.ukforex.co.uk	OFX Foreign Exchange Services
www.bis.org	Bank for International Settlements
www.FT.com	The Financial Times
www.bankofengland.co.uk	Bank of England
www.currenex.com	Currenex
www.bgcpartners.com	Brokerage company
www.ecb.int	European Central Bank
www.euronext.com	Euronext Exchange
www.fxconnect.com	Execution venue
www.imf.org	International Monetary Fund
www.cmegroup.com	Chicago Mercantile Exchange
www.theice.com	International Exchange
financial.thomsonreuters.com	FXAll
uk.finance.yahoo.com	Yahoo finance
www.ssgloballink.com	State Street Global Markets
uk.reuters.com	Reuters
www.oanda.com	OANDA. FX market maker and data provider
www.wto.org	World Trade Organisation
www.oecd.org	Organisation for Economic Co-operation and Development
www.cls-group.com	CLS group (Continuous linked settlement)

Video presentations

Bank and financial organisation chief executives and other senior people describe and discuss policy and other aspects of their operations in interviews, documentaries and webcasts at www.merchantcantos.com – free to view.

Self-review questions

1 Describe the difference between the spot and forward currency markets.

2 Explain through a simple example how the forward market can be used to hedge against a currency risk.

3 Define the following in relation to foreign exchange:
   a   transaction risk;
   b   translation risk;
   c   economic risk.

4 What are the advantages and disadvantages of responding to foreign exchange risk by: a invoicing in your currency; b doing nothing?

5 Draw out the difference between netting and matching by describing both.

6 What is a money market hedge, and what are leading and lagging?

7 How does a currency future differ from a currency forward?

8 Compare hedging using forwards with hedging using options.

9 Describe how you would manage translation and economic risk.

10 Explain the purchasing power parity (PPP) theory of exchange-rate determination.

11 Describe the relationship between spot rates and forward rates under the interest rate parity (IRP) theory.

12 What is the expectations theory?

Questions and problems

Answers to most questions can be found at www.pearsoned.co.uk/arnold.

Answers to questions marked with an asterisk are to be found only in the Lecturer's Guide.

1   Answer the following given that the rate of exchange between the Japanese yen and sterling is quoted at ¥/£188.869 – 189.131:

   a   How many pounds will a company obtain if it sold ¥1m?
   b   What is the cost of £500,000?
   c   How many yen would be received from selling £1m?
   d   What is the cost of buying ¥100,000?

2   On 1 April an Australian exporter sells A$10m of coal to a New Zealand company. The importer is sent an invoice for NZ$11m payable in six months. The spot rate of exchange between the Australian and New Zealand dollars is NZ$1.1/A$.

   Required

   a   If the spot rate of exchange six months later is NZ$1.2/A$ what exchange rate gain or loss will be made by the Australian exporter?
   b   If the spot rate of exchange six months later is NZ$1.05/A$ what exchange rate gain or loss will be made by the Australian exporter?
   c   A six-month forward is available at NZ$1.09/A$. Show how risk can be reduced using the forward.
   d   Discuss the relative merits of using forwards and options to hedge forex risk.

3   Describe the main types of risk facing an organisation which has dealings in a foreign currency. Can all these risks be hedged, and should all these risks be hedged at all times?

4* (*Examination level*)
   a   A UK company exports machine parts to South Africa on three months' credit. The invoice totals R150m and the current spot rate is R7.46/£. Exchange rates have been volatile in recent months and the directors are concerned that forex rates might move so as to make the export deal unprofitable. They are considering three hedge strategies:
      i   forward market hedge;
      ii   money market hedge;
      iii option hedge.

   other information:

   • three-month forward rate: R7.5/£;
   • interest payable for three months' borrowing in rand: 2.5% for the three months (not an annual rate);
   • three-month American-style rand put, sterling call option is available for R150m with a strike price of R7.5/£ for a premium payable now of £400,000 on the over-the-counter market.

   Required

   Show how the hedging strategies might work. Use the following assumed spot rates at the end of three months in order to illustrate the nature of each of the hedges:

            R7.00/£.
            R8.00/£.

   b   Explain why it may not always make sense for a company to hedge forex risk.

5   British Steel suffered greatly as a result of the high value of sterling because it is a major exporter (as are many of its customers). Consider the range of approaches British Steel could have taken to reduce both its transaction and economic exposure.

6   Describe how foreign exchange changes can undermine the competitive position of the firm. Suggest some measures to reduce this risk.

7 a   A basket of goods sells for SFr2,000 in Switzerland when the same basket of goods sells for £1,000 in the UK. The current exchange rate is SFr2.0/£. Over the forthcoming year inflation in Switzerland is estimated to be 2% and in the UK, 4%. If the purchasing power parity theory holds true what will the exchange rate be at the end of the year?

   b   What factors prevent the PPP always holding true in the short run?

8 a   The rate of interest available on a one-year government bond in Canada is 5%. A similar-risk bond in Australia yields 7%. The current spot rate of exchange is C$1.02/A$. What will be the one-year forward rate if the market obeys the interest rate parity theory?

   b   Describe the expectation theory of foreign exchange.

9* (*Examination level*) Lozenge plc has taken delivery of 50,000 electronic devices from a Malaysian company. The seller is in a strong bargaining position and has priced the devices in Malaysian dollars at M$12 each. It has granted Lozenge three months' credit.

   The Malaysian interest rate is 3% per quarter.

   Lozenge has all its money tied up in its operations but could borrow in sterling at 3% per quarter (three months) if necessary.

Forex rates	Malaysian dollar/£
Spot	5.4165
Three-month forward	5.425

A three-month sterling put, Malaysian dollar call currency option with a strike price of M$5.425/£ for M$600,000 is available for a premium of M$15,000.

Required

Discuss and illustrate three hedging strategies available to Lozenge. Weigh up the advantages and disadvantages of each strategy. Show all calculations.

10 The spot rate between the euro and the US dollar is €1.77/US$ and the expected annual rates of inflation are expected to be 2% and 5% respectively.

   a   If the purchasing power parity theory holds, what will the spot rate of exchange be in one year?

   b   If the interest rates available on government bonds are 6% in the Eurozone and 9% in the USA, and the interest rate parity theory holds, what is the current one-year forward rate?

11 The spot rate of exchange is Won1,507/£ between Korea and the UK. The one-month forward rate is Won1,450/£. A UK company has exported goods to Korea invoiced in Won to the value of Won1,507m on one month's credit.

   To borrow in Won for one month will cost 0.5%, whereas to borrow in sterling for one month will cost 0.6% of the amount borrowed.

Required

   a   Show how the forward market can be used to hedge.

   b   Show how the money market can be used to hedge.

Assignments

1 Examine a recent import or export deal at a company you know well. Write a report detailing the extent of exposure to transaction risk prior to any hedge activity. Describe the risk-reducing steps taken, if any, and critically compare alternative strategies.

2 Write a report for a company you know well, describing the extent to which it is exposed to transaction, translation and economic risk. Consider ways of coping with these risks and recommend a plan of action.

Appendices

Appendix I

Future value of £1 at compound interest

Interest rate

Periods	1	2	3	4	5	6	7	8	9	10	11	12	13	14	15	
1	1.0100	1.0200	1.0300	1.0400	1.0500	1.0600	1.0700	1.0800	1.0900	1.1000	1.1100	1.1200	1.1300	1.1400	1.1500	1
2	1.0201	1.0404	1.0609	1.0816	1.1025	1.1236	1.1449	1.1664	1.1881	1.2100	1.2321	1.2544	1.2769	1.2996	1.3225	2
3	1.0303	1.0612	1.0927	1.1249	1.1576	1.1910	1.2250	1.2597	1.2950	1.3310	1.3676	1.4049	1.4429	1.4815	1.5209	3
4	1.0406	1.0824	1.1255	1.1699	1.2155	1.2625	1.3108	1.3605	1.4116	1.4641	1.5181	1.5735	1.6305	1.6890	1.7490	4
5	1.0510	1.1041	1.1593	1.2167	1.2763	1.3382	1.4026	1.4693	1.5386	1.6105	1.6851	1.7623	1.8424	1.9254	2.0114	5
6	1.0615	1.1262	1.1941	1.2653	1.3401	1.4185	1.5007	1.5869	1.6771	1.7716	1.8704	1.9738	2.0820	2.1950	2.3131	6
7	1.0721	1.1487	1.2299	1.3159	1.4071	1.5036	1.6058	1.7138	1.8280	1.9487	2.0762	2.2107	2.3526	2.5023	2.6600	7
8	1.0829	1.1717	1.2668	1.3686	1.4775	1.5938	1.7182	1.8509	1.9926	2.1436	2.3045	2.4760	2.6584	2.8526	3.0590	8
9	1.0937	1.1951	1.3048	1.4233	1.5513	1.6895	1.8385	1.9990	2.1719	2.3579	2.5580	2.7731	3.0040	3.2519	3.5179	9
10	1.1046	1.2190	1.3439	1.4802	1.6289	1.7908	1.9672	2.1589	2.3674	2.5937	2.8394	3.1058	3.3946	3.7072	4.0456	10
11	1.1157	1.2434	1.3842	1.5395	1.7103	1.8983	2.1049	2.3316	2.5804	2.8531	3.1518	3.4785	3.8359	4.2262	4.6524	11
12	1.1268	1.2682	1.4258	1.6010	1.7959	2.0122	2.2522	2.5182	2.8127	3.1384	3.4985	3.8960	4.3345	4.8179	5.3503	12
13	1.1381	1.2936	1.4685	1.6651	1.8856	2.1329	2.4098	2.7196	3.0658	3.4523	3.8833	4.3635	4.8980	5.4924	6.1528	13
14	1.1495	1.3195	1.5126	1.7317	1.9799	2.2609	2.5785	2.9372	3.3417	3.7975	4.3104	4.8871	5.5348	6.2613	7.0757	14
15	1.1610	1.3459	1.5580	1.8009	2.0789	2.3966	2.7590	3.1722	3.6425	4.1772	4.7846	5.4736	6.2543	7.1379	8.1371	15
16	1.1726	1.3728	1.6047	1.8730	2.1829	2.5404	2.9522	3.4259	3.9703	4.5950	5.3109	6.1304	7.0673	8.1372	9.3576	16
17	1.1843	1.4002	1.6528	1.9479	2.2920	2.6928	3.1588	3.7000	4.3276	5.0545	5.8951	6.8660	7.9861	9.2765	10.7613	17
18	1.1961	1.4282	1.7024	2.0258	2.4066	2.8543	3.3799	3.9960	4.7171	5.5599	6.5436	7.6900	9.0243	10.5752	12.3755	18
19	1.2081	1.4568	1.7535	2.1068	2.5270	3.0256	3.6165	4.3157	5.1417	6.1159	7.2633	8.6128	10.1974	12.0557	14.2318	19
20	1.2202	1.4859	1.8061	2.1911	2.6533	3.2071	3.8697	4.6610	5.6044	6.7275	8.0623	9.6463	11.5231	13.7435	16.3665	20
25	1.2824	1.6406	2.0938	2.6658	3.3864	4.2919	5.4274	6.8485	8.6231	10.8347	13.5855	17.0001	21.2305	26.4619	32.9190	25

Periods	16	17	18	19	20	21	22	23	24	25	26	27	28	29	30	
1	1.1600	1.1700	1.1800	1.1900	1.2000	1.2100	1.2200	1.2300	1.2400	1.2500	1.2600	1.2700	1.2800	1.2900	1.3000	1
2	1.3456	1.3689	1.3924	1.4161	1.4400	1.4641	1.4884	1.5129	1.5376	1.5625	1.5876	1.6129	1.6384	1.6641	1.6900	2
3	1.5609	1.6016	1.6430	1.6852	1.7280	1.7716	1.8158	1.8609	1.9066	1.9531	2.0004	2.0484	2.0972	2.1467	2.1970	3
4	1.8106	1.8739	1.9388	2.0053	2.0736	2.1436	2.2153	2.2889	2.3642	2.4414	2.5205	2.6014	2.6844	2.7692	2.8561	4
5	2.1003	2.1924	2.2878	2.3864	2.4883	2.5937	2.7027	2.8153	2.9316	3.0518	3.1758	3.3038	3.4360	3.5723	3.7129	5
6	2.4364	2.5652	2.6996	2.8398	2.9860	3.1384	3.2973	3.4628	3.6352	3.8147	4.0015	4.1959	4.3980	4.6083	4.8268	6
7	2.8262	3.0012	3.1855	3.3793	3.5832	3.7975	4.0227	4.2593	4.5077	4.7684	5.0419	5.3288	5.6295	5.9447	6.2749	7
8	3.2784	3.5115	3.7589	4.0214	4.2998	4.5950	4.9077	5.2389	5.5895	5.9605	6.3528	6.7675	7.2058	7.6686	8.1573	8
9	3.8030	4.1084	4.4355	4.7854	5.1598	5.5599	5.9874	6.4439	6.9310	7.4506	8.0045	8.5948	9.2234	9.8925	10.6045	9
10	4.4114	4.8068	5.2338	5.6947	6.1917	6.7275	7.3046	7.9259	8.5944	9.3132	10.0857	10.9153	11.8059	12.7614	13.7858	10
11	5.1173	5.6240	6.1759	6.7767	7.4301	8.1403	8.9117	9.7489	10.6571	11.6415	12.7080	13.8625	15.1116	16.4622	17.9216	11
12	5.9360	6.5801	7.2876	8.0642	8.9161	9.8497	10.8722	11.9912	13.2148	14.5519	16.0120	17.6053	19.3428	21.2362	23.2981	12
13	6.8858	7.6987	8.5994	9.5964	10.6993	11.9182	13.2641	14.7491	16.3863	18.1899	20.1752	22.3588	24.7588	27.3947	30.2875	13
14	7.9875	9.0075	10.1472	11.4198	12.8392	14.4210	16.1822	18.1414	20.3191	22.7374	25.4207	28.3957	31.6913	35.3391	39.3738	14
15	9.2655	10.5387	11.9737	13.5895	15.4070	17.4494	19.7423	22.3140	25.1956	28.4217	32.0301	36.0625	40.5648	45.5875	51.1859	15
16	10.7480	12.3303	14.1290	16.1715	18.4884	21.1138	24.0856	27.4462	31.2426	35.5271	40.3579	45.7994	51.9230	58.8079	66.5417	16
17	12.4677	14.4265	16.6722	19.2441	22.1861	25.5477	29.3844	33.7588	38.7408	44.4089	50.8510	58.1652	66.4614	75.8621	86.5042	17
18	14.4625	16.8790	19.6733	22.9005	26.6233	30.9127	35.8490	41.5233	48.0386	55.5112	64.0722	73.8698	85.0706	97.8622	112.4554	18
19	16.7765	19.7484	23.2144	27.2516	31.9480	37.4043	43.7358	51.0737	59.5679	69.3889	80.7310	93.8147	108.8904	126.2422	146.1920	19
20	19.4608	23.1056	27.3930	32.4294	38.3376	45.2593	53.3576	62.8206	73.8641	86.7362	101.7211	119.1446	139.3797	162.8524	190.0496	20
25	40.8742	50.6578	62.6686	77.3881	95.3962	117.3909	144.2101	176.8593	216.5420	264.6978	323.0454	393.6344	478.9049	581.7585	705.6410	25

Appendix II

Present value of £1 at compound interest

Interest rate

Periods	1	2	3	4	5	6	7	8	9	10	11	12	13	14	15	
1	0.9901	0.9804	0.9709	0.9615	0.9524	0.9434	0.9346	0.9259	0.9174	0.9091	0.9009	0.8929	0.8850	0.8772	0.8696	1
2	0.9803	0.9612	0.9426	0.9246	0.9070	0.8900	0.8734	0.8573	0.8417	0.8264	0.8116	0.7972	0.7831	0.7695	0.7561	2
3	0.9706	0.9423	0.9151	0.8890	0.8638	0.8396	0.8163	0.7938	0.7722	0.7513	0.7312	0.7118	0.6931	0.6750	0.6575	3
4	0.9610	0.9238	0.8885	0.8548	0.8227	0.7921	0.7629	0.7350	0.7084	0.6830	0.6587	0.6355	0.6133	0.5921	0.5718	4
5	0.9515	0.9057	0.8626	0.8219	0.7835	0.7473	0.7130	0.6806	0.6499	0.6209	0.5935	0.5674	0.5428	0.5194	0.4972	5
6	0.9420	0.8880	0.8375	0.7903	0.7462	0.7050	0.6663	0.6302	0.5963	0.5645	0.5346	0.5066	0.4803	0.4556	0.4323	6
7	0.9327	0.8706	0.8131	0.7599	0.7107	0.6651	0.6227	0.5835	0.5470	0.5132	0.4817	0.4523	0.4251	0.3996	0.3759	7
8	0.9235	0.8535	0.7894	0.7307	0.6768	0.6274	0.5820	0.5403	0.5019	0.4665	0.4339	0.4039	0.3762	0.3506	0.3269	8
9	0.9143	0.8368	0.7664	0.7026	0.6446	0.5919	0.5439	0.5002	0.4604	0.4241	0.3909	0.3606	0.3329	0.3075	0.2843	9
10	0.9053	0.8203	0.7441	0.6756	0.6139	0.5584	0.5083	0.4632	0.4224	0.3855	0.3522	0.3220	0.2946	0.2697	0.2472	10
11	0.8963	0.8043	0.7224	0.6496	0.5847	0.5268	0.4751	0.4289	0.3875	0.3505	0.3173	0.2875	0.2607	0.2366	0.2149	11
12	0.8874	0.7885	0.7014	0.6246	0.5568	0.4970	0.4440	0.3971	0.3555	0.3186	0.2858	0.2567	0.2307	0.2076	0.1869	12
13	0.8787	0.7730	0.6810	0.6006	0.5303	0.4688	0.4150	0.3677	0.3262	0.2897	0.2575	0.2292	0.2042	0.1821	0.1625	13
14	0.8700	0.7579	0.6611	0.5775	0.5051	0.4423	0.3878	0.3405	0.2992	0.2633	0.2320	0.2046	0.1807	0.1597	0.1413	14
15	0.8613	0.7430	0.6419	0.5553	0.4810	0.4173	0.3624	0.3152	0.2745	0.2394	0.2090	0.1827	0.1599	0.1401	0.1229	15
16	0.8528	0.7284	0.6232	0.5339	0.4581	0.3936	0.3387	0.2919	0.2519	0.2176	0.1883	0.1631	0.1415	0.1229	0.1069	16
17	0.8444	0.7142	0.6050	0.5134	0.4363	0.3714	0.3166	0.2703	0.2311	0.1978	0.1696	0.1456	0.1252	0.1078	0.0929	17
18	0.8360	0.7002	0.5874	0.4936	0.4155	0.3503	0.2959	0.2502	0.2120	0.1799	0.1528	0.1300	0.1108	0.0946	0.0808	18
19	0.8277	0.6864	0.5703	0.4746	0.3957	0.3305	0.2765	0.2317	0.1945	0.1635	0.1377	0.1161	0.0981	0.0829	0.0703	19
20	0.8195	0.6730	0.5537	0.4564	0.3769	0.3118	0.2584	0.2145	0.1784	0.1486	0.1240	0.1037	0.0868	0.0728	0.0611	20
25	0.7795	0.6095	0.4776	0.3751	0.2953	0.2330	0.1842	0.1460	0.1160	0.0923	0.0736	0.0588	0.0471	0.0378	0.0304	25
30	0.7419	0.5521	0.4120	0.3083	0.2314	0.1741	0.1314	0.0994	0.0754	0.0573	0.0437	0.0334	0.0256	0.0196	0.0151	30
35	0.7059	0.5000	0.3554	0.2534	0.1813	0.1301	0.0937	0.0676	0.0490	0.0356	0.0259	0.0189	0.0139	0.0102	0.0075	35
40	0.6717	0.4529	0.3066	0.2083	0.1420	0.0972	0.0668	0.0460	0.0318	0.0221	0.0154	0.0107	0.0075	0.0053	0.0037	40
45	0.6391	0.4102	0.2644	0.1712	0.1113	0.0727	0.0476	0.0313	0.0207	0.0137	0.0091	0.0061	0.0041	0.0027	0.0019	45
50	0.6080	0.3715	0.2281	0.1407	0.0872	0.0543	0.0339	0.0213	0.0134	0.0085	0.0054	0.0035	0.0022	0.0014	0.0009	50

Periods	16	17	18	19	20	21	22	23	24	25	26	27	28	29	30	
1	0.8621	0.8547	0.8475	0.8403	0.8333	0.8264	0.8197	0.8130	0.8065	0.8000	0.7937	0.7874	0.7812	0.7752	0.7692	1
2	0.7432	0.7305	0.7182	0.7062	0.6944	0.6830	0.6719	0.6610	0.6504	0.6400	0.6299	0.6200	0.6104	0.6009	0.5917	2
3	0.6407	0.6244	0.6086	0.5934	0.5787	0.5645	0.5507	0.5374	0.5245	0.5120	0.4999	0.4882	0.4768	0.4658	0.4552	3
4	0.5523	0.5337	0.5158	0.4987	0.4823	0.4665	0.4514	0.4369	0.4230	0.4096	0.3968	0.3844	0.3725	0.3611	0.3501	4
5	0.4761	0.4561	0.4371	0.4190	0.4019	0.3855	0.3700	0.3552	0.3411	0.3277	0.3149	0.3027	0.2910	0.2799	0.2693	5
6	0.4104	0.3898	0.3704	0.3521	0.3349	0.3186	0.3033	0.2888	0.2751	0.2621	0.2499	0.2383	0.2274	0.2170	0.2072	6
7	0.3538	0.3332	0.3139	0.2959	0.2791	0.2633	0.2486	0.2348	0.2218	0.2097	0.1983	0.1877	0.1776	0.1682	0.1594	7
8	0.3050	0.2848	0.2660	0.2487	0.2326	0.2176	0.2038	0.1909	0.1789	0.1678	0.1574	0.1478	0.1388	0.1304	0.1226	8
9	0.2630	0.2434	0.2255	0.2090	0.1938	0.1799	0.1670	0.1552	0.1443	0.1342	0.1249	0.1164	0.1084	0.1011	0.0943	9
10	0.2267	0.2080	0.1911	0.1756	0.1615	0.1486	0.1369	0.1262	0.1164	0.1074	0.0992	0.0916	0.0847	0.0784	0.0725	10
11	0.1954	0.1778	0.1619	0.1476	0.1346	0.1228	0.1122	0.1026	0.0938	0.0859	0.0787	0.0721	0.0662	0.0607	0.0558	11
12	0.1685	0.1520	0.1372	0.1240	0.1122	0.1015	0.0920	0.0834	0.0757	0.0687	0.0625	0.0568	0.0517	0.0471	0.0429	12
13	0.1452	0.1299	0.1163	0.1042	0.0935	0.0839	0.0754	0.0678	0.0610	0.0550	0.0496	0.0447	0.0404	0.0365	0.0330	13
14	0.1252	0.1110	0.0985	0.0876	0.0779	0.0693	0.0618	0.0551	0.0492	0.0440	0.0393	0.0352	0.0316	0.0283	0.0254	14
15	0.1079	0.0949	0.0835	0.0736	0.0649	0.0573	0.0507	0.0448	0.0397	0.0352	0.0312	0.0277	0.0247	0.0219	0.0195	15
16	0.0930	0.0811	0.0708	0.0618	0.0541	0.0474	0.0415	0.0364	0.0320	0.0281	0.0248	0.0218	0.0193	0.0170	0.0150	16
17	0.0802	0.0693	0.0600	0.0520	0.0451	0.0391	0.0340	0.0296	0.0258	0.0225	0.0197	0.0172	0.0150	0.0132	0.0116	17
18	0.0691	0.0592	0.0508	0.0437	0.0376	0.0323	0.0279	0.0241	0.0208	0.0180	0.0156	0.0135	0.0118	0.0102	0.0089	18
19	0.0596	0.0506	0.0431	0.0367	0.0313	0.0267	0.0229	0.0196	0.0168	0.0144	0.0124	0.0107	0.0092	0.0079	0.0068	19
20	0.0514	0.0433	0.0365	0.0308	0.0261	0.0221	0.0187	0.0159	0.0135	0.0115	0.0098	0.0084	0.0072	0.0061	0.0053	20
25	0.0245	0.0197	0.0160	0.0129	0.0105	0.0085	0.0069	0.0057	0.0046	0.0038	0.0031	0.0025	0.0021	0.0017	0.0014	25
30	0.0116	0.0090	0.0070	0.0054	0.0042	0.0033	0.0026	0.0020	0.0016	0.0012	0.0010	0.0008	0.0006	0.0005	0.0004	30
35	0.0055	0.0041	0.0030	0.0023	0.0017	0.0013	0.0009	0.0007	0.0005	0.0004	0.0003	0.0002	0.0002	0.0001	0.0001	35
40	0.0026	0.0019	0.0013	0.0010	0.0007	0.0005	0.0004	0.0003	0.0002	0.0001	0.0001	0.0001	0.0001	0.0000	0.0000	40
45	0.0013	0.0009	0.0006	0.0004	0.0003	0.0002	0.0001	0.0001	0.0001	0.0000	0.0000	0.0000	0.0000	0.0000	0.0000	45
50	0.0006	0.0004	0.0003	0.0002	0.0001	0.0001	0.0000	0.0000	0.0000	0.0000	0.0000	0.0000	0.0000	0.0000	0.0000	50

Appendix III

Present value of an annuity of £1 at compound interest

$$\dfrac{1-{}^{1}\!/(1+i)^{n}}{i}\times A$$

Interest rate

Periods	1	2	3	4	5	6	7	8	9	10	11	12	13	14	15
1	0.9901	0.9804	0.9709	0.9615	0.9524	0.9434	0.9346	0.9259	0.9174	0.9091	0.9009	0.8929	0.8850	0.8772	0.8696
2	1.9704	1.9416	1.9135	1.8861	1.8594	1.8334	1.8080	1.7833	1.7591	1.7355	1.7125	1.6901	1.6681	1.6467	1.6257
3	2.9410	2.8839	2.8286	2.7751	2.7232	2.6730	2.6243	2.5771	2.5313	2.4869	2.4437	2.4018	2.3612	2.3216	2.2832
4	3.9020	3.8077	3.7171	3.6299	3.5460	3.4651	3.3872	3.3121	3.2397	3.1699	3.1024	3.0373	2.9745	2.9137	2.8550
5	4.8534	4.7135	4.5797	4.4518	4.3295	4.2124	4.1002	3.9927	3.8897	3.7908	3.6959	3.6048	3.5172	3.4331	3.3522
6	5.7955	5.6014	5.4172	5.2421	5.0757	4.9173	4.7665	4.6229	4.4859	4.3553	4.2305	4.1114	3.9975	3.8887	3.7845
7	6.7282	6.4720	6.2303	6.0021	5.7864	5.5824	5.3893	5.2064	5.0330	4.8684	4.7122	4.5638	4.4226	4.2883	4.1604
8	7.6517	7.3255	7.0197	6.7327	6.4632	6.2098	5.9713	5.7466	5.5348	5.3349	5.1461	4.9676	4.7988	4.6389	4.4873
9	8.5660	8.1622	7.7861	7.4353	7.1078	6.8017	6.5152	6.2469	5.9952	5.7590	5.5370	5.3282	5.1317	4.9464	4.7716
10	9.4713	8.9826	8.5302	8.1109	7.7217	7.3601	7.0236	6.7101	6.4177	6.1446	5.8892	5.6502	5.4262	5.2161	5.0188
11	10.3676	9.7868	9.2526	8.7605	8.3064	7.8869	7.4987	7.1390	6.8052	6.4951	6.2065	5.9377	5.6869	5.4527	5.2337
12	11.2551	10.5753	9.9540	9.3851	8.8633	8.3838	7.9427	7.5361	7.1607	6.8137	6.4924	6.1944	5.9176	5.6603	5.4206
13	12.1337	11.3484	10.6350	9.9856	9.3936	8.8527	8.3577	7.9038	7.4869	7.1034	6.7499	6.4235	6.1218	5.8424	5.5831
14	13.0037	12.1062	11.2961	10.5631	9.8986	9.2950	8.7455	8.2442	7.7862	7.3667	6.9819	6.6282	6.3025	6.0021	5.7245
15	13.8651	12.8493	11.9379	11.1184	10.3797	9.7122	9.1079	8.5595	8.0607	7.6061	7.1909	6.8109	6.4624	6.1422	5.8474
16	14.7179	13.5777	12.5611	11.6523	10.8378	10.1059	9.4466	8.8514	8.3126	7.8237	7.3792	6.9740	6.6039	6.2651	5.9542
17	15.5623	14.2919	13.1661	12.1657	11.2741	10.4773	9.7632	9.1216	8.5436	8.0216	7.5488	7.1196	6.7291	6.3729	6.0472
18	16.3983	14.9920	13.7535	12.6593	11.6896	10.8276	10.0591	9.3719	8.7556	8.2014	7.7016	7.2497	6.8399	6.4674	6.1280
19	17.2260	15.6785	14.3238	13.1339	12.0853	11.1581	10.3336	9.6036	8.9501	8.3649	7.8393	7.3658	6.9380	6.5504	6.1982
20	18.0456	16.3514	14.8775	13.5903	12.4622	11.4699	10.5940	9.8181	9.1285	8.5136	7.9633	7.4694	7.0248	6.6231	6.2593
25	22.0232	19.5235	17.4131	15.6221	14.0939	12.7834	11.6536	10.6748	9.8226	9.0770	8.4217	7.8431	7.3300	6.8729	6.4641
30	25.8077	22.3965	19.6004	17.2920	15.3725	13.7648	12.4090	11.2578	10.2737	9.4269	8.6938	8.0552	7.4957	7.0027	6.5660
35	29.4086	24.9986	21.4872	18.6646	16.3742	14.4982	12.9477	11.6546	10.5668	9.6442	8.8552	8.1755	7.5856	7.0700	6.6166
40	32.8347	27.3555	23.1148	19.7928	17.1591	15.0463	13.3317	11.9246	10.7574	9.7791	8.9511	8.2438	7.6344	7.1050	6.6418
45	36.0945	29.4902	24.5187	20.7200	17.7741	15.4558	13.6055	12.1084	10.8812	9.8628	9.0079	8.2825	7.6609	7.1232	6.6543
50	39.1961	31.4236	25.7298	21.4822	18.2559	15.7619	13.8007	12.2335	10.9617	9.9148	9.0417	8.3045	7.6752	7.1327	6.6605

Periods	16	17	18	19	20	21	22	23	24	25	26	27	28	29	30
1	0.8621	0.8547	0.8475	0.8403	0.8333	0.8264	0.8197	0.8130	0.8065	0.8000	0.7937	0.7874	0.7812	0.7752	0.7692
2	1.6052	1.5852	1.5656	1.5465	1.5278	1.5095	1.4915	1.4740	1.4568	1.4400	1.4235	1.4074	1.3916	1.3761	1.3609
3	2.2459	2.2096	2.1743	2.1399	2.1065	2.0739	2.0422	2.0114	1.9813	1.9520	1.9234	1.8956	1.8684	1.8420	1.8161
4	2.7982	2.7432	2.6901	2.6386	2.5887	2.5404	2.4936	2.4483	2.4043	2.3616	2.3202	2.2800	2.2410	2.2031	2.1662
5	3.2743	3.1993	3.1272	3.0576	2.9906	2.9260	2.8636	2.8035	2.7454	2.6893	2.6351	2.5827	2.5320	2.4830	2.4356
6	3.6847	3.5892	3.4976	3.4098	3.3255	3.2446	3.1669	3.0923	3.0205	2.9514	2.8850	2.8210	2.7594	2.7000	2.6427
7	4.0386	3.9224	3.8115	3.7057	3.6046	3.5079	3.4155	3.3270	3.2423	3.1611	3.0833	3.0087	2.9370	2.8682	2.8021
8	4.3436	4.2072	4.0776	3.9544	3.8372	3.7256	3.6193	3.5179	3.4212	3.3289	3.2407	3.1564	3.0758	2.9986	2.9247
9	4.6065	4.4506	4.3030	4.1633	4.0310	3.9054	3.7863	3.6731	3.5655	3.4631	3.3657	3.2728	3.1842	3.0997	3.0190
10	4.8332	4.6586	4.4941	4.3389	4.1925	4.0541	3.9232	3.7993	3.6819	3.5705	3.4648	3.3644	3.2689	3.1781	3.0915
11	5.0286	4.8364	4.6560	4.4865	4.3271	4.1769	4.0354	3.9018	3.7757	3.6564	3.5435	3.4365	3.3351	3.2388	3.1473
12	5.1971	4.9884	4.7932	4.6105	4.4392	4.2784	4.1274	3.9852	3.8514	3.7251	3.6059	3.4933	3.3868	3.2859	3.1903
13	5.3423	5.1183	4.9095	4.7147	4.5327	4.3624	4.2028	4.0530	3.9124	3.7801	3.6555	3.5381	3.4272	3.3224	3.2233
14	5.4675	5.2293	5.0081	4.8023	4.6106	4.4317	4.2646	4.1082	3.9616	3.8241	3.6949	3.5733	3.4587	3.3507	3.2487
15	5.5755	5.3242	5.0916	4.8759	4.6755	4.4890	4.3152	4.1530	4.0013	3.8593	3.7261	3.6010	3.4834	3.3726	3.2682
16	5.6685	5.4053	5.1624	4.9377	4.7296	4.5364	4.3567	4.1894	4.0333	3.8874	3.7509	3.6228	3.5026	3.3896	3.2832
17	5.7487	5.4746	5.2223	4.9897	4.7746	4.5755	4.3908	4.2190	4.0591	3.9099	3.7705	3.6400	3.5177	3.4028	3.2948
18	5.8178	5.5339	5.2732	5.0333	4.8122	4.6079	4.4187	4.2431	4.0799	3.9279	3.7861	3.6536	3.5294	3.4130	3.3037
19	5.8775	5.5845	5.3162	5.0700	4.8435	4.6346	4.4415	4.2627	4.0967	3.9424	3.7985	3.6642	3.5386	3.4210	3.3105
20	5.9288	5.6278	5.3527	5.1009	4.8696	4.6567	4.4603	4.2786	4.1103	3.9539	3.8083	3.6726	3.5458	3.4271	3.3158
25	6.0971	5.7662	5.4669	5.1951	4.9476	4.7213	4.5139	4.3232	4.1474	3.9849	3.8342	3.6943	3.5640	3.4423	3.3286
30	6.1772	5.8294	5.5168	5.2347	4.9789	4.7463	4.5338	4.3391	4.1601	3.9950	3.8424	3.7009	3.5693	3.4466	3.3321
35	6.2153	5.8582	5.5386	5.2512	4.9915	4.7559	4.5411	4.3447	4.1644	3.9984	3.8450	3.7028	3.5708	3.4478	3.3330
40	6.2335	5.8713	5.5482	5.2582	4.9966	4.7596	4.5439	4.3467	4.1659	3.9995	3.8458	3.7034	3.5712	3.4481	3.3332
45	6.2421	5.8773	5.5523	5.2611	4.9986	4.7610	4.5449	4.3474	4.1664	3.9998	3.8460	3.7036	3.5714	3.4482	3.3333
50	6.2463	5.8801	5.5541	5.2623	4.9995	4.7616	4.5452	4.3477	4.1666	3.9999	3.8461	3.7037	3.5714	3.4483	3.3333

Appendix IV
Future value of an annuity of £1 at compound interest

$$A\left[\frac{(1+i)^n - 1}{i}\right]$$

Periods	Interest rate																				
	1	2	3	4	5	6	7	8	9	10	12	14	16	18	20	25	30	35	40	45	50
1	1.0000	1.0000	1.0000	1.0000	1.0000	1.0000	1.0000	1.0000	1.0000	1.0000	1.0000	1.0000	1.0000	1.0000	1.0000	1.0000	1.0000	1.0000	1.0000	1.0000	1.0000
2	2.0100	2.0200	2.0300	2.0400	2.0500	2.0600	2.0700	2.0800	2.0900	2.1000	2.1200	2.1400	2.1600	2.1800	2.2000	2.2500	2.3000	2.3500	2.400	2.4500	2.5000
3	3.0301	3.0604	3.0909	3.1216	3.1525	3.1836	3.2149	3.2464	3.2781	3.3100	3.3744	3.4396	3.5056	3.5724	3.6400	3.8125	3.9900	4.1725	4.3600	4.5525	4.7500
4	4.0604	4.1216	4.1836	4.2465	4.3101	4.3746	4.4399	4.5061	4.5731	4.6410	4.7793	4.9211	5.0665	5.2154	5.3680	5.7656	6.1870	6.6329	7.1040	7.6011	8.1250
5	5.1010	5.2040	5.3091	5.4163	5.5256	5.6371	5.7507	5.8666	5.9847	6.1051	6.3528	6.6101	6.8771	7.1542	7.4416	8.2070	9.0431	9.9544	10.9456	12.0216	13.1875
6	6.1520	6.3081	6.4684	6.6330	6.8019	6.9753	7.1533	7.3359	7.5233	7.7156	8.1152	8.5355	8.9775	9.4420	9.9299	11.2588	12.7560	14.4834	16.3238	18.4314	20.7813
7	7.2135	7.4343	7.6625	7.8983	8.1420	8.3938	8.6540	8.9228	9.2004	9.4872	10.0890	10.7305	11.4139	12.1415	12.9159	15.0735	17.5828	20.4919	23.8534	27.7255	32.1719
8	8.2857	8.5830	8.8923	9.2142	9.5491	9.8975	10.2598	10.6366	11.0285	11.4359	12.2997	13.2328	14.2401	15.3270	16.4991	19.8419	23.8577	28.6640	34.3947	41.2019	49.2578
9	9.3685	9.7546	10.1591	10.5828	11.0266	11.4913	11.9780	12.4876	13.0210	13.5795	14.7757	16.0853	17.5185	19.0859	20.7989	25.8023	32.0150	39.6964	49.1526	60.7428	74.8867
10	10.4622	10.9497	11.4639	12.0061	12.5779	13.1808	13.8164	14.4866	15.1929	15.9374	17.5487	19.3373	21.3215	23.5213	25.9587	33.2529	42.6195	54.5902	69.8137	89.0771	113.330
11	11.5668	12.1687	12.8078	13.4864	14.2068	14.9716	15.7836	16.6455	17.5603	18.5312	20.6546	23.0445	25.7329	28.7551	32.1504	42.5661	56.4053	74.6967	98.7391	130.162	170.995
12	12.6825	13.4121	14.1920	15.0258	15.9171	16.8699	17.8885	18.9771	20.1407	21.3843	24.1331	27.2707	30.8502	34.9311	39.5805	54.2077	74.3270	101.841	139.235	189.735	257.493
13	13.8093	14.6803	15.6178	16.6268	17.7130	18.8821	20.1406	21.4953	22.9534	24.5227	28.0291	32.0887	36.7862	42.2187	48.4966	68.7596	97.6250	138.485	195.929	276.115	387.239
14	14.9474	15.9739	17.0863	18.2919	19.5986	21.0151	22.5505	24.2149	26.0192	27.9750	32.3926	37.5811	43.6720	50.8180	59.1959	86.9495	127.913	187.954	275.300	401.367	581.859
15	16.0969	17.2934	18.5989	20.0236	21.5786	23.2760	25.1290	27.1521	29.3609	31.7725	37.2797	43.8424	51.6595	60.9653	72.0351	109.687	167.286	254.738	386.420	582.982	873.788
16	17.2579	18.6393	20.1569	21.8245	23.6575	25.6725	27.8881	30.3243	33.0034	35.9497	42.7533	50.9804	60.9250	72.9390	87.4421	138.109	218.472	344.897	541.988	846.324	1311.68
17	18.4304	20.0121	21.7616	23.6975	25.8404	28.2129	30.8402	33.7502	36.9737	40.5447	48.8837	59.1176	71.6730	87.0680	105.931	173.636	285.014	466.611	759.784	1228.17	1968.52
18	19.6147	21.4123	23.4144	25.6454	28.1324	30.9057	33.9990	37.4502	41.3013	45.5992	55.7497	68.3941	84.1407	103.740	128.117	218.045	371.518	630.925	1064.70	1781.85	2953.78
19	20.8109	22.8406	25.1169	27.6712	30.5390	33.7600	37.3790	41.4463	46.0185	51.1591	63.4397	78.9692	98.6032	123.414	154.740	273.556	483.973	852.748	1491.58	2584.68	4431.68
20	22.0190	24.2974	26.8704	29.7781	33.0660	36.7856	40.9955	45.7620	51.1601	57.2750	72.0524	91.0249	115.380	146.628	186.688	342.945	630.165	1152.21	2089.21	3748.78	6648.51
25	28.2432	32.0303	36.4593	41.6459	47.7271	54.8645	63.2490	73.1059	84.7009	98.3471	133.334	181.871	249.214	342.603	471.981	1054.79	2348.80	5176.50	11,247.20	24040.7	50500.3
30	34.7849	40.5681	47.5754	56.0849	66.4388	79.0582	94.4608	113.283	136.308	164.494	241.333	356.787	530.312	790.948	1181.88	3227.17	8729.99	23221.6	60501.1	154107	383500
35	41.6603	49.9945	60.4621	73.6522	90.3203	111.435	138.237	172.317	215.711	271.024	431.663	693.573	1120.71	1816.65	2948.34	9856.76	32422.9	104136	325400	987794	2912217
40	48.8864	60.4020	75.4013	95.0255	120.800	154.762	199.635	259.057	337.882	442.593	767.091	1342.03	2360.76	4163.21	7343.86	30088.7	120393	466960	1750092	6331512	22114663
45	56.4811	71.8927	92.7199	121.029	159.700	212.744	285.749	386.506	525.859	718.905	1358.23	2590.56	4965.27	9531.58	18281.3	91831.5	447019	2093876	9412424	40583319	167933233
50	64.4632	84.5794	112.797	152.667	209.348	290.336	406.529	573.770	815.084	1163.91	2400.02	4994.52	10435.6	21813.1	45497.2	280256	1659761	9389020	50622288	260128295	1275242998

z	0.00	0.01	0.02	0.03	0.04	0.05	0.06	0.07	0.08	0.09
0.0	0.0000	0.0040	0.0080	0.0120	0.0160	0.0199	0.0239	0.0279	0.0319	0.0359
0.1	0.0398	0.0438	0.0478	0.0517	0.0557	0.0596	0.0636	0.0675	0.0714	0.0753
0.2	0.0793	0.0832	0.0871	0.0910	0.0948	0.0987	0.1026	0.1064	0.1103	0.1141
0.3	0.1179	0.1217	0.1255	0.1293	0.1331	0.1368	0.1406	0.1443	0.1480	0.1517
0.4	0.1554	0.1591	0.1628	0.1664	0.1700	0.1736	0.1772	0.1808	0.1844	0.1879
0.5	0.1915	0.1950	0.1985	0.2019	0.2054	0.2088	0.2123	0.2157	0.2190	0.2224
0.6	0.2257	0.2291	0.2324	0.2357	0.2389	0.2422	0.2454	0.2486	0.2517	0.2549
0.7	0.2580	0.2611	0.2642	0.2673	0.2704	0.2734	0.2764	0.2794	0.2823	0.2852
0.8	0.2881	0.2910	0.2939	0.2967	0.2995	0.3023	0.3051	0.3078	0.3106	0.3133
0.9	0.3159	0.3186	0.3212	0.3238	0.3264	0.3289	0.3315	0.3340	0.3365	0.3389
1.0	0.3413	0.3438	0.3461	0.3485	0.3508	0.3531	0.3554	0.3577	0.3599	0.3621
1.1	0.3643	0.3665	0.3686	0.3708	0.3729	0.3749	0.3770	0.3790	0.3810	0.3830
1.2	0.3849	0.3869	0.3888	0.3907	0.3925	0.3944	0.3962	0.3980	0.3997	0.4015
1.3	0.4032	0.4049	0.4066	0.4082	0.4099	0.4115	0.4131	0.4147	0.4162	0.4177
1.4	0.4192	0.4207	0.4222	0.4236	0.4251	0.4265	0.4279	0.4292	0.4306	0.4319
1.5	0.4332	0.4345	0.4357	0.4370	0.4382	0.4394	0.4406	0.4418	0.4429	0.4441
1.6	0.4452	0.4463	0.4474	0.4484	0.4495	0.4505	0.4515	0.4525	0.4535	0.4545
1.7	0.4554	0.4564	0.4573	0.4582	0.4591	0.4599	0.4608	0.4616	0.4625	0.4633
1.8	0.4641	0.4649	0.4656	0.4664	0.4671	0.4678	0.4686	0.4693	0.4699	0.4706
1.9	0.4713	0.4719	0.4726	0.4732	0.4738	0.4744	0.4750	0.4756	0.4761	0.4767
2.0	0.4772	0.4778	0.4783	0.4788	0.4793	0.4798	0.4803	0.4808	0.4812	0.4817
2.1	0.4821	0.4826	0.4830	0.4834	0.4838	0.4842	0.4846	0.4850	0.4854	0.4857
2.2	0.4861	0.4864	0.4868	0.4871	0.4875	0.4878	0.4881	0.4884	0.4887	0.4890
2.3	0.4893	0.4896	0.4898	0.4901	0.4904	0.4906	0.4909	0.4911	0.4913	0.4916
2.4	0.4918	0.4920	0.4922	0.4925	0.4927	0.4929	0.4931	0.4932	0.4934	0.4936
2.5	0.4938	0.4940	0.4941	0.4943	0.4945	0.4946	0.4948	0.4949	0.4951	0.4952
2.6	0.4953	0.4955	0.4956	0.4957	0.4959	0.4960	0.4961	0.4962	0.4963	0.4964
2.7	0.4965	0.4966	0.4967	0.4968	0.4969	0.4970	0.4971	0.4972	0.4973	0.4974
2.8	0.4974	0.4975	0.4976	0.4977	0.4977	0.4978	0.4979	0.4979	0.4980	0.4981
2.9	0.4981	0.4982	0.4982	0.4983	0.4984	0.4984	0.4985	0.4985	0.4986	0.4986
3.0	0.4987	0.4987	0.4987	0.4988	0.4988	0.4989	0.4989	0.4989	0.4990	0.4990

1 a £124 **b** £125.97

2 a £26,533 **b** £163,665

3 a 14.2 years **b** 4.96 years

4 Present values of the four options:

   a £1,000,000
   b £1,104,883
   c £1,500,000
   d £1,283,540

Given the time value of money of 9 per cent per annum and certainty about the future (e.g. that you will live to enjoy the perpetuity) then the official answer is c. You may like to question whether this is what you would really go for. If you prefer another option, try to explain what that option says about your time value of money.

5 6%

6 £675

7 14.93%

8 a £32.20 **b** £31.18

9 £4,731

10 £6,217, 8.24%

11 Present value of a ten-year £800 annuity = £4,711. Therefore you could invest £4,711 @ 11% and receive £800 per year for ten years. Reject Supersalesman's offer.

12 £6,468

Glossary

'A' shares Sometimes the 'A' shares are the ordinary shares that carry fewer or no votes. However, in many companies 'A' shares carry more votes than the 'B' shares. The shares may also differ with regard to the size of dividend.

Abandon The choice made by a holder of a warrant or option to allow it to expire without exercise.

Abnormal return (residual return) A return greater than the market return after adjusting for differences in risk.

Absolute advantage A firm, person, organisation or country has an absolute advantage if it can obtain a benefit at a lower cost than other firms, people, organisations or countries. For example Costa Rica has an absolute advantage in growing bananas *vis-à-vis* Europe.

Acceptance credit (bank bill) An institution (e.g. bank) commits itself to the payment of a sum of money in the future as stated in the acceptance credit document. The borrower is given this document (which can be passed on to a supplier) in return for a promise to pay a sum on the maturity date to the institution. The acceptance credit can be sold in the discount market to obtain funds for the borrower (or to pass on to a supplier).

Accounting rate of return (ARR) A measure of profitability based on accounting numbers. Profit divided by assets devoted to the activity (e.g. project, entire business) as a percentage.

Accounting standards A set of formal rules and conventions set by the accounting profession to calculate accounting numbers.

Accounts payable Short-term debts owed by a firm to its creditors for goods and services received. In the UK 'creditors' is often used.

Accounts receivable Customer debts to this company. In the UK 'debtors' is often used to mean the same.

Acid test *see* Quick ratio.

Acquisition premium – *see* bid premium

Additivity Ability to add up.

Administration An administrator, 'administrative receiver' takes over the running of a distressed company to help it survive and avoid liquidation. This follows the company's failure to abide by loan agreements. Administrators often keep the business running as a going concern, but may conclude they have no alternative to liquidation to release money for creditors.

Adverse selection problem When there is an opportunity or incentive for some firms/individuals to act to take advantage of their informational edge over others then the firms/individuals doing that activity will be disproportionately those taking advantage rather than being truly representative of the population as a whole, e.g. the tendency for poorer-than-average risks to continue with insurance. This will raise the cost of insurance for the whole group, including those of less-than-average risk. This is caused by asymmetric information in which the poorer-than-average risk policyholder knows more about their risk level than the insurer does.

Affirmative covenants Loan agreement conditions that require positive action on the part of the borrower, e.g. a statement that a bond will pay regular dividends, or that the borrower will distribute information regularly.

Ageing schedule The total debtor/payables figure is broken down to show how long invoices have been outstanding (i.e. have remained unpaid).

Agency Acting for or in the place of another with his/her/their authority.

Agency costs Costs of preventing agents (e.g. managers) pursuing their own interests at the expense of their principals (e.g. shareholders). Examples include contracting costs and costs of monitoring. In addition there is the agency cost of the loss of wealth caused by the extent to which prevention measures have

not worked and managers continue to pursue non-shareholder wealth goals.

Agent A person who acts for or in the place of another with that other person's authority (the '**principal**').

Aggressive shares Shares having a beta value greater than 1.

AGM *see* Annual general meeting.

AIM admission document The document needed for a company to be quoted on the Alternative Investment Market in the first instance. It is similar to a prospectus.

Allocation of capital (or resources) The mechanism for selecting competing investment projects leading to the production of a mixture of goods and services by a society. This can be influenced by the forces of supply and demand; and by central authority direction. The term may also be used for selection of securities (e.g. shares) by investors or business units and activities by managers.

Allocational efficiency of markets Efficiency in the process of allocating society's scarce resources between competing real investments.

Allotment In a new issue of shares, if more shares are demanded at the price than are available, they may be apportioned (allotted) between the applicants.

All-paper deal When a bidder offers to buy shares in a target the payment is entirely in the form of shares in the bidder.

Alpha (Alpha coefficient, α) A measure of performance greater than or less than the market as a whole after allowing for beta in the capital asset pricing model (q.v.). That portion of a share's return that cannot be explained by its responsiveness to moves in the market as a whole. Sometimes called stock-specific return.

Alternative Investment Market (AIM) The lightly regulated share market operated by the London Stock Exchange, focused particularly on smaller, less well-established companies.

Alternative investments Outside the mainstream, e.g. art, stamps, coins, wine, hedge funds, venture capital.

American Depositary Receipts (ADRs) Depositary receipts issued in the USA.

American-style option (American option) An option which can be exercised by the purchaser at any time up to the expiry date.

AMEX The American Stock Exchange. Trades equities, options and exchange-traded funds. It is now part of the NYSE group.

Amortisation (i) The repayment of a debt by a series of instalments. (ii) The gradual writing off from the balance sheet of intangible assets such as goodwill.

Analyst A researcher of companies' prospects and predictor of their share price performance. Also analyses other securities.

Angel *see* Business angels.

Annual equivalent annuity (AEA) A regular annual amount which is equivalent, in present value terms, to another set of cash flows.

Annual equivalent rate (AER) *see* Annual percentage rate.

Annual general meeting (AGM) A limited company must hold in each calendar year an annual general meeting. It is an opportunity for shareholders to meet and talk with each other and with those who run the company on their behalf. The managers give an account of their stewardship. All shareholders are entitled to attend and vote. Election of directors may take place.

Annual percentage rate (APR) The true annual interest rate charged by a lender. It takes full account of the timing of payments of interest and principal.

Annual results Annual company accounts. This term is often used for the preliminary results.

Annuity An even stream of payments (the same amount each time) over a given period of time with a fixed frequency of payments, usually annually.

Annuity due An annuity where the cash flows occur at the start of each period rather than at the end – the first payment is due now, not in one year's time.

Arbitrage The act of exploiting price differences on the same instrument or similar securities by simultaneously selling the overpriced security and buying the underpriced security.

Arbitrage pricing theory (APT) A type of multi-factor model which relates return on securities to various non-diversifiable risk factors. The expected return on any risky security is a linear combination of these factors.

Arithmetic mean or average The average of a set of numbers equals the sum of the observations divided by the number of observations.

Arrangement fee A fee for agreeing and setting up a financial transaction such as a bank loan.

Articles of association Internal rules governing a company. Can be unique to a company if true to company law.

Asset In the financial markets an asset is anything that can be traded as a security, e.g. share, option, commodity, bond.

Asset allocation An investment methodology, which specifies the proportion of funds to be invested in different asset classes, e.g. property, shares, bonds.

Asset-backed securities (ABS) *see* Securitisation.

Asset backing The value of the assets held in the business – often measured on a per share basis.

Asset class Asset types, e.g. bonds, shares.

Asset liquidity The extent to which assets can be converted to cash quickly and at a low transaction cost.

Asset lock-up In a hostile takeover situation, the target sells to a friendly firm those parts of the business most attractive to the bidder.

Asset securitisation *see* Securitisation.

Asset transformers Intermediaries who, by creating a completely new security – the intermediate security – mobilise savings and encourage investment. The primary security is issued by the ultimate borrower to the intermediary, who offers intermediate securities to the primary investors.

Associated company A company in which an investor (usually a holding company) holds a participating interest and exercises significant influence over the entity. 'Interest' includes shares, options and convertible securities. 'Participating' means the interest is held on a long-term basis and there is significant influence. Usually a 20% or more holding of the shares is presumed to be participating.

Asymmetric information One party in a negotiation or relationship is not in the same position as other parties, being ignorant of, or unable to observe, some information which is essential to the contracting and decision-making process.

At-the-money option The current underlying price is equal to the option exercise price.

Audit committee A group of independent non-executive directors responsible for validating financial figures by for example working with external auditors.

Auditor Auditors determine whether the company's financial statements are misleading and whether the accounts show a true and fair view.

Authorised but unissued ordinary share capital Shares that have not yet been sold by the company to investors. However, they have been created (authorised by shareholders) and may be sold or given to existing shareholders or sold to new shareholders.

Authorised share capital The maximum amount of share capital that a company can issue. The limit can be changed by a shareholder vote.

Average collection period (ACP) The average number of days it takes to collect debts from customers. The total debtors outstanding divided by the average daily sales.

Back office That part of a financial institution which deals with the settlement of contracts, accounting, regulatory matters and management information processes.

Back-to-back loan Company A and Company B lend to each other the same amount with the same maturity but in different currencies. The purpose is to hedge against currency fluctuations.

Bad debts Debts that are unlikely to be paid.

Bad growth When a company increases investment in an area of business that generates returns less than the opportunity cost of capital.

Balance of payments A record of the payment for goods and services obtained by a country and other transfers of currency from abroad and the receipts for goods and services sold and other transfers of currency abroad. The balance on the current account (visible trade and invisible trade) is the difference between national income and national expenditure in the period. The capital account is made up of such items as the inward and outward flow of money for investment and international grants and loans.

Balance sheet Provides a picture of what a company owned, what it owes and is owed on a particular day in the past. It summarises assets, liabilities and net worth (capital).

Balance sheet hedge To counter the risk of forex (q.v.) translation or economic exposure a company may hedge (q.v.) by borrowing in the same currency as the denomination of the assets.

Balloon repayment on a loan The majority of the repayment of a loan is made at or near the maturity date, with the final payment substantially larger than the earlier payments.

Ballot In a new issue of shares when a company floats on a stock exchange if the demand is greater than the supply, the shares are allocated to some applicants but not others, selected at random.

Bancassurance Companies offering both banking and insurance.

Bank bill *see* Acceptance credit.

Bank covenants *see* Covenant.

Bank for International Settlements (BIS) Controlled by central banks, the BIS was established to assist international financial co-ordination. It promotes international monetary co-ordination, provides research and statistical data, co-ordination and trusteeship for intergovernmental loans and acts as a central bank for national central banks, accepting deposits and making loans.

Bank of England The central bank of the United Kingdom, responsible for monetary policy. It oversees the affairs of other financial institutions, issues banknotes and coins, manages the national debt and exchange rate, and is lender of last resort.

Banker's draft A payment drawn upon the bank itself rather than the customer. It is therefore very reassuring to the supplier, because of the higher probability of being paid compared with a standard cheque.

Bankruptcy Commonly used to describe an individual or company that cannot meet its fixed commitments on borrowing which leads to legal action. However, technically, in the UK individuals become

bankrupt whereas firms become insolvent.

Barriers to entry The obstacles that a company entering a market for the first time has to overcome to do well in that market.

Base-case strategy A continuation of current strategy.

Base rate The reference rate of interest set by banks but influenced by the Bank of England that forms the basis for interest rates on bank loans, overdrafts and deposit rates.

Basic (FRS 3) earnings per share Includes deductions from profit of one-off exceptional items and goodwill amortisation.

Basis point (bp) One-hundredth of 1%, usually applied to interest rates.

Bear An investor who takes the view that prices are likely to fall.

Bear fund Designed to do well when shares are falling in price.

Bearer bond The ownership of a bond is not recorded on a register. Possession of the bond is sufficient to receive interest, etc.

Bells and Whistles Additional features placed on derivatives or securities, such as bonds, that are designed to attract investors or reduce issue costs.

Benchmark A financial security or index of financial securities the returns or levels of which is considered to be a suitable reference rate for other securities, e.g. the interest rate on a ten-year gilt is a reference benchmark for corporate bond interest.

Benefit–cost ratio A measure of present value per £ invested. Benefit–cost ratio = Net present value (NPV) (q.v.) divided by Initial outlay.

Beta A measure of the systematic risk of a financial security. In the capital asset pricing model (q.v.) it is a measure of the sensitivity to market movements of a financial security's return, as measured by the covariance between returns on the asset and returns on the market portfolio divided by the variance of the market portfolio. In practice a proxy (e.g. FTSE 100 index) is used for the market portfolio.

Bid–offer spread ('Bid–ask spread' in USA) The difference between the market maker's buy and sell prices.

Bid premium The additional amount an acquirer has to offer above the pre-bid share price in order to succeed in a takeover offer.

Bid price The price at which a market maker will buy shares or a dealer in other markets will buy a security or commodity.

Bid yield The yield to maturity on a bond given the market price at which the market makers will buy from investors.

Bill A legal document with a promise to pay or a demand for payment.

Bill of exchange A document setting out a commitment to pay a sum of money at a specified point in time, e.g. an importer commits itself to paying a supplier. Bills of exchange may be discounted – that is, sold before maturity for less than face value.

BIMBO A buy-in management buyout. A combination of a management buyout and a buy-in. Outside managers join forces with existing managers to take over a company, subsidiary or unit.

Bird-in-the-hand fallacy The belief that dividends received earlier are discounted at a lower annual rate than those received in more distant years.

Black Monday 19 October 1987, the date of a large fall in stock market prices (also Monday 28 October 1929 in USA).

Black Wednesday 16 September 1992, a day of severe currency turbulence when sterling and the Italian lira devalued significantly and were forced to leave the Exchange Rate Mechanism.

Blue chip A company regarded as of the highest quality; regarded, often mistakenly, as safest.

Board of Directors People elected by shareholders to run a company.

Bond A debt obligation with a long-term maturity (more than one year), usually issued by firms and governments.

Bond covenant *see* Covenant.

Bonus issue *see* Scrip issue.

Bookrunner *see* Book-building

Book value Balance sheet value. Can be expressed on a per share basis.

Book-building A book runner (lead manager) invites major institutional investors to suggest how many shares (or other financial securities) they would be interested in purchasing and at what price in a new issue or secondary issue of shares (or other financial securities). This helps to establish the price and allocate shares.

Book-to-market equity ratio The ratio of a firm's balance sheet net asset value to the total market value of its shares.

Bootstrapping game *see* Price-earnings ratio game.

Borrowing capacity Limits to total borrowing levels imposed by lenders, often determined by available collateral.

Bottom line Profit attributable to the shareholders produced by a company over a period of time, e.g. one year.

Bought deal An investment bank (the 'lead manager', perhaps together with co-managers of the issue), buys an entire security issue (e.g. shares) from a client corporation raising finance. The investment bank usually intends to then sell it out to institutional clients within hours.

Bourse Alternative name for a stock exchange. A French word, but used in other countries, particularly in Continental Europe.

Break-even analysis Analysing the level of sales at which a project, division or business produces a zero profit (accounting emphasis).

Break-even NPV The point at which when a single variable is changed, the net present value (NPV) (q.v.) of a proposed project switches from positive to negative (or vice versa).

Break-up value The total value of separate parts of the company if the parts are sold off to the highest bidder.

British Bankers Association (BBA) Trade association of British banks. Sets model contracts, publishes interest rates, e.g. interbank rates, advocates on behalf of banks.

Broker/brokerage Assists in the buying and selling of financial securities by acting as a 'go-between', helping to reduce search, transaction and information costs.

Broker-dealer An individual acting as agent for buyers and sellers, but who, at the same time, trades for his own account and may also be a market maker.

Bubble An explosive upward movement in financial security or other asset prices not based on fundamentally rational factors, followed by a sharp decline (a crash).

Budget (national) Sets out government expenditure and revenue for the financial year. In the UK it is presented by the Chancellor of the Exchequer to the British Parliament.

Buffer stock Stock (raw material, work-in-progress or finished goods) held to reduce the negative effects (stock-out costs) of an unusually large usage of stock.

Building society A UK financial institution, the primary role of which is the provision of mortgages for home purchase. Building societies are non-profit-making mutual organisations. Funding is mostly through small deposits by individuals.

Bulge bracket A leading investment bank.

Bull An investor taking the view that prices will rise.

Bulldog A foreign bond issued in the UK.

Bullet bond A bond where all the principal on a loan is repaid at maturity.

Business angels (Informal venture capitalists) Wealthy individuals prepared to invest about £10,000–£250,000 in a start-up, early-stage or developing firm. They often have managerial and/or technical experience to offer the management team as well as equity and debt finance. Medium- to long-term investment in high-risk situations.

Business risk The risk associated with the underlying operations of a business. The variability of the firm's operating income, before interest: this dispersion is caused purely by business-related factors and not by the debt burden.

Buy-back *see* Share repurchase.

Buy-side Investors, and those who act or advise on their behalf (e.g. investment institutions such as unit trusts, private equity funds, pension funds and hedge funds) who purchase securities and the services offered by the sell-side institutions.

BVCA British Private Equity and Venture Capital Association. The UK industry body and public policy advocate for the private equity and venture capital industry.

CAC 40 (Compagnie des Agents de Change 40 Index) A stock market index of French shares quoted in Paris.

Cadbury report The Committee on the Financial Aspects of Corporate Governance chaired by Sir Adrian Cadbury made recommendations on the role of directors and auditors, published in 1992.

Call-back features *see* Call option.

Call option This gives the purchaser the right, but not the obligation, to buy a fixed quantity of a commodity, financial instrument or some other underlying asset at a given price, at or before a specified date.

Called-up (issued) share capital The total value of shares sold by a company when expressed at par or nominal value.

Cap (1) An interest rate cap is a contract that effectively gives the purchaser the right to set a maximum level for interest rates payable. Compensation is paid to the purchaser of a cap if interest rates rise above an agreed level. (2) (Derivatives) Any feature that sets a maximum return, payout or cost.

Capex *see* Capital expenditure

Capital (1) Funding for a business – can be equity only or equity plus debt. (2) Another term for net worth – total assets minus total liabilities.

Capital Asset Pricing Model (CAPM) An asset (e.g. share) pricing theory which assumes that financial assets, in equilibrium, will be priced to produce rates of return which compensate investors for systematic risk as measured by the covariance of the assets' return with the market portfolio return (i.e. beta).

Capital budgeting The process of analysing and selecting long-term capital investments.

Capital expenditure (capex) The purchase of long-lived (more than one year) assets (that is, fixed assets).

Capital gain A financial gain made when an asset has increased in value and is then sold (a realised capital gain) or retained (unrealised capital gain).

Capital gearing The extent to which the firm's total capital is in the form of debt.

Capital lease *see* Finance lease and Leasing.

Capital market Where those raising finance can do so by selling financial securities to investors, e.g. bonds, shares.

Capital rationing When funds are not available to finance all wealth-enhancing (positive NPV) projects.

Capital reconstruction (restructuring) Altering the shape of the firm's liabilities. E.g. increases/ decreases in the amount of equity; increases/ decreases in debt; lengthening/ shortening debt maturities.

Capital structure The proportion of the firm's capital which is equity or debt.

Capitalisation (1) An item of expenditure is taken on to the balance sheet and capitalised as an asset rather than written off against profits. (2) Short for market capitalisation (q.v.).

Capitalisation factor A discount rate.

Capitalisation issue *see* Scrip issue.

Capitalisation rate Required rate of return for the class of risk.

Capped bonds The floating interest rate charged cannot rise above a specified level.

Captives A venture capital organisation that raises its capital from one institution (or a small group of institutions).

Cartel A group of otherwise competing firms entering into an agreement to set mutually acceptable prices, output levels and market shares for their products.

Cash-conversion cycle The stock-conversion period plus the debtor-conversion period minus the credit period granted by suppliers. It focuses on the length of time between the company's outlay on inputs and the receipt of money from the sale of goods.

Cash cow A company with low growth and stable market conditions with low investment needs. The company's competitive strength enables it to produce surplus cash.

Cash dividend A normal dividend by a company, paid in cash rather than a scrip dividend.

Cash flow statement The formal report of a company's cash movements over a period.

Cash settled In the derivatives market some contracts are physically settled at expiry date (e.g. copper is delivered in return for cash under the derivative contract). However, many derivatives are not physically delivered; rather, a cash difference representing a gain or loss on the closed derivative position changes hands.

Causal ambiguity A potential imitator is unable to see clearly which resource is giving the sustainable competitive advantage to a firm or it is difficult to identify the way in which the extraordinary resource was created in the first place.

CBOT *see* Chicago Board of Trade.

CEO (Chief Executive Officer) The director with the highest power over the actions of the firm.

Central bank A bankers' bank and lender of last resort, which controls the credit system of an economy, e.g. controls note issue, acts as the government's bank, controls interest rates and regulates the country's banking system.

Central Securities Depository, CSD A financial institution that holds shares on behalf of investors so that ownership can be transferred quickly through changing the electronic book entry rather than transferring physical certificates.

Central Counter-party (CCP) clearing house *see* Clearing house.

Certainty equivalent The value of a risk-free cash flow that would make the investor indifferent as to the choice between this safe cash flow or an alternative risky cash flow.

Certificate of deposit (CD) A deposit is made at a bank. A certificate confirming that a deposit has been made is given by the bank to the lender. This is normally a bearer security. Most CDs can then be sold in the secondary market whenever the depositor (firm or investor) needs cash.

Chapter 11 In the US companies in financial difficulties can gain some protection under chapter 11, intended to allow the company to continue in operation while an attempt is made to negotiate with lenders and suppliers to restructure the finances.

CHAPS (Clearing House Automated Payment System) The UK same-day interbank clearing system for sterling payments (computer based).

Challenger banks Banks which currently only operate in a few towns or only on the Internet, that are determined to draw customers from the established giants of the industry.

Characteristic line The line that best relates the return on a share to the return on a broad market index.

Chartism Security analysis that relies on historic price charts (and/or trading volumes) to predict future movements.

Chicago Board of Trade (CBOT) The futures and options exchange in Chicago, USA – the world's oldest (established 1848). Now part of CME Group.

Chicago Board Options Exchange (CBOE) The largest options exchange in the world, trading options on shares, indices and interest rates.

Chicago Mercantile Exchange (CME) *see* CME.

Chief executive officer (CEO) The manager/director in overall charge of the running of the business.

Chief executive's review (operational review) A comment, contained in a company's annual report and accounts, on performance, strategy and managerial intentions.

Chinese walls Barriers within a financial service company designed to prevent sensitive information being passed on to another branch of the organisation.

CHIPS (Clearing House Interbank Payment System) The US system for settling US dollar payment the same day between banks.

Circle of competence The business areas that an individual thoroughly understands and is equipped to analyse.

City Code on Takeovers and Mergers Provides the main governing rules for UK-based companies engaged in merger activity. Self-regulated and administered by the Takeover Panel.

City of London A collective term for the financial institutions located in the financial district to the east of St Paul's Cathedral in London (also called the Square Mile). However, the term is also used to refer to all UK-based financial institutions, wherever they are located.

City Panel on Takeovers and Mergers The organization that provides and enforces rules governing behaviour in companies engaged in merger activity in the UK. The rules apply to unquoted and quoted public companies. Often shortened to 'The takeover Panel' or 'The Panel'.

Clawback Existing shareholders often have the right to reclaim shares sold under a placing as though they were entitled to them under a rights issue.

Clean price On a bond the prices are generally quoted 'clean', that is without taking account of the accrued interest since the last coupon payment.

Clearing a trade The stock exchange (or other market clearer) ensures that (1) all reports of a trade are reconciled to make sure all parties are in agreement as to the number of shares traded and the price; and (2) the buyer and seller have the cash and securities to do the deal.

Clearing bank Member of the London Bankers' Clearing House, which clears cheques, settling indebtedness between two parties.

Clearing house An institution which registers, monitors, matches and settles mutual indebtedness between a number of individuals or organisations. The clearing house may also act as a counterparty or central counterparty, that is act as a buyer to every seller and as a seller to every buyer.

Clientele effect In dividend theory the level of dividend may be influenced by shareholders preferring a dividend pattern which matches their consumption pattern and/or tax position.

Closed-end funds Collective investment vehicles (e.g. investment trusts) that do not create or redeem shares on a daily basis in response to increases and decreases in demand. They have a fixed number of shares for lengthy periods.

Closing out a futures position Taking a second action in the futures market (say, selling the future) which is exactly opposite to the first action (say, buying the future). Also called reversing the trade.

CLS bank *see* Continuous linked settlement.

CME An exchange which trades a wide range of currency futures and options, interest rate futures and options, community futures and options and share index futures and options. Within the CME group are CME, CBOT, NYMEX and COMEX.

Code *see* City Code on Takeovers and Mergers

Coefficient of determination, R-squared For single linear regression this is the proportion of variation in the dependant variable that is related to the variation in the independent variable. A measure of the 'goodness of fit' in a regression equation.

Co-lead manager The title given to an underwriter (e.g. for a bond sale) who has joint lead manager status and may sometimes be engaged in structuring the transaction. Usually part of the selling group. Usually does not act as a bookrunner.

Collar A ceiling and floor interest rate placed on the variability of interest payable on a debt, often achieved by the simultaneous purchase of an interest rate cap and sale of an interest rate floor.

Collateral Property and/or other assets pledged by a borrower to protect the interests of the lender – they may be seized if the borrower reneges.

Collective funds *see* Pooled funds.

Combined Code of Corporate Governance A set of guidelines for best practice corporate governance (e.g. the majority of the board to be independent non-executive directors). The UKLA requires compliance with the Code or an explanation for non-compliance.

Commercial banking A range of banking services undertaken, including taking deposits and making loans, chequing facilities, trustee services, securities advisory services. For retail and corporate clients.

Commercial bill (bank bill or trade bill) A document expressing the commitment of a borrowing firm to repay a short-term debt at a fixed date in the future.

Commercial paper (CP) An unsecured note promising the holder (lender) a sum of money to be paid in a few days – average maturity of 40 days. If they are denominated in a foreign currency and placed outside the jurisdiction of the authorities of that currency then the notes are Eurocommercial paper.

Commitment fee A fee payable in return for a commitment by a bank to lend money at some future date. In some cases the fee is only payable on the undrawn portion of the loan, in others the fee also applies to funds already drawn down under the arrangement.

Commodity price swap Each counterparty agrees to make regular payments to the other where one of the payments is determined by the varying price of a commodity or an index of commodities.

Commodity (commoditized) product (1) Undifferentiated compared with competitor offerings in any customer-important way by factors such as performance, appearance, service support, etc. For example, many personal computers are said to be commodity products. (2) Raw materials and foodstuffs.

Common stock The term used in the USA to describe ordinary shares in a company.

Companies Acts The series of laws enacted by Parliament governing the establishment and conduct of incorporated business enterprises. The Companies Act 2006 consolidated the Acts that preceded it.

Companies House The place where records are kept of every UK company. These accounts, etc. are then made available to the general public.

Company registrar *see* Registrar.

Comparative advantage A firm or a country has a comparative advantage in the production of good X if the opportunity cost of producing a unit of X, in terms of other goods forgone, is lower, in that country compared with another country, or in that firm compared with another firm.

Competition and Markets Authority This UK organisation may obtain any information needed to investigate possible monopoly or other anti-competitive situations resulting in a substantial lessening in competition leading to the detriment of buyers of goods and services. It may then block anti-competitive action.

Competitive advantage (edge) The possession of extraordinary resources that allow a firm to rise above the others in its industry to generate exceptional long-run rates of return on capital employed.

Competitive floor Where shareholders receive a rate of return that only just induces them to put money into the firm and hold it there. This minimal rate of return occurs because of the high level of competition in the market for the firm's product, or because of value being reduced to the minimum by one or more of the other of Porter's five forces.

Competitive position The competitive strength of the firm *vis-à-vis* rivals, suppliers, customer and substitutes in a product market.

Complementary product One that is generally bought alongside the product in question.

Compliance Methods of ensuring that financial market operators meet any legal and supervisory requirements.

Compound interest Interest is paid on the sum which accumulates, whether or not that sum comes from principal or from interest received at intermediate dates.

Compound return The income received on an investment is reinvested in the investment and future returns are gained on both the original capital and the ploughed-back income. Usually measured as an annual percentage return.

Concert party A group of investors who, pursuant to an agreement or understanding (whether formal or informal), co-operate to obtain or consolidate control of a company or to frustrate the successful outcome of a takeover offer for a company.

Conflict of preferences There is a conflict of preferences between the primary investors wanting low-cost liquidity and low risk on invested funds, and the ultimate borrowers wanting long-term risk-bearing capital.

Conglomerate A holding company with subsidiaries with operations in different business areas.

Conglomerate bank A bank with a wide range of activities, products and markets.

Conglomerate merger The combining of two firms which operate in unrelated business areas.

Consideration The price paid for something.

Consolidated (group) accounts All the income, costs, assets and all the liabilities of all group companies, whether wholly or partially owned, are brought together in the consolidated accounts. Consolidation must take place if 50% or more of a subsidiary's shares are held by the parent. If less than 50% of the shares are held consolidation may still be required.

Consolidation of shares The number of shares is reduced by the company and the nominal value of each remaining share rises.

Consumer price index (CPI) A measure of general inflation.

Consumer credit firms Offering credit; this may be in a variety of ways, e.g. hire purchase, term loan, credit card, payday loan, pawnbrokers.

Continuing obligations Standards of behaviour and actions required of firms listed on the London Stock Exchange, enforced by the United Kingdom Listing Authority (q.v.).

Continuous Linked Settlement (CLS) A system designed to reduce the risk of failure of one counterparty to a foreign exchange transaction to fulfil an obligation. Payment of the two sides of the currency deal is made the day after the deal, organised by the CLS Bank.

Continuous order book Throughout the trading day orders are automatically matched and executed against one another.

Contract for differences (CFD) The buyer and seller agree to pay, in cash, at the closing of the contract, the difference between the opening and closing price of the underlying shares, multiplied by the number of shares in the contract.

Contractual theory Views the firm as a network of contracts, actual and implicit, which specify the roles to be played by various participants. Most participants bargain for low risk and a satisfactory return. Shareholders accept high risk in anticipation of any surplus returns after all other parties have been satisfied.

Contrarian Taking the opposite position to the generality of investors.

Control premium – *see* bid premium

Controlling shareholder Any shareholder able to control the composition of the board of directors and therefore the direction of the company. Strictly speaking this is 50%, but even a 30% shareholder can exercise this degree of power, and therefore 30% is used as the cut-off point for some purposes.

Conventional cash flows Where an outflow is followed by a series of inflows, or a cash inflow is followed by a series of cash outflows.

Convergence The coming together of the futures price and the underlying price as the final trading day of a futures contract approaches.

Conversion premium With convertible bonds, it is the difference between the current share price and the conversion price, expressed as a percentage of the current share price.

Conversion price The share price at which convertible bonds may be converted.

Conversion ratio (1) The nominal (par) value of a convertible bond divided by the conversion price. The number of shares available per bond. (2) The ratio of the number of warrants that must be held and exercised in order to buy or sell a single unit of the asset (e.g. one share).

Conversion value The value of a convertible bond if it were converted into ordinary shares at the current share price.

Convertible bonds Bonds which carry a rate of interest and give the owner the right to exchange the bonds at some stage in the future into ordinary shares according to a prearranged formula.

Convertible currency A currency that may be exchanged into another with no or few restrictions on individuals, companies or institutions, such as government prohibitions.

Convertible loan stock Same definition as Convertible bond.

Convertible preferred stock A preferred share that can be changed into another type of security, e.g. an ordinary share, at the holder's option.

Corporate adviser These professional financial service firms advise companies gaining a quotation for their shares on the UK's NEX Exchange to ensure knowledge and compliance with the rules and responsibilities of being on NEX. They provide reassurance to investors that the company meets certain basic standards of financial record keeping, reporting and corporate governance.

Corporate bond A bond issued by a company.

Corporate acquisition *see* Takeover (acquisition).

Corporate broker Stockbrokers that act on behalf of companies quoted on an exchange. For example, they may provide advice on market conditions or may represent the company to the market. Corporate brokers are knowledgeable about the share and other financial markets. They advise companies on fund raising (e.g. new issues). They try to generate interest amongst investors for the company's securities. They stand prepared to buy and sell companies' shares.

Corporate finance department of investment banks The department assisting firms in raising funds (e.g. rights issues, bond issues) and managing their finances.

Corporate governance The system of management and control of the corporation.

Corporate Governance Code Guidelines of best practice for companies regarding the powers and responsibilities of directors, shareholders and senior managers.

Corporate raider An organisation that makes hostile takeover approaches for quoted companies.

Corporate Social Responsibility, CSR Taking into account the effects of the organisation's impact on the environment and social wellbeing. Going beyond regulatory requirements in taking action to improve, say communities, the environment, human rights and employee welfare, even at the expense of near term profits.

Corporate value The present value of cash flows for the entire corporation within the planning horizon plus the present value of cash flows after the planning horizon plus the saleable value of assets not required for cash flow generation. Includes cash flows attributable to equity and debt holders.

Corporate venturing Large companies fostering the development of smaller enterprises through, say, joint capital development or equity capital provision.

Corporation tax A tax levied on the profits of companies.

Correlation coefficient A measure of the extent to which two variables show a relationship, expressed on a scale of −1 to +1. A correlation of −1 implies that two share prices, two markets, etc., move in opposite directions by the same percentages.

Correlation scale A scale between −1 and +1 showing the degree of co-movement of two variables, e.g. the return on two shares. A value of −1 indicates exact opposite movement, a value of +1 indicates perfect movement in the same direction.

Cost leadership strategy Standard no-frills product. Emphasis on scale economies and other cost advantages.

Cost of capital The rate of return that a company has to offer finance providers to induce them to buy and hold a financial security.

Cost of sales The expense incurred for brought-in raw materials and components.

Counterparty The buyer for a seller, and the seller for a buyer.

Counterparty risk The risk that a counterparty to a contract defaults and does not fulfil its obligations.

Country risk Risk to transactions overseas or assets held abroad due to political, legal, regulatory or settlement changes or difficulties, e.g. nationalisation or law forbidding repatriation of profits.

Coupons An attachment to bond or loan note documents which may be separated and serve as evidence of entitlement to interest. Nowadays it refers to the interest itself: the nominal annual rate of interest expressed as a percentage of the principal value.

Covariance The extent to which two variables move together.

Covenant A solemn agreement.

Cover Offsetting one position in a financial security with an equal and opposite transaction in the same or linked (e.g. derivative) security.

Covered call option writing Writing a call option on an underlying when the writer owns at least the number of underlying securities included in the option.

Covered warrants The same as warrants except that financial institutions issue them, selling the right to buy or sell shares in industrial and commercial companies.

Creative accounting The drawing up of accounts which obey the letter of the law and accounting body rules but which involve the manipulation of accounts to show the most favourable profit and balance sheet.

Credit derivative An instrument for which the payoff is linked to changes in the underlying's credit standing or default, e.g. if the credit rating changes on a bond issued by a company from BBB− to D the holder will receive a payout on a credit derivative (sold by a financial institution) which takes as its underlying that particular company's bond.

Credit facility or Credit line A short-term borrowing arrangement with a bank or other lender under which borrowing may fluctuate at the behest of the borrower up to a fixed total amount, e.g. overdraft, revolving facility.

Credit insurance (1) An insurance policy that pays out on trade debts held by the firm when customers fail to meet their obligations. (2) An insurance policy that pays out in the event of default on a debt instrument.

Credit period The average length of time between the purchase of inputs and the payment for them. Equal to the average level of creditors divided by the purchases on credit per day.

Credit rating An estimate of the quality of a debt from the lender's viewpoint in terms of the likelihood of interest and capital not being paid and of the extent to which the lender is protected in the event of default. Credit-rating agencies are paid fees by companies, governments, etc. wishing to attract lenders.

Credit risk The risk that a counterparty to a financial transaction will fail to fulfil its obligation.

Credit risk premium or credit spread The additional yield (over, say, reputable government bonds) on a debt instrument due to the borrower's additional perceived probability of default.

Credit union A non-profit organisation accepting deposits and making loans, operated as a co-operative.

Creditor One to whom a debt is owed.

Creditors (accounts payable, or payables) Amounts owed by a company to suppliers and others.

Crest or CREST An electronic means of settlement and registration of shares and other securities following a sale on the London Stock Exchange, operated by CRESTCo.

Crowdfunding (crowd financing or crowd sourced capital) Many websites connect entrepreneurial firms seeking equity or debt capital with investors in the crowdfunding sector. Potential investors can look online at a range of companies pitching to raise a few hundred thousand or millions from hundreds of investors putting in amounts ranging upwards from just a few hundred pounds.

Crown jewels defence In a hostile merger situation, the target sells off the most attractive parts of the business.

Cum-dividend (1) When an investor buys a government bond (q.v.) when it is still designated cum-dividend or cum-coupon he/she is entitled to the accrued interest since the last coupon was paid. (2) A share (q.v.) designated cum-dividend indicates that the buyer will be entitled to a dividend recently announced by the company.

Cum-rights Shares bought on the stock market prior to the ex-rights day are designated cum-rights and carry to the new owner the right to subscribe for the new shares in the rights issue.

Cumulative If a payment (interest or dividend) on a bond (q.v.) or share (q.v.) is missed in one period those securities are given priority when the next payment is made. These arrears must be cleared up before shareholders received dividends.

Currency option A contract giving the right but not the obligation to buy or sell currency on specified terms.

Currency swap *see* Swap.

Current account deficit *see* Balance of payment.

Current asset value (net) Current assets (cash, accounts receivable, inventory) minus current liabilities (also called working capital).

Current assets Cash and other assets that can be turned into cash within days or weeks. Includes inventory (stocks) of raw materials, partially finished goods and finished goods, receivables (debtors) and investments expected to be sold within one year.

Current liabilities Amounts owed that the company expects to have to pay within the next year.

Current ratio The ratio of current liabilities to the current assets of a business.

Current yield (flat yield, income yield or running yield) The ratio of the coupon (q.v.) on a bond (q.v.) to its current market price.

Cyclically adjusted price/earnings ratio (CAPE) Current market price of a single company's share (or the market as a whole) divided by average earnings over the past ten years.

Cyclical companies (or industries, or shares) Those companies in which profits are particularly sensitive to the growth level in the economy, which may be cyclical.

Daily Official List (DOL) The daily record setting out the prices of all trades in securities conducted on the London Stock Exchange.

Dark pool A trading venue where large orders can be placed anonymously to reduce the effect of the trade on market prices.

Darling A stock market darling is one which receives a lot of attention and is regarded as very attractive.

Dawn raid An acquirer acts with such speed in buying the shares of the target company that the raider achieves the objective of a substantial stake in the target before its management has time to react.

DAX 30 (Deutsche Aktienindex) A stock market index of German shares quoted on Deutsche Börse (q.v.).

Debentures Bonds issued with redemption dates a number of years into the future or irredeemable. Usually secured against specific assets (mortgage debentures) or through a floating charge on the firm's assets (floating debentures). In the USA and Canada debenture means an unsecured debt with a fixed coupon.

Debt An obligation to pay.

Debt capital Capital raised with (usually) a fixed obligation in terms of interest and principal payments, e.g. loans and bonds.

Debt maturity The length of time left until the repayment of principal on a debt becomes due.

Debt rating A rating given by one of the credit rating agencies to bonds or borrowers.

Debt restructuring Negotiating with lenders to vary the terms of the debt in time of difficulty.

Debt-to-equity ratio The ratio of a company's long-term debt to shareholders' funds.

Debtor One who owes a debt.

Debtor conversion period The average number of days to convert customer debts into cash. Equal to the average value of debtors divided by the average value of sales per day.

Debtors (accounts receivable, receivables) When goods are sold by a company on credit its customers owe it money. They are debtors or trade debtors.

Declining (reducing) balance method of depreciation The amount by which an asset is depreciated declines from one year to the next

as it is determined by a constant percentage of the asset's depreciated value at the start of each year.

Deep discounted bonds Bonds sold well below par value, usually because they have little or no coupon.

Deep discounted rights issue A rights issue price is much less than the present market price of the old shares.

Default A failure to make agreed payments of interest or principal, or failure to comply with some other provision in a loan agreement.

Defensive industries Those industries where profits are not particularly sensitive to the growth level in the economy.

Defensive shares Having a beta value of less than 1.

Deferred ordinary shares (1) Rank below preferred ordinary shares for dividends. So, if profits are low deferred ordinary holders may not receive a dividend, but in a good year the holders (often founders) may receive a large share of the profit (2) The right to the dividend is deferred for a set period, after which the holders rank equal with ordinary shareholders.

Deferred tax In drawing up a set of company accounts there are some deductions that can be made for calculating taxable profits, thus lowering tax paid for that period, which not deductible (to the same extent) for accounting profits. However, there will be future tax consequence because the expense cannot be used again, thus there is a prospect of raised tax payable in a future year. For example, with a fixed (non-current) asset the writing down allowance, which can be used to reduce current tax payable, is often greater than the depreciation charge as determined by the company's accounting policy. The differences is called a timing difference. A deferred tax provision is the difference between (i) the corporation tax actually payable on the taxable trading profit and (ii) the tax that would have been payable if the taxable trading profit is the same as the accounting profit (using normal depreciation not writing down allowance).

Dematerialisation Traditionally the evidence of financial security ownership is by written statements on paper (e.g. share certificates). Increasingly such information is being placed on electronic records

and paper evidence is being abandoned.

Demerger The separation of companies or business units that are currently under one corporate umbrella. It applies particularly to the unravelling of a merger.

Depletion A reduction in the value of a natural resource, e.g. oil in the ground, owned by a company.

Depositary receipts Certificates, representing evidence of ownership of a company's shares (or other securities) held by a depository. Depositary Receipts (DRs) are negotiable (can be traded) certificates which represent ownership of a given number of a company's shares which can be listed and traded independently from the underlying shares. There are a number of forms of DRs including American Depositary Receipts (ADRs), Global Depositary Receipts (GDRs), Euro Depositary Receipts (EDRs) and Retail Depositary Receipts (RDRs).

Depository Person or firm, often a large bank, entrusted with safekeeping of funds, securities, or other valuable assets. They can transfer ownership of shares/bonds etc., from one investor's account to another, reducing paperwork for executing a trade and speeding up the transfer process.

Depreciation The reduction in the stated value of assets with a useful life of more than one year that are not bought and sold as part of normal trading. The reduction may be due to wearing out, using up, effluxion of time or obsolescence.

Derivative A financial asset (instrument), the performance of which is based on (derived from) the behaviour of the value of an underlying asset.

Deutsche Börse AG The German Stock Exchange based in Frankfurt.

Development capital Second stage finance (following seed finance – *see* Seedcorn capital or money *and* Early-stage capital) to permit business expansion.

Differentiated product One that is slightly different in significant ways from those supplied by other companies. The unique nature of the product/service offered allows for a premium price to be charged.

Diluted earnings per share Takes into account any additional shares that may be issued in the future under executive share option schemes and other commitments.

Dilution The effect on the earnings and voting power per ordinary share from an increase in the number of shares issued without a corresponding increase in the firm's earnings.

Diminishing marginal utility Successive equal increments in quantity of a good (money) yield smaller and smaller increases in utility.

Direct foreign investment The cross-border purchase of commercial assets such as factories, industrial plant or whole companies for productive purposes.

Directors' dealings Directors' purchase or sale of shares in their own company. This is legal (except at certain times of the company's year). Some investors examine directors' dealings to decide whether to buy or sell.

Directors' report Information and commentary on company performance and other matters contained in a company's annual report and accounts.

Dirty price, full price, invoice price On a bond a buyer pays a total of the clean price and the accrued interest since the last coupon payment.

Disclosure of shareholdings If a stake of 3% or more is held by one shareholder in a UK public company, then this has to be declared to the company.

Discount (1) The amount below face value at which a financial claim sells, e.g. bill of exchange or zero coupon bond. (2) The extent to which an investment trust's shares sell below the net asset value. (3) The amount by which a future value of a currency is less than its spot value. (4) The action of purchasing financial instruments, e.g. bills, at a discount. (5) The degree to which a security sells below its issue price in the secondary market. (6) The process of equating a cash flow at some future date with today's value using the time value of money. (7) A deduction from the normal price or value, the opposite of premium.

Discount house An institution that purchases promissory notes and resells them or holds them until maturity.

Discount market deposit Originally it was money deposited with a London discount house. However, there is now a collection of UK institutions and dealers in money market instruments such as trade bills. These are normally repayable at call or very short term. Clearing banks are the usual depositors.

Discount rate (1) The rate of return used to discount cash flows received in future years. It is the opportunity cost of capital given the risk class of the future cash flows. (2) The rate of interest at which some central banks lend money to the banking system.

Discounted cash flow Future cash flows are converted into the common denominator of time zero money by adjusting for the time value of money.

Discounted payback The period of time required to recover initial cash outflow when the cash inflows are discounted at the opportunity cost of capital.

Discounting The process of reducing future cash flows to a present value using an appropriate discount rate.

Disintermediation Borrowing firms bypassing financial institutions and obtaining debt finance directly from the market.

Disinvest To sell an investment.

Distress A company is suffering financial problems which could lead to bankruptcy.

Diversifiable risk *see* Unsystematic risk.

Diversification To invest in varied projects, enterprises, financial securities, products, markets, etc.

Divestiture (Divestment) The selling off of assets or subsidiary businesses by a company or individual.

Dividend That part of profit paid to ordinary shareholders, usually on a regular basis.

Dividend cover The number of times net profits after tax available for distribution exceed the dividend actually paid or declared. Earnings per share divided by gross dividend per share *or* Total post-tax profits divided by total dividend payout.

Dividend discount model *see* Dividend valuation models.

Dividend payout ratio The percentage of a company's earnings paid out as dividends.

Dividend per share The total amount paid or due to be paid in dividends for the year (interim and final) divided by the number of shares in issue.

Dividend policy The determination of the proportion of profits paid out to shareholders over the longer term.

Dividend reinvestment plan (DRIP) A shareholder receives shares in lieu of a cash dividend. This avoids the cost and trouble of receiving cash and then reinvesting.

Dividend valuation models (DVM) These methods of share valuation are based on the premise that the market value of ordinary shares represents the sum of the expected future dividend flows, to infinity, discounted to present value.

Dividend yield The amount of dividend paid on each share in the most recent year as a percentage of the share price.

Divisible projects It is possible to undertake a fraction of a project.

Divorce of ownership and control In large corporations shareholders own the firm but may not be able to exercise control. Managers often have control because of a diffuse and divided shareholder body, proxy votes and apathy.

Domestic bonds Bonds which are issued and traded in the country of their currency.

Dominance When one (investment) possibility is clearly preferable to a risk-averse investor because it possesses a better expected return than another possibility for the same level of risk.

Dow or Dow Jones Industrial Average (DJIA) The best known index of movements in the price of US stocks and shares. There are 30 shares in the index. (It is not strictly an index, but an average of raw prices.)

Drawdown arrangement A loan facility is established and the borrower uses it (takes the money available) in stages as the funds are required.

Dual-class Shares in the USA and in some other countries which divide into two or more classes, each with different degrees of voting rights.

Due diligence When a transaction is contemplated, such as a merger or a loan, a detailed investigation of the company is carried out, usually by specialists, to ensure that it is in a satisfactory condition for the purpose of the transaction. E.g. a merger candidate might be examined by accountants, lawyers, bankers, consultants etc., to reveal risks and other information.

Duopoly Two companies dominate the supply of goods or services in an industry.

E-money Also known as electronic money, as e-currency, electronic cash, digital currency, cyber money. Money transferred by electronic means.

Early-settlement discount The reduction of a debt owed if it is paid at an early date.

Early-stage capital Funds for initial manufacturing and sales for a newly formed company. High-risk capital available from entrepreneurs, business angels and venture capital funds.

Earn-out The purchase price of a company is linked to the future profits performance. Future instalments of the purchase price may be adjusted if the company performs better or worse than expected.

Earning power The earning (profit) capacity of a business in a normal year. What the company might be expected to earn year after year if the business conditions continue unchanged.

Earnings Profits, usually measured after deduction of tax.

Earnings guidance A company guiding analysts to estimates of profits for the current period.

Earnings multiple Price–earnings ratio.

Earnings per share (EPS) Profit after tax and interest divided by number of shares in issue.

Earnings yield Earnings per share divided by current market price of share.

EBIT A company's earnings (profits) before interest and taxes are deducted.

EBITDA Earnings before interest, taxation, depreciation and amortisation. Or as cynics have it: Earnings Before I Tricked The Dumb Auditor.

Economic book value A term used by Stern Stewart & Co. It is based on the balance sheet capital employed figure subject to a number of adjustments.

Economic exposure *see* Economic risk.

Economic franchise Pricing power usually facilitated by strong barriers to entry for potential new firms in that product market. The strength and durability of an economic franchise are determined by (1) the structure of the industry; and (2) the ability of the firm to rise above its rivals in its industry and generate exceptional long-run rates of return on capital employed.

Economic profit (EP) For a period the economic profit is the amount earned by a business after deducting all operating expenses and a charge for the opportunity cost of the capital employed.

Economic risk The risk that a company's economic value may decline as a result of currency movements causing a loss in competitive strength.

Economic value added (EVA) Developed by Stern Stewart & Co. A value-based metric of corporate performance which multiplies the invested capital (after adjustments) by the spread between the (adjusted) actual return on capital and the weighted average cost of capital (q.v.). The adjustments are to the profit figures to obtain the actual return and to the balance sheet to obtain the invested capital figure.

Economies of scale Larger size of output often leads to lower cost per unit of output.

Economies of scope The ability to reduce the unit costs of an item by sharing some costs between a number of product lines, e.g. using the same truck to deliver both ketchup and beans to a store.

Effective annual rate *see* Annual percentage rate.

Efficient market hypothesis (EMH) The EMH implies that new information is incorporated into a share price (1) rapidly and (2) rationally. *See also* Efficient stock market.

Efficient portfolio A portfolio that offers the highest expected return for a given level of risk (standard deviation) and the lowest risk for its expected return.

Efficient stock market Prices rationally reflect available information. In an efficient market no trader will be presented with an opportunity for making an abnormal return, except by chance. *See also* Efficient market hypothesis.

EGM *see* Extraordinary general meeting.

EIS Enterprise Investment Scheme. A UK tax benefit for investing in young companies.

Electronic Communication Network (ECN) An alternative trading venue for shares quoted on US and European stock exchanges.

Electronic funds transfer at a point of sale (EFTPOS) A computerised system allowing the automatic transfer of money from a buyer to a seller of goods or services at the time of sale.

Electronic settlement Transferring shares from sellers to buyers without certificates – it is a computer entry only.

Emerging markets Security markets in countries with relatively low/middle incomes but with rapid economic growth, or in countries with fairly high income levels but relatively underdeveloped stock markets

and limited internationalisation of financial markets.

Employee share ownership plans (ESOPs) Schemes designed to encourage employees to build up a share-holding in their company.

Endowment policies (savings schemes) Life insurance schemes with the additional feature of a lump sum is payable, either at the end of the term of the policy or on death.

Enfranchisement Granting voting rights to holders of non-voting shares.

Enterprise investment scheme (EIS) Tax relief is available to investors in qualifying company shares (unquoted firms not involved in financial investment and property).

Enterprise value The sum of a company's total equity market capitalisation and borrowings minus the cash it holds. Some analysts add pension provisions, minority interests and other claims on the business.

Enterprise value to EBITDA ratio (EV/EBITDA) The total of the market value of equity plus debt minus cash divided by earnings before deduction of interest, tax, depreciation and amortisation.

Entrepreneur Defined by economists as the owner-manager of a firm. Usually supplies capital, organises production, decides on strategic direction and bears risk.

EONIA (Euro Overnight Index Average) Overnight interest rate of the euro in the Eurozone.

Equilibrium in markets When the forces of supply and demand are evenly balanced.

Equities, Equity, Equity capital An ownership share of a business, each equity share (of the same class) represents an equal stake in the business. Capital invested in the business in the form of shares is not set to be repaid by the company, but owners can sell their shares to other investors, or vote for liquidation of all the firm's assets to release the capital to them after meeting all other obligations.

Equitisation An increasing emphasis placed on share (equity) finance and stock exchanges in economies around the world. A growing equity culture.

Equity approach An economic profit approach to value measurement that deducts interest from operating profit as well as tax. From this is deducted the required return on equity funds devoted to the activity only (i.e. does not include required return for debt capital).

Equity indices Baskets of shares indicating the movement of the equity market as a whole or sub-sets of the markets.

Equity kicker (sweetener) The attachment to a bond or other debt finance of some rights to participate in and benefit from a good performance (e.g. to exercise an option to purchase shares). Often used with mezzanine finance (q.v.) and high-yield bonds.

Equity-linked bonds A bond with features of both debt and equity. It contains an option to purchase, or exchange a bond for, an equity stake in the issuer, its parent or another company. This option can be by way of a right to convert the bond into equity (convertible bond) or by way of a warrant attached to the bond giving the right to purchase shares.

Equity option The right but not the obligation to buy or sell shares at a pre-arranged price in the future.

Equity premium *see* Equity risk premium.

Equity risk premium The additional average annual rate of return for an averagely risky share over the return on a risk-free asset (e.g. a reputable government bond). It is the average extra return over many decades.

Equity shareholders' funds *see* Shareholders' funds.

Equity warrants A security issued by a company that gives to the owners the right but not the obligation to purchase shares in the company from the company at a fixed price during or at the end of a specified time period. It is the company itself that sells the right to purchase.

EURIBOR (Euro Interbank Offered Rate) Short-term interest rates in the interbank market (highly stable banks lending to one another) in the currency of the euro.

Euro The name of the single European currency in use since 1999 in the eurozone.

Euro medium-term notes (EMTN) *see* Medium-term note.

Eurobond Bond sold outside the jurisdiction of the country in whose currency the bond is denominated. For example, a bond issued in yen outside Japan.

Eurocommercial paper *see* Commercial paper.

Eurocredit A market in credit outside the jurisdiction of the country in whose currency the loan is denominated. (Borrowers can gain access to medium-term bank lending, for 1–15 years.)

Eurocurrency Currency held outside its country of origin, for example, Australian dollars held outside Australia. Note: this market existed long before the creation of the currency in the eurozone. It has no connection with the euro.

Eurocurrency banking Transactions in a currency other than the host country's currency. For example, transactions in Canadian dollars in London. No connection with the currency in the eurozone.

Eurocurrency deposits Short-term wholesale money market deposits made in the eurocurrency market.

Eurodeposit account Short-term wholesale money market deposits are made into an account set up for that purpose made in the eurocurrency market.

Eurodollar A deposit or credit of dollars held outside the regulation of the US authorities, say in Tokyo, London or Paris. No connection with the currency in the eurozone.

Euromarkets Informal (unregulated) markets in money held outside the jurisdiction of the country of origin, e.g. Swiss francs lending outside the control of the Swiss authorities – perhaps the francs are in London. No connection with the euro, the currency in use in the eurozone. Euromarkets began in the late 1950s and now encompass the eurocurrency, eurocredit and eurobond markets as well as over-the-counter derivatives and commodity markets.

Euronext The combined financial stock market comprising the French, Dutch, Belgian and Portuguese bourses.

Euronotes A short-term debt security. These are normally issued at a discount to face value for periods of one, three and six months' maturity. They are tradable once issued and are bearer securities. They are issued outside the jurisdiction of the currency stated on the note. They are backed up by a revolving underwriting facility which ensures that the issuer will be able to raise funds.

European Central Counterparty A pan-European clearing and settlement service for financial transactions.

European Monetary Union (EMU) A single currency with a single central bank having control over interest rates being created for those EU member states which join. The process of moving towards a monetary union began in 1999.

European-style options (or European options) Options which can only be exercised by the purchaser on a predetermined future date.

Euro-security markets Informal (unregulated) markets in money held outside the jurisdiction of the country of origin, e.g. Swiss franc lending in London, outside the control of the Swiss authorities. Financial securities such as bonds, commercial paper, ordinary shares, convertibles, floating rate notes, medium-term notes, and promissory notes offered on or traded in these euromarkets.

Eurosterling Sterling traded in the eurocurrency market.

Eurosterling bond A bond issued in sterling outside of the control of the UK authorities.

Euro Swiss francs Swiss francs traded in the eurocurrency market.

Euroyen Japanese yen traded in the eurocurrency market.

Eurozone Those countries which joined together in adopting the euro as their currency.

Event risk The risk that some future event may negatively affect the return on a financial instrument, e.g. an earthquake event affects returns on Japanese bonds or the resignation of a CEO endangers the company.

Ex-ante Intended, desired or expected before the event.

Exchange trading Trading of financial instruments on regulated exchanges.

Ex-coupon A bond sold without the right to the next interest payment.

Ex-dividend When a share or bond is designated ex-dividend a purchaser will not be entitled to a recently announced dividend or the accrued interest on the bond since the last coupon – the old owner will receive the dividend (coupon).

Ex-post The value of some variable after the event.

Ex-rights When a share goes 'ex-rights' any purchaser of a share after that date will not have a right to subscribe for new shares in the rights issue.

Ex-rights price of a share The theoretical market price following a rights issue.

Exceptional items Gains or costs which are part of the company's ordinary activities but either are unusual in themselves or have an exceptionally large impact on profits that year.

Excess return (ER) (1) The return above the level expected given the level of risk taken. (2) A value metric that examines the amount of capital invested in previous years and then charges the company for its use over the years. It also credits companies for the returns shareholders can make from the money paid to them (e.g. as dividends) when reinvested in the market. Excess return expressed in present value terms equals actual wealth expressed in present value terms minus expected wealth expressed in present value terms.

Exchange controls The state controls the purchase and sale of currencies by its residents.

Exchange rate The price of one currency expressed in terms of another.

Exchange rate risk The possibility of losing money because the exchange rate moves adversely, affecting say the value of foreign income in your home currency.

Exchange Market Size – *see* Normal Market size.

Exchange Traded Fund, ETF These funds are set up as companies issuing shares to investors, and the money raised is used to buy a range of securities such as a collection of shares in a particular stock market index or sector.

Exchange trading Trading of financial instruments on regulated markets.

Exchangeable bond A bond that entitles the owner to choose at a later date whether to exchange the bond for shares in a company. The shares are in a company other than the one that issued the bond.

Exclusive franchise *see* Economic franchise.

Execution-only brokers A stockbroker who will buy or sell shares cheaply but will not give advice or other services.

Executive directors Manage day-to-day activities of the firms as well as contributing to boardroom discussion of company-wide policy and strategic direction.

Exercise price (strike price) The price at which an underlying will be bought (call) or sold (put) under an option contract.

Exit (1) The term used to describe the point at which a venture capitalist can recoup some or all of the investment made. (2) The closing of a position created by a transaction, e.g. a previous purchase of bonds is exited by selling the bonds.

Exit barrier A factor preventing/inhibiting firms from stopping production in a particular industry.

Exotic A term used to describe an unusual financial transaction, e.g. exotic option, exotic currency (i.e. one with few trades).

Expansion capital Capital needed by companies at a fast-development phase to increase production capacity, working capital and capital for the further development of the product or market. Venture capital is often used.

Expectations hypothesis of the term structure of interest rates (yield curve) Long-term interest rates reflect the market consensus on the changes in short-term interest rates.

Expectations theory of foreign exchange The current forward exchange rate is an unbiased predictor of the spot rate at that point in the future.

Expected return The mean or average outcome calculated by weighting each of the possible outcomes by the probability of occurrence and then summing the result.

Experience curve The cost of performing a task reduces as experience is gained through repetition.

Expiry date of an option The time when rights to buy or sell the under the option contract cease.

External finance Outside finance raised by a firm, i.e. finance that it did not generate internally, for example through profits retention.

External metrics Measures of corporate performance which are accessible to individuals outside the firm and concern the performance of the firm as a whole.

Extraordinary general meeting (EGM) A meeting of the company (shareholders and directors) other than the annual general meeting (q.v.). It may be convened when the directors think fit. However, shareholders holding more than 10% of the paid-up share capital carrying voting rights can insist on the directors calling a meeting (if at least 12 months have elapsed since the last general meeting, the request may be made by only 5% of shareholders). If the directors do not call a meeting as properly requested, the members who requested it (or half of them by voting rights) may call the meeting themselves.

Extraordinary resources Those that give the firm a competitive edge.

A resource which when combined with other (ordinary) resources enables the firm to outperform competitors and create new value-generating opportunities. Critical extraordinary resources determine what a firm can do successfully.

Extrapolate To estimate values beyond the known values by the extension of a curve or line.

Face value *see* Par value.

Factor model A model which relates the returns on a security to that security's sensitivity to the movements of various factors (e.g. GDP growth, inflation) common to all shares.

Factor risk/Non-factor risk A factor risk is a systematic risk in multi-factor models describing the relationship between risk and return for fully diversified investors. Non-factor risk is unsystematic risk in multi-factor models.

Factoring To borrow from factors against the security of trade debtors. Factoring companies also provide additional services such as sales ledger administration and credit insurance.

Fair game In the context of a stock market this is where some investors and fund raisers are not able to benefit at the expense of other participants. The market is regulated to avoid abuse, negligence and fraud. It is cheap to carry out transactions and the market provides high liquidity.

Fair value (Fair-market value) The amount an asset could be exchanged for in an arm's-length transaction between informed and willing parties.

Fallen angel Debt which used to rate as investment grade but which is now regarded as junk, mezzanine finance (q.v.) or high-yield finance.

FEER The Fundamental Equilibrium Exchange Rate (FEER) is the exchange rate between two currencies that results in a sustainable current-account balance. The exchange rate is expected to move (in theory) so as to achieve current-account balance.

Federal funds rate (Fed funds) The rate at which US financial institutions will lend to each other overnight.

Filter approach to investment A technique for examining shares using historic price trends. The trader focuses on the long-term trends by filtering out short-term movements.

Final dividend The dividend announced with the annual accounts. The final dividend plus the interim dividend make the total dividend for the year for a company that reports results every six months.

Finance house A financial institution offering to supply finance in the form of hire purchase, leasing and other forms of instalment credit.

Finance lease (also called capital lease, financial lease or full payout lease) The lessor expects to recover the full cost (or almost the full cost) of the asset plus interest, over the period of the lease.

Financial assets (securities, instruments) or Financial claim Contracts that state agreement about the exchange of money in the future, e.g. shares, bonds, bank loans, derivatives.

Financial bidder Acquiring companies are often private equity firms and other financial institutions looking for undervalued targets with potential to generate higher cash flows, often after a reorganisation or by combining with other industry firms owned by the private firm. Not a strategic bidder, with an expectation of gaining synergy by combining business operations.

Financial Conduct Authority (FCA) The regulatory body overseeing financial services, responsible for investor protection, market supervision and regulation. It oversees exchanges, conducts market surveillance and monitors transactions on many financial markets.

Financial distress Obligations to creditors are not met or are met with difficulty.

Financial gearing (leverage) see Gearing.

Financial instrument A real or virtual document representing monetary value, e.g. bond, share, option, certificate of deposit, etc.

Financial intermediaries Organisations that put finance providers and those looking for finance in touch with each other, or create intermediate securities.

Financial Reporting Council (FRC) The UK's independent regulator responsible for ensuring high quality corporate reporting, accounts and governance.

Financial risk The additional variability in a firm's returns to shareholders and the additional risk of insolvency which arises because the financial structure contains debt.

Financial Services and Markets Act The 2000 Act (and orders made under it) form the bedrock of financial regulations in the UK.

Financial slack (Financial flexibility) Having cash (or near-cash) and/or spare debt capacity available to take up opportunities as they appear.

Financing gap The gap in the provision of finance for medium-sized, fast-growing firms. Often these firms are too large or fast growing to ask the individual shareholders for more funds or to obtain sufficient bank finance. Also they are not ready to launch on the stock market.

Financing-type decision In an investment project the initial cash flow is positive.

Finished goods inventory period The number of days for which finished goods await delivery to customers. Equal to the average value of finished goods in stock divided by the average goods sold per day.

Fintech A term to denote new technology companies focused on financial services.

Fisher's equation The money rate of return m is related to the real rate of return h and the expected inflation rate i through the following equation: $(1 + m) = (1 + h)(1 + i)$.

Fixed assets (non-current assets) Those not held for resale, but for use in the business.

Fixed charge (e.g. fixed charged debenture or loan) A specific asset(s) assigned as collateral security for a debt.

Fixed cost A cost that does not vary according to the amount of goods or services that are produced. Those business costs that have to be paid regardless of the firm's turnover and activity.

Fixed exchange rate The national authorities act to ensure that the rate of exchange between two currencies is constant.

Fixed interest (Fixed rate) Interest on a debt security is constant over its life.

Fixed-interest securities Strictly, the term applies to securities, such as bonds, on which the holder receives a predetermined interest pattern on the par value (e.g. gilts, corporate bonds, eurobonds). However, the term is also used for debt securities even when there is no regular interest, e.g. zero-coupon bonds (q.v.), and when the interest varies, as with floating rate notes (q.v.), for example.

Fixed-rate borrowing (fixed interest) The interest rate is constant throughout the loan period.

Flat rate The rate of interest quoted by a hire purchase company (or other lender) to a hiree which fails to reflect properly the true interest rate being charged as measured by the annual percentage rate (APR) (q.v.).

Flat yield see Yield.

Float (1) The difference between the cash balance shown on a firm's chequebook and the bank account. Caused by delays in the transfer of funds between bank accounts. (2) An exchange rate that is permitted to vary against other currencies. (3) An issuance of shares to the public by a company joining a stock market. (4) For insurance companies it is the pool of money held in the firm in readiness to pay claims.

Floating charge The total assets of the company or an individual are used as collateral security for a debt. There is no specific asset assigned as collateral.

Floating exchange rate A rate of exchange which is not fixed by national authorities but fluctuates depending on demand and supply for the currency.

Floating-rate notes (FRNs) Notes issued in which the coupon fluctuates according to a benchmark interest rate charge (e.g. LIBOR – q.v.). Issued in the euromarkets generally with maturities of 7 to 15 years. **Reverse floaters** Those on which the interest rate declines as LIBOR rises.

Floating-rate borrowing (floating interest) The rate of interest on a loan varies with a standard reference rate, e.g. LIBOR.

Floor An agreement whereby, if interest rates fall below an agreed level, the seller (floor writer) makes compensatory payments to the floor buyer.

Floor trading A place where members of a stock or commodity market come face to face to trade. Strangely, the term has been extended to 'electronic trading floors' for the buying and selling of shares, bonds, commodities, etc.

Flotation The issue of shares in a company for the first time on a stock exchange.

Focus strategy The selection of a segment in the industry to serve to the exclusion of others.

'Footsie' Nickname for FTSE 100 index. Trademarked.

Foreign banking Transactions in the home currency with non-residents.

Foreign bond A bond denominated in the currency of the country where it is issued when the issuer is a non-resident.

Foreign exchange control Limits are placed by a government on the purchase and sale of foreign currency.

Foreign exchange markets (Forex or FX) Markets that facilitate the exchange of one currency into another.

Foreign exchange swap (FX swap) A single deal with two parts to it. First, there is the actual exchange of two currencies on a specific date at a rate agreed at the time of the conclusion of the contract – this is usually a spot exchange but it can be a forward. Secondly, there is a reverse exchange of the same two currencies at a date further in the future at a rate agreed at the time of the contract. The rates of exchange are usually different in the two parts.

Forex A contraction of 'foreign exchange'.

Forfaiting A bank (or other lender) purchases a number of sales invoices or promissory notes from an exporting company; usually the importer's bank guarantees the invoices.

Forward A contract between two parties to undertake an exchange at an agreed future date at a price agreed now.

Forward agreement *see* Forward.

forward market The forward market is the over-the-counter financial market where contracts for future delivery are agreed.

Forward PER Current share price divided by the anticipated earnings for the current year.

Forward-rate agreement (FRA) An agreement about the future level of interest rates. Compensation is paid by one party to the other to the extent that market interest rates deviate from the 'agreed' rate.

Founders' shares Dividends are paid only after all other categories of equity shares have received fixed rates of dividend. They usually carry a number of special voting rights over certain company matters.

Free cash flow Cash generated by a business not required for operations or for reinvestment. Profit before deducting depreciation, amortisation and provisions, but after interest, tax, capital expenditure on long-lived items and increases in working capital necessary to maintain the company's competitive position and accept all value-generating investments.

Free float (Free capital) The proportion of a quoted company's shares not held by those closest (e.g. directors, founding families) to the company who may be unlikely to sell their shares.

Frequency function (probability or frequency distribution) The organisation of data to show the probabilities of certain values occurring.

Friendly mergers The two companies agree to a merger.

Friendly Society A mutual (co-operative) organisation involved in saving and lending.

FRS 3 *see* Basic (FRS 3) earnings per share.

FTSE 100 share index An index representing the UK's 100 largest listed shares. An average weighted by market capitalisation.

FTSE Actuaries All-Share Index (the 'All-Share') The most representative index of UK shares, reflecting about 600 companies' shares.

FTSE Eurofirst300 An index of European shares.

FTSE All-World Index An index of share price movements around the world.

FTSE International (originally owned by the *Financial Times* and the London Stock Exchange) This organisation calculates a range of share indices published on a regular (usually daily) basis.

Full-payout lease *see* Leasing and Finance lease.

Fully paid The holder of shares has paid the full price and does not owe another instalment(s)

Fund management Investment of and administering a quantity of money, e.g. pension fund, insurance fund, on behalf of the fund's owners.

Fund of funds A fund that invests the money it raises from investors in a range of funds (e.g. hedge funds).

Fund raising Companies can raise money through rights issues, etc.

Fundamental analysts Individuals that try to estimate a share's true value, based on future returns to the company. Data from many sources are used, e.g. company accounts, economic trends, social trends, technological changes, etc.

Fundamental beta An adjustment to the risk premium on the average share, which amalgamates a number of operating and financial characteristics of the specific company being examined.

Fundraising Companies can raise money through a rights issue, IPO or bond sales, etc.

Fungible Interchangeable securities; can be exchanged for each other on identical terms.

Future A contract between two parties to undertake a transaction at an agreed price on a specified future date.

FX A contraction of 'Foreign exchange'.

GAAP Generally accepted accounting principles for reporting company results.

GDP (nominal, real) Gross domestic product, the sum of all output of goods and services produced by a nation. Nominal means including inflation, and real means with inflation removed.

Gearing (financial gearing) The proportion of debt capital in the overall capital structure. Also called leverage. High gearing can lead to exaggeratedly high returns if things go well or exaggerated losses if things do not go well.

Gearing (operating gearing) The extent to which the firm's total costs are fixed. This influences the break-even point and the sensitivity of profits to changes in sales level.

General inflation The process of steadily rising prices resulting in the diminishing purchasing power of a given nominal sum of money. Measured by an overall price index (e.g. RPI and CPI) which follows the price changes of a 'basket' of goods and services through time.

General insurance Insurance against specific contingencies, e.g. fire, theft and accident. The term excludes life insurance.

Geometric mean The geometric mean of a set of n positive numbers is the nth root of their product.

Gilts (gilt-edged securities) Fixed-interest UK government securities (bonds) – a means for the UK government to raise finance from savers. They usually offer regular interest and a redemption amount paid years in the future.

Globalisation The increasing internationalisation of trade, particularly financial product transactions. The integration of economic and capital markets throughout the world.

GNP *see* gross national product.

Goal congruence The aligning of the actions of senior management with the interests of shareholders.

Going concern A judgement as to whether a company has sufficient financial strength to continue for at least one year. Accounts are usually drawn up on the assumption that the business is a going concern.

Going long Buying a financial security (e.g. a share) in the hope that its price will rise.

Going public Market jargon used when a company becomes quoted on a stock exchange (the company may have been a public limited company, plc, for years before this).

Going short *see* Short selling.

Golden handcuffs Financial inducements to remain working for a firm.

Golden parachutes In a hostile merger situation, managers will receive large pay-offs if the firm is acquired.

Golden shares Shares with extraordinary special powers over the company, e.g. power of veto over a merger.

Good growth When a firm grows by investment in positive-performance-spread activities, i.e. the expected rate of return is greater than the required rate of return (calculated as the opportunity cost of capital).

Goodwill An accounting term for the difference between the amount that a company pays for another company and the sum of the fair value of that company's individual assets (after deducting all liabilities). Goodwill is thus an intangible asset representing things like the value of the company's brand names and the skills of its employees.

Grace period A lender grants the borrower a delay in the repayment of interest and/or principal at the outset of a lending agreement.

Greenbury Committee report Recommendations on corporate governance (1995).

Greenmail Key shareholders try to obtain a reward (e.g. the repurchase of their shares at a premium) from the company for not selling to a hostile bidder or becoming a bidder themselves.

Greenshoe An option that permits an issuing house, when assisting a corporation in a new issue, to sell more shares than originally planned. They may do this if demand is particularly strong.

Grey Knight During a merger bid process a second bidder, who is a rival to the initial hostile bidder, launches a bid. The rivalry may produce a higher takeover price.

Grey market A market in shares where the shares have not yet come into existence, e.g. in the period between investors being told they will receive shares in a new issue and the actual receipt they may sell on the expectation of obtaining them later.

Gross dividend yield Gross (before tax) dividend per share as a percentage of the share price.

$$\frac{\text{dividend per share}}{\text{Share price}} \times 100$$

Gross domestic product *see* GDP.

Gross margin *see* Gross profit margin.

Gross national product A measure of the value of all goods and services produced in a country in a period.

Gross present value The total present value of all the cash flows, excluding the initial investment.

Gross profit Turnover less cost of sales.

Gross profit margin (gross margin) Profit defined as sales minus cost of sales expressed as a percentage of sales.

Gross redemption yield (Gross yield to redemption) A calculation of the redemption yield (*see* Yield) before tax.

Group accounts *see* Consolidated accounts

Growth industries Those industries which grow almost regardless of the state of the economy.

Growth stock/share Where the company has performed better than average (in growth of earnings per share) for a period of years and is expected to do so in the future. Some speculators call some companies growth stocks even though there is no history of good performance growth.

Guaranteed loan stock (bond) An organisation other than the borrower guarantees to the lender the repayment of the principal plus the interest payment.

Haircut (1) A loss of value of a debt instrument due to some form of default (2) A margin imposed on the collateral of a repurchase agreement to protect the buyer from fluctuations.

Half-yearly report *see* Interim report

Hampel report A follow-up to the Cadbury (1992) and Greenbury (1995) reports on corporate governance. Chaired by Sir Ronald Hampel and published in 1998.

Hang Seng Index Main index for Hong Kong shares.

Hard capital rationing Agencies external to the firm will not supply unlimited amounts of investment capital, even though positive NPV projects are identified.

Hard currency A currency traded in a foreign exchange market for which demand is persistently high. It is unlikely to depreciate by large percentages. The major currencies (e.g. US dollar, euro and sterling) are considered hard currencies.

Headline (underlying, adjusted or normalised) earnings per share Directors produce these profit per share numbers by excluding one-off costs, exceptional items and goodwill amortisation to show underlying profit per share trend (or just to make the managerial performance look better).

Hedge or Hedging Reducing or eliminating risk by undertaking a countervailing transaction.

Hedge fund A collective investment vehicle that operates relatively free from regulation allowing it to take steps in managing a portfolio that other fund managers are unable to take, e.g. borrowing to invest, shorting the market.

Her Majesty's Revenue and Customs (HMRC) The principal tax collecting authority in the UK.

Herstatt risk In 1974 the German bank Herstatt was closed by the Bundesbank. It had entered into forex transactions and received deutschmarks from counterparties in European time, but had not made the corresponding transfer of US dollars to its counterparties in New York time. It is the risk that arises when forex transactions are settled in different time zones.

Higgs Committee report Recommendations on corporate governance published in 2003.

High-frequency trading (HFT) Ultrafast internet trading using computers programmed with algorithms to buy and sell automatically in a fraction of a second.

High Growth Segment Companies can be admitted to this part of the London Stock Exchange's Main Market only subject to the EU minimum standards and the HGS rulebook issued by LSE, e.g. only 10% of shares need to be in a free float.

High-yield debt *see* Mezzanine finance or Junk bonds.

High-yield shares (yield stocks, high yielder) Shares offering a high current dividend yield because the share price is low due to the expectation of low growth in profits and dividends or because of perceived high risk. Sometimes labelled 'value shares'.

Hire purchase (HP) The user (hiree) of goods pays regular instalments of interest and principal to the hire purchase company over a period of months. Full ownership passes to the hiree at the end of the period (the hiree is able to use the goods from the outset).

Historical PER (P_0/E_0) Current share price divided by the most recent annual earnings per share.

Holding company *see* Parent company.

Holding period returns Total holding period returns on a financial asset consist of (1) income, e.g. dividend paid; and (2) capital gain/loss – a rise/fall in the value of the asset.

Homemade dividends Shareholders creating an income from shareholdings by selling a portion of their shareholding.

Horizontal merger The two companies merging are engaged in similar lines of activity.

Hostile merger The target (acquired) firm's management is opposed to the merger.

Hurdle rate The required rate of return. The minimum return required from a position, making an investment or undertaking a project.

Hybrid finance A debt issue or security that combines the features of two or more instruments, e.g. a convertible bond is a package of a bond with an option to convert. Also used to indicate that a form of finance has both debt risk/return features (e.g. regular interest and a right to receive principal at a fixed date) and equity risk/return features (e.g. the returns depend to a large extent on the profitability of the firm).

ICE, Intercontinental Exchange Operates leading regulated exchanges (e.g. the New York Stock Exchange), trading platforms and clearing houses. Deals in shares, futures and derivatives.

ICE Futures Europe An electronic exchange trading in a variety of derivative instruments.

Idiosyncratic risk An alternative name for unsystematic risk.

Impact day The day during the launch of a new issue of shares when the price is announced, the prospectus published and offering is officially announced.

Impairment The writing down of assets and goodwill in the balance sheet if they are judged to have become permanently impaired (not expected to earn at least a satisfactory return). Impairments may also impact the profit and loss account.

Imperfect hedge The hedge position will partly, but not exactly, mirror the change in price of the underlying.

In-the-money option An option with intrinsic value. For a call option (q.v.) the current underlying price is more than the option exercise price. For a put option (q.v.) the current price of the underlying is below the exercise price.

Income gearing (income leverage) The proportion of the annual income streams (i.e. pre-interest profits or cash flow) devoted to the prior claims of debt holders. The reciprocal of income gearing is the interest cover.

Income reinvested The performance of shares, other securities or portfolios is usually expressed as 'total return' including both capital gains or losses and the accumulated benefit of periodic reinvestment of income distributions in further shares or securities of the same kind as the original investment.

Income statement Alternative title for profit and loss account.

Income yield *see* Yield.

Incorporation The forming of a company (usually offering limited liability to the shareholders), including the necessary legal formalities.

Incremental cash flow The new cash flows that occur as a result of going ahead with a project.

Incremental effects Those cash flows indirectly associated with a project, e.g. the cash flows on an existing project are boosted if the new project under consideration goes ahead.

Incremental fixed capital investment Investment in fixed assets which adds to the stock of assets and does not merely replace worn-out assets.

Incubators Organisations established to assist fast-growing young firms. They may provide finance, accounting services, legal services, offices, etc.

Independent director One that is not beholden to the dominant executive directors. Customers, suppliers or friends of the founding family are not usually regarded as independent.

Independents A venture capital organisation that raises its capital from the financial markets – it is not owned by one institution.

Independent variables The two variables are completely unrelated; there is no co-movement.

Index *see* Market index.

Index option An option on a share index, e.g. FTSE 100 or Standard & Poor's 500.

Index funds (trackers) Collective investment funds (e.g. unit trusts) which try to replicate a stock market index rather than to pick winners in an actively managed fund.

Index-linked gilts (stocks) The redemption value and the coupons rise with inflation over the life of the UK government bond.

Indicative offer – *see* Virtual bid

Indices *see* Market index.

Industry attractiveness The economics of the market for the product(s), part of which is determined by the industry structure.

Industry structure The combination of the degree of rivalry within the industry among existing firms; the bargaining strength of industry firms with suppliers and customers; and the potential for new firms to enter and for substitute products to take customers. The industry structure determines the long-run rate of return on capital employed within the industry.

Inevitables Companies that are likely to be dominating their field for many decades due to their competitive strength.

Inflation The process of prices rising resulting in the fall of the purchasing power of one currency unit.

Inflation-linked Usually refers to investment securities. The returns go up equivalent to the rise in inflation.

Inflation risk The risk that the nominal returns on an investment will be insufficient to offset the decline in the value of money due to inflation.

Informal venture capitalist An alternative name for business angel (q.v.).

Information asymmetry One party to a transaction (e.g. loan agreement) has more information on risk and return relating to the transaction than the other party.

Information costs The cost of gathering and analysing information, e.g. in the context of deciding whether to lend money to a firm.

Informed investors Those that are highly knowledgeable about financial securities and the fundamental evaluation of their worth.

Initial margin An amount that a derivative contractor has to provide to the clearing house when first entering upon a derivative contract.

Initial public offering (IPO) (New Issue) The offering of shares in the equity of a company to the public for the first time.

Insider trading (dealing) Trading shares, etc. on the basis of information not in the public domain.

Insolvent (a) A company unable to pay debts as they become due. (2) Having liabilities in excess of a reasonable market value of assets.

Instalment credit A form of finance to pay for goods or services over a period through the payment of principal and interest in regular instalments.

Institutional neglect Share analysts, particularly at the major institutions, may fail to spend enough time studying small firms, preferring to concentrate on the larger 100 or so.

Institutionalisation The increasing tendency for organisational investing, as opposed to individuals investing money in securities (e.g. pension funds and investment trusts collect the savings of individuals to invest in shares).

Instrument A general term for all types of financial documents, such as shares, bonds, commercial paper, etc.

Insurable risk Risk that can be transferred through the payment of premiums to insurance companies.

Intangible assets Those that you cannot touch – they are non-physical, e.g. goodwill.

Interbank brokers Brokers in the forex markets who act as intermediaries between buyers and sellers. They provide anonymity to each side.

Interbank market The wholesale market in short-term money and foreign exchange in which banks borrow and lend among themselves. It is now extended to include large companies and other organisations.

Interest cap *see* Cap.

Interest rate cap *see* Cap.

Interest cover The number of times the income (profit or cash flow) of a business exceeds the interest payments made to service its loan capital.

Interest rate parity (IRP) of exchange rate determination The interest rate parity theory holds true when the difference between spot and forward exchange rates is equal to the differential between interest rates available in the two currencies.

Interest rate risk The risk that changes in interest rates will have an adverse impact.

Interest rate swap *see* Swap.

Interest-withholding tax Tax is deducted before the investor receives interest.

Interest yield *see* Yield.

Interim dividend A dividend related to the first half-year's (or quarter's) trading.

Interim report A statement giving unaudited profit figures for the first half of the financial year, shortly after the end of the first half-year.

Intermediaries offer A method of selling shares in the new issue market. Shares are offered to financial institutions such as stockbrokers. Clients of these intermediaries can then apply to buy shares from them.

Intermediate debt *see* Mezzanine finance or Junk bonds.

Intermediate security To help solve the conflict of preferences between savers (investors) in society and the ultimate borrowers' intermediaries (e.g. banks) create intermediate securities (e.g. bank account) offering the characteristics attractive to investors, i.e. high liquidity, low risk and the ability to deal in small amounts.

Internal finance Funds generated by the firm's activities, and available for investment within the firm after meeting contractual obligations.

Internal metrics Measures of corporate performance available to those inside the company. They can be used at the corporate, SBU (q.v.) or product-line level.

Internal rate of return (IRR) The discount rate that makes the present value of a future stream of cash flows equal to the initial investment(s).

Internalisation of transactions By bringing together two firms at different stages of the production chain in a vertical merger, an acquirer may achieve more efficient co-ordination of the different levels.

International banking Banking transactions outside the jurisdiction of the authorities of the currency in which the transaction takes place.

International bonds Some people use the term to mean the same as Eurobonds, others extend the definition to encompass foreign bonds as well.

International Capital Market Association (ICMA) A self-regulatory organisation designed to promote orderly trading and the general development of the Euromarkets.

International Financial Reporting Standards (IFRS) Accounting standards issued by the International Accounting Standards Board (IASB) adopted by dozens of countries. Companies listed on London's Main Market and on AIM have to adopt IFRS.

Interpolation Estimating intermediate data points on a set of data where observed points are at intervals.

Intrinsic value (company) The discounted value of the cash (owner earnings) that can be taken out of a business by the shareholders during its remaining life.

Intrinsic value (options) The payoff that would be received if the underlying is at its current level when the option expires.

Introduction A company with shares already quoted on another stock exchange, or where there is already a wide spread of shareholders, may be introduced to the market, without underwriting costs. This allows a secondary market in the shares even though no new shares are issued.

Inventory *see* Stock.

Investing-type decision In an investment project the initial cash flow is negative.

Investment bank or Merchant bank Banks that carry out a variety of financial services, usually excluding high street banking. Their services are usually fee based, e.g. fees for merger advice to companies.

Investment grade debt Debt with a sufficiently high credit rating (BBB – or Baa and above) to be regarded as safe enough for institutional investors that are restricted to holding only safe debt.

Investment trusts (investment companies) Collective investment vehicles set up as companies selling shares. The money raised is invested in assets such as shares, gilts, corporate bonds and property.

Invoice An itemised list of goods shipped, usually specifying the terms of sale and price.

Invoice discounting Invoices sent to trade debtors are pledged to a finance house in return for an immediate payment of up to 80% of the face value.

Invoice finance A method of receiving finance secured by receivables (trade debtors). A finance house advances funds to a firm. When a customer pays on the invoice the company pays the finance house with interest.

IOU A colloquialism intended to mean 'I owe you'. The acknowledgement of a debt.

IRR *see* Internal rate of return.

Irredeemable, perpetual Financial securities with no fixed maturity date at which the principal is repaid.

Irrelevancy of the dividend policy proposition (by Modigliani and Miller) If a few assumptions can be made, dividend policy is irrelevant to share value.

Islamic bonds Bonds which comply with Islamic low (e.g. no interest).

Issued share capital That part of a company's share capital that has been subscribed by shareholders, either paid up or partially paid up.

Issuing house *see* Sponsor.

Joint stock enterprise The ownership (share) capital is divided into small units, permitting a number of investors to contribute varying amounts to the total. Profits are divided between stockholders in proportion to the number of shares they own.

Joint venture A business operation (usually a separate company) is jointly owned by two or more parent firms. It also applies to strategic alliances between companies where they collaborate on, for example, research.

Junior debt (junior security) *see* Subordinated debt.

Junk bonds Low-quality, low credit-rated company bonds. Rated below investment grade (less than BBB− or Baa). Risky and with a high yield.

Just-in-time stock holding Materials and work-in-progress are delivered just before they are needed and finished goods are produced just before being sent to customers.

Key performance indicators (KPIs) Most companies include a number of KPIs in their reports and accounts, comparing actual performance against targets and against previous year's outcomes, accompanied by a discussion of aspirations and achievements. Examples: return on capital employed, customer satisfaction ratings.

Kicker *see* Equity kicker.

Lagging The postponement of a payment beyond the due date. A tactic used in international trade when the debtor expects the relative value of the currency in which the debt is expected to fall.

Laissez-faire The principle of the non-intervention of government in economic affairs.

LCH Settles mutual indebtedness between a number of organisations. It settles ('clears') trades for equity traders, forex traders, derivative traders, bond traders, energy traders, and guarantees all contracts. It acts as a central counterparty to all trades on an exchange.

Lead manager In a new issue of securities (e.g. shares, bonds, syndicated loans) the lead manager controls and organises the issue. There may be joint lead managers, co-managers and regional lead managers.

Lead steer A term used to describe a dominant person with the power to induce others to follow.

Lead time The delay between placing an order with a supplier and the order being delivered.

Leading The bringing forward from the original due date of the payment of a debt.

Leasing The owner of an asset (lessor) grants the use of the asset to another party (lessee) for a specified period in return for regular rental payments. The asset does not become the property of the lessee at the end of the specified period. *See also* Finance lease and Operating lease.

Lender of last resort This is usually the central bank, which provides a group of financial institutions with funds if they cannot otherwise obtain them.

Lessee The user of an asset under a lease.

Lessor The provider of an asset under a lease.

Leverage (1) Borrowing or obtaining a large exposure to the movement on an underlying asset's price with only a small amount initially committed, as in a derivative deal. (2) The proportion of debt capital in the overall capital structure.

Leveraged buyout (LBO) The acquisition of a company, subsidiary or unit by another, financed mainly by borrowings.

Leveraged recapitalisation The financial structure of the firm is altered in such a way that it becomes highly geared.

Liability An obligation to pay a debt.

LIBOR (London Interbank Offered Rate) The rate of interest offered on loans to highly rated (low-risk) banks in the London interbank market for a specific period (e.g. three months). Used as a reference rate for other loans.

Lien A right is given to a lender to seize possession of assets belonging to a borrower under the lien until the loan is repaid.

Life cycle stage of value creation The longevity of competitive advantage and favourable industry economics can be represented in terms of a life cycle with four stages: development, growth, maturity and decline. In the early stages superior long-term value performance is expected because of a sustainable competitive advantage and favourable long-term industry economics.

Life insurance or life assurance Insurance under which the beneficiaries receive payment upon death of the policyholder or other person named in the policy. Endowment policies offer a savings vehicle as well as cover against death.

LIFFE (London International Financial Futures and Options Exchange) The main derivatives exchange in London – now part of Intercontinental Exchange group.

Limit bid/order In a book-building exercise a potential institutional investor states that it will buy a given number of shares at a particular price.

Limit order/prices A type of buy or sell order instruction given by an investor to a broker to buy a specified quantity of a security at or below a specified price, or to sell it at or above a specified price.

Limited companies (Ltd) 'Private' companies with no minimum amount of share capital, but with restrictions on the range of investors who can be offered shares. Limited liability for the debts of the firm is granted to the shareholders. They cannot be quoted on the London Stock Exchange.

Limited liability The owners of shares in a business have a limit on their loss, set as the amount they have committed to invest in shares.

Line of credit *see* Credit facility.

Line of least resistance Taking the path with the least hassle.

Liquidation value *see* Liquidation of a company.

Liquidation of a company The winding-up of the affairs of a company when it ceases business. This could be forced by an inability to make payment when due or it could be voluntary when shareholders choose to end the company. Assets are sold, liabilities paid (if sufficient funds) and the surplus (if any) is distributed to shareholders.

Liquidity The degree to which an asset can be sold quickly and easily without loss in value.

Liquidity-preference hypothesis of the term structure of interest rates The bond yield curve is predominately upward sloping because investors require an extra return for lending on a long-term basis.

Liquidity risk (1) The risk that an organisation may not have, or may not be able to raise, cash funds when needed, (2) For an equity investor (and other security holders) liquidity risk may arise because it becomes difficult to sell a holding quickly without moving the price against you.

Listed companies Those on the Official List (q.v.) of the United Kingdom Listing Authority.

Listed Private Equity (LPEQ) Funds which are companies invested in unquoted companies, but which have their own shares quoted on an exchange. A subset are private equity investment trusts.

Listing agreement The UK Listing Authority (q.v.) insists that a company signs a listing agreement committing the directors to certain standards of behaviour and levels of reporting to shareholders.

Listing particulars *see* Prospectus.

Listing Rules The regulations concerning the initial flotation of a company on a regulated stock exchange and the continuing requirements the company must meet.

Lloyd's Insurance Market A medium-sized insurance business in London founded over two centuries ago. 'Names' supply the capital to back insurance policies. Names can now be limited liability companies rather than individuals with unlimited liability to pay up on an insurance policy.

LME London Metal Exchange.

Loan stock A fixed-interest debt financial security. May be unsecured.

Local authority bills/deposits Lending money to a local government authority.

London Metal Exchange (LME) Trades metals (e.g. lead, zinc, tin, aluminium and nickel) in spot, forward and option markets.

London Stock Exchange (LSE) The London market in which securities are bought and sold.

Long bond Often defined as bonds with a time to maturity greater than 15 years, but there is some flexibility in this, so a 10-year bond is often described as being long.

Long-form report A report by accountants for the sponsor of a company being prepared for flotation. The report is detailed and confidential. It helps to reassure the sponsors when putting their name to the issue and provides the basis for the short-form report included in the prospectus.

Long position A positive exposure to a quantity – if the market rises the position improves. Owning a security or commodity; the opposite of a short position (selling).

Long-range structural analysis A process used to forecast the long-term rates of return of an industry.

Long-term incentive plan (LTIP) A scheme designed to motivate senior managers and directors of a company by paying bonuses if certain targets are surpassed (e.g. share price has risen relative to the market index).

Lot (piece) A standard number of units when trading securities as set out by convention or the exchange of trading, e.g. 100 shares or $100,000 bonds or 1,000 shares as the underlying in a traded option contract or £62,500 in a currency futures contract.

Low-grade debt *see* Mezzanine finance or Junk bonds.

Low-yield shares (stocks) Shares offering a relatively low dividend yield expected to grow rapidly. Often labelled 'growth stocks'.

LPEQ *See* Listed private equity

LSE *See* London Stock Exchange

Ltd *see* Private limited company.

M & A Merger and acquisition.

Macroeconomics The study of the relationships between broad economic aggregates: national income, saving, investment, balance of payments, inflation, etc.

Main Market The Official List of the London Stock Exchange, as opposed to the Alternative Investment Market (qq.v.).

Maintenance margin (futures) The level of margin that must be maintained on a futures account (usually at a clearing house). Daily marking to market of the position may reveal the need to put more money into the account to top up to the maintenance margin.

Making a book Market makers offering two prices: the price at which they are willing to buy (bid price)

and the price they are willing to sell (offer price).

Management buy-in (MBI) A new team of managers makes an offer to a company to buy the whole company, a subsidiary or a section of the company, with the of taking over the running of it themselves. Private equity organisations often provide the major part of the finance.

Management buyout (MBO) A team of managers makes an offer to its employers to buy a whole business, a subsidiary or a section so that the managers own and run it themselves. Private equity organisation money is often used to finance the majority of the purchase price.

Managementism/Managerialism Management not acting in shareholders' best interests by pursuing objectives attractive to the management team. There are three levels: (1) dishonest managers; (2) honest but incompetent managers; (3) honest and competent but as humans, subject to the influence of conflicts of interest.

Managing director (MD) An executive responsible for running a business.

Mandatory bid If 30% or more of the shares of a company are acquired the holder is required under the Takeover Panel rules to bid for all the company's shares.

Margin call A demand by a clearing house for a futures position taker to top up the margin held at the clearing house as the underlying moves unfavourably for the position holder.

Margin (futures) Money placed aside to back a futures purchase or sale. This is used to reassure the counterparty (the clearing house in most cases) to the future that money will be available should the purchaser/seller renege on the deal.

Margin (market makers) The difference between the bid and offer prices announced by market makers.

Market capitalisation The total value at market prices of the ordinary shares in issue for a company (or a stock market, or a sector of the stock market).

Market entry Firms that previously did not supply goods or services to this industry now do so.

Market equilibrium When the forces of supply and demand are evenly balanced.

Market in managerial control Teams of managers compete for control of corporate assets, e.g. through merger activity.

Market index A sample of shares is used to represent a share (or other) market's level and movements as a benchmark against which individual shares are judged.

Market makers Organisations that stand ready to buy and sell shares (or other securities) from investors on their own behalf (at the centre of a quote-driven system of share trading). Also known as dealers.

Market portfolio In finance theory it is a portfolio which contains all assets. Each asset is held in proportion to the asset's share of the total market value of all the assets. A proxy for this is often employed, e.g. the FTSE 100 index.

Market power The ability to exercise some control over the price of the product.

Market risk *see* Systematic risk.

Market risk premium *see* Equity risk premium.

Market segmentation hypothesis of the term structure of interest rates The yield curve is created (or at least influenced) by the supply and demand conditions in a number of sub-markets defined by maturity range.

Market-to-book ratio (MBR) The market value of a firm divided by capital invested. ('Capital invested' is usually taken to be balance sheet net assets.)

Market value added The difference between the total amount of capital put into a business by finance providers (debt and equity) and the current market value of the company's shares and debts.

Marking to market The losses or gains on a derivative contract are assessed daily in reference to the value of the underlying price.

Matador A foreign bond issued in the Spanish domestic market.

Matched-bargain systems *see* Order-driven trading system.

Matching The company matches the inflows and outflows in different currencies covered by trade, etc., so that it is only necessary to deal on the currency markets for the unmatched portion of the total transactions.

Matching principle The maturity structure of debt matches the maturity of projects or assets held by the firm. Short-term assets are financed by short-term debt and long-term assets are financed by long-term debt.

Maturity (Maturity date, Final maturity or Redemption date) The time when a financial security (e.g. a bond) is due to be redeemed and the par value is paid to the lender.

Maturity structure The profile of the length of time to the redemption and repayment of a company's various debts.

Maturity transformation Intermediaries offer securities with liquid characteristics to induce primary investors to purchase them or deposit funds. The money raised is made available to the ultimate borrowers on a long-term, illiquid basis.

Maximisation of long-term shareholder wealth The assumed objective of the firm in finance. It takes into account the time value of money and risk.

Mean (1) arithmetic mean: a set of numbers are summed, and the answer is divided by the number of numbers; (2) geometric mean: calculated as the nth root of the product of n number, e.g. the geometric mean of 2 and 5 is $\sqrt{2 \times 5} = \sqrt{10} = 3.16$.

Mean reversion *see* Reversion to the mean.

Mean-variance rule If the expected return on two projects is the same but the second has a higher variance (or standard deviation) (qq.v.), then the first will be preferred. Also, if the variance on the two projects is the same but the second has a higher expected return, the second will be preferred.

Medium-term note (MTN) A document setting out a promise from a borrower to pay the holders a specified sum on the maturity date and, in many cases, a coupon interest in the meantime. Maturity can range from nine months to 30 years (usually one to five years). If in a foreign currency they are called euro medium-term notes.

Memorandum of Association Lays down the rules which govern a company and its relations with the outside world, e.g. states the objective of the company.

Merchant bank *see* Investment bank.

Merger The combining of two business entities under common ownership.

Metric Method of measurement.

Mezzanine finance Unsecured debt or preference shares offering a high return with a high risk. Ranked behind secured debt but ahead of equity. It may carry an equity kicker (q.v.).

Mid-market price A price between the bid and offer prices set by a market maker(s) at which shares (or other financial securities) can be sold or bought.

Minority shareholder A shareholder who owns less than 50% of a company's ordinary shares.

Mobilisation of savings The flow of savings primarily from the household sector to the ultimate borrowers to invest in real assets. This process is encouraged by financial intermediaries.

Model Code for Directors' Dealings UK Listing Authority rules for directors and senior staff dealing in shares of their own company if listed on say the Main Market of the London Stock Exchange, e.g. no dealing in the period of 60 days immediately preceding a preliminary announcement of the company's annual results.

Modified internal rate of return (MIRR) The rate of return which equates the initial investment with a project's terminal value, where the terminal value is the future value of the cash inflows compounded at the required rate of return (the opportunity cost of capital).

Momentum investing Buying shares (or other securities) that have recently risen and selling those that have recently fallen.

Monetary policy The deliberate control of the money supply and/or rates of interest by the central bank.

Money cash flow All future cash flows are expressed in the prices expected to rule when the cash flow occurs.

Money markets Wholesale financial markets (i.e. those dealing with large amounts) in which lending and borrowing on a short-term basis takes place (<1 year). Examples of instruments: banker's acceptances, certificates of deposit, commercial paper, treasury bills.

Money rate of return The rate of return which includes a return to compensate for inflation.

Monopoly One producer in an industry. However for Competition and Markets Authority purposes a monopoly is defined as a market share of 25%.

Moral hazard The presence of a safety net (e.g. an insurance policy) encourages adverse behaviour (e.g. carelessness). An incentive to take extraordinary risks (risks that tend to fall on others) aimed at rectifying a desperate position. The risk that a party to a transaction is not acting in good faith by providing misleading or inadequate information.

Mortgage debentures Bonds secured using property as collateral.

Mortgage-style repayment schedule A regular monthly amount is paid to a lender which covers both interest and some capital repayment. At first most of the monthly payment goes towards interest. As the outstanding debt is reduced, the monthly payment pays off a larger and larger amount of the capital.

Musharakah, A form of Islamic finance where a joint enterprise is established by the bank and borrower. Both contribute capital plus management and labour (although some parties, e.g. banks, contribute little other than capital). Profit (loss) is shared in pre-agreed proportions – there is a prohibition against a fixed lump sum for any party. All partners have unlimited liability.

MTN *see* Medium-term note.

Multilateral Trading Facility (MTF) An alternative trading venue for shares quoted on US and European stock exchanges.

Mutual funds A collective investment vehicle for shares or other financial securities. Many investors hold units in the mutual fund which then invests in securities.

Mutually owned organisations Organisations run for the benefit of the members (usually the same as the consumers of the organisation's output) and not for shareholders. Examples include some insurance organisations, building societies and the co-operative societies.

Naked (or uncovered) Long or short positioning in a derivative without an offsetting position in the underlying. *See also* Uncovered call option writing.

NASDAQ (National Association of Securities Dealers Automated Quotation system) A series of computer-based information services and an order execution system for the US over-the-counter securities (e.g. share) market.

National Savings Lending to the UK government through the purchase of bonds, and placing money into savings accounts.

NAV Net asset value

Near-cash (near-money, quasi-money) Highly liquid financial assets but which are generally not usable for transactions and therefore cannot be fully regarded as cash, e.g. treasury bills.

Negative (restrictive) covenants Loan agreements conditions that restrict the actions and rights of the borrower until the debt has been repaid in full.

Negotiability (1) Transferable to another – free to be traded in financial markets. (2) Capable of being settled by agreement between the parties involved in a transaction.

Net asset value (NAV), Net assets (Net worth) A company's total assets minus all the liabilities. Fixed assets, plus stocks, debtors, cash and other liquid assets, minus long-and short-term liabilities.

Net book value The original cost of an asset minus the accumulated depreciation for tangible assets or minus the amortisation for intangibles since their acquisition. Can also be used for the totality of the balance sheet as an alternative phrase to net asset value.

Net current assets The difference between current assets and current liabilities (qq.v.).

Net interest yield Gross yield on a debt instrument less the tax payable on that interest.

Net present value (NPV) The present value of the expected cash flows associated with a project or other investment after discounting at a rate which reflects the value of the alternative use of the funds.

Net profit (Net income) Profit after interest, tax and extraordinary charges and receipts.

Net realisable value What someone might reasonably be expected to pay less the costs of preparing for the sale.

Net worth (Net asset value) Total assets minus total liabilities.

Netting When subsidiaries in different countries settle intra-organisational currency debts for the net amount owed in a currency rather than the gross amount.

Neuer Markt German stock exchange for smaller young companies. Now closed due to financial scandals and loss of confidence among investors.

New entrant A company entering a market area to compete with existing players.

New issue The sale of securities, e.g. debentures or shares, to raise additional finance or to float existing securities of a company on a stock exchange for the first time.

NEX Exchange Companies that do not want to pay the costs of a flotation on the London Stock Exchange can gain a quotation on London-based NEX Exchange (formerly ICAP Securities & Derivatives Exchange (ISDX)). By having their shares quoted on NEX Exchange companies provide a service to their shareholders, allowing them to buy and sell shares. It also allows access to capital, for example, by selling more shares in a rights issue.

Niche company A fast-growing small to medium-sized firm operating in a specialist business with high potential.

Nikkei index or Nikkei 225 Stock Average A share index based on the prices of 225 shares quoted on the Tokyo Stock Exchange.

Nil paid rights Shareholders may sell the rights to purchase shares in a rights issue without having paid anything for these rights.

Noise trading Uninformed investors buying and selling financial securities at irrational prices, thus creating noise (strange movements) in the price of securities. 'Noise' is derived from natural science: random interference in physical processes.

Nomad *see* Nominated Adviser

Nominal return (or nominal interest rate) The return on an investment including inflation. If the return necessary to compensate for the decline in the purchasing power of money (inflation) is deducted from the nominal return we have the real rate of return.

Nominal value *see* Par value.

Nominated adviser (Nomad) Each company on the Alternative Investment Market (q.v.) has to retain a nomad. They act as quality controllers, confirming to the London Stock Exchange that the company has complied with the rules. They also act as consultants to the company.

Nominated brokers Each company on the Alternative Investment Market (q.v.) has to retain a nominated broker, who helps to bring buyers and sellers together, comments on the firm's prospects and advises the company on investor relations and market conditions for fund raising.

Nominee accounts An official holder of an asset is not the beneficial owner but merely holds the asset in a nominee account for the beneficiary. In the stock market, the most common use of nominee accounts is where execution-only brokers act as nominees for their clients. The shares are registered in the name of the broker, but the client has beneficial ownership of them.

Non-executive director, NED (Outside director) A director without day-to-day operational responsibility for the firm.

Non-recourse A lending arrangement, say in project finance, where the lenders have no right to insist that the parent company(s) pay the due interest and capital should the project company be unable to do so.

Non-voting shares A company may issue two or more classes of ordinary shares, one or more of which may be of shares that do not carry any votes.

Normal market size, NMS The threshold below which market makers are obliged to buy/sell shares at the prices they posted on the London Stock Exchange systems without modification. They are 'firm prices', but they have the freedom to adjust prices after deals are completed, at the price quoted. The term Exchange Market Size, EMS, is an alternative.

Normal rate of return A rate of return that is just sufficient to induce shareholders to put money into the firm and hold it there.

Normalised earnings per share *see* Headline earnings per share.

Note (promissory note) A financial security with the promise to pay a specific sum of money by a given date, e.g. commercial paper, floating rate notes. Usually unsecured.

Note issuance facility (Note purchase facility) A medium-term arrangement allowing borrowers to issue a series of short-term promissory notes (usually 3–6 month maturity). A group of banks guarantees the availability of funds by agreeing to purchase any unsold notes at each issue date while the facility is in place.

NYSE The New York Stock Exchange.

Objective probability A probability that can be established theoretically or from historical data.

Off-balance-sheet finance Assets are acquired in such a way that liabilities do not appear on the balance sheet, e.g. some lease agreements permit the exclusion of the liability in the accounts.

Offer as unconditional *see* Unconditionality.

Offer document (1) A formal document sent by a company attempting to buy all the shares in a target firm to all the shareholders of the target setting out the offer. (2) The legal document for an offer for sale in a new issue (IPO).

Offer for sale A method of selling shares in a new issue. The company sponsor offers shares to the public by inviting subscriptions from investors. (1) Offer for sale by fixed price – the sponsor fixes the price prior to the offer. (2) Offer for sale by tender – investors state the price they are willing to pay. A strike price is established by the sponsors after receiving all the bids. All investors pay the strike price.

Offer price (1) The price at which a market maker in shares will sell a share, or a dealer in other markets will sell a security or asset. (2) The price of a new issue of securities, e.g. a new issue of shares.

Official List (OL) The daily list of securities admitted for trading on highly regulated UK markets such as the London Stock Exchange. It does not include securities traded on the Alternative Investment Market (AIM) (q.v.).

Offshore investment Outside investors' home country jurisdiction and financial regulation, usually in tax havens.

Oligopoly A small number of producers in an industry.

Onshore fund A fund authorised and supervised by the financial regulator in the investor's home country.

Open-ended funds The size of the fund and the number of units depends on the amount investors wish to put into the fund e.g. a unit trust. The manager adds to or liquidates part of the assets of the fund depending on the level of purchases or sales of the units in the fund.

Open-ended investment companies (OEIC) Share-issuing collective investment vehicles with one price for investors. OEICs are able to issue more shares if demand increases from investors, unlike investment trusts. OEICs invest the finance raised in securities, primarily shares.

Open interest The sum of outstanding long and short positions in a given futures or option contract. Transactions have not been offset or closed out, thus there is still exposure to movements in the underlying (q.v.).

Open offer New shares are sold to a wide range of external investors (not existing shareholders). However, under clawback provisions, existing shareholders can buy the shares at the offer price if they wish.

Open outcry Where trading is through oral calling of buy and sell offers and hand signals by market members.

Operating gearing *see* Gearing.

Operating lease The lease period is significantly less than the expected useful life of the asset and the agreed lease payments do not amount to a present value of more than 90% of the value of the asset.

Operating margin *see* Operating profit margin.

Operating profit (operating income) The accounting income remaining after paying all costs other than interest and tax.

Operating profit margin (operating margin, trading margin) Operating profit as a percentage of sales.

Operational efficiency of a market Relates to how the market minimises the cost to buyers and sellers of transactions in securities on the exchange.

Operational risks The risks that come from the business activity itself rather than from, say, financial risks such as interest rates changing.

Opportunity cost The value forgone by opting for one course of action; the next best use of, say, financial resources.

Opportunity cost of capital The return that is sacrificed by investing finance in one way rather than investing in an alternative of the same risk class, e.g. a financial security.

Option A contract giving one party the right, but not the obligation, to buy or sell a financial instrument, commodity or some other underlying asset at a given price, at or before a specified date.

Option premium The amount paid by an option purchaser (holder) to obtain the rights under an option contract.

Order book system *see* Order-driven trading system.

Order-driven trading system (matched-bargain or order book system) Buy and sell orders for securities are entered on a central computer system, and investors are automatically matched according to the price and volume they entered – SETS is an example (q.v.).

Ordinary resources Those that give the firm competitive parity. They provide a threshold competence.

Ordinary shares The equity capital of the firm. The holders of ordinary shares are the owners and are therefore entitled to all distributed profits after the holders of preference shares, debentures and other debt have had their claims met. They are also entitled to control the direction of the company through the power of their votes – usually one vote per share.

Organic growth Growth from within the firm rather than through mergers.

Out-of-the-money option An option with no intrinsic value. For a call option (q.v.) the current price of the underlying is less than the exercise price. For a put option (q.v.) the current price of the underlying (q.v.) is more than the exercise price.

Over-allotment issue Same as Greenshoe (q.v.).

Over-capacity An industry or company has significantly more capacity to supply a product than is being demanded.

Over-subscription In a new issue (IPO) of securities investors offer to buy more securities (e.g. shares) than are made available.

Over-the-counter trade (OTC) Securities trading carried on outside regulated exchanges. These bilateral deals allow tailor-made transactions.

Overdraft A permit to overdraw on an account (e.g. a bank account) up to a stated limit; to take more out of a bank account than it contains. This arrangement is usually offered for a period, say six months or one year, but most banks retain the right to call in the loan (demand repayment) at any time.

Overhang Blocks of securities or commodities that are known to be available for sale. This can lead to share (or commodity) price depression due to the anticipated sale of the large block of shares (or the commodity).

Overhead The business expenses not chargeable to a particular part of the work or product: a cost that is not directly associated with producing the merchandise.

Overnight Lending or borrowing of cash or securities in the financial markets which is repaid within 24 hours.

Overtrading When a business has insufficient finance to sustain its level of trading (turnover). Too much cash is tied up in stocks and debtors, and too little is available to pay creditors and meet day-to-day expenses. A business is said to be overtrading when it tries to engage in more business than the investment in working capital will allow. This can happen even in profitable circumstances.

Owner earnings Earnings plus depreciation, depletion, amortisation and certain other non-cash charges less the amount of expenditure for plant and machinery and working capital, etc. that a business requires to fully maintain its long-term competitive position, its unit volume and to invest in value-generating opportunities.

PacMan defence or strategy In a hostile merger situation the target makes a counterbid for the bidder.

Paid-up capital The amount of the authorised share capital that has been paid for or subscribed for by shareholders.

Panel on Takeovers & Mergers *see* Takeover panel.

Paper A term for some securities, e.g. certificates of deposit, commercial paper.

Paper bid In a merger the acquirer offers shares in itself to buy shares in the target.

Par value (nominal, principal stated book or face value) A stated nominal value of a share or bond. Not related to market value which fluctuates.

Parent company (Holding company) The one that partially or wholly owns other companies.

Partnership An unincorporated business formed by the association of two or more persons who share the risk and profits.

Pathfinder prospectus In a new issue of shares a detailed report on the company is prepared and made available to potential investors a few days before the issue price is announced.

Payables (accounts payable) Trade credit received from suppliers.

Payback The period of time it takes to recover the initial cash put into a project.

Payment services institutions Financial organisations offering payment transactions, e.g. credit transfers, direct debits, payment cards, money remittance to another country and foreign exchange services.

Payment-in-kind (PIKs) notes and loans High risk debt offering a very high rate of return (900 basis points over LIBOR or more). They do not pay out a coupon; they pay out in the form of more bonds or loans.

Payout ratio The percentage of after-tax profit paid to shareholders in dividends.

Pecking order theory of financial gearing Firms exhibit preferences in terms of sources of finance. The most acceptable source of finance is retained earnings, followed by borrowing and then by new equity issues.

Peer-to-peer lending Raising finance directly from savers via the internet, e.g. small businesses raising money from individuals and financial institutions, or small businesses selling unpaid invoices to provide working capital.

Pension funds/schemes These manage money on behalf of members to provide a pension upon the member's retirement. Most funds invest heavily in bonds and shares.

Pension holiday When a pension fund does not need additional contributions for a time, it may grant the contributors, e.g. companies and/or members, a break from making payments.

PER *see* Price-earnings ratio.

Perfect competition (perfect market) Entry to the industry is free and the existing firms have no bargaining power over suppliers or customers. Rivalry between existing firms is fierce because products are identical. The following assumptions hold: (1) There is a large number of buyers. (2) There is a large number of sellers. (3) The quantity of goods bought by any individual transaction is so small relative to the total quantity traded that individual trades leave the market price unaffected. (4) The units of goods sold by different sellers are the same – the product is homogeneous. (5) There is perfect information – all buyers and all sellers have complete information on the prices being asked and offered in other parts of the market. (6) There is perfect freedom of exit from the market.

Perfect hedge Eliminates risk because the movements in the value of the hedge (q.v.) instrument are exactly contrary to the change in the value of the underlying (q.v.).

Perfect market *see* Perfect competition.

Perfect negative correlation When two variables (e.g. returns on two shares) always move in exactly opposite directions by the same proportional amount.

Perfect positive correlation When two variables (e.g. returns on two shares) always move in the same direction by the same proportional amount.

Performance spread The percentage difference between the actual rate of return on an investment and the required rate given its risk class.

Permanent capital Capital, such as through the purchase of shares in a company which cannot be withdrawn.

Perpetuity A regular sum of money received at intervals forever.

Personal guarantee An individual associated with a company, e.g. director, personally guarantees that a debt will be repaid.

Personal/private pension A pension scheme set up for an individual by that individual. Contributions to the fund are subject to tax relief in the UK.

Personal membership of CREST Investors hold shares in their own accounts with CREST rather than in a broker's nominee company or in a certified form.

Physical delivery/settlement Settlement of a futures contract by delivery of the underlying (q.v.) rather than cash settlement based on price movement during the holding of the open position.

Pip The smallest FX trading variation, equal to one ten-thousandth of one unit of currency e.g. 0.0001% of $1.

Placing, place or placement A method of selling shares and other financial securities in the primary market. Securities are offered to the sponsors' or brokers' private clients and/or a narrow group of institutions.

Plain vanilla A bond that lacks any special features such as a call or put provision.

Planning horizon The point in the future after which an investment will earn only the minimum acceptable rate of return.

plc Public limited company.

Poison pills Actions taken, or which will be taken, which make a firm unpalatable to a hostile acquirer.

Political risk Changes in government or government policies impacting on investment or business returns and volatility of returns.

Pooled funds Organisations (e.g. unit trusts) that gather together numerous small quantities of money from investors and then invest in a wide range of financial securities.

Portfolio A collection of investments.

Portfolio approach to merger integration *see* Preservation approach to merger integration.

Portfolio investment (1) Investment in a variety of instruments; (2) (in national accounting) investment made by firms and individuals in bonds and shares issued in another country. An alternative form of foreign investment is direct investment, buying commercial assets such as factory premises and industrial plant.

Portfolio optimiser A computer program designed to select an optimal portfolio in terms of risk and return.

Portfolio planning Allocating resources within the company to those strategic business units (q.v.) and product/customer areas offering the greatest value creation, while withdrawing capital from those destroying value.

Portfolio theory Formal mathematical model for calculating risk-return trade-offs as securities are combined in a portfolio.

Post-completion audit The monitoring and evaluation of the progress of a capital investment project through a comparison of the actual cash flows and other benefits with those forecast at the time of authorisation.

PPP *see* Purchasing power parity.

Precautionary motive for holding cash This arises out of the possibility of unforeseen needs for cash for expenditure in an unpredictable environment.

Pre-emption rights The strong right of shareholders of UK companies to have first refusal to subscribe for further issues of shares. *See* Rights issue.

Preference share These normally entitle the holder to a fixed rate of dividend but this is not guaranteed. Holders of preference shares precede the holders of ordinary shares, but follow bond holders and other lenders, in payment of dividends and return of principal. *Participating preference share*: share in residual profits. *Cumulative preference share*: share carries forward the right to preferential dividends. *Redeemable preference share*: a preference share with a finite life. *Convertible preference share*: may be converted into another type of security, e.g. ordinary shares.

Preferred ordinary shares Rank higher than deferred ordinary shares for an agreed rate of dividend or share of profits. Not the same as preference shares.

Preliminary annual results (Preliminary profit announcements, prelims) After the year-end and before the full reports and accounts are published, a statement on the profit for the year and other information is provided by companies quoted on the London Stock Exchange.

Premium (1) (On an option) The amount paid to an option writer to obtain the right to buy or sell the underlying. (2) (Foreign exchange) The forward rate of exchange stands at a higher level than the current spot rate. (3) (Investment trusts) The amount the share price exceeds the net asset value per share. (4) (Insurance) An amount paid (usually annually) to ensure against risk.

Premium listing on the London Stock Exchange Most companies on the Main Market of the LSE have a premium listing where they are subject to particularly strict rules, e.g. on flotation a minimum three years of audited accounts. Premium listing companies are required to meet the UK's super-equivalent rules, which are more strict than the EU minimum requirements. Complying with higher standards of regulation, disclosure of information and corporate governances leads to a lower cost of capital through building greater investor confidence.

Present value The current worth of future cash flows when discounted.

Preservation approach to merger integration Little is changed in the acquired firm in terms of culture, systems or personnel. General management skills might be transferred from the parent along with strict financial performance yardsticks and demanding incentive schemes.

Press Collective name for newspapers and periodicals.

Pre-tax margin *see* Pre-tax profit margin.

Pre-tax profit Profit on ordinary activities before deducting taxation.

Pre-tax profit margin (pre-tax margin) Profit after all expenses including interest expressed as a percentage of sales.

Price discovery (price formation) The process of forming prices through the interaction of numerous buy and sell orders in an exchange.

Price-earnings ratio (PER, Price-earnings multiple, PE multiple, PE ratio, P/E ratio) *Historical (or Trailing):* Share price divided by most recently reported annual earnings per share. *Forward (prospective):* share price divided by anticipated annual earnings per share.

Price-earnings ratio game (bootstrapping) Companies increase earnings per share by acquiring other companies with lower price-earnings ratios than themselves. The share price can rise despite the absence of an economic value gain.

Price formation *see* Price discovery

Price limit The maximum price an investor is willing to pay to buy, or the minimum a seller is willing to accept.

Price-sensitive information That which may influence the share price or trading in the shares.

Price-to-book ratio (market-to-book ratio) The price of a share as a multiple of per share book (balance sheet) value.

Price-weighted index An index of a collection of financial (e.g. shares) or other assets (e.g. houses) which measures through time the average price of the constituents.

Pricing power An ability to raise prices even when product demand is flat without the danger of losing significant volume or market share.

Primary investors The household sector contains the savers in society who are the main providers of funds used for investment in the business sector.

Primary listing The main stock exchange where a publicly traded company's stock is bought and sold, e.g. a company may have a primary listing on the London Stock Exchange and a secondary listing on the Australian Stock Exchange, where share trades can take place.

Primary market A market in which securities are initially issued to investors rather than a secondary market in which investors buy and sell to each other.

Prime grade *see* Investment grade debt.

Principal (1) The capital amount of a debt, excluding any interest. (2) A person acting for their own purposes accepting risk in financial transactions, rather than someone acting as an agent for another. (3) The amount invested.

Principal–agent problem In which an agent, e.g. a manager, does not act in the best interests of the principal, e.g. the shareholder.

Private client brokers Stockbrokers acting for investors in the buying and selling of financial instruments and providing other investment-related services for investors.

Private equity Share capital invested in companies not quoted on an exchange.

Private Equity Investment Trusts (PEIT) Investment vehicles allowing investors to buy into an established private equity fund run by an experienced management team investing in unquoted companies. The investor buys PEIT shares which are traded on the London Stock Exchange.

Private investors (private clients) Investors buying and selling small quantities of shares and other securities on their own account rather than institutions buying and selling for funds or the financial organisation's own account.

Private limited company (Ltd) A company which is unable to offer its shares to the wider public.

Privatisation The sale to private investors of government-owned equity (shares) in state-owned industries or other commercial enterprises.

Pro forma earnings (a) Projected or forecast earnings, (b) Earnings estimates prepared by the directors so as to exclude those items they regards as unusual or nonrecurring for a recent past period. These are not audited and may be unreliable.

Profit and loss account (income statement) Records whether a company's sales revenue was greater than its costs.

Profit margin Profits as a percentage of sales.

Profitability index A measure of present value per pound invested.

Project An investment within the business requiring medium- to long-term commitment of resources.

Project appraisal The assessment of the viability of proposed long-term investments in real assets within the firm.

Project finance Finance assembled for a specific project. The loan and equity returns are tied to the cash flows and fortunes of the project rather than being dependent on the parent company/companies.

Promissory note A debtor promises to pay on demand or at a fixed date or a date to be determined by circumstances. A note is created stated this obligation.

Proprietary transactions (Proprietary trading) A financial institution, as well as acting as an agent for a client, may trade on the financial markets with a view to generating profits for itself, e.g. speculation on forex (q.v.).

Prospectus A document containing information about a company (or unit trust/OEIC – q.v.), to assist with a new issue (initial public offering, IPO) by supplying detail about the company and how it operates.

Provision (1) Sum set aside in accounts for anticipated loss or expenditure when the amount is uncertain or the date the loss/liability become due is uncertain. (2) A clause or stipulation in a legal agreement giving one party a right.

Provisional Allotment Letter (PAL) In a rights issue shareholders receive PALs which are temporary documents of title showing each shareholder the number of shares they can apply for. To accept the shareholder fills in and returns the PAL with a cheque or banker's draft.

Proxy votes Shareholders unable to attend a shareholders' meeting may authorise another person, e.g. a director or the chairman, to vote on their behalf, either as instructed or as that person sees fit.

Prudential Regulatory Authority (PRA) A subsidiary of the Bank of England supervising and regulating financial institutions, banks, insurers and brokers for micro-prudential (systemwide) risk – seeking to enhance the safety and soundness of individual institutions, as opposed to the macroprudential view which focuses on the welfare of the financial system as a whole.

Public limited company (plc) A company which may have an unlimited number of shareholders and offer its shares to the wider public (unlike a limited company – q.v.). Must have a minimum share value of £50,000. Some plcs are listed on the London Stock Exchange.

Public-to-private (PTP) The management of a company currently quoted on a stock exchange may return it to unquoted status with the assistance of private equity finance.

Purchasing power parity (PPP) theory of exchange rate determination Exchange rates will be in equilibrium when their domestic purchasing powers at that rate of exchange are equivalent. Movements in exchange rates will be a function of the differential in the two currencies' inflation rates.

Put features *see* Put options.

Put option This gives the purchaser the right, but not the obligation, to sell a financial instrument, commodity or some other underlying asset at a given price, at or before a specified date.

Qualitative analysis Relying on subjective elements to take a view, e.g. valuing shares by judging quality of management and strategic position.

Quant (Quantum) analysis Quantitative analysis using complex mathematical models.

Quantitative analysis Using statistics and mathematics to measure financial performance.

Quick asset value (net) Current assets minus stock minus current liabilities (qq.v.).

Quick ratio (acid test) The ratio of current assets, less stock, to total current liabilities (qq.v).

Quota Quantitative limits placed on the importation of specified goods.

Quote-driven trading system Market makers post bid and offer prices on a computerised system.

Quoted Those shares with a price quoted on a recognised investment exchange (RIE) or AIM (e.g. the Official List of the London Stock Exchange (qq.v.)).

R&D Research and development

Random walk theory The movements in (share) prices are independent of one another; one day's price change cannot be predicted by looking at the previous day's price change.

Ranking (debt) Order of precedence for payment of obligations. Senior debt receives annual interest and redemption payments ahead of junior (or subordinated) debt. So, if the company has insufficient resources to pay its obligations the junior debt holders may receive little or nothing.

Rappaport's value drivers The seven key factors which determine value are: (1) Sales growth rate. (2) Operating profit margin. (3) Tax rate. (4) Incremental fixed capital investment. (5) Incremental working capital investment. (6) The planning horizon. (7) The required rate of return.

Rating *see* Credit rating.

Raw materials stock period The average number of days raw materials remain unchanged and in stock. Equal to the average value of raw materials stock divided by the average purchase of raw materials per day.

Real assets Assets used to carry on a business. These assets can be tangible (e.g. buildings) or intangible (e.g. a brand) as opposed to financial assets.

Real cash flows Future cash flows are expressed in terms of constant purchasing power.

Real option An option to undertake different courses of action in the real asset market (strategic and operational options), as opposed to a tradable option on financial securities or commodities.

Real rate of return The rate that would be required (or obtained) in the absence of inflation. The nominal return minus inflation.

Realised gain A gain (increase in value) made when a deal has been completed and money released.

Recapitalisation A change in the company's financial structure, e.g. in debt to equity ratio by say selling more shares or bond holders swapping bonds for shares.

Receivable (Accounts receivable) A sum due from a customer for goods delivered: trade credit.

Receiver A receiver takes control of a business if a creditor successfully files a bankruptcy petition. The receiver may then sell the company's assets and distribute the proceeds among the creditors.

Recognised Clearing House (RCH) A financial institution approved by regulators to act as a clearing house in the UK

Recognised investment exchange (RIE) A body authorised to regulate securities trading in the UK, e.g. the London Stock Exchange.

Recourse If a financial asset is sold (such as a trade debt), the purchaser could return to the vendor or guarantor for payment in the event of non-payment by the borrower.

Redeemable preference shares *See* Preference shares

Redemption The repayment of the principal amount, or the par value, of a security (e.g. bond) at the maturity date resulting in the retirement and cancellation on the security.

Redemption yield *see* Yield.

Registered bond A bond where the owner's details are kept on a register open to the company and the authorities.

Registrar An organisation that maintains a record of share (and other securities) ownership for a company. It also communicates with shareholders on behalf of the company.

Regulated exchange market A market where there is a degree of supervision concerning market behaviour or other controls on the freedom of participants.

Regulatory Information Services (RIS) Companies on UK stock exchanges are required to announce quickly any price sensitive information. They do this by making an announcement electronically via one of the Regulatory Information Services approved by the Financial Conduct Authority. The RIS then disseminates the news very quickly to dozens of financial websites and other places.

Regulatory News Service (RNS) A system for distributing important company announcements and other price-sensitive financial news run by the London Stock Exchange.

Reinvestment rate The rate of return on the periodic cash flows generated by a project when invested.

Relationship banking A long-term, intimate and relatively open relationship is established between a corporation and its banks. Banks often supply a range of tailor-made services rather than one-off services.

Rembrandt A foreign bond issued in The Netherlands.

Remuneration committee A group of directors of a company, all of which are independent of management, decide the remuneration of executive directors.

Repayment holiday *see* Grace period.

Reporting accountant A company planning to float on the London Stock Exchange employs a reporting accountant to prepare a detailed report on the firm's financial controls, track record, financing and forecasts.

Repurchase of shares A company which has prospered, or no better use for its cash, buys back some of its shares.

Required return The minimum rate of return given the opportunity cost of capital.

Rescheduling, restructuring finance Rearranging the payments made by a borrower to a lender – usually as a result of financial distress.

Rescue rights issue A company in dire trouble, in danger of failure, carries out a rights issue to raise capital.

Residual income An alternative term for economic profit.

Residual theory of dividends Dividends should only be paid when the firm has financed all its positive NPV projects.

Resistance line A line drawn on a price (e.g. share) chart showing the market participants' reluctance to push the price below (or above) the line over a period of time.

Resolution A proposal put to the vote at a shareholders' meeting.

Resolution of uncertainty theory of dividends The market places a greater value on shares offering higher near-term dividends because these are more certain than more distant dividends.

Restructuring costs The costs associated with a reorganisation of the business, e.g. closing factories, redundancies.

Retail banking Banking for individual customers or small firms, normally for small amounts. High-volume, low-value banking.

Retail brokers *See* Private client brokers

Retail investor (individual investor, small investor) One who is not considered experienced enough to be regarded as a professional or expert. Under the Financial Conduct Authority rules retail investor receive regulatory protection and rights to compensation.

Retail Price Index (RPI) An index measuring the cost of a basket of retail goods and services over time to estimate inflation.

Retail Service Providers (RSPs) Automated computer dealing services to brokers and investors.

Retained earnings That part of a company's profits after deduction of tax not paid as dividends.

Retention ratio Retained profits for the year as a proportion of profits after tax attributable to ordinary shareholders for the year.

Return on capital employed (ROCE); Return on assets (ROA); Return on investment (ROI); Return on invested capital (ROIC) Traditional measures of profitability. Profit return divided by the volume of resources devoted to the activity. Resources usually includes shareholders' funds, net debt and provisions. Cumulative goodwill, previously written off, may be added back to the resources total. *See also* Accounting rate of return.

Return on equity (ROE) Profit attributable to shareholders as a percentage of equity shareholders' funds. Calculated by dividing net profit after tax by equity capital in balance sheet.

Revaluation reserve A balance sheet entry that records accumulated revaluations of fixed assets.

Revenue reserves (retained earnings, profit and loss reserves) Profits retained by the company from previous year's profits plus the gains made when non-current assets are sold (after tax deduction and losses on non-current asset sales). These are available to pay cash dividends.

Reverse floater *see* Reverse floating-rate notes.

Reverse floating-rate notes *see* Floating-rate notes.

Reverse takeover The acquiring company is smaller than the target in terms of market capitalisation and offers newly created shares in itself as consideration for the purchase of the shares in the acquirer. So many new shares are created that the former shareholders in the target become the dominant shareholders in the combined entity.

Reversing the trade *see* Closing out a futures position.

Reversion to the mean The behaviour of financial markets is often characterised as reverting to the mean, in which an otherwise random process of price changes or returns tends over the medium to long term to move towards the average.

Revolving credit, revolving credit facility (RCF) An arrangement whereby a borrower can draw down short-term loans as the need arises, to a maximum over a period of years.

Revolving underwriting facility (RUF) A bank(s) underwrites the borrower's access to funds at a specified rate in the short-term financial markets (e.g. by issuing euronotes) throughout an agreed period. If the notes are not bought in the market the underwriter(s) is obliged to purchase them.

Reward-to-variability ratio Alternative name for Sharpe ratio (q.v.).

Reward-to-volatility ratio An alternative name for Treynor's ratio (q.v.).

Rights issue An invitation to existing shareholders to purchase additional shares in the company in proportion to their existing holdings.

Risk A future return has a variety of possible values. Sometimes measured by standard deviation (q.v.).

Risk arbitrage Taking a position (purchase or sale) in a security, commodity, etc., because it is judged to be mispriced relative to other securities with similar characteristics. The comparator securities are not identical (e.g. shares in Unilever and in Procter & Gamble) and therefore there is an element of risk that the valuation gap will widen rather than contract. An extreme form of risk arbitrage is to take a position hoping to make a profit if an event occurs (e.g. a takeover). If the event does not occur there may be a loss. The word 'arbitrage' has been stretched beyond breaking point, as true arbitrage should be risk free.

Risk averter Someone who prefers a more certain return to an alternative with an equal expected return but which is more risky.

Risk lover (seeker) Someone who prefers a more uncertain alternative to an alternative with an equal but less risky outcome.

Risk management The selection of those risks a business should take and those which should be avoided or mitigated, followed by action to avoid or reduce risk.

Risk premium The extra return, above the risk-free rate for accepting risk.

Risk transformation Intermediaries offer low-risk securities or arrangements to primary investors to attract funds (e.g. bank account deal), which are then used to purchase higher-risk securities issued by the ultimate borrowers (e.g. the bank buys a corporate bond).

Risk-free rate of return (RFR) The rate earned on riskless investment, denoted r_f. A reasonable proxy is short-term lending to a reputable government.

Risk-return line A line on a two-dimensional graph showing all the possible expected returns and standard deviation combinations, available from the construction of portfolios from two assets. This can also be called the two-asset opportunity set or feasibility set.

Roadshow Companies and their advisers make a series of presentations to potential investors, usually to entice them into buying a new issue of securities.

Rolled-over overdraft Short-term loan facilities are perpetuated into the medium and long term by the renewal of the overdraft facility.

Rolling settlement Shares and cash are exchanged after a deal has been struck a fixed number of days later – usually after two or three days – rather than on a specific account day.

RPI (retail price index) A UK measure of general inflation.

R-squared, R^2 *see* Coefficient of determination.

Running yield *see* Yield.

Safe haven A more secure investment in time of trouble, such as major financial turmoil. UK or US government bonds and treasury bills, for example, are usually regarded as safe havens.

Sale and leaseback Assets (e.g. land and buildings) are sold to another firm (e.g. bank, insurance company) with a simultaneous agreement for the vendor to lease the asset back for a stated period under specific terms.

Sale and repurchase agreement *see* Repurchase agreement.

Sales ledger administration The management of receivables (trade debtors): recording credit sales, checking customer creditworthiness, sending invoices and chasing late payers.

Samurai A foreign bond, yen-denominated, issued by a non-Japanese entity in the domestic Japanese market.

S&P 500 Standard & Poor's index of 500 leading US shares.

Satisficed When a contributor to an organisation is given just enough of a return to make their contribution, e.g. banks are given contracted interest and principal, and no more.

Scaledown In a new issue, when a company floats on a stock exchange, if demand is greater than supply at the offer price the applicants receive less than they applied for, according to a prearranged formula.

Scenario analysis An analysis of the change in NPV (q.v.) brought about by the simultaneous change in a number of key inputs to an NPV analysis. Typically a 'worst case scenario', when all the changes in variables are worsening, and a 'best case scenario', when all variable changes are positive, are calculated.

Scheme of arrangement A relatively quick and cheap way of combining two companies whereby target managers and acquiring managers agree to allow the target shareholders to vote on a merger. If three-quarters vote in favour, and the arrangement is sanctioned by a court the scheme is binding on all shareholders. All target shareholders are then required to sell to the acquirer. Thus the acquirer can avoid having a rump minority hanging on to their shares.

Scrip dividends Shareholders are offered the alternative of additional shares rather than a cash dividend.

Scrip issue The issue of more shares to existing shareholders according to their current holdings. Shareholders do not pay for these new shares. Company reserves are converted into issued capital.

SDR *see* Special drawing rights.

SEAQ (Stock Exchange Automated Quotation System) A real-time computer screen-based quotation system for securities where market makers on the London Stock Exchange report bid-offer prices and trading volumes, and brokers and other traders can observe prices and trades.

Search costs The cost of finding another person or organisation with which to transact business/investment.

Seasoned Equity Offerings (SEOs) Companies that have been on a stock exchange for some time selling new shares, e.g. via a rights issue.

Second lien loans Low ranking loans paying high rates of return. The owners of the loans are in line behind senior secured creditors in a liquidation.

Secondary buy-out (sale) A company that has been backed by private equity finance is then sold to another private equity firm(s).

Secondary listing Some companies choose to make the London Stock Exchange their secondary listing with their primary (most important) listing on another exchange.

Secondary market Securities already issued are traded between investors.

Secondary market trading facility A system to allow current holders of shares or other securities to trade between themselves.

Second-tier markets Financial trading markets established as more lightly regulated markets alongside main highly regulated markets. This allows companies with say a short trading history to obtain a quotation for their shares.

Securities and Exchange Commission (SEC) The US federal body responsible for the regulation of securities markets (exchanges, brokers, investment advisers, etc.).

Securities house This may mean simply an issuing house. However, the term is sometimes used more broadly for an institution concerned with buying and selling securities or acting as agent in the buying and selling of securities.

Securitisation Financial assets (e.g. a claim to a number of mortgage payments) which are not tradable can be repackaged into other securities (e.g. bonds) and then sold. These are called asset-backed securities.

Security (1) A financial asset, e.g. a share or bond. (2) Asset pledged to be surrendered in the event of a loan default.

Security market line (SML) A linear (straight) line showing the relationship between systematic risk and expected rates of return for individual assets (securities). According to the capital asset pricing model (q.v.) the return above the risk-free rate of return (q.v.) for a risky asset is equal to the risk premium for the market portfolio multiplied by the beta coefficient.

SEDOL, Stock Exchange Daily Official List. A journal published daily giving prices and deals for shares on London's Official List. Companies are given SEDOL numbers to identify them.

Seed Enterprise Investment Scheme, SEIS The UK government provides tax benefits for investors in small, early stage companies with fewer than 25 employees and gross assets under £200,000.

Seedcorn capital or money (Seed capital or money) The financing of the development of a business concept. High risk; usually provided by venture capitalists, entrepreneurs or business angels.

Self-amortising A reduction in the amount outstanding on a loan by regular payments to the lender.

Self-regulation Industry participants regulate themselves within a light-touch legislated framework.

Sell-side Organisations in the securities business that help create and trade securities and also sell their services to buy-side institutions and individuals (examples of sell-side organisations are investment banks, analysts, brokers and securities firms).

Selling the rights nil paid In a rights issue existing shareholders are entitled to sell the rights to the new shares without the need to purchase the new shares.

Semi-annual Twice a year at regular intervals.

Semi-captives A venture capital organisation that raises its capital from the financial markets, but is dominated by the participation of an organising institution.

Semi-strong efficiency Share prices fully reflect all the relevant, publicly available information.

Senior debt *see* Subordinated debt.

Sensitivity analysis An analysis of the effect on project NPV of changes in the assumed values of key variables, e.g. sales level, labour costs. Variables are changed one at a time. It is a 'what-if' analysis, e.g. what if raw material costs rise by 20%?

Separate legal person A company is a legal entity under the law. It is entitled to make contracts and be sued, for example, separately from the owners of the company.

Separation principle The decision on asset allocation can split into (1) selecting the optimum market portfolio on the efficiency frontier, and (2) allocating wealth between the optimum portfolio and the risk-free asset.

Serious Fraud Office (SFO) Investigates and prosecutes crimes of serious or complex fraud and corruption exceeding £1m in the UK.

SETS (Stock Exchange Electronic Trading System) An electronic order book-based trading system for the London Stock Exchange. Brokers input buy and sell orders directly into the system. Buyers and sellers are matched and the trade executed automatically. The system is used for the largest UK shares.

SETSqx (Stock Exchange Electronic Trading Service – quotes and crosses) A share trading system run by the London Stock Exchange with a focus on lightly traded shares (few trades per day).

Settlement The completion of a transaction, e.g. upon the sale of a share in the secondary market cash is transferred as payment, in return ownership is transferred.

Settlement price The price calculated by a derivatives exchange at the end of each trading session as the closing price that will be used in determining profits and losses for the marking-to-market process for margin accounts.

Shadow banking system Powerful non-bank bodies that move money and risk without involving banks e.g. money market funds, hedge funds, private equity funds.

Share Companies divide the ownership of the company into ordinary shares. An owner of a share usually has the same rights to vote and receive dividends as another owner of a share. Also called equity (q.v.). Shares other than ordinary shares may also be created which carry different rights, e.g. preference shares (q.v.).

Share buy-back, share repurchase The company buys back a proportion of its shares from shareholders.

Share certificate A document showing ownership of part of the share capital of a company.

Share markets Institutions which facilitate the regulated sale and purchase of shares; includes the primary and secondary markets.

Share option scheme Employees are offered the right to buy shares in their company at a modest price some time in the future.

Share premium account A balance sheet entry represented by the difference between the price received by a company when it sells shares and the par value of those shares.

Share split (stock split) Shareholders receive additional shares from the company without payment. The nominal (par) value of each share is reduced in proportion to the increase in the number of shares, so the total book value of shares remains the same.

Shareholder value analysis A technique developed by Rappaport (q.v.) for establishing value creation. It equals the present value of operating cash flows within the planning horizon *plus* the present value of operating cash flows after the planning horizon *plus* the current value of marketable securities and other non-operating investments *less* corporate debt.

Shareholder wealth maximisation The maximising of shareholders' purchasing power. In a pricing efficient market, it is the maximisation of the current share price.

Shareholders' funds (Equity) The net assets of the business (after deduction of all short- and long-term liabilities and minority interests) shown in the balance sheet.

Sharia, Shari'ah law Islamic law governing, among other things, financial dealings.

Sharpe's ratio A measure relating risk and return. The extent to which a portfolio's (or share's) return has been greater than a risk-free asset divided by its standard deviation (q.v.).

Shell company A company with a stockmarket quotation but with very little in the way of real economic activity. It may have cash but no production.

Short position In a derivative contract the counterparty in a short position is the one that has agreed to deliver (e.g. sell) the underlying (q.v.).

Short selling The selling of financial securities (e.g. shares) not yet owned, in the anticipation of being able to buy at a later date at a lower price.

Short-term sterling interest rate future (colloquially known as short sterling) The three-month sterling interest rate future contract traded on ICE Futures Europe (q.v.). Notional fixed-term deposits for three-month periods starting at a specified time in the future.

Short-termism A charge levelled at the financial institutions in their expectations of the companies to which they provide finance. It is argued that long-term benefits are lost because of pressure for short-term performance.

Shorting Same as Short selling.

Shorts Bonds, e.g. gilts, with less than five years to maturity.

Sight bank account (current account) cheque/check account One where deposits can be withdrawn without notice.

Sigma A measure of dispersion of returns, standard deviation (q.v.).

Signalling Some financial decisions are taken to be signals from the managers to the financial markets, e.g. an increase in financial gearing, or a change in dividend policy.

Simple interest Interest is paid on the original principal; no interest is paid on the accumulated interest payments.

Simple yield *see* Yield.

Sinking fund Money is accumulated in a fund through regular payments in order eventually to repay a debt.

Small firm effect (Size effect) The tendency of small firms to give abnormally high returns on the stock market observed in some academic studies, but not in others.

Soft capital rationing Internal management-imposed limits on investment expenditure.

Solvency The ability to pay legal debts.

South Sea Bubble A financial bubble (*see* Bubble) in which the price of shares in the South Sea Company were pushed to ridiculously high levels on a surge of over-optimism in the early eighteenth century.

Sovereign debt Debt (e.g. a bond) issued by a government.

Sovereign wealth fund A collective investment funds set up and managed by a government on behalf of their people for the long term. It might receive money from say oil income and use that to invest in shares and other assets around the world.

Special dividend An exceptionally large dividend paid on a one-off basis.

Special purpose vehicle or entity (SPV, SPE) Companies set these up as separate organisations (usually as limited companies) for a particular purpose. They are designed so that their accounts are not consolidated with those of the rest of the group.

Special resolution A company's shareholders vote at an AGM or EGM with a majority of 75% of those voting for it to be carried. Normally special resolutions are reserved for important changes in the constitution of the company. Other matters are normally dealt with by way of an ordinary resolution (50% or more of the votes required).

Special drawing rights (SDRs) A composite currency designed by the International Monetary Fund (IMF). Each IMF member country is allocated SDRs in proportion to its quota.

Specialist Fund Market The London Stock Exchanged launched this in 2007 to creates a market in shares of closed-ended investment funds such as hedge funds, emerging market funds, specialist property.

Specific inflation The price changes in an individual good or service.

Specific risk *see* Unsystematic risk.

Speculative grade Bonds with a credit rating below investment grade.

Speculative motive for holding cash This means that unexpected opportunities can be taken immediately.

Speculators Those that take a position in financial instruments and other assets with a view to obtaining a profit on changes in their market price.

Sponsor Lends its reputation to a new issue of securities, advises the client company (along with the issuing broker) and co-ordinates the new issue process. Sponsors are usually investment banks or stockbrokers. Also called an issuing house.

Spot market A market for immediate transactions (e.g. spot forex market, spot interest market), as opposed to an agreement to make a transaction some time in the future (e.g. forward, option, future).

Spot rate of interest *see* Spot market.

Spread The difference between the price to buy and the price to sell a financial security. Market makers quote a bid–offer spread for shares. The lower price (bid) is the price an investor receives if selling to the market maker. The higher (offer) price is the price if the investor wishes to buy from the market maker.

Square mile The medieval boundary of the City of London, enclosing roughly a square mile. Now the world's leading financial centre.

Stakeholder A party with an interest (financial or otherwise) in an organisation, e.g. employees, customers, suppliers, the local community.

Standard & Poor's A leading credit rating agency.

Standard and Poor's 500 An index of leading (largest) 500 US shares listed in the New York Stock Exchange. Companies are weighted by market capitalisation of the NYSE.

Standard deviation A statistical measure of the dispersion around an average. A measure of volatility. The standard deviation is the square root of the variance. A fund or a share return can be expected to fall within one standard deviation of its average two-thirds of the time if the future is like the past.

Standard listing on the London Stock Exchange A few companies have chosen this less onerous form of listing on the LSE than the premium listing. A standard listing regime does not necessarily require three years of figures on flotation and is far less tough on a number of other quality indicators and ongoing restraints, such as requiring shareholder approval for significant transactions.

Standard variable rate The base or standard rate of interest charged by a bank or other institution to retail borrowers.

Start-up capital Finance for young companies which have not yet sold their product commercially. High risk; usually provided by venture capitalists, entrepreneurs or business angels.

Statement of financial position The term for balance sheet under International Accounting Standards.

Statistically independent shares The movement of two variables is completely unrelated (e.g. the returns on two shares are unrelated).

Statutory Established, regulated or imposed by or in conformity with laws passed by a legislative body, e.g. Parliament.

Sterling bonds Corporate bonds which pay interest and principal in pounds sterling.

Stock (1) Another term for inventory of raw materials, work-in-progress and finished items. (2) US term for share.

Stockbroker (1) A regulated professional who arranges the buying and selling of shares and other securities for investors. (2) (Corporate broker) Assists corporations in representing themselves to the financial markets, advises on finance raising and rules of markets. May match buyers with sellers of the client firm's securities.

Stock exchange A market in which securities are bought and sold. In continental Europe the term bourse may be used.

Stock Exchange Automated Quotations *see* SEAQ.

Stock Exchange Electronic Trading System *see* SETS.

Stock futures Futures in particular company shares. Also called single stock futures.

Stock market *see* Stock exchange.

Stock-out costs The cost associated with being unable to draw on a stock of raw material, work-in-progress or finished goods inventory (loss of sales, profits and goodwill, and also production dislocation).

Stocks and shares There is some lack of clarity in the distinction between stocks and shares. Shares are equities in companies. Stocks are financial instruments that pay interest, e.g. bonds. However, in the USA shares are also called 'common stocks' and the shareholders are sometimes referred to as the stockholders. So when some people use the term stocks they could be referring to either bonds or shares.

Stock split *see* Share split.

Straight bond One with a regular fixed rate of interest and without the right of conversion (to, say, shares) or any other unusual rights.

Straight-line depreciation A fixed (non-current) asset is depreciated by the same amount each year over its useful life.

Strategic analysis The analysis of industries, products and markets served by the firm and the company's competitive position within the industry.

Strategic bidder In a merger the bidder is a company in a related field of business, such as a competitor, supplier or customer which looks for targets offering long-term operational synergies (i.e. not a financial bidder).

Strategic business unit (SBU) A business unit within the overall corporate entity which is distinguishable from other business units because it serves a defined external market where management can conduct strategic planning in relation to products and markets.

Strategic objectives These goals are used as the criteria to guide the firm, e.g. market share targets. However, they may not always be good indicators of whether shareholder wealth is being maximised.

Strategic position A firm's competitive position within an industry and the attractiveness of the industry.

Strategy Selecting which product or market areas to enter/exit and how to ensure a good competitive position in those markets/products.

Strategy planes chart Maps a firm's, SBU's or product line's position in terms of industry attractiveness, competitive advantage and life cycle stage of value potential.

Strike bid In a book-building exercise a potential institutional investor states that it will buy a given number of shares within the initial price range.

Strike price (1) In the offer for sale by a tender it is the price selected that will sell the required quantity of shares given the offers made. (2) The price paid by the holder of an option when/if the option is exercised – *see* Exercise price.

Strong form efficiency All relevant information, including that which is privately held, is reflected in the security (e.g. share) price.

Subjective probability Probabilities are devised based on personal judgement of the range of outcomes along with the likelihood of their occurrence.

Subordinated debt A debt which ranks below another liability in order of priority for payment of interest or principal. Senior debt ranks above junior (subordinated) debt for payment.

Sub-prime mortgage A mortgage designed for borrowers with a low credit rating charged at an interest rate above the rate levied on prime borrowers.

Subscription rights A right to subscribe for some shares.

Subsidiary A company is a subsidiary of another company if the parent company holds the majority of the voting rights (more than 50%), or has a minority of the shares but has the right to appoint or remove directors holding a majority of the voting rights at meetings of the board on all, or substantially all, matters or it has the right to exercise a dominant influence.

Sukuk A form of Islamic bond.

Summary financial statement Companies often send small investors a summary of the financial statements rather than the full report and accounts. This suits many investors and saves the company some money. However, an investor is entitled to receive a full annual report and accounts. It may be necessary to make a request for this.

Sunk cost A cost the firm has incurred or to which it is committed that cannot be altered. This cost does not influence subsequent decisions and can be ignored in, for example, project appraisal.

Super normal returns A rate of return above the normal rate.

Survivorship bias In empirical studies of share price performance the results may be distorted by focusing only on companies which survived through to the end of the period of study. Particularly poor performers (i.e. liquidated firms) are removed from the sample, thus biasing the results in a positive direction.

SVR *see* Standard variable rate.

Swap An exchange of cash payment obligations. An interest rate swap is where one company arranges with a counterparty to exchange interest rate payments. In a currency swap the two parties exchange interest obligations (receipts) for an agreed period between two different currencies.

Swaption or swap-option An option to have a swap at a later date.

Sweep facility Automatic transfer of funds from one bank account to another account. Usually done to take advantage of higher interest rates.

Symbiosis type of post-merger integration Large differences between acquired and parent firms in culture, systems, etc., are maintained. However, collaboration in communications and the cross-fertilisation of ideas are encouraged.

Syndicated loan A loan made by one or more banks to one borrower.

Synergy A combined entity (e.g. two companies merging) will have a value greater than the sum of the parts.

Systematic (Undiversifiable or market or residual) risk That element of return variability from an asset which cannot be eliminated through diversification (q.v.). Measured by beta (q.v.). It comprises the risk factors common to all firms.

Systemic risk The risk of failure within the financial system causing a domino-type effect bringing down large parts of the system.

Take-out Market expression of bid made to a seller to 'takeout' his position – e.g. venture capital backed companies are bought allowing the venture capitalist to exit from the investment.

Takeover (acquisition) Many people use these terms interchangeably with merger. However, some differentiate takeover as meaning a purchase of one firm by another with the concomitant implication of financial and managerial domination. Usually applied to hostile (without target management approval) mergers.

Takeover Panel The committee responsible for supervising compliance with the (UK) City Code on Takeovers and Mergers (q.v.).

Tangible assets Those that have a physical presence.

Tariff Taxes imposed on imports.

Tax allowance An amount of income or capital gain that is not taxed.

Tax avoidance Steps taken to reduce tax that are permitted under the law.

Tax evasion Deliberately giving a false statement or omitting a relevant fact. Illegal.

Tax haven A country or place with low rates of tax and less (or more flexible) regulation.

Tax shield The benefit for a company that comes from having some of its capital in debt form, the interest on which is tax deductible, resulting in a lower outflow from the company to the tax authorities.

Taxable profit That element of profit subject to taxation. This frequently differs from reported profit.

techMARK The London Stock Exchange launched techMARK in 1999. It is a subsection of the shares within the LSE's Official List (q.v.). It is a grouping of technology companies. It imposes different rules on companies seeking a flotation from those that apply to the other companies on the Official List (e.g. only one year's accounts are required).

Technical analysis Analysis of share price movements and trading volume to forecast future movements from past movements.

Tender offer A public offer to purchase securities.

Term assurance Life assurance taken out for less than the whole life – the insured sum is paid only in the event of the insured person dying within the term.

Term loan A loan of a fixed amount for an agreed time and on specified terms, usually with regular periodic payments. Most frequently provided by banks.

Term securities Securities that have a set length of maturity, with a penalty for early withdrawal.

Term structure of interest rates The patterns of interest rates on bonds with differing lengths of time to maturity but with the same risk. Strictly it is the zero coupon implied interest rate for different lengths of time. *See also* Yield curve.

Terminal value The forecast future value of sums of money compounded to the end of a common time horizon.

Three-day rolling settlement (T + 3) After a share transaction in the stock exchange investors pay for shares three working days later.

Tick The minimum price movement of a security or derivative contract.

Tier one ratio of core capital That part of a bank's capital defined as shareholders' equity.

Tiger economies (or countries) The first four industrialised economies in Asia excluding Japan: Taiwan, South Korea, Singapore and Hong Kong (also referred to as dragon economies).

'Time adjusted' measures of profitability The time value of money is taken into account.

Time deposit, term deposit, fixed deposit, savings account Money deposited for a set time or for which a lengthy notice to withdraw must be given. Money cannot be withdrawn on demand.

Time loan Loans with a specific maturity (US usage).

Time value That part of an option's value that represents the value of the option expiring in the future rather than now. The longer the period to expiry, the greater the chance that the option will become in-the-money before the expiry date. The amount by which the option premium exceeds the intrinsic value.

Time value of money A pound received in the future is worth less than a pound received today – the present value of a sum of money depends on the date of its receipt.

Total (or market) capitalisation *see* Market capitalisation.

Total shareholder return (TSR) or Total return The total return earned on a share over a period of time: dividends per share plus capital gain divided by initial share price expressed as a percentage.

Touch prices *see* Yellow strip.

Tracker An investment fund which is intended to replicate the return of a market index. Also called an index fund or passive fund.

Trade acceptance *see* Acceptance credit.

Trade credit (payables) Where goods and services are delivered to a firm for use in its production and are not paid for immediately.

Trade receivables (debtors) Amounts owing by customers of a firm for goods and services delivered.

Trade debtor A customer of a firm who has not yet paid for goods and services delivered.

Trade sale A company buys another company in the same line of business.

Traded option An option tradable on a market separate from the underlying (q.v.).

Trading floor A place where traders in a market (or their representatives) can meet to agree transactions face to face. However investment banks often have 'trading floors' where they 'meet' counterparties on other trading floors to conduct transactions via the telephone or computer.

Trading margin *see* Operating profit margin.

Traditional option An option available on any security but with an exercise price fixed as the market price on the day the option is bought. Bilateral contracts between the option buyer and the option writer rather than exchange-traded instruments. All such options expire after three months and cannot be sold to a secondary investor.

Transaction risk The risk that transactions already entered into, or for which the firm is likely to have a commitment in a foreign currency, will have a variable value in the home currency because of exchange-rate movements.

Transactional banking Banks compete with each other to offer services at the lowest cost to corporations, on a service-by-service basis.

Transactional motive for holding cash Money is used as a means of exchange; receipts and payments are rarely perfectly synchronised and therefore an individual or business generally needs to hold a stock of money to meet expenditure.

Translation risk This risk arises because financial data denominated in one currency are then expressed in terms of another currency.

Treasury UK government department responsible for financial and economic policy.

Treasury bill A short-term money market instrument issued (sold) by the central bank, mainly in the UK and the USA, usually to supply the government's short-term financing needs.

Treasury bond Long-term (maturity > 10 years) government bonds.

Treasury management To plan, organise and control cash and borrowings so as to optimise interest and currency flows, and minimise the cost of funds. Also to plan and execute communications programmes to enhance investors' confidence in the firm.

Treynor's ratio or index (reward-to-volatility ratio) A measure relating return to risk. It is the return on a portfolio (or share) minus the risk-free rate of rate of return divided by beta.

TRRACK system A system to assist the analysis of a company's extraordinary resources under the headings: tangible; relationships; reputation; attitude; capabilities; and knowledge.

Trust deed A document specifying the regulation of the management of assets on behalf of beneficiaries of the trust.

Trustees Those that are charged with the responsibility for ensuring compliance with the trust deed.

Tulipmania A seventeenth-century Dutch bubble in which the price of tulip bulbs were bid up because people expected to be able to sell to someone else at an even greater price. *See* Bubble.

Turnover (revenue or sales) (1) Money received or to be received by the company from goods and services sold during the period. (2) In portfolio management, the amount of trading relative to the value of the portfolio.

Turquoise trading platform majority owned by LSE. Trades in equities, options, futures and derivatives.

Two-day rolling settlement (T + 2) After a share transaction in the stock exchange investors pay for the shares two working days later.

UKLA *see* United Kingdom Listing Authority.

Ultimate borrowers Firms investing in real assets need finance which ultimately comes from the primary investors.

Uncertainty Strictly (in economists' terms), uncertainty is when there is more than one possible outcome to a course of action; the form of each possible outcome is known, but the probability of getting any one outcome is not known. However, the distinction between risk (the ability to assign probabilities) and uncertainty has largely been ignored for the purposes of this text.

Unconditionality In a merger (q.v.), once unconditionality is declared, the acquirer becomes obliged to buy. Target shareholders who accepted the offer are no longer able to withdraw their acceptance.

Unconventional cash flows A series of cash flows in which there is more than one change in sign.

Uncovered (naked) call option writing Writing a call option (q.v.) on an underlying (q.v.) when the writer does not own the underlying securities included in the option.

Underlying The asset (e.g. share, commodity) that is the subject of a derivative contract.

Underlying earnings per share *see* Headline earnings per share.

Underwriters (1) These (usually large financial institutions) guarantee to buy the proportion of a new issue of securities (e.g. shares) not taken up by the market, in return for a fee. (2) These assess, insurance risks and set the amount and terms of the premium.

Undifferentiated product One that is much the same as that supplied by other companies.

Undiversifiable risk *see* Systematic risk.

Uninformed investors Those that have no/little knowledge about financial securities and the fundamental evaluation of their worth.

Unique risk *see* Unsystematic risk.

Unit trust An investment organisation that attracts funds from individual investors by issuing units to invest in a range of securities, e.g. shares or bonds. It is open ended, the number of units expanding to meet demand.

United Kingdom Corporate Governance Code Following a number of financial scandals, guidelines of best practice in corporate governance were issued which are guidelines of best practice for companies regarding the powers and responsibilities of directors, shareholders and senior managers.

United Kingdom Listing Authority (UKLA) This organisation is part of the Financial Conduct Authority (q.v.) and rigorously enforces a set of demanding rules on companies at the time when they join the stock market and in subsequent years.

Universal banks Financial institutions involved in many different aspects of finance including retail banking and wholesale banking.

Unlisted Shares and other securities not on the United Kingdom Listing Authority's acceptance list to be traded on a highly regulated market (usually the Main Market of the London Stock Exchange) are described as unlisted.

Unquoted firms Those shares with a price not quoted on a recognised investment exchange, RIE (e.g. the Official List or AIM of the London Stock Exchange – qq.v.).

Unsecured A financial claim with no collateral or any charge over the assets of the borrower.

Unsystematic (unique or diversifiable or specific) risk That element of an asset's variability in returns which can be eliminated by holding a well-diversified portfolio.

Utility (1) The satisfaction, pleasure or fulfilment of needs derived from consuming some quantity of a good or service. (2) A business involved in basic goods and services, e.g. water, electricity.

Valuation risk (price risk) The possibility that, when a financial instrument matures or is sold in the market, the amount received is less than anticipated by the owner.

Value action pentagon This displays the five actions for creating value: (1) Increase the return on existing capital. (2) Raise investment in positive spread units. (3) Divest assets from negative spread units to release capital for more productive use. (4) Extend the planning horizon. (5) Lower the required rate of return.

Value chain The interlinking activities that take place within an organisation or between organisations in the process of converting inputs into outputs. Identifying these activities and finding ways to perform them more efficiently is a way for companies to gain competitive advantage over their rivals.

Value creation The four key elements are: (1) Amount of capital invested. (2) Actual rate of return on capital. (3) Required rate of return. (4) Planning horizon (for performance-spread persistence).

Value creation profile An analysis of the sources of value creation within the firm from its products and market segments, which maps value creation against the proportion of capital invested.

Value drivers Crucial organisational capabilities, giving the firm competitive advantage. Different from Rappaport's value drivers (q.v.).

Value investing The identification and holding of shares which are fundamentally undervalued by the market, given the prospects of the firm.

Value-based management A managerial approach in which the primary purpose is long-term shareholder wealth maximisation. The objective of the firm, its systems, strategy, processes, analytical techniques, performance measurements and culture have as their guiding objective long-term shareholder wealth maximisation.

Vanilla bond *see* Straight bond.

Variable costs Costs that rise or fall with product output and sales.

Variable rate bond (loan) The interest rate payable varies with short-term rates (e.g. LIBOR six months).

Variance A measure of volatility around an average value. It is the square of the standard deviation.

Variation margin The amount of money paid after the payment of the initial margin required to secure an option or futures position, after it has been revalued by the exchange or clearing house. Variation margin payments may be required daily to top the account up to the maintenance margin level.

Vendor placing Shares issued to a company to pay for assets, or issued to shareholders to pay for an entire company in a takeover are placed with investors keen on holding the shares in return for cash. The vendors can then receive the cash.

Venture capital (VC) Finance provided to unquoted firms by specialised financial institutions. This may be backing for an entrepreneur, financing a start-up or developing business, or assisting a management buyout or buy-in. Usually it is provided by a mixture of equity, loans and mezzanine finance. It is used for medium-term to long-term investment in high-risk situations.

Venture capital trusts (VCTs) An investment vehicle introduced to the UK in 1995 to encourage investment in small and fast-growing companies. The VCT invests in a range of small businesses. The providers of finance to the VCT are given important tax breaks.

Vertical merger Where the two merging firms are from different stages of the production chain.

Virtual bid (indicative offer) When a proper merger offer by one company for another has not been made, but the potential acquirer has raised the possibility of making a bid for the target firm without any commitment.

Volatility The speed and magnitude of price movements over time, measured by standard deviation or variance (qq.v.).

Volume transformation Intermediaries gather small quantities of money from numerous savers and repackage these sums into larger bundles for investment in the business sector or elsewhere.

Wall Street Originally describing the location of the New York Stock Exchange and some financial institutions, it is now a term used to mean securities trading and financial markets/services generally in the USA.

Warrant A financial instrument which gives the holder the right but not the obligation to purchase shares (or bonds) in the company from the company at a fixed price at some time in the future (during or at the end of a specific time period).

Weak-form efficiency Share prices (or other securities) fully reflect all information contained in past price movements. This precludes the possibility of studying past price movements to successfully predict future movement sufficiently well to systematically outperform the stock market after allowing for different risk levels.

Wealth added index (WAI) A value metric devised and trademarked by Stern Stewart & Co. It measures the increase in shareholder's wealth through dividend and capital gains over a number of years after deducting the cost of equity capital, defined as the return required for shares of that risk class.

Weighted average cost of capital (WACC) The weighted average cost of capital (the discount rate) is calculated by weighting the cost of debt and equity in proportion to their contributions to the total capital of the firm.

White knight A friendly company which makes a bid for a company that is the subject of a hostile takeover bid. The white knight's bid is welcomed by the directors of the target company.

Whole-of-life policies Life assurance that pays out to beneficiaries when the insured dies (not limited to, say, the next 10 years).

Wholesale bank One that lends, arranges lending or supplies services on a large scale to corporations and within the interbank market, as opposed to retail banks dealing in relatively small sums for depositors and borrowers.

Wholesale financial markets Markets available only to those dealing in large quantities. Dominated by interbank transactions.

Winding-up The process of ending a company, selling its assets, paying its creditors and distributing the remaining cash among shareholders.

Winner's curse In winning a merger battle, the acquirer suffers a loss in value because it overpays.

Withholding tax Taxation deducted from income by the payer of that income (e.g. company paying interest or dividends) and then sent to tax authorities.

Work-in-progress period The number of days to convert raw materials into finished goods. Equal to the average value of work-in-progress divided by the average cost of goods sold per day.

Working capital The difference between current assets and current liabilities – net current assets or net current liabilities (qq.v.).

Working capital cycle Typically, investment in raw materials, work-in-progress and finished goods is followed by sales for cash or on credit. Credit sales funds are usually collected at a later date. Investment is needed at each stage to finance current assets. The cycle may be expressed in terms of the length of time between the acquisition of raw materials and other inputs and the flow of cash from the sale of goods.

Write down (Write off) Companies change the recorded value of assets when they are no longer worth the previously stated value.

Writer of an option The seller of an option contract, granting the right but not the obligation to the purchaser.

Writing-down allowance (WDA) (Capital allowance) Reductions in taxable profit related to a firm's capital expenditure (e.g. plant, machinery, vehicles). A portion of the value is a tax-deductible expense in the year.

Xetra DAX A stock market index of German shares quoted on the Deutsche Börse.

Yankees A foreign bond, US dollar-denominated, issued by a non-US entity in the domestic US market.

Yellow strip The yellow band on a SEAQ or SETSqx screen which displays the highest bid and the lowest offered prices that competing market makers are offering in a security. It is known colloquially as the 'touch' or 'yellow strip' prices.

Yield The income from a security as a proportion of its market price. The flat yield (current yield, interest yield, simple yield, running yield and income yield) on a fixed interest security is the gross interest amount, divided by the current market price, expressed as a percentage. The redemption yield or yield to maturity of a bond is the discount rate such that the present value of all cash inflows from the bond (interest plus principal) is equal to the bond's current market price.

Yield curve A graph showing the relationship between the length of time to the maturity of a number of bonds with the same risk and the interest rate.

Yield stock *see* High yield shares.

Yield to maturity *see* Yield.

Z statistic A measure of the number of standard deviations away from the mean (average) value a point (say an NPV outcome) is.

Zero-cost option A combination of option purchase and option writing. The price of the written option (premium) is the same as the price (premium) paid for the option that is purchased, so the net cost is zero.

Zero coupon bond (or zero coupon preference share) A bond (or preference share) that does not pay regular interest (dividend) but instead is issued at a discount (i.e. below par value) and is redeemable at par, thus offering a capital gain.

Bibliography

Abdeen, A.M. and Haight, T. (2011) 'A fresh look at economic value added: Empirical study of the fortune five-hundred companies', *Journal of Applied Business Research,* 18(2).

Abraham, A. and Ikenberry, D. (1994) 'The individual investor and the weekend effect', *Journal of Financial and Quantitative Analysis,* June.

Acemoglu, D., Johnson, S. and Mitton, T. (2009) 'Determinants of vertical integration: financial development and contracting costs', *Journal of Finance,* LXIV(3), pp. 1251–90.

Adams, R.B., Licht, A.N. and Sagiv, L. (2011) 'Shareholders and stakeholders: How do directors decide?' *Strategic Management Journal,* 32(12).

Adebambo, B.N. and Yan, X. (2016) 'Momentum, reversals, and fund manager overconfidence', *Financial Management* (Wiley-Blackwell), 45(3), pp. 609–39.

Aggarwal, R. (2001) 'Using economic profit to assess performance: A metric for modern firms', *Business Horizons,* Jan/Feb, pp. 55–60.

Aggarwal, R., Erel, I., Stulz, R. and Williamson, R. (2010) 'Differences in governance practices between U.S. and foreign firms: measurement, causes, and consequences', *Review of Financial Studies,* 23(3), pp. 3131–69.

Ahern, K.R. and J. Harford (2014) 'The importance of industry links in merger waves', *Journal of Finance,* 69(2), pp. 527–76.

Ahmad, W. and Jelic, R. (2014) 'Lockup Agreements and Survival of UK IPOs', *Journal of Business Finance & Accounting,* 41(5) & (6), 717–42, June/July 2014.

Aktas, N., de Bodt, E. and Roll, R. (2013) 'Learning from repetitive acquisitions: Evidence from the time between deals', *Journal of Financial Economics,* 108, pp. 99–117.

Al-Ali, J. and Arkwright, T. (2000) 'An investigation of UK companies' practice in the determination, interpretation and usage of the cost of capital', *Journal of Interdisciplinary Economics,* 11, pp. 303–19.

Alexander, G.J., Bailey, J.V. and Sharpe, W.F. (2008) *Investments.* 6th edn. Upper Saddle River, NJ: Prentice-Hall.

Alkaraan, F. and Northcott, D. (2006) 'Strategic capital investment decision-making: a role for emergent analysis tools? A study of practice in large UK manufacturing companies', *British Accounting Review,* 38, pp. 149–73.

Almazan, A., De Motta, A., Titman, S. and Uysal, V. (2010) 'Financial structure, acquisition opportunities and firm locations', *The Journal of Finance,* LXV (2), pp. 529–58.

Al-Rjoub, S.A.M., Varela, O. and Hassan, M.K. (2005) 'The size reversal in the USA', *Applied Financial Economics,* 15, pp. 1189–97.

Alti, A. (2006) 'How persistent is the impact of market timing on capital structure?' *Journal of Finance,* 61(4), August, pp. 1681–710.

Alzahrani, M. and Laffer, M. (2012) 'Investor protection, taxation, and dividends', *Journal of Corporate Finance,* 18, pp. 745–62.

Ambrose, B.W. and Megginson, W.L. (1992) 'The role of asset structure, ownership structure, and takeover defences in determining acquisition likelihood', *Journal of Financial and Quantitative Analysis,* 27(4), pp. 575–89.

Ami, E., Kama, I. and Levi, S. (2015) 'Conditional persistence of earnings components and accounting anomalies', *Journal of Business Finance & Accounting,* Sep/Oct 2015, 42(7/8), pp. 801–25.

Amihud. Y., Hameed, A., Kang, W. and Zhang, H. (2015) 'The illiquidity premium: International evidence', *Journal of Financial Economics,* 117, pp. 350–68.

Amran, M. and Kulatilaka, N. (1999) *Real Options: Managing Strategic Investment in an Uncertain World.* Boston, MA: Harvard Business School Press.

Andersen, T.J. (2006) *Global Derivatives: A Strategic Management Perspective.* Harlow: FT Prentice Hall.

Anderson, K. and Brooks, C. (2006) 'The long-term price–earnings ratio', *Journal of Business Finance and Accounting,* 33(7) & (8), pp. 1063–86.

Anderson, A.M., Bey, R.P. and Weaver, S.C. (2005) 'Economic Value Added® adjustments: Much ado about nothing?' Working Paper. Bethlehem, PA: Lehigh University.

Anderson, R.C., Mansi, S.A. and Reeb, D.M. (2003) 'Founding family ownership and the agency cost of debt', *Journal of Financial Economics,* 68, pp. 263–85.

Andor, G. et al. (2015) 'Capital budgeting practices: a survey of Central and Eastern European firms', *Emerging Markets Review,* 23: 148–72.

Andrade, G. and Kaplan, S. (1998) 'How costly is financial (not economic) distress? Evidence from highly leveraged transactions that became distressed', *Journal of Finance,* 53, pp. 1443–93.

Andreadakis, S. (2012) 'Enlightened Shareholder Value: Is it the new modus operandi for modern corporations?' In S. Boubaker et al. (eds), *Corporate Governance,* Springer-Verlag, Berlin.

Andrikopoulos, P., Daynes, A., Latimer, D. and Pagas, P. (2008) 'Size effect, methodological issues and "risk-to-default": evidence from the UK stock market', *European Journal of Finance,* 14(4) pp. 299–314.

Ang, J., Cole, R. and Lin, J. (2000) 'Agency costs and ownership structure', *Journal of Finance,* 55(1), pp. 81–106.

Anthony, R.N. (1960) 'The trouble with profit maximisation', *Harvard Business Review,* Nov.–Dec., pp. 126–34.

Antoniou, A., Petmezas, D. and Zhao, H. (2007) 'Bidder gains and losses of firms involved in many acquisitions', *Journal of Business Finance and Accounting*, 34(7), (8), pp. 1221–44.

Ap Gwilym, O., Seaton, J., Suddason, K. and Thomas, S. (2006) 'International evidence on the payout ratio, earnings, dividends and returns', *Financial Analysts Journal*, 62(1) pp. 36–53.

Arikan, A.M. and Stulz (2016) 'Corporate acquisitions, diversification, and the firm's life cycle', *Journal of Finance*, 71(1), pp. 139–94.

Armitage, S. (2010) 'Block buying and choice of issue method in UK seasoned equity offers', *Journal of Business Finance & Accounting*, 37(3), (4), pp. 422–48.

Armitage, S., Dionysiou, D. and Gonzalez, A. (2014) 'Are the discounts in seasoned equity offers due to inelastic demand?' *Journal of Business Finance & Accounting*, 41(5) & (6), 743–72, June/July 2014.

Arnold, G. (2000) 'Tracing the development of value-based management'. In Glen Arnold and Matt Davies (eds), *Value-based Management: Context and Application*. London: Wiley.

Arnold, G. (2009) *The Financial Times Guide to Value Investing: How to become a disciplined investor.* 2nd edn. Harlow: FT Prentice Hall.

Arnold, G. (2011) *The Great Investors*. Harlow: FT Prentice Hall.

Arnold, G. (2012a) *Modern Financial Markets and Institutions*. Harlow: FT Prentice Hall.

Arnold, G. (2012b) *The Financial Times Guide to Financial Markets*. Harlow: FT Prentice Hall.

Arnold, G. (2014a) *The Financial Times Guide to Investing*. 3rd edn. Harlow: FT Prentice Hall.

Arnold G. (2014b) *The Financial Times Guide to Banking*. Harlow: FT Prentice Hall.

Arnold, G. (2015) *Financial Times Guide to Bond and Money Markets*. Harlow: FT Prentice Hall.

Arnold, G. (2017) *The Deals of Warren Buffett, Vol. 1 The First $100m*. Harriman House, Petersfield, Hampshire.

Arnold, G.C. and Baker, R.D. (2007) 'Return reversal in UK shares', Salford Business School Working Paper 107/07.

Arnold, G.C. and Davies, M. (eds) (2000) *Value-Based Management*. London: John Wiley & Sons.

Arnold, G.C. and Hatzopoulos, P.D. (2000) 'The theory–practice gap in capital budgeting: Evidence from the United Kingdom', *Journal of Business Finance and Accounting*, 27(5) and (6), June/July, pp. 603–26.

Arnold, G. and Shi, J. (2005) 'Profitability of momentum strategies in UK bull and bear market conditions', University of Salford Working Papers.

Arnold, G.C. and Xiao, Y. (2007) 'Financial statement analysis and the return reversal effect'. Salford Business School Working Paper 108/07.

Arnott, R.D. and Asness, C.S. (2003) 'Surprise! Higher dividends = higher growth', *Financial Analysts Journal*, January, 59, pp. 71–87.

Arnott, R. and Bernstein, P. (2002) 'What risk premium is normal?', *Financial Analysts Journal*, March/April.

Arya, A., Fellingham, J.C. and Glover, J.C. (1998) 'Capital budgeting: some exceptions to the net present value rule', *Issues in Accounting Education*, 13(3), August, pp. 499–508.

Aslan, H. (2016) 'Do lending relationships affect corporate financial policies?' *Financial Management*, Spring, 45(1), pp. 141–73.

Asness, C.S., Israelov, R. and Liew, J.M. (2011) 'International diversification works (eventually)', *Financial Analysts Journal*, 67(3), pp. 24–38.

Asness, C.S., Moskowitz, T.J. and Pedersen, L.H. (2013) 'Value and momentum everywhere', *Journal of Finance*, LXVIII(3), pp. 929–85.

Association for Finance Professionals (2011) 'Current trends in estimating and applying the cost of capital', www.afponline.org.

Atanassov, J. and Kim, E.H. (2009) 'Labor and corporate governance: international evidence from restructuring decisions', *Journal of Finance*, 64(1), pp. 341–74.

Baba, N. and Packer, F. (2009) 'Interpreting deviations from covered interest parity during the financial market turmoil of 2007–08', *Journal of Banking and Finance*, 33, pp. 1953–62.

Baghai, R.P., Servaes, H. and Ane, A. (2014) 'Have rating agencies become more conservative? Implications for capital structure and debt pricing', *Journal of Finance*, 69(5), pp. 1961–2005.

Bailey, D.H., Borwein, J.M., López de Prado, M. and Qiji Jim Zhu (2014) 'Pseudo-mathematics and financial charlatanism: the effects of backtest overfitting on out-of-sample performance', *Notices of the American Mathematical Society*, 61(5), pp. 458–71.

Baker, A. and Wurgler, J. (2002) 'Market timing and capital structure', *Journal of Finance*, 62(1), February, pp. 1–32.

Baker, M. and Wurgler, J. (2004) 'A catering theory of dividends', *Journal of Finance*, 59(3), June, pp. 1125–65.

Baker, M., Bradley, B. and Wurgler, J. (2011) 'Benchmarks as limits to arbitrage: understanding the low-volatility anomaly', *Financial Analysts Journal*, 67(1) pp. 40–54.

Baker, H.K., Powell, G.E. and Veit E.T. (2002) 'Revisiting managerial perspectives on dividend policy', *Journal of Economics and Finance*, 26(3), pp. 267–83.

Ball, R. and Kothari, S.P. (1989) 'Nonstationary expected returns: Implications for tests of market efficiency and serial correlation in returns', *Journal of Financial Economics*, 25, pp. 51–94.

Ball, R., Gerakos, J., Linnainmaa, J.T. and Nikolaev, V. (2016) 'Accruals, cash flows, and operating profitability in the cross section of stock returns', *Journal of Financial Economics*, 121, pp. 28–45.

Ball, R., Kothari, S.P. and Shanken, J. (1995) 'Problems in measuring portfolio performance: An application to contrarian investment strategies', *Journal of Financial Economics*, May, 38, pp. 79–107.

Baltazar, M. (2008) *The Beginners Guide to Financial Spread Betting*, 2nd edn. Harriman House.

Bancel, F. and Mittoo, U. (2004) 'Cross-country determinants of capital structure choice: A survey of European firms', *Financial Management*, 33, 103–32.

Bancel F. and Mittoo, U. (2011) 'Survey evidence on financing decisions and cost of capital'. In H.K. Baker and Martin, G. (Eds.), *Capital Structure and Corporate Financing Decisions – Theory, Evidence, and Practice* (pp. 229–48). Hoboken, New Jersey: John Wiley, Ch. 13.

Banerjee, S., Dasgupta, S. and Kim, Y. (2008) 'Buyer–supplier relationships and the stakeholder theory of capital structure', *The Journal of Finance*, LXIII (5), pp. 2507–52.

Bank for International Settlements (2016) *Triennial Central Bank Survey of Foreign Exchange and OTC derivatives markets in 2016*. Available at www.bis.org/publ/rpfx16.htm

Banz, R. (1981) 'The relationship between return and market value of common stock', *Journal of Financial Economics*, 9, pp. 3–18.

Banz, R.W. and Breen, W.J. (1986) 'Sample-dependent results using accounting and market data: Some evidence', *Journal of Finance*, 41, pp. 779–93.

Barber, B.M. and Odean, T. (1999) 'The courage of misguided convictions', *Financial Analysts Journal*, 55, November–December, pp. 41–55.

Barber, B.M. and Odean, T. (2000) 'Trading is hazardous to your wealth: The common stock investment performance and individual investors', *Journal of Finance*, 55(2), April, pp. 773–806.

Barberis, N., Shleifer, A. and Vishny, R.W. (1998) 'A model of investor sentiment', *Journal of Financial Economics*, 49, pp. 307–43.

Barclays Capital, *Equity Gilt Studies*. London: Barclays.

Barker, R. (2001) *Determining Value: Valuation models and financial statements*. Harlow: Financial Times Prentice Hall.

Barroso P. and Santa-Clara, P. (2015) 'Momentum has its moments', *Journal of Financial Economics*, 116, pp. 111–20.

Barry, C.B., Peavy J.W. (III) and Rodriguez, M. (1998) 'Performance characteristics of emerging capital markets', *Financial Analysts Journal*, January/February, pp. 72–80.

Bar-Isaac, H. and Shapiro, J. (2013) 'Rating quality over the business cycle', *Journal of Financial Economics*, 108, pp. 62–78.

Basu, S. (1975) 'The information content of price-earnings ratios', *Financial Management*, 4, Summer, pp. 53–64.

Basu, S. (1977) 'Investment performance of common stocks in relation to their price/earnings ratios: A test of the efficient market hypothesis', *Journal of Finance*, 32(3), June, pp. 663–82.

Basu, S. (1983) 'The relationship between earnings' yield, market value and return for NYSE stocks – Further evidence', *Journal of Financial Economics*, June, pp. 129–56.

Baumol, W.J. (1952) 'The transactions demand for cash: An inventory theoretic approach', *Quarterly Journal of Economics*, November, 66(4), pp. 545–56.

Bebchuk, L., Cohen, A. and Ferrell, A. (2009) 'What matters in corporate governance?' *Review of Financial Studies*, 22(2), pp. 783–827.

Becht, M., Mayer, C. and Rossi, S. (2010) 'Returns to shareholder activism: evidence from a clinical study of the Hermes UK Focus Fund', *Review of Financial Studies*, 23(3), pp. 3093–129.

Becker, B., Ivković, Z. and Weisbenner, S. (2011) 'Local dividend clienteles', *Journal of Finance*, 66(2), pp. 655–83.

Bena, J. and Li, K. (2014) 'Corporate innovations and mergers and acquisitions', *Journal of Finance*, October, 69(5), pp. 1923–60.

Benartzi, S. and Thaler, R. (1995) 'Myopic loss aversion and the equity premium puzzle', *Quarterly Journal of Economics*, 110(1), pp. 73–92.

Bennouna, K., Meredith, G.G. and Marchant, T. (2010) 'Improved capital budgeting decision making: evidence from Canada', *Management Decision*, 48(2), pp. 225–47.

Berg, T., Saunders, A. and Steffen, S. (2016) 'The total cost of borrowing in the loan market: don't ignore the fees', *Journal of Finance*, June 2016, 71(3), pp. 1357–92.

Bergman, J. and Van Cieaf, M, (2012) 'Total Shareholder Return (TSR) and management performance: a performance metric appropriately used, or mostly abused?' *Rotman International Journal of Pension Management*, 5(2), pp. 26–33.

Berle, A.A. and Means, G.C. (1932) *The Modern Corporation and Private Property*. New York: Macmillan.

Bernard, V. (1993) 'Stock price reaction to earnings announcements', in Thaler, R. (ed.) *Advances in Behavioural Finance*. New York: Russell Sage Foundation.

Bernard, V.L. and Thomas, J.K. (1989) 'Post-earnings-announcement drift: Delayed price response or risk premium?', *Journal of Accounting Research*, 27 (Supplement 1989), pp. 1–36.

Bernstein, P.L. (1996) *Against the Gods: The Remarkable Story of Risk*. Chichester: John Wiley & Sons, Inc.

Bessembinder, H. and Zhang, F. (2013) 'Firm characteristics and long-run stock returns after corporate events', *Journal of Financial Economics*, 109, pp. 83–102.

Bevan, A.A. and Danbolt, J. (2004) 'Testing for inconsistencies in the estimation of UK capital structure determinants', *Applied Financial Economics*, 14, pp. 55–66.

Bhalla, V.K. (2006) *Working Capital Management*. Anmol Publications Pvt.

Bharath, S., Dahiya, S., Saunders, A. and Srinivasan, A. (2007) 'So what do I get? The bank's view of lending relationships', *Journal of Financial Economics*, 85, pp. 368–419.

Bhattacharya, H. (2009) *Working Capital Management: Strategies and Techniques*. 2nd edn. New Delhi PHI Learning.

Bhattacharyya, S. and Nain, A. (2011) 'Horizontal acquisitions and buying power: A product market analysis', *Journal of Financial Economics*, 99, 97–115.

Bhide, A. (1993) 'The causes and consequences of hostile takeovers', in Chew, Jr, D.H. (ed.), *The New Finance: Where Theory Meets Practice*. New York: McGrawHill.

Bierman, H. and Smidt, S. (2006) *The Capital Budgeting Decision*, 9th edn. London: Routledge.

Bierman, H. and Smidt, S. (2006) *Advanced Capital Budgeting*. London: Routledge.

Bigelli, M. and Sanchez-Vidal, J. (2012) 'Cash Holdings in Private Firms', *Journal of Banking and Finance*, 36(1), pp. 26–35.

Black, F. (1972) 'Capital market equilibrium with restricted borrowing', *Journal of Business* (July), pp. 444–55.

Black, F. (1976) 'The dividend puzzle', *Journal of Portfolio Management*, 2, pp. 5–8.

Black, F. (1986) 'Noise', *Journal of Finance,* 41(3), July, pp. 529–34.

Black, F. (1993) 'Beta and return', *Journal of Portfolio Management,* 20, Fall, pp. 8–18.

Black, F. and Scholes, M. (1973) 'The pricing of options and corporate liabilities', *Journal of Political Economy,* May/June, pp. 637–59.

Black, F., Jensen, M.C. and Scholes, M. (1972) 'The Capital Asset Pricing Model: some empirical tests', in M. Jensen (ed.), *Studies in the Theory of Capital Markets.* New York: Praeger.

Blanco, B., Garcia Lara, J.M. and Tribo, J.A. (2015) 'Segment disclosure and cost of capital', *Journal of Business Finance & Accounting,* Apr/May, Vol. 42, pp. 367–411.

Block, S. (2007) 'Are "Real Options" Actually Used in the Real World?' *The Engineering Economist,* 52(3), 255–68.

Blokdyk, G. (2017) *Treasury management Complete Self-Assessment Guide,* 5STARCooks

Blume, M.E. (1971) 'On the assessment of risk', *Journal of Finance,* 26(1), March, pp. 1–10.

Blume, M.E. (1975) 'Betas and their regression tendencies', *Journal of Finance,* 30(3), June, pp. 785–95.

Blume, M. and Friend, I. (1973) 'A new look at the Capital Asset Pricing Model', *Journal of Finance,* March, pp. 19–33.

Boardman, C.M., Reinhard, W.J. and Celec, S.G. (1982) 'The role of the payback period in the theory and application of duration to capital budgeting', *Journal of Business Finance and Accounting,* 9(4), Winter, pp. 511–22.

Bodie, Z., Kane, A. and Marcus, A.J. (2017) *Investments.* 11th edn. New York: McGraw-Hill.

Bonini, S., Dallocchio, M., Raimbourg, P. and Salvi, A. (2016) 'Do firms hedge translation risks?', *Journal of Financial Management,* Markets and Institutions, 4(2), 155–78.

Booth, L., Aivazian, V., Demirgue-Kunt, A. and Maksimovic, V. (2001) 'Capital structures in developing countries', *Journal of Finance,* 61(1), February, pp. 87–130.

Botsari, A. and Meeks, G. (2008) 'Do acquirers manage earnings prior to a share for share bid?' *Journal of Business Finance and Accounting,* 35(5), (6), pp. 633–70.

Bouwens, J. and Lent, L.V. (2007) 'Assessing the performance of business unit managers', *Journal of Accounting Research,* 45(4), pp. 667–97.

Bragg, S.M. (2010) *Treasury Management: The practitioner's guide.* Chichester: John Wiley and Sons.

Brav, O. (2009) 'Access to capital, capital structure, and the funding of the firm', *The Journal of Finance,* LXIV (1).

Brav, A., Graham, J.R., Harvey, C.R. and Michaely, R. (2005) 'Pay-out policy in the 21st century', *Journal of Financial Economics,* 77, pp. 483–527.

Brealey, R.H., Myers, S.C. and Allen, F. (2017) *The Principles of Corporate Finance,* 12th edn. Boston: McGraw-Hill.

Brennan, M. (1971) 'A note on dividend irrelevance and the Gordon valuation model', *Journal of Finance,* December, pp. 1115–21.

Brennan, M.J. and Schwartz, E.S. (1985) 'Evaluating natural resource investments', *Journal of Business,* 58, pp. 135–57.

Brennan, M.J. and Trigeorgis, L. (eds) (2000) *Project Flexibility, Agency, and Competition: New Developments in the Theory and Application of Real Options.* Oxford, New York: Oxford University Press.

Breuer, W., Rieger, M.O. and Soypak, K.C. (2014) 'The behavioural foundations of corporate dividend policy: A cross-country approach', *Journal of Banking and Finance,* 42, pp. 247–65.

Brierley, P. and Bunn, P. (2005) 'The determination of UK corporate capital gearing', *Bank of England Quarterly Bulletin,* Autumn, pp. 356–66.

Brigham, E.F. and Ehrhardt, M.C. (2016) *Financial Management: Theory and Practice.* 15th edn. Cengage Learning.

British Private Equity and Venture Capital Association, London (www.bvca.co.uk).

Brock, W., Lakonishok, J. and LeBaron, B. (1992) 'Simple technical trading rules and the stochastic properties of stock returns', *Journal of Finance,* 47, December, pp. 1731–64.

Bromwich, M. and Bhimani, A. (1991) 'Strategic investment appraisal', *Management Accounting,* March.

Brounen, D., de Jong, A. and Koedijk, K. (2004) 'Corporate finance in Europe: Confronting theory with practice', *Financial Management,* Winter, pp. 71–101.

Brunnermeier, M.K. and Nagel, S. (2004) 'Hedge funds and the technology bubble', *Journal of Finance,* LIX (5), October, pp. 2013–40.

Brusa, J., Liu, P. and Schulman, C. (2003) 'The weekend and 'reverse" weekend effects: An analysis by month of the year, week of month, and industry', *Journal of Business Finance and Accounting,* 30(5) and (6), June/July, pp. 863–90.

Buckley, A. (2004) *Multinational Finance.* 5th edn. Harlow: FT Prentice Hall.

Buffett, W. (1982) Letter to Shareholders accompanying the Berkshire Hathaway Annual Report. Omaha, NE. www.berkshirehathaway.com.

Buffett, W. (1984) *Berkshire Hathaway Annual Report.* Omaha, NE: Berkshire Hathaway.

Buffett, W.E. (1984) 'The superinvestors of Graham-and-Doddsville', an edited transcript of a talk given at Columbia University in 1984.

Buffett, W. (1995) Letter to Shareholders accompanying the Berkshire Hathaway Annual Report. Omaha, NE. www.berkshirehathaway.com.

Buffett, W.E. (2000) Letter to shareholders included with the 2000 Annual Report of Berkshire Hathaway Inc: www.berkshirehathaway.com.

Bulan, L. and Yan, Z. (2009) 'The pecking order theory and the firm's life cycle', *Banking and Finance Letters,* 1(3), pp. 129–140.

Bulan, L. and Yan, Z. (2011) 'Firm maturity and the pecking order theory', *International Journal of Business and Economics,* 9(3), pp. 179–200.

Bulan, L., Mayer, C. and Somerville, S.T. (2009) 'Irreversible investment, real options and competition: evidence from real estate development', *Journal of Urban Development,* May, 65(3), pp. 237–51.

Bunn, R. and Young, G. (2004) Corporate capital structure in the United Kingdom: Determinants and adjustment. Bank of England Working Paper 226 (www.bankofengland.co.uk/wp/index.html).

Buono, A. and Bowditch, J. (2003) *The Human Side of Mergers and Acquisitions.* Beard Books, US.

Burkert, M. and Lueg, R. (2013) 'Differences in the sophistication of Value-based management – The role of top executives', *Management Accounting Research,* 24(1), 3–22.

Burnside, C., Eichenbaum, M., Kleschelski, I. and Rebelo, S. (2006) 'The returns to currency speculation', NBER Working Paper No. 12489. Available at www.nber.org/papers/w12489.

Capaul, C., Rowley, I. and Sharpe, W.F. (1993) 'International value and growth stock returns', *Financial Analysts Journal,* 49, January–February, pp. 27–36.

Cartwright, S. and Cooper, C. (2005) *Mergers and Acquisitions: The Human Factor.* Jaico Publishing House.

Caylor, M.L., Christensen, T.E., Johnson, P.M. and Lopez, T.J. (2015) 'Analysts' and Investors' Reactions to Consistent Earnings Signals', *Journal of Business Finance & Accounting,* Nov/Dec 2015, 42(9/10), pp. 1041–74.

Cerqueiro, G., Ongena, S. and Roszbach, K. (2016) 'Collateralization, bank loan rates, and monitoring', *Journal of Finance,* 71(3), pp. 1295–322.

Chambers, D. and Dimson, E. (2009) 'IPO underpricing over the very long run', *Journal of Finance,* LXIV(3).

Chan, A. and Chen, A.P.L. (1996) 'An empirical re-examination of the cross-section of expected returns: UK evidence', *Journal of Business Finance and Accounting,* 23, pp. 1435–52.

Chan, L.K.C. and Lakonishok, J. (2004) 'Value and growth investing: review and update', *Financial Analysts Journal,* January/February, pp. 71–86.

Chan, L.K.C., Hamao, Y. and Lakonishok, J. (1991) 'Fundamentals and stock returns in Japan', *Journal of Finance,* 46, pp. 1739–64.

Chan, L.K.C., Jegadeesh, N. and Lakonishok, J. (1996) 'Momentum strategies', *Journal of Finance,* 51, December, pp. 1681–713.

Chava, S. and Roberts, M.R. (2008) 'How does financing impact investment? The role of debt covenants', *Journal of Finance,* LXIII(5), Oct, pp. 2085–121.

Chemmanur, T.J., Loutskina, E. and Xuan Tian (2014) 'Corporate venture capital, value creation, and innovation', *The Review of Financial Studies,* 27(8), pp. 2433–73.

Chen, Y., Truong, C. and Veeraraghavan, M. (2015) 'CEO risk-taking incentives and the cost of equity capital', *Journal of Business Finance & Accounting,* Sep/Oct, 42(7/8), pp. 915–46.

Cheremushkin, V.S. (2008). What's wrong with the Economic Value Added? [Online] Available: http://ssrn.com/abstract=1120917.

Childs, P.D., Ott, S.M. and Triantis, A.J. (1998) 'Capital budgeting for interrelated projects: a real options approach', *Journal of Financial and Quantitative Analysis,* 33(3), pp. 305–34.

Chisholm, A.M. (2009) *An Introduction to International Capital Markets.* 2nd edn. Chichester: J. Wiley and Sons.

Chittenden, F. and Darregia, M. (2004) 'Capital Investment decision making: some results from studying entrepreneurial businesses', www.icaew.co.uk.

Choi, N., Fedenia, M., Skiba, H. and Sokolyk, T. (2017) 'Portfolio concentration and performance of institutional investors worldwide', *Journal of Financial Economics,* 123, pp. 189–208.

Chopra, N., Lakonishok, J. and Ritter, J.R. (1992) 'Measuring abnormal performance: Do stocks overact?', *Journal of Financial Economics,* 31, pp. 235–68.

Chordia, T., Goyal, A., Sadka, G., Sadka, R. and Shivakumar, L. (2009) 'Liquidity and the post-earnings-announcement drift', *Financial Analysts Journal,* 65(4) pp. 18–32.

Chordia, T., Subrahmanyam, A. and Tong, Q. (2014) 'Have capital market anomalies attenuated in the recent era of high liquidity and trading activity?' *Journal of Accounting and Economics,* 58: 41–58.

Choudhry, M., Joannas, D., Landuyt, G., Periera, R. and Pienaar, R. (2010) *Capital Market Instruments: Analysis and valuation,* 3rd edn. London: Palgrave Macmillan.

Chui, A.C.W., Titman, S. and Wei, K.C.J. (2010) 'Individualism and momentum around the world', *The Journal of Finance,* LXV(1), Feb. pp. 361–92.

Churchill, N.C. and Mullins J.W. (2001) 'How fast can your company afford to grow?', *Harvard Business Review,* 79(5) pp. 135–43.

Clare, A. and Thomas, S. (1995) 'The overreaction hypothesis and the UK stock market', *Journal of Business Finance and Accounting,* 22(7), October, pp. 961–73.

Clarke, R., de Silva, H. and Thorley, S. (2006) 'Minimum-variance portfolios in the US equity market: reducing volatility without sacrificing returns', *The Journal of Portfolio Management,* Fall, pp. 10–24.

Cochrane, J.H. (2001) *Asset Pricing.* Princeton, NJ, and Oxford: Princeton University Press.

Coffey, N., Hrung, W.B. and Sarkar, A. (2009) 'Capital constraints, counterparty risk, and deviations from covered interest rate parity', Federal Reserve Bank of New York Staff Reports, no. 393 (September).

Collis, D.J. and Montgomery, C.A. (2005) *Corporate Strategy: A resource-based approach.* 2nd edn. New York: McGraw-Hill.

Conn, R.L., Cosh, A., Guest, P.M. and Hughes, A. (2005) 'The impact on UK acquirers of domestic, cross-border, public and private acquisitions', *Journal of Business Finance & Accounting,* 32(5) and (6), June/July.

Cooper, I. and Kaplanis, E. (1994) 'Home bias in equity portfolios, inflation hedging and international capital market equilibrium', *Review of Financial Studies,* 7(1), pp. 45–60.

Coopers & Lybrand and OC & C (1993) *A Review of The Acquisition Experience of Major Uk Companies.* London: Coopers & Lybrand.

Copeland, T. and Antikarov, V. (2001) *Real Options: A Practitioner's Guide.* New York: Texere.

Copeland, T. and Tufano, P. (2004) 'A real-world way to manage real options', *Harvard Business Review,* March, pp. 1–11.

Corhay, A., Hawawini, G. and Michel, P. (1987) 'Seasonality in the risk-return relationship: some international evidence', *Journal of Finance,* 42, pp. 49–68.

Cosh, A., Guest, P.M. and Hughes, A. (2006) 'Board share ownership and takeover performance', *Journal of*

Business Finance & Accounting, 33(3/4), Apr/May pp. 459–510.

Coulthurst, N.J. (1986) 'The application of the incremental principle in capital investment project evaluation', *Accounting and Business Research*, Autumn.

Coulthurst, N.J. (1986) 'Accounting for inflation in capital investment: state of the art and science', *Accounting and Business Research*, Winter, pp. 33–42.

Cowling, K., Stoneman, P. and Cubbin, J. et al. (1980) *Mergers and Economic Performance*. Cambridge: Cambridge University Press.

Cronqvist, H., Siegel, S. and Yu, F. (2015) 'Value versus growth investing: Why do different investors have different styles?' *Journal of Financial Economics*, 117, pp. 333–49.

Crossland, M., Dempsey, M. and Moizer, P. (1991) 'The effect of cum- to ex-dividend changes on UK share prices', *Accounting and Business Research*, 22(85), pp. 47–50.

Cuñat, V., Gine, M. and Guadalupe (2012) 'The vote is cast: The effect of corporate governance on shareholder value', *Journal of Finance*, 67, pp. 1943–77.

Cuthbertson, K. (2004) *Quantitative Financial Economics*, 2nd edn. Chichester: Wiley.

Damodaran, A. (2008) 'What is the risk free rate?' Working paper, available at http://papers.ssrn.com/sol3/papers.cfm?abstract_id=1317436

Damodaran, A. (2009) 'Equity risk premiums (ERP): determinants, estimation and implications – a post-crisis update', *Financial Markets, Institutions & Instruments*, 18(5), pp. 289–370.

Damodaran, A. (2012) *Investment Valuation*. 3rd edn. New York: John Wiley & Sons.

Damodaran, A. (2014) *Applied Corporate Finance*, 4th edn. New York: John Wiley & Sons.

Damodaran, A. (2015) *Applied Corporate Finance: A User's Manual*. 4th edn. New York: John Wiley & Sons.

Damodaran, A. (2017) 'Equity Risk Premiums (ERP): Determinants, Estimation and Implications – The 2017 Edition.' Available at SSRN: https://ssrn.com/abstract=2947861

Daniel, K. and Moskowitz, T.J. (2016) 'Momentum Crashes', *Journal of Financial Economics*, 122, pp. 221–47.

Daniel, H. and Titman, S. (1997) 'Evidence on the characteristics of cross-sectional variation in common stock returns', *Journal of Finance*, 52, pp. 1–33.

Daniel, H. and Titman, S. (2006) 'Market reactions to tangible and intangible information', *Journal of Finance*, 61(4), pp. 1605–43.

Daniel, K., Hirshleifer, D. and Subrahmanyam, A. (1998) 'Investor psychology and security market under- and overreactions', *Journal of Finance*, 53(6), pp. 1839–85.

Danis, A., Daniel, A.R. and Whited, T.M. (2014) 'Refinancing, profitability, and capital structure', *Journal of Financial Economics*, 114, pp. 424–43.

Daunfeldt, S.O. and Hartwig, F. (2014), 'What determines the use of capital budgeting methods? Evidence from Swedish listed companies', *Journal of Finance and Economics*, 2(4), pp. 101–12.

Davies, M. (2000) 'Lessons from practice: VBM at Lloyds TSB', in G.C. Arnold and M. Davies (eds) (2000)

Value-Based Management. Chichester: John Wiley & Sons.

Davies, M., Arnold, G.C., Cornelius, I. and Walmsey, S. (2000) *Managing for Shareholder Value*. London: Informa Publishing Group.

Davis, J.L., Fama, E.F. and French, K.R. (2009) 'Characteristics, covariances, and average returns: 1929 to 1997', *The Journal of Finance*, LV(1), pp. 389–406.

Dawson, E.R. and Steeley, J.M. (2003) 'On the existence of visual technical patterns in the UK stock market', *Journal of Business Finance and Accounting*, 30(1) and (2), January–March, pp. 263–97.

Dean, J. (1951) *Capital Budgeting*. New York: Columbia University Press.

De Bondt, W.F.M. and Thaler, R.H. (1985) 'Does the stock market overreact?', *Journal of Finance*, 40(3), July, pp. 793–805.

De Bondt, W.F.M. and Thaler, R.H. (1987) 'Further evidence on investor overreaction and stock market seasonality', *Journal of Finance*, 42(3), pp. 557–81.

Dekker, H. C., Groot, T., Schoute, M. and Wiersma, E. (2012) 'Determinants of the use of value-based performance measures for managerial performance evaluation', *Journal of Business Finance & Accounting*, 39(9), 1214–39. doi:10.1111/jbfa.12004

Dellavigna, S. and Pollet, J.M. (2009), 'Investor inattention and Friday earnings announcements', *The Journal of Finance*, LXIV(2), pp. 709–49.

De Long, J.B., Shleifer, A., Summers, L.H. and Waldmann, R.J. (1989) 'The size and incidence of the losses from noise trading', *Journal of Finance*, 44(3), July, pp. 681–96.

De Long, J.B., Shleifer, A., Summers, L.H. and Waldmann, R.J. (1990) 'Noise trader risk in financial markets', *Journal of Political Economy*, 98, pp. 703–38.

De Wit, B. and Meyer, R. (2015) *Strategy: Process, Content, Context*. 5th edn. Andover: Cengage.

Degeorge, F., Martin, J. and Phalippou, L. (2016) 'On secondary buyouts', *Journal of Financial Economics*, 120, pp. 124–45.

Deloof, M., De Maeseneire, W. and Inghelbrecht, K. (2009) 'How do investment banks value initial public offerings (IPOs)?' *Journal of Business Finance and Accounting*, 36(1), (2) pp. 130–60.

Demaria, C. (2013) *Introduction to Private Equity: Venture, Growth, LBO and Turnaround Capital*, Chichester: John Wiley and Sons.

Desai, M.A. (2004) 'Foreign exchange markets and transactions', Harvard Business School note. (Available at Harvard Business School website.)

Desai, M. and Jin, L. (2011) 'Institutional tax clienteles and pay-out policy', *Journal of Financial Economics*, 100, pp. 68–84.

Dhanani, A. (2005) 'Corporate dividend policy: The views of British financial managers', *Journal of Business Finance and Accounting*, 32(7) and (8), Sept/Oct, pp. 1625–72.

Dhrymes, P.J., Friend, I. and Gultekim, N.B. (1984) 'A critical reexamination of the empirical evidence on the arbitrage pricing theory', *Journal of Finance*, 39, June, pp. 323–46.

Dimson, E. (ed.) (1988) *Stock Market Anomalies*. Cambridge: Cambridge University Press.

Dimson, E. and Marsh, P.R. (1986) 'Event study methodologies and the size effect: The case of UK press recommendations', *Journal of Financial Economics,* 17, pp. 113–42.

Dimson, E. and Marsh P.R. (1999) 'Murphy's law and market anomalies', *Journal of Portfolio Management,* 25(2), pp. 53–69.

Dimson, E., Marsh, P.R. and Staunton, M. (2001) *The Millennium Book II: 101 Years of Investment Returns.* London: ABN AMRO and London Business School.

Dimson, E., Marsh, P. and Staunton, M. (2002) *Triumph of the Optimists: 101 Years of Global Investment Returns.* Princeton, NJ: Princeton University Press.

Dimson, E., Marsh, P. and Staunton, M. (2006) The Cap Worldwide Equity Premium: A smaller puzzle (7 April 2006), EFA 2006 Zurich meetings papers available at SSRN: http://ssrn.com/abstract=891620

Dimson, E., Marsh, P. and Staunton, M. (2008) *ABN AMRO Global Investment Returns Yearbook 2009.* ABN AMRO, Royal Bank of Scotland and London Business School.

Dimson, E., Marsh, P. and Staunton, M. (2009) Credit Suisse Global Investment Returns Yearbook 2009. Credit Suisse Research Institute, available at http://publications.credit-suisse.com/

Dimson, E., Marsh, P. and Staunton, M (2011) 'Equity risk premia around the world', Available at SRN: https://ssrn.com/abstract=1940165 or http://dx.doi.org/10.2139/ssrn.1940165

Dimson, E., Marsh, P. and Staunton, M. (2017) Credit Suisse Global Investment Returns Yearbook 2017. Credit Suisse Research Institute, available at http://publications.credit-suisse.com/

Dimson, E., Marsh, P., Staunton, M., Kersley, R. and O'Sullivan, M. (2017) *Credit Suisse Global Investment Returns Yearbook 2017- slide deck.* London: Credit Suisse.

Dissanaike, G. (1997) 'Do stock market investors overreact?', *Journal of Business Finance and Accounting,* 24(1), January, pp. 27–49.

Divecha, A.B., Drach, J. and Stefek, D. (1992) 'Emerging markets: a quantitative perspective', *Journal of Portfolio Management,* Fall, pp. 41–50.

Dixit, A. and Pindyck, R. (1994) *Investment Under Uncertainty.* Princeton, NJ: Princeton University Press.

Dixit, A.K. and Pindyck, R.S. (1995) 'The options approach to capital investment', *Harvard Business Review,* May–June. (Also reproduced in J. Rutterford (ed.) *Financial Strategy.* New York: John Wiley, 1998.)

Doidge, C., Andrew Karolyi, G. and Stulz, R. (2007) 'Why do countries matter so much for corporate governance?' *Journal of Financial Economics,* 86(1), pp. 1–39.

Dolvin, S.D. and Jordan, B.D. (2008) 'Underpricing, overhang, and the cost of going public to preexisting shareholders', *Journal of Business Finance & Accounting,* 35(3), (4), pp. 434–58.

Donaldson, G. (1961) *Corporate Debt Policy and the Determination of Corporate Debt Capacity.* Boston: Harvard Graduate School of Business Administration.

Donaldson, G. (1963) 'Financial goals: Management vs. stockholders', *Harvard Business Review,* May–June, pp. 116–29.

Donaldson, G. (1969) *Strategy for Financial Mobility.* Boston: Harvard University.

Donghui L., Moshirian, F., Pham, P. and Zein, J. (2006) 'When financial institutions are large shareholders: the role of macro corporate governance environments', *Journal of Finance,* 61(6), pp. 2975–3007.

Dreman, D. (1998) *Contrarian Investment Strategies: The Next Generation.* New York: John Wiley & Sons.

Dreman, D. (2007) *Contrarian Investment Strategies: The psychological edge.* New York: Simon & Schuster.

Dreman, D. and Berry, M. (1995) 'Overreaction, underreaction, and the low P/E effect', *Financial Analysts Journal,* 51, July/August, pp. 21–30.

Drobetz, W., Grüninger, M. and Hirschvogl, S. (2010) 'Information asymmetry and the value of cash', *Journal of Banking and Finance,* 34, pp. 2168–84.

Duc Hung Tran (2014) 'Multiple corporate governance attributes and the cost of capital – Evidence from Germany', *The British Accounting Review,* 46, pp. 179–97.

Duchin, R. and B. Schmidt (2013) 'Riding the merger wave', *Journal of Financial Economics,* 107, pp. 69–88.

Duke, L.K. and Upadhyay, A. (2006) 'Drivers of investment and marketing performance: Implications for mutual fund management', *Journal of Investing,* 15(2), pp. 107–11.

Dyck, A. and Zingales, L. (2004) 'Private benefits of control: an international comparison', *Journal of Finance,* 59(2), pp. 537–600.

Easterbrook, F.H. (1984) 'Two *agency-cost* explanations of dividends', *American Economic Review,* 74(4), September pp. 650–60.

Edelena, R.M., Ince, O.S. and Kadlecc, G.B. (2016) 'Institutional investors and stock return anomalies', *Journal of Financial Economics,* 119, pp. 472–88.

Eiteman, D.K., Stonehill, A.I. and Moffett, M.H. (2015) *Multinational Business Finance, Global Edition.* 14th edition. Pearson.

Eiteman, D.K., Stonehill, A.I. and Moffett, M.H. (2015) *Multinational Business Finance.* 14th edn. Pearson.

Ekanem, I. (2005) '"Bootstrapping": the investment decision-making process in small firms', *British Accounting Review,* 37, pp. 299–318.

Elgharbawy, A. and Abdel-Kader, M. (2013) Enterprise governance and value-based management: A theoretical contingency framework. *Journal of Management & Governance,* 17(1), 99–129.

Elmassria, M.M., Harris, E.P. and Carter, D.B. (2016) 'Accounting for strategic investment decision-making under extreme uncertainly', *The British Accounting Review,* 48(2), pp. 151–68.

Elton, E.J., Gruber, M.J. and Brown, S.J. (2014) *Modern Portfolio Theory and Investment Analysis,* 9th edn. New York: Wiley.

Elton, E.J., Gruber, M.J. and Mei, J. (1994) 'Cost of capital using arbitrage pricing theory: a case study of nine New York utilities', *Financial Markets, Institutions and Instruments,* 3, August, pp. 46–73.

Elton, E.J., Gruber, M.J. and Rentzler, J. (1983) 'A simple examination of the empirical relationship between dividend yields and deviations from the CAPM', *Journal of Banking and Finance,* 7, pp. 135–46.

Elton, E.J., Gruber, M.J., Brown, S.J. and Goetzmann, W.N. (2014) *Modern Portfolio Theory and Investment Analysis,* 9th edn. Chichester: John Wiley & Sons.

Elton, E.J., Gruber, M.J., Brown, S.J. and Goetzmann, W.N. (2017) *Modern Portfolio Theory and Investment Analysis,* 9th edn. New York: Wiley.

Emmanuel, C., Harris, E. and Komakech, S. (2010) 'Towards a better understanding of capital investment decisions', *Journal of Accounting and Organizational Change,* 6(4), pp. 477–504.

Epstein, M.J. (2005) 'The determinants and evaluation of merger success', *Business Horizons,* 48, pp. 37–46.

Espinoza R.D. (2014) 'Separating project risk from the time-value of money: A step toward integration of risk management and valuation of infrastructure investments', *International Journal of Project Management,* 32, pp. 1056–72.

EY (annually). Annual Report on the Performance of Portfolio Companies. www.bvca.co.uk.

Faelten, A., M. Gietzmann and Vitkova, V. (2014) 'Naked M&A Transactions: How the lack of local expertise in cross-border deals can negatively affect acquirer performance – and how informed institutional investors can mitigate this effect', *Journal of Business Finance & Accounting.* 41(3/4), pp. 469–506.

Fama, E.F. (1965) 'The behaviour of stock market prices', *Journal of Business,* January, pp. 34–106.

Fama, E.F. (1970) 'Efficient capital markets: A review of theory and empirical work', *Journal of Finance,* May, pp. 383–417.

Fama, E.G. (1978) 'The effects of a firm's investment and financing decisions', *American Economic Review,* 68(3), June, pp. 272–84.

Fama, E.F. (1980) 'Agency problems and the theory of the firm', *Journal of Political Economy,* Spring, pp. 288–307.

Fama, E.F. (1981) 'Stock returns, real activity, inflation and money', *American Economic Review,* 71 (Sept.), pp. 545–64.

Fama, E.F. (1991) 'Efficient capital markets II', *Journal of Finance,* 46(5), December, pp. 1575–617.

Fama, E.F. (1998) 'Market efficiency, long-term returns, and behavioural finance', *Journal of Financial Economics,* 49, September, pp. 283–306.

Fama, E.F. and French, K.R. (1988) 'Permanent and temporary components of stock prices', *Journal of Political Economy,* 96, pp. 246–73.

Fama, G. and French, K. (1992) 'The cross-section of expected stock returns', *Journal of Finance,* 47, June, pp. 427–65.

Fama, E.F. and French, K.R. (1993) 'Common risk factors in the returns on stocks and bonds', *Journal of Financial Economics,* 33, pp. 3–56.

Fama, E.F. and French, K.R. (1995) 'Size and book-to-market factors in earnings and returns', *Journal of Finance,* 50(1), March, pp. 131–55.

Fama, E.F. and French, K.R. (1996) 'Multifactor explanations of asset pricing anomalies', *Journal of Finance,* 50 (1), March, pp. 55–84.

Fama, E.F. and French, K.R. (1998) 'Value versus growth: The international evidence', *Journal of Finance,* 53(6), December, pp. 1975–99.

Fama, E.F. and French, K.R. (2002) 'The equity premium', *Journal of Finance,* 57(2), April, pp. 637–59.

Fama, E.F. and French, K.R. (2005) 'Financing decisions: Who issues stocks?', *Journal of Financial Economics,* 76, pp. 549–82.

Fama, E.F. and French, K.R. (2006) 'The value premium and the CAPM', *Journal of Finance,* LXI (5) October, pp. 2163–85.

Fama, E.F. and French, K.R. (2008) 'Average returns, B/M, and share issues', *The Journal of Finance,* LXIII(6), December, pp. 2971–95.

Fama, E.F. and French, K.R. (2015) 'The five-factor asset pricing model', *Journal of Financial Economics,* 116, pp. 1–22.

Fama, E.F. and French, K.R. (2016) 'Dissecting anomalies with a five-factor model', *The Review of Financial Studies,* 29(1).

Fama, E.F. and MacBeth, J. (1973) 'Risk, return and equilibrium: empirical test', *Journal of Political Economy,* May/June, pp. 607–36.

Fama, E.F. and Miller, M.H. (1972) *The Theory of Finance.* New York: Holt, Rinehart & Winston.

Fama, E.F., Fisher, L., Jensen, M.C. and Roll, R. (1969) 'The adjustment of stock prices to new information', *International Economic Review,* 10(1), February, pp. 1–21.

Fang, L., Ivashina, V. and Lerner, J. (2015) 'The disintermediation of financial markets: Direct investing in private equity', *Journal of Financial Economics,* 116, pp. 160–78.

Faulkender M. and Smith J.M. (2016) 'Taxes and leverage at multinational corporations', *Journal of Financial Economics,* 122(1), pp. 1–20.

Fee, C.E. and Thomas, S. (2004) 'Sources of gains in horizontal mergers: Evidence from customer, supplier, and rival firms', *Journal of Financial Economics,* 74(3), Dec., pp. 423–60.

Feldman S.J. (2005) *Principles of Private Firm Valuation.* New Jersey: John Wiley & Sons.

Fernández, P. (2001a) 'Valuation using multiples: How do analysts reach their conclusions?' Available at SSRN: http://papers.ssrn.com/sol3/papers.cfm?abstract_id=274972.

Fernández, P. (2001b) 'Optimal capital structure: Problems with the Harvard and Damodaran Approaches', IESE Business School Working Paper.

Fernández, P. (2001c) 'EVA and cash value added do NOT measure shareholder value creation', available at http://papers.ssrn.com/sol3/papers.cfm?abstract_id=270799

Fernández, F. (2002) 'Valuation methods and shareholder value creation'. Available as download from www.sciencedirect.com/science/book/9780122538414 or http://books.google.co.uk/.

Fernández, P. (2002) *Valuation and Shareholder Value.* San Diego, CA: Academic Press. Available electronically at Amazon.co.uk (free).

Fernández, F. (2003) '80 common and uncommon errors in company valuation', a paper available on SSRN http://papers.ssrn.com/.

Fernández, P. (2004) 'Discounted cash flow valuation methods: Examples of perpetuities, constant growth and general case.' Available at SSRN: http://papers.ssrn.com/sol3/papers.cfm?abstract_id=743229.

Fernández, P. (2007a) 'Equity premium: historical, expected, required and implied.' Working paper published on SSRN, available at www.ssrn.com/

Fernández, P. (2007b) 'Company valuation methods: The most common errors in valuations.' IESE Working Paper No. 449.

Fernández, P. (2007c) 'Valuing companies by cash flow discounting: Ten methods and nine theories', *Managerial Finance*, 33(11), pp. 853–76.

Fernández, P. (2008a) 'Are calculated betas worth anything?' Working paper published on SSRN, available at http://ssrn.com/abstract=504565

Fernández, P. (2008b) 'Three residual income valuation methods and discounted cash flow valuation', available at http://papers.ssrn.com/sol3/papers. cfm?abstract_id=296945

Fernández, P. (2008c) 'Valuation of brands and intellectual capital.' Available at SSRN: http://papers. ssrn.com/sol3/papers.cfm?abstract_id=270688.

Fernández, P. (2008d) 'Cash flow is fact. Net income is just an opinion.' Available at SSRN: http://papers.ssrn. com/sol3/papers.cfm?abstract_id=330540.

Fernández, P. (2009) 'Betas used by professors: A survey with 2,500 answers.' Working paper published on SSRN, available at http://papers.ssrn.com/sol3/papers. cfm?abstract_id=1407464

Fernández, F. (2010) 'WACC: definition, misconceptions and errors', a paper available on SSRN http://papers. ssrn.com/sol3/papers.cfm?abstract_id=1620871.

Fernández, P. and Bermejo, V. (2009) 'Beta = 1 does a better job than calculated betas.' Working paper on SSRN, available at http://ssrn.com/abstract=1406923

Fernández, P., Aguirreamalloa, J. and Corres, L. (2010) 'Shareholder value creators in the S&P 500: 1991–2010', available at www.ssrn.com

Fernández, P., Ortiz Pizarro, Alberto and Fernández Acín, Isabel (2016) 'Market Risk Premium Used in 71 Countries in 2016: A Survey with 6,932 Answers.' Available at SSRN: https://ssrn.com/abstract=2776636

Ferris, S.P., Noronha, G. and Unlu, E. (2010) 'The more, merrier: An international analysis of the frequency of dividend payment', *Journal of Business Finance and Accounting*, 37(1), (2) pp. 148–70.

Fich, E.M. and Shivdasani, A. (2006) 'Are busy boards effective monitors?' *Journal of Finance*, LXI(2), April.

Fifield, S.G.M., Power, D.M. and Sinclair, C.D. (2005) 'An analysis of trading strategies in eleven European stock markets', *European Journal of Finance*, 11(6) pp. 531–48.

Figelman, I. (2007) 'Interaction of stock return momentum with earnings measures', *Financial Analysts Journal*, 63(3), pp. 71–8.

Finance and Leasing Association (FLA) Annual Report. London: FLA.

Finnie, J. (1988) 'The role of financial appraisal in decisions to acquire advanced manufacturing technology', *Accounting and Business Research*, 18(70), pp. 133–9.

Firth, M. (1980) 'Takeovers, shareholders' returns and the theory of the firm', *Quarterly Journal of Economics*, 94, March, pp. 235–60.

Firth, M. (1991) 'Corporate takeovers, stockholder returns and executive rewards', *Managerial and Decision Economics*, 12, pp. 421–8.

Fischer, E., Heinkel, R. and Zechner, J. (1989) 'Dynamic capital structure choice', *Journal of Finance*, 44, 19–40.

Fisher, I. (1930) *The Theory of Interest*. New York: Macmillan.

Flannery, M.J. and Rangan, K.P. (2006) 'Partial adjustment toward target capital structures', *Journal of Financial Economics*, 79, pp. 469–506.

Floyd E., Li, N. and Skinner D. (2015) 'Pay-out policy through the financial crisis: The growth of repurchases and the resilience of dividends', *Journal of Financial Economics*, 118(2) pp. 299–316.

Foster, G., Olsen, C. and Shevlin, T. (1984) 'Earnings releases, anomalies, and the behaviour of security returns', *Accounting Review*, 59(4), October, pp. 574–603.

Fox, J. (2009) *The Myth of the Rational Market*. London: HarperBusiness.

Fox, J. and Lorsch, J.W. (2012) 'What good are shareholders?' *Harvard Business Review*, July–August, pp. 48–57.

Francis, G. and Minchington, C. (2000) 'Value-based Metrics as Divisional Performance Measures', in Arnold, G.C. and Davies, M. (eds) *Value-Based Management*. Chichester: John Wiley & Sons.

Frank, M.Z. and Goyal, V.K. (2003) 'Testing the pecking order theory of capital structure', *Journal of Financial Economics*, 67, pp. 217–48.

Franks, J. and Harris, R. (1989) 'Shareholder wealth effects of corporate takeovers: The UK experience 1955–85', *Journal of Financial Economics*, 23, pp. 225–49.

Franks, J. and Mayer, C. (1996) 'Hostile takeovers and correction of managerial failure', *Journal of Financial Economics*, 40, pp. 163–81.

Franzini, A. and Pedersen, L.H. (2014) 'Betting against beta', *Journal of Financial Economics*, 111, pp. 1–25.

Frazzini, A. (2006) 'The disposition effect and underreaction to news', *Journal of Finance*, LXI (4), August, pp. 2017–46.

Frehen, R.G.P., Goetzmann, W.N. and Rouwenhorst, K.G. (2013) 'New evidence on the first financial bubble', *Journal of Financial Economics*, 108, pp. 585–607.

Frezatti, F., et al. (2013) 'Investment decisions on long-term assets: integrating strategic and financial perspectives', *European Accounting Review*, 22(2): 297–336.

Friedman, M. (1970) 'The social responsibility of business is to increase its profits', *New York Times Magazine*, 30 Sept.

Froot, K.A. and Dabora, E. (1999) 'How are stock prices affected by the location of trade?', *Journal of Financial Economics*, 53, pp. 189–216.

Frost, P.A. and Savarino, J.E. (1986) 'Portfolio size and estimation risk', *Journal of Portfolio Management*, 12, Summer, pp. 60–4.

Fuller, R.J., Huberts, L.C. and Levinson, M.J. (1993) 'Returns to E/P strategies, higgledy-piggledy growth, analysts' forecast errors, and omitted risk factors', *Journal of Portfolio Management*, Winter, pp. 13–24.

Fu, F., Lu, L. and Officer, M.S. (2013) 'Acquisitions driven by stock overvaluation: Are they good deals?' *Journal of Financial Economics*, 109, pp. 24–39.

Gadella, J.W. (1992) 'Post-project appraisal', *Management Accounting*. March, pp. 52 and 58.

Galbraith, J. (1967) 'The goals of an industrial system' (excerpt from *The New Industrial State*). Reproduced in H.I. Ansoff, *Business Strategy*. London: Penguin, 1969.

Galitz, L. (2012) *Financial Times Handbook of Financial Engineering*. 3rd edn. London: FT Prentice Hall.

George, T.J. and Hwang, C. (2007) 'Long-term return reversals: overreaction or taxes?' *The Journal of Finance*, LXII(6), pp. 2865–96.

Ghosh, A. (2004) 'Increasing market share as a rationale for corporate acquisitions', *Journal of Business Finance & Accounting*, 31(1) & (2), January/March, pp. 209–47.

Ghoshal, S. (2005) 'Bad management theories are destroying good management practices', *Academy of Management's Learning and Education*, 4(1), pp. 75–91.

Girerd-Potin, I., Jimenez-Garcès, S. and Louvet, P.J. (2014) 'Which dimensions of social responsibility concern financial investors', *Journal of Business Ethics*, 121(4), pp. 777–98.

Goergen, M. and Renneboog, L. (2004) 'Shareholder wealth effects of European domestic and cross-border takeover bids', *European Financial Management*, 10(1), pp. 9–45.

Goetzman, W.N., Lingfeng, L. and Rouwenhorst, K.G. (2005) 'Long-term global market correlations', *Journal of Business*, 78(1), pp. 1–38.

Gompers, P., Kaplan, S. and Mukharlyamov, V. (2015) 'What private equity investors think they do for the companies they buy', *Harvard Business Review*, 18 June.

Gompers, P., Kaplan, S. N. and Mukharlyamov, V. (2016) What do private equity firms say they do? *Journal of Financial Economics*, 121, pp. 449–76.

Gorbenko, A.S. and Malenko, A. (2014) 'Strategic and financial bidders in takeover auctions', *Journal of Finance*, 69(6), pp. 2513–55.

Gordon, M.J. (1959) 'Dividends, earnings and stock prices', *Review of Economics and Statistics*, 41, May, pp. 99–105.

Gordon, M.J. (1962) *The Investment, Financing and Valuation of the Corporation*. Homewood, IL: Irwin.

Gordon, M.J. (1963) 'Optimal investment and financing policy', *Journal of Finance*, May.

Gordon, L.A. and Myers, M.D. (1991) 'Post-auditing capital projects', *Management Accounting* (US), January, pp. 39–42.

Gordon, M.J. and Shapiro, E. (1956) 'Capital equipment analysis: The required rate of profit', *Management Science*, III, pp. 102–10.

Gorton, G., Kahl, M. and Rosen, R.J. (2009) 'Eat or be eaten: A theory of mergers and firm size', *Journal of Finance*, LXIV(3), pp. 1291–344.

Graham, B. (1973, 2003) *The Intelligent Investor*. Revised edition updated by Jason Zweig. New York: Harper Business Essentials.

Graham, B. and Dodd, D. (1934) *Security Analysis*. New York: McGraw-Hill.

Graham, J.R. and Harvey, C.R. (2001) 'The theory and practice of corporate finance: Evidence from the field', *Journal of Financial Economics*, 60(2–3), May, pp. 187–243.

Graham, J.R. and Harvey, C.R. (2016) The Equity Risk Premium in 2016. Available at SSRN: https://ssrn.com/abstract=2816603 or http://dx.doi.org/10.2139/ssrn.2816603

Graham, J.R. and Kumar, A. (2006) 'Do dividend clienteles exist? Evidence on dividend preferences of retail investors', *Journal of Finance*, 61(3), June, pp. 1305–36.

Graham, J. and Leary, M. (2011) 'A review of empirical capital structure research and directions for the future', *Annual Review of Financial Economics*, 3, pp. 309–45.

Gregory, A. (1997) 'An examination of the long-run performance of UK acquiring firms', *Journal of Business Finance and Accounting*, 24(7–8), Sept., pp. 971–1002.

Gregory, A. (2005) 'The long run abnormal performance of UK acquirers and the free cash flow hypothesis', *Journal of Business Finance & Accounting*, 32(5) & (6), June/July, pp. 777–814.

Gregory, A. and Rutterford, J. (1999) 'The cost of capital in the UK: a comparison of industry and the city'. CIMA monograph, May.

Gregory, A., Guermat, C. and Al-Shawawreh, F. (2010) 'UK IPOs: long run returns, behavioural timing and pseudo timing', *Journal of Business Finance & Accounting*, 37(5), (6), pp. 612–47.

Gregory, A., Harris, R.D.F. and Michou, M. (2001) 'An analysis of contrarian investment strategies in the UK', *Journal of Business Finance and Accounting*, 28(9) and (10), November–December, pp. 1193–228.

Gregory, A., Harris, R.D.F. and Michou, M. (2003) 'Contrarian investment and macroeconomic risk', *Journal of Business Finance and Accounting*, 30(1) and (2), January–March, pp. 213–55.

Gregory, A., Rajesh, T. and Christidis, A. (2013) 'Constructing and Testing Alternative Versions of the Fama-French and Carhart Models in the UK', *Journal of Business Finance & Accounting*. Jan/Feb 2013, 40(1/2), pp. 172–214.

Grinblatt, M. and Han, B. (2005) 'Prospect theory, mental accounting and momentum', *Journal of Financial Economics*, 78, pp. 311–39.

Grullon, G. and Michaely, R. (2002) 'Dividends, share repurchases, and the substitution hypothesis', *Journal of Finance*, 57(4), pp. 1649–84.

Guo, S., Hotchkiss, E.S. and Song, W. (2011) 'Do buyouts (still) create value?', *Journal of Finance*, 66(2), pp. 479–517.

Gustavo, G. and Roni, M. (2004) 'The information content of share repurchase programs', *Journal of Finance*, April, 59(2), pp. 651–80.

Haislip, A. (2011) *Essentials of Venture Capital*. Chichester: John Wiley & Sons, Inc.

Hajdasinski, M.M. (1993) 'The payback period as a measure of profitability and liquidity', *Engineering Economist*, 38(3), Spring, pp. 177–91.

Hall, J. and Millard, S. (2010) 'Capital budgeting practices used by selected listed South African firms', *South African Journal of Economics Management Science*, 13(1), pp. 85–97.

Hamberg, M. and Novak, J. (2010) 'Accounting conservatism and transitory earnings in value and growth strategies', *Journal of Business Finance & Accounting*, 37(5), (6), pp. 518–37.

Hampden-Turner, C. and Trompenaars, F. (2000) *Building Crosscultural Competence*. Selfpublished.

Hann, R.N., Ogneva, M. and Ozbas, O. (2013) 'Corporate diversification and the cost of capital', *Journal of Finance*, October, 68(5), pp. 1961–99.

Hansen, H., Huhn, W., Legrand, O., Steiners, D. and Vahlenkamp, T. (2009) *Capex Excellence: Optimising fixed asset investing*. Chichester: John Wiley and Sons.

Han Xia (2014) 'Can investor-paid credit rating agencies improve the information quality of issuer-paid rating agencies?' *Journal of Financial Economics,* 111, pp. 450–68.

Harchaoui, T.M. and Lasserre, P. (2001) 'Testing the option value theory of irreversible investment', *International Economic Review,* February, 42(1), pp. 141–66.

Harding, D., Rovit, S. and Corbett, A. (2005) 'Three steps to avoiding merger meltdown', *Harvard Management Update,* March, pp. 1–5.

Harford, J. (2005) 'What drives merger waves', *Journal of Financial Economics,* 77(3), pp. 529–60.

Harris, A. (1996) 'Wanted: Insiders', *Management Today,* July, pp. 40–1.

Harris, M. and Raviv, A. (1991) 'The theory of capital structure', *Journal of Finance,* 46, pp. 297–355.

Hart, O.D. (1995a) *Firms, Contracts and Financial Structure.* Oxford: Oxford University Press.

Hart, O.D. (1995b) 'Corporate governance: some theory and implications', *Economic Journal,* 105, pp. 678–9.

Harvey, C.R., Lins, K.V. and Roper, A.H. (2004) 'The effect of capital structure when expected agency costs are extreme', *Journal of Financial Economics,* 74, pp. 3–30.

Hasbrouck, J. (1985) 'The characteristics of takeover targets: q and other measures', *Journal of Banking and Finance,* 9, pp. 351–62.

Haspeslagh, P. and Jemison, D. (1991) *Managing Acquisitions.* New York: Free Press.

Hawawini, G.A. and Michel, P.A. (eds) (1984) *European Equity Markets, Risk, Return and Efficiency.* Garland Publishing.

Hawawini, G. and Klein, D.B. (1994) 'On the predictability of common stock returns: Worldwide evidence', in Jarrow, R.A., Maksinovic, V. and Ziembas, W.T. (eds) *Finance.* Amsterdam: North-Holland.

Hayek, F.A. (1969) 'The corporation in a democratic society: in whose interests ought it and will it be run?' Reprinted in H.I. Ansoff, *Business Strategy.* London: Penguin, 1969.

Headley, J.S. and Tufano, P. (2001) 'Why manage risk?' Harvard Business School Note. Available from Harvard Business Online.

Hellmann, T. and V. Thiele (2015) 'Friends or foes? The interrelationship between angel and venture capital markets', *Journal of Financial Economics,* 115, pp. 639–53.

Hengelbrock, J., Theissen, E. and Westheide, C. (2013) 'Market Response to Investor Sentiment', *Journal of Business Finance & Accounting,* Aug/Sept 2013, 40(7/8), pp. 901–17.

Hertz, D.B. (1964) 'Risk analysis in capital investment', *Harvard Business Review,* January/ February, pp. 95–106.

Hertz, D.B and Thomas, H. (1984) *Practical Risk Analysis: An Approach through Case Histories.* Chichester: Wiley.

Hickman, B.G. (1958) 'Corporate bond quality and investor experience', *National Bureau of Economic Research,* 14, Princeton.

Hicks, J.R. (1946) *Value and Capital: An Inquiry into some Fundamental Principles of Economic Theory.* 2nd edn. Oxford: Oxford University Press.

Hillert, A., Jacobs, H. and Müller, S. (2014) 'Media Makes Momentum', *Review of Financial Studies,* Dec, 27(12), pp. 3467–501.

Hillier, F.S. (1963) 'The derivation of probabilistic information for the evaluation of risky investments', *Management Science,* April, pp. 443–57.

Hirshleifer, J. (1958) 'On the theory of optimal investment decision', *Journal of Political Economy,* 66 (August), pp. 329–52.

Hirshleifer, J. (1961) 'Risk, the discount rate and investment decisions', *American Economic Review,* May, pp. 112–20.

Hirshleifer, D., Lim, S.S. and Teoh, S.H. (2009) 'Driven to distraction: extraneous events and underreaction to earnings news', *The Journal of Finance,* LXIV(5), pp. 2289–325.

Ho, S.M. and Pike, R.H. (1991) 'Risk analysis techniques in capital budgeting contexts', *Accounting, and Business Research,* 21(83), pp. 227–38.

Hoffmann, N. (2013) 'Discounted cash flow valuation for small cap M&A integration', *Journal of Applied Corporate Finance,* Spring, 25(2), pp. 116–21.

Hodgkinson, L. and Partington, G.H. (2008) 'The motivation for takeovers in the UK', *Journal of Business Finance and Accounting,* 35(1), (2), pp. 102–26.

Hofmann, E., Maucher, D., Piesker, S. and James, P. R. (2011) *Ways Out of the Working Capital Trap: Empowering Self-Financing Growth,* Springer.

Hoffmann, N. (2013) 'Discounted cash flow valuation for small cap M&A integration', *Journal of Applied Corporate Finance,* Spring, 25(2), pp. 116–21.

Hon, M.T. and Tonks, I. (2003) 'Momentum in the UK stock market', *Journal of Multinational Financial Management,* 13, pp. 43–70.

Hong, H. and Sraer, D.A. (2016) 'Speculative betas', *Journal of Finance,* Oct, 71(5), pp. 2095–144.

Hong, H. and Stein, J.C. (1999) 'A unified theory of underreaction, momentum trading and overreaction in asset markets', *Journal of Finance,* 54(6), pp. 2143–84.

Hovakimian, A., Kayhan, A. and Titman, S. (2012) 'Are corporate default probabilities consistent with the static trade-off theory?' *Review of Financial Studies,* 25, pp. 315–34.

Howell, S., Stark, A., Newton, D., Paxson, D., Cavus, M. and Pereira, J. (2001) *Real Options: Evaluating Corporate Investment Opportunities in a Dynamic World.* Harlow: Financial Times Prentice Hall.

Hull, J.C. (2017) *Option, Futures and Other Derivatives, Global Edition.* 9th edn. Harlow: Pearson Education.

Ikenberry, D., Lakonishok, J. and Vermaelen, T. (1995) 'Market under reaction to open market share repurchases', *Journal of Financial Economics,* October–November, pp. 181–208.

Ikenberry, D., Rankine, G. and Stice, E. (1996) 'What do stock splits really signal?', *Journal of Financial and Quantitative Analysis,* 31, pp. 357–75.

Invest Europe (www.investeurope.eu).

Irwin, D. and Scott, J.M. (2010) 'Barriers faced by SMEs in raising bank finance', *International Journal of Entrepreneurial Behaviour and Research,* 16, pp. 245–59.

Isenberg, D. and D. Lawton (2014) 'How to finance the scale-up of your company', *Harvard Business Review,* 18 August, pp. 2–4.

Ishii, J. and Xuan, Y. (2014) 'Acquirer-target social ties and merger outcomes', *Journal of Financial Economics*, 112, pp. 344–63.

Ismail, T. and Cline, M. (2005) 'Investment appraisal under conditions of continuous and discrete cash flows and discounting', *Managerial Auditing Journal*, 20(1), pp. 30–35.

Israel, R. and Moskowitz, T.J. (2013) 'The role of shorting, firm size, and time on market anomalies', *Journal of Financial Economics*, 108 pp. 275–301.

Jacobs, M.T. and Shivdasani, A. (2012) 'Do you know your cost of capital?' *Harvard Business Review*, July–August, pp. 118–24.

Jaffe, J., Keim, D.B. and Westerfield, R. (1989) 'Earnings yields, market values and stock returns', *Journal of Finance*, 44, pp. 135–48. US data, 1951–86.

Jagannathan, M., Stephens, C.P. and Weisbach, M.S. (2000) 'Financial flexibility and the choice between dividends and stock repurchases', *Journal of Financial Economics*, 57(3), September, pp. 355–84.

Jagannathana, R., Matsaa, D.A., Meier, I. and Tarhan, V. (2016) 'Why do firms use high discount rates?' *Journal of Financial Economics*, 120, pp. 445–63.

Jegadeesh, N. and Titman, S. (1993) 'Returns to buying winners and selling losers: Implications for stock market efficiency', *Journal of Finance*, 48, March, pp. 65–91.

Jensen, M.C. (1968) 'The performance of mutual funds in the period 1945–64', *Journal of Finance*, 23, May, pp. 389–416.

Jensen, M.C. (1986) 'Agency costs of free cash flow, corporate finance and takeovers', *American Economic Review*, 76, pp. 323–9.

Jensen, M.C. (1989) 'Eclipse of the public corporation', *Harvard Business Review*, September–October, pp. 61–74.

Jensen, M.C. (2001) 'Value maximisation, stakeholder theory, and the corporate objective function', *Journal of Applied Corporate Finance*, 14(3), Fall.

Jensen, M.C. and Meckling, W.H. (1976) 'Theory of the firm: Managerial behavior, agency costs and ownership structure', *Journal of Financial Economics*, Oct., 3, pp. 305–60.

John, K., Litov, L. and Yeung, B. (2008) 'Corporate governance and risk-taking', *Journal of Finance*, 63(4), pp. 1679–1728.

Johnson, G. and Scholes, K. (2017) *Exploring Corporate Strategy*. 11th edn. Harlow: Pearson Education.

Jorion, P. (1992) 'Portfolio optimisation in practice', *Financial Analysts Journal*, 48, January/February, pp. 68–74.

Jorion, P. and Goetzmann, W.N. (1999) 'Global stock markets in the twentieth century', *Journal of Finance*, LIV(3) June, pp. 953–80.

Jotikasthira, C., Le, A. and Lundblad, C. (2015) 'Why do term structures in different currencies co-move?' *Journal of Financial Economics*, 115, pp. 58–83.

Kahnemann, D. (2012) *Thinking fast and slow*. Penguin.

Kahnemann, D. and Tversky, A. (2000) *Choices, Values and Frames*. Cambridge: Cambridge University Press.

Kahneman, D., Slovic, P. and Tversky, A. (1982) *Judgment under Uncertainty: Heuristics and Biases*. Cambridge: Cambridge University Press.

Kama, I. (2009) 'On the market reaction to revenue and earnings surprises', *Journal of Business Finance & Accounting*, 36(1), (2), pp. 31–50.

Kaplan, R.S. and Atkinson, A.A. (2013) *Advanced Management Accounting*, International Edition (3rd edition), Pearson.

Kaplan, R. and Norton, D.P. (1996) *The Balanced Scorecard*. Boston, MA: Harvard Business School Press.

Kaplanis, E. and Schaefer, S. (1991) 'Exchange risk and international diversification in bond and equity portfolios', *Journal of Economics and Business*, 43, pp. 287–307.

Kay, J. (1993) *Foundations of Corporate Success*. New York: Oxford University Press.

Kay, J. (2004) 'Forget how the crow flies', *Financial Times Magazine*, 17–18 January, pp. 17–21.

Kay, J. (2009) *The Long and Short of It*. London: The Erasmus Press.

Kay, J. (2010) *Obliquity: Why our goals are best achieved indirectly*. London: Profile Books.

Kayhan, A. and Titman, S. (2007) 'Firms' histories and their capital structures', *Journal of Financial Economics*, 83, pp. 1–32.

Keane, S. (1974) 'Dividends and the resolution of uncertainty', *Journal of Business Finance and Accountancy*, Autumn.

Kee, R. and Bublitz, B. (1988) 'The role of payback in the investment process', *Accounting and Business Research*, 18(70), pp. 149–55.

Keim, D.B. (1983) 'Size-related anomalies and stock return seasonality: Further empirical evidence', *Journal of Financial Economics*, 12, pp. 13–32.

Keim, D.B. (1988) 'Stock market regularities: A synthesis of the evidence and explanations', in Dimson, E. (ed.) *Stock Market Anomalies*, Cambridge: Cambridge University Press, and in Lofthouse, S. (ed.) (1994) *Readings in Investment*, Chichester: Wiley.

Keim, D.B. and Ziemba, W.T. (eds) (2000) *Security Market Imperfections in World Wide Equity Markets*. Cambridge: Cambridge University Press.

Kelly, S. (2016) 'Making strides with the help of technology', Treasury and Risk Management: New York, April.

Kendall, M. (1953) 'The analysis of economic time-series prices', *Journal of the Royal Statistical Society*, 96, pp. 11–25.

Kennedy, A. and Mills, R. (1990) *Post Completion Audit of Capital Expenditure Projects*. London: CIMA. Management Accounting Guide 9.

Kennedy, A. and Mills, R. (1992) 'Post completion auditing: a source of strategic direction?', *Management Accounting* (UK), May, pp. 26–8.

Kennedy, A. and Mills, R. (1993a) 'Post completion auditing in practice', *Management Accounting*, October, pp. 22–5.

Kennedy, A. and Mills, R. (1993b) 'Experiences in operating a post-audit system', *Management Accounting*, November.

Kerins, F., Kutsuna, K. and Smith, R. (2007) 'Why are IPOs underpriced? Evidence from Japan's hybrid auction-method offerings', *Journal of Financial Economics*, 85, pp. 637–66.

Kerr, W. R., Lerber, J. and Schoar, A. (2014) 'The consequences of entrepreneurial finance: evidence from angel financings', *The Review of Financial Studies*, 27(1), pp. 20–55.

Kester, G. and Robbins, G. (2011) 'The capital budgeting practices of listed Irish companies' insights from

CFOs on their investment appraisal techniques', *Accountancy Ireland*, 43(1), pp. 28–30.

Keynes, J.M. (1936) *The General Theory of Employment, Interest and Money.* London: Harcourt, Brace and World.

Kim, K., Kitsabunnarat-Chatjuthamard, P. and Nofsinger, J. (2007) 'Large shareholders, board independence, and minority shareholder rights: evidence from Europe', *Journal of Corporate Finance,* 13(5), pp. 859–80.

Kindleberger, C.P. and Aliber, R.Z. (2011) *Manias, Panics and Crashes: A History of Financial Crises,* 6th edn. New York: Macmillan.

Kisgen, D.J. (2006) 'Credit ratings and capital structure', *Journal of Finance,* 61(3), June, pp. 1035–72.

Klein, A. and Zur, E. (2009) 'Entrepreneurial shareholder activism: hedge funds and other private investors', *Journal of Finance,* LXIV(1), pp. 187–229.

Knauer, A., Lahmann, A., Pflücke, M. and Schwetzler, B. (2014) 'How much do private equity funds benefit from debt-related tax shields?' *Journal of Applied Corporate Finance,* 26(1), Winter, pp. 85–93.

Koch, A.S. and Sun, A.X. (2004) 'Dividend changes and the persistence of past earnings changes', *Journal of Finance,* 59(5), October, pp. 2093–116.

Korajczyk, R.A. and Levy, A. (2003) 'Capital structure choice: Macroeconomic conditions and financial constraints', *Journal of Financial Economics,* 68, pp. 75–109.

Kothari, S.P., Shanken, J. and Sloan, R.G. (1995) 'Another look at the cross-section of expected stock returns', *Journal of Finance,* 50(1) March, pp. 185–224.

KPMG (2016) Cost of Capital Survey 2016. KPMG London (https://assets.kpmg.com/content/dam/kpmg/ch/pdf/cost-of-capital-study-2016-en.pdf)

Kraus, A. and Litzenberger, R. (1973) 'A state-preference model of optimal financial leverage', *Journal of Finance,* 28, pp. 911–22.

Krüger, P., A. Landier and D. Thesmar (2015) 'The WACC fallacy: The real effects of using a unique discount rate', *Journal of Finance.* June, 70(3), pp. 1253–85.

Lakonishok, J., Shleifer, A. and Vishny, R. (1994) 'Contrarian investment extrapolation and risk', *Journal of Finance,* 49, pp. 1541–78.

Lamont, O.A. and Thaler, R.H. (2003) 'Can the market add and subtract? Mispricing in tech price equity carve-outs', *Journal of Political Economy,* 111 (2 April), pp. 227–68.

La Porta, R. (1996) 'Expectations and the cross-section of stock returns', *Journal of Finance,* 51(5), December, pp. 1715–42.

La Porta, R., Lakonishok, J., Shleifer, A. and Vishny, R. (1997) 'Good news for value stocks: Further evidence on market efficiency', *Journal of Finance,* 52(2), pp. 859–74.

La Porta, R., Lopez-de-Silanes, F., Shleifer, A. and Vishny, R. (2000) 'Investor protection and corporate governance', *Journal of Financial Economics,* 58(1/2), pp. 3–27.

Larrain, B. and F. Urzúa I. (2013) 'Controlling shareholders and market timing in share issuance', *Journal of Financial Economics,* 109, pp. 661–81.

Lawrence, A.G. and Myers, M.D. (1991) 'Post-auditing capital projects', *Management Accounting,* January, pp. 39–42.

Leary, M.T. (2009) 'Bank loan supply, lender choice, and corporate capital structure', *The Journal of Finance,* LXIV (3), pp. 1143–85.

Leary, M.T. and Roberts, M.R. (2005) 'Do firms rebalance their capital structures?', *Journal of Finance,* 60(6), December, pp. 2575–619.

Lee, D.R. and Verbrugge, J.A. (1996) 'The efficient market theory thrives on criticism', *Journal of Applied Corporate Finance,* 9(1), pp. 3–11.

Lefley, F. (1997) 'The sometimes-overlooked discounted payback method', *Management Accounting* (UK), November, p. 36.

Lefley, F. (2013) 'The appraisal of ICT and non-ICT capital projects: A study of the current practices of large UK organisations', *International Journal of Managing Projects in Business, Bingley,* 6.3, pp. 505–33.

Lel, U. and Miller, D.P. (2015) 'Does takeover activity cause managerial discipline? Evidence from international M&A laws', *Review of Financial Studies,* 28(6), pp. 1588–622.

Lerman, A., Livnat, J. and Mendenhall, R.R. (2007) 'Double surprise into higher future returns', *Financial Analysts Journal,* 63(4), pp. 63–71.

Lerner, J. (2013) 'Corporate Venturing', *Harvard Business Review,* October, pp. 87–94.

Lerner, J., Hardymon, F. and Leamon, A. (2012) *Venture Capital and Private Equity: A Casebook.* 5th edn. Chichester: John Wiley & Sons, Inc.

Lerner, J., Sorensen, M. and Strömberg, P. (2011) 'Private equity and long-run investment: The case of innovation', *Journal of Finance,* 66(2), pp. 445–77.

Lerner, J., Sorensen, M. and Strömberg, P. (2013) 'Private equity and investment in innovation: Evidence from patents', *Applied Corporate Finance,* 25(2), Spring, pp. 95–102.

Leuz, C., Lins, K. and Warnock, F. (2009) 'Do foreigners invest less in poorly governed firms?' *Review of Financial Studies,* 22(8), pp. 3245–85.

Lev, B. (1992) 'Observations on the merger phenomenon and a review of the evidence'. Reprinted in J.M. Stern and D. Chew (eds), *The Revolution in Corporate Finance.* 2nd edn. Oxford: Blackwell.

Levich, Richard M (2011) 'Evidence of financial globalisation and crises: interest rate parity', In *The Encyclopedia of Financial Globalization.* Edited by Gerard Caprio. Amsterdam: Elsevier Publishing.

Levine, P. and Aaronovitch, S. (1981) 'The financial characteristics of firms and theories of merger activity', *Journal of Industrial Economics,* 30, pp. 149–72.

Levis, M. (1989) 'Stock market anomalies: A reassessment based on UK evidence', *Journal of Banking and Finance,* 13, pp. 675–96.

Levis, M. (1990) 'The winner's curse problem, interest costs and the underpricing of initial public offerings', *Economic Journal,* 100, March, pp. 76–89.

Levy, R.A. (1971) 'On the short-term stationarity of beta coefficients', *Financial Analysts Journal, November–December,* pp. 55–62.

Levy, H. (1978) 'Equilibrium in an imperfect market: a constraint on the number of securities in the portfolio', *American Economic Review,* September, pp. 643–58.

Lewellen, J. (2004) 'Predicting returns with financial ratios', *Journal of Financial Economics,* 74, pp. 209–35.

Lewellen, W.G., Stanley, K.L., Lease, R.C. and Schlarbaum, G.G. (1978) 'Some direct evidence of the dividend clientele phenomenon', *Journal of Finance,* December, pp. 1385–99.

Lewis, K. (1996) 'Consumption, stock returns, and the gains from international risk-sharing', *NBER Working Paper,* No. 5410, January.

Li, X. (2015) 'Accounting conservatism and the cost of capital: An international analysis', *Journal of Business Finance & Accounting.* June, 42(5/6), pp. 555–82.

Li, X. and Wang, S. (2015) 'Post-Earnings-Announcement Drift in Global Markets: Evidence from an Information Shock', *Review of Financial Studies,* 28(4), pp. 1242–83.

Li, X., Brooks, C. and Miffre, J. (2009) 'The value premium and time-varying volatility', *Journal of Business Finance & Accounting,* 36(9), (10), pp. 1252–72.

Lim, J., Minton, B.A. and Weisbach, M.S. (2014) 'Syndicated loan spreads and the composition of the syndicate', *Journal of Financial Economics,* 111, pp. 45–69.

Lintner, J. (1956) 'Distribution of income of corporations among dividends, retained earnings and taxes', *American Economic Review,* 46, May, pp. 97–113.

Lintner, J. (1965) 'The valuation of risky assets and the selection of risky investments in stock portfolios and capital budgets', *Review of Economics and Statistics,* 47, February, pp. 13–37.

Lister R. (2005) 'Cost of capital: The case for the prosecution', *Investment Management and Financial Innovations,* 2, pp. 142–57.

Lister, R. (2006) 'Cost of capital is beyond our reach', *Accountancy,* December, pp. 42–3.

Litzenberger, R.H. and Ramaswamy, K. (1979) 'The effect of personal taxes and dividends on capital asset prices: Theory and empirical evidence', *Journal of Financial Economics,* 7, pp. 163–95.

Litzenberger, R. and Ramaswamy, K. (1982) 'The effects of dividends on common stock prices: Tax effects or information effects?', *Journal of Finance,* May, pp. 429–43.

Liu, B. and McConnell, J.J. (2015) 'CEOs, abandoned acquisitions, and the media', *Journal of Applied Corporate Finance,* 27(3), Summer, pp. 113–20.

Liu, W., Strong, N. and Xu, X. (1999) 'The profitability of momentum investing', *Journal of Business Finance and Accounting,* 26(9) and (10), November–December, pp. 1043–91.

Liu, W., Strong, N. and Xu, X. (2003) 'Post-earnings-announcement drift in the UK', *European Financial Management,* 9(1), pp. 89–116.

Liu, Y., Szewczyk, S.H. and Zantout, Z. (2008) 'Underreaction to dividend reductions and omissions?' *The Journal of Finance,* LXIII(2), pp. 987–1020.

Lo, A. (2017) *Adaptive Markets: Financial evolution at the speed of thought.* Princeton.

Lo, A.W. and Hasanhodzic, J. (2010) *The Evolution of Technical Analysis: Financial Prediction from Babylonian Tablets to Bloomberg Terminals.* New York: John Wiley and Sons.

Lo, A.W. and Mackinley, A.C. (2001) *A Non-random Walk Down Wall Street.* Princeton, NJ: Princeton University Press.

London, S. (2003) 'The long view: lunch with the FT, Milton Friedman', *Financial Times Magazine,* 7–8 June, pp. 12–13.

Longmore, D.R. (1989) 'The persistence of the payback method: A time-adjusted decision rule perspective', *Engineering Economist,* 43(3), Spring, pp. 185–94.

Loughran, T. and McDonald, B. (2013) 'IPO first-day returns, offer price revisions, volatility, and form S-1 language', *Journal of Financial Economics,* 109, pp. 307–26.

Loughran, J. and Vijh, A.M. (1997) 'Do long term shareholders benefit from corporate acquisitions?', *Journal of Finance,* 52(5), pp. 1765–90.

Loughran, T., Rutter, J.R. and Rydqvist, K. (1994, Updated 2015) 'Initial public offerings: International insights', *Pacific-Basin Finance Journal,* 2, pp. 165–99.

Louis, H. (2004a) 'Earnings management and the market performance of acquiring firms', *Journal of Financial Economics,* 74(1), Oct., pp. 121–48.

Louis, H. (2004b) 'The cost of using bank mergers as defensive mechanisms against takeover threats', *Journal of Business,* 77(2) pt.1, pp. 295–310.

Lowe, J. (1997) *Warren Buffett Speaks.* New York: John Wiley & Sons.

Lowe, J. (1999) *The Rediscovered Benjamin Graham.* New York: John Wiley & Sons.

Lowenstein, L. (1991) *Sense and Nonsense in Corporate Finance.* Reading, MA: Addison Wesley.

Lueg, R. and Schäffer, U.J. Betriebswirtsch (2010) 'Assessing empirical research on value-based management: Guidelines for improved hypothesis testing', *Journal für Betriebswirtschaft,* 60: 1.

Luehrman, T.A. (1997) 'Using APV: A better tool for valuing operations', *Harvard Business Review,* 75 (May–June), pp. 145–54.

Lumijärvi, O.P. (1991) 'Selling of capital investments to top management', *Management Accounting Research,* 2, pp. 171–88.

Lutz, F.A. and Lutz, V.C. (1951) *The Theory of Investment in the Firm.* Princeton, NJ: Princeton University Press.

Lynch, P. (1990) *One Up on Wall Street* (with John Rothchild). New York: Penguin Books. (Originally published by Simon & Schuster, 1989.)

Lynch, P. (1994) *Beating the Street* (with John Rothchild). New York: Simon & Schuster.

Madura, J. (2018) *International Financial Management,* 13th edn. London: Thompson.

Magee, J.F. (1964a) 'Decision trees for decision making', *Harvard Business Review,* July/August, pp. 126–38.

Magee, J.F. (1964b) 'How to use decision trees in capital investment', *Harvard Business Review,* September/October, pp. 79–96.

Maksimovic, V., Phillips, G. and Yang, L. (2013) 'Public and private merger waves', *Journal of Finance,* LXVIII(5), October, pp. 2177–216.

Malkiel, B.G. (2016) *A Random Walk Down Wall Street.* 11th Revised Edition. New York: W.W. Norton & Co.

Mancini-Griffoli, T. and Ranaldo, A. (2011) 'Limits to Arbitrage During the Crisis: Funding Liquidity Constraints and Covered Interest Parity.' Available at SSRN: https://ssrn.com/abstract=1569504 or http://dx.doi.org/10.2139/ssrn.1569504

Manso, G. (2013) 'Feedback effects of credit ratings', *Journal of Financial Economics,* 109, pp. 535–48.

Manson, S., Stark, A. and Thomas, H.M. (1994) 'A cash flow analysis of the operational gains from takeovers', *Research Report 35.* London: Chartered Association of Certified Accountants.

Marco-Izquierdo, J.A. (2015) 'CEOs don't care enough about Capital Allocation', *Harvard Business Review Digital Articles* 4/16/2015, pp. 2–4.

Markowitz, H.M. (1952) 'Portfolio selection', *Journal of Finance*, 7, pp. 77–91. Pioneering theory.

Markowitz, H. (1959) *Portfolio Selection*. New York: Wiley.

Markowitz, H.M. (1991) 'Foundations of portfolio theory', *Journal of Finance*, June.

Markowitz, H.M. (2005) 'Market efficiency: a theoretical distinction and so what?', *Financial Analysts Journal*, Sept/Oct, pp. 17–30.

Marsh, P. (1982) 'The choice between equity and debt: An empirical study', *Journal of Finance*, 37, March, pp. 121–44.

Martin, J.D. and Petty, J.W. (2000) *Value Based Management: Corporate response to the shareholder revolution*. Boston, MA: Harvard Business School Press.

Martikainen, T. and Puttonen, V. (1996) 'Finnish days-of-the-week effects', *Journal of Business Finance and Accounting*, 23(7), September, pp. 1019–32.

Masulis, R., Wang, C. and Xie, F. (2009) 'Agency problems at dual-class companies', *Journal of Finance*, 64(4), pp. 1697–727.

Matsa, D.A. (2010) 'Capital structure as a strategic variable: Evidence from collective bargaining', *Journal of Finance*, 65(3), pp. 1197–232.

Matti, K., Linnainmaa, J. T. and Nyberg, P. (2016) 'Return Seasonalities', *Journal of Finance*, 71(4), pp. 1557–90.

Mauboussin, M.J. and Callahan, D. (2014) 'Capital allocation: Evidence, analytical methods and assessment guidance', *Journal of Applied Corporate Finance*, 26(4), pp. 98–74.

Maury, B. (2006) 'Family ownership and firm performance: Empirical evidence from Western European corporations', *Journal of Corporate Finance*, 12(2), pp. 321–41.

McBrady, M.R., Mortal, S. and Schill, M.J. (2010) 'Do firms believe in interest rate parity?'. *Review of Finance*, 14(4), (October), pp. 695–726.

McClatchey, C. (2011) 'Using EVA as a decision metric in capital budgeting', *Journal of Applied Business Research*, 20(4).

McDaniel, W.R., McCarty, D.E. and Jessell, K.A. (1988) 'Discounted cash flow with explicit reinvestment rates: Tutorial and extension', *The Financial Review*, August.

McDonald, R.L. (2013) *Derivatives Markets*. 3nd edn. Harlow: Pearson.

McKinsey and Company: Koller, T., Goedhart, M. and Wessel, D. (2015) *Valuation*. 6th edn. New York: John Wiley & Sons Ltd.

McKinsey (Koller, T., Goedhart, M. and Wessel, D.) (2011) *Value: The four cornerstones of corporate finance*. New York: John Wiley & Sons.

McLaney, E., Pointon, J., Thomas, M. and Tucker, J. (2004) 'Practitioners' perspectives on the UK cost of capital', *European Journal of Finance*, 10, April, pp. 123–38.

McLean, R.D. and Pontiff, J. (2016) 'Does academic research destroy stock return predictability?' *Journal of Finance*, 71(1), pp. 5–32.

McTaggart, J.M., Kontes, P.W. and Mankins, M.C. (1994) *The Value Imperative*. New York: Free Press.

Mehra, R. (2003) 'The equity premium puzzle?' Why is it a puzzle? *Financial Analysts Journal*, 59, pp. 54–69.

Mehra, R. and Prescott, E.C. (1985) 'The Equity Premium: A Puzzle', *Journal of Monetary Economics*, 15, pp. 145–61.

Mehra, R. and Prescott, E. (2006) 'The equity premium: what have we learned in 20 years?' in R. Mehra (ed.) *Handbook of Investments: Equity risk premium* in the Handbook of Economics and Finance Series. Amsterdam: Elsevier.

Merton, R.C. (1998) 'Application of option-pricing theory: twenty-five years later', *American Economic Review*, June, No. 3, pp. 323–49.

Merton, R.C. (2005) 'You have more capital than you think', *Harvard Business Review*, November, pp. 1–10.

Metrick, A. and Yasuda, A. (2010) *Venture Capital and the Finance of Innovation*. 2nd edn. Chichester: John Wiley & Sons, Inc.

Michaely, R., Thaler, R. and Womack, K. (1995) 'Price reaction to dividend initiations and omissions: Overreaction or drift?', *Journal of Finance*, 50, pp. 573–608.

Michaud, R.O. (1989) 'The Markowitz optimization enigma: Is "optimized" optimal?', *Financial Analysts Journal*, 45, January–February, pp. 31–42.

Michaud, R.O., Bergstorm, G.L., Frashure, R.D. and Wolahan, B.K. (1996) 'Twenty years of international equity investment', *Journal of Portfolio Management*, Fall, pp. 9–22.

Michou, M. (2009) 'Is the value spread a good predictor of stock returns? UK evidence', *Journal of Business Finance & Accounting*, 36(7), (8), pp. 925–50.

Miles, D. and Timmermann, A. (1996) 'Variations in expected stock returns: Evidence on the pricing of equities from a cross-section of UK companies', *Economica*, 63, pp. 369–82.

Miller, M.H. (1977) 'Debt and taxes', *Journal of Finance*, 32, May, pp. 261–75.

Miller, M.H. (1997) *Merton Miller on Derivatives*. New York: Wiley.

Miller, M.H. (1988) 'The Modigliani–Miller propositions after thirty years', *Journal of Economic Perspectives* (Fall). Also reproduced in Chew, D.H. (ed.) (2001) *The New Corporate Finance*. New York: McGraw-Hill. 3rd edn.

Miller, M.H. (1991) 'Leverage', *Journal of Finance*, 46, pp. 479–88.

Miller, M.H. and Modigliani, F. (1961) 'Dividend policy, growth and the valuation of shares', *Journal of Business*, 34, October, pp. 411–33.

Miller, M.N. and Orr, D. (1966) 'A model of the demand for money by firms', *Quarterly Journal of Economics*, 80, August, pp. 413–35.

Mitchell, M.L. and Lehn, K. (1990) 'Do bad bidders become good targets?', *Journal of Political Economy*, 98(2), pp. 372–98.

Modigliani, F. and Miller, M.H. (1958) 'The cost of capital, corporation finance and the theory of investment', *American Economic Review*, 48, June, pp. 261–97.

Modigliani, F. and Miller, M.H. (1963) 'Corporate income taxes and the cost of capital: A correction', *American Economic Review*, 53, June, pp. 433–43.

Modigliani, F. and Miller, M.H. (1969) 'Reply to Heins and Sprenkle', *American Economic Review*, 59, September, pp. 592–5.

Moel, A. and Tufano, P. (2002) 'When are real options exercised? An empirical study of mine closings', *The Review of Financial Studies,* Spring, 15(1), pp. 35–64.

Moeller, S.B., Schlingemann, F.P. and Stulz, R.M. (2004) 'Firm size and the gains from acquisitions', *Journal of Financial Economics,* 73, pp. 201–28.

Moeller, S.B., Schlingemann, F.P. and Stulz, R.M. (2005) 'Wealth destruction on a massive scale? A study of acquiring firm returns in the recent merger wave', *The Journal of Finance,* LX(2), April, pp. 757–82.

Montier, J. (2002) *Behavioural Finance: Insights into Irrational Minds and Markets.* London: John Wiley & Sons.

Montier, J. (2007) *Behavioural Investing.* Chichester: John Wiley & Sons.

Montier, J. (2009) *Value Investing: Tools and Techniques for Intelligent Investment.* Chichester: John Wiley & Sons Ltd.

Montier, J. (2010) *The Little Book of Behavioral Investing.* Chichester: John Wiley & Sons, Inc.

Morgan, G. and Thomas, S. (1998) 'Taxes, dividend yields and returns in the UK equity market', *Journal of Banking and Finance,* 22, pp. 405–23.

Morosini, P. and Steger, U. (eds) (2004) *Managing Complex Mergers: Real world lessons in implementing successful cross cultural M&As.* Harlow: Financial Times Prentice Hall.

Mossin, J. (1966) 'Equilibrium in a capital asset market', *Econometrica,* 34, October, pp. 768–83.

Mougoué, M. and Rao, R.P. (2003) 'The information signalling hypothesis of dividends: Evidence from cointegration and causality tests', *Journal of Business Finance and Accounting,* 30(3) and (4), April/May, pp. 441–78.

Mulcahy, D. (2013) 'Six myths about venture capitalists', *Harvard Business Review,* May, pp. 81–83.

Mullins, J. (2014) 'VC funding can be bad for your start-up', *Harvard Business Review,* 4 August, pp. 2–4.

Mussweiler, T. and Schneller, K. (2003) '"What goes up must come down" – how charts influence decisions to buy and sell stocks', *The Journal of Behavioral Finance,* 4(3), pp. 121–30.

Myers, S.C. (1974) 'Interaction of corporate financing and investment decisions – implications for capital budgeting', *Journal of Finance,* 29 (March), pp. 1–25.

Myers, S.C. (1984) 'The capital structure puzzle', *Journal of Finance,* 39, July, pp. 575–82. Myers, S.C. (1996) 'Fischer Black's contributions to corporate finance', *Financial Management,* 25(4), Winter, pp. 95–103.

Myers, S. and Majluf, N. (1984) 'Corporate financing and investment decisions when firms have information investors do not have', *Journal of Financial Economics,* June, pp. 187–221.

Neff, J. (1999) *John Neff on Investing* (with S.L. Mintz). New York: John Wiley & Sons.

Ngatuni, P., Capstaff, J. and Marshall, A. (2007) 'Long-term performance following rights issues and open offers in the UK', *Journal of Business Finance & Accounting,* 34(1), (2), pp. 33–64.

Nichols, N.A. (1993) 'Efficient? Chaotic? What's the New Finance?', *Harvard Business Review,* March–April, pp. 50–8.

Nissim, D. and Ziv, A. (2001) 'Dividend changes and future profitability', *Journal of Finance,* 56(6), pp. 2111–33.

Novy-Marx, R. (2013) 'The other side of value: The gross profitability premium', *Journal of Financial Economics,* 108, pp. 1–28.

Novy-Marx, R. and Velikov, M. (2016) 'A taxonomy of anomalies and their trading costs', *The Review of Financial Studies,* 29(1), pp. 104–47.

Oded, J. and Michel, A. (2008) 'Stock repurchases and the EPS enhancement fallacy', *Financial Analysts Journal,* 64(4), pp. 62–75.

Ofcom UK (telecommunications and media regulator) (www.ofcom.org.uk).

Ofgem (UK energy regulator) (www.ofgem.gov.uk).

Ofwat (UK water regulator) www.ofwat.

Outram, R. (1997) 'For what it's worth', *Management Today,* May, pp. 70–1.

Palepu, K.G. (1986) 'Predicting takeover targets: A methodological and empirical analysis', *Journal of Accounting and Finance,* 8, pp. 3–35.

Park, C-H. and Irwin, S.H. (2007) 'What do we know about the profitability of technical analysis?' *Journal of Economic Surveys,* 21(4), pp. 786–826.

Pastor, L. and Veronesi, P. (2009) 'Technological revolutions and stock prices', *American Economic Review* 99, 1451–83.

Passov, R. (2003) 'How much cash does your company need?' *Harvard Business Review,* November, pp. 1–8.

Perotti, P. and Wagenhofer, A. (2014) 'Earnings quality measures and excess returns', *Journal of Business Finance & Accounting,* 41(5/6), pp. 545–71.

Pettit, R.R. (1977) 'Taxes, transaction costs and clientele effects of dividends', *Journal of Financial Economics,* December.

Phalippou, L. (2008) 'Where is the value premium?' *Financial Analysts Journal,* 64(2), pp. 41–8.

Pike, R.H. (1983) 'A review of recent trends in formal capital budgeting processes', *Accounting and Business Research,* Summer, pp. 201–8.

Pike, R.H. (1983) 'The capital budgeting behaviour and corporate characteristics of capital-constrained firms', *Journal of Business Finance and Accounting,* 10(4), Winter, pp. 663–71.

Pike, R.H. (1996) 'A longitudinal survey of capital budgeting practices', *Journal of Business Finance and Accounting,* 23(1), January.

Pike, R.H. (1988) 'An empirical study of the adoption of sophisticated capital budgeting practices and decision-making effectiveness', *Accounting and Business Research,* 18(72), pp. 341–51.

Pilbeam, K. (2018) *Finance and Financial Markets,* 4th edn. London: Palgrave.

Piotroski, J.D. (2000) 'Value investing: The use of historical financial statement information to separate winners from losers', *Journal of Accounting Research,* 38, Supplement, pp. 1–51.

Pitman, B. (2003) 'Leading for value', *Harvard Business Review,* April, pp. 41–6.

Pohlman, R.A., Santiago, E.S. and F. Lynn Markel (1988) 'Cash Flow Estimation Practices of Large Firms', *Financial Management,* 17(2), pp. 71–9.

Pontiff, J. and Schall, L.D. (1998) 'Book-to-market ratios as predictors of market returns', *Journal of Financial Economics,* 49, pp. 141–60.

Porter, M.E. (1980) *Competitive Strategy.* New York: Free Press.

Porter, M.E. (1985) *Competitive Advantage*. New York: Free Press.

Poterba, J.M. and Summers, L.H. (1988) 'Mean reversion in stock prices: Evidence and implications', *Journal of Financial Economics*, 22, pp. 27–59.

Powell, R.G. and Stark, A.W. (2005) 'Does operating performance increase post takeover for UK takeovers? A comparison of performance measures and benchmarks', *Journal of Corporate Finance*, 11(1 & 2), March, p. 293–317.

Powell, R.G. and Thomas, H.M. (1994) 'Corporate control and takeover prediction', Working paper 94/07 (Department of Accounting and Financial Management, University of Essex).

Prahalad, C.K. and Hamel, G. (1990) 'The core competence of the corporation', *Harvard Business Review*, 68(3), May–June, pp. 79–91.

Puetz, A. and Ruenzi, S. (2011) 'Overconfidence among professional investors: Evidence from mutual fund managers', *Journal of Business Finance & Accounting*, Jun/Jul, 38(5/6), pp. 684–712.

Pukthuanthong-Le, K., Levich, R.M. and Thomas III, L.R. (2007) 'Do foreign exchange markets still trend?', *The Journal of Portfolio Management*, Fall, pp. 114–52.

Pukthuanthong-Le, K. and Thomas III, L.R. (2008) 'Weak-form efficiency in currency markets', *Financial Analysts Journal*, 64(3), pp. 31–52.

Quigg, L. (1993) 'Empirical testing of real option pricing models', *Journal of Finance*, 48(2), pp. 621–40.

Raiyani, J.R. and Joshi, N.K. (2011) 'EVA based performance measurement: A case study of SBI, HFDC Bank', *Management Insight*, 7(1), June, pp. 31–43.

Rapp, M.S., Schellong, D., Schmidt, M. and Wolff, M. (2011) 'Considering the shareholder perspective: Value-based management systems and stock market performance', *Review of Managerial Science*, 5(2–3), pp. 171–94.

Rappaport, A. (1998) *Creating Shareholder Value*. (Revised and updated version.) New York: Free Press.

Rappaport, A. (1999) *Creating Shareholder Value*. New York: Free Press. Revised and updated.

Rappaport, A. (2006) 'Ten ways to create shareholder value', *Harvard Business Review*, September, pp. 66–77.

Rappaport, A. (2011). *Saving Capitalism from Short-termism: How to build long-term value and take back our financial future* (1st edn). New York: McGraw-Hill.

Rappaport, A. and Mauboussin, M.J. (2002) 'Valuation matters', *Harvard Business Review*, 1 March.

Rau, P.R. and Vermaelen, T. (1998) 'Glamour, value and the post-acquisition performance of acquiring firms', *Journal of Financial Economics*, 49(2), pp. 223–53.

Ravenscraft, D. and Scherer, F. (1987) *Mergers, Sell-Offs and Economic Efficiency*. Washington, DC: Brookings Institution.

Reimann, B.C. (1989) *Managing for Value*. Oxford: Basil Blackwell.

Reinganum, M.R. (1981) 'Misspecification of capital asset pricing: Empirical anomalies based on earnings' yields and market values', *Journal of Financial Economics*, 9, pp. 19–46.

Reinganum, M.R. (1982) 'A direct test of Roll's conjecture on the firm size effect', *Journal of Finance*, 37, pp. 27–35.

Reinganum, M.R. (1988) 'The anatomy of a stock market winner', *Financial Analysts Journal*, March–April, pp. 272–84.

Rendleman, R.J., Jones, C.P. and Latané, H.E. (1982) 'Empirical anomalies based on unexpected earnings and the importance of risk adjustments', *Journal of Financial Economics*, November, pp. 269–87.

Rhodes-Kropf, M. and Viswanathan, S. (2005) 'Market valuation and merger waves', *Journal of Finance*, 59, pp. 2685–718.

Rhodes-Kropf, M., Robinson, D.T. and Viswanathan, S. (2005) 'Valuation waves and merger activity: The empirical evidence', *Journal of Financial Economics*, 77(3), pp. 561–603.

Rigopoulos, G. (2014b) 'Real options adoption in capital budgeting: a highlight of recent literature', *Journal of Economics and Business Research*, 20.2, pp. 41–51.

Rigopoulos, G. (2015) 'A review on Real Options utilization in Capital Budgeting practice', *International Journal of Information, Business and Management*, 7(2).

Roberts, H.V. (1959) 'Stock market "patterns" and financial analysis: Methodological suggestions', *Journal of Finance*, March, pp. 1–10.

Roll, R. (1977) 'A critique of the Asset Pricing Theory's tests: Part 1: On past and potential testability of the theory', *Journal of Financial Economics*, 4 March, pp. 129–76.

Roll, R. (1981) 'A possible explanation for the small firm effect', *Journal of Finance*, September.

Roll, R. (1986) 'The hubris hypothesis of corporate takeovers', *Journal of Business*, 59(2), pt. 1, April, pp. 197–216. Also reproduced in R. Thaler (ed.) (1993) *Advances in Behavioral Finance*. New York: Russell Sage Foundation.

Roll, R. (1994) 'What every CFO should know about scientific progress in financial economics: What is known and what remains to be resolved', *Financial Management*, 23(2) (Summer), pp. 69–75.

Roll, R. and Ross, S.A. (1980) 'An empirical investigation of the Arbitrage Pricing Theory', *Journal of Finance*, 35, December, pp. 1073–103.

Rosenberg, B. and Rudd, A. (1986) 'The corporate uses of Beta', in J.M. Stern and D.H. Chew (eds), *The Revolution in Corporate Finance*. Oxford: Basil Blackwell.

Rosenberg, B., Reid, K. and Lanstein, R. (1985) 'Persuasive evidence of market inefficiency', *Journal of Portfolio Management*, 11, Spring, pp. 9–16.

Ross, S.A. (1974) 'Return, risk and arbitrage', in I. Friend and J.L. Bicksler (eds), *Risk and Return in Finance*. New York: Heath Lexington.

Ross, S.A. (1976) 'The arbitrage theory of capital asset pricing', *Journal of Economic Theory*, 13, December, pp. 341–60.

Ross, S. (1977) 'The determination of financial structure: The incentive-signalling approach', *Bell Journal of Economics*, 8, pp. 23–40.

Ross, S.A. (1995) 'Uses, abuses, and alternatives to the net-present-value rule', *Financial Management*, 24(3), Autumn, pp. 96–102.

Rouwenhorst, K.G. (1998) 'International momentum strategies', *Journal of Finance*, 53(1), February, pp. 267–84.

Rouwenhorst, K.G. (1999) 'Local return factors and turnover in emerging stock markets', *Journal of Finance*, 54(4), August, pp. 1439–64.

Rouwenhorst, K.G., Heston, S. and Wessels, R.E. (1999) 'The role of beta and size in the cross-section of European stock returns', *European Financial Management*, 4.

Roy, A. D. (1952) 'Safety first and the holding of assets', *Econometrica*, 20(3), July, pp. 431–49.

Rutterford, J. (2000) 'The cost of capital and shareholder value', in Arnold, G.C. and Davies, M. (eds) *Value-Based Management*. Chichester: John Wiley & Sons.

Ryan, H.E. and Trahan, E.A. (2007) 'Corporate financial control mechanisms and firm performance: The case of value-based management systems', *Journal of Business Finance & Accounting*, 34(1–2), 111–38.

Sabol, A. and Sverer, F. (2017) 'A Review of the Economic Value added Literature and Application.' Special issue, *UTMS Journal of Economics*, 8(1): 19–27.

Sagi, J.S. and Seasholes, M.S. (2007) 'Firm-specific attributes and the cross-section of momentum', *Journal of Financial Economics*, 84, pp. 389–434.

Sangster, A. (1993) 'Capital investment appraisal techniques: A survey of current usage', *Journal of Business Finance and Accounting*, 20(3), April, pp. 307–33.

Saunders, A. and Cornett, M.M. (2015) *Financial Markets and Institutions*. International edition. 6th edn. Boston, MA: McGraw-Hill.

Savor, P.G. and Lu, Q. (2009) 'Do stock mergers create value for acquirers?' *Journal of Finance*, LXIV(3), pp. 1061–97.

Schoenburg, E. (1990) 'Stock price prediction using neural networks', *Neurocomputing*, 2, pp. 17–27.

Scholes, M. (1972) 'The market for securities: Substitution versus price pressure effects of information on share prices', *Journal of Business*, April, pp. 179–211.

Schwartz, E.S. and Trigeorgis, L. (eds) (2001) *Real Options and Investment Under Uncertainty: Classical Readings and Recent Contributions*. London, Cambridge, MA: MIT Press.

Serdar, D.I. and Erel, I. (2013) 'Economic nationalism in mergers and acquisitions', *Journal of Finance*, Dec., 68(6), pp. 2471–514.

Sharma, A.K. and Kumar, S. (2010) 'Economic value added: Literature review and relevant issues', *International Journal of Economics and Finance*, 2(2), May, pp. 200–20.

Shahrur, H. (2005) 'Industry structure and horizontal takeovers: Analysis of wealth effects on rivals, suppliers, and corporate customers', *Journal of Financial Economics*, 76, pp. 61–98.

Sharpe, W.F. (1963) 'A simplified model for portfolio analysis', *Management Science*, 9, pp. 277–93.

Sharpe, W.F. (1964) 'Capital asset prices: a theory of market equilibrium under conditions of risk', *Journal of Finance*, 19, September, pp. 425–42.

Sheen, A. (2014) 'The real product market impact of mergers', *The Journal of Finance* 69(6), August 2014.

Shefrin, H. (2000) *Beyond Greed and Fear*. Boston, MA: Harvard Business School Press.

Shefrin, H.M. and Statman, M. (1984) 'Explaining investor preference for cash dividends', *Journal of Financial Economics*, 13, pp. 253–82.

Shiller, R.J. (1981) 'Do stock prices move too much to be justified by subsequent charges in dividends?', *American Economic Review*, 71, pp. 421–36.

Shiller, R.J. (2000) *Irrational Exuberance*. Princeton, NJ: Princeton University Press.

Shinoda, T. (2010) 'Capital budgeting management practices in Japan – a focus on the use of capital budgeting methods', *Economic Journal of Hokkaido University*, 39, no. 2010, pp. 39–50.

Shivakumar, L. (2006) 'Accruals, cash flows and the post-earnings-announcement drift', *Journal of Business Finance and Accounting*, Jan–Mar, 33(1), pp. 1–25.

Shleifer, A. (2000) *Inefficient Markets: An Introduction to Behavioural Finance*. Oxford: Oxford University Press.

Shon, J. and Zhou, P. (2010) 'Do divergent opinions explain the value premium?' *The Journal of Investing*, Summer, pp. 53–62.

Shu, Tao (2013) 'Institutional investor participation and stock market anomalies', *Journal of Business Finance and Accounting*, 40(5) & (6), pp. 695–718.

Shyam-Sunder, L. and Myers, S.C. (1999) 'Testing static trade off against pecking order models of capital structure', *Journal of Financial Economics*, 51, pp. 219–44.

Siegal, J.J. (2005) 'Perspectives on the equity risk premium', *Financial Analysts Journal*, Nov./Dec., pp. 61–73.

Silva, A. and Bilinski, P. (2015) 'Intended use of proceeds, underwriter quality and the long-run performance of SEOs in the UK', *Journal of Business Finance and Accounting*, 42(9) & (10), November/December, pp. 1282–309.

Singh, A. (1971) *Takeovers*. Cambridge: Cambridge University Press.

Singh, S., Jain, P.K and Yadav, S.S. (2012) 'Capital budgeting decisions: Evidence from India', *Journal of Advances in Management Research*, 9(1), pp. 96–112.

Simon, H.A. (1959) 'Theories of decision making in economics and behavioural science', *American Economic Review*, June.

Simon, H.A. (1964) 'On the concept of organisational goals', *Administrative Science Quarterly*, 9(1), June, pp. 1–22.

Sirower, M.L. (2008) *The Synergy Trap: How Companies Lose the Acquisition Game*. New York: Free Press.

Smith, A. (1776) *The Wealth of Nations*. Reproduced in 1910 in two volumes by J.M. Dent, London.

Smith, C. (1986) 'Investment banking and the capital acquisition process', *Journal of Financial Economics*, 15, pp. 3–29.

Smithers, A. (2009) *Wall Street Revalued: Imperfect markets and inept central bankers*. Chichester: John Wiley & Sons.

Solomon, E. (1963) *The Theory of Financial Management*. New York: Columbia University Press.

Solomons, D. (1965) *Divisional Performance: Measurement and control*. Reproduced 1983. Connecticut: M. Wiener Publishing.

Solnik, B.H. (1974) 'Why not diversify internationally rather than domestically?', *Financial Analysts Journal*, July–August, pp. 48–54.

Solnik, B.H. and McLeavey, D. (2003) *International Investments*, 5th edn. Boston, MA: Pearson Education.

Solomon, E. (1963) *The Theory of Financial Management*. New York: Columbia University Press.

Sorensen, M., Neng Wang and Jinqiang Yang (2014) 'Valuing Private Equity', *The Review of Financial Studies*, 27(7), pp. 1977–2021.

Soros, G. (1987) *The Alchemy of Finance*. New York: John Wiley & Sons. (Reprinted in 1994 with a new preface and a new foreword.)

Soros, G. (1995) *Soros on Soros*. New York: John Wiley & Sons.

Soros, G. (1998) *The Crisis of Global Capitalism*. New York: Public Affairs.

Soros, G. (2009) *The Crash of 2008 and What It Means*. New York: Public Affairs.

Spiedell, L.S. and Sappenfield, R. (1992) 'Global diversification in a shrinking world', *Journal of Portfolio Management*, Fall, pp. 57–67.

Statman, M. and Sepe, J.F. (1984) 'Managerial incentive plans and the use of the payback method', *Journal of Business Finance and Accounting*, 11(1), Spring, pp. 61–5.

Steele, R. and Albright, C. (2004) 'Games managers play at budget time', *MIT Sloan Management Review*, Spring, pp. 81–4.

Stephens, G. and Funnell, J. (1995) 'Take your partners . . .', *Corporate Finance*, London: Euromoney monthly journal, July.

Stern, J. (1998) 'The capital structure puzzle', *Journal of Applied Corporate Finance*, II(I), Spring, pp. 8–23.

Stern, J.M., Stewart, G.B. and Chew, D.H. (2001) 'The EVA® financial management system', in Chew, D.H. (ed.) *The New Corporate Finance*. New York: McGraw-Hill/Irwin.

Stewart, G.B. (1991) *The Quest for Value*. New York: HarperBusiness.

Stewart, G.B. (2001) 'Market myths', in *The New Corporate Finance*. 3rd edn. Edited by Donald H. Chew, New York: McGraw-Hill/Irwin.

Stewart, G.B. (2014) 'The role of the cost of capital in EVA and in corporate value-based management', in Pratt, S.P. and Grabowski, R.J. (eds) *Cost of Capital: Applications and Examples*, John Wiley & Sons, Inc., Hoboken, New Jersey.

Stoff, I. and Braun, R. (2014) 'The evolution of private equity fund terms beyond 2 and 20', *The Journal of Corporate Finance*, 26(1), Winter, pp. 65–75.

Strong, N. and Xu, X.G. (1997) 'Explaining the cross-section of UK expected stock returns', *British Accounting Review*, 29(1), pp. 1–23.

Sudarsanam, S. (2010) *Creating Value from Mergers and Acquisitions: The challenge*. 2nd edn. Harlow: Financial Times Prentice Hall.

Sudarsanam, S. and Mahate, A. (2003) 'Glamour acquirers, methods of payment and postacquisition performance: The UK evidence', *Journal of Business Finance and Accounting*, 30(1 & 2), pp. 299–341.

Sudarsanam, S., Holl, P. and Salami, A. (1996) 'Shareholder wealth gains in mergers: Effect of synergy and ownership structure', *Journal of Business Finance and Accounting*, July, pp. 673–98.

Sullivan, R., Timmermann, A. and White, H. (1999) 'Data-snooping, technical trading rule performance, and the bootstrap', *Journal of Finance*, 54(5), pp. 1647ff.

Swalm, R.O. (1966) 'Utility theory – insights into risk taking', *Harvard Business Review*, November/ December, pp. 123–36.

Tallman, S. (2016) 'Capabilities and capability development', *Wiley Encyclopaedia of Management*, 6(1–3).

Taylor, F. (2010) *Mastering Derivatives Markets*. 4th edn. London: FT Prentice Hall.

Thaler, R. (ed.) (1993) *Advances in Behavioural Finance*. New York: Russell Sage Foundation.

Thaler, R.H. (2005) *Advances in Behavioural Finance*. Volume II. Princeton, NJ: Russell Sage Foundation.

Thaler R.H. (2015) *Misbehaving: The making of behavioural economics*. Penguin Random House.

Thaler, R.H. and C.R Sunstein (2009) *Nudge: Improving decisions about health, wealth and happiness*. Penguin.

The Economist (2005) 'A survey of corporate social responsibility', 22 January.

The Economist (2015) 'The business of business', 21 March.

The Economist (2017) 'Six sects of shareholder value', 21 January.

The Treasurer (a monthly journal). London: Euromoney. www.treasurers.org/thetreasurer

The Treasurers Wiki, Association of Corporate Treasurers.

Tirole, J. (2006) *The Theory of Corporate Finance*. Princeton: Princeton University Press.

Titman, S. J. Wei and Feixue Xie (2004) 'Capital investments and stock returns', *Journal of Financial and Quantitative Analysis*, 39, pp. 677–700.

Tobin, J. (1958) 'Liquidity preference as behaviour toward risk', *Review of Economic Studies*, February, 26, pp. 65–86.

Torres, N. (2015) 'What angel investors value most when choosing what to fund', *Harvard Business Review*, 6 August, pp. 2–5.

Treynor, J. (1965) 'How to rate management of investment funds', *Harvard Business Review*, January–February.

Triana, P. (2009) *Lecturing Birds on Flying: Can Mathematical Theories Destroy the Financial Markets?* Hoboken, NJ: John Wiley & Sons.

Triantis, A. and Borison, A. (2001) 'Real Options: State of the Practice', *Journal of Applied Corporate Finance*, 14(2), 8–24.

Triantis, A.J. and Hodder, J.E. (1990) 'Valuing flexibility as a complex option', *Journal of Finance*, 45, pp. 545–66.

Tricker, R.I. (2015) *Corporate Governance: Principles, Policies, and Practices Paperback*. Third Edition. Oxford University Press.

Trigeorgis, L. (1996) *Real Options: Managerial Flexibility and Strategy in Resource Allocation*. Cambridge, MA: MIT Press.

Truong X. Duong, R. Singh and Eng-Joo Tan (2015) 'Costly self-insurance of rights offerings', *Journal of Business Finance and Accounting*, 42(9) &(10), November/December, pp. 1251–81.

Tse, C-B, (2005) 'Use dividends to signal or not: An examination of the UK dividend pay-out patterns', *Managerial Finance*, 31(4), pp. 12–33.

Tyrrall, D.E. (1998) 'Discounted cash flow: Rational calculation or psychological crutch?', *Management Accounting* (UK), February, pp. 46–8.

UK Corporate Governance Code (2016) Available at the Financial Reporting Council website (www.frc.org.uk).

Van der Wielen, L., van Alphen, W., Bergen, J. and Lindow, P. (2006) 'International cash management. Riskmatrix.

Van Nieuwerburgh, S. and Veldkamp, L. (2009) Informational immobility and the home bias puzzle, *Journal of Finance*, 64, pp. 1187–215.

Van Putten, A. B. and MacMillan I.C. (2004) 'Making real options really work', *Harvard Business Review*, December, pp. 1–8.

Vayanos, D. and Woolley, P. (2011) 'An institutional theory of momentum and reversal.' London School of Economics Working Paper.

Veronesi, P. (2011) *Fixed Income Securities: Valuation, risk and risk management*. New Jersey: John Wiley and Sons.

Wagner, W.H. and Lau, S. (1971) 'The effects of diversification on risk', *Financial Analysts Journal*, November–December.

Wai-Ming Fong and Kevin C. K. Lam (2014) 'Rights offerings and expropriation by controlling shareholders', *Journal of Business Finance and Accounting*, 41(5) & (6), June/July, pp. 773–90.

Watson, R. and Wilson, N. (2002) 'Small and medium size enterprise financing: A note of some empirical implications of a pecking order', *Journal of Business Finance and Accounting*, 29(3) and (4) April/May, pp. 557–78.

Weaver, S.C. (2001) 'Measuring Economic Value Added®: A survey of the practices of EVA® proponents', *Journal of Applied Finance*, Fall/Winter, pp. 7–17.

Wei, K.D. and Starks, L.T. 'Foreign exchange exposure, elasticity and financial distress', *Financial Management* (Wiley Blackwell), Winter 2013, 2(4), pp. 709–35.

Welch, I. (2004) 'Capital structure and stock returns', *Journal of Political Economy*, 112(1), pp. 106–31.

Welch, I. (2011) 'Two common problems in capital structure research: The financial debt-to-asset ratio and issuing activity versus leverage changes', *International Review of Finance*, 11, 1–17.

Wen, S. and Zhao, J. (2011) 'Exploring the rationale of enlightened shareholder value in the realm of UK company law – the path dependence perspective', *International Trade and Business Law Review*, XIV, pp. 153–73.

West, K.D. (1988) 'Bubbles, fads and stock price volatility tests: A partial evaluation', *Journal of Finance*, 43(3), pp. 639–56.

Westerman, W. and von Eije, H. (2005) 'Multinational cash management in Europe towards centralisation and disintermediation: the Philips case', *Management Finance*, 31(10), pp. 65–74.

Weston, J.F., Mitchell, M.L. and Mulherin, J.H. (2013) *Takeovers, Restructuring, and Corporate Governance*. Pearson.

Westwick, C.A. and Shohet, P.S.D. (1976) 'Investment Appraisal and Inflation', ICAEW Research Committee, Occasional Paper, No. 7.

Wilkes, F.M. (1980) 'On multiple rates of return', *Journal of Business Finance and Accounting*, 7(4).

Williamson, O. (1963) 'Managerial discretion and business behaviour', *American Economic Review*, 53, pp. 1033–57.

Wilson, N. and Summers, B. (2002) 'Trade credit terms offered by small firms: Survey evidence and empirical analysis', *Journal of Business Finance and Accounting*, 29(3) and (4), April/May, pp. 317–51.

Wnuk-Pel, T. (2014) 'The practice and factors determining the selection of capital budgeting methods – evidence from the field', *Procedia – Social and Behavioral Sciences*, 156, pp. 612–16.

Wooley, S. (2009) *Sources of Value: A practical guide to the art and science of valuation*. Cambridge University Press.

Wright, S., Mason, R., Satchell, S., Hari, K. and Baskaya, M. (2006) Smither's and Co.'s report on the cost of capital provided to Ofgem (www.ofgem.gov.uk).

Xiao, G.B. and Gregory, A. (2011) 'Stock market driven acquisitions versus the Q theory of takeovers: The UK evidence', *Journal of Business Finance and Accounting*, 38(5), (6), pp. 628–56.

Xiao, Y. and Arnold, G. (2008) 'Testing Benjamin Graham's Net Current Asset Value Strategy in London', *Journal of Investing*, 17(4), Winter, pp. 11–19.

Yang, C.C. (2015) 'The integrated model of core competence and capability', *Total Quality Management and Business Excellence*, 26(1–2).

Yi, B., El-Badawi, M.H. and Lin, B. (2008) 'Pre-issue investor optimism and post-issue underperformance', *Financial Analysts Journal*, 64(5), pp. 77–87.

Young, S.D. and O'Byrne, S.F. (2001) *EVA® and Value-based Management: A practical guide to implementation*, New York: McGraw-Hill.

Zaima J.K. (2008) 'Portfolio investing with EVA', *The Journal of Portfolio Management*, Spring, pp. 34–40.

Zietlow, J.T., Hill, M. and Maness, T.S. (2016) *Short-Term Financial Management*. 5th edn. Cognella Academic Publishing.

Zimmerman, J.L. (2010) *Accounting for Decision Making and Control*, 7th edn. Boston: Irwin/McGraw-Hill.

Index